CUBA
HANDBOOK

CUBA
HANDBOOK

CHRISTOPHER P. BAKER

MOON
TRAVEL
HANDBOOKS

CUBA HANDBOOK
FIRST EDITION

Published by
Moon Publications, Inc.
P.O. Box 3040
Chico, California 95927-3040, USA

Printed by
Colorcraft Ltd.

Please send all comments,
corrections, additions,
amendments, and critiques to:

**CUBA HANDBOOK
MOON TRAVEL HANDBOOKS
P.O. BOX 3040
CHICO, CA 95927-3040, USA
e-mail: travel@moon.com
www.moon.com**

Printing History
1st edition—November 1997

ISBN: 1-56691-095-1
ISSN: 1092-3330

Editors: Karen Bleske, Emily Kendrick, Bill Newlin, Patricia Reilly, Don Root
Map Editor: Gina Wilson Birtcil
Copy Editors: Asha Johnson, Gregor Krause
Production & Design: David Hurst, Rob Warner, Carey Wilson
Cartographers: Chris Folks and Mike Morgenfeld
Index: Asha Johnson

Front cover photo: Tropicana Dancer, Havana, by Christopher P. Baker

Distributed in the United States and Canada by Publishers Group West
Printed in China

To Daisy
and the indomitable
Cuban people

CONTENTS

METROPOLITAN HAVANA . . . . 340~360

SPECIAL TOPICS

HAVANA PROVINCE . . . . 361~371

SPECIAL TOPICS

PINAR DEL RÍO . . . . 372~402

SPECIAL TOPICS

MAPS

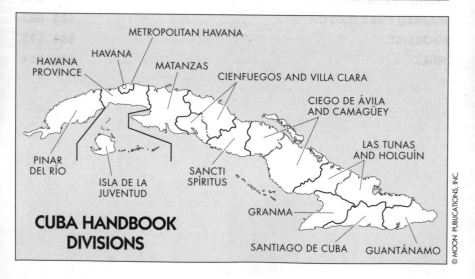

METROPOLITAN HAVANA

HAVANA

HAVANA
PROVINCE

MATANZAS

CIENFUEGOS AND VILLA CLARA

CIEGO DE ÁVILA
AND CAMAGÜEY

LAS TUNAS
AND HOLGUÍN

PINAR
DEL RÍO

ISLA DE LA
JUVENTUD

SANCTI
SPÍRITUS

GRANMA

**CUBA HANDBOOK
DIVISIONS**

SANTIAGO DE CUBA   GUANTÁNAMO

© MOON PUBLICATIONS, INC.

MAP SYMBOLS

▬▬ Superhighway	∷∷∷ Unpaved Road	☐ Highway Shield
▬▬ Primary Road	○ City	▪ Other Location
▬▬ Secondary Road	○ Town	▲ Mountain
▬▬ Tunnel	★ Point of Interest	✗ International Airport
─ ─ ─ Trail	● Accommodation	≟ ≟ Swamp
├──┼ Railroad	▾ Restaurant/Bar	▓ Water

LET US HEAR FROM YOU

Inevitably, a book of this size and scope is a long time in the making. While every effort has been made to keep abreast of the rapid pace of change and development in Cuba, some information may already be out of date by the time you read this book. A few inaccuracies are also inevitable. You—the reader—are a valuable resource in ensuring that future editions contain the most up-to-date and accurate information. Please let us know about any price changes, new accommodations or restaurants, map errors, travel tips, etc.

To assist future travelers, feel free to photocopy maps in this book: while sightseeing, mark the exact locations of new hotels and other travel facilities, and cross off those that may have closed down. Mail your revised map, along with any information you wish to provide (including, if possible, a business card, brochure, and rate card for hotels) to:

Cuba Handbook
c/o Moon Publications
P.O. Box 3040
Chico, CA 95927-3040
USA
e-mail travel@moon.com

ACKNOWLEDGMENTS

Heartfelt thanks are due to many individuals who assisted in the research of this book. First, thanks to Osmany Cienfuegos, Cuba's Minister of Tourism, and Juan Pardo, of Publicitur. I especially appreciate the support of Medea Benjamin and Pamela Montaro at Global Exchange, and Sandra Levinson of the Center for Cuban Studies. Thanks, too, go to my dear friends Jim and Ginny Craven, Jorge Coalla Potts and his family, Emilio Falcón of Havana's Hotel Plaza, Eric Jarneberg of *Jevericka,* Alex Klip of Cubalink Canada, Abe Moore and Sue McManus of SuperClubs Varadero, Tom Miller, Marta Rojas, Wayne Smith, Jorge Tabio, Sebastian Tickle of Caribic Vacations, Robert Walz of Expediciones de la Última Frontera, all my friends and acquaintances who kindly forwarded clips on Cuba, and all others who, through my thoughtlessness or senility, have not been acknowledged. *Gracias amigos,* too, to countless Cubans who displayed selfless hospitality, welcoming me into their hearts and homes and otherwise aiding in times of need—and to *all* Cubans, whose unequaled verve, virtue, charity, and grace taught me that I, and the world, have much to learn from them.

The author also wishes to express appreciation to a number of area specialists from whose writings he has drawn heavily, notably Tom Miller *(Trading with the Enemy: A Yankee Travels Through Castro's Cuba)* and Tad Szulc *(Fidel: A Critical Portrait).*

Lastly, and above all, I offer my deepest gratitude and a lifelong *abrazo* to Daisy Frómeta Bartólome, whose gaiety, love, and affection filled my time in Cuba with sunlight and tropical warmth. Cuba will never be the same without her.

PREFACE

In October 1959, Fidel Castro spoke to the American Society of Travel Agents (ASTA) convention, held that year in the old Blanquita Theater (now the Karl Marx) in Havana. "We have sea," said Castro. "We have bays, we have beautiful beaches, we have medicinal waters in our hotels, we have mountains, we have game and we have fish in the sea and the rivers, and we have sun. Our people are noble, hospitable, and most important, they hate no one. They love visitors, so much in fact that our visitors feel completely at home."

Normal relations with United States still existed back then, and the US ambassador, Philip Bonsai, also lauded Cuban tourism at the ASTA convention: "Cuba is one of the most admirable countries in the world from the point of view of North American tourism and from many other points of view."

Four decades have passed. Nothing has changed but the politics.

Cuba won its independence from Spain at the turn of the century only to be occupied militarily, politically, and economically by the United States. It was an uncertain independence: never fully under the United States' thumb, but never fully out from under it, either, until the Revolution wrote another chapter in Cuban history. Castro & Co. made a beautiful revolution but, alas, spun off into Soviet orbit and got trapped in the Cold War. Three decades later, Cuba and the US remain separated by 90 miles of shimmering ocean churned into a watery no-man's land by political enmity. Today, the Straits of Florida are the widest, deepest moat in the world.

Travelers visiting Cuba today do so at a fascinating historical moment, as Cuba is unwinding from its Marxist cocoon. A new Cuba, with different priorities and viewpoints on what it means to be a member of the Cold War family of nations, is emerging. It is extending its hand to the rest of the world and inviting us to visit. Four decades after Cuba closed its doors to outsiders, tourism is booming again.

Sadly, the US government isn't listening, although an increasing number of US citizens are circumventing the travel restrictions by entering Cuba through Canada, Mexico, or other Caribbean nations. It's remarkably easy to do. Cubans play their part by abstaining from stamping passports, so Uncle Sam need never know. Most *yanquis* harbor the misimpression that it's illegal for US citizens to visit Cuba. It's not; it's merely illegal to spend dollars there. In any event, no US tourist has ever been prosecuted merely for visiting Cuba.

Cuba is made for tropical tourism: the diamond-dust beaches and bathtub-warm seas the colors of peacock feathers; the bottle-green mountains and jade valleys full of dramatic formations; the ancient cities, especially Havana and Trinidad, with their flower-bedecked balconies, rococo churches, and elegant plazas; and, above all, the sultriness and spontaneity of a country called "the most emotionally involving in the Western hemisphere."

The country is blessed with possibility. Divers are already delirious over Cuba's wealth of deep-sea treasures. Sportfishing is also relatively advanced, with several dedicated resorts and far more fish than fishhooks. Laguna del Tesoro, part of the swampy Zapata Peninsula National Park, is one of several premier birdwatching arenas. There are crocodiles, too, lurking leery-eyed in well-preserved Everglades. Horseback riding options abound. Spa and health tourism is booming. Cuba is being eyed as a prime destination for bicycle touring. And hikers can head for the foothills of the Sierra del Rosario or tread trails trod by Che Guevara and Fidel Castro in the Sierra Maestra.

Cuba's greatest, most enigmatic appeal is that traveling through it you sense you are living inside an unfolding drama. Cuba is still intoxicating, still laced with the sharp edges and sinister shadows that made Federico García Lorca, the Spanish poet, write to his parents, "If I get lost look for me in Cuba," and that made Ernest Hemingway want "to stay here for ever."

Alas, thirty-odd years of propaganda and negative media reports have led many visitors to expect the worst—a fossilized shell of a country with a population cowed and sullen, their lips glued shut in fear. Yet those who simply point out Cuba's negatives—the inept bureaucracy, the shortages, the muffled press—do not see the smiling children, or notice the educated youths eager to dissect Voltaire or challenge you to a game of chess. Cuba rightly brags about its educational network and its health system, which provides free care for everyone and has reduced infant mortality and raised life expectancy to a par with developed nations. And after several decades of not being caught up in the monied economy, there is a distinct lack of hype, an environment in which success is not measured by the level of consumption (although this is changing). Cubans can still take ample pleasure in rocking on a veranda watching laughing kids chase a hoop down a dusty street. Even the young retain fond memories of days before the Soviet Union collapsed, when Cubans had become accustomed to a quality of life that has only recently been pulled from under their feet.

Nevertheless, today there is general agreement that things have gone terribly wrong and the future is full of uncertainty. The current crisis is severely testing the Cubans' faith in human cooperation, a situation exacerbated by the tourism boom, which has hallmarks of a Faustian bargain. In the 1950s, Cuba was considered the playground of the United States. The revolutionaries, however, scorned tourism for its bourgeois decadence—the gambling, prostitution, live sex acts, and drugs. Things are now coming full circle with the rise of tourism in the 1990s, as the inequity between the dollar and the peso has created an inverted economy in which bellhops and *jiniteras* (prostitutes) make far more money than surgeons and college professors. An economic elite is once again becoming visible. So are resentments and tensions.

Cuba today drifts somewhere between communism and capitalism. A new breed of relatively young, pragmatic, and market-savvy political leaders is seeking a homespun paradigm of socialism-cum-free-market economy that would restore economic growth while preserving social benefits and avoiding upheaval. The challenge is how to create greater economic and political freedom without allowing the authority of the state to collapse, opening the door to widespread lawlessness, a possible invasion, and massive bloodshed.

Washington seems oblivious to this dilemma. Since 1961, Cuba has been subjected to a punishing embargo that the US government says is done in the name of democracy but which most Cubans consider a dictatorial violation of their sovereignty that only adds to their misery. Meanwhile, in Florida, paramilitary groups of Cuban expatriates simulate war games in the Everglades, training for what could be an eventual assault on their "homeland," while politically ambitious and wealthy right-wing Cuban-Americans who underwrite them wait lustfully in the wings.

The majority of Cubans (those who haven't left on rafts; since 1959, one tenth of the Cuban population has sought opportunity across the Florida Straits) are reluctant to blame Castro entirely for the country's troubles. Despite the economic crisis, Fidel retains his tactical skills and—whatever Washington would like to think—the grudging affection of his people. Demonized by the US, *El Comandante* remains for Cubans a symbol of national dignity. True, Cubans desire change—even a change of leadership—but not the kind that the US government would like to impose. When Cubans talk of "change," they speak of greater efficiency, more food on the table, a greater freedom to live their lives as they wish—but without compromising the accomplishments of their Revolution.

To the international visitor, the frustrations of life for the average Cuban need be no more than a slight inconvenience. Tourists are free to go wherever they wish, and there are few visible hallmarks of a totalitarian system (the secret police lurk deep in the shadows). And yet the "real" Cuba is not easy to fathom, and the casual visitor is easily beguiled. Tourists riding in comfortable Toyota minivans may wind up with little more than a canned experience of the country. An open-minded visitor is torn two ways; Cuba is both disheartening and uplifting. You'll most probably fall in love with the country, while being thankful you don't have to live in it.

After all, you don't have to respect a government to fall in love with a country or its people, and it is hard to believe that the US government's Trading with the Enemy Act is directed at these compellingly warm-hearted people.

Cubans relish a passion for pleasure despite (or because of) their hardships. Salsa and irresistible rumbas pulse through the streets, and throngs of people congregate at nightclubs and cabarets, including the Tropicana, the open-air extravaganza now in its sixth decade of stiletto-heeled paganism. Cubans you have met only moments previously may invite you into their homes, where rum and beer are passed around and you are lured to dance by narcotic rhythms. How often have I been carried away, laughing, flirting, dancing as it were with the enemy?

Everywhere, Cubans embrace and welcome you into their arms. Everything touches your heart. You come away feeling like my friend Stephanie Gervassi-Levin, who on her first visit to Cuba began dancing uncontrollably in a *casa de la trova*. The Cubans formed a line and, "like a diplomat," took her hand, kissed her cheek. As I set out to write this book, she implored, "Chris, bring your genuine feeling into your pages. Breathe the innocence and beauty of Cuba without castrating Castro and his revolution."

Ernest Hemingway, who loved Cuba and lived there for the better part of 20 years, once warned novice writer Arnold Samuelson against "a tendency to condemn before you completely understand. You aren't God, and you never judge a man," Hemingway said. "You present him as he is and you let the reader judge."

BOB RACE

INTRODUCTION

THE LAND

Cuba lies at the western end of the Greater Antilles group of Caribbean islands, which began to heave from the sea about 150 million years ago. Curling east and south like a shepherd's crook are the much younger and smaller Lesser Antilles, a cluster of mostly volcanic islands that bear little resemblance to their larger neighbor.

Long and narrow, Cuba is by far the largest of the Caribbean islands—at 114,524 square km (44,218 square miles), it's about half again as big as all the other Caribbean islands combined. It is only slightly smaller than the state of Louisiana, half the size of the United Kingdom, and three times the size of the Netherlands.

Cuba lies just south of the Tropic of Cancer at the eastern perimeter of the Gulf of Mexico, 150 km (90 miles) south of Key West, Florida, 140 km (87 miles) north of Jamaica, and 210 km (130 miles) east of Mexico's Yucatán peninsula. It is separated from Hispaniola to the east by the narrow, 77-km-wide Windward Passage, or Old Bahamas Channel, a major shipping lane between the North Atlantic Ocean and Caribbean Sea.

Cuba is actually an archipelago with some 4,000-plus islands, islets, and cays dominated by the main island (104,945 square km), which is 1,250 km (777 miles) long and between 31 and 193 km (18 and 120 miles) wide; it averages 80 km (50 miles) wide, broadening from Cabo de San Antonio in the west to Punta Maisí in the east. Likened in shape to everything from an alligator to a phallus, Cuba is a crescent running northwest to southeast, convex to the north.

Slung beneath the mainland's underbelly is the Isla de la Juventud (2,200 square km), the westernmost of a chain of smaller islands—the Archipiélago de los Canarreos—which extends eastward for 110 km across the Golfo de Batabanó. Farther east, beneath east-central Cuba, are a shoal group of tiny coral cays sprinkled with diamond-dust beaches and that poke up a mere four or five meters from the sapphire sea—the Archipiélago de los Járdines de la Reina.

The central north coast, too, is rimmed by a necklace of coral jewels: dark green, ringed by an oval of crushed-sugar sand and bright turquoise shallows, with surf pounding on the reef edge. It's enough to bring out the Robinson Crusoe in anyone, perhaps with the trail of a

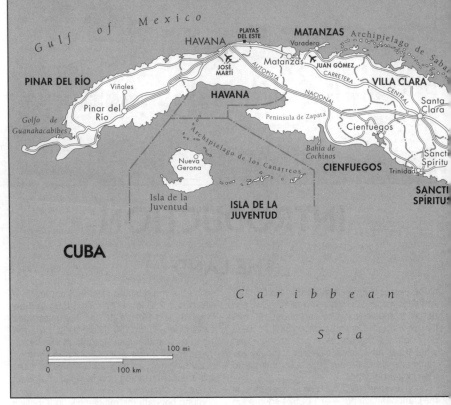

tiny lizard leading up toward the scrubby pines as the only sign that any living creature has been here before.

TOPOGRAPHY

Cuban landscapes are soft and calming, epitomized by sensual waves of lime-green sugarcane undulating like a great swelling sea—landscapes that Kenneth Tynan described in *Holiday* magazine in 1961 as "of soft Pissarro and Cézanne color, and the tropical intensity of Gauguin." Emerald greens flow into burning golds; soft, faded pastels and warm ochers are relieved periodically by brilliant tropical colors, flower petals as red as

lipstick, pavonine waters shading through dazzling jade, and, always, the chartreuse of the canefields.

And yet it is rarely dramatic. Extended flatlands and rolling plains cover almost two-thirds of the island. Indeed, Cuba is the *least* mountainous of the Greater Antilles, with a median elevation of less than 100 meters above sea level. Its topography is dominated by *llanos,* the flatlands that at times seem to stretch forever, level as football fields and just as green, smothered in swampland inhabited by crocodiles or parceled into a checkerboard quilt of banana groves, pineapple farms, citrus orchards, rice paddies, and ubiquitous fields of sugarcane rippling in the breeze like folds of green

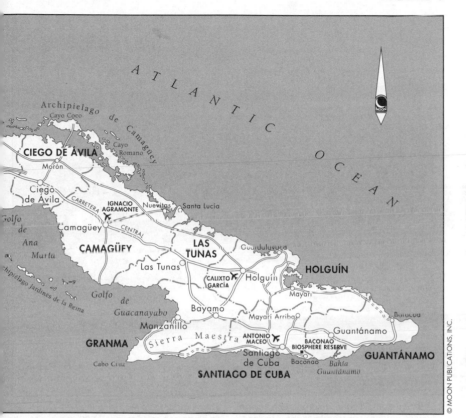

silk. (In contrast, the upland plains of east-central Cuba are relatively infertile and the habitat of Cuban cowboys—*vaqueros*—who tend hardy cattle.)

Cuban Highs

The monotonously fecund flatlands are disjoined by three mountain zones, where the air is cool and inviting and the roads dip and rise through very untropical-looking countryside. Each of the three *alturas* (altitudes) offers its own compelling beauty, with cool pine forests and sparkling lakes.

The westernmost is the slender, low-slung Sierra del Rosarios and Sierra de los Órganos that together constitute the **Cordillera de Guaniguanico** forming a backbone along the length of northern Pinar del Río province and rising to 692 meters atop sugarloaf-shaped Pan de Guajaibón. In their midst is the striking Valle de Viñales, a classic karst landscape of sheer-faced knolls called *mogotes* (see the special topic "Mogotes"). The theatrical formations rise abruptly from the plain and were formed by the collapse of vast underground caverns. The antediluvian morphology is riddled with caves.

The compact **Sierra Escambray** rise steeply from the coast of west-central Cuba, dominating eastern Cienfuegos and southern Villa Clara provinces, with slender fingers extending east into Sancti Spíritus Province.

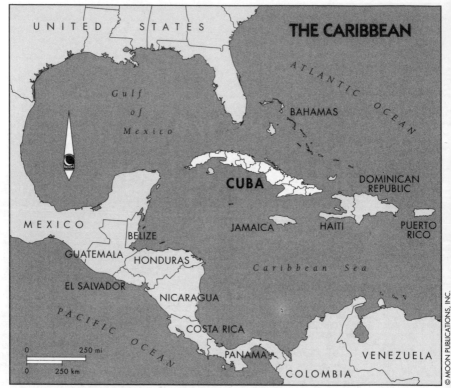

THE CARIBBEAN

UNITED STATES

Gulf of Mexico

ATLANTIC OCEAN

BAHAMAS

CUBA

DOMINICAN REPUBLIC

MEXICO

BELIZE

JAMAICA

HAITI

PUERTO RICO

GUATEMALA

HONDURAS

Caribbean Sea

EL SALVADOR

NICARAGUA

PACIFIC OCEAN

COSTA RICA

PANAMA

VENEZUELA

COLOMBIA

0   250 mi
0   250 km

© MOON PUBLICATIONS, INC.

A third mountain zone, incorporating several adjacent ranges, overshadows the provinces of Granma, Santiago de Cuba, and Guantánamo and spills over into Holguín province. To the west, the precipitous ranges of the Sierra Maestra rise steeply from the sea, culminating atop Pico Turquino at 1,872 meters (6561 feet). They extend from Cabo Cruz eastward 250 km to Guantánamo Bay, interrupted only by the small depression and bay in which nestles the city of Santiago de Cuba. To the east, the folded ranges of the Cuchilla de Toa, Sierra de Puriscal, and Sierra de Cristal are separated from the Sierra Maestra by the Nipe Plateau.

Earthquakes are common in eastern Cuba. The trees move as in a high wind, the birds stop calling, and huge chunks of unstable mountain cleave off and avalanche down the steep slopes.

These mountains are rising in some places as much as one meter every 3,000 years, a result of the upheaving that has been going on for at least 150 million years, when the Caribbean plate (a free-floating piece of the earth's crust), drifting northeastward at about 10 cm a year, first crumpled into the much larger, slow-moving North American plate, forcing the leading edge of the former under the latter and heaving up great amounts of volcanic material.

Down by the Shore
Depending on who is counting, Cuba has more than 400 beaches. They come in shades of oyster white, mulatto dark, golden, and taupe, and range in texture from talcum-fine to coarse-grained. The most breathtakingly beautiful are along the north shore, where some beaches

are a dozen miles long, especially those on the ocean side of the infinitesimal number of coral cays beaded like pearls off the coast. Other beaches are unappealing, especially those of the south coast, despite being touted on tourist maps with tempting umbrella symbols; notable exceptions include Playa Girón and Playa Ancón. Only a few are developed for tourism.

What virtually all have in common is sandy bottoms shelving gently into lagoons protected by offshore coral reefs. The shallows are bright green, turning to aqua, azure, and then sapphire the farther out you go. Beyond that, the ocean gleams a deep indigo.

The coast is indented by dozens of huge bays shaped like deep flasks with narrow inlets. They are havens for shipping today as they were for pirates and Spanish galleons years ago (Cuba has 13 ports listed in the *World Port Index* as offering "excellent" shelter). Not least of these is Bahía de Habana, on whose western shores grew Havana.

Rivers

Cuba has over 500 rivers, most of them short, shallow, and unnavigable. The principal river, the 370-km-long Río Cauto, which originates in the Sierra Maestra and flows northwest, is navigable by boat for about 80 km, fed by heavy rains in the mountains. On the flatlands, especially those of the southern plains, the rivers loop lazily to the sea through a morass of mangroves and lagoons.

Most rivers dwindle to trickles in the dry season, then often swell to rushing torrents, flooding extensive areas on the plains when the rains come (80% falls in summer). To assuage the deluge, Cuba is now studded with huge man-made reservoirs that help control waterflow.

CLIMATE

Cuba lies within the tropics, though its climate—generally hot and moist (average relative humidity is 78%)—is more properly semi- or subtropical. There are only two seasons: wet (May to November) and dry (December to April), with regional variations.

The island is influenced by the warm Gulf Stream currents and by the North Atlantic high-pressure zone that lies northeast of Cuba and gives rise to the near-constant *brisa*, the local name for the prevailing northeast trade winds that caress Cuba year-round. Indeed, despite its more southerly latitude, Havana, wrote Ernest Hemingway, "is cooler than most northern cities in those months [July and August], because the northern trades get up about ten o'clock in the morning and blow until about five o'clock the next morning."

The newspaper *Granma* prints a weather forecast.

Temperatures

Cuba's mean annual temperature is 25.2° C

CUBA'S CLIMATE

AVERAGE TEMPERATURES Temperatures are listed in degrees Celsius.

JAN.	FEB.	MARCH	APRIL	MAY	JUNE	JULY	AUG.	SEPT.	OCT.	NOV.	DEC.
National Average											
26	26	27	29	30	31	32	32	31	29	27	26
Havana											
22	22.5	23	25	26	27	28	28	27.5	26	24	22.5

DAYS WITH RAINFALL

Havana											
6	4	4	4	7	10	9	10	11	11	7	6

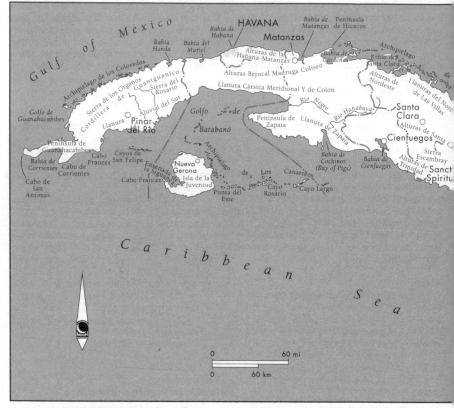

(77° F), with an average of eight hours of sunshine per day throughout the year. There is little seasonal variation, with an *average* temperature in January of 22° C (67° F), rising (along with humidity) to an average of 27.2° C (81° F) in July. Nonetheless, in summer the temperature can rise to 32° C (90° F) or more, and far higher in the Oriente, especially the lowlands of Guantánamo Province (the hottest part of the country), where the thermometer rises inexorably until you may be "forced to take off your flesh and sit in your bones."

The southern coast is generally hotter than the north coast, which receives the trades. Hot winds sometimes rip across the central plains in summer, drawn by the rise of hot air off the land.

Midwinter temperatures can take a sharp dip, infrequently falling below 50° F, when severe cold fronts sweep down into the Gulf of Mexico. Atop the higher mountains temperatures may "plunge" at night to 5° C (40° F).

Sea temperature rises from 26° C (75° F) in winter to 28° C (80° F) in summer, although the northern coastal waters are often cooler due to varying influence of the Gulf Stream.

Rainfall

Years of relative drought are common, when the cattle and sugarcane suffer. When it rains hard, sheets of water collect in the streets, waves crash over the Malecón, power snaps off, telephone lines go down, and taxis are im-

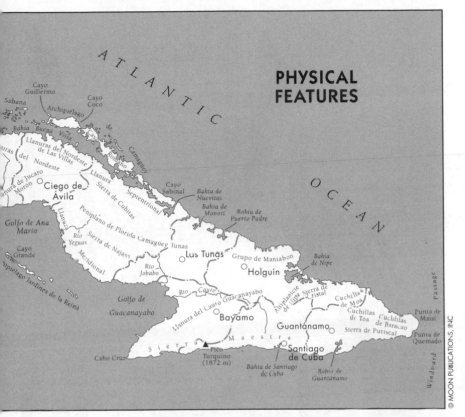

PHYSICAL FEATURES

possible to find.Some rain falls on Cuba an average of 85-100 days a year, totalling an annual average of 132 cm (52 inches). Almost two-thirds falls during the May-October wet season, which can be astoundingly humid. Summer rain is most often a series of intermittent showers interspersed with sunshine, but lingering downpours and storms are common.

Central and western regions experience a three- to five-month dry period known as *La Seca*. February through April and December are the driest months. Nonetheless, heavy winter downpours are associated with cold fronts sweeping south from North America.

The Atlantic coast tends to be slightly rainier than the southern coast. The mountains receive the highest rainfall, especially the uplands of eastern Oriente (up to 400 cm fall in the Cuchillas de Toa). The mountains, however, produce regional micro-climates, forming rain shadows along the southeast coast, so that pockets of cacti and parched scrub grow in the lee of thick-forested slopes.

Hurricanes

Cuba lies within the hurricane belt. August through October is hurricane season, but freak hurricane-force storms can hit Cuba in other months, too. The **"Storm of the Century,"** for example, struck Cuba on 12 March 1993 and destroyed or damaged 40,000 homes and caused (by United Nations estimates) US$1 billion in damage.

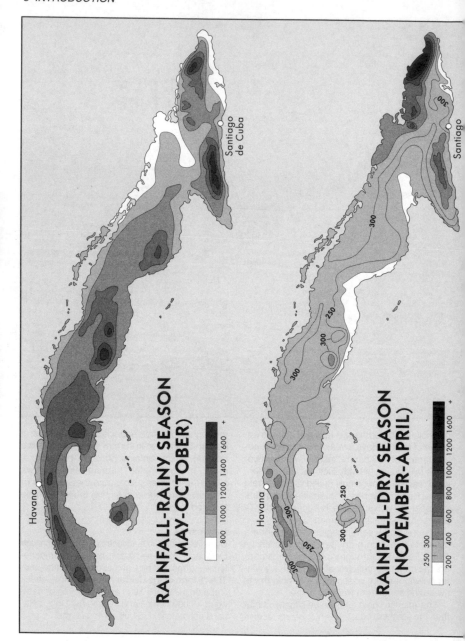

RAINFALL-RAINY SEASON
(MAY-OCTOBER)

800 1000 1200 1400 1600 +

Havana

Santiago
de Cuba

RAINFALL-DRY SEASON
(NOVEMBER-APRIL)

200 250 300 400 600 800 1000 1200 1600 +

Havana

Santiago

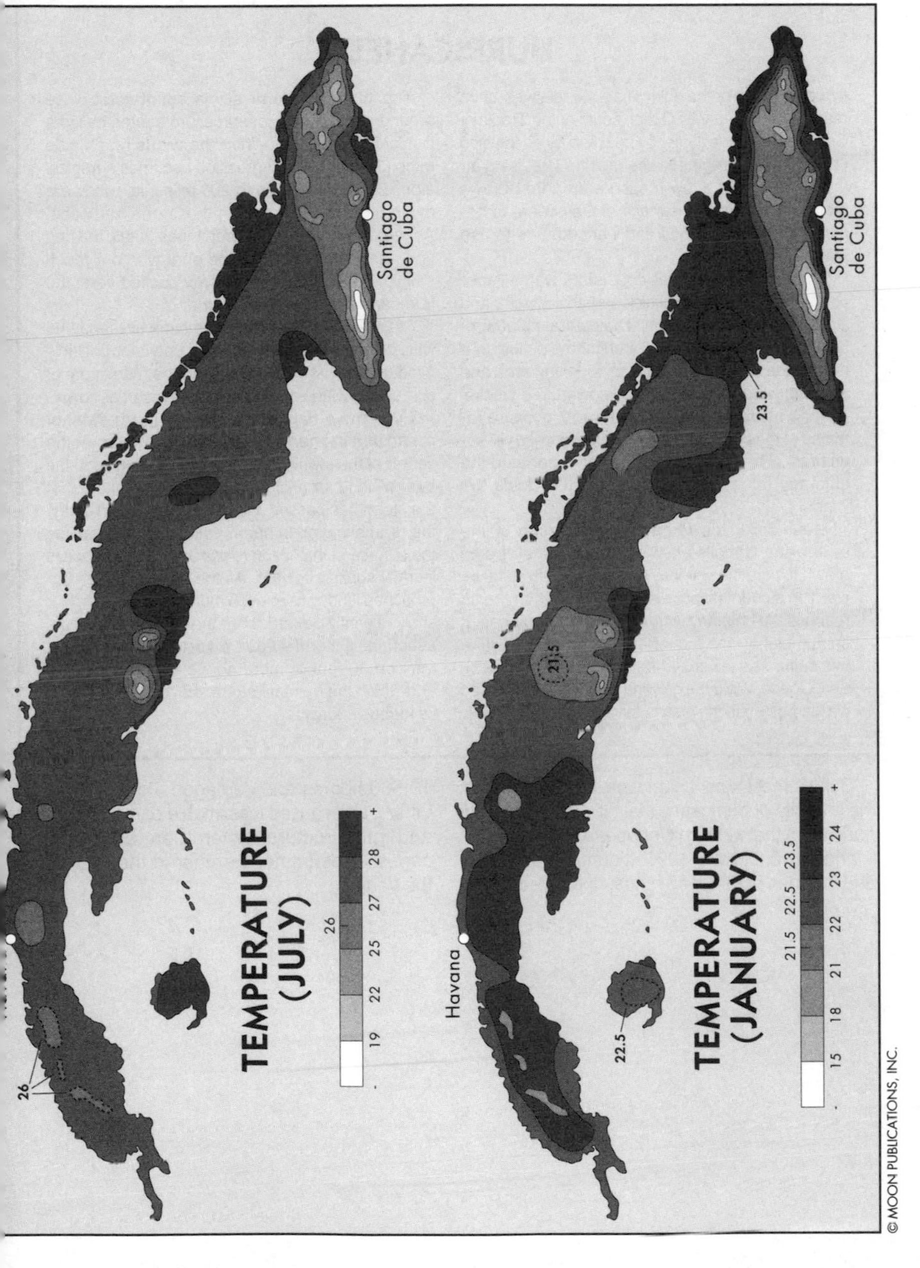

TEMPERATURE
(JULY)

19   22   25   27   28   +
      26

Santiago
de Cuba

26

Havana

TEMPERATURE
(JANUARY)

15   18   21   22   23   24   +
           21.5 22.5 23.5

21.5

22.5

23.5

Santiago
de Cuba

© MOON PUBLICATIONS, INC.

HURRICANES

In the warm air of the doldrums—the relatively calm reaches of the Atlantic Ocean south of the Tropic of Cancer—air made lighter by heat and by an infusion of water vapor begins to rise rapidly. The rising air leaves behind it a low-pressure area that draws more air in along the surface of the ocean, to become further moistened and warmed, and to rise skyward in its turn.

The rising air gradually cools. Its water vapor condenses into clouds, which spread outward, and sink toward the sea again. The central column of upwelling air thus acts like a chimney, pulling in a draft at the bottom from an ever-widening area and spewing warm air and moisture upward like smoke. As long as the source of warmth and moisture remains at the center of the storm, the process will accelerate. The condensing of water vapor atop the chimney releases heat, which further fuels the winds.

Meanwhile, the force of the spinning of the earth—the Coriolis effect—acts on the air being drawn toward the chimney and causes it to spiral inward, in a counterclockwise direction. When the air reaches the chimney, where the winds converge, it spirals higher and higher around an area of relative calm. The inward-wheeling air has been gathering speed, while the growing whirlwind has moved ponderously into the path of the eastern trade winds.

The brewing storm swirls counterclockwise around a deepening low-pressure center, called a tropical depression. When the winds reach gale force (39 mph), the depression becomes a tropical storm. With a width up to 200 miles, its winds are much more dispersed than those of a hurricane. As pressure at the center continues to fall, the ring contracts, concentrating the energy into a much smaller diameter. At the energy-packed core, the hurricane's fury reigns supreme.

Several days before the hurricane hits land, the winds ahead of it begin to push up water until it is piled up against the shore. Then the maelstrom of screaming winds and churning waves bear down.

Even more dangerous is the bulging swell of ocean that the hurricane carries at its heart. At the center of the swirling maelstrom is a calm spot, the eye, which can mislead people into thinking that the storm has passed. Here, beneath the chimney, the dramatic drop in barometric pressures causes the surface of the ocean to rise: the sea's surface is literally sucked upward. As the dome of water approaches land, it rises even more as the ocean floor shelves gently upward. Then the great welling pours ashore as a storm surge—a vast wall of water that may be 30 feet or more above normal sea level and which the monster storm shoves along with all its furious energy.

Cuba's most recent hurricane, Lili, which—like the majority of hurricanes that hit Cuba—moved north from the western Caribbean, battered the island on 18 October 1996. It dumped as much as 18 inches of rain in 48 hours, destroyed some 10,500 homes and damaged at least 145,000 others, and caused inestimable damage to crops and infrastructure. When there are no hurricanes, midsummer weather is the best of all the year.

FLORA

Cuba's ecosystems are less varied and remarkable than those of many smaller destinations. Yet it touts the most impressive species diversity of any Caribbean island. Despite four centuries of devastating deforestation, extensive tracts remain cloaked in a dozen shades of tropical green. Coastal mangrove and wetland preserves, dry forest, scrubby pine forest, pockets of rainforest, and even montane cloud forest, almost desert-dry terrain supporting cacti, and other wild places are strewn like isles within an isle.

Cuba boasts more than 6,370 higher-plant species, of which some 3,180 (nearly 51%) are endemic and about 950 are endangered.

TREES

Indigenous tree species include mahogany, cedar, pine, rosewood, ebony, lignum vitae, cottonwood, logwood, majagua, jagüey (a relative of the weeping willow), and the deciduous, silvery yagruma, which shimmers as if frosted and bursts forth with huge lily-like blooms. Cuban craftsmen highly prize these timbers, many of which are now in short supply following centuries of logging to supply the furniture makers of Europe and to clear the land for King Sugar. The mountain ranges still have ecosystems typical of original Antillean vegetation.

Other archetypal species include the swollen baobab, which looks like it has its roots in the air (for which it is sometimes called the "upside-down tree") and the white-trunked kapok, or silk cotton, and revered ceiba, both of which have wide-spreading boughs.

The bully of trees is the strangler fig. It sprouts from the tops of trees from seeds dropped by birds or bats. It then sends roots to the ground, where they dig into the soil and provide a boost of sustenance. Slowly—it may take a full century—the roots grow and envelop the host tree, choking it until it dies and rots away, leaving the hollow, freestanding fig tree.

There are fruit trees, too, such as the alligator pear tree; the big, dark green aguacates; and the zapote, whose pulpy red fruit is the queen of Cuban fruits. One of Sierra del Rosarios' endemic species, Psidium guayabita, produces a berry from which sweet licor de Guayabita and dry Guayabita seca brandy are made. Sea grape trims the island's shores, as does the coastal manchineel, whose poisonous sap and tiny apple-like fruits should be avoided.

Many woody species are exotics, imports from far-off lands—the eucalyptus from Australia, for example, and the cola-nut, from Africa.

Palms

Visually, the predominant species are the palms, of which Cuba has more than 30 types, including the rare cork palm, found in the western part of Cuba, and the bulging barrigona, or belly palm, so named because of its remarkable ability to store water, as if with child. The coconut palm is severely outnumbered, although it holds its own in northeast Cuba around Baracoa, where an

THE ROYAL PALM

The majestic royal palm (palma royal in Spanish) grows singly or in great elegant clumps. Its smooth gray trunk, which can tower 25 meters, resembles a great marble column with a curious bulge near the top. Long leaves droop sinuously from the explosive top, blossoming afresh with each new moon.

The royal palm is as useful as it is stately. Its fronds (pencas) make good thatch, and the thick green base—the yagua—of the penca, being waterproof, also makes an excellent roof or siding material. The trunk itself makes excellent timber. Bees favor palm honey; and pigs seem to like the seeds, which are used for pig-feed. Humans devour the delicious, succulent palm-heart (palmito) from the center of the trunk. And birds love its black fruit and carry the seeds (palmiche) all over the country.

BOB RACE

Granma Province

CHRISTOPHER P. BAKER

entire local cuisine has evolved from the nut.

The king of palms is the ubiquitous *Roystonea regia,* the royal palm, the indisputable symbol of Cuba (it's even part of the national emblem). It is protected by law, despite its ability to thrive almost anywhere. The **Jardín Botánico Soledad,** at Pepito Tey, 10 km east of Cienfuegos, has the island's most complete collection of Latin American palms, including the endangered cork palm. The **Jardín Botánico Nacional,** in the southern suburbs of Havana, has palms from around the world.

Mangroves

Cuba's shorelines are home to five species of mangrove, which together cover four percent of Cuba. These pioneer land builders thrive at the interface of land and sea, forming a stabilizing tangle that fights tidal erosion and reclaims land from the water. The irrepressible, reddish-barked, shrubby mangroves rise from the dark water on interlocking stilt roots. Small brackish streams and labyrinthine creeks wind among them like snakes, sometimes interconnecting, sometimes petering out in narrow culs-de-sac, sometimes opening suddenly into broad lagoons. A few clear channels may run through the rich and redolent world of the mangroves, but the trees grow so thickly over much of it that you cannot force even a small boat between them.

Mangroves—most wonderfully seen in Zapata or the northern cays—are what botanists call halophytes, plants that thrive in salty conditions.

Although they do not require salt (in fact they grow better in fresh water), they thrive where no other tree can. Cuba's rivers carry silt out of the mountains onto the coastal alluvial plains, where it is trapped by mangroves. The nutrient-rich mud generates algae and other small organisms that form the base of the marine food chain. Food is delivered to the estuaries every day from both the sea and the land so those few plants—and creatures—that can survive here flourish in immense numbers. And their sustained health is vital to the health of other marine ecosystems. The preservation of the mangroves has been taken on by the **Instituto de Ecológia y Sistemas** (Ecology and Systems Institute), Carretera de Varona Km 3.5, Capdevila, Havana, tel. 44-6335.

Mangrove swamps are esteemed as nurseries of marinelife and havens for water birds—cormorants, frigate birds, pelicans, herons, and egrets—which feed and nest here by the thousands, producing guano that makes the mangroves grow faster.

A look down into the water reveals luxuriant life: oysters and sponges attached to the roots, small stingrays flapping slowly over the bottom, and tiny fish in schools of tens of thousands. Baby black-tipped sharks—and other juvenile fish, too—spend much of their early lives among mangrove roots, out of the heavy surf, shielded by the root maze that keeps out large predators. High tide brings larger diners—big mangrove snappers and young barracudas hang motionless in the water.

Mangroves build up the soil until they strand themselves high and dry. In the end they die on the land they have created.

EPIPHYTES AND PARASITES

On higher ground, palms and large-leafed undergrowth such as the "everlasting plant," whose large leaves form habitats for other plants, give way to ferns (including the ground frond, which curls away at your touch), bracken, pine trees, feathery-leafed *palo de cotorra* (parrot tree), and parasitic *conde de pino* (Count of the Pine) vine, whose bright red berries add color to the trunks of its pine tree hosts. The vine—a kin of the mistletoe—lives off the pine by sending its roots into the vascular tissue of the host, seldom killing it but nonetheless rendering it more susceptible to disease by draining it of life-giving nutrients.

Many trees play hosts, too, to epiphytes, arboreal nesters (epiphytes comes from the Greek, "upon plants") that attach themselves to tree trunks or branches. The epiphytic environment is a kind of nutrient desert. Thus bromeliads—brilliantly flowering, spiky leafed "air plants" up to 120 cm across—have developed tanks or cisterns that hold great quantities of rainwater and decaying detritus in the whorled bases of their stiff, tightly overlapping leaves. The plants gain nourishment from dissolved nutrients in the cisterns. Known as "tank epiphytes," they provide trysting places and homes for tiny aquatic animals high above the ground.

The Sierra Maestra mountains are one huge botanical garden, profusely smothered in everything from delicate orchids to prehistoric ferns. Above 2,000 meters, the vegetation changes abruptly to cloud forest. Some wind-battered elfin woods on exposed ridges are dwarfed, whereas more protected areas have majestically tall trees festooned with bromeliads, lichens, mosses, yellow-flowering *palo de cruz* vine, and all manner of lianas and creepers.

FLOWERS AND GARDENS

Monet Colors
The forests and grasslands flare with color, some flamboyantly, for plants like to advertise the delights and rewards they have to offer, including

the ultimate bribe—nectar. Begonias, anthuriums, "Indian laburnum," oleander, anthurium, and poinsettia are common. Trees such as the vermilion African flame-of-the-forest, purple jacaranda, blue rosewood, and almost fluorescent yellow *corteza amarillo* all add their seasonal bouquet to the landscape.

Cuba's national flower is the brilliant white, heady-scented *mariposa,* a native species of jasmine that became a symbol of rebellion and purity at the time of the independence wars. Other common flowering plants are the sensitive mimosa, anthuriums, hibiscus, blossoming hydrangea, bright pink morning glory, and bougainvillea in its rainbow assortment of riotous colors.

African golden trumpet is found everywhere. Water hyacinths, with their white and purple blooms, crowd the freshwater lakes. The brilliant scarlet Cupid's tears *(Lagrimas de Cupido)* spookles green meadows. Congea clambers up over houses. Fence posts cut from the piñon tree grow from a stick in the ground and burst into bright pink efflorescent blossom. And jasmine, orange *jubia d'oro,* and azalea flank major thoroughfares and run down the central divides.

Many plants play out the game of love and reproduction in the heat of the tropical night, when they emit their irresistible fragrances designed to attract specific insects. Other flowering species employ markings on their petals to locate the exact placing of the rewards insects seek. Many orchid species, for example, are marked with lines and spots like an airfield, to show the insect where to land and in which direction to taxi. Others display colors invisible to the human eye, yet clearly perceptible by insects whose eyesight spans the ultraviolet spectrum.

Many herbs also grow wild in Cuba, though surprisingly few find their way into local stores and, hence, into cooking. An exception is mint *(yerba buena),* cultivated on the island since at least 1535. Pimento is an important cash crop that finds its way into local hot sauce. And locally produced vanilla flavors Coppelia ice cream.

Orchids
Cuba has several hundred known species of orchids, and countless others await discovery. In 1990, the purple Ames orchid (thought to be extinct) was discovered, as was another variety, *Marathrum cubanun,* which has no

common name. At any time of year you're sure to find dozens of species in bloom, from sea level to the highest reaches of the Sierra Maestra.

Not only are orchids the largest family of flowering plants, they're also the most diverse: poke around with magnifying glass in hand and you'll come across species with flowers less than one millimeter across. Others have pendulant petals that can reach more than half a meter. Some flower for only one day. Others will last several weeks. The greatest diversity exists in humid—not wet—mid-elevation environments, where they are abundant as tropical epiphytes (constituting 88% of orchid species). While not all orchids lead epiphytic lives—the Spanish called them *parasitos*—those that do are the most exotic of epiphytes, classics of their kind, so heartachingly beautiful that collectors can't resist their siren call.

If you're serious in your study, check out *Flowers of the Caribbean,* by G. W. Lennox and S. A. Seddon, or *Native Orchids of the Eastern Caribbean,* by Julian Kenny; both are published by Macmillan Caribbean, Basingstoke, England.

Botanical Gardens
The **Jardín Botánico Nacional,** near Parque Lenin outside Havana, features dozens of orchid species. You'll find a splendid **Orquideria** (orchid garden) at Soroa, in Pinar del Río Province. There's also a large botanical garden outside Santiago de Cuba. Farther east, in Baconao, is a cactus garden, and set high atop Gran Piedra, at **Ave de Paraísos,** mists swirl through a series of gardens divided by topiary hedges. Here, bird of paradise *(ave de paraíso),* dahlias, chrysanthemums, and dozens of other colorful species are grown for domestic use.

A large collection of native plants can also be seen in the Zapata Swamp, the largest such ecosystem in the Caribbean. Close to one million hectares in size, the swamp is a repository for the greatest diversity of species in the island—750 botanical varieties, 116 native to Cuba, and six found only in Zapata.

FAUNA

No one is quite sure how many species of fauna Cuba possesses, although it is certainly more than 13,000. The vast majority are invertebrates (mostly insects), with a great many species endemic to specific regions. Researchers from the American Museum of Natural History, Cuba's Museo Nacional de Historia Natural, and other institutions have been conducting studies of the island's biodiversity. They found dozens of new species and subspecies, including a large blue lizard and a pupfish, plus primate fossils about 19 million years old—the oldest such remains ever found in the West Indies.

Cuba claims both the world's smallest frog *(Sminthillus limbatus)* and smallest bird (the bee hummingbird, also called the *pájaro mosco*—fly bird—for its diminutive size, and the *zunzuncito* for the swish of its wings); an endemic crocodile species; and unique, beautiful colored snails of the genus *Polymita,* most commonly found in northeast Oriente, around Baracoa.

BIRDS

Cuba has at least 388 species of birds, of which 21 are native to Cuba. About half the birds to be seen in Cuba never venture the 90 miles north to the United States. Many, however, are occasionals, who fly in for the winter. Birds that have all but disappeared in other areas still find tenuous safety in protected pockets of Cuba. The nation offers hope for such rare jewels of the bird world as the ivory-billed woodpecker, found in Cuchillas de Toa, in Holguín Province.

Cuba is a major stopover for migratory waterfowl, and more than a score of species of dove, duck, quail, mallard, snipe, and pigeon flock seasonally to the country's freshwater lakes and coastal lagoons. Spoonbills and flamingos are also common on the cays and among marshy lagoons. White egrets *(coco blanco)* are commonly found around canefields and water flats, and their cousins the *coco negro,* or ibis, and blue heron (locally called *garza*) are also easily seen picking at a buffet of fresh delicacies that extends for miles. Black frigate birds, with their long scimitar wings and forked tails, hang like sinister kites in the wind and from this airborne perch harry other seabirds until the latter release their catch (birders have a name for such thievery: kleptoparasitism). *Gaviotas,* or gulls, needless to say, also prefer maritime regions, as does the oft-seen *gincho* (the sea osprey), who performs aerial acrobatics. The *codorniz,* or diver, lives beside freshwater lakes, where it is frequently found alongside the *yagauza,* a cross between a goose and a duck. The shimmering kingfisher prefers moving water.

Of terrestial species, the marabou stork can be seen in scrub areas. Such areas are also favored by the *cararia,* a goose-stepping ocher, black, and white hawk-like relative of the Senegalese snakebird. Listen at night for the hoot of the barn owl, called the *susundamba* in Africa, whose peoples brought a great fear and respect for the owl to Cuba, where they worked magic with her. Pygmy owls, with their old women's voices, perch in sapodilla trees. Like the owl, the endemic *siju* can rotate its head through 360°.

The *tocororo* (a member of the trogon family) is the national bird, perhaps because its brilliant blue, white, and red plumage copies that of the national flag. It wears a scarlet sash across its breast, like the one worn by the King of Spain, and for that reason, negro slaves were forbidden by plantation owners from looking at the bird. Listen for its tell-tale call: *có, co, có, co, có, có.*

Other birds you might expect to see in the open include boobies, pelicans, the yellow-necked green finch, the wedge-tailed chuchinguaco, or the aura vulture wheeling and sliding on the thermals, Everglade kites soaring in hunt of carrion, and common house sparrows and blackbirds (Ernest Hemingway, in *Islands in the Stream,* wrote of the "flight of blackbirds going in towards Havana where they flew each night from all the countryside to the south and east, converging in long flights to roost, noisily, in the Spanish laurel trees of the Prado").

Tanagers, oropendolas, and woodpeckers brighten the forests. The woodpeckers' short, stubby wings enable it to swerve and dodge at high speed through the undergrowth as it chases

insects. Alas, the island's parrot population has been severely depleted. There were so many parrots and macaws in the New World 500 years ago that the Americas were shown on maps as *Terra Psittacorum,* land of the free parrot. Even Columbus took home as a pet a Cuban red parrot (now on the road to extinction). The best place to spot parrots is the Los Indios forest reserve on Isla de la Juventud. Inhabited by 153 species of migratory and endemic birds, including the Cuban grulla or sandbill crane, but most notably by the Cotorro, the Cuban parrot, emerald green with red throat, foreneck, and cheeks, a white spot on its head, blue primaries, and a maroon abdomen.

The Zapata Peninsula is also a tremendous spot for birding (18 of the nation's 21 endemic species can be seen here), as is Sierra Maestra National Park (favored by the *rabijunco,* a rare migratory bird that settles in these mountains).

Seeing them is relatively easy. Depending on season, location, and luck, you can expect to see many dozens of species on a good day. Few tour companies as yet offer guided bird-study tours.

Hummingbirds
Of all the exotic bird species in Cuba, the hummingbirds beat all contenders. More than 300 species of New World hummingbirds constitute the family Trochilidae, and Cuba has 16. All are stunningly pretty and easy to spot among the scarlet hibiscus blossoms. Their magnificent emerald and purple liveries shimmer iridescent in the sunlight as they sip nectar from the blooms and twirl in midair, their wings a filmy blur. Some males are beplumed with long streamer tails and glistening mustaches, beards, and visors.

These tiny high-speed machines are named after the hum made by the beat of their wings. At up to 100 beats per second, a hummingbird's wings move so rapidly that the naked eye cannot detect them. Alone among birds, they can generate power on both the forward and backward wing strokes, a distinction that allows them to fly sideways, hover, rise straight up, propel themselves upside down, and, remarkably, even fly backwards.

Typically loners, hummingbirds bond with the opposite sex only for the few seconds it takes to

THE WORLD'S SMALLEST BIRD

Imagine a bird that tips the scales at a mere two grams—less than a penny! It is easy to be fooled into thinking of *Mellisuga helenae* as an insect. In fact, it's the world's smallest bird, about the size of a large bee (hence its colloquial name: the bee hummingbird). This tiny jewel is endemic to Cuba.

Only the 1.5-inch-long male ranks as smallest bird in the world. The female is about one-quarter inch longer, on a par with the vervain hummingbird, also found in Jamaica and Hispaniola. The female's cotton-soft nest is barely bigger than a doll's teacup.

The solitary hummer guards its territory with a ferocity remarkable for its diminutive size. One scientist records having a seen a bee hummer "explode with rage" when a vulture had the nerve to perch too close. "The furious hummer attacked it so relentlessly that within minutes the chastened vulture flew off."

It forages on tiny spiders, flies, and other insects, but also takes nourishment from the nectar of plants such as trumpetvines, which depend symbiotically on the bird for pollination.

Columbus' expeditionaries were the first to take note of Cuba's diminutive hummingbird. They sent word back to Spain of a glittering animal of diminutive size and quick movement that seemed to be part bird and part insect. The bird's range has since been gradually depleted, and it is now considered endangered.

mate. Many are fiercely territorial. With luck you might witness a spectacular aerial battle between males defending their territories (if two hummers go zipping by, they're probably in a dog-fight). Nests are often no larger than a thimble. Inside, the female will lay two eggs no larger than coffee beans.

Hummers earned a place in the mythology of the Taino Indians, who called them *colibri,* meaning "god bird." They symbolized rebirth, since the Indians believed that the creature died when the weather turned dry and was born again when the rains came. They worshiped the bird as a *zemi,* a fetish idol representing the path of the sun across the sky. The Taino also thought the hummingbird introduced their ancestors to tobacco, which had both magical and curative properties. Legend lives on in folklore—

some Cubans still believe that the most effective love potion is one made from hummers that have been dried and ground up.

Flamingos

For casual birders, seeing flamingos is a highlight of exploring the cays and lagoons of Cuba. There are six species of flamingos worldwide (four in the New World, and two in Africa). Standing over four feet tall, the roseate is the largest of the New World species. The ungainly yet beautiful bird—locally called the *Cabellero d'Italia* (Italian wig)—can be seen feeding in groups of dozens or even scores at Cayo Coco, Zapata, and other enclosed lagoons where evaporation keeps salinity much higher than in the sea. The supersalty soup teems with larval brine flies and diatoms, blue-green algae—favorite foods of *Phoenicopterus ruber,* the roseate, or West Indian, flamingo. Their food supply contains canthaxanthin, a substance that give the birds their soft pink color (flamingos raised in zoos are fed synthetic canthaxanthin so as not to disappoint visitors).

The flock retreats en masse at the approach of a visitor. One step too far and the birds take off, webbed feet stamping the water surface to foam as the scarlet wings beat for lift in their ungaily take-off, when 10,000 flame-pink birds may suddenly be poured into the blue bowl of sky. Flamingos resemble the Concorde in flight, with reaching head and neck and trailing legs outstretched to counterbalance each other.

flamingo

Flamingos do not breed every year. When they breed, they do so en masse. The mating instinct, once sparked, gathers steam until hundreds or even thousands of birds may be displaying in a tumult, parading up and down, marching stiff-necked in great columns. Ocassionally an individual will break step, stand bolt upright, and shoot out its wings, while others fluff up their feathers and drop their heads as surely as if their necks had been broken.

The birds build nests by ladeling wet mud into miniature volcanoes, which the sun then hardens. Soon the forest of legs conceals tiny youngsters swaddled in gray fluffy plumage.

AMPHIBIANS AND REPTILES

The most common reptiles you'll see are any of 46 lizard species, especially the bright-green Lagartija lizard, with its vermilion wattle, the comical curly-tailed lizard, chameleons, and quaint geckos— everyone's mosquito-eating friend.

With luck, you may spot the dragonlike iguana (particularly on Cayo Largo and other offshore cays), which seems to have little fear of man and can grow to two meters in length. It can be seen in coastal areas crawling through moist deciduous forest leaf litter or basking on branches that hang over water—its preferred route of escape when threatened. There's no mistaking this reptilian nightmare for any other lizard. Its head—the size of a man's fist—is crested with a frightening wig of leathery spines, its heavy body encased in a scaly hide, deeply wrinkled around the sockets of its muscular legs. Despite its menacing *One Million Years B.C.* appearance, it is quite harmless, a nonbelligerent vegetarian.

Aquatic turtles (terrapins) are also common, particularly in the Zapata peninsula, where you can see them basking in rows on partially submerged logs.

The **amphibians** are primarily represented by the frogs and toads, most of which you're probably more likely to hear than to see—especially the horny bullfrogs, croaking their lusty two-tone serenade through the night. Spelunkers might even spot the axolotl, a blind, albino cave-dwelling newt.

Cuba is also home to 14 species of neotropical **snakes,** which inhabit a wide range of Cuban environments. None of Cuba's snakes are poisonous. Among the more common snake species are the wide-ranging boas, which you might spot crawling across a cultivated field or waiting patiently on a bough of a tree in wet or dry tropical forest, savannah, or dry thorn scrub. The Cuban boa can grow to four meters in length. Its converse is the 20-cm-long pygmy boa, found solely in the caves of the Valle de Viñales. Wild boas vary in temperament. Larger ones are aggressive and quite capable of inflicting serious damage with their large teeth. Heaven forbid a full-grown adult should sink its teeth in sufficiently to get its constricting coils around you.

Crocodiles and Caimans

In Cuba, it's easy to spot crocodiles and caimans—the croc's modest-sized relative. The speckled caiman is still relatively common in parts of Cuba's wet lowland—and in fact may be the most abundant in existence today. It is no more than two meters long—one of the smallest of western crocodilians. Another species, the nonnative caiman or *babilla,* is found on the Isla de la Juventud.

The scales of the caiman take on the blue-green color of the water it slithers through. Such camouflage and even the ability to breathe underwater, through raised nostrils, have not protected it. Their nests are heavily disturbed by dogs, foxes, lizards, and humans. And increasingly they are being sought for their skins, which are turned into trivia. Ironically, this is easing the pressure on the crocodiles, which are fast disappearing elsewhere as humanity takes their hides and habitats.

An endemic crocodile species, the rare yellow and black *Crocodylus rhombifer,* is found only in the Zapata peninsula but is being reintroduced to the Lanier swamps, Río Cuato estuary, and other native areas. The crocodile, with a lineage going back 250 million years, was hunted to near extinction during colonial days and today has the most restricted geographical range of any crocodile species in the world. *Lagarto criollo* (as the Cuban croc is colloquially known) is much more aggressive than its cousin, the placid American crocodile, which inhabits many of the estuaries and coastal mangroves around the island and which had interbred with the Cuban crocodile, adding to the latter's woes. Since the

Revolution, Cuba has had an active and highly successful breeding program to save the indigenous species. Today the population is abundant and healthy (about 6,000 exist in the wild). In 1995, the Cuban government was authorized by the Convention of International Trade in Endangered Species to market the skins of the rare animals worldwide to be turned into shoes and handbags, with the money to be plowed back into conservation (only crocs in the captive-breeding program will be culled).

The creatures, which can live 80 years or more, spend much of their days basking on mudbanks. At night, they sink down into the warm waters of the river for the hunt. While the American species is a fish eater, the omnivorous Cuban crocodile occasionally likes meat—wild boars, the occasional deer, unsuspecting fishermen. Pugnacious full-grown males will strike at humans. Crocodiles, who prefer stealth, can run very fast in short bursts. Crocs cannot chew. They simply snap, tear, and swallow. Powerful stomach acids dissolve everything, including bones. A horrible way to go! Beware that toothy leer.

As it moves between its nest and its pond and along its trails through the aquatic vegetation, it helps keep the water open and clear. Enriched by the crocs' droppings and by the remains of its meals, the waters around the holes support a rich growth of algae and higher plants, which in turn support a profusion of animal life. The croc also helps maintain the health of aquatic water systems by weaning out weak and large predatory fish.

Mating season begins in February. The polygamous males (who form harems) will defend their breeding turf from rival suitors with bare-toothed gusto. When estrous females approach, the ardent male gets very excited and goes through a nuptial dance, roaring intensely and even kicking up clouds of spray with his lashing tail. A curtsey by the damsel and the male clasps her ardently with his jaws, their tails intertwine, and the mating is over before you can wipe the steam from your camera.

A female crocodile selects a spot above the high-water mark and exposed to both sunlight and shade, then makes a large nest mound out of sticks, soft vegetation, and mud, which she hollows out to make room for her eggs (usually between 30 and 70). She will guard the nest and keep it moist for several months after laying. The rotting vegetation creates heat, which incubates the eggs. When they are ready to hatch, the hatchlings pipe squeakily and she uncovers the eggs and takes the babies into a special pouch inside her mouth. She then swims away with the youngsters peering out between a palisade of teeth. The male assists, and soon the young crocs are feeding and playing in a special nursery, guarded by the two watchful parents (only 10% of newborn hatchlings survive in the wild; 90% survive in captive breeding programs). For all their beastly behavior, crocodiles are devoted parents.

Despite being relics from the age of the dinosaurs, croc brains are far more complex than those of other reptiles. They are sharp learners. They also have an amazing immune system that can even defeat gangrene. Cuba is looking at the commercial potential, including extraction and development of potential medicines and, purportedly, aphrodisiacs.

Marine Turtles

Marine turtles—notably the hawksbill and, to a lesser degree, the green—nest on Cuban beaches, mostly on Isla de la Juventud and southern cays.

One hundred years ago, turtles were as abundant throughout the Caribbean as the bison once was on the North American plains. They were highly prized for their meat by indigenous peoples, who netted and harpooned them. And British and Spanish fleets, buccaneers, and whalers counted on turtle meat to feed their crews while cruising in New World waters. They're easy to catch and easy to keep alive for weeks on their backs in a space no bigger than the turtle itself. The end of colonialism offered no respite. Large-scale green turtle export occurred about the turn of the century, when turtle soup became a delicacy.

Most of the important nesting sites in Cuba are now protected (such as the beaches of Isla de la Juventud), and access to some is restricted. Despite legislation outlawing the taking of turtle eggs or disturbance of nesting turtles, adult turtles continue to be captured for meat by Cuban fishermen. Hawksbills are also hunted illegally in Cuba for the tourist trade—one often sees stuffed turtle specimens for sale, and shells are used in jewelry and ornaments.

Mother Nature, too, poses her challenges. Of the hundreds of eggs laid by a female in one season, only a handful survive to reach maturity. (As many as 70% of the hatchlings are eaten before they reach the water.)

Turtles have hit on a formula for outwitting their predators, though, or at least for surviving despite them. Each female turtle normally lays an average of 100 eggs. Some marvelous internal clock arranges for most eggs to hatch at night when hatchlings can make their frantic rush for the sea concealed by darkness. Often baby turtles will emerge from the eggs during the day and wait beneath the surface of the beach until nightfall. They are programmed to travel fast across the beach to escape the hungry mouths. Even after reaching the sea they continue to swim frantically for several days—flippers paddling furiously—like clockwork toys.

No one knows where baby turtles go. They swim off and generally are not seen again until they appear years later as adults. Turtles are great travelers capable of amazing feats of navigation. Greens, for example, navigate across up to 1,500 miles of open sea to return, like salmon, to the same nest site, guided presumably by stars and currents from their faraway feeding grounds.

FISH AND SHELLFISH

Since scuba diving and sportfishing are popular throughout Cuba, a word on undersea life is in order.

The warm waters off Cuba's coast are populated by more than 900 species of fish and crustaceans—from octopus, crabs, turtles, and spiny lobsters the size of house cats to sharks, tuna, and their cousins the billfish, which aerodynamically approach swimming perfection with their long pointed snouts, tapered bodies, and crescent-shaped tails. Some billfish grow as large as 12 feet long and weigh as much as as 650 kg, with eyes contoured so as not to bulge and interrupt the smooth streamlined head. These creatures breathe not with gills but by taking in huge amounts of water through wide open mouths. Thus they swim at high speed in order to breathe. The sailfish (a type of billfish) has been timed swimming over short distances at 110 kph—which is faster than the cheetah, the fastest

land mammal. Unlike other fish, they are also warm-blooded, with temperatures considerably higher than those of the water around them.

The lucky diver may also spot whale shark (the largest fish in the world) and manta rays, which swim close to the surface and whose wings can be up to seven meters across. The manta ray uses the water for support, much as gliders use air. It flaps its wings and thus sails slowly through the water, gathering floating crustaceans and tiny fish by filtration in its immense, slot-like mouth.

Smaller fish are as strikingly bejeweled as the damsels of an exotic harem: sapphire fins attached to sulfur bodies, chocolate-brown spots scattered on a vermilion flank, sage-green scales individually rimmed with ringlets of red, white, and black. The entire spectrum has been tapped in audacious permutations. Around the coral reefs, where variety and richness of life is most abundant, individual species have evolved the most vivid liveries to assist in identification.

Fish to avoid include the fatally toxic and heavily camouflaged stonefish and the beautiful, orange and white striped lion fish, whose long spines can inflict a killer sting. The bulbous Jimenea and the puffer fish, which can blow itself up to the size of a baseball, are also poisonous. Jellyfish are also common, including the lethal Portuguese man-of-war. And don't go probing around inside coral, where moray eels make their home—their bite can take your fingers off.

The sea's sandy bottoms are home to conch—snails the size of baseballs—betrayed by their beautiful horn-studded, pink-lined, ceramic-like shell. The animal oozes along the sea floor at a snail's pace, its golden eyes peeping from the ends of long stalks. The islanders enthusiastically eat the tasty conch (they pound the heck out of the flesh, then marinate it in vinegar until it acquires the taste and texture of veal). Other shelled species include the trumpet-like tritons, twirled *liguus,* and spiky *murex.*

Tempting as they are, leave them alone. Collecting shells—and coral—is against both Cuban and international law. Shellfish in Cuba have already suffered over-harvesting (ostensibly, it is for this reason that private restaurants are not allowed to serve lobster, crab, or shrimp).

Inland, Lago de Tesoro harbors the rare *manjuarí,* the Cuban "alligator gar."

Coral Reefs

Coral reefs rim much of Cuba at a distance of usually no more than one km offshore. The reefs are an aquatic version of the Hanging Gardens of Babylon. On the sea floor sit the massive brain corals and the delicate, branching sea fans and feathers; nearer the surface are elkhorn corals, frond-like gorgonians spreading their fingers upward toward the light, lacy outcrops of tubipora like delicately woven Spanish mantillas, and soft flowering corals swaying to the rhythms of the ocean currents.

Coral cays are prodigal places. Here, amid sprawling thickets of bright yellow staghorn, great rosettes of pale mauve brain coral, and dazzling blue tubastras almost luminescent in the bright sunlight, a multicolored extravaganza of polka-dotted, piebald, zebra-striped fish protect their diminutive plots of liquid real estate among the reef's crowded underwater condominiums.

Coral reefs are the most complex and variable community of organisms in the marine world.

Corals are animals that secrete calcium carbonate (better known as limestone). Each individual soft-bodied coral polyp resembles a small sea anemone and is surrounded by an intricately structured calyx of calcium carbonate, an external skeleton that is built upon and multiplied over thousands of generations to form fabulous and massive reef structures.

The secret to coral growth is the symbiotic relationship with single-celled algae—zooxanthellae—which grow inside the cells of coral polyps and photosynthetically produce oxygen and nutrients, which are released as a kind of rent directly into the coral tissues. Zooxanthellae must have sustained exposure to sunlight to photosynthesize. Hence, coral flourishes close to the surface in clear, well-circulated tropical seawater warmed to a temperature that varies between 70° and 80° F. The Caribbean's clear waters expose the submerged coral gardens to a long and fruitful growing season for the algae and other plants that form the base of the food chain in this fertile world.

The reef is a result of a balance between the production of calcium carbonate and a host of destructive forces. Though stinging cells protect it against some predators, coral is perennially gnawed away by certain snails and fish (such as the colorful parrot fish), surviving by its ability

FROM DE BRY, "PETITS VOYAGES," 1601

Imaginations ran rampant after early explorers returned from the Americas. A whale with ears has two spouts, while scissor-tailed frigate birds and flying fish convoy a school of porpoises and seals.

to repair itself and at the same time provide both habitat and food for other fauna.

MAMMALS

Given the diversity of Cuba's ecosystems, it may come as a surprise that only a few dozen mammal species live here—and half of them are bats. Wild boar are common in many wild regions, including the northern cays, Lanier swamps of Isla de la Juventud, and Peninsula de Guanahacabibes, all areas where a small species of deer is also found.

Much of the wildlife is glimpsed only as shadows, such as the *jutia,* a large forest rodent related to the guinea pig and coypu of South America. It is edible and has been hunted for meat since indigenous times. Today it is endangered though found islandwide, as are various smaller relatives, such as the *Captomis garridon,* found only on remote southern cays.

A well-known indigenous animal that you are *not* likely to see is the solenodon, a rare and primitive insectivorous mammal. The solenodon was thought to have become extinct early this century, but a sole female was spotted in the 1970s, prompting creation of a protected reserve in the Cuchilla de Toa mountains. This ratlike mammal (also called the *almiqué*) has large padded feet, large claws, and a long proboscis good for sucking up ants.

Bats

It won't take you long to discover that bats are by far the most numerous mammals throughout Cuba. You may easily come across them slumbering by day halfway up a tree or roosting in a shed and at night swooping between treetops or urban nests to take insects on the wing. In true Dracula fashion, most bats are lunarphobic—they avoid full moon. On nights one week before and after the full moon, they suspend foraging completely and stay in their roosts while the moon is at its peak.

Most species of these—like the **Cuban flower bat** and the giant **Jamaican fruit bat,** with a wingspan of more than 20 inches—are frugivores or insectivores and quite harmless. Weighing in as the smallest bat in the world is Cuba's butterfly or moth bat.

The **vampire bats** are a different matter: they inflict much damage on domestic farm animals by transmitting rabies and other diseases. The vampire bat's modus operandi is almost as frightening as Bram Stoker's Count Dracula. It lands on or close to a sleeping mammal, such as a cow or even an unsuspecting human. Using its two razor-sharp incisors, it then punctures the unsuspecting beast and, with the aid of an anticoagulant saliva, merrily squats beside the wound and laps up the blood while it flows.

Marine Mammals

Cuba, like most neotropical countries, has few marine mammals. Several species of dolphins are common and seven species of whales are occasionally seen in Cuban waters. Otherwise, the only endemic species of any significance is the endangered manatee.

Anyone venturing to the coastal zones of southern Cuba will no doubt be hopeful of seeing a West Indian manatee, a member of the Sirenia family—the only aquatic mammals to subsist entirely on vegetation. This herbivorous critter has long been hunted for its flesh, which is supposedly tender and delicious, and for its very tough hide, which was once used for machine belts and high-pressure hoses.

The heavily wrinkled beast looks like a tuskless walrus, with small beady eyes, fleshy lips that hang over the sides of its mouth, and no hind limbs—just a large, flat, spatulate tail. Now endangered, only a few remain in the most southerly waters of the US and isolated pockets of the Caribbean. Zapata, where the endangered animals are legally protected, has one of the few significant populations. Apparently, jail sentences are mandatory for killing a manatee.

They are not easy to spot, for they lie submerged with only the nostrils showing (your best chance is near the Río Hatiguanico). Watch for rising bubbles in the water—manatees suffer from flatulence, a result of eating up to 100 pounds of water hyacinths and other aquatic flora daily. The creatures (distant cousins of elephants) can weigh up to 2,000 pounds and reach 14 feet in length.

INSECTS

Cuba's long isolation has enabled countless butterflies, moths, ants, termites, wasps, bees, and other tropical insects to evolve in profusion on the island, which boasts over 10,000 species in all. The most brilliantly painted insects are Cuba's 185 species of butterflies and moths, some quite tiny and obscure, others true giants of the insect kingdom, dazzlingly crowned in gold and jewel-like colors. In drier regions, hundreds of species of bees, moth larvae, and tiger beetles make an appearance in the early dry season. When the first rains come, lightbulbs are often deluged with adult moths, beetles, and other insects newly emerged from their pupae.

Then there are all the insects that mimic other things and are harder to spot, such as those that look like rotting leaves. Many insect species are too small to see. The hummingbird flower mite, for example, barely half a millimeter long, is so small it can hitch rides from flower to flower inside the nostrils of hummingbirds. You may detect other insects by their sound. Male crickets, for example, produce a very loud noise by rubbing together the overlapping edges of their wing cases. At dusk, the air trills with the sound of cicadas *(cigarra),* while fireflies flit by all atwinkle with phosphoresence.

Of course, a host of unfriendly bugs also exists: chiggers, wasps and bees, mosquitoes, and the famous "no-see-ums." All four insects can inflict irritating bites on humans.

Butterflies

With almost 200 identified species (at least 28 endemic), Cuba is a lepidopterist's paradise.

You can barely stand still for one minute without checking off a dozen dazzling species: the transparent Cuban clear-wing butterfly, metallic gold monarchs, delicate black-winged heliconius splashed with bright red and yellow, the scintillating yellow orange-barred sulphur, and huge swallowtails fluttering and diving in a ballet of stupendous color.

The marvelously intricate wing patterns are statements of identity, so that individuals may recognize those with whom mating may be fruitful. However, not all the elaboration has a solely sexual connotation. Some butterflies are ornately colored to keep predators at bay. The bright white stripes against black on the zebra butterfly (like other members of the Heliconid family), for example, tell birds that the butterfly tastes acrid; they can even adjust their coloration to fit a changed environment, like chameleons.

Some perfectly tasty butterfly species mimic the Heliconid's colors, tricking predators to disdain them. Others use their colors as camouflage so that at rest they blend in with the green or brown leaves or look like the scaly bark of a tree.

The best time to see butterflies is in the morning, when most species are active, though you may spot a few at dawn and dusk.

CONSERVATION

Cuba has been likened to the setting of Ernest Callenbach's novel *Ecotopia,* about an egalitarian and environmental utopia where the streets are clean, everything is recycled, and nothing is wasted; where there are few cars and lots of bicycles; where electricity is generated from methane from dung; where free health and education services reach the farthest rural outpost; and where city dwellers tend agricultural plots designed to make the island self-sufficient in food and break its traditional dependence on cash crops for export.

Though simplistic, there's truth in this vision. Cuba, a leader in second-generation human rights (to food, shelter, education, and good health) can claim to be a standard-bearer in the quest for third-generation rights to a clean and safe environment. Although McDonald's, ATMs, and home-shopping television programs haven't reached Cuba, the Cubans are ahead of the times in coping with ecological problems the entire world will eventually face.

Indeed, during the Rio Earth Summit in Brazil in 1993, Cuba was one of only two countries worldwide to receive an A+ rating for implementation of sustainable development practices.

Cuba: Red or Green?

One of the first proposals of Cuba's revolutionary government in the early 1960s was to create a greenbelt around Havana. Volunteers spent weekends planting trees, flowers, and ornamental shrubs before the plan died on the vine. In 1978, the government established the National Committee for the Protection and Conservation of Natural Resources and Environment, with responsibility to manage natural resources and wildlife and control air and water pollution.

Much of Cuba's advances are recent, however, necessitated by the collapse of the Soviet bloc. The fuel shortage caused Cubans to relinquish their cars in favor of a more environmentally sound mode of transportation—the bicycle. Everything from solar power (neglected, despite the perfect climate) to windmills (encouraged since the mid-1970s) are now being vaunted as alternatives to fossil fuels. For example, more than 100 of Cuba's 160 or so sugar mills are now powered by *bagasse* (waste from cane processing), saving the island the equivalent of 3.5 million tons of oil. In 1995, almost 30% of Cuba's energy supply came from biomass conversion (experts suggest that with appropriate technology, Cuba could generate twice the electricity from sugar cane that it currently gets from burning oil).

In the 1980s, Cuba began to edge away from debilitating farming systems. It initiated sustainable organic farming techniques and an enormously successful soil conservation program (see the special topic "The Organic Revolution"), while experiments were undertaken to determine which plants had medicinal value (herbal medicine—known as "green" medicine in Cuba—is today a linchpin in the nation's besieged health system, and *curanderos* and their homegrown remedies are no longer scorned).

Today, red and green are complimentary colors. In November 1990, Cuba held its first conference to discuss environmental problems. Cuba even has its own ecologically minded pressure group—**Sendero Verde** (Green Path)—a small dissident organization. And Law No. 33/81 has been passed, declaring that "State agencies, businesses and their affiliates, farm cooperatives, political, social and mass organizations . . . should take measures to protect the environment and guarantee the rational use of natural resources." Nonetheless, there is a lack of public education about ecological issues, and few qualified personnel to handle them.

Despite fairly adequate environmental laws, Cuba *does* suffer from horrific waste and pollution. Industrial chimneys cast deathly palls over parts of Havana, Moa, and other nickel-processing towns of Holguín province. Then there are the Hungarian-made buses that, in Castro's words, "fill the city with exhaust smoke, poisoning everybody. We could draw up statistics on how many people the Hungarian buses kill." And Havana harbour is indisputably one of the most polluted bodies of water in the world (a cleanup effort is said to be in the offing), as are the bays around Moa.

Environmental sensitivity has been lacking, too, in urban planning, which throughout the Revolution has been almost entirely limited to imported designs from Eastern Europe —highly inefficient and sinfully ugly units that show little harmony with the environment, fostering anomie among the inhabitants.

The nonprofit organization **Global Exchange,** 2017 Mission St. #303, San Francisco, CA 941110, tel. (415) 255-7296, offers study tours to explore Cuba's environmental advances and ecology.

Deforestation and Conservation

When Christopher Columbus arrived in Cuba, more than 90% of the island was covered in forest. Some 467 years later, on the eve of the Revolution, only 14% of the land was forested. Seven million hectares had been felled for sugar and cattle, most within this century! During 1945-60, indiscriminate logging reduced forested areas from more than 40% to less than 10% of Cuba's land area.

José Martí said that "a region without trees is poor. A city without trees is sickly, land without trees is parched and bears wretched fruit." Thus, the revolutionary government undertook a reforestation program in the mid-1960s; by the late 1970s, the program had increased the total wooded area to almost 20%.

Since the collapse of the Soviet bloc, Cuba has had to replace more than 300,000 cubic meters of imported timber by felling its own trees. Castro called for a reinvigorated reforestation program. The government announced the Manatí Plan, named for the eastern province where the program was initiated. Since its inception, about 697,000 hectares have been planted (Cuba is one of the few countries in the world to have increased the amount of forested land area in recent decades). Virtually the entire reforestation program, however, is in firs, not diverse species. There is little effort to regenerate primary forest. Nonetheless, large swaths of the country have been spared degradation and are protected within reserves throughout the island.

National Parks and Nature Reserves: In 1963, Cuba established four nature reserves: **El Verayl** and **Cabo de Corrientes** on the Peninsula de Guanahacabibes, in Pinar del Río Province; **Jaguaní,** in Holguín; and **Cupeyal del Norte,** in Guantánamo. A fifth reserve, **Cayo Caguanes,** was established in the north of Sancti Spíritus province in 1968. The parks—Cuba's first—covered four percent of Cuba and were created under the auspices of the Cuban Academy of Sciences. Hunting and logging were banned inside the park's perimeters. Supposedly, over 100 other reserves are planned (as yet, only a few dozen have made it onto the statute books).

In addition, UNESCO has declared four regions to be biosphere reserves: **Sierra del Rosarios** and **Guanahacabibes** in western Piñar del Río province and **Cuchillas del Toa** and **Baconao** in eastern Cuba—constituting an especially vital preserve of important forest watersheds (Desembarco de Granma National Park, for example, is 80% covered with endemic woodland). Other habitats, such as the vast swamplands of the Zapata Peninsula (the largest such ecosytem in the Caribbean), are also protected as vital havens for dozens of endemic species.

Cuba recently created a **National Ecotourism Group** to promote and develop the reserves as ecotourism destinations.

HISTORY

Cuba has a sunny geography shadowed by a dark, brooding history. The Castroite Revolution, which toppled Batista, is part of a continuum in the struggle for freedom from oppression and tyranny that began with the Indian chief Hatuey's revolt in 1513, evolved through the wars of independence in 1868 and 1895 to the Revolution of 1933. A sound knowledge of the island's history is therefore integral to understanding Cuba today. To gloss over the nuance of detail is to easily misread the march of events. It is as fascinating a tale of pathos as that of any nation on earth—perhaps keener, suggests Frank Tannebaum, "because nature has been kind to the island."

PRE-COLUMBIAN HISTORY

Europeans settled Cuba less than 500 years ago—a drop in the bucket compared to the 3,500-year-long tenure of indigenous peoples. The aborigines numbered no fewer than 100,000 (and some estimates suggest as many as 500,000) when the Genoese explorer Christopher Columbus chanced upon the island in 1492 under the service of Spain. The Spaniards who claimed the island lent the name *Arahuacos,* or Arawaks, to the indigenous peoples, but there were several distinct groups that had left the Orinoco basin of the South American

THÉVET, 1558

An Indian smoking rolled tobacco leaf inhaled through the nose.

mainland and island-hopped their way up Caribbean islands over the course of many centuries.

The earliest to arrive were the **Gauana-jatabeys,** hunter-gatherers who lived in the west, in what is now Pinar del Río province. They were followed by the **Ciboneys,** who settled along the south coast, where they established themselves as farmers and fishermen. Mostly, it appears, they lived in caves. Little is known of these pre-Ceramic peoples (3,500 B.C.-A.D. 1,200).

The pre-Ceramic tribes were displaced by the **Taíno,** who first arrived from Hispaniola around A.D. 1100 and again, in a second wave, in the mid-15th century, when they were driven from their homeland on Hispaniola by the barbarous, cannibalistic Caribs and leap-frogged northward through the island chain with the ferocity of a forest fire.

A Peaceable Culture
The Taíno were a sophisticated people. They lived in *bohios,* thatched circular huts designed to withstand the severe storms and hurricanes that frequently lashed the island. Villages, which allied with one another, consisted of 15 or so families governed by a *cacique,* or clan leader.

Since the land produced everything without the aid of the United Fruit Co., the indigenous peoples were able to live well and peaceably, dedicated to the production of children (the parents put pressure on the soft skulls of newborn infants to induce broad, flat foreheads, esteemed as a mark of beauty in adults). They cusped fish from the rivers (often using *guaican* sucker fish tethered on lines to bait larger fish) and culled birds from the trees, which also produced tropical fruits and nuts in abundance: papaya, oranges, mangos, coconuts, and almonds. The Taíno were also an ecologically minded folk who used advanced farming techniques to maximize yields. They grew yucca (also called *manioc*) and corn, which they called *mahis* (maize), as well as yams and peppers. Latter-day Cuban revolutionaries took a leaf out of the aborigines book, for the latter were "the first and purest socialists," in the words of a contemporary Cuban historian: they shared property and looked after the ill and less fortunate.

Although the men went naked, the Taíno were skilled weavers who slept in tightly woven cotton nets—*hammocks*—strung from poles (the Spaniards would later use native labor to weave sailcloth). They were also skilled potters and boatbuilders who hewed canoes from huge tree trunks. It seems they had evolved at least basic astronomical charts, which can still be seen painted on the walls of caves islandwide.

BOB RACE

Christopher Columbus

Columbus "Discovers" Cuba

After making landfall in the Bahamas in 1492 during his first voyage to the New World, Columbus took on indigenous guides and, with a brisk northeasterly at his back, threaded the maze of islets and shallows that lay to the southwest. On the evening of 27 October 1492, Columbus first set eyes on the hazy mass of Cuba.

The explorer voyaged along the north coast for four weeks, touching land at various points and finally dropping anchor on 27 November 1492 in a perfectly protected harbor near today's Gibara, in Holguín Province (Baracoa, at the easternmost point of the island, also claims the distinction of being the explorer's first landfall). The bay that Columbus named Puerto Santo he described by its distinctive, tall, flat-topped mountain, which Cubans now call *El Yunque* (The Anvil). According to legend, he left a wooden cross that today can be seen in Baracoa.

"They are the best people in the world," Columbus recorded of the Indians, "without knowledge of what is evil; nor do they murder or steal . . . . All the people show the most singular loving behavior . . . and are gentle and always laughing."

The Spaniards would change that forever.

THE SPANISH TAKE OVER

In 1493, the Pope granted to Spain control of the lands Columbus had found and ordered that the Indians be converted to Christianity. In 1509, King Ferdinand gave Christopher Columbus's son, Diego, the title of Governor of the Indies with the duty to organize an expedition to further explore Cuba. To lead the expedition, he chose a distinguished and wealthy soldier, Diego Velásquez de Cuellar.

In 1511, four ships from Spain arrived carrying 300 settlers under Diego Columbus and his beautiful wife, María de Toledo (grandniece of King Ferdinand). Also on board was tall, portly, blond Velásquez, the new governor of Cuba, and—very dashing in a great plumed hat and a short velvet cloak tufted with gold—his secretary, young Hernán Cortéz, who later set sail from Havana for Mexico to subdue the Aztecs.

Velásquez founded the first town at Baracoa in 1512, followed within the next few years by six other crude *villas*—Bayamo, Puerto Principe (today's Camagüey), San Cristóbal de la Habana, Sancti Spíritus, Santiago de Cuba, and Trinidad—whose mud streets would eventually be paved with cobblestones shipped from Europe as ballast aboard the armada of vessels now bound for the Americas.

A Sordid Beginning

The Spaniards were not on a holy mission. Medieval Spain was a greedy, cruel, uncultured civilization that foreshortened its cultural lessons with the sword and musket ball. The Spaniards had set out in quest of spices, gold, and rich civilizations. Thus, the once-happy indigenous island cultures—considered by the Spaniards to be a backward, godless race—were subjected to the Spaniards' ruthless and mostly fruitless quest for silver and gold. (Velásquez attempted to take a census, but, according to the leftist cartoonist Rius, "it was impossible to count the Indians: they wouldn't stay still. So the Spanish patented a system which the Yankees later copied, and after counting all the cadavers they discovered that there had been more than a million Indians in Cuba.")

A priest named Bartolomé de las Casas accompanied Velásquez and recorded in his *History of the Indies:*

> *The Indians came to meete us, and to receive us with victuals, and delicate cheere . . . the Devill put himselfe into the Spaniards, to put them all to the edge of the sword in my presence, without any cause whatsoever, more than three thousand soules, which were set before us, men, women and children. I saw there so great cruelties, that never any man living either have or shall see the like.*

Slavery was forbidden by papal edict, but the ingenious Spaniards immediately found a way around the prohibition. Spain parceled its new conquests—Hispaniola and Cuba—among the *conquistadores.* The Indians were turned into *peones*—serfs. Each landowner was allotted from 40 to 200 Indian laborers under a system known as the *encomienda* (from the verb to entrust). Those Indians not marched off to work in mineral mines were rounded up and placed on plantations, where they were forced to labor under the guise of being taught Christianity. Since the Indians were supposed to be freed once converted, they were literally worked to death to extract the maximum labor.

Understandably, word of the brutal treatment—first applied on Hispaniola—spread throughout the Indies. Thus, when Velásquez landed near Guantánamo Bay, he was surprised at the ferocity of the Indians' reception. At one point, at Nuestra Señora de la Asunción, a wooden fort built by earlier colonists near today's Baracoa, the Spanish were held under siege for almost three months.

The Indian resistance was led by Hatuey, an Indian chieftain who had fought the Spanish on the island of Hispaniola and fled to Cuba after his people were defeated. Hatuey was the first in a long line of Cuban rebels—down to Fidel Castro—who learned how to use the mountains for guerrilla warfare. Eventually the Spaniards captured the heroic Indian chief and burned him at the stake on 2 February 1512. As the flames crackled around Hatuey's feet, Father Juan de Tesín offered to baptize him, promising the chieftain that he would then go to heaven. Hatuey asked the priest whether the Spaniards also went to heaven when they died. When Tesín replied, "Yes," Hatuey scornfully replied that he did not want to go where there were "such cruel and wicked people as the Christians." Thus, the Spaniards, in their inimically cruel fashion, provided Cuba with its first martyr to independence. His death rang the death knell for Cuba's native peoples.

The indigenous culture was quickly choked by the stern hand of Spanish rule—condemned that Jehovah and Mammon might triumph over the local idols. The 16th century witnessed the extinction of a race. Those Taíno not put to the sword or worked to death fell victim to exotic diseases. Measles, smallpox, and tuberculosis also reaped the Taínos like a scythe, for the Indians had no natural resistance to European diseases. Within 100 years of Columbus' landfall, virtually the entire indigenous Cuban population had perished (Indian blood, however, still courses through the veins of several thousand Cubans near Baracoa).

The Key to the New World

The Spanish found little silver and gold in Cuba. They had greater luck in Mexico and Peru, whose indigenous cultures flaunted vast quantities of precious metals and jewels. Cuba was set to become a vital stopover and the hub of trade and shipping for Spanish galleons and traders carrying the wealth of the Americas back to Europe. Havana's sheltered harbor became the key to the New World. With the establishment of Havana as capital in 1607, a political structure began to take shape: the country was divided into municipalities, each with a town council. To supply the fleets, the forests were felled, making room for cattle and tobacco (and, later, sugar) for sale in Europe. Meats, hides, and precious hardwoods were shipped to Europe alongside gold and silver.

With the Indian population devastated, the Spanish turned to West Africa to supply its labor.

SLAVE SOCIETY

The majority of slaves that were shipped to Cuba came from highly developed West African tribes such as the Fulani, Hausa, and Yoruba (they came mostly from Senegal, Gambia, and Guinea at first, and later from Nigeria and the Congo). Distinct ethnic groups were kept together (unlike in North America); as a result, their traditions and religions and languages have been retained and passed down.

After being rounded up and herded to African ports, slaves were loaded onto ships where they were scientifically packed like sardines. Space meant profit. Chained together body-to-body in the airless, dark, rancid hold, they wallowed in their own excrement and vomit on the nightmare voyage across the Atlantic. Dozens died from sickness and starvation.

Once ashore, the Africans were herded into *barracoons* to be stored until sold to plantation owners or to work in grand mansions. To avoid the expense of advertising, the Havana *barracoons* were located near the governor's summer palace at the western end of Pasco (now Avenida Salvador Allende), where citizens out for a stroll could view the merchandise like zoo-goers. No attention was paid to family relationships. Parents, children, and siblings were torn asunder forever.

House slaves, while treated poorly, experienced better conditions than slaves in the country, where plantation life was exceedingly cruel. Even so, urban slaves were not spared harsh punishment, which was carried out in public by trained experts. Agonized screams emanated at all times of day from the designated whipping place near Havana's Punta.

Plantation Life

Most slaves lived in *barracoons*, where they were laid out in rows. They had only mud floors and little, if any, ventilation. The huts swarmed with fleas and ticks. A hole in the ground served as a communal toilet.

The slaves were awakened at 4:30 a.m. By 6 a.m. they were marching in file to the fields, where they worked until sunset, with only brief pauses for rest. At 8:30 p.m., the silence bell was rung, and everyone had to go to sleep. Slaves stopped working when they reached 60 years of age.

Men were issued sturdy, coarse linen clothes, and the women blouses, skirts, and petticoats. The women also wore gold jewelry and earrings bought from Moorish tinkers who traveled between plantations. Chinese peddlers also made the rounds, selling sesame seed cakes and other items. Small private plots were the slaves' salvation. Here, they could grow sweet potatoes, gourds, beans, yucca, and peanuts and raise pigs and chickens, which they often sold to whites who came out from the villages. Some plantation owners even allowed slaves to visit nearby taverns, where they were able to trade, drink rum, and play wager games such as "the biscuit," which was played by putting "hard salt biscuits on a counter and striking them with your prick to see who could break them," recalls Estefan Montejo, who related his life as a slave and runaway *(cimarron)* in 1963 at the age of 105. His *Autobiography of a Runaway Slave* is the most comprehensive account of plantation life.

Sunday was rest day. The drums began about midday, and the slaves dressed in their Sunday outfits

and danced. Slaves were not allowed to marry and raise families: pregnant women cost money to feed and were useless for work. Slave owners bred slaves like cattle. Strong males were picked out to mate with the healthiest women, who were expected to produce healthy babies every year. Wet nurses looked after the *criollitos*, who sometimes never saw their parents again.

(continues on next page)

SLAVE SOCIETY
(continued)

Many white men took mistresses among the slave populations. Their children were usually granted their freedom. Havana's free mulattas soon found their way to Europe and North America, where their combination of African exoticism and grace and Spanish hauteur found favor with discerning males. Occasionally a black mistress would be particularly favored and treated well, although their were limits to their upward mobility. (Read Cirilo Villaverde's marvelous and tragic novel *Cecilia Valdés*, whose namesake heroine's passion to be accepted in Havana's upper social echelons ends in a violent denouement).

Rebellions and Runaways
Understandably, rebellion was always around the corner. Slaves were considered dangerous barbarians (Victor Patricio Landaluze's representations of 19th-century life, which hang in Havana's Palacio de Bellas Artes, vividly portray how Africans were regarded at the time, as do the series of 19th-century cigarette labels on display in Havana's national library). The first slave revolt occurred in 1532 in Oriente. A few years later, Havana was sacked by slaves in the wake of an attack by French pirates. Many slaves chose suicide (particularly the Lucumí, for they believed that after death they would return to Africa).

Other slaves chose to run away and flee to the mountains. While runaways on other islands developed fiercely independent communities, such as the Maroons of Jamaica, Cuba's *cimarrones* tended to be independent; runaways often captured and sold other runaways.

To track down runaways, the authorities used posses of *ranchadores*, cruel white peasants with specially trained hunting dogs. When caught, it was standard procedure to cut off one ear as a warning to other slaves.

Nonetheless, slaves had the legal right to buy their and their relatives' freedom. Once free, they could even own and sell property. Most free slaves set up small businesses or hired themselves out as domestic staff.

The first slaves had arrived in 1513 from Hispaniola. By the turn of the century, an incredibly lucrative slave trade had developed. After being herded into ships, slaves were shackled below and endured the most deplorable conditions at sea. They arrived in Cuba diseased and half-starved, and after being sold were worked as beasts of burden, blasting and pummeling stone for gold, and cutting sugarcane beneath the searing sun.

Cuba grew rich. The wealth from sugar and slavery grew exponentially, as did that from the Spanish treasure fleets, which seemed to multiply in Havana harbor year by year. Landowners, slave traders, merchants, and smugglers were in their heyday (the Spanish Crown heavily taxed exports, which fostered smuggling on a remarkable scale). The Spaniards tried to regulate the slave trade, but it was so profitable that it resisted control. Daring foreigners—such as John Hawkins and his nephew Francis Drake—cut in on the trade. Cuba was a plump plum ripe for plucking.

The Period of Piracy
Lured by Cuba's vast wealth, pirates followed in the Spaniards' wake. In 1521, a ship laden with Aztec treasure was captured by the Florentine pirate Ciovanni da Verrazano; the next year, corsair Jean Florin seized a ship full of gold. As early as 1526, a royal decree declared that ships had to travel in convoy to Spain (the crown had a vested interest; it received one-fifth of the treasure). En route, they gathered in Havana harbor. In 1537, Havana was raided. One year later, Jacques de Sores sacked the capital and demanded a ransom. When a bid by the Spaniards to retake the city faltered, de Sores put men, women, and children to the sword before razing the city. French corsairs preyed mercilessly on smaller cities and plantations across the island.

Great fortresses arose to protect the cities, but to no avail. As daring leaders emerged among the pirates, they organized into powerful groups that were soon encouraged and eventually licensed by the governments of France, Holland,

and England to prey upon Spanish shipping and ports as a prelude to challenging Spanish dominance in the Americas.

In 1587 King Philip of Spain determined to end the growing sea power of England and amassed a great armada to invade her. Francis Drake, Hastings, and Sir Walter Raleigh assembled a fleet and destroyed the armada, breaking the power of Spain in the Old World. The humbling defeat left Spain powerless to control the slave trade or prevent a vast bootleg trade that grew around it.

No city was safe; Cuba was so narrow that pirates could easily ransack towns in the center of the island. There were hundreds of raids every year, severely disrupting the economy. Spain was impotent. In 1662, Henry Morgan, a stocky Welshman and leader of the Buccaneers (a motley yet disciplined group of pirates that would later operate under British license from Port Royal in Jamaica) ransacked Havana, pilfered the cathedral bells, and left with a taunt that the Spanish weren't equal to the stone walls that Spain had built: "I could have defended Morro Castle with a dog and a gun."

Only when the pirate attacks began to ease up, towards the end of the 17th century, were the Spanish colonizers able to settle down to raise cattle, tobacco, and sugar.

The Spanish Crown treated Cuba as a cash cow to milk dry as it pleased. It had monopolized tobacco trading by 1717. The restriction so affected farmers' incomes that that year the *vegueros,* (tobacco growers) marched on Havana and deposed the administrators, and burned the fields of growers who cooperated with the Crown. The rebellion, the first against Spain, was brutally crushed. In 1740, Spain created the Real Compañia, with a monopoly on all trade between Cuba and Spain (it bought Cuban products cheaply and sold necessities from Europe at inflated prices).

England Takes Over

While Spain repressed its colony, it had entered a war against a more enlightened nation: England. In 1762, an armada of 200 English warships landed 20,000 troops at Cojímar outside Havana, which fell to the English on 12 August after a 44-day seige. The English immediately

opened the island up to free trade (including unrestricted trade in slaves). Foreign merchant vessels flocked, and Cuba witnessed surging prosperity as a trading frenzy ensued.

Alas, within a year the British traded Cuba for Florida (sugar planters in Jamaica had pressured England to cede back to Spain what would otherwise become a formidable rival for the English sugar market). Meanwhile, Spain had acquired a more enlightened king, Charles III, who adopted a free-trade policy. The boom continued, encouraged a decade later when the newly independent United States began trading directly with Cuba. The North Americans' collective sweet tooth fostered the rapid expansion of sugar plantations in Cuba.

KING SUGAR RULES

Vast fortunes were being made in sugar—and therefore also in slaves. Wealthy Cuban and US slave merchants funded planting of new lands in sugar by granting loans for capital improvements, all meant to foster an increasing need for slaves. Land planted in sugar multiplied more than tenfold by the turn of the 18th century. For the first time, sugar outstripped tobacco in importance. Cuba's future was being writ in the fields.

The massive expansion was significantly boosted with the revolution in 1791 and subsequent demise of the sugar industry on Saint Domingue (Haiti), at that time the dominant sugar producer in the world. About 30,000 French planters washed up in Cuba, bringing their superior knowledge of sugar production.

Cuba's slave population had been slow to develop compared to that of neighboring Caribbean islands. The short tenure of British rule in 1765 sent the slave trade soaring. British slave traders established themselves in Havana and remained thereafter to profit in the booming trade alongside Habaneros. Between 1791 and 1810, over 100,000 slaves arrived (and countless more undocumented slaves were brought in illegally). A royal decree in 1818 opened Cuba's ports to free trade; the sudden explosion in the sugar trade and production saw more than 500,000 slaves imported in the ensuing decade; by 1840, slaves constituted 45% of the population.

In 1817, Spain signed a treaty with England to abolish the slave trade. However, Cuban officials "from the governor down to the harbormaster" were so enriched by bribes from slave traders that the industry continued unabated for most of the century (legislation passed by Spain in 1789 to improve the harsh treatment of slaves also went entirely unheeded). The British government sent emissaries to ensure compliance, but they "might as well have tried to catch mercury in a sieve." By 1835, when the British and Spanish governments agreed by treaty that any ship carrying slaves could be seized, as many as 2,000 vessels a year were arriving in Havana with slaves (to outwit the British navy, the slave traders merely adopted foreign flags; others simply unshackled the incriminating evidence and tossed it overboard). Only in 1888 was slavery in Cuba abolished, and then only because of a crisis in the sugar industry.

The unrivaled prosperity encouraged development of the island. By 1760, Havana was already larger than New York or Boston. The first University of Havana had been established in 1728, the first newspaper in 1763, and the postal service in 1764. Cuba's citizenry were growing vastly wealthy on trade with North America, with the difference that now much of the prosperity flowed back to Cuba, changing the face of Havana, Santiago de Cuba, and other cities. Monuments and parks were erected, alongside public libraries and theaters. Streets were paved, and beautiful colonial homes were erected. Until 1790, even in Havana, when night fell, blackness kept Cubans off the streets except those who were there for no good purpose. That year, street lamps went up in the city.

THE REVOLUTIONARY ERA

Spain, however, continued to rule Cuba badly. Spain's colonial policy, applied throughout its empire, was based on exploitation, with power centralized in Madrid, and politics practiced only for the spoils of office and to the benefit solely of peninsulares—native-born Spaniards. Spain's monopoly laws encouraged the migration to Cuba of a kind of Spanish carpet-bagger. Cuban-born criollos resented the corrupt peninsulares who denied them self-determination.

No Cuban could occupy a public post, set up an industry or business, bring legal action against a Spaniard, or travel without military permission. The criollos increasingly felt Cuban, not Spanish (most carried some black blood in their veins). By the early 19th century, a new generation of young Cuban intellectuals and patriots began to make their voices heard.

The American Revolution had a profound affect on the incipient desire for freedom among the criollos. Nationalist feelings were fueled, aided by Thomas Paine's Rights of Man, which was then being surreptitiously passed around the island. The French Revolution added to the liberation zeal, as did the slave revolution on neighboring Saint Domingue (although that uprising caused the Spanish government to adopt harsher measures to prevent a similar conflagration in Cuba, where slave rebellions were erupting with increasing frequency).

Following the Napoleonic Wars in Europe, Spain's new royal family—the Bourbons—took over a weakened country. Spain's New World territories were wracked by wars of independence led by Simón Bolívar. By 1835, only Cuba and Puerto Rico had not gained independence from Spain. While the Americas were swept with liberation momentum, Cuba remained loyal (the criollos withheld their support for Bolívar for fear of inspiring civil war at home). Nonetheless, many criollos were talking of autonomy. The Spanish initiated brutally repressive policies throughout the island to quell all rumblings of self-rule.

In 1843, Miguel Tacón became governor. The Spanish noble ordered the streets cleaned, drove out criminals, and whipped the idle and unemployed into action. He built fountains and a great theater, paved the streets, and began the first Cuban railway. But Tacón would brook no foolish sentiments for independence. He suppressed patriotic sentiment and exiled leading nationalists. Many criollos were shot for treason. Others suspected of self-rule sentiments were lashed to La Escalera (the staircase or the ladder) and whipped, often until they died.

Spain clung to its colony with despairing strength and the support of wealthy criollos (concentrated in Western Cuba), who feared that abolitionist sentiments in Europe would lead to abolition of slavery in Cuba. They looked to the

United States, where slavery was thriving, for support. In 1850, they were answered by a Venezuelan, Narciso López, who found financial support in the United States for an invasion of Cuba. He arrived with a ragtag force of 500 mercenaries from Kentucky and Mississippi and landed near today's Varadero in 1850. Instead of supporting the invaders, the citizenry notified the Spanish officials. López had to flee ignominiously back to the US. He returned the following year and put up an equally pathetic showing. Among those executed by the Spanish was the nephew of the governor of Kentucky. Not for the last time, the North American press whipped up public sentiment for an invasion of Cuba.

Uncle Sam Stirs

Annexation sentiment in the United States had been spawned by the Louisiana Purchase of 1803. The Mississippi River became the main artery of trade and Cuba's position at the mouth of the Gulf of Mexico took on added strategic importance: the US government was eager to neutralize any threat Cuba posed under the control of hostile powers.

Thus, in 1809 Thomas Jefferson wrote "I candidly confess that I have ever looked upon Cuba as the most interesting addition that can be made to our system of States, the possession of which would give us control over the Gulf of Mexico and the countries and isthmus bordering upon it." In 1808, Jefferson had attempted to purchase Cuba from Spain (he was the first of four presidents to do so). John Quincy Adams thought Cuba a fruit that would ripen until it fell into the lap of the United States. And President James Monroe, writing to Jefferson in 1823, stated that "I have already concurred with you in the sentiment, that too much importance could not be attached to the Island, and that we ought if possible, to incorporate it into our union, availing ourselves of the most favorable moment for it, hoping also it might be done, without a rupture with Spain or any other power."

Sentiment didn't come into it. By 1848, 40% of Cuba's sugar was sold to the US market; manufactures began flowing the other way. Yankees yearned for expanded trade. Thus President James Polk (1845-49) offered Spain US$100 million for Cuba. President Franklin Pierce (1853-57) upped the ante to US$130 million. His successor, James Buchanan, tried twice to purchase Cuba for the same price. But Spain wasn't selling.

The US government, of course, did *not* want to see Cuba gain independence. If the United States couldn't have Cuba, it preferred to see it in the feeble but safe hands of Spain rather than in the hands of more powerful France or England. And an independent Cuba may possibly have been ruled by blacks—a potential stimulus of discontent for the southern slave states. Overnight, the American Civil War changed the equation. With slavery in the US ended, it became impossible for Spain to keep the lid on Cuba. In 1868, the pot boiled over.

The Wars for Independence

The planters of western Cuba were determined to forestall the abolition of slavery in Cuba. But the relatively poor, backward, and nationalistic eastern planters had little to lose. It was expensive to maintain a slave population that was largely redundant for half the year. Their estates were going bankrupt and falling into the hands of rapacious Havana moneylenders. On 10 October 1868, a lawyer, poet, and planter named Carlos Manuel de Céspedes freed the slaves on his plantation at La Demajagua, near Manzanillo, in Oriente. Fellow planters rushed to join him by freeing their slaves, and as the dawn broke over the dewy plantations of Oriente, they raised the *Grito de Yara* (Shout of Yara), the cry of liberty heard throughout the island. Within a week, 1,500 men had flocked to his calling. (Céspedes was eventually elected president; after later being deposed in an internal feud, he was killed in battle in 1873). The Spanish called them the *Mambí*, a Congolese word meaning "despicable." The Mambí quickly captured the town of Bayamo. When Spanish forces arrived to retake the town, the rebels razed it. For the next 10 years, Cuba would be roiled by the bitter First War of Independence in which white and black *criollo* fought side by side against 100,000 troops shipped from Spain.

Guerrilla warfare seized the island. Led by two brilliant generals—one a white, General Maximo Gómez, and the other a *mulatto*, Antonio Macéo —the rebels liberated much of the island and seemed on the verge of victory. However, the movement collapsed and in 1878 the forces signed the Pact of Zanjón. The rebels were given a general amnesty (slaves who had fought with the rebels were also given freedom) in exchange for surrender. The long, bloody war claimed the lives of 250,000 Cubans and 80,000 Spaniards. At least 100,000 Cubans were forced to flee; their lands were expropriated and given to loyalists. Among those arrested was a teenager named José Martí y Pérez. After a brief imprisonment, the young, gifted orator, intellectual, poet, and political leader was exiled to Spain.

Although US President Ulysses Grant (1868-77) was sympathetic to the rebels' cause and shared his predecessors' enthusiasm for seeing Cuba in US hands, he gave the Cuban patriots no assistance, thereby sowing early seeds of anti-American discontent. (To ensure that Spain would be bound by international law to protect US assets, the US government had declined to recognize a state of belligerency.)

The Cuban economy had been devastated by the war, and huge tracts of land lay abandoned. Amid the chaos, North American investors stepped in and bought up the ravaged sugar plantations and many of the sugar mills at ludicrously low rates (by some accounts, as much as US$100 million was invested in the wake of the war). Meanwhile, the Spanish reverted to the same old recipe of tyranny. Independence, the one dignified solution refused the *criollos*, was the cause which united the whole revolutionary population of Cuba.

Martí's Martyrdom

José Martí had been born in Havana in 1853. As a lad of 15 he had startled his mother, reportedly, with the words "To many generations of slaves must succeed one generation of martyrs." Somewhere in his boyish brain he tucked away that foreboding notion. Following his exile to Spain, the journalist and political thinker traveled to the United States, where he settled and through his writings and indefatigable spirit became the acknowledged "apostle" and "intellectual author" of independence. In 1892 he formed the Cuban Revolutionary Party, and from New York, Tampa, Florida, and elsewhere he rallied support for his *compañeros* in Cuba.

Though ill and gaunt, Martí was determined to return to Cuba undercover, wearing his trade-

mark black frock coat and tie. In 1895, Martí joined General Maximo Gómez in the Dominican Republic. Together they sailed to Cuba. On 11 April, they pulled away from their steamer and rowed ashore, landing amid a storm at a village called Playitas, at the eastern end of the island. Martí kissed the Cuban soil he had not seen for 16 years. From here, they linked up with the great Cuban general Antonio Macéo and his ragtag army of blacks, peasants, and landowners.

Barely one month after returning from exile, Martí martyred himself on 19 May 1895, at the age of 42. His motto was, "To die for the fatherland is to live."

Martí's death left Cuba without a spiritual leader. But the Cubans were determined to seize their freedom. Generals Gómez and Macéo led an army of 60,000 the full length of Cuba, smashing Spanish forces en route through guerrilla tactics and occasional face-to-face battles. Macéo's brilliant tactics earned worldwide acclaim until he was finally killed in battle in December 1896 (his father and 10 of his brothers also died for the cause of independence).

After Macéo's death, the struggle degenerated into a destructive guerrilla war of attrition. In a desperate bid to forestall independence, the Spanish governor, Valeriano Weyler—a ruthless general known as The Butcher—began a rural pacification program in which virtually the entire *campesino* population was either slaughtered or herded off their land and into concentration camps called protectorates, where thousands starved to death (the vicious campaign, which claimed the lives of 10% of Cuba's population, was called the *reconcentración*). Weyler erected barbed wire fences, entrenchments, and small forts across the entire width of Cuba. In turn, the rebels torched the sugarcane fields of Oriente and kept them burning until the conflagration licked the suburbs of Havana.

In 1896, Weyler banned exports from Cuba in an attempt to ruin supporters of the Mambí. When, the following year, a more liberal administration took over in Spain, Washington finally forced the Spanish government to recall Weyler (he later stated contemptuously that if he had been given another six months, he would have pacified Cuba).

JOSÉ MARTÍ

He is the most revered figure in Cuban history. His name has been appropriated by the Castro government *and* the fiercely anticommunist exiles in Florida. He is José Martí, avatar of Cuba's independence spirit and the "deological architect of the Cuban Revolution. There is not a single village or town in Cuba that does not have a street, a square or a major building named in his honor.

Martí was born in 1853 in a small house on Calle Paula in Habana Vieja. Martí came from peninsular stock. His father was from Valencia, Spain; his mother was from the Canary Islands. He spent much of his youth in Spain before his parents returned to Cuba. When the War of Independence erupted in 1868, Martí was 15 years old. Already he sympathized with "the cause."

At the age of 16, he published his first newspaper, *La Patria Libre.* He also wrote a letter denouncing a school friend for attending a pro-Spanish rally. The letter was judged to be treasonous, and Martí was sentenced to six-years' imprisonment, including six

months hard labor at the San Lázaro stone quarry in Havana. In 1871, he was exiled to Spain, where he earned a law degree and gravitated to the revolutionary circles then active in Madrid.

In 1878, as part of a general amnesty, He was allowed to return but was then again deported. He traveled through France and, in 1881, to the US, where he settled for the next 14 years with his wife and son, working as a reporter in New York.

The Pen and the Sword

Dressed in his trademark black suit and bow tie, with his thick moustache waxed into pointy tips, Martí devoted more and more of his time to winning independence for Cuba. He wrote poetry heralding the liberation of his homeland during a "time of fervent repose," the years following the Ten Years' War. His writing wedded the rhetoric of nationalism to calls for social justice, fashioning a vision of a free Cuba that broke through class and racial barriers.

Prophetically, Martí's writings are full of invocations to death. It was he who coined the phrase *La Victoria o el Sepulcro* (Victory or the Tomb), which Fidel Castro has turned with great success into a call for *Patria o Muerte* (Patriotism or death).

Martí's voluminous writings are littered with astute critiques of US culture and politics. He despised the expansionist nature of the US, arguing that US ambitions toward Cuba were as dangerous as the rule of Spain. "It is my duty . . . to prevent, through the independence of Cuba, the USA from spreading over the West Indies and falling with added weight upon other lands of Our America. All I have done up to now and shall do hereafter is to that end."

Theory into Action

In 1892, Martí met with leading Cuban exiles and presented his "Fundamentals and Secret Guidelines of the Cuban Revolutionary Party," outlining the goals of the nationalists: independence for Cuba, equality of all Cubans, and establishment of democratic processes. That year, Martí began publishing *Patria.* Through dint of passion and idealism, Martí had established himself as the acknowledged political leader. He melded the various exile factions together, formulated a common program, and managed to integrate the cause of Cuban exile workers into the crusade (they contributed 10% of their earnings to his

tomb of José Martí, Santiago

CHRISTOPHER P. BAKER

(continues on next page)

JOSÉ MARTÍ
(continued)

cause). He founded a revolutionary center, Cuba Libre (Free Cuba), and La Liga de Instrucción, which trained revolutionary fighters.

In 1895, Martí presented the *Manifesto de Montecristi*, outlining the policy for the war of independence that was to be initiated later that year. Martí was named major general of the Armies of Liberation, while General Máximo Gómez was named as supreme commander of the revolutionary forces.

On 11 April 1895, Martí, Gómez and four followers landed at Playitas, in a remote part of eastern Cuba. Moving secretly through the mountains, they gathered supporters and finally linked up with Antonio Maceo and his army of 6,000. The first skirmish with the Spanish occurred at Dos Rios on 19 May 1895. Martí was the first casualty. He had determined on martyrdom and committed sacrificial suicide by riding headlong into the enemy line. Thus, Martí brought the republic to birth "carrying a cadaver around its neck."

THE SPANISH-CUBAN-AMERICAN WAR

The ideal of *Cuba libre!* (Free Cuba!) had genuine support among the US populace, which saw echoes of their own struggle for independence a century earlier. Popular sentiment in the US was stirred by the suffering. United States sugar and business interests also favored intervention. Thus, President William McKinley, seeing his chance to take possession of Cuba—in the name of liberation—entered negotiations to cajole Spain into selling Cuba to end the war. Spain refused.

The public hungered for information about the war, feeding sales of newspapers throughout North America. The *New York World* and *New York Journal* (owned by, respectively, Joseph Pulitzer and William Randolph Hearst) started a race with each other to see which newspaper could first reach one million subscribers. The press took on the job of inflaming Yankee patriotism and fanning war fever based on fabrication and lies. While Hearst's hacks made up stories from Cuba, the magnate himself worked behind the scenes to orchestrate dramatic events. He sent the artist Frederic Remington to Cuba in anticipation of the US's entering the war. At one point Remington wired Hearst: "There will be no war. I wish to return." Hearst hastily replied: "Please remain. You furnish the pictures and I'll furnish the war."

Remember the *Maine*!
Responding to public (and perhaps private) pressure, McKinley sent a warship—the USS

Maine—to Havana, supposedly to protect US citizens living there. On 5 February 1898, the ship mysteriously exploded and sank in Havana harbor, killing 258 people. No one knows whether this was an accident or the work of the Spanish, Cuban nationalists, or, as is thought likely, US agents, but Hearst had his coup and rushed the news out in great red headlines and beating the *World* to the one million mark. He blamed the Spanish, and so did the public. His *New York Journal* coined the phrase "Remember the Maine, to hell with Spain." The paper belabored the jingoistic phrase day after day. The reaction in the US was furious; it was taken for granted that Spain was responsible. The public, egged on by Hearst and Pulitzer, was convinced that might was on the side of right.

Other North Americans were eager to test their mettle, too, especially the army and navy, which hadn't seen action in more than three decades and had modern equipment to put to the test. Theodore Roosevelt, then Assistant Secretary of the Navy, also fanned the flames, seeing the venture as "good for the navy."

Thus, on 25 April 1898, Congress declared war against Spain (US forces also invaded Guam, Puerto Rico, and the Philippines, which they captured in one day). The managing editor of the *World* boasted "Between the *World* and the *Journal,* we barked President McKinley into a war that was none of our business."

The Cavalry Arrives
The US government claimed it was fighting to liberate Cuba. The Cuban General, Máximo Gómez, did not want US troops, however. He

wanted arms and ammunition. The revolutionaries were on the verge of victory and would have undoubtedly won their independence before the close of the century. To placate the Mambí, the Teller Amendment was added to the war declaration. This smokescreen stated that US intentions were to restore peace—"That the United States hereby disclaims any disposition or intention to exercise sovereigny, jurisdiction or control over said island except for pacification thereof, and asserts its determination, when that is accomplished, to leave the government and control of the island to its people."

Cuban freedom fighters soon found themselves forced into the back seat and mostly restricted to manual labor away from the brief fighting, which was restricted to Oriente. The Yanks thought the Cubans a dirty and decrepit lot—most of whom weren't even *white!* "A collection of real tropic savages," reported Hearst journalist Stephen Crane. Where the Mambí did fight, heroically, their part was dismissed, as at the pivotal engagement at San Juan Hill in Santiago de Cuba, where, on 1 July 1898, a cavalry charge ostensibly led by Theodore Roosevelt (who had resigned from government service to volunteer) sealed the war. Spain surrendered her fleet to the US fleet in Santiago harbor on 3 July. On 17 July, Spain surrendered. The Spanish flag was lowered and the Stars and Stripes raised, ending one of the most foolishly run empires in the world. The Secretary of State called it "a splendid little war."

Victors always write the history books. Virtually no credit was given to the years of heroic fighting on the part of the valiant Cubans. In an act of gross arrogance, the US military leaders refused to invite the Mambí to the victory ceremony and parade; the Cuban troops were even ordered to surrender their weapons. The Cuban people have never forgotten the slight; the bitterness still rankles. (It is all the more remarkable that North America should disdain the strength of feeling, having waged its own struggle against English absentee landlordism.)

Cuba ended the century as it had begun—under foreign rule.

Uncle Sam Takes Over

The US government hoped that the Cubans would ask to be admitted to the Union. Opinion in North America was divided. Washington could have annexed Cuba but chose not to. Instead, it "granted" Cuba "independence"—at the end of a short leash.

The US military occupation formally began on 1 January 1899, when 15 infantry regiments, one of engineers and four or artillery arrived to "pacify" Cuba. They would remain for four years. Washington dictated the peace terms embodied

destruction of the US battleship Maine *in Havana Harbor*

JOSEPH BOGGS BEALE

landing of US troops in Cuba

in the Treaty of Paris, signed on 11 April 1899. Even the Cuban Constitution was written by Washington, in 1901, ushering in a period known as the Pseudo-Republic. Rubbing salt in the wound of Cuban sensibilities was a clause called the Platt Amendment, named for Senator Orville H. Platt of Connecticut but written by Elihu Root, Secretary of War. Through it, Uncle Sam acquired the Guantánamo naval base and the right to intervene whenever the US deemed it necessary. Cubans understood that the amendment was an instrument of domination to be applied at Washington's discretion. Although the professed aim was to ensure law and order and stability, the US had actually served to protect its own economic interests and, perhaps unintentionally, the vested interests of the ruling Cuban elite. Even the governor-general, US Army General Leonard Wood, wrote President McKinley that "there is, of course, little or no independence left in Cuba under the Platt Amendment."

The Cuban Congress expressed its dissatisfaction with the Constitution. US officers who spoke no Spanish, had never lived in a hot country, and had no notion of Spanish or Cuban history and ideals found themselves in charge of a tired, starving people and a devastated land wrecked by war.

On Ascencion Day (20 May) 1902, the Stars and Stripes was lowered and the lone-star flag of Cuba, designed by Narciso López, rose into the sunny sky. Havana broke out in a three-day spree of rejoicing. "It's not the republic we dreamed of," said Máximo Gómez. Storm clouds loomed ahead.

THE ERA OF "INDEPENDENCE"

The pseudo-republic was an era of insidious Yankee colonization and domestic acquiescence. Economically, North America held sway over the lives of Cubans through its control of the sugar plantations. Politically, Washington called the shots—and maintained a revolving door to the increasingly corrupt Cuban presidency.

Under General Wood, the US authorities set up schools, started a postal system, established a judiciary and civil service, organized finances, and managed within a few years to eradicate yellow fever in a campaign based on the discovery by a Cuban physician, Dr. Carlos Finlay, that the fever was spread by mosquitoes. "It would have been a poor boon to Cuba to drive the Spaniards out and leave her to care for herself, with two-thirds of her people unable to read and write, and wholly ignorant of the art of self-government," stated Elihu Root.

Washington's intentions seemed at least partly honorable: it firmly wanted to establish a stable, democratic government in the US tradition. The United States installed its first president—Tomás Estrada Palma (the first in a long line of US puppets)—who received his salary, as well as instructions, directly from Washington. Palma, though re-elected in 1905, was too honest and weak to hold greedy politicians in check. Unfortunately, Uncle Sam chose an Anglo-Saxon system unsuited to the Cuban mentality: the centuries of corruption and graft could not be eradicated overnight. (As Machiavelli said, "A corrupted people, having acquired liberty, can maintain it only with the greatest difficulty." After independence, politics "became a cynical game among dishonest men.") Political office was not sought in order to serve the newly independent country but rather to get rich—an idea heartily endorsed by powerful US business interests, who also profited. The US government was constantly influenced to support this or that Cuban who had given, or would give, opportunities to US investors or had borrowed from North American banks. Year by year, Cuba sank more deeply into its old corrupt ways.

The sordid system would last six decades, until a bearded young rebel came down from the mountains to oust the *ancien regime.*

Sinking into Iniquity

Each Cuban president forged new frauds of their own, handed out sinecures (which the Cubans called *botellas*—milk bottles given to babies) to cronies. Through the successive administrations of José Miguel Gómez (1909-13), General Mario Menocal (1913-21), and Alfredo Zayas (1921-25), Cuban politics sank deeper into iniquity.

For the next half-century, Washington discouraged any changes in the status quo; the country's efforts at political and economic reform must first benefit North American investors. "Dollar Diplomacy" it was called (a phrase coined by President Howard Taft). When US economic interests were threatened, Uncle Sam sent in troops. The US landed Marines In 1906 to "restore order" when an armed rebellion attempted to topple the re-elected Estrada regime; in 1912, when black rage exploded into open revolt; and again in 1917, when workers called a general strike (that time, the troops remained until 1923). Dollar diplomacy was blind to the corruption, state violence, and poverty plaguing the country.

A US Colony

The opening years of the Cuban republic were a time of great opportunity for everyone except Cubans—whose economy was in shambles. Agriculture was devastated; industry had been destroyed. Everything was up for grabs. A phenomenal amount of US capital flowed into Cuba. Within the first three years of independence, over 13,000 land speculators and investors descended on Cuba and bought up an estimated 60% of the countryside. In short order, every major industry—tobacco, railroads, utilities, mining, and, above all, sugar—were US owned (the Du Pont estate would grow so enormous it had its own private customs officer). US interests in the sugar industry increased almost overnight from 15% to 75%. Often, land was acquired through legal suits in corrupt or prejudiced courts that robbed tens of thousands of Cuban smallholders of their lands. Cuba had become a giant Monopoly board controlled by Uncle Sam.

The upper classes prospered immensely. The wealthy class kept getting richer, and the mass of poor people kept on struggling to survive.

United States sugar companies bought out small farms and plantations in every direction. Acres of coconut palms, precious forests, and agriculture lands were cut down or plowed up to plant sugar. Up and down the island, tall, brilliant green cane dusted by delicate white blossoms shimmered under the blazing tropical sun.

Since sugar land was so valuable, the allotment for living space was meager. The sugar colonies had no schools, no churches, and no doctors. Although the sugar workers had no other way of earning a living, the sugar companies paid them wages for only half a year. Employment lasted only as long as the dry season—usually until May, when the rains and the downtime began. With no money, a decreased diet, and depressed life, the workers and their families suffered miserably for half the year.

Profits from sugar were so great that Cubans sold out their other properties and poured their money into the Industry. Land that should have produced pineapples, bananas, and yams for the Cubans to eat was planted in sugar to sweeten the desserts of the world. In Havana, rich speculators built great stucco houses and even marble palaces.

The peak of the sugar boom—the "dance of the millions"—lasted from 1915 to 1920, when the price of sugar climbed to 22.5 cents a pound. Then came the crash. By 1921, the price had plummeted to 3.625 cents a pound. In 1924, Cuba produced more than 4.5 million tons of sugar. The next year it produced a million tons more—but the sugar sold for less one cent a pound.

Sugar money had paid for the plush mansions then blossoming in the Vedado district of Havana. The capital city—jewel of the Caribbean—wore a new luster. Nightclubs and casinos had opened. Prostitution was rampant. As Prohibition and a wave of morality swept through the United States, Yankees flocked to Cuba where they wallowed up to their noses in cocaine and sex.

The Machado Epoch

In 1924, president Alfredo Zayas, having made his millions, declined to run for re-election. General Machado y Morales Gerardo, who had cut his teeth as a cattle rustler, stepped into the breach. At first, Machado acted on his promises to construct schools, highways, and a health care system. However, he was also a uniquely corrupt man susceptible to *la mordida* (literally, the bite—bribes), which undercut law and order. In 1928, Machado manipulated a phony election. Although he won, the move triggered a wave of opposition. Machado became a tropical Mussolini, supported by a personal police force of 15,000. His politics was to make himself rich and to protect US investments. His method was to assassinate anyone who opposed his government. Thousands of Cubans were imprisoned, tortured, and executed. Cuba was mired in deep unrest and violence.

When the Great Depression hit, Cuba's one-crop economy was dealt a deathblow, bringing misery throughout the country. Meanwhile, the US had raised its import tariffs on sugar, exacerbating Cuba's plight. The Cuban economy collapsed, and the nation soon disintegrated into mayhem and violent madness. Havana and other cities were swept by random bombings and assassinations. When a radio incorrectly announced that Machado had resigned, thousands of people poured into the streets to celebrate. Machado's henchmen taught them the truth with bullets.

Machado responded to a growing number of hunger marches, strikes, and antigovernment demonstrations with greater repression. The dictator even closed schools and universities and forbade public gatherings.

Machado remained in power only because he was supported by US financial interests. President Calvin Coolidge, of course, thought that "under Machado, Cuba is a sovereign state . . . her people are free, independent, in peace, and enjoying the advantages of democracy." Finally, in the summer of 1933, a general strike brought the whole country to a halt. On 11 August, Machado fled the country—carrying a suitcase full of gold.

Batista Days

Diplomat Sumner Welles, sent to Cuba earlier that summer by Franklin D. Roosevelt, appointed Carlos Manuel de Céspedes (son of the hero of the Ten Years War) as Cuba's provisional president. Within the month he had been overthrown by an amalgam of students (a potent political force) and army officers, including a pivotal 32-year old sergeant named Fulgencio Batista y Zaldivar. Batista was at

GENERAL BATISTA

Fulgencio (he was christened Rubén) Batista y Zaldívar was born out of wedlock and into dire poverty in 1901 at Veguitas, near Banes, a backyard region of Oriente. His father was a sugarfield worker (and the son of an indentured Chinese laborer), his mother black. He enlisted and became a professional soldier and, after learning stenography, was promoted to sergeant.

Batista, an insecure "fiery little bantam of a fella," rose to the top during a *golpe* in 1933, when Fidel Castro was only seven. He became chief of staff of the army and, as such, took over the government. The general brutally suppressed the opposition and began a 25-year tenure as the most powerful man in Cuba. He ruled through a series of puppet presidents before winning the 1940 presidential election himself (Batista was himself a puppet, whose puppeteers lived in Washington).

Batista, who ruled during a period of prosperity, was at first popular with the masses, perhaps because of his lowly origins but also because he enacted progressive social reforms and a new, liberal constitution—and he was blackballed by the elite for being *mulatto*.

In 1944, he retired to Florida, having accummulated US$20 million during his 11-year tenure. Batista missed the limelight, however, and, after working out a deal with the Mafia, returned to Cuba, venal and gluttonous. In March 1952, he pulled off his second coup. The general had come back to power to commit grand larceny hand in hand with the Mob.

At midnight on New Year's Eve 1958, Batista fled with a group of followers. He eventually settled in Spain, where he lived a princely life until his death in 1973. The poor cane-cutter died as one of the world's wealthiest men—he had milked Cuba of almost US$300 million.

Camp Columbia in Havana on 4 September, the day he led other noncommissioned officers in a *golpe* (coup) called the Sergeant's Revolt, which ousted the senior officers. They handed power to a five-man civilian commission that named a leftist university professor, Dr. Ramón Grau San Martín, president.

Grau's slogan was "Cuba for Cuba." When Grau unilaterally revoked the Platt Amendment, the US government refused to recognize him. Grau lasted only four months. His proposed worker's compensation law and regulation of utility rates were far too reformist for Washington. Batista, self-promoted to Colonel and chief of the army, was under no illusions as to the intentions of the United States, which sent 30 naval warships to Cuba as a warning. On 14 January 1931, Batista ousted Grau and seized the reins of power. The upstart sergeant wielded control behind a veil of stooge presidents whom he selected and deposed in quick succession. Batista would have center stage until driven from power in 1959.

Impressed by Batista's fealty to Washington, in 1934 the US agreed to annul the Platt Amendment—with the exception of the clause regarding the Guantánamo naval base. In exchange, they established the Recipocal Trade Agreement, which gave the US total control over Cuba's market. Following promulgation of a new and progressive constitution in 1940, Batista ran for the presidency himself on a progressive platform. Cuban voters gave him a four-year term (1940-44) in what was perhaps the nation's first clean election.

Despite his personal ambitions, Batista displayed relative benevolence and good sense. He maintained enlightened attitudes on elections, civil liberties, public welfare, and workers' rights. The Cuban labor movement attained considerable power during Batista's early tenure. The Cuban Communist Party, founded in 1925, had grown popular among trade unions and played a significant part in the resistance against Machado, who had outlawed the *Partido Comunista de Cuba*. For pragmatic reasons, Batista legalized it, and two leading communists—Juan Marinello and Carlos Rafael Rodríguez—became ministers in his 1940-44 government. (The influence of the Communist Party ebbed and flowed during the next two decades; intriguingly, it opposed Fidel Castro's revolution, and Castro

was never associated with the party until he usurped it following the Revolution.) Batista, however, sold the country short by agreeing to sell the entire 1941 sugar crop to the US for three cents a pound

In the 1944 election, Batista's hand-picked successor lost to Ramón Grau San Martín, the president Batista had deposed. Batista retired to Florida, leaving his country in the hands of a man that Roosevelt had decried as a Communist. Although they were from the professional middle classes, Grau (1944-48) and his democratically elected successor, Carlos Prío Socarrás (1948-52), betrayed the public trust, allowing their administrations to sink into chaos and corruption. Violence again roamed the land. Two rival gangster groups—the Socialist Revolutionary Movement (M.S.R.) and Insurrectional Revolutionary Union (U.I.R.)—ruled the streets (there were 64 political assassinations during Grau's 1944-48 administration). Street demonstrations erupted, organized on behalf of the opposition *Ortodoxo* party led by Senator "Eddy" Chibás, revered for his rare honesty. His public suicide on 5 August 1951 brought together a broad spectrum of Cubans fed up with corruption and gangsterism.

In 1952, Batista again put himself up as a presidential candidate in the forthcoming elections. It soon became clear that he wouldn't win. On 10 March, only three months before the election, he upended the process with a bloodless pre-dawn *golpe*. Batista dissolved the congress and canceled the election. One of the reform-minded candidates for congress whose political ambitions were thwarted by Batista's coup was a dashing young lawyer with a predilection for stylish suits and baseball. His name was Fidel Castro. In 1952, the 25-year-old had risen to great prominence as the most outspoken critic of corrupt government and was being hailed as an incorruptible future president.

To his shame, Harry Truman immediately recognized the infant regime. By recognizing the illegal government, the United States lost any semblance of moral influence. Had Truman acted with greater rectitude there may never have been a Revolution in 1959.

Batista had foresaken his interest in the Cuban people. He had lingered too long in Miami with *mafiosi* and returned spoiled with ambition and greed. His rule was so widely hated that it unified the Cuban people. "The character of the Batista regime in Cuba made a violent popular reaction almost inevitable," concluded a State Department White Paper in 1961.

Gangsters began to take over the hotels and casinos with Batista's blessing (for a cut of the proceeds, of course). As the Batista epoch progressed, US corporations also strengthened their hold on the Cuban economy. Meanwhile, Havana degenerated into an immoral sinkhole where visitors flocked to carouse with "glamorous, lissome Latin lasses, black-eyed señoritas, langorously, enticingly swaying" in the words of one vintage tourist brochure selling "nighttime in Havana." North Americans arrived by plane or aboard the *City of Havana* ferry from Key West to indulge in a few days of sun and sin. They went home happy, unaware that behind the scenes chaos and corruption were rife.

Batista got himself *elected* president in November 1954. But it made no difference. He maintained his empire with a brutal police force. Throughout this sordid period, the United States supported Batista. Neither Washington nor Batista understood the revolutionary forces at work. In the towns, Batista's secret police tortured suspected opposition members and hung them from trees. In the countryside, night fell with a blackness made creepier by the awareness of mysterious forces. "The President's regime was creaking dangerously towards its end," wrote Graham Greene in *Our Man in Havana.*

THE GATHERING STORM

Almost immediately following Batista's *golpe,* Fidel Castro began to plot Batista's denouement. Castro possessed a vision of his place in Cuba's future that seemed pre-ordained. He was also ruthlessly focused. His plan: street protests and legal challenges to the Batista regime (the basis for justifying the planned revolution as a legal act against an illegal regime) and a secret conspiracy simmering underneath. Castro's powerful personality drew the politically disaffected to him. They realized that here was a man who would act. As Tad Szulc wrote, Castro "was now personally at war with the Batista dictatorship . . . Castro would never relent."

After the secret police came to arrest him within 24 hours of Batista's coup, Castro was forced underground. He organized the Movement (later known as the 26th of July Movement) and ran it with military discipline. With a hard core of perhaps one dozen members, the Movement's membership was composed mostly of intellectuals, students, labor-union leadership, and, later, poor workers. Washington's support of Batista ostensibly revolved around the issue of Communism—an entirely irrelevant question with regard to Cuba at the time. Castro had shunned the Communist Party, whose members were automatically excluded from the Movement. Even Castro's Communist brother, Raúl, was kept out for a time. Instead, political instruction centered on the nationalist philosophy of José Martí.

Soon the Movement was an army in training.

The Attack on the Moncada Barracks

Castro, then 26 years old, launched his revolution on 26 July 1953 with an attack on the Moncada barracks in Santiago de Cuba. Castro's plan was to seize arms. A simultaneous attack was planned on Bayamo barracks using 30 men. Since Batista's reinforcements would most likely come from Holguín, Castro figured on blowing up the bridges over the Río Cauto, isolating Oriente Province as a "liberated zone." Meanwhile, other members of the Movement would seize key radio stations and appeal for a national uprising against Batista (Castro's manifesto, called *The Cuban Revolution,* would offer the nation a nine-point plan of salvation).

Castro chose 26 July for the attack because the city would be caught up in Carnival on that day and most of Batista's troops would be away on weekend passes. The rebels relied on surprise, not firepower (they attacked using shotguns and a miscellany of aging rifles and submachine guns). Unfortunately, everything conspired to go wrong the moment the attack began. It quickly collapsed in a hail of bullets, as did the Bayamo attack.

Batista declared a state of emergency. His propaganda machine went to work to convince the nation that the rebels had committed all kinds of atrocities. Unknown to Batista, however, the torture and assassination of 64 rebels who had been captured had been photographed. When the gruesome photos were published, a wave of revulsion swept the land (thousands of Cubans attended a Mass for the dead martyrs). The Catholic hierarchy stepped in and negotiated a guarantee of the lives of any future captives.

Castro was eventually captured by an army detachment whose commander—tall, 53-year-old, black Lieutenant Pedro Sarría—disobeyed orders to kill Castro on sight (Batista later jailed Sarría, but Sarría would go on to become a captain in Fidel's Revolutionary army and a hero of the Revolution). Once in Santiago jail, Fidel was safe from murder because of his enormous public stature. Reporters were even allowed to interview the prisoner, who told them in detail of the rationale for the Moncada attack—a public relations coup that sowed the seeds of future victory. Amazingly, Fidel was allowed to broadcast his story over the national radio to demonstrate to the Cubans how subversive he was ("Imagine the imbecility of these people!" Fidel later said; "At that minute, the second phase of the revolution began").

History Will Absolve Me

Castro, who acted as his own attorney, was sentenced in a sealed court that opened on 21 September 1953 (he scored an instant coup by demanding that his manacles be removed; the chief judge agreed). Castro's goal was to establish the legitimacy of the Moncada attack—it was, he argued, the rebels' *duty* to overthrow the illegal Batista dictatorship. Castro never attempted to defend against the charges leveled at him and his fellow conspirators. He relied solely on attacking Batista's regime, and proudly defended his own actions. When asked who was the "intellectual author" of the attack—in Cuban law, the instigator of an armed assault against the state was as liable as the perpetrator—Castro splendidly answered, "José Martí!")

Gradually, the trial turned as evidence of the brutal tortures mounted. Castro had become the accusing counsel. Batista determined to do away with Fidel. He was held in jail. The court was informed that Castro was ill, but the ever-wily rebel managed to smuggle a letter to court informing the judges that he was perfectly okay and that the jailers were plotting to kill him. The judges moved to protect him.

Castro was sentenced on 16 October in a tiny closed room at the Santiago de Cuba hospital. The prosecutor spoke for two minutes. Castro spoke for two hours in a mesmerizing

oratory in which he devastatingly denounced the Batista regime, citing history's precedents for taking up arms against tyrants, and ending with the words, "Condemn me, it does not matter. History will absolve me!"

Just as the attack on Moncada was a milestone in modern Cuban history, his brilliant defense speech was a watershed that earned him immense national sympathy and legitimacy as the foremost opponent to the dictator. His speech proved that words were mightier than the sword—they became a basic document of the Cuban Revolution, and this call to social justice would become Castro's justification for all future revolutionary acts. He was cheered as he was led away in handcuffs to serve 15 years in jail on the Isle of Pines (now Isla de la Juventud, or Isle of Youth).

Plotting from Prison

Fidel was imprisoned with 25 other companions of the 26 July attack. (José Martí had also been imprisoned on the Isle of Pines, adding to Castro's symbolic association with the original revolutionary hero.) Fidel immediately organized the Abel Santamaría Ideological Academy to teach history, philosophy, political economics, classics, and languages to his fellow revolutionaries. The classes devoured hundreds of books.

Fidel was removed to solitary confinement after leading the prisoners in singing a revolutionary song to goad Batista when the dictator visited the prison in February 1954. Nonetheless, Castro maintained secret communications with fellow inmates, at times using sign language, which they all learned. Fidel even managed to smuggle out of jail the entire text of his "History Will Absolve Me" speech, which he had written using lemon juice as an invisible ink. (Meanwhile, the Cuban courts accepted three lawsuits brought by Castro against the Batista regime.)

The media gave wide coverage to Castro, whose stature increased with each day in jail. A nationwide campaign to free Castro added to his now-lustrous sheen.

In November 1954, Batista won the national presidential election. Though the elections were rigged, Washington quickly embraced the "constitutional" regime. In May 1955, Batista bowed to mounting public pressure and signed an amnesty bill passed by congress. Castro and the Moncada prisoners were free. When the train carrying Fidel reached Havana, he was hoisted aloft by a huge crowd and carried through the streets.

Immediately Castro launched his anti-Batista campaign. Soon, Castro was banned from making public addresses, and newspapers that printed his articles were closed down. Inevitably, Fidel was forced to move constantly for his own safety. On 7 July 1955, he boarded a flight to Mexico. "From trips such as this, one does not return or one returns with the tyranny beheaded at one's feet," he stated in a message printed in the *Bohemia* newspaper.

Castro's Exile

Castro's goal in exile was to prepare a guerrilla army to invade Cuba. Fidel's enthusiasm and optimism were so great that he managed to talk aged revolutionaries such as Alberto Bayo, a hero of the Spanish Civil War, into giving up their careers and businesses to train his nascent army—now known as MR-26-7 *(Movimiento Revolucionario 26 Julio)*—in guerrilla warfare.

In a brilliant coup, Fidel sent a powerful message to the congress of the *Ortodoxo* party, in which he called for the 500 delegates to reject working with Batista through congressional elections and to take the high road—"called revolution." The delegates jumped to their feet chanting "Revolution! Revolution!" Castro had won over the organization. The Communists continued to shun him—the "objective conditions" defined by Karl Marx didn't exist.

Castro also authored the Movement's "Manifesto No. 1 to the People of Cuba," laying out the revolutionary program in detail: "The outlawing of the *latifundia,* distribution of the land among peasant familes . . . The right of the worker to broad participation in profits . . . Drastic decrease in all rents . . . Construction by the state of decent housing to shelter the 400,000 families crowded into filthy single rooms, huts, shacks, and tenements . . . Extension of electricity to the 2,800,000 persons in our rural and suburban sectors who have none . . . Confiscation of all the assets of embezzlers acquired under all past governments . . . " It was a long list.

In July 1955, Castro first met Ernesto "Che" Guevara, an Argentinian doctor, intellectual, and revolutionary. Their destinies merged.

Castro's plan called for a long-term war in both countryside and urban areas (Castro, however, always eschewed terrorism—random violence against the public—as immoral). To raise money for the endeavor, he toured the United States, speechmaking to thousands of Cuban exiles and Yankees alike, inspiring them by invoking Martí's legend. Meanwhile, violent opposition to Batista was mounting in Cuba. Castro remained constant headline news in Havana. In August 1956, he signed the "Mexico Letter" with the Cuban Students' Revolutionary Directorate (DR) to organize armed resistance to Batista's regime ahead of the invasion to establish a revolutionary climate.

When an attempt to purchase a patrol torpedo boat replete with torpedoes and 40-mm cannon failed (the MR-26-7 lost US$20,000 in the transaction), Castro bought a 38-foot-long wooden luxury cruiser to launch his invasion. In the wee hours of 25 November, the *Granma* slipped out of Tuxpán harbor.

The *Granma* Landing

The near-disastrous crossing lasted seven days. Huge swells whipped the boat, and soon the 82 heavily armed men were violently seasick. (The vessel had been designed to carry only 25 people). One engine failed. The boat began to take on water. And the food and water rations ran out; for two days the men had neither. Finally, two days overdue, the boat ran aground in mud at Los Cayuelos, near Niquero in Oriente Province, one mile south of the beach where Castro had planned. The men had to abandon their heavy armaments and supplies and wade ashore through dense mangroves. Che Guevara called it a "shipwreck."

On 2 December 1956, Castro and 81 men were ashore, ready to take on Batista's 40,000-strong armed forces, newly equipped with US armaments. An uprising in Santiago de Cuba, timed to coincide with the planned landings, had failed two days prior, providing Batista with ample warning that an invasion was imminent. Batista was informed of the landing almost as soon as the *Fidelistas* reached dry ground— the *Granma* had been spotted by a passing ship. On 5 December, after a forced march through arduous terrain, the utterly exhausted column halted at a place called Alegría de Pío.

Here they were ambushed by Batista's Rural Guard. The Rebel Army was destroyed. Only 16 men survived, including, remarkably, Castro, Che Guevara, Raúl Castro, Camilo Cienfuegos, and other key leaders. "There was a moment when I was Commander in Chief of myself and two others," Castro later recalled.

THE CUBAN REVOLUTION

On New Year's Day 1957, the Rebel Army was composed of 29 men. Soon peasants began joining the Rebel Army. Castro wasn't proposing a peasant revolution, although guerrilla warfare with peasant support lay at the center of his plan. On 16 January, his modestly armed force struck an army post for the first time since the attack on Moncada.

Batista responded with a ruthless campaign against the local peasantry—torturing and murdering dozens, while B-26 bombers and P-47 fighter planes supplied by the US strafed the Sierra Maestra. Batista managed to alienate the peasantry upon whom Castro's forces relied, while the Rebel Army displayed its kinship with them (they cemented the *guajiros'* support by assisting with the coffee harvest in May 1957).

Much of the Rebel Army's success was due to Celia Sánchez, a middle-class revolutionary who organized the peasant support network that supplied arms, food, and volunteers. It was Sánchez who guided journalist Herbert I. Matthews into the Sierra Maestra in 1957 for his famous interview with Castro that broke like a bombshell in the *New York Times* (24 February, 1957), along with a photo showing the bearded guerrilla leader. Castro managed to fool Matthews into believing that he had many camps, scores of soldiers, and complete mastery of the mountains by putting on a Potemkin theater. "From the look of things, General Batista cannot possibly hope to suppress the Castro revolt," wrote Matthews.

Washington, meanwhile, continued to supply arms and full support to Batista, unaware of the implications of the portentous developments. The US government helped secure Castro's anti-American rage by stupidly awarding the head of Batista's air force a Legion of Merit for its Sierra Maestra campaign. Remarkably, at the same time, the CIA was channeling funds (at least US$50,000) to Castro's Movement! Its clandestine operation is still classified by the US government, and few tidbits have trickled out.

"Jorge is afraid that if the rebels win they'll throw out the Americans and that he'll lose his job before he can get his pension. But I tell him that there'll be more for everyone when they throw that thief out of the palace."

—Letter from Celia to Gustavo
in *Dreaming in Cuban,*
by Cristina García

War in the Cities and Countryside

While the Rebel Army nibbled away at its foes in the mountains, a war of attrition spread throughout the countryside and cities. Sugarcane fields were razed; army posts, police stations, and public utilities were destroyed. On 13 March, an attack on the presidential palace in Havana by the Student's Revolutionary Directorate—acting independently of Castro—failed (35 students died in the attack). Castro, far off in the mountains of Oriente, increasingly found himself in a battle for revolutionary leadership with the Movement's urban wings. Castro considered it the latter's duty to *support* the guerrilla war; the urban revolutionaries felt that they deserved equal say in conducting the fight to oust Batista. On 12 July, Castro committed himself to "free, democratic elections"—the central point of his Sierra Maestra Manifesto, designed to assuage the growing leadership crisis.

By spring, the rebels controlled almost all the mountain regions of Oriente province. The rebel army "was being turned into the cutting edge of the revolutionary process" (the soldiers were "social revolutionaries"). "We didn't speak of Marxism and communism in those days," Castro told biographer Tad Szulc, "but of a social revolution, of a true revolution, of the role of imperialism in our country." Not until several years later did Castro identify his revolution with socialism (Raúl's rebel group, however, was indoctrinated in communist philosophy as part of its guerrilla training). To forestall a deal behind

A PARTIAL SYNOPSIS OF US ANTI-CASTRO ACTIVITY

Dwight Eisenhower; 1959; Triumph of the Cuban Revolution (1 January 1959). Eisenhower orders a CIA campaign to overthrow the Cuban government. Warplanes flying from the US attack sugar mills in Pinar del Río and Camagüey and a passenger train in Las Villas. Battalions of Cuban-Americans are formed, led by ex-Batista army officers; training begins for an invasion of Cuba.

1960; Belgian munitions freighter *Le Coubre* explodes in Havana harbor, killing more than 100 sailors and workers; the CIA is implicated. Training camps set up in Guatemala for the Cuban invasion. Eisenhower cancels sugar-trade agreement with Cuba. Cuba nationalizes US business property; casinos are closed and the US-Cuban Mafia expelled. Eisenhower imposes partial embargo.

John F. Kennedy; 1961; The US breaks diplomatic ties with Cuba. Kennedy imposes travel restrictions to Cuba for US citizens. B-26 bombers piloted by CIA-paid pilots attack Cuba as prelude to Bay of Pigs invasion by 1,200 Cuban exiles. The Cuban militia and army repel the invasion. Castro announces that Cuba is henceforth a socialist state; the Revolution is consolidated. Exodus of disaffected Cubans to US accelerates. Kennedy authorizes Operation Mongoose—a coordinated series of sabotage, propaganda, and paramilitary operations against Cuba.

1962; CIA supplies counterrevolutionary armies in Escambray and Sierra del Rosarios mountains. At US behest, the Organization of American States (OAS) expels Cuba. Kennedy widens the embargo to include foreign products containing Cuban materials; US ports barred to vessels trading with Cuba. Castro turns to the Soviet Union. Soviet missiles deployed in Cuba, spawning the Missile Crisis. U-2 spy plane shot down. Kennedy orders a naval blockade of Cuba and expands the trade embargo.

Lyndon Johnson; 1963-9; CIA continues to sponsor hit-and-run attacks by air and boat. Counterrevolutionary rebels finally defeated. Assassination teams infiltrated into Cuba. CIA plots to kill Castro fail; bombing campaigns initiated in Latin America to discredit Cuba. US Supreme Court overturns travel restraint but rules that US citizens must uphold Treasury Department restrictions on spending money in Cuba.

Richard Nixon; 1969-74; Radical Cuban exile groups begin terrorist campaign. Bombs explode at Cuban embassies in Jamaica, Mexico, Peru, and Spain. Omega 7 claims responsibility for bombings in New Jersey and at the Venezuelan Mission to the U.N.

Gerald Ford; 1974-77; Luciano Nieves, a Cuban exile, is assassinated for advocating dialogue with the Castro government. Cuban-American CIA agent Orlando Bosch founds CORU (United Revolutionary Organization), an umbrella organization for Cuban-exile terrorist groups. Bombings target Cuban embassies, Cubana Airlines' aircraft and offices in New York, Costa Rica, Jamaica, Panama, and Madrid. Bombs in Miami and Portugal kill two Cuban officials. A Cubana Airlines' passenger plane explodes after taking off from Barbados, killing 73 passen-

---

his back, Castro issued a manisfesto affirming the Movement's choice of a respected liberal judge, Manuel Urrutia Lleó, to head a provisional government after Batista's fall. Urrutia promptly left for exile in the US, where he was instrumental in Eisenhower's decision to stop arming Batista publicly (however, Washington kept shipping arms secretly—a fact Castro discovered and which made him furious).

Although he still had only 300 men at arms, on 1 April, Castro declared "total war" on the regime, including the demand that Cubans refuse to pay taxes (an "unpatriotic and coun-

terrevolutionary" action). A general strike was called for 9 April. More than 100 Cubans were killed by police. The strike collapsed and with it the last potency of moderate elements. Castro reorganized the Movement's top command, leaving himself paramount.

Batista met the increasing storm with brutal violence (his henchmen killed almost 20,000 Cubans, far more lives than two years of guerrilla warfare in the Sierras). Finally, he decided to launch an all-out offensive in the Sierra Maestra with 14 battalions and 10,000 men—Operation FF *(Fin de Fidel)*. The 320 or so *Fidelistas*, how-

gers; Orlando Bosch later arrested in Venezuela and charged with the bombing.

Jimmy Carter; 1977-79; Carter lifts travel restrictions to Cuba for US citizens. Omega 7 bombs Cuba's UN Mission, plus New Jersey office of Almacén el Español, a humanitarian organization sending supplies to Cuba; the group later bombs Madison Square Garden to protest presence of Cuban boxers, and Lincoln Center, where Cuban musicians are performing. In 1979, Omega 7 claims responsiblity for bomb attacks that include New York's Kennedy airport, the Cuban Interests Section in Washington, and the Cuban and Soviet Missions to the UN. Omega 7 also claims responsiblity for assassinations of Carlos Muñiz Varela, president of Viajes Varadero, a Puerto Rican travel agency that offers family-reunification trips to Cuba; and of Eulalio José Negrin, who promoted dialogue with the Cuban government. Carter reimposes travel restrictions.

Ronald Reagan; 1981-82; Reagan proposes naval blockade of Cuba. Bombs explode at Mexican consulates in Miami and New York; Cuban exile groups claim responsibility. Cuba's representative to the UN is assassinated. Omega 7 bombs the Venezuelan embassy in Miami to protest imprisonment of Orlando Bosch.

1983; Reagan cancels charter flights between Miami and Havana; orders invasion of Grenada to forestall Cuban influence on Maurice Bishop government (24 Cubans are killed).

1984-88; Bombings and assassinations continue. Congress approves funds for Radio Martí; begins transmitting anti-Castro programs to Cuba. Reagan imposes further restrictions on travel for US citizens.

George Bush; 1989-91; Bush signs the Mack Amendment, making it unlawful for foreign subsidiaries of US companies to trade with Cuba; medicines and food items are now banned. President of Marazul Tours (the only US travel operator with a license to arrange travel to Cuba) is killed by bomb.

1992; Bush signs the Torricelli Cuban Democracy Act further tightening the embargo and putting in effect "Track II," an effort to subvert the Castro government by sponsoring dissidents in Cuba. Bush pardons Orlando Bosch following his extradition to the US. The Cuban-American terrorist organization Alpha 66 attacks tourist resorts in Varadero.

Bill Clinton; 1993-94; Clinton administration grants unofficial trade missions to Cuba, relaxes travel restrictions. Commandos of National Democratic Unity Party invade Cuba by speedboat and kill one Cuban. Disaffected Cubans storm the Peruvian embassy in Havana and demand asylum. Castro permits unrestricted departure, resulting in *balsero* crisis; over 85,000 Cubans leave. Clinton tightens travel restrictions for US citizens. Clinton and Castro sign immigration agreement. US authorities arrest two anti-Castro paramilitary groups for plotting to invade Cuba; both groups are released uncharged. José Basulto, a Bay of Pigs veteran, founds Brothers to the Rescue; Cuban-American pilots violate Cuban airspace to drop subversive literature on Havana.

1996; Two civilian paramilitary aircraft flown by Brothers to the Rescue are shot down by Cuban MiGs in international waters; four Cuban-Americans die. Clinton signs Helms-Burton legislation.

---

ever, beat back the 76-day offensive (Castro broadcast revolutionary and patriotic songs at Batista's army using loudspeakers tied to trees to reduce morale among the government troops) and even captured two tanks and huge quantities of modern weapons. Radio Rebelde broadcast the victories to the rest of the nation from La Plata, Castro's secret headquarters.

In July, Castro and eight leading opposition groups (excluding the communists—Castro decided to co-opt the communists separately) signed the Caracas Pact—an agreement to create a civic coalition and calling on the US to cease all aid to the Batista regime. The writing now on the wall, Washington began negotiations with Castro while maneuvering to keep him from power. In September, Castro—fueled by massive contributions of finances and arms from the Venezuelan government—led an offensive to take Santiago de Cuba. On 30 December, Che Guevara captured Santa Clara. The scent of victory was in the air.

The Revolution Triumphs
Washington prompted Batista to hand over power to a civilian-military junta led by General

Eulogio Cantillo. At midnight on New Year's Eve, Batista and his closest supporters boarded a plane for the Dominican Republic. On 1 January, Cantillo announced his junta. Castro immediately responded over Radio Rebelde, informing the country that "the history of 1898 will not be repeated," an allusion to the usurpation of Cuban independence by US forces. On 2 January, the same day that the Rebel Armies of Camilio Cienfuegos and Che Guevara entered Havana, Castro's army took over Santiago de Cuba. That night he delivered a televised victory speech.

On 3 January 1959, the triumphant guerrilla army began a five-day Romanesque victory march to Havana, with crowds cheering Castro atop a tank, all of it televised to the nation. Finally, he entered Havana and was mobbed by euphoric throngs. That night, 8 January, Castro bathed in spotlights while delivering his victory speech before the nation. Two white doves suddenly appeared, and one miraculously flew down to rest on his shoulders—a stupefying event that fulfilled an Afro-Cuban superstition (doves in Santería mythology represent life) and granted Fidel the protection of the gods. It was "one of those rare, magical moments when cynics are transformed into romantics and romantics into fanatics," wrote photojournalist Lee Lockwood.

Castro—now the "Maximum Leader"—was intent from day one on turning the old social order upside down. He played his cards close to his chest.

Fidel moved cautiously but vigorously to solidify his power under the guise of establishing a pluralist democracy (the first act was a purge that sent thousands of military men and Batista supporters to the firing squad). Although Manuel Urrutia had been named president and a coalition cabinet had been formed, Castro—the real power-holder—immediately set up a "parallel" government behind the scenes. He began secretly negotiating with the Communists, working to co-opt them and build a Marxist-Leninist edifice. Castro recognized that the Cuban people were not yet ready for communism; first he had to prepare public opinion. (Many of his wartime *compadres* who resigned over this issue were jailed for treason). He also had to avoid antagonizing the United States into intervention. Castro began to manipulate Urrutia, first by getting

himself named Prime Minister with power to direct government policy. With that, he had consolidated his *de jure* position as premiere.

Uncle Sam Decides to Oust Castro

Castro had conjured a storm and, like the sorcerer's apprentice, it soon became unclear whether he was directing it or being controlled by it.

Castro—determined to assert Cuba's total independence—feared the possibility that US Marines would steal his revolution as they had stolen independence at the end of the Spanish-Cuban-American War in 1898. He saw conspiracy plots in every move Uncle Sam made. Moreover, an antagonistic relationship between a Castroite Cuba and the United States was inevitable. History pre-ordained it. The Revolution was born when the east-west balance of power was at its zenith, a circumstance that caused the Revolution "to be used as a Cold War weapon and joined it to the side that turned out to be the loser."

There was no way Uncle Sam could tolerate a revolution beyond its control only 90 miles from Florida, especially one that presented ominous potential for US economic and national interests (this was, after all, the nation of which John Foster Dulles said, "The United States doesn't have friends; it only has interests"). Although the US government had recognized the new Cuban government on 4 January 1959 (a recognition that has never been officially withdrawn), barely two months later the National Security Council had determined to oust Castro behind a veil of cooperation and had already authorized the CIA to mount a paramilitary operation.

Just as Washington became obsessed with the Communist issue without understanding or taking into account Cuban nationalism, Castro allowed himself to become obsessed with the United States and its Plattist mentality.

Cuban sovereignty was no longer an issue in which Uncle Sam had a say—a theme that underlay Castro's visit to the United States in March 1959. Vice President Nixon met with Castro and badly misread the Cuban leader (he considered Castro to be controlled by the Communists), with profound implications. Castro disingenuously promised not to expropriate foreign-owned prop-

THE CIA'S DIRTY TRICKS

The CIA's attempts (now defunct) to oust Castro were set in motion by President Eisenhower as early as March 1959. In *Inside the Company: CIA Diary*, ex-CIA agent Philip Agee describes how the dirty-tricks campaign included bombings of public venues meant to discredit Cuba. The agency also invented protest demonstrations, sowed discord in Cuban intelligence by fingering top officials as CIA agents, and even recruited Cuban embassy staff by "dangling stunning beauties . . . exceptionally active in amorous adventures."

The bitter taste left by the CIA's botched Bay of Pigs invasion led to an all-out secret war against Castro, an effort code-named Operation Mongoose, headed by Bobby Kennedy. Mongoose eventually involved 500 case workers handling 3,000 anti-Castro Cubans at an expense of more than $100 million a year.

The CIA's plans read like a James Bond novel . . . or a comedy of errors. Some plots were straightforward, like the attempt to kill Castro with a bazooka. The CIA's Technical Services Division (TSD) was more imaginative. It impregnated a box of cigars with botulism (they were tested on monkeys and "did the job expected of them") and hoped—in vain—to dupe Castro into smoking one. No one knows whether they reached Castro or whether some innocent victim smoked them.

The spooks also tried to damage Castro's image by sprinkling his shoes with thallium salts (a strong depilatory), hoping that his beard would fall out. An-

other box of Castro's favorite cigars was contaminated with a chemical that produced "temporary disorientation."

Eventually, the CIA turned to the Mob. It hired assassins hand-picked by Johnny Rosselli, who had run the syndicate's Sans Souci casino in Havana. The killers were on both the FBI's 10-most-wanted-criminals list and Bobby Kennedy's target list of organized crime figures. The marksmen disguised as Marxmen didn't fool Castro, who correctly assumed the CIA would hire assassins, whom he considered inefficient (an assassin "does not want to die. He's waiting for money, so he takes care of himself"). Several assassins were caught and executed.

Meanwhile, defoliants were dropped on Cuba, canefields set ablaze, Santiago de Cuba's oil refinery was attacked, Havana's El Encanto department store blown up (along with a Cubana Aviation plane, killing all 82 passengers), and terrorist organizations such as Operation 40 were funded and armed.

All this, of course, backfired miserably. The secret war to oust Castro caused the Russians to increase their military commitment to Cuba. In the end it provoked the missile crisis, bringing the world to the brink of nuclear disaster.

Havana's **Museo of the Ministry of the Interior,** Avenida 5ta y Calle 14, is dedicated to the inept deeds of the CIA. Also check out *CIA Targets Fidel. The Secret Assassination Report* (Ocean Press, 1996).

erty and repeated the mantra, "We are not Communists." He also affirmed that elections would *follow* "democracy," which he publicly defined as when all Cubans were employed, well fed, well educated, and healthy. "Real democracy is not possible for hungry people," he said. Though treated cautiously by Washington, Castro received adulation from US crowds.

Let the Reforms Begin!
On 6 March 1959, all rents in Cuba were reduced by 50%. Two months later, Cuba enacted an Agrarian Reform Law (acclaimed by the U.N. as "an example to follow"). The iniquitous *latifundia* (large estates) system was toppled. The law established 966 acres as the maximum permissible holding (even one-half of the Castro

family's 1,920 acres were seized, along with 24,000 acres that the Castros rented from adjoining US-owned sugar estates). To achieve it, Castro created the National Institute of Agrarian Reform, or INRA, which became an immensely powerful political tool headed by the rebel army.

The agrarian reform significantly upped the ante in the tensions between Cuba and Washington. It proved a direct threat to US property interests. The interests of Spanish, British, French, Canadian, and Dutch citizens were all affected. Over time, all claims with those governments were settled through bilateral agreements. Everyone who had their lands expropriated was offered payment with government bonds paying 4.5% interest.

The Cuban peasants were ecstatic at the reforms (many would be less so a few years later, when a second Agrarian Reform transferred all tracts over 67 hectares to the state). Understandably, however, Miami received a flood of unhappy exiles. At first, these were composed of corrupt elements escaping prosecution—pimps, politicos, thugs, assassins, henchmen, political hacks and their accomplices, mafiosi, and the thousands of underlings that support a corrupt regime. As the reforms extended to affect the upper and middle classes, they, too, began to make the 90-mile journey to Florida. The trickle turned into a flood. About 250,000 Cubans left by 1963, most of them white, urban professionals—doctors, teachers, engineers, technicians, businesspeople, and others with entrepreneurial skills. (As Castro's Revolution turned blatantly communist, many of his revolutionary cohorts also began to desert him. Later, intellectuals and homosexuals were persecuted and they, too, joined the flood.)

On 13 July 1959, President Utturia denounced the growing communist trend. Castro resigned as prime minister, then played a typically brilliant gambit. Castro understood that the key to the revolution was Cuban sentiment. At the time of Uturria's resignation, Castro had arranged for peasants to be brought to Havana from all over Cuba to celebrate the anniversary of the attack on Moncada. Castro then appeared on television and denounced Utturia, selling the Revolution through direct appeals to the masses. The streets of Havana erupted in calls for the President's resignation and pleas for Castro's return. He had carried out the world's first coup d'etat by TV! On 1 May 1960, Castro defaulted on his promise to hold elections within a year. The "people," he proclaimed, had declared them unnecessary, rationalizing the suspension of the Constitution and refusal to seek a popular mandate.

Into Soviet Orbit

The Kremlin had shared the Cuban Communists' views that Castro was his own man. He was too unreliable. By 1960, however, Cuba seemed like a perfect strategic asset. Castro obviously needed the Soviets to survive in the face of growing US antagonism. So Castro and Kruschev signed a pact. It is unclear, however, whether Castro fully understood the geopolitical consequences of flirting with the Soviet bear.

The emerging Havana-Moscow axis chilled Washington. Ever fearful of a US invasion and unsure as yet of the depth of Soviet assistance, Castro had decided to make the peasantry the basis of Cuba's defense. Hence, he initiated a massive militia training program, while emissaries began to purchase arms overseas. Although the US government pressured the Europeans not to sell arms to Cuba, the first shipment arrived from Belgium on 4 March 1960 aboard the French ship *Le Coubre*. One week later, the steamship exploded in Havana harbor with 700 tons of arms and munitions still in the hold. Over 82 Cubans were killed. No one claimed responsibility, but the CIA is considered the culprit. If true, the CIA had managed to rally the Cuban people around Castro at a time when he was facing increasing domestic opposition.

During the funeral ceremony for the victims, Castro uttered the rallying cry that would later become the Revolution's supreme motto: ¡Patria o muerte! Recalls Nobel Laureate Gabriel García Márquez:

"The level of social saturation was so great that there was not a place or a moment when you did not come across that rallying cry of anger, written on everything from the cloth shades on the sugar mills to the bottom margin of official documents. And it was repeated endlessly for days and months on radio and television stations until it was incorporated into the very essence of Cuban life."

When Soviet oil began to arrive in May 1960, US-owned refineries (under direct pressure from Washington) refused to refine it. In response, the Cuban government took the refineries over. The United States then hit Cuba where it hurt most: in July, President Eisenhower refused to honor a purchase agreement for Cuban sugar. Cuba's biggest market for virtually its entire source of income had slammed the door. Washington couldn't have played more perfectly into the hands of the Soviet Union, which happily announced that it would purchase the entire Cuban sugar stock.

Hit with Eisenhower's right cross, Castro replied with a left hook: he nationalized *all* Yankee property, including 36 sugar mills, two utility companies, and two nickel mines. In October, the Eisenhower administration banned exports to Cuba. (In March 1961, President Kennedy extended the embargo to include Cuban imports—the beginning of a trade embargo that is still in effect.)

By slamming the door to Cuban sugar and American goods, the US had severed Cuba's umbilical cord. The island faced economic collapse. During that period of intense Cold War, there were only two routes for underdeveloped nations. One way led West, the other East. Lock one door and there ceases to be a choice. "That's stupid, and it's a result of the howls of zealous anticommunists in the United States," said Kruschev. "Castro will have to gravitate to us like an iron filing to a magnet."

Once the fateful step had been taken, Cuba's future was sealed. To give up Soviet assistance would condemn the island again to the domination of the United States and the Revolution to failure.

The Counterrevolution

Meanwhile, internal opposition to Castro was growing. Bands of counterrevolutionary guerrillas had set up a front in the Sierra del Escambray with the backing of the CIA. Castro, with his highly efficient intelligence operation, knew about the CIA's secret plans for an invasion of Cuba by Cuban exiles and correctly figured that the invading force would attempt to link up with these groups. In mid-1960, Castro began to suppress the independent press. He also established the Committees for the Defense of the Revolution (CDRs)—a countrywide information network for "collective vigilance."

Uncle Sam couldn't resist the urge to depose Castro. It's easy to understand why. The Iron Curtain was an impenetrable reality in 1961. The Cold War was part of the climate, and Cuba was embracing the Soviet Bear.

On 31 December 1960, Castro ordered a general mobilization to defend Cuba against military attack. When President Kennedy banned travel by US citizens to Cuba, Castro knew the invasion was imminent. Since any invasion would rely on local support, Cuba's State Security began a nationwide sweep against suspected counterrevolutionaries (about 30,000 suspects

were arrested in Havana alone; many more were arrested in the wake of the invasion).

Kennedy (who in 1960 had recognized in his book *The Strategy of Peace* that "Castro is part of the legacy of [Simón] Bolívar [and] . . . of that earlier revolution which won its war against Spain but left largely untouched the indigenous feudal order") said, "Our objection is not to the Cuban revolution. It is to the fact that Castro has turned it over to the Communists." In January 1961, the Kennedy administration broke diplomatic ties with Cuba. Kennedy pressured Latin American governments to follow suit through the Alliance for Progress, using the carrot and stick (the promise of US$25 billion in aid, and the threat of taking it away). Every Latin American country except Mexico fell in line.

The Bay of Pigs Fiasco

President Kennedy was assured that the Cuban people would rise up in arms. They did, and within 72 hours they had defeated the CIA-backed invasion at the Bay of Pigs on 17 April 1961.

Senator J. William Fulbright, chairman of the Senate Foreign Relations Committee, had warned, "To give this activity even covert support is of a piece with the hypocrisy and cynicism for which the United States is constantly denouncing the Soviet Union . . . The point will not be lost on the rest of the world." It wasn't. The Bay of Pigs was a smashing public relations coup for Cuba. Arthur Schlesinger predicted that it would "fix a malevolent image of the new Administration in the minds of millions."

The invasion brought a new sense of unity to Cuba. United States ambassador Bonsal declared that the Bay of Pigs "consolidated Castro's regime and was a determining factor in giving it the long life it has enjoyed." As Castro admitted: "Our Marxist-Leninist party was really born at Girón; from that date on, socialism became cemented forever with the blood of our workers, peasants, and students." US politicians still can't seem to understand what has always been clear to Castro: that the threat of external danger strengthens the Revolution because of the powerful impact of nationalism on popular reactions.

The debacle not only solidified Castro's tenure but also provoked a repressive housecleaning of anyone thought to be too indepen-

sign proclaiming
"Socialism or Death"
in front of US army
base at Guantanamo

CHRISTOPHER P. BAKER

dent or deviant. As Castro saw it, you were either for the Revolution or against it. By 1965, at least 20,000 political prisoners—including homosexuals, practicing Catholics, and other "social deviants"—toiled in labor camps or languished in jails.

The Cuban Missile Crisis

The Bay of Pigs fiasco also unquestionably led to the Cuban missile crisis in October 1962. If the US had not been thoroughly defeated by Cuban forces on the beaches in 1961, Nikita Kruschev almost certainly would not have dared to precipitate the crisis.

On 1 December 1961, Castro informed Cuba and the world that Cuba was officially a Marxist-Leninist state. The news was a bombshell to the Kennedy administration, which in March 1962 launched Operation Mongoose—a six-phase program to oust Castro by instigating an open revolt (400 CIA agents were assigned full-time to the operation in Washington) and any other means possible.

Kennedy's threat to do away with socialist Cuba virtually obliged Fidel (who, ironically, has always admired Kennedy and still holds him in the highest esteem) to ask the Soviets for rockets to defend Cuba in the event of a US invasion. The Soviets were pleased to assist. In August, Soviet personnel and MiG fighter-bombers began to arrive. Kennedy had warned the Soviets that the US would not tolerate the installation of missiles. Kruschev promised

Kennedy that no "offensive weapons" were being supplied to Cuba. His deceit had near-calamitous consequences.

The crisis not only brought the world to the brink of a nuclear holocaust; it was a black mark for Castro in the eyes of much of the rest of the world. However, to Cubans, Castro personified the heroic confrontation with Yankee imperialism.

Castro had correctly calculated that the threat of nuclear conflict could save him from a nonnuclear attack. The crisis had ended with a guarantee from Kennedy that the US would not invade Cuba (though there is no public record of an *explicit* commitment by Kennedy). Castro was now free to move forward with his socialist revolution.

MAKING THE REVOLUTION

"The real question," said Sen. J. W. Fulbright in 1961, "is whether Castro can in fact succeed in providing a better life for the Cuban people."

Castro's government poured its heart and soul into improving the lot of the Cuban people. First came health and education, where instant gains could be seen. Castro, for example, dubbed 1961 the Year of Education. On the eve of the Revolution, 43% of the population was illiterate according to government statistics (other sources suggest that as many as 80% of the population was literate, however) and half a million Cuban children went without school. In 1960, "literacy brigades" were formed of university stu-

THE CUBAN MISSILE CRISIS

The Cuban Missile Crisis, which Cubans refer to as the Caribbean Crisis, was the result of the escalating tensions of the deepening Cold War. The Soviet Union felt severely threatened by the American deployment of intermediate-range ballistic missiles on the Turkish border with the USSR. To the Soviets, the Bay of Pigs fiasco provided an opening for them to establish bases at equally close range to the US, which could then be used as bargaining chips for a reduction of US bases in Turkey.

Castro feared that the US was planning to invade Cuba. Thus, the Soviets told him they had intelligence confirming his fears. Fidel accordingly requested "strategic defensive weapons." The Soviets began their military build-up in Cuba in early 1962, then pressured the Cuban government to formally request that the Soviet Union install nuclear missiles.

Cuban ports were closed and a curfew enacted while the missiles were brought in. They were a public secret—everyone knew, including Cubans leaving the island for Florida. Soon enough, on 14 October, a U-2 spy plane over western Cuba discovered missile sites. President Kennedy demanded that they be removed. Kruschev refused.

On October 22, Kennedy ordered the US military to go from DefCon (Defense Condition) 5 to DefCon 3. That night, Kennedy went on national TV and announced, "I have directed . . . initial steps to be taken immediately for a strict quarantine on all offensive military equipment . . . . It shall be the policy of this nation to regard any nuclear missile launched from Cuba as an attack by the Soviet Union on the United States, requiring full retaliatory response on the Soviet Union."

As he began speaking, 54 Strategic Air Command (SAC) bombers took to the air, Polaris submarines put to sea, and the SAC prepared 136 Atlas and Titan ICBMs for firing. A US naval task force set out to intercept Soviet vessels and blockade Cuba. That day, *Revolución* published the banner headline *US Prepares Invasion Of Cuba*.

A volatile exchange of messages between Kennedy and Khruschev followed. Tensions mounted. On October 24, the US military went to DefCon 2—for the first and only time in history. The two superpowers verged on full-scale nuclear war.

Rogue Elephants

Although Kennedy was unaware of it, Thomas Powers, commander of SAC, had the "authority [granted

by Curtis LeMay, USAF Chief of Staff] to order retaliatory attack . . . if time or circumstance would not permit a decision by the President." Missiles in 1962 did not have the locking and security mechanisms of modern times, and such an unauthorized launch was entirely feasible.

While Kennedy was looking at the regional implications, Powers and LeMay were thinking of—and apparently hoping for—a preemptive war. Powers and LeMay knew that the US and USSR were moving toward a policy of mutual deterrence based on a pact of "no first-strike," a policy the two figures publicly abhorred. Their missiles would then be a "wasting asset." They pushed Kennedy to bomb Cuba and take out the missiles, believing the Soviets wouldn't dare to respond (at the time, the USSR had only 44 ICBMs and 155 heavy bombers, compared to the US's 156 ICBMs, 144 Polaris submarine-launched missiles, and 1,300 strategic bombers).

At the height of the crisis, on 26 October, Powers ordered an unsanctioned and potentially cataclysmic launch of an ICBM from Vandenburg Air Force Base. Although it was launched across the Pacific and hit the missile test range in Kwajalein atoll in the Marshall Islands, it was still a deliberate provocation. After Khruschev complained that U-2 spy planes flying over Siberia "could be easily taken for a nuclear bomber, which might push us to a fateful step," Powers ordered SAC bombers to deliberately fly past their turnaround points into Soviet airspace. They were recalled at the eleventh hour when Kruschev relented and ordered the missiles removed.

Rogue President

Fidel—always the gambler—may have been equally reckless. According to Carlos Franquí, editor of *Revolución* at the time, Fidel "drove to one of the Russian rocket bases, where the Soviet generals took him on a tour [the missile sites were Russian territory]. . . . At that moment, an American U-2 appeared on a radar screen, flying low over the island. . . . The Russians showed him the ground-to-air missiles and said that with a push of a button, the plane would be blown out of the sky.

"Which button?" Fidel reportedly asked.

"This one," a general replied.

At that, says Franquí, "Fidel pushed it and the rocket brought down the U-2. Anderson, the American pilot, was the only casualty in that war. The

(continues on next page)

THE CUBAN MISSILE CRISIS
(continued)

Russians were flabbergasted, but Fidel simply said, 'Well, now we'll see if there's a war or not.'"

Castro has vigorously denied that he (or any Cuban) had shot down the U-2 on 27 October. "It is still a mystery how it happened," he claims.

What If . . . ?
The majority of Cubans remained on combat alert for a month, prepared to face down the atomic bomb with rifles. "A New York telephone operator, at that time, told a Cuban colleague that people in the United States were quite alarmed over what might occur," recalls Nobel Laureate Gabriel García Márquez. "'We, on the other hand, are quite calm,' replied the Cuban operator. 'After all, the atomic bomb doesn't hurt.'" Maurice Halperin, in *Return to Havana*, recalls living in Havana in October 1962: "Unbelievably, the popular mood was defiance. '¡Patria o Muerte!'

Fidel shouted, and the masses seemed almost eager to take on the Yankees. There was an air of celebration in the city . . . Havana was throbbing."

A conference sponsored by the Center for Foreign Policy Development at Brown University and held in Havana in January 1992, revealed that the Soviets had 45 nuclear missiles readily deployable in Cuba, including nine tactical missiles to be used at the discretion of Soviet field commanders in the event of a US invasion of the island. The US was by then fully mobilized for invasion. Once the invasion began, Soviet generals would have repelled it with the nine tactical missiles, which in turn would have spurred a US nuclear strike against the Soviet Union. (Or maybe not; Franquí, writing in 1984, made the remarkable claim that the Russians never tried to run the nuclear warheads through the US blockade and, therefore, the missiles were entirely harmless.)

---

dents and high school seniors, who left the cities and fanned out over the countryside with the goal of teaching every single Cuban to read and write. Within two years, the regime had added 10,000 classrooms. By the end of its first decade, the number of elementary schools had nearly doubled, from 7,567 in 1958 to 14,753 in 1968. The number of teachers had more than tripled, from 21,806 to 68,583.

Cuba had a huge middle class spread throughout the island (constituting between one-quarter and one-third of the population). Shops were full of produce cheap enough for mass consumption. The island's per capita rankings for automobiles, literacy, and infant mortality (32 per 1,000 live births) suggest that it was comparatively advanced in socioeconomic terms. But five million Cubans also lived without light, water, or sewage. Poverty was endemic, and tens of thousands of Habaneros lived by begging and prostitution. Castro set up special schools for the indigent, the blind, deaf, and mute, and ex-prostitutes. Electricity, gas, and public transport fees were dramatically lowered, as were rents and other fees. Price controls were instituted on goods sold on the free market. The government poured money into health care. And the Revolution brought unparalleled gains in terms of racism and social relations.

Unfortunately, Cuba's far-reaching social programs had a price tag that the national economy could not support. Cuba's infant socialism was living off the fat accumulated by Cuban capitalism.

Mismanaging the Economy
The young revolutionaries badly mismanaged the Cuban economy, swinging this way and that as Castro capriciously tacked between Soviet dictate and misguided personal whim. In 1960, Castro had created JUCEPLAN, a central planning agency modeled on the Soviet's GOSPLAN. Few of its concepts were given a chance to mature—Fidel kept jumping in. In confusedly searching for "truly original socialism," Castro committed economic errors that were worsened by bureaucratic mismanagement and abrupt reversals in direction. Sound economic decisions were sacrificed to revolutionary principles intended to advance the power of the state over private initiative. Che Guevara, Minister of Industry, sought to replace trained managers with communist cadres and market forces with "moral incentives."

The awesome brain drain, a lack of foreign exchange, CIA sabotage, bad administration, lack of economic incentives, and naive policy all conspired to reduce production. Gradually, inventories of imported goods and cash at hand were exhausted. As machinery wore down or broke down, no replacements could be ordered from the United States because of the trade ban enacted in 1961. Raw materials could not be bought. Soon the economy was in appalling shape. In 1962, rationing was introduced. The black market began to blossom.

Sugar was a bitter reminder of US imperialism; monoculture was held to blame for many of Cuba's ills. Castro and Che Guevara decided to abandon a sugar-based economy and industrialize. When the attempt to diversify away from sugar failed, Castro switched tack and mobilized the entire workforce to achieve a record sugar harvest: 10 million tons a year by 1970 (the all-time previous record was only 6.7 million tons). To achieve the goal, the country went onto a war footing. Tens of thousands of inexperienced "voluntary" workers left their jobs in the cities and headed to the countryside. Holidays were abolished. Every inch of arable land was turned over to sugar in the quest for a Pyrrhic victory. Castro was everywhere, leading the charge (one journalist likened him to the overseer of a huge cane plantation, "sticking his Hellenic nose into everything and enjoying it. Power is fun, and if it is absolute, it is absolute fun").

Nonetheless, the effort was a failure: only 8.5 million tons was harvested. And the economy was left in chaos; production elsewhere had been severely disrupted and output declined. (Castro blamed technical reasons for the mammoth failure. Unable to accept his blunder, he repeated the same mistake with other products, notably milk.) Cuba was kept afloat by massive amounts of Soviet aid.

By 1968, the Cuban economy was coming apart at the seams. To make matters worse, that year Castro nationalized the entire retail trade still in private hands. More than 58,000 businesses—from corner cafés and ice cream vendors to auto mechanics—were eliminated in the "Great Revolutionary Offensive," part of the plan to create the "New Man." As a result, even the most basic items disappeared from the shelves. Rationing became more severe.

Again, the Soviets saved the day. Bit by bit, Castro was forced to follow Soviet dictates (the relationship was always hot and cold; Castro's iconoclastic nature rubbed the Kremlin the wrong way). In 1976, Cuba joined COMECON, the Soviet bloc's economic community. Cuba would henceforth supply sugar to the European socialist nations in exchange for whatever the island needed; sugar was even rationed in Cuba to meet obligations! Castro's zealous experimentations gave way to a period of enforced pragmatism.

That year, the First Communist Party Congress initialed a new constitution that recognized Marxist-Leninism as the state's official ideology, and the party as the sole representative of the people. Fidel Castro's tenure as head of state was written into the Constitution.

Adventurism Abroad

The Cuban economy limped along, with shortfalls made up by the Eastern bloc. Cuba received about half of all Soviet economic and military aid to the Third World. Oil, consumer goods, and foodstuffs were plentiful. Things looked rosier and rosier.

Meanwhile, Castro could give more attention to world affairs. He was committed to exporting his Revolution abroad. This adventurism rankled the more cautious Soviet leadership, which tried to bring Castro to heel. But the US invasion of the Dominican Republic in April 1965 to aid the rightist generals was a splendid propaganda coup for Fidel's "anti-imperialism" adventures.

Thus, at the Organization of Latin American Solidarity conference in Havana in August 1967, Castro launched his Fifth International, to "create as many Vietnams as possible" in defiance of the Soviet Union's policy of co-existence with the US. Said Castro: "The duty of every revolutionary is to make the Revolution." Communist parties worldwide denounced the Fidelista line. Cuban troops had already been sent to countries as far afield as Algeria and Zaire. Soon, revolutionary fighters from Angola, Mozambique, and elsewhere were being trained at secret camps on Isla de la Juventud.

By the 1970s, Castro, aspiring to Third World leadership, was shipping troops abroad in a mission of "near Napoleonic dimensions." In Ethiopia and Angola, Cuban troops fought alongside Marxist troops in the civil wars against "racist imperialism" (in Ethiopia they shored up a ruthless regime), and in Nicaragua, Cubans trained, armed, and supported the Sandinista guerrillas that eventually toppled the Somoza regime.

THE IMPLACABLE CUBAN~AMERICANS

"We see, then, how vain the faith and promises of men are who are exiles from their own country. . . . They naturally believe many things that are not true, and add many others on purpose. . . . They will fill you with hopes to that degree that if you attempt to act upon them you will incur a fruitless expense, or engage in an undertaking that will involve in your ruin. . . . A Prince therefore should be slow in undertaking any enterprise upon the representations of exiles, for he will generally gain nothing by it but shame and serious injury."
—Niccoló Machiavelli, *Discourses*

There were over 737,000 Cuban-born US citizens in summer 1995, concentrated in Dade County, Florida (over 500,000), and New Jersey. Their capital is Miami, just 140 miles from Havana—a distance protracted by a generation of despair, hubris, and bile. Their ambition, entrepreneurship, and investments have made Miami the gateway to Latin America. Along the way, Cuban-Americans have moved up through the political hierarchy and gained an inordinate amount of political clout.

The majority of Cuban-Americans fled Cuba shortly after the Revolution, where they formed the white wealthy and middle classes. (Later migrants, still predominantly white, were mostly motivated by that dream of immigrants to the USA—the hope of a better life—rather than political considerations.) Most still dream of a Cuba that no longer exists—and maybe never did exist in the way they recall it. Many have grown militant with distance and time, cultivating delusion "like hothouse orchids," in the words of Cristina Garcia. Nonetheless, fully 70% of Miami Cubans say they will never return to Cuba.

Cuban Americans are torn over the best approach to dealing with Fidel Castro. Moderates, such as *Cambio Cubano* (Cubans for Change) and the **Cuban Committee for Democracy,** want to see a measured policy, including direct negotiations with Castro to encourage phased-in democracy and avoid a period of anarchy and civil war. These centrist groups have limited influence however; they cannot get Washington's ear because the right wing has out-organized and outspent them.

The politically implacable **Cuban-American National Foundation** (CANF), the largest and by far the richest and most powerful of the exile groups, considers itself the Cuban government in exile and is more or less treated as such by US administrations (it was created by the Reagan administration). Critics portray the CANF as vengeful and greedy extremists intoxicated by a cult of nostalgia and drunk on a dream of "liberating" Cuba. Many of the CANF's well-heeled leaders (who come from the cream of Miami's Cuban-American elite) have ties to the Batista regime.

CANF's powerful founder and chairman, Jorge Mas Canosa, makes no secret of his desire to be president of post-Castro Cuba. Mas Canosa, who participated in the Bay of Pigs invasion and whose father was a major in Batista's army, is listed as the sixth-richest Latino in the United States. The *Miami Herald* has called Mas Canosa "Cuba's dictator-in-waiting."

The CANF has campaigned relentlessly for a US military intervention and for an embargo meant to wreak havoc on the Cuban people in the hope that they will finally rise up in arms against Castro (they also have let foreign corporations doing business with Castro's Cuba know that they will no longer be welcome in their post-Castro Cuba). The hope is for a bloody revolution or a total collapse of the country, reminding one of Saint-Just, Robespierre's disciple, who thought the only way to build the republic was to destroy everything opposing it.

Cuba became an international power. More than 377,000 Cuban troops were rotated through Angola during the 15-year war (the last troops came home in May 1991), proportionally far greater than the US troop commitment in Vietnam. Tens of thousands of Cuban doctors and technical specialists were also sent to more than two dozen Third World countries to assist in development (more than 50,000 Cuban civilians were rotated through Angola alone). While Cubans were, and still are, highly critical of the military efforts abroad, Castro, who devoted much time to the cause of development, was lauded throughout the Third World (in 1979 he was named Chairman of the Nonaligned Movement).

About the time that Castro launched his African initiatives, Washington was looking at rap-

Hardball Politics

Contemporary US policy toward Cuba is largely shaped by this hard-nosed constituency. Republicans have come to rely on partisan support from CANF and on generous campaign contributions from the foundation's millionaires (between 1981 and 1996, the CANF contributed over US$1 million to congressional candidates, including key Democrats). Democrats attempt to win their votes by appearing more anti-Castro than the Republicans. For example, during the 1992 presidential campaign, Clinton managed to outflank Bush by endorsing proposed legislation to tighten the trade embargo; grateful Cuban Americans chipped in with US$125,000. Bush, who had withheld support for the Torricelli bill, swiftly changed his tune.

Polls show that more than 40% of Cuban-Americans want open dialogue with Cuba. However, the CANF is dead-set against any wide-ranging US dialogue and works hard to keep Washington from cutting a deal with Castro.

Extremist right-wing Cuban-American groups regularly intimidate individuals who favor a softer approach to the Castro government. According to a report in May 1996 by the New York-based Human Rights Watch, the atmosphere for dissenting views "remains marked by fear and danger." Anti Castro terrorist groups such as Omega 7 and, more recently, Alpha 66 have been responsible for a spate of bombings and assassinations in the United States since the 1970s. Anyone opposing *la causa* (the cause—i.e., the overthrow of Fidel Castro) is a potential target.

The political power of the Cuban-American lobby is such that prosecutions are rarely made. Charges are routinely dropped, and Human Rights Watch charged Dade County's Cuban-American government officials and police with being "derelict" in prosecuting offenders.

The View from Cuba

The Cuban government has been reaching out to exiles in recent years. In 1994, it initiated the first of several conferences on democracy in Havana for exiles to examine measures for normalizing relations. Wooing the exile community has become one of Castro's top priorities: *gusanos* (worms) have become *mariposas* (butterflies), and Cuba's Foreign Ministry has even launched a new quarterly magazine, *Correo de Cuba* (Mail from Cuba) for Cubans living abroad.

Castro has been very successful in convincing Cubans that the extreme Batistiano element in Miami means trouble if they ever return. Cubans are fully versed in the antics of the CANF and blame them for the embargo that worsens their lives. No Cubans see Mas Canosa defending free health or education or the interests of the elderly and poor.

Many Cubans also fear that their homes and land will be sold from under them if the ultra-conservative exiles ever return to power. It's a well-founded fear. Many Cuban-Americans are determined to seize back what they left behind (they maintain a register of properties) and seem eager to make money from selling off Cuban assets; a favorite T-shirt among Cuban-Americans in Miami shows the Malecón lined with fast-food joints.

In Cuba, the exiles are remembered as the top rung of a class structure that left a racist society and carried their prejudice with them (CANF's 50 directors are all white). The wealthy who left Cuba were almost entirely white, while about 58% of Cuba's 11 million people are black, mulatto, or some shade in between.

For an intriguing, satirical look at the "mythomania" of the Miami exile community, read Roberto Fernandez's *Raining Backwards.* I also recommend *Thicker Than Blood,* by Sandra Levison (Henry Holt & Co., 1997), which tells how Cuban families torn apart after the Revolution have evolved separate identities; and Cristina García's *Dreaming in Cuban* is a splendid, almost surreal novel on a similar theme.

prochement with Cuba, beginning with the Ford administration, which worked out several agreements with the Castro government (a gradual lifting of the embargo was sanctioned). Castro's adventurism cooled Uncle Sam's enthusiasm. President Carter also eased the embargo, including lifting the travel restrictions. When Carter announced that the US welcomed Cuban political refugees with "open arms," Castro, in "a gesture of supreme personal rage," slammed the door shut by concocting the Mariel Boatlift.

The Mariel Boatlift

In 1980, 12 Cubans walked through the gates of the Peruvian embassy in Havana and asked for asylum. When the Peruvians refused to hand them over, Castro removed the embassy guards. Within 72 hours, 11,000 Cubans had sought shelter in the embassy. When the foreign press gave the case prominence, Castro decided to allow them to leave. He also seized the opportunity to empty his prisons of dissidents, hardened criminals, homosexuals, and other "antisocial elements." Many were coerced to leave. The Cuban government called them *escoria* (scum), much as Goebbels called Jews *Ungeziefer* (vermin). Thus, Castro disposed of more than 120,000 critics.

The Carter administration was forced to accept the *Marielitos*. (In November 1987, Cuba agreed to take back about 2,500 *Marielitos*—those with histories of mental illness or criminal records—plus almost 4,000 Cubans convicted of crimes since their arrival in the United States.)

In the 1980s, President Ronald Reagan took a much harder line. Castro's adventurism received its first bloody nose in 1983, when President Reagan ordered US marines to storm the Caribbean island of Grenada to topple Maurice Bishop's Cuban-backed socialist regime. The Reagan administration also spawned the Cuban-American National Foundation to give clout to the right-wing Cuban-American voice. In 1985, he established Radio Martí, to broadcast anti-Castro propaganda into Cuba, where Castro, having been shocked by a demonstration of disaffection in 1980, had loosened up by permitting farmers to sell their goods on the free market.

THE BUBBLE BURSTS

Meanwhile, Mikhail Gorbachev had become leader of the Soviet Union and was initiating fateful reforms—just as Castro turned more sharply toward communist orthodoxy.

Castro's program of Rectification of Errors and Struggles Against Negative Tendencies was initiated in 1986 in response to Cuba's faltering economy. The decision resulted in the closure of the highly successful free farmers' markets, which had led to an increase in the food supply and placed unobtainable items, such as garlic, back on kitchen tables. Castro, however, expressed fear that capitalism was rearing its ugly head (he was alarmed at "millionaire garlic growers"). The basic structure of Soviet-style planning and management would

not be altered. It was Castro's first warnings that *glasnost* and *perestroika,* Gorbachev's "heresies," would not be tolerated in Cuba.

By the late 1980s, dissent was sweeping through the Soviet Union and Eastern Europe, where the Communist order was crumbling. Castro, obsessed with the changes occurring in Eastern European countries, reverted to revolutionary purity: the achievements of North Korea's Kim Il Sung were suddenly praised in the media.

In 1989, the Berlin Wall collapsed and the communist dominoes came tumbling down. However, the news in Cuba was dominated by a political show trial that made it clear that reform was not in the cards. General Arnaldo Sánchez Ochoa, a powerful and charismatic national hero with impeccable credentials going back to the Sierra Maestra, was accused of colluding with the Colombian drug cartel to smuggle drugs to the US via Cuba. After a closed trial, Ochoa and 13 other high-ranking officers were convicted of treason and corruption. Ochoa and three others were executed. A massive purge followed, notably of the Ministry of the Interior (MININT), but also of dissidents and private entrepreneurs. Rumors swept the island that Ochoa, who had been espousing reformist discontent, had been conspiring to oust Castro.

The Special Period
With the collapse of Eastern Europe, goods began to disappear from Cuban shelves. When East German powdered milk ceased to arrive, Cuba eliminated butter; when Czechoslovakian malt no longer arrived, Cuban beer disappeared. Soaps, detergents, deodorants, toilet paper, clothing . . . everything vanished.

In January 1990, Castro declared that Cuba had entered a Special Period in a Time of Peace. He also announced a draconian, warlike austerity plan. A new slogan appeared throughout Cuba: *¡Socialismo o muerte!"* (Socialism or death!). Inevitably, rising political discontent boiled over, on 21 April 1991, when clashes erupted between *roqueros* (rock-music fans) and police—the first act of spontaneous rebellion since 1959.

Then, on 18 August 1991, on the last day of the highly successful Pan-American Games in Havana (which Cuba won with 140 gold medals), the Soviet Union began its dizzying unraveling. Boris Yeltsin—an economic reformer who had infuriated Castro by meeting with right-wing Cuban exiles (the CANF and Yeltsin consolidated a close relationship)—took power. Subsidies and supplies to Cuba virtually ceased. The same year, General Noriega was ousted in Panama—Cuba's main source for Western goods. Cuba was cast adrift, a lone socialist island in a capitalist sea.

With the umbilical cords severed, Cuba's economy slipped into coma. Nonetheless, at the Fourth Congress of the Cuban Communist Party, in October 1991, Castro announced a "sacred" duty to save the Revolution. Hopes of reform were dashed. Although the politburo was expanded, with reformers holding half the seats, a new resolution granted the Central Committee absolute powers to overrule any other government body in "unpredictable situations," thereby legally empowering the committee to overrule any legislative vote to oust Castro.

Believing that Cuba was on the verge of collapse, Uncle Sam tightened the screws. In April 1992, President Bush closed US airports and ports to third-country vessels "guilty" of carrying Cuban goods or passengers. Later that year, Congress passed the Cuban Democracy Act, which reduced economic assistance to countries trading with Cuba; increased punitive action against individuals breaking the embargo; and prohibited US subsidiary companies abroad from trading with Cuba.

The Reagan administration had placed four conditions on improved relations with Cuba: a halt to Cuban support of revolution in Central America, withdrawal of its troops from Angola, a reduction of ties with the Soviet Union, and improved human rights. Cuba met all these conditions, to which the Bush administration responded with a new set of imperatives, including the development of a market economy, a reduction of Cuba's armed forces, and internationally supervised elections. The message was: Washington is not interested in improved relations.

By 1993, with riots breaking out on the streets of Havana, it was clear that things couldn't continue the way they were. While dissidents were being rounded up and jailed, the growing reformist movement found an unexpected ally in Raúl Castro, who argued for deregulating key sectors of the economy. Market-savvy reformers were elevated to positions of power and scrambled to nail together a long-term economic recovery plan led by tourism. The Revolution's ideological principles were turned on their head. Possession of the dollar was legalized. Private enterprise was permitted. Even *Playboy*—long banned—was invited to shoot a pictorial photographed in various resorts, while tourist posters flaunted bikini-clad *Cubanas* and the slogan: "Cuba, come and be tempted."

In February 1993, long-promised elections for the National Assembly were held. They were the first elections by secret ballot in four decades, but candidates had been nominated by party-controlled organizations; 95.2% of the Cuban populace endorsed the government ticket. In March 1993, the new Assembly re-elected Castro to another five-year term as president.

But the economic situation had deteriorated so much that malnutrition had reappeared. A growing human tide had begun washing across the Straits of Florida.

The *Balsero* Crisis

Leaving Cuba without an exit permit was illegal; Cubans were rarely granted such visas. The US also routinely denied requests for entry visas. However, the US *guaranteed* residency to any Cuban refugee who stepped foot on US soil.

On 5 August 1994, crowds gathered along the Malecón in response to a rumor that a major exodus was to be permitted and that a flotilla of boats was en route from Florida. When police attempted to clear the boulevard, a riot ensued. Passions were running dangerously high, and two police officers were killed and 35 people injured. Castro saw a chance to defuse a dangerous situation and benefit. He declared that Cuba would no longer police the US borders: if the US would not honor its agreement to allow people to migrate legally, then Cuba would no longer try to prevent anyone from going illegally. The US was hoist on its own petard as thousands of *balseros* fled Cuba on makeshift rafts.

During the next three weeks, at least 20,300 Cubans had been rescued at sea and shipped to Guantánamo naval base, which was expanded to eventually house up to 65,000 refugees. President Clinton's major goal, at almost all costs, was to avoid a replay of the 1980 Mariel

Boatlift. The US was forced to negotiate an immigration accord with Cuba. By 9 September, when the two countries agreed to measures "to ensure that migration between the two countries is safe, legal, and orderly," another 11,060 Cubans had been rescued. Henceforth, the Coast Guard would intercept Cubans heading for the US and return them to Cuba.

Meanwhile, a Miami-based volunteer group called Brothers to the Rescue led by José Basulto had been operating rescue missions. When the flood of *balseros* stopped, pilots of the organization began buzzing Havana and dropping "leaflets of a subversive nature." Cuban authorities complained to the US government on several occasions. Washington warned the organization to stop, although no legal action was taken.

On 24 February 1996, three Brothers to the Rescue Cessnas took off from Opalocka airfield near Miami, Florida. The civilian-paramilitary planes, led by Basulto, were cleared to fly to the Bahamas. Once airborne, they diverted to Cuba. Cuban jet fighters shot two Cessnas down, killing both pilots. The Cuban government claimed that the aircraft came down in Cuban territorial waters. An investigation by the independent International Civil Aviation Organization (ICAO) confirmed that Basulto, who had separated from the other two planes, *did* violate Cuban airspace. But it also confirmed that two Cessnas were downed 10.3 and 11.5 miles *north* of Cuban airspace (ICAO also found that the US government had prior knowledge of the flights and that several US agencies had been carefully monitoring the flights).

Cuban-American exiles and Republican presidential candidates campaigning for the mid-March Florida primary erupted in fury. The incident scuttled the Clinton administration's carefully calibrated policy on Cuba of promoting democratic change.

The Helms-Burton Legislation

In 1995, Sen. Jesse Helms and Rep. Dan Burton had introduced the Cuban Liberty and Democratic Solidarity Act, which would significantly tighten the embargo and punish foreign companies doing business with Cuba. The Helms-Burton Bill was certain to be vetoed by Clinton,

who was sensitive to growing pressure from US businesses to lift the embargo.

Riding on a wave of anti-Castro sentiment in Miami and Washington, Helms steered the legislation through Congress. Clinton caved in. By signing the bill, Clinton significantly limited his own power to change US policy toward Cuba in the future. He, and future presidents, must now seek congressional approval—a near impossible task, given the strength of the anti-Castro lobby—if they seek to modify or lift the embargo. Incredibly, Clinton surrendered his authority to Helms, Chairman of the Senate Foreign Relations Committee and one of the Senate's most recalcitrant reactionaries.

Many experts on Cuba believe the whole event was manipulated—perhaps by right-wing interests, perhaps by Fidel Castro, or perhaps by both. (The day before the incident, a Brothers to the Rescue pilot defected *back* to Cuba; he turned out to be working for Cuban Intelligence. Did he help set the whole thing up in a quid pro quo with Basulto, a former CIA operative?)

The Cuban-American lobby was fearful that Clinton might seek a rapprochement with Cuba. It has been suggested that Basulto may have deliberately led the two other planes to their destiny, knowing that an international incident with Cuba during the run-up to the Florida primaries would secure passage of the Helms-Burton bill. Castro, too, it is claimed, wanted to ensure passage of the bill and forestall a lifting of the embargo, his ultimate ally. "To save his scapegoat," suggested *The Washington Times,* Castro "found the means in the small, civilian planes that had been buzzing Cuba for months. He shot two down on the assumption that doing so would send Congress and the White House into a frenzy of anti-Castro rhetoric and embargo tightening." Clinton's saber rattling allowed Castro to revive flagging anti-Yankeeism and consolidate his tenure at home by jailing dissidents in the face of a new threat from US imperialism.

The Helms-Burton law is also a major propaganda coup for Castro who, it is claimed, knew it would create nothing but headaches for Uncle Sam. The law has seriously disrupted relations with important US trading partners, who have wholeheartedly taken the Cuban side.

THE HELMS-BURTON BILL

Sometimes Castro gets Uncle Sam so furious, the US winds up socking itself in the jaw. Thus, we have the Cuban Liberty and Democratic Solidarity Act, commonly called the Helms-Burton Bill, sponsored by Sen. Jesse Helms (R-N.C.) and Rep. Dan Burton (R.-Ind.). The bill became law in March 1996, with draconian and far-reaching consequences.

First, the law codified all executive orders in effect relevant to the embargo, which will remain in place until a "transition government" is in place in Cuba that meets US criteria. It also eliminates the power of the president to respond to political and economic changes, arrogating Cuba policy to Congress.

The bill also withdraws funding from any international institution providing humanitarian aid to Cuba; provides for a $50,000 civil fine for any US citizen who travels to and "trades with" Cuba; denies entry into the US territory to anyone who has "trafficked" in or done business with people or businesses that have trafficked in property confiscated from US nationals; and bars US banks from loaning to these companies.

Finally, Helms-Burton will allow any US citizen whose property was confiscated after the Revolution to sue any foreign corporation that has "benefited" from the property or from its use. This holds true even if the claimant was *not* a US citizen at the time of expropriation—a requisite of international law. The result could be a blizzard of litigation against those "trafficking" in expropriated Cuban property.

For travelers: The Helms-Burton Act imposes civil fines of up to US$50,000 for US citizens who visit Cuba at their own expense without the US government's permission. At press time, the law was being challenged, and it is unclear whether its provisions against travelers will be implemented.

A Cash Cow for Cuban-Americans

Behind the bluster about toppling Castro, the law really represents the interests of very wealthy Cuban-Americans, such as the Bacardi Corporation and the Fanjul family (the legislation put a $50,000 minimum value on the property lost before a suit can be filed; you had to be *very* rich in 1959 to own $50,000 worth of property). In fact, the legislation—dubbed by some the "Bacardi Rum Protection Law"—was drafted with the help of lawyers representing Bacardi, the National Association of Sugar Mill Owners of Cuba, and the Cuban Association for the Tobacco Industry. Under the Helms-Burton Bill, for example, Bacardi, whose rum distilleries were nationalized, can sue Pernod Ricard, the French liquor company that distributes rum now made in those distilleries; more importantly, it can sue for the right to the lucrative "Havana Club" trademark.

"A Blunderbuss . . . Aimed Squarely at Our Own Foot"

A conspiracy theorist might think the law was written by Castro, who figured out that Helms-Burton creates more problems for the US than for Cuba. Former president Jimmy Carter said, "I think of all the things that have ever been done in my country, this is the stupidest."

The law has been well publicized in Cuba, where it is widely discussed. Helms-Burton has united Cubans behind the Castro government as nothing has done in years.

The law has also earned the wrath of the United States' leading allies, who have wholeheartedly taken the Cuban side. Thus, Canada has enacted retaliatory legislation, including provisions to countersue for any damages incurred under the Helms-Burton provisions. In July 1996, the 15-nation European Union followed suit (Spain's *Sol Meliá,* thumbing its nose at Uncle Sam, even decided to cancel plans to invest in Orlando and Miami, while pressing ahead in Cuba). The law has been condemned by everyone from the Pope to the Organization of American States—"a stunning defeat for the United States," reported the *New York Times*—and clearly violates international law, including the General Agreements on Tariffs and Trade (GATT).

Cuba Calls . . . We Must Answer is a 30-minute documentary video on the US economic blockade and its impact on the lives of the Cuban people. You can order copies (US$20) from the **Cuba Information Project,** 198 Broadway #800, New York, NY 10038, tel. (212) 227-3422. A 90-minute video of the June 1994 Congressional hearings on the Free Trade with Cuba bill is available from **CUBA Update Video,** 124 West 23rd St., New York, NY 10011; $20 plus $2 postage/handling.

GOVERNMENT

Cuba is an independent socialist republic. The Cuban Constitution, adopted in 1975, defines it as a "socialist state of workers and peasants and all other manual and intellectual workers." Dr. Fidel Castro Ruz is head of both state and government.

All power and initiative are in the hands of the Communist Party, which controls the labyrinthine state apparatus. There are no legally recognized political organizations independent of the party, which the Constitution recognizes as "the highest leading force of the society and of the state."

The Constitution, copied largely from the Soviet Constitution of 1936, guarantees the "freedom and inviolability of the individual" as well as freedom of speech, press, and religion—as long as these conform to the "goals of socialist society." In reality, no dissent is permitted.

STATE STRUCTURE

The Central Government
The Council of Ministers: The highest-ranking executive body is the Council of Ministers, headed by Fidel Castro and comprising several vice presidents and ministers. The council is empowered to conduct affairs of the state and draw up bills for submission to the Assembly. The Executive Committee of the Council of Ministers administers Cuba on a day-to-day basis.

According to the Constitution, the council is accountable to the National Assembly of People's Power, which "elects" the members at the initiative of the head of state. The council has jurisdiction over all ministries and central organizations and effectively runs the country under the direction of Fidel Castro.

The National Assembly: The Asemblea Nacional (National Assembly of People's Power) is invested with legislative authority but exercises little legislative initiative. It mostly approves decisions handed down from higher state and party organs. The Assembly is a stepping stone for ambitious individuals, whose political future depends on going along with leadership decisions. Discussion is usually restricted to sub-

jects introduced from the leadership. It is mostly a rubber-stamp legislature.

The Assembly is elected for a five-year term but meets only twice annually (members are part-timers and are not full-time legislators). There were 589 deputies in the 1993-98 *quinquenio* (five-year term). Prior to 1993, deputies were elected by the provincial assemblies. In 1993 they were elected directly by voters, although candidacies must first be approved by the Communist Party. Most deputies are drawn from the party bureaucracy and are predominantly male and white. The Assembly elects high government officials and ratifies executive appointments.

The Council of State: The Council of State is modeled on the Presidium of the former Soviet Union, and functions as the Executive Committee of the National Assembly when the latter is not in session. It is presided over by Fidel Castro.

The Cuban Communist Party
The sole political party is the *Partido Comunista de Cuba* (PCC), of which Fidel Castro is head and his brother Raúl vice secretary. It is closely modeled on the party of the former Soviet Union,

The Party's goal is "to guide common efforts toward the construction of socialism." In Marxist theory, the construction of socialism proceeds through the "dictatorship of the proletariat" toward the communist utopia. En route, the working class takes the reins of state power and governs in its own name. The party assumes unto itself the leadership role and ostensibly represents the "vanguard of the proletariat" or "institutional expression of the people." The PCC determines the direction in which society is to move, and the state provides the mechanism for moving in that direction.

The PCC occupies the central role in all government bodies and institutions. It is led by the Buró Politico (Politburo), which is made up, at press time, of 25 individuals (the number keeps changing). Steering the party, however, is the Comité Central (Central Committee) of the PCC, whose members are selected by Castro. The Comité "elects" members of the Politburo. It now meets every six months (prior to 1980, it

Revolutionary wall in Manzanillo

CHRISTOPHER P. BAKER

met infrequently) and is the principal forum through which the party leadership disseminates Party policy to lower echelons. The committee—comprising 225 members in 1996—is organized into departments, such as the Department of Economy. Less than 20% of members are women; the share of the military has declined from 32% to 12% since 1975.

At the base of the PCC chain is the party cell of 10 members organized at work and educational centers. The cells recruit new members, who go through a six-month scrutiny as to their ideological purity. The youth organizations are the most common avenue for passage into the PCC. Current membership is about 600,000 (about five percent of the population).

The party was formed in 1965. Most of the original 100 committee members were only nominally communists; but all were ardent *Fidelista* loyalists. (In the early years following the Revolution, Castro purged old-school communist militants from the bureaucracy and political institutions, subordinating both in 1963 to the newly formed *Partido Unificado de la Revolución Socialista*—United Party of the Socialist Revolution—which was in turn replaced by the PCC.)

Castro has since drawn from "the elite of the elite" of the party to maintain his government. All top Cuban officials had to be graduates of the Ñico López Central School of the Cuban Communist Party, a university offering teaching in Marxist theory. (Various schools were established under the umbrella of Ñico López as early

as 1959; within two years, 30,000 Cubans had passed through the indoctrination programs. The schools were kept virtually secret in the early years. The upper tiers of government include many cultivated and highly intelligent men (there are few women at this level).

Key positions in government have been occupied by loyal revolutionaries from the ranks of M-26-7, which has become a kind of elite club. Raúl Castro, Carlos Rafael Rodríguez, and Osmani Cienfuegos, all veterans of the Revolution, are the triumvirate at the top of the power structure (even most Cubans are not aware of who constitutes the inner circle and how it works).

Policy emanates from Fidel Castro, who has used his own charismatic qualities and inordinate tactical skills to consolidate almost hegemonic authority. Although the Council of State and Council of Ministers ostensibly make the decisions, Castro shapes those decisions (it is claimed that no official in his right mind dares to criticize Castro and that constructive discussion is virtually impossible). The PCC has no program—Castro defines the flavor of the day.

In December 1975, the First Congress of the Communist Party adopted a new constitution (ratified in February 1976), which established the *permanent* character of the state and ruled out any ideological or structural changes in the future. It became unconstitutional to challenge Fidel Castro, who was effectively named leader for life. Total power was legally vested in him as first secretary of the Communist Party, president of the Republic, chairman of the State Council, chairman of the Council of Ministers, and commander in chief of the armed forces. (He is normally referred to as *Comandante-en-Jefe,* Commander in Chief.) His younger brother, Raúl, was named first vice president of both the Council of State and the Council of Ministers, the second secretary of the Communist Party, defense minister, and General of the Army.

Local Government

The country is divided into 14 provinces and 169 municipalities *(municipios),* dominated by the city of Havana (a separate province), with its population of two million people. Each province and municipality is governed by an Assembly of Delegates of People's Power, representing state bodies at the local level. Traditionally, the councils elected members of the Provincial Assemblies; since 1992, members have been elected by popular ballot and serve two-and-a-half-year terms.

The first experiment in "elected" local government—*poder popular* (popular power)—began in 1974 and was designed to improve public administration through limited decentralization. The organs of Poder Popular also serve as forums for citizens' grievances and deal with problems such as garbage collection, housing improvement, and running day-care centers. When new legislation is pending, local officials go out to "discuss it with the people." They are not autonomous bodies, however, and are hampered by dependence on the vertical structure of economic planning. The Communist Party closely monitors their performance.

The country is also unofficially divided into three areas that are sometimes still referred to colloquially by their colonial titles: Occidente (the western region), Las Villas (the center), and Oriente (the east)

Committees for the Defense of the Revolution

The linchpins in maintaining the loyalty of the masses and spreading the Revolution at the grassroots level are the *Comités para la Defensa de la Revolución* (CDRs), created in 1960 as neighborhood committees designed to protect the Revolution from internal enemies. There are 15,000 CDRs in Havana, and 100,000

throughout the island (66% of the population are members). Every block has one.

On one hand, the CDRs perform wonderful work: they collect blood for hospitals, take retired people on vacations, discourage kids from playing hooky, organize graduation parties, and patrol at night to guard against delinquency. But they are also the vanguard in keeping an eye on the local population, watching and snitching on neighbors (the CDRs are under the direction of MININT, the Ministry of the Interior). Anyone nay-saying the Revolution, mocking Castro, or dealing on the black market (economic crimes are political crimes, seen as a security threat to the state), is likely to be reported by the block warden, a loyal revolutionary, who records what he or she hears from colleagues and neighbors.

People face harsh retribution if they cross the line into political activism. In 1991, Rapid Response Detachments were formed, ostensibly made up of volunteers from local CDRs but under the purview of MININT, to deal with public expressions of dissent. This they do through distasteful pogroms called *actos de repudios,* beating up dissidents, much as did Hitler's *Blockwarts.* Like Nazi street gangs, the brigades are said to be a spontaneous reaction of outraged Cubans.

Other Mass Organizations

Citizen participation in building socialism is manifested through a number of mass organizations controlled by the PCC. Prominent among them are the **Federation of Cuban Women,** the **Confederation of Cuban Workers, Organization of Small Farmers,** and the **Union of Communist Youth.** Although ostensibly representing the interests of their members, the bodies subordinate these to national goals. Thus, for example, strikes are banned and workers have learned to subordinate their autonomy in return for benefits (pensions, holidays, guaranteed employment, etc.) from the state.

Membership in various mass organizations is a virtual prerequisite for getting on in Cuban society. Promotions, access to university, even to vactions and material incentives for the average citizen rely upon being a "good revolutionary" through participation in an organization. Those who are not members become social outcasts. Over 80% of Cuban citizens are members (in contrast, a majority of those who have left Cuba were not members).

> *"'Now for the evidence,' said the King, 'and then the sentence.' 'No!' said the Queen, 'first the sentence and then the evidence!' 'Nonsense!' cried Alice, so loudly that everybody jumped, 'the idea of having the sentence first . . . !'"*

The Judiciary

The highest court in the land is the People's Supreme Court in Havana. Its president and vice president are appointed by the head of state; other judges are elected by the National Assembly. There are seven courts of appeal, 14 provincial courts, and 169 municipal courts for minor offenses. The provinces are divided into judicial districts with courts for civil and criminal cases.

Courts are a fourth branch of government and are not independent. The judiciary is not charged with protecting individual rights but rather, according to Article 121 of the Constitution, with "maintaining and strengthening socialist legality." Thus they are subject to interference by the political leadership. The Council of State, for example, can overturn a judicial decision. And interpretation of the Constitution is the prerogative solely of the National Assembly, not the courts.

Private practice of law is not permitted, and the accused are denied recourse to defense counsel other than state-appointed officials. The penal code accepts a defendant's confession as sufficient proof of his guilt (there are many cases of individuals pressured into confessing to crimes they did not commit). Revolutionary Summary Tribunals enjoy wide powers. Due process is systematically flouted in political cases, according to the apolitical Washington-based human-rights group American Watch.

Cuba, however, has a policy of criminal rehabilitation. In meting out punishment, the penal system allows for amends and guarantees an individual's job upon release from prison (assuming he or she has not been jailed for political crimes). People considered a menace to society receive harsh sentences. Capital punishment by firing squad remains.

The Military and Security Apparatus

For thirty-odd years, the Kennedy-Kruschev "agreement" honored by both superpowers (but disavowed by subsequent US administrations) has guaranteed Cuba's territorial integrity. However, the threat of invasion has at times seemed a distinct possibility, and Cuba is well prepared to repel a US invasion.

Cuba boasts a formidable military under the aegis of the Fuerzas Armadas Revolucionarias (FAR), commanded by Raúl Castro. Its military and militia are replete with battle-tested soldiers (as many as 350,000 Cuban troops served on active duty in Angola and Ethiopia during the 1970s and '80s). In 1993, over 180,000 men and women were on active duty (including 13,500 in the navy and 22,000 in the air force), although this has since been scaled back. In addition, Cuba has 130,000 reservists supplemented by about 100,000 in the "youth labor army," 50,000 in the civil defense force, and 1.3 million in the territorial militias. All males between the ages of 16 and 45 are subject to conscription (conscripts complete a basic training program and are assigned to one of the regular armed forces). Women between 17 and 35 may volunteer for military service.

The key to defense, however, is the "Guerra de Todo el Pueblo" (War of All the People). In the event of an attack, the *entire* population of Cuba will be called into action. To this end, regular defense exercises are conducted for all segments of the civilian population. All Cuban citizens undergo compulsory military training one Sunday—called "Red Sunday"—each month, and while traveling through Cuba do not be surprised to see young women in high heels or old ladies with their hair in curlers tossing grenades and taking pot-shots at imaginary GIs. Small military training grounds are scattered along the roadsides throughout the island.

Spending for the armed forces fell from US$2.24 billion—the highest ever—in 1988 to US$1.83 billion in 1989; since then, the figure has continued to drop sharply. In 1991, the military was re-engineered to help the economy—a return to the model of the "civil soldier," who assists in construction and agriculture. As a result of the economic crisis, the military is largely obliged to earn its way by virtue of what it produces (in 1995, FAR funded 30% of its 701 million peso budget from its investments in tourism, agriculture, and industry).

As recently as 1991, the Soviet Union maintained about 11,000 military personnel in Cuba; by mid-1993 every one had returned to the former Soviet Union. The Russians maintain a handful of staff at the former Soviet electronic surveillance facility at Lourdes.

State security is the responsibility of the Ministry of the Interior, which operates a number of intelligence-related services, plus the National Revolutionary Police (PNR), with paramilitary and military units under its umbrella. Other intelligence units are operated by the Department of State Security and the General Directorate of Intelligence. There are more security-linked officials than meet the eye (as many as one in 27 Cubans, including informers, according to Guillermo Cabrera Infanta, the former editor of *Revolución*).

GOVERNMENT BY PERSONAL WHIM

Cuba is really a *Fidelista* state, one in which Marxist-Leninism has been loosely grafted onto Cuban nationalism, then tended and shaped by one man. The Cuban leader likes to leave his development choices wide open, allowing a flexible interpretation of the correct path to socialism. Ideological dogma is subordinated to tactical considerations. Castro's emotions, what Castro biographer Tad Szulc calls his *caudillo* temperament (that of a modernizing but megalomanical political strongman), are powerful factors in his decision-making.

Castro makes decisions about the minutest aspects of government (it was he, for example, who decided that nurses should wear trousers, not skirts, because a nurse in skirt leaning over a patient, he suggested impishly, might cause a man lying in a bed behind her to have a heart attack). Even minor decisions are delayed until they have received Castro's blessing.

In consequence, too, most Cuban managers in the state-run economy lack the courage to make decisions, a massive obstacle to the development of an efficient economy. Government officials must study Castro's speeches intently to stay tuned with his forever-changing views. The fear of repercussions from on high is so great

that the bureaucracy—Cubans call it a "*burrocracy*"—has evolved as a "mutually protective society" (Cubans joke that the island *is* a two-party state—the Communist Party and the Bureaucratic Party).

The result—besides an "endless labyrinth of errors committed and about to be committed" (in a speech in early 1987, Castro said, "We must correct the errors we made in correcting our errors")—is minimal accountability. Castro has been quick to admit the shortcomings of the system, which he blames on irresponsible managers, lack of discipline, and greed and corruption in high places (making, suggests Maurice Halperin, "the noticeable exception of his own performance").

Castro has built a new privileged ruling class based around top-level government officials, the security apparatus, and the military. Access to privilege has fostered a struggle to obtain political position; for every inept or corrupt bureaucrat, however, are many highly capable and dedicated communists who have not taken advantage of their powerful positions to aggrandize themselves. The early years of the Revolution were marked by gross bureaucratic disorganization. Decision-making came from the top and went to the bottom, leaving organizations such as the Central Planning Board (JUCEPLAN) out of the loop.

"The fundamental problem," says Tad Szulc, "remains Fidel Castro's psychological inability, rather than conscious refusal, to let go of any power . . . a state of affairs that paralyzes all initiative at lower levels." Political rivalry—even criticism—isn't welcome. Purges within the party and government are occasionally aimed against individuals allegedly trying to establish their own power bases or expressing disaffection. And apocalyptic slogans such as "Socialism or Death!" indicate that on the surface, Castro prefers obduracy over consent and political change.

"Direct Democracy"

Fidel Castro runs Cuba as much by charismatic as through institutional leadership: *personalismo* is central in *Fidelismo*. Castro has called Western democracies "complete garbage." He prefers what he calls "direct democracy"—his appeals ("popular consultations") to the people. Castro has relied on his ability to whip up the crowds at mass rallies and elicit mass support through direct appeals to the Cuban people.

Castro uses persuasive arguments to keep revolutionary ardor alive. Images of destitution in neighboring countires are standard fare, as is the threat from the United States, which has spent four decades assiduously trying to undermine Castro and the Cuban Revolution.

A State of Acquiescence

Castro has engineered a state where an individual's personal survival requires a display of loyalty and adherence to the Revolution. A margin of public criticism is allowed, to vent political pressure. The headiest steam is periodically allowed to leave for Florida on rafts and inflated innor tubes. Otherwise jail or "spontaneous" acts of repudiation by gangs of "citizens" quickly silence the dissident and serve to put others on notice.

The government maintains a file on *every* worker, a labor dossier that follows him or her from job to job. Cubans have to voice—or fake—their loyalty. To become *integrado* (integrated) is essential to get by. Transgressions are reported in one's dossier. It's advantageous to be a member of the Union of Young Communists or a similar organization in order to prove loyalty to the government. Most workplaces convene meetings in which workers discuss government policies and their effects on the people. Complaints are relatively few, to avoid inviting trouble. If "antisocial" comments are noted, the worker may be kicked out of his or her job, or blackballed.

Nonetheless, dissidence and vocal opposition to both the state of affairs and the Castro government have grown markedly in recent years. An increasing number of Cubans are tired of sacrifice, foolhardy experiments, and the paternalism that tells them how to live their lives. The constant opening and closing of society has taken its toll, raising and then dashing Cubans' hopes. In August 1993, *Newsweek* reported a sudden spate of formerly unheard-of rock-throwing attacks on state-owned properties at night. Even the local Communist Party headquarters in San Cristóbal (80 km southwest of Havana) was burned down.

Popular discontent finally boiled over during riots in Havana in August 1994. One riot doesn't make a revolution. And this one was tame by US standards (although dozens of people were hurt and scores of plate-glass windows broken). But the riot was by far the most violent protest in Cuba in the almost four decades since Castro took power.

Rising social discontent and divisions at the grassroots level have prompted the government to broaden and invigorate its structures to attract and maintain support and keep revolutionary fervor alive. Meanwhile, harassment and jailing of dissidents rose sharply in 1992; again in September 1994, following the *balsero* crisis; in July 1995 and again in spring 1996, when police initiated a crackdown on Cubans having contact with foreigners.

From Marx to Martí

The sudden collapse of the Soviet bloc sent severe ideological shock waves through Cuba and forced Castro to make political changes that marked a break with the past. In March 1990, Castro called for the Fourth Communist Party Congress and initiated a grassroots program to collect recommendations from the populace—the first national public opinion survey in post-1959 history. More than 3.5 million Cubans attended meetings and spoke their minds before the meetings were called off. More than one million suggestions were documented and tabulated. The people expressed overwhelming desire for reform.

Castro recognized that the top-down process was out of sync with the social base. He embarked on his own version of the "Chinese model" for the survival of socialism: creating a market economy with the aid of foreign investment, while maintaining political control. Rather than move towards a multi-party system, Castro aimed to make the present one-party system more democratic and responsive to people's needs. Major political reform was out of the question: Castro believes that the Soviet Union collapsed because Mikhail Gorbachev allowed both economic and political reforms.

Fidel, who perhaps had convinced himself that socialism really would triumph over capitalism, was clearly shaken by events in Eastern Europe and, it is said, seemed to lose his self-confidence and footing. To the average Cuban it began to look like Raúl had taken over

FIDEL CASTRO

Whatever you think of his politics, Fidel Castro is unquestionably one of the most remarkable and enigmatic figures of this century, thriving on contradiction and paradox like a romantic character from the fiction of his Colombian novelist friend Gabriel García Márquez.

Fidel Castro Ruz, child prodigy, was born on 13 August 1926 at Manacas *finca* near Birán in northern Oriente, the fifth of nine children of Ángel Castro y Argiz. Fidel's mother was the family housemaid, Lina Ruz González, whom Ángel married after divorcing his wife. (Fidel's father was an émigré to Cuba from Galicia in Spain as a destitute 13-year-old. In Cuba, he gradually rose to become a modestly wealthy landowner who employed 300 workers on a 26,000-acre domain; he owned 1,920 acres and leased the rest from the United Fruit Company, to whom he sold cane.) Fidel weighed 10 pounds at birth—the first hint that he would always be larger than life. The early records of his family are sketchy, and Castro, who seems to have had a happy childhood, likes to keep it that way—much as he attempts to suppress the notion that he comes from a bourgeois family.

As a boy he was extremely assertive, rebellious, and combative. He was a natural athlete and grew especially accomplished at track events and baseball. He was no sportsman, however; if his team was losing, he would often leave the field and go home (Gabriel García Márquez has said, "I do not think anyone in this world could be a worse loser"). It became a matter of principle to excel—and win—

at everything. His Jesuit teachers identified what Richard Nixon later saw in Castro: "that indefinable quality which, for good or evil, makes a leader of men." His school yearbook recorded that he was *excelencia* and predicted that "he will fill with brilliant pages the book of his life."

Star Rising

Fidel enrolled in Havana University's law school in October 1945, where he immediately plunged into politics and gained the limelight as a student leader. Castro earned his first front-page newspaper appearance following his first public speech, denouncing President Grau, on 27 November 1946. In 1947, when the foremost political opposition figure, Edward Chibás, formed the *Ortodoxo* party, Castro, at the age of 21, was sufficiently well known to be invited to help organize it. He stopped attending law school and rose rapidly to prominence as the most outspoken critic of the Grau government, including as head of his own revolutionary group, Orthodox Radical Action.

The period was exceedingly violent: armed gangs roamed the campus, and Fidel never went anywhere without a gun. As organizer of the street demonstrations calling for Grau's ouster, Castro was soon on the police hit list, and several attempts were made on his life. In February 1949, Fidel was accused of assassinating a political rival, Manolo Castro (no relation). After being arrested and subsequently released on "conditional liberty," he went into hiding.

He remained determined to stay in the limelight, however. In March, he flew to Bogotá to attend the Ninth Inter-American Conference, where foreign ministers were destined to sign the charter of the Organization of American States. Soon enough, Castro was in the thick of student demonstrations opposing the organization as a scheme for US domination of the hemisphere. One week later, while he was on his way to meet Jorge Eliécer Gaitán (the popular leader of the opposition Progressive Liberal Party), Gaitán was assassinated. Bogotá erupted in spontaneous riots—the *Bogotázo*. Castro was irresistibly drawn in and, arming himself with a tear-gas shotgun and police uniform stolen from a police station, found himself at the vanguard of the revolution—with a police detachment under his command. Inevitably, Castro again made headline news.

BOB RACE

On 12 October 1949, Castro married a pretty philosophy student named Mirta Díaz-Balart, and they honeymooned for several weeks in the United States. (The couple divorced in 1954; she left for the USA, then Spain.) Back home, Castro was once again in the thick of political violence. Gangsterism had soared under President Prío. In November, Fidel gave a suicidal speech in which he denounced the gangster process, admitted his past associations with gangsterism, then named all the gangsters, politicians, and student leaders profiting from the "gangs' pact." Again in fear for his life, Fidel left Cuba for the United States.

He returned four months later to cram for a multiple degree. In September 1950, Castro graduated with the titles of Doctor of Law, Doctor of Social Sciences, and Doctor of Diplomatic Law (in the press, Fidel is often referred to as Dr. Castro). He then launched into a law practice, concentrating on "lost causes" on behalf of the poor (most of his legal work was offered pro bono publico—free).

Congressional Candidate
By 1951, Castro was preparing for national office. Fulgencio Batista, who had returned from retirement in Florida to run for president, even asked to receive Castro to get the measure of the young man who in January 1952 shook Cuba's political foundation by releasing a detailed indictment of President Prío. His campaign was far ahead of his time. The dizzyingly imaginative 25-year-old utilized mass mailings and stump speeches with a foresight and veracity theretofore unknown. His personal magnetism, his brilliant speeches, and his unquestioned honesty aroused the crowds, who cheered him deliriously (Fidel had championed the cause of the urban poor and had no problem earning their loyalty).

Castro was certain to be elected to the Chamber of Deputies. It was also clear that Batista was going to be trounced in the presidential contest. Batista couldn't stomach defeat, so, at dawn on 10 March 1952, he effected a *golpe* (military coup) and, next day, moved back into the presidential palace he had vacated eight years before.

Says Tad Szulc: "Many Cubans think that without a coup, Castro would have served as a congressman for four years until 1956, then run for the Senate, and made his pitch for the presidency in 1960 and 1964. Given the fact that Cuba was wholly bereft of serious political leadership and given Castro's rising pop-

ularity . . . it would appear that he was fated to govern Cuba—no matter how he arrived at the top job."

The rest, as they say, is history.

A Communist *Caudillo?*
At 30 years old, Castro was fighting in the Sierra Maestra, a disgruntled lawyer turned revolutionary who craved Batista's job. At 32, he had it. He was determined not to let go. When he came down from the mountains, he was considered a "younger, bearded version of Magwitch: a tall outlaw emerging from the fog of history to make Pips of us all," wrote Guillermo Cabrera Infante, a brilliant novelist who, like thousands, supported Castro but later soured on him. "The outlaw became a law unto himself." It is a claim that many have made: that Fidel used the Revolution to carry out a personal *caudillista* coup (a *caudillo* is a Spanish strongman leader).

Castro has since led Cuba through four decades of "dizzying experience." He has outlasted nine US presidents, each of whom predicted his imminent demise and plotted to hasten it by fair means or foul. He shows no sign of relinquishing power and has said he will never do so while Washington remains hostile—a condition he thrives on (Graham Greene determined that Castro was "an empirical Marxist, who plays Communism by ear and not by book").

Castro is consummately machiavellian (masking truth to reach and maintain power). He is not the saint his ardent admirers portray, nor is he the evil oppressor described by Washington. He deserves full credit for the extraordinary gifts of social justice, dignity, and advances in health and education that the Revolution has bestowed upon Cuba and wishes to share with the underprivileged world. Castro—who knew he could never carry out his revolution in an elective system—believes disease, malnutrition, illiteracy, economic inadequacy, and dependence on the West are criminal shames and that a better social order can be created through the perfection of good values. Despite the turn of events, Castro clings to the thread of his dream: "I have no choice but to continue being a communist, like the early Christians remained Christian . . . If I'm told 98% of the people no longer believe in the Revolution, I'll continue to fight. If I'm told I'm the only one who believes in it, I'll continue."

A Hatred of Uncle Sam
Castro turned to Communism mostly for strategic, not ideological, reasons, but his bitterness towards

(continues on next page)

FIDEL CASTRO
(continued)

the United States undoubtedly also shaped his decision. He has been less committed to Marxism than to anti-imperialism, in which he is unwavering. He has cast himself in the role of David versus Goliath, in the tradition of José Martí, who wrote "my sling is the sling of David." Castro sees himself as Martí's heir, representing the same combination of New World nationalism, Spanish romanticism, and philosophical radicalism. His trump card is Cuban nationalist sentiment.

His boyhood impressions of destitution in Holguín province under the thumb of the United Fruit Company and, later, the 1954 overthrow of the reformist Arbenz government in Guatemala by a military force organized by the CIA and underwritten by United Fruit, had a profound impact on Castro's thinking. Ever since, Castro has viewed world politics through the prism of anti-Americanism. During the war in the Sierra Maestra, Castro stated, "When this war has ended, a much bigger and greater war will start for me, a war I shall launch against them. I realize this will be my true destiny."

He brilliantly used the Cold War to enlist the Soviet Union to move Cuba out of the US orbit, and was thus able—with Soviet funds—to bolster his stature as a nationalist redeemer by guaranteeing the Cuban masses substantial social and economic gains.

Castro, however, has no animosities towards North Americans. His many close personal contacts range from media maverick Ted Turner to actor Jack Lemmon and even the Rockefeller clan.

Many Talents

Castro has a gargantuan hunger for information, a huge trove of knowledge (Fidel is an avid speed-reader), and an equally prodigious memory (he never forgets facts and figures, a remarkable asset he nourished at law school, where he forced himself to depend on his memory by destroying the materials he had learned by heart).

There is a sense of perfection in everything he does, applied through a superbly methodical mind and laser-clear focus. He has astounding political instincts, notably an uncanny ability to predict the future moves of his adversaries (Castro is a masterly chess player). Castro's "rarest virtue," says his intimate friend Gabriel García Márquez, "is the ability to foresee the evolution of an event to its farthest-reaching consequences."

Castro is also a gambler of unsurpassed self-confidence. (Says Infante, "Castro's real genius lies in the arts of deception and while the world plays bridge by the book, he plays poker, bluffing and holding his cards close to his olive-green chest.") His daring and chutzpah are attributed by some observers to his Galician temperament—that of an anarchist and born *guerrillero* (guerrilla fighter). He has stood at the threshold of death several times and loves to court danger. For example, in 1981, he chose to run to the Mexican port of Cozumel in a high-speed launch just to see whether the US Navy—then patrolling the Gulf of Mexico to stop Cuban arms shipments to Nicaragua—could catch him.

Castro's vanity is monumental (Fidel never laughs at himself unless he makes the joke). Fidel wears glasses but dislikes being seen in public in them, considering them a sign of weakness. His beard is also more than a trademark; he likes to hide his double chin.

He nurtures his image with exquisite care, feigning modesty to hide his immense ego. "I am not here because I assigned myself to this job . . . I am here because this job has been thrust upon me," Castro said in 1994. He also claims that his place in history does not bother him: "All the glory in the world can fit into a kernel of corn." Yet in the same breath he likens himself to Jesus Christ (one of his favorite allusions).

Castro's revolutionary concept has been built on communicating with the masses (whom he sees and treats as his "children"), and he conducts much of his domestic government through his frequent public speeches (usually televised in entirety). He understood at an early stage that he and television were made for each other. Castro—"one of the best television actors in the world"—is masterfully persuasive, an amazingly gifted speaker who holds Cubans spellbound with his oratory.

His early speeches often lasted for hours; today he is more succinct. (Fidel's loquaciousness is legendary. When he and Raúl were imprisoned together on the Isle of Pines in 1954, Raúl complained that his elder brother "didn't let me sleep for weeks . . . he just talked day and night, day and night.") He is not, however, a man of small talk; he is deadly serious whenever he opens his mouth. He also listens intently when the subject interests him; he is a great questioner, homing immediately to the heart of the matter.

Adored or Hated?

A large segment of Cubans see Castro as a ruthless dictator who cynically betrayed the democratic ideals that he used to rally millions to his banner. To Miami exiles especially, *El Líder* is just a common tyrant. Nonetheless, Castro's longevity and success are due in great measure to the admiration of a majority of the Cuban people, to whom he was and remains a hero. There persists an adulation for *El Máximo* or *El Caballo* (the horse—an allusion to the Chinese belief that dreams represent numbers to place bets on, and that the horse is number one).

Castro has consistently proven his concern for honesty and social justice in a nation mired for five centuries in corruption and inequality. Traveling through Cuba you'll come across countless families who keep a framed photograph of him. You'll even hear of women offering themselves to Fidel, "drawn by his power, his unfathomable eyes."

Cubans' bawdy street wisdom says that Castro has various domiciles—a sane precaution in view of the CIA's numerous attempts on his life—so that he can attend to his lovers. Certainly, many highly intelligent and beautiful women have dedicated themselves to Castro and his cause, but Fidel saves his most ardent passions for the Revolution. Nonetheless, he is a "dilettante extraordinaire" in esoteric pursuits, notably gourmet dining (but not cigars; Fidel quit smoking in 1985). His second love is deep-sea fishing. He is also a good diver and often flies down to spear-fish at his tiny retreat on Cayo Piedra, where he dines on an offshore barge and sleeps in a rustic old caretaker's home while guests relax more luxuriously in a modern guesthouse.

Castro retains the loyalty of millions of Cubans, but he is only loyal to those who are loyal to him. He feels that to survive he must be "absolutely and undeviatingly uncompromising." In 1996, his biographer Tad Szulc wrote, "He is determined not to tolerate any challenge to his authority, whatever the consequences." You are either for the Revolution or against it. Castro does not forget, or pardon; his heart is made of both gold and steel. Thus, while he has always shown solicitude for those who have served him or the Revolution, his capacity for fury is renowned, and it is said that no official in his right mind dares criticize him. (Paradoxically, he can be extremely gentle and courteous, expecially towards women, in whose company he is slightly abashed.) Cubans fear the consequences of saying anything against him, discreetly stroking their chins—an allusion to his beard—rather than uttering his name.

Castro denies that a personality cult exists. Yet Castro lives, suggests Szulc, "bathed in the absolute adulation orchestrated by the propaganda organs of the regime." The first page of newspapers and the lead item on the evening television news are usually devoted to Castro's public acts or speeches. His quotations were even printed at the bottom of every page of the old Havana telephone directory. And, although there are no streets or public edifices named for him, on May Day and other special holidays posters and billboards are adorned with his face.

Given his innate conviction of destiny and unquenchable thirst to lead, the indefatigable Cuban leader, who turned 70 in 1996 and has outlasted all the leaders of his time but King Hussein of Jordan, could be around for many years. His hair and beard have grayed and his skin is dotted with sunspots, but in 1996 author Gay Talese found him "in fine health. His facial skin is florid and unsagging, his dark eyes dart around the room with ever-alert intensity, and he has a full head of lustrous gray hair not thinning at the crown." Doctors say Castro maintains a mostly vegetarian diet and works out every day on an exercise bicycle.

from his elder brother, who virtually disappeared from public view. Political analysts began to talk of Fidel having become a figurehead while others carried out the necessary reforms he found repugnant. Raúl, for example, replaced half the Communist Party's first secretaries in the provinces in mid-1994 with young, pro-reformist yet staunch party men. Others speculate it is a crafty move: if the reforms fail, Fidel will be better insulated and able to step back into the breach.

While Cubans aired their grievances, the Soviet Union collapsed. As a result, the Fourth Congress—held in October 1991—ended up concentrating on how to save socialism, declaring its faith in the existing system, instead of how to embark on the next stage of the Revolution. The Congress closed with an announcement that Cuba would live under wartime conditions. Hopes for liberalization of the economy were dashed.

CUBA'S VITAL STATISTICS

Area: 114,478 square km (42,804 square miles)

Population: 10,900,000 (1993)

Annual Population Growth: 0.9% (1990-95)

Urbanization: 75%

Capital: Havana, pop. 2,090,000

Religion: secular; most of those who practice religion are Roman Catholic, but traditional Afro-Cuban paganism has a large following.

Language: Spanish

Climate: subtropical, with a wet season from May to October and a dry season from November to April. Average annual temperature is 24° C (75° F), with little variation. January and February are the coolest months.

Time: GMT -5. Daylight saving time operates Apr.-Oct.

Currency: peso (official rate of exchange is 1.32 to US$1; unofficial exchange rate is approximately 100 to US$1)

Business Hours: Government offices: Mon.-Fri. 8:30 a.m.-12:30 p.m. and 1:30-5:30 p.m., alternate Saturdays 8 a.m.-5 p.m.; National Banks: Mon.-Fri. 8.30 a.m.-noon and 1.30-3 p.m.; Saturday 8.30-10.30 a.m.

Literacy: 98%

Life Expectancy: 75 years

Birth Rate: 17 per 1,000 (1992)

Mortality Rate: 7 per 1,000 (1992)

Infant Mortality: 9.4 per 1,000 (1993)

Nonetheless, the Congress enacted several key reforms. Elections by voice vote within the Communist Party were replaced by confidential ballots (leading to the first-ever votes—three—against Fidel Castro), and religious believers were again welcomed into the party. Secret ballots replaced voice votes for local party leadership. And delegates to Cuba's National Assembly would henceforth be elected by direct vote, rather than the indirect system in which provincial delegates elect national delegates. Officials also acknowledged that "mass organizations" such as the neighborhood CDRs—top-down bodies

for transmitting edicts from above—needed reform to give people a greater say in national issues and revitalize grassroots support. Direct elections for the presidency were not debated.

Meanwhile, the Communist Party had trimmed the fat from its bloated bureaucracy and reorganized the powerful Central Committee Secretariat. The reforms led to more ideological discussion, and the government briefly relaxed its control over the scope of intellectual and political debate.

The result? The ideological values of Marxism-Leninism have been diluted, usurped by a new prominence for the ideas of José Martí: "patriotic" education and duty have been placed ahead of Communist tenets. Likewise, law and ideology have been separated. New laws no longer necessarily reflect Marxist-Leninist ideology—a prerequisite for the welcoming of capitalist methods and (heavens!) even the endorsement of foreign private-property owners. The Cuban government ostensibly now acknowledges the family, not the state, as "society's fundamental cell."

Several mass organizations, such as the Union of Young Communists (no longer under the direction of the Communist Party), have gained a limited measure of increased autonomy. New governmental institutions, such as the People's Councils (Consejos Populares), have assumed new responsibilities for solving grassroots problems. The population has been given avenues to express discontent, including outspoken phone-in programs on local radio and television. Independent organizations have evolved (many erstwhile state-employed journalists, for example, have formed their own union). And the right of Cuban nationals to travel abroad has been extended (in mid-1991, the government lowered the age eligibility for a Cuban passport to 20, though the document costs US$800).

Also in 1991, more than half of the 225 members of the Central Committee were replaced in a dramatic shakeup meant to inject youthful energy and new wisdom. Young charismatic reformers from within the Communist Party, such as Roberto Robaino, have been elevated to important portfolios. The "best and the brightest" were going to organize things. Castro and the new breed of intellectually capable reformers are preparing for a post-Castro Cuba.

Going to the Ballot Box

In December 1992, for the first time since 1952, Cubans went to the ballot box to vote in municipal elections. Turnout for the elections, according to official figures, reached 97.2%. However, up to 35% of voters invalidated their ballots or left them blank according to one source (the official figure was 7.2%). In February 1993, legislative elections were the first in which voters also cast ballots directly for candidates to the provincial and national assemblies. All Cubans 16 years of age or older can vote.

It wasn't democracy as Westerners know it. Candidates were not allowed to campaign beyond having their names and resumes published in the offical press. Candidates are barred from proposing programs to deal with specific issues (on the pretext that such campaigning encourages "demagoguery and false promises"). And the candidate selection process is largely party-controlled: nominations are decided by the party. And only the Communist Party is legally permitted to distribute propaganda or organize political meetings.

Still, the National Assembly went through an 84% turnover. "Only" two-thirds of candidates were Communist Party members; hence, the new legislature has a large contingent of non-Communist legislators, including two Protestant ministers. The election of Assembly members has no bearing on the selection of high government officials, which is two stages removed from popular accountability.

In April 1994, another major reorganization took place. The State's 21 Ministries, nine Committees, and 10 Institutions were reduced to 27 Ministries and five Institutions. Each had to reorganize internally to reflect current conditions and adapt to the evolving enterprise system. Reforms were also made further down as part of

INTO THE NEXT CENTURY

Fidel Castro turned 70 in August 1996. He may last another decade, but he can't live forever. What comes next?

Fidel's four-years-younger brother, Raúl Castro, the armed forces minister and number two in the Communist Party, is his hierarchical successor. However, he has none of his brother's charisma and is far less popular than Fidel, from whom he derives his political strength.

The prominent rise of influential young politicians suggests that Fidel may prefer his successor to be drawn from their ranks. The foremost contender is Roberto Robaina, who, at 37 years old, was elevated to the post of Foreign Minister in 1993. Other possibilities include Ricardo Alarcón, the National Assembly president and top emissary in dealings with the US, and Carlos Lage, the economics czar and vice president of the Council of State.

They face the challenge of keeping the revolutionary flame alive while cautiously moving towards a quasi-market economy. "Our project," says Robaina, "is to preserve the basic conquests of the Revolution—our sovereignty, independence, health care, and education. Everything else is negotiable." Cuban leaders have even begun to talk of allowing opposition parties—if the US would lift its embargo. Cuba claims that it cannot afford the potential instability of a multi-party system while the US continues to undermine the current government. Castro recently said that he, too, would step down if the conditions were right ("Time goes by, and even marathon runners get tired"), but never while the US maintains its aggressive posture.

A Cuban human rights movement has evolved as the most viable organized opposition to the current regime; it is treated by the government with a mixture of tolerance, repression, and scorn. Most dissident leaders want to see a transition based on reforms that mobilize the system in the direction of social democracy. "Our system is so sick with hatred that any attempt to overthrow the current system would have a terrible effect. Blood would run in the streets," says Elizardo Sanchez, head of the Cuban Commission of Human Rights and National Reconciliation, a leading dissident group within Cuba.

A 674-page report commissioned in 1993 by the US State Department and prepared by 17 academics concluded that "Cuba's future will be grim, no matter what is the name of its ruler or the form of its political regime . . . The most optimistic conclusions set the date for an appreciably more liberal, more democratic, and more prosperous Cuba no sooner than the beginning of the millennium."

The Potential for Civil War

A change of leadership could be traumatic. In a

(continues on next page)

INTO THE NEXT CENTURY
(continued)

classified warning in August 1993, the CIA predicted that "tensions and uncertainties are so acute that significant miscalculations by Castro, a deterioriation of his health, or plotting in the military could provoke regime-threatening instability."

The situation has improved since 1993, but Castro's leadership is so central to the regime's viability that his absence will create unprecedented dilemmas. The initial succession crisis will probably lead to political turmoil. The party may split into factions, while the populace may take to the streets to vent its pent-up desire for change. The potential for bloodshed is considerable—the island is saturated with weapons and virtually every adult knows how to use them.

The role of the military could be decisive. The military top brass is made up of loyal communists (purges get rid of the rest), but it is unknown where the military's loyalties may lie in Fidel's absence.

More US Intervention?

Alas, Cuba is caught between the devil and the deep blue sea. The US holds the key to Cuba's destiny. Since 1996, embodied in US law is the *demand* that Cuba constitute a transition government and, within a year of establishing that government, hold "free and fair" democratic elections. In effect, the US policy is aimed at destabilizing Cuba without

concern for establishing a viable alternative to the revolutionary regime (which would entail shifting support from ultra-right Cuban opposition groups in Miami to more moderate opposition groups with whom the Castro regime has begun to talk).

Once Pandora's box is opened, the US government may feel compelled to intervene; the Clinton administration has already taken steps to deal with the ensuing chaos and confusion, which it considers "inevitable." At that point, the US might also assist radical Cuban-Americans in returning to Cuba to "liberate" their homeland—a scenario that is anathema to everyone now living in Cuba, including the opposition groups, and would doubtless be resisted tooth and nail. US government studies suggest an invasion of Cuba would cost at least 50,000 US casualties. "If they come, they'll experience another Vietnam!" warns Fidel.

It could happen. Since 1994, right-wing politicians led by Sen. Jesse Helms, Chairman of the Senate Foreign Relations Committee, have firmly taken the reins of US policy toward Cuba. Helms, an unrepentant Cold Warrior who has threatened to take Castro out—either "in a horizontal or vertical position"—says, "Forget Haiti. Invade Cuba!" He may not mean it, but Florida's politically ambitious Cuban-American clique is working hard to bring the issue to a head.

streamlining the People's Power System, intended to do away with duplicate functions, more clearly delineate who is responsible for what, and give more clout to local municipal assemblies. Local elected officials are now required by law to meet with voters and report back on what is being done to solve their problems.

RETRENCHMENT?

Cuba is not rushing to embrace the capitalist model, however much the US government would wish it. They are trying to find a third way. For now, things are shaping up towards a "market dictatorship" (dubbed *capitalismo frío,* or cold capitalism) while behind the scenes a power play is occurring between hard-liners and reformers over the pace of reform in Cuba.

The Cuban hierarchy fears losing control. It also fears that Cuba's dignity and sense of purpose has been lost, leading to a crisis of values. By 1995, as the Cuban economy began to rebound, hard-liners in the government expressed fears that change has come too quickly—too much too soon.

The full Central Committee of the Cuban Communist Party met in March 1996 (for only its sixth time ever) and signaled a retrenchment of communist ideals. The meeting confirmed that Cuba would continue its economic planning according to the tenets of Marxist-Leninist theory, while reaffirming its will to resist the Clinton administration's "Track II" policy of undermining the Castro regime through academic exchanges, support for dissidents, and other "fifth column" activities. Nongovernment bodies and the self-employed sector came in for keen criticism, and rigorous efforts to suppress "the negative effects" of free enterprise were called for. The boom in tourism was considered a kind of Trojan Horse that also spreads negative influences, including "the ideas of consumer society" (US dollars aren't clean—they come tainted by decadent cultural values).

The convocation concluded that while harmful, economic changes are necessary under existing circumstances, while the need to protect social-ism was paramount to maintain "revolutionary purity." Thus, a harsh crackdown on political dissidents was implemented in spring 1996.

Nonetheless, Fidel clearly realizes that the age of Marxism-Leninism is gone forever and has concluded that it is time to concentrate on the future. The continued hard-line rhetoric is for public consumption while behind the scenes a new, more progressive stage set is erected and secured.

THE ECONOMY

THE PREREVOLUTIONARY ECONOMY

Ostensibly, in 1958 Cuba was relatively prosperous—fourth among the 20 Latin American nations on a per capita basis, with a large middle class and a mature market economy and banking sector. Yet the wealth was highly concentrated, and the vast majority of the Cuban people were poor.

According to the 1946 census, the last taken before the Revolution, 71% of the land was in the hands of only eight percent of the population. Most of the best land—the sugar land—was owned by US corporations (almost 80% of sugarcane was grown by *colonos,* share-croppers, under contract to the *centrales*).

Dependency on Uncle Sam

US corporations virtually owned the island. Yankee assets in Cuba amounted to over a billion dollars. Most of the cattle ranches, more than 50% of the railways, 40% of sugar production, 90% of mining and oil production, and almost 100% of telephone and utility services were owned by US companies.

Beginning in 1934, every year the US Congress established a preferential quota for Cuban sugar. In exchange for a guaranteed price that was two cents above the world market price—in effect, a "subsidy" to protect US domestic sugar producers—Cuba had to guarantee tariff concessions on US goods sold to Cuba (the island's manufacturers thereby found it impossible to compete with US imports).

The agreement kept Cuba tied to the US as a one-commodity economy. It also bound Cuba to US goods. Cuba was a classic case of a dependent nation. It exported sugar but was forced to import confections. It exported tomatoes but had to buy tomato paste. It supplied the fruits it later had to buy back in cans and the tobacco it had to purchase as cigarettes. In 1958, the US imported more than 75% of all Cuban exports (mostly sugar) and supplied the island with more than 80% of its imports.

US corporations were able to indemnify themselves against taxes on corporate profits. What revenues found their way into state coffers soon disappeared into personal pockets.

Castro inherited a depleted treasury.

COMMUNISM ON STEROIDS

Castro and Che Guevara, who became the Minister of Industry, might have been great revolutionaries, but they didn't have the sharply different set of skills and understanding necessary to run an efficient economy, which they had swiftly nationalized.

There were few coherent economic plans in the 1960s—just grandiose schemes that almost always ended in near ruin. The revolutionaries had zero experience in marketing, financing, and other mercantilist skills. Worse, they tried to buck the law of supply and demand. They replaced monetary work incentives with "moral" incentives, set artificially low prices, and got diminishing supplies in return.

The minimum wage allowed Cubans to buy all available necessities, but there was nothing else to purchase. Thus, there was no incentive to earn more. Rationing inhibited the work incentive that would in turn permit the elimination of rationing. Socialism had nationalized wealth but, says Guillermo Cabrera Infante, in a "Hegelian capriole" it "socialized poverty" too.

Dependency on Comrade Joe

Fortunately, the Soviet Union was more than delighted to step in as Cuba's benefactor. Says P.J. O'Rourke, "The Cuban got the luxury of running their economy along the lines of a Berkeley commune, and like California hippies wheedling their parents for cash, someone else paid the tab."

The reemphasis on sugar production in the late 1960s represented a shift from a disastrous policy of rapid industrialization designed to diversify the economy. Eventually the reimposition of Soviet planning and management mechanisms allowed the Cuban economy to recover during the 1970s.

With the assistance of massive Soviet aid, estimated at more than US$3 billion annually (the Soviet Union also sustained the Cuban economy by buying 85% of its foreign exports "at reasonable market prices"), Cuba's economic growth averaged 7.3% annually in the early 1980s. The annual national budget was also roughly in balance—about US$10.8 billion in both revenue and expenditure.

On the eve of the collapse of the Soviet Union, 84% of Cuba's trade was with the Soviet Union and Eastern Europe.

The End of Subsidies

After the fall of the Berlin Wall, imports from Eastern Europe fell by half in 1990 and virtually ceased in 1991. Imports from the Soviet Union fell from US$5.52 billion in 1989 (including 13 million tons of petroleum) to US$1.31 billion in 1991 (the October coup in Russia severed the gasoline pipeline; no oil whatsoever was delivered in December). By 1992, trade with Cuba's former communist partners had shriveled to seven percent of its former value.

To compound the problem, the world market price of sugar (which in the 1980s accounted for 80% of Cuba's export earnings) also plummeted. In 1989, one ton of sugar bought seven tons of oil; in 1993, a time when Cuba *desperately* needed oil, it would buy just 1.3 tons.

With the supply of fertilizers and pesticides also curtailed, the sugar harvest plummeted from

8.1 million tons in 1989-90 to 4.2 million tons in 1992. In 1993, the harvest—the lowest in 50 years—produced only 3.3 million tons (with an export value of only $965 million, down from $5 billion in 1986). It was an unmitigated disaster.

The Soviet Union's collapse cut Cuba's "rustbucket" economy adrift. Between 1990 and 1994, the economy shrank 34% according to the Cuban government (estimates from nongovernment sources suggest the figure may have been as high as 60%). By the end of 1994, half the country's industrial factories had closed, as had 70% of its public transport network. Sugar mills were shut down and cannibalized for parts to keep more efficient mills operating. Power outages further disrupted industrial production. Lunch breaks were eliminated so that office workers could leave early to save on electricity. Ominously, inflation was running at 80-90%. Unemployment stood at 40%. The work force was left idle.

A FAREWELL TO MARXISM

Castro scorned the shock therapy adopted by other Latin American countries. Still, Cuba clearly would have to do an about-face to survive.

Thus, Castro elevated so-called "yummies"—young, upwardly mobile Marxists—to senior positions in government ministries. The yummies believed they had the New Age quasi-Marxist ideas to restore health to the ailing economy without sacrificing the advances of the Revolution.

In October 1991, the Cuban Communist Party Congress adopted a resolution establishing profit-maximizing state-owned Cuban corporations that operate independently of the central state apparatus. They're free to engage in multinational commerce, and they enjoy total independence in purchasing, marketing, and negotiating with foreign investors. Together they established a joint corporation constituted for a period of 25 years with a one-time option for a 25-year extension. Government subsidies are also history; each company must establish its own profit margin (they give to the state any profits remaining after reinvesting and paying dividends to shareholders). Foreign investors are exempted for 10 years from taxes on income—and, most important, they can repatriate all profits.

CUBAN CIGARS

"There is no substitute for our tobacco anywhere in the world. It's easier to make good cognac than to achieve the quality of Cuban tobacco."

—Fidel Castro

It seems ironic that Cuba—scourge of the capitalist world—should have been compelled by history and geography to produce that blatant symbol of capitalist wealth and power, the cigar. Yet it does so with pride. The unrivaled reputation of Cuban cigars as the best in the world transcends politics, transubstantiating a weed into an object capable of evoking rapture. And Cubans guard the unique reputation scrupulously.

"Havana" cigars are not only a source of hard currency—they're part and parcel of the national culture. Although Fidel gave up smoking in 1985 (after what he called a "heroic struggle"), Cubans still smoke 250 million cigars domestically every year. Another 65 million are exported annually through Habanos, S.A. (exports were 100 million annually in the late 1980s but fell to 50 million in 1994 before beginning to rebound). Although some 20% of Cuban cigars are machine-made, only hand-rolling can produce the best quality.

An Early Beginning

This cigar tradition was first documented among the indigenous tribes by Christopher Columbus. The Taino Indians made monster cigars (at the very least, they probably kept the mosquitoes away) called *cohiba* (the word "cigar" originated from *sikar*, the Mayan word for smoking, which in Spanish became *cigarro*).

The popular habit of smoking cigars (as opposed to tobacco in pipes, first introduced to Europe by Columbus) began in Spain, where cigars made from Cuban tobacco were first made in Seville in 1717. Demand for higher-quality cigars grew and *Sevillas* (as Spanish cigars were called) were superseded by Cuban-made cigars. King Ferdinand VI of Spain encouraged production—a state monopoly—in the Spanish colony. Soon, tobacco was Cuba's main export.

After the Peninsula Campaign (1806-12) of the Napoleonic wars, British and French veterans returned home with the cigar habit, which soon became fashionable in their home countries.

By the mid-19th century, there were almost 1,300 cigar factories throughout Cuba.

A US Addiction

Israel Putnam, an officer in the British Army (later an American general in the Revolutionary War), introduced the cigar to North America in 1762, when he returned from Cuba to his home in Connecticut with a selection of Havana cigars. Soon, Cuban cigars were being imported. Domestic cigar production also began, using Cuban tobacco (even the American cigars were known as Havanas, which by then had become a generic term). By the late 19th century, several US presidents practiced the habit and helped make cigar smoking a status symbol.

The demand fostered a full-fledged cigar-making industry in the United States (by 1905 there were 80,000 cigar-manufacturing businesses in the US, most of them mom-and-pop operations run by Cuban émigrés). But it was to Cuba that the cognoscenti looked for the finest cigars of all. "No lover of cigars can imagine the voluptuous pleasure of sitting in a café sipping slowly a strong magnificent coffee and smoking rhythmically those divine leaves of Cuba," wrote American pianist Arthur Rubenstein.

Bundled, Boxed, and Boycotted

Cuban cigars were sold originally in bundles covered with pigs' bladders, later in huge cedar chests. The banking firm of H. Upmann initiated export in cedar boxes in 1830, when it imported cigars for its directors in London. Later, the bank decided to enter the cigar business, and the embossed cedar box complete with colorful lithographic label became the standard form of packaging. Each specific brand evolved its own elaborate lithograph, while different sizes (and certain brands) even evolved their own box styles.

The Montecristo was the fashionable cigar of choice. In the 1930s, any tycoon or film director worth the name was to be seen with a whopping Montecristo A in his mouth. Half of all the Havanas sold in the world in the 1930s were Montecristos, by which time much of Cuba's tobacco industry had passed into US ownership.

Among the devotees of Cuban cigars was President Kennedy, who smoked Petit Uppmans. In 1962, at the height of the Cuban missile crisis, Kennedy asked his press secretary Pierre Salinger to obtain as many Uppmans as he could. Next day, reported Salinger, Kennedy asked him how many he

(continues on next page)

CUBAN CIGARS
(continued)

had found. Twelve hundred, replied his aide. Kennedy then pulled out and signed the decree establishing a trade embargo with Cuba. Ex-British premier Winston Churchill also stopped smoking Havanas and started smoking Jamaican cigars, but after a time he forgot about politics and went back to Havanas. During World War II, the Cubans had made him a gift of 10,000 top-quality cigars. His brand was Romeo y Julieta.

The embargo dealt a crushing blow to Cuba's cigar industry. Castro nationalized the cigar industry and founded a state monopoly, Cubatabaco. Many dispossessed cigar-factory owners emigrated to the Dominican Republic, Mexico, Venezuela, and Honduras, where they started up again, often using the same brand names they had owned in Cuba (today, the Dominican Republic produces 47% of the handmade cigars imported into the US). Experts agree, however, that these foreign "Cuban" brands are inferior to their Havana counterparts (perhaps this is why cigar sales in the US have declined from nine billion cigars in 1970 to two billion today).

A Finer Choice

At the time of the Revolution, about 1,000 brands and sizes of Havanas existed. There are now about 35 brands and 500 cigar varieties. Only eight factories make handmade export-quality cigars in Cuba today, compared to 120 at the beginning of the century. All cigar factories produce various brands. Some factories specialize in particular flavors, others in particular sizes—of which there are no fewer than 60 standard variations, with minor variations from brand to brand.

Fatter cigars—the choice of connoisseurs—are more fully flavored and smoke more smoothly and slowly than those with smaller ring gauges. As a rule, darker cigars are also more full-bodied and sweeter. The expertise and care expressed in the cigar factory determines how well a cigar burns and tastes, and a visit to a factory is a must for anyone wishing to gain a true appreciation of Havana cigars.

Cigars, when properly stored, continue to ferment and mature in their boxes—an aging process similar to good wines. Rules on when to smoke a cigar don't exist, but many experts claim that the prime cigars are those aged for six to eight years. Everyone agrees that a cigar should be smoked either within three months of manufacture or not for at least a year (the interim is known as a "period of sickness").

For a complete synopsis of individual cigar brands and types, refer to the *Cigar Companion: A Connoisseur's Guide,* by Anwer Bati (Running Press, 125 S. 22nd St., Philadelphia, PA 19103), or *Rudman's Complete Pocket Guide to Cigars,* by Theo Rudman (Good Living Publishing, Helderberg, South Africa). Two books—*Holy Smoke,* by Guillermo Cabrera Infante, and *Cuban Counterpoint,* by Fernando Ortíz—tell the tale of Cuban cigars. Other good resources are the quarterly *Cigar Aficionado* (M. Shanker Communications Inc., 387 Park Ave. S., New York, NY 10016), and the German language *European Cigar Cult Journal* (im Falstaff-Verlag, Opernring 1/E/4, A10/10 Wien, Austria).

By 1993, a clearly defined model had evolved. The old Central Planning Board, which piloted the state-run economy, was abolished. Cuba stood between "an unworkable socialism and a voracious market economy, searching for alternatives in the midst of crisis," noted Cuban scholar Gail Reed.

Wooing Foreign Investors

The process began slowly and cautiously but has snowballed in recent years. In April 1994, the government created a Foreign Investment Ministry to more aggressively woo foreign investors. In September 1995, the Cuban National Assembly passed a law allowing foreigners to have wholly owned businesses in all sectors of the economy except defense, national security, education, and public health. Foreigner corporations (but not individuals) can even buy buildings (but not land, which is leased).

In 1996, Castro signed a deal initiating duty-free zones around Havana and Santiago de Cuba with special tax, banking, tariff, and other incentives for foreign corporations. It has even begun to sell off state entities and is even looking at creating industrial parks.

After 1990, Havana began handing over large chunks of the economy to the military, which in July 1987 had begun sweeping experiments in the management of its enterprises, including Western-style management techniques; military leaders began taking seminars on entrepreneurial methods, quality control, and worker incentives. Today, generals in civilian clothes run quasi-private corporations such as Gaviota (which is partially owned by foreign investors), some of whose resort hotels are built by the army's construction company, Unión de Empresas Constructoras. TRD Caribe, a subsidiary of Gaviota, even runs a chain of department stores.

Reinventing Capitalism

Cuba has sent some of its best and brightest abroad for crash courses in capitalist business techniques. The University of Havana has adapted its economics courses to include courses on capitalism. And an International Business Center of Havana opened in June 1993 to teach marketing and management seminars. That ultimate symbol of *Yanqui* capitalism, advertising, has also returned to Cuba (revenue from advertising made it possible for Cuba's state-run *Tele Rebelde* to televise the World Cup soccer games in 1994).

In the summer of 1993, Castro opened up the service sector and agriculture to private enterprise on an individual basis. State farms were to be converted to private cooperatives run on the basis of profitability, individual citizens could lease land and cultivate it on their own, and produce markets were permitted.

The government also legalized self-employment for plumbers, electricians, tailors, cobblers, barbers, photographers, and dozens of others who could—upon registration (self-employed people need a permit from the State Labor and Social Security Committee)—ply their trades freely. The government even planned to rent out hundreds of vacant *cafeterías* and storefronts to private individuals. In late 1995, Minister for Economy and Planning José Luís Rodriguez said that private and state-run small and medium-sized business would soon become part of the scene. By mid-1995, 210,000 Cubans (about five percent of Cuba's labor force) had officially registered as self-employed individuals. Another 200,000 or so were engaged in similar activities without bothering about the legalities.

By January 1994, 69% of state-run companies were operating in the red, kept from bleeding to death by massive state subsidies. The government proposed to cut its massive deficit by slashing subsidies, eliminating 700,000 jobs, imposing price increases, and reducing a huge excess of liquidity by taking up to nine billion pesos out of circulation (in 1994, 12.5 billion pesos were in circulation in Cuba).

When dollars were legalized, in 1993, the peso—which officialy is at parity with the dollar but floats at market value on the black market—crashed, bottoming out at 150 to the dollar in 1994. It was essential to end the dual economy, whereby the dollar and peso circulate side by side, like hot and cold ocean currents. For now, the Cuban government is attempting to replace dollars in circulation with "convertible" pesos equal to the dollar (but not actually convertible).

By 1995 the peso had rebounded to 20 to US$1, a sure sign of a stronger economy.

Meanwhile, the government desperately needed to get hold of foreign currency floating freely in the black market (economics minister Carlos Lage estimated that up to US$300 million in foreign currency circulates illegally each year, usually coming into the country as aid from relatives abroad or as tips from foreign tourists). In

selling lighter fluid refills

CHRISTOPHER P. BAKER

mid-1993, therefore, Cuba legalized that paramount capitalist tool, the *yanqui* dollar

The government hoped to drain dollars from the booming black market, relieve shortages by allowing more foreign goods into mainstream Cuban society, and attract more money from the million-plus Cuban "exiles" in the US

To soak up the dollars, the government opened up "foreign exchange recovery stores." Every item imaginable—from gasoline and toothpaste to Japanese TVs—was made available. The dollar's legalization opened up a huge internal market, igniting trade that has fueled the economy: in 1994, Cubans spent an estimated US$1 billion in 600 state-run hard-currency stores across the island.

In September 1995, the government also announced that Cubans could open interest-bearing savings accounts (which the Communists had theretofore discouraged) or purchase certificates of deposits with dollars (the National Bank of Cuba will pay the market interest rate). And, for the first time, loans would be available to self-employed people.

Cuba even introduced its first investment fund—the Beta Gran Caribe Fund—in fall 1995, on the Irish Stock Exchange. (The old Havana Stock Exchange is—and is likely for the foreseeable future to remain—a workers' canteen.)

In 1994, the National Assembly of People's Power approved the first tax law in Cuba—a bitter pill to swallow, since Cubans had not been subject to taxation since 1967. In addition, parliament approved fees for a range of items that had been free, such as school lunches and sporting events. In January 1996, personal foreign exchange income and various "profitable activities" became subject to taxation at rates from 10% to 50%, payable in pesos or hard currency, depending on how taxpayers made their income. Taxes are targeted primarily at the self-employed, who must pay a fixed monthly payment (and, at the end of the year, a progressive amount based on their actual income). To collect taxes, a new entity, the National Office of Tax Administration (ONAT), was created.

Back from the Brink

As a result of all these reforms, Cuba halted the slide. In 1993, long-depressed sugar and nickel prices began rising, and Cuba's energetic attempts to reinsert itself into the world market were beginning to pay off.

The government reported that the economy grew 0.7% in 1994 and 2.7% in 1995 (when exports rose 14%). GDP for 1996 increased 7.8%. State revenues were up 25% and subsidies to inefficient state enterprises down 40%. The deficit was reduced from 33% of GDP in 1993 to 2.4% in 1996.

Meanwhile, foreign debt has risen from US$2.8 billion in 1983 to US$9 billion in 1995. Much of the debt is extremely high-cost short-term loans. Imports have thus required payment in cash, forcing Cuba to interrupt payments on existing debt.

As radical as these changes appear, Cuban authorities have hesitated about wholesale economic reforms. The state has no intention of ceding control of the economy to its citizens. The question is whether the tentative steps towards *capitalismo frio* will prove too slippery a slope for the government to turn back. Already the activities of the foreign joint ventures, the new farmers' markets, the new self-employed sector, and the vast black market are far larger and more vibrant than the official, socialist economy.

Fidel wants capitalists but not capitalism. In fall 1995, Castro warned that the economic reforms "do not signify a return to capitalism, much less a crazy and uncontrolled rush in that direction. . . . We have swept away the capitalist system, and it will never return as long as there is a communist, a patriot, a revolutionary in Cuba . . . . Our main objective is to preserve the revolution, our independence, and the achievements of socialism"—and, he might have added, the single-party system or his own rule.

In the wake of Castro's displeasure, legislators have leaned away from further reforms. After opening a Pandora's box, in 1995 the government began reversing itself on some of the reforms. A period of "consolidation" was judged necessary.

While foreign capitalists are welcome to join hands with Cuban state-owned corporations, Cuba's self-employed are increasingly finding Cuban-style capitalism bruising in the face of growing government regulation and taxation. Each modest reform is hedged with restrictions. The government keeps businesses on a short leash. There is zero tolerance for those who try to

WHAT US CITIZENS CAN DO TO HELP END THE EMBARGO

Since 1996, the US embargo has been embodied in law. However, times (and laws) change. US citizens who oppose the embargo can make their views known to representatives in Washington. The following suggestions are offered by the Center for Cuban Studies:

Contact Your Senator or Representative in Congress: US Congress, Washington, D.C. 20510, tel. (202) 225-3121—House switchboard—or (202) 224-3121 for the Senate switchboard. Write a simple, moderate, straightforward letter to your representative that makes the argument for ending the embargo and requests he/she co-sponsor a bill to rescind the Helms-Burton legislation.

Write or Call President Clinton: President Clinton, The White House, Washington, D.C. 20500, tel. (202) 456-1414. Also call or fax the **White House Comment Line,** tel. (202) 456-1111, fax (202) 456-2461, **National Security Advisor,** tel. (202) 456-2255, fax (202) 456-2883, and the **Secretary of State,** tel. (202) 647-6575, fax (202) 647-7120.

Publicize Your Concern: Write a simple, moderate, straightforward letter to the editor of your local newspaper as well as any national newspapers or magazines and make the argument for ending the embargo.

Senators and Representatives and their staffs religiously read and heed letters to the editors in hometown and home-state publications. Every letter on an important issue is deemed to express the views of 500 other constituents who don't take the trouble to write.

Support Solidarity Organizations: Humanitarian and solidarity organizations that work to normalize relations with Cuba are underfunded and welcome donations (see chart "Organizations" for a complete list of organizations). In addition, consider joining the Center for Cuban Studies ($40 per year, including a subscription to *Cuba Update;* 124 West 23rd St., New York, NY 10011, tel. (212) 242-0559, fax (212) 242-1937.

---

bend the rules; budding entrepreneurs find themselves in a constant ballet with the government.

In fall 1995, the self-employed were no longer allowed to sell their products near schools, hospitals, tourist areas, government establishments, or on major streets. Nor can state enterprises buy their goods or services from the self-employed. The government reserves unto itself the right to limit self-employment where there is a local labor shortage. An individual may sell only what he or she produces—no filthy middlemen! No one may hire workers. And university graduates are not allowed to work on their own account.

The state occasionally purges entrepreneurs it considers too prosperous by seizing their cars, motorcycles, and other assets gained from "excess profits." Instead, many Cubans fear that the Cuban government is moving to quash free enterprise altogether as the Cuban economy regains its vigor and posture.

AGRICULTURE

"'There must be much hunger,'" says one of Ernest Hemingway's characters in *Islands in the Stream.* "'You cannot realize it,'" comes the reply. "No I can't, Thomas Hudson thought. I can't realize it at all. I can't realize why there should ever be any hunger in this country ever." Traveling through Cuba, you'll also sense the vast potential that caused René Dumont, the outstanding French agronomist, to say that "with proper management, Cuba could adequately feed five times its current population."

Before the Revolution, Cuba certainly couldn't feed itself: the best arable lands were planted in sugarcane for export. Alas, the revolutionary government hasn't managed agriculture efficiently either. Thoughts of self-sufficiency were sacrificed to satisfy the Soviet sweet tooth. And management of agriculture has been dumbfoundingly inept.

Prior to the 1960 Agrarian Reform Law, about 16% of the land was owned by individual farmers; the balance was held in large estates, many owned by large, US-owned sugar companies. After the Revolution, the lands were organized in a system of centralized, inefficient state farms dedicated to monoculture. Large farms supplanted small ones, machines replaced laborers, and Cuba followed "modern" agricultural practices, utilizing imported pesticides and fertilizers. Food distribution was also centralized and highly inefficient (in 1991, "for every peso of fruits and vegetables on the stand, 23 cents were lost to spoilage," reported journalist Gail Reed).

Over 1.6 million hectares are given to sugarcane and 2.5 million to pasture. Only 1.5 million hectares are set aside for other crops. A mere 12% of the land under cultivation is planted in food crops; the rest is dedicated to export crops. More than 60% of Cuba's rice, grains, and other staples are imported.

Cuba's major obstacle to recovery remains agricultural production, which in the early 1990s collapsed due to a combination of factors, including lack of machinery, fertilizers, and labor incentives, plus a series of alternating droughts and torrential storms that conspired with a series of pest-plagues to devastate crop harvests. Unfortunately, too, deteriorating living conditions induced farmers and agricultural workers to put down their hoes to move in with better-off city cousins, leaving fewer and fewer laborers toiling in the fields. To forestall the movement, the virtues of returning to an agrarian lifestyle are being extolled. And new rural towns are planned to lure urbanites (in January 1996, it was announced that 120,000 new houses would be built in the countryside).

The "National Food Self-Sufficiency Program"
In 1991-94, Cuba's population faced malnutrition on a massive scale. Cuba's number-one priority was to increase food production. Ground zero in the battle is the fertile agricultural land around Havana, where large tracts of land have been switched from export crops to food crops. Vacant land, such as that along roadsides, was cultivated. And vegetable gardens—previously a rare sight—sprouted in the urban centers. (In early 1992, the government claimed that there were 30,000 such gardens in Havana, and nearly one million across the country. This is surely an exaggeration.)

Legions of "volunteers" and laid-off workers were shipped to the countryside to help boost production. The massive mobilization of cityfolk to farmlands did not solve the problem. The "national food self-sufficiency program" failed to meet basic needs, especially for vegetables and fruits. More dramatic reforms were called for.

The Breakup of State Farms
In September 1993, Cuba made dramatic changes in the organization of its agriculture. Prior to this, state farms and about 180 agro-industrial complexes cultivated 82% of Cuba's arable land. Cooperatives farmed an additional 10%, with the balance farmed by private farmers. The new law—Resolution 357—authorized the establishment of autonomous cooperatives (unidades basicas de producción cooperativa) on land set aside "for an indefinite period" by the state. These cooperatives own their production, administer their own resources, open their own bank accounts, elect their own managers, develop their own budgets, purchase their own equipment, and pay their own taxes. They farm government land but own the crop they harvest (by contrast, traditional cooperatives pool their plots for common land ownership). However, they are still obliged to follow state directives and sell all their production to the state at prices fixed by the latter.

In addition, the law authorized the transfer of idle land to private owners. In 1994, 12,000 hectares of tobacco land were turned over to 5,835 families. Families have been granted land in mountainous areas. And small plots (less than half a hectare) of idle land have been leased to pensioners and others whose circumstances prevent them participating in "systematic" farming. Private farms currently utilize about 20% of Cuba's cultivable land (they, too, are obliged to sell 80% of their produce to the state).

As a result of the reforms, only 5.5% of sugarcane farmlands are now in state farms. In addition, agricultural subsidies fell from three billion pesos in 1993 to 1.7 billion in 1994 and less than 500 million in 1995. Food production increased 11% in 1995.

Reverting to Traditional Agriculture
The need for foreign exchange still dictates that priority must go to production for export. But large tracts of land have been switched from export-oriented cash crops to food crops. More importantly, massive experiments in farming are taking place, based on traditional practices such as increased use of oxen (since 1990, 100,000 bulls have been domesticated to plow the fields) and old-fashioned mulching combined with organic fertilizers such as fermented cane runoff.

Today, Cuba is at the forefront of historic efforts to apply ecologically sound agricultural

THE ORGANIC REVOLUTION

Prior to the Special Period, Cuba's agricultural system was dominated by large-scale, capital-intensive monoculture more similar in many ways to the Central Valley of California than to the typical Latin American *minifundio* (small-scale farm). Cuban farming became dependent on mechanization, artificial fertilizers, insecticides, and other costly inputs channeled virtually cost-free through the Soviet umbilical cord. When the Soviet bloc collapsed, food imports plummeted along with chemical subsidies.

Compounding the problem, during the early 1980s Cuba had pushed toward the extremes of capital-intensive farming without regard to the consequent problems. Insecticides devastated natural insect predators, while many pests became resistant (and Cuba began to see infestations of "super pests"). Meanwhile, soils had been salinized by excessive irrigation and sterilized by fertilizers and pesticides and no longer produced a concomitant increase in yields.

Converting to Sanity

Today, Cuba is undergoing the world's most ambitious and far-reaching conversion from chemical-intensive agriculture to organic and semi-organic farming using integrated pest management, crop rotation, soil conservation practices, organic fertilizers, intercrops, and oxen in place of tractors.

Cuba has rediscovered traditional peasant methods and invented its own alternative technologies. An "alternative agriculture" movement had taken hold as early as 1982, including an ambitious research program in biological control using biopesticides. Today it has over 200 artisanal centers that produce biopesticides nationwide, headed by farmers trained in universities (while farmers in other Latin American countries are marginalized, in Cuba they are at the center of things and enjoy access to leading technology).

Cuban scientists are releasing parasitic and predatory insects en masse; bacterial and fungal diseases of insect pests are also being applied to crops in lieu of chemical insecticides; the Mechanization Institute, which once developed tractor-drawn plows, now builds innovative implements pulled by oxen; and the use of biofertilizers (for example, legumes as green manures and free-living bacteria that make atmospheric nitrogen available for other crops) is said to be unrivaled in the world.

By 1995, Cuba was beginning to see chemical-free food production rising to levels attained before the organic revolution.

"The future elsewhere in the world will require Cuba's new model," says Dr. Peter Rosset, director of California's Institute for Food and Development Policy (popularly known as Food First), which has a collaborative project with the Cuban Association for Organic Farming and the Advanced Institute for Agricultural Sciences of Havana.

For further reading, check out *The Greening of Cuba: A National Experiment in Organic Agriculture* by Peter Rosset and Medea Benjamin.

Study Tours

Global Exchange, 2017 Mission St. Suite 303, San Francisco, CA 94110, tel. (415) 255-7296 or (800) 497-1994, offers study tours of Cuba's organic farming and agricultural development. A typical one-week tour costs US$1,300 including round-trip airfare.

Food First, 398 60th St, Oakland, CA 94618, tel. (510) 654-4400 or (800) 888-3314; e-mail food-first@igc.apc.org, also has occasional study tours featuring visits to agricultural cooperatives, biopesticide production centers, "organoponic" food gardens, and the Havana Agricultural University in San José de las Lajas.

techniques. "Cuba has made what is proably the world's most immediate and far-reaching changeover from chemical-dependent agriculture to low-input, sustainable agriculture," says Medea Benjamin, co-author of *The Greening of the Revolution.*

The Cubans began experimenting with alternative farming in the early 1980s. The demise of the Soviet Union has forced them to plunge in headlong, assisted by the U.N. Food and Agricultural Organization.

Biological agents such as fungi and nematodes have been harnessed as pest control agents. A small worm-eating fly now guards the yucca crop; zillions of wasps are being bred to attack the sugarcane borer; and ants have been unleashed in the banana and sweet potato crops.

The Food Research Institute of Havana has

also developed a technology for the production of food products (such as milk and yogurt) from soybeans. Fortunately, soy food products are much less expensive to produce than meat and dairy products. Nutritionists have come up with a soy-enriched ground beef as a solution to the beef shortage. They've also invented Cerelac, a powdered milk substitute that today has replaced the liter of milk a day that every child once received. The government had to convince Cubans to eat the stuff (Cubans roll their eyes at the mere mention of soy—they do *not* like it).

Global Exchange, 2017 Mission St. #303, San Francisco, CA 94110, tel. (415) 255-7296, offers study tours to explore how Cuba is restructuring its food system to emphasize self-sufficiency and sustainability.

Cattle

Cattle numbered more than 5.9 million on the eve of the Special Period. Cuba has always had a strong cattle industry, particularly in the central provinces centered on Camagüey, which has been famous for beef and dairy production since before the Revolution. Castro has taken a lively interest in the field, so to speak, especially in the development of sturdier strains and artificial insemination. The central uplands are a center for genetic breeding of cattle, such as Cuba's home-grown Charolais, Santa Gertrudis, and F1 strains. Zebu from India, for example, have been crossed with Canadian Holstein, well adapted to the tropics yet capable, reportedly, of giving a whopping 20 or more pints of milk a day.

Development is hindered by a lack of water and nutritious feed; cattle forage on natural grasses, but owing to deforestation and a change to a more arid climate over the past 400 years, these have evolved to the point where they are no longer nutritious. Cuba has made advances in alternative cattle feeds (such as from bagasse), but not sufficient to sustain notably greater yields.

Unfortunately, the dairy industry was reliant on imported feed grain. In 1990, Cuba could no longer afford to import feed for domestic livestock. Consequently, milk production fell to 335 million liters in 1992. (In 1994, the state therefore had to curtail the milk ration for children over seven. In mid-1995, it limited rations to children under three and a half years old.)

Citrus

In 1990, Cuba—the world's 14th-largest producer—exported 460,000 tons of citrus (the target had been 1.5 million tons), mostly to the Soviet Union and Eastern Bloc countries. Cuba's citrus fruits are not of sufficient quality to compete on world markets, and the vast majority of fruits grown serve the domestic market for fruit juice.

Many of the citrus plantations are now overgrown with weeds, but considerable effort is now being made to upgrade them, with technical assistance from Chile and Israel. A 115,000-acre citrus operation at Jagüey Grande is the world's largest under one management; it is operated by an Israeli company as part of a US$22 million joint venture. The Jagüey Grande project produced about 600,000 tons of oranges, grapefruits, limes, and tangerines in 1995, equivalent to less than one percent of total US production (an Israeli engineer working on the project informed me that Cuban plantation managers vastly exaggerate the production figures). An estimated 150,000 tons of citrus was lost in October 1996, when Hurricane Lili socked it to Cuba.

Coffee

Cuba produces excellent coffee. (Japan and France account for almost 80% of Cuba's coffee exports.) The finest quality is the Crystal Mountain variety, grown mainly in the Sierra del Escambray.

Last century, Cuba was one of the world's leading coffee producers. In 1827, there were 2,067 coffee plantations *(cafeteles).* Most, however, were destroyed during the 10-year War of Independence. The introduction of a tariff to protect Cuban coffee in 1927 prompted a revival, and Cuba enjoyed modest exports on the eve of the Revolution. The exodus of workers from the land in recent years, however, has had an impact on coffee production, which has declined over the past decade. Yields and total production have dropped even more markedly since 1990 (exports—the responsibility of the firm Cubaexport—fell from 12,000 tons to 9,200 tons between 1990 and 1994). A plan—*Plan Turquino*—was therefore conceived to motivate farmers and their families to remain in the mountains and train young people in coffee cultivation. Most coffee is grown on small plots worked by hand.

SOYA WANNA INVEST IN CUBA?

Before the economic crisis, Cuba provided all children under the age of 14 with one liter of dairy milk per day. At press time, the country could only provide milk for children under seven. The government's goal was to substitute soy yogurt for children between ages seven and 14.

To help Cuba realize its potential, Global Exchange launched the Campaign to Exempt Food and Medicines from the Embargo (under existing US law, trade in food and medicines to Cuba is illegal) by creating ¡Soy Cubano! in association with the Cuban Institute for Basic Research in Tropical Agriculture. ¡Soy Cubano! has entered into a joint venture with a Cuban factory that produces soy yogurt, soy ice cream, and soy cheeses. The joint venture directly contravenes the US embargo—and is meant to do so—by encouraging US citizens to invest in a Cuban enterprise that

works towards ensuring that Cuban children receive a healthy, protein-rich diet.

By the close of 1996 ¡Soy Cubano! had raised US$45,000 and had more than 700 shareholders around the world. The money will fund the purchase of raw materials and equipment, research, and the construction of soy factories in each province of Cuba, with the aim of producing two liters of soy yogurt drink per week for Cuban children who can no longer receive their previously guaranteed liter of milk per day due to the economic crisis.

Shares can be purchased by contacting the ¡Soy Cubano! Company, c/o Food and Medicine Campaign, P.O. Box 401116, San Francisco, CA 94140, tel. (415) 558-9490, fax (415) 255-7498.

A persuasive half-hour documentary video—*Soy Cubano*—explains the issues and costs US$25 (US$50 to institutions).

Sugar

¡Azúcar! The whole country reeks of sweet, pungent sugar, Cuba's curse and her blessing. The Cuban landscape is one of endless cane fields, lorded over by the towering chimneys of great sugar mills. Sugar is Cuba's bondsman. The nation's bittersweet calvary has been responsible for curses like slavery and the country's almost total dependence on not only the one product, but, as history as proven, on single imperial nations: first Spain, then the United States, and most recently the Soviet Union.

Due to Cuba's soil and climate, sugar thrives here as nowhere else in the world. The unusual depth (up to seven meters) and fertility of Cuba's limestone soils are unparalleled in the world for producing sugar—sugar plants can be raised without replanting for up to 20 years, a longer period than anywhere else in the world. And the sucrose content of Cuban sugar is higher, too.

Four decades ago, the World Bank wrote of "the diabetic dangers of the dominance of sugar in her economic bloodstream." Cuba's economy reverberated whenever world sugar prices fell. Periods of prosperity were followed by periods of depression. Even when world sugar prices boomed, only a handful of speculators and investors profited. When prices were low, every Cuban suffered.

Cuba had one of the highest rates of unemployment in the world, and no other country in the world had quite the same problem—an entire rural underclass thrown out of work for eight months of the off-season. Many workers and their families were forced to subsist on *sopa de gallo* (rooster soup), a mixture of brown sugar and water.

Dreams of breaking Cuba's dependence on monoculture were shattered in the 1960s by the island's shift of economic dependence from the United States to the Soviet Union. Cuba's newfound colonial role was to feed sugar to the Soviet bear. (The Soviets showed little interest in promoting Cuban diversification.) Cuba's traditional dependence on sugar exports changed little during three decades of socialism: sugar represented about 75% by value of Cuban exports on the eve of the Revolution; in 1989, it was about 80%. Production rose gradually from about 5 million tons a year in the early 1970s to an impressive 7.5 million tons on average in the late 1980s.

About one-quarter of production went to capitalist markets to earn Cuba hard currency. Alas, world sugar prices fell from 20 cents in 1980 to a measly four cents in 1985—comparable to prices in the depression year of 1932. Cuba's sugar-dependent economy is still on a treadmill; it has had to produce more and more sugar

ZAFRA—THE SUGAR HARVEST

With the onset of the dry season, Cuba prepares for the *zafra,* the sugar harvest, which runs from November through June. Then, the temperatures soars into the 90s and the harvesters *(macheteros)* are in the fields from dawn until dusk, wielding their short, wide, blunt-nosed machetes.

First, the cane stalks are burnt at ground level to soften them for the cut. The *macheteros* grab the three-meter-tall stalks, which they slash close to the ground (where the sweetness concentrates). Then, they cut off the top and strip the dry leaves from the stalk.

Before the introduction of mechanical cane cutters in the 1970s, 350,000 laborers were required for the harvest, and workers used to come by tens of thousands from Haiti and Jamaica just for the season. In 1989, when three-quarters of the crop was harvested mechanically, only 60,000 workers were needed. The Cuban-designed combine-harvester can cut a truckload of cane (about 15,000 pounds) in 10 minutes, three times more than even the most skilled *macheteros* can cut by hand in a day.

Harvesters rumble and sputter through the night, their paths illuminated by floodlights. The cut cane is then delivered to one of the approximately 150 sugar mills in Cuba, which operate 24 hours a day. Here, the sugarcane is fed to the huge steel crushers that squeeze out the sugary pulp called *guarapo* (drunk by Cubans cold or with rum), which is boiled, clarified, evaporated, and separated into molasses and sugar crystals. The molasses makes rum, yeast, and cattle feed. *Bagasse,* the fibre left after squeezing, fuels boilers or is shipped off to mills to be turned into paper

BOB RACE

sugarcane

and wallboard. The sugar is shipped by rail to bulk shipping terminals, such as the huge Tricontinental in Cienfuegos, for transport to refineries abroad.

---

to generate the same income. Moreover, Cuba has faced growing competition from Brazil and new producers such as India and the increasingly more efficient sugar *beet* producers. Between 1969 and 1985, Cuba's share of total sugar imports by capitalist countries declined from 13% to under nine percent.

The collapse of the Soviet bloc rendered a triple whammy to Cuba's sugar industry. Not only did its main market collapse, but preferential prices guaranteed by the Soviet Union also vanished, forcing Cuba to sell its sugar at world market prices. The sugar fields also had to go without fertilizer and herbicides, while a lack of

fuel and spare parts rendered harvesters (the harvest is 80% mechanized) and sugar processing plants useless. From seven million tons in 1991, the harvest plummeted in 1994 to a 50-year low of 3.3 million tons.

In 1993, the government reorganized the industry. Most state farms were abolished. Workers now work in cooperatives, earning profits for cane produced over state-set quotas. In November 1994, the Cuban government spoke of allowing foreign investors back to revitalize the sugar industry. Cuba also hopes to attract foreign investors to build sugar refineries (the country has traditionally exported raw sugar to countries that process the sugar in their own refineries; much of world demand is for refined sugar, which sells at a higher price). Sure enough, international banks and commodities brokers are now investing in Cuba's sugar industry.

By May 1996, the harvest had attained the year's goal of 4.5 million tons. Should the Cuban sugar harvest recover, several million tons of sugar that were once price-indexed to Soviet oil imports will spill onto the world market, driving prices down.

Ironically, sugar isn't easy to find in Cuba and is rarely available at government stores.

Tobacco

Tobacco has traditionally been Cuba's second most important agricultural earner of foreign exchange. About 50,000 hectares are given to tobacco, which is grown in rich valleys and slopes throughout Cuba, but predominantly in a 90-mile-long, 10-mile-wide valley—Vuelta Abajo—in Pinar del Río, incomparably the best spot in the world to grow tobacco. Cuban tobacco is grown on small properties, many privately owned by the farmers (the average holding is only 25 acres).

Annual production attained about 50,000 metric tons in the mid-1970s before a blight of blue mold infected the tobacco fields. Production gradually recovered and reached about 40,000 tons in 1990 (enough for 90 million cigars, worth about US$100 million). Unable to afford fertilizers and fungicides, and hit by adverse weather, Cuba has since experienced a series of disastrous harvests. Production fell by 50% in 1993 and markedly again in 1995. European importers rushed in to protect their source by offering short-terms loans.

It worked. The 1996 harvest yielded 32,000 tons (70 million cigars' worth), up 25% from 1995. Foreign investment continues.

INDUSTRY

The Castro regime has invested considerable money in metal processing, spare parts industries to service equipment installed prior to the US embargo, and factories turning out domestic appliances (albeit of shoddy quality). Cement, rubber, and tobacco products, processed foods, textiles, clothing, footwear, chemicals, and fertilizers are the staple industries.

The government is now keen to stimulate domestic manufacturing, funded by foreign capital. While other factories were closing around it, for example, the Antillana Steel Plant began operating in 1992, producing around 460,000 tons a year (doubling Cuba's steel production). The first bottling plant for natural juices and milk opened in November 1993, when Cuba announced plans for an electric motor factory, to be set up with assitance from China. It also opened its first paper-producing factory in April 1994 (much of the production is earmarked for export), when it also launched its first animal feed factory with a planned output of 730 tons a day.

One of Cuba's greatest hopes for increasing export earnings is in pharmaceuticals, where its investments in biotechnology are beginning to pay off (US biotechnology expert Sam Dryden calls the Cuban program "world class").

In late 1994, the government also launched Coral Container Lines (with 65 merchant vessels) to expand its maritime links. The country is well served by eight major ports and 44 minor ports. Havana, with about 50 docks with full loading facilities, accommodates almost 40% of all cargo, including most grain and oil shipments.

Cuba's deep-sea fishing fleet consists of small independent operators banded into cooperatives. Many boats departed during the Mariel boatlift in 1980 and never returned. The fleet has dwindled ever since.

Mining

Cuba boasts an array of mineral resources, and most have yet to be exploited. Cuba is particularly wealthy in deposits of chromite, cobalt, and iron (up to 3.5 billion tons of ore), gold and silver (up to 600,000 tons), plus copper, manganese, lead, and zinc, all concentrated in northeastern Cuba. In February 1996, the Golden Hill Mining Co. of Canada announced "spectacular" results after drilling for gold in east-central Cuba. In recent years, Cuba has granted at least a dozen foreign companies prospecting rights.

By far the most important mineral is nickel, traditionally Cuba's second-largest foreign exchange earner. Cuba is the world's fourth-largest producer of nickel and has about 37% of the world's estimated reserves (about 19 million tons). The reserves are relatively easy and cheap to mine.

Despite the US government's attempts to disrupt Cuba's nickel sales to Europe, exports have quadrupled since 1990, mostly to Germany, Italy, and Sweden, as well as to India, Canada, and China. Mining has attracted 30% of all foreign business ventures on the island. Cuba does a particularly booming business in nickel with Sherritt Gordon of Canada, the largest foreign investor in Cuba.

TOURISM

One thing was clear at the 16th Cuba Tourism Convention held in May 1996 at Havana's Palacio de Convenciones: the US government's attempts to pressure the international travel and tourism trade into staying home are disdained abroad. More than 200 journalists and almost 1,100 delegates showed up to take notes and sign deals. Even Japanese tourism representatives were on hand to learn about and negoti-

CUBA'S BLACK GOLD

In April 1960, the Soviet ship *Chernovci* arrived with a 70,000-barrel load of oil—the beginning of a 10,000-kilometer petroleum pipeline that was maintained for three decades. Cuba traded nickel, citrus, and sugar to the Soviet Union in return for 10-12 million tons of crude oil and petroleum per year (as much as half of this was re-exported for hard currency to purchase necessities on the world market; by the mid-1980s, oil surpassed sugar as the island's major money-maker). Spared the hardship of oil shocks and price swings, Cuba became addicted to cheap oil and failed to divert its energy supply. Oil was Cuba's Achilles heel.

Russia's decision to halt supplies of subsidized oil in 1991 triggered Cuba's desperate crisis. Between 1989 and 1992, the supply of Soviet oil dropped from 13 million to 6.1 million tons. The inability to convert oil into cash was a crisis in itself. Worse, Russia now demanded hard currency for its oil—at world prices.

A Crude Solution

The collapse of oil imports forced Cuba to take a closer look at its own natural resources. Fortunately, Cuba *does* have oil, and crude is currently being pumped from 20 oil fields. The five main producers are along the north coast concentrated near Varadero, which has estimated reserves of one billion barrels. Production began in 1988 and has risen steadily, from 882,000 tons in 1992 to 1.475 million in 1996—enough to cover one-eighth of the island's oil needs. Foreign experts say they expect to find enough domestic reserves for Cuba to become self-sufficent.

In 1990, foreign oil companies were invited to explore and invest, and Cubapetróleo formed Commercial Cupet S.A. to enter into contracts with foreign investors. Cuba's hopes to attract significant investments from the world's oil giants were scotched by threats from Washington. Nonetheless, at least 12 companies—from Canada, France, Germany, Sweden, Mexico, Brazil, and the UK—had invested in oil exploration as of mid-1996. Production contracts are for 25 years. Cuba's foreign partners can sell their portion of the petroleum to the island at world market prices; they can also sell it freely on the world market if they wish. Under the risk contracts, the foreign companies supply all the capital and technology for exploration. If oil isn't found, the company withdraws without any benefits.

Russia has also resumed bartering oil for sugar on the basis of 2.5 million tons of oil for one million tons of sugar through a triangulation deal whereby Russia delivers oil to Venezuelan-owned refineries in Europe, Venezuela ships an equivalent amount of its own oil to Cuba, and Cuba pays Russia with sugar.

Cuba's crude oil is heavy, with a high sulfur content that makes it hard to process. The majority is used unrefined for electricity generation. Most of Cuba's power plants use energy-inefficient Eastern European systems that require high-grade crude oil. Cuba has thus embarked on upgrading its technology to take advantage of heavier, domestic high-sulfur fuel.

The drastic reduction in crude oil imports also left Cuba's four refineries idle (Cuba has an 11-million-ton refining capacity). The government hopes that oil-rich states like Colombia, Mexico, and Trinidad and Tobago will use its excess capacity. The Cuban government has even discussed selling the refineries to foreign companies.

ate a piece of Cuba's robust tourism pie.

How robust? According to Eduardo Rodríguez de la Vega, deputy minister of tourism, Cuba posted a 16.1% *average* annual growth 1990-95, compared to 4.7% for the Caribbean as a whole (visitors from the US account for 52.4% of all arrivals in the Caribbean; Cuba, of course, receives virtually no tourism from the US). For 1996, first-quarter visitors were up an astounding 45% over the spring of 1995, and tourist arrivals for the year were expected to top one million, generating revenues of US$1.2 billion (in 1996, tourism employment exceeded 125,000).

Before 1959, Cuba was one of the world's hottest tourist destinations. The US public was fascinated with the exotic new possession just offshore.

When Batista was ousted, most Americans (85% of foreign tourists before 1959) stayed home—visitation declined from 272,226 in 1957 to a scant 12,000 in 1974. Havana's former hot spots gathered dust. Apart from a handful of Russians, the beaches belonged to the Cubans throughout the 1960s and '70s, when tourism contributed virtually nothing to the nation's coffers.

Cuba's Comeback

Havana's view of tourism has profoundly shifted since the demise of the Soviet Union. Forsaken by his sugar daddy, Fidel established a no-holds-barred tack force to bandage Cuba's hemorrhaging economy with hard currency culled from a once toxic source—Western consumer culture. The challenge is whether Cuba can sell its sun and sand without selling its soul. Between 1989 and 1992, the Cuban government spent over US$500 million to put a new gleam on its tourist infrastructure and lure foreigners to the "new" Cuba. Its five-year tourism industry plan for 1996-2000 calls for investments of US$1.376 billion in hotel rooms!

Cuba is successfully beating its swords into timeshares. It has quickly emerged as a major force in attracting non-US tourists and is already well on the way to recapturing its 30% pre-Castro share of the Caribbean market.

In 1984, Cuba received 207,000 tourists and US$84 million. In 1995, the island received 740,000 visitors, good for approximately US$1 billion, and an 18.2% increase over the previous year, despite the negative media reports surrounding the *balsero* crisis.

Cuba is gearing up to receive as many as 2.5 million tourists—good for an estimated US$3.12 billion in hard-currency revenue—by 2000. An independent study by Price Waterhouse—*An Assessment of Tourism Developments and Opportunities in Cuba* (December 1994; see bibliography)—predicted actual arrivals would be at least 1,434,000 in the year 2000—under the most adverse conditions and with the US embargo still in place—and possibly as high as 3.5 million assuming the embargo is lifted (and these figures *exclude* cruise-ship arrivals). The island has set itself an ambitious long-term goal of 10 million tourists annually by 2010! Says *Condé Nast Traveler:* "The goal will likely be met," thanks largely to packages that are immensely competitive. It's even cheaper for Mexicans to vacation in Cuba than Cozumel or Cancún; in 1993, Mexican tourists represented 10.3% of Cuba's visitors. That year, 43.5% of tourists came from Europe (Germany, Spain, and Italy are the prime sources, in that order), 22.9% from Latin America, and 21.1% from Canada.

US visitors made up only 2.6 percent of Cuba's tourist arrivals in 1991, when 15,000 US citizens—mostly Cuban-Americans—visited the island legally. Estimates vary for the past few years but by all accounts at least 60,000 visited Cuba in 1996.

The Future *Yanqui* Invasion

A 1993 study by Ernest Preeg, of the Center for Strategic and International Studies, estimated the effects of ending the US embargo and painted a picture of a virtual tourism gold rush. Preeg projected as many as four million arrivals annually within five years of the repeal of existing travel restrictions (half would be stay-over visitors; half would be cruise passengers).

The Cuban government plans on having 49,556 rooms available by the turn of the millennium, by far the largest capacity in the Caribbean. As of January 1996 it had 23,467 rooms (of which perhaps 15,000 were of "international quality"); of other Caribbean islands, only the Dominican Republic had more.

Currently, priority is being given to construction of new hotels and to refurbishment of existing hotels that don't meet international standards. Business, like nature, abhors a vacuum, and foreign companies are rushing in where Uncle Sam fears to tread. In May 1995 some 178 negotiations were under way with foreign companies for new joint-venture agreements with Cuba's five major tour and hotel entities—Cubanacán, Gaviota, Gran Caribe, Horizontes, and Islazul. Barely a month goes by without another deal being announced. And in a move sure to have profound implications, the Minister of Tourism indicated that the underground tourist economy—such as rooms-for-hire—will soon be legalized and regulated. The government is even taking steps to promote residential tourism, including a new law permitting real estate investment and usufruct.

Cuba's Tourism Development Master Plan is specifically designed to avoid overbuilding and overdeveloping key areas. Although 67 areas have been earmarked for tourist development, the plan focuses on eight regions: the city of Havana (number one in tourist visits), Varadero (a stunning peninsula beach resort in Matanza province and number two in visitors), Cayo Largo (the largest island of the Canarreos archipelago), Cayo Coco (slated to be Cuba's second Varadero, with US$1.6 billion projected investment), Santiago de Cuba (a splendid colonial city in the lee of the Sierra Maestra), Trinidad (another colonial gem named a UNESCO World Heritage Site), and both Santa Lucí and Northern Holguín (where pretty beaches are being milked for their resort potential). Ground zero in the quest for hard currency is Varadero, where winter occupancy rates have been running well above 90%.

The new Ministry of Tourism is positioning and promoting Cuba as a Caribbean destination offering diversity and value for money. New marketing efforts are focusing on higher-income travelers and on promoting broader vacation packages that expand beyond single locales. Cuban tourism operators are being encouraged to implement cooperative promotion campaigns. All-inclusive vacations, yacht-charter programs, full-service scuba diving centers, fly-drive vacations, ecotourism, and incentive travel are all destined to receive high priority. And the strategy gives a strong emphasis to developing multi-destination vacations hand in hand with neighboring islands and foreign tour operators.

Cruise terminals are also planned, as well as marinas, airport expansion, at least four new golf courses, and the replacement of Cubana's aging air fleet. And the US-Cuban immigration accord signed in May 1995 will allow Cuba to focus more attention on developing its watersports infrastructure (previously, the Castro regime feared that the boats and jet-skis would be used by Cubans eager to flee to Florida). Plans call for mitigating other weak links in the tourism industry—a shortage of "standalone dining and entertainment facilities," limited domestic air transportation, substandard service quality, and a lack of variety of food.

Cuba's Tourism Structure

In April 1994, Cuba announced sweeping reforms in its tourism industry. The top-heavy National Tourism Institute (INTUR) was dissolved and replaced by the Ministry of Tourism, headed by Osmani Cienfuegos (brother of Camilio Cienfuegos, the revolutionary martyr). New Cuban enterprises have arisen from the ashes of INTUR. Each operates autonomously and within a system of self-management and "healthy competition" that includes the authority to form associations with foreign capital.

The muscle behind Cuba's tourist trade is Cubanacán, which operates over 50 hotels and has shown significant profits since its founding (it also owns restaurants, marinas, 350 buses, and more than 500 rental cars, and has been at the forefront of the island's efforts to strike lucrative joint-venture deals with foreign, principally European companies). Gaviota has developed far more specialized programs than Cubanacán, including one of the fastest-growing areas in tourism to Cuba—health tourism for wealthy foreigners. It has also positioned itself as a provider of VIP services. Many of its hotels are former R&R facilities enjoyed by the military until 1989. The company, which works with almost 100 tour operators in 26 countries, also uses former military planes and helicopters to move tourists around the island.

The other three are separate hotel groups: Gran Caribe for four-and five-star hotels; Horizontes, for three-star and less; and Islazul for domestic hotels that don't take tourists. In addition, a corporation called Rumbos was created to outfit tourist areas with facilities and services with everything from restaurants, coffee shops, and highway rest stops, to airport services, excursions, and scooters for rent.

THE CUBAN PEOPLE AND SOCIETY

It is a rare visitor to Cuba who, exploring beyond the tourist circuit, does not at some time break down in tears. Everyone, everything, touches your heart. It is the way the Cubans embrace you with global innocence, how their disarming charm and irrepressible gaiety amid the heartrending pathos of their situation moves you to examine the meaning of life.

"It is not easy to describe the strength and enthusiasm of the Cubans," wrote Angela Davis after attending the 1962 World Youth Peace Festival in Helsinki, when the Revolution was only three years old. The cultural presentation given by the Cuban delegation illustrated for Davis the "infectious dynamism" that moves so many visitors to tears.

At the end of their show, the Cubans did not simply let the curtain fall. Their "performance" [which satirized the way US capitalists had invaded Cuba and robbed it of sovereignty], after all, had been much more than a mere show. It had been life and reality. Had they drawn the curtain and bowed to applause, it would have been as if their commitment was simply "art." The Cubans continued their dancing, doing a spirited conga right off the stage and into the audience. Those of us openly enthralled by the Cubans, their revolution, and the triumphant beat of the drums rose spontaneously to join their conga line. And the rest—the timid ones, perhaps even the agents—were pulled bodily by the Cubans into the dance. Before we knew it we were doing this dance—a dance brought into Cuban culture by slaves dancing in a line of chains—all through the building and on into the streets. Puzzled Finns looked on in disbelief at hundreds of young people of all colors, oblivious to traffic, flowing down the streets of Helsinki.

DEMOGRAPHY

The population of Cuba is approximately 10.8 million (the 1989 census identified 10.5 million), of which 73% is classified as urban; 19.9% live in the city of Havana, with a population of about 2,110,000 (Santiago de Cuba, the second-largest city, has 346,000 people). The annual average growth rate is 0.88%, down from 2.3% from 1953 to 1970 and 1.1% in the 1980s. Almost two million Cubans have left the island since 1959.

Cuba's family-planning policies have helped the country reduce its birth rate from 4.2% in 1960 to 1.9% in 1991—about the same as in the US. Cuba is in the company of the world's developed nations, both in respect to its aging population and low birth rates. Fertility rates are 1.9 children per woman, compared to 1.8 in both the US and Great Britain, 1.7 in Canada and Japan, and 1.6 in Spain. Only 19 countries have lower fertility rates, according to 1990 statistics.

The declining birth rates are due to the population's heightened cultural levels, the increased percentage of women engaged full-time as workers, and increased access to health care, including abortion services (88% of adults use contraceptive methods). Cuban men and women alike shun Kohinoor, the heavy-duty Cuban-made condoms locally called *el quitasensaciones* (the killjoy)—which are hard to come by anyway. Instead, Cuban women use abortion as a birth control (Cuba has a staggering 56.6 abortions for every 100 live births). The government has introduced a national "pro-infancy" program and increased sex education classes and is distributing contraceptives with the aim of reducing the abortion rate by half by the year 2000.

Cuba's marriage rate is the world's highest: 17.7 per 1,000 people each year. Its divorce rate is also high: 4.2 per 1000, compared to 4.8 for the US and 0.4 for Italy. Nonetheless, 60% of births are to unmarried mothers (Cuba has a high incidence of teenage pregnancy). This carries no social stigma, as the Family Code 1974 abolished the concept of illegitimacy. (About one-quarter of children were born out of wedlock on the eve of the Revolution, simply because many people could not afford the marriage fees, or the fees to register their children. Both Fulgencio Batista and Fidel Castro were born out of wedlock.)

An Aging Population

The reduced birth rate could lead to a real population reduction by the year 2022. The low birth and mortality rates and high life expectancy also mean a rapidly aging population (the United Nations considers a population aging when elderly people constitute over seven percent of the population). In early 1992, 12% of the population was 60 years or older—an enormous social security burden for the beleaguered government.

The number of elderly will triple by 2030, when the nonworking population will equal the working population.

In 1980, according to the Ministry of Health, the suicide rate was 21.6 per 100,000 Cubans—the greatest cause of death between the ages of 15 and 45—double that of the United States.

The Ethnic Mix

The 1993 census reports that, officially, about 66% of the population are "white," mainly of Spanish origin. About 12% are black, and 22% are mulattoes of mixed ethnicity. In reality, the percentage of mulattoes is far greater (Cuban lore claims there is some African in every Cuban's blood). Chinese constitute about 0.1%.

While there are no pure-blood native Indians left in Cuba, in the east—especially around Baracoa—genetic traces recall the ancient culture. (Cubans—in fact, all Latin Americans—resent the way North Americans take to themselves the word America. "We, too, are Americans," they'll remind you.)

The population has grown markedly darker since the Revolution. About 10% of Cuba's population has emigrated since 1959, and the vast majority of exiles were from the wealthy and educated white classes (98% of Miami's Cuban-exile community is white).

Race Relations

Slavery has burdened many countries of the Americas with racial and social problems still unresolved today. But Cuba has gone further than any other to untangle the Gordian knot. Cuban society is more intermixed than any other on earth. Racial harmony is everywhere evident (the kind of racial strife that afflicts the US and United Kingdom is entirely absent). Cubans feel proud of the racially liberating Revolution that has achieved what appears to be a truly colorblind, multiracial society.

Despite slavery, by Caribbean norms Cuba has been a "white" society, whose numbers were constantly fed by a steady inpouring of immigrants from Spain. After emancipation in 1888, the island was spared the brutal segregation of the American South and, as in the US, a black middle class evolved. There was significant mobility and opportunity.

old man and boy

CHRISTOPHER P. BAKER

Nonetheless, legal racial segregation remained the norm in Washington's Caribbean protectorate as it was in the United States in the first half of the 20th century. The white caste retained control. Capitalist Cuba boasted "whites only" clubs, restaurants, schools, hotels, beaches, recreation centers, housing areas and, of course, discrimination in job hiring. Racism was so endemic among the elite that when dictator Fulgencio Batista—who was a mixture of white, black, and Chinese—arrived at the exclusive Havana Yacht Club, they turned the lights out to let him know that although he was president, as a mulatto he was not welcome. Most blacks lived as described by Ernest Hemingway in *Islands in the Stream:* "The lean-to was built at a steep slant and there was barely room for two people to lie down in it. The couple who lived in it were sitting in the entrance cooking coffee in a tin can. They were Negroes, filthy, scaly with age and dirt, wearing clothing made from old sugar sacks." Not surprisingly, a strong, separate black culture evolved, with its own social clubs, restaurants, and literature.

Cuba's revolutionary government swiftly outlawed institutionalized discrimination and vigorously enforced laws to bring about racial equality. Castro said "we can't leave the promotion of women, Blacks, and mestizos to chance. It has to be the work of the party: we have to straighten out what history has twisted."

There is no doubt that the Cuban government has achieved marvelous things. By replacing the social structures that allowed racism to exist, the Revolution has made it virtually impossible for any group to be relegated forever to racial servitude. Afro-Cubans are far healthier, better educated, and more skilled and confident than blacks in Brazil, Colombia, Panama, Jamaica, Haiti, or the urban underclass of the US. They enjoy the lowest rate of infant mortality in Latin American and the Caribbean—one vastly superior, it should be added, to that of blacks in the United States. Hence, blacks are, on the whole, more loyal to Castro than whites.

The social advantages that opened up after the Revolution have resulted in the abolition of lily-white scenes. Mixed marriages no longer raise eyebrows in Cuba. Everyone shares a Cuban-ness. Black novelist Alice Walker, who knows Cuba well, has written, "Unlike black Americans, who have never felt at ease with being American, black Cubans raised in the Revolution take no special pride in being black. They take great pride in being Cuban. Nor do they appear able to feel, viscerally, what racism is."

A negative perspective is offered by Carlos Moore, an Afro-Cuban writer who left Cuba in 1963, in his *Castro, the Blacks, and Africa* (Center for Afro-American Studies, University of California, Los Angeles, 1988).

Behind the Veil
There are still cultural barriers and discrimination, however. Few blacks are employed in the tourist industry (other than as maids). Some social venues attract an almost exclusively white crowd, while others are virtually all-black affairs (blacks still retain their religion, their bonds, their worldview). The most marginal Havana neighborhoods still have a heavy preponderance of blacks. Most Cuban blacks still work at menial jobs and earn, on average, less than whites. And blacks are notoriously absent from the upper echelons of government.

Nor has the Revolution totally overcome stereotypical racial thinking and prejudice. Black youths, for example, claim to be disproportionately harassed by police. You do still hear racist comments, and many Cuban mulattoes still prefer to define their racial identity with whites rather than with blacks (prior to the Revolution, it was common for mulattoes with lighter skin to be referred to as *mas adelantados*—more advanced).

CHARACTER, CONDUCT, AND CUSTOMS

In a world full of cynicism and anomie, the Cubans' refreshing innocence and disarming charm is uplifting. Although a clear Cuban identity has emerged, Cuban society is not easy to fathom. Cubans "adore mystery and continually do their damnedest to render everything more intriguing. Conventional rules do not apply," thought author Juliet Barclay. "When it came to ambiguity, Cuba was the leader of the pack," added author Pico Iyer. "An ironist can have a field day."

The Cubans are somewhat schizoid. In the four decades since the Revolution, most Cubans have learned to live double lives. One side is spirited, inventive, irrepressibly argumentative and critical, inclined to keep private shrines at home to both Christian saints and African gods, and profit however possible from the failings and inefficiencies of the state. The other side commits them to be good revolutionaries and to cling to the state and the man who runs it.

The Cubans value context, their philosophical approach to life differs markedly from North American or northern European values. Thus, attempts to analyze Cuba through the North American value system is bound to be wide of the mark. Most importantly, most North Americans don't understand what the "Revolution" means. When Cubans speak of the "Revolution," they don't mean the toppling of Batista's regime, or Castro's seizure of power, or even his and the country's conversion to communism. They mean the ongoing process of building a society where everyone benefits. Their philosophical framework is different. Most Cubans, regardless of their feelings for Castro, take great pride in the "Revolution," and a large percentage seem happy to accept the sacrifice of individual liberties for the sake of improving equality.

For example, the *average* Cuban is not particularly concerned about whether Cuba has democracy as defined by US administrations. Cuban people are more committed to social justice and equality, and the idea that democracy includes every person's right to guaranteed health care, education, and culture is deeply ingrained in their consciousness. This has less to do with an innate Cuban characterstic than with *Fidelismo,* whose tenets—an anithesis of decades of greed and corruption—call for puritanism and morality, which after four decades have seeped into the masses.

The spartan effort reached extremes, as the following news story shows:

premier Fidel Castro has decided to revise the rules of baseball, it was disclosed today.

Last Sunday, after cutting cane at a nearby sugar mill, Dr. Castro pitched a sandlot game. But when a runner stole second base from him, the Premier ordered him back to first.

"In the revolution," Dr. Castro said, "no one can steal—even in baseball."

As such, Cubans are not concerned with the accumulation of material wealth. Unlike North Americans, they are not individual "consumpto-units." Most Cubans are more interested in sharing something with you than getting something from you. (Cubans call each other *compañero* or *compañera,* which has a "cozy sound of companionship.") They are unmoved by talk of your material accomplishments. Thus, when Cuba's most famous doctor, Rodrigo Alvarez-Cambras, was given one million dollars for removing a malignant tumor from Iraqi leader Saddam Hussein, the esteemed black surgeon and dedicated socialist donated his gift to the Cuban state.

It is more important that everyone has more than the basic minimum—more important, too, to live life. Indeed, four decades of socialism has not changed the hedonistic culture of Cubans: the traditional Afro-Cuban tropical culture has proved resistant to puritanical revolutionary doctrine. They are sensualists of the first degree. Judging by the ease with which couples neck openly, wink seductively at strangers, and spontaneously slip into bed, the dictatorship of the proletariat that transformed Eastern Europe into a perpetual Sunday school has made little headway in Cuba. The state may promote the family, but Cubans have a notoriously indulgent attitude to casual sex—the national pastime.

Cubans also retain a pride and lack of pretension. Cubans are also notoriously toilet- and fashion-conscious. Even the poorest Cuban manages to keep fastidiously clean and well dressed. It has been said that "to take away their soap would be Castro's greatest folly. Almost anything else can be tolerated, but take away their soap and the regime would fall!"

The women are astute and self-assured, and the men are very sentimental. The struggles of the past four decades have fostered a remarkable sense of confidence and maturity. As such, there's no reserve, no emotional distance, no holding back. Cubans engage you in a very intimate way. They're not afraid of physical contact; they touch a lot. They also look you in the eye: they don't blink or flinch but are direct and assured. They're alive and full of emotional intensity. You sense that Cubans are so chock-full of verve and chutzpah that Cuba will surely remain the same, though regimes may come and go.

The economic crisis and demise of socialism elsewhere in the world, however, has fostered an identity crisis; even the most dedicated communists admit their fears about the future, particularly that a loss of values, morals, and solidarity is eroding the principles of the New Man. Many people are alternately sad and high-spirited. Conditions are often heartbreaking, yet most Cubans don't get beaten down. They never seem to lose their sense of humor, reminding me of a statement by the 18th-century Englishman Oliver Edwards: "I have tried in my time to be a philosopher, but I don't know how, cheerfulness was always breaking in."

Social Divisions

The Revolution destroyed the social stratification inherited from Spanish colonial rule. Distinct delineations among the classes withered away. Not that prerevolutionary Cuba was entirely rigid—it was unusual in Latin America for its high degree of "social mobility" (Castro's father, for example, was a poor farm laborer when he emigrated from Spain but rose to become a wealthy landowner in Cuba). Prerevolutionary life was not simply black and white, rich and poor. There was a huge middle class, although it has been argued that there was no characteristically middle-class way of life—no conscious middle-class ideal. As an agrarian-populist movement pitted against Havana-based middle sector interests, *Fidelismo* warred against the middle class and destroyed it. (The old privileged class was replaced, however, by a *nueva clase* of senior Communist Party members who enjoy benefits unavailable to other Cubans; the old underclass has been replaced by a class of outcasts who do not support the revolutionary government and have thereby been deprived of social benefits.)

Cubans lack the social caste system that makes so many Europeans walk on eggshells. Education (and, in this regard, the Revolution) has made them free. There is absolutely no deference, no subservience. Cubans accept people at face value and are slow to judge others negatively. They are instantly at ease, and greet each other with hearty handshakes or kisses. Women meeting for the first time will embrace like sisters. A complete stranger is sure to give you a warm *abrazo*, or hug. Even the most fleeting acquaintances will offer you a meal, or go out of their way to help you however they can. As a foreigner, you'll meet with the warmest courte-

sies wherever you go. Every Cuban wants to open his or her home and is eager to please, uncommonly generous, extremely courteous and gracious, and self-sacrificing to a fault. (Cubans can't understand why foreigners are always saying, "Thank you!" Doing things for others is the expected norm. Cubans rarely say "thank you" when they receive gifts—which you, the wealthy foreigner, are expected to provide.)

In the current crisis, society is unraveling, a stratified society is emerging, and the values and ethics are becoming strained. Prostitution is once again rampant. Bourgeois privilege has returned. An economic elite of *masetas* (rich Cubans) is becoming visible, and so are class resentments and tensions. And corruption and theft have raised their ugly heads.

Cuban Curiosity

A sense of isolation and a high level of cultural development have filled Cubans with intense curiosity. One reason why so many Cubans ask foreigners *"¿Qué hora es?"* is to strike up a conversation (another reason is that they really do need to know the time in a country where time stopped years ago). They will guess at your nationality and quiz you about the most prosaic matters of Western life, as well as the most profound. Issues of income and costs are areas of deep interest, and you may be questioned in intimate detail. Sexual relations arouse equally keen interest, and Cubans of both genders are often excited to volunteer their services to help guide Cupid's arrow.

On the street, you'll be approached constantly: Cubans want to know about the outside world. They pepper you with questions. They watch

---

WHAT'S IN A NAME?

Spanish surnames are combinations of the first surname of the person's father, which comes first, and the mother's first surname, which comes second. Thus, the son of Ángel Castro Argiz and Lina Ruz González is called Fidel Castro Ruz.

Women do not take their husbands' surnames after marriage; instead, their surnames remain the same.

Hollywood movies and cable TV and often converse with a surprising mix of wordly-wise erudition and naivete.

If you tell them you are a *Yanquí,* most Cubans light up. They are genuinely fond of US citizens. "Why do Americans not like us?" they'll ask you, before expressing their hope that Cuba and the US might soon again be friends.

Although Cubans thrive on debate, they are hesitant to discuss politics openly, except behind closed doors. Occasionally, someone will open up to you with sometimes unexpected frankness.

An independent Gallup poll found in November 1994 that 20% of Cubans had attended church in the previous month, 36% had attended a political meeting, and 36% answered "every week" when asked how often they gathered with friends to dance or listen to music.

Humor

Despite their hardships, Cubans have not lost the ability to laugh. Their renowned humor is called the "yeast for their buoyant optimism about the future." Stand-up comedy is a tradition in Cuban nightclubs. And *chistes*—jokes—race around the country.

Cubans turn everything into a *chiste,* most of which are aimed at themselves. Theirs is a penetrating black humor that spares no one—the insufferable bureaucrat, *jiniteras,* the Special Period. There are no sacred cows. Not even Fidel (perhaps *especially* not *El Jefe*) is spared the barbs, although his name is never used. (The silent reference is usually communicated by the gesture of a hand stroking a beard.) Other favorite targets of scorn are Russian-made Lada cars and Hungarian buses, which every Cuban agrees are all lemons and which the Hungarian government stopped making after selling the fleet to Cuba—hence, no spare parts.

Like the English, Cubans also boast a great wit. They lace their conversations with double entendres and often risque innuendo. The Spanish-speaking foreigner is often left behind by subtle inflections and Cuban idioms.

The Nationalist Spirit

Cubans are an intensely passionate and patriotic people united by nationalist spirit and love of country. They are by culture and tradition politically conscious. The revolutionary government has engaged in consciousness raising on a national scale. Innumerable museums teach Cubans—a people used to being underlings—that they can have pride as a nation whose national character is shaped by passionate struggles and a turbulent history rich in violent conquest, slavery, rebellions, dictatorships, revolution, and invasion.

Cubans are nationalists before they are socialists or even incipient capitalists. Cubans had not expected socialism from the Revolution but they could accept it, not simply because so many benefited from the social mobility the Revolution had brought but because, as Maurice Halperin suggests, "it came with nationalism, that is, an assertion of economic and political independence from the United States, the goal of Cuban patriots for a half century." This reality provides Cubans with a different perspective and viewpoint on history.

Labor and the Work Ethic

Cubans are distinct from all their Caribbean neighbors in one important respect. They combine their southern joy of living with a northern work ethic that makes them unique achievers. Through the centuries, Cuba has received a constant infusion of the most energetic Spanish people in the Caribbean, what author James Michener calls "a unique group, one of the strongest cultural stocks in the New World": the wealthier, better-educated, and most motivated colonizers fleeing rebellion and invasion on Haiti, Santo Domingo, and Jamaica. The entrepreneurial spirit isn't dead, as attested by the success of *paladares* and the makeshift enterprises of street vendors who gaudily display their wares as in a traveling show. In consequence, there is a major turnaround in society as Cubans are finding a newfound belief in themselves as self-reliant individuals.

The vast majority of Cubans work for the state. With few exceptions, the state dictates where an individual will work. Thus, the degree of anomie is great. Many Cubans ask their doctor friends to issue *certificados* (medical excuses) so that they can take a "vacation" from the boredom of employment that offers little financial reward and little hope of promotion. (*Socio* is the buddy network, used to shield you from the demands of the state. *Pinche* and *mayimbe* are your high-level contacts, those who help you get around the bureaucracy, such as the doctor who writes a false note to relieve you of "voluntary" work in the countryside.)

The vast improvements in the standards of living among rural families in recent decades has not been enough to keep the younger generation on the land. There has been a steady transfer of workers from agricultural to industrial and service-oriented jobs. Since the Special Period, the migration from the *campos* has accelerated (although Cuba has been spared the mass migrations to the cities that have plagued other Third World counties).

To make up for the labor shortfall, Castro invented "volunteer" brigades. Urban workers, university students, and even schoolchildren are shipped to the countryside to toil in the fields. Workers who refuse to work on *microbrigades* are subject to recrimination. Although the legal minimum working age is 17, the Labor Code exempts 15- and 16-year-olds to allow them to fill labor shortages.

Volunteer workers get an *estimulo,* a reward, such as priority listing for apartments. Nonetheless, very little work gets done in the fields (groups spend much of the day in dalliance, often carnally, until the time comes to go home). There are moral rewards and material rewards—perhaps a week at Varadero, or the right to buy a refrigerator—for other workers.

Cuba has 6.6 million people of working age, of which 67% are in the labor force. Wages are according to a salary scale of 22 levels, with the top level getting six times that of the lowest. Highly trained professionals share the same struggles as unskilled workers. Though paid slightly more, doctors and engineers and lawyers are not a separate "class" as they are in the U.S., Europe, or even the rest of the Caribbean. Life is little different for those who earn 350 pesos a month and those who earn 850.

Cuban Passivity

Cubans nationwide say that things cannot go on as they are: "We must have change!" When you ask them how change will come, most roll their eyes and shrug. Politically, the majority of Cubans—those not firmly committed to the political apparatus—are weighed down with passivity. Open demonstrations against the government are extremely rare.

Silence, congruity, and complicity—pretending to be satisfied and happy with the system—are cultural reflexes that have been called indicative of cultural decay. Jacobo Timerman's *Cuba: A Journey* provides a baneful look at this passivity.

Homosexuality

Cuban gays must find pleasing irony that the heart of the homosexual world is Castro Street in San Francisco. It is assuredly not named in El Jefe's honor, as gays—called "queens," *maricónes,* or *locas* in the Cuban vernacular—were persecuted following the Revolution. Castro (who denies the comment) supposedly told journalist Lee Lockwood that a homosexual could never "embody the conditions and requirements of . . . a true revolutionary." Before 1959, the most visible expression of homosexuality was in prostitution (economic necessity forced many men to prostitute themselves to US tourists and the Cuban bourgeoisie), which led to support for the Stalinist notion that homosexuality was a product of capitalist decadence. Thus, homosexuals were among the groups identified as "undesirable."

Castro says that such prejudices were a product not of the Revolution but of the existing social milieu. "We inherited male chauvinism—and many other bad habits—from the conquistadores," he told Tomás Borge in *Face to Face with Fidel Castro* (Ocean Press, 1992). "That historical legacy . . . influenced our attitude toward homosexuality." And it is true enough that the gay rights movement had not yet been born in the US and the same prejudices which the revolutionaries inherited about homosexuals were prevalent elsewhere in the world, too.

Thus, gays and lesbians met with "homophobic repression and rejection" in Cuba, just as they did in the US. In Cuba, however, it was more systematic and brutal. The pogrom began in earnest in 1965; homosexuals were arrested and sent to agricultural work and reeducation camps—UMAP (Units for Military Help to Agricultural Production)—which gay filmmaker Néstor Almendros revealed in his documentaries *Improper Conduct* and *Nobody Listened.* (Echoing Auschwitz, over the gate of one such camp in Camagüey was the admonition: "Work Makes You Men.")

Many brilliant intellectuals lost their jobs because they were gay (or accused of being gay through anonymous denunciation). Homosexuality was also considered an aberration of nature that could weaken the family structure. Hence homosexuals were not allowed to teach, become doctors, or occupy positions from which they could "pervert" Cuban youth.

Although UMAP camps closed in 1968 (later, those who had lost their jobs were reinstated and given back pay), periodic purges occurred throughout the 1970s and early 80s. Understandably, many homosexuals left—or were forced to leave—on the Mariel boatlift. However, by the mid-1980s, Cuba began to respond to the gay-rights movement that had already gained momentum worldwide. Officially, the new position was that homosexuality and bisexuality are no less natural or healthy than heterosexuality. Families are encouraged to go to therapy to learn to accept homosexuality within the family. In 1987, a directive was issued to police to stop harassment. And an official atonement was made through the release at the 1993 Havana Film Festival of *Vidas paralelas* (Parallel Lives) and *La Bella de Alhambra* (The Beauty at the Alhambra), and the hit movie *Fresa y Chocolat* (Strawberry and Chocolate), which dealt sympathetically with homsexuality. *Fresa y Chocolat,* which deals with the persecution of gays in Cuba and the government's use of informers, was officially approved by Cuba's Film Institute (headed by Alfredo Guevara, a homosexual and close confidante of Castro), offering proof that the government was exorcising the ghost of a shameful past.

Nonetheless, prejudice still exists throughout society, and there is still a restriction on gays joining the party. The gay community does not have representative organizations, although the first gay men's group on the island, Cubans in the Struggle Against AIDS, was recently formed.

Gay Cuba, by Sonja de Vries, is a documentary film that looks candidly at the treatment of gays and lesbians in Cuba since the Revolution. You can order copies from Frameline, 346 Ninth St., San Francisco, CA 94103, tel. (415) 703-8654, fax (415) 861-1404; e-mail, frameline@aol.com, or http://www.frameline.org. Also check out *Machos, Maricones, and Gays: Cuba and Homosexuality,* by Ian Lumsden (Philadelphia, PA: Temple University, 1996) for a study of the relationship between male homosexuality and Cuban society.

LIFE IN CUBA

Many Americans who visit Cuba complain that life there is hard. And it is. But they do not seem adequately impressed by the fact that poverty has been eliminated, or that nearly all the people can read: that a 300,000-copy printing of a new book can be sold out in days. They do not seem awed by a country that provides free medical care to all its citizens and labors daily to provide decent housing for everyone. They do not say (as I feel) that a hard life shared equally by all is preferable to a life of ease and plenty enjoyed by a few. Standing in line for hours to receive one's daily bread cannot be so outrageous if it means every person will receive bread, and no one will go to bed hungry at night.

—Alice Walker,
My Father's Country is Poor (1977)

On the eve of the Revolution, Cuba was a semideveloped country with more millionaires than anywhere south of Texas, a rapidly evolving capitalist infrastructure, and an urban labor force that had achieved "the eight-hour day, double pay for overtime, one month's paid vacation, nine days sick leave, and the right to strike." On the other hand, Cubans who drove Cadillacs and gambled in the casinos were as remote culturally as they were economically from the mass of their countrymen. In 1950, a World Bank study team reported that 40% of urban dwellers and 60% of rural dwellers were undernourished (rural dwellers relied on *malanga,* a nutritious—albeit tough—root, corn, sweet potatoes, plantains, and sugar; even beans and rice were beyond reach of the rural dweller, as were most vegetables). Over 40% of Cuban people had never gone to school; only 60% had regular full-time employment. The city orphanage in Havana even had a drop-chute with flaps to facilitate the abandonment of babies by mothers who couldn't afford to bring them up.

The Revolution immeasurably improved the human condition of millions of Cubans, eliminating poverty and gross disparities, although at the cost of destroying the middle classes and imposing a general paucity. But at least everyone had the essentials. The government provided five crates of beer as a wedding present, and birthday cakes for kids under 10. And everyone enjoyed two two-week vacations a year at the beach.

The 1990s have been devastating for a population accustomed to a much higher standard of living. In 1991, when Castro warned his people that they were entering a "special period," he was warning that their society was about to experience a special kind of collapse, and they were about to feel a special kind of pain. The worst year, 1993, was "so hard, so difficult, so terrible," said Castro. Only in 1995 did things begin to improve.

The Bare Essentials

Row upon row of citrus trees grow just 30 miles from Havana, but it is impossible to find an orange for sale. Vast acres of state farms and cooperatives go unfarmed, while cultivated land goes virtually untended. What happens to the food produced is a mystery. Hospitals, schools, and works canteens get priority, but almost nothing reaches the state groceries (almost 40% of produce is stolen as it passes through the distribution system known as *acopio*). The *campesinos* do okay. But many urban dwellers go without.

So much is allowed per person from the state grocery store per month—six pounds of rice, eleven pounds of beans, four ounces of coffee, four ounces of lard—but only when available. Candles, kerosene, and matches all appear in the ration books but are hardly ever in stock. Nor are cooking oil, household detergent, or soap—the items most direly felt (in some places, a bar of soap is more valued than a bar of gold). A wait for a new bra can take years!

Today, Cubans are focused on issues of everyday survival. Conversations are laced with an obsession for food items many Cubans can only dream about. Few Cubans can eat in the dollars-only restaurants where the good food is served. Not because they're Cubans (that's a myth). But because they don't have dollars. Most Cubans rely on the underground economy—*los bisneros*—doing business illegally; on theft or fortuitous employment; or, for the exceedingly fortunate, a wealthy relative or a lover abroad.

The Black Market and *Resolviendo*

The black market, known as the *bolsa* (the exchange), resolves the failings of the State controlled economy. For four decades it has touched all walks of life. Gas-station attendants sell gasoline "stretched" with kerosene (the good stuff is siphoned off and sold on the black market), while store managers routinely set aside part of the state-supplied stock to sell on the *bolsa*.

Cubans have always survived by *resolviendo*—the Cuban art of barter, the cut corner, the gray market where much of Cuba's economy operates. By 1992, the average Cuban was spending more than 50% of his or her income on informal or black market purchases. What the black market couldn't provide, the Cubans took for themselves. Offices were plundered for lightbulbs. Restaurants had to chain the tableware to the table to stop it walking off.

In 1993, the government had no option but to legalize both farmers' markets *(mercados agropecuarios)* and the dollar. As a result, black market prices tumbled in response to the law of supply and demand, but market prices are high, and a typical Cuban salary can disappear in two or three trips. The average monthly wage is about 350 pesos (about US$17 at black market exchange rates), yet meat in the farmers' market can cost 25 pesos a pound, and black beans nine pesos (fortunately, rent, food, and utilities are so heavily subsidized that they are virtually free).

A few years ago a peso income had some value. Today it is virtually worthless. Life has become organized around a mad scramble for dollars. The lucky ones have access to family cash, known as *fula,* sent from Miami. Cuban economists reckon that only about 25% of the population has regular access to dollars. The rest, including the professionals (doctors, engineers, architects, white-collar workers) are experiencing downward mobility, replaced by a new breed of upper class—a motley collection of black marketeers, part-time prostitutes, waiters, and criminal entrepreneurs. Without access to US dollars, Cubans must rely on their wits and faith (Cubans joke about getting by on *fe,* Spanish for faith, but

LIFE IN THE "SPECIAL PERIOD"

Life turned grim under what the Cubans call the "Special Period," which began when the Berlin Wall crashed and Cuba's Soviet lifeline was severed. Cuba went from down to destitute. Old problems resurfaced, such as the *buzos*—people who live off garbage bins. The hardship of the Special Period caused a rupture in the nation's ethics. Crime rose swiftly, and envy and anomie filled the vacuum left by the collapse of the egalitarian promise.

The lights went out on the Revolution—literally. After the last Soviet tanker departed, in June 1992, the government began electricity blackouts. There was no air conditioning, no fans, refrigeration, or lights. There was no fuel for transportation. Buses and taxis gave way to *coches*—homemade, horse-drawn carts. Everywhere, human and animal labor replaced oil-consuming machinery. Without oil or electricity to run machines, or raw materials to process, or spare parts to repair machinery, factories closed down and state bureaucracies began transferring laid-off workers to jobs in the countryside. Nightclubs, restaurants, and hotels that were once full all closed. Gaiety on the streets was replaced with a forlorn melancholy.

Harvests simply rotted in the fields for want of distribution, undermining one of Castro's bedrock promises—that all Cubans would have enough to eat. People accustomed to a government-subsidized food basket guaranteeing every person at least two high-protein, high-calorie meals a day were stunned to suddenly be confronting shortages in almost every staple. The scarcities were manifest in long lines for rationed goods, a phenomenon that had nearly disappeared by the mid-1980s. A kind of line organizers' mafia evolved, selling places *(turnos)* in the queue *(la cola)*. Cubans spent their days standing and waiting.

What began as inconveniences turned into real hardships as domestic purchasing power declined from an estimated US$8.6 billion to US$2.2 billion.

Monthly allotments were greatly reduced. Even cigarettes were rationed—to three packs a month. First toiletries, then meats and other staples disappeared. Cubans had to resort to making hamburger meat from banana peels and steaks from grapefruit rinds. Many Cubans began rearing *jutías,* ratlike native rodents—and the most desperate resorted to rats. Black marketeers were said to be melting condoms and passing the rubber off as cheese on pizzas. Cuba, the only country in Latin America to have eliminated hunger, began to suffer malnutrition.

When state-owned restaurants closed, unauthorized restaurants in private homes—*paladares*—began offering a black-market supply of meals cooked from food "borrowed" by staffers at tourist hotels or purchased from enterprising farmers who sold surplus produce.

By 1994, a cautious sense of optimism began to emerge, an anticipation that things might soon change for the better. The awful *apagónes* (blackouts) had been trimmed from 18 hours in duration to four. Food crops no longer rotted in the fields. The legal availability of dollars eased life for those Cubans who had access to greenbacks, and farmers' markets eased life for those without.

Nonetheless, Cuban officials began criticizing the "excessive egalitarianism" of the system as a way of softening up the public for the next hardship phase, including the possibility of eliminating state-rationed foodstuffs and essentials, the introduction of taxation, a devaluation of the peso, and the introduction of charges for sacred goods and services such as educational materials, museums and art exhibitions, and perhaps even health services.

For powerful descriptions of the harrowing living conditions during the Special Period, read Jacobo Timerman's *Cuba: A Journey,* Maurice Halperin's *Return to Havana,* or Andres Oppenheimer's *Castro's Final Hour.*

---

today an acronym for *familia extranjera*—family abroad). The majority of Cubans have to simply *buscar la forma,* find a way.

Barter is common. So are time payments, verbal contracts for future delivery, and a hundred variations on the theme. Those with a few dollars might buy scarce products and then barter them to other Cubans who have no link to the dollar economy. One neighbor might bring another canned goods in exchange for fish. A third can get his car engine fixed in exchange for peanut butter.

Every morning, people prepare to cobble together some kind of normalcy out of whatever the situation allows them. Cubans are masters at making the best of a bad situation. *Resolver*—to resolve, to overcome obstacles with ingenuity, spontaneity, and humor—is one of the most commonly used verbs on the island.

Cubans have learned to laugh about their hardships. Nonetheless, having sacrificed for the Revolution for three decades, many Cubans are exhausted. Frustrations have set in. It's a remarkable testament to the spirit of the people that they have been able to withstand the upheavals without grave social and political consequences.

Simple Pleasures

Cuba has no *fiesta* tradition. The Cubans are too industrious for that—too busy playing volleyball or baseball or practicing martial arts while the other half whiles away the long, hot afternoons in the cool shade of arcaded balconies, playing dominoes or eking out a meager living mending cigarette lighters or resoling shoes. At night, everyone gathers around the TV to watch *Te Odio, Mi Amor*—an immensely popular Brazilian *telenova* (soap opera) dubbed into Spanish—and life on the dimly lit streets disappears except for the occasional courting couple. In rural areas, pleasures are simple: cockfights, rodeos, fiestas, cheap rum, and sex. Urban life is more urbane, offering movies, art galleries, trovas, discos, cheap rum, and sex.

Cuban social life revolves around the family (social obligations dictate that if you make money, you are expected to support family members) and, to a lesser degree, friends and neighbors. Cubans are a gregarious people, and foreigners are often amazed by the degree to which Cubans exist in the public eye, carrying on their everyday lives behind wide-open windows open to the streets as if no one were looking. To Cuban passersby, this is nothing remarkable, but the foreigner cannot resist the same insatiable curiosity that seizes you when your neighbors at home forget to draw their curtains at night.

For all its musical gaiety and pockets of passionate pleasure, life for the average Cuban is dreary, even melancholy—the food, the literature, daily events. Vitality is limited to Havana and Santiago. Elsewhere, in general, life for the majority is reduced to making do and making out. Socialist equality can begin to look dismal as you contemplate Cubans rocking on their porches, waiting for something to happen.

Living Conditions

Until the Revolution, government expenditures were concentrated mostly in and around Havana. The provinces were neglected and had few sewers or plumbing, few paved roads or electricity. Rural housing was basic. According to the 1953 census, only two percent of rural houses had piped water, 54% had no toilet whatsoever (85% of the rural population relied for their water on rivers and streams—many polluted), and 43% had no electricity.

Since the Revolution, the government has concentrated its energies on developing the countryside and replacing urban shantytowns with apartment housing. Today, virtually every house on the island has electricity, although a large percentage do not have hot water. (Households are metered separately for use of elec-

playing dominoes in Old Havana

tricity. Payments for this are made directly to state authorities.) By law, no renter can pay more than 10% of his or her salary in rent. However, almost 80% of Cubans own their own homes ("Mrs. Thatcher's vision of a homeowners' society come true in communist Cuba," Martha Gellhorn noted, wryly. "Rents pile up like down payments year after year, until the sale price of the flat is reached, whereupon bingo, you become an old-fashioned capitalist owner"). Those who owned houses before the Revolution have been allowed to keep them (those who fled Cuba forfeited their property to the state). Cubans can swap their houses without state approval but cannot sell them.

The typical country house is a low, one-story structure with thick walls to keep out the heat, built of adobe or porous brick covered with stucco painted blue, pink, green, or buff, and roofed with red tiles. It's often whitewashed within and has high ceilings; tall, barred, glassless windows; and cool stone or tile floors. The very poorest people—and a few remain, despite the Revolution—build light shacks of wood, woven bamboo, or other fiber, like a basket, with a thick thatched roof.

Conditions in the cities vary markedly, particularly in Havana, where much prerevolutionary housing is deteriorated to a point of dilapidation. However, there *are* many fine, well-kept houses (Havana's Miramar is one exemplary location for seeing them). Fifty percent of Havana's housing is rated "poor" to "bad," and the housing shortage is so critical that many Habaneros live in a *barbecue,* a room divided in two. Due to lack of space, the high-ceilinged rooms of many old colonial buildings have been turned into two stories by adding new ceilings and wooden staircases.

Interiors often belie the dour impression received on the street. Rooms everywhere are kept spic and span and furnished with typically Cuban decor: family photos, kitschy ceramic animals, plastic flowers, and other effusive knick-knackery—and frequently a photo of Fidel, Che, or Camilo Cienfuegos. Always there is a large refrigerator (Russian or prerevolutionary Yankee) and at least one TV.

Most housing built since the Revolution (in both town and country) is concrete apartment block units of a standard Bulgarian design—the ugly Bauhaus vision of uniform, starkly func-

tional workers' housing, which had the advantage of being cheap to build and, in theory, easy and cheap to maintain. Most have not been maintained. And, boy, do they need it! Most were jerry-built by unskilled volunteer labor, adding salt to the wound of the aesthetic shortfall.

Why is there no paint? Because the centralized planning process is intent on meeting production quotas, not on allocating scarce resources for maintenance and repair, which are not foreseen in their plans. Spare parts aren't ordered to maintain sewers or electrical boxes, so, over time, everything is jerry-rigged. Until 1993, it was illegal for Cubans to freelance as electricians, plumbers, or construction workers, so everyone relied on the state, which gave home and public-utility repair low priority.

Since the Special Period, Cuba has become littered with half-finished structures like the bones of dinosaurs. Materials are simply no longer available to finish the jobs. Today, in a deteriorating situation, as many as one million Cubans are "ill-housed" (compared to as many as five million inhabitants before the Revolution). Squatting is common, and homelessness has begun to appear. The National Housing Institute planned to build 50,000 units in 1996 (up from 35,000 in 1995) and to increase restoration of existing housing threefold.

CHILDREN AND YOUTH

One of the simplest pleasures for the foreign traveler is to see smiling children (Cuban children are always smiling) in school uniforms so colorful that they reminded novelist James Michener of "a meadow of flowers. Well nourished, well shod and clothed, they were the permanent face of the land." And well behaved, too! About 35% of the population are below 16 years of age.

Children are treated with great indulgence by the state as much as by family members. The government has made magnificent strides to improve the lot of poor children. Never have I seen a neglected child in modern Cuba.

Once, when asked about the sister who turned her back on the Revolution, Fidel told TV interviewer Barbara Walters, "We have the same mother and father, but different ideas. I am a committed socialist. She is an enemy of so-

---

TURNING FIFTEEN

Four decades of socialism have killed off many traditional celebrations—but not *las fiestas de quince*—the birthday parties for 15-year-old girls. There is nothing like a *quince* party (a direct legacy of Spanish heritage) for a young *Cubana*.

Parents will save money from the day the girl is born to do her right with a memorable fifteenth—the day on which the *quinceañera* may openly begin her sexual life without family recrimination. A whole arsenal might be involved, from the hairdresser and dressmaker (a special dress resembling wedding gowns or a knock-'em-dead Scarlett O'Hara outfit is de rigueur) to the photographer and the classic American car with chauffeur to take the young woman and her friends to the party.

---

cialism and that is why she says [bad] things about me. But let me tell you. I have five million brothers and sisters and between us we have millions of children. We love these children." There is no doubt he is sincere.

Children are sworn in at the age of six to become communist pioneers.

Cuban youth have grown up in a mature Revolution—more than 60% of the Cuban population were born after the Revolution. The older generation had attempted to make the Revolution, had faced down the threat of US invasion, had witnessed astounding social achievements—all through collective endeavor. Although there is respectful communication between generations, clashes are becoming more common. Where their parents use "we," Cuba's youth use "I"—I want to do so and so. The majority are bored by the constant calls for greater sacrifice and tired of being treated as if they were stupid. They want to enjoy life.

Cuban youth are in a confusing limbo where neither the socialist role model nor its complete rejection is appropriate to the current circumstances. Young people growing up in the current era of hardship and economic opening are not necessarily abandoning revolutionary principles (although the war in Angola—Cuba's Vietnam—was a misadventure that left many of the young angry and disaffected). But the methods and ideas many

are adopting alarm the authorities. As the quest for US dollars tightens its grip, an increasing number of Cuban youth are asking, "What's the point in studying?" They are more concerned with their future than with the party's. Many youths realize they can get further through their own work and savvy and are going into business for themselves as *jiniteros* and *cuenta propistas* (freelancers), making a buck doing anything from driving taxis to repairing tire punctures.

The government worries that the increased association with foreign tourists helps foster nonconformism, such as the growing number of long-haired youths—*roqueros* and *frikis*—who sport ripped jeans and would look at home at a Metallica concert.

Cuban youth are expressing their individuality—they want to be themselves, which today means showing a marked preference for anything North American, especially in clothing. They wouldn't be caught dead in a guayabera, the traditional tropical shirt favored by older men; instead, young women dress in the latest fashion—tight jeans, halter tops, mini-skirts, short shorts, and diaphanous blouses, flared pants, and trendy shoes. Young men follow suit, though more conservatively, and as well as their budgets allow. "Egotism" is flourishing. Consumerism is capturing the imagination of Cuban youth, spawned by the notion that the only way to advance is by making money. Teenagers are becoming sexually promiscuous at an earlier age, and their casual attitude to sex is fueling a rapid rise in prostitution.

More and more, youth feel there is no future in Cuba. "We can't wait forever," they say. Still, few youths feel a hatred for Fidel Castro. Rather, they see him as "a benevolent idealist whose program has run out of steam."

Youth are served by their own newspapers, such as *Pioniero* and *Juventud Rebelde (Rebel Youth)*.

Global Exchange, 2017 Mission St. #303, San Francisco, CA 94110, tel. (415) 255-7296, offers study tours to explore Cuban youth culture. Also look for a copy of *Cuba Va!,* a splendid hour-long documentary—released in 1993—in which Cuban youth express their fears and hopes; US$95; Cuba Va Video Project, 12 Liberty St., San Francisco, CA 94110, tel. (415) 282-1812, fax (415) 282-1798.

WOMEN AND MACHISMO IN CUBAN SOCIETY

According to Saul Landau, Cuba is the only "unisex" country in the world. The country has an impressive record in women's rights. A United Nations' survey ranks Cuba among the top 20 nations in which women have the highest participation in politics and business. Women make up 50% of university students and 60% of doctors (a review of the University of Havana yearbooks shows that women were well represented *before* the Revolution also), although they are still poorly represented in the upper echelons of government.

Cuba's solid achievements in the past four decades reflect Castro's own faith in the equal abilities of women, and the belief that the Revolution cannot be called complete until women share full opportunities. Women workers' rights are protected by Law 1263, passed in 1974, which guarantees women the same salaries as men. In addition, women receive 18 weeks of paid maternity leave—six before the birth and the remainder after. Working mothers have the right to one day off with pay each month, or the option of staying home and receiving 60% of their full salary until the child reaches the age of six months. And every woman and girl can get birth control assistance, regardless of marital status.

Equality of the sexes is also given legal guarantees through the Cuban **Family Code,** which codifies that the male must share household duties. The Spanish heritage is patriarchal (under the Spanish Civil Code, which was extended into the Cuban Republic, the husband had exclusive rights to property, finances, and, legally, the obedience of his wife and children). The strict Spanish pattern has been broken down by the Revolution, but it still colors family life.

Prejudices and stereotypical behaviors still exist. Male machismo continues, and pretty women walking down the street are often bombarded with comments ranging from *piropos* (witty compliments) to forthright invitations to sex. And though the sexes may have been equalized, the Revolution has not been able to get the Cubanness out of Cuban women who,

regardless of age, still adore coquetry.

Few Cuban women simply put on a dress and go out. Instead, they make a great show of expressing their bodily beauty. "Cuban women don't walk, they sway," Naty Revuelta, one of Castro's former mistresses (and the mother of his daughter), has said. "When they walk, everything is in motion, from the ankle to the shoulder. The soldiers had a terrible time in the beginning, trying to teach them to march in the militia. They just couldn't get the sway out of them." Even the most ardent revolutionaries still paint their faces and attempt a toilette to heighten the femme fatale effect, as in their preference for minimalist and tight-fitting clothing. Women still routinely shorten and take in their uniforms to show their legs, outline their backsides, and be noticed.

Overt appreciation of the female form may seem sexist to "politically correct" North Americans, but in Cuba, rear ends have a value and meaning much more significant than in other cultures. Cuban literature overflows with references to *las nalgas cubanas*—the Cuban ass—usually plump and belonging to a well-rounded *mulatta*. Tom Miller synthesizes the longstanding fascination with *el culo*—the butt—in his marvelous travelogue, *Trading with the Enemy*. "I found enough material to keep a culophile busy for months."

Of course, these stereotypes belie the ongoing debate within Cuba about the "correct" role of women. A nongovernmental organization called **Association of Women Communicators, MAGIN,** Calle 11 #160 e/ K y L, Vedado, Havana, tel. 32-3322, fax 33-3079, organizes workshops designed to build self-esteem and develop a greater understanding of the concepts of gender and feminism. Likewise, **Casa de las Américas,** Avenida 3ra y G, Vedado, Havana, tel. 32-3587, fax 32-7272, e-mail casa@tinored.cu, works to broaden the area of women's studies in Cuba and, it, too, sponsors workshops and seminars on the status of women.

Women's interests are also represented by the **Cuban Federation of Women** (Federación de Mujeres Cubanas), Paseo #250, Havana, tel. 30-6043, headed by Vilma Espín, wife of Raúl Castro and known as the First Lady of Cuba. It was founded to rouse women to be good revolutionaries but in recent years has devoted more effort to women's issues and rights, particularly the fight against a rising tide of teenage pregnancy (the *average* Cuban girl begins sexual activity at 13 and has her first baby at 18).

The June 1995 issue of *Cuba Update* focuses on "Women's Lives" in Cuba (US$6; Center for Cuban Studies, 124 West 23rd St., New York, NY 10011)

RELIGION

Cuba is officially an atheist country, and proselytizing is illegal. Nonetheless, a recent government survey found that more than half of all Cubans are *creyentos,* believers of one sort of another.

Christianity

Cubans have always been lukewarm about Christianity, and the church has never been strong in Cuba. In colonial times, there were few churches in rural districts, where it was often usual for a traveling priest to call only once a year, usually to perform baptisms and marriages. Even in towns, most Cubans would respond to the bell only on special occasions, usually when it pealed for births, marriages, and maybe Easter morning, when men milled by the door, piously half in and half out. The Catholic Church sided with the Spanish against the patriots during the colonial era. After independence, the constitution therefore provided for separation of church and state, depriving the former of its political influence and state support.

Later, the Catholic Church had a quid pro quo with the corrupt Machado, Grau, and Batista regimes—You keep out of our business and we'll keep out of yours." When the Revolution triumphed, many of the clergy left for Miami along with the rich to whom they had ministered.

The Catholic Church grew concerned as the Revolution moved left. When Fidel nationalized the church's lands, it saw red (kind of). The church became a focus of opposition. In August 1960, the Catholic bishops issued a pastoral letter formally denouncing the Castro government; a second pastoral letter later that year urged Fidel to reject communism. Fidel saw red, too. Many priests were expelled when the Vatican opposed the revolutionary government (few Cubans entered the priesthood; the Vatican had to look abroad for three-quarters of its priests in Cuba).

Although the Castro regime has never banned the practice of religion, the church was allowed to engage in only marginal social activities. Church attendance came to be considered antisocial. Religious education was eliminated from the school curriculum. Practicing Catholics were banned from the Communist Party. In 1965, Holy Week was even re-christened "Playa Girón Week." Consequently, religious believers have declined from more than 70% of the population to less than 30% and attendance plummeted. The Cuban Conference on Bishops estimates that only about one percent of the population goes to church at least twice a year. Churches have had to close down due to disrepair (many priests resorted to holding services in private homes).

In 1986, Fidel Castro performed an about face: religion was no longer the opiate of the masses. In 1990, he admitted that "believers" had been unjustly treated. That year, tor only the second time in more than 30 years, radio and television stations began transmitting religious music and songs. The following year, the Communist Party opened its doors to believers, and security agents disappeared from churches. It was a timely move, co-opting the shifting mood. The collapse of the Soviet Union proved the adage that "when the earth moves under the people's feet, they naturally look up to the sky." The collapse left a spiritual vacuum that has fed church attendance, while the number of seminarians has also skyrocketed. The trendiest piece of jewelry these days is a gold cross.

Castro recognizes that the accelerating religious revival reflects a massive loss of faith in government. He has attempted to go with the rising tide, while recognizing, too, that the church has a valuable role to play in upholding ethical values in the face of flagging enthusiasm and growing doubt. The Cuban government and Protestant Church initiated a dialogue aimed at finding a strategy to unite atheists and believers (though Protestantism was only introduced at the turn of the century, prerevolutionary Cuba evolved the highest percentage—almost 15%—of Protestants of any Latin American nation).

Skirmishes continue, however. In spite of warming relations with the Protestant Church, the Catholic Church hierarchy has continued to be highly critical of the Castro government. In summer 1994, Cuba's 11 Catholic bishops issued a pastoral letter criticizing the government's monopoly on power and calling for reforms that take into account Cuba's panoply of ideas. It was the strongest criticism of Castro to date (Castro called it a "stab in the back"). The bishops have also condemned right-wing Cuban émigrés, the US embargo, and US interference in Cuban affairs, even though the embargo specifically exempts relief shipments to "non-governmental organizations"—in effect, the church (such support permits the church to usurp the state's role as provider).

Papal emissaries began visiting Cuba in 1990—part of the Pope's agenda to help save Cuba from the dangers of a violent and bloody power transition. On 19 November 1996, Castro met with Pope John Paul II in Rome. The pontiff agreed to visit Cuba the following year in the hope that a papal embrace magnified by television exposure might defuse much of the internal opposition.

Santería

Santería, or saint worship, has been deeply entrenched in Cuban culture for 300 years. The cult is a fusion of Catholicism with the Lucumí religion of the African Yoruba tribes (several other Afro-Cuban cults emerged during the slave era, most notably the Bantu tribes' Palo Monte and the Abakuá secret societies). Since slave masters had banned African religious practice, the slaves cloaked their gods in Catholic garb and continued to pray to them to preserve a shred of their souls and strengthen them against the indignities.

Thus, in santería, Catholic figures are avatars of the Yoruban orishas (divine beings of African animism worshiped in secretive and complex rituals that may feature animal sacrifices along with chanting, dancing, and music). Gods change their sex at midnight: by day, adherents may pray in front of a figure of Santa Barbara and at night worship the same figure as Changó. There are several hundred gods in the pantheon, but only about 20 are honored in daily life.

It is thought that the orishas control an individual's life (a string of bad luck will be blamed on an orisha) and must therefore be placated.

The gods are believed to perform all kinds of miracles on a person's behalf and are thus consulted and besought. They're too supreme for mere mortals to communicate with directly. Hence, santeros or babalaos (priests) act as go-betweens to honor the saints and interpret their commands.

Cubans are superstitious people. It's said that if you scratch a Cuban, Catholic or non-, you find a santería believer underneath. Almost every home has a statue of a santería god and a glass of water to appease the spirits of the dead. Even Fidel Castro, a highly superstitious person, is said to be a believer. He had triumphed on 1 January, a holy day for the orishas. The red and black flag of the revolutionaries was that of Elleguá, god of destiny. Then, on 8 January 1959, as Fidel addressed the nation from Camp Columbia, suddenly two doves flew over the audience and circled the brightly lit podium; miraculously, one of the doves alighted on Fidel's shoulder, touching off an explosion from the ecstatic onlookers: "Fee-del! Fee-del! Fee-del!" In santería, doves are symbols of Obatalá, the Son of God. To Cubans—and perhaps Fidel himself—the event was a supreme symbol that the gods had chosen Fidel to guide Cuba.

Over ensuing years, Castro's dogma of scientific communism attempted to convert santería into a folkloric movement. Religious rites were restricted. As Marxism lost its appeal in the late 1980s, santería bounced back, offering relief from the "propogandistic realism" of the socialist world. The desperate conditions of the Special Period have caused millions to visit their babalaos. In 1990, the Castro government began to co-opt support for the faith—it is said that Castro also encourages santería as a counterpoint to the rising power of the Catholic Church—by economically and politically supporting the babalaos (reportedly, many babalaos have been recruited by MININT, for they above all know people's secrets).

Santería is a sensuous religion. It lacks the arbitrary moral prescriptions of Catholicism—the orishas let adherents have a good time. The gods themselves are fallible and hedonistic philanderers, such as the much feared and respected Changó, god of war, fire, thunder, and lightning, whose many mistresses include Oyá (patroness of justice) and Ochún, the sensuous black goddess that many Cuban women identify as the *orisha* of love in an erroneous syncretism with Venus.

Throughout Cuba, you'll see believers clad all in white, having just gone through their initiation rites. Each person is "guarded" by a particular god. Followers of Changó wear collars decorated with red and white plastic beads; followers of Ochún wear yellow and white beads. Each saint also has his or her own dance. Each, too, has his or her "altar," such as the ceiba tree in the corner of Havana's Plaza de Armas, where good charms and bad (fruits, rum-soaked cakes, pastries, and coins) are strewn near its trunk and the stirred earth near its sacred roots bulges with buried offerings. At other altars, caged pigeons await their fate at the end of a knife.

Organized Tours: The government has set up *diplosanterías* where foreign visitors can consult with santería priests for dollars. **Rumbos** offers an excursion to witness santería in Regla, al Santuario #13, tel. 90-0812. Reservations can be made through any Infotur office (US$22). **Havanatur,** Calle 2 #17 e/ 1 y 3, Miramar, Havana, tel. 33-2273 or 33-2161, fax 33-2877, offers a weeklong tour ("Rendezvous with the Orishas"), which includes visits to Regla, Guanabacoa, and Santa María del Rosarío.

Judaism

Cuba's Jewish community once thrived. Today it is thought to number only about 1,300, about five percent of its prerevolutionary size, when Havana's Jewish community supported five synagogues, several schools, and a college.

The first Jews are thought to have traveled to Cuba with Columbus and were followed in the 16th century by Sephardic Jews escaping persecution at the hands of the Spanish Inquisition (many Jews fled to the Caribbean under assumed Christian identities). Later, Jews coming from Mediterranean countries felt at home in Cuba. They concentrated in southern Habana Vieja (Old Havana), many starting out in Cuba selling ties and cloth and gaining a monopoly based around Bernaza and Muralla Streets and across the bay in Guanabacoa. They were joined at the turn of this century by Jews from Florida, who founded the United Hebrew Congregation. Other Ashkenazic Jews emigrating from Eastern Europe passed through Cuba en route to the United States in significant numbers until the US slammed its doors in 1924, after which they settled in Cuba. Arriving during a time of destitution, they were relatively poor compared to the earlier Jewish immigrants and were disparagingly called *polacos*. Many were sustained by the largesse of the United Hebrew Congregation.

Sephardic Jews came as families and were profoundly religious. They formed social clubs, opened their own schools, and married their own. By contrast, Ashkenazim most often were single men who went on to marry Cuban (Catholic) women and eventually were assimilated into Cuban society, says Robert M. Levine in his book *Tropical Diaspora: the Jewish Experience in Cuba* (University Press of Florida, 1993). The Ashkenazim were fired with socialist ideals and were prominent in the founding of both the labor and Cuban communist movements.

Cuba seems to have been relatively free of anti-Semitism (Batista was a friend to Jews fleeing Nazi Europe). Levine, however, records how during the late 1930s, the US government bowed to isolationist, labor, and anti-Semitic pressures at home and convinced the Cuban government to turn back European Jews. It is a sordid chapter in US history, best told through the tragic story of the SS *St. Louis* and its 937 passengers trying to escape Nazi Germany in 1939. The ship languished in Havana harbor for a week while US and Cuban officials deliberated on letting passengers disembark; tragically, entry was refused, and the ship and passengers were sent back to Europe and their fate.

By the 1950s, Cuban Jews had prospered in the clothing trade and enjoyed a cosmopolitan life. The Revolution "had elements of tragedy for the Jewish community," writes Rosshandler, author of the autobiographical novel *Passing Through Havana* (St. Martin's Press, 1984). Castro gave them "the option of staying and keeping their homes. But they had devoted their energy to business and they could not bear to live in a society that looked down on what they prized." Jews became part of the Cuban diaspora, and only perhaps as many as 2,000 remained (a few joined the Castro government; two became early cabinet members).

"Castro's Jews" say that Jews have been better treated in Cuba than anywhere else in the world. Jewish religious schools were the only parochial schools allowed to remain open after the Revolution (the government provided school buses). The Cuban government has always made matzoh available and even authorized a kosher butcher shop in Habana Vieja to supply meat for observant Jews. The Jewish community also has its own cemetery, atop a hill in Guanabacoa, east of Havana, dating from 1910.

A renaissance in the Jewish faith is occurring. Synagogues are being refurbished and new ones opened. In 1994, the first bar mitzvah took place in over 12 years and the first formal bris in over five years. And the recently reopened Hebrew Sunday School (for children and adults) in the Patronato (the Jewish community center on the ground floor of the synagogue in Vedado) teaches Hebrew and Yiddish.

To learn more, look for screenings of the documentary film *Havana Nagila: the Jews of Cuba* (57 minutes, 1995), directed by Laura Paull, which traces the history of Jews in Cuba from their immigration in the early 1900s to the current resurgence of Jewish life. Also look for screenings of *Next Year in Havana,* a documentary by Lori Beraha about Havana's Jewish community; you can order copies from Caribbean Music and Dance Programs, 1611 Telegraph Ave. #808, Oakland, CA 94612, tel. (510) 444-7173.

The **Cuban-Jewish Aid Society,** P.O. Box 2101, Mill Valley, CA 94942, tel. (415) 388-2418, fax (415) 550-8009; and 44 Mercury Ave., Colonia, NJ 07607, tel. (908) 499-9132, sends medicines, humanitarian aid, and religious articles to Cuba. Donations should be sent to the New Jersey address. The society is licensed to take US citizens on its annual tours of Cuba. Adela Dworin, the doyenne of Patronato, says help has come from around the world—but never from Cuban-American Jews in Miami until 1993 when, defying elders of the Jewish community in South Florida, Eddie and Xiomara Levy formed a group called **Jewish Solidarity** to deliver humanitarian aid. It leads group study tours to Cuba.

EDUCATION

Despite its restrictions on individual liberty, Cuba has attempted to maximize its human potential, and its education system is justifiably a source of national pride. The country enjoys one of the greatest proportions of university graduates in the world, and it is a joy to hear everywhere the intelligent voices of an educat-

ed and evocatively philosophical people. In general, Cubans are highly knowledgeable, often displaying an astonishing level of intellectual development and erudition. Their conversations are spiced with literary allusions and historical references. Even in the most remote Cuban backwater, you'll come across bright-eyed children laden with satchels, making their way to and from school in pin-neat uniforms colored according to their grades (younger ones wear short-sleeved white shirts, light-blue neckerchiefs, and maroon shorts or mini-skirts; secondary school children wear white shirts, red neckerchiefs, and ocher-yellow long pants or mini-skirts all the way up to their . . . twelfth grade. The neckerchiefs show that they are Pioneers, similar to Cub and Boy Scouts.)

It wasn't that way before the Revolution, when education was the privilege of the middle and upper classes.

During Spanish colonial times, no country in Latin America spent less on education and more on its army (not a single state-supported library existed on the eve of independence). Better ed-

students at the University of Havana

ucation was one of the prime motivations for the Revolution that overthrew General Machado in 1933, but education made little progress in the post-war decades. And though the constitution of 1940 expressed lofty ideals—the budget of the Ministry of Education should not be smaller than that of any other ministry—educational funds simply became a huge source of graft (Aureliano Sánchez Arango, who took office in 1948 as a rare honest Minister of Education, described his ministry as a cave of entrenched bandits). Those who could afford to sent their children to private schools while the majority went unversed. World Bank statistics reveal that in 1958 over half of all Cuban children were without *any* schooling (compared to 36% for Latin America as a whole). In the countryside, books and pencils were as rare as silk pajamas.

The Great Literacy Campaign

In December 1960, the government announced a war on illiteracy. On 10 April 1961, 120,000 literacy workers—*brigadistas*—of all ages spread throughout the Island to teach reading and writing to one million illiterates. Overnight, Cuba's illiteracy rate dropped from 24% to three percent. (To learn more about the literacy campaign, check out the **Literacy Museum** in Havana's Marianao district.)

The government followed up by establishing about 10,000 new classrooms in rural areas and introducing traveling libraries. Today, literacy is about 98.5%. According to UNICEF statistics, nine out of 10 Cuban children complete four years of primary schooling—the minimum required for a child to have a chance of being literate and numerate (the US average is 9.6; Costa Rica 8.4; Chile 7.5; Haiti 1.2). School is compulsory to age 15 (ninth grade). Children may then choose to continue three years pre-university study or at technical schools. Anyone who has ever visited a Cuban classroom must remark on the enthusiasm displayed by willing, lively pupils. In rural areas, few schools have a library or gym or laboratory, yet teachers get on with the job. All education is free.

The *average* Cuban has received nine years of schooling. One in every 15 people is a college graduate. And about four percent—more than 400,000 people—hold university degrees, while another 1.3 million have graduated from technical

schools. Cuba has four universities, plus 85 research centers. Opportunity is there for all children, but even Cuba's educational system is competitive. Children with special talents may opt to attend specialist schools that foster particular skills in art, music, or sports. The best pupils go to highly prized vocational schools—assuming, of course, that they display the correct behavioral attitudes.

Before the Special Period, all schoolchildren went on two camping trips every year. They also spent a week at Varadero or a similar beach resort (top students from every school also spent a month together at Varadero as a reward for their efforts). Sadly, those days have ended. And truancy and illiteracy are rising.

The Downside

As the Brazilian economist Roberto Campos said, statistics are like bikinis: they show what's important but hide what's essential. For one, the hyper-educated population is hard pressed to find books, and not simply because of a shortage of paper, which has meant a dearth of children's textbooks. The literary panorama is severely circumscribed: only politically acceptable works are allowed. Cubans' understanding of world affairs is shaped by a system evolved following the Revolution to foster socialist thinking. In the hands of the state, schooling has been a key tool in promoting the "communist formation" of the next generation and the creation of the "New Man." The Marxist-Leninist conception of things is embodied in education through Article 38 of the Constitution.

Schooling stresses linguistic and arithmetic skills at primary level and vocational and technical abilities at secondary level. (There is no doubt that Cuba's schools produce a people with inordinate literary abilities; gain a Cuban pen pal and you'll understand what I mean.) Many senior students, however, have little choice of professional study. A close friend, given no choice but to study civil construction, told me how she and her classmates hated the subject. Those who didn't want to study or wanted to flunk, were allowed to volunteer to work on construction projects. No wonder Cuban construction is so bad!

Work-Study

What is unique about the Cuban education system is its emphasis on combining learning with

TURNING OUT CHAMPIONS

Tiny Cuba is one of the top five sports powers in the world, excelling in baseball, volleyball, boxing, and track and field. At the 1993 Caribbean and Central American Games, in Puerto Rico, Cuban athletes won 275 gold medals—75 more than the rest of the nations combined.

Cuba's international success is credited to its splendid educational system. When the Revolution triumphed, sports became a priority alongside land reform, education, and health care. In 1964, the Castro government opened a network of sports schools—Escuelas de Iniciación Deportiva (EIDE)—as part of the primary and secondary education system, with the job of preparing young talent for sports achievement. There are 15 EIDE schools throughout Cuba. The island also has 76 sports academies and an athletic "finishing" school in Havana (the Escuela Superior de Perfeccionamiento Atlético).

School Games are held islandwide every year. These mini-Olympics help Cuba identify talent to be selected for specialized coaching (for example, María Colón Rueñes was identified as a potential javelin champion when she was only seven years old; she went on to win the gold medal at the Moscow Olympics). Many of Cuba's sports greats have passed through these schools—track and field stars such as world-record-holding high jumper Javier Sotomayor, world-record sprinters Leroy Burrel and Ana Fidelia Quirot, and volleyball legends such as Jel Despaigne and Mireya Luís.

Cuba was the undeniable winner of the Seventh World Boxing Championship in Berlin in May 1995, when the tiny nation scooped up four of the 12 gold medals, plus two silver and three bronze, crushing Germany (which placed second), Russia, and the United States. At the 1992 Olympic Games, Cuban boxers swept the field with gold medals in seven divisions (heavyweight Félix Savó was chosen as outstanding boxer of the games).

Amateurs or Professionals?
Sports figures are considered workers and "part of the society's productive efforts." As such, sports stars are paid a salary on a par with other workers, although most national team members also receive special perks. However, the Cuban government recently approved professional endorsements for track-and-field team members, and manufacturers such as Adidas now sponsor Cuba's top athletes. The hope is that Cuban boxers may go the same way, and baseball players may not be far behind.

Most Cuban sports stars are genuinely motivated by the love of accomplishment, representing the Revolution's model of a "new man." Alberto Juantorena, the only person to win Olympic 400- and 800-meter golds, demonstrates the unselfish attitude and fierce loyalty to his beleaguered island so typical of Cuba's athletes. Like dozens of Cuban superstars, he has turned down offers to earn big money abroad.

Cuba has a Sports Hall of Fame, in the **Sala Polivente Ramón Font** sports hall on Avenida Independencia, tel. 81-4296.

work. Cuban children are expected to be *estudiantes hoy, trabajadores mañana, soldados de la patria siempre*—students today, workers tomorrow, soldiers always—fulfilling José Martí's dictum: "In the morning, the pen—but in the afternoon, the plow."

The "Schools in the Countryside" program began in 1971. Secondary schoolchildren spend time each summer working in the countryside, where they live in boarding schools attached to 1,250-acre plots of arable land and boasting names such as "the Juvenile Column of the Centenary." Half of all intermediate-level children also attend a rural boarding school for at least some of their education. Here, time is equally divided between study and labor, the latter most often in citrus plantations, where the kids bring in the harvest. Here, too, unintended by the state, children learn to be lovers. Promiscuity is a staple in the fields.

HEALTH

In prerevolutionary Havana, only the monied class could afford good medical care. There were only 6,250 physicians in all of Cuba on the eve of the Revolution. Of these, 70% were in Havana (as were 60% of all hospital beds). Most people in rural areas went without medical services of any kind. Alas, half of Cuba's entire medical staff had fled the island by 1961, leaving Cuba critically short of doctors.

From the beginning, health care has assumed an inordinately prominent place in revolutionary government policies (in 1989, the government spent 12% of its budget on health care—four times the prerevolutionary figure—and whereas there was one medical school in Cuba in 1959, albeit a world-class facility, today some 21 medical schools churn out 4,000 doctors each year). In 1978, Fidel Castro predicted that Cuba would become the bulwark of Third World medicine, put a doctor on every block, become a world medical power, and surpass the US in certain health indices. In all four, he has been vindicated.

As a result, UNICEF puts Cuba four notches behind the United States in health indices and ahead of all other developing nations (despite the fact that Cuba's per capita GNP is only one-twentieth that of the US). Cuba's life expectancy of 73.9 years is the highest in Latin America (Argentina and Chile—the two countries considered the most developed in Latin America—have twice the mortality, with life expectancies of 36 and 32, respectively; Mexico has 47, Guatemala 57), and its infant mortality rate the lowest. Cuba has made major efforts to lower its infant mortality below 15 per 1,000 live births. In 1987, it achieved 13.7, compared to 11.5 for the United States and an average of 90 for other Third World countries. In mid-1996, Cuban authorities reported an infant mortality rate of 8 per 1,000 births (compared to 11 for Great Britain). Today, a child born is Havana is *twice* as likely to survive as a child born in Washington, D.C.

The Revolution's amazing accomplishment is due to its emphasis on preventive medicine and community-based doctors. The immediate need in 1959 was to stem the epidemics, infections, and parasitic diseases then plaguing Cuba. The first effort was to provide health services to poor rural areas that were without them. It has been notably successful. A near 100% immunization rate has ensured the total eradication of several preventable contagious diseases. The Pan American Health Organization declared Cuba the first polio-free country in the Americas. Cuba has the highest rate of immunization against measles in the world—better than the US—says UNICEF, which uses the measles immunization rate as the most reliable barometer of a country's commitment to bringing basic medical advances to its people. Cuba has also eradicated malaria and diphtheria. And, reportedly, no one has died from tuberculosis since 1979 (the incidence of the disease was reduced to 0.7 per 100,000 in 1983).

Family Doctor Program

Castro also set out to train doctors en masse. By 1984, Cuba's ratio of doctors per 10,000 inhabitants was double the Latin American ratio, and its ratio of nurses was seven times higher than the norm. That year, the government established the family doctor program, calling for 75,000 doctors and 20,000 nurses to provide primary care—on every city block and in every hamlet—by the year 2000. In mid-1996, the country had one doctor for every 200 inhabitants, with over 61,000 doctors nationwide (the program now covers more than 70% of Cuba)—*twice* as many per capita as the United States, which has one for every 405 inhabitants. (Dental care lags behind: in 1993, there was one dentist for every 1,278 inhabitants.) The vast majority of people from Mexico south to Tierra del Fuego would weep with joy to have such medical care.

The idea is for every Cuban to have his or her own doctor trained in comprehensive general medicine close by, living and working in the neighborhood, combining the duties of a family doctor and public health advocate (the doctor maintains the medical history of every community member and prepares a preventive medicine schedule based on each patient's needs). Foreign visitors are welcome to peek inside the three-story *casa del medico* (the family doctor's home), with a clinic on the ground floor, living quarters for the doctor's family on the second floor, and quarters for the nurse's family above.

Medical services are free to all citizens, regardless of medical attention and care required. Cubans have no fear of being turned away because they cannot pay. "We do not want to have private medicine because we have created a healthy system which has rendered extraordinary results," Castro has said. "And we do not want to destroy it. It would be a historic crime to do so."

CUBA'S FLYING DOCTORS

Since 1963, when Cuba sent 56 doctors to newly independent Algeria, the country has provided medical assistance to Third World countries regardless of its own economic straits. In 1985, the New York Times dubbed Cuba's international medical aid program "the largest Peace Corps-style program of civilian aid in the world." That year, Cuba had 16,000 doctors, teachers, agronomists, and other technical specialists serving in 22 Third World countries, including more doctors than the World Health Organization.

Cuba has also offered free medical care in Cuba for Third World patients, most famously for child victims of the Chernobyl nuclear disaster in the Soviet Union. In addition, prior to the Special Period, Cuba offered more than 20,000 international scholarships a year to Third World medical students (many times the number offered by the US), all of whom were required to return to their home countries upon completion of their training (three-quarters of foreign medical students who enter US medical schools never return to their home countries). Cuba has even donated entire hospitals to Third World countries.

Every town and village also has a hospital, plus a maternity home and a home where the elderly can spend their days being cared for while sons and daughters work (the government also runs day-care centers for children 45 days to six years old throughout the island). Fifteen mobile laboratories travel the country performing pre-clinical diagnostics for breast cancer. All women get pap smears and, if pregnant, extensive prenatal care. Virtually the entire population has been screened for AIDS. And local clinics even provide sex education for youngsters and exercise classes for elderly persons.

Beyond Primary Care

Cuba also commands the kind of technology that most poor countries can only dream about: ultrasound for obstetricians, CAT scans for radiologists, stacks of high-tech monitors in the suites for intensive care. Cuba has performed heart transplants (since 1985), heart-lung transplants (since 1987), coronary bypasses, pacemaker implantations, microsurgery, and a host of other advanced surgical procedures. A 1988 Pan-American Health Organization assessment of Cuba's foremost hospital, the Hospital Hermanos Ameijeiras, concluded that it "conducts research and uses technology at the international cutting edge in the 38 specialties in which services are rendered." In 1992, Science magazine rated the Ibero-Latin American Center for Nervous System Transplants and Regeneration as the world's best for the treatment of parkinsonism through transplanting fetal nervous brain tissue.

In addition, prior to the Special Period, the homegrown pharmaceutical industry supplied 80% of Cuba's needs. Cuba has made notable leaps in advancing the field of molecular immunology. It even manufactures interferons for AIDS treatment; a meningitis vaccine first "discovered" at the Finlay Institute; even a cure for the skin disease vitiligo, discovered by Cuban doctor Carlos Miyares Cao. Alas, the collapse of the Soviet Union and the increasingly restrictive US embargo have prevented Cuba from being able to obtain the raw materials, equipment, or spare parts for their high-tech industry. The entire world is poorer for it.

Many observers note that quality of service has been sacrificed to quantity, that the quality of medical services before the Revolution were far superior to that of most other Latin American nations, and that the improvements since 1959 have been built on accelerating gains made in the 1940s and '50s. True, most hospitals and clinics are basic by Western standards. But they are there, and fully manned. And Cuba's remarkable health indices have been attained with average health expenditures per capita of US$65, compared to US$589 in the US

Cuba's Medical Crisis

Cuba's admirable health system has suffered a catastrophic setback since the collapse of the Soviet bloc. Even before the Special Period, Cuba's health system faced severe shortages and long waiting lists for operations. Since 1991, services have been vastly curtailed. Dissemination of medicines has plummeted by over half. Nonessential operations have been postponed, and priority is given to those in most urgent need.

Doctors are writing prescriptions that the local pharmacy can no longer fill (the Cuban pharmaceutical industry has had to export many of its more sophisticated products to obtain funds to buy oil). Critical medicines are in such short supply that doctors are resorting to herbal remedies. Herbal teas substitute for sedatives. Aloe is given as an anti-inflammatory. Doctors have had to turn to acupuncture to anesthetize patients. Lacking sutures, many surgeons have had to sew using hemp. Materials for diagnostic tests have virtually disappeared. Faced with a severe shortage of X-ray film, radiologists have turned to more dangerous fluoroscopy. The absence of sulfa drugs, antibiotics, antibacterial medicines, and disinfectants has turned routine health problems into serious illnesses. Shortages of soap, toilet paper, chlorine, and other water treatment chemicals have made many drinking water supplies unsafe and brought a rise in diarrhea and hepatitis in health facilities and countrywide. And many hospitals even tell their patients to bring their own towels and bed sheets.

In addition, Cubans' average caloric intake fell from 2,845 calories a day in 1989 to 1,780 in 1994, leaving the population more susceptible to disease (the healthy norm is 2,500-3,000, depending on a person's weight). The incidence of babies born with low birth weights and of anemia among expectant mothers have risen. Beriberi (caused by Vitamin B deficiency), scurvy, typhoid, and tuberculosis— all eradicated since the Revolution—have reappeared. And in 1993, about 50,000 Cubans were diagnosed with optic neuritis, a mysterious eye and nerve disorder leading to gradual blindness attributable to malnutrition and vitamin deficiency. (*Granma* even featured a story recommending that Cubans eat flowers, leaves, and seeds from pumpkins, sweet potatoes, beets, and manioc to supplement their vitamin intake).

Foreign public health experts say that the impact of the Special Period could have been catastrophic had Cuba not had such a superb health system nationwide.

COMPUTERS FOR CUBAN HEALTH

Dr. José Santos, of Havana's main heart hospital, used to read 15 international medical journals every month. Now the hospital has *none*.

In 1994, Cuba's Ministry of Public Health lost its US$1 million budget for purchasing medical journals and books (Santos says he hasn't had a new textbook since 1990). Thus, it turned to computer communication with the help of the United Nations. Havana's Center for Medical Sciences Information (CNICM) initiated INFOMED to link outlying doctors and rural clinics with regional and provincial hospitals, research centers, and medical schools, which, in turn, are connected to a central database in Havana.

The UN provided Type 4986 servers. But Cuba is desperately short of end-user terminals at its key medical centers.

Project INFOMED collects old PC-XT or PC-AT computers for shipment to Cuba. If you have an old IBM-compatible machine collecting dust in your attic, why not donate it to INFOMED and allow it to be reincarnated as a life-saving instrument? Financial contributions are also needed to cover shipping costs. And medical supplies are welcome.

Contact Project INFOMED, Peace for Cuba Task Force, P.O. Box 450, Santa Clara, CA 95052, tel. (408) 243-4359, fax (408) 243-1229; e-mail jreardon@igc.apc.org; or via the caravan's web site at http://www.igc.org/laborquotes /cubasoli.html.

Uncle Sam's Shame

The situation was worsened in 1992, when the US Congress passed the Torricelli Act, which banned all shipments of foods and medicines to Cuba except humanitarian aid (these items had previously been exempt from the embargo). Prior to the bill's passage, 70% of US subsidiary trade with Cuba was in food and medicines. By barring such trade, the embargo forces Cuba to import medicines and medical supplies from Europe and Asia at vastly inflated prices. In addition, all medical equipment and supplies manufactured in the US or under US patent cannot be exported to Cuba by third-country companies without a license from the US Commerce Department. Such licenses are routinely denied.

In 1994, a team from the American Public

Health Association reported that the embargo is contributing to death and disease in Cuba. The fact-finding tour concluded that "the embargo has exacerbated an already difficult situation in which nutritional deficiencies, unsafe water, deteriorating sanitation, overcrowding, and an absence of crucial medicines and supplies have attacked the formerly healthy population."

ON THE ROAD

SIGHTSEEING HIGHLIGHTS

Havana

Habana Vieja: Atmospheric historic district comprising castles, palaces, and mansions dating back centuries, including the **Plaza de la Catedral, Plaza de Armas, Castillo de la Real Fuerza, Convent of San Francisco, José Martí's Birthplace,** and **La Bodeguita del Medio** and **El Floridita,** two bars popularized by Ernest Hemingway. Replete with museums. Two days minimum.

Museum of the Revolution: Former presidential palace now tells the tale of the Revolution. Includes the *Granma* **Memorial,** featuring the vessel that brought Fidel Castro, Che Guevara, and fellow revolutionaries from exile to initiate the Revolution.

Martí Monument and Museum: Towering marble and granite statue dominates Plaza de la Revolución. All-around views of Havana from the *mirador.* Contains a splendid museum honoring Cuba's National Hero.

Napoleonic Museum: Memorabilia of Napoleon Bonaparte in a well-preserved colonial mansion.

Maqueta de Habana: Detailed 1:1,000 scale model of Havana. Provides a bird's-eye perspective of the entire city.

Tropicana Nightclub: Spectacular cabaret with more than 200 performers—predominantly tall mulattas in fantastical costumes.

Metropolitan Havana

Hemingway Museum (Finca Vigía): "Papa's" former home on a hill southeast of Havana is preserved as it was on the day he died. His sportfishing boat—the *Pilar*—stands in the grounds.

Cojímar: Old fishing village where Ernest Hemingway berthed the *Pilar:* A memorial to Hemingway and the Las Terrazas bar and restaurant recall his presence.

Havana Province

Puente Bacunayagua: Stunning views over a dramatic gorge from Cuba's tallest bridge.

Pinar del Río Province

Valle de Viñales: Beautiful valley dominated by dramatic limestone formations. Includes the **Mural de Dos Hermanos, Cuevas del Indio,** the spa of **San Vicente,** and the adjacent **Valle de Ancón.** Quintessential rural landscapes. Center of tobacco farming.

Las Terrazas: Intriguing rural community with a top-notch hotel. Local artists' studios, hik-

BEACHES

Camagüey: About 10 beaches on both north and south coasts. Those on the north are spectacular, with fine white sand; the southern beaches are ugly. Archipiélago de los Járdines de la Reina lies offshore, with splendid beaches. *Best beaches:* Santa Lucía and Cayo Sabinal.

Cayo Largo and Isla de la Juventud: About 16, with fine white sand. *Best beaches:* Bibijagua (Isla de la Juventud), Playa Sirena and Playa Blanca (Cayo Largo), Cayo Rico (Archipiélago de los Canarreos).

Ciego de Ávila: About 10 spectacular white sand beaches on the north shore, particularly on Cayo Coco and Cayo Guillermo. Both cays have resorts. Spectacular beaches, too, on the cays of the Archipiélago de los Járdines de la Reina. *Best beaches:* Cayo Coco and Cayo Guillermo.

Cienfuegos: Although not known for quality beaches, it has several small beaches boasting fine white sand. *Best beaches:* Playa Rancho Luna.

Granma: Few beaches. Most are coarse dark sand. *Best beaches:* Marea del Portillo.

Guantánamo: About 15 beaches, primarily with coarse white sand. Most are on the south shore. *Best beaches:* Maguana, near Baracoa.

Havana: About 34, mostly with fine white sand, concentrated east of the capital, centered on Playas del Este. Beaches along the south coast are disappointing. *Best beaches:* Santa María del Mar, Tarará, Jucáro.

Holguín: Guardalavaca is the most developed beach—one of about 20 with fine white sand. *Best beaches:* Guardalavaca, Don Lino, Estero Ciego, and Cayo Saetía.

Las Tunas: The north shore has at least seven fine white sand stretches. *Best beaches:* Covarrubias and Playa Uvero.

Matanzas: About 10, all with fine white sand. Most are on the north shore, including Varadero, the most popular and developed beach in Cuba. *Best beaches:* Varadero, Playa Girón.

Pinar del Río: About 20, evenly distributed between north and south coasts. *Best beaches:* María la Gorda and Cayo Levisa.

Sancti Spíritus: About eight white sand beaches, all on the south coast. *Best beaches:* Playa Ancón, near Trinidad.

Santiago de Cuba: More than 20, from fine dark sand in the west to coarse, white sand in the east. *Best beaches:* Playas Siboney, Bucanero, Bacajagua, and Sigua.

Villa Clara: Most of the 15 or so fine white sand beaches are associated with the hard-to-reach offshore cays. *Best beaches:* Playas Santa María and Los Ensenachos, on Cayo Fragoso and Cayo Francés.

ing trails, an ecology center, coffee farm (now a restaurant), and mineral springs and cascades.

Isla de la Juventud
Presidio Modelo: Somber prison—now derelict—where Fidel Castro and other revolutionaries were imprisoned in 1953. The hospital and Fidel's solitary cell contain a museum.

Matanzas Province
Museo de Playa Girón: Small but excellent museum celebrates the victory at the Bay of Pigs.

Cienfuegos and Villa Clara Provinces
Remedios: Beautiful colonial town centered on **Iglesia Bien Viaje,** with the **Museo de Parrandas** honoring the annual fireworks festivals.

Sierra del Escambray: Scenic uplands are lushly forested and good for birding.

Sancti Spiritus Province
Playa Ancón: Superb, miles-long white sand beach with scuba diving offshore. Good hotel. Trinidad close at hand.

Trinidad: Singularly the most important and appealing attraction outside Havana. Intimate colonial city set on a hill, preserved intact as a living museum. Charming plazas, cobbled streets, and architectural treasures. Equally appealing for its traditional life. Two days minimum.

Central Cuba
Cayo Coco: Superb white sand beaches. Top-notch resort hotel. Birdlife includes flamingos. Dramatic drive along *pedraplen* land bridge.

Camagüey: Provincial capital with notable colonial heritage. Highlights include **Catedral Nuestra Señora de la Merced,** a cigar factory, the **Teatro Principal,** and cobbled plazas such as **Plaza San Juan de Díos.** Partly restored.

Las Tunas and Holguín Provinces
Grupo de Maniabon: Upland region with quintessential Cuban scenery. Traditional *campesino* lifestyle.

Finca Mayabe: Hilltop *finca* with fighting cocks and other traditional peasant attractions. Swimming pool, restaurant, and villas perched on cliff face. Pancho the donkey entertains by guzzling beer.

Granma Province
Pico Turquino: Cuba's highest peak, accessible by a steep, well-worn trail. Bust of José Martí at the top, which offers staggering views over Oriente. For the fit and hearty.

Marea del Portillo to Chivirico: Long, lonesome drive along cacti-covered shore in lee of Sierra Maestra. Unpaved road. An adventure.

La Comandancia de la Plata: Fidel Castro's headquarters in the Sierra Maestra are preserved. Reach it via a dramatic drive, then hike along a forested mountain ridge.

Santiago Province
Gran Piedra National Park: Mountain reserve protecting flora and fauna, within Baconao Biosphere Reserve. Steep winding road leads to Gran Piedra. Dramatic views.

Moncada Barracks: Ground zero of the Revolution. Old army barracks (today a school) attacked by Fidel Castro and followers in 1953. Splendid museum.

Museo Bacardi: Splendid collection of colonial artifacts and weaponry, plus art gallery and small ethnographic museum of the Americas.

Morro Castle: Great stone bulwark perched dramatically atop the cliffs at the entrance to Bahía de Santiago de Cuba. Contains the **Museum of Piracy.**

Santa Ifigenia Cemetery: Chock-full of figures of historical import entombed in theatrical array of mausoleums and graves. José Martí mausoleum.

Valle de Prehistória: Jurassic Park in stone. Large collection of kitschy, life-size concrete dinosaurs. Excellent little museum of natural history.

Guantánamo Province
Baracoa: Remote town with heaps of charm. Places of note include a small cigar factory, **Museo Matachón,** in the Matachón fortress, and **Catedral Nuestra Señora de la Asunción,** containing the **Cruz de la Parra** supposedly left in Cuba by Christoper Columbus. Sensational views from El Castillito (today a pleasant hotel). Fascinating cultural life. Regional cuisine.

La Farola: Suspenseful road snaking up and over the Sierra del Purial mountains. Incredible views.

RECREATION

BICYCLING

The occasional sweat and effort make Cuba's spectacular landscapes and serenity all the more endearing from the seat of a bike saddle. Sure, you'll work for your reward—but you'll never get so close to so much beauty in a car.

Bicycle touring offers a chance to explore the island alongside the Cubans themselves. Since the demise of the Soviet Union severed the gasoline pipeline, the Cubans have taken to bicycling with zeal. The roads are little trafficked, although potholes and stray animals are a consistent problem (a helmet is a wise investment). Repairs are never a problem: you'll find a well-stocked bicycle shop in virtually every town, and scores of Cubans now make a living repairing bicycles and punctures *(poncheras)*. You should nonetheless bring essential spares.

Airlines generally allow bicycles to be checked free of charge (properly packaged) with one piece of luggage. Otherwise, a small charge may apply. Leave your racing bike at home and bring a touring bike or, better yet, a mountain bike. You can also rent a bicycle from **Panataxi** in Havana (see "Getting Around" in the Havana chapter), if you don't mind cruising around on a single-gear Chinese pachyderm.

If you're interested in joining groups of Cuban students, mostly English-speaking, contact the **Club Ciclocaribe Olímpico,** Comité Olímpico Cubano, Calle 13 #601 esq. C, Vedado, Havana, Cuba CP 10400, or **Club de Cicliturismo "Gran Caribe,"** c/o Ignacio Valladares Rivero; home tel. 98-9193 in Guanabacoa, or tel. 78-3941 at the Estadio Juan Abrantes. Ignacio and fellow students welcome foreigners to join them on weekend cycle trips into the countryside surrounding Havana.

A good resource for cycling information is Cuba's **Federación de Ciclismo,** tel. 68-3776 or 68-3661, in Havana.

Organized Tours

In the UK, **Hazel Pennington Bike Tours,** P.O. Box 75, Bath, Avon BA1 1BX, England, tel. 01225-480130, fax 01225-480132, offers 14-day bicycle tours each March, November, and December (£685, or £1,070 including roundtrip airfare from Stansted). The itinerary, which includes some challenging rides (an a/c coach is available if you want to skip the hard bits), takes in the Sierra de Escambray, Trinidad, Cienfuegos, the Sierra del Rosarios, Viñales, and Havana.

In Canada, **Adventures Unlimited,** 65 Front St. East #304, Toronto, Ontario M5E1B5, tel. (416) 360-6603 or (800) 567-6286, fax (416) 363-1522, offers one- and two-week cycling trips (C$1,699 and C$2,699, from Toronto) with monthly departures Oct.-April. The well-planned itinerary begins and ends in Varadero, with visits to the Bay of Pigs, Cienfuegos, Trinidad, Sancti Spíritus, Santa Clara, and Cárdenas the first week and via Havana to Soroa, Viñales, and Pinar del Río the second.

MacQueen's Bicycle Shop & Travel, 430 Queen St., Charlottestown, Prince Edward Island, Canada C1A 4E8, tel. (902) 368-2453 or (800) 969-2822, fax (902) 894-4547; e-mail biketour@peinet.pe.ca, also offers bicycle guided tours in Cuba. In 1997, it had two eight-day itineraries in Oriente, one from Manzanillo in Granma Province and the other from Santiago de Cuba and including Gran Piedra and Baconao National Park (C$1,599, including roundtrip airfare from Toronto). Both concentrate on exploring Granma Province and the Sierra Maestra. The company supplies Canadian-made bicycles. Distances average 50 km daily, but a support van is available also. The company has a homepage at http://www.peinet.pe.ca/PEI-homepage/pei_biz/macqueen/mcqtext.html.

In the US, **Wings of the World,** 1200 William St. #706, Buffalo, NY 14240, tel. (800) 465-8687, offers eight-day escorted bicycling tours to Cuba every month. The trip includes a warm-up ride through the colonial streets of Havana, then seven days venturing through eastern Cuba, where highlights include the Sierra de Nipe, the Baconao Reserve, Santiago de Cuba, and Guantánamo. The tour costs US$1,895. Daily cycling distances average about 50 km. Participants can bring their own bicycles or use a cycle supplied by the company. An a/c support bus accompanies the tours.

BIRDWATCHING

Wherever you travel in Cuba, you're sure to be surrounded by the calls and whistles of dozens of exotic species. Much of the Cuban landscape is relatively open and scrubby, making birds more easy to spot. Your best bet for seeing and learning about different species is to hire a qualified guide. Bring binoculars, although you can also buy them (expensive!) at Optica Miramar, Avenida 7ma and Calle 24, Miramar, Havana, tel. 33-2990, fax 33-2893.

The swampy Zapata Peninsula is one of the best birdwatching arenas in the Caribbean—87% of the island's 380-plus bird species (22 of them endemic) can be seen here—and has an **International Birdwatching Center** at Playa Larga. With luck you might spot the smallest hummingbird in the world (the *pájaro mosca*), the *tocororo* or Cuban trogon, and flamingos, which can also be seen on the northern cays. The cays are also favored nesting sites for scores of migratory species. Isla de la Juventud has Cuba's largest population of parrots. The Sierra del Rosarios and mountains of Oriente are also superb birding sites, especially Baconao Biosphere Reserve and Cuchillas de Toa Biosphere Reserve, created when the endangered ivory-billed woodpecker was discovered there a few years ago.

The state agency **Cubatur,** Calle 23 #156, Vedado, Havana, tel. 32-4521, fax 33-3104, publishes a birdwatching brochure and recently introduced birding excursions.

Wings of the World, 1200 William St. #706, Buffalo, NY 14240, tel. (800) 465-8687, offers eight-day birding tours in January, February, and March (US$2,295). The tours visit Zapatas and Treasure Lake, the Long Point Bird Observatory, and La Güira National Park in Pinar del Río.

FISHING

So few anglers have fished Cuba during the past three decades that the fish populations are jostling for space. Cuba is a sleeper, with freshwater lakes and lagoons that almost boil with tarpon, bonefish, snook, and bass. And so many gamefish run offshore, streaming through the Gulf Stream that Ernest Hemingway called his great blue river, that deep-sea fishing here has been compared to "hunting elk in the suburbs."

Freshwater Fishing
Cuba offers freshwater fishing in five of its 14 provinces, mostly in man-made lakes. The star of the show is largemouth bass, the freshwater fish that is most attractive to millions of US sport fishermen. Bass fishing is best at Lake Hanabanilla and neighboring Lake Granizo in the Sierra del Escambray; Lake Cuyaguatoje in Pinar del Río; and Lake Zaza in Sancti Spíritus province. Nearby Lake Legrije, and Lake Redonda, near Morón in Ciego de Avila province, are other good sites.

Americans fishing home waters apparently catch, on average, only one bass every two days of fishing. "During those same two days, a bass fisherman fishing at Lake Zaza in Cuba might expect to catch 100 bass of incredible quality," claims Dan Snow, a fishing expert who has spent more than a decade fishing in Cuba. "There's a good chance that a world record bass exists in Cuba," says Snow. "A man living near Lake Hanabanilla claimed to have caught a 26-pound bass." The current record, recognized by the International Game Fish Association and set in 1932, stands at 22 pounds four ounces.

Trout fishing is particularly good at Presa Alacranes, in Villa Clara. The record catch at this freshwater reservoir is 15.7 pounds. Lake Zaza and Lake La Redonda, which has the highest concentration of trout per square kilometer, are also good.

Maspotón, a dedicated hunting and fishing resort on the south shore of Pinar del Río, is a popular spot to catch tarpon, as are Laguna del Tesoro and the brackish coastal lagoons of Zapata Peninsula. These "silver rockets" can reach up to 75 kg, and you're sure to have your hands full: no other fish jumps, leaps, twists, and turns like the tarpon. When you tire of wrestling these snappy fighters, you can take on snook—another worthy opponent.

As for bonefish, few (if any) destinations can compare. Angling maestro Joe Brooks wrote glowingly of fishing Cuba's Isle of Pines (today's Isla de la Juventud) in the 1950s, when he and his angling pals, bonefish experts all, landed 31 bones on their best day. In 1995, an inexperienced angler named Oddvar Sessions landed 26 bonefish at Zapata—before 3:30 p.m. and in off-season! In 1996, two other anglers caught 103 bonefish in one day in shallow flats during bad weather (one, Ricardo Setec, reported that the fish swam between his legs and were not alarmed unless he made sudden movements). Light-tackle enthusiasts will also find shallow-water bonefish and tarpon in abundance off Cayo Largo, and in the Járdines de la Reina archipelago south of Ciego de Ávila province.

Several hotels cater to anglers and hunters. **Cubatur** and **Horizontes** publish brochures on fishing in Cuba and can arrange licenses and fishing guides (compulsory), included in the price of your fishing package.

Dan Snow publishes **CubaNews,** P.O. Box 5484, Kingwood, TX 77325, tel. (713) 358-2262, a monthly newsletter on fishing; subscription $50 per year. **Pan-Angling Travel,** 180 N. Michigan Ave., Chicago, IL 60601, tel. (312) 263-0328, fax (312) 263-5246, publishes a newsletter with regular articles on fishing in Cuba; it also arranges fishing trips to Zapata. In Canada, **Magna Outdoors,** 50 Alness St. #200C, Downsview, Ontario M3J 2G9, tel. (416) 665-7174 or (800) 387-3717, fax (416) 665-8448, offers fishing trips.

The best months for bass fishing are the colder months, when the temperature drops to an average of 77° F. Tarpon and snook are caught year-round.

Several US companies (Tarponwear, Orvis, Fenwick, and Patagonia, among others) sell fishing and hunting clothing designed specifically for the tropics. Supplex-based garments are cool, and dry quickly when wet. You'll also need a wide-brimmed hat and a lightweight rainsuit, plus neoprene wading shoes if you plan on wading the flats. You should take your own rods, reels, and tackle.

Deep-Sea Fishing

You'll discover far more fish than fishhooks off the coast of Cuba, where snagging the *really* big one comes easy. Hardly a season goes by without some IGFA record being broken.

There is much to learn about tactics in fighting big fish, and no fishermen was ever so knowledgeable as Ernest Hemingway, who returned to Cuba year after year and reputedly became the first sportsman to fish marlin with rod and reel in Cuban waters.

Every year, the big run of marlin begins in May, when they swim against the Gulf Stream current close to the Cuban shore. In places, the stream begins only a quarter-mile offshore with the depth sounder reading 1,000 feet; another quarter-mile and the bottom plummets another 5,000 feet.

Fishing expeditions for barracuda and spearfish are offered from Marina Hemingway, Playas del Este, Varadero, and other marinas along the north coast. Other good spots are the Los Canarreos Archipelago (which includes Isla de la Juventud and Cayo Largo).

Spearfish such as the dorado, marlin, and striped tuna bite best on beetles. The barracuda, however, is so rapacious it will "even go for a shoestring." Not so the coronado, the grouper, or the *macabí,* which are more cautious eaters. Barracuda run year-round. The best months for spearfish are May-August.

Puertosol, Calle Cobre #34404, e/ 2da y 4ta, Villa Marina, Tarará, Havana, tel. 33-3510, fax 33-5501, offers sportsfishing excursions from most of its 18 marinas islandwide. Typical four-hour light-tackle excursions *(pesa a fondo)* cost US$15-30 per person; four-hour deep-sea excursions cost US$150-250 for up to four passengers. Likewise, **Clubnaútica,** Paseo 309 #2B e/ 13 y 15, Vedado, Havana, tel. 33-4546, fax 33-4545, offers excursions from Marina Hemingway, Varadero, Cayo Largo, and Marina Tarará. Its four-hour "Fishing the Hemingway Route" package from Havana's Marina Hemingway costs US$360 for four passengers, including lunch and drinks.

Fishing Tournaments

Cuba hosts several sportfishing tournaments. The big three competitions are based in Havana's Marina Hemingway: **The Currican Tournament** is held the first or second week of April, when the surface species take to Hemingway's "great blue river." **The Ernest Hemingway International Marlin Tournament** is the granddaddy of tournaments. It's held each May or June and offers trophies for the biggest marlin and the highest score. The Ernest Hemingway Cup may well be the world's most sought-after fishing trophy. **The Blue Marlin Tournament** also entices fisherfolk from around the world each August or September.

Wings of the World, 1200 William St. #706, Buffalo, NY 14240, tel. (800) 465-8687, offers eight-day fishing trips timed to coincide with each of the three tournaments. The US$2,495 price includes air, hotel, entrance fee, and all other aspects of competing—and their trips are fully legal for all US citizens!

GOLF

Cuba is investing in its future as a golfing destination. For now, you would visit Cuba to golf merely as a curiosity. The existing nine-hole course at Varadero is third-rate, and only one of four courses in Havana remains from prerevolutionary days. The **Havana Golf Club,** Carretera de Vento, Km. 8, Capdevila Havana, tel. 44-4836 or 44-8227, is also a nine-hole course. An additional nine holes may be finished by late 1997, however, A resident pro Jorge Dulque—gives lessons (US$10 per hour). Caddies and clubs can be rented, but the pro shop is almost bare.

At least four 18-hole courses are slated to be built in the next few years by Spanish developers.

Annual golf tournaments are hosted at the Havana Golf Club and Las Américas Golf Club at Varadero.

Wings of the World 1200 William St. #706, Buffalo, NY 14240, tel. (800) 465-8687, offers occasional golf tours.

HIKING

Cuba has the potential to be a hiker's paradise. For now, organized hiking is almost totally undeveloped. There are only a handful of trails developed specifically for hiking; a notable exception is the full-day climb of Cuba's highest mountain, Pico Turquino, in the Sierra Maestra. Diehards can head for the foothills of the Sierra del Rosarios, and Sierra Maestra and Cuchillas de Toa in Oriente, where trails lace the mountains. Pinares de Mayarí (in Holguín province), El Saltón (in Santiago province), and Moka Hotel (in Pinar del Río) are all eco-resorts with hiking trails.

Camping wild is frowned on by authorities. You should have no problem finding accommodation with locals you meet.

Don't forget to carry plenty of water and a shade hat. And you should stock up on snacks before setting out. You may be able to buy local produce from farmers, who'll generously offer whatever they have out of the goodness of their hearts. Common courtesy dictates that you should pay for hospitality.

HUNTING

Cubans are big hunters, and the island has many hunting reserves and facilities, albeit relatively basic. Most hunting is for white-crowned pigeon, mourning dove, white-winged dove, quail, migrant ducks, common snipe, American coot, and guinea fowl. Most reserves are located near lakes, coastal lagoons, and offshore cays. Guanahacabibes, in Pinar del Río, plus Cayo Sabinal, Cayo Romano, and Baconao also offer hunting for deer and wild boar. Cayo Saetia even has African game animals, first introduced to answer the demands of Communist Party officials.

Most hunting reserves provide field guides, rent shotguns, and sell cartridges. Hunters are allowed to bring their own guns (caliber 12-20 shotguns) and up to 100 shells. You must re-

---

HUNTING RESERVES

Aguachales de Falla: Ciego de Avila

Alonso de Rojas: Pinar del Río

Cayo Saetía: Holguín

Cerro de Caisimú: Granma

El Indio: Santiago

El Taje: Sancti Spíritus

Florida: Camagüey

Guanahacabibes: Pinar del Río

La Vibora: Pinar del Río

Los Caneyes: Villa Clara

Manatí Hunting Preserve: Sancti Spíritus

Maspotón: Pinar del Río

Sur de Ciego de Avila: Ciego de Avila

Sur del Jíbaro: Sancti Spíritus

Yariguá: Cienfuegos

quest a permit to import a gun no fewer than seven working days before proposed trip date. Good-quality ammunition can also be purchased in Cuba; a 25-cartridge box costs US$10. You *must* have a proper hunting permit (US$20) and hunt only with a guide.

Horizontes, Calle 23 #156, e/ N y O, Vedado, Havana, tel. 33-4142, fax 33-3161, which operates hunting lodges and hotels in or near key hunting reserves, publishes a brochure on hunting. Horizontes will take care of obtaining your permit and guides.

Cuba's hunting season runs from October 31 to March 15, with hunting allowed from dawn to dusk seven days a week. The season for mourning dove starts on September 15, for white-crowned pigeon and fulvous tree duck on August 1. Daily limits are dependent on species and specific reserve.

Organized Tours

A Canadian company, **Magna Outdoors,** 50 Alness St. #200C, Downsview, Ontario M3J 2G9, tel. (416) 665-7174 or (800) 387-3717, fax (416) 665-8448, offers weeklong hunting trips featuring two days at El Taje Lodge, three at Manatí Hunting Preserve, and time to relax at Varadero.

SAILING

The Cuban coastline extends 5,746 km, or 3,102 nautical miles, of which 2,400 km are along the 10-fathom line. The **northeast** coast is indented with deep, flask-shaped bays with modest marina facilities. The **central north** coast is a maze of coral cays and islets with sheltered coves, with the resort of Varadero to the west; much of the water is too shallow for boating. West of Havana, the **coast of Pinar del Río** is more easily navigated, with a few pocket bays and cays dispersed off the coast (but only one marina). The **south coast** has a handful of meager marinas, plus the attraction of scores of cays, most notably Cayo Largo (a good base for forays to or from the Cayman Islands). Along the entire **southeast coast,** surf pounds the base of dramatic steep mountains; there are tiny harbors evenly spaced.

For cruising, you'll need to register your boat upon arrival and receive a cruising permit called a *Permiso Especial de Navegación* (US$50 or more, depending on the length of your boat). You'll need an official clearance—a *despacho*—to depart for your next, and each and

MARINA SERVICES

	AQUA	PARADISO	COLONY	CAYO LARGO	JAGÚA	ANCÓN
Location	Varadero	Varadero	Isla Juventud	Cayo Largo	Cienfuegos	Casilda
Latitude	23° 08'	23° 08'	21° 38'	21° 38'	22° 07'	21° 44'
Longitude	81° 18'	81° 18'	82° 59'	81° 34'	80° 27'	79° 59'
Mooring capacity	110	29	30	20	15	4
Electricity	110/220	110/220	110/220	110/220	110/220	110/220
Water	Yes	Yes	Yes	Yes	Yes	Yes
Watchman	Yes	Yes	Yes	Yes	Yes	Yes
Diesel	Yes	Yes	Yes	Yes	Yes	Yes
Gas	Yes	Yes	Yes	Yes	Yes	Yes
Tourism bureau	Yes	Yes	Yes	Yes	Yes	Yes
Sanitary service	Yes	Yes	Yes	Yes	Yes	Yes
Showers	Yes	No	No	No	No	No
Accommodation	Yes	Yes	Yes	Yes	Yes	Yes
Telephone	Yes	Yes	Yes	Yes	Yes	Yes
Laundry	Yes	Yes	Yes	Yes	Yes	No
Shop	Yes	Yes	Yes	Yes	Yes	Yes
Currency exchange	Yes	Yes	Yes	Yes	Yes	Yes
Propane gas	Yes	Yes	No	No	Yes	No

every, stop. Authorities will usually ask for a planned itinerary, but hold to your guns and insist on flexibility to cruise at random toward your final destination. A *Permiso de Salida* will be issued listing your final destination and possible stops en route. Simon Charles, in his *Cruising Guide to Cuba,* reports that the Ministry of the Interior (MINREX) have never denied or modified his requests; he recommends noting on the *permiso* any plans to scuba dive or anchor offshore at any of Cuba's zillion cays. Be patient! Official proceedings are always courteous but time consuming.

Puertosol Marinas de Cuba, Calle Cobre #34404, e/ 2da y 4ta, Villa Marina, Tarará, Havana, tel. 33-3510, fax 33-5501, operates 18 marinas and dive centers, including 11 new "full-service" marinas currently being developed at Cienfuegos, Caibairiín, Cayo Francés and Santa María, Cayo Coco, Santiago de Cuba, and Baracoa. However, only two marinas—those in Havana and Varadero—are up to international par. Some are very basic. All marinas offer freshwater, 110-volt electrical hook-ups, plus diesel and gasoline. The price of diesel varies (in early 1996, it cost 70 cents per liter in Cienfuegos, but US$1 in Cayo Largo). Berthing fees range from 25 cents to 45 cents a foot per night. Marina staff usually bend over backwards to assist foreign yachters.

See "Getting There" in this chapter for information on sailing *to* Cuba.

Warning: Beware fishermen's nets, especially in the Gulf of Batabanó.

The famous **US-Havana Regatta,** which was held every March from 1930 to 1959, was revived in 1994 when 84 yachts competed in a race from Sarasota, Florida, to Marina Hemingway, in Havana. The International Nautical Club of Havana hosts the annual race, whose date and start point varies year by year. Since Cuba foots the bill for docking and other fees, US participants are not in violation of US law. For information on future regattas, contact the Sarasota Sailing Squadron, tel. (941) 388-2355, or the Nautical Club at Marina Hemingway, tel. 33-6715, ext. 701.

Yacht Charters

Clubnaútica, Paseo 309 #2B e/ 13 y 15, Vedado, Havana, tel. 33-4546, fax 33-4545, has facilities in Holguín, Varadero, Cayo Largo, and Marina Tarará. Its low season weekly charter rates range from US$2,100 for an Elan 43 to US$4,690 for an Oceanis 500 or similar. It also has catamarans for charter, as well as powerboats, such as Zuiderzee 30s (US$2,660). A deposit of US$2,000 or US$,3500 is required, depending on size of boat. Skippers cost US$65 a day plus meals. A hostess is US$50 extra. Bedding and cleaning service is provided. Diving equipment can be rented additionally. Deposits (35% on signing) can be paid by Euro-traveler's check, credit card, or in cash. Rates increase as much as 60% in peak season (mid-December through mid-January).

Puertosol Marinas de Cuba, Calle Cobre #34404, e/ 2da y 4ta, Villa Marina, Tarará, Havana, tel. 33-3510, fax 33-5501, rents yachts at most of its 18 marinas islandwide. Typical rates begin at about US$1,540 per week for small vessels in low season. Puertosol has established a **Tarará International Nautical Club** that offers members discounts of 45% on "sail navigation course for beginners," 35% on wharfage fees, 25% on scuba diving packages, 20% on nautical activities, and 15% off the cost of lodging and meals. Membership costs US$10 monthly (plus US$15 initiation fee) and is restricted to diplomats, businessmen, and foreign press.

SCUBA DIVING

Cuba is a diver's paradise. It is compared to the Cayman Islands 20 years ago, with sites as fabulous and the quality of dive operations as high as almost anywhere in the Caribbean. There are dozens of Spanish galleons and even U-boats sunk off the south coast. Many of the sites, particularly to the south, are unexplored. The best diving is on the south side, although the north coast has some splendid sites, including the 40-km-long reef off Santa Lucía, with extensive coral reefs and countless cays and islets. Visibility ranges from 15 to 35 meters. Water temperatures average 80° F to 85° F.

The traditional critters of the Caribbean abound: barracuda, rays, sharks, tarpon, and turtles. The star-studded cast also includes angels, bigeyes, butterflies, damsels, drums, gobies, groupers, grunts, jacks, parrotfish, snappers, triggerfish, and wrasses, all of which seem perfectly content to ignore the human presence.

Dozens of morays peer out from beneath rocky ledges.

Spearfishing is strictly controlled. Spearguns and gigs are *not* allowed through customs.

Cuba has developed four principal dive areas: the **Archipiélago de los Colorados,** on Cuba's extreme northwest shore; the **Sabana and Camagüey archipelagos,** two extended islet clusters centrally located on the northern coastline; **Járdines de la Reina,** a group of coralline limestone cays on the southeast coast; and the **Isle of Youth** (Isla de la Juventud). Many sites are also being explored near **Cayo Largo.** The so-called **"Blue Circuit"** east of Havana also has prime sites. And the waters off the tip of **Cabo de Corrientes,** at the westernmost point of Cuba, offer fantastic diving with dozens of sites accessible from the modest **María la Gorda International Diving Center.**

The preeminent site is Isla de la Juventud, one of the top dive destinations in the Caribbean with the **International Scuba Diving Center.**. A compression chamber is located within 20 minutes of the Hotel Colony, the main dive resort. Shipwrecks and shallow reefs are prime attractions, but the main appeal is the abrupt drop-off from the island shelf into the Gulf of Mexico, with huge formations of black coral at about 20 meters.

A second international diving center opened in 1994 in the Santa Lucía beach resort area in Camagüey province. At least 30 other beaches have scuba facilities, and there are 11 decompression chambers (including three mobile chambers), with more planned (in Havana, the chamber is at Hospital Luís Díaz Soto, Habanas del Este, tel. 60-2804; in Santiago de Cuba, it's at the José Castillo Duany Military Hospital).

Scuba diving is available at virtually every resort site, and many large beachside hotels offer diving programs and certification courses. Many also have modestly equipped dive shops. The

BEISBOL: CUBA'S NATIONAL PASTIME

Beisbol (or *pelota*) is as much an obsession in Cuba as it is in the US —more so, in fact; in 1909, Ralph Estep, a salesman for Packard, journeyed through Cuba and thought it "baseball crazy." The first officially recorded baseball game was played in Cuba, in 1874, at what is now the world's oldest baseball stadium still in use.

Just watch Cuban kids, playing, writes author Randy Wayne White, "without spikes, hitting without helmets, sharing their cheap Batos gloves, but playing like I have never seen kids play before. It wasn't so much the skill—though they certainly had skill—as it was the passion with which they played, a kind of controlled frenzy." No wonder Cuba traditionally beats the pants off the US team in the Olympic Games.

Needless to say, the US professional leagues are well aware of this enormous talent pool. Players who make the Cuban national team and barnstorm the Olympics earn about 400 pesos a month—about the same as the average laborer—and it's not surprising that many are tempted by the prospect of

Juan Abrahantes baseball stadium, Havana

CHRISTOPHER P. BAKER

standard of equipment is good. Nonetheless, it's a good idea to bring your own equipment (leave tanks and weight belts at home, as all scuba diving centers have steel 12- or 15-liter tanks).

If you need to replace O-rings, batteries, straps, etc, most supplies are available. Tank fittings and equipment in Cuba are both European and North American.

You can even dive from Fidel Castro's protocol ship, the *Coral Negro,* a live-aboard which takes 20 passengers and is fully equipped.

Cuban divemasters are all trained by internationally recognized organizations and are highly skilled.

Publicitur publishes a 60-page booklet, *The Cuban Caribbean: Scuba-Diving Guide,* by Feliberto Garrié Fajardo. However, serious divers should consult *Diving and Snorkeling Guide to Cuba,* by Diana Williams (Houston: Pisces Books, 1996), which provides detailed accounts of major dive-sites.

Organized Tours
In Canada, the **Fuji Incentive Group,** 463 Adelade, Toronto, Ontario M5V 1S7, tel. (416) 777-0098, fax (416) 777-0099, offers diving tours in Cuba. **Hooked on Diving,** tel. (514) 843-8873, fax (514) 843-9439, also offers weeklong packages to Cayo Largo. In the UK, **Aquatours,** Milboa Lodge, Portsmouth Rd., Thames Ditton, Surrey KT7 0ESI, tel. (0181) 339-0040, fax (0181) 339-0080, has scuba tours to Cuba.

In the US, **Wings of the World,** 1200 William St. #706, Buffalo, NY 14240, tel. (800) 465-8687, offers weeklong diving packages to Isla de la Juventud.

SPORTS

Cuba is a world superstar in sports and athletics—out of all proportion to its diminutive size. In 1971, the Cuban government formed the National Institute for Sports, Physical Education,

riches in the US. Rene Arocha, now a star pitcher for the St. Louis Cardinals, split from the Cuban team during a stopover in Miami in July 1991. In September 1995, Cuban pitcher and national team member Osvaldo Ferná left Cuba and signed a $3.3 million deal with the San Francisco Giants. That same year, Livan Hernandez left and was snatched up for $4.5 million by the Florida Marline. And Cuban pitcher Rolando Arrojo defected during the 1996 Olympics.

Still, not every player is eager to leave. In 1995, Omar Linares, slugging third baseman for the Pinar del Río team and considered by many the best amateur baseball player in the world, rejected a $1.5 million offer to play for the New York Yankees (he was reportedly offered even more money by a Japanese team). "My family and country come first," said Linares. "I'm aware of what a million-and-a-half dollars means, but I'm faithful to Fidel."

Ah, yes, Fidel. Cuba is led by a sports fanatic. In the early years of power, Castro would often drop in at the Cerro stadium in the evening to pitch a few balls at the Sugar Kings' batters. And everyone knows the story of how Fidel once tried out as a pitcher for the old Washington Senators. How different history might have been had his curveball curved a little better!

Cuba's stars play more than 100 games a season on regional teams under the supervision of the best coaches, sports doctors, and competition psychologists outside the US big leagues. Each province has a team on the national league *(Liga Nacional),* and two provinces and the city of Havana have two teams each, making 18 teams in all. The last game of every three-game series is played in a *pueblo* away from the provincial capital so that fans in the country can see their favorite team play live. The season runs Dec.-June. After the regular season, East and West divisions compete in National Series playoffs, and eight teams are consolidated for the *Serie Selectiva* (Selective Series), from which the best players are culled to represent Cuba in postseason international games.

Stadiums are oases of relaxation and amusement. There are no exploding scoreboards or dancing mascots, and beer and souvenir hawkers are replaced by old men wandering among the seats with thermoses, selling thimble-size cups of sweet Cuban espresso. Spam sandwiches replace hot dogs in the stands, where the spectators, being good socialists, also cheer for the opposition base-stealers and home-run hitters. The balls are even returned from the stands, because everyone understands they're too valuable to keep as souvenirs.

and Recreation. The state invested huge sums in bringing sports to the Cuban people. Sports training is incorporated into every school curriculum and many adult education programs. Baseball, chess, dominoes, and martial arts are the real national pastimes, but virtually every conceivable sport and recreation is available, too.

Rough, often weed-covered basketball courts are everywhere, and most towns have a baseball stadium, gymnasium, and athletic facilities. Boxing is a passion for Cubans, and almost every town has a boxing gym and even open-air bouts. Only a few tourist hotels have gyms. In Havana, the best is at the Hotel Cohiba. Most facilities are basic by North American standards, but, hey, it's the results that count—and in that, Cuba is David to the US's Goliath.

There have been several international motorcycle races recently, and a cross-island car rally. **Watersports:** most large tourist resorts provide jet skis, Hobie-cats, banana-boat rides, and miscellaneous other watersports.

Cuba Deportes, Calle 20 #705, Marianao, Havana, tel. 22-2073, manages Cuban sports and access to them for foreigners.

Organized Tours
US Tour Companies: Coaches, trainers, and sports enthusiasts can learn the secrets of Cuba's amateur sports success on an eight-day study tour offered by **Wings of the World,** 1200 William St. #706, Buffalo, NY 14240, tel. (800) 465-8687. Basketball, volleyball, baseball, and boxing are all featured, including visits to the Sports Medicine Institute, the national baseball training center in Cienfuegos, plus visits to various national sports schools, where training sessions and formal matches are held. Monthly departures are offered. The tours cost US$1,795.

Last Frontier Expeditions, 4823 White Rock Circle, Suite H, Boulder, CO 80301, tel. (303) 530-9275, fax (303) 530-9275, offers a trip to the **Ernest Hemingway International Sports Classic** *(Clásico Internacional Hemingway),* a 10K race through Habana Vieja that the company helped initiate in 1995. The race occurs each May and is part of "national sports week," which includes baseball, basketball, and volleyball, symposia on sports, and visits to sports-medicine clinics.

ARTS AND ENTERTAINMENT

Since the Revolution, the government's sponsorship of the arts has yielded a rich harvest in every field. The **Centro Nacional de Escuelas de Arte** (National Center of Schools of Art), created in 1960, has 41 schools under its umbrella, including the national Escuela de la Música, a national folkloric school, two ballet schools, two fine arts schools, and a school of modern dance, plus schools at the provincial level.

Cuba's Ministry of Culture works to expose every Cuban to as full a range of cultural offerings as possible. Visit a cigar factory and you'll hear the *lector* reading from the works of Ernest Hemingway, Nicolas Guillén, or Gabriel García Márquez. Neither is it unusual to hear of ballet being performed in factories, or for a traveling puppet theater group to perform in a mountain village.

Cuba's wealth of arts venues is unrivaled within the Caribbean except, perhaps, for Venezuela. (Unfortunately, many venues have been closed or now operate on a threadbare budget since the Special Period; others, to which entrance was once free, now charge.) Every city has a

Casa de la Trova, where you can hear traditional music and dance, and a *Casa de la Cultura,* where movies, art exhibitions, and other cultural events are hosted. Major cities have ongoing music concerts, choral recitals, and art and sculpture exhibits. And virtually every town also has a theater, a movie house, and at least one disco or *centro nocturno.* Still, cultural life away from big cities is drab.

Cuba is one of the few tropical countries to have produced a *modern* culture of its own. During the first years of the Revolution, Castro enjoyed being the "bohemian intellectual." Artists and writers enjoyed relative freedom. As the romantic phase of the Revolution passed into an era of more dogmatic ideology, hard-line Marxists took over the Culture Council. In 1961, the government invited intellectuals to a debate on the meaning of cultural liberty at which Castro offered his "Words to the Intellectuals," which he summed up with a credo: "Within the Revolution, everything. Against the Revolution, nothing!" (It is ironic that one of the most brilliant of Cuban intellectuals should have so stifled intellectual freedom.) The government acquired full control of the mass media. Many talented intellectuals, writers, and artists were intimidated into ideological straitjackets. Thousands chose to leave Cuba.

Many talented individuals stayed, of course, and produced rich and lively works. But these were dark years of a relative spiritual vacuum. Social (socialist) analysis was always woven into the artistic tapestry. No politically incorrect works were allowed. The carryover is felt today, although it is no longer a punishable crime to possess music by the Beatles!

Despite ideological restraints, there is a genuine commitment on the part of the Cuban government to culture and the arts. Unfortunately, since the Special Period, many clubs and social forums that were a staple for cultural life have been forced to close, although by 1996 the situation had begun to improve. And schools have been affected immensely, suffering great shortages of instruments, sheet music, leotards, dance shoes, paints, brushes, and other materials. *Donations are welcome!*

At one level, conditions have facilitiated a renaissance since the 1980s. Buoyed by commercial possibilities opened by tourism, artwork and entertainment are now taking wing, indeed soaring. Tourists are generally inured to the drought. Most major hotels, for example, have bars and discos. Take your pick between dollars-only haunts, where drinks will set you back at least US$3 a pop, to earthy discos (called cabarets) for locals, where *one peso* will buy a beer. At some places, only couples are admitted; many discos have a strange policy of not letting single women in (the opposite of Western discos). Few discos get in the groove before midnight; most go on until 4 a.m. or dawn.

The casinos and strip clubs, of course, were closed years ago.

Resources

In Havana, look for the weekly tourist newspaper *Cartelera,* which publishes information on exhibitions, galleries, and performances. It's available in many hotel lobbies. *Granma* also lists the forthcoming week's events.

The Ministry of Culture sponsors a bimonthly magazine, *Revolución y Cultura,* containing interviews, fiction, poetry, essays, photography and profiles on the arts, plus news on cultural

events. It is hard to come by today (past issues—US$3 each—can be obtained from the Center for Cuban Studies, 124 West 23rd St., New York, NY 10011).

Paradiso: Promotora de Viajes Culturales, Calle 19 #560, esq. C, Vedado, Havana, tel. 32-6928, fax 33-3921, promotes artistic and cultural events, festivals, courses, seminars, workshops, and conferences in arts, sciences, and technology. It also arranges participatory courses for foreigners in cultural courses (see "Culture," under "Special Activities," later in this chapter).

Idea Bank Z (BIZ) is a nonprofit group of artists, writers, and intellectuals that champions Cuban culture. For example, it publishes limited editions of unpublished writers (incorporating visual art), among them *Libros-Arte* and *Libros-Fventos Especiales.* BIZ is preparing a databank of contemporary Cuban art (donations can be sent to Banco de Ideas Z, Calle 19, No. 1362, Apto. 15, e/ 24 y 26, Vedado, Havana 4, C.P. 10400, tel. 3-7327).

Art-Pals, P.O. Box 87, Redding Ridge, CT 06876, has initiated an exchange of artwork between primary-grade children in Danbury, Connecticut, and Alamar, on the outskirts of Havana. It hopes to expand the program to help bring about a better understanding and awareness of the children's respective societies. The organization collects donations of art materials, paper, and school supplies for distribution in Cuba.

In towns, look for the **Casa de la Cultura, Casa de la Trova,** and the **Bien Fonda Cultura,** where forthcoming events are posted.

FESTIVALS

Folkloric and traditional music fiestas and specialist festivals are held throughout the island, ranging from "high culture," such as the **International Ballet Festival,** to purely local, down-to-earth affairs, such as the year-end *parrandas* of Remedios, Zulueta, Placetas, and Camajuani in Villa Clara province, where the townsfolk indulge in a massive fireworks battle.

Some of Cuba's annual festivals are world renowned, among them the *Havana Jazz Festival,* the **International Lyric Festival,** the **Guitar Festival,** Havana's **International Contemporary Music Festival,** and the **International Festival of New Latin-American Cinema,** held in Havana in mid-December. For information, contact the Instituto de Cinematografía in Havana, tel. 33-4634, fax 33-3281, or the Center for Cuban Studies, tel. (212) 242-0559.

The Special Period, however, has taken its toll. Prior to the 1990s, popular festivals and cultural celebrations were far more common. "Street parties" and carnivals such as those celebrating the beginning of the Revolution (25-27 July) and the triumph of the Revolution (1 January) have been curtailed. However, festival life is rebounding, as with the newly rejuvenated **Cabildos** festival on 6 January, when the streets of Habana Vieja resound with festivities recalling the days when *cabildos* danced through the streets in vivid costumes and painted faces (for information, contact the City Historian's office at Calle Tacon #1, tel. 53-7-33-8183). **Carnaval in Havana!** and **Carnival in Santiago,** too, were revived in 1995 after a five-year hiatus. Traditional *comparsas* once again parade through the streets, and the island's hottest salsa and jazz groups give outdoor concerts along the Malecón. The carnivals traditionally have been performed in July following the *zafra,* sugar harvest, but the Havana carnival is now held in February. (*Comparsas*—music and dance originally tied to slaves' tribe of origin—are still practiced and performed in local *barrios* throughout Havana and Cuba. Check with the local Casa de la Trova for locations and times of rehearsals and performances.)

When 1 May rolls around, the whole of Cuba takes to the streets to honor "workers" at **May Day Parades.** *The* place to be that day is the Plaza de la Revolución in Havana, where you'll be surrounded by one million people waving colorful banners and placards and wearing T-shirts painted with revolutionary slogans. The sensation is uplifting as you are swept along in the tide making its way to the plaza to witness the military parade and to hear Fidel Castro and other leaders exhort Cubans to greater sacrifice. Scores of buses bring workers and children in from surrounding regions. Similar scenes are repeated islandwide.

Cuba, though nominally atheist, hosts a number of religious parades, such as the **Procession of the Miracles** each 17 December when hundreds of pilgrims—many of them dragging stones or crawling on their knees—make their way to the Santuario de San Lazaro, the "leper of the miracles," to give thanks to the saint (known as Babalu Aye in *santería*) for miracles they imagine he has granted. The sanctuary, a national monument, is at Rincón, on the outskirts of Santiago de las Vegas in Havana Province.

A US organization, **Caribbean Music and Dance Programs,** 1611 Telegraph Ave. #808, Oakland, CA 94612, tel. (510) 444-7173, fax (510) 444-5412, e-mail caribmusic@igc.apc.org, offers weeklong study packages to the carnival (US$1,475, including roundtrip airfare from Cancún or Nassau).

¡**Afrocubanismo!** is a major annual festival and workshop of Afro-Cuban music and dance hosted each August/September in Banff, Canada. Contact **The Banff Center for the Arts,** Office of the Registrar, P.O. Box 1020, Station 28, 107 Tunnel Mountain Dr., Banff, Alberta, Canada T0L 0CO, tel. (403) 762-6180.

MUSEUMS AND GALLERIES

Few cities in Latin America can match Havana's showcase museums and galleries. Havana has almost 40 museums and at least 14 major art galleries and countless minor ones. Other museums and galleries are scattered throughout the province. You'll find many natural history museums and "decorative arts" museums, but by far the majority are dedicated in one form or another to the glories of the Revolution. Entrance for foreigners usually costs US50 cents to US$3. Almost always, you are accompanied by a guide, who either trails a short distance behind or offers a sometimes stirring, sometimes turgid, précis of socialism. Many museums support a variety of cultural activities, such as theater and ballet.

A few museums are outstanding, such as the National Arts Museum in Havana's Palacio de Bellas Artes, which houses a tremendous collection of both classical and modern art featuring works by Renoir, Picasso, Rodin, and other masters.

Even entire cities are living museums, notably Habana Vieja and Trinidad, both UNESCO World Heritage Sites, with cobblestone streets, castles, palatial mansions, and colonial plazas.

THEATER

Havana has seven major theaters; Santiago de Cuba has eight. There are about 30 provincial theaters. Nonetheless, Cuba is *not* a thespian's dream. Theater is the least developed of Cuba's cultural media. Many theaters host little drama and are used mostly for operatic, symphonic, and other concerts. Theater was usurped by the Revolution as a medium for mass consciousness raising. As such, it became heavily politicized (the Teatro Escambray, for example, took to the hills to convey revolutionary ideals to the peasantry). In recent years, an avant-garde theater offering veiled political criticism has begun to evolve.

MUSIC AND DANCE

Author Norman Mailer scolded President Kennedy for the Bay of Pigs defeat by asking, "Wasn't there anyone around to give you the

Gran Teatro de La Habana

lecture on Cuba? Don't you sense the enormity of your mistake—you invade a country without understanding its music." Cuba's musical influence reverberates around the world, from Kinshasa to Tokyo.

Music—the pulsing undercurrent of Cuban life—is everywhere. Dance, from the earliest *guaguanco* to the *mambo* craze, has always been a potent expression of an enshrined national tradition—Cuban sensualism. Girls are whisked onto the dance floor and whirled through a flurry of complicated steps and sensuous undulations, the intensity of which makes their North American counterparts look like butlers practicing the waltz. Young or elderly, every Cuban undulates with coquetry, swaying to the rhythm just a little closer than cheek to cheek. It's a wonder the birth rate isn't higher.

Cubans even enjoy the anguished, melancholy verses of the tango, which sprang from Buenos Aires' brothels almost a century ago but perfectly fits Cuba's mood today. Many Cubans listen to the radio broadcasts of María Luisa Macbeth—devoted to tango. Havana has two tango clubs, and you may find others around the country.

The development of Cuban music styles since 1800—from *contradanza, danzón, habanera,* mambo, and *son* to *nueva trova*—is the story, writes Erroll McDonald, "of a swinging dialectic between West African choral and percussive genius and European melodic and harmonic sophistication."

Folkloric Music and Dance

The earliest influence was Spanish. The colonists brought the melodies (such as the *bolero*), guitars, and violins from which evolved early *criollo* folk music. Most of Cuba's folk music, or *guajira* (such as the all-important *danzón,* the *punto,* and the *zapateo,* all popular in past centuries among white country people and accompanied by small accordions, kettledrums, gourds, and calabashes) is European music that has been influened through contact with black culture.

You can still witness such *punto campesinas* being performed in country towns, including the slow and sensual *yambú* and (especially in Matanzas province) the *columbia,* a solo men's dance performed blindfolded with machetes.

The melancholic love song *Guantanamera* is undoubtedly the most famous of Cuban *guajiras,* recorded by everyone from Pete Seeger to Julio Iglesias. Look for performances by the **Conjunto Folclórico Nacional** (National Folklore Dance Group), which performs nationwide. The group was founded in 1962 to revive Cuban folk traditions because it was thought that the populace had lost touch with its folkloric past. Every major city has a performance group supported by the national umbrella body.

From Europe, too, came the *trovas,* poetic songs concerned with great historical events and, above all, with love. *Trovas,* which were descended from the medieval ballad, were sung in Cuba throughout the colonial period. *Trovadores* performed for free, as they still do at Casas de la Trova. The Matamoros Trio is perhaps the best-known in the genre. This century has seen the evolution of *trovas nuevas,* songs about contemporary life. The movement has ties to the American folk-protest song movement of the 1960s and often includes outspoken criticism of current situations. The contemporary works of Pablo Milané and Silvio Rodríguez, for example, echo the revolutionary dreams and restlessness of the current generation.

The African Influence

Almost from the beginning, the Spanish guitar (from the tiny *requinto* to the nine-stringed *tres*) joined the hourglass-shaped African *bata* and *bongo* drum, *claves* (two short hardwood sticks clapped together), and *chequerí* (seed-filled gourds) to give Cuban music its distinctive form. Slaves played at speakeasies in huts in the slaves' quarters. Their jam sessions gave birth to the *guaguancó,* a mix of flamenco guitar and African rhythm that is the mother of Cuban dance music. Later, slaves would take the *guaguancó* a few steps further to create the sensuous rumba, a sinuous dance from the hips (the rumba has African roots, but the melody is very Spanish) and from which tumbled most other forms of Cuban music; and the *tumba francesa,* a dance of French-African fusion.

Rumba remains deliriously popular. On Saturday afternoons, crowds of Cubans flock to Rumba Sabado (Rumba Saturday). Havana's Atarés neighborhood have embarked on a project to revive the rumba and has revitalized the typical street dance group, Los Marquesas.

Watch for performances by **Los Muñequitos de Matanzas** (literally, the dolls of Matanzas but signifying the "kings of rumba")—who tour worldwide but whose base is Matanzas, where you might catch them at the Casa de la Trova.

From rumba, which evolved around the turn of the century, came *son,* originally a sugar-workers' dance adopted by urban musicians for their large percussion and horn sections. Such contemporary groups as Los Van Van have incorporated the *son,* which has its own variants, such as the fast, infectious, overtly sexual *son changüí* from Guantánamo province, typified by the music of Orquestra Revé.

The **mambo,** like the cha-cha, which evolved from it, is a derivative of the *danzón,* jazzed up with rhythmic innovations. Mambo is a passé but still revered dance, like the jitterbug in the US, danced usually only by older people. Created in Cuba by Orestes López in 1938, mambo stormed the United States in the 1950s, when Cuban performers were the hottest ticket in town. Though the craze died, mambo left its mark on everything from American jazz to the old Walt Disney cartoons where the salt and pepper shakers get up and dance. People were titillated by the aggressive sexual overtures required of women in the elegant but provocative dance. Captivated by the earthy break from the more modest swing, Americans created a simpler but equally risqué spin-off—"dirty dancing."

A few years ago, the movie *The Mambo Kings* (a tale of two Cuban-American musician brothers in New York, who live in a state of obsessive nostalgia for the highly sentamentalized Havana of their memories) fueled the popularity of Cuban danceterias across the US. Such clubs, however, lack the building sexual energy that fuels the dance in tattered, peeling Havana (check out the Club Río, still known as Johnny's, in honor of its owner before the Revolution).

The mix of Cuban and North American sounds created blends such as *filin* ("feeling") music, as sung by Rita Montaner and Nat King Cole, who performed regularly in Havana; and *Cu-bop,* which fused bebop with Afro-Cuban rhythms, epitomized by Benny Moré—*el bárbaro de ritmo* (the Barbarian of Rhythms)—a theatrical showman who was considered the top artist of Cuban popular music. His more famous tunes include *Rebel Heart* and *Treat Me as I Am.*

Modern Sounds

The Revolution put a crimp in the music scene. Foreign performers stayed away, while many top performers left Cuba, such as Celía Cruz, "queen of salsa." **Salsa** (a derivative of *son*) has flourished since the 1980s, when the government began to lighten up. It is the heartbeat of most Cuban nightlife and a musical form so hot it can cook the pork. Los Van Van—one of Cuba's hottest big, brassy salsa-style bands—and Irakere have come up with innovative and explosive mixtures of jazz, classical, rock, and traditional Cuban music that have stirred commotion in the music and entertainment circles. They regularly tour Europe and Latin America, earning the country scarce hard currency.

For a long time, the playing of **jazz** in Cuba was completely discouraged (it was seen as "representative of Yankee imperialism, the music of the enemy"). Cuban musicians missed out on the Latin Jazz effervescence of the 1960s. Paquito D'Rivera, for example, was discouraged from playing jazz when he became director of the Orquestra Cubana de Música Moderna in 1970. Today, Cuba boasts wonderful jazz players of every stripe, though there is still a paucity of places where jazz can be heard.

Cuban jazz zigzags from bebop to fusion and European classical to Afro-Caribbean rhythms. It is "a bravura, macho form of jazz; trumpeters playing the highest notes and pianists going as fast as they can go." Cuban jazz musicians are admired the world over for their unique creativity and spirit. "When this is over and the musicians start coming out of Cuba, we'll all have to go back to school to catch up," says North American jazz maestro Tito Puente. Many leading international stars are Cuban. Celebrated trumpeter Arturo Sandoval left Irakere and Cuba in 1990, and D'Rivera left Cuba for New York in 1980. Like many artists, however, his departure had nothing to do with politics. "I fell in love with being a jazz musician in New York since first listening to a Benny Goodman record," he says. (Nonetheless, both groups' music was pulled from the shelves in Cuba. Those who leave Cuba take their *cubanidad* with them; they become nonpersons at home.)

Watch for a terrific jazz-fusion group called Cuarto Espacio, a jazz singer named Xiamara, and pianists Chucho Valdés and Gonzalo Rubalcava.

The **International Havana Jazz Festival** is held in mid-February, highlighted by an "All Stars Concert" at José Echeverria Stadium, plus concerts in the Palacio de Salsa (Hotel Riviera) and Casa de la Cultura de Plaza (Calle Calzada, esq. 8, Vedado).

Rock and roll was once officially banned. Today, it is usurping salsa as the music of choice. You'll see many long-haired youths—*roqueros*—wearing Led Zeppelin and Metallica T-shirts (heavy metal fans are known as *metálicos,* while "hippies" are called "freakies"). In recent years, the Young Communists have lassoed the popularity of modern-music to corral disaffected youth. Hence the state sponsors rock concerts, and state television and radio generously broadcast pirated videos of everyone from Nirvana to Sinéad O'Connor. However, the government keeps its own rock musicians (such as heavy-metal group Zouo) on short leashes. Playing unofficial venues can get *roqueros* arrested. To a large degree, the state decides what music can be played. Electricity rationing also sometimes pulls the plug on rehearsals and concerts, which are advertised through the grapevine.

Many Cubans are also avid fans of American rap artists, and they can gracefully execute M.C. Hammer's trademark whirling-dervish, hip-hop steps. You'll find many reggae fans sporting dreadlocks (such as Carlos Alfonso Valdés, tho leader of a popular Cuban funk band, Sintesis, with dreadlocks nearly down to his waist) and Bob Marley T-shirts (Cuban youth have scarce resourses but possess a dead-on fashion sense gleaned from MTV).

Classical Music

"In the realm of classical music Cuba has been an inspirational locale rather than a breeding ground for great composers and instrumentalists," says noted pianist Daniel Fenmore. Nonetheless, it is astounding how many contemporary Cubans are accomplished classical musicians. Everywhere you go, you will come across violinists, pianists, and cellists serenading you for tips while you eat.

Cuba boasts several classical orchestras, notably the **National Symphony Orchestra,** under the baton of Manuel Duchesne Cuzán. It first performed in November 1960 and has a repertoire ranging from 17th-century works to the most contemporary creations, with a special em-

TUNING WITH THE ENEMY

When Benjamin Treuhaft first visited Cuba, he marveled at the ability of young musicians to raise beautiful sounds from decrepit pianos—Wurlitzer short uprights from the turn of the century, unpromising 1970s Russian Tchaikas, and pre-1959 US instruments eaten by salt air and termites.

Treuhaft, a piano tuner who has tuned on behalf of Steinway, vowed to collect pianos and ship them to Cuba. His mission of musical mercy, however, struck a dissonant note with the US Commerce Dept., which declared that pianos are not humanitarian aid and were therefore barred. When Treuhauft replied in jest that the Cubans might use the pianos for military purposes, the case was shifted to the department's Office of Missile and Nuclear Technology! Due considerations were presumably given to piano throw weights and trajectories before official permission was given to ship his pianos, providing that they were not "used for the purpose of torture or human rights abuse"—proof that US policy toward Cuba is overdue for its own major tuning.

The first 22 pianos (plus an organ and half a ton of spare parts) reached Havana on 20 December 1995, to be dispersed to deserving students and teachers by the Instituto Cubano de la Musica (Cuban Institute of Music). Alas, when he returned from Cuba, Treuhaft, who charges US$1 per repair in Cuba, was informed by the Treasury Dept. that he would be fined US$10,000 for "earning income derived from Cuban nationals."

Treuhaft needs piano wire, tuning pins, and tools, but most of all that old piano (in rebuildable condition) languishing in your basement. Monetary donations are also requested (make checks payable to Hava-

piano). Treuhaft plans to create a tuner's school in Cuba and leads "tuners' brigades" to tune and teach workshops. Contact Benjamin Treuhaft, Underwater Piano Shop, 2005 Stuart St., Berkeley, CA 94703, tel./fax (510) 843-3823, e-mail blt@igc.apc.org.

Ben Treuhaft

phasis on popularizing works by Latin American and Cuban composers, such as Amadeo Roldán and Alejandro García Caturla. It may not be on a par with the London Philharmonic or the San Francisco Symphony Orchestra, but a performance is stirring nevertheless. Watch, too, for performances by Frank Fernández, Cuba's finest classical pianist.

One of Cuba's premier choral groups, **Schola Cantorum Coral,** known also as Coralina, trains children and youth in chorale.

Ballet
Cubans love ballet, which is associated in Cuba with one name above all—Alicia Alonso. Alonso

was a prima ballerina with the American Ballet Theater since its inception in the 1940s. She returned to Cuba and, sponsored by Batista (who hated ballet but considered her star status a propaganda bonus), founded the **National Ballet of Cuba** in 1948. Alonso was outspoken in her criticism of the "Sordid Era," and she went into exile in 1956 when Batista withdrew his patronage. The Revolution later adopted her. Her company is renowned worldwide for its original choreography and talent. The season runs all year and Havana's Grand Theater and National Theater are regular venues for performances. The National Ballet company spends much of its time touring at home and abroad.

The **Camagüey Ballet**—founded since the Revolution by Alicia's husband, Fernando Alonso—is also renowned for its innovative streak, as is the Santiago-based **Ballet Folklórico de Oriente,** which lends contemporary interpretations to traditional themes.

Cabarets

Cabarets are a staple of Cuban life and cater mostly to Cuban couples. Every town has at least one. The entertainment varies, but singers, magicians, acrobats, and comedians are usually featured (Ela Calvo is a popular cabaret songstress who travels from town to town). Sometimes, the term "cabaret" merely refers to a disco. More frequently, it refers to *cabarets espectáculos,* highlighted by long-legged women (usually mulattas) in high heels and skimpy costumes with lots of sequins, feathers, and frills and who gyrate their glistening copper-colored bodies into an erotic frenzy. Usually, they are accompanied by smaller dance troupes of bare-chested male performers who occasionaly lift the mulattas over their heads. Cuban couples delight in these shows.

Cabarets have also become a tourist staple. The largest and showiest, involving dozens of performers, are reserved for the upscale hotels. Outshining them all is the Tropicana, Cuba's premier Las Vegas-style nightclub, boasting over 200 performers. It has two outlets—one each in Havana and Santiago de Cuba—and is a *de riguer* night out for *every* tourist. Entrance to local clubs for Cubans cost about five pesos; tourist venues cost US$5-55.

ARTS AND CRAFTS

Cuba has a prominent place in the world of arts. You'll find an incredible array of art, sculpture, and photo exhibitions—especially in Havana but also nationwide. The shows often draw top international artists as well as Cubans of stature: an exhibition of sculptures by the famous English genius Henry Moore was set for early 1997, for example. In Havana, you can pick up a bimonthly program **(Galerías de Arte Programacion)** from the Centro de Desarrollo de las Artes Visuales, San Ignacio #352, Plaza Vieja, Havana 1. As for crafts, I'm in constant awe of the range and quality. And Cuba's poster and mural art is perhaps unrivaled in the world.

Cuba has made great efforts to display art from other countries, notably the Caribbean and Latin America, as for example the **Art of Our Americas** collection, housed in Havana's Casa de las Américas, a nongovernmental institution that has studied and promoted every aspect of Latin American and Caribbean culture since 1959. Similar institutions can be found islandwide. For example, the **Casa de la Artesanía Latinoamericana** in Varadero displays pottery, woodcarvings, metalworks, and weavings from throughout the Americas. Even entire villages, such as **El Oásis** near Santiago, exist as art communities.

If you can, time your vist to coincide with the prestigious **Havana Biennale,** an annual art show hosted by the Havana's Centro Wilfredo Lam each May.

To learn more about Cuban art, get hold of a copy of *Everyday Art,* a portrayal of Cuba's folkloric traditions and contemporary art scene. This 50-minute video focuses on the everyday life of Cuban musicians, dancers, and artists and reflects the strong presence of folk art in social institutions such as religion and education. You can order it for US$30 from Caribbean Music and Dance Programs, 1611 Telegraph Ave. #808, Oakland, CA 94612, tel. (510) 444-7173, fax (510) 444-5142.

The Center for Cuban Studies, 124 West 23rd St., New York, NY 10011, tel. (212) 242-0559, maintains the **Cuban Art Space,** the largest collection of contemporary Cuban art in the United States, with more than 800 paintings, drawings, and graphics, plus about 5,000 posters. Originals and reproductions are offered for sale.

See "Shopping" for regulations regarding purchasing and exporting works of art.

The Artist in Cuba

Cuban artists express an intense Afro-Latin Americanism in their passionate, visceral, colorful, socially engaged art. Painters and other artists imaginatively stretch their limited resources to produce widely interpretive modern and postmodern works. The work is eclectic, but there is energy in it all.

In the late 1960s, the government tried to compel Cuban artists to shun then-prevalent decadent abstract art and adopt the realistic style of the party's Mexican sympathizers such as Diego Rivera and David Alfaro Siqueiros, who turned

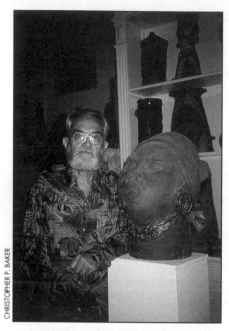

CHRISTOPHER P. BAKER

Roberto Fernández Martinez in his studio

from easel painting to wall murals because, in the words of Siqueiros: "While it is technically possible to play a revolutionary hymn on a church organ, it is not the instrument one would prefer." The artists who grew up *after* the 1959 revolution—the "generation of the '80s"—have been given artistic encouragement, reflecting Cuba's liberal notion that artists are no less socially useful than masons, storekeepers, and bus drivers.

Cuba has 21 art schools, organized regionally with at least one per province. The **Instituto Superior de Arte** (Higher Institute of Art), Calle 120 #1110, Cubanacán, Havana, tel./fax 33-6633, Cuba's premier art school, remains key as an educational center and gateway to the world of Cuban art.

The art educational system is both traditional and modern, with fundamental classical drawing and painting techniques at its core. The Cuban state has always fostered academic training in still life, landscape, and figure form (the nobility of sugarcane cutters and factory workers, of course, was emphasized). On attaining mastery of these skills, artists are encouraged to depart on experiments in expression to the extent of their imaginations (and without overstepping Castro's 1961 dictum to think more of the message than the aesthetic). As a result, says critic Tina Spiro, "most Cuban artwork, regardless of its style, is informed by a precision of line and a beautiful technical finish."

Upon matriculation from art school, artists receive the support of the **Fondo Cubano de Bienes Culturales,** Muralla #107, esq. San Ignacio, Habana Vieja, tel. 33-8005, fax 33-8121, in marketing and presenting their work to the public. The Cuban Cultural Fund is organized regionally by province and offers gallery exhibitions, cataloging services, shipping, and transportation. It is currently trying to transform itself into a more marketing-oriented entity.

Until recent years, artists were employed by various Cuban state institutions and received a small portion of receipts from the sale of their work. In 1991, the government finally recognized that copyright belongs with the artist. It has created independent profit-making, self-financing agencies, such as ARTEX, to represent individual artists on a contractual basis whereby the agency retains 15% of sales receipts. New regulations provide that artists (including performers) can, ostensibly, retain up to 85% of earnings from the sale or licensing of copyrights abroad. A portion of the retained earnings goes to the Ministry of Culture's **Fund for Educational and Cultural Development,** which provides resources for arts training and public arts programs.

The artists themselves are increasingly shaking off their clichés and conservatism. In 1980, when the Cuban government began to loosen up, it even sponsored a show of avant-garde work influenced by international formats. Artists began holding unofficial exhibitions in their homes. By the late 1980s, the artists were overstepping their bounds (*The Orgasm on the Bay,* by Tomás Esson, for example, depicted an ejaculating cigar in Castro's mouth). Armando Hart, Minister of Culture, decided that the Cuban artists' enthusiasm should be promoted from afar. Mexico City was selected and a community of deported artists has evolved—quixotically, with official Cuban sponsorship. (Florida's Cuban-American community has been hostile to the new generation of contemporary artists for not sharing their fanatically right-wing position. Miami's Cuban Museum of Art and Culture, for example, has been bombed twice for showing works by artists still living in Cuba.) In recent years, Cuban artists have taken the Western art world by storm. Says *Newsweek,* "Like the German and Italian neoexpressionists who took over the scene in the '70s and '80s, the Cuban artists may be on the brink of changing the face of contemporary art."

A new religious element is also taking root in art (where Afro-Cuban faith was basic to art in the 1980s, religious art today is inclining toward Roman Catholicism). And much of current art subtly criticizes the folly of its socio-political environment, but usually in a politically safe, universal statement about the irony in human existence—for example, Juan-Carlos Amador Machado has broken through the restrictions and paints the world of rotting Habana Vieja outside his door, expressing the hardships of daily life in a dark, surreal way. Within limits, this artistic dissent is not censored. Armando Hart has maintained this policy throughout his lengthy tenure from the Revolution to the present day.

Among Cuba's most revered contemporary artists is Alfredo Sosabravo—a painter, draftsman, engraver, and ceramist born in 1930—and the most versatile and complete artist among those making up the plastic-arts movement in Cuba today. He's also perhaps the most prolific: you'll come across his works (and influence) everywhere, including a permanent exhibition at Havana's Museo Nacional and the Palacio de Bellas Artes. He is dramatically present in hotel lobbies and other touristed spots. Look, too, for the erotic art of Chago Armada and the sensual landscapes of Lester Campa, painted in almost hallucinogenic detail.

Carving and Crafts

You'll find many artists producing fantastic sculptural ceramics, such as those of Teresita Gomez or Roberto Fernández, whose works—often totemic—are heavily influenced by African myths. Look, too, for the works of women artists such as Antonio Eiriz and Amelia Peláez, and US-born Jacqueline Maggi, now professor of engraving at the Advanced Institute of Art, in Havana, who "tackles the problem of women" in her woodcarvings and sculptures.

Lovers of Tiffany lamps should look for Gilberto Kindelán's transparent art nouveau lamps with bucolic landscapes featuring butterflies, which Kindelán describes as very visual and lending themselves well to poetry and movement in glass. The artist gets his glass, pewter, copper, and bronze from old mansions, recycling pieces rescued from beneath the wrecking ball.

You'll also find a resurgence of Cuban jewelry, some of which is quite stunning.

The **Handicrafts Association of Cuba** sponsors crafts.

LITERATURE

Cubans are incredibly literate. They are avid readers, and not just of home-country writers. The works of many renowned international authors are widely read throughout Cuba: Ernest Hemingway, Tennessee Williams, Gabriel Gar-

WILFREDO LAM

Wilfredo Lam, a Cubist and student of Pablo Picasso, was one of the greatest painters to emerge from Cuba during this century. His heritage was a mixture of Cuban, African, and Chinese blood. He was born in 1902, in Sagua La Grande, and studied at Havana's San Alejandro School of Painting. In 1936, he traveled to Paris and developed close ties with the surrealists. Picasso took Lam under his wing and offered the young Cuban his studio to work in. Lam lived briefly in Marseilles before returning to Havana. In 1956, he returned to Europe, although he continued to visit Cuba periodically. He died in Paris on 11 September 1982.

Lam's work distills the essence of Afro-Antillean culture. He broke with the traditional rules and created his own style using the myths, rituals, customs, and magic of his background to explore a world of Caribbean negritude. His most important works are considered to be *La Silla,* painted in 1941, and *La Jungla,* painted in 1943. Many of his etchings, sketches, and canvases are exhibited in Havana's Bella Artes museum. His *La Manigua,* painted in Haiti in 1956, hangs in the Museum of Modern Art in New York. And one of his paintings, *La Mañana Verde,* sold at Sotheby's in 1995 for US$965,000.

cía Márquez, Günter Grass, Isabel Allende, Jorge Amado (one 21-year-old Cuban told me she enjoyed reading Agatha Christie, Tennessee Williams, and even Anne Rice).

Cuba's goals and struggles have been a breeding ground for passions and dialectics that have spawned dozens of literary geniuses whose works are clenched fists that cry out against social injustice. Says writer Errol Mc-Donald, "The confluence of the struggle against Spanish and American imperialism, the impact of the cultivation of sugar and tobacco, a high appreciation of the 'low-down' sublimities of Afro-Cuban and Hispanic peasant life, a deep awareness of European 'high' and American popular culture, and the shock of the revolution has resulted in a literature that is staggering for its profundity and breadth—its richness."

Cuba's early literary figures were mostly essayists and poets. Indeed, poets were being published in Cuba 100 years before the *Mayflower* landed in Massachusetts in 1620. The tensions of the 19th century produced some astounding writers, most notably José Martí, perhaps the greatest prose writer in Spanish during this period (his mastery of English is also astonishing).

Cuban literature was born in exile. The most talented Cuban writers, such as Cirilo Villaverde (whose spellbinding novel *Cecilia Valdés* was written in exile in the 1880s), José María Heredia (1803-39), Julián del Casal (1863-93), and Alejo Carpentier, all produced their best works abroad. The promiscuous Cuban 19th-century woman of letters, Gertrudis Gómez de Avellaneda y Artega (1814-73), also flourished as a writer in exile. So, too, more recently, Virgilio Piñera, a brilliantly mordant literary man whose extraordinary brutal lyricism and grim evocation of the simple facts of life are captured in *Cold Tales*. Piñera was cast into purgatory in the 1960s, among the first intellectuals who became "contagious political bacteria" during the Revolution.

Although post-revolutionary Cuba has had its literary figures of note, it has not produced a definable literature of its own. The "debate" in 1961, when Castro dictated that only pro-revolutionary works would be allowed, evoked a vacuum. For the next three decades, the degree of "social responsibility" determined who got published (as well as who speaks on radio or television). Writers, suggests Jacobo Timerman, "were crushed and immobilized by a tombstone."

The "Gray Five Years"

The ice age lasted for a very long decade and came to a climax 1970-76, a period euphemistically called "the gray five years" *(quinquenia gris)*. Then, the communists attempted to force Cuba into the mold of Eastern European "socialist realism" to the detriment of Cuba's rich national culture.

Most of the boldest and best writers (many of whom had been devoted revolutionaries) departed into exile. Among them were Carlos Franquí, Guillermo Cabrera Infante, Huberto Padilla, Severo Sarduy, and playwright Antón Arrufat.

"What good is teaching millions to read when only one man decides what you read?" asks Infante, who was one of the first to leave and one of the greatest of Cuba's 20th-century writers. In the first years of the Revolution, literary magazines such as *Lunes* and *Casa* attained an extraordinary dynamism. In 1961, Castro reacted. The newspaper *Revolución* became a powerful organ that, says Infanta, "literally blasted many writers into submission—or oblivion" (later it was reborn as *Granma*. The worst years ended when the Ministry of Culture was founded in 1976, ushering in a period of greater leniency.

Post-Revolutionary Literature

Although much of the cream of the crop left Cuba, the country still maintained a productive literary output. Some contemporary novelists were uncritically complicit in Castroism. But the limitations imposed by strictures of orthodoxy have, for the most part, stifled emotion, sensibility, and a rich, fertile language. Five notable exceptions are Alejo Carpentier (1904-80); José Lezama Lima (1912-76), author of *Paradiso,* which was later made into a successful film; Nicolás Guillé (1902-86), the mulatto, communist, and literary grandee of the Cuban revolution who, in the 1920s, wrote *poesía negra* (black poetry) and whose later works are encapsulated in *The Great Zoo & Other Poems,* political poems of the common man; Dulce María Loynaz, Director of the Cuban Academy of Language and acclaimed as the leading Cuban poet; and the poet Eliseo Diego, who won Cuba's National Literature Award in 1986 and Mexico's Juan Rulfo International Prize for Latin American and Caribbean literature before he died in 1994.

Carpentier (his name is pronounced in the French style) is known for his erudite and verbally explosive works. My favorite is "Journey Back to the Source," a brilliant short story chronicling the life of Don Marcial, Marqués de Capellanías, but told chronologically backwards from death to birth. Carpentier was born in Havana to a French father and Russian mother. In 1946, during the violent excesses of the Batista era, he had to flee Cuba for Venezuela where he wrote his best novels (one year before, he published a seminal work called *Music in Cuba*). When the Castro revolution triumphed, the gifted novelist and revolutionary patriot returned as an honored spiritual leader. Alas, Carpentier became a bureaucrat and sycophant; under his influence, the National Printing Press even reworked *Moby Dick* to make it palatable to the socialist masses (Captain Ahab, Ishamel, and Queequeg were still there but, says Infante, "you couldn't find God in the labyrinth of the sea").

Many young writers born since 1959 have pushed the boundaries of expression further than ever before. Such writers as Reinaldo Arenas and José Camillo de la Cera also fled Cuba and became well known abroad. Others struggled on, facing harassment for their efforts. There were no independent publishing houses. Therefore, many splendid writers found it difficult to get their books published because their works were too radical. Iginio Barrere Causse, who has won international awards (the checks have never arrived), has six unpublished manuscripts. Some authors have resorted to sending manuscripts with foreigners. Others become "official writers."

The New Thaw

The past few years have seen a considerable thaw. It's no longer as in the 1960s and '70s, when all you could write was, "Viva Cuba, Viva la Revolución." The transitional nightmare is over. The current Cuban cultural policy is to salvage those artists and writers who, having produced significant works, were never allowed to publish. Now-dead writers of note are invoked and homage is paid to them, while those who remain alive now see their works dusted off, published, and awarded honorifics. Many writers previously reduced to "nonpersons" are now being treated with kindness and, often, postmortem canonization.

Ironically, this new openness coincides with the hardships of the Special Period, which have caused a severe paper shortage affecting Cuba's publishing industry. By 1993, books were beginning to get as scarce as the food. Many state-employed writers found themselves among the ranks of the unemployed. Prompted by the economic and political openings of the early 1990s, they banded together to form the **Union of Freelance Writers and Artists.** Alas, Cuba's political climate runs hot and cold. In spring 1996, the government began to cool authors down a bit, and freelancers reported a new tug on the leash.

Besides national literature, Cubans are fond of international classics. Among the most widely read authors are Ernest Hemingway, Mark Twain, Raymond Chandler, and Dashiell Hammett.

Resources

Virtually every town has a library *(biblioteca)*, albeit usually stocked with books solely of a politically correct flavor. The National Library in Havana contains more than 530,000 volumes. Literary and poetry readings are common events in Havana and other municipalities (most are free). Most towns also have at least one bookshop, where works are severely proscribed. The entire, often paltry, stock is usually limited to books by Fidel Castro, Che Guevara, José Martí, and other communists, internationalists, or Cuban nationalists, and those that offer a sympathetic viewpoint of communism. English-language works are hard to come by.

An excellent resource is the **Unión Nacional de Escritores y Artistas de Cuba,** UNEAC, Calle 17 #351, Vedado, Havana, tel. 32-2391, the Writer's Union, housed in a beautiful old mansion not far from the Habana Libre. The mansion's porch is now the union's cafe, where you may mingle with Cuba's literati. UNEAC publishes a bimonthly magazine, *La Gaceta,* and subscriptions (US$40) are available through Pathfinder, 410 West St., New York, NY 10014, tel. (212) 741-0690, fax (212) 727-0150.

The **Havana Book Fair,** organized by the Cuban Book Institute and the Cuban Book Chamber, is usually held in February, attracting exhibitors, publishers, and booksellers. For information, contact either the Center for Cuban Studies, tel. (212) 242-0559, or Cámara Cubana del Libro, Feria Internacional del Libro Habana,

THE NEW MAN

The "New Man" is the very essence of the Revolution. In a sense, he—or she—is what the Cuban Revolution is all about. The New Man is a person whose social conscience prevails over selfish material interest: an unalienated being, unsullied by the profit motive, living to serve his community, and preferring a virtuous existence over indulgent ways.

Che Guevara believed that the selfish motivations that determine behavior in a capitalist system would become obsolete when collective social welfare became the stated goal. Che set out his thoughts in an essay, "Man and Socialism in Cuba," in which he explained the difference in motivation and outlook between people in capitalist and socialist societies. He believed that the notion of material value lay at the root of capitalist evil. Man himself became a commodity. Meanwhile, liberty eroded moral values: individualism was selfish and divisive and essentially detrimental to social development.

To build socialism, a new ethos and consciousness must be built. By removing market forces and profit or personal gain, replacing these with production for the social good and planning instead of market "anarchy," a new individual would emerge committed to a selfless motivation to help shape a new society. Castro agreed with Guevara, and a revolution to create the New Man was launched. It called for collective spartanism shaped by Castro's personal belief in sacrifice.

The government moved to censure work for personal benefit. Bonuses and other financial incentives were replaced with "moral incentives"; consumerism was replaced by the notion of "collective and individual satisfaction" from work. Private enterprise and trade were banned. Ideological debate was quelled. Apathy was frowned on. And psychological and other pressures bore down on anyone who refused to go along with the new values imposed from above.

For many Cubans, the idea of the New Man struck a resonant chord, because the Revolution came from the people themselves, not against their will or in spite of them. This nourished the concept of collective responsibility and duty, subordinating liberty (to do as one wishes) for the common good. There was nothing the Cubans wouldn't do. The state didn't even need to ask. "No one worked from eight to five," a 59-year-old woman told reporter Lynn Darling. "You worked around the clock. The horizons were open. We had a world to conquer, a world to give to our grandchildren."

An intrinsic sense of egalitarianism and dignity was nourished and seeped into the Cuban persona, as many individuals strove to embody the New Man ideal. Cubans spread their spirit throughout the Third World, helping the poor and the miserable.

Tragically, Cuba today is a suffering and anxious nation, subject to the same horrendous forces that have caused the Third World such despair. Cuba is coming up for sale and in the quest for survival has been forced to turn back to the entrepreneurial spirit it once eschewed. The *jiniteras,* the petty thieves on the streets, the children who are now taught to beg: all these things are the result of Cuba's poverty. The New Man—one of the greatest gifts of the Revolution—is slowly dying. "The world is poorer for the loss of that intangible, optimistic, altruistic spirit," says Saul Landau. Indeed it is.

Calle 15 #604, Vedado, Havana, Cuba. US citizens involved in the publishing industry or otherwise with a vested interest in books and informational materials—and intent on visiting the fair *legally*—should request a license to attend the fair from the US Treasury Department.

FILM

Cubans are passionate moviegoers and the entire island is blessed with cinemas, including many of prerevolutionary art-nouveau grandeur. Entrance usually costs a single peso (foreigners are rarely charged in dollars), and the menu is surprisingly varied and hip. Leading Hollywood productions (classic and contemporary) and cartoons are shown, as are westerns, kung-fu flicks, and other foreign productions, particularly those of socially redeeming quality. Movies are often subtitled in Spanish (others are dubbed, to enjoy which you'll need to be fluent in Spanish). Adult films are banned, as are certain politically "offensive" movies (one movie you will not see in Cuba, for instance, is *The Wonderful Country,* starring Robert Mitchum; it was banned because the villains were called the Castro brothers).

In 1959, Cuba established a high-quality cinema institute to produce feature films, documentaries, and newsreels with heavy revolutionary content. All movies in Cuba—their making, importation/exportation, and distribution—are under the control of the **Instituto de Cinematografía,** Film Institute, Calle 23 #1109, Vedado, Havana, tel. 33-4634, fax 33-3281.

Undoubtedly the most respected of Cuba's filmmakers is Tomás Gutiérrez Alea, one of the great masters of Cuban cinema, whose work is part of a general questioning of things—part of the New Latin American Cinema. The Film Institute has granted a relative laxity to directors such as Gutiérrez, whose populist works are of an irreverent picaresque genre. For example, *Memorías del Subdesarrollo* (Memories of Underdevelopment), made in 1968, traced the life of the bourgeoisie disrupted by the Revolution. He followed it with *Death of a Bureaucrat,* a satire on the stifling bureaucracy imposed after the Revolution; and *La última cena* (The Last Supper), which dealt with a member of the upper class confronting the emerging social phenomenon that was about to topple them.

Gutiérrez's finest film, a true classic of modern cinema, is *Fresa y Chocolate* (Strawberries and Chocolate), which when released in 1994 caused near-riots at cinemas in Cuba, for the crush for entry was so great. The provocative but humane comedy tolls of the difficulties faced by a macho, homophobic Communist Party member in befriending a homosexual. It portrays the marginalization of intellectuals, the implementation of prejudices, the idealization of "norms" of behavior, the struggles to be different in a rigid revolutionary context. It is less an indictment than a social analysis of the purge against homosexuals that climaxed in the 1970s, when many actors and directors were fired. (The purge swept university classrooms, publishing, and public offices, profoundly affecting Cuba's cultural movement. Extremely talented homosexual artists languished in the anonymity of minor jobs. The Cuban theater, which had attained broad prestige, has never recovered in spite of strong support from the government in recent years.)

Fresa y Chocolat is understood as a universal plea for tolerance. It could not have been produced without official approval, and therefore exemplifies an acknowledgement of how the prejudice against homosexuals harmed Cuba's cultural life.

One of my favorite movies is *Soy Cuba* (I Am Cuba), Soviet director Mikhail Kalatozov's agonizingly serious black and white early-'60s, Cold War agitprop made when the idealism and the promise of the Cuban Revolution were genuine. A classic of its kind, the movie depicts events of the Cuban Revolution through the eyes of one of Russia's most acclaimed directors and the words of leading Russian poet, Yevgeny Yovtushenko. Intended as the *Battleship Potemkin* of the 1960s, it brims with tales of oppressive reality and kitschy imagery of Americans pawing scantily clad Cuban beauties. The deep-focus cinematography of the Cuban landscape is stunning. Nonetheless, Cubans apparently despised the film after its 1964 release in Havana. It was booed and swiftly disappeared, resurfacing in 1993 at the San Francisco International Film Festival to a stunned and delighted audience. Cuba never looked so fantastically exotic as through the radical camera techniques and surreal imagery à la Eisenstein. You can obtain copies of *Soy Cuba* from New York-based Milestone Film & Video, tel. (800) 603-1104.

The annual **Havana Film Festival,** held in December, is esteemed throughout the world. The famous all-night parties with top Cuban performers were replaced in 1994 by more serious all-night conversations. But this is *the* event to see and be seen at in Cuba. Fidel is often on hand, schmoozing with Hollywood actors and directors in the lobbies of the Hotel Nacional and Habana Libre.

ACCOMMODATIONS AND CAMPING

HOTELS

The Institute of Physical Planning has developed a master plan that suggests Cuba can attain more than 150,000 hotel rooms; it plans to have 50,000 rooms in service by the year 2000, up from 23,467 in January 1996. The vast majority of hotels are concentrated in the major tourism zones. Outside these areas, hotels tend to be of poor quality, though not below tolerable levels. In the boondocks, you will have minimal choice.

Cuban hotels are graded by the conventional star system, although the rating is rather generous. Prior to 1987, virtually all hotel construction was for the use of Cubans (before the Special Period, every worker received two paid vacations a year, each of two weeks). Most such hotels rate as one- or two-star on the international scale and are usually dreary post-Stalinist properties described as having "all the plaintiveness of an Olympic facility two decades after the games have ended." However, Cuba *does* have a handful of world-class hotels, with more coming online every month.

Most cities have at least one or two older hotels (usually basic, with faded charm) around the central park, and a larger, cement Bauhaus-era hotel on the outskirts. Following the Revolution, the Soviets infected the entire island with their architectural blight, melancholic enough to dampen even the most optimistic traveler's spirits. (You wonder if the architects have ever visited the sites; faceless factotums in Havana have, for example, ordered frosted glass for windows in rooms that would otherwise offer staggering views.)

Many of these Bulgarian-designed structures have been given a facelift, with potted plants, fresh paint, and new furnishings. Others, however, retain lumpy beds and dour utility furniture, despite the remake. The cash-strapped government continues to upgrade its hotels.

Hotels built in recent years reflect standards necessary to attract a foreign clientele (most would be rated three- or four-star). Since 1994, when six hospitality enterprises were created, niche hotels have begun to appear, including many five-star deluxe properties, especially in Havana. International hotel companies have made inroads in joint ventures with the Cuban hotel groups. Spain's Group Sol, for example, operates several deluxe hotels under the Meliá label. Other companies, such as Germany's LTI and Canada's Delta Hotels and Resorts, manage upscale properties on a par with hotels elsewhere in the Caribbean. Even Club Med is in Cuba, having opened a 600-room luxury resort in Varadero in late 1996.

Rooms are generally small by North American standards. Carpeting is rare; cool, tiled floors are the norm. Lighting tends to be subdued (usually because the wattage is low). Virtually every hotel room has air-conditioning. Most hotels have both a "regular" restaurant (usually with buffet service) and a specialty restaurant. A swimming pool is usual, most often with a bar. Most hotels also supply towels and soap, and the most deluxe ones usually provide shampoo, conditioner, and body lotion. Bring your own sink plug, however, especially for less expensive accommodations.

Many of the new upscale hotels have state-of-the-art energy-management and security systems, plus a panoply of services commensurate with first-rate hotels elsewhere in the Caribbean. That said, even the more upscale hotels are not entirely free of Cuban quirks.

Fawlty Towers?

Cuba's hotel foibles conjure up déjà vu for viewers of *Fawlty Towers,* the BBC's hilarious sitcom. Most hotels have a few petty annoyances. For example, after a hot, sticky day you return to your room to find no hot water—a plight for which you're supposed to get 10% off your bill. No running water at all? Twenty percent off. Ah! The water is running—but, alas, there's no plug. In theory, you're entitled to a well-defined refund for each such contingency. A sorry mattress is worth a 10% discount according to the State Prices Commission.

The number of faults is usually in inverse proportion to price: at cheaper places, you'll find gurgling pipes, no toilet seat (quite likely), no bathplugs (virtually guaranteed), sunken mattresses (guaranteed). You'll fare better at the newer, more expensive hotels.

Be prepared for cold showers. You'll soon get used to it and may even come to look forward to a refreshingly cool shower. Even hot water may only be tepid—and available at certain times of day. Shower units are often powered by electric heater elements, which you switch on for the duration of your shower. Beware! It's easy to give yourself a shock from any metal objects nearby.

Though many of the staff are mustard-keen, far too many hotels have abysmal service (Castro agreed: "Cubans are the most hospitable, friendly, and attentive people in the world. But as soon as you put a waiter's uniform on them, they become terrible.") Sometimes the opposite is true. Chambermaids, for example, often rearrange your belongings until you can no longer find them—which may be the whole point (I've "lost" several items of clothing this way).

Cuba is aggressively addressing the deficiencies and has set up hotel management training schools run by Austrians—world leaders in the hospitality industry. However, hotel management still leaves much to be desired, and there rarely seems to be a manager on site. It's enough to make you wonder if Basil Fawlty is running the show.

Prices and Reservations

Your accommodation will probably be your biggest-ticket item in Cuba: prices range from US$15 to US$100 and more. Hotels in this book are classified as: **Budget** (less than US$10), **Inexpensive** (US$10-25), **Moderate** (US$25-50), **Upscale** (US$50-80), and **Deluxe** (US$80 and above).

To keep costs down, consider buying a charter package tour with airfare and hotel included (tour operators usually buy hotel rooms in bulk and pass the savings on to you). Also consider a villa (usually well-furnished and an excellent bargain when sharing with other people) or, my recommendation, a *casa particular*.

Prices at many hotels vary for low and high season. Usually low season is May-June and Sept.-Nov., high season is Dec.-April and June-Aug. However, this varies. Some hotels have four rates according to peak high-season and low low-season. Usually, single rooms cost about 20% less than double rooms. There is no hotel occupancy tax. If you book your hotels from abroad, you'll be issued hotel vouchers that you exchange upon arrival in Cuba for a coupon (usually through the Cubatur representative at the airport), or present at your hotel.

Usually, the desk clerk in your hotel will be happy to call and make reservations for your next hotel. Finding a hotel room without a reservation is hardly ever a problem. Still, many of the best hotels book solid at Christmas, New Year, and during Carnaval in Havana in mid-February and in Santiago de Cuba in July.

Officially, it's *de rigeur* to book at least one night's accommodation prior to arrival, which

Hotel Castillo, Baracoa

you can do abroad through accredited tour agencies. Usually you won't be asked about this; I've arrived in Cuba without advance accommodations on several occasions and never had a problem. You can give a private address if you have an apartment to rent. However, you *may* be directed to the tourist information booth to secure a reservation.

The following Cuban agencies operate hotels.

Horizontes, Calle 23 #156, e/ N y O, Vedado, Havana, tel. 33-7818, is the largest group, with more than 60 hotels (mostly in the two- and three-star categories). **Gran Caribe,** Avenida 7ma, e/ 42 y 44, Miramar, Havana, tel. 33-0259, operates about 30 hotels (mostly in Havana), including several five-star properties. **Cubanacán,** Avenida 146 e/ 11 y 13, Playa, Havana, tel. 33-6043, has about 60 hotels from modest to luxury (representing 80% of all five-star hotels in Cuba). **Gaviota,** Calle 16 #504, e/ 5 y 7, Miramar, Havana, tel. 22-7670, has about 15 hotels. **Islazul,** Malecón y G, Vedado, Havana, tel. 32-9660, has 2,000 hotel rooms, primarily for national tourism. Local municipalities operate an additional 6,500 rooms. Most of the latter are very basic (many are also rapidly deteriorating).

The Cuban corporations all publish hotel directories available through Cuban tourist offices abroad. You may need to double-check telephone numbers, which change frequently (plus, much of the literature contains incorrect numbers, the result of shoddy typing).

Hotel Booking Agents: In Canada, **My Favorite Sunset,** 35 The Links Rd., Suite 203, Toronto, Ontario M2P 1T8, tel. (416) 225-2200, fax (416) 225-2580, is a hotel reservation network specializing in Cuba and the Caribbean. In the UK, **Regent Holidays,** 15 John St., Bristol BS1 2HR, tel. 0272-211711, fax 0272-254-866, acts as a booking agent for hotels throughout Cuba.

Havanatur's international offices also act as booking agents. See chart.

Security

Security is an issue, especially in budget hotels. Before accepting a room, ensure that the door is secure and that your room can't be entered by someone climbing in through the window. *Always* lock your door.

Most tourist hotels have safe deposit boxes at the front desk, or in your room. Be sure to use it for any valuables, especially your passport, camera, and money. Petty thefts from hotel rooms are frequent. The most popular items to walk seem to be clothing. Consider locking *all* your items in your suitcase each time you leave your room (valuables, of course, should still go in the hotel safe).

Tarjetas de Huespedes

You'll be issued a *tarjeta de huesped* (guest card) at each hotel, identifying you as a hotel guest. The card must be presented when ordering and signing for meals and drinks, when changing money, and often when entering the elevator to your room. *Don't lose it!*

Cuban Guests

The presence of young women seeking foreign husbands or at least a temporary arrangement became a fixture of most hotel lobbies in the early 1990s. In 1995, the government began to clear them out, and there are now strictures against young Cuban women (and men) entering hotel lobbies alone, and hotel staff are often on guard to prevent Cubans slipping upstairs with foreign guests.

It's not strictly true, however, that Cubans are not allowed in hotels. For example, outside major tourist areas, most hotels are run by Islazul and the clientele is *primarily* Cuban; foreigners and Cubans generally come and go and interact without restriction. However, the policy is in flux as the government finesses its handling of *jiniteras* (good-time girls) and *jiniteros* (illicit marketeers) in hotels.

At press time, Cubans were not allowed in guests' rooms with foreigners unless they are also registered as guests. This is true regardless if your "guest" is visiting for five minute or five hours. If you want a guest in your room, you'll have to register him or her at reception and pay the double rate. Some hotels require that a Cuban wishing to stay with a foreigner do so for a minimum number of nights, usually three. However, some hotels make no exception—no Cubans!

In the event that you find a lover, the chances are strong that your hotel concierge may turn your partner away (unless he or she possesses a *tarjeta huesped* or is listed on yours). It's possible that a US$5 bill casually slipped into a palm may resolve things, but don't count on it.

If you and your partner encounter problems at the hotel, consider moving to a *casa particular,* a room rented in a private home (or even the entire house). Many Cuban couples even rent rooms by the hour in someone else's home to consummate their love unions. This is accepted practice, especially in overcrowded Havana, where several families often share the same apartment and lovers need a place of coital convenience. No one blinks an eye.

Of course, the government is sensitive to the needs of every man and woman and has created "Love Hotels."

"Love Hotels"
State-run, 24-hour love hotels, or *posadas,* exist to provide relief for the large percentage of Cubans who live together with aunts, uncles, parents, and even grandparents along with the children, often in conditions in which rooms are subdivided by curtains. At these hotels, couples can enjoy an intimate siesta together. Most couples are married, sometimes to each other.

Most towns have at least one. In most, conditions are modest to say the least. More upscale, congenial facilities have gardens, a/c, and music in the rooms, such as El Monumental (12 km west of Havana), which is favored by government officials.

Rooms are usually rented for three hours, typically for five pesos (25 cents), for which the state thoughtfully provides a bottle of rum by the bed.

Aparthotels
Aparthotels, often linked to regular hotels, offer rooms with kitchens or kitchenettes (pots and pans and cutlery are provided), and sometimes small suites furnished with sofas and tables and chairs. One- or two-bedroom units are available. Aparthotels are particularly economical for families. Most are characterless: it's all a matter of taste.

Peso Hotels
Peso hotels cater to Cubans and are extremely cheap—usually the equivalent of less than US$1. Although a few are quite attractive, most

are dour by Western standards. The worst are little more than mildewed nests of foul bedclothes.

You cannot book peso hotels through any state tourism organization; you will have to do this face-to-face in Cuba. Every town has a *carpeta* (central booking office, usually used by Cubans) where hotel reservations are made. They'll make bookings by telephone for a small charge. Many peso hotels refuse to accept foreigners; others charge a minimal dollar rate; some will take your pesos. Don't believe it if you're told that a pesos-only hotel is full. That's a standard answer given to foreigners. Be persistent. Be creative. Be nice about it. If the receptionist warms to you, a room can magically be found. But don't count on it.

CASAS PARTICULARES

One of the best ways to go is to seek out a *casa particular*—a privately rented room, often in a family home. For US$10 to US$30 a day, you can rent a room, often with breakfast and dinner included. I've taken apartments with some wonderful Cubans. Some families even rent their entire homes as bed-and-breakfasts. You may even meet whole families who are willing to move out of their homes on a moment's notice!

Since the triumph of the Revolution, the Urban Reform Law has explicitly prohibited the rent of housing. However, a new tax code introduced in 1996 includes a resolution that covers taxation of revenue from renting rooms. (Until then, only one town—Trinidad—permitted residents to rent rooms legally.) Cubans are now permitted to rent out up to two rooms. *Casas particulares* have been growing in popularity in recent years, especially since the crackdowns on *jiniteras*. *Casas particulares* are easy to find in major cities, where touts work on commission and will approach you on the street. Alternately, ask a private taxi driver. He's sure to know.

In October 1996, police in Havana had begun regulating *casas particulares* to ensure that those renting out their houses "fulfill their social duty" (roughly translated as: pay taxes and not permit *jiniteras*). Your host now has to record your passport number and the particulars of any of your guests.

CAMPING

Cuba is not geared for camping. That said, Cuba is replete with *campismos,* basic holiday camps built for Cubans. Today the majority are run-down and dour, with very few clients. Many will accept foreigners. Accommodation is usually in basic cabins, but a few also have tents. At most, you'll be allowed to pitch a tent. Expect to pay between 10 and 20 pesos or US$10-20. Toilet facilities are often basic, and water supply may or may not work. Sites are operated by **Campismo Popular,** which has offices *(carpetas)* in most towns. Some have basic *cafeterías,* but few were open as recently as 1996.

El Abra is the *only* tent site of international quality; it's midway between Havana and Varadero. You will require permission to camp "wild." Don't expect to find fresh water or food available at most places where you'll probably be tempted to pitch a tent. Pack in *everything* you think you'll need.

FOOD AND DRINK

A standing joke is: What are the three biggest failures of the Revolution? Breakfast, lunch, and dinner. Cuba may be a culinary adventure but not one that will usually have you, like Oliver, asking for more. You're not going to Cuba to put on weight.

Before the Revolution, Cuba boasted many world-class restaurants (many Cubans will tell you of the wealth of fine international restaurants four decades ago). Alas, after 1959, many of the middle-and upper-class clientele fled Cuba along with the restaurateurs and chefs, taking their custom, knowledge, and entrepreneurship with them.

Today, all but a handful of restaurants are state-owned, and the blasé socialist attitude to dining, tough economic times, and general inefficiencies of the system are reflected in boring menus, poor standards, and lack of availability (don't be fooled by extensive menus, as many items will probably not be available). State-run restaurants come in grades one to seven, one being the best.

Havana is an exception to the culinary rule; there, you'll find wide options. There are usually plenty of local eateries in towns, but even here it can be a wearying experience trying to find somewhere with palatable food. In rural areas (ironically), eating can be a real challenge. Shortages are everywhere (a refrigerator in Cuba is called a *coco* because it has a hard shell on the outside and nothing but water inside). You may even feel twinges of capitalist guilt when asking a waitress for milk to go with your coffee. (Before the Special Period, everyone had access to milk and eggs, but Cuba had come to rely on varieties of cattle and chickens that are grain fed. With the collapse of the Soviet bloc, grain supplies ceased and production of milk and eggs plummeted.)

Rationing has become a permanent fixture of the past three decades. The collapse of the Soviet Union only made a bad situation much worse, since in 1989 an estimated 40% of rationed items were supplied by the former Soviet bloc. (Depending on your viewpoint, Cuba's rationing system proves either that the government is inept or that it is just. To critics, it is "the most conspicuous indicator of a prolonged, systemic economic failure." Others point out that prior to the "Special Period," rationing had guaranteed the entire population sufficient proteins, carbohydrates, minerals, and vitamins to maintain good health. The Cuban government likes to blame the US embargo, but after a sustained tour of the island you're likely to conclude that without the profit motive to oil the wheels, the inefficient communist system is mostly to blame. Whatever, the paucity is a constant source of exasperation for foreigners traveling independently.) Fortunately, everywhere you eat you're sure to be serenaded by troubadors to add cheer to even the dreariest meal.

If you spend much time touring in the countryside, expect to lose some weight. In the Oriente, restaurant food tends to be particularly unpalatable. Throughout the island you'll pass mile after mile of rich cultivated land growing produce, but when you arrive at your hotel you'll often find that the only vegetables on the menu are canned. Bite the bullet! As a tourist, you're privileged to get the best that's available. When touring, you should plan ahead. Stock up on sodas, biscuits, and other pre-packaged snacks at dollars-only stores (there's always one at Cupet gas stations) before setting out each day.

Take a sweater—many restaurants have the a/c cranked up to freezing. And be relaxed about dining; expect service to take much longer than you may be used to. Sometimes, the service is swift and friendly, sometimes protracted and surly. For a lunchtime pizza you can wait 10 minutes for a waiter, another half-hour for the pizza to arrive, 15 minutes for the bill, and another 10 for the change. Plan up to two hours for dinner in a state-run restaurant. Oh, and please don't take the cutlery. There may be a "cutlery guardian" sitting at a special table by the door to prevent ne'er-do-goods from smuggling out the precious flatware, even if it is made of base metal.

Most places serve *criollo* (traditional Cuban) food, but only a few restaurants truly excel in native Cuban cuisine. The more expensive places tend toward "continental" cuisine, at which even fewer excel. International cuisines are poorly represented. There are some reasonable Spanish and Chinese restaurants, though none that come close to winning awards. Reservations for the best restaurants are recommended.

State-run *merenderos* (lunch counters) and roadside snack stalls display their meager offerings in glass cases. A signboard indicatoo what's available, with items noted on strips that can be removed as particular items sell out.

Eating in Cuba doesn't present the health problems associated with many other destinations in Latin America. I've *never* gotten sick eating in Cuba.

Most tours to Cuba include breakfast and usually some dinners in the cost of the tour. Refunds are not made for meals not taken.

Now the Good News

Cuba *does* have some splendid restaurants, notably in Havana. The country is beginning to invest in culinary (and management) training in order to resolve the deplorable inadequacy of restaurant food. Cuba has even introduced a chain of drive-in fast-food eateries—El Rápido—including some (in Havana) where you're served by waitresses on roller-skates.

The way to go, however, is to eat at *paladares,* private restaurants whose owners often meld entrepreneurship with a sense for experimentation and culinary flair. Here you can fill up for US$5-10. Usually, the price includes a salad and dessert and, often, beer.

Look for Christmas lights (the *paladares's* unofficial advertisement) hanging outside.

Breakfasts

There are virtually no places to breakfast other than hotel restaurants, most of which serve variations on the same dreary buffets: ham, Spam, cheese, boiled eggs, and an array of fruits and unappetizing cakes and biscuits. (Note that hotel room rates don't usually include breakfast.) Fruits—mangoes, papayas, pineapples—are most often frozen overnight and thawed (barely) for breakfast, thereby destroying the pulp and flavor. Top-class hotels usually do a bit better. Nonguests are usually welcome; prices range US$4-12. In cheaper hotels in the boondocks, you may even find that the only thing available for breakfast is a Spam sandwich *(bocadillo).* Ugh!

In more remote areas, you'd be wise to have a large breakfast—finding food during the day may be a withering chore. Don't leave breakfast (normally served 7-10 a.m.) until the last thing or you'll arrive to find only crumbs (I'm not kidding).

Many hotels offer an *oferta especial* (special offer) that grants guests a discount up to 25% on buffet meals.

Hotel Food

The majority of hotels have amateurs in the kitchens. With few exceptions, food quality seems to decline with distance from Havana. Away from tourist centers, hotels are often "oases in a consumer desert," and even the local populace flock to feast on meals of dubious quality. Fortunately, the situation is beginning to improve as Cuba focuses on training its culinary staff and the worst food deficiencies of the Special Period are overcome (even tourist hotels are not spared the shortages imposed by the Special Period).

In general, hotel fare leans heavily towards pork, eggs, canned vegetables, and baked goods. Smorgasbord (*mesa sueca*—Swiss table) buffets are popular. The variety is usually limited by Western standards, and presentation often leaves much to be desired. *À la carte* menus are offered in specialty restaurants in top-class hotels (meals here are rarely included in package prices). Many hotels have *Noches Cubana* (Cuban nights), featuring typical Cuban specialties.

Self-Catering

Shopping for food for the average Cuban is a dismal activity. There are scant groceries, no roadside 7-Elevens. Rarely will you find fruits and vegetables for sale, and during 11,000 km of travel through Cuba, I saw *one* place serving fresh milk for pesos (I couldn't buy any because I didn't have a container).

The state-run groceries, called *puestos,* where fresh produce—often of questionable quality— is sold, can make Westerners cringe. Cuba's best fruits and vegetables are exported for hard currency or turned into juices. Meat is equally scarce. As a result, most Cubans are forced to rely on the black market.

Since 1994, when free trading was legalized for farmers, Cuba has sprouted **produce markets** or farmers' markets *(mercados agropecuarios),* where fruits, vegetables, and meats are sold. Every town has at least one, though it will often be hidden away, off the beaten track.

You can purchase Western goods at dollars-only stores, open to foreigners and Cubans alike and stocked with packaged and canned goods from all over the world. Havana even has a few supermarkets, though these are rare outside the capital. Cupet gas stations usually have dollars-only stores attached, where Western snack goods are sold.

Most towns have bakeries serving sweet and tasty confections and Cuba's infamously horrible bread (most often served as buns or twisted rolls), which Maurice Halperin found, whether toasted or not, "formed a sticky mass difficult to dislodge from between cheek and gum." I disagree—usually it's dry as a bone. (Cuba's reputation for lousy bread pre-dates the Revolution. "Why can't the Cubans make decent bread?" Che Guevara is reported to have asked. Of course, Cubans eat rice, not bread, as they have since the early 19th century, when it became the staple food of black slaves; only well-to-do Cubans ate bread.) To be fair, some hotels and restaurants serve excellent bread, and the situation may now improve with the signing of a contract with a French company, scheduled to build a factory to supply pastries and breads to the tourist.

Paladares

I feel sorry for the package tourists, force-fed at their communal troughs when, at least in major cities, privately run *paladares* are at hand (the word means "palate," and the places are named for a popular Brazilian soap opera). With the onset of the Special Period, the food shortage became so desperate that enterprising Cubans began operating illicit eateries. In September 1994, the government legalized home restaurants, allowing them to serve up to 12 people at one seating. (Under Cuba's restrictive self-employment laws, relatives can assist, but the owners cannot hire salaried workers. Initially, the government charged a US$20 monthly licensing fee; in early 1996, it upped the fee to a staggering US$600.)

The owners put great energy into their enterprises, many of which are open 24 hours. Most serve both Cubans (often for pesos) and foreigners (always for dollars) and display an inventiveness in preparing good food and service that Fidel himself has often complained about. However, Castro says that the *paladares* are "enriching" their owners and has refused to dine at them.

Typical meals cost from US$3 upward, often with tremendous helpings. Restaurant owners are legally barred from serving shrimp and lobster. Many owners defy the ban, and it's easy enough to find a huge lobster meal for US$10, including beer or soft drink.

WHAT TO EAT

Cuban Dishes

Ninety times out of a hundred, your options are *criollo, criollo,* or *criollo.* Cuban food is mostly peasant fare, usually lacking in sauces and spices.

Pork *(cerdo)* and chicken *(pollo)* are the two main protein staples, usually served with rice and black beans *(frijoles negros)* and fried banana or plantain *(platanos). Cerdo asado* (succulent roast pork) and *moros y cristianos* (Moors and Christians—rice and black beans) and *arroz congrí* (rice with red beans) are the most popular and widely dispensed dishes. Another national dish is *ajíaco,* (hotchpotch), a stew of meats and vegetables.

By far the most common dish is grilled chicken *(pollo asado)* or variants. Several restaurants prepare chicken, often marinated, by their own splen-

lunch, Cayo Sabinal

did recipes. Grilled pork chops are also common. Beef is rare outside the tourist restaurants, where filet mignons and prime rib are often on the menu. Most beef dishes tend to be far below Western standards—often overcooked and fatty.

Another favorite dish is *conejo,* rabbit (it's commonly on the menu but unavailable; where they get rabbits from I don't know, as I've never seen one in Cuba). Meat finds its way into snacks, such as *empanadas de carne,* pies or flat pancakes enclosing meat morsels; *ayacas,* a kind of tamale, corn tortilla filled with meat and spices; *piccadillo,* a snack of spiced beef, onion, tomato; and *bistec de palomilla,* fillet of steak, often cooked as an *empanada.* Crumbled pork rinds find their way into *fufu,* mixed with cooked plantain, a popular dish in Oriente. And ham and cheese, the two most ubiquitous foods, find their way into fish and stuffed inside steaks as *bistec uruguayano.*

Fish had never been a major part of the Cuban diet and has made its way onto the national menu only in recent years. As food shortages increased following the Revolution, Castro himself appealed to Cubans to eat fish; he said he would be seen eating only fish on TV until Cubans understood its nutritional value.

Sea bass *(corvina),* swordfish *(filet de emperador),* and *pargo* (red snapper) are the most commonly eaten species. You can find some splendid fish dishes, but all too often Cuban chefs murder your fish steak. Dry, leathery, and zealously overcooked is the norm, with lots of bones for good measure.

Lobster is readily available virtually everywhere. What a bargain! If you avoid the expensive touristy haunts, you can enjoy a whole-lobster meal with trimmings and beer for US$10. Also look for *coctel de ostiones*—oyster cocktail.

International Influences

Cuba's culinary landscape has suffered for lack of international connections during four decades. (Let's face it: what could the Soviets offer?) Cuba's Chinese population fled the island after the Revolution, along with most other foreigners.

Chino descendants still operate Chinese restaurants, however. You'll find one in almost every town, making do as best they can in the food shortages. With luck, you'll also come across Spanish restaurants serving seafood *paella* (Las Terrazas in Cojímar and Hostal Valencia in Havana are two).

Italian restaurants are growing in popularity, although their menus are mostly limited to spaghetti bolognese and pizzas. You'll find pizzerias serving local custom everywhere in Cuba (you can buy a slice for five pesos), including at hotels. However, most Cuban pizzas are dismal by North American standards—usually with a bland base covered with a thin layer of tomato paste and a smattering of cheese and ham (English people will recognize it). Likewise, hamburgers are popular, cheap, and usually not much worse than North American fast-food burgers (though some, to be sure, *are* much worse).

Vegetables

Cubans consider vegetables "rabbit food." Fresh vegetables rarely find their way onto menus, other than in salads. Mixed salads *(ensaladas mixta)* usually consist of a plate of lettuce or cucumbers *(pepinos)* and tomatoes (often served green, yet sweet) with oil and vinagrette dressing. *Palmito,* the succulent heart of palm, is also common as a salad. Often, you'll receive canned vegetables as a salad. Sometimes you'll receive shredded cabbage *(col),* often alone. Beetroot is also common. So is yucca, which closely resembles a stringy potato in look, taste, and texture. It is prepared and served like a potato in any number of ways. A popular side dish is *boniato* (sweet potato), and other root vegetables such as *malanga,* a bland root crop rich in starch grown by the native Indian population and a staple of rural families before the Revolution.

Vegetables are most often used in soups and stews, such as *ajíaco,* a popular and tasty soup made with yucca, malanga, turnips, and herbs. Another common soup is garbanzo.

Beans are the most common vegetable and are used in many dishes. *Congrí oriental* is rice and red beans cooked together (the term refers to the Congo). *Frijoles negros dormidos* are black beans cooked and allowed to stand till the next day.

Fruits

Cuba's rich soils and amicable climate nourish a panoply of fruits . . . at least, they should. Elsewhere in the Caribbean and Latin America, you can't drive around a bend without having someone selling a bunch of ripe bananas or handfuls of papayas, mangoes, or coconuts. Not so in Cuba. Fruits are rare jewels outside hotel restaurant buffets. You'll pass many fields of pineapples, although rarely will you find any available outside hotel restaurants, and the same is true of melons. Even oranges and grapefruits, grown widely in Cuba, are about as common as gold nuggets. Virtually the entire fruit harvest goes to produce fruit juice. To buy fruits, head to the local *mercado agropecuario* (farmers' market).

The most common fruit is the *platano,* a relative of the banana but used as a vegetable in a variety of ways, including as *tostones,* fried green plantains eaten as a snack, much like thick chips or English crisps.

Surprisingly, coconuts are rare in the nation, except in eastern Cuba, around Baracoa, where the juice and meat finds its ways into the cuisine peculiar to the region (eastern Cuba boasts the nation's only real regional cuisine).

In addition to well-known fruits such as papayas, look for such lesser-known types as the furry *mamey colorado,* an oval, chocolate-brown fruit with a custardy texture and taste; the cylindrical, orange-colored *marañon,* the cashew-apple, whose seed grows *outside* the fruit; the oval, coarse-skinned *zapote,* a sweet granular fruit most commonly found in Oriente; and the large, irregular-shaped *guanábana,* whose thick skin is covered with briars (the pulp, however, is sweet and "soupy," with a hint of vanilla). *Canitel* (familiar to travelers to Jamaica as ackee) is also grown, through rarely found.

Count yourself lucky to get your hands on mangoes, whose larger versions are referred to in the feminine gender, *mangas,* because of their size.

Be careful with the word *papaya.* Habaneros refer to the papaya fruit as *fruta bomba* because in Cuba, "papaya" is a slang term for vagina.

Desserts

Cubans make great desserts, often available for a few centavos at bakeries *(panaderias)* islandwide. Hotel confections tend toward biscuits and sponge cakes (usually rather dry) topped with jam and canned cream. *Flan,* a caramel custard, is also popular (a variant is a delicious pudding called *natilla),* as is marmalade and cheese.

Also try *tatianoff,* chocolate cake smothered with cream; *chu,* bite-size puff pastries stuffed with an almost bitter cheesy meringue; and *churrizo,* deep-fried doughnut rings sold at every bakery and many streetside stalls, where you can also buy *galletas,* ubiquitous sweet biscuits sold loose.

The many coconut-based desserts include *coco quemado* (coconut pudding), *coco rallady y queso* (grated coconut with cheese in syrup), and the *cucurucho,* a regional specialty of Baracoa made of pressed coconut and cocoa.

Of course, the best dessert of all is Cuban **ice cream,** most notably that made by Coppelia. Most cities have a Coppelia outlet. Before the Revolution, Baskin-Robbins' 28 flavors was the brand of choice (all ice cream was imported from the United States). Fidel, however, had promised to outdo the Yanks with 29 flavors, a boast Cuba failed to achieve. In 1996, after five years of the Special Period, Coppelia was managing only two flavors a day.

Cubans use specific terms for different kinds of scoops. *Helado,* which means "ice cream," also means a single large scoop; two large scoops are called *jimagua;* several small scoops is an *ensalada;* and *sundae* is ice cream served with fruit. Want more? Ask for *adicionál.*

DRINKING

Nonalcoholic Drinks

Christopher Columbus noted the quality of Cuba's water in 1494 on his second voyage to the New World: "The water is so cold and of such goodness and so sweet that no better could be found in the world." Sure enough, water is potable virtually everywhere, although many towns in central Cuba had their water supplies disrupted and contaminated by Hurricane Lili in October 1996. Bottled mineral water is widely available and usually delivered to your table automatically if you ask for water. It's normal when you ask for water to receive bottled water, usually Ciego Montero Agua Mineral, produced by Cubagua. (It comes from Manatial de Ciego Montero, in Palmira in Cienfuegos province, and "stimuates the digestion and facilitates the urinary elimination of uric acid," says the label.)

Coca-Cola and Pepsi (or their Cuban-made equivalent, Tropicola), Fanta (or Cuban-made Najita), and other soft drinks are readily available at hotels, restaurants, and dollar-stores—which demonstrates how ridiculous the US embargo is (says Jesse Jackson, "While I was in Cuba, I drank a Coca-Cola that Germany had imported from France to ship to Cuba—a Coke that could have come directly from Miami or Atlanta"). *Malta Caracas* is a popular nonalcoholic drink from Venezuela that resembles a dark English stout but tastes like root beer.

Far more thirst quenching and energy-giving, however, is *guarapo,* fresh-squeezed sugarcane juice, sold cold at roadside *guaraperias* throughout the countryside (you won't find any in Havana). Sugar even finds its way into water:

agua dulce, a popular *campesino's* drink made of boiled water and brown sugar gives one energy for field labor.

There's no shortage of canned fruit drinks produced locally (virtually the entire Cuban fruit crop is pulped for juices). All the native juices that can possibly be adapted end up in cans or cartons. Occasionally you'll come across small bars selling fresh-squeezed orange juice (usually 20-50 centavos a glass) and *agua natural* (natural water; usually free). Another great way to beat the heat is by downing *batidos,* delicious and refreshing fruit drinks blended with milk and ice, and *refrescos,* chilled fruit juices that you can buy at roadside stalls, usually for 50 centavos or one peso. Many *refrescos* are made from exotic fruits, such as the seed of the baobab, which lends a sherbet-like fizz to sugared water.

Coffee: Cubans take frequent coffee breaks, and no home visit is complete without being offered a *cafecito.* Coffee also ends each meal. Cubans love it thick and strong, like espresso, served black in tiny cups and heavily sweetened. *Delicious.* Unfortunately, most of the pre-revolutionary *cafeterías*—coffee stands—that used to make coffee on every corner have vanished. A few remain, as do tea shops (*Casas de Té* or *Casas de Infusiones*), often on main squares.

Much Cuban domestic coffee has been adulterated—*café mesclado*—since the Special Period with other roasted products, usually chicory. The best export brand is Cubita, sold vacuum-packed.

Café con leche (coffee with milk) is served in tourist restaurants, usually at a ratio of 50:50, with hot milk. Don't confuse this with *Café americano,* which is usually diluted Cuban coffee.

Alcoholic Drinks

Beers: Cuba makes several excellent German-style beers, usually served just a little above freezing (US75 cents-US$2, depending on where you drink). Hatuey is full-flavored lager. Cristal, Manacas, and Lagarto are lighter. Bucanero is a heavy-bodied lager. All are sold nationally, but you'll also find regional beers as well as the inexpensive and duller *Clara,* the rough-brewed beer for domestic consumption (typically one peso).

MOJITO: THE BODEGUITA'S CLASSIC DRINK

Here's the official version of how to make a killer *mojito*, as prepared by the barmen at the Bodeguita del Medio:

Combine half a teaspoon of sugar and the juice of half a lime in a highball glass. Add a sprig of *yerba buena* (mint), crushing the stalk to release the juice; two ice cubes; and 1.5 oz. of Havana Club Light Dry Cuban rum. Fill with soda and stir. *Salud!*

Before the Special Period, most villages had *cervecerias,* beer dispensaries that were boisterous social centers. Many have since died. In some rural areas you may still find roadside dispensers where you can buy beer in paper cups for a few centavos.

You'll also find Heineken, Labatts, Ice, some US brands, and Mexican brands such as Tecate for sale in dollar stores and tourist hotel bars. Prices range from US$1-3.

Rum: Cuba's specialty is rum and rum-based cocktails. Cuban rums resemble Bacardi rums—which is not surprising, since several key rum factories in Cuba were originally owned by the Bacardi family—and come in three classes: light and dry *(ligero y seco) Carta Blanca,* aged for three years and also known as *tres años;* golden and dry *(dorado y seco) Carta de Oro* rums, aged for five years *(cinco años);* and dark seven-year-old *Añejo* rums *(siete años).* There are several brands, most notably the Habana Club label. Try the *Pati-Cruzada* label; its cheaper, but some people prefer it.

A bottle of quality rum costs US$5-10 at **Tiendas Panamericanos** and hotel stores. In touristy nightclubs, the same bottle can set you back US$20 or more. In nontouristy clubs, you can buy a shot of rum for US50 cents and in peso joints, for 50 *centavos.*

Golden and aged rums are best drunk straight (although *campesinos* drink *tragos*—shots—of overproof *aguardente,* cheap white rum). White rum is ideal for cocktails, such as a *piña colada,* an *Isla de Pinos,* a *Manhattan,* a *Presidente,* a *Cuba Bella,* and, most notably, the *daiquiri* and the *mojito*—both favorites of Ernest Hemingway, who helped launch both drinks to world fame. The *daiquiri* is a mix of light rum, lime juice, and ice, blended and served semi-frozen. The *mojito* is rum with sugar, lime juice, soda, a dash of Angostura bitters, and a sprig of mint, served on the rocks.

Recalling the Andrews sisters' song, "Drinking Rum and Coca-Cola," you'll surely want to try a *Cuba Libre* on its home turf. Dark rums are also used in cocktails such as the appropriately named *Mulata,* with lime and cocoa liqueur.

Other Alcoholic Drinks: Certain regions are known for unique liqueurs, such as *guayabita,* a brandy-like drink made from rum and guava and exclusive to Pinar del Río.

Wine lists have improved in recent years, and imported Chilean and French wines are no more expensive than elsewhere in the Caribbean. Some places even serve Californian wines. Avoid *vino quinado,* a sweet and unsophisticated Cuban wine. The most memorable thing about it is the hangover. Imported wines aren't cheap. Expect to pay US$4 and upward for a tiny glass, US$15 for a bottle.

Forget hard liquors, which are readily available in touristy bars but usually very expensive. You can buy bottles of your favorite imported tipple at *diplotiendas.*

GETTING THERE

BY AIR

Cuba's tourism boom is fueling an increase in air traffic to Cuba. About 40 airlines service Cuba. Charters account for about 90% of arrivals. Leading international carriers have regular scheduled service from from Europe, Canada, and Central and South America, and more are being added. If you want flexibility, choose your airline carefully—some are notoriously accommodating, others not. The US government bans flights between the US and Cuba, and all flights to and from Cuba are forbidden from using US airspace.

Cuba has a well-developed air transport network, with six international airports: Camagüey (Ignacio Agramonte), Cayo Coco, Havana (José Martí International), Holguín (Frank País Airport), Santiago de Cuba (Antonio Maceo Airport), and Varadero (Juan Gualberto Gómez). Most flights land at either Havana or Varadero, with Santiago and Holguín (which serves the beaches of Guardalavaca and Santa Lucía) of secondary importance.

Fares

Airline fares are in flux in these days of deregulation. The cheapest *scheduled* fares are APEX (Advance-Purchase EXcursion), which you must buy at least 21 days before departure and which limit your visit. From Europe, you must stay a minimum of 14 days and return within 180 days. Penalties usually apply for any changes after you buy your ticket. Generally, the further in advance you buy your ticket, the cheaper it will

CUBANA OFFICES IN CUBA

Baracoa: Calle Martí #181, tel. (021) 42171

Bayamo: Calle Martí #58, esq. Parada y Rojas, tel. (023) 423916

Camagüey: Calle República #400, esq. Correa, Camagüey, tel. (0322) 92156 or 91338

Ciego de Ávila. Calle Chico Valdéz #83, Carretera Central e/ Maceo y Honorato Castillo, tel. (058) 25316

Guantánamo: Calle Calixto García e/ Aquilera y Prado 817, tel. (021) 34533 or 34789

Havana: (National) Calle Infanta, esq. Humboldt, Plaza, tel. 70-5961 or 33-4949, (International) Calle 23 #64, Vedado, Havana, tel. 78-4961 or 33-4949

Holguín: Calle Libertad, esq. Martí, Policentro, tel. (024) 425707; Aeropuerto Frank País, tel. (024) 462512

Las Tunas: Calle 24 de Febrero esq. Lucas Ortiz, tel. (031) 42702

Manzanillo: Calle Maceo #70 e/ Villuenda y Merchá, tel. (023) 2800

Moa: Avenida del Puerto Rpto. Rolo, Monterrey, Moa, tel. (024) 67916; Aeropuerto Capitán Orestes Acosta, tel. (024) 7370

Nueva Gerona Calle 39 #1415 e/ 16 y 18, Nueva Gerona, Isla de la Juventud, tel. (061) 6122531 or 6124259

Santiago de Cuba: Calle Félix Pena #671 e/ San Basilio y Heredia, tel. (0226) 24156, 20898, or 22290; Aeropuerto Antonio Maceo, tel. (0226) 91014 or 91865

Varadero: Hotel Iberostar Barlovento, Calle 9 esq. 1ra, tel. (05) 667593; Aeropuerto Juan Gualberto Gómez, tel. (05) 62133 or 63016

be. Buy your return ticket before arriving in Cuba, as flights are often full and one-way tickets purchased in Cuba tend to be expensive (note, too, that if you miss a Cubana charter flight, you'll forfeit 100% of the fare and need to purchase a new ticket).

Keep your eyes open for introductory fares.

The cheapest fares are usually on direct flights to Cuba, but you can also find cheap fares to Miami, from where you can take a flight to the Bahamas and then to Cuba. If you fly to a US gateway on a US carrier en route to Cuba, you must have your ticket for the Cuban portion issued on a separate ticket stock.

If you're flexible, consider traveling **standby,** where you do not make a reservation but instead turn up at the airport and hope for an empty seat, preferably at a last-minute discount rate.

Charter packages that include airfare and accommodations are often cheaper than many flight-only options; since you don't *have* to use the hotel portion, they can be the cheapest way to get to Cuba. Certain restrictions apply.

In England, you may be able to save money by buying your ticket through a **"bucket-shop"** (similar to a **"consolidator"** in North America), which sells discounted tickets on scheduled carriers. Consolidators usually have access to a limited number of tickets, so book early.

Practicalities

Ensure that you make your reservation as early as possible (several months in advance would be ideal), especially during peak season, as flights are often oversold. Always reconfirm your reservation within 72 hours of your departure (reservations are frequently canceled if not reconfirmed, especially during Dec.-Jan. holidays), and arrive at the airport with at least two hours to spare. Avoid reservations that leave little time for connections—baggage transfers and Customs and immigration procedures may take more time than planned.

I recommend using a travel agent for reservations (most do not charge a fee, but instead derive their income from commissions already figured into the airlines' fee). The agent's computer will display most of the options, usually including seat availability and current fares, and they have the responsibility to chase down refunds in the event of overbooking, cancellations, etc.

Cubana de Aviación

Cuba's national airline is Cubana de Aviación, which celebrated its 67th anniversary in 1996. Cubana's flights to the US were discontinued in 1962 and have not been revived. After the US embargo was imposed, the airline's vintage Bristol Britannia planes were replaced by Soviet-made aircraft, including 32-passenger Yak-40s, 120-passenger Yak-42s, 156-passenger TU-154s, and 168-passenger IL-62s. They're adequately comfortable, if a little rough around the edges (and smelly; I've even seen cockroaches on board), with the same space between seats as on Western jets, which they copy. Cubana recently added several 44-passenger Fokker-27s, plus two 309-passenger DC-10s. The airline's only First Class *(Clase Tropical)* service is on its DC-10s.

At press time, Cubana offered regular scheduled service between Cuba and Barcelona, Berlin, Bogotá, Brussels, Buenos Aires, Cancún, Caracas, Fort de France, Frankfurt, Guayaquíl, Kingston, Las Palmas, Lima, Lisbon, London, Madrid, Mendoza, Mexico City, Montreal, Moscow, Panama City, Paris, Puerto Pitre, Rio de Janeiro, Rome, San José (Costa Rica), Santiago de Chile, Santiago de Compostela (Spain), Sao Paulo, and Toronto. Additional services are slated. Cubana offers charter flights between Cuba and Buenos Aires, Cologne, Gran Cayman, Guadalajara, Lisbon, Madrid, Mexico City, Montego Bay, Montevideo, Nassau, Paris, Quito, Santiago de Chile, Santo Domingo, Toronto, and Veracruz.

Cubana's attitude toward scheduled departures is cavalier—flight times change frequently. But its safety record is good. Ensure that you check in on time on your day of departure; the airline is notorious for disposing of seats of passengers who arrive after the scheduled check-in time.

Overhead bins are smaller than in US- and European-made planes. Often, you'll find people smoking on nonsmoking flights.

Cubana's fares are generally lower than other airlines'.

From the USA

At press time, no flights were permitted between the US and Cuba. Nor can any US airline, tour operator, or travel agent make arrangements for flights to Cuba without a license from the Treasury Department. And under the terms of the embargo, US citizens showing an airline reservation which includes an *onward flight* to Cuba will be refused boarding on the flight out of the US. It is essential to have completely separate tickets and reservations for your travel into and out of Cuba from any third country.

Nonetheless, thousands of US citizens take advantage of the many scheduled commercial airline services to Cuba from third countries. In reality, getting to Cuba from the US is no more difficult than flying, say, from Buffalo, New York, to Portland, Oregon. The most popular routes are through Canada or the Bahamas for East Coast residents and through Mexico for West Coast residents.

Marazul Tours, Tower Plaza Mall, 4100 Park Ave., Weehawken, NH 07087, tel. (201) 319-9670 or (800) 223-5334, fax (201) 319-9009, is the only travel agency currently authorized to book flights, procure visas from the Cuban government, and make other arrangements for individual travel.

The Miami-based commuter carrier Gulfstream International Airlines operates one flight a week to Havana for the US Interests Section. Unfortunately, no, you cannot get on.

"Secret" Charters: Prior to February 1996, when President Clinton banned flights to Cuba, licensed charter flights operated to Havana from Miami—the only permitted gateway. The semi-

US LAW AND TRAVEL TO CUBA

Contrary to popular belief, US law does *not* prohibit US citizens from visiting Cuba. However, tourism is effectively banned by the Trading With the Enemy Act, which prohibits US citizens from spending money there.

The Cubans have no restrictions on US tourists. On the contrary; they welcome US visitors with open arms. The Cubans are savvy—they won't stamp your passport. As many as 80,000 US citizens visited Cuba in 1995; only about 20% did so legally, while the rest slipped in through third countries.

The regulations change frequently. For the latest provisions, contact the Office of Foreign Assets Control (OFAC), US Department of the Treasury, Washington, D.C. 20200, tel. (202) 622-2520. Request the *Cuban Assets Control Regulations*. The Treasury Department maintains an online home site describing the various categories at www.cn-traveler.com/code/cuba.html.

The following regulations applied to US citizens and residents at press time (the text is reprinted verbatim from a US State Department bulletin issued in March 1996):

The US Department of the Treasury's Cuban Assets Control Regulations . . . require that persons subject to US jurisdiction traveling to and within Cuba need a Department of the Treasury license in order to buy goods (a meal at a hotel, for example) or services (an airline ticket, tour package, or hotel room).

The following categories of travelers are permitted to spend money for Cuban travel without the need to obtain special permission from the US Treasury Department:

Official Government Travelers. US and foreign government officials, including representatives of international organizations of which the United States is a member, who are traveling on official business.

Journalists regularly employed in such capacity by a news reporting organization.

Persons who are visiting to visit close relatives in Cuba in circumstances of extreme humanitarian need. This authorization is valid without a specific license from the Office of Foreign Assets Control only once every 12 months.

Special licenses may be issued by the Office of Foreign Assets Control on a case by case basis authorizing travel transactions by persons in connection with the following travel categories:

Humanitarian Travel. Persons traveling to Cuba (1) to visit close relatives in cases involving extreme hardship, such as terminal illness or severe medical emergency, (2) persons traveling to Cuba to accompany licensed humanitarian donations (other than gift parcels), or (3) persons traveling in connection with activities of recognized human rights organizations investigating specific human rights violations.

Travel in connection with professional research or similar activities, for clearly defined educational or religious activities, or for purposes related to the exportation, importation, or transmission of informational materials, including provision of telecommunications services. *(continues on next page)*

US LAW AND TRAVEL TO CUBA
(continued)

Except as specifically licensed by the Office of Foreign Assets Control, payments in connection with any other travel to Cuba are prohibited, whether travelers go directly or via a third country such as Mexico, Canada, or another Caribbean island.

"Fully hosted" travel to Cuba is not restricted, provided that the travel is not aboard a direct flight between the United States and Cuba. A fully hosted traveler may pay for transportation only if aboard a non-Cuban carrier. Travelers whose expenses are covered by a person not subject to US jurisdiction may not bring back any Cuban origin goods, except for informational materials.

Vessels: All persons on board vessels, including the owner, must be an authorized traveler, as listed above, to engage in travel transactions in Cuba. If you are not an authorized traveler, you may not purchase meals, pay for transportation, lodging, dockage, or mooring fees, and you may not bring any Cuban origin goods back to the United States. Any payments to the Marina Hemingway International Yacht Club would be considered a prohibited payment to a Cuban national and therefore in violation of the Regulations. Vessel owners are prohibited from carrying travelers to Cuba who pay them for passage if the owner does not have a specific license from OFAC authorizing him to be a Service Provider to Cuba.

What You May Buy: Money may be spent only for purchases of items directly related to travel such as hotel accommodations, meals, and goods personally used by the traveler in Cuba at a rate not to exceed $100 per day or for the purchase of $100 worth of Cuban merchandise to be brought into the United States as accompanied baggage. Purchases of services related to travel, such as nonemergency medical services, are prohibited . . . The purchase of publications and other informational material is not restricted in any way.

A Range of Options
Many ordinary US citizens and residents can also

qualify for official travel status as "researchers." The law states that "Specific licenses for transactions related to travel to, from, and within Cuba may be issued for persons engaging in professional research and *similar activities*" (my italics). Several organizations are licensed to offer educational trips and can assist you to meet qualification requirements.

In addition, "Specific licenses will be issued to persons for travel to Cuba for clearly defined educational activities . . . attendance at a meeting or conference . . . activities related to study for an undergraduate or graduate degree sponsored by a college or university located in the United States."

Prior to October 1995, when the process became even more politicized as to who would be granted licenses, freelance journalists could travel to Cuba without asking Uncle Sam's permission. Now they, too, need a license, thereby allowing the US government to veto the entry of particular journalists.

If you want to go it alone and try the "journalist" or "researcher" angle, write to the Licensing Division, **Office of Foreign Assets Control,** Department of the Treasury, 1331 G Street NW, Washington, D.C. 20220, tel. (202) 376-0922. The Treasury Department requires a *written statement* of why your proposed trip falls within the rules for permissible travel. If your story is convincing, you should get approval in two or three months.

You may also travel legally by booking a prepaid, all-inclusive package with companies such as Wings of the World.

A far simpler alternative—the route chosen by the vast majority of US visitors to Cuba—is to forget the legal restrictions and simply go!

Will You Be Fined?
Trading with Cuba is good for up to a US$250,000 fine and 10 years in prison, but arresting people for merely vacationing in Cuba is not high on the US government's list of priorities. To my knowledge, *no one* has been prosecuted merely for going to Cuba and spending money there as a tourist.

---

secret flights still operate twice weekly—via Cancún (US$399 roundtrip). The flights aren't listed, and you are led to the plane as if a spy swap were taking place.

Before the ban, **Marazul Charters,** tel. (305) 232-8157 (also see Marazul Tours, above), flew three Boeing 727s weekly to Havana at 90% capacity. Other brokers included **Airline Brokers**

Company, tel. (305) 871-1260, fax (305) 447-0965, e-mail tfre97a@prodigy.com, and **C&T,** P.O. Box 996091, Miami, FL 0351, tel. (305) 876-7660, fax (305) 871-1260. Charter operators are only authorized to carry properly documented passengers as permitted by the US Treasury Dept. Individuals who are hosted by the Cuban government are barred from taking charter flights through Miami and must travel on a non-Cuban carrier from outside the US.

If direct flights have been resurrected by the time you read this, expect to pay US$225-255 roundtrip, plus US$45 airport taxes (US$185 one-way).

By Private Aircraft: Owners of private aircraft, including air ambulance services, who intend to land in Cuba must obtain a temporary export permit for the aircraft from the US Department of Commerce prior to departure.

You must contact the **Instituto de Acronáutica Civil de Cuba,** Calle 23 #64, Vedado, Havana, tel./fax 33-4571, at least 10 days prior to arrival in Cuba and at least 48 hours before an overflight.

From Canada

Over 200,000 Canadians visited Cuba in 1996, and there are plenty of flights between the two countries. Most traffic is on a charter-package basis. The bulk of Canadian charters fly to Varadero (a three-and-a-half-hour flight from Toronto). Toronto-based tour operators are the driving force of the trade. You might find cheap airfares—about C$400 roundtrip—through **Travel Deals,** tel. (416) 236-0125 or **Wholesale Travel Group,** tel. (416) 366-1000.

Cubana, tel. (514) 871-1222, has scheduled departures from Montreal and Toronto to Havana and Varadero on Sunday (from C$500). **Air Canada Vacations,** tel. (514) 422-5788, a division of Air Canada, offers packages to Varadero and has twice-weekly flights to Havana. Seven-night packages range from C$499 to C$1,099. **Air Transat,** tel. (416) 485-3377 or 233-8228, and **Canada 3000,** tel. (416) 674-2661, offer roundtrip fares to Varadero and Cienfuegos ranging in cost from C$399 (low-season) to C$499 (high-season). Fares to Havana are approximately C$449, C$469 to Santiago de Cuba. **Regent Holidays,** 6205 Airport Rd., Bldg. A, Suite 200, Mississauga, Ontario L4V 1E1, tel. (416) 673-3343, fax (416) 673-1717, offers roundtrip airfares to both Santiago and Varadero for as low as C$369 using Air Transat. First-class cabins cost about C$100 more. **Magna Holidays,** 50 Alness St. #200C, Downsview, Ontario M3J 2G9, tel. (416) 665-7330, specializes in Cuban vacation packages from Toronto and Montreal. It offers air-only from C$429 aboard Cubana.

Adventure Tours, 111 Avenue Rd., Suite 500, Toronto, Ontario M5R 3J8) offers a range of all-inclusive air-and-hotel packages in Varadero, Bucanero (near Santiago de Cuba), and Santa Lucía. Its affiliate, **Fiesta Sun,** has a broader range of one-week air-hotel packages from C$499. ITH's **Adventure Fiesta,** tel. (416) 967-1510, offers weekly winter packages to Varadero, Santiago de Cuba, Cayo Coco and other Cuban resort destinations; prices begin at C$499. And **Conquest Tours,** 85 Brisbane Rd, Downsview,

CANADIAN CHARTER FLIGHTS

CARRIER	FROM	DESTINATION	DAY OF WEEK	SEASON
Royal Airlines	Toronto	Varadero	Sunday	Sep.-Dec
Royal Airlines	Toronto	Varadero	Monday	mid-Dec.-July
Canada 3000	Toronto	Varadero	Thursday	mid-Dec.-mid-April
Royal Airlines	Ottawa	Varadero	Saturday	mid-Dec.-March
Royal Airlines	Toronto	Camaguey	Thursday	mid-Dec.-July
Royal Airlines	Toronto	Cayo Largo	Monday	mid-Dec.-April
Air Transat	Toronto	Santiago	Monday	Nov.-June

Ontario M3J 2K3, tel. (416) 665-9255, fax (416) 665-6811, has charter packages from Halifax to Santa Lucía on Thursday Feb.-April.

Other companies include **Canadian Holidays,** tel. (416) 620-8687; **Bel-Air Inc.,** Montreal, tel. (514) 871-8330; **Cubanacán Tours,** 1255 University, Suite 211, Montreal, Quebec H3B 3B2, tel. (514) 861-4444; **Cubanacán Canada International,** 372 Bay St., Suite 1902, Toronto, Ontario M5H 2W9, tel. (416) 601-0343, fax (416) 601-0346; **Club Voyage,** Montreal, tel. (514) 284-3406; **P. Lawson Travel,** Toronto, tel. (416) 862-0607; **Royal Adventure,** tel. (416) 967-1510; and **Wings of the World,** 653 Mt. Pleasant Rd., Toronto, Ontario M4S 2N2 tel. (416) 482-1223 or (800) 465-8687, fax (416) 486-4011.

Canadian Universities Travel Service, Travel Cuts, 187 College St., Toronto, ON M5T 1P7, tel. (416) 979-2406, sells discount airfares to students and has 25 offices throughout Canada.

From Europe

Several airlines fly direct to Cuba from Europe (or with a refueling stop at Gander, in Canada, en route). American Airlines, British Airways, Continental, United Airlines, and Virgin Atlantic fly from London to Miami, where you can connect with an airline to the Bahamas, and from there to Cuba (see "From the Caribbean," below). Note, however, that if flying aboard a US carrier, you will have to make your reservation for the Bahamas-Cuba leg separately.

From the UK: Until November 1996, **Cubana,** 49 Conduit St., London W1, tel. (171) 734-1165, fax (171) 437-0681, flew from Stansted using a DC-10 leased from France's AOM airline, departing Thursday, and returning from Havana on Wednesday (£360 roundtrip; flight time is nine hours). However, at press time, Cubana was scheduled to transfer operations to Gatwick. Tickets are supposedly valid for two weeks only, and dates are not changeable. In spring 1996, **Journey Latin America,** 14-16 Devonshire Rd., London W4 2HD, tel. (0181) 747-3108, fax (0181) 742-1312, offered roundtrip between London and Havana for £358/424 (low/high-season).

All-Jamaica, 130 Bury New Rd., Whitefield, Manchester M45 6AD, tel. (0161) 796-9222, fax (0161) 796-9444, promotes UK-Jamaica-Cuba trips using Air UK Leisure. It has charters to Montego Bay from Manchester on Sunday and from Gatwick on Monday, connecting with flights to Cuba. You can also connect with flights to Cuba from Jamaica using **British Airways** or **Air Jamaica** from Heathrow. (At press time, British Airways was considering launching direct flights to Havana.)

You can also nip over to Amsterdam on Air UK and connect with Martinair's nonstop flight to Holguín. Alternately, you could fly to Ireland with Aer Lingus and take **Aeroflot,** 69-72 Picadilly, London W1V 9HH, tel. (171) 491-1764; in Cuba, Calle 23 #54, esq. Infanta, Vedado, Havana, tel. 33-3200 or 70-6292, fax 33-3288, to Havana from Shannon for £445 on Saturday, Monday, or Wednesday, returning one day later. The ticket is valid for one month only. You can also take **Iberia** from Heathrow via Madrid (£549 during low season; check to see if they still have a companion fare, which was recently £295). You'll need to change planes in Madrid (the airline may pay for any requisite overnight stay). You can also fly **Viasa Airlines** from Heathrow with a change of aircraft in Caracas (£460 in low season). It departs Tuesday and Saturday, returning Monday and Friday. **Air UK Leisure** has a charter flight to Camagüey and Varadero.

"Bucket shops" advertise in London's *What's On, Time Out,* and leading Sunday newspapers. **Trailfinders,** 42 Earl's Court Rd., London W8 6EJ, tel. (181) 747-3108, specializes in cheap fares throughout Latin America. **STA Travel,** 74 Old Brompton Rd., London SW7, tel. (171) 937-9971, fax (171) 938-5321, specializes in student fares. STA also has offices at 25 Queens Rd., Bristol; 38 Sydney St., Cambridge; 75 Deansgate, Manchester; and 19 High St., Oxford. Alternately, try **Council Travel,** 28A Poland St., London W1V 3DB, tel. (171) 437-7767.

From Spain: Cubana flies direct to Havana from Madrid on Monday and Friday, from Barcelona on Saturday, and from Santiago de Compostela on Monday using a DC-10. **Iberia,** tel. 587-8785, also flies to Havana from Madrid, daily except Friday.

From Germany: Cubana operates a DC-10 to Havana from Frankfurt on Saturday and from Berlin via Brussels on Sunday. It also flies from Frankfurt to Santiago de Cuba on Saturday and has charter service from Cologne to both Holguín and Havana on Friday. **LTU,** tel. 0190-211767, fax (0211) 927-0000, Internet address http://www.ltu.de, operates charters from Dusseldorf to Havana on Friday, Holguín on Wednesday, and Varadero on Monday (from Frankfurt on Sunday) for about DM1,470; or about £450 roundtrip with a connecting flight from London and a three-month maximum stay). **Condor,** tel. (061) 07-755440, fax (061) 07-7550, also operates charters from Germany.

From Elsewhere in Europe: Cubana flies direct to Havana from Paris on Sunday and via Santiago de Cuba on Saturday, Las Palmas on Tuesday and Friday, Lisbon on Thursday, Moscow on Tuesday, and Rome on Monday. It also has charter flights to Havana, Holguín, and Varadero.

Aeroflot, 69-72 Picadilly, London W1V 9HH, tel. (171) 491-1764; in Cuba, Calle 23 #54, esq. Infanta, Vedado, Havana, tel. 33-3200 or 70-6292, fax 33-3288, flies to Havana from Luxembourg, Moscow, and Shannon (Fire), with connecting service to Lima, Managua, Moscow, Panama City, and Santiago de Chile.

Finnair operates DC-10 service between Helsinki and Holguín. **KLM** has flights to Havana from Amsterdam on Wednesday and Sunday (£550 from London, low-season). **Martinair** flies to Holguín and Varadero from Amsterdam on Saturday, serving the Dutch-run hotels of Guardalavaca (from £540 from London; an open-jaw arrangement allows you to return from Varadero). **Lauda Air** has service from Austria.

Discount Fares: In Germany, discount fares are available through **Council Travel** in Dusseldorf, tel. 2113-29088, and Munich, tel. 0898-95022; and from **STA Travel,** tel. 6943-0191, fax 6943-9858, in Frankfurt. In France, try **Uniclam,** 63 rue St. Augustin, Paris 75002, tel. (1) 4266-2087; or **Voyages Découvertes,** 21 rue Cambon, Paris, tel. (1) 4261-0001. In Dublin, Ireland, contact **Concord Travel,** tel. 763232, **Cubatravel,** tel. 713422, or **Smurfit Travel,** 38 Dane St., Dublin 2, tel. 774211, fax 01793436.

From Central and South America

In the 1960s, Latin American airlines suspended scheduled flights to Cuba under US pressure. Today, the rush is on, and flights—many of which are booked solid—serve Cuba from a dozen destinations. Reservations cannot be booked through US travel agencies and tour operators.

From Mexico: Mexicana, tel.(5) 325-0990, and **Aeromexico,** tel. (5) 207-6311, both operate scheduled service to Cuba from Mexico City (about US$280 one-way, US$420 roundtrip).

Cubana offers service from Mexico City on Wednesday and Saturday and from Cancún daily; in Mexico City, Temistocles #246 B esq. Av. Homero, Colonia Polanca, tel. (5) 255-3776, fax (5) 255-0835; in Cancún, Av. Yazchilán #23 SM-24 M-22, Retorno 3 e/ Nir-Cheaven y Tan-Chacte, tel. (87) 73-33. It also has service from Cancún to Varadero on Monday. Fares from Cancún begin at about US$180 roundtrip, plus US$24 tax.

Taíno Tours, 9330 Ignacio Comonfort St, Tijuana, tel. (66) 84-7001, operates five-hour flights between Tijuana and Havana aboard a MD-80 chartered from Aeromexico. The roundtrip flight costs US$399; departures are every Saturday. The company also has weeklong package tours from US$650.

Several companies offer charter flights and packages from Cancún and Mérida, including **Divermex,** Plaza Americas, Cancún, tel. (98) 842325, (98) 845005, fax (98) 842325, **Exper-Tours,** tel. (98) 474-08, and **Yucatán Tours,** Merida, tel. 299-282-582, fax 266-319. One-week packages, including airfare, begin at about US$350. **Aero Caribbean** has service between Mérida and Havana on Friday and Sunday; in Mexico, c/o Merihabana, Calle 59 #508, esq. 62, Hotel Reforma, Mérida, tel./fax 23-6612. Also try **Cubanatours,** Baja California 255, Edificio B, Despacho 103, Colonia Hipódromo Condesa, Mexico D.F., CP-06100, tel.(5) 264-2107, fax (5) 264-2865.

Warning: Ostensibly, you need to buy a Cuban visa before boarding the aircraft; Mexican operators have you at their mercy and gouge accordingly—sometimes asking US$50 or more! (They'll also try to insist that you make reservations for at least two nights' accommodation.) Note that, for the return leg, you must obtain your tourist card for Mexico *before* arriving at Havana airport, where tourist cards are *not* issued; you can obtain one from the Mexican embassy at Calle 12 #518, Miramar, Havana, tel. 33-0856.

From Central America: LACSA in Costa Rica, tel. (506) 232-3555, fax (506) 232-4593, flies from San José to Havana on Monday, Wednesday, and Friday, returning next day (US$484 roundtrip). **Cubana** operates flights from San José on Wednesday and Sunday, and from Panama City on Sunday (US$499). **COPA,** c/o Havanatur, Calle 23, No. 64, Vedado, Havana, tel. 33-1758, flies to Havana from Panama

City every Monday and Friday. **Aero Caribbean** operates flights between Havana and Managua, Nicaragua, on Wednesday (in Nicaragua, c/o Aero Segovia, Rpto. Bosques de Altamira #158, Managua, tel./fax 67-8102, for about US$380 roundtrip.

From South America: Cubana has service to Havana from Sao Paolo (Friday), Rio de Janeiro (Friday), Santiago de Chile (Monday), Lima (Saturday—continuing to Varadero), Quito (Saturday), and Bogotá (Friday). It also serves Ciego de Ávila from Buenos Aires on Thursday. **Viasa,** tel. 21125, and **Aeropostal,** tel. 509-3666, fax 509-4080, also operate from Venezuela; and **Ladeco,** tel. 639-5053, fax 639-7277, flies to Havana from Santiago de Chile. Cubana also operates charter flights to Havana from Guayaquil and Quito in Ecuador (Saturday) and Caracas (Saturday).

From the Caribbean
From the Bahamas: Cubana offers charter flights to Havana from Nassau on Tuesday, Wednesday, Friday, and Sunday. You can book through **Majestic Tours,** tel. (809) 328-0387, and **Bahatours** (also known as **Havanatur Nassau),** P.O. Box N-10246, Nassau, Bahamas, tel. (809) 322-2796, fax (809) 361-1336, which offer charter flights for US$120 one-way or US$192 roundtrip, plus two- to seven-night packages to Havana and Varadero beginning at US$199 (two nights) including roundtrip airfare, transfers, and accommodations. Departure times change frequently.

Returning from Cuba, you pass through Bahamian immigration (there is no in-transit lounge). *Don't* mention to Bahamian Customs that you're in transit from Cuba, as they go "on notice" and will likely search your bags. The departure terminal for flights to the US is next door (to the left of the exit from the arrivals hall). You must pass through US Immigration and Customs here. If you're a US citizen, they won't know that you've been in Cuba unless you tell them (although I suspect that the immigration forms handed in to Bahamian officials may be passed on to US immigration). However, US officials will ask you where you stayed in the Bahamas and how long. If you choose to tell the truth, expect to be searched (and to have your Cuban purchases confiscated); if you choose not to tell the truth, you'll be expected to name the Bahamas hotel where you stayed; any hesitation may give the game away. US Customs officials can be snide and peevish—one of my friends had all her Cuban cigars snapped in two before her eyes!

From the Cayman Islands: Eddy Tours, P.O. Box 31097, Grand Cayman, tel. (809) 949-4606, fax (809) 949-4095, operates charters using Cubana (Friday and Sunday).

From the Dominican Republic: Cubana has charter service to Havana from Santo Domingo on Thursday (via Santiago) and Sunday. **Aero Caribbean,** Avenida 23 #64, e/ P y Infanta, Vedado, Havana, tel. 78-6813, fax 33-5016; in the Dominican Republic, c/o Agencia Coturca, Avenida Sadalha #200, Plaza Milton, Santiago de los Caballeros, tel. 971-0041, and **AeroGaviota,** Avenida 47 #2814 e/ 28 y 34, Reparto Kohly, Playa, Havana, tel. 81-3068, fax 33-2621, also operate twice-weekly flights between Puerto Plata and Santiago and Havana.

From Jamaica: Cubana has scheduled flights to Havana from Kingston on Wednesday and Saturday and charter service to Varadero and Havana from Montego Bay on Friday and Sunday. Several Jamaican tour companies utilize these flights.

Caribic Vacations, 69 Gloucester Av., Montego Bay, tel. (809) 979-0322, fax (809) 979-3421, offers charter flights from Montego Bay to Varadero and Havana on Friday and Sunday. Roundtrip flights cost US$199 (US$179 one-way). Flight times change with seasons; check for latest details. At press time it planned on replacing Yak-41s with Boeing 737s.

InterCaribe, 11½ Ardenne Rd., Kingston 10, tel. (809) 978-2150, fax (809) 978-2686, has a charter flight to Santiago de Cuba from Kingston on Friday, returning on Sunday. It also has flights to Havana from Kingston, departing on Wednesday. **Sunholiday Tours,** P.O. Box 531, Montego Bay, St. James, Jamaica, tel. (809) 952-5629, fax (809) 979-0725, in the US, tel. (800) 433-2920, also has flights departing Montego Bay for Havana on Saturday, and for Santiago de Cuba (US$148 one-way, US$165 roundtrip) on Thursday.

CUBANA AIRLINES OFFICES OUTSIDE CUBA

Berlin: Frankfurter Tor 8-A, 1034 Berlin, tel. 589-3409; Airport, tel. 678-8185

Bogotá: Carrera 14 #7920, Bogotá, tel. 621-0793, fax 621-0793

Brussels: Avenie Louise #272, BTE1, Brussels, tel. 640-2050, fax 640-0810

Buenos Aires: Sarmiento #552 e/ Florida y San Martin, tel. 326-5291, fax 326-5294; Airport, tel. 620-0011

Cancún: Av. Yaxchilan #23, SM-24 M-22 retorno 3, e/ Nit-Cheaven y Tanchacte, Cancún, tel. 860192, fax 877373

Caracas: Av. Rómulo Gallegos con Primera, Edificio Pascal Torre B #133, Palos Grandes, Caracas, tel. 289-3548, fax 285-6313

Cologne: Flughafen Kolh-Bonn Postfach 980213, 5000 Koln, tel. 02203-402190

Frankfurt: An der Hauptwache 7, 60313 Frankfurt am Main, tel. 069-913-0980

Gander: Gander Airport, Canada, tel. 709-651-2489

Guayaquíl: Centro Comercial Las Vitrinas, Local No.61, Calle H La Kenedy, tel. 390727, fax 289911

Kingston: 22 Trafalgar Road #11, Kingston 10, tel. 978-3410, 978-3406

Las Palmas: Calle Galicia #29, Las Palmas, Gran Canaria, tel. (928) 272408, fax (028) 272419

Lima: Jiron Tarata #250, Miraflores, Lima 18, tel. 410554, fax 471363

London: 49 Conduit St., London W1R 9FB, tel. 171-734-1165, fax 171-437-0681

Madrid: Calle Princesa #25, Edificio Exágono, 28008 Madrid, tel. 542-2923, fax 541-6642; Airport, tel. 205-8448

Mexico City: Temistocles #246 esq. Homero, Colonia Polanco, C.P. 11550 Deleg. Manuel Hidalgo, Mexico D.F., tel. 255-3770, fax 255-0835; Airport, tel. 571-5368

Montevideo: Boulevar Artigas 1147 #504, Montevideo, Uruguay, tel. 481402

Montreal: 4 Place Ville Marie #405, Montreal, Quebec H3B 2E7, tel. 514-871-1222, fax 514-871-1227

Moscow: Karovit Val 7, Corpus 1, Seccion 5, Moscow, tel. 237-1901, fax 207-0391, Airport, tel. 578-7650

Panama: Calle 29 y Av. Justo Arosemena No.4-14, tel. 507-227-2122 or 27-2291, fax 507-272-2241

Paris: Tour Maine Montparnasse, 33 Avenue de Maine, B.P. 171, 75755 Paris Cedex 15, tel. 4538-3112, fax 4538-3110; Airport, tel. 4884-4060

Quito: Avenida de los Shyris y 6 de Diciembre, Edificio Torre Nova Oficina 1A, Quito, tel. 5939-227463

Rio de Janeiro: Rua Teofilo Otono 81, CJ 901, CEP 20080, Rio de Janeiro, tel. 021-233-0960

Rome: Via Barberini 86, 4 Piano, Rome, tel. 474-1104, fax 474-6836

San José: De Canal 7, Carretera á Pavas, San José, tel. (506) 290-5095, fax 290-5101

Santiago de Chile: Calle Fidel Oteiza 1971 #201, Providencia, Santiago de Chile, tel. 274-1819, fax 274-8207

Santo Domingo: Av. Tiradente esq. 27 de Febrero, Plaza Merengue, Local 209, tel. 809-227-2040; Airport, tel. 809-549-0345

Sao Paulo: Rua da Consolacao 232, Conjunto 1009, Centro Sao Paulo, tel. 2144571, fax 255-8660

Toronto: Lester B. Pearson Airport, tel./fax 416-676-4723

Vienna: Vienna International Airport, Flughafen Wien, Betriebsges MBH, Postfach 1, A-1300, Wien Flughafen, Austria C-206, tel. 71110 ext. 5671

The national commuter airline, **Air Jamaica Express,** was considering opening routes to Cuba in 1996. For the latest information, contact Air Jamaica, tel. (800) 523-5585 in the US; in Jamaica, tel. (809) 929-0834, fax (809) 929-0833.

From Elsewhere: Cubana operates charter service between Havana and St. Maarten, Fort-de-France in Martinique (Friday), and Pointe-a-Pitre in Guadeloupe (Friday). And it plans to add service to Bridgetown (Barbados). In late 1995, **BWIA** opened talks with Cubana about code-sharing arrangements that would see Cubana using Trinidad as a hub for South America routes. **Aero Gaviota** also offers charter flights from the Caribbean and Central and South America.

From Asia

From Hong Kong, one of the easiest routes is with **Iberia** nonstop from Macau to Madrid and then on to Havana. Flying nonstop to Los Angeles, then to Mexico City, Tijuana, or Cancún is also easy. Alternately, fly United or Malaysia Airlines to Mexico City (20 hours) and catch a flight next day to Havana (three hours). A roundtrip economy ticket is about HK$16,340, depending on the agent.

A company called **Travel Network,** 11th Floor, On Lan Centre, 11-15 On Lan St., Central, Hong Kong, tel. (852) 2845-4545, fax (852) 2868-5824, has experience booking travel to Cuba Ask for Alene Freidenrich. The company custom-designs packages for individuals. It also offers a six-day trip (US$1,700 plus airfare). Alene can arrange visas, or contact the Cuban Honorary Consul, tel. (852) 2525-6320; allow seven working days (HK$250).

From Australia

You'll find no direct flights to Cuba, nor any bargain fares. The best bet is to fly to Los Angeles and then to Cuba via Mexico, or to Miami and then via the Bahamas. A route from Sydney via Buenos Aires or Santiago de Chile and then to Havana is also possible. Specialists in discount fares include **STA Travel,** 220 Faraday St., Carlton, Melbourne, Victoria 3053, tel. (03) 347-4711 or (03) 347-6911, fax (03) 347-0608; or 1A Lee St., Railway Sq., Sydney 2000, tel. (02) 212-1258. In New Zealand, contact STA at 10 High St., Auckland, tel. (09) 309-9723, fax (09) 309-9829; 10 O'Connell St., Wellington, tel. (09) 309-9191; or—get this— 207 Cuba St., Wellington, tel. (04) 385-0561.

Cubatours, 235 Swan St., Richmond, Victoria 3121, tel. (3) 9428-0385, specializes in air-land packages to Cuba, as does Melbourne-based **Cuba World,** tel.(3) 9867-1200.

BY CRUISE SHIP

The US embargo has restricted the cruise industry's access to Cuba. No US company can operate cruises to Cuba, and because foreign-owned vessels cannot dock in the US within six months of visiting Cuba or carrying Cuban passengers or goods, even foreign companies have shunned Cuba—until recently.

The Italian company Costa Crociere initiated cruises to Cuba in October 1995 by forming a separate company—**Costa Cruceros,** Costa Crociere, Via D'Annunzio, 2-16121 Genova, Italy, and repositioning its *Ocean Pearl,* a 500-passenger vessel which it renamed *Costa Playa.* The vessel departs from Puerto Plata in the Dominican Republic every Tuesday at 8 p.m. and stops at Montego Bay, Jamaica, Santiago de Cuba, Havana, and Nipe, in Cuba. The cruises are operated in association with the French cruise company Paquet. You can also take the eight-day cruise package starting from and returning to Havana (departures every Friday). Per person rates begin at US$1,190 (low-season), US$1,350 (middle), US$1,511 (high), and US$1,748 (Christmas and New Year). Suites begin at US$1,961. Prices are all-inclusive (even tips are included), which means that *US citizens can legally take the cruise,* so long as they don't spend money in Cuba or tip the ship's Cuban staff. Shore excursions are additional. Air-sea packages are offered from Madrid each Tuesday, year-round.

Likewise, in November 1996, Cuba launched the *Meliá Don Juan,* with 203 staterooms and nine deluxe suites. The vessel is operated under a management contract by Spain's **Meliá Hoteles,** in Cuba, tel. 53-5-667013, fax 55-5-667162; in Italy, tel. 016-701-1692, fax 039-605-8063; in Germany, tel. 01-302301, fax, 02131-63467; in the UK, tel. 800-282720, fax 171-916-3431. It departs Cienfuegos each Friday for a three-day cruise to Cayo Largo and Grand Cayman (Cayman Islands), and each Monday for a four-day cruise to Cayman Brac (Cayman Islands), Santiago de Cuba, and Montego Bay (Jamaica).

CRUISING THROUGH SOCIALIST SEAS

The seas around Cuba have all the makings of a premier cruise region. With scores of beaches and dozens of colonial cities, the possible itineraries are endless.

In 1993, 8.5 million people took a cruise in the Caribbean, saturating Caribbean ports of call. With almost 30 new cruise ships being introduced by the year 2000, cruise companies have set their sights on Cuba to relieve the pressure.

US cruise companies are still barred from operating to Cuba. Although foreign-owned cruise ships are free to call, they fear the repercussions of the 1992 Torricelli Act, which prevents foreign vessels that berth in Cuba from berthing in US territory within 180 days. Nonetheless, industry pundits predict Havana will once again become one of the world's busiest cruise ports, replacing Nassau as the most visited port in the Caribbean.

Cuba's strategic location 90 miles south of Florida makes it a natural cruise hub. A cruise ship sailing from south Florida in late afternoon could be in Havana by sunrise the following morning.

Cruise-ship companies hungry for a virgin destination are tripping over themselves to be first into Cuba. At least one company is studying the prospect of ferry service between Miami and Havana. Florida East Coast Industries even has plans to operate a rail-barge across the 90-mile-wide straits. And in April 1992, the Port of Miami released details of a plan to build six new cruise-ship terminals in anticipation of the inevitable boom.

Cuba, too, is planning to embrace the cruise industry in a big way. The island already has eight major ports and 44 minor ports capable of handling cruise ships. Port facilities are described by one cruise industry official as "not wonderful, but they're functional for cruise ships." To accommodate the anticipated influx, the Cuban government is committing resources for the development of state-of-the-art cruise passenger terminals (see "Terminal Sierra Maestra," under "Getting There. By Sea" in the Havana chapter).

Italy's Costa Crociere line closed its Florida-based Pearl Cruises and initiated cruises to Cuba in October 1995 by repositioning its 500-passenger *Ocean Pearl* to the Dominican Republic. In 1996, it was followed by the *Meliá Don Juan*, operated by Meliá Hoteles and based in Cienfuegos.

You can take the weeklong cruise, and even board the vessel in Grand Cayman on Saturday or in Montego Bay on Thursday, o/o JTL Jamaica Tours, tel. (809) 953-3132, fax (809) 953-2107. Meliá plans to begin basing a second cruise ship to Havana.

Information

Cuba Cruise Watch is an occasional newsletter published by Vacations at Sea, 4919 Canal St. #102, New Orleans, LA 70119, tel. (318) 482-1572 or (800) 749-4950. The **Cruise Line Industry Association** may be able to provide the latest information on cruises to Cuba, 500 5th Ave. #1407, New York, NY 10110, tel. (212) 921-0066.

BY YACHT

Until a few years ago, most yachters kept a safe distance from Cuban shorelines. Understandably: Cuban authorities kept a keen eye out to make sure anti-Castro exiles weren't attempting one of their guerrilla attacks. Word on the grapevine was that foreign boats might be seized. Whatever the foundation of early fears, Cuba today offers a warm reception to visitors arriving by sea. Yachts from many countries bob at anchor at marinas and coves around the island. Many cruisers come from other Caribbean islands, Europe, or Canada. But as Simon Charles reports in his excellent *Cruising Guide to Cuba*, "the vast majority of foreign boats cruising Cuban waters have transited from Florida."

The US State Dept. advises that "US citizens are discouraged from traveling to Cuba in private boats" and permits such travel "only after meeting all US and Cuban government documentation and clearance requirements."

Scores of sailors—including US citizens in US-registered vessels—sail to Cuba each year without incident and without breaking the law (which for US citizens means no spending money there; ostensibly, you'll need to find a non-US citizen to pay your berth fees, and I presume you will cater yourself with food brought from the US. Get the picture?).

BOB RACE

Note: An executive order signed by President Clinton in spring 1996 states that vessels leaving Florida with the intention of entering Cuban territory may be confiscated by US authorities. The act was aimed at dissuading anti-Castro radicals from rash acts. Check with skippers who've recently sailed to Cuba to find out how this translates in reality. Most US skippers I've spoken to have had no problems when they return to the US—as long as they don't have their holds full of Cuban cigars!

Many guidebooks report that you must request permission at least two weeks in advance from Cuban authorities to call in. This is wrong. *No advance permission is required.* (Anyone planning on sailing to Cuba should obtain a copy of Simon Charles' book; see the Booklist.)

Yacht Charters and Crewing

US citizens should refer to Treasury Department regulations regarding chartering vessels for travel to Cuba. Charter companies in the Bahamas may permit travel to Cuba. Try **Nassau Yacht Haven,** tel. (809) 393-8173. In the UK, contact Alan Toone of **Compass Yacht Services,** Holly Cottage, Heathley End, Chislehurst, Kent BR7 6AB, tel. (181) 467-2450. Alan arranges yacht charters and may be able to assist in finding a crewing position.

Maps and Charts

You'll need accurate maps and charts, especially for the reef-infested passage from the Bahamas. British Admiralty charts, US Defense

Mapping Agency charts, and Imray yachting charts are all accurate and can be ordered from **Bluewater Books & Charts,** 1481 S.E. 17th St., Causeway, Ft. Lauderdale, FL 33316, tel. (305) 763-6533 or (800) 942-2583. In Havana, you can purchase nautical charts from **El Navigante** in Habana Vieja, Calle Mercaderes #115, Habana Vieja; Cuba CP 10100, Gaveta Postal 130, tel. 61-3625, fax 33-2869.

Your Reception in Cuba

I've cruised to and from Cuba, have spent considerable time at Cuban marinas, and can vouch that your reception in Cuba will most likely be thoroughly welcoming. However, I've heard one horrifying tale from two English crew members who claim to have had their yacht impounded by corrupt officials in Cuba after they ran aground. At the present time, the United States and Cuba do not have a Coast Guard agreement. Therefore, although the Cuban authorities have usually proven to be exceedingly helpful to yachters in distress, "craft developing engine trouble or other technical difficulties in Cuban territorial waters cannot expect assistance from the US Coast Guard." Cuba's territorial waters extend 12 miles out.

Traveling with Private Skippers

A surprising number of skippers ferry passengers to Cuba. It's possible to find private skippers sailing to Havana from Florida, New Orleans, and other ports along the southern seaboard, as well as from the Bahamas. Boats leave all the time from marinas along the Florida Keys. You can call various marinas for recommendations.

In the US, if you plead your case sufficiently well, you might try a humanitarian organization called **Basta!**, 7 Higgs Ln., Key West, FL 33049, tel./fax (305) 294-6940, e-mail jitters@aol.com or jjyoung@igc.apc.org. It has 38 registered vessels on call to carry humanitarian aid under license from the Treasury Department. Note, however, that they do *not* take ordinary citizens looking for a way to sneak into Cuba.

If you don't arrange a return trip with the same skipper, you'll find plenty of yachts flying the Stars and Stripes at Marina Hemingway in Havana. There'll ususally be a skipper willing to run you back to Florida. Be flexible. Pinpointing exact vessel departure dates and times is nearly impossible, especially in winter. As Ernest Hemingway wrote, "Brother, don't let anybody tell you there isn't plenty of water between Key West and Havana!" A nasty weather front can delay your departure as much as a week or more.

Warning: There's nothing illegal if passengers don't spend money in Cuba and if skippers don't charge for passage to or from Cuba. You may be questioned about this by US Customs or Immigration, who'll take a dim view of things. If a skipper asks for money, legally you must decline. Consider negotiating a *free* passage; of course, diesel fuel is expensive, so you may feel charitably inclined (vessels seem to use anywhere from US$200 to US$400 worth of fuel for a trip across the Straits of Florida).

ORGANIZED TOURS

Joining an organized tour offers certain advantages over traveling independently, such as the learning passed along by a knowledgeable guide. Tours are also good bets for those with limited time: you'll proceed to the most interesting places without the unforeseen delays and distractions that can be the bane of independent travel. Everything is usually taken care of from your arrival to your departure, including transportation and accommodations. The petty bureaucratic hassles and language problems you may otherwise not wish to face are eliminated, too. And several companies buy hotel rooms and airline seats in bulk, then pass the savings on to you.

Most organized tours to Cuba focus on the cultural and historical experience, although a growing number focus on special-interest travel. Check the tour inclusions carefully to identify any hidden costs such as airport taxes, tips, service charges, extra meals, and entertainment. Most tours are priced according to quality of accommodation, from deluxe to budget.

Most US organizations that offer trips to Cuba are *not* accredited tour and travel operators and do not offer consumer-protection programs. However, all operators in Canada and the United Kingdom offering tours to Cuba must by law guarantee full repayment in the case of default. Consider trip cancellation insurance. Paying for your tour by credit card is a good idea; in the event of a serious complaint you can challenge the charge.

Within Cuba, there are several state-run tour agencies that offer organized excursions and tours to all the major sites and attractions. Most are up to Western levels of efficiency and service. English-speaking guides, private transportation, meals, and accommodations are standard inclusions. This gives you the added flexibility of making your own tour arrangements once you've arrived in Cuba and gained a better sense of your options and desires.

US Citizens Traveling to Cuba
Fortunately, US citizens *can* legally travel to Cuba on certain organized tours. Organizations that arrange trips to Cuba are required to obtain special government authorized licenses.

Most programs are "study" tours that provide a deep immersion in particular aspects of Cuban life and issues. While the focus of most tours is educational, there's usually plenty of time for relaxation. By joining such groups you'll enjoy the advantage of coming to understand a little more of Cuba, perhaps, than would the average tourist. Participants usually have to demonstrate serious interest in the subject of study; in reality, this often proves a formality, especially in the realm of "arts," where the State Dept. accepts that it is difficult for artists to make a living as professionals.

Conventional Tours from the UK
Havanatur UK, Interchange House, 27 Stafford Rd., Croydon, Surrey CRO 4NG, tel. (0181) 681-3613, fax (0181) 760-0031, has the widest range of packages from England, with one- and

A NOTE FOR US TRAVEL AGENTS AND TOUR OPERATORS

US law states, "US travel service providers, such as travel agents and tour operators, who handle travel arrangements to, from, or within Cuba must hold special authorizations from the US Treasury Department to engage in such activities."

However, "It is possible to provide travel services to US persons legally able to travel to Cuba for family visits, professional research, or news gathering," says Michael Krinsky, a partner in the law firm of Rabinowitz, Boudin, Standard, Krinsky and Lieberman, which represents the Cuban government in the United States.

US travel agencies can also provide services to third countries, from where a traveler makes his or her own arrangements for travel to and within Cuba. They may also be able to provide services, such as travel arrangements to Jamaica, where a component includes an excursion to Cuba. Treasury Department regulations do not "show a clear penalty against travel agents who book travel this way." *Travel agents should double-check the regulations*, however, with the US Department of the Treasury, or with Krinsky, 740 Broadway, New York, NY 10003, tel. (212) 254-1111, fax (212) 674-4614, e-mail mkrinsky@igc.apc.org.

Cuba publishes a complete English-language tourism guide for travel agents and tour operators. The 350-page illustrated *Cuba Tourist Directory*, US$18 including postage, can be ordered from Publications Exchange, 8306 Mills Drive, Suite 241, Miami, FL 33183, tel. (305) 256-0162, fax (305) 252-1813. Another 250-page *Technical Guide on Cuba for Travel Agents* is published by Nexo Editores, P.O. Box 10119, 28080 Madrid, Spain, tel. (91) 531-9742, fax (91) 531-9856.

---

two-week packages to Havana, Varadero, and Santiago using Cubana from Stansted. Havanatur also has escorted motorcoach tours, and ecology and scuba diving packages. Prices depend on date of departure and hotel selected. A one-week package at the Hotel Deauville in Havana, for example, starts at £575, depending on the season. All holidays are fully flexible and you can mix and match resorts. A 2.25% service charge applies if you pay using a credit card. Alternately, contact **Cubanacán UK,** Skylines, Unit 49, Limeharbour, Docklands, London E14 9TS, tel. (0171) 537-7909.

Regent Holidays, 15 John St., Bristol BS1 2HR, tel. 0272-211711, fax 0272-254866, specializes in customizing tours for independent travelers. It also has a two-week package tour with one week each in Havana and Varadero (from £165/170 s/d low season, £235/240 high season). **VE Tours** has two-week packages from £529, including roundtrip flights from Stansted, 37-39 Great Marlborough St., London W1V 1HA, tel. (0171) 437-7534.

Journey Latin America, 14-16 Devonshire Rd., London W4 2HD, tel. (0181) 747-3108, fax (0181) 742-1312, offers a nine-day "Cuban Discovery" every Saturday using Iberia from Heathrow (from £499, including airfare) and a two-week "Cubana Libre" trip departing fortnightly from Stansted (from £477). It also offers a 15-day "Gaviota" program taking in Havana, Santiago de Cuba, Cienfuegos, Trinidad, and Varadero (from £965), plus two-week fly-drive packages.

Cuba trips are also a specialty of **Travel-Coast,** 26 Crown Rd., Twickenham TW1 3EE, tel. (181) 891-2222, fax (181) 892-9588; **Latin American Travel,** 7 Buckingham Gate, London SW1E 6JX, tel. (171) 630-0070, fax (171) 630-9900; the **Latin American Travel Centre,** 51 High St., Reigate, Surrey RH2 9RT, tel./fax 01737-222250; and **Travel South America,** The White House, Chantry Lane, Bishopthorpe, York YO2 1QF, tel. 01904-70443, fax 01904-704147. Other companies offering tours to Cuba include **Ashley Holidays,** 35 Wood Lane, Wickersley, Rotherham, S Yorks S66 0JT, tel. 0709-543626; **Progressive Travel,** 12 Porchester Place, Marble Arch, London W2 2BS, tel. (171) 262-1676; **Union Travel,** tel. (171) 493-4343; **Page & Moy,** tel. 0533-542000; **South American Experience,** 47 Cuaston St, London SW1 4AT, tel. (171) 379-0344; **Island Holidays,** tel. 0764-70107; and **Mazorca,** Hackney Business Centre, Studio 8, 277 Mare St., London E8 1EB, tel. (181) 533-5432.

Conventional Tours from Other Countries
(See the information on charter airlines this section for companies offering tour packages from Canada, Mexico, and other destinations.) In Germany, contact **Pegasus Havanna** (it also has an office in Havana at Avenida 7, Calle 44, tel. 33-1903, fax 33-1904). In Switzerland, try **Jelmoli Reisen,** tel. (1) 211-1357, and in France, **Havanatur,** tel. (1) 4742-5858.

Excursions from Jamaica are very popular with US citizens. **Caribic Vacations,** 69 Gloucester Ave., Montego Bay, tel. (809) 979-0322, fax (809) 979-3421, offers two-, five-, and seven-night packages with guided city tours plus a choice of hotels in either Havana or Varadero. Packages begin at US$289. **InterCaribe,** 11½ Ardenne Rd., Kingston 10, tel. (809) 978-2150, fax (809) 978-2686, offers three- and seven-night packages to Santiago de Cuba and Havana from Kingston for as little as US$239. **Sunholiday,** P.O. Box 531, Montego Bay, St. James, Jamaica, tel. (809) 952-5629, fax (809) 979-0725, in the US tel. (800) 433-2920, has "Cuba for a Day" excursions for US$179, including airfare and sightseeing, plus a "Weekend in Havana" for US$269.

HEALTH TOURISM

The need for foreign currency has resulted in some health-care resources being diverted to "health tourism" (originally developed for an Eastern bloc clientele), where foreign patients come to Cuba for advanced treatment.

Cuba offers everything from spas and health resorts offering "stress breaks" to advanced treatments such as eye, open-heart, and plastic surgery. It is acknowledged as a world leader in orthopedics, and the **Frank País Orthopedic Hospital** recently had to double the capacity of its 40-bed ward for foreigners to meet demand. Cuba has even established the **International Placental Histotherapy Center** for treating vitiligo. And the **International Neurological Restoration Center** is claimed to be the only center in the world devoted entirely to the field of "neuro-restoration" (it offers treatments for Parkinson's disease, Alzheimer's disease, multiple sclerosis, epilepsy, etc.).

Cuba's "sun and surgery" program is run by **Servimed,** Calle 18 #4304 e/ 43 y 47, Playa, Habana, tel. 33-2658 or 33-2023, fax 33-2948 or 33-1630, a division of Cubanacán.

Sanatoriums

Treatment for stress, asthma, hypertension, obesity, and alcohol control are provided at Basic Self-Curative Training Centers at **Casa del Valle,** in the Yumurí Valley, and the **Pan-American Village,** just east of Havana. Both specialize in personalized 7-, 14-, and 21-day programs designed specifically for each patient's needs. The teams are made up of a general medicine specialist, a psychologist, therapist, and nurses and technicians. Everything from tai-chi and yoga to stress workshops, acupuncture, and respiratory exercises are incorporated.

Excursions to sites of scenic and natural beauty are usually part of the program.

Spas

Cuba has many mineral and medicinal hot springs, as well as brines and muds that have been used for centuries for their curative effects. Existing facilities—many of which have become run down in recent years—were inspired by Cuba's flirtation with the Soviet Union.

The largest facility is at **Topes de Collantes,** in the Sierra del Escambray. **Spa San Vicente,** near Viñales, was being remodeled in 1996 to offer physiotherapy, massage, acupuncture, medicinal mud therapy, etc. The sulfurous waters here average 31° C and are claimed to have curative properties for respiratory, gastrointestinal, and dermatological problems. **Spa Elguea,** outside Corralillo near Cárdenas, is renowned for its treatment for rheumatism. It, too, is being remodeled. Both spa hotels are operated by **Horizontes,** Calle 23 #156, e/ N y O, Vedado, Havana, tel. 33-4142, fax 33-3161.

San Diego de los Baños, in Pinar del Río, was recently remodeled, with treatments offered at the charming Mirador Hotel.

Organized Tours

Weeklong study programs are offered monthly by **Wings of the World,** 1200 William St. #706, Buffalo, NY 14240, tel. (800) 465-8687, with a focus on exploring Cuba's medical sciences and facilities.

Ecotours

Cuba has clichéd beaches, but it also has bush. Ecotourism has come late to the Caribbean, and not least to Cuba, which depends heavily on resort-based, sun-seeking tourists. Despite its vast acreage in national parks and the diversity of its landscapes, Cuba's ecotourism potential remains virtually untapped. Cuba has very few naturalist guides. And so-called "eco-lodges" are mostly merely lodges set in wilderness areas. But a beginning has been made, such as at the stunning **Moka Eco-Hotel** in Pinar del Río province. Ecotourism is beginning to rise on the neap of an eco-sensitive tide.

A newly formed entity, **Cubamar,** Hotel Plaza, 5th Floor, Habana Vieja, tel. 33-8317, is focusing on developing camping and ecotourism. **Alcona S.A.,** Calle 42 #514, esq. Avenida 7, Playa, Habana, tel. 22-2526, fax 33-1531, has a series of weeklong eco-tour packages to the Cayos de San Felipe; nature reserves in the Sierra del Rosarios mountains; Los Indios Nature Reserve on Isla de la Juventud; Desembarco del Granma National Park; and Pico Turquino National Park.

Wings of the World, 1200 William St. #706, Buffalo, NY 14240, tel. (800) 465-8687, offers an 11-day eco-trip, "From Mountains to Forest." Departures are offered the third Sunday of each month (US$2,695). The tour visits the Sierra de Nipe mountains, Pinares de Mayarí, Baconao Biosphere Reserve, Zapata, Viñales, and Las Terrazas in Pinar del Río. **Global Exchange,**

HERMANA Á HERMANA/ SISTER TO SISTER

Hermana á Hermana/Sister to Sister, 2017 Mission St. #303, San Francisco, CA 94110, tel. (415) 255-7296, fax (415) 255-7498, e-mail: globalexch@igc.apc.org, is a hemispheric initiative to create "peaceful and just relations between the US and Cuba." The project was initiated in 1996 by a coalition of Canadian, Mexican, and Caribbean women's groups and promotes cultural, professional, religious, and education exchanges between US, Latin American, Caribbean, and Cuban women. It also leads women's delegations to Cuba.

2017 Mission St. #303, San Francisco, CA 94110, tel. (415) 255-7296 or (800) 497-1994, e-mail globalexch@igc.org., offers study tours that provide insights into Cuba's sustainable development projects. The trips focus on sustainable agriculture, traditional medicines, and renewable energy.

Delta Cuba Hotels & Resorts, 350 Bloor St. East #300, Toronto, Ontario M4W 1H4, tel. (416) 926-7800 or (800) 268-1133, fax (416) 926-7846; in Cuba, Calle 248 y Avenida 5, Santa Fe, Havana, tel. 33-6336, offers an all-inclusive seven-day eco-tour utilizing four eco-lodges in Oriente. Highlights include a jeep ride into the Sierra Maestra and Sierra de Nipe for hiking and horseback riding.

Heritage and Culture Tours

Every moment in Cuba is a fascinating study in cultural anthopology. Nonetheless, you can make a more serious study of things on numerous organized tours.

In Cuba, **Paradiso: Promotora de Viajes Culturales,** Calle 19 #560, esq. C, Vedado, Havana, tel. 32-6928, fax 33-3921, arranges visits and participation in cultural courses and programs, such as children's book publishing (five days, US$300) at the Instituto Cubano del Libro, theater criticism in Cuba (five days, US$60), and contemporary visual art (seven days, US$200). Its catalog of events and festivals for 1995 included classes and studies in ballet and modern dance, the International Benny Moré Festival, the International Hemingway Colloquium, and the Artisans' Fair.

The **Cuba Information Project,** 198 Broadway, Suite 800, New York, NY 10038, tel. (212) 227-3422, fax (212) 227-4859, offers 10-day study tours such as health care in Cuba, the Spanish legacy in Trinidad and Sancti Spíritus, and childcare in rural Cuba (US$1,200). They also offer language study courses.

Global Exchange, 2017 Mission St. #303, San Francisco, CA 94110, tel. (415) 255-7296 or (800) 497-1994, e-mail globalexch@igc.org, sponsors study tours to Cuba focusing on different aspects of Cuban life, including health care, art, culture and education, religion, agriculture and ecology, Afro-Cuban culture, women's issues, and music and dance. Most trips are 10 days long and cost an average of

ORGANIZATIONS TO KNOW

IN THE US

The **National Network on Cuba** is an umbrella organization with over 70 member groups, including the following.

All People's Congress
2489 Mission St., No. 28, San Francisco, CA 94110
tel. (415) 821-6545
Organization works to foster people-to-people ties between US citizens and the people of Cuba through alternative trade.

Association for Free Trade With Cuba
Dunn's Bldg., 725 Washington St., Suite 300, Oakland, CA 94607
tel. (510) 268-8427, fax (510) 839-9857, e-mail viasco@acl.com
This group is dedicated to lifting the US embargo against Cuba and has formed a lobbying body to represent business interests that want to see a normalization of relations.

Center for Cuban Studies
124 W. 23rd St., New York, NY 10011
tel. (212) 242-0559, fax (212) 242-1937
Supports educational forums on Cuba, publishes the splendid quarterly *Cuba Update,* organizes study tours, and distributes a wide range of books and videos on Cuba. It also has an art gallery and the largest research library on Cuba in North America.

The Cuba Group
501 Brickell Key Dr., Suite 200, Miami, FL 33131
tel. (305) 381-8685, fax (305) 372-1089
A consulting and advisory firm providing information on the Cuban business, trade, and investment environment. It publishes a monthly newsletter, *The Cuba Report.*

Cuba Information Project
198 Broadway #800, New York, NY 10038
or One Union Square West #211, New York, NY 10003
tel. (212) 366-6703, fax (212) 227-4859
Provides information on legislation and lobbying and publishes the quarterly *Cuba Action.* Organizes monthly study tours on a variety of subjects and runs the **US+Cuba Medical Project,** which ships humanitarian aid to Cuba.

Cuba Policy Project
Johns Hopkins University, Cuban Studies Program, 1740 Massachusetts Ave. NW, Washington, D.C. 20036
tel. (202) 663-5732
Publishes the monthly *Cubainfo* newsletter, conducts research on Cuba, and operates academic exchanges with Cuba.

Cuban American Alliance Education Fund
P.O. Box 491, Hayward, CA 94543
tel./fax (510) 538-9694, e-mail delfern@igc.apc.org
Represents moderate Cuban-Americans who wish for dialogue with Cuba. In particular, it sponsors efforts at family reunification and an end to travel restrictions imposed by Washington on Cuban-Americans wishing to visit Cuba. It also has a program to assist in the physical rehabilitation needs of children at the Julito Díaz Hospital (donations of medicines and medical equipment are needed).

(continues on next page)

ORGANIZATIONS TO KNOW
(continued)

Cuban American Committee
1601 Connecticut Ave. NW, Washington, D.C. 20009
tel. (202) 667-6367
Works with the Cuban-American community and media to normalize relations.

Cuban American Women of the United States
1130 Stanford Ave., Garden Grove, CA 92642
tel. (310) 634-6189, fax (310) 607-0690
Lobbies to exclude medicines and medical equipment from the US embargo. It provides humanitarian, apolitical assistance and supposed bicultural education, including through travel to Cuba.

Global Exchange
2017 Mission St. #303, San Francisco, CA 94110
tel. (415) 255-7296, fax (415) 255-7498
Organizes monthly study tours to Cuba on an eclectic range of themes and also produces educational literature. Global Exchange has launched a Campaign to End the Cold War Against Cuba, designed to lift the blockade and normalize relations with the country (the campaign involves public education, legislative pressure, exchanges, and material aid in the form of medicine), and the Campaign to Exempt Food and Medicines from the Embargo. Other Cuba-related projects include **Soy Cubano!** and **Hermana á Hermana.** Has also sponsored "Freedom to Travel Challenge" tours for those who want to challenge the legality of US travel restrictions.

IFCO/Pastors for Peace
402 West 145th St., New York, NY 10031
tel. (212) 926-5757, fax (212) 926-5842
Organizes the US-Friendshipment Caravans to Cuba, challenging the embargo by traveling with vehicles filled with donations of humanitarian aid. Also has study tours and organizes work brigades to assist in community projects in Cuba.

International Peace Walk
4521 Campus Drive #211, Irvine, CA 92715
tel./fax (714) 856-0200
Organizes "walks" in Cuba dedicated to sponsoring communication, understanding, and peace by "bringing down the walls of righteousness and ignorance that divide the human family."

National "Hands Off" Cuba Coalition
P.O. Box 21560, Washington, DC 20009
tel. (202) 234-2000; New York affiliate, tel. (212) 601-4751
Ad hoc coalition of organizations opposing US policy toward Cuba. The lobbying and educational organization publishes the newsletter *¡Baragua!* and sends medicines.

Peace for Cuba Task Force
P.O. Box 450, Santa Clara, CA 95052
tel. (408) 243-4359, fax (408) 243-1229, e-mail jreardon@igc.apc.org or dwald@igc.apc.org
Devoted to improving relations with Cuba. It sponsors speaking forums and accepts donations of medicines, foodstuffs, and educational materials for the US-Cuba Friendshipment Caravans. It also runs Project INFOMED to supply desperately needed computers to medical centers in Cuba. Donations of computers and peripherals are requested.

US-Cuba Medical Project
One Union Square West #211, New York, NY 10003
tel. (212) 227-5270, fax (212) 227-4859
Provides medical and humanitarian aid to Cuba, working through the Cuban Red Cross. It has accom-

plished noteworthy relief following natural disasters such as Hurricane Lili (October 1996). Its directors include actor/singer Harry Belafonte and novelist Alice Walker.

US-Cuba Trade and Economic Council
30 Rockefeller Plaza, New York, NY 10112
tel. (212) 246-1444, fax (212) 246-2345, e-mail uscubatr@ios.com
A nonpartisan business organization that publishes the newsletter *Economic Eye on Cuba.* It claims not "to take positions with respect to US-Republic of Cuba political relations," but it favors trade.

Va por Cuba
c/o Peter Gellert, Xola 181 piso 4, Colonia Alamos, 03400 Mexico
tel./fax 52-5-782-2564
Ships gasoline to Cuba to ease the transport crisis. Contributions are accepted by bank transfer.

Venceremos Brigade
P.O. Box 7071, Oakland, CA 94601
tel. (510) 267-0606
National solidarity organization, organizes educational and work trips to Cuba.

IN THE UNITED KINGDOM

Cuban Solidarity Campaign
CSC, The Red Rose Club, 129 Seven Sisters Rd., London N7 7QG
tel. (171) 263-6452
Works to provide information and resources to Cuba and works for rational and just relations. Membership ranges from £4 to £50, depending on your status.

Club Clandestino
11 Kensington High St., London
Meets in Bar Cuba the first Sunday of every month.

Club Cubana
The Cat House, Brown St., Glasgow
Hosts a Cuba Solidarity Campaign meeting first Friday of the month.

UK Cuba Friendship Association
3 Bridge Cottages, Downside Road, Cobham, Surrey KT11 3PL
tel. (0932) 864149

IN EUROPE

Cuba Sí France
20 rue Denis Papin, 94200 Ivry-Sur-Seine, France
tel. (1) 451-51143
This solidarity organization arranges for shipment of hospital beds and medicines.

AND ON THE RIGHT . . .

Cuban American National Foundation
1000 Thomas Jefferson St., Suite 505, Washington, DC 20007
tel. (202) 265-2822
An ultra-conservative lobbying group dedicated to the overthrow of Fidel Castro and replacement by a self-appointed government formed of CANF leaders, many with ties to the Batista regime.

Movement for an Independent and Democratic Cuba
10020 S.W. 37th Terrace, Miami, FL 33165
tel. (305) 551-8484, fax (305) 599-9365
This lobby group operates the Institute for Economic Development of Cuba.

US$1,300, including roundtrip airfare from Mexico or the Bahamas. Occasionally it offers unusual trips such as "Paths to Freedom," a two-week tour retracing the path that Che Guevera, Fidel Castro, and other young rebels made during their guerrilla war in the Sierra Maestra Mountains. The organization also collects medical supplies and donations for distribution to Cuba's organization of disabled people, the America Arias Maternity Hospital, and the William Soler Children's Hospital. And it was the spearhead of the Freedom to Travel Campaign, an effort to assert US citizens' constitutional rights to travel to Cuba and bring an end to restrictions.

The **Center for Cuban Studies,** 124 West 23rd St., New York, NY 10011, tel. (212) 242-0559, fax (212) 242-1937, has fact-finding tours on a monthly basis for members of the center (US$800). The weeklong trips focus on education and health care, urban issues, welfare, etc., and include meetings with experts. It also offers frequent "seminar tours" for nonmembers on a wide variety of themes. Recent offerings have included Cuban art, the public health system, "Coping With the Crisis," "Caribbean Cultural Festival," African roots of Cuba Culture, sexual politics in Cuba, architecture and preservation, and attendance at the Havana Film Festival. Most trips are a week to 10 days in duration and cost from US$900 to US$1,400, including roundtrip airfare from Miami or Nassau.

Wings of the World, 1200 William St. #706, Buffalo, NY 14240-0706; or 1636 3rd Ave. #232, New York, NY 10128, tel. (800) 465-8687, fax (416) 486-4001, actively—and legally—promotes its Cuban "cultural adventures" to all US citizens. Because the company's tours are "fully hosted and totally prepaid," including personal amenities, participants ostensibly "neither exchange nor spend money while in Cuba." Available are 10- and 12-day tours of Cuba, departing from Nassau (Bahamas) or Cancún (Mexico). The tours include Havana, two days each in Varadero and Santiago de Cuba, plus a day in the Cienfuegos mountains. Trips start at US$2,495, excluding airfare. The company also offers a wide range of special tours, including a one-week "Golf Tournament in Havana" tour in late October, plus a Hemingway tour to coincide with the annual Hem-

ingway Colloquium in Havana. The company claims that "not one of our American travelers has had any problems with the State Department" as the company "abides by all the legal requirements."

Cabas Associates, 4915 Broadway, Suite 41, New York, NY 10034, tel. (319) 354-3189 or (800) 446-1234, fax (319) 337-2045, offers study tours of contemporary Cuban society. The one-week itinerary includes visits to Havana, Matanzas, Varadero, and Trinidad (from US$895).

Queers for Cuba, 3543 18th St. #33, San Francisco, CA 94110, tel. (415) 995-4678, operates an annual "solidarity and education delegation" to Cuba each December. The trip focuses on expanding understanding and expressing solidarity with Cuba's gay and lesbian population.

Expediciones de la Última Frontera, 4823 White Rock Circle, Suite H, Boulder, CO 80301-3260, tel. (303) 530-9275, fax (303) 530-9275, offers packages for cigar lovers and to sports-related events such as the Ernest Hemingway International Sports Classic 10K race and the Ernest Hemingway Sportfishing Tournament.

Jewish Heritage Tours

The **Cuban-Jewish Aid Society,** P.O. Box 2101, Mill Valley, CA 94942, tel. (415) 388-2418, fax (415) 550-8009; or 44 Mercury Ave., Colonia, NJ 07067, tel. (908) 499-9132, offers annual trips. Participants engage with Cuban Jews and help dispense medicines and other items in regional cities. Eight-day programs cost US$1,500, including airfare from Nassau or Cancún.

Caribbean Music & Dance Programs (see "Music and Dance Tours," below, for address and contact numbers) has an annual weeklong trip—"Next Year in Havana"—to celebrate Passover with Cuban Jews each March/April (US$1,500 including roundtrip airfare from Nassau or Cancún). The **Center for Cuban Studies,** 124 West 23rd St., New York, NY 10011, tel. (212) 242-0559, fax (212) 242-1937, also offers an annual weeklong Jewish heritage tour in January (US$1,450), as does **Wings of the World,** 1200 William St. #706, Buffalo, NY 14240, tel. (800) 465-8687, which also has a panoply of Cuban "cultural adventures" open to all US citizens.

Music and Dance Tours

Cuba's performing arts are unrivaled within the Caribbean, and it is difficult to imagine a more vital country in which to enjoy music and dance. Consider timing your visit for **Carnaval** or one of the major folkloric and traditional music festivals held throughout the island. In December 1994, Nidia Berengeuer, director of the **Academia de Arte de Cuba** initiated an academic program to coordinate international courses in the country.

The **Conjunto Folclórico Nacional** (National Folklore Dance Group) and **Danza Contemporánea de Cuba** offer twice-yearly, two-week courses in Afro-Cuban music and dance (contact **ARTEX,** Avenida 5ta #8010 esq. 82, Miramar, Havana, tel. 33-2276 or fax 33-2033). ARTEX also sponsors other courses in the arts and literature, including seminars in *cutumba* (Franco-Haitian-Cuban song and dance) plus courses at the Cuban School of Ballet (La Escuela Cubana de Ballet), the Instituto Superior de Arte, and the National School of Art (Centro Nacional de Escuelas de Arte).

Caribbean Music and Dance Progams, 1611 Telegraph Ave., Suite 808, Oakland, CA 94612, tel. (510) 444-7173, fax (510) 444-5412, e-mail caribmusic@igc.apc.org, or http://www.arana.com /caribmusic, offers a variety of study courses in Cuba. Each February, the organization offers a two-week Cuban Popular Music & Dance Workshop in association with the Havana Jazz Festival (a one-week trip to the jazz festival costs US$1,100, including seminars—US$800 outside the US). Courses are taught at the prestigious Escuela Nacional de Arte (ENA). The dance workshop—taught at the Escuela de la Música, 13013 Calle 9 y 149, Miramar, Havana—is open to everyone from beginners to professionals and includes lively tuition in *danzón, son,* cha-cha-chá, mambo, rumba, salsa, *larueda,* and the hip-swiveling *despolote.* Many of Cuba's leading musicians teach the music workshop, with instruction in percussion, drumset, piano, bass, guitar, trumpet, trombone, flute, saxophone, violin, and vocals. Chucho Valdes and Irakere, Juan Formell and Los Van Van, Changuito, and legendary flautist Richard Esqúes are among the faculty who provide one-on-one tuition. Imagine learning guitar from Eric Clapton and you have the idea. The cost is US$1,650 (US$1,350 from outside the US).

The same organization also offers a workshop in Afro-Cuban folkloric music and dance hosted by the legendary groups Los Muñequitos and Grupo AfroCuba, in Matanzas (US$1,350, US$1,100 joining in Havana). You can also explore the roots of *son* in Oriente province on a two-week tour in mid-summer (US$1,550, US$1,250 joining in Santiago de Cuba). Santiago is also the venue for a "Cuban & Haitian Folkloric Dance & Music Workshop" and one-week packages to the "Festival of Fire" carnival (US$1,100, US$800 joining in Santiago). All prices include airfare from Nassau or Cancún.

The **Center for Cuban Studies,** 124 West 23rd St., New York, NY 10011, tel. (212) 242-0559, fax (212) 242-1937, also has a one-week seminar on Cuban music in February in collaboration with the Cuban Music Institute and Music Museum (US$1,250, including airfare). **Wings of the World Travel,** 1200 William St. #706, Buffalo, NY 14240, tel. (800) 465-8687, offers an annual weeklong tour (US$2,195) to the Havana Jazz Festival that includes roundtrip flights from Nassau (Bahamas), two jazz workshops, reserved seating at jazz concerts, plus sightseeing. US citizens can *legally* join the tours.

In the UK, **Festival Tours International,** 96 Providence Lane, Long Ashton, Bristol BS18 9DN, tel./fax 01275-392953, offers packages to Carnaval and the Havana Jazz and Film Festivals. Also contact the **Britain-Cuba Dance Student Exchange,** Weekends Arts College, Interchange Studios, Dalby St., London NW5 3NQ. Zurich-based **Danzamania** (in Havana, tel. 32-1476, fax 33-3722) offers study tours in music and dance in Cuba.

Veterans Tours

Yes, believe it or not, even US veterans are catered to! The **Vietnam Veterans of America Foundation,** c/o Jim Long, VVNA, 2327 31st Ave., San Francisco, CA 94116, tel. (415) 780-5156 or (415) 665-2670, or (800) 800-4NET, fax (415) 780-5033, e-mail jimlong@sf.com, offers an annual trip to Cuba for US veterans. The trips depart in early November and are timed to celebrate Veterans Day in the company of Cuban *combatientes* and military veterans. Past programs have included visits to Guantánamo and the Bay of Pigs; military ceremonies honoring the war dead; plus meetings with Cuban military figures, such as General Tamayo, who once went into space with Soviet cosmonauts. In 1995, trip members were able to look down upon the US naval base at Guantánamo from a special arena with restaurant reserved for VIPs.

The trips feature meetings with Cuban veterans of the Spanish Civil War, the Revolutionary war, the Bay of Pigs, and the Angolan, Ethiopian, and Nicaraguan conflicts, as well as meetings with members of **Instituto Cubana Amistad con los Pueblos,** a veterans organization that performs social work on behalf of incapacitated members of Cuban society. The trips are open to veterans and veterans' groups, regardless of political leanings. They are operated through a provision in US legislation that permits such tours to be hosted by the Cuban government.

Volunteer Programs

The **American Friends Service Committee,** Human Resource, 1501 Cherry St., Philadelphia, PA 19102, tel. (215) 241-7000, is a Quaker organization which in the past has offered youth from the US and other countries a chance to engage with Cuban youth on three-week summer programs. The program was not offered in 1995 and 1996 but may be resurrected. The program involves summer work camps and conferences in which Christians and communists come together. Participants should be between 18 and 28 years old and fluent in Spanish.

International Peace Walk, 4521 Campus Drive, #211, Irvine, CA 92715, tel. (714) 856-0200, fax (714) 856-0200, e-mail om@igc.org, a group founded to help bring peace between the US and USSR, may offer 12-day "peace walks" in Cuba featuring study programs, working alongside Cubans, news-gathering, delivering humanitarian aid, etc. The 1994 trip (US$1,400, including airfare from Mexico) was canceled by the Cubans.

Pastors for Peace-IFCO, tel. (612) 378-0062, organizes regular **US-Cuba Friendshipment Caravans,** in which participants openly defy the embargo and assist in delivering medicines and aid to Cuba *without* a license. The caravans travel through the US collecting donations for transhipment. Since the first caravan, in 1992, more than 1,000 volunteers have delivered over 500 tons of aid.

VOLUNTEERING FOR WORK IN CUBA

To help the ailing economy, Cuba welcomes volunteer teams to work for 20-day stints in the countryside. The work is hard—mostly it consists of cutting sugar cane. Contact the Havana-based **Cuban Institute of Friendship with the Peoples** (Instituto Cubano de Amistad con los Pueblo), ICAP, Calle 17 #301 e/ H y L, Vedado, Habana, Cuba, tel.´ (537) 32-8017.

In the UK: The **Cuban Solidarity Campaign,** The Red Rose Club, 129 Seven Sisters Road, London N7 7QG, tel. (171) 263-6452, sends international work brigades to help in the sugar harvest. In 1996, three-week trips cost £600, including travel, meals, accommodation, and visa.

In the USA: **Venceremos Brigade,** P.O. Box 7071, Oakland, CA 94601, tel. (510) 267-0606, organizes work trips to Cuba, as does the **Brigada Antonio Maceo,** P.O. Box 248829, Miami, FL 33124, a Cuban-American organization.

Warning: US law prohibits US citizens from receiving remuneration for work in Cuba. You are permitted to work in Cuba if fully hosted.

Similar tours are offered by **Volunteers for Peace,** c/o International Work Camp, 43 Tiffany Rd., Belmont, VT 05730, tel. (802) 259-2759, fax (802) 259-2922. Participants from throughout the world work alongside Cubans to assist with community development. The three-week trips—US$1,200 (US$850 for non-US citizens, meeting in Havana)—are hosted by the Cuban Institute for Friendship with the People (ICAP) but coordinated by people in local communities.

England's **Cuban Solidarity Campaign,** 44 Morat St., London SW9 ORR, tel. (171) 820-9976, offers work brigades, including visits to hospitals and schools. Participants work in construction and agriculture. The organization also publishes the *CubaSí* newsletter. Subscriptions cost £4 (unwaged), £12 (waged), or £15-50 (organizations).

Work and Study Exchanges

US citizens are prohibited by US law from working in Cuba in any capacity. However, in October

INTERNATIONAL TOUR COMPANIES

The following companies offer tours to Cuba.

ARGENTINA

Guamatur: Paraguay #610, Buenos Aires, tel. 312-0503, fax 311-0509.
Holland Travel: Corrientes #753, Buenos Aires, tel. 322-4725, fax (541) 311-05079.

AUSTRIA

Pegasus: Seilergasse 16, 1010 Vienna, tel. 515450.

BAHAMAS

Havanatur Nassau: West Hill St., P.O. Box 10246, Nassau, tel. 322-2796, fax 328-7980.

BELGIUM

Havanatour Benelux: Rue van Arteveldestraat 46, 1000 Brussels, tel. 250-20700, fax 250-23475.

BRAZIL

Cubanacán do Brasil: Edifico Italia 21 Andar, Conjuto 212-A, São Paulo, tel. (11) 2596712.

CANADA

Cubanacán Tours: 1255 Université, Suite 211, Montroal, Quebec H3B 3B2, tel. 861-4444.
Cubanacán Canada International: 372 Bay St., Suite 406, Toronto, tel. (416) 601-0343, fax (416) 601-0346.
Hola Sun Holidays: 146 W. Beaver Creek Rd., Richmond Hill, Ontario L4B 1C2, tel. 882-9445, fax 882-5184.
Magna Tours: 61 Alness St., Suite 203, Downview, Toronto, Ontario M3J 2H2, tel. (416) 665-7330, fax (416) 665-8448.

CHILE

Guamatur Chile: Moneda 812 OF 1101, Santiago, tel. 383725.

COLOMBIA

Caribe Representaciones: Calle 19 #4-74, 2101 Bogotá, tel. 284-0162, fax 286-6427.

COSTA RICA

Tikal Tours Apdo. 6398, San José 1000, tel. (506) 223-2811, fax (506) 223-1916

DOMINICAN REPUBLIC

Emely Tours: Calle San Rco. de Macoris #58, Santo Domingo, tel. (809) 687-7114.

IRELAND

Cubatravel: 11 S. Anne St., Dublin 2, tel. (01) 713422.

FRANCE

Havanatur: 24 Rue Quatre, Septembre 75002, Paris, tel. (1) 47-42-5858, fax (1) 42-65-1801

GERMANY

Air Conti: Neuhauser Str 34, D-8000 Munich, tel. 089-55179, fax 089-55179362
Aquarius: Oberanger 36, D-8000 Munich, tel. 89-269065, fax 49-69552526.
Avione: Sternwaldstrasse 26, postach 1430, D-7800 Frieburg, tel. 0761-31393.
Caribbean Tours: Hamburger Strasse 131/8 O.G. 200, Hamburg 76, tel. 0401-29194
Intratours: Faszinnationsreisen GMBH, Eiserne Hand no. 19, Frankfurt, tel. 597-0011.
IT Reisen: Habsburgerring 818-20, 500 Koln 1, tel. 221-256572, fax 49-221-253220.
Nautilus Tours: Feilitzcstrasse 24-D-8000, Munich 40, tel. (089) 333091.

(continues on next page)

INTERNATIONAL TOUR COMPANIES

(continued)

Tropicana Touristik: Berlinerstrasse 161/100, Berlin 31, tel. (030) 8537041, fax 8534070.
TTW: Grosse Spillingsgasse 15, 6000 Frankfurt M60, tel. 69-468091, fax 49-69-454091.
Wessel Tours: Walter Kolb Strasse 9/11, D-6000 Frankfurt M70, tel. 49-696-22972, fax 49-69-628042.

GUATEMALA

Viajes Espacio: Edif. El Triángulo, Oficina A-X, 7ma Avenida 6-53, Zona 4, Guatemala, tel. 316722.

ITALY

Cubanacán Italia: Via Fabio Filzi, 33, 20124, Milano, tel. (39-2) 6671-1219, fax (39-2) 6671-0839)
Havanatur Italia: tel. (3911) 669-0632, fax (3911) 650-4608

JAMAICA

Caribic Vacations: 69 Gloucester Ave., Montego Bay, tel. (809) 952-5013, fax (809) 952-0981
InterCaribe: 11^{1}/2 Ardenne Rd., Kingston 10, tel. (809) 929-7865, fax (809) 926-6607

JAPAN

Kyoei Havanatur: Sanno Grand Bldg., 14-2-2 Chome, Nagata-Cho, Chiyoda-ku, Tokyo, tel. (03) 3581-7451, fax (03) 3581-4725.

MEXICO

Cubanatours: Baja California 255, Edif. B, Despacho 103 Colonia, Hipódromo Condesa, Mexico D.F., tel. 574-4921.
Havanatur Mérida: Calle 60 #448 e/ 49 y 51, Dpto. 113, Col Centro, Mérida.
Taino Tours: tel. 52-5-559-3907, fax 52-5-559-3951
Viajes Divermex: Av. Coba #5, Centro Comercial Plaza América, Local B-6 Cancún, Quintana Roo, tel. 52-988-75487
Viñales Tours: Oaxaca 80, Colonia Roma, México D.F., tel. 208-9900.
Viñales Tours: Av. López Mateos Nte. 1038-9, Plaza Florencia CP 44680, Guadalajara, tel. 419347.

NETHERLANDS

Cubanacán International BV: Visseringlaa 20 2288, ER Rijswijk, Netherlands, tel. (31-70) 390-5152, fax (31-70) 319-3452.

NICARAGUA

Serviajes: Km. 4, Carretera Masay, Apto. 2910, Managua, tel. 671894, fax 670387.

PANAMA

Atlantis Tours: Edif. Malina, Local No. 3, P. Baja, Ap. Postal 55-2173, Paitilla, tel. (507) 64-4466, fax (507) 64-8370.
Guamatour: Centro Comercial, Bal-Harbour, Punta Paitilla, tel. 69-5726.

PORTUGAL

Prestige: R. Pascoal de Melo, 133-1° esq., tel. (3) 525513, fax (3) 540961.

PUERTO RICO

Viajes Antillas: Arzuaga #201, Río Piedra, tel. (809) 763-7280.

RUSSIA

Mar Cuba: Petrovka 15 #22, 103031 Moscú, tel. (095) 208-1033, fax (095) 921-7698.

SPAIN

Guama S.A.: Paseo de la Habana 28, Primero Izquierda, Madrid 28036, tel. 4-11-20-48, fax 4-11-34-47.

SWITZERLAND

Baumeler Reisen: Zinggentorstrasse 1, Postfach CH-6002, Luzern, tel. (041) 509900.
Imholz-Jelmoli: Birmensdorferstrasse 108, Postfach, CH-8036, Zürich, tel. (01) 462-6240.

VENEZUELA

Ideal Tours: Centro Capriles P.V., Locales 10 y 11, Plaza Venezuela, Caraca 1050, tel. 781-9101.

1995, President Clinton expanded the categories of individuals allowed to visit Cuba by creating a category for academic exchange. The law allows US undergraduates to enroll in Cuban universities and US universities to establish study programs in Cuba. Check the latest situation, as this may have been nixed by passage of the Helms-Burton legislation.

Wayne Smith, former chief of the US Interests Section In Havana (and an outspoken critic of US policy toward Cuba), heads the **Cuba Exchange Program** offered through the School of Advanced International Studies at Johns Hopkins University, 1740 Massachusetts Ave. N.W., Washington, D.C. 20036, tel. (202) 663-5732,

PASTORS FOR PEACE

The Minneapolis-based Pastors for Peace delivers humanitarian aid to Cuba through the annual **US-Cuban Friendshipment Caravan.** The Caravan moves through, and gathers aid in, 150 cities from the West Coast to Washington D.C., before traveling to Canada or Mexico, where the aid is shipped to Cuba.

Pastors for Peace also supports community development projects in Cuba through the Martin Luther King Memorial Center in Havana.

Send donations to Pastors for Peace, 620 West 28th St, Minneapolis, MN 55408, tel. (612) 670-7121 or (612) 378-0062, fax (612) 870-7109 or (612) 378-0134, e-mail p4p@igc.apc.org; or c/o Inter-Religious Foundation for Community Organization, tel. (212) 926-5757, fax (212) 926-5842.

The organization also operates Work Brigades in which volunteers work to help construct houses. The weeklong trips cost US$850, including roundtrip airfare from Cancún. Research trips are also offered in which participants live in a working-class *barrio* in Havana as fully hosted guests (US$900).

fax (202) 663-5737. Smith escorts scholars on learning programs. Also try **CamBas Association,** tel. (319) 354-3189, fax (319) 338-3320, associated with the University of Iowa. Tulane University and Bates College in Maine also sponsor programs to Cuba—the perfect liberal arts laboratory.

Mercadu S.A., Calle 13 #951, Vedado, Havana, tel. 33-3893, fax 33-3028, arranges study visits for foreigners at centers of higher learning throughout Cuba and spanning a wide range of academic subjects. It also arranges working holidays and runs a summer school at the Universities of Havana, Matanzas, and Pinar del Río, with over 100 courses listed in its catalog.

If you're interested in the arts, consider one of the courses arranged by the Instituto Superior de Arte's **Oficina de Relaciones Internacionales,** Calle 120 #11110, Playa, Havana, tel. 21-6075, fax 33-6633, e-mail isa@reduniv.edu.cu, whose menu spans the gamut of the art world. Besides short-term courses, it also accepts foreigners for full-year study beginning in September (from US$2,000 for tuition). The **Escuela Internacional de Cine,** Apdo. 4041, San Antonio de los Baños, Provincia de la Habana, tel. 0650-3152, fax 33-5341, on the outskirts of Havana, offers courses for broadcasting professionals. And the **Centro Nacional de Conservación,** Calle Cuba #610, Havana, tel. 61-5043, offers courses in architectural and art restoration.

Similarly, in Santiago de Cuba, **Promotur Cultural,** Casa de la Cultura, Calle 13 #154, Vista de Alegre, Santiago de Cuba, tel. 4-2285, fax 4-2387, offers study courses in Cuban culture from one week to one month, with a special emphasis on music and dance.

Language Courses
The **Grupo de Turismo Científico Educacional,** Avenida 3 #402, Miramar, Havana, tel./fax 33-1697, offers intensive Spanish lan-

guage courses at the **José Martí Language Center for Foreigners,** Calle 16 #109 in Miramar. They arrange accommodations at Hostal Icemar.

You can also sign up for two-week to four-month Spanish language and Cuban culture courses offered by Mercadu S.A., Calle 13 #951, Vedado, Havana, tel. 33-3893, fax 33-3028. The 14-day package costs US$480 double occupancy, including tuition, basic accommodation, and two meals daily; a one-month program costs US$580; the four-month course costs US$2,300. Single rooms cost US$10 extra per day.

In the US, **Global Exchange,** 2017 Mission St., Suite 303, San Francisco, CA 94110, tel. (415) 497-1994 or (800) 497-1994, fax (415) 255-7498, offers language study at the José Martí Language Center. In the UK, the **School of Latin American Spanish,** Docklands Enterprise Centre, 11 Marshalsea Rd., London SE1 1EP, tel. (171) 357-8793, offers seven-week regular and intensive summer language courses in Cuba.

GETTING AROUND

Cuba is deceptively large. The easiest—albeit most expensive—way to explore it is to take organized excursions, which are offered islandwide by any number of Cuban tour agencies. However, you'll travel with other tourists, shielded from the people and much of the nation's harsher realities. The most *rewarding* way to explore is independently. Contrary to popular notion, you can tour the island on your own without restriction.

Public transport, however, is unpredictable. Bus transportation can be a nightmare. At least on trains, tourists are graciously given first crack at whatever's available. Having your own wheels is preferable. Want to hire a car? No problem. Travel by bicycle? Go for it. I even shipped my *motorcycle* to Cuba and traveled 11,000 km without a hiccup or raised eyebrow.

Since 1995, gasoline has been readily available again, and the dire transportation problems of the early 1990s are receding.

As a rule of thumb, make reservations as far ahead as possible.

BY AIR

The fastest way to get around is to fly. Fortunately, Cuba's air network is relatively well developed, and flying is economical. Most of Havana's main cities have an airport, and virtually every major tourism destination is within a two-hour drive of an airport. (Facilities at Havana, Santiago de Cuba, Ciego de Avila, and Varadero are good, with adequate restaurants, bars, and retail stores. Regional airports are smaller and have limited facilities.)

There are four domestic carriers: Aero Caribbean, Aero Gaviota, Cubana (the most important), and ENSA. All utilize rather beaten-about Russian aircraft, although Cubana also has Fokker F-27s.

Aero Caribbean, Calle 23 #113, Vedado, Havana, tel. 79-7524, operates charter flights from Havana to most of the popular tourist destinations, including Isla de la Juventud (US$18 one-way)—on Wednesday, Friday, and Sunday—and Holguín (US$65) and Santiago (US$75), both on Wednesday and Sunday. It also serves Cayo Largo. **AeroTaxi,** Calle 27 #102, e/ M y N, Vedado, Havana, tel. 32-4460 utilizes 12-passenger biplanes, mostly for excursion flights. It has facilities at most airports. **Aero Gaviota,** Avenida 47 #2814 e/ 28 y 34, Raparto Kohly, Playa, Havana, tel. 81-3068, fax 33-2621, offers charter flights in 30-passenger Yak-40s and 38-passenger Antonov-26s and "executive" service in eight-seat helicopters. **Cubana,** Calle Infanta esq. Humbolt, Havana, tel. 33-4949, the largest carrier, has service be-

AERO CARIBBEAN OFFICES

HAVANA

Calle 23 #64 esq. P, Vedado, tel. 33-4543, fax 33-5016
Aeropuerto Wajay, tel. 45-3013 or 45-1135, fax 33-5017

VARADERO

Aeropuerto Juan Gualberto Gómez, tel./fax 66-7096

tween all the major airports. Its fares are 25% cheaper if booked in conjunction with an international Cubana flight.

Reservations

Transportation is limited by lack of aircraft, so flights are frequently fully booked (regular domestic flights operate at almost 100% occupancy year-round), especially in the Aug.-Dec. peak season, when Cubans take their holidays. The most solidly booked routes are Havana-Santiago, Havana-Trinidad, Santa Lucía-Trinidad, and Varadero-Cayo Largo. Often you must make a reservation a week in advance. Fortunately, foreigners with dollars are usually given priority on waiting lists. Reservations usually have to be paid in avance and are normally nonrefundable. Forego telephone reservations: make your booking *in person* at the airline office or through one of the major tour agencies. Better still is to make reservations before arriving in Cuba (you'll be given a voucher that you exchange for a ticket upon arrival in Cuba).

Delays, flight cancellations, and changes in schedule are common. And don't expect luxury—be happy if you get a Spam-and-cheese sandwich. More likely, since flights are short, you'll receive a boiled sweet.

Be sure to arrive on time for check-in; otherwise your seat will likely be given away. If that happens, *don't expect a refund,* and bear in mind that you may not even be able to get a seat on the next plane out.

BY RAIL

Exploring by train is the next step down the travel ladder—a great way to meet Cubans and see the country at a slow pace, but relatively unpredictable and, at times, uncomfortable.

Cuba was one of the few Latin American countries with a well-developed railway system in 1959 that reached into virtually every corner of the country (the lines were laid by the great sugar companies to carry sugarcane to the mills and then to port; the first steam train was introduced in the 1830s). Some 5,300 km of the 14,640-km system constitute main line public service railways.

Rail transport, which was nationalized following the Revolution, has been largely ne- glected since 1959 in favor of truck transport. A major upgrading occurred in the 1970s, when the Central Railroad was rebuilt. New diesel locomotives (all of them relatively fuel inefficient) were imported from the Soviet Union, Czechoslovakia, and Argentina.

One main rail axis spans the country, connecting all the major cities, with major ports and secondary cities linked by branch lines. There is no rail service *within* cities, although quaint commuter trains (a little like the dinky English or Swiss two-carriage trains) called *Ferro-Ómnibus* provide suburban rail service for towns such as Santa Clara and Las Tunas.

The loss of oil and spare parts since the collapse of the Soviet Bloc reduced the state-run railroad system to shambles. The four daily trips between Havana and Santiago de Cuba, for example, were reduced to one per day in 1991. Fortunately, at press time, most of the services seemed to be up and running. The schedule is no way firm, so double-check days and times given in this book. Also check the arrival time at your destination carefully and plan accordingly, as many trains arrive (and depart) in the wee hours of the morning. Few trains run on time.

Two services operate between Havana and Santiago de Cuba: the fast *especial,* which takes 16-20 hours for the 860-km journey, and the slow *regular.* The *especial* (which has a poorly stocked *cafetería* wagon, comfy seats, and bone-chilling a/c) stops at all the major cities en route; the other (far less salubrious, but lazy and quite adequate) is colloquially called the *lechero*—the "milkman"—because it stops at virtually every village.

Bicycles are allowed on most trains. You usually pay (in pesos) at the end of the journey.

Reservations

Most trains are sold out several days or weeks ahead. Cubans pay in pesos. Foreigners must pay an equivalent fare in dollars at the ticket offices of **Ladis,** (formerly Ferrotur, by which it is still more commonly known). You may still find a ticket agent in the boonies willing to charge you in pesos, but don't count on it. Your greenback allows you to skip the line; it also buys a guaranteed seat. Fortunately, you can normally walk up to the Ladis office at the station, buy your ticket, and take a seat on board within an hour. In Havana, the main Ladis ticket office, tel. 62-

1770, is outside the main railway at Calles Arsenal and Cienfuegos (open 7 a.m.-7 p.m.). Ladis offices in the provinces are less efficient: buy your ticket as far in advance as possible. (A discreet gift such as a slab of chocolate may melt away problems.) Don't trust being able to book consecutive journeys "down the line" in advance—make a habit of buying your ticket for the next leg of your journey upon arrival in each destination.

Reservations can also be made through Palacio de Turismo offices islandwide, which saves the bother of waiting in line at the station. Some tour agencies will also make your booking for you.

Reservations for local services can't be made. You'll have to join the *cola* (queue) and buy your ticket on the day of departure (sometimes the day before; each station usually lists the allotted time for ticket purchase). To identify the last person in line ahead of you, ask who is *el último*.

Classes

Foreigners paying dollars are now expected to travel on the *especial,* which has reclining cushioned seats. Service in this "luxury class" includes a basic meal (usually fried chicken or beans and rice with soda to wash it down). Regardless, take snacks and drinks!

Most branch line services are *clase segunda* (second class) only, which, though inexpensive, is arduous for long journeys and best suited to hardy travelers—they're typically dirty and overcrowded, with uncushioned wooden seats. Most branch lines offer second-class only. *Clase primera* (first class) is only marginally better, with padded seats, though still crowded and hardly comfortable. Some routes offer *clase primera especial,* which provides more comfort and, often, basic boxed meals.

Nonsmoking compartments haven't yet made it to Cuba.

BY BUS

For stoics with *lots* of time, there is public bus travel. Few foreign travelers opt to ride on the noisy, rickety old Cuban- or Hungarian-made buses, with their jammed windows, noxious exhaust fumes, and (often) arse-numbing seats.

Fortunately, there are two classes of buses for long-distance travel: a/c *especiales* are faster and more comfortable than *regulares.*

Cuba's bus system serves almost every nook and cranny of the island. Virtually the entire population relies on the bus system for travel within and between cities. The demand so exceeds supply that there is often a waiting line in excess of one month for the most popular long-distance routes. Inter-city buses rarely have a spare seat. Hence, Cuban bus stations have been called "citadels of desperation." Most towns have *two* bus stations for out-of-town service: a **Terminal de Ómnibus Intermunicipales,** for local and municipal service, and a **Terminal de Ómnibus Interprovinciales,** for service between provinces.

Usually, no advance reservations are available for the short-distance **intermunicipal services.** You'll have to join the queue, but be prepared for a mad scrum as soon as the bus arrives. At other times, you'll be issued a *tike* (a slip of paper, not a ticket) that records your destination and position in line. You board when your number is called, so don't wander off—and don't dally once it's called (you should learn Spanish numerals by heart; alternately, ask a neighbor to help identify when it's your turn). Fares are collected on board. Since buses are often full, try to board the bus at its originating point. Most intermunicipal terminals are chaotic. Buses are asphyxiatingly crowded and interminably slow. Intra-provincial buses don't cross provincial boundaries; hence, you may be put down at a border in the middle of nowhere and have to mill around with everyone else, hoping that a connecting bus shows for the rest of the journey.

The state agency **Empresa Ómnibus Nacionales,** Avenida Independencia #101, Havana, tel. 70-6155, operates all **interprovincial services,** which are more comfortable, usually with reclining seats. Reservations are essential; expect to wait at least several days before being able to get a seat (do *not* expect to show up at the station and simply board a bus). At press time, a policy of giving foreigners preferential treatment seemed to be in effect. You can always try checking at the *fallo* counter, which handles cancellations and dishes out seats on a kind of standby basis. Good luck! Only one-way tickets are available. Don't forget to book any return trip also as far in advance as possible.

Don't rely on the validity of published schedules. Information about bus schedules is fragmentary. There are no published schedules; instead, they are normally written in chalk at bus stations. The main bus station in Havana has a full list of services and fares. Beware pickpockets, and don't display wads of money when purchasing your ticket. Normally, you'll first receive a *número de espera,* a ticket that indicates your position on the waiting list (the list—*lista de espera*—is posted in the waiting room and includes the numbers). Get there at least an hour before departure for long-distance buses. Often the rush to get aboard can be furious.

Some buses have room for storage below; others do not, in which case luggage space will be limited to overhead racks. Stops on *regular* buses are frequent. Everyone seems to have a chicken and a couple of cardboard boxes to load aboard. *Travel light!* Consider leaving some luggage at your hotel in Havana.

If possible, sit toward the front. Conditions can get very cramped and very hot; the back tends to get the hottest (and often smelliest—from exhaust fumes). Aisle seats usually provide more legroom. You'll want some water to guard against dehydration, but don't drink too much coffee or other liquids—toilet stops can be few and far between. *Bring plenty of snacks.* Long-distance buses make food stops, but often there isn't sufficient food for everyone. Likewise, Cubans will rush to the bathroom, where a long line may develop.

Cubans relinquish their seats gladly to pregnant women, the handicapped, elderly people, and mothers with small children. Set a good example: do the same.

If a bus doesn't go to the particular destination you desire (boy, you're *really* in the boonies), then take a bus to the nearest town and from there take a taxi or hire a private car.

Most routes have shelters. Locals will direct you to the correct bus stop if you ask.

Within Towns
Most large towns have intra-city bus service. Usually, they are cloyingly overcrowded. At least they only cost 10 centavos (the standard fare), which you normally drop into a fare box next to the driver. Many Cubans board through the rear door (although technically this is illegal), in which case, if the bus is jam-packed like a sardine can, you can pass your fare to the front via other passengers. Be prepared for the *cola* to disintegrate when the bus arrives.

To stop the bus, shout *¡Parada!*

Tourist Buses
The tourist boom hasn't spawned many bus shuttle services between points on the tourist circuit, but you can book yourself onto an excursion bus operated by one of the state-run tour agencies. Usually these are modern a/c buses up to the best international standards. Most agencies offer transfers. **Havanatur,** Calle 6 #117 e/ 1ra y 3ra, Miramar, Havana, tel. 33-2712 or 33-2090, fax 33-2601, and other Cuban tour agencies offer seats on tour buses serving Varadero, Trinidad, and other key destinations. Take a sweater; some buses are overly air-conditioned.

A shuttle service within Havana has been introduced.

Makeshift "Buses"
Stoics among stoics can travel the Cuban way. The Special Period has had such a traumatic effect on the transportation system that the populace now relies on anything that moves. In many areas, flatbed trucks have been converted and have basic wooden seats welded to the floor. Often there are no seats, and the local "bus" might be a converted cattle truck or a flatbed pulled by a tractor, with passengers crammed in and standing like cows. If you're hitchhiking, this is for you.

BY TAXI

Cuba has a good taxi system, including long-distance taxis. Taxis serving tourists charge in dollars; those serving the local population—peso taxis—charge in pesos. During rainy periods, taxis are in high demand.

Tourist Taxis
Tourist taxis are inexpensive by US or European standards, so much so that they're a viable option for short-haul touring, especially if you're traveling with two or three other people. Generally, taxis will go wherever a road leads. Most *turistaxis* (those serving tourists for dollars) in Havana and leading cities are radio-dis-

patched, although you can also find them at designated pick-up points and at tourist hotels. Most *turistaxis* are modern Japanese cars or Mercedes. Jeep-taxis (usually Mercedes or Toyotas) are common in more remote areas and on Isla de la Juventud.

In Havana, **Panataxi** provides efficient radio-dispatched taxi service (mostly for Cubans but also for tourists) using Lada, the Russian-made Fiat described as "tough as a Land Rover, with iron-hard upholstery and, judging by sensation, no springs." They are far more economical than *turistaxis*.

You can hire a *turistaxi* by the hour or day; the cost normally compares favorably to hiring a car for the day. By law, Cuban drivers must use their meters (not all taxis outside the main cities have meters). If you want to get the price down, you might be able to strike a bargain with the driver. Here's the deal. Your driver will stop the meter at so many dollars and you give him a slightly greater amount. Since his dispatcher records the destination, mile for mile, usually a dollar per mile, the taxi driver splits the excess with the dispatcher. Most taxi drivers are un-scrupulously honest with passengers. If you think you're being gouged, contest the fee.

Outside Havana, you'll normally find taxis around the main squares of small towns. You do not normally tip Cuban taxi drivers.

At press time, official rates were pegged to distance. In towns, you can get almost any-where for less than US$10. Nighttime fares cost about 20% more. Long journeys are usually charged at a pre-agreed fare.

Long-Distance Taxis: Infotur provides a long-distance taxi service. You can book through any of their Palacios de Turismo nationwide. Although relatively expensive, they are a value option for three or four passengers sharing the cost. Or you can try using peso taxis.

Peso Taxis

Taxis—deprecatingly called *los incapturables* (uncatchable)—also serve the local population, usually along fixed routes and charging in pesos at ludicrously low rates. You'll normally find them around the main squares, although they are as-signed to airports, hotels, and other key sites. Peso taxis (also called ***colectivos***) are not sup-posed to give rides to foreigners, but many do so, especially for a dollar gratuity. They usually

take as many passengers as they can cram in and are not supposed to pick up passengers between their designated departure and return points. Look for a light lit up above the cab—it signifies if the taxi is *libre* (free). You should change dollars for pesos beforehand.

The base fare is one peso. Each km costs 25 centavos (35 centavos at night).

Maquinas, the inter-city taxis, are usually big Yankee cars that hang around outside railway and bus terminals. Again, they're not supposed to take foreigners, but a deal can usually be arranged. Often they won't depart until they fill up with passengers. Count on traveling about three km per peso.

Freelance Cabs

So you want a little more class, eh? Don't mind the possibility of breaking down in the boonies? Many Cubans with classic cars from the hey-day of Detroit treat their prized possession as exotic cash cows—they rent them out (mostly illegally) for guided tours. Says Cristina García, "Twenty dollars buys gas enough for a decent

ciclotaxis, *Havana*

ADDRESSES

In most Cuban cities, addresses are given as locations. Thus the Havanatur office is at Calle 6 e/ 1ra y 3ra, Miramar, Havana, meaning it is on Calle 6 between (e/ is for entre—between) First and Third Avenue (Avenida 1ra y 3ra).

Street numbers are occasionally used. Thus, the Hotel Inglaterra is at Prado #416 esq. San Rafael, Habana Vieja; at the corner (esq. for esquina) of Prado and Calle San Rafael, in Old Havana (Habana Vieja).

Piso refers to the floor level (thus, an office on Piso 3ra is on the third floor).

Most cities are laid out on a grid pattern centered at a main square or plaza (usually called Plaza Central, Parque Central, or Plaza Mayor), with parallel streets (calles) running perpendicular to avenues (avenidas). Some towns, however, have even-numbered calles (usually north-south) running perpendicular to odd-numbered calles (usually east-west).

Note that in most cities, many streets have at least two names: one predating the Revolution (and usually the most commonly used colloquially) and the other a post-revolutionary name. For example, in Havana, the Prado is the old (and preferred) term for the Paseo de Martí. On maps, the modern name takes precedence, with the old name often shown in parentheses.

spin. Seventy dollars gets you a day in a top-of-the-line Cadillac convertible with fins so big they block the rear-view mirror. Forget about renting from Hertz or Avis ever again."

Your fare is negotiable, so ask around. Agree on the fare before getting in. Make sure you know whether this is one-way or roundtrip. Don't be afraid to bargain. You may get a better deal if you speak Spanish and know local customs.

Horse-Drawn Cabs

The clip-clop of hooves echoes through virtually every town and resort in Cuba (Havana excepted). Horse-drawn cabs (coches) have been dusted off and given a new lease on life since the Special Period. In Varadero and other beach resorts, elegant antique carriages with leather seats are touted for sightseeing (US$1-2 will get you anywhere). Elsewhere, they're a utility and are often decrepit carts with basic bench seats pulled by fittingly scrawny mules (one

peso is a standard fare). Coches usually congregate around bus and rail stations.

You don't tip the driver, but please buy some food for the emaciated mule.

BY CAR

A growing number of foreign tourists to Cuba now rent a car. Exploring the island by car allows total freedom of movement (there are no restrictions on where you can go), plus you can cover a lot of turf without the time delays of public transport.

You can travel the entire length and breadth of the country in about two weeks. A drive from Havana into Pinar del Río, then east to the Zapata peninsula and Trinidad, then back through the Sierra del Escambray allows you to see much of the nation's splendid scenery, history, and culture along with enough hairpins, dirt roads, and mountain passes to give drivers a sense of adventure. From Santiago, a route east to Guantánamo and Baracoa, then via Holguín, Bayamo, Manzanillo, and Chivirico should suffice for a one- to two-week drive.

Cuba has some 31,000 km (19,260 miles) of roads, of which about 15,500 km (9,700 miles) are paved. Virtually every town, airport, and harbor is accessible by paved road, as are all the more popular beach destinations. In more remote areas, especially in the mountains and distant coastal regions, access is by unpaved road that can shake both a car and its occupants until their doors and teeth rattle. In the rainy season, such roads become quagmires or even totally flooded. Here you'll need a 4WD. The worst roads I encountered were in the mountains of Guantánamo province.

Cuba is a great place to drive. Outside Havana, the city blurs, thins, and finally vanishes behind you along with the traffic. There are so few vehicles on the roads that you can travel all day and sometimes pass only a half dozen other vehicles.

True, many of the roads are in a poor state of repair, often with huge potholes (the government admits that 60% of the road network is in "regular or bad repair"). But for the most part, the roads are in reasonably good condition, especially compared to those of neighboring islands To bolster the road-repair budget, tolls—the first since the Revolution—were introduced in 1996 for specific roads, including the Matanzas-Varadero Expressway and the Cayo Coco bridge. Foreigners pay US$2 per vehicle (buses and trucks pay US$4).

The main highway is the **Carretera Central** (Central Highway), built during the reign of General Machado. It runs along the island's spine for 1,200 km (760 miles) from one end of the country to the other. (Its construction, announced in 1926, was a classic tale of corruption. Chase National Bank financed the project to the tune of US$100 million, benefitting contractors, General Machado, and his cronies immensely. The US construction company, Warren Bros., lobbied heavily to prevent the US government from ousting Machado.) The road is an ordinary two-lane highway which leads through dozens of sleepy rural towns.

For maximum speed and minimum sightseeing, take the A-1, the country's main highway—six-lanes wide and fast. Construction of the **Autopista Nacional** (National Expressway; sometimes called the *Ocho Vías*—eight-ways) came to a halt with the Special Period and has not been resumed. About 650 km have been completed, from Pinar del Río to a point just east of Santa Clara, and from Santiago de Cuba about 30 km northwestward. Travel time between Havana and Santa Clara is about four hours. Food stops, signs, and gas stations are limited.

Be cautious on the Autopista, where you can travel at high speed. At least two railway lines cross the highway in depressions that can bend your wheel if you hit 'em at high speed.

Traffic Regulations

To drive in Cuba, you must be 21 years or older and hold either an International Drivers' License (IDL) or a valid national driver's license. You must also have at least one year's driving experience. In North America, you can obtain an IDL through any American Automobile Association office; and in the UK from the AA, Fanum House, Basingstoke, Hampshire RG21 2EA, or RAC, P.O. Box 100, 7 Brighton Rd., Croydon CR2 6XW.

Traffic drives on the right, as in the US. The speed limit is 100 kph (61 mph) on freeways, 90 kph (55 mph) on highways, 60 kph (37 mph) on rural roads, 50 kph (30 mph) on urban roads,

and 40 kph (25 mph) in children's zones. Speed limits are vigorously enforced by an efficient highway patrol. If you receive a traffic fine, it will be deducted from the deposit for your rental (there's a space for fines provided on the rental-car papers).

Seat belt use is not mandatory, nor are motorcyclists required to wear helmets. Insurance—a state monopoly—*is* mandatory. Note that's its illegal to 1) enter an intersection unless you can exit, 2) make a right turn on a red light unless indicated by a white arrow or traffic signal *(Derecha con Luz Roja),* or 3) overtake on the right. Cars coming uphill have right of way.

Driving Safety

Driving is of as high a standard as you will find anywhere in the Caribbean or Latin America, partly due to the very difficult driving test (all Cuban drivers attend a two-month driving course that includes four weeks of theoretical classes). I don't share Ernest Hemingway's sense of "the illogical and neurotic Cuban traffic." Cubans rarely display typical Latin tendencies behind the wheel. They drive relatively slowly (far *too* slowly sometimes, but you can't blame them in their four-decade-old clunkers). They also obey traffic signals, mostly, and for the most part are respectful.

Keep your speed down. The main cause of traffic deaths in Cuba is collisions with bicycles and wayward livestock. The Autopista is favored by huge Brahma bulls and other beasts that wander freely onto the highway. On virtually any road, you'll pass cattle grazing the margins on each side. Oxen, farmers driving ox-carts, and bicyclists all have a tendency to turn into your path at the moment you decide to pass (Cubans in the boonies are not used to seeing other traffic, so it isn't on their minds). Driving at night is perilous—most roads are unlighted and few have siderails or painted markings at the margins.

Watch out for sticks jutting up in the road. These usually indicate a huge pothole. Slow down if you see the sign *topes* or *túmulos,* meaning "road bumps." The first time you barrel over them heedlessly will serve notice to respect the warning next time.

Even on the darkest of days, with torrential rains falling, Cubans will forego using headlights. Use yours! (Remember that in Scandinavia and Canada, where use of headlights is now mandatory at all times, vehicular accidents have been significantly reduced.) If you use your headlights by day, every second Cuban you pass will raise their hands and make a motion like a quacking duck to let you know. You'd think it was a social sin. Quack! quack!

Vamos por el camino corecto—in essence, "Drive Safely!"

Accidents and Breakdowns
One of the most common sights in Cuba is to see a car stalled in the road with females sitting stoically to the side while the males toil to jerry-rig a repair. If your car breaks down, there will be no shortage of Cubans willing to offer advice and consummate fix-it skills. If the problem is minor, fine. However, rental car agencies usually have a clause to protect against likely damage to the car from unwarranted re-

---

CUBA'S VINTAGE AMERICAN CARS

"Magnificent finned automobiles cruise grandly down the street like parade floats. I feel like we're back in time, in a kind of Cuban version of an earlier America."
—Cristina García, *Dreaming in Cuban*

Fifties nostalgia is alive and well on the streets of Havana. Stylish Chevrolets, Packards, and Cadillacs weave among the sober Russian-made Ladas and Moskovitchs, their large engines guzzling precious gas at an astonishing rate. Automotive sentimentality is reason enough to visit Cuba—the greatest living car museum in the world.

American cars flooded into Cuba for 50 years. During Batista's days, Cuba probably imported more Cadillacs and Buicks and DeSotos than any other nation in the world. Then came the Cuban Revolution and the US trade embargo. In terms of Ameri-

can automobiles, time stopped when Castro took power.

Still, relics from Detroit's heyday are everywhere, ubiquitous reminders of that period in the 1950s when American cars—high-finned, big-boned, with the come-hither allure of Marilyn Monroe—seemed tailor-made for the streets of prerevolutionary Havana.

Imagine. A '57 Packard gleams in the lyrical Cuban sunlight. Nearby, perhaps, sits a 1950 Chevy Deluxe, a '57 Chevrolet Bel Air hardtop, and an Oldsmobile Golden Rocket from the same year, inviting foreigners to admire the dashboard or run their fingers along a tail fin. More numerous are staid Chrysler New Yorker sedans, Ford Customlines, and Buick Centuries.

Lacking proper tools and replacement parts, Cubans adeptly cajole one more kilometer out of
(continues on next page)

CHRISTOPHER P. BAKER

Auto Museum, Baracoa

CUBA'S VINTAGE AMERICAN CARS
(continued)

their battered hulks. Their intestinally reconstituted engines are monuments to ingenuity and geopolitics—decades of improvised repairs have melded parts from Detroit and Moscow alike. (Russian Gaz jeeps are favorite targets for cannibalization, since their engines were cloned from a Detroit engine.)

One occasionally spots a shining example of museum quality. The majority, though, have long ago been touched up with housepaint and decorated with flashy mirrors and metallic stars, as if to celebrate a religious holiday. Some are adorned with multicolored flags to invoke the protection of Changó or another *santería* god.

The mechanical dinosaurs are called *cacharros*. Normally, the word means a broken-down jalopy, but in the case of old Yankee classics, the word is "whispered softly, tenderly, like the name of a lost first love," says Cristina García in the introduction to *Cars of Cuba,* a beautiful little photo-essay book published by Harry N. Abrams, New York, 1995.

Wings of the World, 1200 William St. #706, Buffalo, NY 14240, tel. (800) 465-8687, occasionally offers a "Classic Car Adventure" in Cuba. The six-day tour (US$2,195 including airfare from New York) includes a chauffeur-driven tour of Cuba by vintage auto.

---

pairs. For major problems, call the rental agency; it will arrange a tow or send a mechanic.

You should also call the agency in the event of an accident. After an accident, *never* move the vehicles until the police arrive. Get the names, license plate numbers, and *cedulas* (legal identification numbers) of any witnesses. Make a sketch of the accident. Then call the **transit police** (in Havana, tel. 82-0116; outside Havana, tel. 116).

Do *not* offer statements to anyone other than the police. In case of injury, call the **Red Cross** (unfortunately, there is no national emergency telephone number to summon an ambulance, although several cities are served by calling 118). Try not to leave the accident scene, or at least keep an eye on your car; the other party may tamper with the evidence. And don't let honking traffic pressure you into moving the cars.

The *tráficos* are usually level-headed. However, as a foreigner with deep pockets, the blame might be assigned to you in the event that in cannot be proved otherwise. Don't expect much help from locals. Cubans are loath to involve themselves where the police are concerned. Show the police your license and car rental documents, but make sure you get them back (if you suspect the other driver has been drinking, ask the policeman to administer a Breathalyzer test—an *alcolemia*). The *tráfico* cannot levy a fine on the spot. If you are issued a ticket, it will normally be taken care of by your

car rental agency, which will usually deduct the sum from your credit card. If someone is seriously injured or killed and you are blamed, you should immediately contact your embassy for legal assistance. **Asistur,** Paseo de Martí #254, Havana, tel. 62-5519, can also offer legal and other assistance.

Gasoline

Gasoline (petrol) is sold at **Servi-Cupet** stations nationwide. You'll rarely have to drive more than 100 km between gas stations. Virtually every town has a Cupet station, plus at least one other station serving gas for pesos to locals. By 1996, the traumatic gasoline shortage of the early 1990s was history; petrol was readily available everywhere. Still, it's wise to not let your gas tank get below half-full, especially since occasional electrical blackouts shut the pumps down. It's a good idea to ask the gas attendant where the next place is that you can fill up. If you run out of gas, there's sure to be someone willing to sell from private stock.

Gasoline costs US90 cents per liter—about US$3.40 a gallon (Cupet stations accept US dollars only; foreigners are no longer issued tourist gasoline vouchers, as they were a few years ago). "Regular" and "Superior" grades are available, but, as yet, unleaded gas is not.

Cubans without dollars have a harder time of things. Gas station attendants do a brisk business by siphoning off a liter of gas here and there for sale on the black market.

24-HOUR GAS STATIONS

CITY	SERVICE STATION	LOCATION
HAVANA PROVINCE		
Havana	Pequeño Gigante	Av. Independencia y 271, Boyeros
Havana	Riviera	Paseo y Malecón, Playa
Havana	El Motor	5ta y 112, Playa
Havana	Havana in Bond	Valle de Berroa
Havana	Tangan	Malecón y 11, Plaza
Havana	Bacuranao	Carretera Monumental, Habana Este
Havana	Gran Vía	Rotonda de Guanabo, Habana Este
Havana	31 y 18	Av. 31 y 18, Playa
Havana	L y 17	Calle L, esq. 17, Playa
Havana	Vento y Santa Catalina	Vento y Santa Catalina, Cerro
Bauta	Bauta	Carretera Central
PINAR DEL RÍO PROVINCE		
Pinar del Río	Siboney	Carretera Central Km. 88, Rpto. 10 de Octubre
MATANZAS PROVINCE		
Matanzas	Bellamar	Calzada General Betancourt y Jagüey
Varadero	Darsena	Carretera via Blanca
Cárdenas	Cárdenas	Km 12 (entrance to town)
Colón	Carretera Central	(opposite Hotel Santiago)
Jagüey Grande	Jagüey	on the *autopista*, one km before the exit for Jagüey
CIENFUEGOS PROVINCE		
Cienfuegos	Ranchón de Aguada	Autopista Nacional, Km. 172
Cienfuegos	Rancho Luna	Road to Trinidad (near Hotel Rancho Luna)
Punta Gorda	Punta Gorda	Calle 37 y Av. 16
VILLA CLARA PROVINCE		
Santa Clara	La Estrella	Carretera Central y Caridad
SANCTI SPÍRITUS PROVINCE		
Trinidad	Trinidad	Carretera Sancti Spíritus (entrance to town)
CIEGO DE ÁVILA PROVINCE		
Ciego de Ávila	El Oeste	Carretera Central este, esq. Circunvalación
Ciego de Ávila	Cupet Norte	road to Morón y Circunvalación
Cayo Coco	Cayo Coco	Tourist Transportation Base
CAMAGÜEY PROVINCE		
Camagüey	Vía Blanca Cupet	Carretera Central y Vista Hermosa
Camagüey	Libertad 1	Carretera Central y Av. La Cariadd
Santa Lucia	Policentro	
LAS TUNAS PROVINCE		
Las Tunas	9 de Abril	Carretera Central y Av. Menocal
Las Tunas	13 de Marzo	Carretera Central (entrance to town)
GRANMA PROVINCE		
Bayamo	El Especial	Carretera Central
Manzanillo	La Bruja	Carratera Manzanillo (Niquero y Circunvalación)

(continues on next page)

24-HOUR GAS STATIONS
(continued)

HOLGUÍN PROVINCE

Holguín	La Loma	Calle Libertad, Carratera Gibara
Holgín	Ciudad Jardín	Carretera Central (entrance to town)
Guardalavaca	Guardalavaca	entrance to tourist center

SANTIAGO DE CUBA PROVINCE

Santiago de Cuba	La Bujía	Carretera Central y Céspedes

GUANTÁNAMO PROVINCE

Guantánamo	Vía Azul	Prado esq. 6 Este
Baracoa	Cubacu	five km east of town

Insurance

If you rent a car you will be responsible for any damage or theft. Hence you should purchase insurance offered by the rental agency. It costs US$8-10 daily with a deductible (you pay the first US$200-500 or so), or US$12-15 for fully comprehensive coverage. Inspect your car thoroughly for damage and marks before setting off; otherwise, you may be charged for the slightest dent when you return. On the diagram you'll be given to sign, note even the most innocuous marks. Don't forget the inside, as well as the radio antenna. Defrosters often don't work (you'll need to bring a rag to wipe the windows, since they will tend to fog up). **Note:** you can use your a/c to clear up condensation only briefly, after which it cools the windows too much, causing condensation. Don't assume the car rental agency has taken care of tire pressures or fluids. Check them yourself before you set off.

If you have your own vehicle, the state-run organization **ESEN,** Calle 18, e/ Avenidas 5 y 7, tel. 29-6510, 33-1763 (ask for Maritza Naranjo), insures automobiles and has special packages for foreigners. It offers a choice of all risks, including theft, roll-overs, "catastrophes," and "partial theft." I insured my motorbike for a premium of US$8,000; the policy cost US$228, including theft, fire, accident, and a small medical premium (my policy was valid for three months, at 40% of the annual premium). You can insure in pesos or dollars and are paid back in the same currency.

Maps and Directions

Cuban roads are very well signposted. However, many signs are where you'd never think of looking or are otherwise obscured. Ask directions whenever you're in doubt. The average Cuban will be delighted to offer assistance.

It's extraordinary how little Cubans know of regions outside their own locale. You may as well ask them directions to the far side of the moon. In the countryside, you'll need to phrase your questions so as not to preempt the answer. For example, rather than asking, "Does this road go to so-and-so?" (which will surely earn you a reply, *"Si, señor!"*), ask "Where does this route go?"

You should acquire as many maps as you can lay your hands on. The best general touring map of Cuba for drivers is *Kuba/Cuba,* published by Cartographia of Budapest. The 1:250,000-scale map is fairly accurate. So, too, is the one published by Freytag & Berndt. Both feature streets maps of leading cities on the reverse sides.

Otherwise, look for *Automapa Nacional,* published by Ediciones Geo and available for sale at many tourist souvenir outlets. Cuba's Instituto Cubano de Geodesia y Cartografía publishes a road map *(Mapa de Carreteras)* for each province. They're quite detailed. Most maps published in Cuba are several years out of date. (Even the best maps show paved roads that are in fact dirt roads.) A series of detailed and accurate city maps for tourists is now also widely available.

Traffic Police

Traffic police, or *tráficos* (mostly motorcycle cops), patrol the main highways. Often there's a cop at the entrance and exit of a town. Oncoming cars will flash their lights to indicate, "Slow down—police ahead." Cuban traffic cops are generally very scrupulous and extremely courteous (they'll usually greet you and send you on your way with a salute).

If you're stopped, the police will ask to see your license, passport, and rental contract. Speeding fines are usually paid through the car rental agency. Don't think you can get away without paying a fine. Delinquent fines are reported to the immigration authorities, who may catch you as you attempt to exit the country. The best advice is: don't speed!

Throughout Havana and a few other cities you'll pass numerous *puntos de control*—control points—manned by police and looking like tiny air-traffic-control towers. You are expected to slow down. Signs give advance warning.

See the chart for telephone numbers of *tráticos* nationwide.

Car Rentals

No, you can't book Avis or Hertz in Cuba. However, all the major Cuban tourism agencies have car rental divisions. The demand is so great that even off-season many rental outlets have no small cars available. If you're planning on traveling to Cuba during peak Christmas and New Year season, you'll absolutely need to make advance reservations (you're also now competing with the upwardly mobile Cubans who have dollars to spare). Make sure you clarify any one-way drop-off fees, late return penalties, etc. If you book from abroad, ask for a copy of the reservation to be faxed to you and take this copy with you to Cuba. Also, be prepared to defend against any mysterious charges that may appear later. The companies accept payment by Visa, MasterCard, Eurocard, Banamex, Carnet, and JCB, as well as in cash and traveler's checks. You will normally be required to pay a deposit of US$500 (perhaps more).

The range of vehicle options is extensive. You can usually choose stick-shift or automatic, although the particular agency (or the specific location where you book) may not have the model you request. Normally it can arrange for the model you want to be delivered. Agencies will de-

CAR RENTAL COMPANIES

CUBANACÁN

Banes	tel. 3-0280
Camagüey	tel. 4-8284
Cayo Coco	tel. 33-5388
Ciego de Ávila	tel. 33-38936
Daiquirí	tel. 24849
Holguín	tel. 3-0243
Marea del Portillo	tel. 2-5901
Santiago de Cuba	tel. 4-1787
Varadero	tel. 6-3259

HAVANAUTOS

Havana (main office)	tel. 33-2369 or 33-2891, fax 33-1416
Baracoa	tel. 43511
Camagüey	tel. 0-322-72015
Ciego de Ávila	tel. 0-332-0013
Cienfuegos	tel. 33-5154
Holguín	tel. 33-5360
Isla de la Juventud	tel. 0-61-2300
Playas del Este	tel. 33-8113/33-5502
Pinar del Río	tel. 0-82-5071
Santiago de Cuba	tel. 33-5062
Trinidad	tel. 0-419-6100
Varadero	tel. 33-7094
Villa Clara	tel. 0-422-26036

NACIONAL RENT-A-CAR

Havana (main office)	tel. 81-0357, 20-6897, or 23-7000
Holguín	tel. 0-24-30102
Santiago de Cuba	tel. 0-226-41368
Trinidad	0-419-4101
Varadero	tel. 0-56-2968
24-hour repair service	tel. 81-0357 or 20-6897

TRANSAUTOS

Havana (main office)	tel. 33-5532 or 33-4038, fax 33-4057
Camagüey	tel. 03227-2328
Santiago de Cuba	tel. 33-5015, ext. 3207
Trinidad	tel. 041-4011
Varadero	tel. 33-7336

See separate chart in Havana chapter for locations of car rental outlets in Havana.

liver and pick up from your hotel (larger upscale tourist hotels have their car rental desks on-site).

Four-Wheel Drive: For most exploring, you probably don't need a 4WD. You'll want one, however, for exploring the Sierra Maestra, Sierra Cristál, Sierra del Purial, and Cuchillas de Toa, many of the roads leading to and along virtually the entire southern shore, the road from Marea del Portillo to Santiago de Cuba, Cayo Sabinal and Cayo Romano, the extreme northwest coast, the Peninsula de Guanahacabibes, and the extreme south of Isla de la Juventud. This is especially true in rainy season, when dirt roads become veritable morasses.

Rates: Expect to pay about US$50-100 per day plus insurance, depending on the size of the vehicle. The largest agency, **Havanautos,** Calle 2 #505 y Avenida 5, Miramar, tel. 33-2369 or 33-2891, fax 33-1416, offers a choice of 14 vehicles, from a small Daewoo Tico (US$45 per day with unlimited mileage) and a midsize Nissan EX salon (US$65) to a luxury Mercedez-Benz C180 (US$139). A Jeep Daihatsu costs US$55 for a soft-top; a Nissan Vanette holding eight passengers costs US$114; and a deluxe, a/c, eight-seat Dodge Caravan costs US$120. "Special Weekend" package rates are offered, but they don't provide any extra savings. (**Insurance** is additional—US$9 per day with US$250 deductible, US$15 with no deductible. **Transautos,** tel. 33-5532 or 33-4038, fax 33-4057, rents Peugeot 205 Juniors for US$45, including insurance and unlimited mileage. The company has a fleet of more than 725 vehicles. However, each time I've inquired, I've been told that no 205s are available. **Rex Limousine Service** rents Volvo sedans for US$125 a day (it has a booth in the arrivals hall of Terminal Two at José Martí airport in Havana).

In the UK, you can book cars in advance through **Havanatur UK,** 27 Stafford Rd., Croydon, Surrey CR0 4NG, tel. (0181) 681-3613, fax (0181) 760-0031. Rates begin at £30 per day for a Daewoo Tico, £37 for a convertible Daihatsu Jeep, and £43 for a Nissan Sentra, based on a one-week rental.

If your car is broken into or otherwise damaged, you must get a police statement—otherwise, you may be charged for the damage (check the fine print on the contract).

Most agencies offer a **chauffeur service** for US$30 a day.

Warning: Note that if you extend over the return period, you'll be billed on an *hourly* basis for additional time (make sure the time recorded on your contract is that for your *departure with the car,* not the time you entered into negotiations). Also check the fuel level carefully *before* setting off. If it doesn't look full to the brim, point this out to the rental agent; otherwise, you could be the victim of an impending scam (if you return the car with the same amount of fuel, you may be charged for the extra gas needed to top up the tank—and the agent will no doubt be pocketing the difference, having recorded a full tank when you rented the car).

Fly-Drive Packages: Hoteles Horizontes, tel. 33-4238, 33-4334 or 33-4361, fax 33-3166, in association with **Nacional Rent-a-Car,** tel. 81-0357, 20-6897, or 23-7000, offers a Flexi Fly & Drive prepurchased package combining car rental and hotel vouchers that offers the freedom to follow your whims. You simply pick up your car at any of the international airports in Havana, Varadero, Holguín, or Santiago de Cuba and hit the road armed with vouchers good at any of Horizontes' 70-plus hotels Islandwide. The standard six- or 13-night package includes a stick-shift plus double room with EP plan. The package offers unlimited mileage and the flexibility of traveling wherever you wish, without hotel reservations (except for the first night, which is reserved in advance). Another benefit is that you can drop the car off at any of the other locations at no additional charge. Nor do you have to pay a deposit for the car rental. Children under 12 travel free. Horizontes provides you with a handy, pocket-size guide to touring Cuba which includes a list of Cupet gas stations. Horizontes has 24-hour service.

Cubacar Car Rental, Avenida 146 e/ 11 y 13, Playa, Apdo. Postal 16046, Havana 11600, tel. 33-1700, fax 33-1656, also offers fly-drive packages, as does **Havanatur,** Calle 2 #17, e/ 1 y 3, Miramar, Havana, tel. 33-2273, fax 33-2877.

In the UK, **Journey Latin America,** 14-16 Devonshire Rd., Chiswick, London W4 2HD, tel. (181) 747-8315, fax (181) 742-1312, offers two two-week fly-drive programs with set itineraries, departing London's Stansted airport on Thursday year-round. The first includes nights in Havana, Sancti Spíritus, Camagüey,

Santiago de Cuba, and Holguín; the second is a shortened version—Havana to Holguín. Options include a Suzuki 4WD or small sedan. The first 1,400 km is included in the price, which ranges from £1,279 to £1,429 per person, double.

Motorcycles and Scooters: At press time, you could not rent motorcycles in Cuba. However, small Japanese scooters can be rented from Rumbos stands at virtually all the main resorts. Rates are about US$30 a day, plus insurance. They're highly unstable, especially in the sand-blown streets of resorts. If you opt for a scooter, drive slowly and cautiously.

Taking your own Motorcycle: Yes, you can take your own motorbike. It's amazingly easy and trouble-free once you get it to Cuba. Outside the US, you can ship your motorcycle air-freight with most scheduled carriers (Cubana charges about US$1,000 one-way from Mexico aboard its DC-10). You would be wise to contact a motorcycle shipping broker, who can usually get better rates and can take care of freighting insurance, etc. In Germany, contact **mhs Motorradtouren GmbH,** Donnersbergerstrasse 32, D-8000 Munich 19, tel. (49) 89-168-4888, fax (49) 89-166-5549.

Getting there from the US is more of a problem. In 1996, I took my motorcycle to Cuba with a private skipper from Florida. Many US sailors take their motorbikes into Cuba, and entering Cuba with a vehicle is a breeze.

Consider freighting by sea from Europe, Canada, or Tampico (Mexico) aboard **Coral Container Lines,** Calle Oficios #170, Havana, tel. 33-8766, fax 33-8123, Cuba's freight service. In Mexico, contact **Raymis,** tel. 14-2376, fax 14-2379.

Documentation in Cuba: Upon arrival in Cuba (presumably at Marina Hemingway), you'll be given a letter from Cuban Customs (make sure it has an official stamp), which grants you one week in which to register with the main Customs office at Terminal Sierra Mastra in Habana Vieja (it was scheduled to move at press time). Here, you're given another offical form that grants you the right to import your motorbike for 30 days (you'll need to return to this office to have it extended, in increments of 30 days). You then go to the main Transit Police office at Avenida 1ra (e/ 12 y 14) in Miramar to have

your motorbike inspected and receive a *chapa* (license plate). You'll need to take a special 10-peso stamp, which you purchase at any post office (the nearest to the *tránsito* office is at Avenida 21 and Calle 42; there's a state-run *casa de cambio* across the road, where you can purchase Cuban pesos). Hence, the whole process will cost 50 cents! The inspectors will make an imprint of your vehicle registration number. (Note that there's a special area in the car park for foreign residents; ask a local to show you.)

If you wish to renew your *chapa* for an additional 30 days, you have to visit the *tránsito* office at Vía Blanca and Aguas Claras, rather than at Avenida 1. First, though, you'll need to receive a 30-day extension from Customs (if you landed your vehicle at Marina Hemingway, you'll need to get a letter from the Customs office there). Fortunately, the extension costs nothing—but it does have to be obtained in Havana.

Returning to the US: Legally, you require an export license from the US Commerce Dept. to take a vehicle to Cuba. Unless you can show sufficient cause, your request will be denied. Hence, if you travel back to the US with a private skipper, you could run afoul of authorities, who could seize your motorbike—a damn good reason to consider freighting via a third country. (US Customs might still seize it if there is Cuban mud on the tires! Make sure your motorbike is scrupulously clean.)

BY BICYCLE

A growing number of visitors to Cuba are showing an interest in cycling tourism, and I've bumped into a handful of foreigners cycling independently through Cuba. One essential item: a sturdy lock! Always take precautions against theft (keep your bicycle in your hotel room). You may even be able to buy a mountain bicycle in Cuba at some dollar stores.

Although they do not have sections on Cuba, *Latin America by Bike: A Complete Touring Guide,* by Walter Sienko (Seattle, WA: The Mountaineers, 1993), and *Latin America by Bike,* by J.P. Panet (New York: Passport Press, 1987) provide good insight into preparing for cycling in the Americas.

THE BICYCLE REVOLUTION

In 1991, when the first shipment of Flying Pigeon bicycles arrived from China, there were only an estimated 30,000 bicycles in Havana, a city of two million people. The visitor arriving in Havana today could be forgiven for imagining he or she had arrived in Ho Chi Minh City. Bicycles are everywhere, outnumbering cars, trucks, and buses twenty to one. The story is the same across the island.

Cynics have dubbed Cuba's wholesale switch to bicycles since the collapse of the Soviet bloc as a socialist failing, a symbol of the nation's backwardness. Others acclaim it an astounding achievement, a two-wheel triumph over an overnight loss of gasoline and adversity. *Granma,* the Cuban newspaper, christened it the "bicycle revolution."

American cars had flooded the island for half a century. Then came the US trade embargo. The 1960s saw the arrival of the first sober-looking Lada and Moskovitch sedans, imported in the ensuing decades by the tens of thousands from the Soviet Union, along with Hungarian and Czech buses, which provided an efficient transport network. The Eastern bloc buses were notorious for their lack of comfort, as were the stunted Girón buses that Cuba began producing in 1967. But they carried millions of Cubans for years despite their defects, most notably their low mileage.

Professor Maurice Halperin, who taught at the University of Havana, does not "recall seeing a single adult Cuban on a bicycle in Havana during the entire period of my residence in the city, from 1962 to 1968."

Goodbye to Gas

The collapse of the Soviet Union severed the nation's gasoline pipeline. Transportation virtually ground to a halt, along with the rest of the Cuban economy.

In November 1990, the Cuban government launched sweeping energy-saving measures that called for a "widespread substitution of oxen for farm machinery and hundreds of thousands of bicycles for gasoline-consuming vehicles." Cuba's program of massive importation, domestic production, and mass distribution, implemented during the past five years, was launched as a "militant and defensive campaign," symbolized on 1 May 1991 when the armed forces appeared on bicycles in the May Day parade.

The government contracted with China to purchase 1.2 million bicycles, and by the end of 1991, 530,000 single-gear Chinese bicycles were in use on the streets of Havana.

Cuba: Bicycle Capital of the Americas

Overnight, Cuba transformed itself into the bicycle capital of the Americas. "The comprehensiveness and speed of implementation of this program," said a 1994 World Bank report, "is unprecedented in the history of transportation." The report noted that about two million bicycles were in use islandwide.

"Today, we can say that the bicycle is as much a part of the Cuban scenario as the palm tree," says Narciso Hernandez, director of Empresa Claudio Arugelles Fábrica de Bicicletas, in Havana. Hernandez's factory is one of five established in 1991 by the Cuban government to supplement the Chinese imports. The government's goal was to produce half a million domestic two-wheelers within five

aboard a ciclobus

CHRISTOPHER P. BAKER

years. Each of the factories produces a different model. Cuba imports parts such as small bolts, chains, spindles, and brakes, but makes the frames, forks and handlebars.

The bicycles are disbursed through MINCIN (Ministerio de Comercial Interior), which parcels them out to schools, factories, and workers' associations. Others are sold at special stores. Lucky recipients can purchase their bicycles outright or pay for them in monthly installments. Workers pay 125 pesos— equivalent to about half the average monthly salary—while students pay 65 pesos. Cuba still can't produce enough bicycles to satisfy the demand, and a thriving black market has arisen.

The Chinese bicycles were cumbersome, hard-to-pump beasts—true antediluvian pachyderms with only one gear. Worse, they weighed 48 pounds. The Cubans redesigned the chunky models with smaller frames, thereby lopping off 15 pounds. In a corner of Fábrica Empresa Claudio Arugelles, I saw a mini-mountain of discarded sheaf-springs. Surely they belonged on cars or trucks? No, said Hernandez, they belonged to some of the 60,000 Chinese cargo tricycles that Cuba imported in 1991 to replace its scuttled truck fleet. "The springs are too heavy, so we eliminate them," he explained. Other Cuban innovations include a tricycle for disabled people, and a "bicibus," a Dr Seuss-worthy contraption made of two bicycles with rows of seats—and pedals—for twelve people in-between. Hernandez proudly pointed out a rugged-looking prototype of an all-chrome, all terrain mountain bike of lightweight metals, with pneumatic suspension at front and rear. "One day soon, Cuba hopes to begin exporting bikes," Hernandez said.

Cubans manage to coax great speed from their sturdy steeds. Young men zigzag through the streets, disdainful of all other traffic, while old men and women pedal painstakingly down the middle of the road with leisurely sovereignty, like holy cattle. During the early phase of the bicycle revolution, hospital emergency rooms were flooded with victims. Most Cubans had never ridden bicycles before. They teetered en masse through the pot-holed streets, often with passengers, even whole families, hanging onto jury-rigged seats and rear-hub extenders. Due to the paucity of cars, cyclists rode the wrong way down major boulevards, which they crisscrossed at will. Few *bicis* had rear reflectors, and the brakes on the Chinese-made models barely worked. Handlebar warning bells chirped incessantly.

Cuban planners like Gina Rey, of the Group for the Integral Development of the Capital, were challenged to reorganize Havana's transportation network to prevent turmoil on the streets. The plan called for many colonial streets in Habana Vieja to be closed to motorized traffic. Bicycle lanes were created. The city government initiated classes in bicycle safety. Bicycle parking lots were cleared throughout the city. Ferry boats threading their way across Havana harbour were equipped for bicycles. And special buses *(Ciclobuses)* were detailed to carry cyclists through the tunnel beneath the bay.

"We've entered the bicycle era," Castro has noted. "But after this Special Period disappears we mustn't abandon this wonderful custom." Bicycles would solve many of the country's energy quandries—and pollution and health problems, too. "With bicycles, we will improve the quality of life in our society," Castro claims. Anyone who has seen Hungarian buses coughing fitfully through the streets of Cuba, belching thick black clouds, would agree.

HITCHHIKING

Hitchhiking in Cuba is a way of life, not an invitation to violence. Hitchhikers have plenty of company; many Cubans rely on it, especially in the boonies, where there are official *botellas* (literally bottles, but colloquially the word signifies hitchhiking posts) on the edges of towns. Here, officials of the state Inspección Estatal, wearing mustard-colored uniforms, are in charge. They wave down virtually any vehicle that moves, and all state vehicles (those with red license plates) *must* stop at *botellas* to pick up hitchers. Many *botellas* even have rain shelters and steps to help you climb into trucks! Early morning is easiest for hitching, when there's more traffic.

A queue system prevails—first come, first served. The Cubans will be honored and delighted by the presence of a foreigner, however, and may usher you to the front of the *(cola)*. You, they realize, have restricted time; they have all the time in the world.

Cuba is probably the safest place to hitch in the world, though it may be excrutiatingly slow going. In Cuba, if buses don't go where you're going, don't expect to see many cars. And sticking out your thumb won't do it. Try to wave down the vehicle—whether it's a tractor, a truck, or a motorcycle. If it moves, in Cuba it's fair game. Open-bed trucks are the most likely vehicles. Bring an umbrella to protect against sun and rain; you could end up standing up—literally like cattle—in an open-bed truck for most of your journey. And you'll normally have to pay a few pesos for the privilege!

If you receive a ride in a private car, politeness and gratitude demand that you offer to pay for your ride *("¿Cuanto le debo?")*—after you're safely delivered. Even Cubans normally pay a few coins, and so should you.

ORGANIZED EXCURSIONS

This is one area where Cuba runs a world-class operation. If your time is limited and you like the idea of a smooth-running itinerary, book an excursion with one of the national tour agencies. Their guides are very good—usually friendly, enthusiastic, well educated, and bilingual. You can book excursions at the tour desk in the lobby of virtually any tourist hotel.

Cuba has a surprisingly large and modern fleet of buses and minibuses for transfers, excursions, and touring. For example, Cubanacán coordinates its ground transportation through **Veracuba,** Casa Matriz, Calle 146 #1002, Miramar, Havana, tel. 33-6619, fax 33-6312, which has 350 buses. **Transtur,** Avenida de Santa Catalina #360, Vibora, Habana, tel. 41-3906, 40-4754, or 41-8571, which has been around for more than 30 years, is the biggest transport provider specializing in ground transportation for tourists.

Havanatur's **Tour & Travel,** Calle 23 y M; or Avenida 5 #8409, e/ 84 y 86, Miramar, Havana, tel. 33-0166 or 33-1549, fax 33-1547, offers a series of day excursions to Soroa (US$30) and Viñales (US$38) in Pinar del Río, Trinidad and Cienfuegos (US$120), and Varadero (US$38). Prices include lunch. **Fantástico,** Avenida 146 e/ 11 y 13, Playa, Apdo. Postal 16046, Habana 11600, tel. 33-1700, fax 33-1656, has a similar range of tours to virtually every destination in the country from major tourist sites.

Guides
You can request a personal guide from any of the Havanatur offices nationwide. Most are familiar with at least two languages. They're also extremely well versed in history. If you want to hire one, contact **Havanatur,** Avenida 5 #8409 e/ 84 y 86, Miramar, Havana, tel. 33-2433 or 33-2595, fax 33-1760.

INFORMATION AND SERVICES

VISAS AND OFFICIALDOM

Tourist Cards
A valid passport is required for entry. However, most foreign visitors do not need a visa to enter Cuba; a tourist card will suffice, except for citizens of France, Italy, Russia, Switzerland, and Eastern European and Scandinavian countries, who can enter with only a passport. (Citizens of Japan, Malaysia, Peru, and Singapore *do* need a visa.) No tourist card is required for a stay of less than 72 hours.

Cuban tourist cards are issued by Cuban consulates and through approved tour agencies and airlines abroad. In a pinch, cards may be issued upon arrival at José Martí International Airport in Havana, but don't rely on it. The card costs US$15

(note that many tour operators in Mexico charge inflated rates)—£10 in the UK. If you apply for a card through a Cuban consulate, it can take six or more weeks (go in person if possible). It is usually better to have the card issued by the airline or tour organization handling your passage to Cuba; they can usually issue it without notice. In the UK, **Regent Holidays,** 15 John St., Briston BS1 2HR, tel. 0272-211711, fax 0272-254866, issues tourist cards for £11. You can also get them through **Havanatur UK,** 27 Stafford Rd., Croydon, Surrey CR0 4NG, tel. (0181) 681-3613, fax (0181) 760-0031, or any of the tour operators listed under "Getting There" in this chapter.

Note: When filling out the tourist card, you should take care about what occupation you claim for yourself. Journalists, police officers, and people in military or government service

CUBA TOURIST BUREAUS

ARGENTINA

Paraguay no. 631, Buenos Aires, tel. 311-5820

BRAZIL

Av. Sao Luis 50-39 Andar, CEP 01046 Sao Paulo SP, tel. (11) 259-3044, fax (11) 258-8818

CANADA

55 Queen St. E, Suite 705, Toronto, Ontario M5C 1R5, tel. (416) 362-0700, fax (416) 362-0702

440 Blvd. René Lévesque Quest, Bureau 1402, Montreal, Quebec H2Z 1V7, tel. (514) 875-8004, fax (514) 875-8006

FRANCE

24 rue du Quatre Septembre, 75002 Paris, tel. 474-25-415, fax 400-70-213

GERMANY

Steinweg 2, 6000 Frankfurt Main 1, tel. 069-28-83-22/23

ITALY

via General Fara 30, Terzo Piano, 20124 Milano, tel. 66-98-14-63169

MEXICO

Insurgentes Sur no. 421, Complejo Aristo, Edif. B, 06100 México D.F., tel. 574-9454

RUSSIA

Hotel Belgrado, Moscow, tel. 248-3262

SPAIN

Paseo de la Habana no. 28, 1ed 28036, Madrid, tel. 411-3097

UNITED KINGDOM

161 High Holborn, London WC1V 6PA, tel. (071) 836-3606, fax (071) 836-2602

---

are suspect and face possible surveillance. "Consultant" is a handy occupation and covers a multitude of sins!

Extensions: Tourist cards are good for one entry only and are valid for up to 30 days but can be renewed for up to six months (US citizens may stay in Cuba for a maximum of three months). Extensions—*parogas*—are issued in 30-day increments (US$25). Simply go to the **Buro de Turismo** in the lobby of the Hotel Habana Libre, at Calles 23 y L, in Vedado. The process takes five minutes. You'll be issued a white piece of paper that you should keep with your passport and original tourist card. In Santiago, go to the immigration office at 412 Calle San Vacilio (e/ Carbarrio y Carniceria).

The law requires that you carry your passport or tourist card with you at all times during your stay. It's a good idea to make photocopies of *all* your important documents, including your passport, and keep them separate from the originals, which you can keep in your hotel safe along with other valuables. It's wise, too, to take half-a-dozen passport-size photographs (you can also have photos taken at most **Photo Services** stores throughout Cuba; in Havana, head to the **Centro de Prensa Internacional**—International Press Center—at Calles 23 y O, in Vedado, tel. 32-0526). In the event of a problem, you should contact your embassy or consulate, plus the **Ministerio de Relaciones Exteriores,** Ministry of Foreign Relations (MINREX), Calzada #360 y Avenida de los Presidentes, Vedado, tel. 30-5031. For the MINREX office that handles tourist cards, visas, and passports, call 32-4908.

Special Visas

Businesspeople, journalists, and individuals born in Cuba but now resident abroad must obtain special visas in advance from a Cuban consulate. Your passport *will* be stamped, and you may be required to report to MINREX upon arrival in Havana.

Journalists can slip into Cuba on an ordinary tourist visa, but if Cuban authorities find out they'll insist you obtain a special visa from the International Press Center, Calles 23 y O, in Vedado, tel. 32-0526. A journalist's visa costs US$60. You'll have to hand over your passport, which finds its way to MINREX. This normally takes up to a week, but you can pay a special fee (US$70) to expedite processing and return.

US Citizens

Officially, US citizens need a visa, although in practice a tourist card is all you'll need. Visas can be obtained in advance from the Cuban Interests Section, 2369 16th St. NW, Washington, DC 20009, tel. (202) 797-8515/8. Visas may take months to obtain. Even then, you're not guaranteed a reply. It is far easier to obtain a tourist card from whichever tour agency, organization, or airline you decide to travel to Cuba with. If you're traveling with a group, the organization will obtain your visa in about two weeks. Marazul Tours, 250 West 57th St., Suite 1311, New York, NY 10107, tel. (800) 223-5334 or (212) 582-9570, can facilitate obtaining a tourist visa.

Cuban Émigrés: US citizens of Cuban origin are required to enter and leave Cuba with Cuban passports (you will also need your US passport to depart and enter the United States). No visa is required, but at press time an entry permit (US$100) valid for a 21-day stay was necessary, issued by tour agencies or the Cuban Interests Section or any other Cuban embassy or consulate. Cuban émigrés who have "not demonstrated any hostile attitude toward Cuba and who do not have a criminal record in their country of residence" can obtain a **Multiple Entry Travel Visa** *(vigencia de viaje)* good for two years and entry to Cuba as many times as desired for periods of up to 90 days. A nonrefundable deposit of US$50 is required, plus a US$150 fee payable upon receipt of the permit (you'll need a valid Cuban passport, six passport pictures, and proof that you do not have a criminal record).

Note, however, that Uncle Sam permits Cuban-Americans to visit Cuba only once per year and only for reasons of extreme family hardship!

(Cuba does not recognize dual citizenship for Cuban citizens who are also US citizens; Cuban-born citizens are—according to the US State Department—thereby denied representation through the US Interests Section in the event of arrest).

Other Documentation and Considerations

All tourists may be required to demonstrate an outbound ticket and adequate finances for their proposed stay upon arrival. This is normally requested of travelers planning on staying 30 days or more.

Cuban officials are sensitive to incursions into the country by CIA agents, right-wing Cuban exiles, and other "antisocial" characters. They are sensitive to your appearance, so be aware that you can help your own cause by looking neat and tidy. If you look like you'd be a "bad influence," you might be turned around and put on the next plane home.

Cuban immigration authorities do not require travelers to show proof of immunizations or an international vaccination card.

USEFUL GOVERNMENT TELEPHONE NUMBERS

MINISTRY OF FOREIGN RELATIONS

Reception	tel. 30-5031
Passports and Visas	tel. 32-4908
Europe	tel. 32-1895
North America	tel. 32-5178
USA	tel. 32-0859

CUBAN INSTISTITUE FOR FRIENDSHIP WITH THE PEOPLE (INSTITUTO CUBANO DE AMISTAD CON LOS PUEBLOS)

Foreign residents (living in Cuba)	tel. 32-7641
Cuban residents abroad	tel. 32-3464
Europe	tel. 32-5405
North America	tel. 32-9561

OTHER ORGANIZATIONS

Federation of Cuban Women	tel. 30-6043
Institute of National Parks	tel. 29-0523
Institute of Sports and Physical Education	tel. 40-3581

The following numbers are for the **international relations** offices of the following ministries:

Communications	tel. 78-2860
Economy and Planning	tel. 81-9354
Education	tel. 61-5147
Foreign Investment	tel. 23-8573
Health	tel. 33-3511
Justice	tel. 30-9915
Science and Technology	tel. 62-6606
Sports and Physical Education	tel. 40-5366
Superior Education	tel. 32-3548
Tourism	tel. 33-0545

turned around at the airport and sent packing. A nominal limit of six rolls of film is rarely enforced.

A Customs declaration need not be filled out. However, if you're carrying particularly valuable items such as laptop computers or high-tech video cameras, you may be asked to provide a written declaration. If for whatever reason you must leave some items with Customs authorities, make sure that you obtain a signed receipt to enable you to reclaim the items upon departure.

In June 1995, everyone entering Cuba was granted the right to import newly acquired objects and articles valued at US$1,000, plus "personal effects" valued at US$100, as well as 10 kilograms of medicine.

Your hand-carried baggage will be X-rayed upon arrival at the Havana airport.

FREEDOM TO TRAVEL

In 1984, the Supreme Court agreed that US citizens have a constitutional right to travel but that the right had to yield to national security concerns. Hence, restrictions on travel to Cuba were upheld within the bailiwick of executive (presidential) privilege. In September 1995, the **Freedom to Travel Campaign** initiated a lawsuit challenging the constitutionality of the restrictions on travel to Cuba as a violation of First Amendment rights. The US Circuit Court of Appeals, however, upheld the 1984 Supreme Court ruling.

The Freedom to Travel Campaign, P.O. Box 401116, San Francisco, CA 94140, tel. (415) 558-9490, was founded in 1993 to challenge the law directly by organizing highly publicized tours to Cuba. The movement garnered enough support to force Washington to set up an Interagency Review team to reconsider the travel restrictions, while Congress passed a resolution reaffirming the right of US citizens to travel for educational, cultural, and humanitarian purposes.

Amnesty International has vowed that it will consider any US citizens convicted for travel to Cuba as "prisoners of conscience" and will launch an international campaign on their behalf.

(Independent travelers are no longer required to report to the Cubatur Individual Tourism Desk at the airport.)

Don't lose your baggage claim tag issued at your originating airport. You'll need to show this upon exiting the airport in Cuba.

CUSTOMS

Travelers arriving in Cuba are allowed to bring in three liters of alcohol, a carton of cigarettes, and personal effects, including a camera or video camera, portable radio, typewriter, sports gear, etc. I've even brought in a laptop computer. You cannot bring in firearms, although hunting guns—which require a license—are permitted. Cuban authorities will seize fruits, weapons, and "counterrevolutionary" or pornographic materials, in which case you may be

---

DRUGS

Cuban law prohibits the possession, sale, or use of narcotic substances, including marijuana. Laws are strictly enforced and Cuba vigorously prosecutes drug traffickers caught in Cuban territory. Whatever your personal beliefs on drug use, Cuba is no place to demonstrate a statement of rights. Be warned that both the US and Cuban governments are attempting to stamp out drug trafficking, and if you're caught, you will receive no special favors because you're foreign. A trial could take many months, in which case you'll be jailed on the premise that you're guilty until proven innocent.

Few countries are so drug-free. You may, rarely, come across homegrown marijuana, but serious drug use is unknown. Be aware that if offered drugs on the street, you may be dealing with a plainclothes policeman.

Looking unkempt and dirty sets alarm bells ringing in the minds of officialdom. If you normally roll your own cigarettes, consider leaving your papers at home. Stick to commercial brands. Better yet, use it as an opportunity to give up smoking.

You should bring with you only medications for personal use as prescribed by a physician (a letter from your physician explaining the need for any prescription drugs in your possession might also be a good idea).

CUBAN CONSULATES/EMBASSIES ABROAD

Australia: 9-15 Bronte Rd. #804, Sydney NSW 2026, tel. (70) 354-1417
Canada: 388 Main St., Ottawa K1S 1E3, tel. (613) 563-0141, fax (613) 540-2066
England: (Embassy) 167 High Holborn, London WC1V 6PA, tel. (171) 240-2488
England: (Consulate) 15 Grape St., London WC2H 8DR, tel. (171) 240-2488
France: 16 rue de Presles, 75015 Paris, tel. (1) 4567-5535, fax (1) 4566-4635
Germany: Kennedy Allee 22-24, 5300 Bonn 2, Godesberg, tel. (228) 885733
Italy: Via Licinia 7, 00153 Rome, tel. (6) 575-5984
Mexico: Presidente Masarik 554, Colonia Polanco, Mexico 5 DF, tel. (5) 259-0045
Netherlands: Prins Mauritslaan 6, The Hague 2582 LRR, tel. (2) 371-5766
Spain: Paseo de la Habana 194, Madrid, tel. (1) 458-2500
Switzerland: Seminarstrasse 29, 3006 Bern, tel. (31) 444-834
USA: (Interests Section) 2630 16th St. N.W., Washington, D.C. 20009, tel. (202) 797-8518, fax (202) 797-8512

The headquarters of Cuban Customs **(Aduana General de la República)** is at Plaza de la Revolución #6, Nuevo Vedado, tel. 81-0022.

Exiting Cuba
Travelers exiting Cuba are charged US$15 departure tax on international flights. No charge applies for travelers leaving by private boat. Cuba prohibits the export of valuable antiques and art without a license, including pre-Columbian artifacts, as well (ostensibly) as endangered wildlife products.

You may not export more than US$5,000 in cash.

Returning to the US
US citizens who have traveled *legally* to Cuba are allowed to bring back no more than US$100 of Cuban goods as accompanied baggage, plus up to US$10,000 of artwork and an unlimited amount of literature, posters, and other informational materials protected under the First Amendment of the Constitution. Sculpture created by Cubans may be licensed for importation provided it is lower than $25,000 in value, and you are also allowed to bring back a "reasonable" amount of Cuban cigars—as long as you purchased them in Cuba. "Reasonable" means up to four boxes per person. Uncle Sam quirkily forbids you to bring cigars back if bought anywhere other than in Cuba. Be sure to get a receipt, even if you buy from a street seller. No goods of Cuban origin may be imported to the US unaccompanied, either directly or through third countries, such as Canada or Mexico.

All other US citizens are liable to have any Cuban goods confiscated, however innocuous and however acquired. Don't tempt fate by flaunting your Cuban T-shirt or shaking your Cuban maracas!

The Office of Foreign Assets Controls publishes a pamphlet, *What You Need to Know about the US Embargo,* US Department of the Treasury, Washington, D.C. 20220, tel. (202) 622-2520. Alternately, contact the US Customs Service, 1301 Constitution Ave. NW, Washington, D.C. 20229.

Citizens of all other countries entering the US after visiting Cuba are immune from Uncle Sam's restrictions.

Returning to Canada
Canadian citizens are allowed an "exemption" of C$300 annually (or C$100 per quarter) for goods purchased abroad, plus 1.1 liters of spirits and 200 cigarettes.

Drugs
It goes without saying that trying to smuggle drugs through Customs is not only illegal but also stupid. Trained dogs are employed to sniff out contraband at US airports as well as at Cuban airports and ports.

SPECIAL CONSIDERATIONS

NOTES FOR MEN

The lures of women is the likeliest source of problems for men.

Cuban women have a reputation for being hot-blooded. They like being romanced but they're also aggressive, displaying little equivocation. Cuban women often call foreign men timid ("They touch you like you're crystal"). Such overt sexuality can be thrilling to males raised in a Protestant or Catholic culture. As such, amorous Mexicans are flocking to Havana for the mulatta women. And on the beaches of Playa del Este and Varadero, langorous Lolitas in tiny *tangas* sashay along the sands in the arms of Italian men. Tourism-generated prostitution is proliferating. So, too, are marriages between Cubans and foreigners. The government takes a glum view of both.

Although there are many exceptions, it is often not any animal magnetism that makes Cuban women want to share your bed. It is the bulge in your pocket—a wallet filled with greenbacks. Many women who seek out foreigners would laugh to be called prostitutes (*jiniteras,* from *jineta*—jockey), the term used for women who hang out at the entrances of hotels and discos or parade the beaches, seeking invitations for drinks, a meal, a taste of the high life, and—*"por Dio!"*—a romantic liaison that may even end, who knows, in a proposal of marriage to a wealthy *pepe* (slang for foreigner). But the Castro regime sees things differently. In 1996, it began a crackdown on *jiniterismo,* including attempts to regulate visits by Cubans in private apartments rented by foreign tourists and the arrest of at least two groups of foreign males involved in "pornogaphy." Circumspection is called for.

Fortunately, Cuba seems free of the kind of scams pulled by good-time girls in other countries, such as muggings by male accomplices, and even drugging and robbery. Nonetheless, any involvement with salacious ladies requires prudence.

Men in "sensitive" occupations (journalists and government employees) should be aware that there is always a possibility that the femme fatale who sweeps you off your feet may be in the employ of Cuba's state security.

NOTES FOR WOMEN

Most women stress the enjoyment of traveling in Cuba. With few exceptions, Cuban men treat women with great respect and, for the most part, as equals. Post-revolutionary political correctness is everywhere. True, Cuba is a mildly macho society, but sexual assault of women is unheard of. It is hard to imagine a safer place for women to travel. This is especially true in the countryside, where the Cuban male is much more conservative than his urban counterpart. *Women Travel: Adventures, Advice, and Experience,* by Niktania Jansz and Miranda Davies (Rough Guides), is full of practical advice for women travelers.

If you do welcome the amorous overtures of men, Cuba is heaven. The art of gentle seduction is to Cuban men a kind of national pastime—a sport and a trial of manhood. They will hiss in appreciation from a distance like serpents, and call out *piropos*—affectionate and lyrical opithets that, in general, Cuban women encourage.

Take effusions of love with a grain of salt; while swearing eternal devotion, your Don Juan may conveniently forget to mention he's married. Be aware, too, that while the affection may be genuine, you are assuredly the moneybags in the relationship. There are even Cuban men who earn their living giving pleasure to women looking for love beneath the palms.

Cuban men are used to Cuban women, who fully express their megaton sexuality. My female friends report that Cuban men are diligent in the role of pleasing a woman.

If you're not interested in love in the tropics, simply pretend not to notice advances and avoid eye contact; a longing stare is part of the game. You can help prevent these overtures by dressing modestly, especially in rural areas where shorts, tube tops, or strapless sundresses invite attention.

SEXUAL MORES IN CUBA

Cuba is a sexually permissive society. As journalist Jacobo Timerman wrote, "Eros is amply gratified in Cuba and needs no stimulation." Cuban men and women alike pervade a joyous eroticism that transcends the hangups of essentially puritanical Europe or North America. Seduction is a national pastime pursued by both sexes—the free expression of a high-spirited people confined in an authoritarian world. After all, Cubans joke, sex is the only thing Castro can't ration.

In *Chronicles of the City of Havana* (1991), Uruguayan journalist Eduardo Galeano tells the following story.

One day at noon, *guagua* 68 screeched to a halt at an intersection. There were cries of protest at the tremendous jolt until the passengers saw why the bus driver had jammed on the brakes: a magnificent woman had just crossed the street.

"You'll have to forgive me, gentlemen," said the driver of *guagua* 68, and he got out. All the passengers applauded and wished him luck.

The bus driver swaggered along, in no hurry, and the passengers watched him approach the saucy female, who stood on the corner, leaning against the wall, licking an ice cream cone. From *guagua* 68, the passengers followed the darting motion of her tongue as it kissed the ice cream while the driver talked on and on with no apparent result, until all at once she laughed and glanced up at him. The driver gave the thumbs-up sign and the passengers burst into a hearty ovation.

Promiscuity is rampant. So are extramarital affairs. Love is not associated with sex. And both genders are unusually bold. Men and women let their eyes run slowly over strangers they find attractive. Long glances—*ojitos*—often accompanied by uninhibited comments, betray envisioned improprieties. Even the women murmur *piropos*—courtly overtures—and sometimes comic declarations of love. "Dark-eyed Stellas light their feller's panatelas," Irving Berlin once wrote of Cuba. And how!

Teenagers become sexually active at an early age: girls at 13 on average, boys at 15, according to Cuba's National Center for Sex Education, which dispenses sex counseling to youths, along with condoms and birth control pills. Males and females and old and young alike insist that promiscuity is a natural attribute. "Cubans like sex," says the director of Baracoa's family planning clinic. "It's part of our daily meal. Here you have girls who at 13 are already experts in sex." More than 160,000 abortions are performed free of charge each year, one-third on teenagers; in 1989, 61% of births were out of wedlock.

A good resource is the **Federación de Mujeres Cubanas,** Cuban Women's Federation, Paseo #260, Vedado, Havana, tel. 30-9931, which sponsors forums and acts to promote the interests of women. In the US, you might find the **Federation of Women's Travel Organizations,** 4545 N. 36th St. #126, Phoenix, AZ 85018, tel. (602) 956-7175, useful.

Global Exchange, 2017 Mission St., Room 303, San Francisco, CA 94110, tel. (415) 497-1994 or (800) 497-1994, fax (415) 255-7498, leads a Women's Delegation to Cuba study tour, in which participants meet women workers and members of women's and neighborhood organizations. Their 1996 trip cost US$1,300, including roundtrip airfare from Cancún. The **Center for Cuban Studies,** 124 West 23rd St., New York, NY 10011, tel. (212) 242-0559, fax (212) 242-1937, also has similar study tours occasionally.

NOTES FOR GAYS AND LESBIANS

Cuba is schizophrenic when it comes to homosexuality. Following the Revolution, homosexuals were treated harshly. During the late 1960s, scores of gays were purged from government posts and sent to work camps, and purges continued sporadically through the next decade. (Even Castro's guest Allen Ginsberg, the homosexual poet, was kicked out of Cuba for remarking that Fidel Castro must have had homosexual experiences as a boy and for stating that he would like to make love with Che Guevara.)

In the past decade, the Cuban government has attempted to make amends. The interior of the country, more wed to traditional machismo and antigay sentiment, is also liberalizing. Discrimination still exists, but there are still instances of police harassment, and derogatory terms persist. Gays, *jineteros,* and Cuban "liberals" who befriend foreigners often fall afoul of the law of *peligrosidad,* which declares as "dangerous" anyone who acts in an antisocial manner and against the norms of socialist morality.

To understand the sociology of Latino homosexuality, readers of Spanish may wish to browse *Hombres que Aman Hombres,* by Jacobo Schifter Sikora and Johnny Madrigal Pana (San José, Costa Rica: Ediciones Illep-Sida, 1992).

Meeting Places

Many Cuban homosexuals remain in the closet. Still, there are an increasing number of gay gathering places in Havana, such as the shorefront on Avenida 1ra and Calle 16 in Miramar, a section on Santa María beach at Playas del Este, Coppelia at Calle 23 and L in Vedado, and the Parque Maceo on the Malecón in Centro Habana. Don Giovanni, on Calle Tacón, is also a gathering spot for gays and lesbians, as is Café O'Reilly in Habana Vieja.

Organizations

I am not aware of any lesbian organization (Cuban machismo is still so strongly entrenched that it is inconceivable to many that lesbianism actually exists). The first gay men's group on the island, called **Cubans in the Struggle Against AIDS,** was recently formed. And gays and lesbians from Cuba and the US joined hands in February 1994 to form a networking group—**Queers for Cuba**—based out of the **Cuban National Commission on Sex Education,** Calle 23 #177, Vedado, Havana, tel. 30-2679, and intended to build solidarity with Cuban lesbians, bisexuals, and gays. It sponsors educational forums about the reality of gays in Cuba and organizes delegations to the island. The group is requesting donations of gay literature, school and office supplies, and safe sex materials. Donations can be sent to Queers for Cuba, 3543 18th St., Box 33, San Francisco, CA 94110, tel. (415) 995-4678, which also offers solidarity trips to the island.

The Center for Cuban Studies, tel. (212) 242-0559, offers occasional "update" study tours of lesbian and gay issues in Cuba. It also requests donations of condoms, safe sex materials, literature, medicines, etc. **MADRE,** 121 West 237th St. #301, New York, NY 10001, also accepts donations of material aid (condoms, literature, etc.) for distribution in Cuba.

Useful resources include the **Gay & Lesbian Travel Services Network,** 2300 Market St. #142, San Francisco, CA 94114, tel. (415) 552-5140, fax (415) 552-5104; e-mail, gaytvlinfo@aol.com; **Odysseus: The International Gay Travel Planner,** P.O. Box 1548, Port Washington, NY 11050, tel. (516) 944-5330 or (800) 257-5344, fax (516) 944-7540; the **International Gay Travel Association,** P.O. Box 4974, Key West, FL 33041, tel. (800) 448-8550; and the **International Gay & Lesbian Association,** 208 W. 13th St., New York, NY 10011, tel. (212) 620-7310, or, in Europe, 81 Rue Marche au Charbon, 1000 Brussels, Belgium, tel. 32-2-502-2471.

NOTES FOR STUDENTS AND YOUTH

Cuban students receive discounts for entry to many museums and other sites. This may apply to foreign students, too. Cuba is becoming more sophisticated in its relations with foreign organizations. By the time you read this, the **International Student Identity Card** (ISIC) could be accepted in Cuba. The card entitles students 12 years and older to discounts on transportation, entrances to museums, and more. When purchased in the US (US$15; tel. 800-GET-AN-ID), ISIC even includes emergency medical coverage (although this won't apply in Cuba) and access to a 24-hour emergency hotline. Students can obtain ISICs at any student union. Alternately, in the US, contact the **Council on International Educational Exchange (CIEE),** 205 E. 42nd St., New York, NY 10017, tel. (212) 661-1414, fax (212) 972-3231. In Canada, cards (C$13) can be obtained through **Travel Cuts,** 187 College St., Toronto, ON, tel. (416) 979-2406. In the UK, students can obtain an ISIC from any student union.

The **Youth International Educational Exchange Card** provides similar benefits for students and for nonstudents under 26. In the US, contact CIEE; in Europe, contact the **Federation of International Youth Travel,** Bredgade 25 H, Copenhagen, DK-1210 Denmark, tel. 45-33-33-9600, fax 45-33-93-9676. However, there is no guarantee the card will be honored in Cuba.

In 1995, President Clinton agreed to permit academic exchanges with Cuba. Students will be permitted to enroll at Cuban universities. The

Cuban Exchange Program, School of Advanced International Studies, Johns Hopkins University, 1740 Massachusetts Ave. NW, Washington, D.C. 20036, tel. (202) 663-5732, fax (202) 663-5737, can provide information.

Transitions Abroad, 18 Hulst Rd., Box 344, Amherst, MA 01004, tel. (413) 256-0373, provides information for students wishing to study abroad. Another handy resource is the *Directory of Study Abroad Programs,* contact Renaissance Publications, 7819 Barkwood Dr., Worthington, OH 43085, tel. (614) 885-9568, fax (614) 436-2793, and **CIEE's Work Abroad Department,** 205 E. 42nd St., New York, NY 10017, tel. (212) 661-1414, ext. 1130.

The **Union de Jovenes Comunistas** (Young Communists' Union) has an international relations office at Calle 17 #252, Vedado, Havana, tel. 32-3906. It also operates a youth hotel, **Hotel Juventud,** on Avenida 7ma, Altahabana, tel. 33-8799. The **Universidad de Habana** (University of Havana), tel. 78-2252, is at Calle L y Colina in Vedado.

NOTES FOR SENIORS

Cuba treats its own senior citizens with honor, and discounts are offered for entry to museums, etc. Again, this may apply to foreign seniors in a few instances.

Global Exchange, 2017 Mission St., Room 303, San Francisco, CA 94110, tel. (415) 497-1994 or (800) 497-1994, fax (415) 255-7498, occasionally offers an "Elders in Cuba" study tour.

Useful resources include the **American Association of Retired Persons** (AARP), 601 E. St., Washington, D.C. 20049, tel. (202) 434-2277, which has a "Purchase Privilege Program" offering discounts on airfares which you may be able to use for flights to a third country en route to Cuba. **Elderhostel,** 80 Boylston St., Suite 400, Boston, MA 02116, tel. (617) 426-7788, offers educational trips for seniors, as does Toronto-based **ElderTreks,** tel. (416) 588-5000. Neither organization offered trips to Cuba at press time, but they may be useful resources.

Other handy sources include *The Mature Traveler,* P.O. Box 50820, Reno, NV 89513, a monthly newsletter; and *The International Health Guide for Senior Citizen Travelers,* by Robert Lange, M.D. (New York: Pilot Books).

NOTES FOR TRAVELERS WITH DISABILITIES

Cuba has made great advances in guaranteeing the rights of the disabled, and Cubans go out of their way to assist travelers with disabilities. However, you'll need to plan your vacation carefully—few allowances have been made in infrastructure.

The **Cuban Association for Physically-Motor Disabled People** (ACLIFIM) can be of assistance. In 1995, it organized the first international Conference on Disabled People's Rights in Havana. You can write ACLIFIM at Ermita #213 e/ San Pedro y Lombillo, Plaza de la Revolución, CP 10600, Havana, tel. 81-5336 or 81-0911, fax 33-3787, e-mail aclifim@informed.sld.cu. Alternately, in the US, contact **Marazul Tours,** Tower Plaza, 4100 Park Ave, Weehawken, NJ 07087, tel. (201) 319-9670 or (800) 223-5334, fax (201) 319-9009, which arranges trips to this and similar conferences.

In the US, the **Society for the Advancement of Travel for the Handicapped,** 347 5th Ave. #610, New York, NY 10016, tel. (212) 447-7284, fax (212) 725-8253, publishes a quarterly newsletter entitled *Access to Travel.* Another handy newsletter is *The Wheelchair Traveler,* 23 Ball Hill Rd., Milford, NH 03055, tel. (603) 673-4539. Don't expect them to have much information on Cuba, however.

TRAVELERS WITH CHILDREN

Generally, travel with children poses no special problems. Cubans adore children and will dote on yours. There are few sanitary or health problems to worry about. However, children's items such as diapers (nappies) and baby foods are very difficult to obtain in Cuba. Bring cotton swabs, diapers (consider bringing cotton diapers; they're more ecologically acceptable), Band-Aids, and a small first-aid kit with any necessary medicines for your child. If you plan on driving around, bring your own children's car seat—they're not offered in rental cars.

Children's hospitals are located in all major cities; Havana has seven children's hospitals, including the **Pediatrico Centro Habana,** Calzada de Infanta y Benjumeda, Centro Habana, tel. 79-6002.

Children under the age of two travel free on airlines; children between two and 12 are offered special discounts (check with individual airlines). Children under 16 usually stay free with parents at hotels, although an extra-bed rate may be charged.

Cuban TV features a few children's programs, and you can find kiddies' books in Spanish at leading bookstores. Many hotels feature children's amusements, including water slides. Some also offer babysitting. There are children's amusement parks **(parques diversiones)** in every town, although most are run-down. Several have carousels, small roller coasters, and other rides.

The equivalent of the Boy and Girl Scouts and Girl Guides is the **Pioneros José Martí,** Avenida de la Presidencia #503, Vedado, Havana, tel. 32-1111, which has chapters throughout the country. Its main focus is instilling youth with revolutionary correctness and civil responsibility. Having your children interact would be a fascinating education.

Travel with Your Children, 45 W. 18th St., New York, NY 10011, tel. (212) 206-0688, publishes the *Family Fun Times* newsletter 10 times a year (US$35 subscription). It also operates an information service. **Great Vacations with Your Kids** (New York: E.P. Dutton), by Dorothy Jordan and Marjorie Cohen, is a handy reference guide to planning a trip with children.

PERSONAL CONDUCT

Cubans are immensely respectful and courteous, with a deep sense of integrity. Politeness is greatly appreciated, and you can ease your way considerably by being both courteous and patient. Always greet your host with *"¡Buenas días!"* (morning) or *"¡Buenas tardes!"* (afternoon). And never neglect to say, *"Gracias."* Honor local dress codes as appropriate. Topless and nude bathing are neither allowed nor accepted (except at Varadero, Cayo Coco, and Cay Largo, where topless bathing is tolerated). For men, short shorts should be relegated to beachwear, although longer shorts are now gaining acceptance on urban streets for men. Cuban women, however, expose a lot of flesh in their everyday dress.

Cubans are extremely hygienic and have an understandable natural prejudice against anyone who ignores personal hygiene.

Respect the natural environment. Take only photographs, leave only footprints.

DEALING WITH OFFICIALS

Bribery and Corruption
Cuba is one of the few places in the world where you can get yourself into serious trouble by offering a bribe. To its credit, Castro's government has differed greatly from other countries receiving billions of dollars in foreign aid—most of which ends up in officials' pockets. It also ended overt corruption, where an elite ruling class plundered the national treasury. Virtually every policemen or official you deal with will be scrupulously honest.

However, during major financial straits, otherwise upright honest people will do unscrupulous things, and the integrity of Cuban officials is beginning to show cracks. Many have turned to the black market to augment their salaries. Castro blames the growth in bribery and corruption on "economic relations with capitalism" (see Andres Oppenheimer's *Castro's Final Hour* for an opposing viewpoint). There have been isolated reports of tourists being shaken down for money, although most corruption seems to be in black-market activities that are hardly likely to affect you.

POLITICAL ACTIVITY

Criticism of the government is defined as "anti-social behavior" and is punishable by law. Given three decades of US efforts to destabilize the country, Cuban authorities understandably do not look favorably on foreigners who become involved in political activity, especially with known dissidents. Avoid making inflammatory comments; otherwise, you could well find yourself on the next plane home.

CHRISTOPHER P. BAKER

Capitolo, Havana

Never pay a policeman money. If a policeman asks for money, get his name and badge number and file a complaint to the Ministry of Foreign Relations.

Police
The **Nacional Revolucionario Policía** (National Revolutionary Police) are a branch of the Ministry of the Interior.

In Havana, you'll see uniformed policemen everywhere. My experiences with uniformed Cuban policemen, who perform the same functions as uniformed police officers in other countries, have been wholly positive. From transit cop to beat cop to tourist cop, I've witnessed great civility and impressive courtesy.

Sure, it's disconcerting to see ordinary Cubans being stopped at random for I.D. checks, but it's a far cry from countries such as Guatemala, Haiti, or El Salvador, where you sense the machine-gun-toting police are there to intimidate.

Police are under instructions *not* to stop or harass tourists unless they have broken, or are suspected of breaking, the law. If you are stopped by policemen wanting to search you, insist on it being done in front of a neutral witness—*"solamente con testigos."* If at all possible, do *not* allow an official to confiscate or walk away with your passport (you should always carry a copy of your passport and tourist card with you at all times to verify your identity). Don't panic! Tell as little as circumspection dictates—unlike priests, policemen rarely offer absolution for confessions. And remember, a bribe offered here can get you into real trouble!

Cuba is a paranoid nation that zealously guards against threats to the state's integrity (with good reason; Uncle Sam is still bent on toppling the Castro regime by fair means or foul). The state security apparatus is fine-tuned to keep an eye on foreigners. Plainclothes policemen and informers are abundant, and the CDRs are also alert. Remember that freedom of speech is relative and does not include the right to go around criticizing the Cuban system or you-know-who. Obey all laws and customs. Reportedly, journalists and others in "sensitive occupations" may be assigned specific rooms—which are bugged—or otherwise kept an eye on. Be circumspect about what you say, especially to anyone you do not implicity trust.

Never attempt to photograph police officers or military figures.

Dealing with Bureaucrats
Most government officials with whom you are likely to deal are there to assist you and, as author Simon Charles suggests, "Unlike those in supposedly more developed countries, he understands that!" Well, kind of. Cuba has an insufferable bureaucracy as portrayed in the trenchant black comedy *Death of a Bureaucrat.* The island is riddled with catch-22s, and working with government ministries (I almost wrote "mysteries") can be a perplexing and frustrating endeavor. Civil servants in Cuba are always civil but usually servants only to their master. Very few people have the power to say, "Yes"—but everyone is allowed to say, "No." Finding the person who can say "Yes" is the key.

HUMAN RIGHTS

Disobedience is the capital sin in Cuba. "It is fair to say that under Castro, Cubans have lost even the tenuous civil and political liberties they had under the old regime," claims Professor Wayne Smith, former head of the US Interests Section in Havana. "Woe to anyone who gets on a soap box in downtown Havana and questions the wisdom of the Castro government." The Cuban penal code states that disrespect for authorities is good for one to seven years in prison, and although Castro is careful not to crack down too hard, free speech is tightly controlled.

Writers and artists suffer systematic persecution for "deviations" and are regularly expelled from UNEAC, the Writers' Union, "as traitors to the revolutionary cause." Dissidents dismissed from their jobs are often put to work as gardeners—it's safer to poison garden insects than Cuban minds. Elizardo Sánchez, today president of the dissident Cuban Commission of Human Rights and National Reconciliation, was expelled from the University of Havana for "defending a version of Marxism that differed from the official one" and has since spent years in and out of jail.

The regime is not above jailing even its most loyal supporters if they renege on the Revolution. Carlos Franquí, leading revolutionary, founder of Radio Rebelde, and editor-in-chief of *Revolución*, was even expunged from photos (airbrushed into nonexistence) and made a nonperson until he was forced to flee surreptitiously to France. Even the most trivial comment or action can bring retribution. Thus, Olga Andreu, the librarian of Casa de las Américas, was removed from her job simply for recommending *Tres Tristes Tigres*, a novel by Guillermo Cabrera Infante, who was forced to flee Cuba in 1963 and became persona non grata.

Plantados (dissidents who remain firm) are often taken to Villa Marista, the state security headquarters, where psychological abuse is said to be common. The unlucky ones are said to end up at either the Combinado del Este penitentiary, south of Havana, or the Carbó Serviá ward at the Mazorra, the Havana Provincial Psychiatric Hospital, where some dissidents have reported electric-shock treatment and other physical abuses. *Against All Hope*, by former *plantado* Armando Valladares, tells of his 22 years behind bars in Cuba.

Signs of Improvement

Contemporary Cuba, however, is a far cry from the 1960s, when crushing sentences were imposed en masse following secret, often puppet, trials. In 1965, when the CIA was doing its best to overthrow the Cuban government, Castro admitted that there were 20,000 "counterrevolutionary criminals" in Cuban jails, including cultural and political dissidents. The true numbers were unquestionably far higher.

The US Department of State's reports on human rights suggest that Cuba's record has improved steadily. By international standards, the numbers of political prisoners is now few; in 1989, the International Red Cross identified 257 Cubans in jail for strictly political offenses (subsequent crackdowns have added several hundred more). This is a stain in itself, but a better record than that of Turkey, El Salvador, and several other countries supported by the US.

How Much is the USA to Blame?

The view that Cuba is an oppressive dictatorship is an oversimplification of a complex situation. Fear does not stalk the streets. The military is even popular. More importantly, a small country persecuted by the most powerful nation on earth and living under a relentless state of siege is not the best ground for freedom to flourish. The UN Special Rapporteur seriously criticized Cuba's human rights record but also condemned Washington's hostility to Castro's government as a contributing factor.

For example, during the late 1980s, dissidents enjoyed unprecedented freedoms, and Castro was grudgingly cooperating with international human rights groups. Washington had long said that any improvement in relations between the two countries depended on Cuba's human rights policies. The Bush administration rejected such an improvement and stepped up its attempts to destabilize Cuba, thereby removing any incentive Castro had to continue his policy of leniency. A crackdown followed. Likewise, the government has grown increasingly concerned about Clinton's Track II attempts to foster internal dissent in Cuba, and *it* initiated a new wave of repression.

In late 1995, some 130 dissident factions—most prominently the intellectual opposition movement Criterio Alternativo (Alternative Criterion Group),

(continues on next page)

HUMAN RIGHTS
(continued)

led by Cuban poet María Elena Cruz Varela—formed an umbrella group called the **Concilio Cubano.** Concilio may represent the most significant political challenge to Castro in four decades; while not seeking to overthrow the government, the or-ganization demands that free speech be permitted. Ironically, even the most persecuted of Cuban dissidents are called traitors by the Miami-based right-wing Cuban American National Foundation if they call for dialogue with the Castro regime.

The most important lesson you should learn: ranting at Cubans gets you nowhere. Getting apopletic with charming-faced Cuban official-dom only results in "negatives given more pos-itively, broader and more regretful smiles, a rue-ful elevation of palms, eyes, and shoulders."

Behind every office door is a desk or counter behind which is a woman—preferably middle-aged and the very "cornerstone of bureaucra-cy"—whose job it is to keep people out. Logical arguments count for little; charm, even romantic *priopos* or a gift of chocolate, seem to work better.

HEALTH AND SAFETY

Cuba has the best health system outside the "developed" world (although facilities and standards are not always up to those of, say, North America, Cuba's health indices—which surpass those of the US in several regards—prove that socialized medicine *can* guarantee everyone good care).

Sanitary standards in Cuba are very high, and the chances of succumbing to illness or serious disease are poor. As long as you take appropriate precautions and use common sense, you're not likely to incur serious illness. If you do, you have the benefit of knowing that the nation has a health-care system that guarantees treatment. There are English-speaking doctors in most cities, and you will rarely find yourself far from medical help. However, medicines are hard to find away from key tourist spots (there are local pharmacies everywhere, but since the Special Period, they are poorly stocked; *turno regulares* are open 8 a.m.-5 p.m., *turnos permanentes* are open 24 hours).

Cuba offers specialized services to foreign tourists. Most major cities and resort destinations have 24-hour **international clinics** *(clínicas internacionales)* and pharmacies staffed by English-speaking doctors and nurses. Several hotels have in-house medical personnel. Payment is made in foreign currency (credit cards are accepted, except if issued in the US).

The Cuban agency **Servimed,** Calle 18 #4304 e/ 43 y 47, Miramar, tel. 33-2658, fax 33-2948, operates facilities throughout Cuba that are geared to providing medical and health services to foreigners, including a wide range of beauty- and spa-related services. In Havana, these include the **Clínica Cira García,** tel. 33-2660, a full-service hospital; **Farmacia Internacional,** tel. 33-2051, a pharmacy stocked with Western pharmaceuticals; **Óptica Miramar,** for spectacles and contact lenses; and **Instituto Pedro Kouri,** which specializes in treatment of HIV/AIDS, hepatitis, and other contagious and parasitic diseases. Servimed even offers such programs as drug rehabilitation and treatment for alcoholism at **El Quinque** health resort, at Los Pedernales,

near Bayamo, in Granma province, tel. 33-5301; and **Tayabito** near Camagüey, tel./fax 33-5548.

However, US citizens should note that Uncle Sam's concern for your welfare is such that even if visiting Cuba legally, payment for "non-emergency medical services" is prohibited. Developing an ingrown toenail? Sorry, buddy . . . endure!

BEFORE YOU GO

Dental and medical checkups may be advisable before departing home, particularly if you intend to travel for a considerable time, partake in strenuous activities, or have an existing medical problem. Take along any medications, including prescriptions for eyewear; keep prescription drugs in their original bottles to avoid suspicion at Customs. If you suffer from a debilitating health problem, wear a medical alert bracelet. Pharmacies can prescribe drugs (be wary of expiration dates, as shelf life of drugs may be shortened under tropical conditions).

A basic health kit is a good idea. Pack the following (as a minimum) in a small plastic container: alcohol swabs and medicinal alcohol, antiseptic cream, Band-Aids, aspirin or painkillers, diarrhea medication, sunburn remedy, antifungal foot powder, calamine and/or antihistamine, water-purification tablets, surgical tape, bandages and gauze, and scissors. **Adventure Medical Kits,** P.O. Box 43309, Oakland, CA 94624, tel. (510) 632-1442 or (800) 324-3517, fax (510) 632-1284, has the most comprehensive range of travel and wilderness medical kits, from a whopping Expedition Kit to specialist kits for sailors, whitewater enthusiasts, and families. The packs come with handy medical booklets.

Information on health concerns can be answered by **Intermedic,** 777 3rd Ave., New York, NY 10017, tel. (212) 486-8974, and the **Department of State Citizens Emergency Center,** tel. (202) 647-5225. In the UK, you can get information, innoculations, and medical supplies from the **British Airways Travel Clinic,** tel. (171) 831-5333, which has branches nationwide, or the **Thomas Cook Vaccination Center,** 3-4 Wellington Terrace, Turnpike Lane, London N8 0PXX, tel. (181) 889-7014.

The **International Association for Medical Assistance to Travellers** (IAMAT), 417 Center St., Lewiston, NY 14092, tel. (716) 754-4883; in Canada, 40 Regal Rd., Guelph, Ontario N1K 1B5, tel. (519) 836-0102; in Europe, 57 Voirets, 1212 Grand-Lancy, Geneva, Switzerland, publishes helpful information, including a list of approved physicians and clinics. A useful pocket-sized book is *Staying Healthy in Asia, Africa, and Latin America,* Moon Publications, P.O. Box 3040, Chico, CA 95927-3040, tel. (800) 345-5473, which is packed with first-aid and basic medical information.

Medical Insurance

Medical insurance is highly recommended. Travelers should check to see if their health insurance or other policies cover for medical expenses while abroad—and specifically in Cuba.

Traveler's insurance isn't cheap, but it can be a sound investment. Travel agencies can sell you traveler's health and baggage insurance, as well as insurance against cancellation of a prepaid tour.

In the US: US citizens are in luck: some insurance programs guarantee coverage for Cuba. These include **American Express,** P.O. Box 919010, San Diego, CA 92190, tel. (800) 234-0375. Also try **Wallach and Company,** Box 480, Middleburg, VA 22117, tel. (703) 687-3166 or (800) 237-6615; **Travelers,** 1 Tower Square, Hartford, CT 06183, tel. (203) 277-0111 or (800) 243-3174; **Access America International,** P.O. Box 90315, Richmond, VA 23286, tel. (800) 284-8300; **International Underwriters,** 243 Church St. W, Vienna, VA 22180, tel. (703) 281-9500; **TravelGuard International,** 1145 Clark St., Stevens Point, WI 54481, tel. (715) 345-0505 or (800) 782-5151; and **Carefree Travel Insurance,** Box 310, 120 Meola Blvd., Mineola, NY 11501, tel. (516) 294-0220 or (800) 323-3149.

In the UK: The **Association of British Insurers,** 51 Gresham St., London BC2V 7HQ, tel. (171) 600-3333, and **Europe Assistance,** 252 High St., Croyden, Surrey CR0 1NF, tel. (181) 680-1234, can provide advice for obtaining travel insurance in Britain. Havanatur UK offers an insurance package using **Extrasure Travel Insurances,** 6 Lloyds Ave., London EC3N 3AX,

tel. (171) 488-9341. Their package covers medical expenses up to £3,000,000 plus a host of other benefits. It costs £39.97 for up to nine days, or £43.05 for up to 17 days for adults 17-69 years of age.

In Cuba: You can obtain insurance once you arrive in Cuba through **ESEN,** Calle 18, e/ Avenida 5ta y 7ra, Miramar, Havana, tel. 29-6510 or 33-1763, which offers medical insurance for foreign travelers (US$10 per US$1,000 of treatment). Another Cuban company, **ESICUBA,** Seguros Internacionales de Cuba, Calle Cuba 340, Havana, tel. 62-5051, fax 33-8038, offers travelers' insurance, although most of its policies are oriented toward the needs of companies, not individuals. ESICUBA insures all kinds of risks. Premiums are expensive and can be paid in any convertible foreign currency (indemnities are paid in the same currency). It's open 8 a.m.-3 p.m. Both ESEN and ESICUBA are independent companies, although the Cuban government is the major shareholder. They're rated by Insurance Solvency International and reinsure through Lloyds and other major insurers.

Cubans insure through the **Empresa del Seguro Nacional,** Lagueruela #54, 10 de Octubre, Havana, tel. 99-3462, which has offices throughout Cuba. **Lloyd's of London** has an agency at Calle Obispo 356 in Habana Vieja, tel. 61-0671, and at Calle B #310 between 13 y 15 in Vedado, tel. 33-4663, fax 33-3837.

MEDICAL EMERGENCIES

In emergencies, call 116 for the police. Unfortunately, there is no single emergency telephone number for the Red Cross or ambulance.

You will never be far from a hospital or Red Cross service in Cuba. All hospitals in the country provide free emergency health care for foreigners. If you select treatment at **Clínica García** or another Servimed facility for foreigners, then you will have to pay by cash or credit card and seek reimbursement from your insurance company once you return home (credit cards issued by US banks are not valid).

A Swiss-based company called **Assist-Card** provides emergency services in Cuba, including arranging doctor's visits to your hotel and even emergency evacuation. It works in conjuction with **Asistur.**

Medical Evacuation

Uncle Sam has deemed that even US emergency evacuation services cannot fly to Cuba to evacuate US citizens without a license from the Treasury Department. Of course, the rules keep changing, so it may be worth checking the latest situation with such companies as **Traveler's Emergency Network,** P.O. Box 238, Hyattsville, MD 20797, tel. (800) 275-4836, and **International SOS Assistance,** Box 11568, Philadelphia, PA 19116, tel. (215) 244-1500 or (800) 523-8930, both of which provide worldwide ground and air evacuation and medical assistance.

VACCINATIONS

No vaccinations are required to enter Cuba unless visitors are arriving from areas of cholera and yellow fever infection (mostly Africa and South America), in which they they must have valid vaccinations. Epidemic diseases have mostly been eradicated throughout the country. Cuba's achievements in eliminating infectious disease are unrivaled in the world. It is the only country to have totally eliminated measles, for example.

Consult your physician for recommended vaccinations. Travelers planning to rough it should consider vaccinations against tetanus and infectious hepatitis.

Infectious hepatitis (hepatitis A) is reported only infrequently in Cuba. Main symptoms are stomach pains, loss of appetite, yellowing skin and eyes, and extreme tiredness. Hepatitis A is contracted through unhygienic foods or contaminated water (salads and unpeeled fruits are major culprits). A gamma globulin vaccination is recommended. The much rarer Hepatitis B is usually contracted through unclean needles, blood transfusions, or unsafe sex.

You do *not* need an **International Certificate of Vaccinations.** Plan ahead for getting your vaccinations.

HEALTH PROBLEMS

Infection

Regardless of Cuba's admirable health records, it *is* a tropical country. Even the slightest scratch can fester quickly in the tropics. Treat promptly and regularly with antiseptic and keep the wound clean.

Intestinal Problems

Cuba's tap water is safe to drink in most places. However, serious deficiencies in water treatment chemicals in recent years have made many regional water supplies unsafe (Hurricane Lili, in October 1996, also seriously damaged many water supplies, especially in Cienfuegos and Villa Clara provinces). If you want to play it safe, drink bottled mineral water *(agua mineral),* which is widely available. Remember, ice cubes are water, too. Always wash your hands before eating, and don't brush your teeth using suspect water.

Food hygiene standards in Cuba are very high. Milk is pasteurized, so you're not likely to encounter any problems normally associated with dairy products. However, the change in diet—which may alter the bacteria that are normal and necessary in the bowel—may briefly cause diarrhea or constipation (in case of the latter, eat lots of fruit). Fortunately, the stomach usually builds up a resistance to unaccustomed foods. Most cases of diarrhea are caused by microbial bowel infections resulting from contaminated food. Common-sense precautions include not eating uncooked fish or shellfish (which collect cholera bugs), uncooked vegetables, unwashed salads, or unpeeled fruit (peel the fruit *yourself*). And be fastidious with personal hygiene.

Diarrhea is usually temporary, and many doctors recommend letting it run its course. Personally, I prefer to medicate straight away with Lomotil or another antidiarrheal. Treat diarrhea with rest and lots of liquid to replace the water and salts lost. Avoid alcohol and milk products. If conditions don't improve after three days, seek medical help.

Diarrhea accompanied by severe abdominal pain, blood in your stool, and fever is a sign of **dysentery.** Seek immediate medical diagnosis. Tetracycline or ampicillin is normally used to cure bacillary dysentery. More complex professional treatment is required for amoebic dysentery. The symptoms of both are similar. **Giardiasis,** acquired from infected water, is another intestinal complaint. It causes diarrhea, bloating, persistent indigestion, and weight loss. Again, seek medical advice. **Intestinal worms** can be contracted by walking barefoot on infested beaches, grass, or earth.

Sunburn and Skin Problems

Don't underestimate the tropical sun. It's intense and can fry you in minutes. It can even burn you through light clothing or while you're lying in the shade. The midday sun is especially potent. Even if you consider yourself nicely tanned already, use a suncream or sunblock at least SPF 8. Zinc oxide provides almost 100% protection. Bring sun lotions with you; they're not always readily available in Cuba, although most hotel stores sell them. If you're intent on a tan, have patience. Build up gradually, and use an aloe gel after sunbathing; it helps repair any skin damage. The tops of feet and backs of knees are particularly susceptible to burning. Consider wearing a wide-brimmed hat, too. Calamine lotion and aloe gel will soothe light burns; for more serious burns, use steroid creams.

Sun glare—especially prevalent if you're on water—can cause conjunctivitis. Sunglasses will protect against this. **Prickly heat** is an itchy rash, normally caused by clothing that is too tight or in need of washing. This, and **athlete's foot,** are best treated by airing out the body and washing your clothes.

Dehydration and Heat Problems

The tropical humidity and heat can sap your body fluids like blotting paper. You'll sweat profusely, especially in the Oriente, where summer temperatures are extreme. Leg cramps, exhaustion, dizziness, and headaches are possible signs of dehydration. Although your body may acclimatize to the heat gradually, at the same time dehydration can develop slowly. Diarrhea will drain your body of fluids swiftly.

Drink regularly to avoid dehydration. Ideally, drink water, but *batidos* or *refrescoes* purchased at streetside stalls are a perfectly refreshing Cuban antidote to dehydration. Avoid alcohol, which processes water in the body.

Excessive exposure to too much heat can cause **heat stroke,** a potentially fatal result of a failure in the body's heat-regulation mechanisms.

scorpion

Excessive sweating, extreme headaches, and disorientation leading to possible convulsions and delirium are typical symptoms. Emergency medical care is essential! If hospitalization is not possible, place the victim in the shade, cover him with a wet cloth, and fan continually to cool him down.

Don't be alarmed if your ankles and legs get puffy. It's the tropical climate. When you rest, keep your feet higher than your head (a cold Epsom salts footbath also helps).

Many tourists come down with colds *(catarro Cubano),* often brought up by the debilitating affects of constantly shifting from icily air-conditioned restaurants and hotels to sultry outdoor heat. A more serious ailment is **bronchitis,** which should be treated with antibiotics.

Snakes, Scorpions, and Crocodiles

Snakes are common in Cuba. Fortunately, they're not poisonous. The worst you'll usually suffer is two puncture marks and some bruising and swelling, but who needs that? You should always watch where you're treading or putting your hands, as a startled snake might bite you.

Scorpions exist in Cuba, although they are not very numerous and you are not likely to see them. Their sting is painful and can cause nausea and fever but is not usually as frightening as the horror stories would have you believe. If you get bitten, drink lots of liquids and take lots of rest. Don't forget to shake out your shoes and clothing each morning. Trying to pick up a scorpion by hand is foolish; if the bugger refuses to leave your room, a hard, hefty object (and something to clean up the mess) is the best defense.

A saucepan, however, won't work on the aggressive Cuban crocodile. Something bigger is called for—like a big stick to jam between top and bottom jaws. Fortunately, most areas inhabited by crocodiles, such as the Zapata swamps, are off-limits to foreigners without guides. Don't go wading in swampland.

Insects and Arachnids

At some stage during your visit to Cuba you'll probably be the victim of rapacious **mosquitoes.** Varadero, the cays, Zapata, and other coastal flatlands are particularly noted for mosquitoes, as is the waterfront region of Miramar, in Havana. Their bites itch, sure, but you need have no fear of malaria—it's not present in Cuba. Fortunately, mosquitoes are mostly nocturnal; when they awake from daylight slumber they are demonically hungry and will drool over your blood-suffused body. To keep them at bay, turn on your a/c or overhead fan as high as is comfortable.

However, mosquitoes (particularly those active by day) *do* transmit **dengue fever,** which *is* present, although extremely rare, in Cuba. The illness can be fatal (death usually results from internal hemorrhaging). Its symptoms are similar to those for malaria, with additional severe pain in the joints and bones, for which it is sometimes called "breaking bones disease." Other symptoms include severe headaches and high fever. Unlike malaria, it is not recurring. Clothing can be sprayed with the insecticide permethrin. There is no cure. Dengue fever must run its course. In the unlikely event you contact it, have plenty of aspirin or other painkillers on hand. Drink lots of water.

Tiny, irritating **"no-see-ums,"** truly evil bloodsucking sandflies about the size of a pinpoint, inhabit a few beaches and marshy coastal areas in Cuba. For some strange reason this nuisance (but what a nuisance!) are active only for a short period around dusk. You can pour sulfur powder on your shoes, socks, and ankles. Above all, avoid the beach just before and during dusk.

Repellent sprays and lotions are a must for coastal areas. Take lotion to apply to the body and aerosol spray for clothing. Avon Skin-So-Soft oil is such an effective bug repellent—especially against "no-see-ums"—that US Marines use it by the truckload ("Gee, private, you sure smell nice—and your skin's so soft!"). The best mosquito repellents contain DEET (diethylmetatoluamide), although it leaves "no-see-ums" unfazed. DEET is quite toxic; avoid using it on small children, and avoid getting it on plastic or lycra—which it will melt. Use mosquito netting at night in the lowlands (you can obtain good hammocks and "no-see-um" nets in the US from **Campmor,** P.O. Box 997, Paramus, NJ 07653, tel. (800) 526-4784. A fan over your bed and mosquito coils (*espirales,* which are rarely sold in Cuba) that smolder for up to eight hours also

help keep mosquitoes at bay. Citronella candles may help, too.

Long-sleeved shirts and long pants will help reduce the number of bites you collect.

There are wasps and bees in Cuba; otherwise, Cuba is relatively free of biting insects, especially in the dry central plains, although flies can be abundant. Even ants are a relative rarity. The most common bugs you'll see will be cockroaches, which are found virtually everywhere. Check your bedding before crawling into bed. Keep beds away from walls. And, for true paranoids, look underneath the toilet seat before sitting down.

Fortunately, only a few people have fierce reactions to insect and spider bites. However, bites can easily become infected in the tropics, so avoid scratching! Treat with antiseptics or antibiotics. A baking-soda bath can help relieve itching if you're badly bitten, as can antihistamine tablets, hydrocortisone, and calamine lotion.

Chiggers *(coloradillas)* inhabit grasslands, particularly in dry areas favored by cattle. Their bites itch like hell. Mosquito repellent won't deter them. If you plan on hiking through cattle pastures, consider dusting your shoes, socks, and ankles with sulfur powder. Sucking sulfur tablets *(azufre sublimado)* apparently gives your sweat a smell that chiggers find obnoxious. **C&C Laboratories,** P.O. Box 7779, Dallas, TX 75209, tel. (214) 748-7953, sells Chigarid, for relief of chigger bites. Nail polish apparently works, too (over the bites, not on the nails) by suffocating the beasts.

Ticks hang out near livestock. They burrow head-first into your skin. Extract a tick by gripping it with tweezers as close to the head as you can get and pulling it gently out. Be careful not to pull the body—you'll snap their bodies off, leaving their heads in your flesh, where they'll fester.

Some insect larvae, once laid beneath your skin, can cause boils (you'll often see a clear hole in the middle of the boil or pimple). Completely cover with Vaseline and a secure Band-Aid or tape and let it dry overnight. All being well, you should be able to squeeze the culprit out next day.

Scabies: Since the onset of the Special Period, the lack of hygeine products and generally harsher conditions under which many Cubans are now forced to live has led to a rapid increase in the incidence of scabies (a microscopic mite) and lice. Infestation is possible if you're staying in unhygienic conditions or sleeping with people already infested. A casual sexual liaison is the most common way to become contaminated. If you're unfortunate enough to contract scabies, you'll need to use a body shampoo containing gamma benzene hexachloride or one percent lindane solution (lindane is a highly toxic pesticide). At the same time, you must also wash all your clothing and bedding in very hot water—and throw out your underwear. Your sexual partner will need to do the same. The severe itching caused by scabies infestation appears after three or four weeks (it appears as little dots, often in lines and sometimes ending in blisters, especially around the genitals, elbows, wrists, lower abdomen, nipples, and on the head of the penis). A second bout of scabies usually shows itself within 48 hours of re-infestation. Treatment in the US is by prescription only. However, you can obtain *Scabisan* from Cuban pharmacies, including the **Farmacia Internacional** in Havana.

Avoid **bees nests.** If you disturb a nest, running in a zigzag is said to help in fleeing. If there's water about, take a dunk and stay submerged for a while.

If any bites you receive become infected, it's best to have them treated locally (and certainly promptly); doctors back home might have difficulty diagnosing and treating the condition.

AIDS and Sexually Transmitted Diseases

The risk of contracting AIDS in Cuba is relatively minor. Since 1983, fewer than 350 cases have been reported, and only about 1,400 Cubans had been diagnosed as HIV-positive (virtually the entire adult population has been tested). The Cuban government conducts an exemplary anti-AIDS campaign. Cuba even manufactures AIDS-diagnostic kits as well as interferons for treatment. However, the incidence of AIDS is already showing signs of rapid increase, a situation likely to get worse in coming years, due to the growing prevalence of sexual liaisons between Cubans and foreigners.

Gonorrhea, syphilis, and other sexually transmitted diseases are fairly common. Avoidance of casual sexual contact is the best prevention. If you do succumb to the mating urge, use condoms, which can be purchased at dollar stores. However, don't rely on condoms *(preservativos)* being available locally. You should purchase a supply before departing for Cuba. Practice safe sex!

Other Problems

Rabies, though rare in Cuba, can be contracted through the bite of an infected dog or other animal. It's always fatal unless treated. You're extremely unlikely to be the victim of a vampire bat, a common rabies carrier that preys on cattle. Still, if you're sleeping in the open, keep your toes covered.

SAFETY

All the negative media hype sponsored by Washington has left many people with a false impression that Cuba is unsafe. Far from it. Few places in the world are as safe for visitors as Cuba is.

Frankly, most visitors are far less likely to run into problems in Cuba than they are in their own backyards. The vast majority of Cubans are supremely honest and friendly people. Rape, mugging, and other violent crime is virtually unknown. However, the hardships imposed by the Special Period have fostered a growing problem of petty theft and corruption. And purse-snatching and even mugging are incipient. Remember, there are far more muggings and murders in San Francisco or London each year than in the whole of Cuba.

Traffic is perhaps the greatest danger, despite a relative paucity of vehicles on the road. Be especially wary when crossing the streets in Havana. Stand well away from the curb—especially on corners, where buses often mount the sidewalk. Cyclists are everywhere, making insouciant turns and weaving with leisurely sovereignty, like Brahmin cattle. And sidewalks are full of gaping potholes and tilted curbstones. Watch your step! Outside Havana, oxen, mules, and other livestock wander along the roads. Use extra caution when passing tractors and trucks (often so laden with sugarcane that if they are fortunate enough to have a mirror, they can't use it), which without warning tend to make sweeping turns across the road.

AIDS IN CUBA

Cuba has one of the world's most aggressive and successful campaigns against AIDS. The World Health Organization (WHO) and the Pan-American Health Organization have praised the program as exemplary.

Cuba's unique response to the worldwide epidemic that began in the early 1980s was to initiate mass testing of the population and a "mandatory quarantine" of everyone testing positive. By 1994, when the policy of *mandatory* testing was ended, about 98% of the adult population had been tested. Voluntary testing continues.

The program has stemmed an epidemic that rages only 50 miles away in Haiti and kept the spread of the disease to a level that no other country can equal. By the turn of 1996, Cuba had recorded 1,196 cases of HIV (up 97 cases over 1995), and 287 people had died of AIDS. A recent report by the WHO's Global Program on AIDS showed Cuba with 7.3 cases per million population; in comparison, the US had 241.2 cases per million. New York City, which has roughly the same population as Cuba (approximately 10 million) had 42,737 cases of full-blown AIDS as of February 1993. Puerto Rico has only one-third Cuba's population but 8,117 reported cases of AIDS.

At first, the purpose was keeping the disease from spreading. The objective was to develop AIDS sanatoriums throughout the island, where people who test HIV-positive could be evaluated medically and psychologically and educated in the ethics and biology of AIDS prevention—then go out and lead a normal life, using the sanatorium as an outpatient facility. Twelve sanatoriums exist on the island. Residents live in small houses or apartments, alone or as couples (straight or gay).

Cuba has defended its sanatorium policy as a way of guaranteeing first-class health care for patients while protecting the rest of the population. "When you think about the amount of money they spend on each of us, and that we don't pay one cent!" an AIDS-positive hemophiliac told journalist Karen Wald, "and apart from that, we receive our complete salary. What other country in the world

has done that? You're asking if the Revolution violates my rights by sending me to a sanatorium? I'm alive because of the Revolution!"

Mandatory confinement was ended in early 1994. Instead, an outpatient program has been implemented. (Anyone who tests HIV-positive has his or her job and salary assured, whether or not he or she is able to work).

The new emphasis is on personal responsibility. The Ministry of Health has established the National Center for Sex Education to offer safe-sex workshops. Even so, health officials fear that Cubans have been given a false sense of security, and although condoms are widely available at pharmacies, the machismo of Latin American cultures inhibits their use by Cuban men.

Unlike the United States, the primary source of contamination in Cuba has been heterosexual relations. Of the 434 cases in 1989, 122 were directly attributable to Cuba's military involvement in Angola and Ethiopia (the rate of reported cases of syphilis in Cuba also increased dramatically, from 7.2 per 100,000 in 1970 to 84.3 per 100,000 in 1987, after the soldiers began returning from Africa). Infection via blood transfusion ended in 1986 after Cuba stopped importing blood products and began testing its entire blood supply. And maternal-feed transmission—one of the fastest-growing sources of infection in the United States (in February 1983, New York reported a newborn infection rate of one out of 61 babies)—is practically nonexistent due to sound prenatal care. Cuba has reported only three HIV-positive children, plus one child who has died of AIDS.

Despite Cuba's laudable success, today it has little money to spend on AIDS programs that go beyond the barest essentials. And the rapid growth of tourism is throwing a new variable into the equation. Cuban health officials fear a massive increase in the incidence of sexually transmitted diseases: WHO statistics show a 150% increase since 1990, a trend strongly implicating the foreign invasion.

There's an AIDS Information Drop-In Center at the National Center for Health Education, Calle 1 #507, Vedado, Havana, tel. 32-1920.

In the countryside, you need to take some basic precautions. Hikers straying off trails can easily lose their way in the mountain forests. Remember that atop the higher mountains, sunny weather can turn cold and rainy in seconds, so dress accordingly. And be extra cautious if crossing rivers; a rainstorm upstream can turn the river downstream into a raging torrent without any warning. Ideally, go with a guide.

Theft

Cuba's many charms can lull visitors into a false sense of security. True, theft pales in comparison to most other destinations. But the country has more than its fair share of economic and social problems, with rising street crime among them. The recent economic crisis has spawned a growing number of petty thieves and purse slashers. Theft from hotel rooms is increasing, although mostly this seems to be items of clothing, not money. Corruption—until very recently virtually unknown in revolutionary Cuba—is rearing its ugly head, too. Most crime is opportunistic, and thieves seek easy targets. Don't become paranoid. A few common-sense precautions, though, are in order.

Crowded places are the happy hunting grounds of crafty crooks. If you sense yourself being squeezed or jostled, don't hold back—elbow your way out of there immediately. Better safe than sorry. Don't leave items on the beach unattended if you go for a swim.

Make photocopies of all important documents: your passport (showing photograph and visas, if applicable), airline ticket, credit cards, insurance policy, driver's license. Carry the photocopies with you, and leave the originals along with your other valuables in the hotel safe where possible. If this isn't possible, carry the originals with you in a secure inside pocket. Don't put all your eggs in one basket. Prepare an "emergency kit," to include photocopies of your documents and an adequate sum of money to tide you over if your wallet gets stolen. If you're robbed, immediately file a police report. You'll need this to make an insurance claim. The Cuban police energetically investigate theft against foreigners.

For credit card security, insist that imprints are made in your presence. Make sure any imprints incorrectly completed are torn up. Don't take someone else's word that it will be done. Destroy the carbons yourself.

Walking streets at night is safe virtually everywhere. However, in Havana and other major cities, be wary of darker back streets at night (very few streets have lights). And note that some local bars can get rowdy after the *aguardente* (cheap rum) has been flowing a while. Cubans are an uncommonly decent lot in general. Drunkenness is not tolerated, although you'll occasionally see drunks. (Far worse are the German tourists—"lager louts"—who hang around Varadero and occasionally get drunk and obnoxious.)

ASISTUR OFFICES

MAIN OFFICE (HAVANA):

Paseo del Prado #254, e/ Animas y Trocadero, Habana Viejo, tel. 33-8527 or 62-5519, fax 33-8087; also a branch at the Hotel Capri, Calle 19 y N

OTHER LOCATIONS

Cienfuegos: Hotel Jagua, Calle 37 #1, Punda Gorda, tel. 432-6362 or 66-6190

Santiago de Cuba: Hotel Santiago, Av. de las Américas y Calle M, tel. 33-5015, ext. 3128, fax 33-5805

Varadero: Calle 31 #101, e/ 1 y 3, tel. 33-7276

If a serious theft occurs, you'll need to report it to the police (Asistur can help). You'll receive a statement *(denuncio)* for insurance purposes (and to replace lost tourist cards, traveler's checks, etc.) and which you should make sure is dated and stamped.

Common-Sense Precautions

Don't wear jewelry, chains, or expensive watches. Leave them with your ego at home. Wear an inexpensive digital watch.

Never carry more cash than you need for the day. The rest should be kept in the hotel safe. If you don't trust the hotel or if it doesn't have a safe, try as best you can to hide your valuables and secure your room. The majority of your money should be in the form of traveler's checks, which can be refunded if lost or stolen.

Never leave your purse, camera, or luggage unattended in public places. And always keep a wary eye on your luggage on public transportation, especially backpacks (sneak thieves love their zippered compartments).

Never carry your wallet in your back pocket. Instead, wear a secure money belt. Alternatively, you can carry your bills in your front pocket. Pack them beneath a handkerchief. Carry any other money in an inside pocket, a "secret" pocket sewn into your pants or jacket, or hidden in a body pouch or an elasticated wallet below the knee. Spread your money around your person.

Don't carry more luggage than you can adequately manage. Limit your baggage to *one* suitcase or duffel. And have a lock for each luggage item. Purses should have a short strap (ideally, one with metal woven in) that fits tightly against the body and snaps closed or has a zipper. *Always* keep purses fully zipped and luggage locked.

Don't leave anything of value within reach of an open window.

Don't leave anything of value in your car.

Don't leave tents unguarded.

Be particularly wary after cashing money at a bank, or if doing a deal with a street-changer or *jinitero.*

Have fun and don't worry!

If Things Go Wrong

Cuba has established an agency—**Asistur: Asistencia al Viajero**—specifically to assist travelers in need. It has offices in Havana, Cienfuegos, Varadero, and Santiago de Cuba; all are open 24 hours year-round. Asistur offers a wide range of services, including coordinating medical assistance, legal advice, liaison with family and insurance companies, and even repatriation if necessary (including the bodies of travelers who die in Cuba). Asistur also helps obtain new travel documents and locate lost luggage and may even indemnify against loss (assuming you already have travelers' insurance). You can even receive an advance of funds if you run out of money. Normally, Asistur pays all costs up front and is reimbursed through your insurance policy (either issued by a company in your home country or through the Cuban insurance company, ESICUBA). You can also pay for services directly. Its **central office** is at Paseo del Prado #254, e/ Animas y Trocadero, Habana Vieja, tel. 33-8527 or 62-5519, fax 33-8087, e-mail asistur@asist.sld.cu.

EMERGENCY HELP

In the event of an emergency, the following may be of help:

Citizen's Emergency Center, US State Department, tel. (202) 647-5225, fax (202) 647-3000.

International SOS Assistance, 8 Neshaminy Interplex, P.O. Box 11568, Philadelphia, PA 19116, tel. (215) 244-1500.

International Legal Defense Counsel, 11 South 15th St., Packard Bldg., Philadelphia, PA 19102, tel. (215) 977-9982.

If things turn dire, contact your embassy or consulate. Consulate officials can't get you out of jail, but they can help you locate a lawyer, alleviate unhealthy conditions, or arrange for funds to be wired if you run short of money. They may even be able to authorize a reimbursable loan while you arrange for cash to be forwarded, or even lend you money to get home (the US Department of State hates to admit this).

US citizens shouldn't expect the **US Interests Section,** c/o Embassy of Switzerland, Calzada e/ L y M, Vedado, tel. 32-0551 or 32-9700, to bend over backward; it exists for political reasons, not to help citizens (nonetheless, depending on your predicament, your plight may be sufficient to ensure assistance). The *Handbook of Consular Services,* Public Affairs Staff, Bureau of Consular Affairs, US Department of State, Washington, D.C. 20520, provides details of such assistance. Friends and family can also call the Department of State's **Overseas Citizen Service,** tel. (202) 647-5225, to check on you if things go awry. Remember, however, that the US does not have *full* diplomatic representation in Cuba, and its tapestry of pullable strings is understandably threadbare. If arrested, US citizens should ask Cuban authorities to notify the US Interests Section. A US consular officer will then try to arrange regular visits, at the discretion of the Cuban government (Cuba does not recognize dual citizenship for Cuban citizens who are also US citizens; Cuban-born citizens are—according to the US State Department—thereby denied representation through the US Interests Section in the event of arrest).

Legal Assistance: The **Consultoría Jurídica Internacional** (International Judicial Consultative Bureau), Calle 18 #120, esq. Avenida 3, Miramar, Havana, tel. 33-2490, fax 33-2303; and Avenida 1 #2008, esq. Calle 21, Varadero, tel. 33-7077, fax 33-7080, provides legal advice and services regarding all aspects of Cuban law—from marriages and notarization to advising on the constitutionality of business ventures. It is not designed to assist travelers.

Americans Traveling Abroad: What You Should Know Before You Go, by Gladson Nwanna (World Travel Institute Press, P.O. Box 32671-1A, Baltimore, MD 21208; $39.99 plus $3 shipping) is an invaluable resource on safety, health, money tips, and so on. It includes a chapter on Cuba.

MONEY

CURRENCY

In a word, dollars! dollars! dollars! Take as much as you want—there is no limit to the amount of convertible currency you can bring into Cuba. All hotels, car rental agencies, resort facilities, restaurants, and other places dealing with international tourists accept *only* US dollars (sometimes called *moneda efectiva*). Most European currencies are also accepted, as are Mexican pesos and Canadian dollars, but having US dollars will make life considerably easier.

But watch out! A large quantity of counterfeit US$100 bills are in circulation (printed in Colombia, apparently), and many Cubans are wary. Supposedly, only post-1962 bills are now legal tender, but you'll find bills going back to the 1930s still circulating. You'll usually be able to change a US$100 bill in any Cuban city, even if someone has to make the rounds to find someone to break it down (your dollars are so precious, no one will ever turn you away). Nonetheless, it's always best to have plenty of small bills, especially for the boonies.

Cuban Currency

The Cuban currency is the peso, which is designated $ and should not be confused with the US $ (to make matters worse, the dollar is sometimes called the peso). Cuban currency is often called *moneda nacional* (national money). Bills are issued in denominations of one (olive), three (red), five (green), 10 (brown), 20 (blue), and 50 (purple) pesos; a one-peso coin is also issued. The peso is divided into 100 *centavos,* issued in coin denominations of one, two, five, 10, and 20 centavos (which is also called a peseta).

Very few state-run entities will accept pesos from foreigners. In reality, there is very little that most foreigners will need pesos for. Exceptions are if you want to travel on Cuban buses, hang out at local bars and restaurants not normally frequented by tourists, or buy *refrescoes, batidos,* or other snacks on the street. Otherwise, spending pesos in Havana is nigh impossible (it's a lot easier, however, in the countryside).

You can also purchase special gold and silver **Cuban Mints** (not candy) at banks, airports, and other locations, including the **Cuban Mint Store,** Calle 18 #306, e/ 3 y 5, Miramar, Havana, tel. 29-6693, fax 22-8345. The bright red three-peso note with Che Guevara's portrait makes a good souvenir (US$3).

Tourist Currency

Sometimes, you'll be given rainbow-colored notes and flimsy coins that look like Monopoly money. They're called *Pesos Convertibles* (convertible pesos), or "B Certificates," and **INTUR coins** that are valid in lieu of dollars for all transactions. This currency is widely accepted. Bills are issued in the following denominations: one, two, five, 10, 20, 50, and 100 pesos, on a par with US dollar denominations. You can use them as you would US dollar bills and can exchange them for hard currency at the airport on the day of departure.

CURRENCY EXCHANGE

The Cuban peso is not traded on international markets as a convertible currency. Nonetheless, the Cuban government establishes its value at parity with the US dollar. However, the *unofficial* exchange rate—the black market rate—is used by almost everyone to set the peso's true value, and that of goods and services. When possession and spending of dollars was legalized for Cubans in 1993, the value of the peso plunged to 150 to the dollar (by August 1995) before climbing back to 25 to one. The rate has remained stable ever since and at press time still stood at about 25 pesos to one US dollar (it trades at about 10% higher outside Havana, however).

All prices in this book are quoted in US dollars unless otherwise indicated.

Exchanging Currency

You can exchange your foreign currency for the necessary US dollars at banks or hotel cash desks (arriving, you can change money at the José Martí International Airport in Havana or at the Antonio Maceo International Airport in Santiago de Cuba).

Legally, foreign currency can be changed for pesos only at a bank or an official *casa de cambio* (exchange bureau). In 1995, the Cuban government legalized currency exchange at the unofficial rate by a new enterprise called **Cadeca** (an acronym for *casa de cambio*). Cadeca established exchange booths at key points throughout Havana and in most large cities. Most are aimed at culling dollars from the local economy, rather than from tourists. Nonetheless, foreigners can exchange dollars for pesos here. In May 1996, Cadeca was buying at 30 pesos and selling at 25 pesos to the dollar—the approximate black market rate. Exchange only small amounts of dollars for pesos as pocket change for local buses etc.

If you exchange pesos legally, you'll be issued a currency control slip for the amount exchanged. You'll need to present the slip when you change pesos back to dollars, which you can only do at the airport on your day of departure. However, note that the maximum amount is a piddling 10 pesos! So spend all your local currency before leaving.

Street Changers
The creation of Cadeca has taken the wind out of the sails of *jiniteros* who change cash illegally on the streets. Still, you'll inevitably be approached, especially in Habana Vieja, along the Prado, and outside the Partagas cigar factory—and in Parque Céspedes in Santiago de Cuba. You'll be offered about the same deal as Cadeca offers.

Travelers illicitly changing money—as well as the *jiniteros*—face heavy fines but are rarely prosecuted, unlike Cubans. Many tourists are ripped off during the deal, so due caution is urged. Even muggings have been reported. A few ripoff artists work as pairs. Always count your pesos before handing over your US dollars; otherwise, you could find yourself holding a bunch of newspaper clippings wrapped inside a wad of real notes. *Jiniteros* on Havana's Prado are notoriously pushy and unsavory. In fact, they're a pain in the ass! Be wary.

Credit Cards
Most hotels, car rental companies, and travel suppliers, as well as larger restaurants, will accept credit card payments, as long as the cards are not issued by US banks (blame Uncle Sam; the US Treasury Department forbids US banks to process transactions involving Cuba). The following credit cards are honored: Access, Banamex, Bancomer, Carnet, Diners Club International, JCB, MasterCard, and VISA International. You can use your credit card to obtain a cash advance up to US$5,000 (US$100 minimum) at the **Banco Financiero Internacional,** tel. 33-4011, in the Hotel Habana Libre in Vedado, Havana (open Mon.-Sat. 8 a.m.-3 p.m.), and at the bank's branches in Varadero and Santiago de Cuba.

US citizens must travel on a cash-only basis. If you have a foreign bank account, you can try to obtain a credit card, which you can then use without restraint (aside from your credit limit). You'll still be breaking US laws, but the Cubans make no distinctions.

Don't rely entirely on credit cards, however, as often you may find that no vouchers are available to process transactions.

Traveler's Checks
Traveler's checks (unless issued by US banks) are accepted in most tourist restaurant and hotels; they can be in any foreign currency, including US dollars. Thomas Cook traveler's checks are best. Avoid American Express traveler's checks. However, in 1995, you could ostensibly get American Express traveler's checks cashed through **Asistur** offices.

You should *not* enter the date or the place when signing your checks—a Cuban requirement.

Banks
The state-controlled **Banco Nacional de Cuba** is the main commercial bank. It has branches throughout the country (most are open weekdays 8:30 a.m.-3 p.m.). In Havana, the branch at Calle M and Linea has a foreign-exchange desk, as does the branch in Varadero. There are also two independent banks—the autonomous, state-run **Banco Financiero Internacional S.A.,** which handles foreign currency transactions, and **Banco Internacional de Comercio,** which handles financing and credit for international trade. Banco Financiero offers currency exchange services at free-market rates. Its main branch is inside the lobby of the Hotel Habana Libre, in Havana.

A number of foreign banks have opened offices in Havana in recent years. However, as of early 1996, foreign banks could not offer banking services to foreign travelers.

Money Transfers

In October 1995, President Clinton granted permission for **Western Union** to open offices in Cuba to help Cuban Americans send money to relatives. The passage of the Helms-Burton legislation in February 1996 seems to have nixed this. In the event that the deal goes ahead, Western Union's office in Havana (still closed at press time) was at Calle Obispo #35, tel. 62-5297 or 62-6985.

Citizens of other countries can arrange money transfers or even a cash advance (in an emergency) from **Asistur,** Pasel del Prado #254, e/ Animas y Trocadero, Habana Vieja, tel. 33-8527 or 62-5519, fax 51-2905. The Cuban agency provides assistance to travelers. You may also be able to arrange a "wire transfer" through the Banco Financiero Internacional in Havana (see above). You'll need to telex your home bank. It's a good idea to carry full details of your home account with you in Cuba, including your bank's telex number. The process can take many days.

In Canada, **Antilles Express,** 9632 Charlton Ave., Montreal, Quebec H2B 2C5, tel. (514) 385-9449, can forward money to Havana in five days (longer elsewhere in Cuba) for a commission.

COSTS

Cuba can be as expensive or inexpensive as you wish, depending on how you travel. If you get around on public transport, rent rooms with Cuban families, dine in local eateries, and keep your entertainment to nontouristy venues, then the truly impecunious may be able to survive on as little as US$20 a day, with your room taking the lion's share. However, by being so frugal you'll have to rough it, have a very flexible itin-

erary, and be prepared for a basic food regimen.

If you want at least a modicum of comforts, then budget upward of US$40 a day. The majority of travelers will need *at least* double this, especially in Havana. Accommodation costs US$25-200 per night in Havana, half that amount outside the capital. Meals average US$3-10 with a beer; lunch or dinner at a *good* restaurant will usually cost upward of US$10 and can run to US$50 or so. Entrance to a cabaret or disco will cost US$5-15, plus drinks (a visit to Tropicana will set you back a minimum US$35). Day tours featuring sightseeing and meals average US$35-50.

Take enough cash to leave deposits for a rental car. And don't forget: if you run out of money, you may have difficulty getting more money forwarded quickly and easily. Bring items you think you'll need; you don't want to start shelling out for toiletries and the like. If you have a Cuban lover or friends, you'll want to treat them to dinners, etc., which can send your budget skyrocketing. And don't forget that you'll want to buy some Cuban cigars, souvenirs, and artwork.

I existed frugally on US$60 a day for four months during my motorcycle journey and over US$100 a day when renting a car, which will cost you at least US$60 plus gasoline.

Note that virtually everywhere on the tourist circuit, where Cubans pay in pesos, you'll be charged at parity in dollars, or even greater.

Discounts

Cuba is not in the business of offering discounts. Market competition isn't that developed! However, **Havanatur UK,** Interchange House, 27 Stafford Rd., Croydon, Surrey RO 4NG, tel. (181) 681-3613, fax (181) 760-0031, offers a **Discount Card** good for a 10% discount on all optional tours and excursions and meals at selected restaurants in Havana, Varadero, Matanzas, Cienfuegos, and Zapata. Keep your eyes peeled while in Cuba for any similar cards.

COMMUNICATIONS AND MEDIA

The **Ministry of Communications,** Avenida de Independencia, Plaza de la Revolución, tel. 82-0088, controls all communications, including mail and telecommunications.

NEWSPAPERS AND MAGAZINES

International Publications

There's no end of publications and coverage on Cuba. Mainstream US publications often report negatively and are unduly influenced by information provided by the US government. Says the much loved newsman Walter Cronkite, "The American people are being denied the free flow of information to and from Cuba that would enable them to intelligently participate in the decisions on our future policy there. The culprit is the US government."

It pays to broaden your reading to gain a truer picture of Cuba—never an easy country to understand.

One of the best sources is *Cuba Update,* published bi-monthly by the Center for Cuban Studies. It covers arts, economics, politics, women's and race issues, and travel and is strongly sympathetic to Cuban perspectives. Contributors include leading experts on Cuban issues, both in and outside Cuba. Subscriptions cost US$35 a year, or US$50 a year including membership in the center.

CubaINFO is a triweekly news digest on US-Cuban relations and economic and foreign affairs, published by the Cuba Exchange Program of the School of Advanced International Studies at Johns Hopkins University. It's indispensable for serious students. Subscriptions cost US$50 individuals, US$200 corporate (add US$25 for international orders). Write SAIS, 1740 Massachusetts Ave. NW, Washington, D.C. 20036-1984, tel. (202) 663-5753, fax (202) 663-5737. In a similar vein is *La Alborada,* a monthly newsletter published by the Cuban American Alliance Education Fund, 1605 John St., Suite 206, Fort Lee, NJ 07024, tel. (201) 363-0212, fax (201) 363-0213, e-mail delfern#igc.apc.org, and representing the perspectives of moderate Cuban-Americans.

The Cuba Report, 501 Brickell Key Dr., Suite 200, Miami, FL 33131, tel. (305) 381-8685, fax (305) 372-1089, is a monthly newsletter covering current economic, business, and financial happenings relating to Cuba. Subscriptions cost a whopping US$395. The publisher, James Whisenand, also periodically publishes *The Cuba Supplement* in magazine format.

Global Exchange, 2017 Mission St. #303, San Francisco, CA 94110, tel. (415) 255-7296 or (800) 497-1994, fax (415) 255-7498, e-mail globalexch@igc.org, publishes an annual *Cuba Reader,* a 100-page compendium of current articles on Cuba's political and economic system, health care, human rights, US relations, etc. (US$0, plus US$1.50 shipping). Global Exchange also publishes books on Cuba's political economy and US-Cuban relations.

In England, the Cuban Solidarity Campaign, 44 Morat St., London SW9 ORH, tel. (171) 820-9976, publishes the *CubaSí* newsletter. Subscriptions cost £4 (unwaged), £12 (waged), or £15-50 (organizations).

General publications to review include the *Latin American Weekly Report,* published weekly; subscription rates on request: 61 Old Street, London EC1V 9HX, England, tel. (071) 251-0012, fax (071) 253-8193. The monthly *Caribbean Update,* 52 Maple Ave., Maplewood, NJ 07040, tel. (201) 762-1565 or (800) 647-9990 (subscriptions only), fax (201) 762-9585, US$188 a year, reports primarily on business and economic issues. *Caribbean Week* is a bi-weekly news magazine covering everything from arts and economics to politics and travel. Its frequent reportage on Cuba is balanced. Subscriptions cost US$30 (Caribbean Communications, Inc., 1320 Route 9, Champlain, NY 12919).

Perspectiva Mundial is a Spanish-language publication with a New Internationalist (leftist) perspective and frequent Cuba coverage. Annual subscriptions cost US$17, Pathfinder, 410 West St., New York, NY 10014, tel. (212) 243-6392, fax (212) 924-6040. Likewise, in English and also available through Pathfinder, is the *New International.* Another Spanish-language publication you can order through Pathfinder is *La Gaceta,* the bimonthly journal of the Union of Writers and Artists of Cuba. Subscriptions cost US$40.

In Cuba, most major hotels' gift stores sell a small selection of leading international newspapers and magazines (including *Newsweek, Time, USA Today, The New York Times, Le Figaro,* and *Das Spiegel*). In Havana, a good source is the **Hotel Victoria**. Most foreign publications are distributed in Cuba through **World Services Publications,** Calle 33 #2003, e/ 20 y 22, Vedado, tel. 33-3002, fax 33-3066, which can steer you in the right direction. Outside Havana, finding Western publications is difficult. Expect to pay up to three times what you'd pay at home.

Cuban Publications

Where US "establishment" media is heavily slanted to profile Cuba negatively, domestic media is subject to what Maurice Halperin refers to as "the self-righteous and congratulatory monotony of the Cuban propaganda machine." As with governments everywhere, Cuba's state-controlled media usually hides as much as it reveals. Nonetheless, much is unbiased reporting that fairly presents the Cuban perspective.

The most important publication is *Granma,* the official Communist Party paper. Founded in 1965, it was published daily until supply shortages caused printing to be cut back. It focuses heavily on profiling a daily succession of victories in the building of socialism; perusing it has been called

HOW CUBANS FEEL ABOUT THE REVOLUTION

The fall of the Berlin Wall and the disintegration of the Soviet Bloc brought expectations of a Ceausescu-like ending for Castro.

Why, then, have Cuba's internal and external crises not produced Castro's downfall? The US State Department and right-wing Cuban-Americans sow the field with stories of a "one-party monopoly," "30 years of brainwashing," and the "grip of fear" imposed on Cubans by "the police state." There is an element of truth in all these assessments, but what they do not take into account are the unifying power of national pride and anti-imperialism, the very real achievements of the Revolution, and, yes, Fidel's unique charisma.

Cubans describe harrowing privation and in almost the same breath profess loyalty to Fidel. A 1992 report by the US Army War College concluded that in spite of the current crisis, Castro still retains a substantial base of popular support among the Cuban public. Those with a hate-hate relation are resigned to sullen silence, prison, or exile. Most Cubans, however, have a love-hate relationship with El Máximo, although they are hesitant to express their negative feelings too openly.

Most importantly, after five centuries of humiliation, Castro was, and remains, a symbol of national dignity. He gave Cuba pride. Unlike Eastern Europe, Cuba's revolution was home-grown, not imposed by Soviet troops. It came from the Cubans themselves. Just as Yankees take pride in the men of 1776, Cubans take pride in *their* revolutionary

heroes: they are the nation's embodiment of independence from Spain and the United States. Fidel is Cuba's George Washington.

Tangible Gains

Belief in the Revolution still runs deep. Most Cubans who support the Revolution do so not from reading Karl Marx but because they know they are infinitely better off than residents of neighboring countries. While it is easy to compare themselves—and to be compared by Westerners—to North America, Cubans prefer to compare Cuba to Mexico, Jamaica, Haiti, and the Dominican Republic—countries beset by true poverty. Conditions in Cuba are hard, but virtually nowhere do you find, as you do in many Latin American and Caribbean countries, hordes of child beggars in squalid slums. Instead, uniformed schoolchildren attend day-care centers and schools. Everyone still eats—even if not well—and medical care is free and available to all. The Cubans are acutely aware of all this.

Cuba has invested 30 years of resources to become one of the few underdeveloped nations with a system that protects all members of society from illiteracy and ill health. The Cuban Constitution guarantees the protection of all workers and their families against any eventual risk or contingency. The retirement age is 55 for women, 60 for men (five years sooner in the case of occupations deemed hazardous), among the lowest in the world. Thus, it is not unusual for citizens to collect pensions for up to 20 years or more.

"a degradation of the act of reading." I find it lucid, in-depth, and well-written—essential reading if you want to get the Cuban side of international events. It even features the occasional article that criticizes the Cuban government. Some of the unsigned editorials in *Granma* are written by Fidel Castro, whose colorful style, highlighted with subtle invective, is unmistakable. A weekly edition is also published in Spanish, English, and French. You'll find it in many hotel gift stores and at the editorial offices, at Avenida General Suárez y Calle Territorial, Plaza de la Revolución, Havana, tel. 81-6265 or 70-6521, fax 33-5176, e-mail granmai@tinored.cu. US subscriptions cost US$40, Pathfinder Press, 410 West St., New York, NY 10014. In Canada, contact Granma, ANPO, P.O. Box 91055, Effort Sq., Postal Outlet, Hamilton, ON L8N 2C3, tel./fax (905) 527-0070. You can also access *Granma* on-line at http://www.cubaweb.cu/granma.

Juventud Rebelde, General Suárez e/ Ayesteran y Territorial, tel. 6-9876, also founded in 1965, is the evening paper of the Communist Youth League. (The Communist Party also publishes the monthly *El Militante Comunista.*)

Many bookstores and hotel gift stores also sell *Prisma,* an English-language, bimonthly magazine covering politics, economics, travel, and general subjects on Cuba and the Americas published by Prensa Latina. For subscriptions in Canada, write Express Magazine, Service d'Abonnement, 4011 boul Robert, Montreal, Quebec H1Z 4H6, tel. (514) 374-9811; $16; in the US, Express Magazine, Service d'Abon-

---

All this has produced mammoth goodwill among the Cuban populace.

Thus, in an independent Gallup poll (the first-ever independent poll held in Cuba) in November 1994, 58% of Cubans said the nation's successes in education and health care outweigh its failures. Eighty percent felt their food needs had been met, 90% felt the same about health, and 96% regarding education. When asked about "the principal failure of the Cuban Revolution," only three percent answered "no liberty" and a similar percentage answered "no rights."

A State of Confusion

Since the onset of the Special Period, Cuba has found it impossible to sustain its cradle-to-grave benefits. "Our real problem," says Ricardo Alarcón, head of the National Assembly, "is comparing ourselves with ourselves five years ago," referring to the "golden years" of the 1980s. The social gains of the Revolution were achieved two decades ago and were taken for granted. Today, a majority of Cubans still support socialism but are tired of the inefficiencies, the endless hardships, and the growing inequalities. A society of haves and have nots has emerged, which many Cubans find increasingly difficult to reconcile with their daily lives. How, for example, can the government explain the US$250,000 charcoal-gray Lamborghini Diablo parked outside Havana's five-star Melia Cohiba hotel?

More and more Cubans complain about Castro but, to an astonishing degree, people have separated their discontent with the way things are from the man in charge. Even members of the disaffected younger generation do not speak with hatred, as East Germans did of Erich Honecker. They speak of Castro with a combination of the respect and anger a son feels for an overbearing father who can't get with the times.

"What Alternative Do We Have?"

The current economic crisis has created palpable discontent, yet many of those who do not actively support Castro see no viable alternative. People understand that their economy is in ruins, but they see no one who could lead them out of their present misery. As they struggle to improve things, people feel that they are on familiar ground with Fidel.

A majority of Cubans are anxious for a return to the market economy, even at the cost of privilege and inequity and risk—but not at the cost of the benefits of the Revolution. There is no opposition in Cuba, and mistrust of those who have fled to the US runs high. "We will never accept a government dictated by Miami," says leading Cuban dissident Elizardo Sánchez. The majority of Cubans want change, but they do not want to open their door to a type of interference that has taught some bitter lessons in the past.

The US embargo is seen by Cubans for what it is: an attempt to starve them into bringing Castro down. Thus, Castro is able to make Uncle Sam the scapegoat for the country's woes. In response to the Gallup poll's question "In your opinion, what is the most serious problem facing Cuba?," the largest group, 31%, answered that it was the US embargo.

nement, P.O. Box 0007, Rouse Point, NY 12979, tel. (800) 363-1310; $20. In a similar vein is the weekly magazine *Bohemia.* You can order copies through the Center for Cuban Studies.

Less easily obtainable are those publications that serve the Cuban populace, such as the daily newspaper *Tribuna de la Habana; Trabajadores,* the newspaper of the trades unions; *Mujeres,* Av. Rancho Boyeros y San Pedro, Havana, tel. 70-1000, a monthly magazine for women; and *Contactos,* published bimonthly by the Chamber of Commerce.

BOOKS

New York's **Center for Cuban Studies** (see "International Publications," above) publishes a catalog of books, posters, and other informational materials available for mail-order purchase. Likewise, several books on Cuba can be ordered through **Global Exchange,** the **Cuba Information Project,** and **Cuban Solidarity Campaign** (also see "International Publications"), including a series of Cuba titles published by Ocean Press, GPO Box 3279, Melbourne, Vicotria 3001, Australia.

Pathfinder Press (see above) publishes leftist books, including a large library of Cuba titles. The company has distributors worldwide, in the UK and Europe, Pathfinder, 47 The Cut, London SE1 8LL, tel. (171) 261-1354, fax (171) 928-7970; in Australia and New Zealand, c/o Baker & Taylor International, 80 Chandos St., St. Leonard, N.S.W. 2065, tel. 2-436-2666, fax 2-436-2170.

The Caribbean Basin Business Directory & Handbook published by Caribbean Communications Inc. is an invaluable resource for businesses. It costs US$400 and can be ordered from Leffert's Place, River Rd., St. Michael, Barbados, tel. (809) 436-1902, fax (809) 436-1904, or e-mail Caribbean-week@caribnet.net.

For a list of recommended reading, see the Booklist.

RADIO AND TELEVISION

The state-owned Instituto Cubano de Radiofusión controls all broadcast media. There are two national TV networks—**Canal 6: Cubavi-** sion and **Canal 2: Tele Rebelde**—and one provincial station in Oriente. Virtually every home has a TV (Cuba has about two million televisions), and Cubans are addicted to television, especially Brazilian *telenovelas* (soap operas), which bring virtually the entire nation to a standstill.

A few jerrybuilt satellite dishes festoon the rooftops, picking up CNN, the Discovery Channel, and other US stations. In March 1995, the government declared private dishes illegal and gave residents 60 days to remove them. However, the Cuban government supposedly pirates foreign cable TV stations by stealing a signal captured by a government satellite dish mounted on the Habana Libre Hotel and retransmitted to other tourist hotels. (Be wary if your hotel advertises that it has "satellite" TV. Normally, you'll receive a half-dozen fuzzy US stations. Cable is offered in some upscale hotels, usually showing HBO, ESPN, Cinemax, CNN, VH1—a rival to MTV—and the international service of TV España.) The Spanish firm MA Publicidad and the Cuban RTV Comerciál signed an agreement in 1995 to set up a Spanish-language cable station—**Multimedia Caribe**—to broadcast 24 hours to the US and South America.

The weekly tourist publication *Cartelera,* available free at hotel newsstands, lists television programming for the coming week. Tele Rebelde features national and international news at 12:30 and 8 p.m. Cubavision shows movies (usually recent Hollywood classics) every Saturday night as well as regular screenings of *Walking in Havana* (a guided tour with the City Historian, Eusebio Leal).

Cuban television stations have some very intelligent programming, with a heavy emphasis on science and culture, sports, Hispanic soaps, and foreign movies. One night I watched a profile on the problems faced by Latin America's indigenous cultures in adjusting to their contemporary setting. Cuban television cartoons are heavily moralistic and aim to teach Cuban youth proper behavior, and educational shows have a broadly internationalist focus. There is none of the mindless violence that seems to dominate comtemporary American cartoons. Cuban television advertisements typically inveigh against abortions *("Aborción no es un metodo anticonceptivo"),* exhort Cubans to work hard, or call for their participation in important festivals.

Cuban has five national radio stations: **Radio Liberación** offers mostly cultural programs; **Radio Musicál** airs classical music; **Radio Progreso** features light entertainment; **Radio Rebelde** and **Radio Reloj** both report news. There are also provincial and local stations. In Havana and along the northwest coast, you can tune in to radio stations from southern Florida; on the south coast, to stations from Jamaica; and in Oriente, to the American Forces Network (AM 1340 or FM 102.1), broadcast from Guantánamo naval base.

Radio Martí and **TV Martí** attempt to broadcast anti-Castro programing into Cuba from the US. The Cuban government manages to block this right-wing propaganda (funded by the US government to the tune of US$20 million a year). The only people able to receive TV Martí are the folks in the US Interests Section! (In 1996, Congress voted to establish an ultra-high-frequency transmission station to override Cuba's jamming system.)

The *Christian Science Monitor* beams into Cuba with greater success, as does the *BBC World Service*, call the Beeb in London for frequencies: tel. (171) 257-2685.

For Tourists

Radio Taíno (AM 1160) is geared for tourists and airs in both English and Spanish 1-3 p.m. daily. It promotes Cuban culture and plays middle-of-the-road music. **TV Taíno** is the television equivalent, aired 7-8 p.m. each Thursday. *Cánal de Sol* is available in many hotels, providing viewing for foreigners (everything from foreign soccer matches to kitschy travelogues).

MAIL

Cuba's mail system may be terminally slow, but otherwise it is relatively efficient. Most of my mail to and from Cuba has made it to its final destination without a hitch. International airmail *(correo aereo)* averages about one month each way (to save time, savvy Cubans usually hand their letters to foreigners to mail outside Cuba). Don't even think about sea-mail! When mailing from Cuba, it helps to write the country destination in Spanish: England is *Inglaterra* (use this for Wales and Scotland also, on the line below either country); France is *Francia;* Italy is *Italia;*

Germany is *Alemania;* Spain is *España;* Switzerland is *Suiza;* and the USA is *Estados Unidos.*

Most tourist hotels sell postage stamps and will accept your mail for delivery. Cuba is well-served by post offices; even the smallest town has one (to buy stamps, go to the *Sellos* counter).

Within Cuba, rates are incredibly low: letters cost from 15 centavos (20 grams or less) to 2.05 pesos (up to 500 grams); postcards cost 10 *centavos.*

Most mail in Cuba is delivered to a street address. Virtually no one rents a mailbox.

Parcels: The Ministerio de Comunicaciones requires that parcels to be mailed from Cuba should be delivered to the post office *unwrapped* for inspection. It is far better to send packages through an express courier service. If mailing to the US, remember that Uncle Sam is ever-vigilant for parcels from Cuba. Don't try mailing Aunt Sally a box of Cohibas for Christmas. They'll go up in smoke all right—on the US Customs 24-hour funeral pyre!

Receiving Mail: Getting incoming mail is time-consuming. You can receive mail in Cuba by having letters and parcels addressed to you using your name as it appears on your passport or other I.D. for general delivery to: "c/o

Espera [your name], Ministerio de Comunicaciones, Avenida Independencia y 19 de Mayo, Habana 6, Cuba." To collect mail *poste restante,* go to the **Ministry of Communications,** tel. 81-8008 or 7-4461, on the northeast corner of the Plaza de la Revolución. The names of people who have received mail are posted. Keep incoming mail simple—parcels are less likely to make it. It may be more efficient to have incoming mail addressed *"Espera" [your name]* at your hotel or embassy.

Note: Uncle Sam restricts what may be mailed to Cuba from the US. Letters and literature can be mailed without restriction. Gift parcels can be "sent or carried by an authorized traveler" to an individual or religious or educational organization if the domestic retail value does not exceed US$200. Only one parcel per month is allowed. And contents are limited to food, vitamins, seeds, medicines, medical supplies, clothing, personal hygiene items, and a few other categories. All other parcels are subject to seizure! Don't think you can skirt around this by sending by DHL. Your package will either be returned or seized.

Express Mail
DHL Worldwide Express has offices in most major cities throughout Cuba. The main offices are in Havana at Avenida 1ra y 42, Miramar, tel. 33-1578 or 33-1876, fax 33-1578, and in Varadero at Avenida 1ra y Calle 64, tel. 62-103. See regional chapters for other locations. The offices are open Mon.-Fri. 9 a.m.-6 p.m. and Saturday 8:30 a.m.-noon. DHL acts as Customs broker and offers daily door-to-door pickup and delivery service at no extra charge. It guarantees delivery in Havana in less than 24 hours. It offers four options: *Express,* for sending documents with no commercial value; *International,* for documents to anywhere in the world; *International Packages,* for commercial samples; and *National* (still in its promotional stage), for sending documents and packages between towns throughout Cuba.

International Charges: An express document to Canada, Mexico, or the US costs US$20; to anywhere else, US$25. A one-kilo document package costs US$47 (or US$57); a five-kilo package costs US$111 (or US$121). Rates are slightly higher for commercial packages. The minimum cost to send *to* Cuba by DHL is US$60.

DHL OFFICES

Havana: (Main Office) Av. 1ra y 42, Miramar, tel. 33-1876, fax 33-1578

Havana: Hotel Yagrumas, tel. 650-4460

Camagüey: Hotel Camagüey, tel. 71542

Ciego de Ávila: Hotel Ciego, tel. 22573

Cienfuegos: Hotel Jagua, tel. 6554

Holguín: Hotel Pernik, tel. 481984

Isla de la Juventud: Calle Martí #2201, tel. 22331

Pinar del Río: Hotel Pinar del Río, tel. 5070 (ext. 251)

Santiago de Cuba: Parque Céspedes, tel. 7795

Varadero: Av. 1ra y 64, tel. 62103, fax 33-7020

Villa Clara: Colón #10 altos, tel. 4626

Domestic Charges: Documents up to three kilos cost US$4 within Havana (US50 cents more for each additional kilo). A similar package to Pinar del Río, Matanzas, Villa Clara, or Cienfuegos province costs US$6; to Sancti Spíritus, Ciego de Ávila, Camagüey, Isla de la Juventud or Cayo Largo, US$8; and to the provinces of Oriente US$10.

Cubapacks, Cubapost, and **Cubanacán** also offer express courier service.

TELECOMMUNICATIONS

Telephones

Cuba has one of the lowest rates of telephones per capita in Latin America: 5.4 per 100 people (about the same as Jamaica). Nonetheless, public phones are all over the country. Much of the telephone network is more than 25 years old and desperately in need of replacement. The AT&T system, installed long before the Revolution, was overhauled in 1964 but soon began to suffer from lack of replacement parts due to the US embargo (telephone communications with the rest of the world remained reliant on a "prehistoric" underwater cable controlled, it is claimed, by US intelligence agencies). Alas, Castro's solution was to pull out the Yankee equipment and convert to "fraternal Hungarian equipment." It was downhill from there.

Service has never been good, and unless you're making a call from an international hotel, calling can still be a dreary adventure. Phones in international hotels and *telecorreos* tend to be moderately up to par; private phones, usually antique, perform like something from a Hitchcock movie. Calls are subject to lengthy delays. Getting a dial tone is the first obstacle. You may get a busy signal (though this does not necessarily mean the line is engaged) or a series of squeaks and squawks. A telephone that is working one minute may simply go dead the next. You just have to keep trying. When an office number is connected, you may experience problems in being transferred to the party you wish to speak to.

Avoid public phone booths if possible; they tend to be on noisy street corners (the 1996 phone directory lists the locations of all public phones in Cuba). Older public phones can only

be used for local calls; they take five centavo coins. When you hear the "time-up" signal (a short *blip*), you must *immediately* put in another coin to avoid being cut off. Newer public phones also take 20-centavo coins and can be used for long-distance calls also (you get any change back when you hang up).

Things have actually improved dramatically in recent years. In 1992, the Cuban government set up a new telephone company—**Empresa de Telcomunicaciones de Cuba** (ETECSA)—to improve and manage long-distance service. ETECSA was partially privatized, selling a 49% stake to the Italian company Italcable and Mexico's Grupo Domos, which agreed to spend nearly US$1.5 billion to modernize the existing 610,000 lines, then install an additional one million, bringing Cuba up to par with Mexico, with 11 telephones per 100 people by 2001. ETESCA plans to replace 90% of Havana's analog network and 70% of the analog network in the rest of Cuba with digital systems by the year 2000 (a fiber-optic network is being installed).

Cubans usually answer the phone by saying either *"¡Oigo!"* (I'm listening!) or *"¡Dígame!"* (Speak to me!). It sounds abrupt, but they're not being rude.

TELEPHONE AREA CODES

If calling to a number outside the area code where you are, dial 0, the city code, then the telephone number. A complete list of city and provincial codes is provided in the national telephone directory.

HAVANA CITY

All numbers use the prefix "7"
Exceptions:
Guanabo: 687
Santiago de las Vegas: 683

PINAR DEL RÍO

Most towns use the prefix "8"
Exceptions:
Bahía Honda: 86
Candelaria: 85
Isabel Rubio: 84
Pinar del Río: 82

LA HABANA

Artemisa: 63
Batabano: 62
Bejucal: 66
Boca de Jaruco: 692
Guines: 62
Jaruco: 64
Mariel: 63
San Antonio de las Vegas: 64
San Antonio de los Baños: 650

ISLA DE LA JUVENTUD

All towns use the prefix "61"

MATANZAS

Most towns use the prefix "5"
Exceptions:
Girón: 59
Jagüey Grande: 59
Matanzas: 52
Pedro Betancourt: 5
Playa Larga: 59

CIENFUEGOS

Most towns use the prefix "43"
Exceptions:
Cienfuegos: 432
Cruces: 433

VILLA CLARA

Most towns use the prefix "42"
Exceptions:
Santa Clara: 422

SANCTI SPÍRITUS

Most towns use the prefix "41"
Exceptions:
Arroyo Blanco: 418
Topes de Collantes: 42
Trinidad: 419

CIEGA DE ÁVILA

Most towns use the prefix "33"
Exceptions:
Morón: 335

CAMAGÜEY

Most towns use the prefix "32"
Exceptions:
Camagüey: 322

LAS TUNAS

All towns use the prefix "31"

HOLGUÍN

All towns use the prefix "23"

GRANMA

All towns use the prefix "24"

SANTIAGO DE CUBA

Most towns use the prefix "22"
Exceptions:
Boniato: 226
Cruce de los Baños: 225
El Caney: 226
Palma Soriano: 225
Santiago de Cuba: 226

GUANTÁNAMO

Most towns use the prefix "21"
Exceptions:
El Jamal: 214
La Maquina: 214

International Calls: Cuba'a international code is 53. When calling Cuba from North America, dial 011 (the international dialing code), then 53 (the country code) followed by the city code and number. AT&T has a "language line" that will connect you with an interpreter, tel. (800) 843-8420; US$3.50 per minute.

Calling *from* Cuba, you can ask your hotel operator to connect you or you can call from a telecommunications booth in most tourist hotels. Alternately, you'll find public telephone centers (telecorreos or centros telefónicos) in most large cities. In Havana, the main centro is in the Hotel Habana Libre.

For direct outbound international calls from Cuba, dial 119, then the country code, followed by the area code and number. The international access code when using direct-dial phones in hotels is 88 (followed by the country code); when dialing from public and all other phones, dial 119. For the international operator, dial 0, wait 30 seconds for the tone, then dial 9. For operator-assisted calls from Havana to the US, dial 66-1212.

Cost per minute is related to four geographic zones: North America (US$2.50), Central America and the Caribbean (US$3.25), South America (US$4.25), and Europe and the rest of the world (US$5.50)—ouch!

Domestic Calls: For local calls in the same area code, simply dial the number you wish to reach. To dial a number outside your area code, dial 0, then the local city code and the number you wish to reach. For the local operator, dial 0. Rates range from US five cents to US$1 per minute, depending on zone (the minimum charge is US30 cents).

Prepaid Phonecards: You can buy prepaid phone cards from telecorreos or from **Intertel,** Calle 33 #1427 e/ 14 y 18, Miramar, Havana, tel. 33-2476, fax 33-2504, in denominations of US$10, US$25 or US$45 for use in a limited number of special phone boxes in major hotels, airports, the Palacio de las Convenciones, and certain tourist centers. They can be used for domestic and international calls. You'll be able to see the diminishing value of the card displayed during your call (if it expires, you can replace it with a new one without interrupting your call by pushing button C and inserting a new card).

Cellular Phones: In mid-1993, cellular phone service was introduced to Cuba under a joint venture agreement between Mexico's TIMSA and Emtelcuba, which joined to form **Cubacel.** You can bring your own cellular phone into the country; Cubacel will activate it and provide you with a local line for US$12. Cubacel also rents cellular phones at a cost of US$7 daily (plus a US$3 one-time activation fee). You also have to pay a US$410 security deposit, plus US$100 per day deposit for use. Air time costs US90 cents per minute in addition to relevant long-distance charges.

As of 1996, service was limited to Havana, Varadero, and Santiago provinces. Cienfuegos and Holguín were scheduled to be added to the network in 1997.

Cubacel's main office in Havana is at 510 Calle 28, e/ 5 y 7, Miramar, tel. 33-2222, fax 33-1737. They also have offices in Havana at the José Martí International Airport, tel. 80-0043, in Varadero at Calle 1, esq. 25, tel. 80-9222, and in Santiago de Cuba at the Hotel Santiago, tel. 8-6199. Open Mon.-Fri. 8 a.m.-5 p.m. and Saturday 8 a.m.-noon.

Telephone Directories: Until 1996, there was no accurate or complete telephone directory; the last directory, issued in 1973, was as rare as kryptonite. In spring 1996, however, ETECSA published four comprehensive regional directories (Ciudad de la Habana, Zona Occidental, Zona Central, and Zona Oriental). You can purchase the gleaming new directories from ETECSA headquarters at Aguila 565 and Dragones in Havana, tel. 60-7409. Ask for Marlene María Orúe Milian, the publicity director. The Havana directory costs US$10; an all-Cuba directory costs US$20.

The hotel switchboards can be helpful in finding telephone numbers, but it often requires time and patience. Call 113 for directory inquiries.

The **Center for Cuban Studies,** 124 West 23rd St., New York, NY 10011, tel. (212) 242-0559, fax (212) 242-1937, has compiled a list of useful telephone and fax numbers and will research a list of up to 50 numbers for a search fee of US$50.

Telex, Fax, and Telegram
You can send telexes and faxes from most tourist hotels, usually for a fee slightly more than the comparable telephone charge. You can also transmit from most telecorreos.

ECTESA offers 24-hour telegram service by calling 81-8844 or going through its telecorreo offices. International telegraphic service is charged per word: 75 centavos to North America, 80 to Europe, 85 to the rest of world. Domestic rates are posted in telecorreos. In Havana, telegrams may be also sent from **Cuba Transatlantic Radio Corporation (RCA),** Calle Obispo y Aguiar. There are also RCA offices in Camagüey, Cienfuegos, and Santiago de Cuba.

CUBA ON THE INTERNET

Cuba-Specific
There are plenty of Cuba sites on the World Wide Web. The Republic of Cuba's WWW site is http://www.unipr.it:80/~davide/cuba/home.html.

Cuba-L is an information service on Cuba run by Nelson Valdés, a sociology professor at the University of New Mexico, Albuquerque, tel. (505) 277-2501; e-mail nvaldes@unm.edu. For US$60 annually, he'll send out a package of Cuba-related news items culled from leading publications, government agencies, tourism bureaus, and think tanks covering the political spectrum.

Travel and Tourism: Tourist information sites include the Cuban government's Home Page (see above). TraveNet! has a Cuba menu at http://www.sky.net/~eric/t/carcub.htm.

General Sites: WWW Virtual Library has links to information on Cuban economic and political matters: http://lanic.utexas.edu/la/ca/cuba.

Another site called Cuba Internet Resources—http://ix.urz.uni-heidelberg.de/~pklee/Cuba—has selected links to sites devoted to information on Cuban society, including US government documents. The host is in Germany, but the site is in English.

PeaceNet's Cuba Gopher—gopher://gopher.igc.org11/peace/cuba—has connections to documents concerned with Cuba. It's the site of the Institute for Global Communications, which offers low-cost communications with Cuba through Web, a Canadian network that serves as a clearinghouse for news services in Cuba, US$10 monthly; IGC, tel. (415) 442-0220, fax (415) 546-1976, e-mail support@igc.apc.org.

Other general information sites include: http://qqq.com:80/dtt/country/cuba/index.html, and http://www.cris.com/~wm/cuba/index.html.

Granma, the official daily newspaper, has a site at http://www.cubaweb.cu/granma. The CIA also provides the *World Factbook,* good for statistics and general information on Cuba (although heavily biased in its interpretations); it also has an index of publications that can be ordered, such as trade statistics on Cuba: http://www.odci.gov/96fact/fb96tpc/fb96toc.html,

or http://www.fedworld.gov/ntis/ntishome.html. Alternately, go to http://www.odci.gov/cia for everything you ever wanted to know about the CIA (well, perhaps not everything).

Other Cuba Sites: http://interhealth.com:80/cuba/tourist.html; http://www.travelxn.com/usstate/ta52.htm; and http://www.charm.net/~ibc/smokin/cuba.html.

French subscribers can access "Tourisme a Cuba: operation survie" at http://pauillac.inria.fr/~maranget/volcans/juin/dossier/cuba.html.

General Travel Interest
Your first hit should be Moon Publications' homepage, which includes an online version of the company's newsletter, *Travel Matters,* at http://www.moon.com/.

CaribNet—at http://www.caribnet.net or http://www.cpscaribnet.com—has information covering tourism, commerce, etc. throughout the Caribbean. For information, call (809) 431-0415 or fax (809) 429-5903, e-mail info@caribnet.net. The **Caribbean Tourism Organization** has a site on TravelFile's web, listing attractions, activities, accommodations, culture, events, etc. Each of the CTO's 34 members is profiled, including Cuba at http://www.travelfile.com/get. The CTO can be reached at 20 East 46th St, New York, NY 10017, tel. (212) 682-0435, fax (212) 697-4258.

News Groups (groups in which anyone with Internet access can participate, like a public bulletin board) via general e-mail exchange include Cuba National Newsgroup at aol.neighborhood.nation.cuba, plus soc.culture.cuba, soc.culture.caribbean, and clari.world.americas.caribbean.

The Global Network Navigator's GNN Travel Center is another good resource: http://www.ora.com/gnn/meta/travel/index.html. In the UK, World Travel Net has a site at http://www.world-travel-net.co.uk; e-mail: worldtravelnet@easynet.co.uk.

Online Service in Cuba
In theory, you can communicate directly with Cuba through e-mail. Few people or organizations, however, have access to a computer or modem. Still, there are numerous computer clubs and formal classes in computer technology in Cuba, centered in the **Palacio Central de**

Computación y Electrónica, tel. 63-3349 or 61-7555, in the old Sears building on Calle Reina No. 2 at Calle Amistad in Centro Havana, which also houses the popular e-mail network, *tinored.* The administrative contact is Pedro Espineira: peter%tinored@apc.org.

Electronic expert Robert Mabley claims that only 10% of his electronic transmissions get through to Cuba. "They seem to be sent with no trouble, but then disappear," he reports. Rumor has it that an "anti-Castro cyber terrorist"

has figured out a way to flag electronic mail to Cuba and hijack it!

CD-ROM
The CIA's *World Factbook* is available on CD-ROM from the National Technical Information Service, tel. (703) 487-4650, fax (703) 321-8547, for US$30. The book includes data on the people, politics, geography, and economies of numerous countries, including Cuba. It can be ordered in Windows or Macintosh versions.

TOURIST INFORMATION

PUBLICATIONS

Maps
One of the most attractive and accurate road maps is a 1:250,000 topographical map produced by Kartografiai Vallalat, of Hungary, and a virtually identical map by Freytag & Berndt. Both show main tourist attractions and feature street maps of key cities. You can buy or order either from travel bookstores in North America and Europe.

SouthTrek, 1301 Oxford Ave., Austin, TX 78704, tel./fax (512) 443-4533, e-mail sotrek @onr.com, specializes in maps of Latin America. It sells a 250:000 scale map of Cuba (US$9.95), including maps of Havana and five other cities. Send for a free catalog. In England, try Stanford's, 12-14 Long Acre, London WC2E 9LP, tel. (171) 836-1321, fax (171) 836-0189.

In Cuba, the Instituto Cubano de Geodesia y Cartografía produces a *Mapa Turístico de Cuba* as well as regional and city maps, plus detailed maps of individual attractions, such as Cemeterio Colón. They vary in scope, but some are extremely accurate and detailed. The institute doesn't sell maps, but you can buy them through Infotur offices and souvenir stalls. Maps of specific sites, such as Parque Lenin, can often be bought at the attraction itself. The institute also publishes a series of provincial road maps *(mapas de carrateras).* Most cost about US$1.

Cuba's Ediciones Geo produces a series of pocket-size tourist maps of regions and cities. They have a handy index and brief information in six languages. Cuban tour and hotel outfits

also produce their own maps. For example, Havanatur produces a handy pocket-size map of Cuba and Havana, and Horizontes has a detailed road map showing the location of its hotels, including details on each.

Detailed maps of the island's infrastructure are produced by the Instituto de Planificación Física, Laparilla 65, Habana Vieja, tel. 62-9330, fax 61-9533. They don't normally sell maps.

Infotur and Rumbos S.A. souvenir stalls in Havana and elsewhere usually have maps for sale. In Havana you should also try Tienda de las Navegantes, Mercaderes 115, Habana Vieja, tel. 61-3625, fax 33-2869, which has the widest array of tourist maps and nautical charts available in Cuba. You can buy a handy *Atlas de Cuba,* albeit a few years old, from the secondhand bookfair held on weekends at Plaza de Armas in Havana. The topographic maps are exquisite, but the road system shown is behind the times.

Magazines and Newsletters
Occasional features on Cuba appear in leading travel magazines such as *Islands* and *Caribbean Travel & Life,* a glossy bimonthly that has feature articles, news reports, and other information on travel throughout the Caribbean. Expect to see more on Cuba; in 1995, the editor made her first trip and was enamored of the place, as reported in the January 1996 issue (P.O. Box 2054, Marion, OH 43305; annual subscriptions cost US$19.95). An equivalent in the UK is *Caribbean World,* Albert Hall Magazines, 84 Albert Hall Mansions, Prince Consort Rd., London SW7 2AQ. This high-quality glossy is

published quarterly and frequently has reports on Cuba. Subscriptions in the UK cost £10; overseas subscriptions cost £21.70.

In Cuba, look for *Cartelera*, a free weekly tourist publication that offers up-to-date listings of the forthcoming week's events, including TV programing, theater, music and dance, and other entertainment. You can pick up a copy at most tourist hotels or from the editorial office at Calle 15 #602 e/ B y C, Vedado, Havana,.tel./fax 33-3732.

Sol y Son, Graphic Publicidad, Calle 14 #113 e/ 1ra y 3ra, Miramar, Havana, tel. 33-2245, fax 33-2186, is the in-flight magazine of Cubana airlines, published in English and Spanish. It's a slick, sophisticated magazine that provides profiles and news information on destinations, culture, and the arts.

Cubanacán publishes the colorful English-language bimonthly *Cubanacán Beach Magazine,* featuring travel, general destination pieces, and cultural profiles on Cuba. You can order it from MediaMar International, Poseidonstraat 9, Curaçao, tel. 599-9-602356, fax 599-9-657826.

Books
Macmillan Caribbean, a division of Macmillan Press, publishes a series of guidebooks and special-interest titles on the region, including a rather cheery *Cuba: Official Guide,* written with the obvious endorsement of the Cuban government. To order a catalog, contact Macmillan Caribbean, Houndmills, Basingstoke, Hampshire RG21 2XS, England, tel. 1256-29242, fax 1256-20109. **West Indies Books Unlimited,** P.O. Box 2315, Sarasota, FL 34230, tel. (813) 954-8601, sells a wide range of books on the Caribbean, including some now out of print.

Americans Traveling Abroad: What You Should Know Before You Go, by Gladson I. Nwanna (World Travel Institute, Baltimore) provides solid general guidelines and tips on health, safety, shopping, visas etc. The chapter on Cuba is a reprint from a bulletin issued by the US State Department and intended to serve as advice—albeit written in language to deter US citizens from travel—to Americans traveling to Cuba. You should double-check US government sources for latest bulletins.

Travel Tips for Travelers to Cuba is an unduly negative pamphlet published by the US State Department's Bureau of Consular Affairs (D.O.S. Publication #9232, D.C.A.). It's available from the

---

ASSIST-CARD INTERNATIONAL

Assist-Card, an international company, 15 rue du Cendrier, Ginebra, Switzerland, tel. (22) 732-0320, fax (22) 738-6305, offers travel assistance with everything from tracking lost luggage and finding medical, legal, and technical services to emergency transfers and repatriation, which you can request 24 hours a day. It has Regional Assistance Centers worldwide, including in Cuba (yes, even for US citizens).

For assistance in Cuba, call 625519 or 638284 (the Cuban agency is Asistur). If you have difficulty, you can call the regional office in Miami, tel. (305) 381-9959.

Assist-Card International has regional headquarters in the following locations:
Spain: Calle Silva 2, Madrid, tel. (01) 559-0500, fax (01) 542-4680.
USA: 1001 South Bayshore Dr. #2302, Miami, FL 33131, tel. (305) 381-9959, fax (305) 375-8135.
Australia: 49 Sherwood Rd., Brisbane, tel. (07) 360-0353, fax (07) 371-9074.

Superintendent of Documents, US Government Printing Office, Washington, D.C. 20402, tel. (202) 783-3283.

The Center for Cuban Studies maintains the **Lourdes Casal Library** at 124 West 23rd St., New York, NY 10011, tel. (212) 242-0559, fax (212) 242-1937. It has a collection of over 5,000 books on Cuba, as well as subscriptions to *Granma, Bohemia,* and other Cuban journals. It's open Mon.-Fri. 10 a.m.-6 p.m. and Saturday by appointment. The Cuban Art Space and Center Bookstore are also here.

For more books on Cuba, see the Booklist.

VIDEOS

There's no shortage of travel videos on Cuba available once you arrive on the island. Prior to traveling, you can get a rosy overview of Cuba by ordering *Cubanacán's Cuba* from **Sam-Sher Enterprises,** 9040 Leslie St., Suite 6, Richmond Hill, Ont. L4B 1G2, tel. (416) 771-9752, fax (416) 771-9741. Other videos, such as *Cuba: A Caribbean Smile* are also available, from

Westminster Communications, tel. (416) 882-8468, fax (416) 737-9491.

Also in Canada, **Martz Travel** has produced a 60-minute video—*Cuba Now*—specifically for travel agents and tourism industry personnel, US$29.95; Cuba Now, Box 2517, Wilkes-Barre, PA 18702, tel. (717) 825-0973 or (800) 733-CUBA.

The **Center for Cuban Studies,** 124 West 23rd St., New York, NY 10011, tel. (212) 242-0559, fax (212) 242-1937, sells from a huge collection of videos on Cuba, Cuban feature films on video, plus short films made by the Cuban Institute of Cinematic Arts and Industries. Most are in Spanish with English subtitles. Send for a free catalog.

TOURIST OFFICES

Cuba's **Ministerio de Turismo,** Calle 19 #710, Vedado, Havana, tel. 33-431, or 33-0545 for international relations, is in charge of tourism. However, Cuba's tourist offices abroad are represented by other state tourism agencies, most notably **Cubatur,** Calle F #157, Vedado, Havana, tel. 3-6733 or 30-1512, but also by Havanatur and Cubanacán. There is no such office in the US; however, **Cubanacán,** 372 Bay St., Suite 406, Toronto, ON M5H 2W9, tel. (416) 601-0343, fax (416) 601-0340, will provide information and mail literature to US citizens.

Within Cuba, **Infotur** (Información Turística), tel. 23-3376 or 63-6960, fax 33-8164, operates **Palacios de Turismo** (tourist information booths) throughout the island.

Publicitur, Calle 19 #16, e/ M and N, Vedado, Havana, tel. 32-3516, fax 33-3422, is the agency responsible for publishing and disseminating tourism literature. **Informacion Nacional** dispenses information about virtually every aspect of Cuba. Its main office is at Calle 23 #358, two blocks west of the Hotel Habana Libre, in Vedado, Havana, tel. 32-1269.

TRAVEL CLUBS

In the UK, the **Latin American Travel Association,** 1-7 Windmill Mews, Chiswick, London W4 1RW, tel. (181) 742-1529, fax (181) 742-2025, promotes Cuba and the rest of Latin America as a tourist destination on behalf of its members, most of whom are tour operators and travel suppliers.

North America is poorly served, for obvious reasons. The **South America Explorer's Club,** 1510 York St., Denver, CO 80206, tel. (303) 320-0388, publishes the quarterly *South American Explorer* magazine, containing a list of guidebooks, maps, trip reports, and resources for sale, as well as feature articles and advice for travelers and explorers. Annual membership costs US$25.

The **Latin American Travel Association,** 6175 N.W. 153rd St., Suite 332, Miami Lakes, FL 33104, tel. (305) 557-5221, is a professional body representing the interests of tour companies and travel suppliers. Likewise, the **South American Travel Association,** c/o Creative Resources, 12830 N.W. 9th St., Miami, FL 33182, is geared to travel industry personnel, though it accepts membership from anyone; it publishes the *News of Latin America* (US$20). Neither is very knowledgeable on Cuba.

Cuba is a member of both the **Caribbean Tourist Organization,** 20 E. 46th St., New York, NY 10017, tel. (212) 682-0435, fax (212) 697-4258, and the **Caribbean Hotel Association,** 18 Marseilles St., Suite 2B, San Juan, PR 00907, tel. (809) 725-9139, fax (809) 725-9108, both of which are barred under US law from promoting Cuba in the United States. In Canada, the **Tourism Industry Association of Canada,** 130 Albert St., Suite 1016, Ottawa, ON K1P 5G4, tel. (613) 238-3883, fax (613) 238-3878, suffers no such restraint.

WHEN TO GO

Cuba has distinct summer and winter periods, despite its subtropical location. The winter period, Nov.-April, is most pleasant, with relatively little rain and temperatures averaging a balmy 75-80° F. Surprisingly cool spells are possible, however, as cold fronts move south from Florida, bringing the chance of brief periods of rain. This is also the busy season, and many hotels in Havana and favored resort destinations can be fully booked, especially during Christmas, New Year, and Easter. Consider making advance reservations for the first few nights during these periods.

Traveling off-season (May-Oct.) has benefits, although you should be prepared for the

NATIONAL HOLIDAYS

1 January	Liberation Day (Día de la Liberación)
2 January	Victory Day (Día de la Victoria)
28 January	José Martí's birthday
24 February	Anniversary of the Second War of Independence
8 March	International Women's Day (Día de las Mujeres)
13 March	Anniversary of the students' attack on the presidential palace
19 April	Bay of Pigs Victory (Victoria del Playa Girón)
1 May	Labor Day (Día de las Trabajadores)
26 July	National Revolution Day (anniversary of the attack on the Moncada barracks)
30 July	Day of the Martyrs of the Revolution
8 October	Anniversary of Che Guevara's death
10 October	Anniversary of the First War of Independence
28 October	Memorial day to Camilio Cienfuegos
2 December	Anniversary of the landing of the *Granma*
7 December	Memorial day to Antonio Maceo

possibility of prolonged rains, severe storms, and even a slim chance of hurricanes. This period is also the hottest, with average temperatures rising to about 85-90° F in midsummer. The hottest weather is in the eastern part of the country, which can be stifling. Some unpaved roads may become impassable for short periods of time due to mud and flooding. Most hotels charge lower rates in the summer low season, usually 20-40% below winter rates, and it often easier to find rooms in the most popular hotels.

Spring and autumn are preferable. *Cartelera,* the weekly tourist newspaper, publishes a weather forecast on page two. Cuban TV newscasts feature weather forecasts (in Spanish).

Also consider whether you want to attend specific festivals and events (many are now timed for the peak season).

WHAT TO TAKE

Pack light! A good rule of thumb is to lay out everything you wish to take—then cut it by half. Most often, I've regretted packing too much, not too little. Remember, you'll need some spare room too for any souvenirs you plan on bringing home. Leave your jewelry at home—it invites theft.

Most important, don't forget your passport, airline tickets, traveler's checks, and other documentation. You'd be amazed how many folks get to the airport before discovering this "minor" oversight.

Many items are scarce in Cuba. You can usually find a full range of Western toiletries available in **Tiendas Panamericanos** (dollar stores stocking Western goods), which you'll encounter in all the main towns islandwide. However, don't depend on it. Take all the toiletries you think you'll need. Don't forget a towel and face cloth—upscale hotels will provide them, but not so less expensive hotels. (Caution: towels are occasionally stolen by chambermaids.) Women should pack extra tampons (those you don't use will make good gifts to Cuban women). T-shirts also make good giveaways. Most Western medicines and pharmaceuticals can be purchased at special pharmacies and clinics for foreigners in Havana and major cities, but you should bring any specific medications you think you'll need.

Independent travelers will find it a good idea to pack at least a half-dozen extra passport photographs for any unforeseen official paperwork that might arise.

The Basic Rules

Limit yourself to *one* bag (preferably a sturdy duffel or garment bag with plenty of pockets), plus a small day-pack or camera bag. If using public transport, note that space on domestic buses and planes is limited. Suitcases are fine for Cuba, where the vast majority of travelers disdain public transportation. If you travel by bus or train, forgo suitcases and backpacks with external frames or appendages—they catch and easily bend or break. One of the best investments you can make is a well-made duffel bag that doubles as a backpack and can be carried by hand or on the back. A small day-pack allows you to pack everything for a one- or two-day journey. You may even be able to leave the rest of your gear in the storage room of a Havana hotel.

Limit the number of changes of clothing. However, remember that you'll sweat often. Pack items that work in various combinations—preferably darker items that don't show the inevitable dirt and stains you'll quickly collect on your travels. Note, though, that dark clothes tend to be hotter than light clothing, which reflects the sun's rays. Pack khakis and subdued greens if you plan on much close-up nature viewing.

Some people recommend packing just two sets of clothes—one to wash and one to wear. Two sets of clothing seems ascetic. Three T-shirts, two dressier shirts, a couple of tank tops, a sweatshirt and sweatpants, a polo shirt, a pair of Levi's, "safari" pants, two pairs of shorts, and a sleeveless "safari" or photographer's jacket with heaps of pockets suffice for me. Women may wish to substitute blouses and mid-length skirts. Don't forget your bathing suit.

Be resigned in advance to the fact that the climate takes the wave out of your hair. Simplify your hair-do before you leave home. A 1950s guide to dressing in Cuba recommends to "forget about stockings completely if your legs are shapely, tanned, and well-groomed." Few Cuban women wear stockings or panty hose (Cuban women also have a curious habit of shaving their legs only as far up as their favorite dress item, so that they appear in public half shaved and half not when wearing shorter items).

Pack plenty of socks and undergarments—you may need a daily change. Wash them frequently to help keep athlete's foot and other fungal growths at bay. Better yet, rely on sandals as much as possible.

Coping with the Climate

Cuba is mostly hot and humid, but it can occasionally get chilly in midwinter and at higher elevations, especially at night. It's always a good idea to pack a sweater and/or a warm windproof jacket. You'll need one to cope with the bone-chilling a/c in hotels and restaurants. Parts of Oriente and the extreme west are parched, hot, and dry most of the year. At higher altitudes, it can get very chilly and wet if clouds set in.

You'll want light, loose-fitting shirts and pants. And if you plan on hiking, a loose-fitting cotton canvas shirt and pants will help protect against thorns and biting bugs.

Note: Here's a handy tip for handling changes in environment. Whenever you move from, say, relatively cool upland areas to hot, humid low-

the author traveling light in Valle de Viñales

lands, *take a shower*. This leaves the human body at the *local* temperature. You'll be amazed at how much more quickly you'll adjust.

In the wet season, plan on experiencing rain. An inexpensive umbrella is best (they're in short supply, so it's best to bring one with you). Raincoats are heavy and tend to make you sweat. Breathable Gore-Tex rainproof jackets work fine. A hooded poncho is also good. Make sure it has slits down the side for your arms and that it is large enough to carry a small day-pack underneath.

Note that denim jeans take forever to dry when wet. I always pack a pair of light cotton-polyester safari-style pants, which are cooler, dry quickly, and have plenty of pockets. Ideally, everything should be drip-dry, wash-and-wear.

If visiting in the wet season, protect your spare clothing in a plastic bag inside your backpack.

Jackets, Ties, and Cocktail Dresses?

Cubans do not stand on ceremony, and most travelers will not need dressy clothes. Cubans dress informally but always very neatly (they rarely go out in the evening without first changing into fresh clothes). Even Cuban business-people and officials dress simply, usually with a *guayabara* shirt worn outside the trousers, even at official functions. Nonetheless, at the very least, pack a pair of slacks and a dressy shirt. You may wish to take a jacket and tie or cocktail dress for dinners in more expensive hotels and restaurants—or, for the lucky few, an impromptu meeting with Fidel or at other diplomatic functions. Shorts are acceptable wear. Save shorter-style runner's shorts for the beach.

Some restaurants and discos have a dress code; T-shirts and shorts are not permissible.

Footwear

You'll need a comfortable pair of low-heeled walking shoes. Lightweight sandals are de rigueur. Normally, sneakers will do double-duty for most occasions. In the wet season—and if you plan on any nature activities—your shoes will get wet. Rubber boots *(botas de hule)* are a godsend on tropical trails. In fact, they're standard wear for *campesinos*. Buying them in Cuba is virtually out of the question, however, so you might want to invest in a pair of waterproof hiking shoes.

Other

If you bring prescription drugs, be sure the druggist's identification label is on the container. Writing materials are extremely hard to come by: take pens, pencils, and notepads (and lots of extras to give away).

FILM AND PHOTOGRAPHY

Cuba is a photographer's dream. Photographer John Kings, who accompanied James Michener to illustrate his book *Six Days in Havana*, called Havana "one of the most photogenic cities in the world. . . . It was captivating and challenging and for the next five days my finger barely left the shutter of my little German eye." You'll agree, so come prepared.

You are never denied access to anything you wish to photograph (except military and industrial installations, airports, and people in uniform).

Equipment and Film

You are allowed to bring two cameras plus six rolls of film into Cuba (don't worry about the official film limit; I've never heard of it being enforced). Film is susceptible to damage by airport X-ray machines. Usually one or two passes through a machine won't harm it, but the effect is cumulative. You should *always* request that your film (including your loaded camera) be hand-checked by airport security.

A 35mm SLR camera is most versatile and will give top-notch results, but an instamatic is fine.

Decide how much film you think you'll need to bring—then triple it! I recommend one roll per day as a minimum if you're even half-serious about your photography. If you do need to buy film in Cuba, check the expiration date; it may be outdated. And the film may have been sitting in the sun for months on end—not good.

Film—almost exlusively Kodak or Agfa—is sold at most tourist hotels and at Photo Service stores, located in towns islandwide. Very rarely will you find slide (transparency) film. Most Photo Service stores also sell a few Nikon, Minolta, and Canon instamatic cameras, as well as a meager stock of batteries. *Take spare batteries* for light meters and flashes. You will *not* be able to buy filters in Cuba.

Keep your film out of the sun. If possible, refrigerate it. Color emulsions are particularly sensitive to tropical heat, and film rolls can also soften with the humidity so that they easily stretch and refuse to wind in your camera. Pack both your virgin and exposed film in a Ziploc plastic bag with silica gel inside to protect against moisture.

Keep your lenses clean and dry when not in use. Silica gel packs are essential to help protect your camera gear from moisture; use them if you carry your camera equipment inside a plastic bag. Cameras are valuable goods. Never turn your back on your camera gear. Watch it at all times.

Film Processing

You can have your print and slide film processed at any Photo Service outlet. It also makes color prints and copies up to 50 by 60 inches and offers framing. However, Cuba faces a chemical shortage, and there is no guarantee that the processing chemicals are clean. For this reason, you should consider waiting until you get home (try to keep your film cool). You can also buy film with prepaid processing—each roll comes with a self-mailer and you can simply pop it in a mailbox; the prints or slides will then be mailed to your home. However, given the visiccitudes of the Cuban mail system, you're more likely to arrive home first (and your film may never show up).

Videos

Video cameras can be imported to Cuba. It's best to ensure that you have fresh batteries before arriving, although camcorder batteries can be found in Havana and major tourist resorts at Photo Service outlets. The same rule holds true for blank tapes, which are not always readily available outside major tourist locales.

Cuba uses the same broadcast standard as North America. However, very few hotel rooms have VCRs.

Photo Etiquette

Cubans of every shade and stripe will ham for your camera and will generally cooperate willingly. In 1991, a group of professional photographers traveled through Cuba to produce a coffee-table book (Five Corners Publications,

HCR 70, Box 7A, Plymouth, VT 05056): "The group consensus was that none of us had ever photographed more beautiful or cooperative subjects."

However, never assume an automatic right to take a personal photograph. If you come across individuals who don't want to be photographed, honor their wishes. It's a common courtesy, too, to ask permission to photograph what might be considered private situations. Use your judgment and discretion. Don't attempt to photograph members of the police or military—they are under strict instructions not to allow themselves to be photographed.

Many children will request money for being photographed. So, too, will the mulattas dressed in traditional costume in Plaza de la Catedral in Habana Vieja. The latter are officially sanctioned to do so, but the government discourages its other citizens from "begging." Whether you pay is a matter of conscience. If they insist on being paid and you don't want to pay, don't take the shot. It is considered a courtesy to buy a small trinket in markets from whomever you wish to photograph. And don't forget to send photographs to anyone you promise to send to.

Warning: Several foreigners have been arrested and deported in recent years for filming pornography. The Cuban government defines it fairly broadly—and keeps a strict watch for such illicit use of cameras.

OTHER PRACTICALITIES

Weights and Measures

Cuba operates on the metric system. Liquids are sold in liters, fruits and vegetables by the kilo. Distances are given in meters and kilometers. See the chart at the back of the book for metric conversions.

Vestiges of the US system and old Spanish systems remain, however, such as the *pulgada* (2.54 cm, or one inch), *cordel* (20.35 meters, or 22.26 yards), or, more commonly, the *caballeria* (about 324 square *cordeles,* deemed sufficient to support a mounted soldier and his family). Old units of weight still heard include the *onza* (about one ounce), *libra* (about one pound), *saco* (a measure of coffee), and *quintal.*

Time

Cuban time is equivalent to US eastern standard time: five hours behind Greenwich mean time, the same as New York and Miami, three hours ahead of the US west coast. There is little seasonal variation in dawn. However, Cuba has daylight saving time May-October.

Business Hours

Hours are flexible. Government offices usually open Mon.-Fri. 8:30 a.m.-12:30 p.m. and 1:30-5:30 p.m. and every second Saturday 8:30 a.m.-noon. Banks are usually open Mon.-Fri. 8:30 a.m.-noon and 1:30-3 p.m. and Saturday 8:30-10:30 a.m. Post offices are usually open Mon.-Sat. 8 a.m.-10 p.m. and Sunday 8 a.m.-6 p.m. Most shops are open Mon.-Sat. 8:30 a.m.-5:30 p.m., although many remain open later, including all day Sunday. Museum opening times vary widely (and change frequently), although most are closed on Monday. Most banks, businesses, and government offices close during national holidays.

Many Cubans still honor the *merienda*, coffee breaks taken usually at about 10 a.m. and 3 p.m.

Cubans like to dine late. Fortunately, many *paladares* are open 24 hours and many tourist restaurants stay open until 11 p.m. However, local eateries serving Cubans often run out of food by mid-evening—don't leave dining too late.

Electricity

Cuba operates on 110-volt A.C. (60-cycle) nationwide, though 220-volt is found in places. Most outlets use US plugs: flat, parallel two-pins, and three rectangular pins. A two-prong adapter is a good idea (take one with you; they're hard to come by in Cuba). **Magellan's,** P.O. Box 5485, Santa Barbara, CA 93150, tel. (800) 962-4932, can supply plugs and adapters, as well as dozens of other handy travel items featured in a free catalog.

At press time, Cuba was still suffering regular electricity blackouts. Take a flashlight and spare batteries. A couple of long-lasting candles are also a good idea (don't forget the matches or a lighter).

If possible, do not allow your personal computer or disks to pass through an airport X-ray machine. The magnets supposedly can wipe out all your data and programs (however, I've never had any such problem). Insist on having it hand-checked. You'll need to turn your computer on to show that it's not a bomb.

HAVANA

INTRODUCTION

Winston Churchill, approaching Havana by sea in 1895, wrote that he felt "delirious yet tumultuous. . . . I felt as if I sailed with Long John Silver and first gazed on Treasure Island. Here was a place where anything might happen. Here was a place where something would certainly happen. Here I might leave my bones."

Countless writers have commented on the exhilarating sensation that engulfs visitors to this most beautiful and beguiling of Caribbean cities. The potency of Havana's appeal is owed to a quality that "runs deeper than the stuff of which travel brochures are made. It is irresistible and intangible," writes Juliet Barclay—as if, adds Arnold Samuelson, recalling his first visit to Havana, in 1934, "everything you have seen before is forgotten, everything you see and hear then being so strange you feel . . . as if you had died and come to life in a different world." The city's ethereal mood, little changed today, is so pronounced that it finds its way into novels. "I wake up feeling different, like something inside me is changing, something chemical and irreversible. There's a magic here working its way through my veins," says Pilar, a Cuban-American character from New York who returns to Havana in Cristina García's novel *Dreaming in Cuban*. Set foot one

time in Havana and you can only flee or succumb to its enigmatic allure. It is impossible to resist the city's mysteries and contradictions.

Walking Havana's streets you sense you are living inside a romantic thriller. You don't want to sleep for fear of missing a vital experience. Before the Revolution, Havana had a reputation as a place of intrigue and tawdry romance. The whiff of conspiracy, the intimation of liaison, is still in the air.

Your first reaction is of being caught in an eerie colonial-cum-1950s time warp. Fading signs advertising Hotpoint and Singer appliances evoke the decadent decades when Cuba was a virtual colony of the United States. High-finned, chrome-spangled dowagers from the heyday of Detroit are everywhere, conjuring images of dark-eyed temptresses and men in Panama hats and white linen suits. Havana, now Communist but still carnal, is peopled in fact as in fiction by characters from the novels of Ernest Hemingway and Graham Greene. All the glamor of an abandoned stage set is here, patinated by age. For foreign visitors, it is heady stuff.

Profile of the City

Havana (pop. 2.2 million), political, cultural and industrial heart of the nation, contains one-fifth of

Cuba's population. It has a flavor all its own; a strange amalgam of colonialism, capitalism, and communism merged into one.

One of the great historical cities of the New World, Havana is a far cry from the Caribbean backwaters that call themselves capitals elsewhere in the Antilles. It is obvious, as you walk tree-lined boulevards and eerily Neapolitan streets that are the most tranquil and unthreatening of any you will find in Latin America, that Cuba was wealthy years ago to a degree that most South American and Caribbean cities were not. Havana is a city, notes architect Jorge Rigau, "upholstered in columns, cushioned by colonnaded arcades."

The Spanish colonial buildings hard up against the Atlantic are handsome indeed. They come in a spectacular amalgam of styles—from the academic classicism of aristocratic homes, rococo residential exteriors, Moorish interiors, art deco and art nouveau public buildings, and "internationalist" housing and other Communist carbuncles that reflect Cuba's gravitation into the Soviet orbit.

At the heart of the city is enchanting Habana Vieja (Old Havana), a living museum inhabited by 60,000 people and containing perhaps the finest collection of Spanish colonial buildings in all the Americas. Baroque churches, convents, and castles that could have been transposed from Madrid or Cádiz still reign majestically over squares embraced by the former palaces of Cuba's ruling gentry and cobbled streets still haunted by Ernest Hemingway's ghost.

Hemingway's house, Finca Vigía, is one of dozens of museums dedicated to the memory of great men and women. And although most of the older monuments—those of politically incorrect heroes—were pulled down, at least they were replaced by dozens of grandiose monuments to those on the correct side of history.

Street names may have been changed, but balmy city streets with walls in faded tropical pastels still smolder gold in the waxing sun. Sunlight still filters through stained-glass *mediopuntos* to dance on the cool marble floors. And time cannot erase the sound of the "jalousies above the colonnades creaking in the small wind from the sea," in the words of Graham Greene. "True, [Havana] was disheveled and shabby," wrote Brenda Loree, "but in the manner of a beautiful woman who had let herself go. You could still tell that she had good bones."

Faded Glory
It has been fashionable among foreign journalists of late to portray Havana as a slum, a crumbling city of "tattered colonnades and peeling paint, shadowed by a somnolent remorse." True enough, Havana aches with penury and pathos. The sultry seductress of prerevolutionary days needs a million gallons of paint (political humorist P.J. O'Rourke has written, "Half an hour in Havana is enough to cure you of a taste for that distressed look so popular in Crate & Barrel stores"). Three decades of official neglect have left Havana's buildings in various stages of decay. But at least they're still standing and

flying the flag

CHRISTOPHER P. BAKER

haven't been swept away by a gaudy wave of tourist hotels, shopping malls, and marinas.

Soon after Castro took power, his government announced a policy emphasizing rural development. The countryside had long been neglected, and a significant portion of the rural population lived in abject poverty. But the putative triumphs of the Revolution in the countryside could not stem migration to the cities, particularly Havana, which suffered ongoing neglect and impoverishment. Little new construction has taken place in the past 30 years. Thus, Havana has faced an acute housing shortage. The Revolution democratized the former haunts of the ruling and middle classes—many of their mansions in the once all-white suburbs of Vedado and Miramar, like the housing in working-class regions, were divided into smaller and smaller apartments.

"The unhealthy shanty towns, which had disappeared during the early years of the Revolution, have reappeared," Castro declared in 1989, speaking of the *ciudadelos,* the decrepit tenements "where families live in one or two little rooms, with very little space." Castro estimated that 300,000 people in Havana live in slum conditions and that only 50% of inhabitants have proper sewage. You can't blame the Revolution. Havana has been "a city in lamentable decline" for more a century.

In certain areas, conditions are now truly depressing. Many Habaneros cling tenaciously to family life behind crumbling façades festooned with makeshift wiring and inside tottering buildings that should have faced the bulldozer's maw long ago. Many buildings have fallen masonry and piles of plaster on the floor, unpainted walls mildewed by the tropical climate, and stairs so dilapidated one is afraid to step onto them. Once pleasant strolls in Cerro and Habana Vieja have become obstacle courses over piles of rubble and beneath wooden braces propping up one building after another. In some areas, garbage collection is now haphazard. Fortunately, most of the sewers still work and although when it rains the streets fill with puddles, they are thankfully free of the pestilent aromas of so many other cities elsewhere in the tropics.

A City Rekindled

Returning to Havana in 1996, I was astounded by the sense of vitality that only a year before had been absent. Streets, plazas, and parks pulsed with humanity moving with renewed purpose. I had the sense that life was returning to some semblance of normality.

Habana Vieja is getting a stunning facelift—a remarkable restoration project has been ongoing for over a decade. The commercial district of Vedado is again on the rise with foreign-funded construction. And scores of mansions in Miramar are being restored to haughty grandeur and turned into posh boutiques and restaurants. Everywhere, local residents are repairing Moorish mosaics and giving their homes fresh coats of paint.

Even gasoline is again plentiful. Reports of Cuba's transport system having come to a virtual standstill are now outdated. Bus service is almost fully functional, and the streets are thrumming to motor traffic. And the notorious power outages that plagued Havana nightly in the early 1990s have now become mere inconveniences.

GEOGRAPHY

Havana lies due south of Florida, on Cuba's far northwest coast. It is built on the west side of a sweeping bay with a narrow funnel entrance—Bahía de Habana—and extends west 12 km to the Río Jaimanitas.

La Ciudad de la Habana (City of Havana) covers 752 square km and 15 municipalities. The city core is divided into three regions of tourist interest: Habana Vieja, Centro Habana (Central Havana), and Vedado and Plaza de la Revolución (Vedado is administratively a part of Plaza). West of the Río Almendares is a fourth important district, Miramar. Outside these four regions are the suburbs, which extend for a radius of about 20 km from the center.

Habana Vieja and Central Havana are mostly flat but slope almost imperceptibly to the southwest. Vedado and Miramar also slope gradually to the south, where Cerro and Plaza de la Revolución extend across gently rolling hills.

East of Havana, a chain of hills runs parallel to the shore, inland of the rocky coast. The coast is indented with coves. About 15 km east of the city, a series of long, white sand beaches—the Playas del Este—prove tempting on hot summer days. The shore west of the city is less appealing, mostly rocky with a few beaches of modest appeal.

HISTORY

Foundation of a City

Today's Havana began life in July 1515 as the westernmost of the seven cities established under Diego Velásquez. The city, called San Cristóbal de la Habana, was first located on the south coast, where Batabanó stands today. The site was an unmitigated disaster. Within four years, the settlers had moved to the north coast, where they erected rough huts at the mouth of the Río Chorrera (now Almendares). A few years earlier, the expeditionary Sebastian de Ocampo had discovered a more promising site—Puerto de Carenas, so named because the site was ideal for careening ships—a few km farther east, and on 25 November 1519, the date of the second founding of San Cristóbal de la Habana, the settlers moved to the shore of a flask-shaped, deep-water bay surrounded by rolling hills and hidden within a cliff-hung narrow channel.

The first houses stood facing the sea in a row between the present sites of the Plaza de Armas and the Plaza de San Francisco. Initially, life was extremely spartan. But Puerto de Carena's proximity to the deep channel between Cuba and the shallow seas of the Bahamas were highly advantageous.

The Early Years

Throughout the 16th century, an ever-increasing number of ships called in Havana's port as the New World began to yield up its riches. Staggering amounts of treasure were transported to Spain. In 1508, the prize amounted to 8,000 ducados; by 1512, it rose to 90,000. When Mexico and Peru were conquered, the quantities rose to astronomical heights. The city gained such prominence that in July 1553 the governor of Cuba, Gonzalo Pérez de Angulo, moved the capital (and his residence) from Santiago de Cuba in the east of the island.

In 1564, a Spanish expedition reached the Philippines. The next year, it discovered the northern Pacific trade winds that for the next 250 years propelled ships laden with Chinese treasure to Acapulco, from where the booty was carried overland to Veracruz, on the Gulf of Mexico, and loaded onto ships bound for Havana and Europe. Oriental perfumes, pearls, silks, and ivories passed through Havana. To these shipments were added silver from Bolivia, alpaca from Peru, and rare woods from central America, plus Cuban tobacco, leather, fruit, and its own precious woods. Havana could never have imagined such wealth! The fleet of 1583 had to leave one million pesos behind because there was no more room in the ships' holds.

Every spring and summer, all the ships returning from the Americas crowded into Havana's harbor before setting off for Spain in an armed convoy. To provision them, an aqueduct was built to bring water down to the harbor, fruit and vegetables came from smallholdings outside Havana, and the citizens made soup and *tasajo* (salted meat) from the vast quantities of crabs and tortoises that overran the city. Havana's air reeked and the city itself overflowed with drunken sailors, packs of wild dogs, cutthroats, and whores—at night, few citizens dared venture out unless heavily armed.

Building for Posterity

While the British went out to their colonies to grow rich and return, the Spanish went to grow rich and stay. They brought a permanence of design and planning to their New World cities that other colonial powers never achieved. "The Spanish built cities where they settled, but the English just let cities grow. The poorest street of Havana had dignity compared to the shanty towns of Kingston," wrote Graham Greene.

By the turn of the 18th century, Havana was the third-largest city in the New World (after Mexico City and Lima). The 17th and 18th centuries saw a surge of pious energy and ecclesiastical construction as the ever-powerful bishops brought their influence to bear in statuary and stone. Most notable of the "builder-bishops" was Diego Evelino de Compostela, a vigorous ecclesiastic who arrived from Spain in November 1687. In short order, he initiated the Convento de Belén, Convento de Santa Clara de Asís, Iglesia Santa Teresa de Jesús, and Iglesia del Santo Ángel Custodio. Compostela's work was continued by an equally dynamic bishop, Gerónimo Valdés, who founded the University of Havana.

The wealth of the Americas helped fill the churches and convents with gold and silver. Ha-

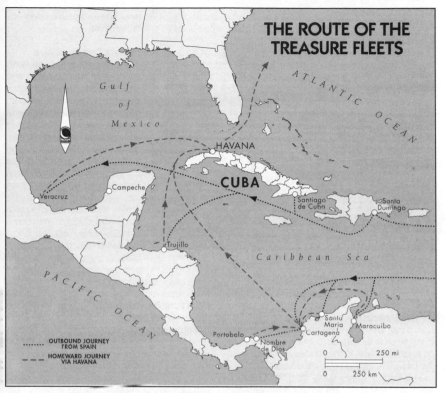

THE ROUTE OF THE
TREASURE FLEETS

Gulf
of
Mexico

ATLANTIC OCEAN

HAVANA

CUBA

Veracruz

Campeche

Santiago
de Cuba

Santo
Domingo

Trujillo

Caribbean Sea

PACIFIC OCEAN

Portobelo

Nombre
de Dios

Santa
Maria
Cartagena

Maracaibo

0   250 mi

0   250 km

········· OUTBOUND JOURNEY
         FROM SPAIN
- - - HOMEWARD JOURNEY
      VIA HAVANA

vana was by now a prosperous city, and became even more so as the tobacco industry prospered from European noses, which reverberated with satisfied sneezes induced by Cuban snuff. Smuggling was endemic (Cubans were not allowed to trade with anyone but Spain). Industries were established, and the city was renowned for building the best galleons in the Indies. The goods of the hinterlands, especially precious leathers and timber, flowed out from the harbor, while the black gold of slaves and the fineries of Europe flowed in.

Spanish ships also unloaded builders and craftsmen, hired to help citizens display their earnings—legitimate and ill-gotten alike—in an outpouring of architectural sophistication. They brought with them a Moorish aesthetic, which they translated into a unique "tropical synthesis of column, courtyard, and chiaroscuro."

The British Take Over

On 4 January 1762, George III of England declared war on Spain. Some years before, the British governor of Jamaica, Charles Knowles, had been hosted on an official visit to Havana, where he spent much of his time reconnoitering the city's defenses. Knowles was consulted, and a plan drawn up for an attack on Havana. It was an audacious plan that would shake Havana, and Cuba, to the core.

Though the city, which by then numbered about 40,000 inhabitants, was heavily defended, its Achilles' heel was the Cabaña, a long ridge overlooking Morro Castle and Havana's harbor. On June 6, a British fleet of 50 warships—carrying 11,000 troops—arrived off Cojímar. The next day, they put ashore—and Havana erupted in panic. The Spanish scuttled three ships in the harbormouth, ineptly trapping their own war-

French pirates attacking Havana

ships inside the harbor. That night, when Spanish guards atop the Cabaña began firing at British scouts, the Spanish warships began blasting the ridge, causing their own troops to flee. The British had taken the ridge and began preparing to lay seige to the city. On July 29, sappers blew an enormous hole in the Castillo de Morro, and the flag of St. George was raised over the city.

The English immediately lifted the trade restrictions, and merchant ships from many nations began a race to Havana, which overnight became what Abbé Guillaume Raynal called the "boulevard of the New World." To his discredit, however, the English commander, George Keppel, Earl of Albermarle, milked the city dry by imposing usurious levies, especially upon the Catholic Church. After the British commandeered the Iglesia San Francisco de Asís for Protestant worship, the church was never again used for service by Havana's citizens.

The citizens were relieved of further indignations on 10 February 1763, when England foolishly exchanged Cuba for Florida in the Treaty of Paris, which ended the war. On 6 July, the last British troops departed Havana. The Spanish lost no time in rebuilding their forts, and between 1764 and 1774 built an enormous fortress—San Carlos de la Cabaña, the largest fortress in the Americas—atop the Cabaña ridge. The British invasion ensured that Havana would never again be neglected by Spain.

Havana Comes of Age

Havana prospered, growing every year more elegant and sophisticated. Under the supervision of the new Spanish governor, the Marqués de la Torre, it attained a new focus and rigorous architectural harmony. The elegant Prado (the first broad boulevard outside the city walls) was laid, great warehouses went up along the harborfront, the Plaza de Armas was reconstructed with the grand dimensions (and a grandiose governor's residence) familiar to visitors today, and a baroque cathedral was built and new buildings erected in the Plaza de Cienaga (today's Plaza de la Catedral). The first public gas lighting arrived in 1768, along with a workable system of aqueducts. Most of the streets—which had by now been given the names they possess today—were cobbled. Fine theaters arose alongside bustling casinos and bars.

Life was lived ostentatiously by those with the means. The wealthy merchants and plantation owners erected beautiful mansions graced with baroque stonework painted in every conceivable combination of pastel colors, "all shimmering and quivering in the hot, glowing air." Inside, they were fitted with every luxury in European style. Most households in Havana were also maintained by slaves—often in great numbers, for the slave trade through Havana had grown astronomically as sugar began to dominate the slave-based agricultural economy, contributing even vaster sums to Havana's coffers.

Whirligig Life on the Streets

Life coursed through Havana's plazas like a storm of sweetpeas: peasants leading mules bearing baskets of fruit and vegetables, farmers adding to the great crush as they drive cattle and pigs to market, acrobats and clowns doing tricks for handouts, musicians serenading, lottery-ticket sellers bearing down on anyone who looked as if they deserved some good luck that day, water vendors hawking foul-smelling water, goats being milked door-to-door, and *volantas*—carriages with light bodies suspended as if in midair between enormous wheels—racing around the streets, each pulled by a well-groomed horse ridden by a Negro *calesero* (postilion) in resplendent livery. (Habana Vieja's system of one-way streets dates to this period. Many of the street signs embedded in the walls of old Habana Vieja still bear a pointing hand in a frilly cuff pointing the way for passing *caleseros*.)

The city must have resembled a grand operatic production—especially at night, with the harbor, crosshatched by masts and spars, shining under the glint of soft moonlight. It must have been a sight, too, to watch the coquettish maidens wearing white ballgowns and necklaces of giant fireflies—*cocullos*—gathering on Sunday for the brilliant masked balls eagerly anticipated by Habaneras.

The City Bursts its Seams

By the mid-19th century, Habana Vieja harbored 55,000 people. New buildings were going up, and the city was bursting with uncontainable energy. Soon there was not a square centimeter left for building within the city walls. In 1863, the walls came tumbling down—less than a century after they were completed. A new upscale district called Vedado rose behind the shore west of Habana Vieja. Graceful boulevards pushed westward into the surrounding hills and countryside, lined with a parade of *quintas* (country houses) fronted by classical columns. The baroque bowed out, as architects harked back farther to the heyday of Greece.

Havana's owes much of its modern face to Governor Miguel Tacón y Rosique, who initiated a brisk program of urban reform that included creation of a fire brigade, a police force, street cleaning, street signs, a drainage system, and unbridled construction. Tacón supported the first railroad in the Spanish colonies, linking Havana with Bejucal in 1837. Fortunately for latter-day tourists, Tacón had a rival: the Conde de Villanueva, the *criollo* (Cuban-born) administrator of the royal estates.

The elitist *Peninsulares* (native Spaniards) ran Cuba as a fiefdom, and *criollos* were allowed no say in administration of the island. Unquenchable animosity had arisen between them, firing the wars of independence but also fueling a contest to erect public and rival edifices as expressions of Spanish and disaffected *criollo* pride. We owe the Templete, the neobaroque Gran Teatro on Parque Central, and the contemporary face of the Prado to this war.

Alas, while Havana matured in grandeur, the surrounding countryside was being laid waste by the wars of independence. Spanish authorities in Havana meted out harsh sentences against anyone who declared himself against Spain. La Cañana became a jail, and many famous nationalist figures, including José Martí, were imprisoned here. By the late 1880s, many of the wealthy land-owning Habaneros were forced to sell their crippled estates to US citizens, many of whom had begun to flock to the island for other pleasures selected from more than 200 brothels.

The US government had long coveted Cuba, and found its pretext on 15 February 1898, when the USS *Maine* exploded in Havana harbor. The hulk of the *Maine* lay in the harbor until 1912, when the rusting symbol of *norteamericano* interference in Cuban affairs was raised, hauled far out to sea, and sunk.

Into the 20th Century

When the war ended, in 1898, the US military administration initiated far-reaching reforms, including a campaign that eradicated the yellow-fever epidemics then common in Havana, and the capital city entered a new era. The Malecón was laid out; wealthy *yanquis* and Cubanos built their posh mansions side-by-side in the western suburbs of Vedado and Miramar, where the first country clubs were opened; the older residential areas settled into an era of decay; and many cherished old buildings were demolished. Apartment buildings and hotels went up, and many of the once-fashionable houses along the Prado and in Habana Vieja were converted for commercial use.

Havana continued to prosper in the wake of World War I. In 1920, the new Presidential Palace was opened, and the presidency of Cuba relocated from the Palace of the Captains-General. In 1929, the ribbon was cut on the statuesque Capitolio, and the legislature took its seats. But Cuban politics had sunk into a spiral of corruption and graft, and in the ensuing decades Havana attracted the good and the bad in about equal measure. Havana, wrote Juliet Barclay, filled with "milkshakes and mafiosi, hot dogs and whores. Yanqui Doodle had come to town and was having martini-drinking competitions in the Sevilla Bar."

THE MOB IN CUBA

For three decades the Mafia had the run of the house. During Prohibition (1920-33), mobsters such as Al Capone had contracted with Cuban refineries to supply molasses for their illicit rum factories. When Prohibition ended, the Mob turned to gambling. The Mafia's interests were represented by Meyer Lansky, the Jewish mobster from Miami who arrived in 1939 and struck a deal with Fulgencio Batista, Cuba's strongman president. Lansky, acting as lieutenant for national crime syndicate boss Salvatore "Lucky" Luciano, took over the Oriental Park race track and the casino at Havana's Casino Nacional, where he ran a straight game that attracted high rollers. The Cuban state was so crooked, the Mob didn't even need to break the law.

World War II effectively put an end to the Mob's business. Lansky returned to Florida, followed (in 1944) by Batista, when he lost to Ramón Grau in the national election.

After the US deported Luciano to Italy in 1946, he immediately moved to Cuba, where he intended to establish a gambling and narcotics operation and regain his status as head of the US Mob. He called a summit in Havana's Hotel Nacional. The US, however, pressured Grau to deport Luciano back to Italy. Before leaving, Luciano named Meyer Lansky head of operations.

Lansky's aboveboard operation had withered, replaced by rigged casinos. Havana had developed a bad reputation. Cuban casinos rented space to entrepreneurs who, says Stephen Williams, ran "wildly crooked games with the only limit to their profit being the extent of their daring."

When Florida voters declined to legalize gambling, the state's casinos were closed down. This was followed by a federal campaign to suppress national crime syndicates. Mobsters decided Cuba was the place to be. A new summit was called at Fulgencio Batista's house in Daytona Beach, attended by Cuban politicians and military brass. A deal was struck: Batista would return to Cuba, regain power, and open the doors to large-scale gambling. In return, he and his crooked pals would receive a piece of the take.

A gift of US$250,000 (personally delivered by Lansky) helped convince President Grau to step aside, and on 10 March 1952, Batista again occupied the Presidential Palace. New laws were quickly enacted to attract investment in hotels and casinos, and banks were set up as fronts to channel money into the hands of Cuban politicos. In the United States, the Mafia faced certain limitations. In Cuba, anything was permissible: gambling, pornography, drugs. Corruption and self-enrichment occurred on a colossal scale. Organized crime became one of the three real power groups in Cuba (the others being Batista's military regime and American business). Together, they established a virtual criminal state.

Four "families" ruled the roost. The first, headed by Cuban-Italian Amleto Batistti, controlled the heroin and cocaine routes to the United States and an emporium of illegal gambling from Batistti's base at the Hotel Sevilla. The "family" of Amadeo Barletta organized the "Black Shirts" in Havana. The third family, headed by Tampa's Mafia boss, Santo Trafficante, Jr., operated the Sans Souci casino-nightclub, plus the casinos in the Capri, Comodoro, Deauville, and Sevilla-Biltmore Hotels. Watching over them all was Lansky, who ran the Montmarte Club and the Internacional Club of the Hotel Nacional.

Lansky again cleaned up the gambling to attract high-stakes gamblers from the States. No frivolities were allowed. Games were regulated and card sharps and cheats were sent packing. Casinos were extensively renovated, and cocaine and prostitutes were supplied to high rollers. (Trafficante claimed to have supplied three prostitutes for Senator John F. Kennedy and then watched the foursome through a one-way mirror—but forgot to film it.)

The tourists flocked. Lansky's last act was to built the ritziest hotel and casino in Cuba—the US$14 million Hotel Riviera, which opened on 10 December 1958. Within three weeks, on New Year's Eve, the sold-out floor show at the Riviera's Copa Room nightclub had 200 no-shows. Batista and his crooked henchmen had fled the country. The casinos were closed down (only after they had paid their employees) and, in June 1959, Lansky, Trafficante, and other "undesirable aliens" were arrested and kicked out of Cuba. Said Lansky: "I crapped out."

When US naval vessels entered Havana harbor, the narrow harbormouth beneath the Morro Castle was "jammed with rowboats full of clamoring prostitutes!" recalls one sailor.

By the 1950s, Havana had acquired skyscrapers such as the FOCSA building and the Hilton (now the Habana Libre). Ministries were being moved to a new center of construction, in the Plaza de la República (today the Plaza de la Revolución), inland from Vedado. Hotels were booming. Gambling found a new lease on life, and casinos flourished. "The future looks fabulous for Havana," said Wilbur Clarke, the croupier who operated the casino in the Hotel Nacional, little knowing what the course of history had in store.

The Post-Revolutionary Era

Fidel Castro arrived in Havana on 9 January 1959 to a tumultuous welcome. One of the first acts of the government was to close the strip clubs, casinos, and brothels. As time unveiled the communist nature of the Castro regime, a mass exodus of the wealthy and the middle class began, inexorably changing the face of Havana.

In 1959, Havana was a highly developed city—one of the most developed in Latin America—with a large wealthy and prospering middle class, and a vigorous culture. Nonetheless, the city faced a tremendous housing shortage. Festering slums and shanty towns marred the suburbs. The government ordered them razed. Concrete high-rise apartment blocks were erected on the outskirts, especially in Habanas del Este. A great plaza—the Plaza de la Revolución—was laid out. Meanwhile, the Presidential Palace and Capitolio—ultimate symbols of the "sordid era"—were turned into museums, while the new government moved into new ministry buildings surrounding the Plaza de la Revolución.

That accomplished, the Revolution turned its back on the city and gave its attention instead to the countryside. Havana's aged housing and infrastructure, much of it already decayed, have ever since suffered benign neglect. Even the Mayor of Havana has admitted that "the Revolution has been hard on the city." On 14 December 1982, UNESCO's Inter-Governmental Committee for World Cultural and Natural Protection named Habana Vieja a "World Heritage Site" worthy of protection and restoration.

SIGHTSEEING

Since the main sights are so spread out, it is best to explore Havana in sections, beginning with Habana Vieja, where the vast majority of historical sites are located. Habana Vieja is best explored on foot, while it's perhaps best to see the rest of the city using taxis, on a sightseeing tour with Havanatur, or by hiring a private car and guide. All touristed areas are well patroled by police, who are usually very helpful and gracious.

A guided city tour is a good way of getting your bearings. **Tour & Travel**, tel. 33-9199, offers guided city tours by minibus daily (US$10). **Agencia Viajes San Cristóbal,** Calle Oficio 110, tel. 33-8693, offers guided walking tours of Habana Vieja.

I also recommend you call in first at the **Maqueta de la Habana** (see "Maqueta" in the "Miramar" section, later in this chapter) to peruse the 1:1,000-scale model that will give you an idea of the city's layout. Next, visit the **José Martí Memorial** to take the elevator to the top of the *mirador,* where you gain a bird's-eye view of the entire city, as if the *maqueta* had come to life. With that, you're ready to begin exploring.

HABANA VIEJA~THE OLD CITY

Habana Vieja (4.5 square km; pop. 105,000) is defined by the limits of the early colonial settlement that lay within fortified walls. Today, the legal boundary of Habana Vieja includes all that lies east of Paseo de Martí, and even Regla and Guanabacoa on the east shores of the bay. Don't underestimate how much there is to see in Habana Vieja. At least two days are required, and one week isn't too much.

Habana Vieja is roughly shaped like a diamond, with the Castillo de la Punta at the east end of the Malecón its northerly point. Its western boundary, Paseo de Martí (colloquially called the Prado) runs south from here to Parque de la Fraternidad. Avenida de la Bélgica runs southeast from here, tracing the old city wall southeastward to the harborfront at the west end of Desamparados. East of Castillo de la Punta, Avenida Carlos Manuel de Céspedes (Avenida del Puerto) runs along the harbor channel that forms the northern boundary as far as Castillo de la Real Fuerza, where Avenida de la Puerto (the eastern flank) begins the smooth curve southward and westward (as Desamparado) along the harborfront.

The original city developed along a polynuclear axis that extended roughly north-south from Castillo de la Real Fuerza to Plaza Vieja. Here are the major sites of interest, centered on two plazas of great stature: the Plaza de Armas and the smaller but more imposing Plaza de la Catedral. The old squares concentrate the past into an essence that is so rich, suggests Barclay, "that it is indigestible unless taken in small sips." Each square has its own unique flavor, which seems to change with the hours and light: melancholic in the rain, bustling and alive in the sun, and "voluptuous when a hot midnight is illuminated by lamps and vibrates with guitar music and the muffled heartbeat of an African drum." The southern half of Habana Vieja, south of Plaza Vieja, is less "touristy," and walking its streets you'll gain a strong feel for the daily lot of Habaneros.

You'll frequently find humble and haughty side by side, since for most of the colonial period areas were socially mixed. Slaves lived in separate quarters or their masters' mansions. Merchants lived above their warehouses, where the slaves also lived. The best stores in colonial days were along Calles Obispo and O'Reilly, seething Oriental bazaars that were once covered in colorful awnings that softened the glare of the sun. They were Aladdin's caves of European fineries, incense, crystal and china, muslin and ribbons, and *piña* cloth, a silky gauze made of pineapple fiber and dyed in radiant colors. Obispo is still the lifeline connecting Centro Habana with Habana Vieja.

The maze of narrow one-way streets is purgatory for anyone with a motor vehicle, so *walk*. In any event, the main plazas and the streets between them are barred to traffic by huge artillery shells in the ground.

CASTILLO DE LA PUNTA TO CASTILLO DE LA REAL FUERZA

The low-slung Castillo de San Salvador de la Punta sits at the west end of Avenida Manuel de Céspedes at the meeting point of the Malecón and Paseo de Martí (the Prado). The fortress was initiated in 1589 directly across the harbor channel from Morro Castle so that the two fortresses might catch invaders in a crossfire. Between them, a great chain was slung each night to secure Havana harbor in colonial days.

The fort holds no appeal, although a restoration was nearing completion at press time.

Its site, however, is pivotal, and from the plaza overlooking the harbor channel (a favorite spot for trysting lovers at night), you may revel in the sweeping vista westward along the Malecón toward the statuesque façade of Vedado, dominated by the Hotel Nacional.

Immediately to the east stands the **Monumento al General Máximo Gómez,** a massive piece of white marble supported by classical columns. The monument, erected in 1835, honors the Dominican-born hero of the Cuban wars of independence who led the Liberation Army as commander-in-chief. Generalissimo Gómez (1836-1905) is cast in bronze atop his horse. The access road to the tunnel that leads to Morro Castle and Habanas del Este curls and nosedives beneath the monument.

East of the monumento, Avenida Manuel de Céspedes runs along the harborfront. It's bordered by a wide, shady park separating Manuel de Céspedes from Tacón, which runs parallel and formed the original waterfront, which was later extended with landfill. At Tacón's western end, facing the Gómez monument, is the **Museo de la Música,** tel. 80-6810, housed in the sober **Casa de Pérez de la Riva,** which was built in Italian Renaissance style in 1905 and which for a short time served as a jail. The museum traces the evolution of Cuban music since early colonial days; many antique instruments are displayed, including a beautiful collection of venerable pianos and the huge collection of drums once owned by Fernando Ortíz, a renowned Africanist. There is even a separate room where you can listen to old scores drawn from the record library. Open Tues.-Sat. 10 a.m.-6 p.m. and Sunday 9 a.m.-noon. Entrance is US$2.

One block east, peek in at the **Palacio Pedroso,** at the foot of Calle Cuarteles. This magnificent mansion was built in Moorish style for a nobleman, Don Mateo Pedroso, around 1780. Pedroso's home—a profusion of patterned tiles and foliate door arches—was a center for Havana's social life well into the 19th century. Today, duly restored, it houses the **Palacio de Artesanía,** with craft shops and a bar where you can soak up live music and soothing rum while enjoying a pronounced whiff of the *Arabian Nights.*

Amazingly, none of the maps or tourist literature make any mention of the splendid fortress a stone's throw east, at the foot of Chacón. This is because the *fortaleza* today houses the transit-police headquarters. Fronting it, in the middle of Tacón, is a watchtower—a rare remnant of the original city wall.

Tacón ends at a tiny *plazuela* at the foot of Empedrado, where a bevy of colorful old fishing boats that could have fallen from a painting by Hockney sit on the cobbled curbside in front of the **Casa de la Miniatura,** a former mansion that now sells exquisite miniature soldiers. Around the corner, on a narrow extension of Tacón that leads to Plaza de Armas, another restored mansion now houses **Bar y Restaurante D'Giovanni,** with a fabulous inner courtyard graced by three tiers of balustraded balconies (note the stunning mural in the entranceway).

Also worth a visit is the building next door, **Gabinete de la Arqueología,** the Archaeological Department of the Office of the City Historian, at Calle Tacón 12. Remarkably, the beautiful mansion (first mentioned in documents in 1644) was inherited in 1700 by a mulatta whose owner, Doña Lorenza de Carvajal, had granted her freedom (Doña Lorenza's own daughter had brought disgrace upon herself by becoming pregnant and was shuttled off to a convent). The mansion's most remarkable feature is a series of eccentric murals depicting life in bold technicolor as it was lived in Havana centuries ago (the murals, painted between 1763 and 1767, were revealed during a recent restoration from beneath 26 layers of paint and whitewash).

Seminario de San Carlos y San Ambrosio

The jewel in the crown of Tacón is this massive seminary, between Chacón and Empedrado, established by the Jesuits in 1721 and ever since a center for young men studying for an ecclesiastical career. Its dramatic baroque façade is missed by most tourists. It is a joy to escape to the serenity of the inner courtyard. The seminary was built in an irregular polygon during the second half of the 18th century with a three-story gallery in varying styles. Note the massive banister of caoba wood with elaborate carvings.

PLAZA DE LA CATEDRAL

You'll find yourself returning again and again to this exquisite cobbled square dominated by the intimate but imposing, decadently baroque 18th-century "Columbus Cathedral"—and, on the other three sides, aristocratic *palacios,* the Casa de Lombillo, Casa del Marqués de Arcos, Casa del Conde Bayona, and Casa de Marqués de Aguas Claras.

This was the last (and finest) square to be laid out in Habana Vieja, for it occupied a lowly quarter where rainwater drained (it was originally known as the Plazuela de la Cienaga—Little Square of the Swamp). Its present texture dates from the 18th century, before which it served as a fish market and watering station. On the southwest corner of the square is the **Callejon de Chorro,** a tiny cul-de-sac with a plaque denoting where a bathhouse was once located at the terminus of the Zanja Real (royal

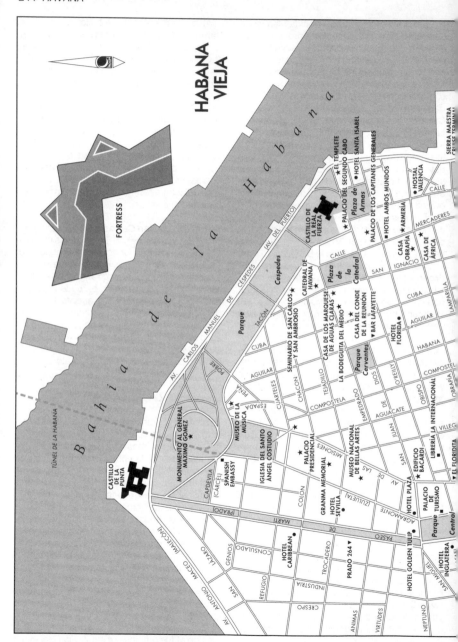

HABANA VIEJA

FORTRESS

TÚNEL DE LA HABANA

B a h i a   d e   l a   H a b a n a

CASTILLO DE LA PUNTA

AV. ANTONIO MACEO (MALECÓN)

GENIOS

CONSULADO

TROCADERO

HOTEL CARIBBEAN ▼

PRADO 264 ▼

SAN LÁZARO

REFUGIO

INDUSTRIA

CRESPO

ANIMAS

VIRTUDES

NEPTUNO

CAPDEVILA

MONUMENTO AL GENERAL MÁXIMO GÓMEZ ★

SPANISH EMBASSY ■

CÁRCEL

COLÓN

IZQUIERDO

AGRAMONTE

PASEO DE MARTÍ (PRADO)

HOTEL GOLDEN TULIP ▼

SAN MIGUEL

HOTEL INGLATERRA ▼

GRANMA MEMORIAL ■

HOTEL SEVILLA

IGLESIA DEL SANTO ÁNGEL COSTUDIO ★

PALACIO PRESIDENCIAL ★

MUSEO NACIONAL DE LAS ARTES ★

MISIÓN

AV. DE AGUACATE

HOTEL PLAZA ■

PALACIO DE TURISMO ■

Parque Central

EDIFICIO BACARDÍ ■

LIBRERÍA LA INTERNACIONAL ■

▼ EL FLORIDITA

AV. CARLOS MANUEL DE CÉSPEDES

Parque TACÓN

Cespedes

AV. DEL PUERTO

CASTILLO DE LA REAL FUERZA ★

CATEDRAL DE HAVANA ★

Plaza de la Catedral

EL TEMPLETE ★

PALACIO DEL SEGUNDO CABO ★

HOTEL SANTA ISABEL ●

Plaza de Armas

PALACIO DE LOS CAPITANES GENERALES ★

HOTEL AMBOS MUNDOS ■

ARMERÍA ★

CASA OBRAPÍA ★

CASA DE ÁFRICA ★

HOSTAL VALENCIA ●

CALLE

SIERRA MAESTRA CRUISE TERMINAL

MERCADERES

SAN IGNACIO

CUBA

LAMPARILLA

HABANA

COMPOSTELA

OBRAPÍA

O'REILLY

OBISPO

VILLEGAS

MUSEO DE LA MÚSICA ★

SEMINARIO DE SAN CARLOS Y SAN AMBROSIO ★

CASA DE LOS MARQUESES DE AGUAS CLARAS ★

CASA DEL CONDE DE LA REUNIÓN ★

▼ BAR LAFAYETTE

LA BODEGUITA DEL MEDIO ★

Parque Cervantes

HOTEL FLORIDA ●

PEÑA POBRE

CUBA

AGUILAR

CHACÓN

TEJADILLO

EMPEDRADO

SAN JUAN DE DIOS

ESPADA

CUARTELES

COMPOSTELA

AGUACATE

AV. DE

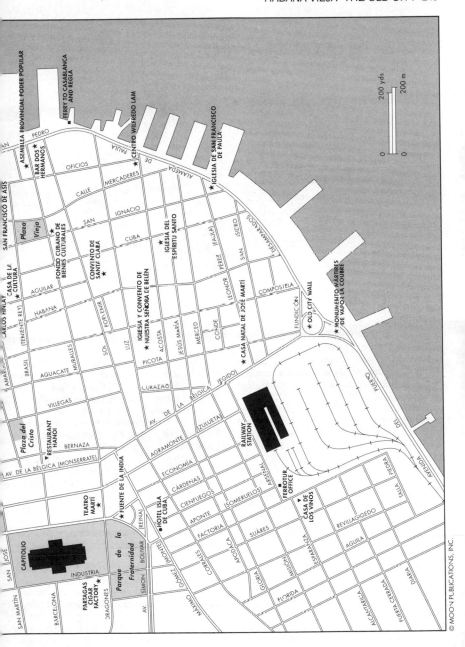

PLAZA DE LA CATEDRAL AND
PLAZA DE ARMAS AREA

ditch—the aqueduct that brought water from distant hills). A small sink and spigot are all that remain. (At the end of Callejon de Chorro is the **Taller Experimental de la Gráfica,** where you can watch art students making impressive prints).

The plaza is roamed by mulattas who will happily preen and pose for your camera for a small fee. By stages, the square has become a week-round gallery for arts and crafts and is today firmly in the grip of commercialism.

For the best view and photos down over the square, ascend the steps to the upper level of **Casa de Luís Chacón,** the simple two-story structure that faces the cathedral. It was built in the 1720s for Governor General Don Luís Chacón and today houses the **Museo de Arte Colonial,** tel. 61-1367. The museum is an Aladdin's cave of colonial furniture, glass, porcelain, Baccarat crystal, ironwork, musical instruments, and other sumptuous artifacts from the colonial period. One room is devoted to the stunningly colorful stained-glass *vitrales* and *mediopuntos* unique to Cuba. There's even an array of chamberpots! Open daily except Tuesday 9 a.m.-5 p.m. and Sunday 9 a.m.-1 p.m.; entrance costs

US$2. (The building is also known as the Casa del Conde Bayona.)

On the plaza's east side is the **Casa de Lombillo.** Built in 1741, this former home of a slave trader still houses a small post office (Cuba's first), as it has since 1821. Note the post-box set into the outside wall; it is a grotesque face— that of a tragic Greek mask—carved in stone, with as its slit a scowling mouth that looks like it might take your fingers or at least spit back your letter. Part of the building (to the left of the post office-cum-souvenir store) is now the **Museo de la Educación** (entrance US$1), dedicated in part to telling the tale of the remarkable and inspirational literacy campaign of 1961, when university students and teachers went to the far corners of Cuba. Almost one million people were taught to read and write during the epochal program.

Casa de Lombillo adjoins the **Casa del Marqués de Arcos,** built in 1740s for the royal treasurer. The mansion today houses the **Nelson Domínguez Experimental Graphics Art Gallery,** its walls virtually obliterated by large canvases by Domínguez, a noted Cuban artist whose exquisite mind seems to be inhabited, suggests City Historian Eusebio Leal Spengler, by "strange officiating priests of myth and religious fantasy."

The two houses are fronted by a wide gallery *(portal)* supported by thick columns and today used as a venue for artists to display their works.

Catedral de la Habana

Known colloquially as Catedral Colón and Catedral de San Cristóbal, this stunner has an official name—Catedral de la Virgen María de la Concepción Inmaculada. The cathedral was initiated by the Jesuits in 1748. The order was kicked out of Cuba by Carlos III in 1767, but the building was eventually completed in 1777.

Describing the cathedral's baroque façade, adorned with clinging columns and rippled like a great swelling sea, Cuban novelist Alejo Carpentier wrote that it was "music turned to stone." The façade is so simple yet magnificent that a royal decree of December 1793 elevated the church to a cathedral because "the beautifully carved stones of the church . . . are clamouring from their walls for the distinction of cathedral." On either side of the façade are mismatched towers (one fatter and taller than the other) containing two bells—one from Matanzas province and one from Spain—supposedly cast with a dash of gold and silver which is said to account for their musical tone. The eastern bell tower has in the past been open to tourists.

Beyond the huge wooden doors, columns divide the church into three naves. The main altar is of Carrara marble inlaid with gold, silver, onyx, and carved wood.

The Spanish believed that a casket which had been brought to Havana with due pomp and circumstance from Santo Domingo in 1796 and resided in the cathedral for over a century held the ashes of Christopher Columbus. Casket and ashes—a "pile of dust and a bit of bone"—were returned to Spain in 1899. All but the partisan Habaneros now believe that the ashes were those of Columbus' son Diego. The stone statue of Columbus that stood outside the cathedral is gone (Graham Greene, in *Our Man From Havana,* thought it looked "as though it had been formed through the centuries under water, like a coral reef, by the action of insects").

At press time, the cathedral was open Mon.-Fri. 9-11 a.m. and 2:30-6 p.m., and for Mass Tuesday and Thursday at 8 a.m. and Sunday at 10:30 a.m. A guided tour is reportedly offered on Saturday afternoons.

Casa de los Marqueses de Aguas Claras

If the heat and bustle of the square get to you, you should settle on the patio beneath the soaring *portal* of this splendid old mansion on the west side of the plaza. Here you can sip a cool beer or heady *mojito* and watch the comings and goings while being serenaded by musicians. The mansion was owned during the 16th century by Governor General Gonzalo Pérez de Angulo and has since been added to by subsequent owners. The inner courtyard, which has a fountain and a grand piano amid lush palms and clinging vines, today houses the Restaurante La Fuente del Patio.

The restaurant extends upstairs, where the middle class once dwelled in apartments (since converted for diners' pleasure, enhanced by *mediopuntos* which by day saturate the floors with shifting fans of red and blue light). Novelist Enrique Fernandez, writing in 1994, recalled being able to look down from his grandmoth-

Plaza de la Catedral

CHRISTOPHER P. BAKER

ERNEST HEMINGWAY AND CUBA

Ernest Hemingway first set out from Key West to wrestle marlin in the wide streaming currents off the Cuban coast in April 1932. Years later, he was to sail to and fro on the Key West-Havana route dozens of times. The blue waters of the Gulf Stream, chock-full of billfish, brought him closer and closer until eventually, "succumbing to the other charms of Cuba, different from and more difficult to explain than the big fish in September," he settled on this irresistibly charismatic island.

Hemingway loved Cuba and lived there for the better part of 20 years. It was more alluring, more fulfilling, than Venice, Sun Valley, or the green hills of Africa. Once, when Hemingway was away from Cuba, he was asked what he worried about in his sleep. "My house in Cuba," he replied, referring to Finca Vigía, in the suburb of San Francisco de Paula, 15 kilometers southeast of Havana.

At first it was the fishing—and the women—that brought Hemingway back to Cuba. When his wife was absent, Hemingway did his best to keep up his bad-boy reputation for booze and broads.

The Cult of Hemingway
Havana's city fathers have leased Papa's spirit to lend ambience to and put a polish on his favorite haunts. Havana's marina is named for the prize-winning novelist. A special rum, "El Ron Vigía" was even introduced to coincide with the author's 95th birthday, on 21 July 1994. Hemingway's room in the Hotel Ambos Mundos and Finca Vigía are preserved as museums. And plans are even underway for a "Friends of Hemingway" club for tourists.

Yet the cult of Hemingway is very real. Cubans worship him with an intensity not far short of that accorded Che Guevara and nationalist hero José Martí. The novelist's works are required reading in Cuban schools. His books are best-sellers. "We admire Hemingway because he understood the Cuban people; he supported us," a friend told me. The Cuban understanding of Hemingway's "Cuba novels" is that they support a core tenet of Communist ideology—that humans are only fulfilled acting in a "socialist" context for a moral purpose, not individualistically. (Many of Hemingway's novels appear to condemn economic and political injustices.)

"All the works of Hemingway are a defense of human rights," claims Fidel, who knows Papa's nov-els "in depth" and once claimed that *For Whom the Bell Tolls,* Hemingway's fictional account of the Spanish Civil War, had inspired his guerrilla tactics. Fidel has said the reason he admires Hemingway so much is that he envies him the adventures he had. In July 1961, after Hemingway's death, his widow, Mary Welsh, returned to Finca Vigía to collect some items she wanted. Fidel came to visit. Recalls Welsh, Fidel "headed for Ernest's chair and was seating himself when I murmured that it was my husband's favorite. The Prime Minister raised himself up, slightly abashed."

The two headstrong fellows met only once, during the Tenth Annual Ernest Hemingway Billfish Tournament in May 1960. As sponsor and judge of the competition, Hemingway invited Cuba's youthful new leader as his guest of honor. Fidel was to present the winner's trophy; instead, he hooked the biggest marlin and won the prize for himself. Hemingway surrendered the trophy to a beaming Fidel. They would never meet again. One year later, the great writer committed suicide in Idaho.

Papa and the Revolution
There has been a great deal of speculation about Hemingway's position toward the Cuban Revolution. Cuba, of course, attempts to portray him as sympathetic (Gabriel García Márquez refers to "Our

BOB RACE

Hemingway" in the prologue to Cuban novelist Norberto Fuente's *Hemingway in Cuba*).

Hemingway's Cuban novels are full of images of prerevolutionary terror and destitution. "There is an absolutely murderous tyranny that extends over every little village in the country," he wrote in *Islands in the Stream*.

"I believe completely in the historical necessity of the Cuban revolution," he wrote a friend in 1960. Papa was away from Cuba all of 1959, but he returned in 1960, recorded *New York Times* correspondent Herbert Matthews, "to show his sympathy and support for the Castro Revolution." Papa even used his legendary 38-foot sportfishing boat, the *Pilar*, to run arms for the rebel army, claims Gregorio Fuentes, the weatherbeaten sailor-guardian of the *Pilar* for 23 years. In his will, the great author dedicated his home and possessions—including his Nobel prize—to the Cuban state; but the *Pilar* he left to Fuentes.

Hemingway's widow, Mary, told the journalist Luís Dáez that "Hemingway was always in favor of the Revolution," and another writer, Lisandro Otero records Hemingway as saying, "Had I been a few years younger, I would have climbed the Sierra Maestra with Fidel Castro." The truth of these comments, alas, can't be validated. But Hemingway's enigmatic farewell comment as he departed the island in 1960 is illuminating: *"Vamos a ganar. Nosotros los cubanos vamos a ganar.* [We are going to win. We Cubans are going to win.] I'm not a Yankee, you know." What would he have made of the outcome?

Organized Tours

Wings of the World, 1200 William St. #706, Buffalo, NY 14240, tel. (800) 465-8687, offers a fully escorted eight-day Hemingway's Trail tour, timed to coincide with the annual **International Hemingway Colloquium,** held at Finca Vigía each July (US$2,495 including airfare from New York). Since the trips are fully prepaid and all-inclusive, they're legal for *any* US citizen.

Paradiso, Calle 19 #560, esq. Calle C, Vedado, Havana, tel. 32-6928, fax 33-3021, offers a five-hour excursion—"Hemingway: the Mystery of a Footprint"—that includes a visit to Finca Vigía and Cojímar (US$35).

---

er's balcony and watch "the goings on in the plaza: the fruit vendors and bootblacks, the elegant men and women in white linen going into the restaurant (which was far too pricey for the second-floor tenants), and at the garishly dressed Americans buying stuffed baby alligators in the tourist shops that festooned the other two *palacios*." You can still steal out onto the rickety balconies to look down on the colorful action; when the crowds disappear, note the patterned cobbles.

Immediately next door, abutting the Casa de Aguas Claras to the south, is the **Casa de Baños,** looking quite ancient but built this century in colonial style on the site of a 19th-century bathhouse erected over an *aljibe*—water reservoir—fed by the Zanja Real. Today it contains the **Galería tor Manuel,** which sells exquisite quality arts.

La Bodeguita del Medio

No visit to Havana is complete without at least one visit to Ernest Hemingway's favorite watering hole, at 207 Calle Empedrado, tel. 62-6121, half a block west of the cathedral. This neighborhood hangout was originally the coachhouse of the mansion next door (that of the Countess de la Reunion). Later it was a bodega, a mom-and-pop grocery store that served drinks and food over the counter. The owner, Martínez, hit upon a brilliant idea: he gave writers credit. The writers, of course, wrote about their newfound hangout, thereby attracting literati and cognoscenti from around the world.

You enter through a saloon-style swinging door. The bar is immediately on your right, with the restaurant behind (note the beautiful tilework along the passageway wall). The bar is usually crowded with tourists, who ebb and flow. Troubadors move among the thirsty *turistas*. Between tides, you can still savor the proletarian fusion of dialectics and rum. (The house drink is the *mojito*, the rum mint julep—US$3—that Hemingway brought out of obscurity and turned into the national drink.)

The rustic wooden bar is carved with names. Miscellaneous bric-a-brac adorns the walls: posters, paintings, and faded black-and-white photos of Papa Hemingway, Carmen Miranda, and other famous visitors. The walls look as if a swarm of adolescents has been given amphetamines and let loose with crayons. The most famous graffiti, of course, is credited to Papa: "Mi

Mojito En La Bodeguita, Mi Daiquiri En El Floridita," he supposedly scrawled on the sky-blue walls. Errol Flynn thought it "A Great Place To Get Drunk."

Casa del Conde de la Reunión

This beautiful house, at Empredado #215, 50 meters west of La Bodeguita, was built in the 1820s, at the peak of the baroque era. The doorway opens onto a courtyard surrounded by rooms in which Alejo Carpentier, Cuba's most famous novelist (and a dedicated revolutionary), once worked. A portion of the home, which houses the **Centro de Promoción Cultural,** is dedicated to his memory as the **Museo Carpentier.** One entire wall bears a display under sloping glass of Carpentier's early works. His Volkswagen Beetle is on display in a first-floor room along with his raincoat, thrown stylishly over his old desk chair. The novelist's widow dedicated his posthumous royalties to establish and maintain the museum.

Parque Cervantes
(Plazuela de San Juan de Díos)

Two blocks west of the cathedral, you'll pass this small, unkempt plaza (between Calles Habana and Aguiar) surrounding a white marble monument—erected in 1906—with a life-size facsimile of Miguel de Cervantes, the great Spanish author of *Don Quixote,* sitting in a chair, book and pen in hand, looking contemplatively down upon rose bushes.

CALLE O'REILLY

Narrow **Calle San Ignacio** leads south from the Plaza de la Catedral to Calle O'Reilly—named not, as you may suspect, for an Irishman but rather for a Spaniard, Alejandro O'Reilly, who arrived to represent the Spanish crown after the British returned the city to Spain in 1763.

O'Reilly was before the Revolution a major commercial thoroughfare: "The bells were ringing in Santo Christo, and the doves rose from the roof in the golden evening and circled away over the lottery shops of O'Reilly Street and the banks of Obispo," wrote Graham Greene in *Our Man in Havana.* Worth a look is the neoclassical **National City Bank of New York,** at O'Reilly and Compostela, where, "passing through great stone portals, which were decorated with four-leaf clovers," Greene's Wormold was reminded of his meager status. In the basement vaults, the **Museum of Finances** today traces the history of banking from the colonial era to the tenure of Che Guevara's reign as the bank's president in the early 1960s.

Half a block west of Calle San Ignacio is **Café O'Reilly,** O'Reilly #205, an atmospheric streetside café with an ornate cast-iron spiral staircase that leads up to a tiny bar where you may sit on a balcony and sip rich Cuban coffee or cappuccino while watching the tide of people flooding O'Reilly.

Two blocks east is the **Empresa Cubana del Tabaco,** O'Reilly #104, tel. 33-8997 or 61-0485, the headquarters of Habanos S.A., which oversees Cuba's production and sale of cigars. Visitors are welcomed into the lobby to admire an exhibition, including display cases of Cuba's finest cigars. Outside, note the plaque at the corner of O'Reilly and Tacón that reads, "Two Island Peoples in the Same Seas of Struggle and Hope. Cuba and Ireland."

You now stand at the northwest corner of the Plaza de Armas.

PLAZA DE ARMAS

The most important plaza in Habana Vieja, and the oldest—originally laid out in 1519—is this handsome square at the seaward end of Calles Obispo and O'Reilly, opening onto Avenida del Puerto to the east. Plaza de Armas was the early focus of the settlement and later became its administrative center. It is still rimmed by four important buildings constructed in the late 18th century, when the capacious square was reconstructed with "buildings appropriate to the grandeur of this city." The square seems still to ring with the cacophany of the past, when military parades, extravagant fiestas, and musical concerts were held under the watchful eye of the governor and the gentry would take their formal evening promenade. The lovely tradition has been revived on Sunday, when by day the plaza hosts a secondhand book fair and, by night, musical concerts. The square is lent a romantic cast by its verdant park shaded by palms and tall trees festooned with lianas and epiphytes and lit at night by beautifully filigreed

RESTORING OLD HAVANA

Old Havana has been called the "finest urban ensemble in the Americas." The fortress colonial town that burst its walls when Washington, D.C., was still a swamp is a 350-acre repository of antique buildings. More than 900 of Habana Vieja's 3,157 structures are of historic importance. Of these, only 101 were built in the 20th century. Almost 500 are from the 19th; 200 are from the 18th; and 144 are from the 16th and 17th.

Only one in six buildings is in good condition. Many are crumbling into ruins around the people who occupy them.

In 1977, the Cuban government named Habana Vieja a National Monument. The following year it formalized a plan to rescue the city from centuries of neglect under the guidance of Eusebio Leal Spengler, the charismatic city historian, thanks to whose efforts Havana was proclaimed a UNESCO World Heritage Site in 1982.

The ambitious plan stretches beyond the year 2000 and concentrates on the five squares, Plaza de Armas, Plaza de la Catedral, Plaza Vieja, Plaza de San Francisco, and Plaza del Cristo. The most important buildings have received major renovations; others are being given facelifts—symbols of triumph over horrendous shortages of materials and money. Nonetheless, the project has been seriously jeopardized by the current economic crisis. Hence, the Cuban government is seeking foreign investors to help salvage the collapsing buildings.

Florida-based Cuban-Americans, including architects and art historians, have formed **The Bridge for Historic Preservation,** 1625 Colony Ave., Kissimmee, FL 34744, tel. (407) 847-7892, fax (407) 847-2986, to assist in Havana's restoration efforts. It requests donations.

Other Cuban-Americans have formed the Miami-based **Cuban National Heritage** as a trust-in-exile that sponsors symposiums with Cuba's architectural historians (but not state agencies) and is developing zoning codes to help fend off powerful southern Florida developers who are hungrily eyeing the island and are likely to bulldoze historic areas.

---

lamps. At its center is a statue of Manuel de Céspedes, hero of the Ten Years' War, with a tall palm at each corner.

East of the square, on Avenida Puerto at the foot of O'Reilly, is a monument to Cuban seamen killed during World War II by Nazi submarines (four Cuban vessels were sunk by German U-boats).

The following buildings are described in clockwise order around the plaza.

Palacio de los Capitanes Generales

Commanding the square is this somber, stately palace fronted by a cool loggia shadowed by a façade of Ionic columns supporting nine great arches. The tall loggia boasts a life-size statue of Fernando VII with a scroll of parchment in one hand—jauntily cocked (pardon the pun) and the butt of ribald jokes—and plumed hat in the other.

Spain's stern rule was enforced from here: the Palacio de los Capitanes Generales was home to 65 governors of Cuba between 1791 and 1898 and, after that, the early seat of the Cuban government (and the US governor's residence during Uncle Sam's occupation). Be-

tween 1920 and 1967, it served as Havana's city hall. Originally the parish church—La Parroquial Mayor, built in 1555—stood here. Alas, the holy structure was destroyed by what insurance agencies like to call an "act of God"—it was demolished when a warship, the ill-named *Invincible,* exploded alongside the wharf down the way, and the mast and spars came through the roof!

The palace is a magnificent three-story structure surrounding a courtyard (entered from the plaza) which contains a statue of Christopher Columbus competing for the light with tall palms and a veritable botanical garden of foliage. Don't be alarmed by any ghoulish shrieks—a peacock lives in the courtyard. Arched colonnades rise to all sides, festooned with vines and bougainvillea. Several afternoons each week an orchestra plays decorous 19th-century dance music, while pretty girls in crinolines flit up and down the majestic staircase, delighting in the ritual of the *Quince,* the traditional celebration of a girl's 15th birthday. On the southeast corner you can spot a hole containing the coffin of an unknown nobleman, one of several graves from the old Cementerio de Espada (a church that once stood

bookfair, Plaza de
Armas

CHRISTOPHER P. BAKER

here was razed to make way for the palace; note the plaque—the oldest in Havana—commemorating the death of Doña María de Cepero y Nieto, who was felled when a harquebus was accidentally fired while she was praying).

Today, the palace houses the **Museum of the City of Havana,** tel. 61-4463 or 62-0400. The entrance is to the side, on Calle Obispo. The great flight of marble stairs leads to high-ceilinged rooms as gracious and richly furnished as those in Versailles or Buckingham Palace. The throne room (made for the King of Spain but never used) is of particularly breathtaking splendor and is brimful of treasures. The countless curiosities include two enormous marble bathtubs in the shape of nautilus shells, Máximo Gómez's death mask, and a cannon made of leather. There is also a Hall of Flags, plus exquisite collections illustrating the story of the city's (and Cuba's) development and the 19th-century struggles for independence. Open daily 9:30 a.m.-6:30 p.m. Entrance costs US$3 tourists (US$2 extra for cameras). You can purchase a US$9 ticket good for *all* museums in Havana.

The museum (1 Calle Tacón) also has a model of an early 20th-century sugar plantation at 1:22.5 scale, complete with steam engine, milling machines, and plantation grounds with workers' dwellings, a church, and a hotel—all transporting you back in time on the world's smallest sugar plantation. A railroad runs through the plantation, with two steam locomotives pulling sugarcane carriers, water tanks, and passenger carriages. Trains depart Mon.-Fri. at 11 a.m., noon, and 2:30 p.m.

Palacio del Segundo Cabo
The quasi-Moorish, pseudo-baroque, part neoclassical Palace of the Second Lieutenant, on the north side of the square, dates from 1770. Its use metamorphosed several times until it became the home of the vice-governor general (Second Lieutenant) and, immediately after independence, the seat of the Senate. Today, it houses the Bien Fondo Cultura and Bella Habana bookstore.

Castillo de la Real Fuerza
This pocket-size castle, tel. 80-0216, finished in 1582, is the oldest of the four forts that guarded the New World's most precious harbor. With walls six meters wide and 10 tall, it forms a square with enormous triangular bulwarks at the corners. The governors of Cuba lived here until 1762. I never cease to marvel at its solidity, simple sophistication, sharp angles (which slice the dark waters of the moat like the prows of galleons), and beauty especially at night, when it is haloed in ghostly light.

Visitors enter the fortress on the northeast corner of Plaza de Armas via a courtyard full of photogenic patinated cannons and mortars. Note the royal coat of arms (of Sevilla in Spain) carved in stone above the massive gateway as you cross the moat by a drawbridge to enter a vaulted interior containing two suits of armor in glass cases.

Stairs lead up to the storehouse and battle-ments, now housing an impressive ceramic art store and the El Meson restaurant, popular with locals. A door to the right immediately after entering the restaurant leads to a courtyard, where you can climb to the top of a cylindrical tower rising from the northwest corner. The tower contains an antique brass bell gone mossy green with age and weather. The bell was rung to signal the approach of ships, with differing notes for friends and foes. The tower is topped by a bronze weathervane called La Giraldilla de la Habana—a reference to the Giralda weathervane in Seville. It's a pathetic looking thing, but much is made of it (it's the symbol of Havana and also graces the label of Havana Club rum bottles). The vane is a copy—the archetype, which was toppled in a hurricane, resides in the city museum. The original was cast in 1631 in honor of Inéz de Bobadil-la, the wife of Governor Hernando de Soto, the tireless explorer who fruitlessly searched for the Fountain of Youth in Florida. Every afternoon for four years she climbed the tower and scanned the horizon in vain for his return. In memory of his widow, the residents of Havana commissioned the weathervane and placed it atop the tower. The Giraldilla is a voluptuous albeit small figure with hair braided in thick ropes, bronze robes fluttering in the wind. In her right hand she holds a palm tree and in her left a cross.

El Templete

A charming copy of a Doric temple sits on the square's northeast corner. It was built in the early 19th century on the site where the first mass and town council meeting were held in 1519, beside a massive ceiba tree. The original ceiba was felled by a hurricane in 1828 and re-placed by a column fronted by a small bust of Christopher Columbus. The tree has since been replanted and today still shades the tiny tem-ple, which wears a great cloak of bougainvillea.

Its interior, with black and white checkerboard marble floor, is dominated by triptych wall-to-ceiling paintings depicting the first Mass, the first town council meeting, and the inauguration of the Templete. In the center of the room is a bust of the artist, Jean Baptiste Ver May, whose ashes (along with those of his wife, who also died—along with 8,000 other citizens—in the cholera epidemic of 1833) are contained in a marble urn next to the bust.

The Southeast Corner

The grand building immediately south of El Templete is the former Palacio del Conde de Santovenia. The conde (count) in question was famous for hosting elaborate parties, most no-toriously a three-day bash in 1833 to celebrate the accession to the throne of Isabel II and which climaxed with an ascent of a gaily deco-rated gas-filled balloon (he was less popular with his immediate neighbors, who detested the reek of oil and fish that wafted over the square from his first-floor warehouses). In the late 19th century, it was bought and sanitized by a colonel from New Orleans who reopened it as a resplendent hotel, Hotel Santa Isabel, a guise it resumes in 1997.

One block east of the hotel, on narrow Calle Baratillo, is the **Casa del Café**, serving all kinds of Cuban coffees, and, next door, the **Taberna del Galeón**, better known as the House of Rum. Inside, where it is as cool as a well, you can taste various rums at no cost, although it is hoped you will make a purchase from the wide selection. The decor is marvelous—shiny hard-woods throughout. The place is popular with tour groups, which ebb and flow like sardines.

Calle Obispo

Calle Obispo is Habana Vieja's bustling thor-oughfare, linking Plaza de Armas with Parque Central. Every visitor to Havana ought to walk its length.

Leading from the southwest corner of Plaza de Armas is one of the most bohemian sections of Havana: a 50-meter-long cobbled section of Calle Obispo, which runs east-west from the plaza to Monserrate. Look closely at the two cannons outside the south side of the Palacio de Capitanes Generales and you'll note the mono-gram of King George III. They're relics of the brief English occupation of Cuba in 1762.

Facing the plaza is **Restaurante Cubano,** housed in a green and ocher 17th-century man-sion that was originally the college of San Fran-cisco de Sales for orphan girls. Its central patio is surrounded by galleries of stocky columns and wide arches enclosing slatted doors and *mediopuntos.* The ground floor is also occupied by the lively **Café Mina,** where you may sit be-neath shady canopies on the sidewalk and sup and nibble while Cuban musicians entertain; and the **Casa del Agua la Tinaja,** next door, which sells mineral water (US25 cents a glass—the source was discovered in 1544, and early explorers made use of the water; in 1831, an aqueduct was built to carry it to the burgeoning town, thereby solving the water shortage).

Adjacent, at Obispo #113, massive metal-studded doorways open into what was once a stable. Today, it contains a bakery—**Dulcería Doña Teresa**—selling custards, ice creams, and other delights. Next door is the **Museo de Plata,** closed for restoration at press time, and then the **Oficina del Historidades de la Ciudad** (office of the city historian; Obispo #117-119), with a copper galleon hanging above its door and an old cannon standing upright outside. Appropriately, this is the oldest house in Havana, dating from around 1570. Inside you'll find books on Cuban history and culture for sale, and, behind a grilled gate, venerable artifacts including a *quitrín,* a two-wheeled conveyance with a moveable bonnet to protect passengers from the elements, made to be pulled by a single horse (usually ridden by a *calesero,* a black slave, who dressed in high boots, top hat, and a costume trimmed with colorful ribbons). With luck, the city historian, Eusebio Leal, may appear to regale visitors with fascinating tales of his restoration plans for the city.

At the end of the cobbled pedestrians-only block is an apothecary—**Boutica Francesa de Santa Catalina**—in a beautiful blue and cream mansion, the former Casa del Marques de Casa Torre (Obispo #121). Fascinating it is, too, with its colorful ceramic jars decorated with floral motifs full of herbs and potions. Next door, on Mercaderes, is the **Casa de las Infusiones,** still selling refreshing cups of tea today as it has since 1841. Opposite, on the corner of Calles Mercaderes and Obispo, is the Hotel Ambos Mundos (see below). Across the street, at the corner of Obispo and Mercaderes, is an **antique bell** held aloft by modern concrete pillars. It, too, has a plaque in Spanish commemorating the fact that this was the original site of the University of Havana, founded in January 1728. The bell once tolled to call the students to class.

Other sites of interest along Calle Obispo include the **Banco Nacional de Cuba,** in a splendid neoclassical building—that of the Comite Estatal de Finaza—fronted by fluted corinthian columns and portals decorated with four-leaf clovers. It's three blocks west of Plaza de Armas,

at Calle Cuba. While here, check out the former Palacio de Joaquín Gómez, now the **Hotel Florida,** with a stunning lobby dating from 1838, catercorner to the bank. Also worth a peek is **La Casa del Consomé La Luz,** five blocks west of the plaza, at Calles Obispo and Havana, another moody apothecary with a white marble floor and old glass cabinets faded with age, filled with chemists tubes, mixing vases, and mortars and pestles and lined with bottles of oils, herbs, and powders.

Hotel Ambos Mundos

This hotel, built in the 1920s, recently reopened after a long restoration. It is conveniently located around the corner from La Bodeguita, Ernest Hemingway's "little shop in the middle of the street," and a 10-minute wobble from El Floridita. Off and on throughout the 1930s, Hemingway laid his head in Room 511, where the plot of *For Whom The Bell Tolls* formed in his mind. After the Revolution, the hotel was turned into a hostelry for employees of the Ministry of Education across the way. Hemingway's room—"a gloomy room, 16 square meters, with a double bed made of ordinary wood, two night tables and a writing table with a chair," recalled Colombian author and Nobel laureate Gabriel García Márquez—was preserved, even down to an old Spanish edition of *Don Quixote* on the night table (entrance US$1). You can easily identify his top-story room when gazing up from street level. The hotel was once painted white; although rose-pink today, the exterior walls of Hemingway's room have been left white to commemorate his presence.

A plaque on the exterior wall reads, "The novelist Ernest Hemingway lived in this Hotel Ambos Mundos during the decade of the 1930s." Another plaque tells you that "In this site, on 3 January 1841, George Washington Halsey inaugurated the first photographic studio" in Cuba.

CALLE OFICIOS TO PLAZA DE SAN FRANCISCO

Calle Oficios leads south from Plaza de Armas three blocks to Plaza de San Francisco. Its newly restored colonial buildings are confections in stone, and walking this street you may fall under a spell from which you may never escape.

The first noteworthy building is **Casa del Árabe** (Arab House) at Oficios #12, tel. 61-8715. This mansion, an appropriately fine example of Moorish-inspired architecture, is the only place in Havana where Muslims can practice the Islamic faith. It now houses a museum dedicated to all things Arabic. You enter into a beautiful place bursting with foliage—a softly dappled courtyard radiating ineffable calm. The prayer hall is decorated with hardwoods inlaid with mother-of-pearl, tempting you to run your fingers across the floral and geometric motifs to sense the tactile pleasure. Please resist! The museum displays exquisitely crafted camel saddles and Oriental carpets, an exact replica of a *souk* (market), models of Arab *dhows,* (the traditional sailing vessels), and a superb collection of Arab weaponry. Open Tues.-Sat. 2:30-6:30 p.m. and 7-9:45 p.m., and Sunday 9 a.m.-1 p.m. Entrance costs US$2 and includes entrance to the auto museum across the street.

At Calle Oficios #13, Havana's **Museo de Autos Antiguo** includes an eclectic range of antique automobiles from a 1902 Cadillac to a 1960s-era Daimler limousine. Che Guevara's jeep is one of several vehicles that once belonged to famous figures. A number of classic Harley-Davidson motorbikes are also exhibited. Open daily 9 a.m.-6.30 p.m. The US$2 entrance includes admission to the Casa del Árabe.

Coin lovers should call in at the **Museo Numismático,** at Oficios #8, next to Casa del Árabe. The fascinating collection of coins dates back to the earliest colonial days and includes "company store" currency printed by the sugar mills. Open Tues.-Sat. 1-8 p.m. and Sunday 9 a.m.-1 p.m.

Around the corner, in the Casa Garibaldi at Calle Justíz #21, is **El Caserón del Tango,** which opened in July 1993 to promote the melancholic Argentinian dance. There's a theater opposite—**Casa de la Comedia** (also known as Salón Ensayo)—in the headquarters for the Teatro Anaquillé, in a former slave quarters. It hosts children's theater and comedy events from 4 p.m. on weekends.

Make sure to call in at **Hostal Valencia,** a picturesque Spanish-style *posada* that looks as if it's been magically transported from some Manchegan village. The hotel, on the corner of Oficios and Obrapia, could have been used as a model by Cervantes for the inn where Don Quixote was dubbed a knight by the bewildered innkeeper. The *hostal* sets out to attract tourists with a liberal coating of green and white paint, various bits and pieces of armor, a handsome bar and courtyard, and a splendid restaurant looking onto Oficios through full-length *rejas*—turned wooden rails. One look and you may want to check in.

PLAZA DE SAN FRANCISCO

The cobbled Plaza de San Francisco, at the foot of Amargua, faces onto Avenida del Puerto and the inner shore of Havana harbour, of which it was once an inlet. At its heart is a beautiful fountain, **Fuente de los Leones**—Fountain of the Lions—erected in 1836, moved to different locations at various times, but finally ensconced where it began life. The muscular five-story neo-classical building on the north side is the **Antigua Lonja del Comercio,** dating from 1907, when it was built as a center for trading in food commodities. It's now sparkling after a complete restoration, again housing offices of international corporations. Note the beautiful dome crowned by a figure of the god Mercury.

Across the way, the **Terminal Sierra Maestra** cruise terminal faces onto the plaza. It's a fantastic location: imagine arriving by sea! No other cruise terminal in the world opens so immediately onto the heart of such an incredible colonial city.

The beautiful colonial buildings on Calle Oficios south of the plaza were nearing the completion of restoration at press time and reminded me, with their fresh coat of paint, of the cobbled mews of Kensington, in London. What a remake! One of the gems is the pink and green **Casa de Carmen Montilla,** 50 meters south of the square. Only the front of the house remains, but the architects have made creative use of the empty shell. Through the breezy doorway you can catch sight of a fabulous 3-D mural by famous Cuban artist Sergio Sabravo at the back of an open-air sculpture garden. Fabulous art is portrayed within, in the two-level art gallery. You may be tempted to pass by the 19th-century building housing the **Asemblea Provincial Poder Popular,** or local government. Enter—the interior lobby is striking for its ornate baroque and neoclassical stucco work.

Iglesia y Convento de San Francisco de Asís
Dominating the plaza on the south is the great church whose construction was launched in 1719. It began humbly but was reconstructed in 1730 in baroque style, with a 40-meter bell tower—one of the tallest in all the Americas, crowned by St. Helen holding a sacred Cross of Jerusalem. The church was eventually proclaimed a Minorite Basilia, and it was from its chapel that the processions of the *Vía Crucis* departed every Lenten Friday, ending at the Iglesia del Santo Cristo del Buen Viaje. The devout passed down Calle Amargura (Street of Bitterness), where stations of the cross were set up and decorated with crucifixes and altars. You can still see one of the stations—Casa de la Cruz Verde—at the corner of Calles Amargura and Mercaderes.

After the Protestant English used the church briefly for worship during their tenure in Havana in 1762, the Catholics refused ever to use it again as a church.

The main nave, with its towering roof, looks as if it will stand for another 500 years. During the restoration, I watched muralists painting the marvelous trompe l'oeil that extends the perspective of the nave. Note the Tiffany grandfather clock (in working order), dating to the 1820s, on the far right. On the left side, inset into the walls, are the morbid remains of Teodoro—a Franciscan brother of high regard—pickled in glass jars next to a statue of St. Francis. You may peer into the crypts through a glass window in the terra-cotta tile floor.

Alas, the sumptuously adorned altars are gone, replaced by a huge crucifix suspended above a grand piano. Yes, the nave has metamorphosed into a concert hall; the music program is posted in the entrance. Performances (usually classical) are given each Saturday at 6 p.m. and Sunday at 11 a.m.

The nave opens to the right onto the cloisters of a convent, to which the church belonged.

HAVANA'S MUSEUMS

Museo de la Educación: (Museum of Literacy) Empredaro #151, Habana Vieja, tel. 61-5468. This museum, in Plaza de la Catedral, traces Cuba's achievements in the Great Literacy Campaign to eradicate illiteracy.

Museo Antropológico Montane: (Anthropological Museum) Calle San Lázaro, Vedado, tel. 79-3488. Contains exhibits on pre-Columbian culture.

Museo y Archivo de la Música: (Music Archives and Museum) Calle Capdevilla #1, e/ Aguiar y Habana, Centro Habana, tel. 80-6810. Exhibits trace the evolution of Cuban musical styles.

Museo de Armas: (Weapons Museum) Calle O'Reilly #2, Habana Vieja, tel. 61-6130. Small arms spanning several centuries are displayed, including many owned (and used) by individuals of historical importance.

Museo de Arte Colonial: (Museum of Colonial Art) Calle San Ignacio #61, Habana Vieja, tel. 62-6440. This fine museum contains stunning period furniture and decorations from the colonial era.

Museo de Artes Decorativas: (Museum of the Decorative Arts) Calle 17 #502, Vedado, tel. 30-8037. A splendid mansion displaying colonial period furniture and decorations.

Museo Casa Abel Santamaría: Calle 25 #154, Vedado, tel. 70-0417. The house where the martyred revolutionary hero lived, and also headquarters for Fidel Castro's nascent M-26-7 movement.

Museo Casa Natal de José Martí: Calle Leon Peréz, Habana Vieja, tel. 61-3778. The birthplace of national hero José Martí records his contributions to the cause of independence.

Museo de Ciencias Carlos Finlay: (Carlos Finlay Museum of Sciences) Calle Cuba #460, Habana Vieja. Honors the achievements of Cuban medical scientist Carlos Finlay and other noted Cubans in the field of science.

Museo de Ciencias Naturales Felipe Poey: (Felipe Poey Natural Sciences Museum) Calle Industria, Habana Vieja, tel. 63-1268. Contains stuffed and pickled exhibits of Cuba's flora and fauna and traces aspects of pre-Columbian culture.

Museo de la Ciudad de Habana: (City Museum of Havana) Calle Tacón #1, Habana Vieja, tel. 33-8183. This museum traces the development of the city from its earliest colonial days. Many fine exhibits from the Spanish period. A must-see.

Museo Nacional de Bellas Artes: (National Fine Arts Museum) Calle Animas, Habana Vieja, tel. 61-

It is now a museum with fabulous silverwork, porcelain, and other treasures of the Spanish epoch, including a room full of ornately gilded hymnals of silver and even mother-of-pearl displayed in glass cases. In the late 1840s, the liberal government expropriated and secularized the property, which became a Customs office, a post office, and, in this century, a warehouse serving the nearby wharfs. A music school occupies part of the building. The church and convent were reopened in October 1994 after a complete restoration. A must-see. Entrance costs US$2.

CALLES MERCADERES AND OBRAPIA

Intimate Calle Mercaderes links Plaza de Armas with Plaza Vieja, four blocks south. Now restored to grandeur, it is brimming with handsome buildings and museums of interest.

The block immediately south of Calle Obispo includes the **Tienda de las Navegantes** (Mercaderes #117), a beautiful wood- and glass-fronted building with a ship's wheel inlaid with a copper galleon above the door. This incongruously positioned store sells maps and nautical charts, including the best selection of road and city maps available in Cuba. A hearse-size glass case contains a three-meter-long scale model of the *Juan Sebastian Elcano,* made in 1928 for La Compañia Transatlantica de Barcelona.

Across the street are the **Casa de Puerto Rico** and **Casa del Tabaco,** both at Mercaderes #120. The latter—the Museum of Tobacco—is upstairs, tel. 62-2258; open Tues.-Sun. 10:30 a.m.-1 p.m. and Sunday 10:30 a.m.-5 p.m.; no entrance charge. The first room, part of which is decorated as a typical middle-class sitting room, with rocking chairs and a cigar displayed on a silver ashtray, contains a collection of lithos from cigar-box covers. Other exhibits include pipes

---

1864. A splendid, if poorly illuminated, collection of Cuban paintings and sculptures, plus important works representing Impressionist and other major styles, as well as Latin America's largest collection of Greek, Roman, and Egyptian treasures. A must see.

Museo Nacional de Música: (National Music Museum) Calle Capdevila #1, Habana Vieja, tel. 61-9846. Instruments and scores spanning several centuries trace the evolution of Cuban music and the contributions of its finest composers and performers.

Museo Napoleónico: (Napoleonic Museum) Calle San Miguel #1159, Vedado, tel. 79-1412. This splendid mansion houses personal possessions of Napoleon Bonaparte and other memorabilia relating to the French Emperor.

Museo Numismático: (Numismatic Museum) Calle Oficios, Habana Vieja, tel. 61-5857. Coins of the realm dating back centuries are displayed.

Museo Postal Filatélico: (Postal/Philatelic Museum) Avenida Independencia, Plaza de la Revolución, tel. 70-5043. Displays a superb collection of Cuban and international stamps.

Museo del Pueblo Combatiente: (Museum of the Fighting People) Avenida 5ta #7201, Miramar, tel. 29-1497. This strangely named museum tells the Cuban government's version of the counterrevolutionary struggles, including the CIA's Operation Mon-

goose and the mass exodus from Cuba in the wake of the Revolution.

Museo de la Revolución: (Museum of the Revolution) Calle Refugio #1, Habana Vieja. Housed in the former Presidential Palace, this museum is Cuba's most complete exhibition on the Revolution, with maps, weaponry, personal articles, photographs, the *Granma,* tanks, and warplanes. A must-see.

Parque Histórico Militar El Morro-La Cabaña: (El Morro-La Cabaña Historical Military Park) Carratera de la Cabaña, Habanas del Este. The Morro Castle and La Cabaña fortress are hulking testaments to Havana's military history. A must-see.

Museo Nacional del Aire: (National Air Museum) Avenida 212 y La Coronela, Cubanacán. A splendid array of military and civilian aircraft, plus models and exhibits recording notable moments in Cuban aviation history.

Museo Ernest Hemingway: San Francisco de Paula, tel. 91-0809. The Nobel novelist's former home, Finca Vigía, has been left as it was when Hemingway died in 1961. A must-see.

Museo Histórico de Guanabacoa: (Historical Museum of Guanabacoa) Calle Martí #108, Guanabacoa, tel. 97-9117. This museum of *santería* profiles the influence of slavery and African cultures on the evolution of Cuban culture and the syncretic Afro-Cuban cults.

and lighters from around the world. Look out for the stunning silver cigar box engraved with script that reads: "To my godfather Dr. Fidel Castro Ruz from Fidel Charles Getto, August 9, 1959." Upstairs you'll find a humidor staffed by store clerks in professional livery. (They must be freezing—bring a sweater!)

At the end of the block, at the corner of Obrapía, the pink building with wraparound wrought-iron balustrade and Mexican flag fluttering above the doorway is the **Casa de Benito Juárez,** housing the Sociedad Cubano Mexicana de Relaciones Culturales, marvelously displaying artwork and costumes from different Mexican states. Entrance costs US$1. The house faces a tiny *plazuela* with a larger-than-life bronze statue of Simón Bolívar atop a marble pedestal. Half a block east, at Obrapia #111, is the **Casa Guayasamú,** housing a museum of plastic arts and photographs from Ecuador, with changing exhibitions of art from other Latin American countries. A huge dugout canoe sits in the entrance lobby (Tues.-Sat. 10 a.m.-5 p.m., US$1).

Interested in firearms? Then check out the **Armería,** one block south at Mercaderes #157, tel. 6-5221. The museum is dedicated to four members of MR-26-7 who were killed in an assault on the armory on 9 April 1959. The displays include dozens of shotguns and rifles of every barrel and bore, plus hunting paraphernalia, stuffed birds, bearskins, and other poor critters bagged for fun. You can buy hunting supplies here. A sign outside reads, "Armaments Company of Cuba, hunting supplies and explosives." The company was a subsidiary of Dupont, the US munitions giant.

Across the street is **Casa Simón Bolívar** housing the Venezuelan embassy and containing the **Museo de Simón Bolívar,** which displays cultural works and art from Venezuela (open Tues.-Sat. 10 a.m.-5 p.m., US$1). Next door, at the corner of Lamparilla, is the diminutive and quaint **Museo de Bomberos,** exhibiting turn-of-the-century firefighters' uniforms plus three vintage fire engines, including a 1901 horse-drawn machine made by Shand, Mason & Co., London.

If heading down to Plaza Vieja, check out the stunning lobby—a mix of art nouveau and neoclassical—with dramatic skylight in the building on the southwest corner of Mercaderes and Amargura.

Casa de la Obra Pía

The splendid mansion with lemon-meringue-yellow walls on the northwest corner of Obrapía and Mercaderes was owned by the Calvo de Puertas family, one of the most important families in Cuba in early colonial days. (The street is named for the *obra pía*—pious act—of Don Martín Calvo de la Puerta, who devoted a portion of his wealth to dowering five orphan girls every year.) It dates from the early 17th century, with additions such as voluptuous moldings and dimpled cherubs as late as 1793 in baroque style. Visitors can see the arms of the Castellón family (who bought the house after Martín Calvo de la Puerto's death), surrounded by exuberant baroque stonework, emblazoned above the carved entrance of regal proportions at Obrapía #158.

As much as any house in Habana Vieja, Casa de la Obra Pía exemplifies the Spanish adaptation of a Moorish inner courtyard, with a serene, scented coolness illuminated by daylight filtering through *mediopuntos* fanning out like a peacock's tail. Open Mon.-Sat. 10:30 a.m.-4:30 p.m.; entrance US$1.

Casa de África

When flung open wide, the large wooden doors at Obrapía #157 reveal breezy courtyards full of African artwork and artifacts, masks, and cloth. On the third floor you'll find a fabulous collection of paraphernalia used in *santería,* including statues of the leading deities in the Yoruban pantheon, dancing costumes of the Abakuá, and *otanes* (stones) in which the *orishas*—the gods of *santería*—are said to reside. Much of the collection was contributed by the 17 African embassies in Havana.

The museum guides are well versed, but for a more in-depth recitation ask for the museum's director, Claudia Mola Fernández, or the curator, Raísa Fornaguera.

Open Mon.-Sat. 10:30 a.m.-4 p.m. and Sunday 9 a.m.-noon, tel. 61-2472. Entrance costs US$2.

PLAZA VIEJA

The last of the four main squares in Habana Vieja is Plaza Vieja, the old commercial square (bounded by Calles Mercaderes, San Ignacio, Brasil, and Muralla), surrounded by mansions and apartment blocks from where residents could look down on processions, executions, bullfights, and wild fiestas. The plaza hosted a market where peasants and free Negroes sold all manner of produce. There used to be a stone fountain at its center, with a wide bowl and four dolphins that gushed "intermittent streams of thick, muddy liquid which Negro water vendors eagerly collected in barrels to be sold throughout the city," recorded a French visitor in the 19th century. Alas, President Machado built an underground car park here in the 1930s, and the cobbles and fountain fell afoul of the wrecking ball.

Time and neglect have brought near-ruin this century, and many of the square's beautiful buildings are in a sorry state of repair. Fortunately, the decay is being reversed as the caring restoration of Habana Vieja has reached into Plaza Vieja. The car park was being torn up in 1997 and soon enough a hotel—Apartotel Santo Angel—and a cinema, café, and shops will open. The square is renowned for its acoustics and is often used for concerts.

On the northwest corner is the **Casa de las Hermanas Cárdenas,** recently restored with faux brickwork and marble. The building—named for two sisters, María Loreto and María Ignacia Cárdenas, who lived here in the late 18th century—houses the **Centro de Desarollo de Artes Visuales,** tel. 62-3533, 62-2611. Through the towering doors, immediately on the left, is a craft workshop where young women can be seen making cloth dolls and naive animals gaudily painted in the pointillist fashion now common throughout the Caribbean. The inner courtyard is dominated by an intriguing sculpture—a kind of futuristic skyscraper in miniature—crafted by Sergio Sabravo. Art education classes are given on the second floor, reached via a wide wooden staircase that leads to the top story, where you'll find an art gallery in a wonderfully airy loft. If the tiny yellow door is locked, ask for the key downstairs.

Next door is the **Casa del Conde de San Estéban de Cañongo,** at San Ignacio #356. This former mansion of a nobleman today houses an intriguing artisans' factory—**Artesanías Para Turismo Taller**—where workers use stems of the *malanbueta* plant to weave baskets, wall hangings, and dozens of other items. The supervisor, Ana Ester García Calbert, will be happy to give you a guided tour (in Spanish). You can watch the acid being squeezed from the

thick reeds, which are pressed into flat yet flexible fibers woven into durable mats on simple looms worked by a foot pedal. Other workers sit to the side conjuring the stems into baskets, purses, *zapatas* (shoes), and intriguing wall hangings depicting scenes of old Havana. Alas, the items are not for sale here, but you'll be directed to various *tiendas artesanias* (including El Travesí, next door to El Floridita restaurant).

The old **Palacio Vienna Hotel** (also called the Palacio Cueto), on the southeast corner of Plaza Viejo, is a phenomenal piece of Gaudiesque art nouveau architecture, fabulously ornate and dating from 1906. The frontage is awash in surf-like waves and ballooning balconies.

Physicians and scientists inclined to a busman's holiday might walk one block west and one north of the plaza and check out the impressive **Museo de Ciencias Carlos Finlay,** at Cuba #460, tel. 6-8006. The building, which once housed the Academy of Sciences, today contains a pharmaceutical collection and tells the tales of various Cuban scientists' discoveries and innovations. Finlay is honored, of course, for it was he who discovered that yellow fever is transmitted by mosquitoes. Open Mon.-Sat. 8-11:30 a.m. and 1:30-5 p.m. Entrance US$1.

Casa de los Condes de Jaruco

On the south side of the square is an impressively restored 18th-century building highlighted by mammoth doors opening into a cavernous entrance hall. The Casa de los Condes de Jaruco houses several magnificent *galerias* and boutiques under the umbrella of the **Fondo Cubano de Bienes Culturales** (BFC), tel. 61-3503, the organization responsible for the sale of Cuban art. The BFC headquarters is upstairs, in rooms off the balcony. Whimsical murals are painted on the walls, touched in splashy color by the undulating play of light through *mediopuntas* and by the play of shadow through *rejas.* Downstairs is occupied by three galleries, including, on the right, the **Galeria Pequeño Formato,** with some fascinating miniature modernist paintings and sculptures. The inner courtyard is surrounded by lofty archways festooned with hanging vines. Here, you can snack at wrought-iron tables.

At last report, the upstairs galleries had disappeared, but I was assured that this was only temporary.

SOUTHERN HABANA VIEJA

The much deteriorated southern half of Habana Vieja is given short shrift by most visitors. Nonetheless, numerous gems are worth a peek. The area east of Avenida de Bélgica and southwest of Plaza Vieja, between Calles Brasil and Merced, was the great ecclesiastical center of colonial Havana and is replete with churches and convents. The most notable are listed below, but there are others as well.

The area around Calle Belén was the site of the first community of Sephardic Jews in Cuba following their expulsion from Castile and Aragon in 1492. A Jewish community became well established, and this century many Polish and Lithuanian Jews settled here after fleeing Nazi persecution. The Cuban government proposes to reconstruct the Jewish settlement.

Havana's waterfront boulevard swings south along the harborfront (overshadowed by portside warehouses and once lined with 24-hour sailors' bars), changing names as it curves: Avenida San Pedro . . . Leonor Pérez . . . Desamparados. Leonor Pérez runs alongside the **Alameda de Paula,** Havana's first promenade lined with marble and iron street lamps. Be sure to call at **Dos Hermanos**—the bar at the foot of Sol favored as a Hemingway haunt—and at the **Centro Wilfredo Lam,** at the corner of Acosta and Oficios, tel. 61-3288. The center, named for the noted Cuban artist, displays works by Lam, other Cuban artists, and artists throughout the Third World. It sponsors workshops and the biennial Havana Exhibition, in which up-and-coming artists have a chance to exhibit. Open Mon.-Fri. and alternate Sundays 8:30 a.m.-4:30 p.m.

Leonor Pérez leads to **Plazuela de Paula,** a small circular plaza with the **Iglesia de San Francisco de Paula** in the middle of the road. This twee little place has long been abandoned as a church and today houses a little museum full of oil paintings and oversize photographs of early-20th-century bands. It is also used for the study of popular Cuban music. Another small, handsome church—**Iglesia y Convento de Nuestra Señora de la Merced**—is hidden one block west and one north, at the corner of Calles Cuba and Merced. Trompe l'oeil frescoes add color to the ornate interior, which con-

tains an alcove lined with fake stalactites in honor of Nuestra Señora de Lourdes. The church has strong Afro-Cuban connections, and it is not unusual to see devotees of *santería* kneeling in prayer. Try to time your visit for 24 September, when scores of gaily colored worshippers cram in for the Virgen de la Merced's feast day. More modest celebrations are held on the 24th of each other month.

Desamparados ends at the **Cortina de la Habana,** a remnant section of the old fortress wall enclosing Habana Vieja in colonial days. Desamparados swings south from here past the docks to the Vía Blanca, the road for San Francisco de Paula, Regla, and Playas del Este. One hundred meters south of the Cortina you'll see a monument made of twisted metal parts—fragments of *La Coubre,* the French cargo ship that exploded in Havana harbor on 4 March 1960 (the vessel was carrying armaments for the Castro government, and it is generally assumed that the CIA or other counterrevolutionaries blew it up). The **Monumento Mártires del Vapor La Coubre** honors the seamen who died.

Avenida de Bélgica runs northwest at a slight gradient from the Cortina to the **Estación Central de Ferrocarril,** the impressive Venetian-style railway station containing, sitting on rails in its lobby, an 1843-model steam locomotive—*La Junta*—said to have been Cuba's first. Bélgica is lined with remnants of the original city walls.

Casa Natal de José Martí

A shining star in Habana Vieja's constellation is this simple house—painted ocher, with green windows and door frames and terra-cotta tile floors—at Leonor Pérez #314 (also called Calle Paula), one block east of Avenida de Bélgica.

The house is a shrine for Cuban schoolchildren, who flock to pay homage to Cuba's National Hero, who was born on 28 January 1853 and spent the first four years of his life here. As you may imagine, the house and museum are splendidly kept.

The entrance lobby displays letters from Martí in glass cases and a beautiful bronze bust on a simple wooden pedestal. Many of his personal effects are here, too, including a beautiful lacquered *escritorio* (writing desk) and a broad-brimmed Panama hat given to him by Ecuadorian President Eloy Alfaro (Panama hats don't come from the country of Panama—they're made next door but one, in Ecuador). Many of his original texts and poems and sketches are displays. There's even a lock of the hero's hair from when he was only four years old!

There are more guides (one per room) than you can shake a stick at. They follow you around eerily, although at a discreet distance. Open Tues.-Sat. 10 a.m.-6 p.m. and Sunday 9 a.m.-12:45 p.m. Entrance US$1.

Iglesia y Convento de Nuestra Señora de Belén

This huge complex, occupying the block between Calles Luz and Acosta and Compostela and Aguacate, was until recently a derelict shell. The convent was built to house the first nuns who arrived in Havana, in 1704. Construction took from 1712 to 1718; this was the first baroque religious structure erected in Havana. It is visited by very few tourists. As you enter, note the ornate façade decorated with a nativity scene set in a large niche framed with a shell.

The United Nations and the Swiss government are helping pay for its restoration. The church will supposedly become a religious community again, while part of the building will house a home for the aged. Part of the cloisters are slated to become a hotel.

Iglesia y Convento de Nuestra Señora de Belén

Convento de Santa Clara de Asís

Two blocks east of Belén, between Luz and Sol, you'll discover a massive nunnery—the first founded in Havana. It also once was a slaughterhouse and later housed hundreds of nuns and slaves. It was a refuge for girls unfortunate enough to possess an insufficient dowry to attract suitors. Only thus could the unfortunate females preserve their self-respect.

It is a remarkable building, with a lobby full of beautiful period pieces and an inner and outer cloistered courtyard awash in divine light and surrounded by columns, one of which is entwined by the roots of a *capulí* tree, whose fruits resemble large golden pearls and taste ambrosial. Steady yourself before gazing up at the breathtaking cloister roof carved with geometric designs. Indeed, stunning wooden carvings abound. The convent has been restored to pristine condition and now, fittingly, houses the **Centro Nacional de Conservación y Museología.** Peek inside the **Salon Plenario,** a marble-floored hall with a lofty beamed wooden ceiling of imposing stature and used to teach classes in international culture. By the time you read this, a restaurant may have been opened in the spacious courtyard.

Open Mon.-Fri. 9 a.m.-3 p.m.; entrance US$1.

Iglesia Parroquial del Espíritu Santo

Havana's oldest church lies two blocks south of Santa Clara de Asís, at the corner of Calles Cuba and Acosta. The church, which dates from 1638 (the circa 1674 central nave and façade and circa 1720 Gothic vault are later additions) was originally a hermitage "for the devotions of free Negroes." Today, visitors are welcome to what is truly one of Havana's most charming gems.

The church reveals many surprises, including a gilded, carved wooden pelican in a niche in the baptistery. The sacristy (where parish archives dating back through the 17th century are preserved) boasts an enormous cupboard full of baroque silver staffs and incense holders. Catacombs to each side of the nave are held up by subterranean tree trunks. While exploring the eerie vault that runs under the chapel, peek between the niches and you will see, almost erased by time and damp, a series of paintings of skeletons crowned with tiaras and holding mitres. They represent the dance of death. One look is enough to send you scurrying to escape this "grim place full of bones, dust and spiders."

The body of Bishop Gerónimo Valdés had been laid to rest in the church. He remained in a kind of limbo, his whereabouts unknown, until he turned up, buried under the floor, during a restoration in 1936. Today, he rests in a tomb beside the nave, which boasts a carved wooden altar. The sturdy tower holds four bells. Steps lead up to the gallery, where you may turn the handle of a carillon.

PASEO DE MARTÍ (PRADO)

Paseo de Martí, colloquially known as the Prado, is a kilometer-long tree-lined boulevard that slopes gently uphill from the Castillo de San Salvador de la Punta to the Capitolio, the massive domed neoclassical building that dominates the skyline of Habana Vieja. The Prado is a smaller but no less courtly version of the Champs-Elysées and a splendid place to linger and watch Havana's life unfold. (Be aware, though, that, being popular with tourists, it attracts lots of *jiniteros* eager to part you from your money.)

The beautiful boulevard just outside the old walled city of San Cristóbal de la Habana was initiated by the Marquis de la Torre in 1772 and completed in 1852. Until the end of the last century, it was Havana's most notable thoroughfare. The mansions of aristocratic families rose on each side, with spacious portals for carriages, and it was a sign of distinction to live on Prado Promenade. In time, the Prado lost its luster as the rich moved into exclusive new neighborhoods. During the "sordid era," the Prado and the area immediately west of it—the infamous Colón borough—became famous for sleazy shows and gambling houses such as La Central, where President Prío held "his infamous nights of white powder and tall showgirls."

The Prado's central median is an elevated walkway. An ornate wall borders the path, with alcoves inset into each side containing marble benches carved with scroll motifs. At night it is lit by old brass gas lamps with big globes atop dark green wrought-iron lampposts in the shape of griffins. Schoolchildren sit beneath the shade trees, listening attentively to history or literature lessons presented alfresco.

Midway down the Paseo, between Calle Colon and Refugio, the shade trees form a gathering place—*Se Permuta* (For Exchange)—for those seeking apartments or homes for swap or rent.

Up and down the Prado you'll see tiled mosaics reflecting the Moorish style that has influenced Havana's architecture through the centuries. Note, for example, the mosaic mural of a Nubian beauty on the upper wall of the **Centro Cultural de Árabe** (between Refugio and Trocadero). Note, too, the façade of the Hotel Regis on the corner of Refugio, combining art nouveau and arabesque flourishes. The most stunning example, however, is the lobby of the **Hotel Sevilla** (at Calle Trocadero), which is like entering a Moroccan medina. The Sevilla was the setting for the comical intrigues of Wormold in Graham Greene's *Our Man in Havana.*

Another noteworthy structure is the **Ciné Fausto,** a simple yet powerful rectangular modernist building with an ornament band on its upper façade harking back to art deco. At #306, on the corner of Animas, is Habana Vieja's **Palacio de Matrimonia,** where wedding ceremonies are performed.

HAVANA'S CITY WALLS

African slaves labored for 23 years to build the 1.4-meter-thick, 10-meter-tall city wall that once ringed Havana. Construction of the walls began on 3 February 1674, when the city was just a small village. It ran along the edge of the bay and, on the landward side, stood between today's Calle Egido, Monserrate, and Zulueta.

The 4,892-meter-long wall was completed in 1697. The damage inflicted by the British artillery in 1762 was repaired in 1797, when the thick wall attained its final shape. It formed an irregular polygon with nine bulwarks and, in its first stage, just two entrances (nine more were added later).

As time went on, the *intramuros* (the city within the walls) burst its confines. In 1841, Havana authorities petitioned the Spanish Crown for permission to demolish the walls. The demolition began in 1863, when African slave-convicts were put to work to destroy what their forefathers had built under hard labor.

Alas, only fragments remain, most notably at the junction of Calle Egido and Avenida del Puerto, near the railway station at Avenida del Puerto and Egido, and at Monserrate and Teniente Rey streets. Sentry boxes still stand in front of the Presidential Palace, between Calles Monserrate and Zulueta, and at the northern end of Calle Cuba.

PARQUE CENTRAL AND VICINITY

At Neptuno, the Prado spills out onto the spacious Parque Central, presided over by stately Royal palms, poinciana, and almond trees shading a statue of José Martí. Buses arrive and depart from the busy square, a center for Havana's social life as it was during the city's heyday before the Revolution. Baseball fanatics gather near the Martí statue at a point called *esquina caliente* (hot corner) to discuss and argue the intricacies of the sport. For travelers, too, Parque Central is ground zero, the social epicenter.

All the action happens in the patio bar of the **Hotel Inglaterra,** which opened as a café in 1843, before the hotel existed. The boulevard in front of the hotel, known as the Acrea del Louvre, was always a gathering point for the youth of Cuba and a focal point for rebellion against Spanish rule. General Antonio Maceo recruited here between the two wars of independence. A plaque outside the hotel entrance honors the "lads of the Louvre sidewalk" who died for Cuban independence. Another imposing hotel, the ocher-colored **Hotel Plaza,** built as a triangle in 1909, sits on the northeast face of the square.

Parque Central was Havana's main social center from the late 19th century onward, with three resplendent theaters. Immediately south of the Inglaterra is the exquisitely detailed **Teatro García Lorca** (also called the Gran Teatro), built in 1837 as a social club for the large Galician community with an exorbitantly baroque façade. It has four towers, each tipped by an angel of white marble reaching gracefully for Heaven. It still functions as a theater for the National Ballet and Opera, and patrons still plump their bums in plush velvet seats. Another albeit less imposing theater, the **Teatro Payret** (built in 1878), faces the square from the south. Today it functions as a cinema. The **Teatro Martí** (dating from 1884) is two blocks south, hidden away on Dragones and Agramonte.

The building on the southeast side of the square with a tower at each of its corners is the **Centro Asturiano,** erected in 1885 and today housing the People's Supreme Court, where a Cuban version of justice is dispensed.

El Floridita

The tiny **Plazuela de Albear,** on Monserrate, one block east of Parque Central at the top of Obispo, is hallowed ground. Not because of the bust to Francisco de Albear, who engineered the Malecón and Havana's first water drainage system last century. Rather, here—on the southwest corner—is the famous bar and restaurant haunted by Ernest Hemingway's ghost. The novelist's seat at the dark mahogany bar is preserved as a shrine. His bronze bust watches over things from its pedestal beside the bar, where Constante Ribailagua once served frozen daiquiris to Hemingway (he immortalized both the drink and the venue in his novel *Islands in the Stream*) and such illustrious guests as Gary Cooper, Tennessee Williams, Marlene Dietrich, and Jean-Paul Sartre.

The restaurant has been serving food at this location since 1819, when it was called Pina de Plata. Its name was later changed to La Florida, and then, more affectionately, El Floridita.

It has been spruced up for tourist consumption with a 1930s art-deco polish. Waiters hover in tux jackets and bow ties. You expect a spotlight to come on and Desi Arnaz to appear conducting a dance band, and Papa to stroll in as he would every morning when he lived in Havana and drank with Honest Lil, the Worst Politician, and other real-life characters from his novels. "When we went to the Floridita bar in those days it wasn't like Orson Welles entering the lobby of the Grand Hotel, as Hotchner described Papa's public excursions in later years," recalls Hemingway's son Gregory. "It was just a nice bar where my father knew the staff and could drink with us and his friends."

They've overpriced the place, even for the package tourist crowd. But, what the hell—sipping a daiquiri at El Floridita is a must!

Sloppy Joe's

When sufficiently heady from one-too-many "Papa Specials," slip back out into the columned streets and follow the cool shade of ancient arcades north to the corner of Animas and Agramonte, where a mosaic on the paving announces your arrival at Sloppy Joe's, "a high-ceilinged, bottle-encrusted, tile-floored oasis" commemorated as Freddy's Bar in Hemingway's *To Have and Have Not*. (Joe Russell served as the model for Freddy, the character later immortalized on screen by Humphrey Bogart.) In spring 1996, it was still shuttered, its interior a dusty shambles awaiting the restoration now sweeping Habana Vieja.

Capitolio

This fabulous building, one block south of Parque Central, dominates Havana's skyline. It was built between 1926 and 1929 as Cuba's Chamber of Representatives and Senate and was obsequiously designed after Washington's own Congress building, reflecting the United States' expanding influence in the early 1900s. The lofty cupola rises 61.75 meters and is topped by a replica of 16th-century Florentine sculptor Giambologna's famous bronze Mercury in the Palazzo de Bargello.

A massive stairway—flanked by neoclassical figures in bronze representing Labor and Virtue—lead steeply up to three tall bronze doors sculpted with 30 bas-reliefs that depict important events of Cuban history up to the Capitolio's inauguration in 1929.

The pristine, recently restored building is constructed of local Capellania limestone. The stunning Great Hall of the Lost Steps, however, is almost entirely of marble, with bronze bas-reliefs all around and massive lamps on tall carved pedestals of glittering copper. Facing the door is a massive bronze statue of Cuba's Indian maiden resembling Liberty and representing the Cuban Republic. She is the world's third-largest indoor statue. Her voluptuous figure gleams sensuously after a recent cleaning. In the center of the floor is a 24-carat diamond that marks km 0—the starting point from Havana for the country's highways. The diamond, alas, is a replica (rumor has it that the original is kept securely in Fidel's office). Above your head is the dome and gilt-covered barrel-vaulted ceiling carved in refulgent relief.

By the time you read this, a collection of historical weapons should be on permanent view in the Arms Room, and the classic Sevilla restaurant will have been reopened, as will the former circular Senate chamber and the former Chamber of Representatives. Entrance is free. You can have your photo taken here by any of several official photographers whose antique cameras sit atop wooden tripods at the base of the staircase.

The Capitolio also houses the **Academia de Ciencias,** tel. 6-7127; entrance US$3, encompassing the **Museo de Ciencias Naturales** (Museum of Natural Sciences) and the **Museo de Ciencias y Técnicas** (Museum of Science and Technology). The entrance to the museums—housing superb collections of Cuban flora and fauna, many in clever reproductions of their natural environments, plus stuffed tigers, apes, and other beasts from afar, as well as a **planetarium** that offers hourly shows each evening—is to the left of the staircase. There's even a re-creation of the Punta del Este cave on Isla de la Juventud, replete with aboriginal pictographs. Open Tues.-Sat. 10:15 a.m.-5:45 p.m. and Sunday 9:15 a.m.-12:45 p.m.

Parque de la Fraternidad
This large, bustling, tree-shaded square immediately south of the Capitolio is a curiosity only for the **Árbol de la Fraternidad Americana**—the Friendship Tree—planted at its center in 1928 to cement goodwill between the nations of the Americas. Each delegate to the Pan-American Conference, held in Havana that year, brought soil from his or her home country. Busts of oustanding American leaders look out over the toings and fro-ings. Worth checking out is the **Palacio de Aldama,** a grandiose mansion considered one of Havana's finest; it's on the park's far southwest corner, on Avenida de Bolívar. Today it houses the **Institute of the History of the Communist Movement and the Socialist Revolution.** Hardcore lefties might get a thrill.

The only monument of interest is the **Fuente de la India Noble Habana,** in the middle of the Prado, 100 meters south of the Capitolio. The fountain, erected in 1837, is surmounted by a Carrara marble statue of *La Noble Habana,* the legendary Indian queen after whom the province is named. She is coyly clad in fringed drapes, a feather headdress, and palm leaves. In one hand she bears a cornucopia, in the other a shield with the arms of Havana. Four great fishes lie at her feet and spout water when the tap is turned on.

The highlight is undoubtedly the **Partagas Cigar Factory,** behind the Capitolio at Industria #502, tel. 33-8060. Here you may see Cuba's premium cigars being hand-rolled for the export trade, as they have been since 1845, when the Partagas cigar firm first occupied the site. The humidor to the right of the entrance serves as an information booth and sales room. Guided tours are offered daily at 10:30 a.m. and 1:30 p.m. (US$5).

The streets around the park are a major start and drop-off point for urban buses.

THE INSIDE STORY ON CIGARS

You'll forever remember the pungent aroma of a cigar factory, a visit to which is de rigeur.

The factories, housed in fine old colonial buildings, remain much as they were in the mid-19th century. Though now officially known by ideologically sound names, they're still commonly referred to by their prerevolutionary names, which are displayed on old signs outside. Each specializes in a number of cigar brands of a particular flavor. Revolutionary slogans exhort workers to maintain strict quality— "Quality is respect for people."

From Leaf to Cigar

The tobacco leaves, which arrive from the fields in dry sheets, are first moistened and stripped. The halves are then graded by color and strength (each type of cigar has a recipe). A blender mixes the various grades of leaves, which then go to the production room where each *tabaquero* and *tabaquera* receives enough tobacco to roll approximately 100 cigars for the day.

The rollers work in large rooms, where they sit at rows of workbenches—*galeras*—resembling old-fashioned school desks. Two workers sit at each desk, with piles of loose tobacco leaves at their sides. The rollers take great pride in their work, and it's a treat to marvel at their manual artistry and dexterity. The rollers' indispensable tool is a *chaveta*, a rounded, all-purpose knife for smoothing and cutting leaves, tamping loose tobacco, "circumcising the tips," and sometimes banging a welcome to factory visitors on their desks in rhythmic chorus like a percussion orchestra.

While they work, a *lector* (reader) reads aloud from a strategically positioned platform or high chair. Morning excerpts are read from newspapers; in the afternoon, the *lector* reads from historical or political books or short stories and novels (Alexander Dumas, Agatha Christie, and Ernest Hemingway are favorites; Dumas' novel *The Count of Monte Cristo* was such a hit in the 19th century that it lent its name to the famous Montecristo cigar). The practice dates back to 1864, when the unique institution was set up to alleviate boredom and help the cause of worker education.

Rolling the Cigar

The cigar roller—*torcedore*—fingers his or her leaves and, according to texture and color, chooses two to four filler leaves, which are laid end to end and gently yet firmly rolled into a tube then enveloped by the binder leaves to make a "bunch."

The rough-looking "bunch" is then placed with nine others in a small wooden mold that is screwed down to press each cigar into a solid cylinder. Next, the *tabaquero* selects a wrapper leaf, which he or she trims to size. The "bunch" is then laid at an angle across the wrapper, which is stretched and rolled around the "bunch," overlapping with each turn. A tiny quantity of flavorless tragapanth gum (made from Swiss pine trees) is used to glue the *copa* down. Now the *tabaquero* rolls the cigar, applying pressure with the flat of the *chaveta*. Finally, a piece of wrapper leaf the size and shape of a quarter is cut to form the cap; it is glued and twirled into place, and the excess is trimmed.

The whole process takes about five minutes. Hence, a good cigar maker can roll about 100 medium-sized cigars a day (the average for the largest cigars is far less).

Cigar rollers serve a nine-month apprenticeship (each factory has its own school). Many fail. Those who succeed graduate slowly from making petit corona cigars to the larger and specialized sizes. Rollers are paid piece rates based on the number of cigars they produce. They receive on average 350-400 pesos for a six-day workweek. In addition, they can puff as much as they wish on the fruits of their labor while working.

Cigars Go to Market

The roller ties cigars of the same size and brand into bundles—*media ruedas*—half-wheels—of 50 using a colored ribbon. These are then fumigated in a vacuum chamber. Quality is determined by a *revisador* according to eight criteria such as length, weight, firmness, smoothness of wrappers, and whether the ends are cleanly cut. *Catadores*, professional smokers, then blind test the cigars for aroma, draw, and burn, the relative importance of each varying according to whether the cigar is a slim panatela (draw is paramount) or a fat robusto (flavor being more important). The *catadores* taste only in the morning and rejuvenate their taste buds with sugarless tea.

Once fumigated, cigars are placed in cool cabinets for three weeks to settle fermentation and re-

(continues on next page)

THE INSIDE STORY ON CIGARS
(continued)

move any excess moisture. The cigars are then graded according to color and then shade within a particular color category.

A trademark paper band is then put on by an *anillado*. (A Dutchman, Gustave Bock, introduced the band to distinguish his cigars from other Havanas last century. Later, bands served to prevent gentlemen smokers from staining their white evening gloves.) Finally, the cigars are laid in pinewood boxes with the lightest cigar on the right and the darkest on the left (cigars range from the very mild, greenish-brown *double claro* to the very strong, almost black *oscuro*.) The boxes are then painstakingly inspected for alignment and uniformity. A thin leaf of cedar wood is laid on top to maintain freshness, and the box is sealed with a green-and-white label guaranteeing the cigars are genuine Havanas, or *puros Habanos* (today *puro* is a synonym for cigar).

HAVANA'S CIGAR FACTORIES

El Laguito
Cuba's premier cigar factory was opened in the mid-1960s as a training school in the former home of the Marquez de Pinar del Río, built in 1910 in a swanky residential neighborhood, Calle 146 #2302, Marianao, Havana, tel. 21-0554.

El Laguito makes Montecristos and the majority of Cohibas, *the* premium Havana cigar. Che Guevara initiated production while in charge of the Cuban tobacco industry. His objective was to make a cigar that surpassed every other prerevolutionary cigar. Since Cohibas are made from only the finest leaves, El Laguito is given first choice from the harvest ("the best selection of the best selection," says factory head Emilia Tamayo). The Cohiba was initially made solely for distribution to foreign diplomats and dignitaries. Since 1982, it has been available for general consumption (bodybuilder-turned-actor Arnold Schwarzenegger prefers Cohibas, as did Fidel before he stopped smoking). Today, 3.4 million Cohibas are produced annually—about one percent of Cuban production. Cohibas, rich, rather spicy cigars that come in 11 sizes, are considerably more expensive than other Havana cigars.

a cigar factory in Havana, circa 1900

El Laguito also makes the best cigar in the world—the Trinidad, a cigar you'll not find in any store. The seven-and-a-half-inch-long cigar is made exclusively for Fidel Castro, who presents them to diplomats and dignitaries. The 2,000 Trinidads produced monthly are, says Tamayo, "the selection of the selection of the selection." In 1996, there were rumors that Trinidads might be sold on the open market.

Laguito was also the first factory to employ women rollers. Today the majority of rollers here are women. They are the best cigar rollers in Cuba. Prior to the Revolution, only men rolled cigars; the leaves were selected by women, who often sorted them on their thighs, giving rise to the famous myth about cigars being "rolled on the dusky thighs of Cuban maidens."

Partagas

The Partagas factory, Calle Industria #520, tel. 33-8060, now named Fábrica Francisco Péez, specializes in full-bodied cigars such as the spicy, strongly aromatic La Gloria Cubana, Ramon Allones, the Montecristo, and, of course, the Partagas, one of the oldest of the Havana brands, started in 1843 by Don Jaime Partagas. The three-story structure was built in 1845 to house the Vilar y Vilar Cigar Factory, one of the main cigar factories of the 19th century. Partagas turns out 5 million cigars a year, among them no fewer than 40 types of Partagas brand (many machine-made and of inferior quality). The factory's classy showroom displays a cigar measuring 50 inches!

Tours are offered daily at 10.30 a.m. and 1.30 p.m. ($5).

H. Upmann

One of the most popular factories for tourists, Upmann (Calle Amistad #407, tel. 62-0081) produces 24 million cigars in 39 varieties. The factory, also known as the José Martí factory, was begun by the erstwhile London-based banking house of H. Upmann in 1844, when it registered its name as a cigar brand (beginning in the 1830s, it had imported Cuban cigars in the first embossed cedar boxes; the firm also introduced the cedar-lined aluminum tube in the 1930s). The Upmann name remains synonymous with the highest quality Havana cigars—mild to medium-flavored, very smooth and subtle, and available in over 30 sizes (not to be confused with H. Upmanns made in the Dominican Republic). Cigar connoisseurs consider that the best Montecristos come from this factory.

Other Factories

Romeo y Julieta specializes in medium-flavored brands such as El Rey del Mundo (King of the World) and, since 1875, the fine Romeo y Julieta. It also makes the heavyweight, high-quality, and limited quantity Saint Luís Rey cigars favored by singer Frank Sinatra and actor James Coburn.

La Corona is immediately west of the entrance to the Museo de Revolución.

Neither is open for visits.

Organized Tours

Wings of the World Travel, 653 Mt. Pleasant Rd., Toronto, Ont. M4S 2N2, tel. (416) 482-1223, or 1636 3rd Ave. #232, New York, NY 10128, tel. (800) 465-8687, fax (416) 486-4001), offers a Cuban Cigar Adventure that includes tours of legendary cigar factories, the tobacco museum, tobacco producing areas, plus general sightseeing.

In the UK, **Intro-Cuba,** 500 High Rd., Woodford Green, Essex IG8 0PN, tel. (181) 505-9656, fax (181) 559-0215 offers a similar 14-day guided Cigar Connoisseur Tour (£1,200, including airfare). Departures are offered in February, October, and November.

Habanos S.A. has its headquarters at **Empresa Cubana del Tabaco,** 104 O'Reilly e/ Tacón y Mercaderes, Habana Vieja, tel. 62-5463; open 7:45 a.m.-3:45 p.m.

PLAZA DEL CRISTO

The tiny, utterly charming **Iglesia de Santo Cristo Buen Viaje** sits in the disheveled Plaza del Cristo at the top (west end) of Amargua, between Lamparilla and Brasil, two blocks east of Avenida de Bélgica (Monserrate). It was here that Wormold, the vacuum-cleaner salesman turned secret agent, was "swallowed up among the pimps and lottery sellers of the Havana noon" in Graham Greene's Our Man in Havana. Wormold and his wayward daughter Millie lived at No. 37 Lamparilla. Alas, the house was fictional.

The church is one of Havana's oldest, dating from 1732, but with a hermitage dating from 1640. Buen Vijae was the final point of the Vía Crucis—the Procession of the Cross—held each Lenten Friday. The church, which has a splendid cross-beamed wooden ceiling, was named for its popularity among sailors and travelers, who used to pray in it for safe voyages.

You can follow Calle Brasil east to Plaza Vieja. Midway, at Compostela, you'll pass the handsome **Iglesia de Santa Teresa de Jesús** (call in on Saturday afternoons, when Afro-Cuban music and dance is hosted in the courtyard) and the **Farmacia Roturno Permanente** (formerly the Drogerría Sarrá), whose magnificently carved wooden shelves seem more fitting as the altarwork for the church across the way. The paneled shelves bear painted glass murals and are stocked with herbs and pharmaceuticals in colorful old bottles and ceramic jars.

PARQUE CENTRAL TO THE MONUMENTO MÁXIMO GÓMEZ

Two roads parallel the Prado and slope gently down from Parque Central to the Monumento de Máximo Gómez and the waterfront: Agramonte (Zulueta), one block east of the Prado, and Avenida de Bélgica (Monserrate), one block farther east. If driving, Monserrate is one-way downhill, Agramonte one-way uphill.

Edificio Bacardi
The uniquely inspired building at the top of Avenida de Bélgica, on the corner of Neptuno, is the old headquarters of the Bacardi rum empire. Finished in December 1929, this magnificent art deco structure is clad in Swedish granite and local limestone. Terra-cotta of varying hues ac-

Monumento Máximo Gómez

cents the design, with motifs showing Grecian nymphs and floral patterns. It is crowned by a Lego-like bell tower topped in turn by a wrought-iron, brass-winged gargoyle that is the famous Bacardi motif. The building is difficult to appreciate at street level. Nip inside the Hotel Plaza, where it is best seen from the *azotea*—the rooftop plaza. Alas, the Edificio Bacardi, surely one of the world's finest art deco inspirations, is in dire need of restoration.

Two blocks north brings you to Trocadero and the national museum.

Museo Nacional de Bellas Artes
The National Museum of Art—Cuba's most important art museum—is housed in the ugly concrete Palacio de Bellas Artes, on Trocadero between Zulueta and Monserrate, tel. 61-2332. From the atrium garden, ramps lead up to two dim floors. The museum contains a fabulous collection of Cuban paintings (on the second floor), plus European collections (ground floor) that include works by Goya, Murillo, Rubens, and Velásquez, as well as the works of impressionists. English painters such as Reynolds, Gainsborough, and Turner are represented. It also boasts Latin America's richest trove of classical antiquities including Roman, Greek, and Egyptian statuary and artworks. Rotating exhibits display the works of Cuba's leading contemporary artists. Open Tues.-Sun. 9 a.m.-5 p.m. (US$2).

Palacio Presidencial
This ornate palace was initiated in 1913 to house the provincial government. Before it could be finished it was earmarked as the Presidential Palace, and Tiffany's of New York was entrusted with its interior decoration. It was from here that a string of corrupt presidents, ending with Fulgencio Batista, spun their webs of dissolution. (Batista narrowly escaped with his life when the palace was attacked on 13 March 1957 by a group of young revolutionaries intent on assassinating the dictator; they didn't know that Batista's apartment was reachable only by a private elevator, and the attack turned into a bloody debacle.) Fronting the palace is a semi-derelict watchtower—**Baluarte de Ángel**—erected in 1680 as part of the fortified wall that once surrounded Habana Vieja. Pointing its barrel guilti-

ly the tower's way is a **SAU-100 Stalin tank,** illuminated at night on its lofty pedestal. To the north is a wide-open park, **Plaza 13 de Mayo,** leading down to Monumento al General Máximo Gómez.

Following the Revolution, the three-story palace was converted into the **Museo de la Revolución.** Open Tues.-Sun. 10 a.m.-5 p.m. and Saturday 10 a.m.-6 p.m.; entrance US$3 (cameras US$5 extra). The marble staircase in the foyer leads upstairs to a massive lobby with a fabulous muraled ceiling. From here, it is necessary to follow the route room by room through the mazelike corridors. Rooms are divided chronologically, from the colonial period to the modern day. Detailed maps describe the battles and progress of the revolutionary war. Hundreds of guns and rifles are displayed alongside grisly photos of dead and tortured heroes. The Moncada Room displays the bloodstained uniforms of the rebels who attacked the Moncada barracks in Santiago in 1953. A room labeled "El Triunfo de la Revolución" bears the red flag of M-26-7 and other revolutionary groups and a photo of an ecstatic Fidel. Che Guevara is there in the form of a lifelike statue, sweating, rifle in hand, working his way heroically through the jungle. (A separate museum—the **Museo de Che**—dedicated to telling the tale of the Argentinian doctor-turned-revolutionary, costs US$1 extra.) Oh, and don't fail to notice Ronald Reagan satirized alongside other notable adversaries of the Cuban state in the museum's "Corner of Cretins."

At the rear, in the former palace gardens, is the **Granma Memorial,** preserving the vessel that brought Fidel Castro, Che Guevara, and other revolutionaries from Mexico to Cuba in 1956. The *Granma,* a surprisingly muscular launch that embodies the powerful, unstoppable spirit of the revolutionary movement, is encased in an impressive glass structure—a simulated sea—with a roof held aloft by great concrete columns. It is surrounded by vehicles used in the revolutionary war: strange armored vehicles, the bullet-riddled "Fast Delivery" truck used in the student commando's assault on the Presidential Palace in 1957, and Fidel's green Land Rover, with *Comandancia General Sierra Maestra* stenciled in red on the door. There's also a turbine from the U-2 spy plane downed during the missile crisis in 1962, a naval Sea Fury, and a T-34 tank supposedly used by Castro himself against the counterrevolutionaries at the Bay of Pigs.

You can take photos of the exhibits from the street, but to get closer to the *Granma* you must enter the museum through the main entrance.

Iglesia del Santa Ángel Custodio

There's a virginal purity to this shimmering white church, with its splendid exterior, on Monserrate, immediately east of the Palacio, atop a rock known as Angel Hill. Actually, the lavishly gothic façade is the rear of the church. The entrance is on the corner of Calles Compostela and Cuarteles. From the rear it looks youthful. The church, however, was founded in 1687 by builder-bishop Diego de Compostela. The tower dates from 1846, when a hurricane toppled the original; the façade was reworked in neo-gothic style in the mid-19th century.

It's immaculate yet simple within. Gray marble floor. Modest wooden gothic altar. Statues of saints all around. Pristine stained-glass windows. Splendid!

Cuba's national hero, José Martí, was baptized here on 12 February 1853. The church has appeared in several movies and was the setting for the tragic marriage scene that ends in the violent denouement on the steps of the church in the 19th-century novel *Cecilia Valdés,* by the nationalist Cirilo Villaverde. A bust of the author stands in the *plazuela* outside the church entrance.

CENTRO HABANA AND CERRO

Centro Habana (Central Havana—pop. 175,000) lies west of Habana Vieja and east of Vedado. Centro is mostly residential, with few sites or sights of note. Many houses along and inland of the Malecón, having been battered by waves and salt-air over decades, are in a tumbledown state. Some transcend sordidness and at first take may remind you of the worst tenements of New York or Glasgow. Walk Centro's streets, however, and you can find scores of residents applying fresh plaster and pots of paint to their otherwise melancholic habitations.

In prerevolutionary days, Centro was the heart of Havana's red-light district, and scores of prostitutes roamed such streets as the ill-named Calle Virtudes (Virtues). Today, Centro is the great commercial heart of the city—if a bit faded from the days when there were more goods to sell. Still, by mid-1996, the main shopping streets of San Rafael, Neptuno, and Galiano were springing back to life. Believe it or not, there's also a small Chinatown—**Barrio Chino**—delineated by Calles Zanja, Dragones, Salud, Rayo, San Nicolás, and Manrique.

South of Centro, the land rises gently to Cerro (pop. 130,000), a separate administrative district (the word means "hill"). During the last century, many wealthy families maintained two homes in Havana—one in town, another on the cooler hill.

The two districts are anchored by Avenida Máximo Gómez (Monte or Calzada de Cerro), surely one of the saddest streets in all Havana. The avenue—lined with colonnaded mansions like an endless Greek temple—ascends gradually, marching backward into the past like a classical ruin.

MALECÓN AND VICINITY

How many times have I walked the Malecón? Twenty? Thirty? Once is never enough, for Havana's seafront boulevard enigmatically seems to represent all of Havana.

Literature buffs may be intrigued by the **Museo Lezama Lima,** three blocks inland from the Malecón at Trocadero #162 e/ Crespo y In-dustria, two blocks west of the Prado. The museum, which opened in 1995, is in the former home of prodigious writer José Lezana Lima, author of *Fresa y Chocolat* and *Paradiso,* both of which were made into renowned movies. The building evokes the rich and varied universe of the writer, variously described as a "fat man with a perennial cigar" and a "deeply mystical influence."

Dominating the Malecón to the west is the massive bronze and marble **Monumento Antonio Maceo,** standing in front of the **Hospital Hermanos Ameijeiras,** whose basement vaults (the building was originally the Banco Nacional de Cuba) are rumored to contain Cuba's meager gold reserves.

CALLE SAN RAFAEL

This lively street leading west from Parque Central is for five blocks a well-kept pedestrian precinct and Havana's major shopping street. The stores still bear prerevolutionary neon signs promoting US brand names. One of the most famous department stores is **Fin de Siglo,** the former Sears store, founded around the 1880s and once beloved of Cuban women. It was once brimful of goods from the far corners of the globe. Today, most of its individual counters are threadbare (those that display items often display one item only, usually in limited sizes). However, the mannequins, naked in 1995, were dressed when I visited again a year later. Life is returning to Havana's old commercial center, which is garnering lively cafes and ice-cream stores.

The pedestrian precinct stretches to Avenida de Italia (Galiano), where it reverts to traffic and the stores give way to residences. Luring you westward to Calzada de la Infanta is the distant warbling of birds, and at the junction you'll discover the **Canary Cultivators of Havana,** displaying their rainbow-hued birds.

Calle Neptuno parallels San Rafael to the south. Fans of tango might check out the **Casa del Tango,** a tiny shop at 303 Neptuno.

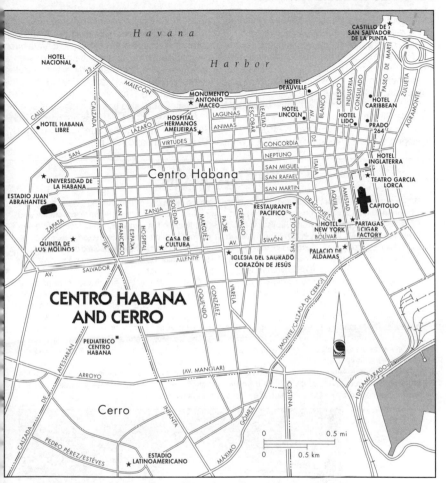

AVENIDA SALVADOR ALLENDE AND SIMÓN BOLÍVAR

This wide boulevard was laid out in the early 19th century by Governor Tacón, when it was known as the Paseo. The governor built his summer house here and was copied by many of Havana's nobility. (One of the mansions, today the **Casa del Cultura Centro Havana,** at Salvador Allende y Arbol Seco, contains the **Galeria Kahlo.**)

On the north side of Salvador Allende, immediately west of Calzada de Infante, are the elegant **Botanical Gardens.** This was a popular recreation spot in colonial days, when it was the site of the pleasure gardens of the governor's summer palace. Slaves newly arrived from Africa were kept here in barracoons, where they could be displayed to passersby. The graceful **Quinta de los Molinos** is reached via a long gladed drive and is named for the royal snuff mills that were built here in 1791 to take advantage of the waters of Zanza Real; you can still see part of the original aqueduct—inaugurated in 1592—to the rear of the *quinta*.

Salvador Allende leads west to the **Castillo del Principe,** built in the 1770s following the English invasion. The castle is off-limits and rarely mentioned in Cuban tourist literature as, apparently, it still houses a prison.

East of Padre Varela, Allende becomes Avenida Simón Bolívar, sloping to Parque de la Fraternidad, with a sweeping view down the scalloped avenue. Simón Bolívar is lined with once-impressive colonial-era structures. The **Iglesia del Sagrado Corazón de Jesús** is a gothic inspiration in stone that could have been transported from medieval England, with a beamed ceiling held aloft by great marbled columns. The stained-glass windows rival the best in Europe. The church, one of the most active in Cuba, also boasts a fabulous soaring altar of carved wood. Services are offered Mon.-Sat. at 7 a.m. and 4:30 p.m. and Sunday at 7 and 9:30 a.m. and 4:30 p.m.

THE MALECÓN

When questioned by an immigration official as to why he had come to Cuba and stayed for 10 years, Costa Rican composer Ray Tico replied, "I fell in love with Havana's seafront drive." The Malecón (embankment) boulevard—designed in 1857 by the Cuban engineer General Francisco de Albear but not laid out until 1902 (by the US governor General Woods)—fronts sinuously and dramatically along the Atlantic shoreline between the Castillo de San Salvador de la Punta and the Río Almendares. "Silver Lamé" was what composer Orlando de la Rosa called it. The metaphor has stuck, although it is today only a ghostly reminder of its former brilliance—what Martha Gellhorn called "a nineteenth-century jewel and a joke."

The Malecón is lined with once-glorious three-story houses, each exuberantly distinct from the next. Unprotected by seaworthy paint, they have proven incapable of withstanding the salt spray that crashes over the seawall in great airy clouds and then floats off in rainbows. Their façades—green trimmed with purple, pink with blue, yellow with orange—are now decrepit, supported by wooden scaffolding, while the broad limestone walkway is now pitted and broken.

All along the shore are the worn remains of square baths—known as "The Elysian Fields"—hewn from the rocks below the seawall, originally with separate areas for men, women, and Negroes. Since the Revolution, they are more democratic.

The boulevard offers a microcosm of Havana life: the elderly walking their dogs, the shiftless looking for tourists, the young passing rum among friends, and scores of couples . . . all through the night, lovers' murmurings mingle with the crash and hiss of the waves.

the Malecón looking toward Vedado

CHRISTOPHER P. BAKER

BARRIO CHINO

After the end of slavery in 1886, landowners imported 150,000 Chinese as indentured laborers to work the fields. The Sino-Cuban descendants of those who worked off their indenture gravitated to Centro Habana, where they settled in the zones bordering the Zanza Real, the aqueduct that channeled water to the city. Here they worked as domestics or opened vegetable shops, laundries, and restaurants and were later joined by Chinese fleeing persecution in California. In time, Havana's Chinese quarter—Barrio Chino—became the largest in Latin America.

During the "sordid era" it was a center of opium dens, prostitution houses, and the infamous Shanghai theater that specialized in pornographic films and to which Wormold took Beatrice in Graham Greene's *Our Man in Havana.*

Today, it is a mere shadow of its former self, with about 400 native born Chinese and perhaps 2,000 descendants still resident in the area. The vast majority of Chinese left Cuba in the years immediately following the Revolution. Barrio Chino has since lost much of its personality along with its colorful characters, who were encouraged to become "less Chinese and more Cuban." Nonetheless, there's enough to remind you of how things once were.

Chinese lanterns still hang outside the doorways, alongside signs written in Chinese. You'll recognize Chinese features, too, in the lively free market held daily (except Wednesday) on tiny Calle Cuchillo. In 1995, the government of China agreed to help rebuild Havana's Chinatown.

The most interesting Chinese buildings are on and around Calle Cuchillo, including **Restaurante Pacifico,** on Calle San Nicolas and Cuchillo. Ernest Hemingway used to eat here, on the top floor of the five-story building to which Fidel Castro is still an occasional visitor. "To get there," recalls Hemingway's son, Gregory, "you had to go up in an old elevator with a sliding iron grille for a door. It stopped at every floor, whether you wanted it to or not. On the second floor there was a five-piece Chinese orchestra blaring crazy atonal music. . . . Then you reached the third floor, where there was a whorehouse. . . . The fourth floor was an opium den with pitifully wasted little figures curled up around their pipes."

If you can, time your visit to coincide with Chinese New Year at the end of January into early February, when the streets are charged with the staccato pop of firecrackers meant to scare away evil spirits and the lion comes out to leap and dance through the streets of Barrio Chino.

AVENIDA MÁXIMO GÓMEZ (MONTE AND CALZADA DE CERRO)

During the 19th century, Cerro developed as the place to retire during the torrid midsummer months. Scores of summer homes were erected in classical style, each more extravagantly Italianate than the next. Many of the luxurious houses went up along Avenida Máximo Gómez (popularly called Monte and Calzada de Cerro), a sinuous street lined with classical stone columns of various styles and materials. Alas, today it looks as Herculaneum must have looked during its decline. Monte's once-stunning arcades are now in desperate condition, and houses are decaying behind lovely façades. To my mind, it is the saddest sight in Havana.

Novelist James Michener, exploring Cerro while looking for a house in which to set the Cuban portion of a novel on the Caribbean, was told "in elegiac tones" by his guide, "The steps went down by decades. 1920s the mansions are in full flower. 1930s the rich families begin to move out. 1940s people grab them who can't afford to maintain them, ruin begins. 1950s ten big families move into each mansion, pay no rent, and begin to tear it apart. 1960s during the first years of the Revolution, no housing elsewhere, so even more crowd in, ruin accelerates. 1970s some of the weakest begin to fall down. 1980s many gone beyond salvation." Heartrending.

A drive along Máximo Gómez will provide a lasting memory. But don't judge Havana by this, for the famous avenue is in the early stage of renovation—most notably at its lower end, near Parque de la Fraternidad. Façades are being renovated and building materials distributed to residents according to the housing conditions. The aim is to restore Monte as one of the city's major shopping streets. Almost two dozen restaurants and shops were reopened here in 1995. And there are plans to establish food stalls around the **Cuatro Caminos** farmers' market (at Manglar and Cristina, also called Avenida de la México), the 19th-century market hall that still functions as such and is well worth a visit for its bustling color and ambience. Watch for pickpockets.

Destilería Bocoy

One of the gems of Máximo Gómez is this venerable home with a two-tone pink façade with the legend "BOCOY" above the wide, handsome door. Its façade is decorated with four dozen handsomely painted cast-iron swans marching wing to wing, "each standing tall and slim, its long neck bent straight down in mortal combat with an evil serpent climbing up its legs to sink its

fangs," wrote James Michener. Michener chose this building for the house in which lived "once-intimate liberal relatives" of a conservative Cuban exile family living in Miami.

Beyond the swan-filled portico, the house contains great oak casks up to seven meters tall hidden in dark recesses—"something out of Piranesi, a ghostly affair with a single unshaded lightbulb"—and containing Cuba's famous Bocoy rums. Bocoy still manufactures one of the choicest rums in Cuba, intended solely as a gift to notable personalities and packaged in a bulbous earthenware bottle inside a miniature pirate's treasure chest labeled La Isla del Tesoro (Treasure Island).

VEDADO AND PLAZA DE LA REVOLUCIÓN

The conclusion of the brief Spanish-American-Cuban War, in 1898, brought US money rushing in—and a new age of elegance to Cuba's capital, concentrated in hilly Vedado, between Centro Habana and the Río Almendares. Fine parks and monuments to generals were added, along with the Malecón, the wide promenade anchoring the waterfront. Large hotels, casinos, department stores, and lavish restaurants sprouted like mushrooms alongside nightclubs displaying fleshly attractions.

Vedado—today's heart of Havana—has been described as "Havana at its middle-class best." The University of Havana is here. So are the fabulous cemetery Cementerio de Colón, many of the city's prime hotels and restaurants, virtually all its main commercial buildings, and block after block of handsome mansions and apartment houses in various states of decay or repair. The streets are lined with trees festooned with strangler figs. (While exploring, watch for stone lions flanking the gates of large mansions. These revered symbols denote the home of a nobleman. Alas, some time late last century, a commoner who had amassed a fortune bought himself a title and erected lions. The proper grandees of Spain were so outraged that they tore theirs down in a protest known as La Muerte de los Leones—the Death of the Lions.)

Vedado is administered as part of Plaza de la Revolución (pop. 165,000), which includes Nuevo Vedado, a distinct district south of Vedado: the area, much of which has been rebuilt

since the Revolution, is centered on the Plaza de la Revolución, surrounded by ministry buildings, the Palacio de la Revolución (the seat of government), and the towering José Martí monument, now containing a fabulous museum.

MALECÓN

This portion of the Malecón is less dramatic than that along the shoreline of Centro Havana. However, there are several important sights, not least the **Hotel Nacional,** dramatically perched atop a small cliff at the junction of La Rampa and the Malecón. This grande dame hotel is worth a peek, not least for its Moorish-influenced architecture.

Just above the hotel, on the shorefront, is the **Monumento ál Maine,** dedicated to the memory of the 260 sailors who died when the US warship exploded in Havana harbor in 1898. Two rusting cannons are laid out beneath great corinthian columns. The monument was desecrated by an angry mob in the days following the Triumph of the Revolution in 1959; they toppled the eagle from its roost and broke its wings. The Castro government later dedicated a plaque that reads, "To the victims of the *Maine,* who were sacrificed by imperialist voracity in its eagerness to seize the island of Cuba."

Three blocks west, at the bottom of Calle L, is the unmarked **US Interests Section,** (formerly the US Embassy) where low-profile US diplomats and CIA agents serve Uncle Sam's whims behind a veil of mirrored-glass windows. Facing it, to the east, is what must be Havana's most photographed site: a huge, brightly painted billboard showing a fanatical Uncle Sam growling menacingly at a Cuban soldier who is shouting, *"Señores Imperialistas: ¡No les tenemos absolutamente ningún miedo!"* ("Mister Imperialists: You don't scare us at all!").

LA RAMPA AND VICINITY

Millionaires, mafiosi, presidents, paupers, and pimps all once walked the five blocks of Calle 23, which rises steeply—and heavily American in style—from the Malecón. La Rampa was the setting of *Three Trapped Tigers,* Guillermo Cabrera Infante's famous novel about swinging-'50s Havana, for it was here that the ritziest hotels, casinos, and nightclubs were concentrated in the days before the Revolution. You may still find yourself enthralled by the verve of La Rampa.

La Rampa's flavor is that of a tree-lined boulevard in Buenos Aires or even Spain, with its candy-stripe awnings shading faded restaurants and nightclubs from the heyday of sin. It is modern, vital, and busy and climbs steadily past the offices of Cubana, Havanatur, the television station, Hotel Habana Libre, and art-deco apartment buildings mingling with high-rise office buildings. Not until the 1950s did it begin to acquire its present look (prior to that, it was a shantytown). In 1963, multicolored granite tiles created by Cuba's leading artists—Wilfredo Lam, René Portocarrero, and others—were laid at intervals in the sidewalks. It is art to be walked on—or not to be, as Hamlet would say.

Anyone interested in Cuba's revolutionary history should step south one block to Calle 25 #164 e/ Infanta y O and the **Casa Abel Santamaría,** where the martyr—brutally tortured and murdered following the attack on Moncada barracks in 1953—once lived. The simple two-room apartment (no. 601) was used prior to the attack as the headquarters of Fidel Castro's nascent revolutionary movement. The original furnishings are still in place.

Catercorner to the Hotel Habana Libre, at the top of the hill at Calle L (the busiest and most important intersection in Havana), is **Parque Coppelia,** an entire block devoted to the consumption of ice cream, of which Cubans are con-

COPPELIA

Coppelia is the name of a park in Havana, the flying saucer-like structure at its heart, and the brand of excellent ice cream served there.

In the good old, bad old days, the trendy area at the top of La Rampa was full of ice-cream parlors. But, it is said, the lower classes and blacks weren't welcome, so in 1966 the government built a big, lush park with a parlor in the middle as the ultimate democratic ice-cream emporium—and surely the biggest ice creamery in the world, serving an estimated 30,000 customers a day.

There's a counter-bar below, and a series of circular rooms above. You can also sit outside, beneath shade trees in any of three open-air sections. Each has its own *cola* (line, queue). Trying to make sense of the lines is a puzzle. People wander off to sit in the shade. The line always magically reforms at the critical moment. Once you're seated, waitresses in red tartan miniskirts provide swift service.

Before the Special Period, you used to be able to choose anything from a one-scoop cone to complex sundaes as well as more than two dozen flavors, including exotic tropical fruits that Ben and Jerry have never heard of.

Supposedly, Coppelia is exclusively for Cubans. But I made it a daily pilgrimage while living in Havana in 1996, when most days only one flavor was available at a time (the flavors may be changed during the day, when a new delivery arrives).

A full bowl—a four-scoop serving—costs a mere $2.50 (US12 cents).

Coppelia is open Tues.-Sun. 10:45 a.m.-1.45 a.m.

summate lovers. The ice cream is excellent and worth the long wait in line.

Universidad de la Habana

Follow Calle L south from La Rampa and you arrive at an immense stone staircase at Calle 27—the famous *escalinata*—that leads up to the university. The 50-meter-wide steps are topped by a porticoed, columned façade beyond which lies a peaceful square surrounded by more columned arcades. The tree-shaded campus was loosely modeled on that of New York's Columbia University. A patinated statue looks down upon the *escalinata,* which in Batista days was famous as a setting for political rallies and riots. The monument across the street at the foot of the steps contains the ashes of Julio Antonio Mella, a student leader (and founder of the Cuban Communist Party) assassinated by the Machado regime in 1929.

The university was founded by ecclesiastics in 1728 and was originally sited on Calle Obispo in Habana Vieja. Admission was based on "purity" of bloodline: Jews, Moors, other non-Christians, and, of course, blacks and mulattoes were barred. The university was secularized in 1842, although admission remained the privilege of the privileged classes.

During this century, the university was composed of 13 schools, each with its own president. The presidents elected the president of the University Students' Federation, the pillar of student political activity and an extremely influential group amid the jungle of Cuban politics. The university was an autonomous "sacred hill," that neither the police nor the army could enter (although gangsters and renegade politicians roamed the campus). Its most notable of many notable students was Fidel Castro, who enrolled in the law school in October 1945.

Fortunately, today it is a peaceful place. Visitors are allowed to stroll the grounds, although peeking into the classes requires advance permission. You can also visit the **Montane Anthropology Museum,** tel. 79-3488, on the second floor of the Felipe Poey Science Building. The museum contains a valuable collection of pre-Columbian artifacts, including carved idols and turtle shells. Downstairs, the **Felipe Poey Museum of Natural History,** tel. 32-9000, displays an excellent array of pre-Columbian artifacts and the inert remains of dozens of endemic species stuffed or pickled for posterity within glass cases. Golly, there's even a pilot whale suspended from the ceiling, while snakes, alligators, and sharks hang in suspended animation on the walls. Open Mon.-Fri. 9 a.m.-4 p.m.

Museo Napoleónico

Who would imagine that so much of Napoleon Bonaparte's personal memorabilia would end up in Cuba? But it is, housed in the splendid Ferrara mansion in the lee of the university, at Calle San Miguel #1159. The collection was the private work of a politician, Orestes Ferrara, who brought back

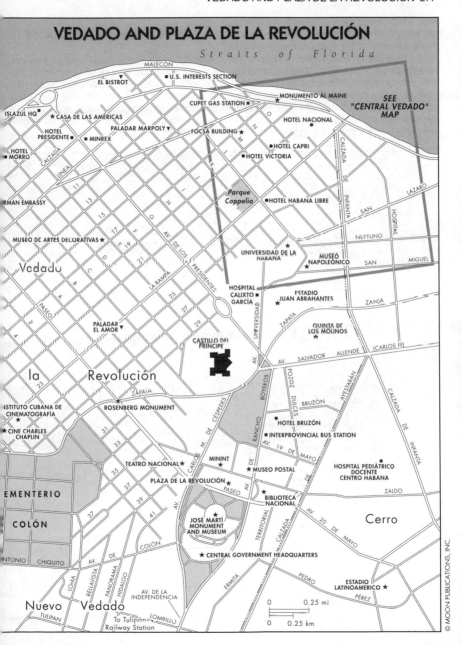

VEDADO AND PLAZA DE LA REVOLUCIÓN

Straits of Florida

MALECÓN

EL BISTROT ▼ ■ U.S. INTERESTS SECTION

SEE "CENTRAL VEDADO" MAP

MONUMENTO ÁL MAINE ★

CUPET GAS STATION ■

ISLAZUL HQ ■

★ CASA DE LAS AMÉRICAS

HOTEL NACIONAL ●

FOCSA BUILDING ★

PALADAR MARPOLY ▼

HOTEL PRESIDENTE ● ■ MINREX

●HOTEL CAPRI

●HOTEL VICTORIA

HOTEL ● MORRO

CALZADA

LINEA

11

RMAN EMBASSY

13

15

CALZADA DE INFANTA

LAZARO

HOSPITAL

Parque Coppelia

●HOTEL HABANA LIBRE

SAN

MUSEO DE ARTES DECORATIVAS ★

17

F

19

D

AV. DE LOS PRESIDENTES

NEPTUNO

Vedado

C

B

21

UNIVERSIDAD DE LA HABANA ★

MUSEO NAPOLEÓNICO ★

SAN

MIGUEL

A

PASEO

23

LA RAMPA

25

27

HOSPITAL CALIXTO ■ GARCÍA ★

ESTADIO JUAN ABRAHANTES ★

ZANJA

2

PALADAR ▼ EL AMOR

29

UNIVERSIDAD

ZAPATA

QUINTA DE LOS MOLINOS ★

CASTILLO DEL PRÍNCIPE

la *Revolución*

23

AV. SALVADOR ALLENDE (CARLOS III)

BOYEROS

POZOZ

DULCES

AYESTARÁN

CALZADA DE INFANTA

ZAPATA

NSTITUTO CUBANA DE CINEMATOGRAFÍA ★

ROSENBERG MONUMENT ★

BRUZÓN

31

33

HOTEL BRUZÓN ■

■ INTERPROVINCIAL BUS STATION

★ CINE CHARLES CHAPLIN

RANCHO

AV. 19 DE MAYO

35

TEATRO NACIONAL ★

MININT

CARLOS M. DE CÉSPEDES

★ MUSEO POSTAL

DE

HOSPITAL PEDIÁTRICO DOCENTE CENTRO HABANA ■

37

PLAZA DE LA REVOLUCIÓN ★

PASEO

BIBLIOTECA NACIONAL ★

ZALDO

EMENTERIO

39

41

AV.

JOSÉ MARTÍ MONUMENT AND MUSEUM ★

TERRITORIAL

CALZADA

AV. 20 DE MAYO

Cerro

COLÓN

★ CENTRAL GOVERNMENT HEADQUARTERS

ERMITA

PEDRO

NTONIO CHIQUITO

AV. DE

COLÓN

LOMA

BELLAVISTA

PANORAMA

HIDALGO

AV. DE LA INDEPENDENCIA

ESTADIO LATINOAMÉRICO ★

PÉREZ

Nuevo *Vedado*

TULIPÁN

To Tulipán Railway Station

LOMBILLO

0   0.25 mi

0   0.25 km

© MOON PUBLICATIONS, INC.

from Europe such precious items as the French emperor's death mask, toothbrush, and the pistols Napoleon used at the Battle of Borodino. The three-story museum is replete with portraits of the military genius. A library on Napoleon is organized chronologically to trace the life of the "Great Corsican." (The large antenna next door is supposedly used to block the signals of TV Martí, beamed from the USA.) Open Mon.-Fri. and alternate Sundays 9 a.m.-noon and 1-4 p.m.

AVENIDA DE LOS PRESIDENTES

Avenida de los Presidentes runs perpendicular to La Rampa and flows downhill to the Malecón. A wide, grassy, tree-lined median runs down its spine. To each side are grand colonial homes in various states of repair and disrepair. Many now function as schools or government departments.

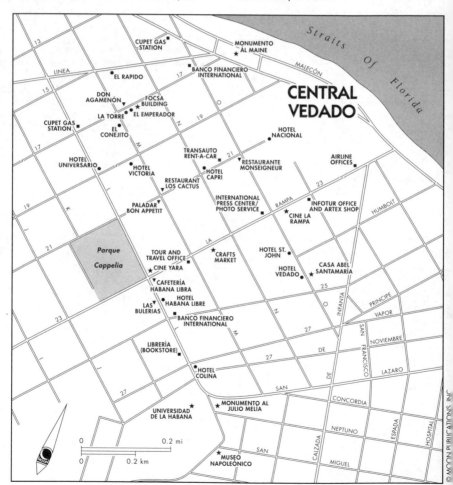

gate to Cementerio de Colón

One of the more extravagant mansions is on Calle 17, two blocks west of Avenida de los Presidentes, c/ D y E. The villa, which formerly belonged to a Cuban countess, now houses the stunning **Museo de Artes Decorativas,** and brims with a lavish collection of furniture, paintings, textiles, and chinoiserie from the 18th and 19th centuries. Most of the furniture, however, is European, not Cuban. No matter, it's staggering in its sumptuous quality. Upstairs, where the landing is festooned with ivory figures, you'll find a boudoir decorated Oriental-style, with furniture inlaid with mother-of-pearl. Highly recommended. Open Tues.-Sat. 11 a.m.-6:30 p.m. and Sunday 9 a.m.-1 p.m. Entrance costs US$1.

If walking the boulevard, pause at #220 to admire the beautiful blue tilework and stucco and the columns like twirled candy sticks. Nearby, at Calle 3ra, is the **Galeria Haydee Santamaría,** containing the Art Collection of New America, comprising more than 6,000 pieces of sculpture, engravings, paintings, photographs, and popular art representing artists throughout the Americas and Caribbean. The gallery contains a silkscreening shop. Concerts, film screenings, and theater and dance programs are hosted. Open Mon.-Fri. 10 a.m.-5 p.m. (Note, too, the handsome bronze statue of Alexandro Rodriguez y Velasco on a granite pedestal, guarded by a bronze figure of Perseus at Calle 9.)

South of Calle 23, the boulevard climbs to the **Monumento al General Máximo Gómez,** topped by nubile figures in classical style.

CEMENTERIO DE COLÓN

Described as "an exercise in pious excesses," Havana's **Necrópolis Cristóbal Colón** is renowned worldwide for its flamboyant mausoleums, vaults, and tombs embellished with angels, griffins, cherubs, and other ornamentation. The cemetery, which covers 56 hectares, has been declared a national monument. It was laid out, between 1871 and 1886, in blocks like a Roman military camp, with a Greek Orthodox-style ocher-colored church at its center—the **Capillo Central.**

Famous *criollo* patricians, colonial aristocrats, and war heroes such as Máximo Gómez are buried here alongside noted intellectuals, merchants, and corrupt politicians (as well, of course, as the rare honest one, too, such as Eduardo Chibás). The list goes on and on: José Raúl Capablanca, the world chess champion; Alejo Carpentier, Cuba's best contemporary novelist; Hubert de Blanck, the noted composer; and Celia Sánchez, Haydee Santamaría, and a plethora of revolutionaries killed for the cause. There are also many collective vaults reflecting Cuba's heterogeneous roots. You could take all day to discover all the gems.

Fortunately, benches are provided beneath shade trees.

The impressive triple-tiered Romanesque entrance gate is at the top of Calle 12 and Calle Zapata, which runs along its north face. The **Buro de Turismo** is to the left of the entrance. The major tombs line the main avenue that leads south from the gate. Guided tours are available free of charge, but tips would be welcome. Open 6 a.m.-6 p.m. Entrance US$1.

PLAZA DE LA REVOLUCIÓN

Havana's largest plaza is a must-see. The plaza itself is a rather ugly tarred square floodlit from atop telegraph poles. It has been accurately described by P.J. O'Rourke as "a vast open space resembling the Mall in D.C., but dropped into the middle of a massive empty parking lot in a tropical Newark."

From Vedado, take bus no. 84 from the bottom La Rampa, at Calle 0 and Humboldt.

To the north and east are government ministries in soulless post-Stalinist style, including, on the northwest side, the tall **Ministerio del Inte-** rior (the ministry in charge of national security) with a windowless wall bearing a fabulous black-metal "mural" of Che Guevara and the words "Hasta la Victoria Siempre." To the west, across Avenida Céspedes, is the modern **Teatro Nacional,** with its glass-plated façade. The theater is well cared for but underutilized—"waiting" as it is, wrote novelist Donald Westlake, "for a theatrical season that had never quite arrived."

To the east of the Ministry of the Interior is the **Ministerio de Comunicaciones** containing the **Museo Postal** (on the ground floor). Serious philatelists will find it fascinating. The well-cataloged collection is kept in sophisticated vertical pull-out glass file drawers. A complete range of Cuban postage stamps (including the first, dating to 1855) is on display, plus a large collection of stamps from almost 100 other countries, including numerous "penny black" and other valuable stamps from England. Check out the little solid-propellant rocket that was launched in 1936 by a group of enthusiastic philatelists eager to promote rocket propulsion to speed up mail delivery! The museum has a well-stocked shop—*filatelica*—selling stamps. Open Mon.-Fri. 9 a.m.-5 p.m. (US$1 entrance).

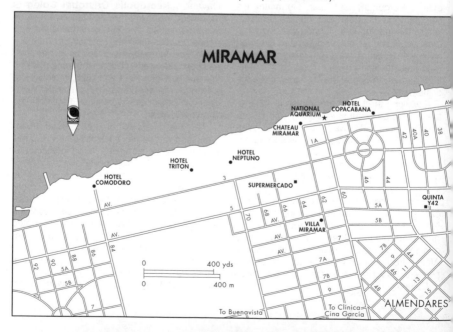

Across Avenida Rancho Boyeros, on the northeast corner of the square, is Cuba's largest library, the **Biblioteca Nacional.** Two blocks north, at the corner of Rancho Boyeros and Bruzón, you'll find the **Museo de Historia del Deportivo,** which tells the history of Cuban sports. Open Tues.-Sun. 10 a.m.-5 p.m. Admission is US$1.

Monumento y Museo José Martí

This spectacular monument, made entirely of gray granite and marble, sits atop a 30-meter-tall base that spans the entire square and acts as a massive reviewing stand and podium from which Fidel tutors, harangues, and encourages the masses. To each side, great arching stairways lead to a huge granite statue of the National Hero sitting in a contemplative pose, like Rodin's *The Thinker.*

Behind looms a slender, 109-meter-tall Babylonian edifice stepped like a soaring ziggurat from a sci-fi movie. The tower—the highest point in Havana—is made entirely of gray marble quarried from the Isle of Youths. The top bristles with antennas. Vultures soar overhead and roost on the narrow ledges, lending an added eerie quality to the scene. Its construction is said to have cost every citizen in Cuba one centavo.

Until early 1996, soldiers barred the way up to the monument, from where sentries surveyed passersby—and often icily shooed them away. The guards have since departed, and the edifice has been opened as a museum dedicated to José Martí, within the base of the tower.

The museum, which opened on 1 February 1996, is splendid, depicting everything you could wish to know about Martí. Among the exhibits are many first-edition works, engravings, drawings, and maps, and reproductions of significant artifacts in Martí's life.

The museum also displays the original plans for the design of the monument and plaza, including a Parthenon-like scheme that seems a copycat version of Washington's Lincoln Memorial. Planning, construction, and urbanization of the area around the plaza is traced with large black-and-white photos that display key moments that have occurred here since the Revolution. New Age music plays in the background, drawing you to a multi-screen broadcast on the wars of independence and the Revolution. One of the four exhibition rooms is dedicated to traveling exhibits, which change every three months.

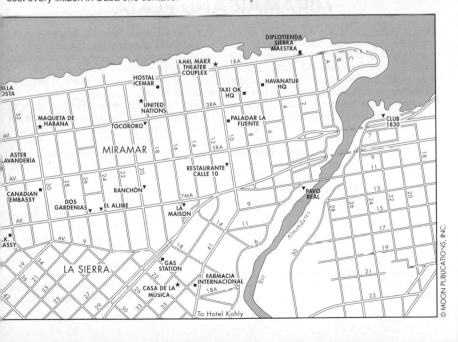

To one side is a small art gallery featuring portraits of Martí by numerous leading artists. The museum is open Tues.-Sat. 10 a.m.-6 p.m. and Sunday 10 a.m.-2 p.m. Entrance costs US$5 (you must pay US$5 extra if you wish to take photographs; US$10 for videos). For an additional US$5, you can take the elevator to a viewing gallery at the top. From above, you can see that the entire structure is designed as a five-pointed star. Each star in the *mirador* contains windows on each side, providing a 360-degree view over Havana. On a clear day it is possible to see 50 miles. Inset in the floor of each point is a compass showing the direction and distance of national and international cities (New York, for example, is 2,100 km away, and the North Pole is 7,441 km away).

Palacio de la Revolución
Immediately behind the José Martí monument is the government building where Castro and the Council of Ministers and their underlings work out policies of state. The labyrinthine, ocher-colored Palace adjoins the buildings of the Central Committee of the Communist Party and is fronted by a broad staircase built by Batista for the Cuban Supreme Court.

An enormous ceramic-tile mosaic of birds, animals, and flowers dominates the reception hall. The artist apparently cast the intricately etched tiles while the architect was still designing the interior, and, through a misunderstanding, the ceiling was built too low. The top two rows wouldn't fit, robbing the mosaic of its crown.

No visitors are allowed.

The Rosenberg Monument
Midway between Plaza de la Revolución and Cementerio de Colón, at the junction of Paseo and Zapata, is a little park with a tree shading an inconspicuous red-brick wall bearing cement doves and an inset sculpture of Julius and Ethel Rosenberg, the US couple executed in 1951 for passing nuclear secrets to the Soviet Union. An inscription reads, "Murdered June 19, 1953." Julius' final words are engraved, too: "For Peace, Bread, and Roses, We Face the Executioners."

MIRAMAR AND PLAYA

West of Vedado stretches a vast and vital region where the wealthy of the '50s lived in high-rise apartments and columned and balustraded mansions. The seaside district of Miramar (part of Playa, which extends to the far west of Havana) is still exclusive—leafy and secluded. The rich who departed left their grandiose homes and classy apartments as valuable gifts to the Revolution. Today, clinics, kindergartens, and clubs occupy the big houses. Those for which no public use could be found were divided up into private apartments.

Miramar is at the forefront of Cuba's quasi-capitalist remake. Its main thoroughfare, the wide fig-tree-lined boulevard called Avenida 5ta, is flanked by mansions that have been restored to an earlier grandeur and leased to foreign corporations—whose neon signs are now everywhere. Avenida 5ta is also "Embassy Row" and Havana's busiest boulevard.

Avenida 1ra (Primera) runs along the seafront. It's a lively spot, popular with Havana's youth. *Balnearios* (bathing areas) are found all along Miramar's waterfront (Playita de 10 y 6 is favored by gays). It's Havana's answer to Santa Monica—without the sand and the pier, but, yes, you may occasionally see girls in skin-tight hot pants being pulled along on roller skates by their dogs.

Mosquitoes can be a problem in the rainy season in Miramar.

Beginning one block south of Avenida 5, at the tunnel under the Río Almendares, Avenida 31 runs south from Miramar to the Tropicana nightclub in the Ciudad Libertad area, beyond which lies the suburban Marianao district.

Farther west is the exclusive Cubanacán district.

Sightseeing
There are few sites of interest. However, I find an enlivening thrill in exploring Miramar, whose many splendid mansions are a joy to behold. A curiosity is the monstrously ugly **Confederation of Independent States' Embassy,** a peculiar Cubist tower—formerly the Soviet Embassy—in the middle of Avenida Quinta between Calles 62 and 66.

And there are two visits you must make. The first is to the **Museum of the Ministry of the In-**

terior, dedicated to the CIA's 30 years of villainy and inept efforts to dethrone Fidel. The seal of the CIA looms over a room full of photos and gadgets—oddities straight from a James Bond movie.

The second is the Maqueta de Habana.

Maqueta de Habana

The *maqueta* (model) is a 1:1,000 scale replica of the city. The 144-square-meter model represents 144 square km of Havana and its environs. It is exquisite—but, more important, a visit here puts the entire city in accessible 3-D perspective, allowing you to understand the layout.

The *maqueta*—one of the largest city models in the world—took nine experts more than 10 years to complete and shows Havana in the most intimate detail. Every contour is included, every building, every bump on every hill, even the balconies on buildings are there! It is color-coded by age: historic buildings are painted crimson; post-revolutionary buildings are in ivory.

The model is made of sections that can be moved on rails to allow access for changes. It is housed in a lofty, hangar-sized, air-conditioned building with a balcony for viewing the city from on high. The building—called the **Pabellón**—

also contains the offices of the **Grupo para el Desarrollo Integral de la Capital,** the government institution responsible for overseeing the integrated development of Havana. The Pabellón also serves as an information center for both Cubans and travelers. Exhibitions on Havana's cultural and social life are sometimes hosted; concerts and social events are hosted in the adjoining garden.

The Pabellón is at Calle 28 #113, e/ Avenida 1 y 3, tel./fax 33-2661, e-mail gdic@tinored.cu. It's open to the public Tues.-Sat. 2-6 p.m. and by advance request Tues.-Sat. 10 a.m.-1 p.m. Entrance costs US$3 (US$1 for students, seniors, and children).

Museo de la Alfabetización

This museum, dedicated to the literacy campaign of 1961, at the junction of Calle 31 and Avenida 100 in Marianao, 100 meters west of the Tropicana nightclub, occupies part of the Cuartel Colombia, the military compound where Batista initiated both his coups. The complex is now a school. Open weekdays 8 a.m.-5 p.m.; US$1. A tower outside the entrance is shaped like a syringe in honor of Carlos Finlay, the Cuban who in 1881 discovered the cause of yellow fever.

ACCOMMODATIONS

Havana is blessed with accommodations of every stripe. The motley and dowdy hostelries of a few years ago are being upstaged by the blossoming of deluxe and boutique hotels. Skyrocketing demand in recent years has fostered the arrival of name-brand hotels.

The Cuban hotel corporations all publish directories available through Cuban tourist offices abroad. You may need to double-check telephone numbers—they change frequently.

The nearest **camping** opportunities are in Playas del Este.

Where to Stay?

Too many hotels are vastly overpriced, so it pays to do your research. The closer you can stay to the main tourist sites, the better. **Habana Vieja** is in the midst of a hotel boom, with many colonial-era mansions and erstwhile

grande dame hotels coming online after splendid makeovers. They have the advantage of superb locations to add to their considerable charms. **Habaguanex,** Oficios #110, e/ Lamparilla y Amargura, tel. 33-8693, fax 33-8697, the state corporation that administers tourist commercial enterprises in Habana Vieja, is slated to open *16* hotels in Habana Vieja in the next few years, beginning with the **Hotel Ambos Mundos** (steeped in Hemingway associations). Keep your eyes out, too, for the reopening of another Hemingway favorite, **Sloppy Joe's,** as a bar and hotel.

Vedado's mid-20th-century offerings tend to be larger and less atmospheric but still well situated for sightseeing. The Hotel Habana Libre, Capri, and Presidente are examples. Here you'll be in the midst of Havana's re-energized night life.

Miramar has a number of hotels popular with

CHE GUEVARA

Ernesto "Che" Guevara was born into a leftist bourgeois family in Rosarío, Argentina, in 1928. He received a medical degree from the University of Buenos Aires in 1953. The footloose doctor then set out on an eight-month motorcycle odyssey through South America that had a profound influence on his radical thinking.

In 1954, he spent a brief period working as a volunteer doctor in Guatemala and was on hand when the Arbénz government was overthrown by a CIA-engineered coup. Guevara helped organize the leftist resistance (the experience left him intensely hostile to the US). He fled Guatemala and went to Mexico, where, in November 1995, he met Fidel Castro and, seeing in him the characteristics of a "great leader," joined the revolutionary cause.

The two had much in common. Guevara was a restless soul who, like Castro, was also daring and courted danger. They were both brilliant intellectuals (Guevara wrote poetry and philosophy and was probably the only true intellectual in Cuba's revolutionary leadership). Each had a relentless work ethic, selfless devotion, and an incorruptible character.

CHRISTOPHER P. BAKER

Although the handsome, pipe-smoking rebel was a severe asthmatic with an acute allergic reaction to mosquitoes, Che also turned out to be Castro's best field commander, eventually writing two books on guerrilla warfare that would become standard texts for Third World revolutionaries. He commanded the Third Front in the Sierra Escambray and led the attack that on 28 December 1958 captured Santa Clara and finally toppled the Batista regime. It was Che Guevara who took command of Havana's main military posts on New Year's Day 1959.

The two men were inseparable during the first years of the Revolution, when Guevara helped steer Castro down the leftist path.

Shaping the Cuban Revolution

The revolutionary regime declared Guevara a native Cuban citizen as an act of gratitude, rendering him legally entitled to hold office in Cuba. He became head of the National Bank of Cuba and Minister of Finance and, in 1961, Minister of Industry. (There is a joke in Cuba about how Che became treasurer of the Republic. At an early meeting of his cabinet, Castro asks who among them is an economist. Che raises his hand and he is sworn in as Minister of Finances. Afterwards, Castro says: "Che, I didn't know you were an economist." Che replies: "I'm not!" Fidel asks, "Then why did you raise your hand when I said I needed an economist?" "An *economist*! I thought you asked for a communist!" Guevara replies.)

Guevara was a "complete Marxist" (he had an obsessive hatred of bourgeois democracy) who despised the profit motive. He supervised the radical economic reforms that swept through Cuba and negotiated the trade deals with the Soviet Union and COMECON countries. However, Guevara was greatly at odds with Castro on fundamental issues. Castro's scheme to institutionalize the Revolution hand-in-hand with the Soviets, for example, ran counter to Guevara's beliefs (Guevara considered the Soviet Union as rapacious as the capitalists).

Although they were intellectual equals, in many ways Che Guevara and Fidel Castro were unmatched. Where Fidel was pragmatic, Che was ideological. Guevara was fair-minded toward Cubans critical of the Castro regime, for instance, unlike Fidel. Guevara gradually lost his usefulness to Fidel's revolution. His frankness eventually disqualified him, forcing him into suicidal exile.

Guevara left Cuba in early 1965. He renounced all his positions in the Cuban government as well as his honorary Cuban citizenship. Guevara apparently severed his ties with Cuba voluntarily, although the reasons have never been adequately explained.

Death and Eternal Glory

Che (the word is an affectionate Argentinian appellation, literally "you" but colloquially meaning "pal" or "buddy") fought briefly in the Congo with the Kinshasa rebels before returning briefly to Cuba. He reemerged in 1966 in Bolivia, where he unsuccessfully attempted to rouse the Bolivian peasantry to revolutionary passions. He was betrayed to the Bolivian Army Rangers by the peasants he had hoped to set free. He died on 9 October 1967, ambushed and executed near Vallegrande along with several other members of the Cuban Communist Party.

Castro has since built an entire cult of worship around Che. He has become an icon, exploited as a "symbol of the purest revolutionary virtue" and lionized for his glorious martyrdom and lofty ideals. Che Guevara became the official role model of the *hombre nuevo*, the New Man, the socialist being

who shuns material rewards and works for moral incentives and the common good. The motto *seremos como Che* ("we will be like Che") is the official slogan of the Young Pioneers, the nation's youth organization.

His image is everywhere, most notably the five-story metal "sculpture" adorning the façade of the Ministry of the Interior in Havana's Plaza de la Revolución. The photographer Korda shot the famous image that will live to eternity—"The Heroic Guerrilla." Guevara is wearing a windbreaker zippered to the neck always in his trademark black beret with five-point revolutionary star, his head tilted slightly, "his eyes burning just beyond the foreseeable future."

Che has been turned into a modern myth the world over. He became a hero to the New Left radicals of the 1960s for his persuasive and purist Marxist beliefs. He was convinced that revolution was the only remedy for Latin America's social inequities ("revolution cleanses men") and advocated peasant-based revolutionary movements. He believed in the perfectibility of man. The ultimate tribute perhaps came from the French philosopher Jean-Paul Sartre, who honored Guevara as "the most complete human being of our age."

tour groups, such as the Comodoro, Copacabana, and Kohly. Most are a considerable distance from sites and attractions.

Reservations

It may be wise to make an advance reservation for your first night, especially considering that many international flights arrive late at night. Currently, with tourism booming, many hotels are fully booked (including the less-expensive hotels that also cater to Cubans). The Christmas and New Year's season is particularly busy. Don't rely on mail to make reservations—it could take several months to confirm. Call direct, send a fax, or have a Cuban state tour agency or a tour operator abroad make your reservation. Normally, a deposit will not be required.

You'll be issued a **guest card** upon registering. You'll usually have to present this to the restaurant staff and, often, to the elevator guard. Any guest accompanying you to your room must have a separate guest card or be listed on yours, and there are now strictures against Cuban women entering hotel lobbies alone.

What Will It Cost?

Hotels are listed by price category: **Budget** US$10 or less; **Inexpensive** US$10-25; **Moderate** US$25-50; **Upscale** US$50-80; and **Deluxe** US$80+. (You can find some wonderful hotels in the "moderate" price range.) Each price category is divided by district: **Habana Vieja, Centro Habana, Vedado, Miramar,** and **Farther Afield.**

Prices were as accurate as possible at time of writing. Cuba imposes no room tax or service charge to guests' bills (this may change, however).

CASAS PARTICULARES

Since the legalization of private room rentals, *casas particulares* (literally, private houses) have sprouted like mushrooms on a damp log. Scores of families rent out rooms to earn a few extra bucks, and you'll have no difficulty finding a place. Some families even vacate their entire homes and go live with relatives for a while.

You should be able to locate a good *casa particular* for US$20-25. Many Habaneros are quick to recommend a particular place, but be aware that touts usually receive a commission. Since conditions vary remarkably, it's important not to agree to a rental arrangement until you've checked a place out.

In Vedado, you'll have the benefit of being in the vital heart of Havana, with a fistful of *paladares* at hand for dining. Vedado, being hilly, is breezy, too, which serves to keep mosquitoes at bay. I've rented four or five *casas particulares* and eventually settled on a splendid unit with a large, well-furnished bedroom, beautifully tiled bathroom with piping hot water, a secure garage for my motorcycle, and the company (whenever I chose) of a wonderful family—for US$25 daily. Contact Jorge Coalla Potts, Calle I #456, Apto. 11, e/ 21 y 23, tel. 32-9032.

Here are a few others to consider: in Habana Vieja, Aguacate #356, e/ Amargura y Lamparilla, tel. 63-7448 (Leonardo Mayor); and in Vedado, Calle B #83, tel. 30-2237 (Eladra Hernandez) and Calle B, e/ 21 y 23, tel. 35-550 (Renaldo González). (I'd like to hear more recommendations from readers.)

BUDGET AND INEXPENSIVE

There are few options for accommodations below US$25. There are a number of "inexpensive" hotels, however. Most serve a primarily Cuban clientele and tend to get full. They usually have two prices: a peso price for Cubans and a dollar price for foreigners. Plumbing tends to be quirky. Petty theft is also a potential problem (check for secure windows and door locks). Few supply bathroom amenities, and you may need to supply your own sink plug.

The following budget hotels, shown on some maps and listed in guidebooks, are closed: Hotel Bristol, Hotel Real, and Hotel Nueva Isla. They may reopen in due course for a Cuban clientele.

Habana Vieja

The best of the bunch is the **Hotel Isla de Cuba,** on Máximo Gómez on the south side of Parque de la Fraternidad, tel. 61-1501 or 62-1031. It is used almost entirely by Cubans and is usually full. Foreigners are accepted for US$11 s, US$14 d, US$18 t. The atmospheric colonial building is aged and gloomy but has antique charm. It is entered through massive 10-meter-tall mahogany doors. Its narrow, soaring atrium has balconies and is surrounded by 64 simple but adequate rooms (two with a/c, the rest with fans). Rooms have telephones and clean bathrooms (with cold water only). *Refresquerías* selling ice cream and sodas lie close at hand, on the corner of Máximo Gómez and Ciengfugos.

Alternately, consider the **Hotel New York,** on Dragones, one block west of Parque de la Fraternidad, tel. 62-7001. It has 75 rooms with ceiling fans, private bathrooms, and cold water (US$11 s, US$15 d, US$19 t); a small bar and restaurant in the lobby; and a popular patio bar and restaurant on the corner outside the hotel.

Centro Habana

The **Hotel Caribbean,** Paseo de Martí #164, on the corner of Colón and Prado, tel. 33-8233 or 62-2071, is a favorite of budget travelers. There's no sign on the hotel door. Look for the sign above the colonnade, which can only be seen from the opposite (east) side of the Prado. It has 40 undistinguished rooms (five with a/c) with TVs and telephones, utility furnishings, and small, dingy bathrooms with quirky plumbing. The top-floor rooms are better. Ask to see several rooms—they vary markedly. There's a coffee shop and tiny restaurant where you can eat for less than US$5. The hotel is overpriced at US$20 s, US$26 d.

Vedado

If you don't mind being a one-hour walk from things, consider the modest **Hotel Bruzón,** between Pozos Dulces and Boyeros, just north of the Plaza de la Revolución, tel. 70-3531. There's nothing particularly appealing about this 46-room hotel, but it will do in a pinch.

The Ministry of Education runs **Hotelito del M.E.S.,** otherwise known as Hotel Universitario, at Calle L y 17, tel. 32-5506, for Cuban and foreign teachers. Walk-in guests are also welcome, although you will probably need to arrange this through an organization such as UNEAC, the writers' union. There are separate dining rooms for Cubans and foreigners.

MODERATE

Habana Vieja

Want to rest your head where Ernest Hemingway found inspiration? Then try the **Hotel Ambos Mundos,** splendidly situated one block west of Plaza de Armas on Calle Obispo, e/ San Ignacio y Mercaderes, tel. 61-4860, fax 33-8697. The hotel, which originally opened in 1920, was scheduled to reopen in 1997 after a terminally long restoration, with 51 a/c rooms and four suites, each with cable TV and international telephone lines. Facilities will include a rooftop restaurant and solarium. Hemingway's room—511—is preserved in suspended animation.

You may be excused for having a flashback to the romantic *posadas* of Spain the moment you walk into **Hostal Valencia,** Oficios #53, e/ Obrapía y Lamparilla, tel. 62-3801, fax 33-8697. Appropriately, this quaint 12-room hotel is owned by a Spanish firm in partnership with the government. The recently restored 18th-century mansion (Casa de Sotolongo) exudes splendid charm, with its lobby—entered through a tall doorway—of hefty oak beams, Spanish tiles, magnificent wrought-iron chandeliers, hardwood colonial seats, and statuettes. The inner courtyard, surrounded by a lofty balcony, is a setting for live music and has a bar that teems with atmosphere and locals enjoying the US$1 beers. The 12 spacious rooms have cool marble floors but are furnished, alas, in modern utility style (US$25-33 s, US$40-44 d, US$57 suite). All have private bathrooms and TVs, telephones, refrigerators, and walls decorated with pretty ceramic plaques. Some have French doors that open onto the street. To the left as you enter is the splendid La Paella restaurant (reservations suggested). Recommended.

Centro Habana

The basic **Hotel Lido,** near the Prado, at Animas and Consulado, tel. 62-5231, is overpriced at US$21/26 s, US$28/35 d low/high season. The modest a/c rooms feature utility furniture, telephones, radios, and tiny balconies. The bathrooms are nicer than in the Hotel Caribbean but have cold water only. Safety boxes are available (use them—the Lido has a reputation for theft) and a bar serves snacks in the dreary lobby. The fifth-floor *azuela* (rooftop) bar has a view over Havana.

A better bet is the *Hotel Lincoln,* Galiano esq. Virtudes, tel. 61-7961. This modest, 139-room hotel is a restored Victorian property whose lobby boasts chandeliers and Louis XVI-style furnishings. It also has 16 suites. The a/c rooms are clean and pleasant and have radios and telephones (US$30 s, US$40 d, US$50 t). Facilities include the elegant Restaurant Colonial, a rooftop terrace bar, and an Asistur Tourist Information booth in the lobby. Both the Lido and Lincoln are favored by Cubans—who pay, of course, in pesos.

A third option—one favored by package-tour groups—is the **Hotel Deauville,** tel. 62-8051, a cement tower journalist Martha Gellhorn called "a postwar, prerevolutionary blight on the Malecón." True enough. Gellhorn "came to dote" on the hideous hotel, though I'm not sure why. It lies in limbo at the foot of Avenida Italia (Galiano), midway between Habana Vieja and Vedado. The 148 a/c rooms have TVs, radios, and telephones (US$38 s, US$50 d, US$60 t). Facilities include a rooftop swimming pool, with an Afro-Cuban cabaret and Haitian folkloric show for entertainment. The service is said to be good, and the views over the city are splendid.

Vedado

If you want to stay in the thick of Vedado, consider the **Hotel St. John's,** on Calle O one block south of La Rampa, tel. 32-9531 or 33-3740. Beyond the coldest lounge in the world, this soulless 14-story property has 96 a/c rooms, each with radio, telephone, and TV (US$25/32 s, US$33/43 d, US$45/54 t low/high season). A cabaret is offered in the Pico Blanco Room (Tues.-Sun.), plus there's a rooftop swimming pool, and a tourism bureau. (The 194-room **Hotel Vedado,** tel. 32-6596, at Calle O e/ 23 y 25, next to the St. John's and of a similar standard, closed for refurbishment in 1996.)

In a similar vein, try the modest 79-room **Hotel Colinas,** on Calle L, two blocks south of the Habana Libre, tel. 32-3535, US$30 s, US$40 d, US$50 t. The rooms are depressingly hokey.

The **Hotel Morro,** at Calles D and 3ra, tel. 32-5907, US$30 s, US$40 d, US$49 t, US$58 q high season, is an adequate yet overpriced property run by Turhoteles. Each of its 20 a/c rooms has a TV, telephone, and refrigerator, and a clean bathroom boasting two rarities: hair driers and plenty of towels. The hotel also offers laundry service. I didn't like either the basic utility furniture or the strange smell in the lobby. Alas, no views through the louvered windows with frosted glass. The small El Faro restaurant and Bar Arrecife are pleasant.

Miramar

Students will fit right in at the **Hostal Icemar,** Calle 16 e/ 1 y 3, tel. 33-0043, operated by MINET, the Ministry of Education, and mostly utilized by foreign students. However, anyone can check into this 1950s Miami-style hotel. It has 54 large a/c rooms with TV and hot water. Check out several rooms, and take one facing the sea; they have more light. Per person rates are US$25/28 s, US$18/21 d, and US$15/18 t low/high-season. It also offers a meal plan. You can also select an apartment across the road for US$80: they're huge (some sleep up to eight people) but rather gloomy and minimally furnished.

Two similar options are **Hotel Universitaria Ispaje,** at Avenida 1 and Calle 22, tel. 23-5370, eight rooms with private baths, US$25 s, US$35 d, including breakfast, and **Villa Universitaria Miramar,** at Calle 62 #508 esq. Avenida 5, tel. 32-1034, 25 rooms with private baths for US$15 s, US$18 d. There's a bar with pool table, popular with Cuban students and expats.

Farther Afield

Cubanacán runs the **Mariposa,** a faceless, uninspired hotel on the Autopista del Medidodía midway between the airport and downtown Havana, in Arroyo Arenas west of the Cubanacán district, tel. 33-6131 or 20-0345. It's handy for the Havana Convention Center but too far out to consider otherwise. The 50-room hotel has four junior suites, US$28 s, US$40 d, year-round.

UPSCALE

Habana Vieja

Wow. What a setting for the **Hotel Santa Isabel,** which was scheduled to open in early 1997 as a posh hostelry—perhaps in the deluxe category—recalling days of yore when it was *the* place to be. The splendid building, facing both westward onto Plaza de Armas and eastward onto the harbor, began life as lodging at the end of the 17th century. It later became a palace of the Countess of Santovenia and, in the second half of the 19th century, the Hotel Santa Isabel. The restored hotel will have 27 rooms (11 of them suites), plus an elegant restaurant, a lobby bar with a fountain, and a rooftop *mirador.* I anticipate Habaguanex will furnish it in period detail. Expect it to sell out.

Parque Central is the privileged location for two good options. The first is the atmospheric and well-run **Hotel Plaza,** Calle Agramonte #267, tel. 63-5730, built in 1909 in the grand old style. The small entrance lobby is quite stunning with its lofty ceiling supported by corinthian columns and festooned with plaster motifs, as if touched by the hand of Grinlin Gibbons. Two squawking parrots fly free in the lobby. A venerable marble stairway leads upstairs to the 186 lofty-ceilinged a/c rooms (18 suites) furnished with dark hardwood antiques and reproductions, TV (with US cable channels), radio, safe deposit box (US$5), and heaps of closet space. The sky-high ceilings help dissipate the heat. Although the rooms are kept spotlessly clean, some are rather gloomy, and rooms facing onto the street can be noisy. The gracious lobby bar is lit by day by four stained glass skylights, and by gilt chandeliers at night when a pianist hits the ivories. The Restaurant Real Plaza serves superior cuisine in a classically chic setting. To the left, tucked away, is another restaurant serving grim breakfasts and set buffet meals. The top (fifth) floor has a terrace restaurant offering views over the city. Service stops at 10 a.m. on the dot, and even the coffee and juice machines are promptly unplugged. The fifth-floor *azuela* has a gift store and a solarium with lounge chairs and a splendid eye-to-eye view of the top of the old Bacardi building. Rates are US$54/68 s, US$72/90 d, US$10 per extra person (low/high season), or US$103 for a suite, including breakfast

Nearby, on the west side of Parque Central, is the **Hotel Inglaterra,** Paseo del Prado #416, tel. 33-8993 or 62-7071, fax 33-8254, with its ornate wedding cake façade. It was a particular favorite of visitors in the 19th century, although travelers' accounts—such as those of Winston Churchill, who laid his head here in 1895—"reverberate with wails about the hard mattresses and the offhand service." The hotel has been named a National Monument. It was recently renovated and, despite recent price hikes (US$39/59 s, US$49/79 d low/high season), remains very popular with younger, independent travelers, for whom it is the unofficial meeting point in Havana. The extravagantly decorated lobby is loaded with atmosphere. Musical interludes emanate from the lobby bar and restaurant, cool havens of stained glass and patterned tiles that whisk you off to Morocco with their arabesque archways and mosaics of green, blue, and gold. Of the 83 a/c rooms, three have panoramic views from their balconies. Noise from the square can be a problem, especially in the early morning. All rooms have telephones, satellite TV, safe deposit boxes, hair driers, and mini-bars. Take time to sip a *mojito* at the rooftop **La Terraza** bar, where cabaret is performed at night. Alas, no swimming pool.

Hostal Conde de Villanueva is an intimate *bogeda*-style hotel for businesspeople and cigar-smokers—due to open in late 1997, which is also when the 150-room **Gran Hotel** is scheduled to open opposite the Capitolio, on the corner of Dragones and the Prado.

Vedado

The **Hotel Habana Riviera,** on the Malecón at the base of Paseo, tel. 30-4051, fax 33-3739, was the Mafia's last and most ambitious attempt to eclipse Las Vegas. Mobster Meyer Lansky owned the hotel but was registered as the kitchen manager to evade taxes (his 20th-floor suite, stripped of memorabilia, is available for US$200 a night). When opened in 1958 it was considered a marvel of modern design. It boasted an egg-shaped, gold-leafed casino and a nightclub whose opening was headlined by Ginger Rogers. The hotel recently underwent restoration to recapture its 1950s ambiance (*sans* casino). The idiosyncratic '50s lobby was replaced in 1995 with contemporary vogue and a pleasant cocktail lounge, although it still features acres of marble and plate glass. It is now operated by Gran Caribe. Alas, the spacious rooms (full of utility furniture, much banged about) still await a renovation worthy of the price. Rooms cost about US$50/60 s/d. The 20-story hotel boasts a large seawater pool, tour desk, boutique, modest restaurant (buffet breakfast costs US$9, buffet dinner costs US$15), coffee shop with excellent service (sandwiches, US$3, Spanish omelette, US$3.50), and the famous Palacio de Salsa nightclub. The hotel rents bicycles (US$3 first hour; US$1 each hour thereafter).

In central Vedado is the charmless **Hotel Capri,** Calle 21 y N, tel. 32-0511. The airy lobby is flooded with light from plate-glass windows, as are the 216 a/c rooms, which are dowdily furnished but have TVs and telephones (low-season rates are US$47/56 s, US$63/76 d, US$76/91 t, standard/"special"; suites cost US$82-151). The 18th-floor *azuela* swimming pool and La Terraza Florenta restaurant both offer spectacular views. The Capri was built by mobster Santo Traficante, Jr. Its gambling casino was, until 1959, run by George Raft, the mobster-movie actor. (A favorite hangout of the Mafia, the Capri was the setting for a scene in Mario Puzo's *The Godfather.*) When revolutionaries arrived on 1 January 1959 to destroy the gaming tables, Raft stood at the door and snarled, "You're not comin' in my casino!" The casino is long gone (it is now a drab dining room), but the hotel features a famous cabaret *espectáculo.* It has an Asistur and tourist information booth.

Farther out, at the foot of Avenida de los Presidentes, is the overpriced **Hotel Presidente,** tel. 32-7521, a tall, slender, art deco-style 1930s property with a maroon exterior and a carnal-red and pink interior lent jaded elegance by its sumptuous Louis XIV-style furnishings and Grecian urns and busts that rise from a beige marble floor. Massages are available (US$10 general; US$5 partial). The 144 a/c rooms, with radio, TV, and telephone, are more simply furnished. Rates run US$49-63 s, US$63-82 d in low season to US$60-77 s, US$78-101 in high season. Suites cost US$101.

Miramar

The **Hotel Kohly,** Avenida 49 esq. 36A, Reparto Kohly, tel. 22-4837, fax 33-1733, is a modest, fairly dreary '70s-style property popular with tour groups. Its out-of-the-way location offers no advantages. The a/c rooms are pleasant enough, nicely though modestly furnished, with spacious showers (US$50 s, US$62 d). The patio restaurant serves excellent rice and beans, pork or chicken, and brothy shallots for US$4. The main restaurant is less appealing. Facilities include a tour desk, car rental, and a bar popular with the local youth, who come for the live music and to play pool on the full-size pool tables and ten-pin bowling in the automated bowling alley.

Another favorite of tour groups is the **Hotel Comodoro,** Avenida 1ra and Calle 84, tel. 22-

5551, fax 33-2028, a Spanish joint venture at the west end of Miramar. If you stay here, expect to fork out plenty of *dinero* for taxi fares into town. It was originally built for the Cuban armed forces, was revamped, and is now a training "school" for apprentice Cuban hotel staff. It has 109 a/c rooms and 15 suites. The ugly 1960s-style exterior belies the appeal of the large a/c rooms, with pleasant modern furnishings plus TV and telephone. Safety boxes cost US$2 per day. It has a bathing area in a natural ocean pool protected by a pier, with its own little beach and spacious, elevated sun terrace shaded by almond trees. Heaps of facilities include a selection of bars and restaurants, and the famous Havana Club disco. There's a travel agency, clothes boutique, Red Cross clinic, and beauty salon. Scuba diving and jet skis are available. Rates are US$67/84 s, US$90/113 d, US$120/143 t, US$140/156 suite low/high season.

Hopefully the lengthy restoration of the **Hotels Neptuno/Triton,** Avenida 3ra y Calle 72, tel. 33-1483 or 33-1606, fax 33-0042, recently upgraded under the label of the Iberostar hotel group, will put some verve into the ugly twin-tower high-rise complex. The tennis courts and large pool and sun terrace with funky plastic furniture aren't particularly appealing, and this part of the rocky shoreline is ugly. Fortunately, the hotel redeems itself a little inside. It has 226 a/c rooms and six suites, all with satellite TV, telephone, radio, safe deposit box, and refrigerator. Rates are US$67/75 s, US$85/105 d, low/high season, US$70/80 s, US$90/110 d with ocean

view). Buffet breakfasts cost US$7, dinners and lunches a steep US$17 each.

Farther Afield
The **Cubanacán Biocaribe,** in Cubanacán at Calle 158 e/ 29 y 31, tel. 21-7141, fax 33-6123, predominantly serves the Havana Convention Center nearby. It's a rather faceless property but has an attractive pool and sundeck, and the 120 a/c rooms (including 15 suites) are pleasingly if modestly furnished. All rooms feature TV, radio, telephone, safe deposit box, and minibar (US$45 s, US$65 d). A full range of facilities includes car rental, tour desk, restaurant, tennis court, and beauty salon.

DELUXE

Habana Vieja
One peek inside the lobby of the **Hotel Sevilla,** Trocadero #55, tel. 33-8560, and it could be love at first sight. The landmark hotel—famous as the setting for Graham Greene's *Our Man in Havana* (Wormold stayed in room 501)—looks splendid after its makeover, with its filigreed balconies and a newly cleaned façade straight out of *1,001 Arabian Nights.* You enter via a lofty arched doorway of Gaudiesque proportions to what may strike you as a Moroccan medina. French louvered windows open fully so that the breeze blows freely, mingling with piped music and the sunlight pouring in through tinted *vitrales.* The hotel, on Trocadero, between the Prado and Zulueta, was built

Hotel Nacional

in 1924. Room rates are US$63/79 s, US$84/105 d, US$105/131 t, low/high season; suites cost US$126-158. The 188 rooms are disappointing despite the renovation—low on light and furnished with tacky, dated furniture. Each has safe, minibar, telephone, and satellite TV. The top-floor restaurant is a sumptuous gem. A tour and carrental desk are on site, as are a small swimming pool, four bars, beauty parlor, and shops.

At press time, the **Golden Tulip Parque Central,** c/o Golden Tulip, tel. 33-0411, fax 33-0413; in The Netherlands, Stationsstraat 2, P.O. Box 619, 1200 AP Hilversum, tel. 35-284588, fax 35-284681; in Canada, tel. (416) 601-0343, fax (416) 601-0346; in the UK, tel. (181) 770-0333, a joint venture of Cubanacán and the Dutch Golden Tulip hotel chain, was due to open in late 1997 at the top of the Prado and Agramonte (Zulueta), on the north side of Parque Central. It will have 200 rooms, a rooftop swimming pool and fitness center, a bar, restaurant, and meeting facilities.

A more intimate and resplendent option is the **Hotel Florida,** in a stunning colonial building—the Casa de Joaquín Gómez, built in 1835 for a wealthy merchant—at Calle Obispo #252 esq. Cuba, tel. 33-8693, fax 33-8697. The 35-room hotel will be opened sometime in late 1997 by Habaguanex. It will be aimed primarily at businesspeople, and you can bet it will be sumptuously furnished.

Vedado

The grandest of Havana's Old World-style hotels is the **Hotel Nacional,** on Calle O, off La Rampa, tel. 33-3564 or 89-2029, fax 33-5054. Luminaries from Winston Churchill and the Prince of Wales to Marlon Brando have laid their heads here. The property recently emerged from a thorough US$15 million restoration that revived the majesty of the 60-plus-year-old neoclassical gem perched haughtily on a cliff overlooking the Malecón with a postcard view of Havana harbor. The hotel was designed by the same architect who designed The Breakers in Palm Beach, which it closely resembles. It is entered via a long, palm-lined driveway. The vast vaulted lobby with mosaic floors boasts Arab-influenced tilework and lofty wood-beamed ceilings, Moorish arches, and extravagant nooks and crannies where whispered confidences were once offered. Most of the 448 a/c rooms (15 are suites) have ocean views. They are large and well-appointed,

with cable TV, telephone, safe, and self-service bar. There's even an Executive Floor, housing 63 specially appointed rooms and suites. Rates are US$125/155 s, US$152/190 d, US$340/420 suite (low/high season), including buffet breakfast. The **Comedor de Aguiar** restaurant serves good Cuban and continental dishes. In 1955, a casino and nightclub was opened and managed by the mobster Meyer Lansky. Today the club—**Le Parisien**—hosts one of the hottest cabarets in town. The top-floor cocktail lounge in the turrets offers a magical view (take the elevator to the eighth floor, then climb the 28 steps). There's a large swimming pool and a full range of facilities, including upscale boutiques, beauty salon, spa, tennis courts, and a tour desk.

Another favorite of business travelers is the small, utterly charming **Hotel Victoria,** splendidly located at Avenida 19 y Calle M, tel. 33-3510, fax 33-3109, a Victorian style, neoclassical building that began life in the 1920s as a small guesthouse. It has only 31 elegant a/c rooms refurbished with hardwoods and beautiful antique reproduction furnishings. I consider it a relative bargain at US$80 s, US$100 d, US$105-130 suite. Relaxation is offered in a small swimming pool and an intimate lobby bar. The elegant restaurant is one of Havana's finest.

The landmark high-rise **Hotel Habana Libre,** at Calles L y 23, tel. 33-4011, fax 33-3141, is synonymous with the heyday of Havana, although I question whether it is truly a "deluxe" hotel. It was built in the '50s by the Hilton chain and soon became a favorite of mobsters and high rollers. Castro set up his headquarters here in early January 1959. Until the recent tourist boom put pep into Havana's hotel scene, the Habana Libre was *the* place to be. It teemed with foreigners—many of them, reported *National Geographic,* "not strictly tourists . . . watched by secret police agents from the 'ministry,' meaning MININT, the Ministry of the Interior." You used to hear that the whole place was bugged. The good ol' bad ol' days are long gone, and it is now managed by the Spanish Tryp group, but the Habana Libre is still popular with foreigners and Cuban VIPs, especially during the annual Havana Film Festival. Prices are high (US$60/$65 s, US$90/$100 d, US$110/$140 t low/high season), the decor in many of the rooms is unimpressive, the plumbing remains capricious, and you can watch your fingernails grow while awaiting the elevators. Nevertheless, the hilltop location is splendid, and the hotel is loaded with facilities—an all-important Infotur desk, bank, airline offices, boutiques, post office and DHL office, international telephone exchange, full-service restaurant, and a patio bar under a futuristic 1950s-era skylight. A renovation was underway at press time.

The **Melía Cohiba,** at the base of Paseo e/ Calles 1 y 3, tel. 33-3636, fax 33-4550, is Havana's first hotel of international deluxe standard, bringing Havana squarely into the 21st century with its handsome postmodern European design and executive services. The 22-story, 462-room hotel—all shining glass and sharp corners—is now *the* hotel of choice for foreign businesspeople, who gather in the **El Relicario** bar. It opened in February 1995 and is run by the Spanish Grupo Sol hotel group. There's no Cuban ambience whatsover, except in the traditional cuisine of the **Abanico de Cristal** restaurant—one of four eateries in the hotel. The spacious lobby hints at the luxe within, with its marble, splendid artwork, and magnesium-bright lighting. The spacious and elegant rooms feature brass lamps, marble floors, Romanesque chairs with beautiful contemporary fabrics, a mellow color scheme of beige, gold, and rust, and mirrored walls behind the bed. The bathrooms are dazzling, with bright halogen lights and huge mirrors. Bidets and hair driers are standard, as are fluffy towels and piping hot water in torrents. There are three standards of suites. Facilities include two swimming pools, a gym, solarium, shopping center, a business center, four restaurants, five bars, and Havana's top disco—Aché. Rates begin at US$150 and run to US$400 for a suite.

Miramar

European tour groups favor the modern **Hotel Copacabana,** Avenida 1ra e/ Calles 34 y 36, tel. 33-1037 or 29-0600, fax 33-3846, whose oceanfront location catches the breezes. The hotel, more of an "upscale" hotel but with "deluxe" prices, was first opened in 1955 by a fervent admirer of Brazil. The atmosphere still has a Brazilian flavor and uses names from that country—the Itapoa steak house, the Do Port pizza and snack bar, the Caipirinha bar and grill. Not surprisingly, the place does a healthy trade with package groups from Brazil and Argentina. The 170 rooms boast hardwood fur-

nishings, floral bedspreads, small TVs, telephones, and safety boxes (US$75-81 s, US$100-108 d, US$27 per extra person). The Restaurant Tucano (prix-fixe meals cost US$15) looks out over the huge swimming pool—popular with Cuban day-visitors—and the ocean. A separate poolside bar serves ham and eggs (US$3), roast chicken (US$6.50), and grilled fish (US$7.50). Take care crossing the dangerously arched bridge over the pool. There's a discotheque, tourism bureau, car-rental office, and boutique. And scuba diving is offered, too.

Chateau Miramar, is a Cubanacán property next to the aquarium on Avenida 7ma at Calle 60, tel. 33-1915 or 33-1952. The five-story, 50-room hotel was recently refurbished. Rooms are neatly furnished. It has nine one-bedroom suites and a seaside pool. The sea spray reaches up to the top-floor windows.

VILLAS, APARTMENTS, AND *PROTOCOLOS*

Self-catering apartments are available for rent, as are fully staffed villas, including *protocolos*—special houses reserved for foreign dignitaries. Most of the *protocolos* are in splendid mansions in the Cubanacán region.

Habana Vieja

You can't go wrong at **Casa Scientifico** at Prado #212, e/ Calles Trocadero y Colón. This lofty-ceilinged old mansion—the old Casa José Miguel Gómez—is like a mini-Versailles, sumptuously adorned with rococo furnishings. Rooms with private bathroom cost about US$20.

Miramar

The **Villa Costa** on Avenida 1ra e/ Calles 34 y 36, just east of the Hotel Copacabana, tel. 29-2250, is a very handsome seafront villa with lots of louvered windows topped by *ventrales* filtering the sunlight into rainbow colors. Caged songbirds chirp and chatter, adding their musical tones. The rooms are simply furnished, though roomy and adequate (US$27, including breakfast). A bargain! You can also choose a nicely furnished a/c suite with a spacious bathroom (US$37). There's a nice lounge with a TV and VCR. It even has a small swimming pool and a sundeck of sorts overlooking the ocean.

The elegant little restaurant serves set meals for US$5.

The most appealing apartment-villas are the **Comodoro Apartments,** in an aesthetically striking Spanish-style village adjoining the Hotel Comodoro on Avenida 1ra and Calle 84, tel. 33-2703, fax 33-2028. Set amid lush foliage are 165 beautiful posada-style, two-story, one-, two-, and three-bedroom villas set around a massive amoeba-shaped swimming pool. Very atmospheric. Rooms have balconies or patios. A bargain at US$120-211 low season, US$150-264 high season, for up to four people.

Also try **Mir Azul,** on Avenida 5ta at Calle 36, tel. 33-0045, in Miramar. This pension (owned by the Ministry of Higher Education) has 10 rooms, a restaurant, pool table, and rooftop sauna. It's popular with expats in the know.

You can also rent attractive two-story waterfront **apartments and villas** in the Cubanacán Paraíso complex in Marina Hemingway, tel. 33-1150, fax 33-1149, US$170 high season. It has 39 houses and 39 bungalows, with one-, two-or three-bedrooms. All have terraces, TVs and video, safe-deposit boxes, and kitchens.

FOOD

Havana is an exception to Cuba's dismal restaurant scene. Even world-class restaurants are beginning to appear. Pierre Cardin, for example, has announced that a **Maxim's** restaurant will open here in 1997. Some are great values (El Aljibe comes to mind). Unfortunately, many restaurants would give the Japanese nasty cases of sticker shock and are also deplorably bad (Restaurante 1830, for example). Some of the best restaurants are in the top-class hotels, which usually have two or more eateries to choose from.

Havana's restaurant scene is in a constant state of flux. Many of the establishments listed below may have changed by the time you read this (so, too, their prices). When I last visited, little streetside snack bars (some pulled by tricycles) had sprouted up all over.

Miramar has some of the finest restaurants in Havana. Many good restaurants are also clustered around Calles M and N, between Calle Linea and La Rampa, in Vedado, where there's also a large crop of private restaurants.

There are great restaurants on the fringes of Havana, too. I particularly recommend Las Terrazas, in Cojímar; Las Ruinas, in Parque Lenin; and La Rueda, in El Chico.

BREAKFAST

Your choice is limited almost entirely to hotel restaurants, which tend to serve dreary buffets. Nonguests are usually welcome (US$4-10). The best buffet breakfast is served in the **Hotel Co-** hiba. Another good option is the **Café La Rampa,** occupying the terrace outside the Hotel Habana Libre, with views over La Rampa and Coppelia. It has a breakfast special of coffee and toast for US$2, with eggs, bacon, coffee, and juice for US$7.

Members of tour groups usually have breakfasts (and most dinners) included in the cost of their tour.

PESO EATERIES

You can find basic *criollo* dishes at pesos-only restaurants frequented by Cubans. Food availability tends to be hit and miss (usually only one or two items are available) and the cuisine undistinguished at best. In some, you may be refused service as a foreigner.

Habana Vieja

To commune with locals, head to **Prado 264** on the Prado at Calle Animas. You can eat a filling meal for 10 pesos (US50 cents). Also try **Casa de los Vinos,** at the corner of Esperanza and Factoria, five blocks south of Parque de la Fraternidad and five west of the railway station. This popular restaurant began life as a workers' canteen in 1911. Today, it is both a restaurant and a bar, popular with Habaneros. With luck, you'll find sausage and bean soup—two of its specialties—although it has fallen on hard times of late. The decor is highlighted by walls inlaid with tiles inscribed with love poems and proverbs.

Vedado

There are two basic pesos-only cafés popular with Cubans on Calle M, one block south of La Rampa: the modern **Marrakais**, serving snacks and sodas, and the streetside *cafetería* above the **Wakamba** nightclub of prerevolutionary fame. Also here is **Club 23**, a basement restaurant on La Rampa e/ O y N. Your best bet, though, are the two restaurants behind Coppelia on Calle 21 and those farther along Calle 23, particularly at the junction with Calle 12.

PALADARES

As everywhere in Cuba, the way to go is to eat at *paladares*, restaurants operated out of Cuban's homes. Vedado is the undisputed *paladar* capital, but you'll also find others scattered around town. Many are open 24 hours; some are closed or operate at restricted hours during the summer off-season. Your Cuban friends will be able to recommend their favorite *paladares*.

At press time, *paladares* were not allowed to sell shrimp or lobster (a state monopoly). Nonetheless, most do, so ask. Most accept pesos and dollars (the former at dollar equivalent), but in cash only.

Habana Vieja

Try *La Rejita Mayéa,* Calle Habana #405, e/ Obispo y Obrapía, tel. 62-6704. It has set meals—basic fare—for US$8. Open daily noon-11 p.m. A friend recommends **EL Rincón de Eleggua** on Calle Aguacate. Apparently it's renowned for its pastries. Also try **Las Tres Carabelas**, at Amargura #56, e/ San Ignacio y Mercaderes.

Vedado

My favorite is **Paladar Marpoly**, a superb restaurant in a colonial home at Calle K 154 (one block north of Linea). It's tricky to get to because of the one-way streets (refer to the map). By day, look for a house with rust-red pillars and a mural of Santa Barbara on the wall; at night, it has a neon sign. The creative menu includes a house special of seafood with pineapple and melted cheese served in a pineapple (US$11, with salad and side dishes). Open noon to midnight.

Another of my favorites is **Paladar El Amor,** on the third floor of an old mansion on Calle 23 e/ B y C, tel. 3-8150. The place is full of fading antiques—porcelain, bronze figurines, silver pieces, and even a grand piano. It's owned by Amor, a young pop singer, and run by the delightful members of her family. Try the superb *pescado agridulce* (battered fish pieces with a sweet-and-sour sauce) served with salad and boiled potatoes for US$4.50. You'll dine off real Wedgewood china. Nearby, in another mansion on Calle B e/ 21 y 23, is **Eddie's,** run by Eddy and his pal, well-known author Reynaldo González. The rooms are full of art.

Another favorite is **El Balcón del Edén,** near Coppelia, on Calle K e/ 19 y 21, tel. 32-9113. It has dining upstairs on an open balcony. Try the superb *marisco enchilada* in spicy tomato sauce (US$10, including accompanying dishes). Servings are plentiful. It's open 24 hours. By the time you read this, the owners may have opened a separate location at the corner of Calle L and Malecón.

For lunch, I frequently eat at **Restaurante Los Cactus,** on Calle 21 e/ Calle K y L, tel. 32-4965. You can dine inside the old mansion or on the breezy, shaded balcony fringed by cacti. It serves simple *criollo* dishes and mediocre pizza, but you can fill up for US$6, including beer. Open 10 a.m.-2 a.m. Catercorner to Los Cactus is **Bon Appetit,** another lunchtime favorite, with a simple menu featuring pizza and spaghetti (US$2). The grilled fish with *congrí* is excellent. A salad, main dish, ice cream, and beer should cost no more than US$5. On the same corner is *Restaurante El Aladino,* claiming to serve *comida árabe* but limited to *criollo* fare.

Also try **El Bistro,** facing the Malecón at the base of Calle K, tel. 32-2708. It's decorated with tasteful artwork and you can dine on a balcony. Ostensibly it serves French food; in reality, it's Cuban cuisine with a quasi-French twist, such as *filete Roquefort* (US$12).

A friend recommended **El Helecho,** at Calle 6 e/ Linea y Calle 11, and the *Festivál* at the corner of Calle D and 27.

Miramar

My favorite here is **Paladar La Fuente,** in an atmospheric old mansion with mezzanine terrace at Calle 10 #303, e/ Avenida 3ra y 5ta, tel. 29-2836. It specializes in superb fish dishes with cheese and ham, including *filete uruguayano* (US$6), but also has spaghettis and pasta (average: US$2). The portions are huge, the preparation is creative, and the food tasty and filling.

Nearby is **Restaurante Calle 10,** in a floodlit mansion on Calle 10, e/ 3ra y 5ta tel. 29-6702. The menu includes pizza (US$2), filete uruguayan (US$7), and fish with ham and cheese (US$5.50). Meals were so-so.

CRIOLLO (CUBAN)

Habana Vieja
A good place to have basic *criollo* dishes is the **Patio Colonial,** in a patio garden on the southeast corner of Plaza de las Armas, at Calles Obispo and Baratillo. Here, grilled chicken with rice, peas, and french fries costs US$4. It's centered on a wooden bar with an umbrella-like roof. It also serves pizzas. The clientele is mostly Cuban, though it charges in dollars.

Nearby, on Avenida de Bélgica (Egido), between Jesús María and Acosta, is **Puerto de Sagua,** tel. 63-6186, a humble yet pleasant restaurant designed on a nautical theme and also beloved of local Cubans.

A favorite of budget travelers is the **Colonial Restaurant,** on the ground floor of the Hotel Inglaterra. It has a wide-ranging menu of Cuban dishes, such as shrimp *en salsa roja* (US$11), *pollo asado* (US$4.50), and fried beef in creole sauce (US$5.25).

No visit to Cuba is complete without a meal at **La Bodeguita del Medio,** 207 Empedrado, one block west of Plaza de la Catedral, tel. 61-8442, a Havana legend favored by Ernest Hemingway. La Bodeguita was honored in 1992 with the "Best of the Best Five Star Diamond Award" by the North American Academy of Gastronomy. At the very least, call in for a *mojito* in the bar. The restaurant specializes in traditional Cuban dishes—most famously its roast pork, steeped black beans, flat-fried bananas, garlicky yucca, and sweet guava pudding—which are, as Nicolás Guillén (Cuba's national poet) once put it, "overflowing with surges of aged rum." You may have to wait for an hour or more to be seated. The service is relaxed to a fault, and the atmosphere bohemian and lively. *Soneros* (popular dance-music performers) and troubadors (poet-musicians) in guayabera shirts entertain. The food is generally fresher at lunch than at dinner, for which you'll pay US$10-20. Reservations are strongly advised.

Virtually every foreigner passing through the Plaza de la Catedral also plonks his or her derriere at the **Restaurante el Patio,** tel. 61-8504, fax 33-8697, if only to enjoy a refreshment in the El Portal patio bar. It's open 24 hours, and in addition to its bar and patio café it has four dining rooms (one a folkloric dining room purportedly specializing in Mexican cuisine). The patio bar serves snacks such as an El Patio sandwich (US$3.50), a hamburger (US$3), and steak palomilla with fries (US$2.75). Drinks are expensive. The main restaurant has three set menus and serves hideously expensive (US$16-28) dishes such as shrimp *al ajillo* (in garlic) and even T-bone steak. But it is well worth the price for the fabulous surroundings and the views over the plaza from upstairs.

La Zaragoza, Calle Monserrate e/ Obispo y Obrapía, tel. 63-1062, open 24 hours, is a dark and moody Spanish-style bodega serving criollo fare, *ceviche peruano* (US$2.50), tortillas (US$3), and pizzas from US$2. Take a sweater! Nearby is the **Castillo de Farnés,** also on Monserrate at #361, esq. Obrapía, tel. 63-1260. This Havana landmark has been famous since its founding as a Spanish restaurant in 1896 (Fidel Castro used to frequent it while a student; he ate here again with Che Guevara on 9 January 1959, following his triumphal entry to Havana).

Vedado
A safe bet is the **Restaurante El Barracón,** in the Hotel Habana Libre, tel. 33-3704. It serves acclaimed *criollo* dishes (especially pork dishes) in atmospheric surroundings, with entrées US$7-15; open noon-midnight. Setting higher standards is the hotel's top-floor **Sierra Maestra** restaurant, tel. 33-3704, offering splendid views over Havana. Food quality is acceptable at a reasonable price. The Barracón closed for renovation in late 1996.

El Conejito, Calle M #206, esq. Avenida 17, tel. 32-4671, is another splendid option, not least for its Old English or Teutonic ambience. A pianist plays while you dine on rabbit *(conejo)* served any of a dozen ways. Entrées average US$7. It also has fish and lobster dishes. Around the corner is the ritzy **Don Agamenón,** in an old mansion on Calle 17, e/ Calle K y L, tel. 33-4529. The neoclassical building has been done up in contemporary decor. It presents Cuban dishes with a flair (US$5-12) and has a special chicken plate for US$12.

Miramar

I find myself returning time and again to **El Aljibe,** Avenida 7ma e/ 24 y 26, tel. 33-1583, open noon-midnight, absolutely my favorite restaurant in Havana. This atmospheric charmer is run by Sergio and Pepe García Macías, former owners of the famous prerevolutionary Rancho Humo restaurant. You dine beneath a soaring bamboo roof. It's very popular with the Havana elite. The chicken *el aljibe* is standard, but far from ordinary—glazed and baked, with fried plantain chips, rice, french fries, and black beans served liberally until you can eat no more. Feel free to take away what may be left over. It's a bargain at US$12 (desserts and beverages cost extra). For dessert, try the flan, coconut pie, or chocolate cake. Check your bill carefully, however—the bread and salad side dish delivered to your table will be charged to your bill even if you didn't order it, and a 10% service charge is automatically billed. The service is prompt and ultra-efficient, so feel free to tip extra.

Next to El Aljibe, at Calle 26, is **Dos Gardenias,** tel. 33-2353, a restored colonial mansion with three restaurants. Downstairs, with its chilly a/c interior or outdoor patio is **Fonda Las Maravillas,** whose quasi-Spanish colonial decor hints at the *criollo* menu. You can enjoy a whole meal for US$4, including bread, salad, beer (or refresco) and main course of chicken, *aporreado de ternera,* or *picadillos à la criolla.* Soups and salads—a plate of cucumber—cost US$1. Dos Gardenias is open noon-midnight.

Suburbs

For views toward Havana—and splendid entertainment—head to **La Divina Pastora,** tel. 62-3886, at the berth for *El Galeón,* 200 meters east of the Morro, directly across the harbor from Castillo de la Real Fuerza. It's housed in a hacienda-style colonial structure and fronted by a battery of cannons. An Afro-Cuban dance troupe (both men and women are topless) performs for diners in the evening. Alas, the *criollo* food is undistinguished. Expect to pay upward of US$10 for a meal. Parking costs US$1. Behind the restaurant, on the harborfront, is a wonderful little bodega-type bar—*Bar la Tasca*—with a breezy balcony offering fabulous views over the harbor. It's a great place to sit on a hot day. It has lances and medieval armor on the walls. The simple menu includes lobster and seafood

dishes from US$8. Not many foreigners find this gem! It's open 12:30 a.m.-11 p.m.

Los Doces Apóstoles, tel. 63-8295, sits at the base of Morro Castle and is similar to La Divina Pastora, though smaller. Open noon-11 p.m.

A more expensive option is the **Ranchón,** in jungly surroundings at Avenida 19 y Calle 140 in Cubanacán, tel. 23-5838. It's acclaimed as one of Havana's best restaurants and serves traditional Cuban cooking, notably grilled fish and meats (the grilled pork chops are particularly good). It has good mixed salads. The food is well prepared and the portions are huge. Open noon-midnight.

INTERNATIONAL

Habana Vieja

Check out the huge, high-ceilinged, marble-floored **Roof Garden Restaurant** atop the Hotel Sevilla—not for the food, which is mediocre, but for the sublime decor. Tall French doors open to balconies overlooking the city. Kemal Kairus, a Lebanese Cuban, plays piano.

The **Restaurante Real Plaza,** on the ground floor of the Hotel Plaza, is very elegant, with gilt light fittings and marvelous high-backed modern chairs. Here I've enjoyed grilled fish for US$7.50.

Vedado

A good bargain is the classy **Restaurante Monseigneur,** opposite the entrance to the Hotel Nacional at the corner of Calle 21. Its elegant decor is aided by violin and piano music. The large menu is heavy with seafoods. Entrées are reasonably priced, with shrimp and lobster at US$12. If you have a few more bucks to spend, try the acclaimed **Comedor de Aguiar,** in the Hotel Nacional, tel. 33-3564. It serves international cuisine, highlighted by shrimp with rum flambé.

Another elegant, albeit expensive, option is the **Restaurante Hotel Victoria,** at Calles 19 and M. The place is conducive to romance, with lots of hardwoods and brass lamps and gilt place settings. The menu—with an extensive wine list—offers grilled lobster (US$22), roasted snapper (US$12), filet mignon (US$11), and spaghetti with seafood (US$4).

The soaring FOCSA Building, at Calle 17 e/ Calles M y N, boasts two acclaimed restaurants. **El Emperador,** tel. 32-4998, on the ground floor, is favored by VIPs. Expect to pay no less than

US$30 for a full-course meal. Reservations advised. The building also boasts the equally costly and overrated **La Torre,** tel. 32-5650, a rooftop restaurant with good views over the city and a separate bar (US$1 entrance). Both restaurants serve Continental cuisine, have lackluster service, and are open noon-midnight. They also have a dress code. You'll get better value elsewhere.

Touted as a dining highlight, **Restaurante 1830,** just east of the Almendares tunnel on Avenida 7ma (Calzada), tel. 3-9907, 3-4504, can be an expensive disappointment. This seaside restaurant is set in a 1920s mansion. You can choose any of four plush dining rooms with huge bay windows overlooking the ocean. Service is often slow and surly, and the food can be equally bad. Open noon-11 p.m. Skip it.

The **Polinesio** restaurant, in the Hotel Habana Libre, tel. 33-4011, has plenty of Tahitian-style ambience, and hints of the South Seas find their way subtly into the menu. The food is mediocre. A meal will run upward of US$20.

Miramar

Prepare yourself for sticker shock if you dine at **Tocororo,** housed in a neoclassical mansion on the corner of Calle 18 y Avenida 3ra, tel. 33-4530. This exquisite restaurant—an elitist luxury where ordinary Cubans can't even think of setting foot—is one of the best in Cuba, known as Gabriel García Márquez's favorite eatery (the Colombian novelist is known for his fondness for fine food). Diplomats and the international business community seem to agree. The lobby is a cross between a museum, an art gallery, and a middle-class Victorian parlor, full of rich treasures. Tocoroco extends out into a garden patio—a delightfully tropical and relaxed place to eat, replete with rattan furniture, Tiffany lamps, and heaps of potted plants, painted wooden toucans and parrots hanging from gilt perches, and real *cotorros* (parrots) in cages. A pianist entertains. The walls bear the signatures of the rich and famous. The food is typical Cuban fare with an international twist. Or is it international with a *criollo* twist? Try the grilled lamb chops and mixed seafood brochette and local favorites such as *frijoles.* But it ain't worth the price (watch for the 10% service charge). Open Mon.-Sat. noon-midnight (sometimes later).

A less-expensive option is **La Cecilia,** Avenida 5ta #11010, e/ 110 y 112, tel. 33-1562, 22-6700,

another elegant and romantic restored mansion in the middle of a large garden. Most of the tables are outdoors and lit by Tiffany lamps surrounded by bamboo. It serves typical Cuban dishes such as *tasajo* (jerked beef), *churrasco* (broiled steak), and *pollo con mojo* (chicken with onion and garlic), as well as grilled lobster. Entrées range US$10 and up. The place has a lengthy wine list at reasonable prices. Open noon-midnight (and Thurs.-Sun. 9:30 p.m.-3 a.m. for cabaret).

In a similar vein is **La Ferminia,** at Avenida 5ta #18207, e/ 182 y 184, tel. 21-0360. The ambience is splendid. The house is full of chandeliers and antiques. It has six private rooms, each in a separate color scheme (the pink room is full of Meissen porcelain). Anthuriums are everywhere. You can dine on an outside patio beneath a timbered roof. The menu includes soups (US$3), grilled chicken (US$8), and fish dishes (US$12); the house specialty is a mixed grill (US$28) with shrimp, lobster, fish, chicken, and scallops. (The chefs seem to have learned their vegetable preparation from the English— they boil the veggies to death.) Open noon-midnight. A soda water and Coca-Cola set me back US$4.

If you'd like to watch a fashion show, try the touristy **La Maison,** Avenida 7ma and Calle 16, tel. 33-1543 or 33-0126. It offers a series of packages that include dinner; the cheapest is US$25 without alcohol. Open Mon.-Sat. 7 p.m.-1 a.m

Suburbs

Las Ruinas, in Parque Lenin, tel. 44-3336, is well worth the drive, if only to admire the fabulous decor and setting. The modern building, which looks like something Frank Lloyd Wright might have conceived, was designed around the ruins of an old sugar mill and features stunning stained-glass panels by the Cuban artist Portocarrero. It is elegant, with linens, crystal, silverware, and classical urns full of flowers. It describes itself as serving international haute cuisine (a lobster bellevue is a specialty). The food has been described as both "reminiscent of school dinners" and "the best in Havana." Take your pick.

ASIAN

Cuba's erstwhile Chinese population has left its culinary legacy on the streets of Havana. A fistful of restaurants boast genuine Oriental decor, although the cuisine is usually disappointing.

Habana Vieja

In Habana Vieja, head first and foremost to **Torre de Marfil,** Mercaderes #121 e/ Oficios y Obrapía, tel. 62-3466, which has all the trappings: the Chinese lanterns, screens, and even a banquet table beneath a mock temple. It's staffed by desultory Chinese waiters, and even the food is authentically Chinese. The menu includes chop suey, chow mein, won ton (US$1.50), and lots of shrimp and lobster dishes. Entrées range US$5-15. It serves a set dinner for US$6.

There's another Chinese restaurant—**La Torre**—on the sidewalk along Tacón, west of the Castillo de Real Fuerza. Also consider **Restaurante Hanoi,** Calle Teniente Rey, e/ Brasil y Bernaza, tel. 63-1681, fax 33-8697, also known as La Casa de la Parre (Grapevine House), named for the luxuriant grapevine growing in the patio. The restaurant—a symbol of friendship with the people of Vietnam—is in one of the oldest houses in Havana. It has rattan furniture, Chinese lanterns, and lacquered wooden wall hangings inlaid with mother-of-pearl. Don't be fooled, however; the menu is more Cuban than Chinese.

Centro Habana

Restaurante Pacífico, on Calle San Nicolas in Barrio Chino, tel. 63-3243, boasts genuine Chinese furniture and Cantonese favorites such as lobster or shrimp chow mein (US$7) and lobster chop suey (US$7). There are restaurants on all five floors, though the main restaurant is on the third. More exclusive guests gather on the fifth (Fidel is an occasional visitor), where Ernest Hemingway used to eat.

Miramar

Your best bet is **Pavo Real,** a little corner of China on Avenida 7ma #205 e/ Calle 2 y 4, tel. 33-2315. Look for the huge Chinese neon sign outside. It also boasts Chinese decor, including stunning art deco stained-glass doors. It serves undistinguished Chinese classics such as chow mein dishes for US$7 and up, plus Japanese tempura (US$9 and up). Try the spring rolls. Open noon-midnight. A better bargain is the **Fonda China,** in Los Gardenias at Avenida 7ma and Calle 26. I recommend the chop suey

de camarones (US$8). Chopsticks—*parritas*—are available. Entrées are US$4-9, complete meals US$8-10.

Hankering for grilled eels, *kim ch'i, chu'sok,* and other Korean specialties? Then head to **El Morambón,** on Avenida 5ta and 32, tel. 23-3336. The cuisine is lackluster and overpriced, but you can eat it until 2 a.m.

OTHER ETHNIC FARE

Arabic

In Habana Vieja are at least two restaurants serving Arabic food. Aiming mostly at tourists is **Restaurante al Medina,** in the Casa de los Árabes on Calle Oficios, one block south of Plaza de Armas, tel. 63-0862. When I first called in, the menu was limited to standard *criollo* items such as fish and rice (US$3), salsa chicken (US$2.50), and vegetarian specialties for US$3. By my last visit, cous-cous and lamb dishes had been added.

You might fare better at the pesos-only **Restaurante Internacional Oasis,** in the Centro Cultural de Árabe on the Prado e/ Calles Refugio y Trocadero. Open 9 a.m.-midnight. Cabarets are hosted nightly (US$5).

Argentinian

Meat lovers might try **La Pampa,** in the Hotel Comodoro, on Avenida 3ra y Calle 84 in Miramar, tel. 33-2028, fax 33-1168. It specializes in Argentinian dishes such as *morcillas* (blood sausage) and *chinchulines* (grilled tripe stuffed with garlic).

Italian

In Vedado, check out the **Terraza Florentino,** the famous rooftop bar of the Hotel Capri. Miramar offers **La Torre del Mangia,** at Avenida 5ta e/ 40 y 42, tel. 33-2450 or 33-2372, perhaps Havana's best place to enjoy Italian food. Supposedly, the chefs were trained in Milan. It's true that their pasta dishes have been the best I've tasted in Cuba, but they remain undistinguished. Entrées cost US$5-15. Open noon-midnight.

Spanish and Mexican

My favorite Spanish restaurant is **La Paella** in the Hostal Valencia on Calle Oficios, one block south of Plaza de Armas in Habana Vieja. It serves various paellas—enough for two people—for

US$7. The *caldo* (soup) and bread is a meal in itself (US$3). You can also choose steak, grilled fish, and chicken dishes (US$4-10) and wash them down with Spanish wines (US$6-13). Try the excellent vegetable house soup. You'll dine beneath colonial chandeliers, surrounded by antique dark-wood furnishings, with large open windows to provide a cooling breeze.

Also in Habana Vieja, try modestly priced **La Tasca,** on the ground floor arcade of the Hotel Sevilla. Its decor replicates a Spanish bodega. The chef will whip up as good an omelette as you've ever had.

In Vedado, the restaurant in **La Chorrera,** the old fortress at the mouth of the Río Almendares at the west end of the Malecón, tel. 33-4504, also reportedly specializes in Spanish cuisine.

I've yet to discover a Mexican restaurant in Cuba serving anything resembling Mexican food. The closest I know is **La Giraldilla,** at Calle 272 e/ 37 y 51 in the La Coronela district of La Lisa, southwest of Havana, tel. 33-6062. It serves everything from tacos to chicken mole, washed down with sangría. Open 11 a.m.-9 p.m.

SEAFOOD

Many restaurants serve seafood dishes, but few specialize in the food of King Neptune. An exception is **La Casa del Escabeche,** at Calles Obiopo and Villegas. As its name suggests, it offers delicious *escovitch* (cube chunks of fish marinated with lime and salsa).

The other must-visit restaurant is **El Floridita,** Monserrate y Obispo, Habana Vieja, tel. 63-1063, the favorite watering hole of one of America's favorite drinkers—Ernest Hemingway—who immortalized the restaurant in *Islands in the Stream*. The restaurant still has a fin de siècle ambience, although today it is rather sterile, cleansed of the heady atmosphere of the days when Papa drank here (it has been called a "glitzy huckster joint" in *Travel & Leisure*). The menu is mostly overpriced seafood. In 1992, El Floridita received the "Best of the Best Five Star Diamond Award" by the North American Academy of Gastronomy. Most of the dishes, alas, are disappointing. The house special is *langosta mariposa* (lobster grilled with almonds, pineapple, and butter) chased with the "Papa special" (a daiquiri). Ex-

pect to pay up to US$60 for two with wine. And even your daiquiri will set you back US$4.

Sharing the same kitchen but serving meals at half the price is the elegant yet simpler **La Pina de Plata,** immediately behind La Floridita.

You should also travel out to Cojímar for a splendid seafood meal at Las Terrazas, a famous Hemingway favorite.

CAFÉS, PIZZERIAS, AND SNACK BARS

In 1995, the government announced plans for a chain of 30 KFC-style, dollars-only fast-food joints called **El Rápido.** At press time, at least a dozen had been completed, including a drive-in just off the Malecón in Vedado, where waitresses on roller skates will serve you fried chicken, fries, and burgers. The quality is fair.

There are dozens of snack bars and cafés throughout Havana. Most cafés double as snacks bars-cum-restaurants; there are few in the purist Parisian tradition.

Habana Vieja
Habana Vieja has several inexpensive places to eat snacks and basic *criollo* fare for US$2-5.

The **Pizzeria Parque Central,** immediately north of the Hotel Inglaterra, is literally a hole in the wall. At least you can pay in pesos. Quality varies.

Doña Isabel Cafetería, on Calle Tacón #4, esq. Empedrado, one block north of Plaza de Armas, tel. 63-3560, serves sandwiches, pizzas, and other snacks. Next door, in a similar vein, is **Don Giovanni,** tel. 63-8560 or 61-4445, a café in a beautiful colonial mansion. It mostly serves snacks but also has a choice of pizzas (US$4-8).

I like **Café O'Reilly,** on O'Reilly one block south of Plaza de la Catedral. It's a great place to relax over coffee and simple snacks (mostly tapas and tortillas) on the upstairs balcony, which looks down over Calle O'Reilly. It's also one of the few places serving cappuccinos (US$1.20) and espresso (US$1); try *café O'Reilly* (coffee with aguardente). Live bands often perform.

While exploring Plaza de Armas, you should call in at **Restaurante La Mina,** on Calle Obispo, tel. 62-0216. Adjoining **Café Mina,** facing onto the square, is the place to sip a cool beer or *mojito* (US$1.50) beneath shady umbrellas. It has good lemonades. Bands and troubadors perform alfresco. Next to it (part of the same complex) is the **Al Cappuccino** coffee house serving homemade pastries and custard for US$1. The **Restaurante Cubano** is at the back in the beautiful patio graced by columns and Tiffany lamps. It serves *criollo* dishes for US$4 and up.

The **Café Paris,** on the corner of Calles Obispo and San Ignacio, is a very lively social scene for both Cubans and tourists. You'll sit at rustic wooden furniture and look out through open trellised windows on life flowing down Obispo. Lively Latin music is usually playing from a jukebox. Fare includes fried chicken (US$2.50), hamburger (US$2), Spanish sausage with potato (US$2.50), and various sandwiches. Beers cost $1.

Another bar-cum-restaurant popular with Cubans is **La Lluvia del Oro,** at Obispo #316, on the corner of Calle Habana. La Lluvia is expressive of the rising bohemian life of the city and remains lively into the wee hours. It's a pleasure to sup at its antique wooden bar, chatting with locals and savoring the music. It serves snack food and pizzas.

Also try **Variedades Obispo,** a 60s-style hamburger joint at Calle Obispo #352.

Centro Habana
La Calesa Cafetería, on Calle San Rafael, is very popular with Cubans. You can sit in the open air beneath a shady canopy and watch the tide of shoppers flooding down San Rafael.

Vedado
The 24-hour **Cafetería Habana Libre,** in the hotel of that name, is sterile but is getting a total facelift and is scheduled to reopen in 1997 in a more pleasant guise. The **Café La Rampa,** outside the Habana Libre, is popular with Cubans and tourists alike.

Miramar
The **El Tucano** snack bar in the Hotel Copacabana has a buffet lunch for US$15. It's nothing to write home about. However, their pizzas (average US$5) are the best I've had in Havana. Try the vegetarian pizza.

ICE CREAM AND DESSERTS

What would Havana be without Coppelia? Cubans are renowned lovers of ice cream, and

farmers' market

there are plenty of *heladerías* to appease lickers' lust. You can buy ice creams for dollars in most tourist hotels, but it's far better to do as Cubans do and appease the heat by buying from *heladerías* on the street.

The granddaddy of 'em all is **Coppelia,** in Coppelia Park in Vedado (catercorner to the Hotel Habana Libre), which serves huge bowls of tasty, rich ice cream which, even last century, traveler Albert Norton "thought especially fine." It's also sold for a pittance. Note, however, that the dollars-only section for tourists has been closed and you *may* be refused service at the other sections when you eventually take your seat after a 20-minute to one-hour wait in line.

Helado Tropical has small outlets throughout Havana, including at Calle Obispo #467, on the corner of Habana (and also on Calle 23, opposite Coppelia). Their ice cream is slushy and nowhere near the quality of Coppelia. Nonetheless, they have the advantage of offering speedy service without lines.

In Habana Vieja, you'll also find *heladerías* on Calle Oficios, attached to Café La Mina; and, in Centro Habana, the **Arlequin Cremeria** on Calle San Rafael, e/ Amistad y Industria.

In Miramar, you can buy delicious pastries, loaves, and iced cakes at **Nonaneli Pandería Dulcería,** a bakery in the Quinta y 42 complex at Avenida 5ta and Calle 42.

OTHER DINING OPTIONS

Meals at Sea

You can even enjoy lunch or dinner aboard **El Galeón,** the replica 18th-century galleon that sails from its berth below Morro Castle (the luncheon cruise costs US$25 and runs 10 a.m.-4 p.m.; the dinner cruise costs US$35 and runs 8:30-11 p.m.). Your hotel tour desk can make reservations; otherwise, call 33-8600, fax 33-8536.

Farmers' Markets

Buying food for yourself, or as a gift to Cuban friends? Then head to the lively markets called **mercados agropecuarios** (farmers' markets), where Cubans sell produce and livestock on the free market. Most take pesos only.

The largest—and most colorful—is **Cuatro Caminos,** in an old Mercado building at Manglar and Cristina (also called Avenida de la Mexico). You may not want to buy a pig strung up alive, or live ducks and chickens trussed on a pole, but if these—or herbs, vegetables, and fresh fruit or fish catch your fancy, you're sure to find it here. Watch for pickpockets.

Other free markets can be found on Avenida de la Bélgica (Egido) between Apodada and Corrales, in Habana Vieja; and in Vedado on Calle 19 e/ A y B, one block east of Paseo.

ENTERTAINMENT

Don't believe anything you've read about communism having killed Cuba's capital city's zest. Habaneros love to paint the town red (so to speak). You can still find as much partying as party line in Havana—a city of spontaneity and the undisputed cultural epicenter of the Caribbean.

At night, the pace quickens and nightclubs pulsate with Latin spirit. The bar scene is dull, but nowhere else in the Caribbean has as many discothèques, cinemas, and cabarets to choose from. Sure, the city has lost the Barbary Coast spirit of prerevolutionary days, when, according to Graham Greene, "three pornographic films were shown nightly between nude dances" in the Shanghai Theater. Many of the famous clubs from the "sordid era," which ended in the 1950s, remain in name, their neon signs reminders of what was. Most are more seedy in decay—albeit without the strippers—than they were three decades ago, and often made more surreal by '50s-era South Seas decor, such as at the Wakamba Club, depicted in the movie *Soy Cuba!* The sauciness of the louche Havana of old keeps peeping through, however.

More cultured entertainment is present aplenty. During the mid-1980s, Cuba was a rest-and-relaxation capital for the Latin Left. (Havana is still popular with South Americans, who flock for the Latin American Film Festival, Havana

Jazz Festival, and other world-class annual cultural extravaganzas, or to polish their reputations as lovers.) Ballet is much appreciated by Habaneros. The only fault to be found is the quality of Cuban theater.

The city is relatively devoid of the kind of lively sidewalk bars that make Rio de Janeiro or Miami hum. You'll find plenty of rather grim local bars and *centros nocturnos,* open-air discotheques, often with laser light shows, serving local populations.

Most hotel bars and sidewalk cafés have live music, everything from salsa bands to folkoric trios. Romantic crooners are a staple, wooing the local crowd. And you can still find traditional ballad-style *trova* (love songs rendered with the aid of guitar and drum), often blended with revolutionary themes.

The weekly tourist newspaper *Cartelera,* available in hotel lobbies, publishes information on exhibitions, galleries, and performances.

FESTIVALS AND EVENTS

Daily Events

Be sure to attend the **Ceremonia del Cañonazo** (Cannon Ceremony), held nightly at 9 p.m. at the Castillo de San Carlos de la Cabaña, when troops dressed in 18th-century military garb, maintaining a tradition going back centuries, light the fuse of a cannon to announce the closing of the city gates.

You can book excursion tours from any hotel tour desk. Several tour agencies combine an excursion to witness the *cañonazo* with dinner and a cabaret show. Rumbos, for example, features dinner at Restaurant 1830, followed by the Cabaret Parisién in the Hotel Nacional. The tour departs leading hotels Friday through Wednesday at 6:30 p.m. Rumbos also offers a cannon-and-cabaret tour *without* dinner nightly except Thursday at 10 p.m. (US$37, including a bottle of rum). **Tropical Travel Agency** has a five-hour excursion that includes a visit to the Cannon Ceremony plus the Cabaret Parisién (US$37).

Annual Festivals and Events

The star-studded annual **International Havana Jazz Festival** is held in mid-February, highlighted by the greats of Cuban jazz, such as Chucho Valdés and Irakere, Los Van Van, Juan Formell, Silvo Rodríguez, and Grupo Perspectiva. Concerts are held at the Palacio de Salsa in the Hotel Riviera, the Casa de Cultura de Plaza (an open-air courtyard with bleacher seating at Calle 7ra esq. 8, in Vedado), and at José Echeverria Stadium, which hosts the All Stars Concert. You can buy tickets in pesos at the Casa de Cultura. Pre-arranged group tours to the festival are offered through **Caribbean Music & Dance Programs,** 1611 Telegraph Ave., Suite 808, Oakland, CA 94612, tel. (510) 444-7173, e-mail caribmusic@igc.apc.org. **Wings of the World Travel,** 1636 3rd Ave. #232, New York, NY 10128, tel. (800) 465-8687, also offers an annual weeklong tour (US$2,195) to the festival. Both programs include jazz workshops and reserved seating at jazz concerts.

In mid-February 1996, thousands of Habaneros celebrated the rebirth of their beloved **Carnival in Havana,** which seems designed to transmit Cubans from reality to fantasy. For an entire week, the Malecón becomes a stage for the island's hottest folkloric, salsa, and jazz groups. Tourists throw inhibitions to the wind and join local residents in colorful pre-Lenten revelry. The party mood is highlighted by outdoor concerts, street fairs, conga lines, and colorful parades. You'll find it impossible not to be caught up in the infectious rhythms. While many folks go lavishly gowned, others ecstatically flaunt their freedom, having cast off customary controls

along with most of their clothing. **Caribbean Music & Dance Programs** (see above) offers seven-day group study programs to Carnival in Havana! (US$1,275, US$1,475 including travel from Mexico or Bahamas).

Literati and bookworms should time their visit to coincide with the **Havana Book Fair,** also held in February, organized by the Cuban Book Institute and the Cuban Book Chamber. For information, contact either the Center for Cuban Studies, 124 West 23rd St., New York, NY 10011, tel. (212) 242-0559, fax (212) 242-1937, or Cámara Cubana del Libro, Feria Internacional del Libro Habana, Calle 15 #604, Vedado, Havana, Cuba, tel. 32-9526, fax 33-8212.

When 1 May rolls around, be sure to head to the Plaza de la Revolución for the **May Day Parade.** Ever been surrounded by one million people waving colorful banners and placards? The feeling is awesome as loyal Habaneros make their way to the plaza to witness the military parade and to hear Fidel Castro and other leaders honor socialism and the workers. Scores of buses bring workers and children in from surrounding regions, and the streets all around are thronged.

In the field of art shows, each May the city hosts the prestigious **Havana Biennale,** hosted by the Wilfredo Lam Center, Calles Oficios y Acosta, Habana Vieja, tel. 61-7008. The show features artists from more than 50 countries around the world (30 artists from the United States were represented in 1995). The show is hosted in almost two dozen venues throughout Habana Vieja. Practical workshops in printmaking and other disciplines are offered, as well as soirées and other activities.

At the **International Festival of New Latin-American Cinema,** a star-spangled guest list is no longer wined and dined at the Cuban State's expense, as in days of yore. And the all-night parties with top Cuban performers for which the festival had earned fame were replaced in 1994 by more sober conversations. But the festival, held in mid-December, is still one of Cuba's most glittering events. Fidel is usually on hand, and famous Hollywood figures gather to schmooze in hotel lobbies. The quality of movies—shown at cinemas across the city—includes films from throughout the Americas and Europe. For further information, contact the Instituto de Cinematografía in Havana, tel. 33-4634, fax 33-3281, or the Center for Cuban Studies, tel. (212) 242-0559.

Every 17 December, devotees of San Lázaro, the "leper of the miracles," make their way to El Rincón, southwest of the city on the outskirts of Santiago de las Vegas. Many of the pilgrims drag stones or crawl on their knees to give thanks to the saint—also known, in *santería,* as Babalú Ayé—for miracles that they believe he granted.

Other annual events include the **Caribbean Cultural Festival** held each June and July. The festival includes dance performances, seminars, films, theater, and art exhibits on Caribbean themes, usually with a distinct focus each year. The Center for Cuban Studies (see above) offers study tours to the festival.

FOLK MUSIC AND DANCE

The capital city fairly vibrates to the pounding of the bongo drum and the strumming of guitars. Many hotels host tourlsty shows on specific days of the week, while virtually any bar worth its salt will feature at least one musician singing *"Guan-tan-a-mera!"*

The **Casa de la Trova,** at San Lazaro #661, in Centro Habana, is especially active on weekends. So, too, the **Casa de 10 Octubre,** at Calzada de Luyanó and Calle Reforma, in the Luyanó district, south of Habana Vieja.

Each district also has its own **Casa de la Cultura,** where traditional music and dance can be heard. One of the more active is that in Habana Vieja at Aguilar #509 esq. Teniente Rey (also called Brasil). Among the regular performances are Afro-Cuban rumba by Grupo Saranbanda on Tuesday (free) and folk music on Friday. The performances, which begin at 8 p.m., are given in the courtyard of the Iglesia San Agustín, where every Saturday at 3 p.m. the Compañia "JJ" Túrarte also performs rumba and popular music and dance. Fantastic—Cuban entertainment at its best. You'll probably be the only tourists there to watch the mulatta dancers dressed in daffodil yellows, flamboyant reds, and morning-sky blues, whirling and shaking to the rhythms of a band dressed in magenta shirts and white shade hats. Entrance costs US$1.

Traditional Afro-Cuban dance is also the focus of **Sábado de Rumba,** held each Saturday afternoon, beginning about 2 p.m., in the inner courtyard of the **Conjunto Folclórico Nacional,** tel. 31-3467, on Calle 4, e/ Calzada y Linea in Vedado. Entrance costs US$1. The **Casa de África,** tel. 61-2472, at Calles Obrapía and Mercaderes also hosts Afro-Cuban performances.

La Divina Pastora restaurant hosts a touristy Afro-Cuban show for diners, famous for being the only topless display in Cuba. Also check out the **Riviera Azúl,** in the Hotel Deauville, on the Malecón and Galiano. The Afro-Cuban folkloric group Oni Ire performs on Friday at 10 p.m., preceding the disco. Entrance costs US$5.

Each Monday and Friday night, Dulce María, an intoxicatingly warmhearted woman singer and songwriter, hosts a soirée called **Encounter With Cuban Music,** at 78 Calle San Ignacio, tel. 61-0412. Climbing a rickety staircase to the very top of the dilapidated three-story building, you emerge on a rooftop of her apartment overlooking the Plaza de la Catedral. Hands are extended. You are hugged warmly by Cubans you do not know. Dulce's band, Son de Cuba, gears up with a rumba. The rhythms of the marimbas, bongos, and a guitar called a *tres* pulse across the rooftops of Habana Vieja. Rum and beer are passed around, and soon you are clapping and laughing while Dulce belts out traditional Cuban compositions, her hips swaying to the narcotic beat. The ice is broken. The infectious beat lures you to dance. It is like the plague—you can only flee or succumb. Each song is introduced by Alicia Pineda, a charming lady who tells of the history and meaning behind the song. The US$5 entrance fee includes a souvenir and beer, but you should also contribute a bottle of rum.

Also check out the Union of Writers and Artists (UNEAC) open-air social club—**El Hurón Azul**—at Calles 17 and H, in Vedado, where *boleros* (ballads) are performed on Saturday night (US$3). It's a great place to meet Cuban intellectuals.

CABARETS

Cabarets are a staple feature of entertainment in Havana for tourists but also for Cubans, who seem to love showy spectacles. However, the term as used by Cubans generally refers to a discotheque. *Cabaret espectáculos* refer to cabarets that feature Las Vegas-style song-and-dance routines. Most of the larger hotels have *espectáculos.* Several tour agencies offer visits to a cabaret in association with the cannon ceremony (see above). You can also book ex-

THE TROPICANA NIGHTCLUB

The Tropicana nightclub, Calle 72 e/ 41 y 45, Marianao, Havana, tel. 20-7507, fax 33-0109, is a *must*. The prerevolutionary extravaganza now in its sixth decade of Vegas paganism—girls! girls! girls!—has been in continuous operation since New Year's Eve 1939, when it opened as the most flamboyant nightclub in the world. The casino has gone, but otherwise neither the Revolution nor the recent economic crisis have ruffled the feathers of Cuba's most spectacular show.

CHRISTOPHER P. BAKER

heat and light at the Tropicana

The "paradise under the stars," which takes place in the open air, begins with the "Dance of the Chandeliers," when a troupe of near-naked showgirls parades down the aisles wearing glowing chandeliers atop their heads. The rest of the show consists of creative song and dance routines and a never-ending parade of tall beauties sashaying and shaking in sequined bikinis, ruffled frills, sensational headdresses, and feathers more ostentatious than peacocks'.

The more than 200 performers are hand-picked from the crème-de-la-crème of Cuba's dancers and singers.

Cubans shake their heads at the concept that this is "sexist." The Tropicana is a favorite venue for Cuban families and couples, who pay 70 pesos entrance or from 232 pesos for a full package including meal and bottle of rum.

The show, enhanced by a fabulous orchestra, takes place in the Salón Bajo Las Estrellas Tues.-Sun. at 9 p.m. (a second, less exuberant show starts at midnight). Entrance costs US$35-55, including a Cuba libre, depending on seating zone (the most expensive is closest to the stage). You're charged US$5 for cameras; US$15 for videos. Cocktails cost US$3. Patrons supposedly get their money back if it rains (if the rains are intermittent, the show merely takes a break, then resumes). You can purchase tickets at the reservation booth 1-8 p.m., but it's best to book in advance through your hotel tour desk or Havanatur, as the show is often sold out (US$40-60 including transfers).

Tropicana also features a discotheque—Arcos de Cristal—until 5 a.m., plus the Bar Restaurante Los Járdines, which remains open until 6 a.m., and Bar Restaurante La Fuente, serving creole cuisine 6 p.m.-midnight (sandwiches cost US$3 and up, a seafood cocktail is US$8, and a bottle of rum will set you back a whopping US$30 or more).

cursions to the cabarets through agencies such as **Tropical Travel Agency,** which charges US$27 for a visit to the Cabaret Parisién. You may need to reserve seats on weekends. Cabarets are usually followed by discos.

The shining star in the cabaret constellation is the **Tropicana.** Every visitor to Cuba should head here once for a jaw-dropping treat.

The most lavish alternative is the **Cabaret Parisién,** in the Hotel Nacional, tel. 7-8980 or 33-3564. Shows are offered Fri.-Wed. 9 p.m.-2:30 a.m. Entrance costs US$20. Although the show ostensibly starts at 9 p.m., you first have to sit through a tedious musical trio; the real show doesn't start until about 10:30 p.m. The wait is worthwhile—the two-hour show is excellent.

Slightly cheaper, but still exotic, is the **Cabaret Capri,** tel. 33-3571, in the **Salon Rojo,** tel. 33-3571, in Vedado's Hotel Capri at N y 21, nightly except Monday at 10 p.m. Another excellent option is the **Cabaret Caribe** (Tues.-Sun. 9 p.m.-2 a.m.), in the Hotel Habana Libre, where the high-kicking showgirls are joined by a gifted magician and a top-notch acrobatic show. It's worth every cent of the US$5 entrance. The cabaret is followed by a disco at 11 p.m., when the place suddenly fills up with Cubans. Also consider the small cabaret in the **Copa Room** (Hotel Riviera, 1ra y Malecón, tel. 32-0511).

Habaneros without dollars to throw around get their cabaret kicks at **El Colmao,** on Calle Aramburu between San José and San Rafael in Centro Habana. The traditional floor show is highlighted by Spanish flamenco. Open 8 p.m.-2 a.m. Cubans pay in pesos but you may be required to pay in dollars. Also check out **Cabaret Las Vegas,** at Infanta, e/ Calles 25 y 27, with a show at 10 p.m. followed by disco (US$5 per couple). Many discos also have cabaret, such as **Club 1830,** which hosts its flurry of flesh and feathers at midnight. Entrance costs US$5.

Aqua Espectáculos

Swimming-pool *espectáculos* are gaining popularity. Choreographed water ballets with son et lumière are on offer at several leading hotels including the Hotel Capri (each Saturday at 10 p.m.), the Hotel Cohiba, and the Hotel Nacional, which offers *Swan Lake* nightly at 9:30 p.m.

DISCOTHEQUES AND NIGHTCLUBS

There's no shortage of discos in dance-crazy Havana. The "best" are money-milking machines serving well-heeled foreigners but also popular with Cubans. Male foreigners can expect to be solicited outside the entrance to these dollars-only discos: Cuban women flood the lobby of the Hotel Riviera, hoping for admission to the Palacio de la Salsa, or take a stranger's arm outside the Club Habana and beg to be escorted in *("por favor!"),* because it costs 10 dollars.

Most of the hotel discos are open 10 p.m.-5 a.m. There's little point in arriving before midnight, when things get going. The best discos go on until well after dawn. Most discos usually play a mix of Latin, techno, and world-beat music. Drinks in the touristy discos can give you sticker shock. The best bet is usually to buy a bottle of rum—but expect to fork out at least US$20 for a bottle!

Don't worry about getting back to your hotel in the wee hours. There are always taxis hovering outside the entrances of the best discos, and freelancers are on hand to run you home for a negotiable fare.

Top of the Pops

If you have money to blow, the classiest disco by far is **Aché,** beside the Hotel Cohiba at the bottom of Paseo in Vedado. It opens at 10 p.m. Professional dancers keep patrons amused until the crowds arrive around midnight. The plush decor is highlighted by a laser light show. Entrance is a steep US$15.

Another elegant option is **Club Habana,** beside the Hotel Comodoro on Avenida 1ra and Calle 84 at the west end of Miramar, tel. 33-2703. Ostensibly it's open 10 p.m.-5 a.m., but it stays open later. Entrance costs US$10. Drinks are outrageously priced (Cokes and beers cost US$5; fruit juices cost US$7; a Cuba libre will set you back US$10). Like the Aché, it attracts a chic in-crowd—mostly a blend of Cubans, Mexicans, and other Latins—who bop to yesterdecade's Abba tunes and MOR pop hits (with a hint of salsa) at top volume.

The **Palacio de Salsa,** tel. 33-4051, in the Hotel Havana Riviera specializes in the Latin beat and often features the top names in live Cuban music. "To walk through the strobe-lit darkness of the disco is to inhabit several simultaneous decades of hand-me-down Hollywood," wrote Lynn Darling in *Esquire.* Nonetheless, this is the place for serious salsa fans. Entrance costs US$10 (half-price on Wednesday)

The **Ipanema,** tel. 29-0601, at the Hotel Copacabana, plays mostly techno music (or it did when I was last there). The clientele is mostly Cuban, and the atmosphere subdued. Entrance costs US$5, but a bottle of rum will set you back a whopping US$33! Also try the **Pico Blanco,** on the top floor of the Hotel St. John's on Calle 0 (US$3). It has salsa on Monday and rumba on weekend afternoons.

For a more laid-back ambience, I recommend the **Club 1830,** on an oceanside terrace behind the Restaurante 1830 (walkways lead through a grotto that includes a Chinese-style pagoda and a mosque-like structure). The disco, which is very popular on weekends, includes a fashion show and undistinguished cabaret *espectáculo.*

Entrance costs US$5. The place doesn't start jumping until well past midnight.

Other spots to consider include **Club Turquino,** on the 25th floor of the Hotel Habana Libre (US$10); **Papa's,** tel. 33-1150, way out west at Marina Hemingway, on Avenida 5ta at Calle 248; and the **Salón Caribe,** tel. 33-4011, in the Hotel Habana Libre (open Wed.-Mon. 9 p.m.-4 a.m.). **La Cecilia,** tel. 33-1562, on Avenida 5ta y 110, in Miramar, also hosts salsa and other music and dance after the restaurant closes (Thurs.-Sun. 9:30 p.m.-2 a.m.).

Jiving with Locals

Cubans without dollars find their fun at such spots as **Juventud 2000 Discoclub,** tel. 30-0720, in the Karl Marx Theater Complex at Avenida 1ra y 10, in Miramar (open Friday, Saturday, and Sunday 9 p.m.-2 a.m.), or the open-air amphitheater on the Malecón, 200 meters west of the Melía Cohiba. This popular spot gets thronged with a mostly black crowd. There is usually a heavy police presence due to the often frequent fights.

Other discos include **La Pampa,** opposite the Torreon de San Lázaro at the Malecón and Vapor (nightly except Monday; US$1, including cabaret); **Palermo,** at San Miguel y Amistad (nightly except Wednesday); and **Club 21,** opposite the Hotel Capri at Calles 21 and N.

Cuban rock fans head to **Patio de María,** on Calle 37 and Paseo, near the Teatro Nacional, where the disco combines Latin sounds with rock on Friday and Saturday nights. Rock concerts are hosted on Sunday evenings.

The tiny **Las Bulerias,** on Calle L opposite the Hotel Habana Libre is a smoky, moody place that's popular mostly with black Cubanas (there are few Cuban males). It doesn't get in the groove until about 11 p.m. Entrance costs US$3; beers are US$1.

Into tango? Check to see if **El Pampero** (also called the Rincón de Tango) has reopened. This club, in the basement of the Hotel Bruzón on Avenida Rancho Boyeros near the Plaza de la Revolución, was famous for highlighting the Argentinian music and dance form. There's another tango club—**Caserón de Tango**—at Calle Justíz #21, one block south of Plaza de Armas in Habana Vieja.

JAZZ VENUES

Despite the fame and popularity of Cuba's jazz musicians, Havana is a far cry from Chicago. There are few dedicated jazz joints. An exception is **Maxim's,** at Calle 3ra y Calle 10, in Vedado, tel. 33981. It's been called seedy, and one writer says that "women should not go unaccompanied." This is overblown, although the place is certainly down-at-heels (yet full of atmosphere). Check your bar bill carefully—the place has a reputation for gouging. Entry is US$1; Cubans pay in pesos; you'll be charged in dollars. Open Mon.-Sat. 3 p.m.-2 a.m. and Sunday noon-2 a.m.

Jazz is also featured nightly at the **Copa** room of the Hotel Riviera. The lobby bar of the Hotel Copacabana also has a jazz trio that performs nightly. And jazz and salsa are staples at the **Jazz Cafetería,** in the Casa Cultura in Vedado at Calle 7 y Avenida 4/6. The Casa Cultura is one of the venues for the annual **International Havana Jazz Festival.**

Cuba's particularly vivacious version of jazz can also be heard at the **Palacio de Salsa,** in the Hotel Riviera, and **Café Turquino Salsa Cabaret,** in the Habana Libre Hotel (the latter features the Cuban salsa group Colé-Colé and its dance troupe).

BARS

You can count good bars on your fingers. Every hotel has a bar, but few are outstanding. The ground-floor bar of the Hotel Cohiba is usually buzzing, as is the patio bar of the Hotel Inglaterra, a meeting point for budget and independent travelers.

Several bars offer superb views of the city: try those at the Hotel Nacional, Hotel Deauville, Hotel Inglaterra, and Hotel Riviera, and La Torre, atop the FOCSA Building at Calles 17 y M (entrance, US$1). Most nights, the rooftop bar of the **Hotel Inglaterra** has live music, often with a small cabaret *espectáculo* (US$5). Weekend evenings are good. The best, perhaps, is the **Turquino,** on the 25th floor of the Hotel Habana Libre—fabulous views! The US$2 admission includes one drink (and you can stay for the cabaret).

Two bars rise above all others, however: **La Bodeguita del Medio** and **El Floridita.** No visit to Havana is complete without sipping a *mojito* in the former and a *daiquiri* in the latter, as Ernest Hemingway did almost daily! As yet unsung in tourist guidebooks (but soon sure to be on tourists' beaten path) is the **Dos Hermanos,** a wharf-front bar where Hemingway bent elbows with sailors and prostitutes. The bar, at San Pedro and Sol, is still down-to-earth (perfect for unpretentious tippling with locals), but at press time Habaguanex had slated it for a spruce up.

For a romantic evening, I recommend the atmospheric **Bar La Tasca,** on the harborfront facing Havana between the Morro and La Cabaña fortresses. It's an intimate oak-beamed place, full of Spanish weaponry, with a friendly barman and a terrace where you can sip your *mojito* while enjoying the views. Nearby, and in a similar vein, are the **Mesón de los Dooo Apóstoles** and **El Polvorín,** below the Morro.

A great place to sample rums is the **Taberna del Galeón,** tel. 33-8061, off the southeast corner of Plaza de Armas. The place, a favorite of tour groups, offers samplers in the hope that you'll purchase a bottle or two. But you can tipple upstairs in solitude, sampling from any of a zillion types of rum (and even Cuban whisky). Try the house special, *puñetazo,* a blend of rum, coffee, and mint.

For a bit of melancholy, head to **Boleros,** in the Dos Gardenias complex on Avenida 7ma and Calle 26. Here, Isolina Carrillo hosts some of the best singers of the *bolero.* Carrillo was a cinema pianist at the age of 10, entered the conservatory at 13, and composed the famous song "Dos Gardenias" after which the complex is named.

More radical youth elements congregate at the **Casa de los Infusiones,** at Calles 23 y G in Vedado, where *aguardente* (neat rum) shots cost US50 cents each.

Draft Beer: Want to quaff a tankard of hoppy Czech brew? Head to the moodily atmospheric wood-paneled **Bar Monserrate,** just south of El Floridita. The place has long been popular with Cubans and is noted for its *Coctel Monserrate* (one teaspoon of sugar, two ounces of grapefruit juice, five drops of grenadine, two ounces of white rum, ice, and a sprig of mint).

CAFÉS

Although Havana is lacking in quality bars, it has plenty of splendid sidewalk cafés. Most are concentrated in Habana Vieja. The most popular is undoubtedly **El Patio Colonial,** on the Plaza de la Catedral. Its appeal is neither its ambience, the drinks, nor musicians, but rather that sitting beneath the cool *portrale* held aloft by tall columns, you can gaze out upon the whirligig of life on the plaza. Expect to be pestered by youngsters begging Chiclets and money.

You'll find plenty of places to sup with locals on Calle O'Reilly. For example, **Café O'Reilly** is an atmospheric spot on O'Reilly and San Ignacio, one block south of the Plaza de la Catedral. It's popular with the gay crowd and has a strong local clientele. Downstairs is a café serving cappuccinos and espressos. Upstairs, there's live music and a balcony where you can sip your rum or *mojito* and watch life on the street below. The place is best enjoyed in late afternoons and early evenings.

Two blocks west, and another favorite of locals, is the **Bar Lafayette,** on Aguilar between O'Reilly and Empedrado. Its house cocktail is rum and tomato juice. Also check out the always buzzing **Café Paris,** on Calle Obispo and San Ignacio. If you follow Obispo west to Villegas, you can even purchase takeout daiquiris for one and a half pesos, served in cardboard cups from a small shop—**El Huevino**—on the corner.

CINEMA

Habaneros are devoted movie buffs. The city is replete with cinemas—by one account more than 170—showing current Hollywood movies (normally within one year of release) plus Cuban films. The latest issue of *Granma* will list what's currently showing.

The **Instituto Cubana De Cinematografía,** next to the Charlie Chaplin movie house on Calle 23 e/ Calles 10 y 12, tel. 33-4634, is in charge of producing and distributing films. It often has preview screenings of new Cuban releases in its studios. The Chaplin has been called the largest theater in the world.

MAIN CINEMAS IN HAVANA

Cine Charles Chaplin: Calle 23 e/ 10 y 12, tel. 31-1101; Daily except Tuesday at 5 and 8 p.m. (box office opens 30 minutes prior). Also here is **Video Charlot** (same times), also showing first run movies.

Cine Payret: Prado and Calle San José, tel. 63-3163

Cine La Rampa: Calle 23 e/ O y P, tel. 78-6146; Daily except Wednesday at 8 p.m. The doors open at 7:30 p.m.; it's best to get there early.

Cine Riviera: Calles 23 y H, tel. 30-9564

Cine Yara: Calle 23 y Calle L, tel. 31-9430

You'll find several movie houses clustered along La Rampa, in central Vedado, among them the **Cine La Rampa, Cine Yara, Cine Riviera,** and, farther west along Calle 23, **Cine Charles Chaplin.** The **Cine Payret,** on the southeast corner of Parque Central, opposite the Capitolio, shows western films.

Age restriction is 16 years. Children and youths can attend screenings at the **Cinemateca Infantil y Juvenil,** at Cinema 23 y 12, every Saturday at 2:30 p.m.

French films are shown on Saturday at 2 p.m. at the **Alliance Française,** at Calle G No. 407 e/ 17 y 19 in Vedado, tel. 33-3370. Entrance is free.

THEATER AND CLASSICAL DANCE

Cubans are enthusiastic lovers of classical music. Audience are known to rise to their feet and yell with delight at the end of concerts. Legitimate or live theater, on the other hand, has yet to take off. *Cartelera* has a complete listing of current performances, including children's theater.

The most important theater is the baroque **Gran Teatro de la Habana,** on the west side of Parque Central, tel. 61-3078 or 61-2360. It is home to the Alicia Alonso Ballet Nacional de Cuba as well as the national opera company. The orchestra is excellent if you excuse the occasional pings of

dropped bows and triangles. The building has two theaters—the **Sala García Lorca,** where ballet and concerts are held, and the smaller **Sala Antonin Artaud,** for less-commercial performances. Jazz and other performances are often given, and most weeks throughout the year you can even see Spanish dance here Thurs.-Sat. at 8:30 p.m. and Sunday at 5 p.m.

Look, too, for performances of the National Symphony and other classical and contemporary performances at the contemporary **Teatro Nacional,** one block west of the Plaza de la Revolución, tel. 79-6011. It also has two performance halls—the **Sala Avellaneda,** for concerts and opera, and the **Sala Covarrubias.** It also hosts important Communist Party functions and revolutionary celebrations.

The **Casa de la Música,** at Calle 17 y E in Vedado, offers concerts by soloists and chamber ensembles—and so does the **Casa de la Música,** on Calle 20 e/ Avenida 33 y 35, in Miramar.

HAVANA'S THEATERS

Gran Teatro: (also known as Teatro García Lorca) Prado (Paseo de Martí) e/ San Rafael y San José, Habana Vieja, tel. 61-3078. Hosts the national ballet, opera, and symphony. Occasional jazz and other concerts are held here.

Teatro Bertold Brecht: Calle 13 y 1ra, tel. 32-9359

Teatro El Sótano: Calle K, e/ Calles 25 y 27, Vedado, tel. 32-0630. **Teatro Guiñol:** Calles M y 19, Vedado, tel. 32-6262. Youth theater.

Teatro Hubert de Blanck: Calzada (Calle 5ra) e/ Calles A and B, Vedado, tel. 30-1011. Known for both modern and classical plays.

Teatro Mella: Linea (Calle 7ra) and Calle A, Vedado, tel. 38-6961. Noted for its contemporary dance and theater, including performances by the **Danza Contemporánea de Cuba.** Many of Cuba's more contemporary and avant-garde plays are performed here.

Teatro Nacional: Paseo y Avenida Céspedes, Plaza de la Revolución, tel. 79-6011. The country's premier theater, used for classical to contemporary shows.

Look out for performances by Xiomara Palacio, a puppet-show artist recognized as Cuba's leading figure in children's theater.

Comedy
Most cabaret shows feature stand-up comedy, but you'll need to be fluent in Spanish to get many giggles out of the shows. You can also head to **Casa de la Comédia** (also called Salón Ensayo), at the corner of Calles Justíz and Baratillo, one block southeast of Plaza de Armas. It hosts comic theater on weekends at 4 p.m., performed by the Teatro Anaquillé.

Comedy is also sometimes performed at the **Café Cantante Mi Habana,** in the Teatro Nacional at Paseo, one block west of the Plaza de la Revolución, tel. 79-6011, and in the bar beside Restaurante Don Amagnemnon, at Calles 17 and M, in Vedado.

OTHER ENTERTAINMENT

Art-Show Openings
Havana offers an abundance of art galleries, where show openings can draw out a variety of entertaining characters. The bimonthly *Galerías de Arte Programación,* available from the **Centro de Desarrollo de las Artes Visuales,** at San Ignacio #352 in Plaza Vieja, lists openings. Typically, you'll find at least 30 major exhibitions in Havana at any one time.

HAVANA ART GALLERIES

Contro Wilfredo Lam: San Ignacio 22 esq. Empedrado, tel. 61-2096; Mon.-Sat. 10 a.m.-5 p.m. Temporary exhibits with contemporary art from the Third World.

Galeria UNEAC: Calle 17 esq. H, Vedado, tel. 32-5781; Mon.-Fri. 9 a.m.-5 p.m. Exhibits by the best contemporary Cuban artists.

Galeria Forma: Calle Obispo #255 e/ Cuba y Aguiar; Mon.-Sat. 10 a.m.-4 p.m. Small-format sculptures by prominent Cuban artists. Also stunning painting by leading artists.

Galeria Habana: Calle Linea e/ E y F, Vedado, tel. 32-7101; Mon.-Sat. 10 a.m.-4 p.m. Paintings, silkscreen prints, and drawings by young Cuban artists.

Galeria La Acacia: Calle San José 114 esq. Consulado y Industria, Centro, tel. 63-9364; Mon.-Sat. 10 a.m.-4 p.m. Fine collection of antiques and works by the great masters of Cuban plastic arts.

Galeria Victor Manuel: Plaza de la Catedral; Mon.-Sat. 10 a.m.-4 p.m. Cuban landscapes, pottery, and applied arts.

Galeria Plaza Vieja: Calle Muralla No.107, esq. San Ignacio, Habana Vieja; Mon.-Fri. 10 a.m.-4 p.m. Specializes in Afro-Cuban influences in the works of celebrities like Manuel Mnedive, Zaida del Río, and Armando Laminaga.

Taller de Seregráfia Rene Portocarrero: Calle Cuba #513, e/ Teniente Rey y Muralla, tel. 62-3276; Mon.-Sat. 10 a.m.-4 p.m. Silkscreen printing workshop; serigraphy applied to art reproduction.

Taller Experimental de la Gráfica: Callejón del Chorro, Plaza de la Catedral, tel. 62-0979; Mon.-Sat. 10 a.m.-4 p.m. Traces the history of engraving. Exclusive pieces for sale.

Galeria Horacio Ruíz: Calle Tacón No.4, esq. Empedrado; Mon.-Sat. 10 a.m.-4 p.m. Leather, metal, glass, papier-mâché, and other materials

Galeria Haydee Santamaría: 3ra y 5ta, Vedado, tel. 32-4653; Mon.-Sat. 10 a.m.-5 p.m. Graphics, prints, drawings, and photography from throughout the Americas.

Galeria Francisco Javier Baez: Plaza de la Catedral; Mon.-Sat. 10 a.m.-4 p.m.

Galeria Roberto Diago: Muralla 107 esq. San Ignacio, Habana Vieja, tel. 33-8005; Mon.-Sat. 10 a.m.-4 p.m. Permanent exhibits of primitive artists.

Fashion Shows

La Maison, Calle 16 #701 esq. Avenida 7ma, Miramar, tel. 33-1550 or 33-1548, fax 33-1585, is touted by Cuban tourist agencies. Fashion shows are held beneath the stars in the terrace garden of an elegant old mansion, on a stage lit by a son et lumière. Live music is provided. It's enjoyable, albeit a bit strained. Reservations are recommended. Entrance costs US$10 (US$15 including transportation and a bottle of rum). You can also dine outside beneath the flame-of-the-forest trees. A disco (in a separate a/c building) begins after the show.

The disco at **Club 1830** also hosts a fashion show, including formal evening wear and see-through wedding gowns (the brides are "dressed" for the honeymoon under their gowns) that would give a vicar a heart attack. The show is included in the US$5 entrance price.

Poetry Readings and Literary Events

The Special Period has had a devastating impact on the publication of Cuban literature. Prior to the Special Period, prominent writers and poets gathered at **La Moderna Poesía** bookstore, at the west end of Calle Obispo, each Saturday at noon to sign copies of their latest releases. I expect these readings may have been resurrected by the time you read this.

Poetry readings are also given at the **Casa de las Américas,** Calle 3 and G, in Vedado, tel. 32-3587; the **Fundación Alejo Carpentier,** at Empedrado No. 215 in Habana Vieja; and **La Madriguera,** a popular hangout for university students, on Avenida Salvador Allende and Calles Luaces. The **Museum of Fine Arts,** on Tracadero and Agramonte (Zulueta), also hosts literary events, as well as film screenings and musical presentations.

National Aquarium

By day, sea lions and other marine mammals provide acrobatic entertainment at the National Aquarium, at Avenida 1ra and Calle 60 in Miramar, tel. 33-1442. Pride of the show are Diana and Ciclón, who belong to the species *Tursiop trucaus,* commonly known as "mule" dolphins. The duo belie that misnomer by performing synchronized leaps through hoops and dances to music. Open daily except Monday 10 a.m.-6 p.m. (US$2, children US50 cents).

Cruises

How about a dinner-and-show cruise aboard a replica pirate ship? **El Galeón,** tel. 33-8600, fax 33-8536, is a mock Spanish galleon fitted out as a restaurant-bar-cum-nightclub. Nightly, it sails around the harbor and along the coast. The dinner cruise (8:30-11 p.m.) includes a disco on board and costs US$35. Special disco cruises are offered Friday and Saturday nights 1:30-3 a.m. (US$10). The drinks are expensive. You can admire the vessel from the Malecón, passing by offshore gaily lit, as if fireflies have settled on the lines and spars.

SPORTS AND RECREATION

Havana has many sports centers *(centros deportivos),* although most are very run down. The largest is the **Panamericano** complex, in Habanas del Este. It includes an Olympic athletic stadium, tennis courts, swimming pool, and even a velodrome for cycling.

Bicycling

The **Club de Cicloturismo "Gran Caribe,"** of the University of Havana, organizes rides each weekend. Call club president Ignacio Valladares Rivero (home tel. 98-9193, or, at Estadio Juan Abrantes, tel. 78-3941) for information.

Golf

Yes, Havana *does* offer golf—at the **Havana Golf Club,** hidden east of the Avenida de la Independencia, at Carretera de Vento Km 8, near Boyeros, about 20 km south of Havana, tel. 44-4836 or 44-8227. Of four courses in Havana in 1959, this is the only one remaining. The nine-hole course—with 18 tees and 22.5 hectares of fairway—was opened in 1948 by the British community and maintained by the British Embassy until given to the Cuban government in 1980. Nine additional holes were being added by a Spanish company and were scheduled to be complete by early 1997. It's not Palm Springs, but it retains the unmistakable air of a private club. There's a minimally stocked pro shop, plus five tennis courts, a swimming pool, and two restaurants set amid landscaped grounds. The pleasant **Bar Hoy 19** (19th Hole), with a small TV lounge, overlooks the greens. The club hosts golf competitions. Membership costs US$70 plus US$45 monthly (US$15 for additional family members). A round costs non-members US$20 for nine holes (US$30 for 18). You can rent clubs for US$10. Caddies cost US$3 per nine holes. A US$3.50 fee is charged to use the pool, US$2 for the tennis facilities. Jorge Dulque is the affable resident golf pro; he charges US$5 per 30 minutes of instruction.

Bowling

You can practice your 10-pin bowling at an alley in the Hotel Kohly or at the Havana Golf Club, tel. 44-4836, way south of town at Carretera de Vento km 8, off Avenida Rancho Boyeros. The club has a fully mechanized two-lane bowling alley and full-size pool tables. They're very popular with local youth.

Horseback Riding

Club Hípico, in Parque Lenin, on the southern outskirts, tel. 33-8203 or 44-1058, fax 33-8166, offers horseback rides plus instruction in riding, jumping, and dressage

Running

The Malecón is a good place to jog, although you need to beware the uneven surface and occasional pothole. I use the bicycle lane. Serious runners might head to the track at the Panamericano complex; the **Estadio Juan Abrahantes,** on Zapata, south of the university; or **Centro Deportivo Claudio Argüellos,** at the junction of Avenida de la Independencia, Avenida 26, and Vía Blanca.

Scuba Diving

The Gulf Stream and Atlantic Ocean currents meet west of the city, where many ships have been sunk through the centuries, among them the wreck of the *Santísimo Trinidad,* off Santa Fé, west of Marina Hemingway. Their wooden and iron hulls make for fascinating exploration. This western shore is known as **Barlovento.**

Marina Hemingway offers scuba diving from **La Aguja Scuba Center,** tel. 33-1150, fax 33-1536, which has professional guides and also rents equipment.

The Hotel Copacabana, at Avenida 1ra e/ Calles 44 y 46 in Miramar, tel. 33-1037, fax 33-3846, offers beginning and advanced scuba diving lessons as well as trips. The water sports concession here rents underwater video and photography equipment.

The so-called **"Blue Circuit"** is a series of dive sites (with profuse coral and shipwrecks) extending east from Bacuranao, about 10 km east of Havana, to the Playas del Este (see "Suburbs" for details). Diving programs are available at several hotels.

Swimming

Most large tourist hotels have pools that are open for the use of nonguests. One of the best is at the Hotel Nacional (US$5 per nonguest). nonswimmers need to beware the sudden steep drop to the deep end, a common fault in the design of Cuban swimming pools. Two other favorites are the pools at the Hotel Copacabana in Miramar and the Hotel Panamericano, at the Complejo Turístico Panamericano.

There are also public swimming pools in Parque Lenin, and also an Olympic pool—**Piscina Olimpica**—at Avenida 99 #3804, in Lotería, southeast of Havana in Cotorro.

However, I recommend a visit to Playas del Este, where you can swim in the warm sea. Forsake joining the locals, who bathe and snorkel in the rough waters and rocky shore of the Malecón. The waters are badly polluted (when the ebbing tide sucks Havana harbor, the sea off the Malecón can seem like pure gasoline), the rocks sharp, and the waters often rough.

Spectator Sports

The **baseball** season runs Dec.-June at the 60,000-seat **Estadio Latinoamericano,** the main baseball stadium, hidden in Cerro on Avenida 20 de Mayo and Calle Pedrosa. Games are played Tues.-Thurs. at 8 p.m., Saturday at 1:30 and 8 p.m., and Sunday at 1:30 p.m. (three pesos). The entrance is at Calle Zequeira. You can also watch games being played at the **Estadio Juan Abrahantes** (also called Estadio

Universitario), below the university at the end of Zanja, at Avenida 27 de Noviembre.

You can watch **boxing and martial arts** at **Sala Polivalente Kid Chocolate** public indoor gymnasium and sports hall on the Prado opposite the Capitolio. It's intriguing to pop inside to watch kids and adults sparring, and playing sports from soccer to volleyball. They may even welcome you onto the court or into the ring! Likewise, martial arts, volleyball, and basketball are hosted at the **Sala Polivalente Ramón**

Fonst in Plaza de la Revolución; and at the **Estadio Universitario Juan Abrantes.**

For **fencing,** head to ExpoCuba (also called Pabexpo; see "Suburbs"). For **hockey,** head to the **Terreno Sintético de Hockey,** in Santiago de las Vegas. The **Complejo de Pelota Vasca Raúl Díaz Argüelles,** at the junction of Avenida de la Independencia, Avenida 26, and Vía Blanca, has a **roller-skating** track. And **soccer games** are played at the **Estadio Pedro Marrero** at Avenida 41 #4409 e/ 44 y 50, in Cerro.

SHOPPING

Havana is a trove of bargain buys. **Tour & Travel,** Avenida 5ta #8409, Miramar, tel. 33-2433, offers a shopping excursion for US$10. It includes visits to La Maison and similar "exclusive goods" stores.

ANTIQUES

Havana's museums and private homes are brimful of invaluable antiques. Alas, there are few antique stores, partly because the government is keen to prevent a wholesale exodus of the country's treasures. Nonetheless, you *can* find antiques for sale. Perhaps the best place is **Galería la Acacia,** 114 San José, Centro Habana, tel. 63-9364, whose trove includes everything from 18th-century ceramics to grand pianos. Some of it is merely kitschy, and much is in a sorry

state. But for the knowledgeable, there are some gems certified by the National Heritage Office. It's open Mon.-Sat. 9 a.m.-4:30 p.m. It accepts Visa, MasterCard, Eurocard, and Banamex.

ARTS & CRAFTS

Souvenir Stores
You'll find **ARTEX** shops throughout the city. All stock postcards, books, music cassettes and CDs, T-shirts, arts and crafts, rum, cigars, and other souvenirs. In Vedado, check out the shop at the junction of Calle L and La Rampa. There are ARTEX stores in all Infotur's **Palacios de Turismo.** You'll also find street stalls selling postcards, guidebooks, maps, and trinkets on all the major squares in Habana Vieja and at other major points of tourist interest in the city.

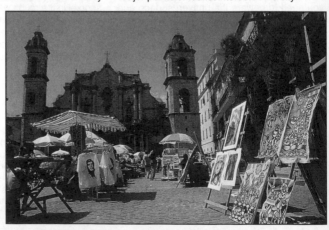

open-air market,
Plaza de la Catedral

WHAT TO BUY

Don't let anyone tell you there's nothing to buy in Cuba; it's a shopper's paradise. True, you don't come here for factory outlets or designer boutiques. But for high-quality art and crafts Havana is unrivaled in the Caribbean . . . at incredible bargain prices. The two big-ticket items are, of course, cigars and rum, readily available throughout the island (top-quality cigars can be purchased for one-third to one-tenth their sale price in North America). And stunning silver and gold jewelry belies Cuba's image as a stodgy vacuum of creativity. Other great bargains include musical instruments (especially drums, maracas, and guitars), saddles, and music cassettes and CDs.

See "Things to Buy" in the Havana chapter, plus regional chapters for information on specific places. For rum and coffee, see the section on "Food," this chapter.

You're not going to find anything of interest in peso stores, half-full of shoddy Cuban-made plastic and other wares. Even before the Special Period, many Cuban stores were notorious for their paucity; since 1990 many have become totally barren, and hence closed for *inventario* (inventory), a euphemism for "closed indefinitely."

Virtually everything of any value to Cubans and foreigners is now sold by the State for dollars at a handful of **diplotiendas** (supermarkets originally intended for diplomats, but now open to all Cubans with dollars) and at **Tiendas Panamericanos,** which every town now has. They're stocked with Western goods . . . from toothpaste to stereos. Credit cards and travellers checks are accepted. Hours are usually 10 a.m.-10 p.m.

Arts and Crafts

Cuba's strong suit is arts and crafts, sold freely for dollars by artisans at street stalls, and also in art and craft stores by state agencies such as the **Fondo de Bienes Culturales** and **ARTEX.** ARTEX has a small store in virtually every town, selling T-shirts, postcards, maps, books and music cassettes and CDs in addition to arts and crafts. Most Intur tourist information office have an ARTEX outlet. (See regional chapters for specifics.)

An **export permit** is now required for all works of art not purchased from state galleries and shops where official receipts are given. If you buy from an independent artist, you'll need to buy a permit (good for up to five works of art) for US$10 from the National Registry of Cultural Goods, Calle 17 #1009 e/ 10 y 12, Vedado. Allow up to two days for processing. Without it, you run the risk of Cuban Customs taking it.

Great imagination is evident in the wares for sale. Cubans are supremely artistic, and the shortest walk through Habana Vieja can be a magical mystery tour of homegrown art. In recent years, art has been patronized by the tourist dollar, and street stalls and ARTEX shops are overflowing with whimsical Woolworths' art: cheap canvas scenes, kitschy rough-hewn erotic carvings, *papier-mâché* masks, and animal figurines painted in pointillist dots. But there is plenty of true-quality art ranging from paintings and tapestries to handworked leather goods, including women's handbags and wall-hangings, and precious wood carvings in Afro-Cuban realism running as high as $400 but representing a solid investment. You'll also see *muñecitas* (dolls) everywhere, mostly of mulattas representing the goddesses of the *santería* religion. Cuban women are great doll collectors, often keeping their childhood dolls into late adulthood.

Cuba doesn't have a strong pottery tradition. However, you'll find everything from small rough clay ashtrays with a clay cigar, and Fidel in figurine form, to creative vases and ceramicware. In Camagüey you can buy simple earthenware jars called *tinajones*. Nuevo Gerona, on the Isle Juventud, has some beautiful ceramic tiles. And the pottery in Varadero sells stunning glazed kitchenware.

Also look for artfully delicate, copper-toned wind chimes made from discarded metal printers' plates; and high-quality graphics by Cuba's top artists printed on recycled paper, including reproductions (US$12-25 average) of classic Cuban painters: Wilfredo Lam, Víctor Manuel, Mariano Rodríguez, and Amelia Peláez. The range of artwork is stunning: keep your eyes peeled for original works by younger, contemporary artists such as Tomás Sanchez, Manuel Mendive and Zaida del Río, with their very Cuban vision of landscapes, myths, and reality.

Posters also make great souvenirs. Cuba is the world leader in political art, and you can find stunning examples for sale for US$2-10 at ARTEX stores nationwide. In Havana, also check out the shop at **Cinemateca,** Calle 23 e/ 10 y 12, Vedado: it sells superb film posters. In North America, you can buy posters from the Center for Cuban Studies, or Inkworks (see the special topic, "Cuban Poster Art").

(continues on next page)

WHAT TO BUY
(continued)

For photos from the revolutionary period, head to **Fototeca** in Plaza Vieja, in Havana.

Artists now freely sell their works on the street, often for unreasonably low prices. Feel free to visit the artists' studios; Calle Obispo in Havana has several, and if heading to Pinar del Río, *do* stop off in Las Terrazas to see the studio of Lester Campa, an artist who recently had his first solo show in the US. You can obtain a list of artists who welcome visitors by contacting the Center for Cuban Studies, 124 West 23rd St., New York, NY 10011, tel. (212) 242-0559.

Bargaining: A limited amount of bargaining is normal at street markets. However, most prices are very low to begin with. Cubans are scratching to earn a few dollars. Be reasonable. Don't bargain simply to win a battle! If the quoted price seems fair—and it usually will—then pay up and feel blessed that you already have a bargain.

Clothing

No doubt you'll want a classically Cuban T-shirt emblazoned with the visage of Che Guevara or revolutionary slogans. You'll find T-shirts for sale at ARTEX stores nationwide, and in the souvenir stores of most tourist hotels.

Another must-buy for men is a guayabera, the quintessential Cuban short-sleeved shirt: double-pleated, four-pocketed, impeccably pressed shirt worn outside the pants. Thought to be of Andalusian descent, it has been standard wear in Cuba since the early 1900s and is today an unofficial government uniform. You can buy them for dollars in ARTEX stores. The best quality bear the Pepe Antonio label.

Women can find tie-dyed fabrics and unique, high-quality Verano dresses at a few dollar-stores such as La Maison in Havana and Santiago, and the Hotel Cohiba in Havana, and you may still find bolts of creative *Telarte* material or clothes made from it. Otherwise, most Cuban-made clothes are of inferior quality.

Cuban factory-made shoes are dowdy and shoddy, but artisans handmake splendid sandals, shoes and cowboy boots that they sell for a song (typically US$8-20) at streetside markets. The quality is incredible given the poor resources many artisans

work with (the island has a long tradition for excellent shoe-craft). Many are very hip in design—often copied from fashion magazines—and play to Cubans' innate sense of fashion. In Havana, check out the fair on the Malecón (see the Havana chapter). Locations change.

Cigars and Cigarettes

Surely you'll want to buy cigars, if only as gifts for friends. After all, they are the finest cigars in the world. See the special topic, "Buying Cuban Cigars."

Opinion is divided on the quality of Cuban cigarettes, which at first hand seem the antithesis of quality. Most Cuban cigarettes are crude, unfiltered, and cheap (50 centavos will buy you a pack of *Popular*). Most smell like sewers. However, some of my smoker friends swear that the export-quality cigarettes, such as Montecristis or H. Uppmann's *Largos,* which have no chemical additives and are pure tobacco, taste far superior to Western cigarettes (US50 cents per pack).

You can always buy packs of Marlboro, Camel, or Winston (and in some establishments, fine-grade English smokes such as Dunhill) at prices below those of North America and Europe.

Music

If you want memories of Cuba to come flooding back after your visit, buy some music cassettes or CDs. Choose from dozens of recordings by jazz and salsa maestros such as Los Van Van, Chucho Valdés and Irakere, Grupo Moncada; and of Cuban folk music *(música tradicional)* by performers such as Conjunto Folclórico Nacional, Los Muñequitos, and Joseíto Fernández. Most of the recordings are unavailable outside Cuba.

Every ARTEX and hotel souvenir store, plus many street markets, sell cassettes and CDs at prices comparable (or slightly higher) to North America and Europe. Musicians who serenade you in restaurants will also approach you to sell their recordings. You can also buy at the last moment at the duty-free stores in airports.

In North America, you can order Cuban music on CDs from **Publications Exchange Inc.,** 8306 Mills Drive, #241, Miami, FL 33183, tel. (305) 256-0162, fax (305) 252-1813.

Manzana de Gómez is a shopping complex immediately south of the Hotel Plaza, east of Parque Central. It contains several souvenir stores selling carvings, leather goods, and intriguing wall hangings, belts, purses, and posters; many are of excellent quality. The store called **Monsieur** is particularly good. The Infotur store, facing Parque Central, has some appalling *cineceros* (ashtrays) made of stuffed frogs doing various acrobatic manoeuvres. *Don't buy these*— doing so contributes to the devastation of Cuba's endemic wildlife.

Several souvenir stores cluster around Plazuela de Albear, immediately east of the Manzana de Gómez.

Open-Air Markets

There are plenty of markets to choose from. The range of goods is generally of surprisingly high quality, and the prices are often ludicrously low. Bargaining is the norm.

The best is undoubtedly the arts and crafts market held in the **Plaza de la Catedral** and spilling into the surrounding streets. Here, you can buy everything from little ceramic figurines of Fidel, miniature bongo drums, and banana-leaf hats to fabulous bronzes and paintings.

An open-air flea market on La Rampa e/ Calle M y L sells woodcarvings, jewelry, shoes, and leather goods. It's open daily 8 a.m.-6 p.m. A better bet is the **Carnaval de la Calle** market, which used to be held every Saturday morning on Avenida de los Presidentes but which has since moved to the Malecón e/ Calles D y E. Some 300 artisans exhibit and sell handicrafts ranging from corals delicately spun into bracelets (note, however, that coral is endangered), beaten copper pieces, quality leather sandals, woodcarvings, paintings, quaint ceramics, carved ox-horns, plates showing 3-D landscapes, and even live parakeets and, alas, stuffed marine turtles and turtle heads.

Galleries

You're spoilt for choice. Havana is home to a dizzying galaxy of galleries, most with both permanent and revolving exhibitions. Pick up a copy of the weekly tourist guide *Cartelera* for complete listings. You can also pick up a bimonthly program—*Galerías de Arte Programación*—from the **Centro de Desarrollo de las Artes Visuales,** at San Ignacio #352 in Plaza Vieja. Its calendar of openings usually lists at least 30 major exhibitions taking place in Havana at any given time. For more complete information on workshops and galleries, contact the **Fondo Cubano de Bienes Culturales,** also in Plaza Vieja at Muralla #107, tel. 33-8005, fax 33-8121. Most galleries are open Mon.-Sat. 10 a.m.-4 p.m.

One of the best places is **Galería la Acacia,** 114 San José, Centro Habana, tel. 63-9364, an art gallery with top-class contemporary works. Expect to pay US$1,000 or more for the best works. Other top-quality art is sold a short distance away at **Galería del Centro Gallego,** next to the Gran Teatro on Parque Central. This Aladdin's cave includes superb bronzes by Joel del Río, imaginative ceramics, some truly stunning silver and gold jewelry, Cuban Tiffany-style lamps, and wooden and papier-mâché animals painted in bright Caribbean colors and pointillist dots, in Haitian fashion. This is high-quality work, priced accordingly. Bring your US$100 bills.

Of a similar standard is the **Galería Victor Manuel,** on the west side of Plaza de la Catedral, displaying fine landscapes and ceramic pieces. Nearby is the **Taller Experimental de la Gráfica,** which traces the history of engraving and has exclusive pieces for sale.

The galleries in the **Casa de los Condes de Jaruco,** on Plaza Vieja, sell work of unparalleled beauty and quality. Upstairs, and most impressive of all, is **Galería de la Casona** with, among its many treasures, fantastic papier-mâché works of a heavily spiritualist nature. Be sure to walk through into the back room, where the works on display include Tiffany lamps, sculpted wooden statues, ceramic pieces, jewelry of truly mesmerizing creativity, and leatherwork among the best I have ever seen. Also upstairs is **Galería de la Plaza Vieja,** where you will find some of the strongest statements in Cuban art. Similarly, you'll find experimental art for sale at the **Centro de Desarrollo de las Artes Visuales,** in the Casa de las Hermanas Cárdenas, on the west side of Plaza Vieja, tel. 62-3533 or 62-2611.

Calle Obispo is famed for its art galleries. The highest quality works are displayed at **Galería Forma,** Calle Obispo #255, tel. 62-0123, fax 33-8121, selling artwork of international standard, including intriguing sculptures and ceramics and copper pieces. The **Taller**

de Pintura, Obispo #312, has a small gloomy room full of paintings of a more explorative, radical nature, including Daliesque paintings and copies of the great Spaniard's works. A gallery at Obispo #366 offers more naive works; that at Obispo #408 has some fantastical ceramics. At Obispo #515, you'll find the studio of experimental ceramist Roberto Fernández Martinez, a lively old man with a spreading white beard who explores the influences of African and Indo-Cuban mythology. His eclectic paintings range through a variety of styles from Klee to Monet. Also on Obispo, on the southeast corner of Plaza de Armas, is an impressive ceramic art store selling works by leading artists such as Alfredo Sosabravo, Amelia Palaez, and Carballo Moreno.

The **Asociación Cubana de Artesana Artistas** has a store on Obispo where individual artists have small booths selling jewelry and arts and crafts. Check out the fantastical, museum-scale wall hangings and fabulous stauettes in the gallery at the rear. Open Tues.-Fri. 1-6 p.m. and Saturday 10 a.m.-4 p.m.

The **Palacio de Artesanía Cubana,** on Calle Tacón, tel. 62-4407, is replete with quality arts and crafts. You can also buy cigars and rum here. Open daily 9 a.m.-6 p.m.

The **Galeria Horacio Ruíz,** in the Palacio del Segundo Cabo, on the north side of Plaza de las Armas, has a large selection of *muñecas* (dolls) and papier-mâché masks.

The **Casa de las Américas,** tel. 32-3587, is a nongovernmental institution—founded by Che Guevara—that studies and promotes Latin American and Caribbean arts and culture. Its Art of Our Americas collection is housed in newly refurbished galleries at the corner of Calle 3 and Avenida de los Presidentes in Vedado (photographic and graphic collections are grouped in the mansion at the corner of Calle 5). Also in Vedado, check out **Galeria Mariano,** on Calle 15 e/ B y C, named in honor of Mariano Rodríguez, a founder of the Cuban school of contemporary art. The small gallery in the lobby of the Hotel Nacional also exhibits and sells paintings by the Cuban masters.

The **Centro Wilfred Lam,** at Calles Oficios and Acosta, tel. 61-7008, exhibits works by the great Cuban master as well as other artists from around the Americas. It hosts the famous Havana Arts Biennial each May.

Jewelry
Joyeria La Habanera, at Calle 12 #505, e/ Avenida 5ta y 7ma in Vedado, tel. 33-2546, fax 33-2529, has an exquisite array of gold and silver jewelery, as do the **Galeria del Centro Gallego** and **Galeria Victor Manuel** (see "Galleries," above).

Most of the open-air markets also have silver-plated jewelry at bargain prices. Check out the weekend market at Calle 25 e/ Calles I y H; some of the simple pieces for sale here (especially the necklaces) display stupendous creativity and craftsmanship, at ludicrously low prices.

Much jewelry, sadly, is of tortoiseshell, in spite of the fact that there's an international ban on the sale and transport of turtle products. *Don't buy it!*

Miniatures
Miniaturists and military buffs will find tiny soldiers and other figurines in the **Casa de la Miniatura,** on Tacón, one block east of Plaza de la Catedral. Many of them are antiques certified by the National Heritage Office.

BOOKS AND POSTERS

Havana is not blessed with good bookstores. Those that exist mostly stock only Spanish-language texts, with a predominant focus on socialist works glorifying the Revolution. Most gift stores sell coffee-table books on Cuba, as well as a range of English-language texts about the Revolution and socialist heroes and, occasionally, novels.

By far the best bookstore is **Librería La Internacional,** at the top of Calle Obispo #528, near El Floridita, tel. 61-3238. It stocks an extensive selection of books, globes, and maps, including a wide range of historical, sociological, and political texts in English, plus a good selection of English-language novels. It's open Mon.-Sat. 9 a.m.-4:30 p.m.

You'll also find a small selection of English-language novels at **La Bella Habana,** in the former Palacio del Segundo Cabo on the north side of Plaza de Armas, tel. 62-8092. Open Mon.-Sat. 9 a.m.-4:30 p.m.

The city's largest bookstore is **Fernando Ortíz,** near the university on Calle L esq. 27, Vedado, tel. 32-9653. Its stock spans the full range of subjects, although almost entirely in Spanish. It sells magazines, including a few in-

CUBAN POSTER ART

Cuba's strongest claim to artistic fame is surely its unique poster art, created in the service of political revolution. Cuban poster art has blossomed thanks to state support—a situation comparable to the United States in the 1930s, when the government paid artists to produce individual work.

The three leading poster-producing agencies—the Organization of Solidarity with the Peoples of Africa, Asia and Latin America; the Cuban Film Institute; and the Editora Política, the propaganda arm of the Cuban Communist Party—have produced over 10,000 posters since 1959. Different state bodies create works for different audiences: artists of the Cuban Film Institute (ICAIC), for example, design posters for movies from Charlie Chaplin comedies to John Wayne westerns; Editora Política produces posters covering everything from AIDS awareness, baseball games, and energy conservation to telling children to do their homework.

Cuba's most talented painters and photographers rejected Soviet realism and developed their own unique graphic style influenced by Latin culture and the country's geography (Cuba is a long way from Bulgaria!). The vibrant colors and lush imagery are consistent with the phyical and psychological makeup of the country, such as the poster urging participation in the harvest, dripping with psychedelic images of fruit and reminisicent of a 1960s Grateful Dead poster.

Cuban posters are typically graceful, combining strong simple concepts and sparce text with ingenious imagery and surprising sophistication. One poster, for example, warns of the dangers of smoking: a wisp of smoke curls upward to form a ghostlike skull.

The vast collection—acclaimed as "the single most focused, potent body of political graphics ever produced in this hemisphere"—provides a lasting visual commentary of the Revolution. Since the onset of the Special Period, however, output has plummeted due to a shortage of materials and money.

The posters kept in Cuba are also, alas, not archivally stable; the country's massive output over 30-plus years was until recently in danger of being lost forever. To save it, Lincoln Cushing—a printer in Berkeley, California—and Virginia-based art director and educator Daniel Walsh founded the **Cuba Poster Project.** Cushing (who was born in Havana in 1953) and Walsh are photographing the complete body of Cuban poster art, transferring it onto CDs, and creating a museum-quality archive. (In 1995, the duo became the first US citizens legally allowed to conduct business with Cuba since the embargo. They sued the US Treasury Dept. in 1986 claiming that the embargo illegally blocked the free exchange of printed materials, which are protected under the First Amendment. After nearly nine years of court battles, the Cuba Poster Project won the case.)

The Cuba Poster Project produces and sells silkscreened T-shirts and note-cards based on Cuba's graphic art, the majority of which is still produced using hands-on methods, without the aid of computers. A portion of the proceeds from Poster Project go back to sponsor Cuban graphic art. You can order your revolutionary T-shirts—or CDs of the posters—from the **Cuba Poster Project,** c/o Inkworks, 2827 7th St., Berkeley, CA 94710, tel. (510) 845-7111.

---

ternational periodicals. Open Mon.-Fri. 10 a.m.-5 p.m. and Saturday 9 a.m.-3 p.m.

Others to check out include **Librería Casa de las Américas,** at Calle G esq. 3ra, Vedado, tel. 32-3587, open Mon.-Fri. 9 a.m.-5 p.m.; **Librería de la UNEAC,** in the Cuban Writers' and Artists' Union at Calle 17 esq. H, Vedado, tel. 32-4551, open Mon.-Fri. 8:30 a.m.-4:30 p.m.; and **Librería Internacional José Martí,** at Calzada #l259 e/ J y I, Vedado, tel. 32-9838, open Mon.-Fri. 9 a.m.-4 p.m.

The **La Moderna Poesia** bookstore, opposite Librería La Internacional on Calle Obispo, promotes works by lesser-known Cuban authors. Readings and book signings are held here on Saturday, although less frequently since the ad-

vent of the Special Period. Also here are the **Librería Cervantes** (a venerable secondhand bookstore) and, next door, the **Librería Maxim Gorky,** which seemed closed at press time.

For books on art and film, check out **Tienda Chaplín,** on Calle 23 e/ 10 y 12, tel. 31-1101; it specializes in works related to the cinema but also has books on art and music, as well as posters and videos. Open Mon.-Sat. 2-9 p.m.

Don't fail to browse the **secondhand book fair** held each weekend at Plaza de Armas. You'll find all kinds of tattered texts, including atlases of Cuba.

Centro de Desarollo de Artes Visuales, in the Casa de las Hermanas Cárdenas on Plaza Vieja, tel. 62-3533, 62-2611, sells artwork, posters, and art and photography books, including *The Unknown Face of Cuban Art* (NCCA, 17 Grange Terrace, Stockton Road, Sunderland SR2 7DF, England) and *Made in Havana: Contemporary Art from Cuba* (Art Gallery of New South Wales, Art Gallery Road, Sydney 2000, Australia).

Posters can be purchased at most ARTEX stores. For reproduction prints, head to **Galería Exposición,** in Manzana de Gómez on Calle San Rafael, tel. 63-8364. It has famous pictures of Che plus a huge range of prints representing works by Cuba's best painters (US$3 to US$10).

The only stationery store I know of is **La Papelería,** at 102 O'Reilly, catercorner to the Plaza de las Armas. It sells pens, paper stock, and other basic office supplies.

CLOTHING AND FASHION ACCESSORIES

Cuba isn't renowned for its fashions. Most likely, if you're male, you'll want to purchase a guayabera, Cuba's unique short-sleeved, patterned shirt worn outside the pants. You can buy these at any ARTEX store or for pesos in the Cuban department stores along Calle San Rafael or Galiano.

Casa 18, also called Exclusividades Verano, at Calle 18 #4106 e/ Calles 41 y 43, tel. 23-7040, sells Cuban-designed clothes, including beautiful one-of-a-kind Verano dresses and straw hats. Nearby, at Calle 6 y Avenida 11, is **La Flora,** which sells fine Cuban crafts and clothing, including guayaberas with the Pepe Antonio label and Verano dresses (other quality items include leatherware, stained-glass lamps, carved statues, ceramic tableware).

The most famous fashion stores are those in **La Maison,** Calle 16 esq. 7ma Avenida, Miramar, tel. 33-1543, a former colonial mansion known for its nightly fashion shows. The rooms have been converted into shops selling upscale imported clothing and deluxe duty-free items such as perfumes and jewelry. There's a shoe and clothes store upstairs. I even bought a beautiful pair of leather sandals here for US$25 (made in Mexico).

For embroideries and lace, head to **El Quitrín,** at the corner of Obrapía and San Ignacio, in Habana Vieja.

You can even buy military uniforms—a Soviet sailor's jacket, perhaps?—at **El Arte,** on Avenida Simón Bolívar, on the east side of Parque de la Fraternidad.

DEPARTMENT STORES AND MARKETS

Diplotiendas sell all manner of Western goods. They originally exclusively served diplomats and other foreigners. Today, Cubans are also welcome—as long as they have dollars to spend.

The huge *supermercado* on Avenida 3ra and Calle 72 (100 meters east of Hotel Triton) in Miramar is Cuba's largest supermarket. It's like walking into a Safeway and has all the same Western consumer goods (at a hefty markup). It has Cuba's best stock of fresh vegetables and fruits, canned goods, and other food items. It's a good idea to stock up here on your favorite snacks for any lengthy touring outside Havana.

Similar supermarkets are springing up all over town, including at a minimall called **Quinta y 42,** at Avenida 5ta and Calle 42, which includes a sporting goods store, toy store, bakery, and general supermarket and the former Hotel Sierra Maestra—now the **Centro Comercial Sierra Maestra**—on Avenida 1ra and Calle 0. Need a TV, microwave oven, or diesel-powered lawn-mower? This is the place to come.

Havana's most important commercial thoroughfares have traditionally been Calles San Rafael and Neptuno, immediately west of Parque Central. This is where the major department stores were located in Cuba's heyday before 1959. They remained open throughout the Revolution, each year growing more dour and minimalist in what they sold. Since the Special Period, they have been threadbare. The vitality is coming back, however, and both streets are thronged again with shoppers hoping to find something worthwhile to buy with their pesos. Foreigners will find little of interest, as the Cuban-made items for sale here are for the most part shoddy in the extreme.

If you need toiletries and general supplies, head for any of the **Tiendas Panamericanos** that serve Cubans with dollars. You'll find them all over Havana, including, in Vedado, outside the Hotel Ha-

BUYING CUBAN CIGARS

Quality cigars can be bought at virtually every restaurant, hotel, and shop that welcomes tourists. A box of 25 top-class cigars will cost as little as US$30. A better bet is to combine your purchase with a visit to a cigar factory. **La Casa del Habano,** in the Partagas factory at Industria #520, e/ Barcelona y Dragones in Habana Viejo, tel. 33-8060, has a massive walk-in humidor. The prices here, however, are higher than elsewhere. The **Palacio de Tabaco** on the ground floor of the Corona factory on Calle Agramonte, is also good.

For the widest selection, visit **Casa del Tabaco,** which has three branches in Havana: Avenida 5ta #1407 esq. 16, Miramar, tel. 29-4040, open Mon.-Sat. 10.30 a.m.-6.30 p.m.; Calle Obispo y Bernaza, Habana Vieja, tel. 63-1242, open daily 10 a.m.-8 p.m., and Residencial Turistico Marina Hemingway, Calle 248 y Avenida 5ta, tel. 33-1154, open Mon.-Fri. 9 a.m.-7 p.m. An option popular with VIPs is **La Casa de 5 y 16,** tel. 29-4040 or 33-11185, also known as "The Temple of the Habano" and selling over 300 varieties of cigars; it's upstairs in a mansion on the corner of Avenida 5 and Calle 16. Also recommended is the **Palacio de Tabaco** at the corner of Avenida 3 and Calle 28; and the **Casa del Tabaco El Corojo,** to the left of the lobby in the Hotel Meliá Cohiba.

The Infotur office on the ground floor of the Casa Manzana de Gomez off Parque Central reportedly stocks some rarer smokes.

Most shops sell by the box only. Due to high demand, cigars are often on back order. Cohibas were rare abroad in 1996 (one major London cigar merchant told me that the Cubans are holding back supply to raise prices). Prices can vary up to 20% from store to store, so shop around. If one store doesn't have what you desire, another surely will.

Buying for Speculation

If you're buying for speculation, buy the best. The only serious collectors' market in cigars is in pre-revolutionary cigars, according to Anwer Bati in *The*

Cigar Companion. Older cigars produced before the 1959 Revolution are commonly described as "pre-Castro." Those made before President Kennedy declared the US trade embargo against Cuba in February 1962 are "pre-embargo."

Pre-Castro or pre-embargo cigars are printed with MADE IN HAVANA-CUBA on the bottom of the box instead of the standard HECHO EN CUBA used today. Since 1985, handmade Cuban cigars have carried the Cubatabaco stamp plus a factory mark and, since 1989, the legend "Hecho en Cuba. Totalmente a Mano" (Made in Cuba. Completely by Hand). If it reads "Hecho a Mano," the cigars are most likely hand-*finished* (i.e., only the wrapper was put on by hand) rather than handmade. If its states only "Hecho en Cuba," they are assuredly machine-made.

In addition, there are styles, sizes, and brands of cigars that have not been made in Cuba since shortly after the Revolution. They're the most valuable (a Belinda corona from the late '30s will sell for $100 or more). And it's not unusual for a box of 100 Montecristo No. 1s from the late 1950s to sell for $4,500 or more.

Today, London is the Havana cigar capital of the world. **Fox/Lewis Cigar Merchants,** 19 St. James's St., London SW1, tel. (171) 930-3787, has the largest stock of Cuban reserves. Also try **Davidoff of London,** 35 St. James St., London SW1, tel. (171) 930-3079.

Street Deals

Street deals are no deal. Everywhere you walk in Havana, *jiniteros* will offer you cigars at discount prices. You'll be tempted by what seems the deal of the century. Forget it! They're virtually guaranteed to be low-quality, machine-made cigars sold falsely as Montecristos or Romeo y Julietas to unsuspecting tourists. Don't be taken in by the sealed counterfeit box, either. It, too, is surely a fake.

You can also buy inferior domestic cigars, called "torpedoes," for about one peso—US$1—in bars and restaurants and on the street.

---

bana Libre, two blocks east on La Rampa, and also two blocks north on Calles 17 and M.

The booklet *La Habana: Touristic and Commercial Guide,* published by Infotur, lists the whereabouts of Tiendas Panamericanos.

MUSIC AND MUSICAL INSTRUMENTS

You'll find cassettes and CDs for sale at every turn. Musicians in restaurants will offer to sell you cassette tapes of their music for US$5-8. However, for the widest selection, head to Miramar and **Max Music,** at Calle 33 #2003 e/ 20 y 22, tel. 33-3002, fax 33-3006; or **Casa de la Música,** at Calle 20 #3309 esq. 35. Both have huge collections of cassettes and CDs running the gamut of Cuban, plus musical instruments. So does the **Tienda de Música,** nearby. You can buy a quality guitar for US$200, or a full-size conga drum for US$100.

Imágenes S.A., 5ta Av. #18008 esq. 182, Reparto Flores, Playa, Havana, tel. 33-6136, fax 33-6168, also has a large stock of CDs and cassettes, plus videos of live performances.

RUM AND CIGARS

Virtually every hotel store sells genuine Cuban cigars, rum, and other Cuban spirits. The widest range of cigars is offered by the **Casa de la Tabaco** and the humidor in the **Partagas** factory. *Don't buy from* jiniteros on the street!

Two stores specialize in rums and offer tastings before you buy. The first is **Casa de Ron,** above El Floridita restaurant at the top end of Calle Obispo, tel. 63-1242. It's open daily 10 a.m.-8 p.m. Alternately, try the **Taberna del**

Galeón, at the bottom of Calle Obispo, on the southeast corner of Plaza de Armas, tel. 33-8061.

Last-minute shoppers find cigars and rums for sale in the duty-free stores in the airport departure lounges.

MISCELLANEOUS

Flowers

Floriarte, at Avenida 5ta and Calle 248, at the entrance to Marina Hemingway 12 km west of downtown, sells locally grown hydrangeas, gladioli, Japanese daisies, and orchids. You may be able to buy export-ready plants. The company plans to open five boutiques selling flowers, handmade ceramics, blown glass ornaments, and costume jewelry.

Gifts For Children

You'll be hard-pressed to find stores catering to children. However, most **Tiendas Panamericanos** sell a limited range of kiddie's toys and supplies. **El Mundo de los Niños** (Children's World) is a small, sparsely stocked children's store on Calle San Rafael and Oquendo, six blocks east of Calzada de Infanta.

SERVICES AND INFORMATION

MONEY

Banks

The most important of the relatively few banks in Havana catering to foreigners is the **Banco Financiero Internacional,** in the Hotel Habana Libre in Vedado, tel. 33-4011. It's at the end of the corridor past the airline offices and is open Mon.-Sat. 8 a.m.-3 p.m. Other BFI branches are located at Linea (Avenida 7ra) #1, Vedado, tel. 33-3003 or 33-3148, fax 33-3006, open Mon.-Fri. 8:30 a.m.-3 p.m.; and at the corner of Linea and Calle 21. The **Banco Nacional** has a branch with a foreign-exchange desk at Calle M and Linea, open Mon.-Fri. 8:30 a.m.-1 p.m.

The **Banco Internacional de Comercio,** Avenida 20 de Mayo and Ayestarán, Habana

6, tel. 33-5115, fax 33-5112, open Mon.-Fri. 8 a.m.-1 p.m., primarily caters to foreign businesses, as does the Dutch-owned **Netherlands Caribbean Banking,** Avenida 5ta #6407, esq. 76, Miramar, tel. 33-0419, fax 33-0472, open Mon.-Fri., 8 a.m.-5 p.m.

Credit Cards and Traveler's Checks

Virtually every restaurant, hotel, and government store will accept payment by credit card and—with somewhat more hesitancy—travelers' checks (as long as they are not issued by a US bank). You can advance cash against your credit card (US$100 minimum; $5,000 maximum) at the **Banco Financiero Internacional** in the Hotel Habana Libre (see above). Visa, MasterCard, Access, Diner's Club, Eurocard, Carnet, and Banamex are accepted.

Traveler's checks can be cashed at most hotel cashier desks, as well as at banks. Many stores also accept them for direct payment.

Moneychangers

There are plenty of moneychangers around farmers' markets *(mercados agropercuarios)*. They're the guys making a strange "hands-on-the-steering-wheel-running-a-chicane" motion. You'll also be approached in touristy areas such as the Prado. If you change money illegally, be cautious of scams.

The government agency **Cadesa** operates several *buros de cambio,* where you can change US dollars and other foreign currency into pesos. The going rate closely follows the black market rate and has taken steam out of the latter. At press time, Cadesa offered 20 pesos for US$1. Most bureaus are located in residential neighborhoods and are clearly designed to soak up US dollars from the local economy. There's a Cadesa booth opposite Cine Yara, outside the

entrance to Coppelia, in Vedado—perfect for paying for Coppelia ice-cream!

COMMUNICATIONS

Postal Service and Courier Mail

Most major tourist hotels have small post offices and philatelic bureaus. Havana is also well served by post offices, which are relatively efficient. If you use those in residential districts, expect a long wait in line (you'll also need pesos). Far quicker is to use the small post office inside the lobby of the Hotel Habana Libre in Vedado (open 24 hours). It also serves as a DHL office. In Habana Vieja, try the post office on the northeast corner of the Plaza de la Catedral; the one on the west side of Plaza de San Francisco; the one at 518 Calle Obispo; the one next to the Gran Teatro on Parque Central; or the one on the north side of the railway station on Avenida de Bélgica.

USEFUL HAVANA TELEPHONE NUMBERS

MEDICAL

Clínica Cira García (international clinic
   and 24-hour pharmacy) . . . . tel. 33-2811
Farmacia Internacional (pharmacy) . . . . tel. 33-2051
Hospital Hermanos Almeijeiras . . . . tel. 70-7721

EMERGENCY

Police . . . . tel. 82-0116
Ambulance . . . . tel. 44-5551/2/3
Asistur . . . . tel. 62-5519

EMBASSIES

Canada . . . . tel. 33-2516, 33-2517
France . . . . tel. 33-0335, 33-2080
Germany . . . . tel. 33-2460
Italy . . . . tel. 33-3378 or 33-3334
Spain . . . . tel. 33-8029
United Kingdom . . . . tel. 33-1771/2
United States (Interest Office) . . . . tel. 32-0551/2/3/4/5/6/7/8/9

TRANSPORTATION

Bus and Rail Agency (Agencia de Ferrocarril y Ómnibus) . . . . tel. 41-4561
Bus Terminal (Terminal de Ómnibus Nacionales) . . . . tel. 79-2456
Railway Station (Estación Central de Ferrocarril) . . . . tel. 62-1920
Terminal de Ferries (for Isla de la Juventud) . . . . tel. 81-1108
Cubana de Aviación Reservations (National) . . . . tel. 70-9391
Cubana de Aviación Reservations (International) . . . . tel. 78-4961
José Martí International Airport . . . . tel. 45-3133 or 45-3308

Most post offices are open weekdays 10 a.m.-5 p.m. and Saturday 8 a.m.-3 p.m. You can send a fax, telex, or telegram at most post offices.

Several courier services are available in Havana. **DHL Worldwide Express** is headquartered at Avenida 1ra y Calle 42, Miramar, tel. 33-1876, fax 33-1578, and operates other offices—in the Hotel Yagrumas, tel. 650-4460; at Calle 40 and Avenida 1; and in the Hotel Habana Libre. All the DHL offices are open weekdays 9 a.m.-6 p.m. and Saturday 9 a.m.-noon.

Other express mail services include **Cubapacks**, Calle 22 #4115, Miramar, tel. 33-2134 or 33-2817, which is open Mon.-Fri. 8:30 a.m.-noon and 1:30-5:30 p.m.; **Cubanacán Express**, Avenida 5ta #8210, e/ 82 y 84, Miramar, tel. 33-2331 or 33-2833, open Mon.-Fri. 8 a.m.-5 p.m.; and **Cubapost**, Avenida 5ta y 112, Playa, tel. 33-6097, fax 33-6098, open Mon.-Fri. 8 a.m.-4 p.m. and Saturday 8 a.m.-2 p.m.

Telephones and Fax Service
Some of the large, upscale tourist hotels now have direct-dial telephones in guest rooms for international calls. Others will connect you via the hotel operator.

At the Hotel Habana Libre, the public can make calls at the telephone exchange in the lobby—a receptionist links you with the international operator (it can take forever, so leave plenty of time). Calls are charged per minute: US$3 to North America, US$4 to Caribbean countries, US$5 to South America, US$6 to Europe and the rest of the world. Calls within Cuba cost US$1-2.75 per minute, depending on zone. Local calls cost US30 cents for the first minute and US10 cents each minute thereafter.

There are also public telephones for international calls in the **International Press Center,** Centro de Prensa Internacional, tel. 32-0526/27/28, on La Rampa and Calle O in Vedado. You can also send faxes or make a telex here (US$2.50 per minute to the US; US$3.50 to the Caribbean, Mexico, and Central America; US$4.25 to South America; and US$5.50 to the rest of the world). It's open 8:30 a.m.-5 p.m.

Cubacel, Calle 28 No.510 e/ 5ta y 7ma, Miramar, tel. 33-0222, fax 33-1737, offers cellular telephone service. If you bring your own phone, the Cubacel office will provide you with linkage. It's a more expensive proposition to rent a cellular phone, but worthwhile if you plan on making lots of international calls. Cubacel also has an office at José Martí International Airport.

Intertel, Compañia Internacional de Telecomunicaciones, at Calle 33 #1427 esq. 18, Miramar, tel. 33-2476, fax 33-2504, handles international services.

GOVERNMENT OFFICES

Immigration and Customs
All immigration issues relating to foreigners are handled by the **Ministerio de Relaciones Exteriores,** Ministry of Foreign Relations, at Avenida 5ta and G, in Vedado, tel. 30-5031.

You can have **passport photos** taken at the International Press Center on La Rampa and Calle O, in Vedado. You can also have photos for visas, passports etc. taken at **Fotógrafa,** Calle Obispo #515, a tiny hole in the wall open 10 a.m.-4 p.m.

The main **Customs** office is on Avenida San Pedro, opposite the Iglesia San Francisco de Asís; it's upstairs, to the right.

Consulates
Most consulates and embassies are located in Miramar (see chart for addresses and phone numbers). The **US Interests Section,** the equivalent of an embassy but lacking an ambassador,

---

US AND CUBAN EMBASSY SURROGATES

In September 1977, Interests Sections—the equivalent of embassies, but without ambassadors—were established in Havana and Washington for the purpose of communications between the two governments, which had severed diplomatic relations. The Interests Sections provide a limited amount of consular services but are mostly geared to serving political agendas.

The US government recommends that its citizens traveling to Cuba register at the Interests Section, located in the Swiss Embassy in the former US Embassy building on Calzada, e/ L y M, in Vedado, tel. 32-0551 or 32-9700. The Cuban Interests Section in Washington serves the same function and is notoriously slow in handling inquiries, if the staff replies at all; 2630 16th St. NW, Washington, DC 20009, tel. (202) 797-8518, fax (202) 797-8521.

EMBASSIES AND CONSULATES IN CUBA

The following nations have embassies/consulates in Havana. Phone numbers and addresses change frequently. Call to confirm address and opening hours.

Argentina: Calle 36 #511, Miramar, tel. 33-2972 or 33-2549, fax 33-2140

Austria: Calle 4 #101, Miramar, tel. 33-2394 or 33-2825, fax 33-1235

Belgium: Avenida 5ta # 7408, Miramar, tel. 33-2410 or 33-2561, fax 33-1318

Bolivia: Calle 26 #113, Miramar, tel. 33-2127 or 33-2426, fax 33-2739

Brazil: Calle 16 #503, Miramar, tel. 33-2026 or 33-2786, fax 33-2328

Bulgaria: Calle B #252, Vedado, tel. 33-3125, 33-3126, or 33-3129, fax 33-3297

Canada: Calle 30 #518, Miramar, tel. 33-2516 or 33-2517, fax 33-1069

Chile: Avenida 33 #1423, Miramar, tel. 33-1222 or 33-1223, fax 33-1694

China, People's Republic of: Calle C #317 e/ 13 and 15, Vedado, tel. 33-3020 or 00-0014, fax 33-3092

Colombia: Calle 14 #515, Miramar, tel. 33-1246 or 33-1247, fax 33-1249

Czech Republic: Avenida Kohly #259, Nuevo Vedado, tel. 33-3105, 33-3467 or 33 3201, fax 33-3596

Denmark: Paseo de Martí #20, Habana Vieja, tel. 33-8128 or 33-8144, fax 33-8127

Ecuador: Avenida 5ta #4407, Miramar, tel. 33-2034 or 33-2820, fax 33-2868

Egypt: Avenida 5ta #1801, Miramar, tel. 33-2441 or 33-2542

Finland: Avenida 7ra #6003, Miramar, tel. 33-2029 or 33-2449, fax 33-2029

France: Calle 14 #312, Miramar, tel. 33-0335 or 33-2080

Germany: Calle B #652, Miramar, tel. 33-2460, fax 33-1586

Greece: Avenida 5ta #7802, Miramar, tel. 33-2995 or 33-2854, fax 33-1784

Hungary: Calle G #458, Vedado, tel. 33-3045, 33-3098, or 33-3365

India: Calle 21 #202, Vedado, tel. 33-3106, 00-3169 or 33-3777, fax 33-3287

Italy: Paseo #606, Vedado, tel. 33-3378

Jamaica: Avenida 5ta #3608, Miramar, tel. 33-2908

Japan: Calle N #62, Vedado, tel. 33-3454 or 33-3355

Mexico: Calle 12 #518, Miramar, tel. 33-0856 or 33-2383, fax 33-2294

Netherlands: Calle 8 #307, Miramar, tel. 33-2511 or 33-2512, fax 33-2059

Nicaragua: Calle 20 #709, Miramar, tel. 33-1025, fax 33-6323

Nigeria: Avenida 5ta #1401, Miramar, tel. 33-2898 or 33-2091, fax 33-2202

Norway: Paseo de Martí #20, Habana Vieja, tel. 33-8128 or 33-8144, fax 33-8127

Palestine: Calle 20 #714, Miramar, tel. 33-2556, fax 33-1159

Panama: Calle 26 #109, Miramar, tel. 33-1673, fax 33-1674

Peru: Calle 36 #109, Miramar, tel. 33-2477 or 33-2632, fax 33-2636

Philippines: Avenida 7maB #6004, tel. 33-1372, fax 33-2915

Poland: Avenida 5ta #4407, Miramar, tel./fax 33-1323

Portugal: Avenida 5ta #6604, Miramar, tel. 33-0149 or 33-2871, fax 33-2593

Romania: Calle 21 #307, Vedado, tel. 33-3325 or 33-3322, fax 33-3324

Russia: Avenida 5ta #6402, Miramar, tel. 33-1080 or 33-1085, fax 33-1038

(continues on next page)

EMBASSIES AND CONSULATES IN CUBA
(continued)

Slovak Republic: Calle 66 #521, Miramar, tel. 33-1884 or 33-1885, fax 33-1883

Spain: Calle Cárcel #51, Habana Viejo, tel. 33-8025 or 33-8093, fax 33-8006

Sri Lanka: Calle 32 #307, Miramar, tel. 33-2649 or 33-2562, fax 33-2183

Sweden: Avenida 31A #1411, Miramar, tel. 33-2563 or 33-2831, fax 33-1194

Switzerland: Avenida 5ta #2005, Miramar, tel. 33-2611 or 33-2729, fax 33-1148

Syria: Avenida 5ta #7402, Miramar, tel. 33-2071, 33-2266 or 33-2434, fax 33-2829

Turkey: Calle 20 #301, Miramar, tel. 33-2933 or 33-2237, fax 33-2899

Ukraine: Avenida 5ta #4405, Miramar, tel. 33-2374 or 33-2586, fax 33-2341

United Kingdom: Calle 34 #708, Miramar, tel. 33-1049, 33-1771, 33-1772, 33-1299,or 33-1286, fax 33-8104

United States: (Interest Office) Calzada e/ L y M, Vedado, tel. 32-0551/2/3/4/5/6/7/8/9

Uruguay: Calle 14 #506, Miramar, tel. 33-2311 or 33-2040, fax 33-2246

Venezuela: Calle 36A #704, Miramar, tel. 33-2497, 33-2662, or 33-2612, fax 33-2773

Vietnam: Avenida 5ta #1802, Miramar, tel. 33-1042, 33-1501, or 33-1502, fax 33-1041

Yugoslavia: Calle 42 #115, Miramar, tel. 33-2607 or 33-2488, fax 33-2982

Zimbabwe: Avenida 3ra #1001, Miramar, tel. 33-2137 or 33-2857, fax 33-2720

---

faces the Malecón at Calzada (Calle 5ta) e/ L y M in Vedado, tel. 33-3551-59.

TRAVEL AGENCIES AND TOURIST ASSISTANCE

Travel Agencies

Most hotels have tour bureaus that can make reservations for excursions, car rental, and possibly air flights. The best dedicated agency is probably **San Cristobal Agencia de Viajes,** on Calle Oficios #110 e/ Lamparilla y Amargura, next to the Habaguanex office on the northwest corner of the Plaza de San Francisco, tel. 33-9585, fax 33-9586.

The main tour agencies also double as general travel agencies. Try **Havanatur,** at Calle 2 #17 e/ Avenida 1ra y 3ra, Miramar, tel. 33-2161, or at La Rampa and Calle P, tel. 70-5284.

Tourist Assistance

Asistur, at Prado #254 e/ Animas y Trocadero, tel. 33-8527 or 62-5519, fax 33-8087, e-mail asistur@asist.sid.cu, provides legal assistance plus other aid to tourists in the event of emergencies. It's open 24 hours. It also has a booth in the lobby of the Hotel Capri, in Vedado.

If you have items stolen, you should report the theft to the nearest police station. At press time, there was no special unit responsible for pursuing thefts from tourists.

Infotur, the government tourist information bureau, has offices (Palacios de Turismo) throughout Havana, including in the arrivals lounge at José Martí International Airport, tel. 45-3542. The staff are friendly and can make reservations for car rentals, accommodations, and transfers. The head office is at Avenida 3ra and Calle 28, in Miramar, tel. 33-8383, fax 33-8164. The Infotur office, Zulueta esq. Neptuno, on the east side of Parque Central, tel. 63-6960, has a good deal of tourist literature, including maps. Likewise, in Vedado you'll find a well-stocked Infotur office at the base of La Rampa and Calle O.

Rumbos operates **Verhabana,** Calle Bernaza #1 at O'Reilly, Habana Vieja, tel./fax 33-8847, an information office specializing in tourism in Havana. Verhabana arranges airport transfers, accommodations, tours, sports and recreation, and restaurant and nightclub reservations. It's open 24 hours year-round. You'll find a **"Magic Window"** offering computerized click-on, click-off information service in the lobby of the Hotel Capri. It uses Windows 95 software to display a visual directory of tourist facilities and attractions in Havana and Varadero.

The office of the Cuban tourism agency, **Cubatur,** at Calle F #157, e/ Calzada y Calle 9 in Vedado, tel. 33-4155, provides information and can make arrangements for independent travelers, as can the headquarters of Havanatur, at Calle 2 #17 e/ 1ra y 3ra, Miramar, tel. 33-2161, and Havanatur's **Tour & Travel,** Avenida 5ta #8409 e/ 84 y 86, Miramar, tel. 33-2433, fax 33-1760. Havanatur's office in Vedado is on La Rampa and Calle P, tel. 70-5284; the staff are very helpful—Julio Ladron de Guevara particularly so (he's also fluent in English).

In Habana Vieja, **Habaguanex,** Calle Oficios #110, on Plaza de San Francisco, tel. 33-8693, fax 33-8697, can provide information on hotels, restaurants, and other places under its umbrella.

Virtually every hotel has a **buro de turismo** In the lobby. Most of the bureaus are geared to selling package excursions, but you'll usually find the staff willing and conscientious, if not always chockfull of information. The best bureau is undoubtedly that in the lobby of the Hotel Habana Libre.

Tourist Guides and Publications

Infotur publishes a compact "touristic and commercial guide" called La Habana, which lists the addresses and telephone numbers of hotels, restaurants, bars, shopping centers, and a full range of services and contains a fold-out map. You can pick it up at any Palacio de Turismo or hotel tour bureau.

Granma is published weekly in various languages, including English. You can usually obtain a copy in hotel lobbies. It features listings of major hotels, restaurants, car rental companies, events, and entertainment in Havana.

MAPS AND NAUTICAL CHARTS

You'll find maps of Havana for sale at most Infotur offices and many hotel gift stores. However, the best source is **Tienda de las Navegantes,** Calle Mercaderes #115, e/ Obispo y Obrapía. Habana Vieja, tel. 61-3625 or 62-3466 (for boaters, VHF channel 16 CMYP3050), which has a wide range of tourist maps of Havana and provinces as well as nautical charts and special-

ized maps such as Cementerio Colón: Map Turístico. If you're planning on touring farther afield, you should definitely head here. Don't count on being able to buy maps covering your destination once you leave Havana.

Two of the best maps are Mapa de La Habana Vieja; Patrimonio de la Humanidad and Ciudad de la Habana: Mapa Turística, both produced by the Instituto Cubano de Geodesia y Cartografía. The road maps are very detailed. The map of Habana Vieja even includes pictures and details of most historic buildings of importance, plus other sites of interest. The Instituto also produces a road map (mapa de carreteras) to La Habana Province, as well as maps of individual tourist attractions such as Parque Lenin. The road map isn't very good.

Look for the excellent little booklet **La Habana Vieja: Guía Turística** (also published by the Instituto Cubano de Geodesia y Cartografía), which contains the most detailed maps of Habana Vieja available. It also features information on key sites of interest, as well as bus routes. You can also pick up a small map of Habana Vieja at the Habaguanex office.

MEDICAL SERVICES

The larger, upscale tourist hotels have nurses on duty. Other hotels will be able to request a doctor for in-house diagnosis and treatment for minor ailments.

Tourists needing medical assistance are usually steered to the **Clínica Cira García,** at Calle 20 #4101 and Avenida 41 in Miramar, tel. 33-2811, fax 33-1633. The gleaming, fully staffed hospital is entirely dedicated to serving foreigners. You pay in dollars—credit cards are acceptable unless they're issued on a US bank (in which case, greenbacks are required, muchas gracias). Similarly, the recently opened **Instituto Pedro Kouri,** in Marianao, is devoted to "international medical care," especially HIV/AIDS, hepatitis, and contagious and parasitic diseases. Contact Servimed (a Spanish acronym for Specialized Medical Services for Health Tourism), Calle 18 #4304 e/ 43 y 47, in Miramar, tel. 33-2658, fax 33-2948.

Low-income patients are served by the 24-story, 1,000-bed **Hospital Hermanos Almeijeiras,** at the corner of Padre Varela and San Lazaro, in Centro Habana, tel. 70-7721.

GENETIC ENGINEERING

Cuba is a biotech minipower. In 1965, there were said to be only 12 research scientists in Cuba; today there are more than 25,000. Under Fidel Castro's personal patronage, Cuba has evolved one of the world's most advanced genetic engineering and biotechnology industries, with large-scale investment coming from public sources such as the Pan American Health Organization and the World Food Program.

The program is led by the Center for Genetic Engineering and Biotechnology, in the Havana suburb of Playa. The center, perhaps the most sophisticated research facility in the Third World, opened in 1986 as one of more than two dozen Cuban institutes dedicated to the biological sciences. Together they supply state-of-the-art health products to the world (sold through the marketing entity Heber Biotec), bringing in over US$100 million annually.

Cuba has developed nearly 200 products, both innovative and derivative. It invented and manufactures vaccines for cerebral meningitis, cholera, hepatitis B, interferon for the treatment of AIDS and cancer, and a skin growth factor to speed the healing of burns. For years, Cuba has touted a cure for the skin diseases vitiligo. Recently it developed PPG, a "wonder drug" that reputedly washes cholesterol out of blood and, incidentally, is said to increase sexual potency (the source of a brisk black market for peddlers selling the drug to tourists). In 1996, CIGB scientists even began testing a vaccine to prevent HIV infection.

Other advances have been made in agriculture and industrial bioengineering. Alas, US law denies these life-saving wonders from being sold in the United States and prohibits the export to Cuba of any product (including foreign-made products bearing a US patent) that might aid the development of medicines and biotechnology on the island.

Clínica Cira García has a 24-hour pharmacy at the rear, tel. 33-2811, ext. 14. It also has a splendid range of Western drugs for not much more than the same price you'd pay in the US. The **Farmacia Internacional,** on the opposite side of Avenida 41, tel. 33-2051, is also well stocked with Western pharmaceuticals and toiletries. It's open Mon.-Fri. 9 a.m.-5:45 p.m. and Saturday 9 a.m.-noon. You may be approached by Cubans outside; they'll give you money to purchase desparately needed medicines inside, as a guard stands at the gate to stop Cubans entering this foreigners-only pharmacy.

Optima Miramar, at Avenida 7ma and Calle 24, Miramar, tel. 33-2990, fax 33-2803, provides full-service optician and optometrist services.

Need an invigorating **massage** or beauty treatment? Try Servimed, which offers various programs for foreigners seeking specialized treatments—everything from orthopedic surgery to spa therapy. Alternately, call **Biotop** at Avenida 7 #2603 in Miramar, tel. 33-2377, fax 33-2378, which has a gymnasium, sauna, and salt and algae baths. It offers health and beauty treatments. Several hotels offer massages and have spas, most notably the **Hotel Cohiba,** at the base of Avenida Paseo in Vedado, tel. 33-3636.

The Hotel Presidente, tel. 32-7521, offers massage services (US$10 general, US$5 local). More specialized massages are also offered by a woman named Dulce María in the Hostal Valencia, on Calle Oficios in Habana Vieja, tel. 61-0412, who offers acupressure and reflexology with an emphasis on special points that stimulate your "sports prowess and sexual functions." A licensed medicinal herbalist operates at Obrapía #212, Mon.-Sat. 9 a.m.-6 p.m.

MISCELLANEOUS SERVICES

Laundromats
The only "self-service" laundry for foreigners I know of is the ultra-modern **Aster Lavandería,** on Calle 34 e/ 3 y 5, in Miramar tel. 33-1622. You can leave your clothes here and pick them up the same day. It costs US$3 per load for wash-and-dry. It's open Mon.-Sat. 8 a.m.-3 p.m. Most upscale hotels offer dry-cleaning and laundry service. It's expensive and usually takes two days. It's easy enough to find locals willing to wash your clothes for a few dollars. Ask around.

The telephone directory lists several dozen other laundries throughout Havana, including more than a dozen self-service *(auto servicio)* locales, most in the Mariano area. Look under the heading: **Tintorerías y Lavanderias.**

Photography

Photo Service stores offer a rapid development service (film processing US$2, slide processing US$5, slide framing US20 cents per slide) and passport photos (six for US$3). The stores also sell cassette tapes, video cassettes, and even a limited range of instamatic and SLR cameras. At press time, film cost: Fujicolor 100 US$4.85, Ektachrome Elite 100 US$10, Kodacolor 100 US$5.45. The main office is inside the International Press Center at Calle 23 y O, Vedado, tel. 33-5031.

Imágenes, Calle 26 #120 esq. Avenida 3ra, Miramar, tel. 33-2469, also rents and sells cameras and film. It's open Mon.-Sat. 8 a.m.-9 p.m.

Libraries

Havana has many libraries. The main one is the **Biblioteca Nacional,** on the east side of Plaza de la Revolución, tel. 79-6091, fax 33-5072. It's open Mon.-Sat. 8 a.m.-6 p.m. You can use the reference room.

There are several specialized libraries, too. The **Biblioteca del Instituto de Literatura y Lingüística,** on Avenida Salvador Allende #710 e/ Castillejo y Soledad, tel. 75405, for example, has a huge collection of novels and foreign-language texts (open Mon.-Fri. 8 a.m.-5 p.m. and Saturday 8 a.m.-2 p.m.). The **Biblioteca Nacional de Ciencias y Tecnología,** in the Academy of Sciences in the Capitolio in Habana Vieja, tel. 60-3411, ext. 1329, has books on sciences and technology. It's open Mon.-Fri. 8:30 a.m.-5 p.m. and Saturday 8:30 a.m.-4 p.m.

GETTING THERE

BY AIR

The vast majority of flights to Cuba arrive in Havana, which in 1996 was served by more than two dozen airlines.

José Martí International Airport

Most visitors to Cuba arrive by air at the José Martí International Airport, 25 km southwest of downtown Havana on Avenida de la Independencia (Avenida Rancho Boyeros), in the Rancho Boyeros district, tel. 33-5177/78/79 or 79-6081. The terminal is stretched to handle the growing volume of passengers. In 1996, the Canadian government agreed to finance construction of a new terminal.

Terminals: The airport has three terminals. They're well apart from each other and accessed by different roads (nor are they linked by a connecting bus service). **Terminal One,** on the south side of the runway, is the most important terminal and handles most international flights plus Cubana domestic flights. **Terminal Two,** on the north side of the runway, also handles international flights, including Aeroflot, Aeromextour, Avianca, Copa, Lacsa, Lanchile, LTU, Mex-icana, and Tame. (Miami charter flights depart and arrive here.) **Terminal Three** (also called Terminal Caribbean), also on the northwest side of the runway (south of the village of Wajay), handles small-plane domestic flights offered by Aero Caribbean. Flights to Cayo Largo also depart from here. *Make sure you arrive at the correct terminal for your departure!*

Immigration and Customs: The immigration procedures are straightforward and no more daunting than when arriving at virtually any other Caribbean destination. Anticipate a long delay, however, as the immigration hall is cramped and long lines often develop (especially at Terminal One). At times, the lines disintegrate into a scrum. Personal carry-on baggage is X-rayed upon arrival. Try to arrive with carry-on baggage only—the wait for checked luggage can take forever. Terminal Two is more efficient.

Tourist Information: Arriving at either terminal, you'll pass a Cubatur and Rumbos tourist information booth that sells guidebooks and maps and arranges accommodations and shuttle transfers into town. You should check in here if you have prepaid vouchers for accommodations or transfers into town. Much has been written about the problems encountered by travelers arriving

AIRLINE OFFICES

The following airlines have their main offices at La Rampa #64 (Avenida 23) between Calles P and Q:

AeroCaribbean: tel. 79-7524/5, fax 33-5016

Aeroflot: tel. 79-6138 or 70-6292, fax 33-3288

Aerovaradero: tel. 33-4126

Air Canada: tel. 33-3730, fax 33-3729

Cubana: (international) tel. 78-4961 or 33-4949, fax 33-3323

Iberia: tel. 33-5041, fax 33-5061

LTU: tel. 33-3542

Martinair: tel. 33-4364 or 33-3730, fax 33-3729

Mexicana: tel. 33-3531

The following also have offices in Havana:

Aerogaviota: Calle 47 #2814, tel. 33-2621

Aeroméxico: José Martí International Airport, tel. 70-7701, fax 33-5169

Cubana: (domestic) Calzada de Infanta #53, tel. 70-5961

Lacsa: Hotel Habana Libre, tel. 33-3114, fax 33-3728

Viasa: Hotel Habana Libre, tel. 33-3130, fax 33-3611

---

without accommodations. However, I've *never* arrived with pre-booked lodging (nor have I ever had any problems at Immigration). I've simply breezed through Immigration and Customs and taken transport into town without a second glance.

For information on arrivals and departures, call 45-3133 or 70-7701.

Getting into Town: Minibus shuttle services are operated by tourist agencies such as Cubanacán. You'll find the buses parked outside the terminals. Normally, they serve arriving tour groups, but they are also happy to act as a shuttle service. Ask the drivers, or look for the Cubatur representative. You'll be charged about US$10 to get to downtown hotels. The buses will drop you at any of several major hotels. Most people arriving on package tours will have been issued prepaid vouchers for the shuttle. Minibus transfers cost US$18 roundtrip to Playas del Este (US$12 one-way) and US$40 roundtrip (US$25 one-way) to Pinar del Río.

By Public Bus: A bus marked "Aeropuerto" departs from Terminal One for Vedado and Parque Central about 15 minutes after the arrival of domestic flights (one peso). Alternately, you can catch buses to Parque de la Fraternidad on the edge of Habana Vieja (no. M-2 from Santiago de las Vegas) from the east side of Avenida de la Independencia—a real hassle! The journey takes about one hour, but the wait can be just as long. Bus service *to* the airport is sporadic.

By Taxi: There are plenty of Turistaxis immediately outside the airport arrivals hall. The fare between downtown and the airport is normally US$13-15. You can also take a private (albeit illegal) taxi for a negotiable fee (usually about US$8); touts will approach you.

Car Rental: Havanautos, tel. 33-5197, and **Transauto Rent-a-Car,** tel. 33-5177, have offices outside the arrival halls of Terminal 1 and Terminal 2, tel. 33-5215. **Cubacar,** tel. 33-5546, also has an office at Terminal 1. The wide, fast Avenida de la Independencia is potholed in places, surprisingly busy during the day (especially with speeding taxis and trucks belching out thick fumes), and poorly lit at night. If arriving with a bicycle, you're best off taking a taxi into town.

BY SEA

At press time, only one passenger vessel called in at Havana. The *Costa Playa* arrives each Saturday at 9 a.m. and leaves about 2 a.m. the following morning on one-week cruises offered year-round from Puerto Plata, in the Dominican Republic. You can also join the ship in Havana for a seven-day cruise to Bahía Nipe, Puerto Plata, Santiago de Cuba, and Montego Bay (Jamaica). The cruises are offered by Costa Cruceros (see "Cruising," under "Getting There" in the On The Road chapter). You can book through hotel tour desks in Cuba. Optional excursions (US$25-60) are offered, including a city tour, a visit to a tobacco factory, the botanic garden and ExpoCuba, the Hemingway Museum and Cojímar, the beaches of Playas del Este, and the Tropicana nightclub.

By the time you read this, additional cruise ships may be calling in Havana, which is destined to become one of the biggest ports-of-call in the world once the US embargo is lifted.

Terminal Sierra Maestra

This is Havana's spanking new cruise terminal, tel. 33-6607, fax 33-6759, inaugurated on 1 December 1995. The facility is a natty conversion of the old Customs building on Avenida San Pedro opposite the Iglesia y Convento San Francisco de Asís. What a setting! Passengers step through the doorways directly onto Plaza de San Francisco and find themselves in the heart of Habana Vieja, a mere stone's throw away.

Only Pier 1 is currently in operation. Two additional piers will be completed as future needs of the cruise industry demand. When complete, the facility will be able to handle four ships at one time (one on each side of Piers 1 and 3).

The skylit facility—owned and operated jointly by Cubanco S.A. (owned by the Cuban Ministry of Transport) and a Curaçao-based Italian company called Milestone—is world-class, combining colonial-style architecture with ultramodern aluminum and plate glass. Pier 1 has two floors, each 8,000 square meters. Downstairs is a parking lot and bus terminal. Passengers are processed upstairs, which has wooden boardwalks outside and hardwood parquet floor inside, and a 1948 Dodge De Luxe D24 and a 1958 Lincoln Continental on display. Facilities include a quality craft and souvenir store. Eventually, Pier 1 will also have an Italian restaurant and disco upstairs.

Immigration and Customs proceedings are swift (10 minutes from the ship to the street). *Ciclotaxis* (pedicabs) and taxis wait outside.

Pier 1 currently serves as a ferry terminal. Future plans include converting the pier at Casablanca, across the bay, into an international ferry terminal serving Florida.

MARINA HEMINGWAY

Havana's marina lies on the western edge of metropolitan Havana, in Barlovento. The marina, Avenida 5ta and Calle 248, Santa Fe, Havana, tel. 33-1831 or 33-1150/1/2/3/4/5/6, fax 33-1831 or 33-1149, is a self-contained village and duty-free port. US dollars are preferred, but all convertible currencies are accepted, as are credit cards (except those issued in the US). If you'd like, you can register your credit card and charge everything to your account.

Position and Orientation

The harbor coordinates are 23° 5'N and 82° 29'W (the seven-beam searchlight located five feet east of the entrance canal is visible for 17 miles). The marina has four parallel canals, each one km long, 15 meters wide, and six meters deep.

Arrival and Departure

You should announce your arrival on VHF Channel 16, HF Channel 68, and SSB 2790 (expect a long wait for the reply). If you plan to dock for less than 72 hours, visas are not required (your passport will suffice). The harbormaster's office will facilitate your entry and exit.

Upon arrival, you must clear Immigration and Customs at the wharf on the left just inside the entrance channel. Be patient!

Arriving and departing skippers should watch for snorkelers and surfers both within and outside the narrow entrance channel.

Docking Facilities and Fees

There are moorings for 100 yachts. Docking fees, which include water, electricity, and custodial services, cost US35 cents per foot per day. Gasoline and diesel are readily available, a mechanic is on hand, and your boat can be hauled out of the water if needed.

Accommodations

El Viejo y el Mar (The Old Man and the Sea) is an upscale contemporary hotel run by Canada's Delta hotel group and used primarily by a business clientele. It has 146 rooms boasting a pleasing maroon and pink color scheme, heaps of red-glazed hardwoods, and splendid modern art. Facilities include a pleasing restaurant, piano bar, and large swimming pool. Rates are US$123 s, US$143 d, US$153 junior suite, US$173 suite.

You can also rent attractive two-story waterfront **apartments and villas** (US$170 s/d high season) along channel C and D and in the Villa Paraíso complex at the end of channel A.

Food

Pizza Nova serves good, bargain-priced pizzas from US$5, although they overcharge for small items, such as milk (US$1.50) in your coffee (US$2.50), and add a whopping service charge. **El Viejo y el Mar** has a reasonable restaurant good for buffet breakfasts. The modishly ritzy **Papa's** (ext. 350), at the end of channel B, specializes in seafoods and has both indoor and outdoor dining, plus a separate café (open 10 a.m.-7 p.m.). Also try **Restaurante Fiesta** (open noon-2 a.m.), which claims to specialize in Spanish cuisine, including a tasty paella. Likewise, the **Restaurante Tosca** at the entrance to channel B, serves Spanish and *criollo* dishes. There are also several cafés and snack bars.

You can buy all manner of Western food items at La Vigía Shopping Center (open 9 a.m.-7 p.m.), at the end of channel B. Skippers can order meals served aboard their vessel (beverages and cigarettes can also be ordered from the ship chandler at a *huge* discount).

Most restaurants are open noon to midnight.

Entertainment
Papa's and **Tasca** both offer a cabaret disco 10 p.m.-4 a.m.

Facilities and Services
The marina has a tourism information center (8 a.m.-8 p.m.) and harbormaster's office in Complejo Turístico Papa, the main service area at the end of channel B. The 24-hour medical post is here, as are a 24-hour laundromat, bathrooms with showers, soda bar, and TV lounge, storage room (full of US-registered motorbikes), plus a beach-volleyball court and four tennis courts.

The post office is at the entrance of channel C (open 24 hours), where you'll also find the Hemingway International Nautical Club, which offers fax and telephone facilities, a bar, and quiet reading room.

Yacht Rental and Watersports
You can rent 27- and 33-foot *Piraña* yachts and larger motorboats, which are also used for crewed excursions. **Jet-skis** can be rented from Complejo Turístico Papa's (8:30 a.m.-4:30 p.m.). The marina even has a **scuba diving** center at the end of channel B.

Getting Around and Away
Many skippers bring their own bicycles, mopeds, or motorbikes to move around the marina and travel into Havana.

You can request a taxi or minibus shuttle by calling 85, 89 or 634.

Car rental is available.

GETTING AROUND

ON FOOT

Having lived in London—a walker's city if ever there was one—I soon learned to disregard the advice of Prime Minister Gladstone, who said, "The way to see London is from the top of a bus, the top of a bus, gentlemen." I walked *everywhere* and grew to know the city intimately. I apply the same rule to Havana, despite its seemingly overwhelming size. You'll probably want to restrict your walking to a single district, such as Habana Vieja—whose compact, narrow, warren-like lanes are no place for vehicular traffic—or the Malecón, or the La Rampa district of Vedado. When traveling beyond and between these districts, you will need transport.

Sidewalks are generally in reasonably good repair, but beware potholes and dog shit underfoot.

BY BUS

Havana's public buses, or *guaguas* (pronounced "wah-wah"), are for stoics. Habaneros are inured and would rather take a bus than walk under almost all circumstances, even if this means traveling like sardines in a can.

Prior to the Special Period, Havana boasted a fine bus system that served the entire city. Then, as the gasoline shortage and lack of spare parts hit home, things ground to a virtual halt—worsened by a general lack of efficiency.

By summer 1996, things had improved dramatically. It seemed that the bus system was almost back to normal. Scores of *Tren Buses* (also called *camelos*—camels) were everywhere. These lengthy, truck-pulled passenger cars sag in the middle, like the rolling stock on US railways. They are numbered with the prefix

M (for Metro-bus). Most leave from Parque de la Fraternidad.

Fares are ridiculously cheap, but most buses have hard, uncushioned seating and are usually packed to the gills, especially during rush hours—7-10 a.m. and 3-6 p.m. Expect to wait in line for from 10 minutes to an hour, depending on the route. Cuban lines (queues, *colas*) are always fluid but tend to reform when the bus appears, so you should follow the Cubans' example and identify the last person in line ahead of you (ask for *el último?*).

Be prepared to push and jostle if the line devolves into a scrum. You'll undoubtedly be the only foreigner aboard and may find yourself being ushered aboard and offered a seat as a honored guest.

Buses stop frequently, but when full the driver may stop only when requested to do so. Bus stops—*paradas*—are usually well marked; most have shelter against rain. Shout *Pare!* (Stop!), or bash the box above the door in Cuban fashion. You'll need to elbow your way to the door well in advance, however. Don't dally, as the bus driver is likely to hit the gas when you're only halfway out.

Schedules and Fares: Most *guaguas* run 24 hours, at least hourly during the day but on reduced schedules 11 p.m.-5 a.m. The standard fare is 10 centavos (exact change only), which you deposit in the box beside the driver. Fares into the suburbs range from 10 to 50 centavos. You'll also find lots of smaller, red and cream-colored, buses called *omnibuses ruteros,* which charge 40 centavos and have the benefit of being uncrowded.

Route Maps: Many maps show Havana's bus routes, but most are out of date (the best maps I know are shown in the booklet *La Habana Vieja: Guía Turística,* published by the Instituto Cubano de Geodesia y Cartografía). Ostensibly, there's a *Rutas de Ómnibus* map, but I've never seen it—and, I suspect, neither will you. Note that many buses follow a loop route, traveling to and from destinations along different streets. Most buses display the bus number and destination above the front window. If in doubt, ask. Many buses arrive and depart from Parque Central and Parque de la Fraternidad in Habana Vieja and La Rampa (Calle 23) in Vedado, especially at Calle L and at Calzada de Infanta.

Be wary of pickpockets on crowded buses.

DANGERS AND ANNOYANCES

You'll face very few hassles while walking the streets of Havana, although the hardships of the Special Period have fostered a rise in petty crime, such as purse snatching (though to nowhere near the degree you'll find in Italy, Brazil, or many other destinations).

Expect to approached by *jiniteros*—hustlers—seeking to sell you cigars or otherwise make a buck. You'll also find a few kids imploring you for pencils and chiclets (*sheek-lays;* Cuba does not make chewing gum). And, if you're male, young women may suggestively wink and press their breasts against your arms. I've found that by totally ignoring them they quickly go away.

The two worst spots for *jiniterismo* are the lower end of the Prado, in Habana Vieja, and the top of La Rampa, outside the entrance to the Hotel Habana Libre. Be cautious and circumspect. Fortunately, there is usually at least one policeman always in sight or sound (certainly outside the Habana Libre).

Take only as much cash with you as you think you'll need for the day or evening. Always carry a photocopy of your passport, too. Leave your valuables in a safe deposit box. If your hotel room doesn't have one, leave your valuables in the safe at the reception desk. Petty theft from rooms is rampant. This is particularly true of clothing. Lock all your possessions in your luggage, and keep all items in rental cars locked out of sight.

Still, don't get paranoid. Havana isn't Naples or Rio de Janeiro, and incidents are still few and far between. Muggings are virtually unknown. Most petty crime is relegated to pickpocketing and, to a limited degree, grab-and-run. Rape is a very rare thing indeed.

Policemen are everywhere, but it pays to be vigilant. There are particular areas to be wary of, particularly at night. These include the dimly lit back streets of Habana Vieja, Centro, and Cerro. When walking at night, stick to the widest, best-lit streets.

BY TAXI

Getting around by taxi is a good bet. There are hundreds of taxis serving both the tourist trade and the local population. True to international form, Havana's taxi drivers are more aggressive on the road than other Havana drivers and are known (as were their *coche*-driving forebears before the invention of the internal-combustion engine) for belting around the street like charioteers.

Note, however, that if you use a taxi four or five times a day, the cost may approach that of renting a car—especially if you're traveling between, say, Miramar and Habana Vieja.

Taxibus Turístico offers scheduled minibus service between major hotels, Habana Vieja, and the Morro Castle for a standard US$2 fare.

Licensed Taxis
Most licensed taxis are operated by state organizations, all of which charge in dollars. The cheapest is **Panataxi,** tel. 81-0153 or 81-4142, which mostly serves Habaneros and mostly uses old Ladas and Moskovitches. Panataxi operates by radio call. It's surprisingly efficient; I've rarely had to wait more than 15 minutes for a radio-dispatched taxi to arrive. You'll also find Panataxi stands on Calle Tacón, one block east of Plaza de la Catedral, and in Vedado at the gas station at Calles 17 and L. A ride from the Hotel Nacional in Vedado to Habana Vieja will cost about US$3.50.

Taxis serving the tourist trade use modern Japanese cars or Mercedes and are operated by **Turistaxi, Transgaviota, Cubanacán,** and **Cubalse.** Virtually every tourist hotel has **Turistaxi** service.

Tourist taxis are about twice as expensive as Panataxi cabs. By international standards, however, Havana's taxis are relatively cheap, and you will rarely pay more than US$10 or so

TAXI FARES FROM HAVANA

The following are sample fares from Havana using Infotur taxis.

DESTINATION	ONE-WAY	ROUNDTRIP
Cienfuegos	US$120	US$220
Matanzas	US$60	US$110
Pinar del Río	US$80	US$150
Soroa	US$45	US$80
Trinidad	US$180	US$300
Viñales	US$90	US$170
Varadero	US$80	US$120

for any journey within town. Taxis are metered, although drivers of licensed taxis are often happy not to use their meters—especially at night—when an advance fare may be negotiated. The meters begin at US$1. Expect to pay about US$5 from La Rampa to Habana Vieja, double that from Miramar. The taxi companies all offer special long-distance and hourly rates.

Peso Taxis, *Colectivos,* and "Gypsy" Cabs
Peso-only taxis serve Cubans and normally don't take tourists. Demand far exceeds supply. Most are Russian Ladas; most also have meters. Be aware that the police may intervene if they see a peso taxi accepting a foreigner. It's worth a try, however. Drivers will probably want you to pay in dollars, in which case negotiate the price (expect to pay about half the fare you'd pay in a Turistaxi). You'll find plenty around Coppelia in Vedado and Parque Central and Parque de la Fraternidad in Habana Vieja.

Colectivos (shared cabs that pick up anyone who flags them down, often until they're packed to the gills) generally run along fixed routes usually using old Yankee cars. They charge in pesos. Ostensibly they're not supposed to pick up foreigners, but in today's climate, your dollars are what count. Most *colectivos* are unmarked, so follow the local example—wave down any large Yankee behemoth coming your way. Avenida 5ta and the Malecón linking Miramar with Habana Vieja are favorite routes.

"Gypsy" cabs driven by freelance chauffeurs are everywhere, too. Most are beat-up Ladas or American jalopies. You'll find freelance driver-guides outside the largest tourist hotels—especially the Hotel Inglaterra on Par-

HAVANA TAXIS

Cubalse . . . . tel. 33-6558
Panataxi . . . . tel. 81-0153 or 81-4142
Taxis OK (Cubanacán). . . . . tel. 33-1446, 29-2323, or 21-7931
Transgaviota . . . . tel. 23-7000, 33-1730, or 81-0357
Turistaxi . . . . tel. 33-5539/40/41/42

que Central, and the hotels Habana Libre, Riviera, and Cohiba in Vedado—and outside discos late at night. Fares are negotiable, and it's often possible to hire a car and driver for the whole day for, say, US$20. Beware scams.

Ciclotaxis

An increasing number of tricycle taxis are plying the streets of Havana, especially along the Malecón. They offer a more relaxing (and cheaper) way of sightseeing and getting around if you're in no hurry. You can go the full length of the Malecón for US$2.

BY CAR

I recommend renting a car if you anticipate touring Havana for an extensive period on your own or you plan on exploring out of town. Virtually every tourist hotel either has a car rental desk or can arrange for a rental car to be delivered. The five state-owned car rental companies have main offices in addition to outlets in leading hotels.

The standard of driving is, in general, admirable (certain taxi drivers excepted). There is relatively little traffic (Havana is probably the only Latin American city without rush-hour traffic—except in certain busy spots, such as Avenida 5ta in Miramar, Avenida Rancho Boyeros,

---

GASOLINE STATIONS IN HAVANA

Cupet-Cimex has 24-hour service centers (dollars only) at:

Habana Vieja, Centro Habana, and Cerro
Vento y Santa Catalina (Cerro)

Vedado and Plaza de la Revolución
Linea y Malecón (Vedado)
Calle L y 19 (Vedado)
Paseo y Malecón (Vedado)
Avenida de la Independencia y Conill (Plaza)

Miramar
Avenida 5ta y Calle 112
Avenida 31 y Calle 18
Avenida 33 y Calle 70 (Tropicana)

Suburbs
Avenida de la Independencia y 271 (Boyeros)
Avenida Dolores (Mirador de Lawton)

CAR RENTAL COMPANIES~ HAVANA LOCATIONS

CUBACAR

Main office . . . . tel. 20-2188 or 33-6312
José Martí International Airport . . . tel. 33-5546
Hotel Comodoro . . . . tel. 33-1706
Marina Hemingway . . . . tel. 33-1707
Hotel Biocaribe . . . . tel. 22-7044

CUBANACÁN

Main office . . . . tel. 20-2188/9

CUBALSE

Main Office, Avenida 3ra #12205,
Náutico, Playa . . . . tel. 33-6568 or 33-6452

HAVANAUTOS

José Martí International Airport
   (Terminal 1) . . . . tel. 33-5197,
   (Terminal 2) . . . . tel. 33-5215
Hotel Colina . . . . tel. 32-3535
Hotel Habana Libre . . . . tel. 33-4011
Hotel Nacional . . . . tel. 33-3192
Hotel Riviera . . . . tel. 33-3577
Hotel Sevilla . . . . tel. 33-8560, ext. 142
Hotel Tritón . . . . tel. 33-2921

TRANSGAVIOTA

Hotel Kolhy . . . . tel. 22-4837 or 33-1730

TRANSAUTO

José Martí International Airport tel. 33-5177/79
Hotel Capri . . . . tel. 33-4038
Hotel Copacabana . . . . tel. 29-0601
Hotel Deauville . . . . . . tel. 62-8051 or 33-8812
Hotel Nacional . . . . tel. 33-3564
Hotel Plaza . . . . tel. 33-8583
Hotel Presidente . . . . tel. 32-7521
Hotel Sevilla . . . . tel. 33-8560
Hotel Neptuno . . . . tel. 29-0881

Transauto also has an office on Calle 21 one block west of the Hotel Nacional.

---

and the Vía Blanca). Traffic police do an efficient job. Most of the traffic lights work—and are even obeyed! Traffic signage is very good. And few of Havana's streets show great deterioration (the roads are far superior to those of most other Caribbean or Latin American cities).

Roads to Avoid: Two notable exceptions to the generally high standards are busy Vía Blanca, which (south of Havana harbor) is in terrible shape and dangerous, and the dual carriageway **Autopista Circular,** or route Calle 100, which forms an almost continous semicircle around the city, linking the arterial highways into Havana. The latter has little traffic and, frankly, it's too far out from the city to serve a useful function unless skirting the city entirely when traveling, say, between Pinar del Río and Matanzas. Be careful! It has treacherous potholes, and some are death-traps—massive hollows invisible until you're upon them. They're usually at intersections.

Parking

A capital city without parking meters? Imagine. Parking is rarely a problem, except in Habana Vieja (you should avoid driving in Habana Vieja, anyway, east of Monserrate). No-parking zones are well marked. Avoid these like the plague, especially if it's an officials-only zone, in which case a policeman will usually be on hand to blow his whistle. Havana has an efficient towing system for the recalcitrant. You can pay your parking ticket through your car rental agency (and be sure to do so before leaving the country).

Note that at Plaza de la Revolución, there's a designated parking zone on the east side of the plaza. Try to park on the plaza or along the road and soldiers will quickly move you along.

Car Repairs

Your car rental company can arrange repairs. However, if you need emergency treatment,

Diplogarage has centers open 24 hours at Avenida 5ta esq. 120, Playa, tel. 33-6159, and at Calle 2 esq. Avenida 7ma, tel. 23-5588, 33-1906.

BY BICYCLE

Habaneros do it—almost one million bicycles wheel through the streets of the Cuban capital—so why not you? **Panaciclo,** Avenida Rancho Boyeros y Santa Ana, near the main bus station in Plaza de la Revolución, tel. 45-3746, 81-0153 or 81-4142, a branch of Panataxi, rents bicycles (US$5 for three hours, US$15 all day—US$10 if rented late in the morning). You can order by phone; they'll deliver to the hotel. The bikes are chunky, one-speeders, uncomfortable and a drag on hills. You may want to bring your own bicycle if you plan on spending considerable time in Havana. Bike locks are provided.

Again, be careful—there are plenty of potholes, and at night many of the streets are unlit. Cuban cyclists are notoriously lackadaisical on the roads, and an average of two cyclists are killed in traffic accidents in Havana every three days. Note that cyclists are not allowed to ride through the tunnel beneath Havana harbor. The municipal government provides specially converted buses—the sky-blue **Ciclobus**—to ferry cyclists through the tunnel. These depart from Avenida de los Estudiantes, where you wait in line to push your *bici* up a ramp onto the bus (10 centavos).

deboarding a
ciclobus

BY FERRY

Tiny ferries (standing only—no seats) bob across the harbor between the Havana waterfront and Regla and Casablanca, on the east side of the bay. The ferry for **Regla** leaves every 15 minutes (10 centavos; five minutes) from a wharf called Muelle Luz on Avenida San Pedro (Avenida del Puerto), at the foot of Calle Santa Clara. The ferry for **Casablanca** has traditionally departed from the foot of Calle O'Reilly but at press time was also operating from the wharf at the foot of Santa Clara.

ORGANIZED TOURS AND EXCURSIONS

City Tours

A city tour is a great way to get an initial feel for Havana. All the hotel tour bureaus offer city tours through the major tour agencies aboard a/c buses. For example, **Tour & Travel,** Avenida 5 #8409, e/ 84 y 86, Miramar, Havana, tel. 33-0166 or 33-1549, fax 33-1547, a division of Havanatur, offers a city tour (US$10) and a shopping tour (US$8). It also has an office in Vedado on La Rampa and Calle O, two blocks downhill from the Hotel Habana Libre. **Tropical Travel Agency** (a division of Rumbos) has a three-and-

a-half-hour city tour departing daily at 9 a.m. and 2 p.m. and including Habana Vieja, Vedado, and Miramar (US$10). And **Agencia San Cristóbal,** Calles Oficios y Amargura, offers guided walking tours of Habana Vieja.

Private Guides: Hotel tour bureaus and tour agencies can arrange personal guided tours. **Cubatur,** Calle F #157, e/ Calzada y Calle 9ra, tel. 33-4155, offers guides for US$25 per day (up to 12 hours) in Havana, US$30 outside Havana. You can also hire a guide weekly (US$200). Again, contact Agencía San Cristóbal.

Harbor Cruises

El Galeón, a replica of an 18th-century Spanish galleon that departs daily from a wharf below the Morro Castle and "sails" (the sails are for show; the vessel is powered by a diesel engine) east past Morro Castle and Cojímar to Tarará, where you can swim, snorkel, and play volleyball. Day trips departing at 10 a.m. (return at 4 p.m.) cost US$45, including a "beach party" and lobster buffet. Three-hour nighttime party cruises are also offered at 7:30 p.m. (also US$45 with lobster buffet and unlimited rum punch; US$25 without dinner). A late-night disco cruise is also offered (US$15).

You can make reservations at your hotel tour desk or via Puertosol, tel. 66-7117 or 33-2161, fax 66-7716 or 33-2877.

You can also arrange excursions along the coast from Marina Hemingway.

GETTING AWAY

All public transport out of Havana to towns far afield are usually booked solid for weeks in advance. Air transport is usually not so bad, but *never* leave things to chance. If you plan on traveling by air, bus, or train, make your reservations as far in advance as possible. Visitors can now look forward to the fact that a certain number of seats are usually reserved for foreigners (Cubans pay in pesos for bus and train travel; you'll pay in dollars).

Note that the **Terminal Aérea y de Ferries,** on Avenida Kohly, opposite the zoo, provides bus transfers only to Batabanó for passengers taking the hydrofoil or ferry to the Isla de la Juventud (see "Batabanó," in the Havana Province chapter).

BY AIR

Most airlines have their main offices at the base of La Rampa (Calle 23), e/ P y Q, in Vedado. These include Aeroflot, Cubana, Iberia, LTU, and Mexicana. Both Lacsa (Costa Rica) and Viasa (Venezuela) have their offices in the lobby of the Hotel Habana Libre, at Calles 23 and L.

The international airlines are linked by computer to their reservations headquarters abroad. However, the Cuban computers "go down" frequently, and confirming and changing reservations may be more time-consuming than you're probably used to. Don't leave things until the last minute. Reconfirm your flight at least 72

SAMPLE DOMESTIC AIRFARES

The following are sample fares to/from Havana at press time. Check for latest fares.

DESTINATION	ONE-WAY	ROUND-TRIP
Baracoa	US$99	US$178
Bayamo	US$80	US$140
Camagüey	US$72	US$124
Ciego de Ávila	US$64	US$108
Guantánamo	US$93	US$166
Holguín	US$80	US$140
Isla de la Juventud	US$37	US$54
Las Tunas	US$77	US$134
Manzanillo	US$80	US$140
Moa	US$93	US$166
Santiago	US$88	US$156
Varadero	US$40	US$60

hours before departure. Cubana is especially notorious for canceling the reservations of those who don't reconfirm on time. It's a good idea to check in in any event, as flight schedules change on a frequent basis.

Cubana, tel. 33-4949 or 33-4446, has a fully computerized reservation system. You can pick up printed timetables of Cubana's domestic and international service at the information desk in the lobby of the Cubana office at Calle 23 #64 (open Mon.-Fri. 8:30 a.m.-4 p.m. and Saturday 8 a.m.-1 p.m.). Double check departure times, which change frequently and at short notice. Tickets for Cubana **charter flights** must be purchased through **Havanatur,** at Calle 6 e/ Avenida 1ra y 3ra, Miramar, tel. 33-2712, or below the Hotel Habana Libre on Calles 23 and M, tel. 33-4082. Don't expect to be able to purchase a ticket at the airport. The Havanatur office upstairs at Terminal Two, for example, is fairly useless. If you miss your flight and want to buy another ticket, you'll have to go to the Miramar or Vedado offices.

Cubanacán Express, Avenida 5 #8210, Playa, Havana, tel. 29-2884, also acts as a reservation agent for domestic and international flights. It also charters aircraft for domestic trips. At a pinch, you may be able to purchase tickets at the airport (you can use your credit card to get a cash advance from the Banco Nacional in the departure lounge), but don't count on it.

José Martí Airport

An expansion was underway at press time at Terminal One and things are in flux (the domestic terminal, formerly to the left of the international terminal, has moved). The check-in area is cramped (Terminal Two is roomier), but the departure lounge is spacious. Both terminals offer a good choice of duty-free shops, plus a bar and restaurant.

The **departure tax** (US$15 at press time) must be paid at a separate counter after you've checked in with the airline.

Listen carefully to the boarding announcements; they are easy to miss, especially over the sound of the live band! Don't linger when your flight is called.

Getting There: Buses marked "Aeropuerto" operate to the airport from the east side of Parque Central in Habana Vieja (the *cola* begins near the José Martí statue). It serves both Terminal 1 and 2 (one peso; US$1). The journey takes about one hour and is very unreliable. Allow plenty of time.

You can also catch bus M-2 from the west side of Parque de la Fraternidad. It goes to Santiago de las Vegas via the airport. Make sure you wait in the line for people wanting seats *(sentados);* the other is for stoics willing to stand. Ask.

A licensed taxi will cost about US$13 (about US$8 for an unlicensed taxi). You can also arrange a shuttle through one of the tour agencies (US$10-15).

BY BUS

Most buses to destinations outside metropolitan Havana leave from the **Terminal de Ómnibus Nacionales** (also called Terminal de Ómnibus Interprovinciales) on Avenida Rancho Boyeros, two blocks north of Plaza de la Revolución at Calle 19 de Mayo. Buses leave from here for virtually every town throughout the country. Most are booked solid weeks in advance, and foreigners get no preference. If long-distance buses are sold out, you can always try stitching together bus service to a number of cities between Havana and your ultimate destination.

Buses to towns near Havana depart from several locations, including the terminal. Most operate on the *último* system—you wait in line without a reservation.

If you plan to travel by bus, you should make your reservation as early as possible either at the bus terminal or at the **Buro de Reservaciones** (also called the Oficina Reservaciones Pasajes), at Calles 21 y 4 in Vedado. It's open Mon.-Fri. 7 a.m.-2 p.m. and Saturday 7 a.m.-noon. It's a Kafkaesque experience. First, there's often a milling mob to contend with, with everyone clamoring to get his or her name on the list. Your name will be scrawled on a decrepit pile of parchment, added to the scores of names ahead of you. Ask to see the sheets for the destination you want so that you can gauge how many days' delay is likely.

On the day of travel, arrive at the terminal at least one hour ahead of departure, otherwise your seat may be issued to people on the waiting list. If you don't have a reservation, you can always try getting on the standby list—*Lista de Fallos*—by showing up at the bus station and hoping you'll be issued the seat of a cancellation or return *(fallo)*. Passengers are granted 22 kg baggage limit (plus one piece of hand luggage), although it seems not to be strictly enforced.

There's an **information booth**, tel. 70-9401, downstairs, plus a post office and small café. A complete list of departures is posted on a blackboard upstairs in the waiting room. A list of tariffs is posted to the left of the blackboard. The tariffs are accurate; the departure times are less so.

Getting There: Bus no. 47 departs the Prado (at Calle Animas) in Habana Vieja to the bus terminal. Bus no. 265 runs from the east side of Parque Central. Buses no. 67 and 84 run there from La Rampa in Vedado.

BY RAIL

Traveling from Havana by train is increasingly a viable option. Rail services, which virtually ceased in 1990-91, continue to be restored to their pre-Special Period schedules as the restored flow of gasoline and diesel fuel grease the wheels of the Cuban economy. Unfortunately, departure times change as often as you change your underwear (frequently, one hopes). Departures are subject to cancellation or delay.

There are three railway stations. The most important is **Estación Central de Ferrocarril,** at Avenida de Bélgica (Egido) and Arsenal, in Habana Vieja, tel. 61-2807 or 61-8382. Trains depart here for most major cities, including Pinar del Río, Cienfuegos, Santa Clara, Sancti Spíritus, Ciego de Ávila, Camagüey, Las Tunas, Santiago and Guantánamo, and Bayamo and Manzanillo. Most trains for Pinar del Río and Havana Province depart from the **Estación 19 de Noviembre** (also called Tulipán), tel. 70-9900, inconveniently located southwest of the Plaza de la Revolución, at Calles Tulipán and Hidalgo. The railcar *(ferro-ómnibus)* to ExpoCuba departs from here.

A third station—the recently renovated **Estación Cristina**—at Avenida de México and Arroyo, on the east side of Cerro Habana, serves outer Havana, including Parque Lenin and, in midsummer only, Playas del Este.

An electric train—the famous **Hershey Train,** tel. 62-4888, also operates from Casablanca to Matanzas. It's a splendid journey (three hours each way), which you can take either with the locals or on a tourist junket.

Purchasing Tickets

The state agency **Ladis** (formerly Ferrotur), tel. 62-1770, handles reservations for all train services. Its office serving foreigners is at Calles Arsenal and Cienfuegos (open daily 7 a.m.-7 p.m.), on the north side of the main railway station in Habana Vieja (look for the "ExpoCuba" sign). You can also purchase tickets and make reservations through Palacio de Turismo offices. Foreigners now pay in dollars. Tickets can be purchased up to one hour prior to departure, but you must purchase your ticket that day for a nighttime departure. (The Tulipán station has no such priority services for dollar-bearing foreigners.)

The ticket office inside the main station was not open last time I stopped by. Instead, reservations are taken at a small doorway on the north side of the station, where there'll be a crowd pushing at the door. If you want to feign being Cuban, or otherwise try to purchase a ticket for pesos, you'll need to put civility aside. Even so, your subterfuge will probably be transparent, in which case you'll most likely be sent to Ferrotur. If your luck holds, don't expect to be able to travel that day. Most likely, your name will be put onto the waiting list for the train you want. You'll receive a *pre-tike,* which you must present on the morning of departure to exchange—God willing—for a reservation slip, which you'll later turn in in exchange for your ticket.

On the day of departure, get there early. The seating in the waiting room is comfortable. You'll need to listen attentively for announcements of departure, as the electronic information board is usually out of order.

Prepare yourself for a relatively uncomfortable journey. Bring snacks and drink.

BY TAXI AND FREELANCE DRIVER

Touring far from Havana by taxi can be inordinately expensive. It's certainly a viable option, however, for places close at hand, such as Cojímar or even Playas del Este. Beyond that you're probably better off renting a car or hiring a private freelance driver.

Try finding a *colectivo* taxi at Parque de la Fraternidad or near the central railway station, where drivers are used to making long-distance runs to Playas del Este or even Pinar del Río and Viñales. You'll need to negotiate a price—be patient and firm. The days when *colectivo* drivers would take pesos from foreigners are almost over. With luck, however, you can still find someone who might run you to Playas del Este for, say, 200 pesos (US$10).

Lots of drivers with their own vehicles are eager to drive you wherever you want to go, and you're sure to be approached almost as soon as you begin looking for a *colectivo*. Again, fares are negotiable. The driver will usually be amenable to any request you make. I've hired a car and driver for as little as US$20 for a full day, plus gasoline (a common courtesy is also to buy your driver his or her lunch), but much depends on the quality of the car—and your negotiating skills.

CAR RENTAL

For lengthy exploring outside Havana, I recommend renting a car for the ease, freedom, and control it grants. Most tourist hotels have a car rental bureau on site, but the main car rental agencies also have main offices. Note that specific locations of the car rental agencies often are booked solid. You may need to hunt around,

DISTANCES FROM HAVANA

All figures represent kilometers.

Baracoa	1,069
Bayamo	842
Camagüey	570
Cárdenas	152
Ciego de Ávila	461
Cienfuegos	336
Guantánamo	971
Holguín	771
Isla de la Juventud	138
Las Tunas	694
Matanzas	101
Pinar del Río	176
Rancho Boyeros	17
Sancti Spíritus	386
Santa Clara	300
Santiago de Cuba	876
Soroa	95
Surgidero de Batabanó	56
Trinidad	454
Varadero	140
Viñales	188

particularly for the smaller models or a 4WD jeep. You can also rent a car at the airport upon arrival. If you're tired or jet-lagged, this is not a good idea. Relax for a day or two, then rent your car.

ORGANIZED TOURS AND EXCURSIONS

The Cuban State tour agencies, such as **Cubanacán,** Calle 164 esq. 17D, Playa, tel. 21-9457 or 33-6044, offer a gamut of excursions and tours to destinations throughout Cuba, as well as multi-destination excursions to Jamaica, the Dominican Republic, the Cayman Islands, and Mexico. You can book most excursions through the tour desk of major hotels.

A typical sampling includes Havanatur's **Tour & Travel,** Avenida 5 #8409, e/ 84 y 86, Miramar, tel. 33-0166 or 33-1549, fax 33-1547, day excursions to Soroa (US$30) and Viñales (US$38) in Pinar del Río, as well as Trinidad and Cienfuegos (US$120) and Varadero (US$38). Prices include lunch. **Tropical Travel Agency** offers a full-day guided excursion to Varadero Beach daily (US$27, US$37 with lunch). It has a similar full-day tour to Trinidad, including a visit to Playa Ancón (US$112, including breakfast and dinner). **Viñales Tours,** Calle 1 #2210 between 22 y 24, Miramar, tel. 33-1051, fax 33-1054, specializes in tours to Pinar del Río province.

You can even go to sea for a week aboard the *Costa Playa* cruise ship, which departs Havana every Saturday night year-round and cruises to the Bahía Nipe, Puerto Plata (Dominican Republic), Santiago de Cuba, and Montego Bay (Jamaica), returning to Havana on Saturday morning.

METROPOLITAN HAVANA
THE SUBURBS

Although the city center of Havana is concentrated in Habana Vieja, Centro Habana, Cerro, Vedado, Plaza de la Revolución, and Miramar, the official metropolitan area of Ciudad de la Habana comprises 727 square kilometers, divided into 15 municipalities. To the east are the beaches of the Playas del Este—a playground for Habaneros and, increasingly, tourists. In addition, a number of metropolitan Havana's prime attractions lie on the city's outskirts and are well worth the drive. The following key sites are described in clockwise order.

LOMA CABAÑA

Looming over Habana Vieja to the north is the rugged cliff face of the Cabaña, dominated by two great fortresses that constitute **Morro-Cabaña Historical Military Park.** It is very windy up here, but the views over Habana Vieja and towards Vedado are spectacular, especially at dawn and dusk.

Castillo de los Tres Reyes del Morro
This handsome, ghost-white castle is built into the rocky palisades of Punta Barlovento, crowning a rise that drops straight to the sea at the entrance to Havana harbor. Canted in its articulation, the fort follows a tradition of military architecture established by the Milanese at the end of the Middle Ages, with stone walls 10 feet thick and a series of batteries stepping down to the shore. It has been marvelously restored to former glory and has lost none of its commanding composure, with plentiful cannons on trolleys in their embrasures. A still-functioning lighthouse was constructed beside the fortress in 1844.

You enter through a long tunnel that leads to a deep moat and drawbridge. The castle contains cisterns, a wine cellar, stables, a church, and dungeons and bomb-proof vaults—which now house the **Museo del Morro, Museo Navigación,** and **Museo de Piratas** (Pirate's Museum). A special treat is the medieval armory, containing a large collection of suits of armor and weaponry that also spans the ancient Arab and Asian worlds. Open Mon.-Sun. 9 a.m.-8 p.m. (entrance US$2, plus $2 for photos, $5 for video).

Below the castle, facing the city, is the **Battery of the Twelve Apostles.**

Castillo San Carlos de la Cabaña
This massive fortress lining Cabaña hill east of the Morro is the largest fort in the Americas. It was built 1764-74 following the English invasion, and

cost the staggering sum of 14 million pesos. The fortress—reached via a massive drawbridge over a 12-meter-deep moat—contains the execution wall known as **El Foso de los Laureles** (Moat of the Laurels), where hundreds of nationalist sympathizers were shot during the wars of independence. It is still used as a military base, and most of the surrounding area is therefore off-limits. However, at press time there were plans to open two museums within the castle.

The gun position overlooking Havana is lined with cannons engraved with lyrical names such as *La Hermosa*. Here, every night at 9 p.m., a small unit assembles in military fashion, dressed in scarlet 18th-century garb and led by fife and drum. Soon enough, you'll hear the reverberating crack of the *cañonazo*—the nightly firing of a cannon, which used to signal the closing of the city gates and the raising of the chain to seal the harbormouth. Today, it causes unsuspecting visitors to drop their drinks.

Food and Services
One of Havana's finest restaurants—**La Divina Pastora**—lies at the berth for *El Galeón*, 200 meters east of the Morro. The beautiful hacienda-style restaurant specializes in *criollo* food (US$5 and up) and offers Afro-Cuban entertainment for the tour groups that flock to the place. Parking costs US$1.

Behind the restaurant, on the harborfront, is a wonderful little bodega-type bar—**Bar la Tasca**—which offers a breezy balcony with fabulous views over the harbor. It's a great place to sit on a hot day. The simple menu includes lobster and seafood dishes from US$8. It's open 12:30 a.m.-11 p.m.

Getting There
Visitors can reach Loma Cabaña via the tunnel that descends beneath the monument to Máximo Gómez off Avenida de Céspedes, at the foot of the Prado (motorcycles are not allowed). Beyond the tunnel, you pass through a toll booth (no toll eastbound). Immediately on your right is an exit for the Morro and Castillo San Carlos.

Many buses from Habana Vieja pass through the tunnel and will drop you by the fortress access road. You can also get there by taking the ferry to Casablanca (see below) and walking uphill—but it's a stiff climb.

Excursions are available to witness the *cañonazo,* usually followed by dinner at La Divina Pastora. You can make reservations through any hotel tour desk or Havanatur.

CASABLANCA

This small village clings to the shore on the northeast side of Havana harbor, in the lee of Castillo San Carlos. The narrow main street is overhung with balconies. and from here tiers of houses rise up the hillside. Today, a few rusting freighters sit in dry dock, and fishing boats bob along the waterfront.

Looming over Casablanca is the domed National Observatory and a great statue of Jesus Christ—**El Cristo de Casablanca**—a 10-minute uphill walk from town. The statue was hewn from Italian Carrara marble by noted Cuban sculptor Jilma Madera. From on high, you have a bird's-eye view of the deep, flask-shaped harbor. The views are especially good at dawn and dusk, and it is possible, with the sun gilding the waters, to imagine great galleons slipping in and out of the harbor, a conduit for the wealth of a hemisphere.

The viewing platform *(mirador)* surrounding the statue is roped off (entrance costs US50 cents), but you can get almost as spectacular a view without passing onto the platform. The Rumbos stand rents binoculars for US50 cents for you to survey Havana more intimately.

Getting There
By Car: Casablanca is reached from the Vía Monumental, east of the tunnel. The road follows the eastern ridge of the *cabaña* and switchbacks down to Casablanca.

By Ferry: A little ferry bobs its way across Havana harbor to Casablanca every 20 minutes or so (10 centavos). It departs from the wharf on the south side of the Terminal Sierra Maestra, at the foot of Calle Santa Clara (from the ferry terminal, the stairway is across the road, to the right).

By Train: You can reach Casablanca from Matanzas aboard the "Hershey Train," a three-car passenger train once belonging to the Hershey-Cuban Railroad. It arrives and departs from the terminal next to the Casablanca ferry termi-

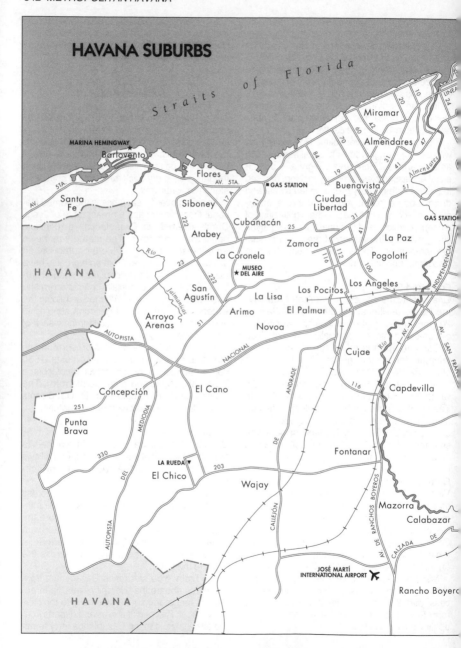

HAVANA SUBURBS

Straits of Florida

MARINA HEMINGWAY
Barlovento

Miramar
Almendares
Buenavista
Flores
AV. 5TA.
GAS STATION
Santa Fe
AV. 5TA.
Siboney
Ciudad Libertad
Cubanacán
Atabey
Zamora
La Paz
La Coronela
Pogolotti
HAVANA
MUSEO DEL AIRE
San Agustín
La Lisa
Los Pocitos
Los Angeles
Arroyo Arenas
Arimo
El Palmar
Novoa
AUTOPISTA
NACIONAL
Cujae
Capdevilla
Concepción
El Cano
Punta Brava
MEDIODIA
Fontanar
LA RUEDA
El Chico
Wajay
Mazorra
Calabazar
AUTOPISTA
CALLEJÓN
AV. DE RANCHOS BOYEROS
JOSÉ MARTÍ INTERNATIONAL AIRPORT
CALZADA
Rancho Boyero
HAVANA
GAS STATION
INDEPENDENCIA
AV. SAN FRAN

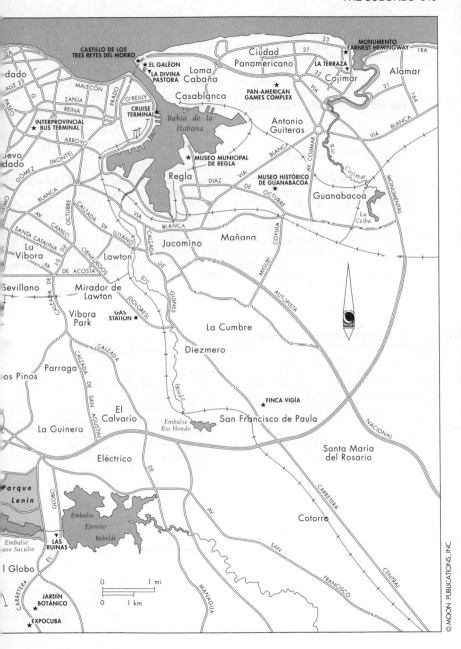

nal. Trains—which make about 40 stops en route!—depart Matanzas at 3:55 and 10:20 a.m. and 2:55 and 9:19 p.m. and arrive Casablanca at 8:27 a.m., 2:52 and 7:32 p.m., and 1:37 a.m. respectively. Trains depart Casablanca for Matanzas at 4:35 and 9:25 a.m. and 3:45 and 8:55 p.m. Tickets cost US$2.80 (you may be able to pay in pesos). Passengers are assigned seat numbers. Ask for a window seat.

CIUDAD PANAMERICANO

Continuing east on the six-lane Vía Monumental, after three km you pass the Pan-American Games complex, built at great cost in 1991. A high-rise village was built to accommodate the athletes, spectators, and press. Today, it is a residential community for Cubans, but it's also pushed prominently in tourist literature. There's no reason to visit unless you have an abiding interest in sports or want a base close to the delightful fishing village of Cojímar nearby.

Accommodations and Food

Jiniteros will probably approach you on the street and offer *casa particulares*. Otherwise, ask around. Expect to pay US$15-25 daily.

The **Hotel Panamericano Resort,** Calle A y Avenida Central, tel. 33-8810, fax 33-8001, features a hotel and two apartment complexes. The hotel offers pleasant rooms with modern (albeit poorly made) furnishings and maroon fabrics. Telephones and TVs are standard. The hotel has a large swimming pool that is a popular social scene on weekends. There's also a large gym plus sauna, car and moped rental, and tourism bureau.

Many travelers choose to rent a modest yet comfortable apartment in either the **Apartotel Las Brisas,** opposite the hotel, or **Apartotel Vista el Mar,** 100 meters west. Together, they offer 421 two- and three-bedroom apartments.

The menu of the hotel's **Restaurante Trópical** features soups (US$2), lobster and shrimp (US$13-21), and a delicious chicken roasted in fruit juices (US$6). Breakfast at the hotel's Mesa Buffet, however, is a lackluster affair.

On the main street, on the right, you'll find **Restaurante El Tapatio,** purportedly serving Mexican food. Despite the mariachi band and the sombreros, the food (and the music) is Cuban *criollo*. It's open 6 p.m.-1 a.m. Try **Restaurante Allegro** for pizzas and spaghetti for less than US$3; it's across the street.

Hidden around the corner from Tapatio, within the courtyard of an apartment complex, is **La Taberna,** tel. 68-411, ext. 129, which bills itself as a "trattoria." The menu features sandwiches and omelettes for under US$2. It's open only until 6 p.m. For ice-cream desserts and shakes, head for the **Cremeria,** 20 meters uphill from Tapatio.

Entertainment and Services

The night spot of choice seems to be the disco of the Panamericano (open 10 p.m. until 6 a.m.). But you can also join the locals in the lively piano bar around the corner at the bottom of the hill.

There's an **Infotur** office, on the corner at the bottom of the main street, tel. 68-2963. It boasts a gift store and small art gallery—**Galería Mariano Rodríguez.** Infotur offers a range of excursions in and around Havana. A Banco Nacional is on the right, 100 meters downhill from the hotel. And you'll find a post office (open 7 a.m.-10 p.m.) at the bottom of the main street.

Getting There and Around

From the Vía Monumental, take the first exit to the right—marked Cójimar—which will take you back over the freeway into the Pan-American complex and the Hotel Panamericano. (Another exit, two km farther, leads directly to the old village). Ciudad Panamericano is well served by buses from Havana. Bus no. 204 arrives and departs from the main street in Ciudad Panamericano, bus M1 from Vía Monumental.

Havanautos has a car rental office near the post office. You can also rent bicycles and scooters, from Club Sauna, tel. 68-2015 or 68-3000 (ask for Rafael or Manuel), the gym adjacent to the hotel. Scooters cost US$12 for two hours, US$15 for three, and US$1 for each additional hour. Bicycles are US$1.50 for the first hour, US$1 for each addtional (tandems are available).

You'll find many *jiniteros* promoting day trips by boat and touting themselves as chauffeurs (you can rent a car and driver for about US$20 per day). The Hotel Panamericano offers a "Hemingway Tour" (US$3, including sandwich), on Monday, Wednesday, and Saturday.

COJÍMAR

For Hemingway fans, a trip to the fishing village of Cojímar is a pilgrimage. For everyone, it's a treat. Here, Ernest Hemingway berthed his legendary sportfishing boat, the *Pilar.*

The forlorn village spreads out along the shore and rises up the hill behind it; an old church on the hilltop has seen better days. The waterfront is lined with weather-beaten, red-tile-roofed cottages with shady verandas. Whitecaps are often whipped up in the bay, making the Cuban flag flutter above **El Torreon,** the pocket-size fortress guarding the cove's entrance. It was here in 1762 that the English put ashore their invasion army and captured Cuba for King George III. The fortress, built in the 1760s to forestall another fiasco, is still in military hands, and you will be shooed away from its steps if you get too close.

Cojímar's most famous resident is Gregorio Fuentes, after whom Hemingway modeled the proud fisherman in *The Old Man and the Sea.* Travelers come from far and wide to hear Fuentes recall his adventures. When I last saw him, in May 1996, the 98-year-old was frail and recovering from a long bout of ill health. He will be delighted to smile for your camera and answer questions; however, please refrain from knocking on his front door at Calle Pesuela #209. The old man can often be found regaling travelers in **La Terraza,** and this is where you should arrange any meeting with him (see "Food," below). He charges $10 for "consultations."

Cojímar is fascinating by night, too, with every house door and window wide open; families sitting on sofas watching TV; dogs roaming for morcolo; figures gently rocking, suffused by the soft glow of 40-watt lights; the moonlight reflecting on the bay. Zig-zagging through these streets one evening, I chanced upon a garden

THE OLD MAN: GREGORIO FUENTES

Gregorio Fuentes, born in 1902, no longer has his sea legs and now walks with the aid of a crutch. But his memory remains keen, particularly when it comes to his old fishing companion, Ernest Hemingway. "His absence is still painful for me," says Fuentes, the now-ancient captain who from 1938 until Hemingway's death was in charge of the writer's boat, the *Pilar.*

Fuentes is considered to be the model for Santiago, the fisheman cursed by *salao* (the worst form of bad luck) in *The Old Man and the Sea,* a simple and profound novel that won Hemingway the Nobel Prize for Literature. Fuentes looks the part: "The old man was thin and gaunt with deep wrinkles in the back of his neck. The brown blotches of the benevolent skin cancer the sun brings from its reflections on the tropic sea were on his cheeks. . . . Everything about him was old except his eyes and they were the same color as the sea and were cheerful and undefeated."

Fuentes started his sea life at Lanzarote, in the Canary Islands, when he was four years old. He came to Cuba at age 10 and met Hemingway in 1931 on Tortuga, in the Bahamas, when the two men were sheltering from a storm (Fuentes was captain of a smack). The two men were virtually inseparable from 1935 to 1960. During World War II, they patrolled the coast for German U-boats. Years

later, says Fuentes, he and Hemingway patrolled the same coast to assist Castro's rebel army. Their birthdays were 11 days apart and, reports Tom Miller, the two would celebrate each other with a bottle of whiskey. Fuentes kept the tradition alive after Hemingway's death by pouring a whiskey over the latter's bust down by the harbor.

CHRISTOPHER P. BAKER

the man himself

full of villagers sitting beneath the stars watching a movie projected onto a house wall.

Monumento Ernest Hemingway

When Hemingway died, every fisherman in the village apparently donated a brass fitting from his boat. The collection was melted down to create the bust of the author that has stared out to sea since 1962 from atop a large limestone block within a columned rotunda at the base of El Torreon. A plaque reads: *"Parque Ernest Hemingway. In grateful memory from the population of Cojímar to the immortal author of* Old Man and the Sea, *inaugurated 21 July 1962, on the 63rd anniversary of his birth."*

The brass bust occasionally receives a spit and polish. The classical rotunda was recently renovated. It is a stirring site, and the royal blue sky and hard windy silence make for a profound experience as you commune alone with Papa.

Accommodations and Food

There are no hotels in Cojímar (the nearest is in Ciudad Panamericano, mentioned above), but you should have no problem renting a room with a local family.

After exploring, you should appease your hunger with fisherman's soup and paella at Hemingway's favorite restaurant, **La Terraza,** tel. 65-3471, on the main street 200 meters south of El Torreon. After Hemingway's death, the restaurant went into decline. Apparently, Fidel, passing through in 1970, was dismayed to learn of its condition and ordered it restored.

The gleaming mahogany bar at the front, accepting dollars only, gets few locals—a pity; what a hangout it could be. You sense that Papa could stroll in at any moment. He is there, patinated in bronze atop a pedestal; adorning the walls in black-and-white, too—sharing a laugh with Fidel. Hemingway's old pal and skipper, Gregorio Fuentes, is often present at lunch times, receiving free meals for regaling tourists with tales of the old days. Regardless, you should toast his good health with a turquoise cocktail appropriately named after Cojímar's venerable homegrown hero.

The food is good, with a wide-ranging menu that includes paella (US$7), grilled shrimp and fish (US$22), fish cocktail (US$2.50), shrimp cocktail (US$8). The "Coctel Fuentes" and tasty appetizers are included in the price. The paella is inconsistent—from sublime to fair.

(If you're feeling impecunious, there's a good *paladar*—**Restaurante Claro de Luna**—a few blocks north of the Hemingway statue.)

Services

The **Infotur** office on the waterfront one block south of the fortress sells tourist gifts, maps, and posters of Papa and has a popular café selling ice cream. The post office is two blocks west on Calle 98; open Mon.-Sat. 8-11 a.m. and 2-6 p.m.

Getting There

The exit from the Vía Monumental is well marked (coming from Havana, take the *second* exit marked Cojímar).

El Torreon and Hemingway bust

You can catch **buses** no. 58, 116, 195, 215 and 217 from the bottom of the Prado, at the junction with Avenida de los Estudiantes (10 centavos). Bus 58 departs from the west side of Parque de la Fraternidad, two blocks west of the Capitolio.

Organized Excursions: Virtually every major hotel in Havana offers excursions to Cojímar through its tour desk. **Paradiso,** Calle 19 #560 esq. Calle C, Vedado, tel. 32-6928, fax 33-3921, includes Cojímar on a five-hour guided excursion—Hemingway: the Mystery of a Footprint— offered daily from Havana at 9:30 a.m.

REGLA

Regla developed into a smugglers' port in colonial days. It was also the setting for Havana's bullfights. Today, the town is a major center of industry. The main electricity-generating plant for Havana is here, along with petrochemical works, both of which pour black and yellow plumes over the town. Regla is also a center of santería, and walking its streets you may note tiny shrines outside many houses. Calle Calixto García has many fine examples. Check out #116 (which has a small madonna enclosed in glass in the wall, with fresh flowers by its side) and #114, whose large altar in the middle of the house is easily seen from the street. A **Fiesta de los Orishas,** a quasi-religious ceremony featuring Afro-Cuban music and dance, is held each Tuesday at 8 p.m. in the **Palacio de Turismo,** at Sanctuario #13, tel. 90-0182.

From the harborfront plaza, the tidy, well-preserved main street (Calle Martí) leads east to **Parque Guaycanamar,** the main plaza fronting a splendidly preserved Georgian edifice with columns. En route you'll pass the **Museo Municipal de Regla,** at #158. It tells the tale of the Virgin of Regla and of the city's participation in revolutionary struggles and presents an intriguing exhibit on Regla's santería associations. Open Tues.-Sat. 9:30 a.m.-6 p.m. and Sunday 9 a.m.-1 pm. Entrance costs $2.

From the park, Calle Calixto García continues east to Guanabacoa, the center of santería in Cuba. (That horrible bad-eggs stench is from the chemical factory on the eastern outskirts of Regla.) You'll pass **Loma de Lenin** (Lenin Hill), where the communist leader's face is carved into the hillside and an olive tree is dedicated to his memory (bus no. 29 will also take you there from the ferry). It's reached via a steep metal staircase and is a good vantage point from which to survey the town.

Iglesia de Nuestra Señora de Regla

This harborfront hermitage, built in 1810, is one of Havana's loveliest churches. I recommend a visit on Sunday, when devout Habaneros flock to pay homage to the black Virgen de Regla, patron saint of sailors (and Catholic counterpart to Yemayá, the African goddess of the sea in the Yoruba religion). The ocher-colored church is well preserved. Its inner beauty is highlighted by a fabulous gilt altar beneath an arched ceiling. On holy days, the altar is sumptuously lit with votive candles. Dwelling in alcoves in the wall are figurines of miscellaneous saints, which devotees reach up to touch while reciting silent prayers. Check out the vaulted niche on the left side of the nave, which contains a statue of St. Anthony leading a wooden suckling pig wearing a dog-collar and a large blue ribbon.

Outside, to the right, presiding over her own private chapel, is the statue of the Virgen del Cobre, Cuba's patron saint, enveloped in a robe adorned with embroidered roses. Nearby is a **"water altar"** with—in miniature—a convoy of tiny ships, plus a wooden rowboat containing tiny effigies of the three Indian fishermen who supposedly found the statue of the black Virgin in Nipes Bay. Another altar is dedicated to St. Barbara, goddess of war. It is adorned with tin soldiers and toy tanks, planes, and other pint-size military hardware—all appropriately painted red—Chango's ritual color. With luck, you may arrive to witness an Afro-Cuban *batá*-drum recital being pounded out beneath the altar.

Masses are held Tuesday and Sunday at 8 and 9 a.m. If you can, time your visit for the seventh of each month, when large Masses are held—or, better yet, 8 September, when the Virgin is paraded through town. The church is open daily 7:30 a.m.-6 p.m.

Food and Information

At Calle Martí and Pereira is a small bar, **Ciboney, La Casa del Daiquirí.** Farther down Martí are **Restaurante Las Américas** and, opposite, **El Criollo Cafetería.** Two pleasant restaurants sit on the southwest corner of Parque Guaycanamar, where an ice cream shop can help you beat the heat.

An **Infotur** office is opposite the the ferry terminal. It displays a map of Regla on the wall and has a gift store and café.

Getting There

The little Regla ferries, bobbing like green corks, are magic carpets across Havana harbor. The ferries run constantly between Regla and the wharf on Avenida San Pedro at the foot of Santa Clara (10 centavos); it's a five-minute crossing. Other ferries depart Regla's wharf for Casablanca.

You can also catch buses from Habana Vieja. Bus no. 6 departs from Agramonte (Zulueta) and Genios; bus no. 106 departs from Agramonte and Refugio.

GUANABACOA

Guanabacoa is a popular pilgrimage site for Habaneros. The town was formally recognized in 1734, but by that time it had already been used as a major landing area for slaves for over a century. A strong Afro-Cuban culture developed. The town, about three km east of Regla, remains Cuba's most important center of santería, and there are plentiful sign of this on the streets.

Before exploring, you should call in at the Infotur office and peruse the map of the city.

The main square is the tree-shaded **Parque de Guanabacoa,** dominated by the columned **Palacio Municipal** and by **Iglesia Parroquial Mayor,** at its center. The recently restored church has a beautiful baroque gilt altar dripping with gold, with pink walls and a lofty wooden roof painted sky blue. The **Museo Histórico de Guanabacoa,** (Historical Museum of Guanabacoa) at Calle Martí #108, between San Antonio y Maceo on the west side of the church, tel. 90-9117, tells the tale of Guanabacoa's development. The 33-room museum outlines the evolution of Afro-Cuban culture, with emphasis on the slave days and santería. Open Mon.-Sat. 8 a.m.-6 p.m. and Sunday 2-6 p.m.

The list of religious sites is endless: **Convento de Santo Domingo,** at Calles Santo Domin-

go and Lebredo; **Iglesia de Santo Domingo,** at Bertemati between Jesús María and Lebredo; **Convento de San Francisco** (still used to train priests, apparently, two centuries after its founding); and **Iglesia Los Escolapios.** Don't forget to check out the **Palacio de Gobierno,** at Pepe Antonio and Jesús María.

Some touted sites are not worth the walk, such as the **Baños de Santa Rita.** Where once stood the colonial *balneario,* today only a few crumbling vestiges remain overlooking a disgustingly littered stream. And the tiny, red-tiled **Hermitage Potosí** and its overgrown cemetery, atop a hill at Calzada Vieja Guanabacoa and Potosí, is in a sad state of neglect, despite its tremendous potential. The hermitage dates back to 1644—one of the oldest in Cuba.

At the corner of San Juan Bosco and San Joaquín is a small shrine to Santo Lazarus beneath a fulsome bougainvillea bower. Pilgrims flock each 17 December bearing flowers and *promesas.* Mirella Acosta, who lives at San Juan Bosco #118, catercorner to the shrine, will happily recite details in Spanish.

If you linger through the afternoon and evening, call in at the **Casa de la Trova,** Martí e/ San Antonio y Versalles, to see if any Afro-Cuban music and dance is happening. Before leaving, also call in at the **Centro Gráfico de Reproducciones Para el Turismo,** at San Juan Bosco and Barreto. It displays ceramics and other artwork.

Accommodations and Food

La Vina (next to the Palacio Municipál) was being renovated at press time and will offer dining alfresco when it opens. Otherwise, try **Pizzería Bambino,** on the northwest corner of the main plaza, where there're also **Coppelia** and **Helado Tropical** outlets for ice cream. On Sunday, about the only place open is the café of Infotur, good for ice cream, sodas, and sandwiches.

Information

The **Infotur** office is on the southeast corner of Iglesia Parroquial Mayor, at Pepe Antonio and Martín Ugarte, tel. 90-6879, open 24 hours daily. Noemi Noallas, the information officer, is superfriendly. The office is stocked with postcards and the usual tourist trinkets and has large maps of the town and surrounding area on the wall.

The **Dirección Municipal de Cultura,** at the juncture of San Andres and Martí, can offer information on the town's culture.

Getting There

Bus no. 3 departs for Guanabacoa from Parque de la Fraternidad in Habana Vieja, and bus no. 95 from the corner of Corrales and Agramonte (Zulueta). From Vedado, you can take bus no. 195; from the Plaza de la Revolución, take bus no. 5.

SAN FRANCISCO DE PAULA

If there is one site you must visit outside Havana, it is **Finca Vigía,** Hemingway's former home in the village of San Francisco de Paula, 12.5 km south of Havana on the Carretera Central (about 20 minutes from Habana Vieja). On 21 July 1994, on the 95th anniversary of Papa's birthday, Finca Vigía reopened its doors as a museum following nearly two years of repairs and remodeling. The house is preserved in suspended animation, just the way the great writer left it. His presence seems to haunt the large, simple home.

The modest street leading to the mansion is lined with small wooden houses where Hemingway's original neighbors still live.

To get there, you must pass through the suburb of Luyano, four km southeast of Habana Vieja. Chugging up Calzada de Luyano when heading

FINCA VIGÍA

In 1939, Hemingway's third wife, Martha Gellhorn, was struck by Finca Vigía (Lookout Farm), a one-story Spanish-colonial house built in 1887 and boasting a wonderful view of Havana. They rented it for $100 a month. When Hemingway's first royalty check from *For Whom The Bell Tolls* arrived, in 1940, he bought the house for US$18,500 because, like his character Ole Anderson in "The Killers," he had tired of roaming from one place to another.

The gateway to the 20-acre hilltop estate is framed by bougainvillea. Mango trees and sumptuous jacarandas line the driveway leading up to the gleaming white house. No one is allowed inside—reasonably so, since every room can be viewed through the wide-open windows, and the temptation to pilfer priceless trinkets is thus reduced. (Two years after Hemingway died, someone offered $80,000 for his famous Royal typewriter which sits on a shelf beside his workroom desk; today, you can buy it for $7—inscribed in gray on a T-shirt that reads "Museo Ernesto Hemingway, Finca Vigía, Cuba").

Through the large windows I could see trophies, firearms, bottles of spirits, old issues of *The Field, Spectator,* and *Sports Afield* strewn about, and more than 8,000 books, arranged higgledy-piggledy the way he supposedly liked them, with no concern for authors or subjects. The dining-room table was set with cut crystal, as if guests were expected.

It is eerie being followed by countless eyes—those of the guides (one to each room) and those of the beasts that had found themselves in the crosshairs of Hemingway's hunting scope. "Don't know how a writer could write surrounded by so many dead animals," Graham Greene commented when he visited. There are bulls, too, everywhere bulls, including paintings by Miró and Klee, photographs and posters of bullfighting scenes, and a chalk plate of a bull's head, a gift from Picasso.

Here is where Hemingway wrote *Islands in the Stream, Across the River and into the Trees, A Moveable Feast* and *The Old Man and the Sea.* The four-story tower next to the house was built at his fourth wife's prompting so that he could write unmolested. Hemingway disliked the tower and continued writing amid the comings and goings of the house, surrounded by papers, shirtless, in Bermuda shorts, with any of 60 cats at his feet as he stood barefoot on the hide of a small kudu.

The sprawling grounds are equally evocative. Hemingway's legendary cabin cruiser, the *Pilar,* is poised loftily beneath a wooden pavilion on the former tennis court, shaded by bamboo and Royal palms. Nearby are the swimming pool where Ava Gardner swam naked and the graves of four of the novelist's favorite dogs.

In August 1961, his widow, Mary, donated the house and most of its contents to the Cuban state, according to Hemingway's will.

The museum, tel. 91-0809, is headed by a trained curator, Gladys Rodríguez. An articulate young guide named Joaquín Bernardo Gó leads free tours. Entrance costs US$3 for foreigners. Open Mon.-Sat. 9 a.m.-4 p.m. and Sunday 9 a.m.-noon. Closed Tuesday and rainy days. A gift shop sells portraits, T-shirts, and other souvenirs.

north, there is a view, off to the left, of El Cerro that reminded Ernest Hemingway's character Thomas Hudson (in *Islands in the Stream*) of Toledo. In Hemingway's day, Luyano was a shantytown so squalid that Hudson carried drink against the shock when passing through. Up until the Triumph of the Revolution, the deplorable shantytowns—there were others ringing the hills—were the most unfortunate spots in Havana.

Getting There

By Car: From Havana, begin at the foot of Calzada de Infante, at its junction with Vía Blanca. From this junction, take Calzada Diez de Octubre south half a km to Calzada de Luyano, which leads east to the Calzada de Güines, the Carretera Central that leads south to San Francisco de Paula. The museum is signed (turn left at Barbería Peluquería).

Alternately, you can take the Circunvalación (Vía Monumental), which circles Havana and runs through San Francisco de Paula, linking it directly with Cojímar, too.

By Bus: Bus no. 7 departs from Parque de la Fraternidad in Habana Vieja. Bus no. 404 departs from Avenida de Bélgica (Monserrate) and Dragones. Both travel via San Francisco de Paula en route to Cotorro and Havana.

By Train: Trains run from the Cristina station at Avenida de México and Arroy, at Cuatro Caminos, in Cerro Habana. Take the train for Cotorro (four times daily) via San Francisco de Paula.

Organized Excursions: Paradiso, Calle 19 #560 esq. Calle C, Vedado, tel. 32-6928, fax 33-3921, offers a five-hour guided excursion (Hemingway: the Mystery of a Footprint) to Finca Vigía (US$35, including lunch). **Cubanacán,** Calle 164 esq. 17D, Playa, Havana, tel. 21-9457, fax 33-6041, also has a "Re-encounter with Hemingway" trip.

PARQUE LENIN

Parque Lenin was created from a former hacienda. The vast complex, open Wed.-Sun. 9 a.m.-10:30 p.m., features wide rolling pastures and small lakes surrounded by forests. Most of the structures, alas, are ungainly Soviet-style concrete designs.

What Parque Lenin lacks in grandeur and stateliness, it makes up for in scale and scope.

You'll need a long study to get an idea of the full scope of Lenin Park, which is laid out around the huge lake, **Presa Paso Sequito.** The park is bounded by the Circunvalación to the north and Calzada de Bejucal to the west. The main entrance to the park is off Calzada de Bejucal. A second road—Calle Cortina de la Presa—enters from the Circunvalación and runs ruler-straight down the center of the park; most sites of interest lie at the south end of this road, south of the lake. Calle Cortina is linked to Calzada de Bejucal by a loop road that passes most of the recreational sites north of the lake.

Prior to 1990, Cuban families flocked to the park for the drive-in movie theater, rodeos, and all the fun of the fair. By 1995, the children's park, with carousels and fairground pleasures, had ceased operation, as had the narrow-gauge railway that circles the park, dropping passengers at various sites (the old steam train, dating to 1915, is preserved under a red-tiled canopy). Hopefully, by the time you read this, the park will have regained its vitality.

Sites, Galleries, and Museums

Begin with a visit to **Galería del Arte Amelia Peláez,** at the south end of Calle Cortina. It displays Paláez's works along with changing exhibitions of other artists. Behind the gallery are a series of bronze busts in rocks.

Nearby is the **Monumento Lenin,** a huge granite visage of the communist leader and thinker in Soviet-realist style. Moving west, you'll pass an **aquarium** displaying freshwater fish and turtles, including the antediluvian garfish *(marijuarí)* and a couple of Cuban crocodiles, Pepe and Rosita. A trail leads from the car park of the aquarium to the **Monumento á Celia Sánchez.** You follow a wide apse of large natural slabs to a broad ampitheater lined with ferns. At its center is a bronze figure of Sánchez ("the most beautiful and endemic flower of the Revolution"), inset in a huge rock. Make sure to peek inside the small museum exhibiting marvelous portraits of the heroine alongside her personal items.

I also recommend a visit to the **Taller Cerámica** (ceramic workshop); **Casa de la Amistad Cubano Soviético** (Cuban-Soviet Friendship House), farther west; and the **Che Guevara Pioneer Palace,** full of stainless-steel sculptures of the revolutionary hero.

Activities, Sports, and Recreation

Equestrian Events: There's an equestrian center—**Club Hípico**—northeast of the entrance off Calzada de Bejucal. It offers riding lessons, horseback trips, competition horse shows, and even trips in a *coche* (colonial horsedrawn coach). The riding club has stables for 30 horses, a training race track and paddock, several dressage paddocks, a smithy, veterinary clinic, changing rooms, showers, and even sauna and massage facilities. Open 9 a.m.-4:30 p.m.

Bicycle and Rowboat Rental: The park is a splendid place to bicycle. There's a bike rental shop, east of Calle Cortina, north of the rodeo, open 9 a.m.-6 p.m. You can also rent rowboats on the lake, 9 a.m.-4:45 p.m.

For Children: The kiddies' areas are concentrated in the northwest quarter and include carousels at **Parque Diversiones,** plus a scenic small-gauge railroad from Terminal Inglesa.

Other Facilities: You may be able to watch cowboys lasso cattle at El Rodeo. There's a doll museum (Colina de los Muñecos), a drive-in movie theater (Ciné Césped), and even a motocross circuit, although many of these facilities were not functioning at last report.

Accommodations, Food, and Services

The modest yet comfortable **Motel La Herradura,** tel. 33-8203 or 44-1058, fax 33-8166, is part of Club Hípico. There's also a **camping** area on the northern fringe of the park.

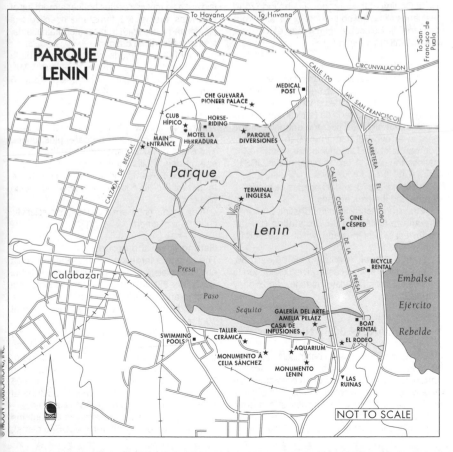

The park boasts the noted **Las Ruinas** restaurant, tel. 44-3336, in an intriguing modern building surrounding the ruins of an old sugar mill. Stained glass and classical urns full of flowers add romantic notes. And the Mexican-style former home of the estate owner now houses a small and pleasing restaurant, the **Casa de Infusiones 1740,** next to the Galeria de Arte. There are several other restaurants, though few were functioning at press time. A medley of soda bars and cafés made of concrete (none of which you'd wish to linger in) are sprinkled around, with attendants waiting for something to develop.

Casa de la Popularidad is an information center with a small bar and restaurant. It's just off Calle Cortina at the junction with the loop road that leads along the north shore of the lake from Calzada de Bejucal. A tourist map of the park (US$1) will prove handy.

Getting There
By car, you can follow the Calzada Diez de Octubre (see "San Francisco de Paula," above) about six km south to the La Vibora district and the junction with Calzada de Bejucal, which runs south about eight km past the entrance of the park at Arroyo Naranjo. From San Francisco, you can take the Circunvalación west; it also passes the park. A taxi will cost about US$12 each way.

Buses no. 31, 73, and 88 operate between La Vibora and the park entrance.

A train runs hourly from the Cristina Station in Havana to Galápago de Oro station (on the northwest side of the park), which is served by bus no. 31.

Tour & Travel, Avenida 5 #8409 esq. 86, Miramar, tel. 33-2433, has a guided excursion to Parque Lenin on Tuesday, Thursday, and Friday (US$25).

JARDÍN BOTÁNICO

This massive (600 hectare) botanical garden, 25 km south of Havana, is worth the drive for enthusiasts. The expansive garden consists mostly of wide pastures planted with copses of trees and shrubs divided by Cuban ecosystems (from coastal thicket to Oriental humid forest) and by regions of the tropical world. Over 100 gardeners

tenderly prune and mulch such oddities as the *satchicha* tree, with pendulous pods that certain African tribeswomen rub on their nipples in the belief that it will give them large breasts.

The highlight is the **Japanese garden,** beautifully landscaped with tiered cascades, fountains, and a jade-green lake full of koi. This little gem was donated by the Japanese government for the 30th anniversary of the Revolution.

The geographic center of the garden has a fascinating variety of palm trees from around the world.

Be sure to walk through the **Rincón Eckman,** a massive glasshouse named after Erik Leonard Eckman (1883-1931), who documented Cuban flora between 1914 and 1924. The glasshouse is laid out as a triptych: cactus house; a room full of epiphytes, bromeliads, ferns and insectivorous plants; and a third with tropical mountain plants, a small cascade, and a pool.

Thirty-five km of roads lead through the park, which was laid out between 1969 and 1984. Open daily 9 a.m.-5 p.m. (in summer, 10 a.m.-6 p.m.). Entrance costs US30 cents.

Food and Services
The glasshouse (which has wheelchair access) boasts a souvenir stall and café, plus toilets. The **Bambú Restaurant** overlooks the Japanese garden. It bills itself as an "eco-restorán" and sells ice creams and sodas. You can buy a tourist map of the garden for US$1 and also hire guides.

A museum, motel, amphitheater, and scientific center are planned.

Getting There and Around
The garden is three km south of Parque Lenin and immediately south of the village of El Globo. Buses no. 88 and 113 leave for the Botanical Garden and ExpoCuba (see below) from the north side of the railway station weekends at 10 a.m., noon, and 3 p.m. and from Havana's Terminal de Ómnibus at 9 and 11 a.m. and 4 p.m. Bus no. 80 also serves the park, from Lawton. A three-car train runs to ExpoCuba, opposite the garden, from the Tulipán station on Calle Tulipán, in Nuevo Vedado, Wed.-Sun. at 9:05 a.m. and 12:35 p.m.; it departs ExpoCuba at 10:50 a.m. and 3:50 p.m. (US$1 one-way).

Private vehicles are *not* allowed through the park. You can park your vehicle (US40 cents), then take a guided tour with a vehicle provided by the garden: reservations can be made by calling 44-8743, Mon.-Fri. 8 a.m.-4 p.m.

Tour & Travel, Avenida 5 #8409 esq. 86, Miramar, tel. 33-2433, has a daily excursion to the garden for US$23.

EXPOCUBA

ExpoCuba, directly opposite the Botanical Gardens at Carretera del Rocío Km 3.5, Arroyo Naranjo, tel. 44-6251, fax 33-5307, is a permanent exhibition of Cuban industry, technology, sports, and culture. It's a popular venue for school field trips and conventioneers—and no wonder—it's impressive.

The facility covers 588,000 square meters and is a museum, trade expo, World's Fair, and entertainment hall rolled into one. It has 34 pavilions, including provincial booths that display the crafts, products, music, and dance of each of Cuba's provinces. There are plenty of other attractions, too. Railroad buffs might check out the vintage rolling stock (including turn-of-the-century carriages) on the entrance forecourt. Booth #9—the maritime booth—displays an armored motor launch, among other vessels. Booth #25 exhibits old carriages and cars.

Food and Services

There's an Asistur information office at the entrance, alongside a bureau de change and a branch of Banco Nacional.

There is a fistful of restaurants and cafés. The best is the elegant **Don Cuba Restaurant,** built around an inner courtyard with neoclassical Roman-cum-Arabic architecture. Flautists and singers perform in the courtyard. I enjoyed a tasty grilled fish with rice and spiced vegetables (US$8).

See "Getting There" under "Jardín Botánico," above, for information on getting to ExpoCuba.

SANTIAGO DE LAS VEGAS

This small town, 20 km south of Havana, is the nearest provincial town to Havana and a worthy destination for an excursion. It straddles Avenida de los Mártires (Avenida Rancho Boyeros), about three km south of the airport. It is steeped in sleepy bucolic charm. Its allure lies in strolling

---

SANTIAGO DE LAS VEGAS USEFUL TELEPHONE NUMBERS

Police . . . . tel. 9-9181
Ambulance . . . . tel. 9-9105
Policlinica . . . . tel. 9-9105

---

the narrow streets lined with red-tile-roofed colonial houses painted in faded pastels.

Immediately southwest of town is the village of Rincón, famed for the **Procession of the Miracles,** which takes place 17 December, when hundreds of pilgrims—up to 50,000 in good years—make their way to the **Sanctuario de San Lazaro,** to give thanks to the saint. On Sunday, Cubans come to have their children baptized, while others fill bottles with holy water from a fountain behind the church (where there's also a leprosy sanatorium).

At **El Cacahual,** between Santiago de las Vegas and El Rincón, General Antonio Maceo—hero of the wars of independence—slumbers in an open-air mausoleum, with a small museum in the adjacent pavilion.

Food and Services

Two pleasing places to eat are **Cafetería Amanecer,** at Avenida 411 #219 ; and **La Tabernita,** a thatched restaurant at the south end of town, on Doble Vía Cacahual, tel. 2033. **Vesuvia Pizzeria** serves slices of pizza for five pesos. Also try the **Mozambique Cafetería,** on the northeast corner of the park, or **Cafetería Cocody,** one block north of the church.

I'm not aware of any hotels.

For **Turistaxi** on General Peraza, tel. 3007.

Getting There and Away

Bus M2 runs from Parque de la Fraternidad in Havana and stops on the southeast corner of the square. The *terminal de autobus* is on the southwest side of town, at Calle 12 and Avenida 17. The main road continues south from here for Bejucal (and San Antonio de los Baños).

CUBANACÁN

This residential region, sloping gently inland west of Miramar, boasts the city's most luxurious residences. Following the Revolution, most of the owners decamped and fled Cuba. Many mansions have since fallen into ruin, reminding novelist James Michener of "an Arthur Rackham painting of a country in which a cruel king has laid waste the mansions of his enemies." (Apparently, after the Revolution, the mansions were dispensed to party officials, many of whom still live in glorious isolation. Alas, others didn't have the resources to maintain them. Many of the mansions were then turned into communal dwellings for multiple families, who turned them into slums.) Others have been splendidly maintained amid neatly trimmed lawns and serve either as "protocol" houses—villas where foreign dignitaries and VIPs are housed during visits to Cuba—or as foreign embassies and immaculately kept ambassadors' homes. Among them is the US Residency.

It is intriguing to cruise Avenida 5—"Embassy Row"—where house #6 (known locally as La Casa de Gabo), with the black Mercedes Benz 280, belongs to Gabriel García Márquez (the Colombian novelist friend of Fidel) and stands next to the mansions given to Robert Redford and Harry Belafonte on their recent visits to Cuba.

The erstwhile exclusive Havana Country Club, complete with 18-hole golf course, was converted following the Revolution to house Cuba's leading art academy. The club building became the Faculty of Music. Additional buildings (most rather grim) were added to house other faculties that together make up the **Instituto Superior de Arte.** Access is via Calle 120.

The **Palacio de las Convenciones**—Havana's impressive convention center—is also here, on Calle 146. It was built in 1979 for the Non-Aligned Conference, and the main hall, seating 2,200 delegates, also hosts meetings of the National Assembly.

Nearby, at Avenida 17 and 180, is **Pabexpo,** with four exhibition halls for hosting trade fairs. Cuba's admirable biotechnology industry is centered here, too. The **Centro de Ingeneria Genética y Biotecnología** is at Avenida 31

and 190, tel. 21-6022, fax 21-8070; the **Centro Nacional de Investigaciones Científicas** is at Avenida 25 and 158, tel. 21-8066. You can arrange visits that will duly impress you with Cuba's phenomenal commitment to—and success with—to cutting-edge research in the field.

Bus no. 32 operates between La Rampa in Vedado and Cubanacán (five pesos).

Museo del Aire
Hidden in the peaceful midst of Cubanacán is the Air Museum, on Avenida 212 and La Coronela. The gamut of civilian and military aircraft displayed includes helicopters, missiles, bombers, and fighter planes, including Soviet MiGs and a turn-of-the-century biplane hanging from the ceiling. The museum also has a restoration program, plus three main rooms that are an Aladdin's cave of aviation mementos. A section dedicated to the Bay of Pigs battle evokes poignant memories; remnants of planes destroyed in the fighting and black-and-white photos speak with mute eloquence of the memory of Cuban pilots who died defending the island. There's also a collection of model aircraft, and a space section honoring Yuri Gagarin and Col. Arnaldo Tamayo Méndez, the first Cuban cosmonaut.

An artisans' shop and a restaurant are planned. Open Tues.-Sun. 9 a.m.-5 p.m. Entrance US$2.

Food
From Cubanacán, the Autopista del Mediodía leads south about five km to the village of El Chico and **La Rueda,** tel. 0684-25, a rustic yet acclaimed restaurant on a Ministry of Agriculture goose farm. The farm is on the Carretera de Guajay, at Calle 294 in the village of El Chico. Not surprisingly, the menu offers goose this and goose that. Be sure to accompany your *foie gras* with the house cocktail of rum and fruit juice. Set meals cost US$20. Despite its distance from the city, the place gets full. Reservations are recommended. Cockfights are hosted. Open noon-8 p.m.

HAVANA TO PLAYAS DEL ESTE

East of the tunnel under Havana harbor, Vía Monumental leads east to Ciudad Panaméricano and Cojímar. One km east of the second

(easternmost) turnoff for Cojímar, Vía Monumental splits. Take the Vía Blanca turnoff marked Playa del Este to reach Playas del Este,

Matanzas, and Varadero (if you continue on Vía Monumental—which appears to head the right way—you'll end up circling Havana on the *circunvalación*). Note that motorcycles are *not* allowed through the tunnel; if you're on two wheels, you'll have to take the Vía Blanca from its origin in Havana, which skirts around the bay and is perhaps the worst-maintained road in the country.

The coastal vistas along the Vía Blanca soon open up with some splendid views to the south as you drive along the coast road between Havana and Matanzas and look down upon wide valleys with rolling hills, tufts of royal palms, and *mogotes* far to the south.

Immediately east of Cojímar, you'll pass a modern, self-contained dormitory city long prized by the Cuban government as an example of the achievements of socialism. Alamar (pop. 100,000) is a sea of ugly concrete high-rise complexes jerry-built almost entirely by micro-brigades of untrained volunteer workers. Alamar extends east to a sister city, **Celimar,** 10 km east of Cojímar. On the western side of Celimar is Bacuranao.

BACURANAO

This small horseshoe cove with white sand beach backed by seagrape and palms is popular on weekends with Habaneros escaping city life for a day by the sea in the sun.

Ernest Hemingway used to berth his *Pilar* here, and it was here that his fishermen in *To Have and Have Not* had squeezed "the Chink's" throat until it cracked.

The area is good for **scuba diving.** The wreck of an 18th-century galleon lies just off the tiny beach and there's another wreck farther out (a popular playpen for turtles). Coral grows abundantly on both sides of the bay, so if you have **snorkeling** gear, bring it.

Buses no. 62 and 162 pass by Bacuranao, departing from Parque Central in Havana.

Accommodations
Villa Bacuranao, is on the eastern shore of the cove, tel. 65-7645, with cabins spread widely amid palm-shaded lawns sloping down to the beach, which angles sharply in a scimitar curve. In low season, the majority of guests

are Cubans; in high season, Italians and Mexicans predominate. The modest yet spacious cabins have utility furniture, TVs, blue linoleum floors, basic kitchens, large bathrooms with hot water, and large, louvered windows (US$15 s, US$20 d in high season, plus US$10 more if you don't have a reservation). It has a pool and a lively bar and cabaret. You can rent bicycles and cars here.

TARARÁ

Two km farther east, you'll cross the Río Tarará and the village of Tarará, which is famous as a summer camp and health resort. Before the Special Period, it was used by Cuban schoolchildren who combined study with beachside pleasures and stayed at Tarará's **José Martí Pioneer City.** Today, Servimed operates Tarará as a health tourism facility.

A pocket-size beach, quiet delightful, forms a spit at the rivermouth. It's popular with locals and has a volleyball court and shady *palapas*. The channel is renowned for its coral—great for snorkeling and scuba diving, as large groupers and snappers swim in and out of the rivermouth.

Accommodations and Food
Most of the 121 modest houses available for rent belong to Cubanacán. Others belong to Puerto Sol, and others to Islazul. They sleep from two to five people and cost US$60/76 (low/high season) for up to four people, US$93/119 for up to six people. Five-bedroom *casas* are also available (US$129/155). Each has a radio, satellite TV, telephone, and private parking.

There are several places to eat. **Restaurante Cojímar** is opposite the marina office, at the corner of Calles 7 and 8. On the same corner is the **Bar Neptune,** opening onto a large swimming pool and sundeck. The tiny yet atmospheric **Restaurante Rio Mar,** 50 meters east of Restaurante Cojímar, offers alfresco dining under palms on the front lawn.

The marina hosts a Cuban Evening with dinner, entertainment, and disco from 9 p.m. onwards.

Marina Tarará
Marina Tarará is behind the spit, on the east side of the river. The marina, which has im-

pressive facilities, is the headquarters for Puertosol marinas nationwide. The marina has 50 berths, with water and electricity hookups, plus diesel and gas. It also has a dry-dock. Contact Club Nautica at Calle 5ta e/ 2da y Cobre, Tarará, Playas del Este, tel. 33-5499 or 33-55-1, fax 33-5500, or via channel VHF 77.

The marina hosts the **Old Man and the Sea Fishing Tournament** each July. Registration costs US$200 for up to three *pescadores* (fishermen). Boats are made available for US$180 - 300 per day, depending on size. It also hosts the **La Hispanidad Fishing Tournament** in October (registration costs US$250, but boat charter fees are the same).

Boat Rental: Yachts can be rented for US$250 for nine hours. You can also rent three live-aboard motorboats. Weekly rentals range from US$2,100 (May-Oct.) to US$2,800 (mid-Dec. to mid-Jan.).

Watersports: Scuba diving trips cost US$27 (one dive) or US$42 (two dives). Initiation dives (three hours) are also offered. You can charter a boat for four hours' **sportfishing** for US$130, including hotel transfers from Havana. Other fishing trips cost US$20. Three-hour **snorkeling** excursions cost US$15 based on a minimum of four people per boat.

Banana boats, jet skis, and catamaran trips are also available.

Yacht Cruises: Excursions are offered, including six-hour "seafaris" aboard the *Faro,* with cocktails, fishing, snorkeling, lunch, and diving (the minimum is four passengers, costing from US$25 per person). A four-hour sunset cruise includes dinner on board, plus nighttime fishing (US$30). Groups can also charter a crewed boat for a two-day voyage to Cayo Paraíso (US$560).

Getting There

Tarará is at Km 17 Vía Blanca, 27 km east of Havana. Coming from Havana, signs for Tarará point left toward the coast, but the unmarked turnoff is the next *right* off the Vía Blanca, just beyond the roadside restaurant. You pass under the autopista and head half a km downhill to the marina.

PLAYAS DEL ESTE

"A sense of the island's racial history and diversity wasn't to be culled from the telephone directory," wrote Carlo Gébler in *Driving Through Cuba,* "but was to be seen at first hand on the sand by the edge of the sea." Cubans are great beachgoers, and nowhere on the island proves the case more than the Playas del Este. On hot summer weekends, all of Havana seems to come down to the beach (well, at least they did before the Special Period, when gas and money were more widely available). The beaches of Playas del Este are temples of ritual narcissism: young Cubans congregate here to meet friends, tan their bodies, play soccer or volleyball, and flirt.

Today, the four Playas del Este (really two beaches separated by the Río Itabo) are being pushed as a hot destination for foreign tourists. The main beach—Playa Santa María—is several km long, with light-golden sand shelving into stunning aquamarine and turquoise waters. A nearly constant tropical breeze is usually strong enough to conjure surf from the warm

turquoise seas—a perfect scenario for lazing, with occasional breaks for grilled fish or fried chicken from thatch-roofed *ranchitas,* where the drinks are strong and you can eat practically with your feet in the water. After a sun-stunned day, everyone seems to curl up for a recuperative snooze in preparation for the reappearance of the bohemian spirit, which stirs around eight.

The beach action concentrates on Playa Santa María, opposite the main hotel, the Tropicoco, where tourists (predominantly European and male) and Cubans (predominantly female) gather lemming-like under *palapas* and palms. It's quite a social scene. Playas del Este is considered by *jiniteras* to be a great place to find single Italian males, for whom the resort has become a virtual colony.

There are several restaurants, bars, and open-air cafes to provide quick relief from hunger or thirst, and two discos for nocturnal pleasures. (The place is relatively dead in the summer off-season now that Cubans no longer flock in the

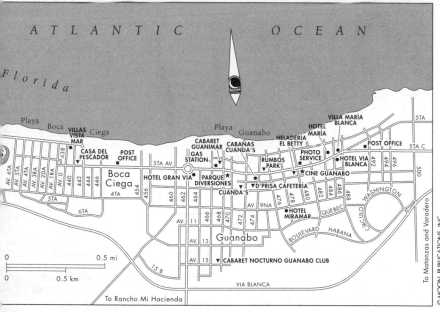

numbers they used to). The hotels are modest, and the beaches have relatively few services and limited watersports, including scuba diving. A coral reef runs offshore at a depth of no more than 20 feet, with lots of brain, elkhorn, and staghorn formations.

Other than the beach itself, forget any hopes of aesthetic appeal. You'll be disappointed if you expect an upscale resort.

Alas, puddles collect in mangroves and pastures on the lowlands inland, forming perfect breeding habitats for mosquitoes. When the rains come, the bloodsuckers are voracious. By day, you're usually okay, but lather up with insect repellent at night.

ORIENTATION AND SETTING

Playas del Este is divided into Mégano and Santa María del Mar to the west of the Río Itabo, with Boca Ciega and Guanabo to the east. Santa María—including Mégano, its western extension—is the main beach and resort. Avenidas de las Terrazas leads downhill from the Vía Blanca to the western point of Playa Mégano. Avenida de las Banderas, one km farther east, leads down to Santa María del Mar.

Playa Boca Ciega is also beautiful, and backed by dunes. It is reached from the Vía Blanca by way of Avenida 462, which runs downhill to Avenida 5ta, the main east-west street, two blocks inland from the shore.

East of Avenida 462 is Guanabo, a Cuban village with many plantation-style wooden homes. Playa Guanabo is the least-attractive beach. Local Cubans use it for recreation, including old men looking like salty characters from a Hemingway novel standing bare-chested, reeling in silvery fish from the surf. It has few restaurants and bars and no hotels to Western standards but is receiving a facelift and slowly accruing tourist facilities.

The village of Santa María Loma is one km inland, atop the hill that parallels the shore. It has many modest rental units.

ACCOMMODATIONS

The Playas del Este have traditionally been the spot of choice for Habaneros on weekends, and despite the rigors of the Special Period many Cubans still find the resources to vacation here. Many places are ugly concrete carbuncles that don't serve current tourism needs well. Some are terribly run-down. Hence, there is a growing trade in private room rentals.

The complex is divided into *zonas,* each with a *carpeta* or reservations office for rental units.

Hotels

Budget: Guanabo is home to several budget hotels that say they no longer normally accept foreigners. Among them are **Hotel María** and **Hotel Vía Blanca,** opposite each other on Avenida 5ta at Calle 486. You may have better luck at the very basic **Villa María Blanca,** with rooms below US$5.

Inexpensive: Cabañas Cuanda's, one block south of Avenida 5ta at Calle 472, tel. 2774, has 37 a/c rooms, most with double beds and showers with tepid water. Rooms are US$25 d.

Moderate: The most popular place in town is the **Hotel Tropicoco,** between Avenidas Sur and Las Terrazas and facing Playa Santa María, tel. 687-2531 or 33-8040, fax 33-5158. The uninspired, communist-style five-story building was recently renovated and is a favorite of Italian and German tour groups. It has 188 a/c rooms with telephones and radio, plus full services: restaurant, bar, tour desk, store, disco, and car rental. Rooms cost from US$35/45 s/d.

Much nicer is the **Hotel Itabo,** Laguna Itabo e/ Santa María del Mar y Boca Ciega, tel. 2580 or 2550, an attractive, secluded property also popular with German and Austrian charters. Itabo is an Indian word meaning "place of water"—the hotel sits on an island surrounded by mangroves. Red-tile-roofed units surround a massive pool and lush lawns with thatched restaurant and bar. Rooms are modest but pleasantly decorated (US$36 s, US$48 d, US$48 suite).

Also check out the modest **Hotel Miramar,** on Avenida 9 and Calle 478 in Guanabo, tel. 2262, with rooms with balconies for US$30 d; the **Hotel Gran Vía,** by the traffic circle at Avenida 5ta and Avenida 462 in Boca Ciega, tel. 2271; and, in Santa María Loma, the **Villa Las Brisas.**

Alas, the best property—**Hotel Club Atlántico Going One,** tel. 2506—is a closed shop—a Gran Caribe property leased entirely for use by an Italian company. Only clients on their packages are allowed.

Villas and Self-Catering *Cabañas*
Horizontes runs the **Aparthotel Atlántico,** on Avenida de las Terrazas, tel. 687-2561, fax 33-5158. Choose from one-, two-, and three-bedroom apartments, or studios. Facilities include a tour desk, car rental, and tennis courts. Another Horizontes option is **Aparthotel Las Terrazas,** Avenida Las Terrazas and Calle 9, tel. 687-4910, fronting the shore. It has 144 a/c apartments with kitchens, TVs, radios, and telephones (US$28 s, US$35 d). There's also a swimming pool.

Villa Mégano, midway down Avenida de las Terrazas, tel. 4441, is a characterless Horizontes property with cabins a 10-minute walk from the beach. Larger cabins cost US$34/44 s, US$46/58 d (low/high season); smaller cabins *(chicas)* cost US$28/36 s, US$38/48 d.

Elegant **Villa los Pinos,** Avenida Las Terrazas y Calle 4, tel. 687-2591 or 687-3320, fax 80-2144, is a Gran Caribe property with 27 two-and three-room villas. Some appear a bit fuddy-duddy, others are impressive; two have private pools. They all have TVs, VCRs, radios, telephones, and kitchens. Rates are US$92-170 for up to four people, including maid service. Other staff are on hand, and baby-sitters can be arranged. **Villas Las Brisas,** on Calle 11, tel. 2469, has 85 rooms for US$20 s, US$28 d in apartments in tropical gardens, plus a restaurant and bar.

If you want a private villa in Boca Ciega, you can book one through **Villas Vista Mar,** on Avenida 1ra and Calle 438 in Boca Ciega, tel. 2771. It has 69 *casas,* from US$44 for a two-bedroom, US$63 for a three-bedroom.

FOOD

Most of the hotels have adequate, albeit uninspired restaurants. Several *palenque* bars and eateries have sprouted on the beach, including two rustic places serving basic *criollo* fare in front of the Hotel Tropicoco. **Bar/Restaurante Bonanza,** on Playa Mégano, has a patio bar and modestly elegant indoor dining, too. You'll pay upward of US$5 for seafoods and the usual creole fare. It also has burgers and pizza noon-5 p.m. Dinner is served 6-9:45 p.m.

Café Pinomar, on Avenida Sur and Calle 5, serves pizzas and burgers and is open 24 hours. Also catering to Italian tastes is **Pizzeria Mi Rinconcito,** one block north, on Avenida de las Terrazas, and **Pizzeria Yara,** on Avenida las Terrazas and Calle 10 (the latter has its own swimming pool).

The most atmospheric place in Boca Ciega is **Casa del Pescador,** a Spanish-style bodega on Calle 5 esq. 442. It has fishing nets hanging from the ceiling. The menu is huge. Fish dishes average US$7, and shrimp and lobster start at US$8. The house specialty is *escabeche* (US$3.50). It's open 10 a.m.-10 p.m.

Two reasonable places in Guanabo are the sparse **Cuanda's**—which serves salads for US80 cents, rice dishes from US$1, and pastas for US$3.50—and **D'Prisa Cafetería,** a modish, pocket-size place serving sandwiches and basic Italian dishes from US$1. Other options include **Rumbos Park,** an open-air café and restaurant on the main street at Calle 474 in Guanabo, and a basic, pesos-only, US-style diner—**Cafetería Hatuey**—on Calle 476.

For ice cream, head to the small **Coppelia,** one block north of Avenida de las Terrazas at the west end of Mégano, or to **Heladería El Betty,** on Avenida 5ta at Calle 480 in Guanabo.

OTHER PRACTICALITIES

Entertainment
There's not much nightlife. The hottest thing is the **Disco Bananarama,** a palenque bar-cum-disco right on the beach in Santa María. The **Hotel Tropicoco** also has a late-night disco (entrance free to hotel guests, US$2 to others).

Several down-to-earth places cater to the local Cuban populace. Try **Centro Nocturno Habana Club,** on Calle 10 e/1 y 3, tel. 3384; **Cabaret Nocturno Guanabo Club,** on Calle 468, tel. 2884; **Cabaret Guanimar,** at Avenida 3 and Calle 468; or **Cabaret Pino del Mar,** on Avenida del Sur e/ Calles 5 y 7, tel. 2729.

Western camp classic films dubbed in Spanish are shown at **Cine Guanabo** on Calle 480, tel. 2440; one peso.

Sports and Recreation
Go-cart racing is offered on a circuitous track at the far western end of Santa María. Each six minutes costs US$5. (There's also a motorcycle racing track and *pista de aeromodelismo*—a model aircraft circuit—south of Avenida Sur, but they don't seem to be in current use.)

You can rent a small boat named *Mi Cayito* (US$12 per hour; 10 a.m.-5 p.m.) to explore the mangroves, where egrets, herons, and other waterfowl can be admired. The little dock is 200 meters west of the bridge over the Río Itabo. **Horses** can be rented on the beach in front of Tropicoco.

If the kids tire of the beach, take them to the basic kiddie's playground—**Parque Diversiones**—on Avenida Quinta and Calle 470 in Boca Ciega. The kids (and adults) can take pot shots at cutouts of soldiers (*yanquis,* perhaps?) at a fairground rifle range one block east, at Calle 472.

Services
You can purchase postage stamps and make international calls at the Hotel Tropicoco. There's also a post office in Boca Ciega, on Avenida 5ta and Calle 448; you'll find another post office in Santa María in Edificio Los Corales, on Avenida de las Terrazas at Calle 11, tel. 4401, open 8 a.m.-1 p.m.

There's a public phone outside Cuanda's, in Guanabo. (The long-distance prefix for Guanabo from elsewhere in Cuba is 0687.)

Servimed operates the **Clínica Internacional**, on Avenida de las Terrazas, one block east of Avenida de las Banderas, tel. 2689. It's open 24 hours. The doctor makes hotel visits if needed (US$40). It boasts a well-stocked pharmacy and even a clinical laboratory and an ambulance. Asistur can arrange credit payment if you're in financial straits. If you need the **Rojo Cruz** (Red Cross), call 4111.

The **Tropical Travel Agency** can advise on and make travel arrangements. It's in Edificio Los Corales, on Avenida de las Terrazas, in Santa María. There's also a tourism desk in the lobby of the Hotel Tropicoco.

Photo Service has two small stores where you can buy instamatic cameras, batteries, and film. The first is on Avenida 5ta in Guanabo, at Calle 480; the other, in Santa María, is on Avenida de las Terrazas just east of Calle 11. There's a **Cupet gas station** on Avenida 5ta, two blocks east of the traffic circle at the foot of Calle 462.

Getting There and Around
Playas del Este is well served by bus from Havana. Buses no. 62, 162, and 262 operate from Parque Central; bus no. 219 departs from the main bus terminal, and bus no. 400 departs from near the railway station, at the junction of Agramonte and Glória (one peso). You can also hire a *maquina* (a *colectivo* taxi) from outside the railway station and at Dragones, in Havana. They'll charge anywhere upward of US$5 to Playas del Este, depending on the number of passengers. A licensed taxi will cost at least US$18 one-way. Ostensibly, a train runs four times daily to Guanabo (July-Aug. only) from Estación Cristina, at Avenida de México and Arroyo in Havana.

You can walk virtually anywhere in Mégano/Santa María or Boca Ciega/Guanabo, although you will want wheels to get between them. The best way is to rent a **bicycle** (US$2 per hour) or **scooter** (US$30 a day) from either the **Rent-a-Moto** booth in front of the Hotel Tropicoco or the bicycle rental agency three blocks east of Cupet gas station in Guanabo.

Transauto Rent-a-Car has three offices: on Avenida de las Terrazas and Calle 11 in Santa María, at the far west end of Avenida de las Terrazas, and beside the traffic circle on Avenida Quinta in Boca Ciega. **Havanauto** has a car-rental office one block farther east.

RANCHO MI HACIENDA

For a break from the beach, head inland to this farmstead-cum-tourist attraction, at Carretera de Jústiz Km 4, at Campo Florido, near Minas, about five km south of Guanabo, tel. 33-5485. The 13-hectare *finca,* raises animals and vegetables used in the ranch's restaurant. It offers horseback riding and boat rides on a lake. Take your camera to record the ferocious yet bloodless cockfights (fortunately, the bird's spurs are covered to prevent them from seriously hurting one another).

Accommodation is provided in six beautiful cabins connected by suspension bridges on the banks of the Rio Itabo, plus three rooms in what was once a posh mansion. Each a/c unit has telephone, satellite TV, and mini-bar. There's a dining hall and swimming pool amid lush gardens. Rancho Mi Hacienda hosts an Afro-Cuban cultural show once a week.

HAVANA PROVINCE

There is comparatively little of interest in the namesake province that extends 65 km east and west and 40 km south of Havana's city limits. Havana is ringed with time-worn, provincial colonial towns, small, yet possessing a dusty charm. Tucked away from the road, hidden in folds of hills, are small fishing and farming villages shaded by royal palms, thorny *marabú* trees, and two-toned *yagruma* trees. Inland, much of the northern province is hilly and pocked with reservoirs that supply fresh water to Habaneros.

Most of Havana province is agricultural, especially the low-lying southern plain—the food basket of the capital city—whose rich red soils feed fruit trees and vegetables. The southern shore is a soggy no-man's-land of swamp and mangroves, where lowly fishing villages are among the most deprived and down-at-heels in Cuba. No road runs along the southern shore. Alas, this area took a direct hit from Hurricane Lili in October 1996, causing much flooding and devastation.

WEST OF HAVANA

ALONG THE COAST

Avenida 5ta leads westward from Havana and becomes the coast road—Autopista La Habana-Mariel (route 2-1-3)—to Pinar del Río province. Just beyond the city limits, you'll pass two places marked on maps as "resorts." Don't be fooled by the umbrella symbols. Neither **Santa Fe,** immediately west of Marina Hemingway, nor **Baracoa** has beaches or facilities of any kind.

Playa Salado, five km farther west, is a tad more appealing. It's a tranquil spot where waves wash up onto a pebbly shore with pocket-size beaches beside a river estuary.

Here, Cubanacán operates **Villa El Salado,** Carretera Panamericano, Km 23.5, Caimito, tel./fax 80-5089. It has 47 a/c bungalows amid palms, casuarinas, and lawns—22 doubles with refrigerators, 25 singles with coolers—all with color TVs, telephones, and safety boxes (US$28 small, US$43 large). Facilities include the La Riviera restaurant, an open-air disco, shop, car rental and tour bureau, a wide swimming pool, and a sundeck.

Beyond Caimito, the sea glows an almost impossibly pavonine blue, as in a Maxfield Parrish painting. The route is lined with fields of spiny sisal. Eventually you'll reach a T-junction, on the outskirts of Mariel. To the right is a huge electricity generating plant—Termoelectricidad Máximo Gómez. To the left, the paved road leads past industrial plants and cement works and heads for Mariel.

MARIEL AND POINTS WEST

This port city, deep inside a flask-shaped bay 45 km west of Havana, is best known as the site of the famous "boatlift" in April 1980, when 120,000 Cubans departed the island and sailed away

to Florida, causing President Carter no end of problems.

MARIEL TELEPHONE NUMBERS	
Police	tel. 9-2441
Ambulance (Cruz Roja/Red Cross)	tel. 9-2568
Policlínica	tel. 9-2506
Terminal de Ómnibus	tel. 9-2104

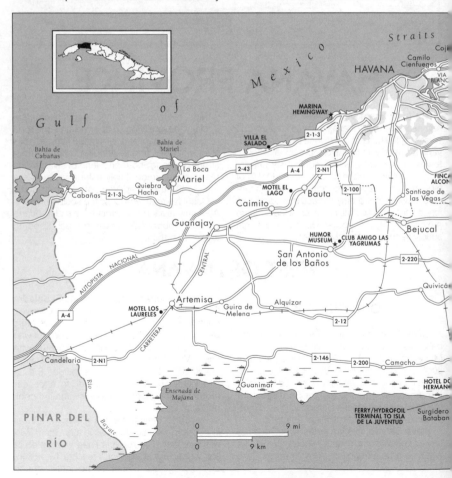

It's a surprisingly small town, as sleepy as most other small Cuban cities despite its port status. Mariel is ringed by docks and factories, including the largest cement factory in Cuba, whose main contribution to the common welfare is to cast a pall of dust over everything for miles around.

The town evolved as a fishing village during the late 17th century. Then the British arrived and established a naval station here in 1762 (there is still a naval academy). Look for the Moorish-inspired building atop the hill on the outskirts north of town, a vision from *Beau Geste* amid the tousled palms. The **Museo Histórico,** Calle 132 # 6926, tel. 9-2554, tells of the city's development

If you decide to overnight, you're limited to the **Motel La Puntilla,** Calle 128, tel. 9-2108, a 21-room peso hotel with swimming pool and bar. For eats, try **Restaurante Resplanador,** next to Agro-Mercado on Calle 132 and Avenida 69; the **Restaurante Wakamba;** or the **Paladar el Dorado.** Buses depart and drop off at a "terminal," on Calle 71, tel. 9-2104.

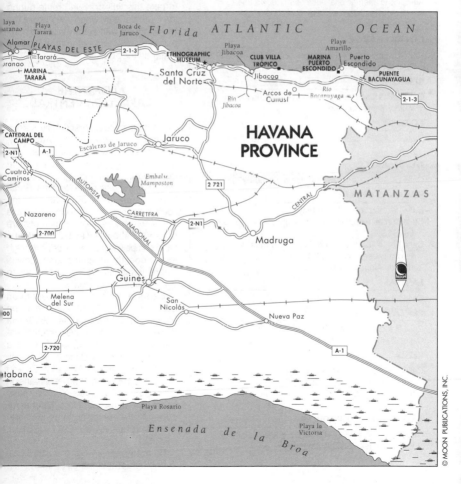

INFOTUR OFFICES IN HAVANA PROVINCE

PLAYA

Palacio de Turismo, Avenida 3ra esq. 28, Miramar, tel. 23-3376 or 23-2608

HABANA VIEJA

Calle Zulueta e/ Neptuno y San Rafael, tel. 63-6960

BOYEROS

Aeropuerto Internacional José Martí, tel. 45-3542
Av. R. Boyeros #353 esq. 315, Galeria de Arte, tel. (0683) 9120

CENTRO HABANA

Calle Galiano #517 e/ Dragones y Zanja, tel. 61-5919 or 33-8634

CERRO

Calle Santa Catalina y Primelle, Av. Rancho Boyeros #128 y Santa Catalina

COTORRO

Calle 33 #3051, Santa María del Rosarío, tel. 0 6820-4254

GUANABACOA

Calle Cadena #7 esq. Pepe Antonio, tel. 90-6879

HABANAS DEL ESTE

Calle 3ra. esq. 164, Alamar Playa
Calle Central #28, Villa Panamericana, tel. 68-2965 or 68-2963
Calle Real #1E2 e/ Chacón, Cojímar Parque Panamericano, tel. 68-3571
Zona 6 de Alamar, tel. 65-7242

LA LISA

Calle 39 esq. 208, tel. 21-696

PLAZA DE LA REVOLUCIÓN

Calle P esq. 23, Vedado, tel. 70-7631 or 70-5284
Calle 12 #570 esq. 25, tel. 33-3726

REGLA

Calle Santuario #13, tel. 90-0182
Calle Alburquerque #151, tel. 90-0297
Calle Central #120 e/ Echarte y San Francisco, tel. 61-8890

SAN MIGUEL DEL PADRÓN

Carretera Central #79 e/ Caraballo y Santo, San Francisco de Paula, tel. 91-2023

Route 2-1-3 continues west to **Cabañas,** beyond which you pass into Pinar del Río province. West of Cabañas, you can look forward to a stunning drive—to my mind, one of the most rewarding in the country. Soon you're amid quintessentially Cuban landscapes, with distant sugar mills *(centrales)* belching out black smoke above sensuously rolling green hills of cane, with mountains—the Sierra del Rosarios—in the distance. It is a special treat to take this little-traveled route during the cane harvest, when you'll share the winding road with creaky wooden carts pulled by oxen, dropping their loads of sugar as they go.

ALONG THE CARRETERA CENTRAL

An alternate route to Pinar del Río is along the freeway known as the Autopista, which begins at Avenida Rancho Boyeros on the southern edge of Havana. The freeway runs clean through the countryside, giving a wide berth to towns. Paralleling the Autopista about five km to the south is the old Carretera Central—route 2-N1—which was the main thoroughfare before the freeway was built. It offers a more compelling journey, passing through four modestly intriguing small towns where vehicular traffic gives way to *campesinos* on horseback.

Bauta has a historical museum on Calle 251 #14613, tel. 2058, and the **Museo Antonio Maceo,** tel. 3533. The **Motel El Lago,** on the Carretera Central just south of town, tel. 3434, is a popular hostelry for Cubans, who flock to the swimming pool. Alas, when I called by in early 1996, the 1950s-era mansion did not accept foreigners. You may have better luck at the dour **Hotel Machurrucuto,** off the Autopista, three km north of Punta Brave, tel. 680-2971, US$10 s, US$20 d.

Caimito is most worth the visit, if only to photograph the intriguing mural displaying a fierce bald eagle painted in the Stars and Stripes voraciously attacking a noble Cuban Indian and peasant. An attractive ocher-colored colonial-era church forms a backdrop.

You might pause in **Guanajay** to peek inside the dramatically baroque theater—Teatro Vicente Mora—on the north side of the town square.

Artemisa

Largest of the four towns is Artemisa, which dates from the early 19th century. The town, 60 km southwest of Havana, has a particularly active **Casa de la Cultura,** and wandering the streets you may come across a number of plaques and a bronze cube monument honoring the many citizens who participated in the attack on the Moncada barracks in Santiago in 1953 (24 of the original 150 Castroite rebels came from Artemisa. Check out the **Museo de Historia,** next to the Casa de la Cultura on Calle Martí, and the **Mausoleo a las Mártires,** east of the Carretera, on Avenida 28 de Enero (open

PLAYING POLITICS WITH IMMIGRATION

A steady trickle of émigrés has journeyed across the Straits of Florida for over a century. Time has passed, but the US has lost none of its allure. (Given the privileged reception enjoyed by Cubans, it is surprising how *few* have migrated to the US—about 10% of the population since 1960, a figure similar to that for most other islands, such as Jamaica, and one-quarter that of Puerto Rico, 40% of whose population now lives in the US.)

At times, the trickle has turned to a flood. In the immediate years following the Revolution, at least 230,000 *gusanos*—worms—left Cuba. A similar number left between 1965 and 1971, when the US government chartered airlines for its Freedom Flights Program. Another 120,000 left in 1980 on the Mariel Boatlift, which ended in immigration accords.

Uncle Sam's Hypocrisy

The US agreed to accept an annual quota of 20,000 Cuban immigrants plus 3,000 former political prisoners and their families. Instead of living up to its end of the bargain, the US government has used immigration policy as a component in its plan to destabilize Cuba.

Most Cubans who petitioned the US for a visa were rejected. From 1984 to 1995, the US averaged 1,227 visas annually out of the 20,000 agreed to. After Cuba relaxed its immigration laws in 1991 and issued thousands of exit visas, the number of visas issued by the US *fell* sharply—to just 864 in 1993. The more difficult the economic circumstances became in Cuba, the fewer legal immigrants were accepted, while the greater the number of *illegals* who were taken in.

The influx of illegals was made possible by the 1966 **Cuban Adjustment Act,** which decreed that any Cuban who had been on US soil for a year and a day qualified for legal residence. The law virtually guaranteed a green card to any Cuban who could reach Florida. Not a single Cuban was turned away, even if they had hijacked a boat or plane. (The law applied only to Cubans—of 23,300 Haitians stopped between 1981 and 1995, only 20 were allowed ashore to seek asylum.)

Cuba claimed, justifiably, that Washington's open-door policy encouraged Cubans to risk their lives. "Clearly this was part of a strategy," claimed Castro. "They thwarted people's efforts to acquire a visa, and deliberately caused discontent; they purposefully left these people disappointed, waiting indefinitely for their visa. They try to invent reasons; that there weren't enough Cubans qualified. How is it that all those who enter illegally have the right qualifications?"

On a Wing and a Prayer

During most of the 1980s, an average of 40 people a year managed the Cuban equivalent of jumping the Berlin Wall. The US Coast Guard reckoned that only half made it to the US (Havana street talk calls the arduous crossing a *paseo de muerte,* a death march). As Cuba's economy nose-dived, the numbers of *balseros* soared. In 1992, a total of 2,553 came to shore. The next year, 3,656 *balseros* found haven in the US.

In 1994, Castro announced that "If the United States does not take measures to stop the incitement of illegal exits from the country, we will feel obliged to tell the Border Patrol not to stop any vessel that wishes to leave Cuba." He was true to his word. Washington and Miami were caught unprepared for the August flood.

In September of 1994, the US slammed the door shut after three decades of an open-door policy for Cubans making the crossing illegally. Henceforth, said President Clinton, the US would honor the immigration accords.

Tues.-Sat. 8 a.m.-5 p.m. and Sunday 8 a.m.-noon). The town's wide main street is colored by the faded pastels of neoclassical houses fronted with verandas supported by Doric and Ionic Greek columns—appropriately, as the town is named for the Greek goddess of fertility, Artemis.

A white marble statue of Artemis guards the ruins of an early-19th-century mansion 18 km west of town, reached along a dirt road. Novelist James Michener used the site, part of an old coffee plantation—**Antiguo Cafetal Angerona,** which went out of business about 1910—as the setting for his sugar plantation in his novel *The Caribbean.* Following a stream, Michener records in *Six Days in Havana,* how he found himself among a collection of "gigantic subterranean cisterns into which the copious supplies of water required in handling coffee beans were collected; it was like a scene from Dante. But it was when I climbed out of the cisterns and onto the plateau above that I came upon the salient fact of this great operation: the immense fenced-in area in which the slaves were kept, an area so vast that five or six football fields could have been fitted in. . . . The mournful place, called a *barracón,* had only one gate, beside which rose a tall stone tower in which men with guns waited

day and night for any sign of incipient rebellion." (You might also consider a visit to the Central Abraham Lincoln, the local sugar mill, to see how King Sugar is processed today.)

Accommodations, Food, and Services: **Hotel Campo Amor** is a basic pesos-only hotel facing the church on the main square, tel. 3-2894. Alternately, try the basic **Motel Los Laureles,** outside town at Carretera Central Km 61, two km west of the bus station, tel. 3-2157. For eats, try **Paladar La Unica,** on Calle 31 and Calle 54, or **Cafetería Las Delicias,** on Calle 52 at the west end of town. You can buy bread at **Panaderia La Parra,** next to Las Delicias. Artemisa even boasts a **photo service** and **post office,** both on Calle 33, the main street. You'll also find a **Banco Nacional** on Calle 43 (Martí), one block north of the church, and a meagerly stocked **pharmacy** on Calle 16, tel. 3-1247.

Getting There: Bus no. 215 operates to Artemisa from Havana's main bus terminal. The **Terminal de Ómnibus** is on the Carretera Central, at Km 58, tel. 3-3527. Trains run four times daily from Havana to the station on Avenida Héroes del Moncada, five blocks west of the plaza (US$2.50). Trains also run regularly to Pinar del Río (US$4).

SOUTH OF HAVANA

The entire landscape of southern Havana province is rich agricultural land, intensively farmed. The area is modestly wealthy, with houses that are comfortable by Cuban standards (there are few rustic *bohíos*) and plenty of cars, a further hint at the regional prosperity. The southern coast is depressingly opposite. Maps show several *playas,* such as **Guanimar** and **Playa del Cajio,** but you can skip them. Guanimar is typical—a down-at-heels, one-street waterfront hamlet that stretches for one km along the marshy waterfront. Despite the promise offered on maps, there's no beach to speak of, just small fishing and rowboats jerry-rigged from aluminum, tin, and polystyrene and as melancholy as the hamlet itself.

A network of roads fans out south from Havana, crisscrossed by minor B-roads that form a complicated spiderweb linking a number of small towns of unpretentious appeal. A coast road

parallels the shore about 10 km inland. East of Batabanó, it passes through miles of banana plantations centered around El Junco, before giving way to sugarcane. Stick to the main road; the secondary road system is an unfathomable labyrinth.

SAN ANTONIO DE LOS BAÑOS

The small town on the banks of the Río Ariguanabo, 30 km south of Havana, is appealing, despite its ramshackle state. There is considerable charm to its tiny triangular plaza, its ocher church, and its main street lined with colonnaded arcades.

The town boasts a **Museo de História,** on Calle 66, tel. 2539, and a **Humor Museum,** in a beautiful colonial home on Calle 60 and Avenida 45. The humor museum opened in 1979, when the city hosted the first **Humor Biennial** as

motorcycle and friends, San Antonio de Los Baños

a tribute to homegrown humorist Marcos Be-hemaras. The festival is still held here every two years. Open Tues.-Sat. 2 7 p.m. and Sunday 9 a.m.-1 p.m. Entrance costs US$1.

The prestigious **International Cinema, Television, and Video School,** sponsored by the New Latin American Cinema Foundation, is also here, presided over the the great Colombian writer and Nobel prize-winner Gabriel García Márquez. The school trains cinema artists from throughout the Third World.

You can hire a rowboat or speedboat at Las Yagrumas for excursions to the **Ojos de Aqua,** the source of dozens of springs that feed the river, and to **Sumidero Cave,** where the river disappears underground beside enormous rocks topped by a huge ceiba (silk-cotton) tree.

Accommodations and Food

One of Cuba's finest provincial hotels, **Club Amigo Las Yagrumas,** overlooks the banks of the Ariguanabo one km northeast of town on the N2-100, the main road that leads south from the Playa district of western Havana, tel.

4460 or, in Havana, 33-5238. This contemporary colonial-style, red-tiled, two-story property is operated as an all-inclusive resort run by Cubanacán. It has 120 pleasantly decorated a/c rooms (US$40 s, US$50 d). Facilities include two grills and a café, a huge pool and sundeck, two tennis courts, two squash courts, a games room, a tour desk, and taxi service. Bicycle and horseback excursions are offered. The resort is popular with tour groups from England and Canada.

A good place to stop for a snack is the **Cuba Libre** restaurant, 200 meters west of the church (it's open Thurs.-Mon. 11:15 a.m.-5:45 p.m.). Equally appealing is **Restaurante Brisas del Caney,** a stone's throw away. Both serve *criollo* food under thatch. The latter has cabaret at night.

Services and Transport

Traditional entertainment is hosted at the **Casa de la Cultura** on Calle 37, tel. 2738, and occasionally at the **Casa de Bienes Culturales,** on Calle 41, tel. 3194. Both are worth the stroll from the hotel. You can arrive or depart by bus; the **Terminal de Ómnibus,** is on Avenida 55, tel. 2737. A livelier scene on weekends is the **Taberna del Tío Cabrera** nightclub on Calle 56 and Avenida 39.

BEJUCAL

This town, about 10 km south of Santiago de las Vegas and a 30-minute drive from Havana,

---

**SAN ANTONIO DE LOS BAÑOS
USEFUL TELEPHONE NUMBERS**

Police	tel. 115
Ambulance	tel. 2781
Hospital	tel. 6-3535
Terminal de Ómnibus	tel. 2737

is perhaps the prettiest in Havana province and well worth an hour or so to admire its freshly painted colonial façades. At its heart is a tidy little square with an ocher-painted colonial church and Cine Martí. There's another attractive square two blocks farther west containing a bronze bust of Martí.

If the heat gets to you, imbibe a cup of refreshing tea at the **Casa Infusiones de Té,** on the main square, where you'll also find *criollo* dishes available at the **El Gallo Restaurant.**

On fine nights, join locals for an outdoor screening on Plaza Martí, the setting for the movie *Paradiso,* based on the novel by José Lezama Lima.

BATABANÓ

Unbelievably, this funky town (pop. 15,000) was the original site of Havana. It was one of the original seven cities, founded in 1515 (by Pánfilo de Narváez, a lieutenant of Diego Velásquez) and named San Cristóbal de la Habana. The settlers lasted only four years before uprooting and establishing a new city on the north coast— today's Havana, 51 km away.

Batabanó is surrounded by ugly suburbs that are dormitories for agricultural fieldhands. I'm hard-pressed to say anything redeeming about it.

About three km south of Batabanó is **Surgidero de Batabanó,** the port town from which the ferries depart for Isla de la Juventud. Surgidero is a run-down, utterly depressing

place. The road from Batabanó divides into a Y as you enter Surgidero; the left fork leads to the ferry terminal, the right to the railway station.

Accommodations, Food, and Services
If you miss the ferry, take a deep breath. The only hotel in town is the **Hotel Dos Hermanos,** close to both the railway station and the ferry terminal at the southern end of Calle 68. It accepts foreigners but gets my vote as the most sordid hotel in Cuba. Fortunately, the price is only 10 pesos (more for a/c), which is about all it's worth.

A small restaurant—**La Perla del Mar**—is around the corner on Avenida 3. In Batabanó, try **Pizzeria La Venecia,** on Calle 64, tel. 8-9675.

There's a **Cupet gas station** in Batabanó, at the junction of Calle 64 (the main street) and Avenida 73.

Getting There and Away
Surgidero de Batabanó is served twice daily by train from Havana's Estación Tulipán. The rail station, whose platform is guarded by a huge cannon from the War of Independence, is at the end of Calle 68. Trains depart for Havana at 8 a.m. and 5 p.m. (two pesos).

The bus station is to the west of Batabanó, inconveniently about two miles from the port. A bus from Havana also serves the ferry terminal in Surgidero; it takes 90 minutes and costs 2.10 pesos.

See the Isla de la Juventud chapter for information on ferry services, or try calling **Navigación Caribe,** tel. 8-4455 or 8-3845.

EAST OF HAVANA

ALONG THE AUTOPISTA

The Autopista (route A-1) runs southeast from Havana almost ruler-straight the whole way to the border with Matanzas province, where it continues east as far as Sancti Spíritus. It's wide, fast, and amazingly devoid of traffic. However, watch for tractors, ox carts, and even cattle crossing the freeway.

The freeway runs parallel to and north of the old Carretera Central (route 2-N1). It skirts the towns and villages that line the old road. The most interesting town is **Santa María del Rosarío,** just

east of the *circunvalación* (Havana's ring-road), on the southeast outskirts of Havana. The town boasts a number of 18th- and 19th-century buildings, many of which were restored by a wealthy patron in the years preceding the Revolution. The town is centered on a large baroque church, a national monument colloquially called the **Catedral del Campo,** with a resplendent carved ceiling and wooden altar dripping with gold leaf. Santa María is served by no. 97 bus from Guanabacoa.

The most important town is **Güines,** an industrial town (pop. 30,000) and major rail junction of no particular charm 35 km southeast of Havana. It sits in the lee of forested hills to the north that include a well-known beauty spot called **Lomas de Amores** (Lovers' Hill).

Tourist maps show a series of beaches along the coast south of Güines: Playa Rosarío, Playa del Caimito, Playa la Victoria. As beach destinations, they have little to offer. Tragically, they took the brunt of Hurricane Lili's wrath in October 1996.

There's a **Cupet gas station** on the main street in Güines, and another (along with a restaurant) at **Servicentro El Jagüey,** on the Autopista 35 km east of Güines, near the border with Matanzas province.

Escaleras de Jaruco

These rolling hills rise east of Havana. They have been named a park and are popular among Habaneros escaping the heat for walks and horseback rides. The hills are composed of limestone terraces denuded in places into rugged karst formations laced with caves. Take the turnoff for **Tapaste** from the Autopista, about 15 km east of Havana. **Parque Escaleras de Jaruco** is six km west of Jaruco village and makes a scenic day trip, especially if you return via Playas del Este.

There are basic campsites (now very rundown), a motel—**Hotel Escaleras de Jaruco**—and two restaurants, most notably a brick-and-tile mansion called **El Árabe,** tel. 3-8285, that sits atop the highest hill and specializes in lamb dishes. In recent years, it has been hardpressed to produce most of the dishes on the menu, such as lamb *en brochette* known as lashe mischwuy. Open Sunday only, in the afternoon.

ALONG THE CARRETERA CENTRAL

The Carretera Central runs southeast through the Havana suburbs of San Francisco de Paulo and Cotorro. About 25 km southeast of Havana, the Autopista crosses the Carretera Central, which you can follow east through the rolling hills of the **Alturas de Habana-Matanzas** to Matanzas via the provincial town of Madruga. There are a few other villages en route with aged churches of interest.

Madruga was the setting in halcyon years for a *santería* procession held each September 12 that would culminate in a wild orgy of dancing and licentious behavior. Take time to stop at the **Ethnographic Museum**—the "House of Fredi"—in the home of the former *Santero Mayor* or *babalawo* (chief priest of the santería religion), where he initiated believers into the mysteries of the *Regla de Ocha.*

Finca Alcona

This farm raises *gallos* (cockerels) for combat. Apparently, buyers come from all over the world to choose a prize Cuban cock. You, too, can visit and watch a cockfight, which are held 25 times daily. A grand **Feria de Gallos de Lidia** is held in early June. *Criollo* cuisine is served in the restaurant **El Gallo de Oro,** where a minstrel band performs popular *campesino* songs.

The farm is 17 km south of Havana, on the Carretera de Managua, outside the village of **Managua.** The easiest route is to take the Carretera Central to Cuatro Caminos, then turn west on the Carretera a Portugaletes for Managua, 15 km west (midway to Santiago de las Vegas). You can book an excursion (US$20, including lunch) direct with Finca Alcona, tel. 22-2526 or 22-2527, fax 33-1532, or with their office on Calle 42 #514 esq. Avenida 7, Miramar.

SANTA CRUZ DEL NORTE

East of the Playas del Este, the narrow volcanic coastal plain is hemmed in by low but steep-faced hills that parallel the shore. Precious, albeit sulfur-rich, oil lies deep underground, and you'll begin to pass small oil derricks bobbing languidly atop the coral clifftops.

Santa Cruz is a ramshackle industrial town steeping in a miasma of photo-chemical fumes and fronted by badly polluted waters. Cuba's largest rum factory (Ronera Santa Cruz) is here, producing the famous Havana Club rums and flavoring the air with its own heady aromas. An even older factory, dating from 1919, stands down by the shore and may also open its doors to visitors eventually.

About four km south of Santa Cruz and worth the detour is the **Central Camilo Cienfuegos,** the old sugar mill of the Hershey Chocolate Company.

The hardy and the impecunious may opt to sleep or dine at the pesos-only **Hotel Río Mar,** overlooking the river in Santa Cruz, tel. 8-4324 or 8-3313.

Buses no. 217 and 70 run from Havana to Santa Cruz del Norte, as does bus no. 699, from Calle Apodaca via Guanabo.

PLAYA JIBACOA

A beautiful little beach lies tucked between cliffs at the mouth of the Río Jibacoa, about three km east of Santa Cruz del Norte. It's popular with Cubans. The waters are of every shade of jade and blue, backed by a tempting white sand beach bracketed by rocky headlands. The beach is reached by a side road at the west end of the bridge or via the Villa Jibacoa Loma, a tourist resort on the hill to the east.

Coral reefs lie close to shore, perfect for snorkeling and scuba diving.

You can reach Jibacoa on bus no. 126 from Santa Cruz, or from Casablanca near Havana (or Matanzas, or points between) on the Hershey Train (get off at Jibacoa Pueblo, about five km south of Jibacoa; anticipate walking to the beach).

Accommodations and Food

You can camp beneath palms behind the beach at **Campamiento Jibacoa.** It has dozens of small, simple cabins, but you can also rent tents (US$10). Meals are served at a basic restaurant (five pesos). There's an indoor recreation room, and a small boatyard where you can rent boats.

Villa Jibacoa Loma is an Islazul property featuring attractive all-stone, two-story bungalows marvelously situated atop the headland overlooking the rivermouth. It's rustic but full of ambience. Facilities include a small pool plus a restaurant. Some villas are modest, with small bedrooms; others are huge, with a pleasing contemporary feel (US$15 s and US$20 d low-season, US$19 s and US$24 d high-season per bedroom). Each features TV, a/c, telephone, refrigerator, and hot water. Some have kitchens. A bargain!

PLAYA AMARILLO AND PUERTO ESCONDIDO

The Vía Blanca moves away from the coast beyond Santa Cruz del Norte. About seven km east, a road leads north five km to a series of white and reddish sand beaches which, prior to the Special Period, were popular holiday spots for Cubans. The widest and whitest beach—**Playa Amarillo**—is the exclusive property of Villa Trópico; the other beaches are pencil thin and less appealing.

Three km east of the turnoff for Trópico, another road leads north to the small coastal village of Puerto Escondido, a "wonderfully cool inlet a few miles down the Cuban coast," where Ernest Hemingway would arrive aboard the *Pilar* to escape the hot summer nights. The spectacular setting—within a wide bend of a deep ravine—is occupied today by the **Puerto Escondido Aquatic Center.** It offers windsurfing, water-skiing, and excursions by yacht and catamaran, plus diving and deep-sea fishing.

Accommodations

Playa Amarillo is dominated by **Club Villa Trópico,** Carretera de Jibacoa, Vía Blanca, Arroyo Bermejo, tel. 8-3551, an all-inclusive resort solely for Italians arriving on package tours run by the Italian company Ventaclub. It has 51 a/c rooms in *cabañas.*

If you don't mind basic facilities and little company, you'll have better luck at **El Abra,** tel. 692-8-3612, a Cuban holiday camp with concrete *cabañas.* It's heavily promoted to foreigners as an "eco-camp" by Cubamar. The run-down facility is still open but draws barely any vacationers. It has comedy shows and movies, plus a huge swimming pool (empty when I last visited). Horseback riding and bicycle rentals are offered. It accepts foreigners and charges US$12 per cabin for the first night, to US$72 for six nights for up to three people (double that for up to six people). There are various categories of cabins, many of them spread east of Playa Amarillo, behind teeny pockets of sand tucked between coral outcrops. Hiking trails lead into the nearby hills.

PUENTE BACUNAYAGUA

Camera at the ready? Then take a deep breath for your stop at this lofty bridge over the River Bacunayagua, 106 km from Havana and five km east of Puerto Escondido (about two km after crossing the Havana-Matanzas provincial boundary). The 313-meter-long bridge, at 112 meters above the river—the highest in Cuba—spans the gorge of the Río Bacunayagua, which slices magically through the narrow coastal mountain chain. The Yumurí valley rolls away to the south, fanning out spectacularly as if contrived for a travel magazine's double-page spread. The views are spectacular, with the valley tufted with royal palms and framed in the hazy distance by dramatic *mogotes* (flat-topped limestone formations). Turkey vultures wheel and slide like kites on the thermals that rise up through the gorge.

The bridge is a favorite stop for tour buses, and there are facilities on the west bank to cater to the hordes. A *mirador* atop the cliff above the bridge offers the best views. There's a bar and restaurant here, plus a souvenir shop.

A road winds downhill to **Villa Turística Bacunayagua,** where there are basic *cabañas* and very minimal facilities beside a rocky cove. You can camp here, but you need to cater for yourself.

It's 14 km from here to Matanzas.

PINAR DEL RÍO
INTRODUCTION

Pinar del Río, the tail of the shark-shaped island, is Cuba's westernmost province. In the valleys here, the world's most exquisite tobacco is nurtured and tenderly harvested on small plots by *guajiros,* the Cuban peasants in straw hats, usually mustachioed, carrying a *machete,* and each with a cigar between his teeth. Oxen are more widely used in the fields of Pinar del Río than elsewhere in the country, transporting you back in time amid quintessentially Cuban landscapes that attain their most dramatic beauty in Viñales Valley, tobacco country par excellence—and one of the most beautiful parts of the country.

Fernando Ortíz, author of *Cuban Counterpoint,* speculates that it is tobacco itself, the region's staple, that has blessed the local culture with a delicate warmth and finesse. Sugar, suggests Ortíz, is utterly masculine and fosters machismo in spite of its sweetness. Tobacco, in contrast, typifies Cuba's gentle, feminine side, despite the phallic shape into which it will be rolled.

But sugar isn't entirely absent here. The eastern lowlands are smothered in endless oceans of green sugarcane billowing like a great ocean, mile upon mile. A sweet, cloying odor of molasses wafts across the countryside, and thick blue-black smoke billows from the tall chimneys of busy *centrales.* Following the Carretera Central or Circuito Norte, you may pass long lines of oxen and carts waiting patiently in the sun for their loads of cane to be unloaded.

Pinar is not a place to seek a beach vacation (with two exceptions) or the grace of colonial cities. Nature-lovers, though, are in for a treat. And there are several sites of historic interest well worth the drive.

Sights
Pinar del Río boasts many timeless villages, none more so than the sleepy town of **Viñales,** one of the most charming in all Cuba. The nearby **Viñales Valley** is also one of Cuba's prime tourist attractions, with incredible limestone formations looming over tobacco fields, plus caves for exploring, and a bucolic setting that Hollywood might have conceived for your camera.

Other attractions in the pine-forested mountains include **Soroa,** known for its orchid garden; **Las Terrazas,** a model community with a first-rate eco-resort, plus artists' and artisans' studios, nature trails, cascades, and the ruins of 19th-century coffee *fincas* (farms) to explore; the thermal spas of **San Diego de los Baños;** and, nearby, **La Gúira National Park,** great for birding and for history buffs investigating the history of Che Guevara.

There are beaches, though few of great appeal. The two star attractions are **Cayo Levisa,** off the central north coast, and **Playa María la Gorda,** in Bahía de Corrientes, at the extreme southwest tip. West of María la Gorda, the **Peninsula de Guanahacabibes** is a nature reserve with a section where hunters may track down wild pig and deer. Fishermen and hunters are also served by several lakes and preserves.

The town of Pinar del Río holds just enough to interest for a one-day visit, including a small cigar factory open for visits.

Land
Pinar del Río, is dominated by a low, ancient mountain chain—the Guanicuanjico—which forms an east-west spine through the province. The chain is divided by the Río San Diego into two mountain ranges—the Sierra del Rosario in the east and the Sierra de los Organos in the west—which cup stunning valleys, such as those of Viñales. The mountains reach a height of 699 meters atop Pan de Guajaibón, in the central Sierra del Rosario.

The mountains edge up close to the narrow, undulating north coast, where a paternoster of cays—the Archipiélago de los Colorados—lies protected by a coral reef.

The broader southern plains are flat and covered with interior soils that support expansive rice plantations, cattle pastures, and swamps that harbor important hunting grounds and lakes stocked with bass and gamefish. A slender pencil of uninhabited land—the Guanahacabibes Peninsula—hangs loosely off the southern tip, jutting west 50 km into the Gulf of Mexico. The peninsula is smothered in dense brush and cactus—a sharp contrast to the pine forests that cover much of the mountain slopes (the Peninsula de Guanahacabibes receives a mere 146 cm of precipitation per year).

History
Pinar was settled by Europeans late in the tenure of Spanish colonial rule, when it was considered Cuba's "Cinderella" province—a label that stuck (unfairly) throughout the years.

The area was inhabited at least 4,000 years ago by the Guanahatabey, the initial aboriginal settlers. Later, the region became a last refuge for the Ciboney Indians, a hunter-gatherer tribe that retreated before the advance of the Taíno Indians and, in turn, devastated the Guanahatabey.

The first Spanish settlement occurred only after 1717, when tobacco growers pulled up stakes in Havana province and moved to the valleys of Pinar del Río. The farmers and citizens were beyond the pale and, guarding their independence jealously, engaged freely in smuggling. Later in the century, French coffee growers established *fincas* on the higher, easterly slopes, while sugar farmers established plantations below. Pinar del Río figured little in the War of Independence and, at the turn of the century, remained Cuba's most backward province.

Following the Revolution, counterrevolutionaries formed bands in the mountains and were suppressed only after several years' fighting. The province has grown modestly prosperous in recent decades, thanks to the government's efforts, to earnings from copper mining in the northwest at Matahambre and Jucaro, and to the valuable tobacco of Viñales and Vuelta Abajo. However, pockets of poverty remain, and modernity overlays a way of life that has changed little this century.

Which Route?
There are three routes from Havana to Pinar del Río. Whichever route you take, you are almost immediately thrust into a quintessentially Cuban landscape of sugarcane, tobacco, and silver-sheathed royal palms, with their swollen upper trunks (those palms with the swollen *lower* trunks are not mutations but *Bearrigona,* "belly palms"). Regardless, you can drive all day and pass no more than a dozen cars. I recommend following a circle, combining two routes.

Most tourists follow the six-lane **Autopista,** the national highway linking the capital city with the town of Pinar del Río. It heads west almost ruler-straight and is in good condition the entire way, except for an occasional and dangerously severe dip in the road. There's relatively little traffic, and the route is pleasingly scenic, with the Sierra del Rosario building off to the north. Be cautious of the many pedestrians seeking rides beside the road (they tend to wander onto the

highway), particularly at night when the Autopista is unlit. There are no towns or gas stations along the entire route and only one roadside refreshment stop. The highway ends at the town of Pinar del Río, a two- to three-hour drive from Havana.

A second, more interesting, option is to follow the old **Carretera Central** through sleepy provincial towns such as Candelaria, Santa Cruz de los Pinos, and Consolación del Sur—towns memorable for their old churches, faded pastel houses, and covered walkways with neoclassical pillars. The two-lane highway parallels the Autopista along the southern edge of the mountains. Both the Carretera and Autopista provide easy access to virtually every place of tourist interest in the province.

A far more scenic route is the lonesome **Circuito Norte,** which follows the picturesque north shore all the way west from Mariel to Mantua. Here's the scoop.

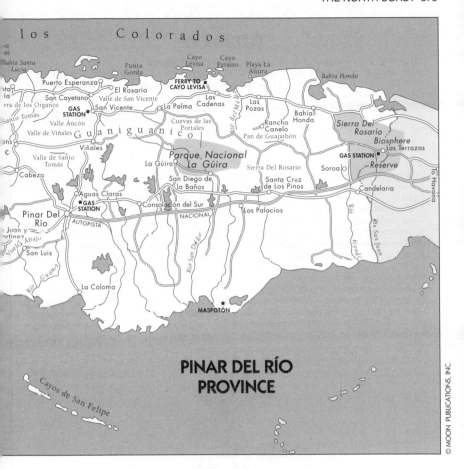

**PINAR DEL RÍO
PROVINCE**

THE NORTH COAST

Few foreigners take time to drive the coast road west from Havana. A pity, for the section between Mariel and San Vicente is one of the most scenic in Cuba: a gentle roller-coaster ride with seductive glimpses of the sea to the north and, to the south, velvety, steep-sided mountains running the length of the mainland.

West of San Vicente, the road is lonesome and dusty, the villages are few and far-between, and there is little to hold your attention except the deep-shadowed Sierras, plump and

rounded, like the hummocky hillocks of southeast Brazil.

The road runs a few miles inland of the coast. Side roads lead north to the shore itself, but there are few, if any, beaches of vital appeal. Side roads also lead inland to Soroa and the Valle de Viñales.

Pinar del Río is reputed to be Cuba's poorest region, and poverty is indeed evident along the north coast, where the fishing villages are down at-heels.

TOBACCO

It is generally acknowledged that the world's best tobacco comes from Cuba (the plant is indigenous to the island), and in particular from the 160-square-mile Vuelta Abajo area of Pinar del Río province. The *vegas* (tobacco fields) of Vuelta Abajo are known to cigar connoisseurs the world over. The choicest leaves of all are grown in about 25 square miles around the towns of San Juan y Martínez and San Luís, where the premier *vegas* are El Corojo and Hoyo de Monterrey, each no bigger than a football field—650 acres given over exclusively to production of wrapper leaves for the world's preeminent cigars.

The climate and rich reddish-brown sandy loam of Vuelta Abajo are ideal for tobacco. Rainfall is about 65 inches a year, but, significantly, only eight inches or so falls during the main growing months of November-February, when temperatures average a perfect 80° F and the area receives around eight hours of sunshine daily.

Most tobacco is grown on small holdings—many privately owned but selling tobacco to the government at a fixed rate. *Vegueros* (tobacco growers) can own up to 150 acres, although most cultivate less than 10 acres.

Raising Tobacco

Tobacco growing is labor-intensive, though, unlike sugarcane, it requires no brutal labor. Cultivation, picking, curing, handling, and rolling tobacco into cigars all require great delicacy.

The seeds are planted around the end of October in flat fields (maize is often grown on the same land outside the tobacco season). Straw is laid down for shade, then removed as the seeds germinate. After one month, the seeds are transplanted to the *vegas*. Buds have to be picked to prevent them from stunting growth. About 120 days after planting, they are ready for harvesting.

There is a range of leaf choices, from *libra de pie,* at the base, to the *corona,* at the top. The art of making a good cigar is to blend these in such proportions as to give the eventual cigar a mild, medium, or full flavor and to ensure that it burns well.

The binder leaf that holds the cigar together is taken from the coarse, sun-grown leaves on the upper part of the plant, chosen for their tensile strength. Dark and oily, they have a very strong flavor and have to be matured for up to three years before they can be used. The finest leaves from the

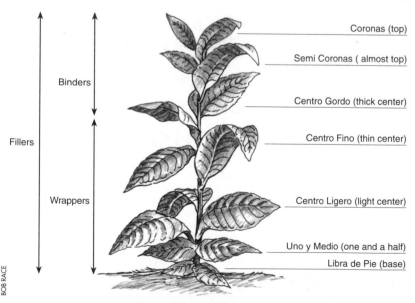

Binders

Fillers

Wrappers

Coronas (top)

Semi Coronas (almost top)

Centro Gordo (thick center)

Centro Fino (thin center)

Centro Ligero (light center)

Uno y Medio (one and a half)

Libra de Pie (base)

BOB RACE

lower part of the plant are used as wrappers; these must be soft and pliable (making it easy for the roller to handle), and must also be free of protruding veins.

Plants designated to produce wrapper for the finest cigars are grown under fine muslin sheets *(tapados)* to prevent the leaves from becoming too oily in a protective response to sunlight. Wrapper leaves grown under cover are classified by color. Those grown under the sun have their own names. Generally, the darker the color, the sweeter the taste.

Leaves are bundled in a *plancha,* or hand, of five leaves and taken to a barn to be cured on poles or *cujes.* (Modern barns are temperature and humidity controlled. Traditional thatched barns face west so that the sun heats one end in the morning and the other in the late afernoon and temperature and humidity are controlled by opening and closing the doors.) Gradually, the green chlorophyll in the leaves turns to brown carotene. After 45-60 days, they are taken down and stacked into bundles, then taken in wooden cases to the *escogida*—sorting house—where they are shaken to separate them, then dampened and aired before being flattened and tied in bunches of 50. These are then fermented in large piles like compost heaps for anywhere up to three months (the wrapper leaves are fermented least). Ammonia and impurities are released. When the temperature reaches 112° F, the pile is "turned" so that fermentation takes place evenly.

The leaves are then graded for different use according to color, size, and quality. They are stripped of their mid-ribs and flattened, then sprayed with water to add moisture. Finally, they are covered with burlap, fermented again, reclassified, and sent to the factories in *tercios*—square bales wrapped in palm bark to help keep the tobacco at a constant humidity. After maturing for up to two years, they are ready to be rolled into cigars.

BAHÍA HONDA

Bahía Honda, 20 km west of Mariel, is very scenic. The town of the same name sits at the head of the bay. You can admire the vista from the hilltop **Motel Punta de Piedra,** tel. 341, north of town. Otherwise, it's basic. Rooms cost US$15-20. A similar option is **Motel La Mulata,** 28 km west of Bahía Honda, with a terrace overlooking the bay.

Playa la Altura is a beach (promoted on tourist maps) at El Morrillo, a small, ramschackle fishing village four km north of the Circuito Norte, some 10 km west of Bahía Honda. The potholed road will transport you past sugarcane fields and deposit you beside a thin and ungainly beach that wears a coat of dried seaweed. Not a place to aim for.

Pan de Guajaibón

Just east of Las Pozas, you may be drawn from the highway to follow a side road south into the Sierra del Rosarios, lured by the sensuously rounded purple peak, Pan de Guajaibón (692 meters; 2,294 feet). The dramatic peak lies within a protected area known as Mil Cumbres (18,160 hectares), part of the Sierra del Rosarios Biosphere Reserve.

The road twists and loops for 15 km, growing ever more scenic as you rise gradually up and over undulating hillocks. Soon you are edging along beneath the *mogotes,* still rising, with slopes now covered with coffee bushes shaded by royal palms, and Pan de Guajaibón looming ahead like the Sugarloaf of Rio de Janeiro. Alas, the road gradually deteriorates and finally fizzles out at the hamlet of **Rancho Canelo,** where there's a small and unkempt military camp. From here its a rough, overgrown track (4WD is recommended) for the final few miles to the soaring mountain.

Continuing along the Circuito Norte, beyond **Las Pozas** the land turns deep rust-red. This is cattle country, with some sugarcane, bananas, and coffee plants for good measure.

Services

There are no gas stations, no stores, nowhere to buy even a soda or bottle of water along the coast road. Keep your eyes peeled for any little roadside stalls with signs for *refrescos* and *batidos.* They're your only chance to buy refreshments.

At Las Pozas, you'll find **Restaurante El Mambí.** It's the first eatery for miles. The pleasant though basic eatery is open 11 a.m.-2 p.m. and 6-8 p.m. It sells sweet, clear natural orange juice *refrescos* (10 centavos), salads, soups, and pork and chicken dishes. A meal and drinks will cost about 10 pesos (US50 cents)!

ARCHIPIÉLAGO DE LOS COLORADOS

West of Las Pozas you'll see the first cays of the Archipiélago de los Colorados beckoning seductively offshore, extending west all the way to the western tip of Cuba and beginning with Cayo Paraíso. Scuba diving is said to be sensational.

Cayo Paraíso

Ernest Hemingway had a fondness for beach-fringed, tousled-palm-shaded Cayo Paraíso. His presence has been venerated by the Provincial Commission of Monuments, which in 1989 erected a small monument beside the small wooden dock. It reads:

> *From the beginning of the 1940s, this place was the refuge of the great North American author Ernest Hemingway, who visited it assiduously, sometimes remaining on the cay for up to 20 days at a time. Here he wrote, rested, roamed the beach, swam, and loved it so much he used it as a base for antisubmarine operations from his yacht the Pilar during the Second World War. In his memory, on the 90th anniversary of his birth.*

A marina is planned at Cayo Paraíso for scuba divers and visiting yachters. The coral is superb, and there's a sunken vessel to explore eight meters down off the northeast of the island. You'll need a boat to get here. Take insect repellent.

Cayo Levisa

About 10 km west of Cayo Paraíso is a larger, more seductive coral cay ringed by 3.5 km of stunning sugar-white beaches two km offshore. It is the only cay in the archipelago that has accommodations. Cayo Levisa is popular with divers for its abundant black coral, lobsters, and other underwater wonders.

There's a 30-meter-long dock on the south side, from where a trail leads through mangroves to the north shore and the hotel.

A boat leaves for Cayo Levisa at 11 a.m. and 5 p.m. (US$10 per person) from the coast guard station at Palma Rubia (the turnoff from the Circuito Norte is 15 km west of Las Pozas, just west of the village of Las Cadenas).

Accommodations

Villa Cayo Levisa is a resort and diving center run by Gran Caribe. It's popular with Italians and Spaniards, particularly in midsummer. The 20 rustic yet pleasantly furnished, a/c *cabañas* face onto the beach (US$41 s, US$80 d). Watersports include sea-kayaking, windsurfing, catamaran boating, and water-skiing. Alberto is the dive guide and scuba instructor. There's also a lively bar, a communal buffet restaurant serving good meals (US$2 breakfast; US$8 lunch and dinner) plus a small boutique. Excursions are offered to Viñales (US$40).

There are plans to expand. Advance reservations are advised. In Havana, contact **Manotur,** tel. 33-1162, fax 33-1164, or **Gran Caribe,** Av. 7 #4210 e/ Calle 42 y 44, Miramar, Havana, tel./fax 33-0238.

WEST OF CAYO LEVISA

Continuing west, you reach **La Palma,** the only town of consequence in the area, with a tiny museum and shops—the first I saw in 200 km! A road leads south from here over the mountains to La Gúira National Park and San Diego de los Baños. The scenery continues to inspire, with lonesome *bohios* and oxen working the palm-studded fields, the sea always two km or so to the north, tantalizingly blue, and—to the south—low rolling hills backed by round-topped *mogotes.*

Ten km west of La Palma is the all-important junction for Viñales and the town of Pinar del Río. Continue straight, though, and you reach **San Cayetano,** boasting a **Servi-Cupet gas station.** A turnoff leads north from here to the little fishing village of **Puerto Esperanza.**

West of San Cayetano, the land begins to takes on a new look, strongly reminiscent of the Gold Country of California, with pine forests and, farther west, where the land flattens out, citrus orchards. From San Cayetano it is 22 km to the small port of **Santa Lucía.** The shallow *esteros* northeast of Santa Lucía are said to attract large numbers of hammerhead sharks in breeding season. Out beyond Bahía Santa Lucía is **Cayo Jutías,** currently being developed for tourism.

West of Baja the road rises straight and as steady as a mathematical equation. The earth is rose pink and swathed in young pines. There's not a soul for miles—no villages, no *bohíos,* though every few km you'll pass *guajiros* standing shellshocked by heat in the shade. Then you arrive at **Dimas,** a pretty hamlet neatly arranged along a single street divided by a central median. At the end is a little pier where lobster boats unload.

Accommodations and Food

In all these miles there is only one restaurant and one hotel, the former at Puerto Esperanza, where a seaside snack bar serves *bocaditos* (sandwiches), *refrescos,* and rice pudding. At El Rosarío, four km east of Puerto Esperanza, there's a villa, **Villa Rosarío,** tel. 93828—a colonial mansion now a modest hotel with four rooms (two with shared bath) and a restaurant where lobster dishes are served.

The only alternative is **Campismo El Copey,** a very basic Cuban holiday camp behind a little beach at Río del Medio, reached via a bumpy road 10 km west of Santa Lucía. It has 30 small, basic bungalows for about 15 pesos.

DIMAS TO MANTUA

South of Dimas you pass around the western edge of the Sierras de los Organos as the road veers south to Mantua. This is a lonesome drive. The parched land is scrub-covered and boring, and gazing upon the azure waters offshore you might wish that you were sailing, not driving. These are prize sailing waters. Scattered wrecks lie offshore, caught amid the coral reefs that scuttled 'em.

Five miles north of Mantua is a T-junction, with Mantua to the left and **Los Arroyos de Mantua** to the right, at the end of a road lined with banana plantations. Los Arroyos is a fishing village whose fleet works the Gulf of Mexico and Gulf of Guanahacabibes. There are no facilities, though the beaches are modestly appealing.

Mantua is a pleasant little town which, in 1896, was the site of a major battle during the War of Independence. The only note of appeal is a square at the south end of town dominated by fig trees surrounding a tall granite column topped by a bronze sculpture of a horse and warrior, *Al Soldado Invasor.* The town has a **bank,** just east of the church, and a **Casa Cultura,** 100 yards farther east, with a restaurant adjacent. Buses arrive and depart in front of the Casa de Cultura.

ALONG THE AUTOPISTA

After leaving Havana, the six-lane concrete highway cuts through rolling plains planted in sugarcane. Then palm-thatch **bohíos** and tobacco fields begin to appear alongside man-made lakes created for irrigation and recreation. Turnoffs lead north into the Sierra del Rosarios, which are replete with attractions.

To the south, the land is as flat as a billiard table. These coastal flatlands can be skipped unless you have an abiding interest in hunting, fishing, or serendipitous exploring. There's nothing of visual appeal and few settlements. Sugarcane quickly gives way to watery meadows dissected by canals and grazed by scrawny cattle—humped zebus—accompanied by their courtesans, snow-white cattle egrets.

About the only place to stop for refreshment is **Las Barrigonas,** on the north side of the Autopista, 27 km east of Pinar del Río. It's popular with tourist buses and features thatched *bohíos* with tourist souvenirs, a café, and a sugarcane *trapiche* for freshly pressed juice. It's backed by tobacco fields.

SIERRA DEL ROSARIOS BIOSPHERE RESERVE

This 25,000-hectare (61,775-acre) reserve covers the easternmost slopes of the Sierra del Rosarios. The mountain slopes had been transformed by logging following the Spanish arrival. As time progressed, erosion and infertility contributed to abandonment of coffee farms and further denudation by impoverished peasants seeking income through logging. Today, the land is given over predominantly to forestry, but raising cattle is also important. The area was named a biosphere reserve by UNESCO in 1985, following a decade of efforts at reforestation by the Cuban government.

Nature trails and ecotourism facilities are meager, though the potentials are great. The reserve protects close to 600 endemic higher plant species and 250 lower plant species (34% of the growth is native to the region). Anyone familiar with the lush rainforests of Dominica or Costa Rica may be disappointed—the reserve is covered by semi-deciduous, mid-elevation montane forest, with bushy and herbaceous zones. There's no denying the beauty, though, in springtime, when the thickly forested slopes blaze with bright red blossoms of *flamboyans,* and *poma rosa* grows wild by the roadside, which is also lined in season with white *yagruma* and the fiery blossoms of *popili.* At any time, the air smells piney fresh.

The forests are replete with wildlife. The 98 bird species (including four of Cuba's eight endemic species) include Cuban trogons, *pedorreras,* nightingales, woodpeckers, hummingbirds, parrots, and the national bird, the *tocororo.* Terrestrial turtles and frogs are common (pack your magnifying glass to search out the smallest frog in the world—*Sminthilus limbatus*). There's an outlandish looking water lizard, found only here, along with bats (five species), deer, and *jutías.*

It can get cool at night—bring a sweater.

SOROA

Most famous of the Biosphere Reserve's attractions is Soroa, an "eco-retreat" set in a valley at about 250 meters elevation and perfect for nature hikes through forests of pine and spruce. Soroa is called the "the Rainbow of Cuba" for its natural beauty, although you need to get above the valley to appreciate the full scope of the setting.

The resort is named for Jean-Paul Soroa, a Frenchman who owned a coffee estate here two centuries ago and whose offspring still bear his name hereabouts. In the 1930s, it became fashionable as a spa with sulfur baths. Since the Revolution, it has gained a new lease on

life, with a hotel and other facilities for tourists.

The road from the Autopista winds uphill until you see plastic signs by the highway pointing to individual attractions, beginning with Baños Romanos and Mirador de Venus, a hilltop lookout, to the right across a tiny bridge. There's a car park by the bridge, next to **Bar Edén,** which overlooks the rippling Río Manantiales, on the opposite side of the road from the Orquideario.

El Salto Cascades

This small, overrated waterfall is reached by a concrete path and stairway that leads down from Bar Edén. From here, they descend 400 meters through fragrant woodlands of pine and wind-bent *coruba* trees to the bottom of the falls, which tumble 35 meters into pools good for bathing—these are the **Baños Romanos.** The waters have medicinal properties and are good for treating respiratory and skin conditions. The cacades are at their most postcard-perfect in the early morning, when the sun shines full force on the glittering waters and you are held spellbound by the misty rainbow, as if by a fairy's wand. Entrance is US$1.

Orquideario Soroa

Soroa's prize attraction is this orchid garden covering three hectares and claiming to be the world's second-largest orchid garden. It enjoys a fabulous hillside setting amid limestone formations, with views down the palm-tufted valley. The garden, nourished by the humid climate and maintained by the University of Pinar del Río, contains more than 20,000 plants repre-

---

THE CORK PALM

This shaggy endemic palm, found only in Pinar del Río, is a souvenir of the Carboniferous era, when this valley was the ocean floor. Somehow, the rare palms managed to stay above the waterline. The living fossil is a member of a family abundant 270 million years ago. It grows to six meters and sheds leaves every other year, leaving a ring around its fuzzy trunk that marks its age. It differs by sex: the masculine and feminine reproductive cells are emitted at different times, thus limiting the plant's propagation.

senting over 700 species—250 of them indigenous to Cuba. Begonias flourish along with other ornamentals beneath the shade of tall palms and towering vine- and ephiphyte-clad trees, such as the peculiarly and aptly named elephant's feet.

The garden was created in 1934 by Spaniard Tomás Felipe Camacho, who built the hilltop house—now a beer garden and *mirador*—and planted the craggy hillside with flowers on behalf of his daughter Pilila. It has been well maintained ever since.

Guided tours are offered daily except Friday 10 a.m.-5:30 p.m. Entrance costs US$3.

There are no signs; turn left 100 yards south of Villas Turística.

Accommodations and Food

La Caridad Campismo, one km uphill from Soroa, has basic cabins (US$12 d). Trails lead directly from the camp into the woods and hills.

Villas Turística Soroa, Carretera de Soroa Km 8, Candelaria, Pinar del Río, tel. 82-2122 or 82-2041, is a delightful resort complex. Stone pathways lead through landscaped grounds to an Olympic-size swimming pool surrounded by 49 small *cabinas* on slopes backed by shade trees and forest. The cabins have refrigerators, a/c, and showers with hot water (US$20 s, US$24 d). The resort also has 10 houses—**Casitas de Soroa**—with kitchenettes, TVs, VCRs, and cassette recorders. Eight have their own private pools! The *casas* are on the hillside above the garden and have fine views over the valley.

The main restaurant (one of three) has bamboo furniture and serves spaghetti dishes (US$2), tortillas and eggs (US$2), and fried chicken creole (US$4.50). Try the superb Daiquirí Soroa, made of grenadine, rum, sugar, and lemon juice. There's also a small nightclub. Spa treatments are no longer offered, but excursions include hiking, birdwatching, horseback-riding, and mountain-biking.

The restaurant at **Castillo de las Nubes,** two km above the orquideario, has been acclaimed for its "chicken Gordon blue." Since the Special Period, alas, the restaurant has lost its luster, and when last I called by, in early 1996, it had been relegated to serving sandwiches and cocktails—and only at lunch. At least the Spanish-style castle in the clouds offers fine views.

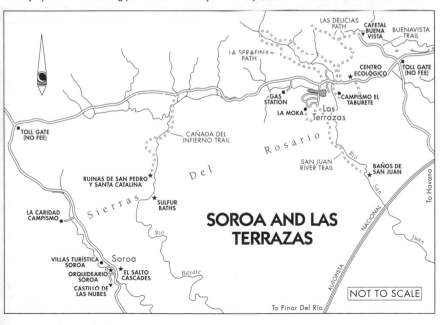

Getting There

Soroa is seven km north of the Autopista. The turnoff is about 80 km west of Havana. You can also reach Soroa from the Circuito Norte, the north coast road. Trains from Havana and Pinar del Río stop at Candelaria, from where you can take a taxi to Soroa, nine km north.

Rumbos has an excursion from Havana for US$29, including lunch. **Tour & Travel,** Av. 5 #8409 esq. 86, Miramar, Havana, tel. 33-2433, also has a one-day excursion for US$30. Soroa is also included in two one-week "ecotour" packages offered by **Hoteles Horizontes,** Calle 23 #156 e/ N y 0, Vedado, Havana, tel. 33-4142, fax 33-3161.

LAS TERRAZAS

This unique agricultural community is a model village that is also touted as one of Cuba's prime ecotourism sites. It's a charmer, and I highly recommend a visit.

Las Terrazas (pop. 1,200) is situated in a narrow valley above the shores of Lago San Juan and beneath palm-fringed, pinnacled mountains. It lies at the heart of a comprehensive rural development project that encompasses 12,355 acres. The village was founded in 1971. From the roadside it looks like a hillside resort. Its occupants are local *campesinos* and their offspring, some of whom work at La Moka, an ecologically principled hotel hidden from view on the forested hills behind the village.

French settlers who fled Haiti in 1792 planted coffee in these hills. After the coffee plantations failed, the local *campesinos,* isolated from education and health services and living amid mountain terrain ill suited for farming, continued to fell the trees for export and eke out a living as charcoal burners. Hillside by hillside, much of the region was turned to deforested wasteland.

In 1967, the government initiated a 5,000-hectare reforestation project, employing the impoverished *campesinos* and providing them with housing in a prize model village designed by architect Osmany Cienfuegos, Cuba's reigning minister of tourism. Las Terrazas is named for the terraces of trees (teak, cedar, mahogany, pine) that were planted two at a time, side by side. Of each pair, only one will live. The other,

destined to die in the struggle for life, will be used for charcoal.

The name is fitting, for the houses of whitewashed concrete with orange doors and and blue shutters are aligned in terraces that cascade down the hillside to the lake, proving that communists can harmoniously blend man with nature.

The village **community center** houses a cinema, dentists' and doctors' offices, a small store, a post office, and a small **museum.** The museum shows pre-Columbian and plantation-era artifacts and tells the tale of Las Terrazas' development. A small *cafetería* sits over the lake, where boats are available for fishing. There's even a rodeo ring where you can watch *guajiros* tussling with stallions and steers.

Looming over the community is **La Loma de Taburete,** a heavily forested, flat-topped mountain where Che Guevara trained his Bolivian guerrillas before his fatal departure for that country in 1965.

Centro Ecológico

This basic ecological center (locally called the Academy of Sciences) gathers scientific information for the reserve. Director Maritza García is in charge of studying and monitoring the different ecosystems. Visitors are welcome. You can rent guides for birding, nature hikes, and the like (US$3 per person per hour for up to three people, US$1 hourly for more than three).

Getting There: There may not be any signs to the center. It's one km west of the road barrier, through the green gates on the north side of the road.

Cafetal Buena Vista

Buena Vista preserves the ruins of a French coffee plantation constructed in 1801, the second-oldest coffee plantation in Cuba. At its peak, in 1828, 125 slaves toiled these slopes.

The buildings have been lovingly restored and are exact reconstructions of the originals. The main building is now a handsome restaurant with lofty beamed ceilings and a steeply angled roof, a legacy of the European tradition of pitching roofs sharply to shed snow. Behind the restaurant are stone terraces where coffee beans were laid out to dry, the remains of the old slave quarters, and, on the uppermost terrace, an ox-powered coffee grinder where coffee beans would be placed in the circular trough, mixed with ashes, then ground to remove the husks. Eventually, it is hoped that the land will be restored to the point that this could again become a working coffee plantation.

It's very breezy up here at 250 meters, with spectacular views over the expansive plains. Guides (US$3 per hour) are available for local hikes. Stone cabins for rent are planned.

Getting There: Turn uphill at the road barrier about three km east of Las Terrazas village. The road winds steeply uphill.

Ruinas de San Pedro y Santa Catalina

About eight km west of Las Terrazas, a dirt track—the **Cañada del Infierno Trail**—follows the Río Bayate south through dense forest to the ruins of San Pedro and the sulfur baths of Santa Catalina. (It's easy to miss the turnoff; look for the bridge over the Río Bayate. You may need a guide—several dirt roads may be confusing). The dirt road follows the river south two km to the ruins of the French coffee plantation. The crumbling remains are overgrown, and climbing figs clamber up the walls.

A faint hint of sulfur lures you downhill to the river, where natural pools encourage swimming. Locals favor the peaceful spot for picnics.

Baños de San Juan

A more enticing spot, these "baths" are reached from the rodeo at Las Terrazas, where a semi-paved road drops south, downhill, about three km to a Y-junction. A turnoff to the left leads to the parking lot. From here, a paved path leads over a small bridge and along the river's edge past deep pools (good for swimming) and sunning platforms to a series of cascades. *¡Que linda!* Thatched ranchitas, including a small bar, sit above the falls, and there are toilets.

The **San Juan River Trail** follows the river valley between the El Salón and El Taburete hills to the San Juan Baths. En route, you'll pass the ruins of La Victoria coffee plantation and sulfide springs.

Trails

Several trails lead into the foothills of the surrounding mountains. Most begin within one km of Las Terrazas. Two that will appeal to nature-

lovers are the **Las Delicias Path** and the **La Serafina Path.** The former climbs Lomas Las Delicias, from where you have a fine view down the valley from the summit. Rare birds that are commonly sighted include the black finch and the sparrow hawk. The trip ends at the Buena Vista coffee plantation. La Serafina (four km) cuts through the Mango Rubio massif and is of particular appeal to birders. The Cuban trogon, the solitaire, woodpeckers, and the Cuban today are common.

The **Buenavista Trail** also leads two km to the coffee plantation.

Accommodations

A basic facility for Cubans—**Campismo el Taburete**—with 54 tiny *cabañas* spreads around the forest edge (11 pesos per person) one km east of the community. Eastern bloc architecture prevails over good taste, with dour concrete structures (It's open daily, but only on weekends for Cubans). The self-contained resort has a bar and restaurant, grocery store, TV room, and ponies for the kids. **Camping** is permitted (tents can be rented).

La Moka, Km 51, Autopista Habana-Pinar del Río, Candelaria, tel. 85-2996 or 85-2921, fax 33-5516, is one of Cuba's showcase hotels—classy, romantic, intimate, and fully deserving of several nights' stay. The hotel, which opened in late 1994, is a contemporary interpretation of Spanish colonial architecture and features a splendid multi-tiered atrium lobby centered on a lime tree with branches disappearing through the skylight. Breezes pour in through columned arches. The two-story accommodations block has magnificent red-barked trees growing up through the balconies and ceiling. The 26 rooms (US$58 s, US$80 d) and one suite (US$150) are designed to international standards and ecological vogue.

Each room has floor-to-ceiling glass window and French door leading onto a spacious terracotta-tiled balcony with tables, reclining chairs, and views through the trees to the lake. Take an upper-story room with high sloping wooden ceilings and antique ceiling fans.

Facilities include a tennis court, small amoeba-shaped pool, sundeck, and lido café and bar reached by a path that winds uphill through lush, landscaped grounds. Renier, the English-speaking in-house guide, is available for hire. You can rent bicycles, and steps lead directly to the lobby from the village. It gets cool here. Bring a sweater.

You can also rent the **Casa del Lago,** a two-bedroom house on the lakeshore, with its own pier, TV, bar, telephone, and kitchenette.

Food

An herb garden supplies the upscale **La Moka** restaurant whose menu (written on huge leaves) includes *filet de imperador* (US$10), chicken supreme (US$7.50), and filet mignon (US$12). I recommend **Terraza de la Fondita,** a restaurant in Unit 9, in the heart of the village. Here, Mercedes Dache cooks fabulous meals (my beef in a tangy sauce with rice and beans, plantain, and pimento, was one of the best I've had in Cuba), which you'll enjoy on a terrace while being serenaded by two young singers, Gladys and Amaury. My dinner cost US$13, including beer and dessert.

Another splendid option is **Cafetal Buena Vista,** where you can dine on a tree-shaded terrace. The restaurant is open only for lunch (noon-4 p.m.), which costs US$10, including coffee, dessert, and a fabulous main dish of rice, lightly boiled potatoes, vegetables, fried bananas, and baked garlic chicken.

Entertainment and Events

There's a **cinema** in the community center, plus a bar down by the lake—great for feeling at home with the locals. There's sure to be someone with a guitar. Impromptu *canturías* featuring country music are often given. The **Dos Hermanos** bar in La Moka is named after one of Ernest Hemingway's favorite bars in Havana (the actual bar here is from the original).

Things to Buy

Local artisan Alberto Gónzalez sells his beautiful kitchen implements hand-crafted of local hardwoods at **Taller de Alberto.** Just up from the rodeo is **Taller de Fibras,** where a women's co-operative makes bargain-priced hats, baskets, and other items of banana leaves and straw. Whether you buy or not, call at **Lester's Art Studio,** in Unit 4. Lester Campa's fabulous works are inspired by deforestation and display staggering detail. Lester was born at Las Terrazas but studied at ENA (Escuela Nacional de Arte), in Havana. He says he needs brushes (especially fine ones) and other art supplies—take a gift. Duporté also has a studio. He specializes in paintings on Cuban flora, especially orchids. There's also a pottery workshop and a serigraphy workshop, where items are on sale.

Services

The gas station is hidden off the main road, 400 meters west of the turnoff into Las Terrazas. There's no sign. Gas costs US$1 per litre.

You can rent horses and mountain bikes at La Moka, and rowboats are available on the lake.

Getting There

Las Terrazas, 75 km west of Havana, is four km north of the Autopista, at Km 51 (there's a

beasts of burden

sign), where a road runs into the mountains. You'll pass a barrier and guardpost en route. You can also reach Las Terrazas north from Soroa. Turn right at the T-junction for Las Terrazas (17 km); if you continue straight at the junction, you'll drop down to Bahía Honda (29 km) on the north coast.

Tour & Travel, Av. 5 #8409 esq. 86, Miramar, Havana, tel. 33-2433, has a one-day excursion to Las Terrazas from Havana (US$31; US$89 with an overnight at Hotel Moka), including lunch at Cafetal Buena Vista.

SAN DIEGO DE LOS BAÑOS

Continuing west along the Autopista or Carretera Central, you'll pass **Los Palacios** (with tempting views of the mountains to the north) to San Diego de los Baños, a small but once-important spa town, 120 km west of Havana and 60 km east of Pinar del Río. The spa waters of the Templado springs were discovered in the 17th century and launched to fame when a leprous slave was supposedly miraculously cured after bathing here. Eminent German scholar and explorer Baron Alexander von Humbolt hyped the San Diego waters. Eminent people flocked, including Napoleon's private doctor. Subsequently, the resort was heavily promoted in the United States as the Saratoga of the Tropics.

The waters—whose temperature hovers at a near constant 37° C to 40° C—brim with magnesium, sulfur, sulfates, and calcides and are an ideal soother for rheumatism, skin disorders, and other ailments. A modern facility was built after the Revolution, with subterranean whirlpool baths. The spa provides treatments from massage (US$7 partial, US$15 full) and electrotherapy (US$5) to acupuncture (US$10) and for everything from stress or obesity to "osteomyoarticulatory" (!) conditions. I was told that the facility receives many foreigners, but the one time I visited I was the *only* visitor. Wheelchairs are provided for the physically impaired.

Accommodations
In the center of town is **Hotel Libertad,** tel. 37820, a nice place with 19 clean and adequate rooms with cold showers, fans, and radios (US$11 s, US$15 d). Another down-to-earth,

much cheaper option is the colonial-era **Hotel Saratoga,** tel. 37821, boasting a columned lobby. It has a restaurant and bar and 39 rooms with Spanish-tiled floors and lofty windows. They, too, have cold showers, radios, and fans. Foreigners may not be accepted. Rates are 7 pesos s, 9 pesos d, 11 pesos t.

Hotel El Mirador, tel. 33-5410, is a supremely attractive property with a beautiful setting above landscaped grounds, with a swimming pool and tiled courtyard. You'll find contemporary flourishes inside the colonial-style 1950s-era structures. The 30 large, a/c rooms feature attractive decor (rattan and pink floral prints), TVs, direct-dial telephones, and hot water in the showers (US$27 s, US$34 d). There's a restaurant lit by Tiffany lamps, a souvenir store, and a cosmetics store. Book rooms through Servimed, Calle 18 #4304 e/ 43 y 47, Miramar, Havana, tel. 33-2658, fax 33-1630.

Food and Services
The classy restaurant of the Hotel El Mirador serves omelettes (US$2-4), spaghetti (from US$2), and fish and steak dishes. At least two *paladares* offer home-cooked meals: **Paladar La Sorpresa,** opposite the Hotel Libertad, and **Paladar El Guerro,** 400 km east of the old town.

There's a post office opposite Hotel Libertad and a telephone office next door. The town also has a cinema and disco.

PARQUE NACIONAL LA GÜIRA

Parque Nacional La Güira protects 54,000 acres of sylvan wilderness that rise to pine forests on the higher slopes of the Sierra de los Organos, northwest of San Diego de los Baños. Though trails are not well developed, the park is a treasure trove for birdwatchers. Timorous deer are also found. And carp, trout, and a native fish called *viahaco* frequent the freshwater streams. The park occupies the former estate of Manuel Cortina, a wealthy landowner who traded in precious woods. Following the Revolution, the land was expropriated and made a preserve for the recreational use of all Cubans.

You enter the park through a mock fortress gate with turrets, beyond which the road rises to Cortina's former mansion, now a **museum,** where his resplendent possessions—antique porcelain, statuary, and tapestries—are preserved. Above the house are a series of modest gardens, including a Japanese garden; a formal English garden with topiary, statuary, and ruins; and a Cuban garden planted profusely with butterfly jasmine and flame trees.

Getting There: The entrance to the park is 200 yards west (left) of the turnoff to the right (east) for San Diego de los Baños when coming from the Autopista. A road leads north through the park and continues to La Palma, on the north coast.

Cuevas de las Portales

This dramatic cave series should be on every tourist's list. Their setting is stunning. Your first sight is of the Río Caiguanabo flowing beneath a fantastically sculpted natural arch that the river has carved through a great *mogote* (a freestanding limestone peak). The great cave, reaching 30 meters high, lies within one wall of the arch. The massive chamber's curved walls and vaulted ceilings are stippled with giant stalagmites and stalactites.

Their remoteness and superb natural position made them a perfect spot for Che Guevara to establish his staff headquarters during the 1962 Cuban Missile Crisis, when he commanded the Western Army. The ever-smiling guide, Gilberto Cruz, will show you the table where Che and his men dined. Steps lead up to a cave within a cave where Che wrote his letters amid heaps of batshit. The cave opens out to the rear, where stands Che's breeze-block office and dormitory, still containing the original table and chairs. Inside, a portal leads to another tiny cave with a floor of rough-hewn boards still supporting Che's narrow, iron bed.

Steps lead down to the fish-filled river through a "botanic garden" of wild philodendrons and strangler figs full of birdsong.

Cuevas de las Portales is on the western edge of the park, four km from the turnoff for Cabañas Los Pinos.

Accommodations and Food

There's a bare-bones *campismo*—**Cajalbana**—at the entrance to Cuevas de las Portales, featuring spartan concrete bungalows. It also has **campsites** with barbecue pits beneath shade trees.

Cabañas de los Pinos is a cottage colony constructed entirely of cedar and pine and set loftily amid the cool pine-fresh forest festooned with epiphytes, a windy seven km uphill drive from the fortress gate. The rustic facility is fantastic. It has 23 wooden, red-tiled treehouses on stilts (12 pesos s/d). The huts have communal showers (cold water only) and minimal furnishings. The air is as sharp as a needle, and it is marvelous to sleep with the wind whistling through the pines. There's a basic restaurant, but bring food in case you have to fend for yourself if you're the only guests, which is likely.

Bar Maracas, about 400 m uphill from the fortress gate, is a down-to-earth eatery serving *criollo* dishes for pesos. About two km uphill from the gate is a larger restaurant, but it, too, has a basic menu. There are brick bungalows here, plus camping.

CLUB MASPOTÓN

Maspotón, 62 km east of the town of Pinar del Río, is a hunting and fishing club located near La Cubana rice plantation, on the southern shores of Los Palacios Municipality, 111 km southwest of Havana. It has 134 square km of lowland marshes and woodlands dotted with lakes and canals bordered with mangroves. The lagoons teem with feisty tarpon ("silver bullets") which give fisherfolk an unbeatable thrill. Since Maspotón lies directly beneath a migratory corridor between North and South America, the air is almost always full of birds settling and taking off. Blue-winged teal, shoveler ducks, pheasants, guinea fowl, snipes, and mourning doves abound.

Maspotón is popular with fishermen for its tarpon, bonefish, and snook in the Río Carragua estuary and for largemouth bass in nearby La Juventud reservoir. You negotiate the still lagoons of black water in flat-bottomed fiberglass boats.

Hunting takes place from boats and 61 blinds built on platforms. Permits are issued on the premises. You'll rise as early as 4 a.m., depending on the bird species you'll set your sights on. You can rent guns and camouflage. Maspotón also sells ammunition (US$10 per 25 rounds) and refrigerates your catch.

Accommodations and Food

The lodge—described accurately by Carlo Gebler in *Driving Through Cuba* as "like a dismal holiday camp"—has 34 a/c rooms in 16 soulless concrete *cabañas* built around a swimming pool and equipped with refrigerators, radios, and private baths. Don't trust the mosquito nets covering the tiny windows; you'll need to splash on the repellent liberally. There's a restaurant and bar, games room with pool table, and TV (US$53 per person, including all meals). Bullfrogs gather beside the lamps that light the pathways at night, when the twinkling of fireflies constitutes the entertainment. I've not eaten here but am informed that the meals are grim—a good incentive to bag your own bird or hook your own fish (take spices and condiments with you). Contact Horizontes Hotels, Calle 23 #156 e/ N y O, Vedado, Havana, tel. 33-4142, fax 33-3161, or write the Club at Granja Arrocera la Cubana, Los Palacios, Pinar del Río (radio tel. COI-26).

Just before Los Palacios is **Restaurante El-tornado,** where I ate one of the best meals I've had in rural Cuba—a superb fish dish with heaps of boiled potatoes and a salted tomato salad. The fish was *tenca,* resembling pilchard. With a *refresco* of fresh-squeezed orange juice, my filling meal cost 11 pesos (US50 cents).

Getting There

Finding Maspotón is half the fun—or frustration. The turnoff from the Autopista is at the sign for **Los Palacios,** a neat agricultural town large enough to have its own small art gallery and bookstore yet described by Carlo Gebler as a "miserable town of wooden shacks, a few stucco-clad buildings in the center, and a rusting railway line running down the main street." Go to the east end of town, cross the railroad tracks to the right, bear immediately left, and take the first right for Maspotón. There are no signs. Follow the zig-zagging, deeply gouged, muddy red track about 12 km until you reach a sign that reads *Club de caza y pesca* pointing to the right. Maspotón is about eight km farther. Just about when you're ready to pack it all in, you arrive.

PINAR DEL RÍO

Pinar del Río, 178 km west of Havana, is the capital of its namesake province. The town (pop. 125,000) is named for the native pine trees that flourished along the banks for the Río Guamá before the Spanish arrived. The first land grants in the area were issued by Spanish authorities in 1544, when the region was called Nueva Filipina. Tobacco farmers established themselves nearby, in Viñales and Vuelta Abajo, and the city prospered on the tobacco trade (the first tobacco factory was founded nearby in 1761). During the 18th and 19th centuries, when sugarcane came to dominate the Cuban economy, tobacco remained Pinar's prime resource, and the city lost much of its early importance. Spanish authorities looked east, neglecting Pinar del Río.

Habaneros consider citizens of Pinar del Río to be backward bumpkins, a legacy of prerevolutionary days, when the city was known by the nickname *Cenicienta* (Cinderella). Tourist literature stretches the truth in touting the city as the "Paradise in the West," but it is well worth an overnight stay.

The town has a pleasant cosmopolitan feel, enhanced by the beauty of the neoclassical historic buildings, many with decorative art nouveau bases supporting columns. By contemporary Cuban standards, Pinar del Río is in a fairly good state of repair. Many houses have recently received coats of fresh paint, there are lots of *paladares,* and the stores along Calle Martí are well stocked with modern goods. Modern concrete apartment blocks, university buildings, a nurses' academy, and the Federico Engels vocational school stand in ugly counterpoint around the city edges.

ORIENTATION

The Autopista slides into town from the east past a row of carob trees. It becomes Calle Martí, a wide boulevard that narrows to two lanes through the city center, dividing the town north and south.

The town is laid out in a rough grid. However, many streets are aligned or curve at odd angles,

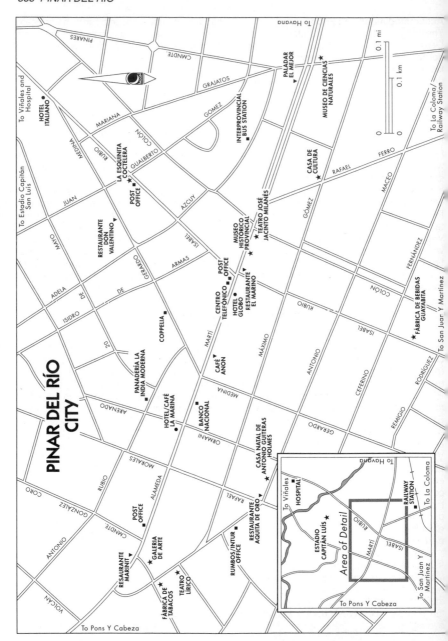

PINAR DEL RÍO CITY

To Havana

To Viñales and Hospital

To Estadio Capitán San Luis

To La Coloma/ Railway Station

To San Juan Y Martínez

To Pons Y Cabeza

To Pons Y Cabeza

PINARES

CMNDTE

GRAJATOS

GOMEZ

MARIANA

COLON

GUALBERTO

AZCUY

RAFAEL

FERRO

MACEO

GÓMEZ

RUBIO

MEDINA

JUAN

MAYO

ADELA

ISIDRO

GERARDO

DE

DE

20

ARENADO

RUBIO

GONZÁLEZ

CMNDTE

ANTONIO

CORO

VOLCÁN

ISABEL

ARMAS

MARTI

MÁXIMO

RUBIO

ANTONIO

ISABEL

COLÓN

FERNÁNDEZ

CEFERINO

GERARDO

REMIGIO

RODRÍGUEZ

MEDINA

ORMANI

ALAMEDA

MORALES

RAFAEL

HOTEL ITALIANO

LA ESQUINITA COCTELERA

POST OFFICE

RESTAURANTE DON VALENTINO

COPPELIA

PANADERÍA LA INDIA MODERNA

HOTEL/CAFÉ LA MARINA

BANCO NACIONAL

CAFÉ AÑON

CENTRO TELEFÓNICO

POST OFFICE

HOTEL GLOBO

RESTAURANTE EL MARINO

MUSEO HISTÓRICO PROVINCIAL

TEATRO JOSÉ JACINTO MILANÉS

CASA DE CULTURA

INTERPROVINCIAL BUS STATION

PALADAR EL MEJOR

MUSEO DE CIENCIAS NATURALES

CASA NATAL DE ANTONIO GUITERAS HOLMES

RESTAURANTE AGUITA DE ORO

RUMBOS/INTUR OFFICE

POST OFFICE

GALERÍA DE ARTE

RESAURANTE MARINIT

TEATRO LÍRICO

FÁBRICA DE TABACOS

FÁBRICA DE BEBIDAS GUAYABITA

0   0.1 mi

0   0.1 km

Area of Detail

To Havana

To Viñales

HOSPITAL

ESTADIO CAPITÁN LUÍS

RAILWAY STATION

To La Coloma

RUBIO

MARTI

ISABEL

To San Juan Y Martínez

To Pons Y Cabeza

and it is easy to lose your direction. Martí is the main street, and most places of interest are here, or along adjacent Calle Máximo Gómez (one block south). The main cross street is Isabel Rubio, which leads north and south to the regions of Viñales and Vuelto Abajo. Unlike most Cuban cities, it has no main central square. The city rises to the west, and at the "top" end of Calle Martí is a small triangular plaza where the most important historic buildings are found.

There's no tourist bureau, but the Ministry of Tourism and Rumbos both have offices at Antonio Maceo #17. You can buy a small but accurate tourist map of Pinar del Río for US$1 from the souvenir shop in the tobacco factory at Calles Antigua Carcel and Ajete.

THINGS TO SEE AND DO

Museum of Natural Sciences
This small and mediocre museum displays the natural history of the province, both extant and extinct. The former includes stuffed mammals, birds, fish, and a collection of seashells. Concrete dinosaurs stand transfixed in the courtyard, including a plesiosaur (a giant marine reptile) and a *Megalocnus rodens* (an extinct oversized rodent once found in Cuba) surrounded by rare cork palms.

The museum is housed in an ornately stuccoed building of Gaudiesque proportion, the Palacio Gausch, built in 1914 by a Spanish doctor to reflect elements from his travels around the world. Thus, the columned entrance is supported by Athenian columns bearing Egyptian motifs, while gothic griffins and gargoyles adorn the façade. The museum is at Calle Martí #202 and Avenida Comandante Pinares. Open Tues.-Sat., 2-6 p.m., and Sunday 9 a.m.-1 p.m. Entrance costs US$1.

Museo Histórico Provincial
This small museum at Calle Martí #58 e/ Calles Isabel Rubio y Colón, traces the history of both the town and the province of Pinar from pre-Columbian days. Aboriginal artifacts (including in a mock cave dwelling) are displayed, along with antique furniture and weaponry. Concerts are sometimes held here; when I called in, a

group called Almendro was playing Brazilian music. It's open Mon.-Sat. 8.30 a.m.-4 p.m. and Sunday 9 a.m.-1 p.m. Entrance costs US$1.

Fábrica de Tabacos
Sometimes referred to as the Tobacco Museum, the quaint little Francisco Donatién cigar factory is housed in the former Antigua Cárcel jail on Calle Antigua Carcel and Ajete. It's an intimate place, where Serbio cigars and five other brands are made for national consumption. You can peer through glass windows to watch the 30 or so *tabaqueros*, who sit in two aisles, sorting their leaves and rolling, trimming, and gluing labels onto cigars. A guided tour costs US$2. You'll savor the beat of *chavetas* (the cigar rollers' rounded, all-purpose knife) being pounded in welcome and have a chance to listen to Segundo Pérez Carrillo reading from novels or *Granma* to keep the rollers amused. Tom Miller describes his visits to the factory in his splendid book, *Trading with the Enemy*. It's open Mon.-Fri. 6:30 a.m.-4:30 p.m. and Saturday 7:30-11:30 a.m. You can buy cigars (including export brands) and souvenirs in a well-stocked shop.

Fábrica de Bebidas Guayabita
The blue building at Isabel Rubio #189, four blocks south of Calle Martí, is Casa Garay, where *guayabita,* a spicy, brandy-like alcoholic drink made from rum and guava, has been produced since 1892. This pleasant liquor is produced exclusively in Pinar del Río. It is made from the fruit of a wild bush—*Psidium guayabita*—that grows only on the sandy plains and pine woods of Pinar del Río. There are two kinds: a sweet *licor de Guayabita* and a dry *Guayabita seca* brandy. Tours are offered. In the tasting room, you can tipple various versions, including *guayabita* served with a shot of crème de menthe. You can buy small bottles for US$5. It's closed on weekends.

Other Sites
The **Teatro José Jacinto Milanés,** at the corner of Calle Martí and Calle Colón, boasts an ornate, circular, tiered interior made entirely of wood and capable of accommodating an audience of 520. The first theater here was dedicated in 1845, though the current theater dates to 1898, when it became a center for social life.

A recent restoration has resurrected its fin-de-siècle splendor. Entrance costs US$1.

Worth a peek, too, is the **Casa Natal de Antonio Guiteras Holmes,** Avenida Maceo #52 e/ San Juan y Ormani Avenado, the former house of a local pharmacist and revolutionary hero brutally murdered in 1935 by the Machado regime. It is now an art gallery. Musical performances are offered in the back courtyard.

ACCOMMODATIONS

The **Hotel La Marina,** on Calle Martí, tel. 2558, ostensibly doesn't accept foreigners, but a sob story may do the trick. Rooms cost 15 pesos. You can make reservations for *campismos* throughout Pinar province at the booking office on Isabel Rubio e/ Isidro de Armas y Adela Azcuy.

The **Hotel Globo,** Calle Martí and Calle Isabel Rubio, tel. 4268, is a moody place with a dark foyer lined with tiles and brightened by intriguing artwork and a stunning mosaic on the stairwell. The 42 rooms have lofty ceilings and are modest but adequate (US$11 s, US$14 d, US$23 t, US$24 suite). Avoid rooms at the front, which pick up noise from the street. A similar option is the **Hotel Italiano** (formerly the Hotel Occidente) on Calle Isabel Rubio, tel. 3049. Its 27 a/c rooms are small and modestly furnished (US$15/18 s, US$20/23 d low/high season). There's a pleasant restaurant downstairs.

If you don't mind staying out of town, I recommend the **Aguas Claras,** on the road to Viñales at Carretera de Viñales Km 7.5, Pinar del Río, tel. 82-2722. It bills itself as an eco-resort and has 50 thatched and modestly furnished a/c bungalows spread amid landscaped grounds with bougainvillea and views through the trees and (down by the river) decks where folkloric shows are performed. Facilities include a swimming pool, restaurant, snack bar, and tourism bureau. Guides are available for hikes, and horses can be rented (US$4 per hour). Chalets cost US$20. **Camping** is also allowed.

Pinar del Río Hotel, Calle Martí Final, tel. 5071, is on the eastern fringe of town. The architecture is depressingly post-Stalinist, though mitigated by the warmth of the relaxed and friendly hotel personnel. The 149 large, a/c rooms are modestly furnished, with private baths, TVs, telephones, and radios. It has a boutique, and a nightclub where cabarets are offered. Other facilities include a restaurant, café, and bar where mosquitoes will thank you for your visit. The swimming pool is a gathering spot for locals on weekends, when the noise might drive you away. Rates are US$20 s, US$28 d low-season and US$25 s, US$34 d, high-season.

FOOD

Pinar del Río has a large selection of restaurants. My favorite is **Restaurante Rumayor,** one km north of town on Carretera Viñales. This fabulous Afro-Cuban restaurant features a huge thatch-and-log dining room decorated with African drums, shields, and religious icons. Seats are of dark woven leather. Service is keen. *Criollo* dishes include the famous house special, *pollo ahumado* (smoked chicken; US$5) and *chirna frita* (fish sautéed with garlic; US$7).

In town, the atmospheric and well-run **Restaurante Aquita de Oro,** tel. 4890, serves steaks from US$4.50. Tall doors offer views onto the street. It features dancing in a courtyard with an arbor of trumpetvine. You'll find chicken and rice (1.20 peso), salads (40 centavos), and more at the **Café La Marina,** a jaded '60s-style diner popular with locals for coffee and ice cream (open 7.30 a.m.-9.30 p.m.). The restaurant in the **Hotel Italiano** is also recommended for basic *criollo* food. **Restaurante La Casona,** opposite the Teatro Milanés, is a large, airy place also popular with locals, as is the lively and modestly elegant **Restaurante Marinit.** The **El Marino** plays on a nautical theme with anchors and chains for rails outside.

Restaurante Don Valentino is a pleasant, if pricey, little *paladar* with soft lighting and carnations on each table. Service can be excruciatingly slow, and the food can be disappointing, though I enjoyed my chicken served with bell pepper and pickled cabbage. Check your bill carefully! Closer to the Hotel Pinar del Río is the **Paladar El Mejor,** opposite the Museum of Natural Sciences.

Seeking vegetarian food? Check out the **Eco-Restaurant Los Caneyes,** three km west of

Pinar on the road to Cabeza. It serves natural health foods under thatch.

Coppelia, on Gerardo Medina, one block east of Martí, has excellent ice cream. It gets crowded; expect to wait in line. There's a bakery—**Panadería La India Moderna**—at Antonio Rubio and 20 de Mayo. It's open 7 a.m.-noon and 5-7 p.m.

Most bars and restaurants in town serve *guayabita,* the local liqueur.

ENTERTAINMENT

Many local restaurants have cabarets at night, ranging from a couple of guys with guitar to *espectáculos* with stiletto-heeled, befeathered mulatta dancers. Don't leave town without checking out the **Rumayor Cabaret,** at the Restaurante Rumayor. This excellent two-hour-long *espectáculo* is offered Thurs.-Sun. and features comedians and other performers. It is followed by a disco. The US$5 entrance includes one drink. The crowd consists almost entirely of young Cuban couples (locals pay 20 pesos). A folklore ensemble performs here on Monday and Tuesday.

The **Casa de Cultura,** on Máximo Gómez #108, has an art gallery plus dances and live music, usually beginning at 9 p.m. The folkloric dances feature the *punta campesina,* in which *guajiros* recite poetry to each other in conversational fashion, each building on the work of the other in a form known as *controversias.* Children's programs are sometimes offered here on weekends at 2 p.m. Kiddie films are also shown at **Sala de Video Satelite,** 50 yards up the hill on the opposite side of the street. Live music is also featured at the **Centro Provicional Artes Plástico Galeria** and **Teatro Lirico.**

The best place to down a few beers with the locals is **La Esquinita Coctelera,** on the corner of Isabel Rubio and Juan Gualberto Gómez. They also serve *guayabita* and the house special, vermouth and rum, to help put the clientele in a singing mood with tunes on the jukebox.

The Vegueros, the local **baseball team,** hosts visiting teams at the Estadio Capitán San Luís, on Calle Capitán San Luís, three blocks west of the Carretera Central for Viñales.

PINAR DEL RÍO USEFUL TELEPHONE NUMBERS

Police	tel. 115 (or 2525)
Hospital	tel. 4443
Terminal de Ómnibus	tel. 2571
Taxis	tel. 2781

INFORMATION AND SERVICES

There's a post office and DHL station in the Hotel Pinar del Río, tel. 5070, ext. 251. The main post office is at the corner of Calle Martí and Isabel Rubio.

The local library—Biblioteca Ramón González Coro—has 90,000 books, including works by Alice Walker and William Faulker (and even braille editions of Castro and Martí), a library of record albums, and a bookbinding room.

The Hospital Provincial is one km north of town, at the junction for Viñales. There's a 24-hour pharmacy next to the Hotel Globo, at the corner of Isabel Rubio, and another—Farmacia El Modernista—next to the Hotel La Marina.

You can purchase toiletries and other essentials at Tienda Panamericano, on Calle Martí.

Cyclists will find a well-stocked bicycle shop near Coppelia, on Calle Gerardo Medina.

THINGS TO BUY

The **Fábrica de Tabacos** has a well-stocked humidor where you can purchase export-quality cigars, plus a souvenir store selling cassettes and T-shirts. Pinar is known for quality ceramics; check out the workshops on Calle Antonio Maceo. And you can buy small bottles of *guayabita* at the factory on Isabel Rubio.

TRANSPORTATION

Getting There

Bus no. 100 departs the main bus station in Havana for Pinar del Río daily at 7:35, 7:50, and 8:25 a.m., noon, and 2:20, 5:30, 6:20, and 7:45 p.m. The route follows the Autopista and takes about three hours (8 pesos); some buses follow the Carretera Central, adding about one hour to the journey. They arrive at the **Terminal de Ómnibus** on Calle Adela Azcuy, between Calle Colón and Comandante Pinares. Buses usually are booked solid weeks ahead.

Rail service has improved dramatically since 1994, when the fuel shortage was still severe. Given the excessive demand for buses, it is a preferable way to travel. Trains depart Havana's Tulipán station daily (US$6.50). The journey ostensibly takes five hours but can take much longer (departure times are subject to change). The station in Pinar del Río is three blocks south of Calle Martí at Calle Comandante Pinares. The second-class service has hard wooden seats. You can make reservations through Ferrotur (see "Getting Away" in the Havana chapter).

Getting Around

Pinar is cozy enough to walk virtually everywhere. However, there are plenty of horsedrawn taxis, which gather on Máximo Gómez between Rafael Ferro and Ciprian Valdes. They're good for traveling short distances within the city. Tourist taxis are based at the Hotel Pinar del Río for trips farther afield.

You can rent cars from Transauto in the Hotel Pinar del Río. The **Cupet gas station** is located two km northeast of town, on the road to Entronque de Ovas, beyond the turnoff for Viñales.

Getting Away

Bus no. 100 leaves for Havana from the **Terminal de Ómnibus Interprovinciales** at 3:30, 4:30, 5:30, 8:30, and 10 a.m., and 1, 2:30, and 4:35 p.m. Buses depart Pinar del Río from the **Terminal de Ómnibus Intermunicipales** (also at Calle Adela Azcuy, e/ Calle Colón y Comandante Pinares) for destinations throughout the province, including Viñales and La Bajada.

Trains for Havana depart at 8:15 a.m. and 11:50 p.m. (US$6.50); for Guane at 7:48 a.m. and 12:16 and 6:30 p.m. (US$1.85); and for Artemisa at 6:25 p.m. (US$3.30). You can buy same-day tickets on a space-available basis.

Aerotaxi, tel. 6-3248, offers flights by Antonov AN-2 biplane to Isla de la Juventud from Pinar's Aeropuerto Àlvaro Barba, two km northeast of town. Departures are Monday, Wednesday, Friday, and Saturday (US$20 one-way). No reservations are taken, so arrive early to sign up for the waiting list.

VIÑALES AND VICINITY

Viñales is a miniature Yosemite, with the most spectacular scenery in all Cuba. Arriving from Pinar del Río takes your breath away. You wind past guava and mango fields, then up through pine-forested hills, climbing past simple *bohios* into the Sierra de los Organos. Atop a steep rise you arrive at Hotel Las Jasmines, where you should park and take in the first jaw-dropping views from above a magnificent valley. The valley (about 11 km long and five wide) is scattered with precipitous knolls the height of skyscrapers towering over a plain of impossibly deep green receding to distant mountains. The setting resembles a Vietnamese or Chinese painting, particularly in the early morning, when mists settle above the valley floor.

The great freestanding rocks are called *mogotes,* isolated, sheer-sloped, round-topped, cone-shaped mounds that are part of the oldest geological formation in Cuba. They are the remnants of a great limestone plateau—part of the Guaniguanico mountain range—that rose from the sea during the Jurassic era, about 160 million years ago. Over the ensuing eons, rain and rivers dissolved and eroded the limestone mass to form classic karst terrain, leaving hummocks as high as 1,000 feet.

Some *mogotes* are laced with holes—canyons, really, hundreds of feet wide—reached often by traipsing through natural tunnels to follow rivers that suddenly disappear down holes in their own valley floors. Pre-Columbian Indians inhabited the caves, and, during the colonial era, runaway slaves built villages amid these lonesome holes.

Between the *mogotes* are *hoyos,* small depressions, filled with deep deposits of rich red soil perfect for growing tobacco. One of the special memories you'll take home is the image of farmers in straw hats ploughing their fields with ox-drawn ploughs—or of standing on high, listening to the sounds from the valley echoing uphill and watching egrets winging across the tobacco fields far below. From January to April, a sweet aroma of tobacco hangs over the fields.

Many species of flora and fauna are found only atop the strange mesas, such as unique varieties of snails. Fauna is so highly endemic that certain mollusks are found only on one or a few *mogotes*. The formations are festooned with rough bush, ferns, and the rare and ancient cork palm *(Mycrocycas calocoma)*, a botanical relic that has been declared a national treasure and grows only here. Below, on the valley floor, grow silk-cotton trees, royal palms, Palmita de Sierra, the *roble caimán* (a relative of the oak), and sweet-smelling mariposa, Cuba's national flower. Other rare, endemic species include a pygmy boa constrictor, the *zunzún* (the world's smallest hummingbird), and the *tomeguín del pinar*, another tiny bird related to hummingbirds.

A good place to capture the valley on film is from the parking lot and *mirador* at Las Jasmines. You'll find a *ranchito* restaurant and gift stalls. If the heat is too much, you can buy a *pipa,* refreshing coconut milk in the husk (US$2).

VIÑALES

The town of Viñales (pop. 10,000), 26 km north of Pinar del Río and 212 km west of Havana, is a rural charmer, justifiably a national monument. In many ways it's still a cowboy town, and its wide main street Calle Salvador Cisnero—is lined with turn-of-the-century, red-tile-roofed cottages and shaded by rows of stately pine trees. The handsome **main square** is shaded by palms and has a bust of José Martí at its center. To one side is a pretty 19th-century church. On the north side, a beautiful arcaded colonial building houses the **Casa de Cultura,** which posts a list of local activities on the door.

Calle Salvador Cisnero has a few other sights of note. The first is **Museo Municipal Adela Azcuy.** It has motley displays telling the history of the region, and, outside, a bronze bust of Adela Azcuy Labrador, a female citizen and captain in the War of Independence. The other local treasure is the **Casa de Don Tomás,** dating to 1822 and now an atmospheric restaurant where you can dine while looking out over the **Hogar Maternidad,** where pregnant women in nightgowns rock gently on the veranda.

Two widows, Carmen and Caridad Miranda, maintain a garden full of fruits, orchids, begonias, and other ornamental and medicinal plants. It is rather grandly called the **Viñales Botanical Garden.** Other villagers seeking herbal remedies consult the two sisters, who are happy to demonstrate for you how the pre-Columbian Indians extracted dyes from plants to paint their bodies.

As elsewhere in Cuba, be prepared for mosquitoes and tiny fleas that pack an irritating punch.

Accommodations

Visitors are blessed with two splendid options—and splendid bargains as well. The first is **Hotel Horizontes Las Ermitas,** Carretera de La Ermita Km 2, Viñales, Pinar del Río, tel. 82-9-3204, fax 1974, one km south of town and magnificently nestled atop the southern scarp of the valley. The gracious contemporary property on a classical theme—hints of ancient Crete blend with Spanish colonial design—wraps around a sundeck and swimming pool with poolside bar where you may settle beneath shady palms to drink—and drink in the heavenly views. The 62 beautifully decorated, a/c rooms are a bargain at US$28 s, US$35 d. Make sure you get a room with a balcony (complete with Adirondack chairs) facing the valley, not the pool. Cockerels on the lawns provide your morning wake-up calls. The restaurant serves sometimes exquisite cuisine, and the heavenly (albeit lethal) local liqueur, *guayabita,* made from pungent, slightly sweet guavas. There's also a well-stocked store.

Equally appealing is **Hotel Horizontes Las Jasmines,** Carretera de Viñales Km 25, Pinar del Río, tel. 829-3265, an older but recently restored Spanish hacienda-style hotel with fancy wrought-iron grillwork and a similar hilltop setting and fabulous vistas. The 16 a/c *cabañas* and 62 rooms (US$25 s, US$36 d) have radios (but no telephones) and gigantic Soviet TVs. The rooms are clean and pleasantly furnished and have balconies facing an Olympic-length ice-blue swimming pool overhanging the cliff. Forty-eight newer rooms are in a separate block. An ornate wooden ceiling and French doors topped with beautiful stained-glass lend an elegance to the second-floor restaurant and bar. The hotel's store is well stocked.

Food
The restaurants at both Hotel La Ermita and Las Jasmines are good bets. The grilled fish at Ermita, for example, is excellent (US$7). *The* place to eat, however, is **Casa de Don Tomás,** an atmospheric wooden colonial charmer at 141 Calle Salvador Cisnero, tel. 93-114. I recommend the house special, *delicias de Don Tomás* (a rice dish with pork, sausage, and lobster), a beef dish called *tasajo a lo campesino,* or paella (US$10), washed down with a *coctel el trapiche* (US$2.50). The Trio Romántico serenades while you eat. It's open daily 10 a.m.-4 p.m. and 6:30-9 p.m.

There are several *paladares,* including **Restaurante Valle,** in the Casa Dago. My favorite, though, is **Mi Casa,** run by José Luís, who has built his beautiful *ranchita* restaurant of bamboo and logs atop stilts. His creole dishes include fish and shrimp (US$6). For local color, try **Restaurante Las Brisas,** one block west of the plaza.

Services and Shopping
There'a a 24-hour pharmacy, one block west of the plaza, tel. 93-169. You'll find a Photo Service next to the police station, tel. 93-124, opposite the plaza on Calle Salvador Cisnero, open 8 a.m.-10 p.m. One block east is a Banco Nacional and the Red Cross. The gas station, 200 meters farther, on the right, won't serve tourists; the nearest **Cupet gas station** is 10 km north of town, at San Cayetano. You can

VIÑALES USEFUL TELEPHONE NUMBERS
Police . . . . tel. 9-3124
Policlinica . . . . tel. 3-8107
Terminal de Ómnibus . . . . tel. 3-8129

make calls from the telephone booth on the southwest side of the main square. The post office is one block south of the plaza.

At the northwest corner of the plaza is a small **Galería de Arte,** where you may buy paintings of moderate quality. There's a souvenir store and a bookstore opposite the plaza, too, next to the police station. Stalls along the block immediately west of the plaza sell baskets and straw goods.

Getting There
By Bus: Bus no. 124 departs for Viñales from the Terminal Ómnibus in Havana at 9:20 a.m. and 1:05 p.m. (10 pesos) and travels via the Autopista. Buses also run along the north coast to San Vicente, where you can catch a bus south to Viñales (you may need to stitch local services together). The bus stop is in front of Photo Service, on the main street.

By Car: From Pinar del Río, take the two-lane Carretera Viñales. Leaving town, take Isabel Rubio for one km and turn left at Hospital Quirúrgico. It's 27 km to Viñales. The road winds uphill through pine forest until you reach a billboard that

Casa de Don Tomás

reads Complejo Turística de Viñales, announcing your arrival above the valley at Hotel Las Jasmines, to the left. The road drops into Viñales town; at the T-junction, the road to the left leads to Los Murales; that to the right leads into town and continues to Las Cuevas and the north coast.

There's also a turnoff for Viñales from the Autopista, eight km east of Pinar del Río; it's a rough road with big potholes (after eight km you'll reach a T-junction, with Aguas Claras to the left and Viñales to the right).

By Taxi: Yes, you can take a licensed taxi from Havana, but be prepared to pay US$100 or more roundtrip. Better to negotiate a price for a private car and driver, which may be as low as US$30 (plus gasoline), depending on the age and reliability of the car.

Organized Tours: Rumbos offers a daylong excursion from Havana departing at 7:30 a.m. (US$39, including lunch) **Tour & Travel,** Avenida 5 #8409 esq. 86, Miramar, Havana, tel. 33-2433, also has a one-day excursion, for US$38. Viñales is also included in a one-week "ecotour" package that also includes Havana, Soroa, and Guamá (in Zapata); it's offered by **Hoteles Horizontes,** Calle 23 #156 e/ N y O, Vedado, Havana, tel. 33-4142, fax 33-3161.

VIÑALES VALLEY NATIONAL MONUMENT

Exploring the Valle de Viñales immerses you in a distinctive yet archetypal Cuban setting. Dominating the valley, of course, are the dramatic *mogotes* in whose shadow *guajiros* in straw hats and white linens lovingly tend their plots of tobacco and maize. Thanks to a very special microclimate of moist nights and cool mornings, tobacco grows well here, dominating the valley economy.

You should take time to talk to farmers, who will be proud and delighted to take you out into their *vegas* and curing sheds to demonstrate the skill of raising tobacco, much of which lies under acres of cheesecloth stretched over the plants to protect against insects and an excess of sun. I have always been welcomed, too, into *bohíos* (thatched rural homesteads) to learn something of rural lifestyles and the benefits that the Revolution has brought.

Nowhere in Cuba will you experience a warmer welcome and balance of pride and humility, or more endearing and timeless scenes, such as the frequent sight of pairs of oxen connected by a yoke pulling two great logs joined in a V and ridden ski-like by a *guajiro*, always with a faithful dog trotting alongside at his heels.

The valley contains several caves of interest. Carretera Puerto Esparanza leads northeast from Viñales to Cueva del Viñales and Cueva del Indio; to the west of town is Caverna de Santo Tomás. There are many other caves, some of which are used for military purposes and are off-limits.

The Valle de Viñales deserves more than daylight perusal, and you should linger after exploring the valley. At dusk, the *mogotes,* now dark and sinister, are often haloed in magenta clouds fringed in gold cast by the setting sun. It's a climactic moment viewed from the lofty Hotel La Ermita or Las Jasmines, from where you look down upon a thin haze of smoke settling in the valley floor from dinners being prepared in *bohíos* (it dissipates shortly after sunup). Buzzards will be riding the last thermals, swooping and sliding like gliders. And the braying of donkeys and clip-clop of hooves far, far below can be heard clearly.

Cuevas del Viñales
This cave, four km north of Viñales, is mostly a curiosity. The cave entrance has been converted into a discotheque replete with laser lights. Bats and swallows nest in nooks and swoop in and out, disturbed by the flashing fandango of the lights and the discordant beat of the disco. Since the Special Period, however, the disco has been hurting for business and the indigenous creatures have earned a reprieve. The dance floor within the cave mouth is overhung with stalactites. Open 8 a.m. until the disco closes in the wee hours! Entrance costs US$1 with a guide (tip the guide).

Cuevas del Indio
Far more interesting is this cave, named for the Indian remains found inside, 1.5 km north of Cuevas del Viñales. The large grotto is entered via a slit at the foot of a *mogote.* You can explore the cave with or without a guide from either of its two entrances. The cave is four km

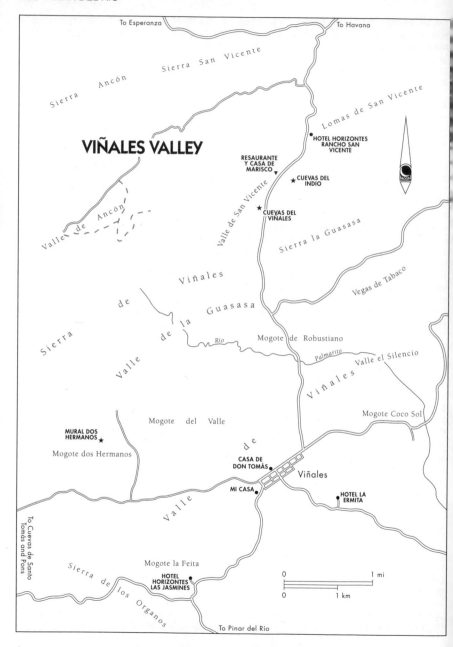

To Esperanza

To Havana

Sierra Ancón

Sierra San Vicente

Lomas de San Vicente

VIÑALES VALLEY

● HOTEL HORIZONTES
RANCHO SAN
VICENTE

RESAURANTE
Y CASA DE
MARISCO ▼

★ CUEVAS DEL
INDIO

Valle de Ancón

★ CUEVAS DEL
VIÑALES

Valle de San Vicente

Sierra la Guasasa

Viñales

Vegas de Tabaco

de

Sierra

de la Guasasa

Valle

Río

Mogote de Robustiano

Palmarito

Valle el Silencio

Viñales

Mogote Coco Sol

Mogote del Valle

de

MURAL DOS
HERMANOS ★

Mogote dos Hermanos

CASA DE
DON TOMÁS ●

Viñales

MI CASA ●

HOTEL LA
ERMITA ●

Valle

To Cuevas de Santo
Tomás and Pons

Sierra de los Organos

Mogote la Feita

HOTEL
HORIZONTES
LAS JASMINES ●

0   1 mi

0   1 km

To Pinar del Río

MOON

long, although you only explore the first km by foot. A flight of steps leads to the main entrance, where you follow a well-lit path (slippery in parts) through the mesmerizing catacomb, which in places has been hollowed to a height of 135 meters. Eventually, you reach an underground pier where a boatman waits to row you on a trip up the subterranean, milky-green river that runs deep beneath the mountain and is a habitat for opaque fish and blind crustaceans. The cave is also inhabited by small bats. In the gloom, it is like a crossing of the Styx! Your guide may point out The Old Man, The Three Musketeers, and other impressive formations, but it is more fun to set your own imagination racing in the Stygian gloom. It's open daily 9 a.m.-5 p.m.; entrance is US$3, including the boat ride.

Valle Ancón
Half a kilometer north of Cueva del Indio, a turnoff from the main road leads west through this dramatic, virtually uninhabited valley. It's six km to the village of Ancón along a steep and winding road lined with pine trees. Beyond Ancón, the dirt road brings you to the valley head, in whose cusp lies a coffee and banana plantation. Serendipity may lure you to follow the road for a cursory glimpse, but don't attempt a complete circle—the meniscus of mountains narrows and you may, as I did, find yourself bogged down in muddy pools.

Dos Hermanas
You've read about it, now go see this much-touted mural painted onto the long, exposed cliff face of one of the largest *mogotes* in the valley, five km west of Viñales. Supposedly, the mural illustrates the process of evolution in the Sierra de los Organos, from mollusk and dinosaur to club-wielding Guanajay Indian, the first human inhabitants of the region. The mural, which measures 200 feet high and 300 feet long, was commissioned by Castro and painted by 25 *campesinos* in 1961 while the artist, Leovigilda González (a disciple of Mexican muralist Diego Rivera), directed from below with a megaphone. The cliff face has recently been repainted in dull, gaudy colors—a red brontosaurus, a yellow tyrannosaurus rex, and a blood-red *Homo sapiens!* What was formerly a modestly appealing curiosity is now a testament to bad taste splotched on the wall of what is otherwise a splendidly beautiful valley. Entrance costs US$1. The restaurant, however, is well worth the visit.

You can walk to Dos Hermanas via a footpath from Viñales village.

Accommodations and Food
Hotel Horizontes Rancho San Vicente, Valle de San Vicente, Viñales, Pinar del Río, tel. 82-9-3200, 200 meters north of Cuevas del Indio, has traditionally specialized in therapeutic massage and spa treatments. There are 29 rooms in

Valle de Viñales

the main building, plus 34 basic a/c *cabañas* spread among forested lawns (US$18-23). All have private bathrooms with hot water. Ask for newer, more pleasing, pretty units. It's very peaceful, with many birds. The lukewarm, 30° C waters and algae-rich mud are good for alleviating rheumatism and other ailments. The dour spa units seemed appropriate for reptilian reproduction when I last dropped by. The rather ugly Spanish-colonial facility was closed for renovation and slated to reopen in 1997.

Restaurante y Casa de Marisco, tel. 93-202, opposite Cuevas del Indio, has two a/c rooms for rent (US$20 s/d). Each is clean and adequate, with radio, two single beds, utility furniture, and private bathroom and hot water. The restaurant specializes in freshwater prawns from the river.

The touristy, glass-enclosed restaurant at the **Cueva del Indio,** tel. 93-202, is nothing special. A better bet is the *ranchita* restaurant by the riverside, 200 meters farther north. It's famous for its *ajiaco* (meat and vegetable stew) and charcoal-grilled chicken.

The rustic thatched restaurant at Dos Hermanas serves excellent *criollo* food (its specialty is grilled pork) and entertains you with musicians. A curiosity is the *organo pinareño,* an antique hand-driven organ fed, like a Jacquard loom, with a belt of cards punched with the musical score. Lunch only. Recommended!

Services
There's a post office 100 meters west of Hotel San Vicente. A Casa de Tabaco was being built at the turnoff for Valle Ancón when I last passed by.

VIÑALES TO PONS

Continuing westward past the turnoff for Dos Hermanas, the road leads to Pons. It's a very beautiful drive for the first few miles, with serrated *mogotes* to the north. Farther west, tobacco gives way to coffee bushes as you rise to El Moncada and the saddle separating the Valle de Viñales and Valle de Santo Tomás, a scrub-covered, uncultivated valley. Don't be tempted to speed down the steep hill to Pons; there's a dangerous section at the bottom with huge potholes and a gravel surface.

At El Moncada, a turnoff leads to **Caverna de Santo Tomás,** which has more than 45 km of galleries, making it one of the largest underground systems in the New World.

At Pons, the road to the right leads via the copper mines of **Matahabre** to Santa Lucía, on the north coast. Or you can turn south and return to Pinar del Río via **Cabeza.** East of Cabeza, the road rises to a crest where there's a staggering view down over the plains. Amid the low-pinnacled, pine-covered mountains, you'd swear you were in the northwestern US. The setting and views are fabulous.

You'll pass **Finca La Guabina,** a 1,560-hectare ranch that lies in the valley of the Río Guamá midway between Cabeza and Pinar del Río. It is surrounded by low mountains foraged by deer and is popular for horseback riding and nature hikes. Rustic accommodations are available. **Alcona S.A.,** Calle 42 #514 esq. Avenida 7, Playa, Habana, tel. 22-2526, fax 33-1532, offers trips to La Guabina, including an eight-day package combining a visit to the Cayos San Felipe (US$780).

WESTERN PINAR DEL RÍO

The region south and west of the town of Pinar del Río is predominantly flat. The climate becomes increasingly drier to the west, and the vegetation correspondingly stunted and harsh. Fish-filled lakes lure anglers. But there is nothing of visual appeal and only one beach worth the drive—María la Gorda, in the Bay of Corrientes to the south of the Peninsula de Guanahacabibes, Cuba's slender westernmost point. The entire peninsula is a nature reserve.

VUELTA ABAJO

About 15 km southwest of the city, you enter rich tobacco country centered on the communities of San Luís and San Juan y Martínez. The area has none of the dramatic beauty of Viñales, but due to a unique combination of climate and soil, the tobacco grown here is considered the finest in the world, better even than that of the Valle de Viñales.

In November, you can see farmers planting fresh tobacco seeds in well-irrigated and fertilized channels. It is planted in patches at different stages to allow for progressive harvesting when every tobacco plant is at its peak, a key to producing the best cigars. The plant grows quickly and is carefully tended, and its flowers are pinched off to prevent its going to seed. Some tobacco is grown under great spreads of cheesecloth ("shade tobacco," as opposed to that grown in open fields, "sun tobacco") to produce a milder leaf. From up high on the plant comes leaves prized for strength; from the middle leaves, aroma; from low down, burnability. By January, the first leaves are ready to harvest, though the main harvest occurs in March and April. The leaves are then cured for about 40 days in drying sheds where they hang like smoked kippers. In Vuelta Abajo, the traditional *bohío* shed has been replaced in recent years by ungainly wooden cubes on stilts, with tin roofs and chimneys, where humidity and temperature can be more strictly controlled.

San Juan y Martínez, 23 km west of Pinar del Río, has a pretty main avenue lined with colorful columned streets. There's a basic pesos hotel—**Motel Yaguan**—one mile east of San Juan y Martínez.

La Coloma

La Coloma is a fishing town at the mouth of the Río Coloma, 25 km south of Pinar del Río town. It also serves the sea-freight and passenger traffic heading for Isla de la Juventud.

Playa Las Cana, immediately west of town and shown on tourist maps as a resort, is not

cigar worker

worth the drive, although you may be intrigued to photograph wooden boats being carvel-planked in the boatyard.

CAYOS DE SAN FELIPE

This small group of 10 lonesome cays lies off the underbelly of Pinar del Río, about 15 km offshore and 30 km northwest of Isla de la Juventud. The cays are inhabited only by a few impoverished fishermen and several unique species of fauna, including a native woodpecker and three endemic species of lizards. There are 16 km of virginal white beaches, with pristine coral reefs. As yet, there are no facilities.

You can take a boat from La Coloma for a few dollars. Alternately, **Alcona S.A.,** Calle 42 #514 esq. Avenida 7, Playa, Havana, tel. 22-2526, fax 33-1532, offers visits to Cayo de San Felipe by boat (including an option for scuba diving) as part of an eight-day package that also includes a visit to Finca La Guabina.

ISABEL RUBIO AND VICINITY

The landscape grows increasingly spartan as you move west from Vuelta Abajo to Isabel Rubio, a small yet relatively prosperous agricultural town that thrives on the harvest of citrus groves shaded from the wind by tall pines.

One km west of Isabel Rubio, beside the main road from Pinar del Río, is **Las Cuevas,** where you can explore a small cave system with stalactites and stalagmites. There's a bar inside, plus (outside the entrance) three little thatched wooden *cabañas* that cost five pesos for three hours. (Yes, it's a *posada,* a "love hotel" for paramours.)

North of town lies **Guane,** at the base of the Cordillera de Guaniguanico, popular with Cubans for hiking and exploring caves from the riverside **Campismo El Salto,** five km north of Guane. Its 46 cabins are basic. Make reservations at the Campismo Popular office in Pinar del Río.

Continuing west from Isabel Rubio, you leave the fresh, well-cultivated land behind and pass through ugly, scrubby countryide via **Sandino,** a planned city built in the early 1960s.

About four km east of Sandino, a turnoff leads south to Laguna Alcatraz Grande and **Cortés,** a small fishing village that lies within a deep, mushroom-shaped bay. The road continues from Cortés, looping around to Isabel Rubio via Laguna Pesquero. The land is as flat as a pancake.

Ten km west of Sandino is **La Fé,** a small, modestly picturesque fishing village nestled in the bay of Juan López at the mouth of the Río Guardiana.

From La Fé, the road loops south to **Manuel Lazo** and the junction for the Peninsula de Guanahacabibes.

Playa Bailén and Playa Boca de Galafre

At Sábalo, 12 km east of Isabel Rubio, separate turnoffs lead south to Playa Bailén, a miles-long golden sand beach, and, immediately east, Playa Boca de Galafre.

Accommodations: Villa Turista Bailén, tel. 33401, is a basic *campismo* designed for Cubans but which accepts foreigners. It is still operating, though with very few guests. It has various standards of accommodation, all basic and slightly dilapidated (from US$12/15 s, US$22/27 d). There's also a three-bedroom villa. The resort has meager facilities. There's a similar, though less substantial, facility at Playa Boca, also with tiny bungalows right on the sand, tel. 33410. It, too, takes foreigners, despite its weatherworn decor and meager facilities (it has two basic restaurants where food may be available, but don't count on it). Either may appeal to budget travelers. If you tire of the beach, there's a crocodile farm to visit nearby.

The train from Pinar del Río to Guane stops at the road, five km from Playa Bailén and also two km from Playa Boca.

Laguna Pesquero
and Embalse Laguna Grande

The area southwest of Isabel Rubio is famous for its lagoons frequented by fishermen. The most popular are Pesquero Lagoon, 10 km south of Isabel Rubio, and Laguna Grande, 25 km west, reached via a turnoff leading north from the main highway. Both are stocked with tilapia and largemouth bass. Waterfowl flock here, but no hunting is allowed.

You can continue north from Laguna Grande

and follow the coast road back to Havana or continue west past citrus fields to **Playa Colorado,** marked on maps (but not worth the drive).

PENINSULA DE GUANAHACABIBES

This willowy peninsula (90 km long and 30 km wide), juts out into the Straits of Yucatán, narrowing down to the tip at Cabo San Antonio. The geologically young peninsula is composed of limestone topped by mile after mile of scrubby woodland. The entire region is uninhabited, save for birds, wild pigs, iguanas, and land crabs that in springtime cross the road en masse, urged along by reproductive hormones and, presumably, the fear of being squashed.

The region became the final refuge for Cuba's aboriginal population as they were driven west by the more advanced and aggressive Taíno Indians. Several important archaeological sites have been uncovered. The few people who live here today eke a meager living from fishing and farming.

There's a military barrier where the road from Manuel Lazo meets the shore at the hamlet of **La Bajada.** The location is idyllic, I'm sure you'll agree, looking out across a huge bay—**Bahía de Corrientes**—lined with mangroves and mile upon mile of white sand beach washed by the coruscating Caribbean Sea. The road to the left swings around the bay and leads 14 km to Cabo de Corrientes and Villa María la Gorda, the area's only hotel; the dirt road to the right leads along the shore of the bay to Cabo San Antonio, the tip of the peninsula, 54 km away.

The cape hooks around to **Punta Cajón,** where there's a small dock for local fishermen. Foreigners are not allowed beyond the lighthouse, though foreign boaters are welcome (you can stock up on fish and ice). The tarpon fishing is said to be good right off the dock. And scuba divers might take a look at the sunken wreck just north of the cape.

The peninsula is said to hold a jail for political prisoners. Hence, the restrictions on entry.

Buses run from Pinar del Río to La Bajada.

Bahía de Corrientes

The deeply indented Bay of Corrientes sweeps around to the east to a cape—**Cabo de Corrientes**—enclosing sparkling waters famed for their cut-glass transparency. Huge whale sharks are commonly seen, as are packs of dolphin and tuna. And the coral reefs are exquisite.

Experienced divers consistently rave about the quality of the diving. There are at least 50 dive sites ranging from vertical walls to coral canyons, tunnels, and caves, and even the remains of Spanish galleons, with cannons and other trinkets scattered about the coral-crusted seabed. Black Coral Valley has 100-meter-long coral walls. Many dive sites are just 200 meters from the María la Gorda International Dive Center, at **Playa María la Gorda,** on the shores of Cabo de Corrientes. Stay clear of the beach around sundown, when a zillion tiny no-see-ums emerge to feast on unsuspecting humans.

The playa is named, according to legend, for a buxom Venezuelan barmaid, María la Gorda (Mary the Fat), who was captured by pirates based in Bahía de Corrientes. When the pirates failed to return from another voyage of plunder, María turned to leasing her body to passing sailors. She prospered on the proceeds of her ample flesh, and her venue became known as *Casa de las Tetas de María la Gorda* (House of Fat Mary's Breasts). The *tetas* in question may actually refer to the two protuberances jutting from the cliffs of nearby Punta Caimán.

María la Gorda International Dive Center has its own compressor, two dedicated dive boats, and four dive-masters. Resort course (initiation) dives cost US$15. Single dives cost US$27, night dives US$30, and US$50 for two dives in a day. The resort also has a 10-dive package for US$200. **Snorkeling** costs US$5.

Private yachters can moor alongside a simple 40-meter-long wharf or in the shallows offshore. **Sportfishing** trips run US$230 for up to four passengers.

Accommodations: Villa María la Gorda, tel. 3121, has 40 a/c rooms with TVs, mini-bars, and private baths. It's rather basic and doesn't live up to the hype of tourist literature. There are two types of accommodations: older, simple cabins and newer, better, but still modest units (both are US$15 per person per night). Rooms have TVs, refrigerators, and private bathrooms. There's a restaurant and a small bar (billed as a "nightclub" in brochures). Several guidebooks have praised the resort for its food, but when I was there the buffet meals were mediocre. The disappointing breakfast costs a whopping US$11, and dinners are a steep US$15. A full-meal plan costs US$30 daily. Car rentals can be arranged with 24 hours notice.

Parque Nacional
Peninsula de Guanahacabibes
The entire low-lying peninsula (nowhere higher than 25 meters above sea level) is encompassed within the Parque Nacional Peninsula de Guanahacabibes, a 101,500-hectare reserve created by UNESCO in 1987 to protect the semi-deciduous woodland, mangroves, and wildlife that live here. At least 14 of the more than 500 woody species are found only on the peninsula. Endemic birds include the tiny *torcaza* and *zunzuncito* hummingbirds. The giant rodents called *jutías* are abundant, as are wild pigs, iguanas, and various species of lizards. A sign warns, *Prohibido Todo Tipo de Interacción Humana* (All Types of Human Interaction are Forbidden—with the animals, that is).

The reserve is split into the El Veral and Cabo de Corrientes nature reserves. Ironically, there's a hunting reserve—**Caza de Guanahacabibes**—within the park, where deer and wild boar can be felled.

There's an **ecological station** at the entrance, just before the military post at La Bajada. Osmany Borrego Fernández, who heads the station, speaks fluent English and will be happy to act as a guide.

Getting There: You must obtain a permit (US$10) from Villa María la Gorda before being granted access to the park. The road is rough *piste,* blazing white, underlain by coral, and covered in sand in places—so drive with care. For most of the way, the route is lined with thick scrub and palms. Stunning beaches lie hidden a stone's throw away, and there are always the calls of birds to enjoy. After 40 km or so, beyond Punta Hollandés, the road opens onto a barren coral platform, with various cactus species and fabulous views across the pellucid Caribbean.

Eventually, you reach Cabo San Antonio, the westernmost point of Cuba, dominated by a lighthouse (Faro Roncali) and a military post.

ISLA DE LA JUVENTUD
INTRODUCTION

Slung below the underbelly of Havana province, in the Gulf of Batabanó, Isla de la Juventud is the westernmost and by far the largest and most important island in the Archipiélago de los Cannareos (Archipelago of the Canaries). Isla de la Juventud (Isle of Youth) is a special municipality, not a province. Barely 70,000 people live on the island, half of them in Nueva Gerona, the administrative center and the only town of significance.

It is hardly an island paradise. There are no striking physical features and no lush tropical vegetation (the island was once smothered with native pine and became known at an early stage as the Isle of Pines). The entire southern half comprises brush and marsh that harbor wild boar, deer, jutias, and *Crocodilus rhombifer,* the endemic Cuban crocodile that is aggressive from the moment it emerges from its egg barely 20 cm long. Turtles also come ashore to deposit the seeds of tomorrow's turtles (if not, you can visit a turtle breeding center near Jacksonville).

The island appeals mostly to travelers seeking an offbeat escape. However, it has some of the finest diving in the Caribbean, several historical sites of importance, untapped nature reserves, and a fascinating contemporary history as the setting for the socialist experiment of International Youth Brigades (hence the island's name). The isle is dotted with boarding schools for foreign students from all over the world, though most are now closed. It's also one of Cuba's main scuba-diving destination (diving centers on the Bay of Siguanea and Punta Francés, on the clawlike southwest extremity of the island).

There is a fitting association between the island's history and the character of its people, who are called *pineros* and *pineras* and who refer to their island affectionately as *la islita.* (Even the local drink—a mix of grapefruit juice, white rum, and ice—is named like a resident, albeit in diminutive form—*pinerito.* It is consumed in the late afternoon as a remedy for the heat, but local lore says it's an aphrodisiac—all the more reason for a second one!) Isla de la Juventud has always had a bit of a Wild West feel, a legacy of its halcyon past as a pirate hangout and, in the mid-20th-century, a haven for the riff-raff, swindlers, and whores who frequented the free port at Neuva Gerona. It still revels in its reputation for going against the grain.

Isla de la Juventud can be explored fully in two days. Nuevo Gerona has plenty of snoozy colonial charm. And there are several sites of interest within a 10-km radius of town. You'll need transport to reach them. The Sierra del Casa, immediately southwest of town, harbor within their low hills three caves—**Cueva el Agua, Cueva El Indio,** and **Cueva del Hondón.** They're worth a peek for their stalagmites and stalactites. The caves were used by pre-Columbian Indians and contain a few faded petroglyphs. Ask a local to accompany you if you wish. He or she can guide you, too, to the nearby site where gray *marmól* (marble) is quarried—the island has Cuba's largest reserves of marble and a long tradition of working it into high-quality crockery and decorative pieces.

LAND

Isla de la Juventud is shaped like an inverted comma. At 3,050 square km, it is about the same size as Trinidad or Greater London. Most of the island is flat, with a hilly central core that reaches 310 meters in elevation. Marmoreal hills—the **Sierra de Caballo** and **Sierra de Casa**—flank the city of Nueva Gerona and rise to 280 and 233 meters, respectively.

The north is predominantly flat or rolling lowland, perfect for raising cattle in the east and citrus (especially pink grapefruit) in the west, where the fertile flatlands are irrigated by streams dammed to create reservoirs. The sweet smell of jasmine floats over the island Jan.-March, when the citrus groves are in bloom (although many were damaged by Hurricane Lili in 1996). Most of the south is composed of limestone smothered in scrubland and the marshy **Lanier Swamp,** which extends the full width of the island and is a habitat for an endangered population of crocodiles, wild pigs, and flocks of ducks and other waterfowl. Beautiful white sand beaches rim the south shore. There are no facilities, however, and your visit will be limited to a day excursion by virtue of legal restrictions.

Note: The entire southern half of the island is a military zone accessed by a single road. You must request a permit to visit any of the sites south of the latitude of Cayo Piedra.

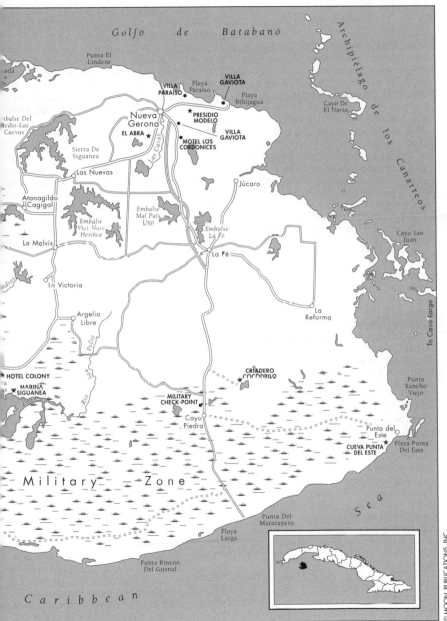

Golfo   de   Batabanó

Archipiélago   de   los   Canarreos

Punta El
Lindero

**VILLA
GAVIOTA**

Playa
Paraíso

**VILLA
PARAISO**

Playa
Bibijagua

Cayo De
El Navío

Nueva
Gerona

★ **PRESIDIO
MODELO**

EL ABRA ★

**VILLA
GAVIOTA**

Embalse Del
Medio-Las
Cuevas

●

**MOTEL LOS
CORDONICES**

Sierra De
Siguanea

Las Nuevas

Atanagildo
Cagigal

Júcaro

Embalse
Mal País
Uno

Cayo San
Juan

Embalse
Viet Nam
Heroíca

Embalse
La Fé

La Melvis

La Fé

To Cayo Largo

La Victoria

Argelia
Libre

La
Reforma

HOTEL COLONY ★

Punta
Rancho
Viejo

**MARINA
SIGUANEA** ★

**CRIADERO
COCODRILO**

**MILITARY
CHECK-POINT** ■

Cayo
Piedra

Punta del
Este

Playa Punta
Del Este

**CUEVA PUNTA
DEL ESTE** ★

Military   Zone

Sea

Punta Del
Maracayero

Playa
Larga

Punta Rincón
Del Guanal

Caribbean

© MOON PUBLICATIONS, INC.

HISTORY

The island was inhabited in pre-Columbian days by the Ciboney, whose legacy can be seen in cave paintings, most elaborately at Punta del Este, on the south coast. The early Indians knew the island as Sigueanea—the first of a dozen or so names given the island over the years. Columbus named it La Evangelista.

The island claims (unconvincingly) to be the setting for Robert Louis Stevenson's *Treasure Island* (not least because Stevenson's sketch-map of Treasure Island resembles the Isle of Youth). Pirates *did* use the isle as a base from which to plunder Spanish treasure ships and raid mainland cities. The southwestern shore is known as the Pirate Coast—a four-mile strip between Point Francés (after the French pirate François Leclerc) and Point Pedernales. The English pirate Henry Morgan even gave his name to one of the island's small towns. The pirates named it the Isle of Parrots, for the many endemic *cotorros*.

Although the Spanish established a fort to protect the passing treasure fleets, it remained a neglected backwater, and the first colony wasn't established until 1826, on the banks of the Río Las Casas. The Spanish military billeted its new recruits on the isle to escape the tropical diseases that plagued them on the mainland, and those already ill were sent here to regain their health at the mineral springs in Santa Fé. After the Santa Rita hotel was built, in 1860, tourists from North America began to arrive, including Samuel Hazard, who came for a bronchial cure in 1862 and wrote *Cuba with Pen and Pencil*.

Throughout the century, the Spanish used the island they had renamed Isla de los Pinos (Isle of Pines) as a prison for Cuban patriots. Its remote locale was convenient for banishing political prisoners, including national hero José Martí, who spent three months in exile here as part of a six-year sentence. This dark period lasted until Model Prison, which opened in 1931, slammed its doors shut in 1961.

Following the War of Independence, the Treaty of Paris, signed in 1898, left the island in legal limbo. Its status was undefined. Although the Platt Amendment in 1902 recognized Cuba's claim on the island, the US forbade any settlement by Cubans and only in 1925 did the island officially became part of the national territory. In consequence, Yankee real estate speculators bought much of the land and sold it for huge profits to gullible midwestern farmers who arrived expecting to find an agricultural paradise. The 300 or so immigrants established small communities and planted the first citrus groves, from which they eked out a meager living. (Settlers of English and Scottish descent from the Cayman Islands also arrived in the 19th century, and founded a turtle-hunting community called Jacksonville on the south coast. The island's intriguing meld also includes Chinese, Japanese, and African settlers.) Many US citizens stayed; their legacy can still be seen in the cemetery and the ruins of their settlement at Columbia, near the Model Prison, which President Gerardo Machado built in 1931 and in which Fidel Castro and 25 followers were later imprisoned following their abortive attack on the Moncada barracks.

The US Navy established a naval base here during World War II and turned the Model Prison into a concentration camp for Axis prisoners. In the postwar years, wealthy Cubans sold land to another generation of US citizens, who used it this time for vacation homes. By the 1950s, the island had become a favored vacation spot (at its peak, 10 flights a day touched down from Miami), and gambling and prostitution were staples. The Hotel Colony (built as a personal investment and private playground by Fulgencio Batista) even had its own abortion clinic.

On the eve of the Revolution, the island's population totaled at most 10,000 people. The Castro government immediately launched a settlement campaign and planted citrus, which today extends over 25,000 hectares, fringed by tall pines and mango trees for windbreaks. (The Revolution, of course, killed the travel trade stone dead.) Thousands of young Cubans went to work "voluntary laborers" in the citrus groves. In 1971, the first of over 60 schools was established for foreign students—primarily from Africa, Nicaragua, Yemen, and North Korea—who formed what were called International Work Brigades and came to learn the Cuban method of work-study. The Cuban government paid the bill (in exchange, the foreign students joined Cuban students in the citrus plantations for the September-December harvest). Together, the young adults helped turn the island into a major producer of citrus. To honor them, in 1978 the Isle of Pines was formally renamed the Isle of Youth. At the height of Cuba's internationalist phase, more than 150,000 foreign students were studying on the island.

The Special Period dealt the international schools a deathblow. The number of foreign students rapidly dwindled, and most of the schools have been abandoned. At press time, the last foreign students were finishing their terms.

NUEVA GERONA AND VICINITY

Nueva Gerona (pop. 30,000) lies a few km inland from the north coast along the west bank of the Río Las Casas. It's a port town and exports primarily marble and citrus. Several times daily, Russian-built hydrofoils come roaring up the mouth of the river, riding high on their thin foils like creations from a Flash Gordon movie. The hydrofoils and daily ferry slice past mangrove-covered cays, then rusting factories and a fist-ful of rickety hydrofoils raised on stilts in dry dock, with others tied at berth alongside a boat up wharf.

The city, however, is surprisingly cosmopolitan for its size and reclusive position and even has a certain air of relative prosperity. The presence of foreign students has lent its own vitality. Despite the relative youth of its edifices, downtown Nueva Gerona is distinctly colonial. The historical core along Calle 39 (Calle Martí) was recently restored with fresh pink tile and pastel paints and is very beautiful.

SIGHTS

Presidio Modelo
The island's most interesting attraction—the Model Prison—is five km east of Nueva Gerona. It was built 1926-31 by President Machado and was designed—on the model of the penitentiary at Joliet, Illinois—on a "panopticon" plan that called for circular buildings that put prisoners under constant surveillance. The prison was designed to house 6,000 inmates in four five-story circular buildings, with 93 cells and two beds in each (considerably more prisoners were crammed in). At the center of each rondel was a watchtower, with slits for viewing prisoners. A fifth circular building, in the center, housed the mess hall, dubbed, because talking was prohibited, The Place of 3,000 Silences. The last prisoner went home in 1967, and only the shells remain.

Nueva Gerona

CHRISTOPHER P. BAKER

Prisoners followed a severe regimen, made worse by the wickedness of trusties, prisoners given preferential treatment and who were permitted all kinds of wanton excesses with fellow inmates. Prisoners were awoken at 5 a.m.; lights out *(silencio)* was at 9 p.m.

The two oblong buildings that now house the museum were used during World War II to intern Japanese-Cubans and Germans captured in Cuban waters. In 1953, one of the buildings housed Fidel Castro and 25 other revolutionaries sentenced to imprisonment here following the attack on the Moncada barracks. They lived apart from the other prisoners and were privileged. Castro used his time here to good effect. Batista foolishly allowed him to set up a revolutionary school—the Abel Santamaría Academy—where the group studied economics, revolutionary theory, and guerrilla tactics. On 15 May 1955, the revolutionaries were released to much fanfare.

You approach an impressive neocolonial façade with a stairway of local marble that leads up to the old administrative building (now a hobby center and school for UJotaCE, the Young Communists). The rondels and museum are in back and are reached by following the perimeter road to the left. Follow it all the way around to the back.

The first wing of the museum contains black-and-white photos and memorabilia from the Machado era. Another wing was the hospital, where Fidel Castro and his 25 compatriots were imprisoned. Their beds are still in place, with a black-and-white photo of each prisoner on the wall. Fidel's bed is next to last, on the left, facing the door as you enter. The school run by Fidel—the Academía Ideológica Abel Santamaría—is cordoned off; it amounts to three long tables and a blackboard. A third wing tells the history of the Moncadistas and Castro's denunciations written while in prison.

Immediately to the left of the entrance is the pastel blue room where Fidel—prisoner RN3859—was later kept in solitary confinement. It's surprisingly large (about 400 square feet), with a lofty ceiling, marble seats, and a spacious marble bathroom with shower of gleaming white tiles. Fidel had it good! A glass case contains some of his favorite books.

The museum is open Tues.-Sat. 9 a.m.-5 p.m. and Sunday 9 a.m.-1 p.m. Entrance costs

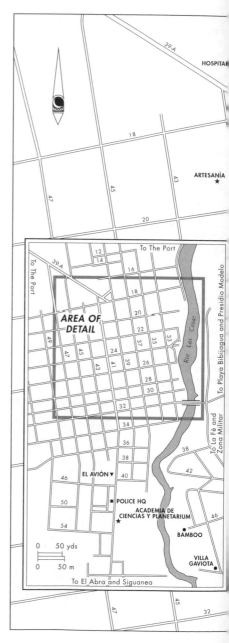

US$1. No photos are permitted inside the museum building.

Around Town

Nueva Gerona proper has no edifices that draw your attention, although Calle 39 is lined with attractive colonial buildings. The node is **Parque Guerrillero Heróico** (between Calles 28 and 30), a wide-open plaza facing a pretty, ocher-colored colonial church, **Nuestra Señora de los Dolores,** erected in 1929 in Mexican colonial style.

The rather grandly named **Academía de Ciencias y Planetarium** is actually a small natural history museum, on Calle 41 one-half mile south of town. It has splendid little displays of endemic flora and fauna in re-creations of native habitats. Watch out—that boa constrictor *(maja de Santa María)* suspended in the tree above your head is over 10 feet long! There's even a small re-creation of the Cueva Punta del Este with crude renditions of humankind's evolution from ape to *Homo sapiens.* The adjoining planetarium hosts occasional demonstrations explaining the heavens. Both the museum and planetarium are open Tues.-Thurs. 8 a.m.-6 p.m., Friday 2-10 p.m., Saturday 1-5 p.m., and Sunday 9 a.m-1 p.m. Entrance costs US$1.

El Pinero is the large and handsome ferry that carried Fidel and his fellow revolutionaries to freedom following their release from imprisonment on the Isle of Pines. The vessel sits on stilts beside the riverbank, between Calles 26 and 28. It lies inert, awaiting the day when it will be restored and opened as a museum.

Near *El Pinero* is a life-size statue of **Ubre blanca,** a locally raised dairy cow that broke world milk-production records and has been immortalized in local marble next to the children's playground (Parque Diversiones) on Calles 28 and 37. Also of interest is the **Centro de Desarrollo de las Artes Visuales,** in a pretty colonial house on Calle 39. Take time to sit in the little plaza next to the *centro;* it features a beautiful ceramic mural and intriguing ceramic seats of a pointillist design. Also worth a visit is the **marble factory** on Calle 24 e/ Calles 55 y 57, where huge gray marble blocks brought down from the nearby mountains are cut and polished.

If you haven't had your fill of revolutionary history, check out the **Museo de los Clandestinos,** at the corner of Calles 24 and 45. It's open Tues.-Sun. 1-9 p.m. and costs US$1.

Playa Bibijagua and Playa Paraíso

Playa Paraíso, five km east of Nueva Gerona, has an attractive white sand beach—overgrown, alas, with seagrass. Another three km brings you to Playa Bibijagua, billed as a black sand beach. It isn't black but rather a narrow sliver of dirty gray sand fringed by a row of palms. The French pirate Latrobe reportedly buried his treasure here, and a chest was, in fact, uncovered here this century—but it was empty. Buses serve the beaches from Nueva Gerona.

El Abra

This farmstead, splendidly nestled in the lee of the Sierra Las Casa two km south of Nueva Gerona, is associated with José Martí, who lived here briefly in 1870 after being sentenced to six years' imprisonment for sedition at the age of 18. After a brief spell in prison on the mainland, Martí was released into the custody of José Sardá (a family friend and respected Catalonian landowner) at El Abra. Martí remained for only three months before departing for exile in Spain in December 1870.

The museum is reached by a long driveway shaded by Cuban oak trees. At the end is the farmhouse, still a family home, with a large bronze bust of Martí outside. The exhibits are in the simple, thatched building to the right and include personal belongings, documents, and other artifacts of Martí's life. The museum is open Tues.-Sat. 9 a.m.-5 p.m. and Sunday 9 am.-1 p.m.

ACCOMMODATIONS

The tourist hotels are outside town. You can easily find a *casa particular* in town, however. I stayed with a wonderful couple in a house near the town center for US$15 a day, including room, filling meals, and superb company. Ask around.

The only hotel in town, the **Hotel La Cubanita,** tel. 23512, is a spartan place. The a/c rooms cost 11 pesos s, 15 d. It has traditionally been adamantly inflexible in not accepting foreigners but will no doubt change now that the students are gone.

About one km southeast of town is **Bamboo**, a run-down facility with basic bungalows centered on a small pool. Rooms cost 15 pesos d.

Your best bet is the **Motel Los Cordonices**, tel. 24981, one of the better hotels geared to Cubans. Its 43 a/c rooms are modest but acceptable, with double beds and telephones (11 pesos s, 15 d, 19 t). I was told that these prices apply for foreigners; if that's true, this is one of the best bargains in Cuba—50 cents a room! There's a restaurant and bar, and cabaret by the pool, which has a wide sundeck. It's five km southeast of Nueva Gerona.

The **Rancho del Tesoro**, near Motel Los Cordonices, used to charge in pesos. It was closed for renovation in spring 1996, and the modest bungalows were being upgraded for tourists.

There's a **Carpeta de Reservaciones Campismo**, tel. 24517, for the *campismo* at Playa Bibijagua. At press time, it didn't accept foreigners, but try your luck. The basic cabins cost seven pesos d, 14 quad.

At Playa Paraíso, **Villa Paraíso** is a basic Cuban *campismo*. The manager says it "might be possible" for foreigners to stay here. The small ranchitas cost 17 pesos s, 25 d. It has a pleasant little restaurant.

Villa Gaviota, Autopista Gerona-La Fé Km 1.5, tel. 23290, two km and a 20-minute walk southeast of town, is an attractive little property. The 20 a/c rooms are pleasingly furnished and look out upon a pool to which Cubans flock on weekends. Each room has marble floors, TV, telephone, refrigerator, and hot water. The staff is friendly. Rates are US$30 s, US$35 d in high season (US$5 less in low season)

FOOD

The town is far better served by restaurants than other provincial towns. You'll find a selection of atmospheric eateries along Calle 39. If you rent a *casa particular*, however, your host will probably feed you—usually far better than you can expect at restaurants.

Restaurante Dragon, on Calle 39 one block north of the church, has a chop suey special (US$6) and other quasi-Chinese dishes. The restaurant has romantic atmosphere with a strong Chinese flavor (the staff are Chinese-Cubans). Continuing south on Calle 39, you reach **Restaurante El Cochinito**, tel. 22809,which specializes in pork dishes, especially roast suckling pig; it's open 2-10 p.m. The **Restaurante El Corderito**, on the corner of Calles 39 and 22, tel. 22400, was closed for restoration at press time. It specializes in lamb dishes.

For an unusual venue, try **El Avión**, Calle 41 e/ Calles 38 y 40, where mediocre snacks and *criollo* meals are served inside an old Cubana aircraft at

On the eastern fringe of town, on the road to Playa Negrita, is **Parque Ahao**, an atmospheric thatched restaurant that serves *criollo* food and has nightly entertainment.

Basic pizzas cost five pesos per slice at **Pizzeria Isola**, at the corner of Calles 30 and 35. Fried chicken and other fast foods are sold in the courtyard of Centro Comercial, on Calle 33. If you're wilting under the heat, head to **Coppelia** (at the corner of Calle 32 and 37) for delicious ice cream. You can pay in pesos or dollars (inordinately more expensive).

You can buy fresh produce from the **mercado agropecuarias** at Calles 24 and 35, and on Calle 41 at the south end of town. Western packaged food items are available from the dollars-only supermarket on Calle 30, one block southeast of the main square.

ENTERTAINMENT AND EVENTS

Nueva Gerona has more night spots than usual in Cuba, thanks to the presence of foreign students. A list of venues offering live music is posted outside the Centro Municipal de la Música, at Calles 18 and 39. Don't forget to lather on the mosquito repellent before venturing out at night.

Watch for performances by Mongo Rivas and his relatives, who form **La Tumbita Crilla**, masters of the compelling dance rhythm *sucusuco*, born here early last century and deeply rooted in the island's culture. The word comes from the onomatopoeic sound of feet moving to its infectious rythm (North American settlers at the beginning of the century called it "shuck-shuck"). The group sometimes welcomes guests at Nuevo Gerona airport and travels the island.

Several venues feature *espectáculo musicales*. **Cabaret El Patio** is the best, with a comedian, singers, and dance routines on a stage made up like a cave with walls of silver foil. The show is a great value at five pesos (beers cost four pesos—US$1 for foreigners). You may be able to slip in for this price, but you should probably expect to have to pay US$5 (for which, however, the waitress kept bringing free beers to my table the last time I went). Also try the **Cabaret Los Luceros,** on Calle 20, beside the river.

Cine Caribe, on the east side of the main square, charges two pesos and shows mostly out-of-date Hollywood movies.

Of bars and discos, one of the liveliest spots is **Club Juvenil,** on Calle 37 e/ Calle 26 y 28. There's a disco most nights in the **Cabaret El Patio** and **Cabaret Los Luceros.**

Casa de las Mieles, on Calle 39 e/ Calles 22 y 24, is a very pretty cocktail bar with a shady terra-cotta terrace; it serves *miel*, aguardiente, and rum drinks. It adjoins the equally attractive **Café Nuevo** (open 10 a.m.-10 p.m.), which has live music.

Local youth gather to socialize around Parque Central, where live salsa and pop bands perform on weekends. Also try **Café de Cuba,** at Calle 39 and 22, where locals get in the groove in the open courtyard, and **Pachanga Pinalera,** at Calles 24 and 35. **Restaurante El Cochinito** also has nightly entertainment, as does **Parque Ahao.**

The **Citrus Festival** (Festival de la Toronja) seems to have died. Traditionally held at Christmas, it featured a carnival atmosphere, with theatrical skits performed by foreign and Cuban students.

SHOPPING

The gallery of **Fonda Cubana de Bienes Culturales,** on Calle 39, sells leather shoes and beautiful ceramics, including the colorful ceramic tiles with relief decorations for which Nueva Gerona's potters are famous. The artisans also create African deities, diminuitive parrots, crocodiles, and exquisite grapefruits in ceramic. Other artists chisel precious majagua, acana, or oak into images of pirates hiding their

booty. You can watch ceramics being made at the workshop at Calles 34 and 55. Another *artesanía*, at Calle 41 e/ Calles 18 y 20, specializes in woodcarvings and jewelry of semi-precious stones.

Librería Frank País, on Calle 39, has the usual stock of Spanish-language books touting socialist theory, but little else.

The dollars-only **Centro Comercial,** on the southeast corner of the main plaza, has a *diplotienda* selling clothing, toiletries, etc. **Photo Service** has a store at 2010 José Martí selling a meager assortment of batteries and film.

INFORMATION AND SERVICES

The old **Buro de Turismo** (still shown on tourist maps), on Calle 39, no longer exists, having been replaced by a tourist office in the Villa Gaviota, outside town.

There's a **Banco Nacional** at the corner of Calles 39 and 18. It's simple to change foreign currency into Cuban pesos on the streets of Nueva Gerona.

The main **post office** is on Calle 39 and Calle 18. **DHL** has an office at Calle 39 #2201, tel. 22331. It's open weekdays 9 a.m.-6 p.m. and Saturday 8:30 a.m.-noon. The Centro Telefónico is on the corner of Calles 41 and 28. You might have to wait in line. Far easier is to make a call from the Villa Gaviota.

The **Hospital Héroes de Baire** is at Calles 18 and 41. It offers no special service for foreigners. For minor ailments, you can seek treatment at the **policlínicos** at Calles 18 and 47 and Calles 24 and 33. There's a **pharmacy** in the hospital

NUEVA GERONA USEFUL TELEPHONE NUMBERS

Police	tel. 116
Ambulance	tel. 2-4170
Hospital	tel. 2-3012
Airport	tel. 2-2300
Rail Reservations (to Havana)	tel. 2-4748
Ferry Reservations	tel. 2-4406
Omnibus Reservations	tel. 2-4425

and another on the corner of Calles 39 and 24. The **police station** is one km south of town, on Calle 41.

There's a **Cupet gas station** on the southest corner of the main square, at Calles 39 and 30.

CRIME AND SAFETY

In 1996, my hosts in Nueva Gerona warned me in earnest not to walk the streets at night: *"Muy peligroso!"* (Very unsafe!). But I had no problems, and I suspect their concerns are mostly unfounded. Nueva Gerona does have a reputation for petty theft, however—partly because of the presence of so many foreign students, many of whom are comparatively wealthy. Avoid unlit alleys at night, and take good care of your wallet in nightclubs.

My hosts seemed particularly concerned about *jiniteras* from the mainland who have flocked to the island to prey on foreign students. It seems that many of the wily women are prone to dispensing *miel* (a sweet honey wine that is a specialty of the island) laced with a knock-out drug. The poor Casanova wakes up to find his valuables gone along, of course, with the woman, who has slipped back to the mainland on the early-morning hydrofoil.

GETTING THERE

Take your passport. You'll need it to travel to the Isle of Youth.

By Air

Cubana operates two flights daily (US$20 one-way) from Havana, at 7:15 a.m. and 7:55 p.m., using 44-seat Russian-built AN-24s. Additional flights depart on Monday and Friday at 9:30 a.m. and Tues.-Thurs. at 6:15 p.m. Flights take 40 minutes and land at Rafael Cabrera Airport, tel. 61-22690, 15 km south of Neuva Gerona. Arrive early for check-in. Demand always outstrips supply, and if you're late, your seat will be given to someone else. For the same reason, it's best to book a roundtrip ticket. **Aerocaribbean** also operates charter flights from Havana and Varadero. And **Aerotaxi** operates flights in Rusian biplanes between Nueva Gerona and Pinar del

Río on Monday, Wednesday, and Friday ($20 one-way). You'll need to arrive early to sign up on the waiting list (no reservations).

On the island, a bus marked *Servicio Aereo* connects flights with downtown Nueva Gerona, stopping at hotels en route (one peso). The bus to the airport departs from outside Cine Caribe.

There's a small airstrip at Siguanea that serves the Hotel Colony. A flight departs daily from Nueva Gerona to Siguanea. **Aerogaviota** offers day excursions from Varadero.

By Sea

By Ferry: A 500-passenger ferry *(barco)* departs Surgidero de Batabanó, on the mainland, 70 km south of Havana, at 7:30 p.m. and arrives Nuevo Gerona about 1:30 a.m. at the ferry terminal on Calle 31 e/ Calles 22 y 24. Officially, the ferry (US$10 one-way) departs on Wednesday, Friday, and Sunday, but it seems to be operating daily in the spring. Your baggage is thoroughly searched before boarding. Horse-drawn taxis wait outside the ferry terminal, which is a 10-minute walk from downtown. You shouldn't pay more than US$1 for a buggy, but with luck you'll be charged in pesos.

You can catch a connecting bus from Havana from the **Terminal de Ferries-Vapores,** at Avenida Kohly and Avenida 26, near the zoo in Nuevo Vedado, tel. 81-1108.

By Hydrofoil: Far quicker is the journey aboard the Russian-built *Kometa* hydrofoil from Surgidero de Batabanó. The sturdy, but time-worn, 106-passenger hydrofoils (called *lanchas cometas* locally and *hidrodeslizadores* officially) depart Batabanó at 10 a.m. and 4p.m. and arrive Nuevo Gerona two hours later. The fare is now a whopping US$15 for foreigners.

Seats are aircraft-type recliners—appropriately, as the journey resembles a turbulent airplane ride. You're served a Spam *bocadito* (sandwich) and a *refresco*.

I strongly recommend buying return *(regreso)* tickets when you purchase your outbound journey *(ida)* tickets. You can buy tickets the same day at the ticket office at the end of the pier in Batabanó, or in advance at the Terminal de Ferries-Vapores. Five seats are reserved for foreigners on the *Kometa,* as are 20 seats on the ferry. However, these are quickly taken up by foreign students commuting to and from the island. If you're foreigner number six, tough luck! Thus you need to ensure you buy your ticket well ahead of time. The ticket office opens at 2:30 p.m. for the *Kometa* and 6 p.m. for the ferry. There's a waiting room and small bar selling *bocaditos*.

By Private Vessel: Private vessels can berth upstream of the hydrofoil terminal, in amongst the rusting tugboats. Few private boats arrive here (most dock at Siguanea), and arrival and departure proceedings are said to be less fluid than other ports.

Taking a Vehicle: You can ship your car or motorbike aboard a flatbed barge towed by a tug (you, however, will have to take either the ferry or *Kometa* and meet the barge in Nueva Gerona). The loading dock is next to the ferry terminal in Batabanó. You'll need to register your vehicle soon after 1 p.m. at the tiny office at the beginning of the pier in Batabanó (the barge sails at 7 p.m., but when I tried to register at 4 p.m. I was turned away and had to return next day). Cars cost US$20 each way, motorbikes US$4.40. The barge arrives in Nueva Gerona at 7 a.m. the following day, docking two km north of the ferry terminal.

GETTING AROUND

Nueva Gerona is small enough that you can walk most places comfortably. Bus service in town is limited, although buses operate to most areas of the island. There are no rail services.

The cheapest way of getting around is by **horse-drawn buggy.** They congregate around the main square and by the ferry terminal when boats arrive. Foreigners are often charged in dollars, but you can often protest to good effect. If not, US$2 will take you anywhere you want to go. **Licensed taxis** (many of them Mercedes jeeps) congregate at the corner of Calles 32 and 39, where a dispatcher controls things, often filling taxis brimful. Demand has eased up in recent years, however, with the improved availability of gasoline, and you can hire a taxi for personal sightseeing quite easily.

Bicycling is a great way to get around town. **Bicycle rentals** are offered at Villa Gaviota. Take plenty of water to combat dehydration. The road network is well developed, and most main roads are in good condition, deteriorating to gravel and dirt towards the boondocks.

Havanautos has a rental car agency next to the Cupet station at the corner of Calles 39 and 32 and another at Villa Gaviota.

On ther other hand, it's easy to transport your own vehicle from the mainland (see above).

GETTING AWAY

By Air
Cubana's flights depart for Havana daily at 8:15 a.m. and 8:55 p.m. (and additionally on Monday and Friday at 12:10 p.m. and Tues.-Thurs. at 5:30 p.m.). Cubana has an office next to the Hotel La Cubanita on Calle 39, tel. 24259. It's open Mon.-Thurs. 8 a.m.-noon and 1-4 p.m. and Friday 1-3 p.m. Although the situation continues to ease, demand exceeds supply. You should book your flight as far in advance as possible.

By Sea
By Ferry: The ferry departs Nueva Gerona at 10 a.m. and arrives Batabanó at 4 p.m. (US$8 one way). The ticket office is inside the ferry terminal, to the right of the entrance. Usually there are two *colas* (although "scrum" might be more correct); the right side is for advance tickets, the left is for same-day tickets.

By Hydrofoil: The hydrofoil leaves Nueva Gerona at 7 a.m. and 1 p.m. Buy your ticket the

Kometa *hydrofoils in dry dock*

day before. If you have to wait, there's a little snack bar that sells sandwiches of puréed ham (yummy!), plus *refrescos* and sweet mint tea.

Shipping Vehicles: The barge carrying cars and other vehicles departs Nueva Gerona at 6 p.m., arriving Batabanó next day at 7 a.m. You'll need to register your vehicle between 2 and 5 p.m.

Bus/Train Connections to Havana: You can buy advance tickets for the connecting bus or train from Batabanó to Havana (US$3) at the ferry terminal in Nueva Gerona. The booth is inside, to the left as you enter the terminal. Advance reservations can be made up to five days in advance in Batabanó or up to two hours prior to departure in the Havana station.

AROUND THE ISLAND

Calle 41 (formerly Avenida Abraham Lincoln) exits Nueva Gerona and leads south past El Abra to Siguanea, 30 km away. En route, you'll pass many international schools and modest agricultural communities surrounded by scrubland, poorly tended citrus orchards, and numerous man-made lakes. (Most of the island's meager rivers were dammed to create reservoirs to provide irrigation for the citrus crops; some are stocked with bass.)

About 10 km south of **Las Nuevas,** a turnoff leads west, ruler-straight via Atanagildo Cagigal to **Playa Buenavista,** a beach shown on maps as a resort but not worth the drive.

Continuing south from Las Neuvas, you pass a turnoff for the new town of **La Victoria.** Beyond **Siguanea** (a small community surrounded by scrubland), the road ends at Playa Rojas, facing the Bahía de Siguanea.

BAY OF SIGUEANEA

This bay is the site of Columbus' landing on 13 June 1494. Later, it was a favored harbor for pirates. There are numerous beaches, but most are hemmed in by mangroves; only **Playa Rojas** is accessible by road. Playa Rojas is the setting for the island's premier resort hotel, the Hotel Colony. In early 1996, sea grasses were taking over, especially below the waterline.

The shores of the bay are almost entirely uninhabited, except by rare wildlife and not-so-rare mosquitoes, which snooze during the day but are hungry and fierce by evening. Take repellent!

Refugio de Fauna los Indios

Much of the shore of the bay is a 4,000-hectare reserve protecting an extremely fragile environment that includes mangroves, savanna, and endemic pines and palms. There are at least 60 endemic floral species, 15 of them limited to this particular spot (14 are endangered, including a species of carnivorous plant). The 153 species of birds include three endemic species, including the endangered Cuban sandbill crane *(Grus canadensis nesiotes),* called *la grulla,* and the lovable *cotorro*—the equally threatened Cuban parrot *(Amazona leucocephala),* which you may recognize from pirate movies, sitting on the shoulders of corsairs—which resides here in greater numbers than anywhere else in Cuba. A good time to visit is May and June, when you can see young parrots learning to fly and chattering endlessly. There are also at least six species of endemic reptiles, plus an endemic bullfrog and tiny frog species. *Jutía* (large guinea-pig-like rodents) are also abundant.

The reserve extends along the shore and inland north of the Hotel Colony and is centered on Punta Los Indios. Rough trails lead into the reserve from La Victoria and Siguanea, but the easiest access is by boat excursion from the hotel (US$25).

Organized Excursions: Alcona S.A., tel. 22-2526, fax 33-1532, includes a one-day visit to Los Indios as part of three-day ecotour package (US$512). Reportedly there's a rustic pensión for visitors.

Scuba Diving

The bay is a renowned scuba-diving site and the setting for the annual Fotosub underwater photography competition. There are 56 dive sites concentrated along **La Costa de los Piratas** (The Pirate Coast), whose tranquil waters are protected from the Gulf Stream currents. The sites extend along a 10-mile axis just offshore between Punta Pedernales and Punta Francés. Off Punta Francés, the basin's wall begins at depths of 60 to 90 feet and plummets into the deeps of the Gulf of Mexico.

Huge coral parapets loom out over the cobalt abyss below. (Site 39 is renowned for the **Caribbean Cathedral,** said to be the tallest coral column in the world.) The wall is laced with canyons, caves, and grottoes. Two sites of particular interest are **Black Coral Wall,** with massive black coral formations, and **Stingray Paradise,** where you may stroke and feed these friendly fish.

Galleons and Wrecks: A naval battle between Thomas Baskerville's pirate ships and a Spanish fleet resulted in many ships being sunk near Siguanea. And a cluster of partially submerged freighters invite exploration amid the shallows. The wrecks were scuttled several decades ago to provide bombing and naval gunnery targets for the Cuban armed forces. Northeast of Punta Francés, between the cape and Cayo Los Indios, are three well-preserved Spanish galleons close together. A local star is Lola, a friendly five-foot-long barracuda that reportedly will even accept food from your hand.

International Scuba Diving Center: The Centro Internacional del Buceo is at Marina El Colony, 1.5 km south of the Hotel Colony. Puertosol offers dives for US$30 (US$56 for two; US$35 for a night dive). A full certification course costs US$175. The hotel also has a special package with 20 dives (two dives daily) for only US$200. It offers specialized courses for beginners, as well as night diving and underwater video courses for experienced divers.

The facility has a large hyperbaric chamber, plus a scuba shop that sells and rents gear. There are 25 boats equipped for diving, and 26 scuba instructors.

If you arrive in your own vessel and have your own scuba gear, you're still required to hire a dive guide, as the bay lies within the military zone (there's supposedly a submarine base).

Wings of the World 1200 William St. #706, Buffalo, NY 14240, tel. (800) 465-8687, offers weeklong scuba diving tours to Isla de la Juventud from the USA (US$1,995 including airfare).

Accommodations

The **Hotel Colony,** Carretera de Siguanea, tel. 98181, is a 1950s-style hotel—it had been open a mere 23 days when Fidel kicked its owner, Fulgencio Batista, out of the country—surrounded by lush vegetation and surrounding an amoeba-shaped pool. It has 77 a/c rooms with private baths, telephones, radios, and TVs. Some guidebooks praise it highly, but I don't find it particularly endearing. Watersports include sea kayaks, banana-boat rides, catamarans (all US$10 per hour), and water-skiing (US$1.50 per minute). A narrow pier leads out to the Mojito Bar, a restaurant of modest appeal. Since you're a captive market, bar drinks are expensive. You can overcome this by buying a bottle of rum at the shop. If you want to go out on the town, there's nothing for miles and miles. Rental cars are available, as are bicycles (US$2.50 per hour) and scooters. Rates vary by season—US$44/53 s, US$56/70 d (low/high season).*Cabañas* cost US$77/88. Suites are US$88/105. Excursions are offered to the crocodile farm (US$12) and by biplane to Cayo Largo (US$89).

Puertosol offers a day excursion to the Hotel Colony from Havana or Varadero for US$79, including snorkeling.

Yachting and Sportfishing

Marina El Colony, tel. 619-8282, fax 33-5212, has 15 berths with electricity, water, gas, and diesel. Berthing fees are about US40 cents per foot. If this is your first international arrival, you'll have a long wait for the officials to travel down from Nueva Gerona. Anyone sailing eastward from Pinar del Río should keep a sharp eye out for lobster pots and fishing nets.

Deep-sea fishing trips are offered from the marina for US$150. You can also fish for bonefish and tarpon in inner waters from a *lancha* (small boat) for US$17.

Puertosol offers "seafaris" to Ranchón (US$15), Los Indios (US$25), and Cayo Coco (US$25). It also has excursions to Pinar del Río (US$149) and elsewhere.

LA FÉ

A fast Autopista runs south from Nueva Gerona to La Fé, an agricultural town that was founded by US citizens and originally called Santa Fé. Some of their plantation-style houses still stand around the main square. The overpowering presence today, however, is the modern concrete two-story apartment blocks of Soviet inspiration (or lack of it).

The road continues east to **La Reforma,** an agricultural center in the midst of dairy cattle country.

CRIADERO COCODRILO

Isla de la Juventud's second worthy attraction is this crocodile breeding farm, which has over 500 crocodiles of varying ages. Head honcho Oneldi Flores will happily lead you around, beginning with the pens for juveniles (the crocs are separated by age, as older crocs are cannibalistic).

A trail leads to natural lagoons where larger boats swim freely amid the water hyacinths. You'll hear them plopping into the water as you approach. Others stick their ground and eye you leerily.

Fortunately, the lagoons are rimmed with wire fences. Be cautious, however, as it's possible to chance upon stray crocodiles on the pathway, and they'll strike at anything that moves rather than turn tail.

The juveniles feast upon the remains of sardines and lobster, while the full grown monsters are fed hacked-up cattle. Vultures sit in the treetops nearby, waiting patiently to seize their share (others pick at the bloody horns laid out for them behind the main facility). Feeding time is usually between 9 and 10 a.m.

The oldest and biggest male is a mean-looking sexagenarian giant who guards his harem jealously. Oneldi will probably prod the big beast with a branch to get him pissed off—have your camera ready to capture the crocodile's lunge!

There are no facilities. Bring your own sodas. Entrance is US$1. Tip your guide.

The farm is 30 km south of Nueva Gerona, about five km north of Cayo Piedra. Look for a blindingly white alabaster road to the left just beyond Pino Alto. Follow the winding dirt road about five km past scrub and swamp. There are no signs.

THE MILITARY ZONE

The entire Isla de la Juventud south of Cayo Piedra along its east-west parallel is a military zone and out of bounds except for permit-holders. There's a checkpoint just south of Cayo Piedra. It's easy, however, to get a permit; they're arranged through the tourist bureau at Villa Gaviota. You'll need to take your permit to the MININT office (dockside in Nueva Gerona, just south of Calle 16) to register and receive an official stamp; otherwise, the guard will turn you back at the checkpoint at Cayo Piedra. It's obligatory, too, to be accompanied by a guide (US$15 per day), which the tourist bureau also arranges.

The entire region is covered in scrawny bush and marshland favored by hunters hoping to bag a wild pig or mourning doves and white-crowned pigeons in hunting preserves south of Siguanea and near Punta del Este. Hunting trips can be arranged through the Villa Gaviota or Hotel Colony.

The south coast is lined with glorious beaches whose sugar-white sands slope down to calm turquoise waters protected by an offshore reef Alas, there's not even a crude *ranchita* restaurant or snack bar. Take lunch and sodas along.

Cueva Punta del Este

From Cayo Piedra, a dirt road leads east 20 km through the Cienaga de Lanier swamp to Punta del Este. The route isn't marked and there are various bifurcations. There's a beautiful beach here, but the main attraction is the group of caves containing important aboriginal petroglyphs on the roofs and walls. The caves are together considered Cuba's Sistine Chapel of rupestrian art—238 pictographs in perfect condition. The paintings date from about AD 800 and are apparently among the most important aboriginal petroglyphs in the Antilles. They weren't discovered until early this century, by a French sailor who was shipwrecked nearby.

The petroglyphs, which display a high level of "geometric abstraction," seem to form a celestial plan thought to represent the passage of days and nights in the cult calendar. Among them are 28 concentric circles of red and black, pierced by a red arrow of two parallel lines and thought to represent the lunar month. Other symbols show crude crosses. Each day the sun's rays enter through the portal of the most important cave. As the sun follows its astral route, it illuminates different sections of the mural. On 22 March, when spring begins, the sun appears in the very center of the cave entrance, revealing a red phallus penetrating a group of concentric circles on the back wall, an obvious allusion to procreation.

Renditions of the petroglyphs are reproduced at the Museum of Natural Science in Havana.

Cayo Piedra to Punta Francés

The road south from Cayo Piedra leads directly to **Playa Larga,** a real stunner of a beach where you may be tempted to linger a lifetime. Five km before the beach is a turnoff to the right that leads west 28 km to Punta Francés, at the tip of the peninsula that forms the claw of Isla de la Juventud. Unfortunately, the road runs inland from the shore for most of the way, with only occasional glimpses of the beautiful shoreline. You should stop off en route at the lighthouse *(faro)* at the very southernmost tip near Punta Rincón del Guanal.

A few isolated farmers and fishermen eke a living from this austere land. Many are descendants of immigrants who arrived from the Cayman Islands over a century ago; a lilting Caribbean English is still spoken.

The road to Punta Francés passes the tiny seaside communities of **Jacksonville,** (named for Atkin Jackson, who founded the hamlet in 1904 and whose descendants still live here), **Cocodrilo,** and **Caleta Grande,** where the English-language tradition remains strong. There's a **Marine Science Station and Turtle Breeding Center** at Caleta Grande. Although Cuba has established stringent regulations on hunting and killing turtles, the laws are rarely honored or enforced (you'll see turtle carapaces and heads for sale all over Cuba). The breeding center is making an effort to save the turtle populations and has about 6,000 green and hawksbill turtles.

Farther west you'll find perfect, lonesome beaches such as **Playa El Francés,** where Spanish galleons and coral formations await scuba divers a short distance from shore.

Getting There: It's a full-day drive from Nueva Gerona and back. A taxi from Nueva Gerona will cost US$65 per day. Alternately you can rent a car from Villa Gaviota or Havanautos for about the same price. Excursions are offered at the Hotel Colony.

ARCHIPIÉLAGO DE LOS CANARREOS

To the east of Isla de la Juventud are several dozen tiny, uninhabited, low-lying islands sprinkled like diamonds across a sapphire sea. Most of the islands in this 160-km-long paternoster are gilt by beaches of purest white and haloed by barrier reefs guaranteeing bathtub-warm waters and endless satisfaction for divers. For now, tourism development is limited to Cayo Largo, the easternmost island—and the only one accessible from the mainland. Cayo Rico, a tiny speckle just west of Cayo Largo, is slated for imminent development. To date, it has only a rustic restaurant serving lobster and seafood.

Cayo Largo is eminently appealing to those seeking a sun, sea, and sand vacation with no interest in interacting with or understanding local culture.

The cays, of course, are a scuba diver's delight. In addition to astounding coral formations, some 200 shipwrecks have been reported in the Canarreos. The Nueva España treasure fleet, for example, foundered in 1563 on the reefs between Cayo Rosarío and Cayo Largo. One of the best sites is Cabeza Sambo, 70 km west of Cayo Largo. The large shallow is strewn with cannons and nautical metallic miscellany. Very little archaeological surveillance has been undertaken, and it is entirely feasible to find coral-encrusted Spanish doubloons.

WILDLIFE

The cays are rich in wildlife. The chief noises are a reptilian hiss and the caterwauling of birds. From a small population of monkeys on Cayo Cantiles to the flamingos inhabiting the salty lagoons of Cayo Pasaje, the Archipiélago de los Canarreos de-

serves a reputation for some of Cuba's best wildlife viewing. The cays have the advantage of being remote and in pristine condition.

Needless to say, with countless hectares of fringing reef, the cays are a potential mecca for divers. Over 800 species of fish gambol among the exquisite coral. Inevitably, where you find fish, you find birds. The cays shelter tens of thousands of seabirds, including crab-eating sparrowhawks perched in the branches; fishing orioles, cormorants, and pelicans that prey on the schools of *manjúas* and sardines; and egrets, majestic white and black herons, and other stilt-legged waders that patrol the shorelines, their heads tilted forward, long bills jabbing at the sand—pick, pick, pick. There are even mockingbirds and endangered parrots—*cotorros*—that flutter about freely on the larger islands.

Lizards, of course, are numerous, darting back and forth, seemingly inured to the sun. Marine turtles are always in the water, particularly during the nesting seasons, when big males hang off the edge of the reef, waiting for the females to return from laying their eggs in coral sand above the high-water mark. And Cayo Iguana, a nature reserve immediately north of Cayo Largo, is noted for its large population of endemic iguanas, as baked and lifeless as the ground they walk on.

IGUANAS

These dragons from the antediluvian dawn are found on many of the cays in the Archipiélago de los Canarreos, where they lie torpid, stewing in the sun, like prehistoric flotsam washed ashore.

It is thought that the reptiles came involuntarily, swept across the ocean on rafts of vegetation or logs. With their watertight skins and tolerance for heat and drought, the iguanas survived without water and food.

The iguanas are draped in Joseph's coats of orange-yellow and ocher-red. They show little fear of man. The creatures are so seemingly tame and docile that they wait patiently for handouts while the sun beats heavily upon their backs. You can get eye-to-eye with them, but they can snap with toothy jaws if you're foolish enough to irritate them!

CAYO LARGO

Cayo Largo, 177 km south of Havana and 120 km east of Isla de la Juventud, is a narrow (three-km-wide), 25-km-long, boomerang-shaped slither of land fringed by the prettiest, emptiest talcum-fine beaches on the planet—an unbroken 20-km stretch of beaches (Blanca, Lindamar, Los Cocos, Tortugas) with sand as blindingly white as Cuban sugar. If all you want to do is laze in the sun, this is the place to be. You won't learn a thing about Cuban life, however, as everything here is a tourist contrivance and you are totally cut off from the mainland and Cubans, other than service staff. (The only Cubans on the island are workers, who live on their own plot on Isla del Sol, north of the airport.) Cayo Largo is favored by Canadians and Europeans, particularly French and, in the words of novelist Pico Iyer, "bronzed Teutons disporting themselves as if in some Aryan holiday camp."

The English privateer Henry Morgan careened his ship here for repairs three centuries ago. Other pirates used Cayo Largo, and there are several galleons and corsairs on the seabed. US firms began building a resort in 1957, but the Revolution brought construction to a close before a single tourist had arrived. The island remained unpopulated except for beasts and birds until 1982, when the Hotel Isla del Sur was begun.

Today, Cayo Largo is one of Cuba's premium resort destinations. Expansion has proceeded within strict ecological limits that protect the reefs and wildlife. Another 450 rooms are planned by the year 2000, bringing the total to 1,200. The Cuban government estimates that the ecology of Cayo Largo can withstand 3,000 rooms, but I suspect it will begin to lose its lustrous sheen.

Cayo Largo is expensive. Expect to pay double what you might on the mainland. Even most watersports must be paid for on an item-by-item basis, despite the suggestion in tourist brochures that jet-skis, windsurfers, etc. are included in the price of your hotel room. Jeez! You even have to rent a sunbed.

Orientation
A single road links the airport, at the northwest end of Cayo Largo, with the resort (three km

away on the island's outer elbow, in an area referred to as Cocodrilo) and the marina and shopping complex immediately north of the airport at Isla del Sol (also called Combinado). The road continues east 14 km as far as Playa Los Cocos. Beaches run the entire length of the seaward side. The leeward side is composed of mangroves and salty lagoons.

Beaches
Cayo Largo has 27 km of serene beaches. The sand's ultra-fine texture and unique crystalline structure prevent it from getting too hot in the midday sun. The beaches merge gently into waters that run from lightest green through turquoise and jade to deep cobalt far out. Topless bathing is tolerated.

The loveliest beach is 2.3-km-long **Playa Sirena,** on the west side of a narrow peninsula—Punta Sirena—that juts up at the western end of the island. The beach is reached by a 10-minute boat ride from the pier at Isla del Sol. Many people justly consider it Cuba's finest beach. It slopes steeply below the waterline (wading is not recommended for children). Jet-skis can be rented, as can windsurfers and catamarans. Volleyball is popular. There are no hotels, but shady wood-and-thatch structures house a souvenir kiosk, toilets, games room, and the Rincón del Castillo Bar. And Cuban dishes are served at **La Parrillada** restaurant to the accompaniment of a music and dance troupe. Open-air courtesy buses chauffeur guests to the harbor, from where ferries run to Playa Sirena.

Red warning flags are sometimes posted when the seas get rough.

Playa Lindamar, setting for the Hotel Pelicano, is a five-km-long, scimitar-shaped beach encompassed by coral. The longest beach is 7.5-km-long **Playa Blanca,** running the length of the foreshore where the villas are located. Immediately east—an unbroken extension of Playa Blanca—are **Playa Los Cocos** and then **Playa Tortuga,** where giant sea turtles come ashore to lay their eggs in the seemingly endless warm sands.

The only beach on the north shore is **Playa Luna,** whose sheltered waters are as soothing as a fresh bath.

Cayo Largo is surrounded by 20 islets (actually large sandbanks), covered with wild grass and scrub and their own shimmering beaches.

Isla del Sol

This tourist village is located just north of the airport, at the tip of Cayo Largo. It features a **Casa de Iso Orishas, El Galeón** jewelry store, ice-cream kiosk, souvenir shop, pharmacy, the atmospheric **Taberna del Pirata** bar, and the **Granja de las Tortugas,** where you can see marine turtles in pools in a small turtle farm. The marina is also located here.

Accommodations

The tourist complex comprises six hotels, each with its own personality and architectural style, from spartan bungalows to deluxe hotel rooms. All are operated by Cuba's Gran Caribe chain and are located between Playa Lindamar and Playa Blanca. They share the same telephone and fax numbers for reservations, tel. 79-4215 or 95-2104, fax 33-2108 or 95-2108. The main desk is at the Isla del Sur Hotel. You can book an all-inclusive package or room(s) only (guests are given colored bracelets to indicate their entitlements).

Villa Capricho, the easternmost property, boasts thatched saddle-roof bungalows of wood and stone aligned along the shore. They're rustic and somewhat jerry-built, yet cozy and full of ambience—perfect if you don't seek deluxe appointments. There are doubles and triples, all with shady porches with hammocks. Larger bungalows have lofty bedrooms and kitchenettes. The 60 a/c rooms even have satellite TVs, which seem out of place. Capricho has a lofty thatch-roofed **Blue Marlin Restaurant**

serving continental breakfasts as well as *paellas* and seafoods for lunch and dinner. Watersports are offered. Rates are US$70 s/d low-season, US$100 s/d high-season.

Villa Iguana has bungalows and 114 a/c rooms in two-story blocks. All have radios, telephones, satellite TVs, and safety deposit boxes. A rustic yet attractive, timber-beamed dining hall serves buffet meals. Watersports are available through the Isla del Sur and Pelícano hotels. Rooms cost US$55 s/d low-season, US$90 s/d high-season.

Villa Coral has 60 rooms in bungalows amid scrubby lawns atop a coral ledge above the beach. Each cottage has two independent guest rooms on each level. A radio, telephone, satellite TV, and safety deposit box are standard. The rooms are satisfyingly simple and center on a half-moon pool with large swim-up bar. An Italian restaurant specializes in pizza lunches (*a la carte* dinners are by reservation). Rooms cost US$60 s/d low-season, US$95 s/d high-season. The facility also includes the single-story bungalows of **Villa Soledad.**

Climbing up the social scale, you may prefer **Isla del Sur,** with 59 a/c rooms with satellite TVs and refrigerators in a twin-level hotel block fronting the beach. All rooms have terraces facing the sea. At its heart is a circular swimming pool. The resort offers a panoply of evening entertainment and has a buffet restaurant, poolside bar, two grills, tourist bureau, and hairdresser. Rooms start at US$80 s/d low-season, US$110 s/d high season.

Pelícano Hotel is a low-rise hotel with 324 rooms, including two suites and 110 bungalows, all with a/c and balconies overlooking the sea. Fifty deluxe rooms have satellite TVs and minibars. Its contemporary design has a strong Spanish-Mexican feel, with appealing moderne decor. There are four restaurants, a café, a piano bar, nightclub, even a gym, a laundry, and dry-cleaning. Recreation includes complete watersports, basketball, volleyball. Same prices as at Isla del Sur.

Food

Eating on Cayo Largo can seriously damage your budget. Meals are inordinately expensive. Even lobster, which is abundant locally, costs US$20 or more in most restaurants. However, the standard of cuisine is better than most other places in Cuba.

The Blue Marlin, in the Villa Capricho, specializes in paellas. Despite its rustic appearance, **La Taberna del Pirata,** at Playa Sirena, serves good seafood dishes, including lobster. Several other restaurants offer *criollo* dishes.

Entertainment and Events

Each September, Cayo Largo hosts two sportsfishing tournaments: the **International Fishing Tournament for the Blind and Visually Impaired,** at the beginning of the month, followed by the **International Marlin Tournament,** under IGFA rules.

A *guateque,* or Cuban country hoe-down, is offered every Saturday at 3 p.m. in the **El Criollo** restaurant. A **Noche Afro-Cubana** is held weekly in the plaza of the Isla del Sol and features performances recalling the dances and rituals of the Yoruba tribe. There's also a *Noche Caribeña* on Playa Sirena.

At night, the airport terminal doubles as the **Blue Lake** disco! A minibus service operates between the hotels and the discotheque, beginning service at 11 p.m.

Watersports

You can choose from every imaginable watersport: banana boats, windsurfing, jet-skiing, snorkeling, sea kayaks, and catamarans.

Sportfishing: The offshore waters teem with gamefish, including white and blue marlin. Bonefish *(macabí)* and tarpon *(sábalo)* are abundant in the shallow waters of the Cayería Los Majáes, immediately northwest of Cayo Largo. Sportfishing excursions can be booked through the Tourism Desk.

Scuba Diving: A barrier reef lies about one km offshore, protecting Cayo Largo from rough seas. The reefs draw rave reviews from scuba divers jaded by the Cayman Islands and Cozumel. There's an absence of currents, and the water never falls below 25° C. Dives are available from the marina for US$35 (single dive) or US$60 (two dives). A 10-dive package costs US$127. Snorkeling costs US$14. Puertosol also has weeklong diving packages from Havana.

A Canadian company, **Hooked on Diving,** tel. (514) 843-8873, fax (514) 843-9439, offers weeklong dive packages on two live-aboard vessels, the MV *Caribbean King* and MV *Lindamar.* The latter sleeps 14 passengers in five a/c cabins; the former sleeps 14 in four a/c cabins. The boats, which are permanently based at Siguanea, are equipped with on-board compressors, aluminum cylinders, portable life-support oxygen, and an auxilary Zodiak. The packages include more remote cays in the Archipiélago de los Canarreos. Weekly departures are offered from Montreal.

Shopping

There's a shopping center opposite the Isla del Sur Hotel, where you can buy everything from fashionwear, beachwear, and sandals to electronic items, music and video cassettes, film, duty-free items, and souvenirs. Check out the **Casa de las Orishas,** which sells dolls and other items associated with santería, the Afro-Cuban religion. Don't buy black coral, stuffed turtles, or other endangered animal products, which are illegal to sell or purchase under international law.

Information and Services

There are medical posts at the Pelícano Hotel and at Villa Coral, plus a policlinico at Isla del Sol. The International Telecommunications Center, opposite the Isla del Sur Hotel, includes a post office, and a telephone and fax office. You can buy international newspapers and magazines here.

There's a tourist bureau and information service in the lobby of the Hotel Isla del Sur. The island has its own cable TV station—Sunshine Channel—which pipes information into hotels.

Getting There

Amazingly, Cayo Largo is a free port, and international travelers can arrive without visa or passport if they have no intention of visiting the Cuban mainland. This is true of sailors arriving by private yacht. Regardless, it's always wise to travel with your passport. You'll need it if you wish to visit the mainland. You can obtain a visa to visit the mainland upon arrival in Cayo Largo.

Most flights arrive midmorning. You are greeted with a welcome cocktail at the thatched-roof, postage-stamp-size airport before being transferred to your hotel. The resort complex is about six km away.

By Air: If you're already in Cuba, the only way to get to Cayo Largo is on a package through Havanatur or a similar tour agency. Cayo Largo is connected by air with Havana (285 km away), Varadero, Isla de la Juventud, Cienfuegos, and Santiago de Cuba. You can book your own flight and separate hotel reservations if you wish, but it is far more expensive than a package deal. It's a 30-minute plane ride from Havana's Terminal Caribbean or from Varadero by Cubana's Yak-40. Aerocaribbean also has flights from the same cities.

International: Charter flights operate directly from Canada, Europe, Mexico, and Grand Cayman. A typical one-week package with **Magna Holidays** costs from C$569 at the Villa Capricho and from C$739 at the Iguana, including roundtrip airfare with **Royal Air,** which flies from Toronto every Saturday. **Fiesta Sun** operates charters from Toronto on Monday.

One-Day Excursions: Most one-day excursions begin with a hotel pick-up about 6 a.m. Charter flights usually depart at 8 a.m. Upon arrival, you are whisked to Isla del Sol for a 15-minute boat ride to Playa Sirena for sunning, watersports, and lunch at La Parrillada Restaurant. In midafternoon, excursion trippers take the boat back to Isla del Sol for shopping before their return flight.

A typical one-day package costs US$150, including the flight. **Puertosol,** Calle Cobre #34404 e/ 2da y 4, Villa Marina, Tarará, Havana, tel. 33-3510, fax 33-5501, offers day excursions from Havana and Varadero for US$94. Similar trips are also offered by **Tour & Travel.** The excursion is a great break for travelers not otherwise able to experience Cuba's beach resorts. It hardly seems worth it, however, if you're planning on taking an excursion from another beach resort.

By Sea: Private yachters can berth at **Marina Cayo Largo,** at Isla del Sol. Simon Charles, in *Cruising Guide to Cuba,* claims that it is "perhaps the best marina-dock in Cuba." It has 20 berths

with 110- and 220-volt electricty, water hooks, and gas and diesel available. The berthing fee is US35 cents per foot. There's a ship's chandler, laundry, and repair service. It's operated by Puertosol S.A., tel. 95-2202/3, fax 51-5056, VHF channel 06.

Eight rooms are available to yachters at **Villa Internacional** (US$40 d, EP).

Getting Around

Car, Motorcycle, Bicycle: The best way to get around is by bicycle or scooter, which you can rent from the Paradiso and Isla del Sur hotels. Many of the finest beach spots can only be reached on two wheels or by hiking. A bicycle tour to Punta Paraíso is offered. Jeep rental is offered through the Pelícano and Isla del Sur hotels, but what's the point? There's only 20 km of road!

Ferries: Ferries leave for Playa Sirena from the pier at Isla del Sol at 8:30 and 10:30 a.m. and 2:30 p.m. They return at 1:30, 3, and 5 p.m. Free bus shuttles will transport you to and from hotels.

Excursions: Excursions are offered to **Cayo Rico** aboard a modern *pirogue* (a yacht with outrigger) for US$35, including a visit to the lobster farm. Excursions to **Cayo Iguana** cost US$12. A full-day excursion to **Cayo Cantiles** costs US$79, including snorkeling and optional fishing for lobster.

Aerotaxi offers a panoramic sightseeing tour by Russian biplane, as well as one-day excursions to Trinidad, Zapata, Pinar del Río, Havana, Varadero, neighoring Grand Cayman, and even Cancún, in Mexico. A sunset cruise is also available, as are horseback trips.

Yachts: Crewed yachts can be rented at the marina. Weeklong charter rates range from US$1,540 in low season (US$2,660 during the Christmas and New Year's period) for an Oceanis 370 to US$3,500 (US$5,180 in high season) for a Kennex 445.

MATANZAS
INTRODUCTION

Matanzas Province has its fair share of attractions of note, including the namesake city of Matanzas. A century ago, Matanzas, a wealthy sugar- and slave-trading port, was known as the "Athens of Cuba" for its literary and artistic vitality. Several structures attest to the cultural life of the city during its colonial heyday.

The coast road linking the city of Matanzas to Havana follows the sharp slope that forms the northern wall of the **Valle de Yumurí,** a huge basin lushly cultivated with sugarcane. It is enfolded by a meniscus of low mountains famed for their mineral springs, most notably at **San Miguel** (alas, they haven't seen action in years and are terribly run-down). East of Matanzas, the broad, scrub-covered plain runs east to the Peninsula de Hicacos and Villa Clara province.

Today, the province's lodestone is **Varadero,** Cuba's trendiest beach town, even for years before the Revolution—when it was a playground for rich Habaneros and Yankees who sunned and sinned here. The resort, occupying the slender Peninsula de Hicacos, 45 km east of Matanzas, is a mini-Cancún in the making. Cuba's premier resort boasts a scintillating 20-km-long beach where almost three-quarters of the island's hotels are located. The beach is a

stunner, but other attractions include a panoply of watersports, scuba diving, boat charters, and good discos and nightlife.

Immediately southeast of Varadero is the historic city of Cárdenas—a timeworn counterpoint to the resort's glitzy contemporary look and a popular, albeit disappointing, excursion destination for vacationers in Varadero.

Central Matanzas is smothered in a vast plain—the Llanura Roja—and its red soils are superbly rich, supporting sugarcane fields (with yields unparalleled elsewhere on the isle) and citrus orchards. The area was Cuba's economic powerhouse in the 19th century.

The city of Matanzas became a center of the slave trade to satisfy the hunger of the labor-intensive sugar plantations, which generated huge wealth for the social elite. Its proximity to Havana lent the region great importance and the area was vigorously contested and devastated in the wars of independence (in 1898, a US general reported seeing nothing but "ruin and starvation").

The southern part of Matanzas province is primarily of interest to nature lovers and history buffs. The entire region is taken up by the low-lying **Zapata Peninsula,** backing a mangrove shore on either side of the Bay of Pigs. This vast and virtually uninhabited marshland system is protected as Cuba's largest nature reserve, harboring fantastic birdlife and a large population of Cuban crocodiles. **Laguna del Tesoro** and **Las Salinas** set a world standard for tarpon and bonefish angling.

In April 1961, the Zapata region was launched from obscurity to fame as the setting for the Bay of Pigs invasion, when Washington met its Waterloo. There are pleasant beaches at Playa Larga and Playa Girón, both major landing sites for the CIA-inspired invasion by Cuban exiles that resulted in "the first defeat of US imperialism in the Americas." Memories of the fiasco—and Cuba's proud moment (they refer to it not as the "invasion" but rather as *la victoria*) are kept alive at a splendid museum. Girón also offers good scuba diving.

Note for Boaters: Private skippers should note that the entire coastline from the Bay of Pigs (21° 45') to Cienfuegos harbor (21° 50') is strictly off-limits. If you're running east-west between Cayo Largo and Cienfuegos or Trinidad, beware a dangerous 36-square-mile submarine pedestal, the **Jagua Bank,** with a four-km radius from 21° 37'N, 080° 39'W.

Routes through the Province
The wide, fast Vía Blanca runs east along the coast from Havana to Matanzas (102 km), and thence to Varadero, 34 km farther east. It's a marvelously scenic drive for much of the way. So is a journey on the historic **Hershey Train,** a venerable electric train that passes through the Yumurí Valley.

The south-central plains are crossed by the Autopista, which skips all towns and runs through flat agricultural lands from Havana to Santa Clara. The winding Carretera Central parallels the Autopista farther north, linking the cities of Matanzas and Santa Clara and passing through dusty old country towns whose luster has faded since the freeway was opened.

MATANZAS AND VICINITY

The city of Matanzas (pop. 98,000) lies within a deep, 11-km-long, five-km-wide bay—the Bahía de Matanzas. The town itself is not especially attractive, although the setting is wonderful—Matanzas rises above the Yumurí and San Juan Rivers, which cut through the center of town, in the cusp of gently rising hills. The wide bay, unusually turquoise, is filled with oil tankers and freighters waiting to be loaded with sugar. Tall chimney stacks rise to the north above the bayfront. They belong to a thermoelectricity plant fueled by hot underground waters, a chemical factory (pouring out insipid, sulfurous fumes), and the country's largest printing works, which today produces a mere fraction of its capacity.

Thousands of foreigners pass through town without stopping. So doing, they miss the faded mansions that line the riverbanks, lending a sense that you have been transported to Venice. Many houses have neoclassical hints, with fluted columns inset into the walls and topped by faux pediments. There is hardly enough of note, however, to hold your attraction for more than half a day.

Los Muñiquitos, perhaps Cuba's best-known folkloric rumba group, hails from Matanzas, a potent center for santería and Afro-Cuban rhythms.

More than 20 Spanish galleons lie at the bottom of Matanzas Bay (Cuba's deepest), sunk by Dutch Admiral Piet Heyn in 1628.

Matanzas translates as "slaughter"; apparently, the name comes from the city's beginnings as a port supplying meats and lard to Spain. A local legend says it was so named after a number of Spaniards, survivors of a shipwreck, were tricked by the local Indians who promised to guide the *conquistadores* to safety but instead ambushed the Spaniards and drowned them. Only four Spaniards survived, one being a beautiful woman whom the Indian chieftain is said to have taken as his own. There may be some truth to the tale—it is recorded by Bernal Días del Castillo, a soldier and chronicler who claimed to have met the four survivors, including the woman, who was later freed and went on to marry a Spaniard.

HISTORY

The city was founded at the end of the 17th century on the site of an Indian village, Yacayo, beside a bay that the indigenous people called Guanima. The Spanish wrought havoc on the Indians and renamed the site San Carlos y San Severino de Matanzas. In 1684, a castle—Castillo de San Severino—was built to guard the bay. A decade later, the land between the Rivers Yumurí and San Juan was surveyed and lots distributed among settlers from the Canary Islands.

During the 18th century, Matanzas grew gradually as a port city exporting beef, salted pork, coffee, and, most importantly, locally grown tobacco. When a royal edict monopolized tobacco production, an exodus left Matanzas almost empty. Fortunately, the rising fortunes of sugar spawned an era of impending prosperity. The town received a huge boost during the free-trade era following the British capture of Cuba in 1762.

During the heyday of sugar in the mid-19th century, the region accounted for more than 50% of national sugar production. Black gold—slaves—came ashore, transported from Africa on ships that returned to Europe laden with the produce of the region. The area witnessed several slave rebellions during the 19th century, most prominently in 1825 and 1843. The Spanish enacted a harsh retribution, and scores of slaves were brutally murdered in an effort to dissuade further rebellions.

Many citizens grew immensely wealthy on the sugar and slave trades, and a fashionable café society evolved. Matanzas sponsored the arts and sciences, attracting poets, artists, and the learned. In 1828, the citizens began printing Cuba's first newspaper. A Philharmonic society and a library were formed, followed by three theaters, and the city quickly acquired its Athens of Cuba moniker.

Matanzas became a battleground during the wars of independence and was even bombarded by the USS *New York*.

ORIENTATION

Matanzas lies on the western shore of the sausage-shaped bay. The town is divided by

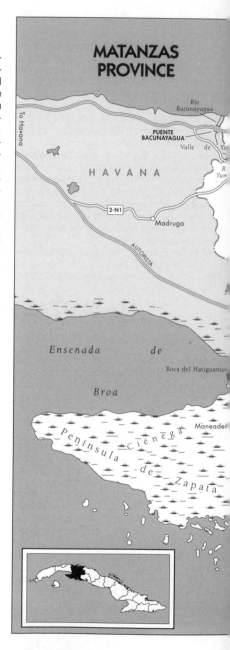

MATANZAS PROVINCE

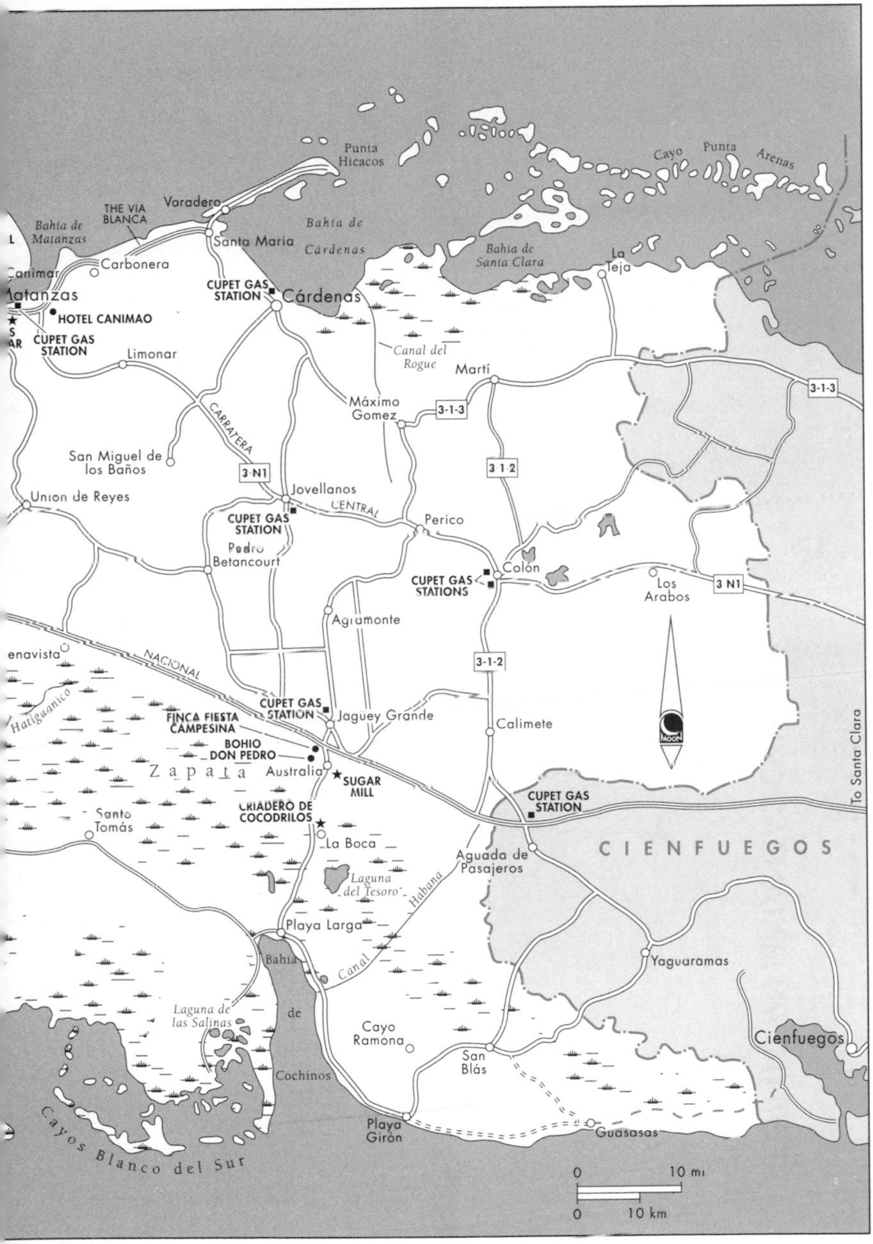

Punta Hicacos

Cayo Punta Arenas

THE VIA BLANCA

Varadero

Bahía de Matanzas

Santa María

Bahía de Cárdenas

Bahía de Santa Clara

La Teja

Canimar

Carbonera

Matanzas

CUPET GAS STATION

Cárdenas

HOTEL CANIMAO

CUPET GAS STATION

Limonar

Canal del Rogue

Martí

3-1-3

Máximo Gomez

3-1-3

CARRATERA

San Miguel de los Baños

3 N1

3 1 2

Union de Reyes

Jovellanos

CENTRAL

Perico

CUPET GAS STATION

Pedro Betancourt

Colón

CUPET GAS STATIONS

Los Arabos

3 N1

Agramonte

3-1-2

NACIONAL

enavista

Hatiguanico

CUPET GAS STATION

Jaguey Grande

Calimete

FINCA FIESTA CAMPESINA

BOHIO DON PEDRO

Australia

SUGAR MILL

Z a p a t a

CUPET GAS STATION

Santo Tomás

CRIADERO DE COCODRILOS

La Boca

C I E N F U E G O S

Laguna del Tesoro

Aguada de Pasajeros

Playa Larga

Bahía

Habana

Yaguaramas

Cienfuegos

Laguna de las Salinas

de

Cayo Ramona

San Blás

Cochinos

Cayos Blanco del Sur

Playa Girón

Guasasas

To Santa Clara

MOON

0   10 mi

0   10 km

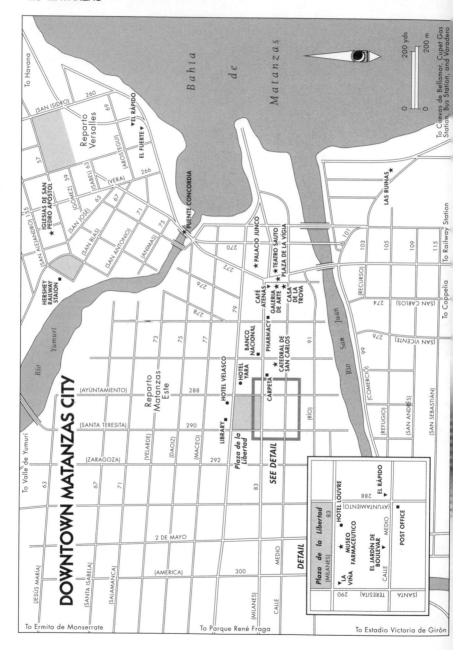

DOWNTOWN MATANZAS CITY

Bahia de Matanzas

To Havana

Reparto Versailles

[SAN ISIDRO]   260
57   69   EL RÁPIDO ▼
              EL FUERTE ▼
59   63 [ISABEL]   [AROSTEGUI]
[SAN ALEJANDRO] 155   [VERA]   266
★ IGLESIAS DE SAN
PEDRO APÓSTOL   [SAN GÓMEZ]
[SAN JOSÉ] 65   PUENTE CONCORDIA
[SAN BLAS] 67   71
[SAN ANTONIO]   75 [ANIMAS]
              270   ★ PALACIO JUNCO

HERSHEY RAILWAY STATION ■
              272   TEATRO SAUTO ★
Río Yumurí   276   Plaza de la Vigía
              79
To Valle de Yumurí   278   ★ CAFÉ ATENAS
              73   GALERÍA ■
              75   DE ARTE
[AYUNTAMIENTO]   77   ★ CASA DE LA TROVA
Reparto Matanzas Este   288   BANCO NACIONAL ■
              ● HOTEL VELASCO   PHARMACY ■
[SANTA TERESITA] 290   91
              ● HOTEL YARA
63 67 71   [VELARDE] [DAOIZ] [MACEO]   ■ CATEDRAL DE SAN CARLOS
[ZARAGOZA]   292   CARPETA ■
[RÍO]
              LIBRARY ■
              Plaza de la Libertad
83   SEE DETAIL
2 DE MAYO
[AMÉRICA]   300

[JESÚS MARÍA] [SANTA ISABELA] [SALAMANCA]   [MILANES] CALLE MEDIO

To Ermita de Monserrate   To Parque René Fraga

Río San Juan

LAS RUINAS ★
              To Railway Station
101
103   To Coppelia
105
[RECURSO] 274 [SAN CARLOS]
109
[SAN VICENTE] 276
115
99 [COMERCIO]
[REFUGIO] [SAN ANDRÉS] [SAN SEBASTIÁN]

To Cuevas de Bellamar, Cupet Gas Station, Bus Station, and Varadero

To Estadio Victoria de Girón

0   200 yds
0   200 m

DETAIL

Plaza de la Libertad
[MILANES]
★ LA VIÑA
★ MUSEO FARMACÉUTICO
● HOTEL LOUVRE
[AYUNTAMIENTO] 288
EL RÁPIDO ▼
EL JARDÍN DE BOULEVAR
CALLE MEDIO
83
290 [TERESITA]
SANTA
■ POST OFFICE

the Rivers Yumurí and San Juan into three distinct sections. To the north is Reparto Versalles, a late colonial addition climbing the gentle slopes. The predominantly 19th-century Pueblo Nuevo extends south of the Río San Juan along flatlands. The historic city center—**Reparto Matanzas**—lies between them and rises gradually to the west. Reparto Playa and its eastward extensions front the bay for several miles.

The Vía Blanca from Havana descends into town from the north to Matanzas Bay. The Vía Blanca skirts the eastern side of the colonial city and continues around the bay en route to Varadero.

The town is laid out in a near-perfect grid. Odd-numbered streets run east-west, even-numbered streets north-south. Many streets have both a name *and* a number. Worse, many of them have *two* names, one old and one post-Revolution. For example, the main shopping street, Calle 79, is also called Calle Contreras, though locals still refer to it as Calle Bonificacio Byrne. Contreras and Calle 83 (Milanés) run west from the Vía Blanca six blocks to the main square, Plaza de la Libertad. Calle Santa Teresita (Calle 290) runs perpendicular to the west, and Calle Ayuntamiento (Calle 288) to the east. Calle Medio, one block south of Milanés, is the main shopping street.

The first three digits of a house number refer to the nearest cross street.

You should be able to handle downtown Matanzas on foot with ease. Sites farther afield will require a bus or taxi. Buses run along most major streets. A few *colectivo* taxis still operate; you should be able to find one at the rail and bus terminals.

SIGHTS

Plaza de la Libertad

The old parade ground (once known as Plaza de las Armas) is a pleasant place to sit under the shade trees and watch the world go by, especially in spring, when the trees are in bloom. At its heart is a granite edifice topped by a bronze statue of José Martí and of the Indian maiden breaking free of her chains. No buildings of architectural note stand out at first sight, but closer scrutiny reveals several historic gems, notably the **Casa de la Cultura** in the former Lyceum Club, and the **biblioteca** (library) in the former Casino Club, both on Bonifacio Byrne. Strolling down Byrne, pause at the private home at number 28203 to admire the ornate iron doors with bold lion door knockers. The former city hall on Calle Ayuntamiento today houses the **Poder Popular**. The **Hotel Louvre** and **La Vina** restaurant are also of historical note.

The most intriguing building by far is the **Pharmaceutical Museum** (Museo Farmacéutico), at the corner of Milanés and Santa Teresa, next to the Hotel Louvre, tel. 3179. The wood-paneled pharmacy is housed in a beautifully restored building dating from 1882. The original pharmacy was opened here in that year by a French pharmacist, Trilet. It functioned as a family-owned pharmacy until 1964, when it metamorphosed into a museum preserving the store just as it was the day it closed—with salves, dried herbs, pharmaceutical instruments, and original porcelain jars neatly arranged on the exquisite carved hardwood shelves. Of the store's 55 prescription registers, one is always kept open for public scrutiny. Take a peek out back, where the laboratory contains a brick oven and copper distilleries and utensils. Note the bright red and orange *ventrales*. Originally they were red, white, and blue—the colors of France—but Spanish authorities insisted that they be replaced with Spain's national colors. Open Mon.-Sat. 10 a.m.-6 p.m., Sunday 9 a.m.-1 p.m. Entrance costs US$1.

Plaza de la Vigía

The city's other plaza of note is four blocks east of Plaza de la Independencia, at the junction of Milanés and Calle 270, immediately north of the **Puente Calixto García** bridge over the Río San Juan. This, the original town plaza has at its heart a marble statue of a freedom fighter during the wars of independence. It also boasts the **Teatro Sauto** (also known as Teatro El Antillano), considered one of Cuba's preeminent neoclassical buildings. It was built in 1863 in classical European theater style at the height of the city's prosperity, and in its heyday it attracted the likes of Sarah Bernhardt. It is easy, staring up at the carved wood and delicate frescoes (representing the muses of comedy, dance, music, theater, and tragedy) to believe you hear the swish of crinoline ball gowns on the marble stairs. The auditorium boasts three tiers with circular balconies supported by thin bronze columns. The theater still hosts performances—mostly on Friday and weekend nights—and is open for guided tours Wed.-Sun. 1-3 p.m. (US$1).

South of the theater is the tiny, neoclassical fire station, **Parque de los Bomberos.** It's worth a visit to marvel at the antique fire engine, pristinely preserved and now on display. Facing the fire station is the **Galería de Arte Provincial** (Monday 9 a.m.-5 p.m. and Tues.-Sat 9 a.m.-6 p.m.; US$1) and, next door, the **Ediciones Vigía,** which produces exquisite handmade books in limited editions and is open weekdays 9 a.m.-6 p.m.; US$1.

On the north side is the **Palacio Junco,** a sky-blue former early-20th-century mansion housing the city's **Museo Histórico Provincial,** tel. 3195. The exhibits trace the city's development, with special attention to its sugar and slave industries during colonial days Open Tues.-Sun. 10 a.m.-noon and 1-6 p.m. (US$1).

Catedral de San Carlos
The Catedral de San Carlos, built in 1878, is tucked off Milanés (Calle 282) one block east of the main square. A recent restoration was partly funded by a German tourist who developed an affection for the church. Today, the opulently frescoed ceiling gleams. The church is usually open weekdays 8 a.m.-noon and 3-5 p.m. and Sunday 9 a.m.-noon. Masses are offered. You may need to rouse the curator, who has an office at the side of the church. She is usually available in the afternoons (except Monday).

Places to View the City
Calle Contreras rises steadily westward from Plaza de la Libertad to **Parque René Fraga,** a dour concrete park. It compensates for its lack of beauty with views over the city. It contains a bronze bust of Bonifacio Byrne, National Poet (1861-1936).

Forsake the park and turn right (north) onto Calle 306 (Domingo Mujica) and follow it uphill to Ermita de Monserrate (Monserrate Hermitage), a *mirador* offering spectacular views over both Matanzas and the Valle de Yumurí, which looks from on high like a smaller version of the

Ngorongoro Crater. Sadly, the hermitage itself is but a shell and has no inherent interest. It is fronted by four pedestals holding aloft very weathered statues of the Muses.

Other Sites of Interest
Note the decorative Babylonian-style columns at each end of **Puente Concordia,** built in 1878 over the Río Yumurí.

Calle 272 crosses the bridge, where to the north is the old **Versalles district,** settled last century by French-Haitian refugees. Worth a peek are the **Iglesia de San Pedro Apóstol,** on the hillside at Calles 57 and 270, and, four blocks east, the **Cuartel Goicuría,** an imposing school—formerly an army barracks, which was assaulted on 29 April 1956 by a band of Castro's rebels.

With a restoration, the **Castillito de San Severino**—northeast of Versalles, reached via the Centro Politécnico on Calles 57 and 230—could be a worthy attraction.

Another tiny fortress, **Las Ruinas,** stands over the Vía Blanca, on the south side of the Río San Juan.

ACCOMMODATIONS

There are three budget, pesos-only hotels in town, each an antique gem. Until recently, they accepted foreigners and charged in the US$15 range. The **Hotel Velasco,** at 28803 Calle 79 and Bonifacio Byrne on the main square, tel. 4443, reminds me of a hotel in New York, circa 1920. Likewise, the slightly run-down **Hotel Louvre,** on the south side of the square, tel. 4074, and the **Hotel Yara,** one block east on Contreras, tel. 4418, are brimful of Spanish antiques and ambience. Alas, all three have recently stopped accepting foreigners, although you might still try your luck. Or try making a reservation through the *carpeta,* on Calle 83, one block east of the main square, tel. 2598 or 4775, which also sells reservations for *campismos* (low-budget holiday camps) throughout the province.

The nearest tourist hotels are the Hotel Valle de Yumurí, about 10 km west of town (see "Yumurí," below), and the Hotel Canimao, about eight km east of town.

Fortunately, many of the citizenry offer private rooms—*casas particulares.* The staff of the above hotels should be able to help. One traveler from Colorado recommends a *casa particular* next to the Hotel Louvre whose owner charges US$5 a night.

FOOD

Matanzas is no better served by eateries than by hotels. The most famous place in town is **La Viña,** at Calles 290 and 83, on the southwest corner of the main square. The rustic colonial ambience is splendid, but the place suffers from a lack of food! The restaurant next door in the Hotel Louvre is said to be adequate, with *arroz y morro* (rice and beans) for about US$1.50. Don't be fooled by the name of the **Salon Mojito,** next to the Hotel Louvre. It serves sodas and mineral water, not *mojitos.*

The nicest place around is **Café Atenas,** opposite the theater on Plaza de la Vigía, with an outdoor patio with shady arbor. It serves sandwiches and other snacks, as does **El Jardín de Boulevar** on Calle Medio, e/ 280 y 290, which also has a patio and bougainvilleas.

There are at least two **El Rápido** fast food cafés that specialize in fried chicken and hamburgers. One is on Calle Medio, behind the cathedral, and the other is on Vía Blanca and Calle 262. Adjoining the latter is another fast-food café, **La Fuerte,** open 24 hours, and offering *bistec* and sandwiches. For US$2, you can fill up on fried chicken and fries. Rumbos operates an open-air dollars-only café and bar in Las Ruinas.

Cuban-Chinese cuisine is served at **Pekin,** on Calle 83, tel. 3902. Meals are said to be of reasonable quality.

You'll find lots of stalls selling snacks and *refrescoes* on Calle 85.

ENTERTAINMENT AND EVENTS

The place to hear Matanzas's famous Afro-Cuban musicians, such as Los Muñequitos—Cuba's premier rumba band—and AfroCuba de Matanzas, is at either of the two **Casas de la Trovas,** one at Calles 83 and 304, west of the main square, tel. 2891, the other on Calles 272

and 121, tel. 4129. Performances are offered on Saturday afternoons and evenings.

Classical concerts, jazz, and dance are offered nightly in the **Teatro Sal José White,** on the main square (one peso). On Friday and weekends, the sumptuous **Teatro Sauto,** on Plaza de la Vigía, tel. 2721, also hosts classical and folkloric performances, plus comedy. Buy your tickets at the theater box office. Group excursions are offered from Varadero, where you can also buy individual tickets from the ARTEX shop at Avenida Primera and Calle 46, tel. 6-3720. The **provincial museum** also hosts classical concerts on Saturday evenings.

The **Centro Nocturno,** at Calles 83 and 268, tel. 2969, offers **cabaret** featuring comedians, musicians, and a dance troupe. It's followed by a disco. The **Cine Velazco,** on the north side of the main square, shows camp classics and recently released English-language movies, dubbed in Spanish (one peso).

The writers' and artists' union at Calle 83 between Matanzas and Magdalena (UNEAC; tel. 4857) sometimes hosts poetry readings, discussions, and music events.

Matanzas' top-ranked baseball team—the Henequeneros (named for those who work with henequen fiber)—play at the 30,000-seat Estadio Victoria a Girón, west of town on Avenida Martín Dihigo. Cuba's first baseball stadium was supposedly built here, in 1874. Games usually take place Tues.-Thurs. 3:30-8 p.m. and Saturday afternoons (one peso).

SERVICES AND INFORMATION

There's no tourist information office.

The main **post office** is on Calle 85 and 290,

MATANZAS USEFUL TELEPHONE NUMBERS

Police	tel. 116
Ambulance	tel. 2337
Hospital	tel. 7011/6
Terminal de Ómnibus	tel. 9-1473 or 9-2701
Railway Station	tel. 9-2409
Taxis	tel. 3970

one block south of the main square, between Santa Teresita and Ayuntamiento. It's open Mon.-Sat. 7 a.m.-8 p.m. The centro telefónico is on Calle 83 and 288, open daily 6:30 a.m.-10 p.m. There's a **Banco Nacional** on Calle Medio one block east of the main square.

Ediciones Geo publishes a pocket-size fold-out map of the city. You can buy it in Havana. The town **library** is on the northwest corner of Parque de la Libertad.

You'll find a **Cupet gas station** on the Vía Blanca, about two km east of town.

GETTING THERE AND AWAY

By Bus

Bus no. 300 ostensibly runs from Havana to Matanzas six times daily at 5:10, 8, and 8:55 a.m. and 2:30, 4:15, and 6:30 p.m. (two hours; five pesos). As usual, the buses are booked days or weeks in advance. Matanzas's chaotic main bus terminal, tel. 7763, is at the junction of Calle 298 and 127. Local buses run from here to downtown and vice versa (take bus no. 16 from Calle 79, one block west of the main square). Long-distance buses operate from the old rail station, now the Estación Ómnibus Nacional, at Calles 131 and 272. Another bus station is located on the Vía Blanca three km east of town.

Return buses to Havana are supposed to leave Matanzas at 5:50, 8:05, and 8:40 a.m. and 1:25, 5:10, and 9 p.m. Buses also leave from here for Varadero (50 centavos) and Cárdenas. You must buy a ticket in advance, then wait for the bus. When the number is called, get ready to join the stampede.

By Train

The new rail station is south of town, at Calle 181. Morning trains depart regularly for Havana, and foreigners are given preferred seating (US$3.50 regular; US$4 express). Trains also depart from here for Camagüey (US$16), Cienfuegos (US$8), Santa Clara (US$7), and Sancti Spíritus, plus Bayamo and Manzanillo. The night express to Santiago (13 hours; US$32) stops at provincial capitals en route.

The Hershey Train leaves from the sky-blue railway station, three blocks northeast of the Río Yumurí bridge at Calle 67, tel. 7254. Trains to

Casablanca depart at 3:55, and 10:20 a.m. and 2:55 and 9:19 p.m. and arrive in Havana at 8:27 a.m. and 2:52, 7:32, and 1:37 p.m. respectively. Tickets cost US$2.80 (foreigners must pay in dollars; Cubans pay 2.80 pesos) and go on sale one hour in advance. Your ticket will have an assigned seat number. Ask for a window seat. Return trains depart Casablanca for Matanzas at 4:35 and 9:25 a.m. and 3:45 and 8:55 p.m., arriving at 9:08 a.m. and 1:54, 8:17, and 1:17 p.m.

Taxis and Tours

A licensed taxi will cost you about US$75 one way from Havana. A taxi to Varadero from Matanzas will cost at least US$30. You can always talk a local driver into taking you for about half the fare.

Tour & Travel, (a division of Havanatur), Avenida Playa #3606 e/ 36 y 37, Varadero, tel. 66-7279, offers a day trip to Matanzas from Varadero for US$15.

Caribbean Music and Dance offers study tours to Matanzas focusing on the region's Afro-Cuban music (see "Special Activities" in the On The Road chapter).

VALLE DE YUMURÍ

Humboldt called it "the loveliest valley in the world." The Cubans call it "the Valley of Delight." The eight-km-wide Yumurí Valley is held in the cusp of 150-meter-high limestone cliffs—the Cuchilla de Habana-Matanzas—to the west of Matanzas. The hills form a natural amphitheater hidden from the modern world. Two rivers, the Yumurí and Bacunayagua, thread their silvered way to the sea through a landscape as archetypally Cuban as any you will find on the island.

Millions of years ago, the valley was underwater, as demonstrated by marine shells and fossils embedded in the valley walls. The cliffs have been eroded and are pocked with caverns, many of them, like **Indian's Cave,** brimful of stalagmites and stalactites, high up on the southern cliff.

Accommodations

Hidden away in the valley bottom is the **Horizontes Casa del Valle Motel,** Km 2, Carretera de Chirno, Valle del Yumurí, Matanzas, tel. 33-

THE HERSHEY TRAIN

Rail journeys hold a particular magic, none more so in Cuba than the Hershey Train, which runs lazily between Havana and Matanzas year-round, four times a day. The diminutive vermilion MU-train locomotive (Ferrocarril de Cuba #20803) looks like it could have fallen from the pages of a story about Thomas, the little "live" engine. The gold-leaf lettering on the two maroon carriages has long since faded—as has the maroon as well.

This fascinating electric railway has its origin in a chocolate bar.

In its heyday, before the Revolution, the Hershey estates belonging to the Pennsylvania-based chocolate company occupied 69 square miles of lush canefields around a modern sugar-factory town (now called Camilo Cienfuegos). At its peak, the estate had 19 steam locomotives. Their sparks, however, constituted a serious fire hazard, so they were replaced with seven 60-ton electric locomotives built especially for the Hershey-Cuban Railroad. Though it was primarily a sugarcane-moving venture, the railroad provided three-car passenger train service between Havana and Matanzas every hour. Today's Hershey Train is the sole working survivor.

A Sugar of a Journey

The train departs Casablanca on the north side of Havana harbor and stops at Guanabacoa and dozens of little way-stations en route to Matanzas. Two minutes before departure, the conductor gives a toot on the horn and a mad rush ensues. Don't expect comfort: the train has only hard wooden seats.

The carriage shudders and begins to thread its way along the narrow main street that parallels the waterfront of Casablanca. The rattle of the rails soon gathers rhythm, with the doors remaining wide open, providing plenty of breeze.

The train winds in and out among the palm-studded hills, speeds along the coast within sight of the Atlantic, then slips between palms, past broad swathes of sugarcane, and through the Yumurí Valley, a region of such beauty that Humboldt, the explorer, called it "the loveliest valley in the world."

On one ride, my fellow passengers and I were treated to a very public attempted seduction involving a young *cubana* dressed in a sexy polka-dot halter top, black baseball shoes, white bobby socks, and Spandex pants. Her unlikely suitor was the conductor, a time-tempered Don Juan who attempted to captivate this coquettish maiden in the steps of the open doorway: he in his ice-blue uniform, down in the stairwell with one leg on the top rung, his arm around her waist, whispering in her ear, she chewing gum nonchalantly, seemingly uninterested yet pressing her body close up into his thigh. When we stopped at Canasi, he helped her onto the platform—still in full view of the passengers looking down—and attempted to kiss her, but the nymphet turned her cheek. Ha! As she began to walk away, he slapped her on the behind in a gesture of fond defeat that caused a ripple of mirth through the carriage. *(continues on next page)*

the Hershey Train

THE HERSHEY TRAIN
(continued)

Two hours into the journey, you'll arrive at a blue station still bearing the Hershey sign. You are now in the heart of the old Hershey sugar factory, where the train pauses sufficiently for you to get down and capture the scene for posterity. Bring some snacks to share with locals, who willingly share from their meager packages unfolded on laps.

After a mesmerizing (albeit tiring) four-hour journey, you finally arrive at the sky-blue Matanzas station.

Trains depart Casablanca for Matanzas at 4:35 and 9:25 a.m. and 3:45 and 8:55 p.m. Trains to Casablanca depart Matanzas at 3:55 and 10:20 a.m. and 2:55 and 9:19 p.m. Tickets cost US$2.80 (you can pay in dollars or pesos) and go on sale one hour in advance. Your ticket will have an assigned seat number. Ask for a window seat.

The Tourist's Version

In 1995, workers of the Camilio Cienfuegos railroad reconditioned a second train (a Brill 3008 that ran for the first time in 1922), with a modified interior for tourists. Thus, there is now a touristy journey (year-round) co-sponsored by Rumbos, featuring visits to the Hershey station, the Camilo Cienfuegos sugar mill, and the Santa Cruz rum factory. Lunch (at El Cayuelo restaurant) is included. January through March, the train also runs special trips for railroad enthusiasts, with a visit to the railroad patio.

7418, a Spanish colonial-style villa dating from 1936 and surrounded by a newer, rather soulless block of rooms facing a swimming pool. The hotel is built atop a sulfurous mineral spring and specializes in treatments for stress, asthma, obesity, and high blood pressure. It offers 7-, 14-, and 21-day stays for those seeking treatments, though it's open to all comers without a minimum-stay restriction. The hotel has 42 modestly furnished but spacious and well-lit a/c rooms with private baths (some share), radios, TVs, telephones, and refrigerators (US$24 s, US$32 d). Far more appealing, however, are the two large bedrooms in the old villa (US$34 s, US$42 d). These have lofty beamed ceilings in Spanish colonial style. One bedroom has 18th-century fabrics and antique chairs in Roman style. The other has a king-size bed and a huge bathroom.

The restaurant is elegant and features quality artwork. The menu offers the usual Cuban fare: grilled chicken, *bistec,* pork, etc.

Other facilities include a two-lane bowling alley and pool table, a poolside bar popular with Cubans, a sauna, and a small gym. Horseback riding is offered, and mopeds are available for rent.

Getting There
The Yumurí Valley is included in a one-week "Rainbow in the Horizon" tour combining sightseeing in Havana and Pinar del Río and offered by **Hoteles Horizontes,** Calle 23 #156 e/ N y O,`

Vedado, Havana, tel. 33-4142, fax 33-3161. The Hershey Train passes through the valley; you can hop off at any of a zillion rural waystops. (For the Hotel Valle de Yumurí, get off at Mena; it's a two-km walk from here.)

THE VÍA BLANCA

The Vía Blanca, also called the Matanzas-Varadero Expressway, hugs the coast, winds past spiky sisal plantations, and cuts inland through scrub-covered hills, with the turquoise sea teasingly appearing between the casuarina trees. Oil derricks by the water's edge nod lethargically, desperately sucking forth black gold atop coral platforms that separate intermittent beaches.

In 1996, a tollbooth was opened at Km 28 (28 km east of Matanzas). Foreigners pay US$2 per vehicle.

Four km east of Matanzas, immediately beyond the bridge over the Río Canimar, a road to the left loops downhill into **Canimar Abajo,** where there's a tiny beach with fishing boats and a pleasant little restaurant. A small fort—**Castillo del Morrillo**—with cannons guards the rivermouth. The castle is now a museum dedicated to revolutionary leader Antonio Guiteras Holmes, who was gunned down in 1935 beneath the mahogany tree near the bridge. The valley is hemmed in by near-vertical limestone cliffs. Small, basic cabins are available for rent (they can be reserved through the *carpeta* of Campismo Popular in Matanzas). Cubamar, tel. 052-615 or 6-1516, offers a 45-minute boat trip from the **Canimar Abajo Aquatic Center.** The journey takes you upriver to Cueva La Eloísa, a flooded cave where you may swim in the pellucid waters. A half-day excursion (US$21) departs at noon and features lunch and a horseback ride. Reservations required. You can also rent rowboats (US$2).

The river is named for Canimao, an aboriginal warrior. According to legend, Canimao's wife, Cibaraya, daughter of the tribal chief, became sick with a life-threatening disease. Canimao called up the Bat God and offered his life in exchange for that of his wife. The Bat God refused. Canimao died anyway—by slitting his throat and casting himself into the river.

Continuing east, you'll pass **Playa El Mamey.** The little beach is a popular spot with Cubans from Matanzas. There are shade trees and a basic restaurant plus kiddies' swings. Camping is permitted, but there are no cabins.

There's a huge cave—**Refugio de Saturno**—whose underground lagoon and dramatic stalagmites and stalactites wait to be explored midway between Matanzas and Varadero, just south of Carbonera. During the War of Independence, a hospital was set up inside. It's popular with scuba divers (excursions are offered from Varadero). Even more appealing are the Cuevas Bellamar.

Cuevas Bellamar

These little-visited caves form one of Cuba's largest cave systems, full of gurgling streams and shimmering flower-like crystal formations (many shaped like crystal goblets without stems) known as dahlias. There are more than 3,000 meters of galleries full of stalactites and stalagmites, including the 80-meter-long, 26-meter-high Gothic Temple. "It seemed the coolest, most magical place on the island," thought Lourdes, a character in Cristina García's novel *Dreaming in Cuban.* The largest stalactite is Columbus's Mantle, plicated like a silken curtain.

The air is thin and the temperature surprisingly high. Open Tues.-Sun. 9 a.m.-5 p.m. Entrance costs US$3 (plus US$2 for cameras, US$4 for video); English-speaking guides are provided. There's a basic restaurant serving mediocre food.

The caves are at Finca La Alcancía, in the hills above Matanzas, about five km southeast of town, reached by turning south from the Vía Blanca onto Calle 226, east of the town center. Bus no. 16 departs Calle 79 and will drop you about 1.5 km below the caves.

Accommodations

Hotel Canimao, west of the bridge over the Río Canimao, tel. 6-1014, is one of Islazul's premier properties. It's an attractive 120-room hotel surrounding a pool amid landscaped grounds. Rooms are modestly furnished (US$17 s, US$22 d low-season and US$21 s, US$28 d high-season). There's late-night cabaret (except Monday), and excursions are offered. Bus no. 16 stops at the Río Canimar bridge (it departs from Calle 300 and 83 in Matanzas).

A more basic option is **Campismo Faro de Maya,** a Cuban holiday camp beside the lighthouse on the eastern side of the Bahía de Matanzas. It has wooden cabins with private bath (cold water) for $10. You can book at the Campismo Popular office in Matanzas.

VARADERO AND VICINITY

INTRODUCTION

Varadero is Cuba's tourist mecca, the artificial Cuba of charter jet packages. Topless blondes recline on equally blonde beaches reading novels in German. The scene could be the Costa Brava. If all you want is sun, sand, sea, and a vital nightlife, then Varadero could be for you.

This former elitist resort, 34 km east of Matanzas and 140 km east of Havana, is fronted by a stunning white sand beach bathed by the warm waters of the Gulf Stream. Flocks of egrets and occasional pelicans fly by, skimming over a sea of pavonine blue.

The resort occupies a narrow peninsula centered on a Cuban village (pop. 15,000) that is fast losing any semblance of Cuban character.

The Cuban government seems hell-bent on developing Varadero as Cuba's Cancún. There are already more than 50 hotels, and the gaps are being filled in. The Mexicans, Germans, Canadians, Italians, French, Jamaicans, and especially the Spanish are pumping money in. A fistful of large-scale, deluxe resorts are under construction (the old Campamento Internacional de Pioneros, which until recently housed Cuban youth, is even being reborn as a hotel). According to the Cuban tourism development master-plan, Varadero alone has a potential capacity for 23,000 hotel rooms—almost as many as exist on the entire island of Jamaica!

Varadero offers snorkeling and scuba diving, although these are somewhat overrated. Watersports abound. Sportfishing is first-rate. And there are heaps of excursions for those who want to explore farther afield. Alas, much of the early promotion efforts concentrated on showing near-naked Cubanas with slogans offering tititlating invitations. As a result, the Cuban government has succeeded in attracting predominantly single males, and *jiniteras* are rife.

Strictly speaking, Varadero is the name of the *beach* area. It lies on the north, ocean-facing side of a 18.6-km-long peninsula called Punta Hicacos (actually a slender island), which encloses Cárdenas Bay and is separated from the mainland by a hairline inlet, the Laguna de Paso Malo. The peninsula is only 1.2 km at its widest point. It slopes to the northeast, where its tip—Hicacos Point—is the northernmost point of Cuba.

The western half of the peninsula is flat. The scrub-covered eastern half is broken by a series of flat-topped mesas—former sand dunes, now turned to stone) and low-lying raised coral platforms pitted with sinkholes and caves full of marine fossils—evidence of uplifting over geological time.

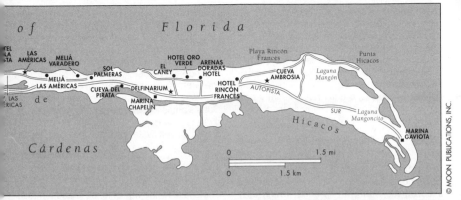

© MOON PUBLICATIONS, INC.

The Beach

"In all the beaches in Cuba the sand was made of grated silver," says a character in Robert Fernández's *Raining Backwards,* "though in Varadero it was also mixed with diamond dust." Who can argue?

The main beach is a virtually unbroken 11.5-km-long swath that widens and improves eastward (where facilities are more upscale), then breaks up into smaller beaches divided by rocky headlands. Most of the deluxe hotels sit over their own "private" beaches. At the far eastern end, beyond the deluxe resorts, a lonesome beach lies unseen and unknown to foreigners. A few Cubans gather here. It is reached from the main causeway by a road just beyond the Hotel Rincón Francés.

Backed by seagrape, oleander, hibiscus, royal poincianas, and palms, the beaches shelve gently into waters the color of a Maxfield Parrish painting. Those shadowed waters conceal a coral reef offshore. Red flags are often posted when seas are rough (there's often a dangerous undertow) or infested by schools of jellyfish, including Portuguese man-of-wars. At night, when the breeze blows offshore, occasional sulphur fumes from the petrochemical works and oil rigs across Bahía de Calderas drift to town, but the effect is not as bad as its reputation.

Semi-nude sunbathing, although illegal, is tolerated at Varadero. Topless bathing is common among European women. (As much as Cuban women love to flaunt their figures—skimpy *tangas* are the norm—I have yet to see a Cubana topless on the beach.)

You can stop in at virtually any hotel or any of the various restaurants fronted by shady ranchitas that line the beach to buy a cooling beer or ice cream. Occasionally, a four-wheel Honda motorcycle putters along selling soda pops and ice

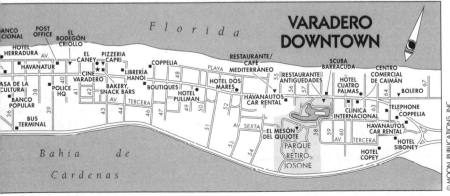

© MOON PUBLICATIONS, INC.

cream, and other hawkers sell papayas, coconuts, and other snacks. A few street vendors of jewelry, carvings, and crafts have their wares laid out on towels on the beach. These include much tortoiseshell and coral pieces to be avoided.

Mosquitoes: Varadero's sole blight is its millions of mosquitoes. Pack insect repellent and calamine lotion, and don't forget to lather up before venturing out for an evening meal.

HISTORY

For around 3,000 years before Christopher Columbus sailed by in 1492, Taino Indians had lived on the Punta de Hicacos, which they named for the *hicacos* trees that grow here. The Spanish settled it as early as 1587, when Don Pedro Camacho developed charcoal and salt-pork enterprises on salt flats and began supplying Spanish fleets. A small community of fisherfolk later sprouted on the south shore, in the village today known as Las Morlas.

Nothing much else happened here until the 1870s, when families from Cárdenas built wooden summer homes and developed the beach for local tourism, with boardinghouses for summer vacationers. In 1883, the families formed a "council," purchased 26 hectares of local land, and four years later presented the town council of Cárdenas with a plan that divided the land into 40 blocks and included plans for the first outdoor baths and other facilities. Rowing regattas developed (the prize was the Cuban Cup), necessitating more lodging, and the first hotel—the Varadero Hotel—opened in 1915.

In 1926, US industrialist Irénée Du Pont bought most of the peninsula beyond the town and built himself a large estate, complete with golf course. Other wealthy Norteamericanos followed, albeit in less grandiose style (Du Pont, of course, who had paid four centavos a square meter, sold them the land—for 120 pesos a square meter). Soon, Varadero was a budding Miami in miniature, with exclusive neighborhoods patrolled by private police. Al Capone bought a house here. So did the dictator Fulgencio Batista.

In the 1950s, US hotels began to spring up, prompted by the building of the Hotel Internacional, which had a casino and was a favored hangout of high-class hookers and mobsters. On the eve of the Revolution, virtually the entire

peninsula was in private hands; villagers who lived within sight of the sugary sands could do no more than stare longingly. After the Revolution, on 17 March 1959, the beach was declared public property and the proletariat were finally able to feel the sand between their toes. Two years later, President Kennedy's "quarantine" put an end to the hotel trade. Varadero, however, remained Cuba's prime tourist asset: Russians quickly arrived to cavort, sun themselves, sip rum, and smoke Cuban cigars just 90 miles from Florida.

ORIENTATION

There is only one way onto the island-peninsula: the bridge over Laguna de Paso Malo, at the extreme west end of the Hicacos Peninsula. Two roads run east along the peninsula from there. The fast Autopista Sur runs along the bayfront all the way to the end. Avenida Primera—the main street—runs along the oceanfront from Calle 8 in the west to Calle L and the Hotel Internacional in the east (west of Calle 8, Avenida Primera becomes Avenida Kawama, which runs through the Kawama district to the Hotel Tryp Paradiso and the westernmost tip of the island).

Cross streets begin at Calle 1, in the Kawama suburb, and run eastward consecutively to Calle 69, in the La Torre area. Farther east, they are lettered, from Calle A to L. The luxury hotel zone begins east of Calle L, where Avenida Primera becomes Avenida de los Américas. Virtually everything of importance is located on Avenida Primera.

There are two nodes of action—around the Centro Comercial El Cacique and Parque Josone, near Calle L, and at the west end, on Avenida Primera between Calles 5 and 13. Most of the action occurs between Calles 1 and 22, east of the Kawama district. The old village of funky wooden houses occupies the central section of town, roughly between Calles 23 and 54. Tourists are usually outnumbered by Cubans between Calles 30 and 54. The west end, centered on Calle 14 and the Kawama district, is very popular with Germans, with a preponderance of younger males.

The eastern tip of the peninsula—Punta Molas—harbors a military base that is strictly off-limits. Nearby is the 26th of July International Pioneer's Camp, where children from all over

SEX AND TOURISM

"'What effect is dollarization having on families and society?' asked one of [the journalists]. Said Maruetti [a Cuban economist], looking bureaucratically oblivious, 'Number One: foreign investment. Two: intensive development of tourism. Three: opening to foreign trade.' Sis had been out hitchhiking and someone made a foreign investment in her. It's all part of Cuba's intensive development of tourism. And, boy, is she open to foreign trade."
—P.J. O'Rourke.

Before the Revolution, Batista's Babylon offered a tropical buffet of sin. Endemic poverty was so great in Cuba during the 1950s that it is said there were more than 100,000 prostitutes in Havana, a city of two million people. In 1959, the revolutionary government closed down the sex shows and porn palaces and sent the prostitutes to rehabilitative trade schools, thereby eliminating the world's oldest trade.

Today, tourism-generated prostitution is proliferating. Reportedly, one Mexico City tour operator even sells weekend "sex packages." The problem is particularly acute in Varadero, where, at night, on dimly lit Avenida Primera, perfumed Cubanas in high heels and tight Spandex call out to unaccompanied males.

Still, the situation is nothing like before the Revolution, when brothels were a dime a dozen and a *yanqui* of impecunious means could get two prostitutes for a dollar!

A Chance to Get Ahead—and Get Away
Today, prostitution in Cuba is mostly an amateur affair. The *jiniteras* (the word comes from *jineta,* or horsewoman, or jockey) who form intimate relationships with tourists are a far cry from the uneducated prostitutes of Batista days. Studies by the Federation of Cuban Women (FMC) have shown that "Most [of the prostitutes] have the benefit of extensive economic and educational opportunity compared to the lot of their sisters before the Revolution. Most are not ashamed [and] few have low self-esteem. . . . *Jiniteras,* with very few exceptions, don't need to practice commercial sexual relations to survive. Instead, what motivates these women . . . is the desire to go out, to enjoy themselves, go places where Cubans are not allowed to go."

Young mulattas hang out by the hotel swimming pools or parade the tourist beaches, seeking invitations to be a part of the high life. A pretty Cubana attached to a generous suitor can be wined and dined and get her entrance paid into the discos, drinks included. Any financial transaction—assuredly, more in one night than she can otherwise earn in a month—becomes a charitable afterthought to a romantic evening out.

Many women hook up with a man for the duration of his visit in the hope that a future relationship may develop. Many succeed in snagging foreign husbands. Their dream is to live abroad—to find a foreign boyfriend who will marry them and take them away.

In 1995, the Congress of the Federation of Cuban Women concluded, too, that the rise in *jiniterismo* has an equal amount to do with Cuban youth's permissive attitudes towards sex. It recognized *jiniterismo* as an expression of a moral crisis and stressed the need to emphasize the role of the family, to help dissuade young women who have discovered the power of their sexuality from living it out to the full.

The Government's Response
The Cuban government has been slow to admit that prostitution is prevalent (some critics even claim that the government sponsored Cuba's image as a cheap-sex paradise to kick-start tourism). "The state tries to prevent it as much as possible. It is not legal in our country to practice prostitution, nor are we going to legalize it. Nor are we thinking in terms of turning it into a freelance occupation to solve unemployment problems. [Laughter.] We are not going to repress it either," Castro told *Time* magazine. Nonetheless, in spring 1996, the government initiated a crackdown. In the first six months of 1996, more than 7,000 women were shipped out of Varadero.

Fortunately, Cuba has not yet come full circle. True, professional prostitution (and pimping) is on the rise, and the first worrisome signs of child prostitution have appeared, with girls as young as 13 hanging around outside the Hotel Habana Libre. But the Cuban situation is not like Asia, where a whole generation is being exploited for commerce by governments hungry for tourist dollars. There are no brothels, and none of the porn palace fiefdoms of Batista days. Nor is it New York, where, in the words of Lynn Darling, "underclass addicts ply their trade under the watchful eye of the men who manage them."

the world used to come to promote future friendship among the peoples.

SIGHTS

A castellated water tower next to the Mesón del Quijote restaurant, atop a rise on Avenida las Américas, looks like an old fortress tower but was, in fact, built in the 1930s. A quaint touch is added by a modernist sculpture of Don Quijote on his trusty steed, lance in hand, galloping across the hillcrest.

There's a tiny **Museo Histórico** in a turn-of-the-century house on Calle 57 and Avenida Playa. Separate sections are dedicated to the local flora, local fauna, and sports in Cuba. Open Tues.-Sat. 10 a.m.-6 p.m. and Sunday 1-6 p.m.

The pocket-size cigar factory—**Fábrica de Tabacos**—at Avenida Primera and Calle 27 is worth a visit.

Las Américas
The most interesting attraction is Las Américas, munitions magnate Irénée Du Pont's colonial Spanish-style mansion at the far eastern end of Avenida las Américas. The green-tile-roofed mansion, which Du Pont named Xanadu, was built in 1926 as a sumptuous winter hideaway (complete with nine-hole golf course) atop the rise on the small headland at the end of the main beach. The Du Pont family lived here until 1959. It has long been a tradition for Cuban girls to have their photographs taken here dressed in ball gowns of a bygone era on their 15th birthdays.

Du Pont fitted his house with Carrara marble floor, great dark wooden eaves and precious timbers, and an organ that could be operated hydraulically or electronically from a separate room. DuPont built a massive wine cellar and wine bar beneath the house. Light pours into the library (where the vast array of volumes went unread). Another room resembles the interior of a captain's cabin, with porthole. On the top floor is a spectacular ballroom and bar decorated in Italian rococo and from which you can gaze longingly along the peninsula. The nine marble-floored bedrooms now house a museum with original furnishings (entrance costs US$3).

A faded tapestry in the dining room poignantly transcribes the lines of Samuel Coleridge's poem that contains the hopes the home once embodied:

In Xanadu did Kubla Khan
A stately pleasure dome decree

Parque Retiro Josone
Varadero's well-kept municipal park, between Calles 54 and 59, is centered on an old mansion furnished with colonial-era antiques. A wealthy sugar mill owner, José Onelia, and his wife lived here in the 1930s. The landscaped park includes a lake with a few flamingos and geese, plus rowboats for rent. There are a swimming pool,

Las Américas, aka Xanadu

CHRISTOPHER P. BAKER

two-lane bowling alley, several outdoor bars, and three restaurants.

Varadero National Park

This 450-hectare patch of scrub and woodland at the eastern tip of the peninsula is hardly an ecotourists' mecca. The area is riddled with limestone caves, many of which contain important aboriginal pictographs, mostly geometric designs such as concentric circles and dotted lines in reds, ochers, and blacks. The most important of these is **Cueva Ambrosia,** in a cliff called Loma La Caseta, on the inner (south) side of the peninsula. The caves contain some 50 or so aboriginal drawings, many excellently preserved. Its subterranean galleries include the "Room of Skylights," named for the openings in the roof through which lights plays down into the shadowed cavern.

ACCOMMODATIONS

There are scores of accommodations to choose from (Varadero hotels collectively provide more than 15,000 rooms), with something for every budget. Many are conversions of dreary cement-block hotels that once catered to Cuban holiday-makers and workers making the most of rewards for high productivity. The older hotels are clustered at the west end of the peninsula. Accommodations tend, in general, to be more upscale as you move east. The luxury resorts are clustered east of the old Du Pont mansion.

Most hotels have a swimming pool and their own restaurants and entertainment. Many offer watersports, including jet skis, water-skiing, and windsurfers. More expensive properties have tourist bureaus, boutiques, and car and bicycle rental facilities. Virtually all properties have a/c and radios in rooms (TVs are not the norm here). Many people who book packages are given apartment units with shared bathrooms and TV rooms; if you want a private bathroom, stress this at the time of booking. The larger resorts usually offer poolside activities, including volleyball and water volleyball games, aerobics classes and evening "animations"—the Cuban phrase for audience-participation entertainment—dance contests, charades, drinking games, etc.

Varadero is still relatively cheap. Still, gone are the days when foreign visitors paid half what similar accommodations would cost elsewhere in the world. Prices rise sharply in peak winter season.

Campgrounds

For a small fee, many local residents will let you pitch a tent on their private plots. Otherwise, there's a very basic campsite at **Centro Turistico Rincón Francés Camismó,** meant for Cubans. It's a 30-minute drive east of Varadero, and you are out on a limb. (The restaurant had no food when I called by.) You can pitch your tent or rent basic wooden cottages (US$15 for up to four people with bath, US$5 without). A bus (signed "Las Morales") runs out here from Varadero.

Casas Particulares

Dozens of locals have taken advantage of the tourism boom to rent rooms. The trade has grown so lucrative that scores of locals have built extensions on their houses. Expect to pay US$20-30. Many are mediocre, but there are some gems. It pays to check out a few until you find one you really like. You may be approached by a tout offering to show you one. If not, ask around.

I recommend an apartment on Calle 27 #207 run by "Tito" Hernández García, tel. 6-3727. It's small but modern and has reliable plumbing and a kitchenette (US$30).

Inexpensive Hotels

If you want an intimate place, try the **Hotel Pullman,** on Avenida Primera y Calle 49, tel. 6-2575. This down-to-earth hotel is in a colonial-style mansion. The 15 rooms are clean, with private bathrooms, hot water, and ceiling fans (US$19 s, US$25 d low-season, US$23 s, US$30 d high-season). The place has by now probably undergone a planned renovation including addition of a/c. It has a small, airy restaurant and a tiny pool. An even better bet is the **Hotel Dos Mares,** Avenida Primera and Calle 53, tel. 62-702, an atmospheric old colonial-style house with 32 large a/c rooms and 24-hour room service (US$23 s, US$28 d, US$39 suite in low season, US$30, US$38, and US$50 in high season).

The **Club Tropical,** Avenida Primera e/ Calle 21 y 23, tel. 6-3915, fax 66-7227, has 255 a/c rooms, each with wicker furniture, TV, phone, and balcony (US$50 s, US$65 d in low season and US$60 s, US$80 d in high season). Some rooms have ocean views. The hotel has a pleasant swimming pool and sundeck. A "deluxe" *casa* with six rooms is also available. There's a rustic beach restaurant, tour bureau, shops, and watersports. In similar vogue, try the **Villa Caribe,** on Avenida de la Playa and Calle 30, tel. 6-3310. It has 124 modestly furnished a/c rooms with an ugly green paint job. The restaurant is elegant. Other facilities include a swimming pool, hairdressers, four bars, disco, and a shop. Rooms have TVs and safe deposit boxes but no telephones (US$23 s, US$30 d low-season and $32 s, $42 d high-season).

Moderate Hotels

A popular option is the **Hotel Aguazul,** Avenida Primera y Calle 13, tel. 60-3918, fax 66-7229, a pleasing three-star property with 78 a/c rooms with satellite TV and telephones, decorated in white and taupe (US$35 s, US$50 d in low season). It also has apartments, for US$28 s, US$38 d.

Nearby, the modern **Hotel Bellamar,** Avenida Primera and Calle 10, tel. 63-014, has 218 a/c rooms with TVs, telephones, and private bathrooms (US$29 s, US$38 d low-season, US$36 s, US$48 d high-season). An additional 64 rooms have shared bathrooms.

Villa Cuba, Carretera Las Américas, tel. 62-975 or 62-966, fax 33-7207 or 66-7207, has 137 a/c rooms in 35 cozy *cabañas,* each with lounge, dining room, and kitchen, and furnished in classy contemporary vogue (US$53/64, low/high season). Other rooms are in a hotel unit (with private bath, US$30 s, US$40 d, US$49 t in low season and US$36 s, US$48 d, and US$59 t in high season; with shared bath, US$37/44 d). You can also rent either of two one-bedroom houses with its own swimming pool, TV, telephone, fax, room safe, and kitchen. A wide range of facilities is on hand, including massage on the terrace (Mon.-Sat. 10 a.m.-6 p.m.; US$5 local, US$7 general), hairdressers, and ice-cream parlor!

The venerable Hotel Internacional has been upgraded since being taken over by the Gran Caribe chain. It is now called the **Resort Internacional,** Carretera Las Américas, tel. 6-3011, fax 33-7246. The hotel is set in pleasing grounds and opens onto what is perhaps the most attractive segment of beach. The '70s-era hotel has several standards of accommodation, including 163 double rooms and two suites. There are also 156 rooms in 66 one- and two-floor *cabañas.* Prices begin at US$31 s, US$41 d low-season (US$37 s, US$49 d high-season). An elegant penthouse is available for US$146 low-season (US$183 high-season). All rooms have a/c, TVs, and attractive furnishings. Facilities include two swimming pools, four restaurants, four grills, a café, six bars, a boutique, bicycle and car rental, tour desk, sauna, hairdressers, and watersports. The Internacional is also venue for the *Sabor Latino* show at the Cabaret Continental.

Hotel Tortuga, Calle 7, e/ Camino del Mar y Bulevar, tel. 62-243, is a modern, 280-room, two-story complex, widespread with lots of open air. The rooms have heaps of light but no TV or telephone (US$30 s, US$40 d, US$48 t low-season, US$39 s, US$52 d, US$63 t high-season). You can also rent villas (US$23 s, US$30 d, US$36 t in low season, US$29 s, US$38 d, US$46 t in high season). It has a tourist bureau and rents mopeds. It's very popular with French Canadian and German package tourists.

Another favorite of Germans is the "three-star" **Hotel Herradura,** Avenida de la Playa e/ Calle 35 y 36, tel. 63-703. It has 79 a/c rooms in apartments (US$29 s, US$38 d in low season, US$35 s, US$47 d in high season). All have telephones and refrigerators. Only 33 have TVs. There's a restaurant and two bars, plus a store and a tourism bureau.

Expensive

My favorite hotel in this category is the highly popular **Hotel Cuatro Palmas,** Avenida Primera, e/ Calle 61 y 62, tel. 66-7044, fax 66-7208, boasting attractive contemporary colonial-era architecture. The hotel is built on the grounds of Fulgencio Batista's summer house and is centered on an attractive swimming pool. It has 222 rooms, all with a/c, satellite TV, hair drierss, radios, and telephones (67 rooms are "standard," 100 have double- and king-size beds); US$84 s, US$120 d low-season, US$90 s, US$128 d high-season). The standard rooms are merely adequate. Villa Cuatro Palmas has 27 a/c rooms in seven houses with living rooms, dining rooms, and kitchens (US$71 s, US$102 d low-season, $84 s, $120 d high-season). A full range of facilities is offered, including cabaret shows beside the pool. It was recently taken over by the Gran Caribe chain and upgraded.

The **Hotel Coral,** tel. 66-7240 or 6-3018, fax 66-7154 is another elegant complex centered on a mammoth, amoeba-shaped pool. The nicely-appointed a/c apartments and rooms feature TVs, telephones and liberal use of glass (US$69 s, US$81 d). It has an arcade of salons and boutiques.

Another good option is the **Hotel Iberostar Barlovento,** Avenida Primera e/ 10 y 12, tel. 33-7140, fax 33-7218, at the west end of Varadero. This modern hotel (a contemporary interpretation of Spanish colonial style) has 171 double rooms, all attractively appointed and with satellite TV, balconies, telephones, and safe deposit boxes (US$75 s, US$96 d). The complex surrounds a large swimming pool.

The **Hotel Riu Las Morlas,** Avenida las Américas, tel. 33-7215, fax 33-7007, or, in Spain, Riu Centre, 07610 Playa de Palma, Mallorca, tel. 26-9111, fax 26-5754, operated by Riu Hotels of Spain, is popular with Germans. Its elegant three-story units boast 157 attractively appointed a/c rooms, each with satellite TV, mini-bar, and terrace with ocean view (US$61 s, US$92 d in high season). The hotel features a weekly gala dinner.

The twin-block, modern high-rise **Hotel Tryp Paradiso Puntarenas,** Avenida Kawama, Varadero, tel. 5-66-71-2024, fax 5-66-7072, stands aloof at the westernmost tip of the peninsula. It's one of Cuba's showcase hotels and has been described in *Condé Nast Traveler* as "euro-trashy, accented by a revolting shade of orange . . ." but "well-maintained, positively glistening with modernity." It is now under Dutch management. The a/c rooms are nicely furnished (US$60 s, US$90 d, US$125 t low-season, US$80 s, US$110 d, US$155 t high-season). The twin towers are divided by a huge sundeck and massive swimming pools with swim-up bars. I find it soulless, despite pleasant decor. The self-contained facility even has a "Children's Club." It also offers massage (Mon.-Sat., US$10) and a motorbike excursion (US$10).

Deluxe

A favorite in this category is **Club Varadero,** Carretera Las Américas Km 3, tel. 33-7030, fax 33-7005, in Canada tel. (800) 553-4320, in the UK tel. 1992-447420, in the US tel. (800) 859-8009, a 270-suite property opened in 1992 as a joint venture of Cubanacán and Jamaica-based SuperClubs. The spacious and handsome suites are in villas and a two-story block. Rooms feature lots of hardwoods, plus private terraces overlooking the ocean and grounds ablaze with plumbago and bougainvillea. Buffet meals are served in a hangar-sized dining room with French doors open to the breezes. Facilities include an impressive aerobics room and gym, and every sport in, on, or under water, including Varadero's most complete scuba training and diving program. Rates—which include all meals, beverages, and activities—average US$200 s, US$260 d for rooms and US$225 s, US$300 for suites, depending on season. (SuperClubs is also developing a second resort, **Cuba Cuba.**)

Next door to Club Varadero is the **Hotel Tuxpán,** Avenida las Américas, tel. 33-5241, fax 33-5242, described as "a bewildering temple to the gods of generic pleasures," perhaps because the 235-room hotel, operated by the German LTI hotel chain, has an atrium lobby loosely modeled on a Mayan pyramid. It's built around a huge, kidney-shaped swimming pool. All rooms have a/c and TVs and are tastefully furnished. Rates begin at about US$85 s, US$95 d.

A sister LTI property—the 330-room **Bella Costa**—features handsome villas in addition to a hotel adjacent to the Tuxpán. It has 306 rooms, all with self-dial telephones, satellite TV, and refrigerators. Most have balconies with ocean views. It shares facilities with the adjacent hotel.

Spain's Grupo Sol operates four luxury hotels under the Meliá trademark. Three are adjacent, and together they take up a mile of beachfront. The **Sol Palmeras** tel. 66-7009, fax 66-7008, is Cuba's largest hotel complex, entered through a lobby with lush foliage, fountains, and caged birds adding a sense of the tropics. It has 375 rooms, 32 suites, and 200 bungalows. A huge pool with a thatched bar lies at its center. Rates range from US$58 s, US$78 d in low season and US$68 s, US$96 d in high season to a hefty US$121 s, US$202 d in peak season (Christmas and New Year's). Bungalows—set in lush grounds, with private terraces looking out over bougainvillea—begin at US$70 s, US$90 d in low season.

The star-shaped **Meliá Varadero,** tel. 66-7013, fax 66-7012, has 483 rooms and seven suites in six arms that fan out from a lofty circular atrium with rooms spiraling upward and vines and ivy cascading down from the balconies. The effect is fabulous—made more so by the chattering of parrots. Rates range from US$61 s, US$84 d in low season to US$124 s, US$208 d in peak season.

The **Meliá Las Américas,** tel. 66-7600, the glitziest of the trio, also boasts a stunning lobby replete with artwork, stained glass, a fountain, and trickling streams. Elegant arched terraces support a beautiful pool and sundeck overlooking its own private beach. Its 225 rooms and 25 suites are in twin-level blocks and feature kitchenettes and small lounge below a mezzanine bedroom with pleasing bamboo and wicker furniture. Bathrooms are equally elegant. Luxury bungalows should also now be available. Rates range from US$63 s, US$88 d in low season to US$126 s, US$212 d in peak season.

Four super-luxury resorts were near completion in mid-1996 farther east—the 200-room **El Caney,** owned by Gaviota; the three-story, 270-room **Hotel Oro Verde;** the 316-room two-story **Arenas Doradas Hotel;** and the 331-room **Hotel Rincón Francés,** a four-story, four-star Cubanacán property.

Club Med Varadero should now also be open. The resort is set to be billed as one of Club Med's "finest" villages, with complete watersports facilities, including scuba diving and deep-sea fishing. Contact Club Med, 2 place de la Bourse, 75083 Paris, tel. (1) 42-96-10-00, fax (1) 40-20-91-44, or, in North America, tel. (800) 453-2582, fax (602) 443-2086.

Apartments and Villas

Many of the hotels listed above also have apartments and villas on site (many of those listed below also have hotel rooms). Most of the Cuban hotel chains operate self-catering units. If you're on a tight budget, try making reservations at **Zona 2: Casa y Apartamento Carpeta,** Avenida Primera, e/ Calles 39 y 40. Suppos-

edly it's not open to tourists, but you never know your luck.

Apartotel Horizontes Varazul, Avenida Primera and Calle 13, tel. 66-7132 or 6-2512, fax 66-7229, next to the Aguazul and part of the same complex, has 69 one-bedroom a/c apartments with kitchens, bathrooms, living rooms, TVs, and telephones (US$36). Horizontes also operates **Apartotel Horizontes Mar del Sur,** Avenida Tercera y Calle 30, tel. 66-7482, with 98 one-room apartments, 48 two-room apartments (plus 42 studios and 130 hotel rooms) billed as a "family hotel."

Cabañas del Sol (part of the Resort Internacional) has small but adequate cabins with a/c and heaps of light pouring in through large louvered windows (US$35 s, US$47 d in low season). The *cabinas* are set in pleasantly landscaped grounds and are served by the beachfront Barbacao Grill.

The most impressive facility is the fully self-contained **Resort Kawama-Punta Blanca,** Hotel Kawama, tel. 66-7156, fax 66-7004, Villa Punta Blanca, tel. 66-7083, fax 66-7004, at the west end of the peninsula. Al Capone would be shocked to see what has become of his former bootlegging headquarters, built in 1934. The facility was recently taken over by Gran Caribe and the villas upgraded and divided into two adjacent properties. The hotel has 202 rooms in 16 houses, 55 *cabañas,* and 84 modules, centered on a hacienda-style main building, with a whole section of the narrow peninsula to itself. The Punta Blanca features 312 rooms in 16 houses and 85 modules. The charming a/c villas are fashioned in quasi-Spanish style and extend along the shore for almost two km. Some are quite splendid. The resort has several bars and restaurants. Havanautos and Havanatur offices are located here. And you can rent bikes and scooters (US$7.50 first hour, US$12 two hours). It's a bargain at US$75 s, US$126 d, all-inclusive of meals, drinks, and activities, including watersports and tennis.

Others to consider include **Villa Sotaveno,** with *casas* with kitchens, TVs, and telephones for US$25 s, US$33 d. The reception desk is in the Hotel Aguazul.

Yachters berthing at the marina can choose to rent bungalows next to Hotel Tryp Paradiso.

FOOD

Varadero has the greatest choice of eateries outside Havana, including many nestled over the beach. The greatest concentration is at the west end of town. It's quite feasible to buy a meal for about US$4, although you should budget twice that for seafood. Lobster begins at about US$12. *Criollo* cuisine predominates. International fare tends to be *criollo* with a hint of foreign lands, so don't set your standards too high. Alas, no one seems to sell the once-famous Varadero punch (made of coconut milk, egg yolks, sugar, and frappé ice).

Private restaurants—*paladares*—aren't permitted in Varadero, but many locals will prepare meals for you on the sly. Expect to pay about US$10 for a filling lobster meal that may be the best you'll eat in all of Cuba.

Some hotels allow nonguests to eat in their restaurants and pool-side grills. The restaurants are reliably among the best in Varadero and offer greater variety than elsewhere (the Tuxpán and Meliá hotels, for example, have gourmet restaurants). Prices in hotels are generally higher than elsewhere. Expect to pay about US$7 for breakfast, US$15 for dinner in upscale hotels.

Cubans patrol the sands selling soft drinks, ice cream, and snacks, and you are never far from somewhere to eat.

Most restaurants have a limited range of French, Spanish, and Chilean wines; some even stock Californian wines.

Fast Food and Snacks

El Rápido, Cuba's version of KFC, has opened three branches: on Avenida Kawama and Calle 7, on Autopista Sur at Calle 30, and on Avenida Primera at Calle 40. It serves fried chicken and fries for about US$2.

El Rincón, on Camino del Mar e/ Calles 11 y 12, is small and intimate, with outside dining on a patio. It serves omelettes (US$3), hamburgers (US$3), and sandwiches (US$1-2) and is open 10 a.m.-10 p.m. **La Colmena** is a pleasingly clean and modern snack bar on Avenida Primera e/ Calle 25 y 36. The **Restaurante/Café Mediterráneo,** tel. 6-2460, is a down-to-earth place opening onto Avenida Primera at Calles 54. It attracts local youth. To the rear is a more

classical restaurant opening onto a shady courtyard; it charges Cubans in pesos (you may be expected to pay in dollars, but give it a try).

For ice cream, head to **Coppelia,** on Avenida Primera e/ Calles 44 y 46, tel. 6-2866. Service to foreigners isn't guaranteed. If your luck holds, a bowl full of superb ice cream will cost 2.40 pesos. Alternately, you can buy Coppelia ice creams for US$1 from any of a zillion streetside snack stands operated by Rumbos. There's also an ice-cream store *(heladería)* in the new mall at Avenida Primera and Calle 43. Also try the liquor store on Calle 63, 100 meters west of the Hotel Cuatro Palmas.

You can order coffee at almost every hotel and restaurant. Coffee shops, however, are a rarity. Try the **Coffee Shop 25,** on Avenida Primera and Calle 25. **Snack Bar Calle 13,** catercorner to the Hotel Aguazul, is a bar serving *criollo* food. It's very popular with young Cubans and is the liveliest hangout in western Varadero.

Criollo

One of my favorite places is **El Meson del Quijote,** tel. 63-522, on a hill above Avenida las Américas. I like its romantic rustic decor, beamed ceiling, metal lamps, brass plaques, and potted plants and climbing ivy on a solarium dining terrace. The menu features a wide range of wines to accompany soups, omelettes, salads, grilled fish, fried chicken, shrimp, and lobster (from US$2-24). Open noon to midnight.

Mi Casita, on Camino del Mar e/ Calles 11 y 12, tel. 6-3787, boasts a beautiful beachfront setting and an elegant a/c dining room with period antiques. A set meal of chicken (US$12), shrimp (US$18), or lobster (US$25) includes soup, salad, dessert, and coffee. It has vegetarian dishes. It's open 7 p.m.-1 a.m.

The romantic **Restaurante Antiguedades,** tel. 6-62044, in Parque Josone, has set dinners, including surf 'n turf, from US$14. **El Bajareque,** tel. 6-3916, is a very rustic, almost Polynesian bar-cum-restaurant also on the grounds of Kawama. Meals cost US$6-20; open noon-12:30am. **El Pollito,** on Avenida Primera e/ 38 y 39, is a rustic bamboo-and-thatch restaurant that also has set meals such as pork chops and fries, with rice and beans, for US$6, including beer. Less expensive alternatives include **Bolero,** a small, rustic, romantic eatery where a beer costs US$1 and grilled chicken is US$3; and **Restaurante El Criollo,** Avenida Primera and Calle 18, tel. 6-3297, a rustic colonial home-turned-restaurant where a burger or grilled chicken costs US$3.

Seafood

The Villa Cuba has the **Barracuda Grill,** a pleasant beachfront bar and restaurant playing Latin music. Here you can buy *mojitos,* screwdrivers, and daiquiris (US$2) to wash down seafood such as "Earth and Sea Brochet" (US$10) and grilled fish (US$7).

The **Restaurante Arrecife,** tel. 6-3918, on the corner of Calle 13 and Camino del Mar, is a pleasant place serving seafood specials, including excellent grilled fish and lobster (US$7-17). A complete special for US$10 includes soup, grilled fish, dessert, and beer. Its outside balcony catches the breezes, and the mood is nice.

The **Mariscada Grill el Anzuelo,** tel. 6-66265, in Parque Josone has been recommended. This seafront restaurant also serves lobster, chicken, and beef dishes. Open 9 a.m.-6 p.m.

Meats

A touristy favorite is **El Bodegón Criollo,** in a rustic old home of limestone at Avenida de la Playa and Calle 40, tel. 62180. It attempts to replicate the famous Bodeguita de Medio in Havana, with classical music and signatures scrawled on the walls. You can dine outside on a shady veranda or inside in a rustic setting with eaves and ships' wheels-turned-lamps hanging from the ceiling. Typical dishes include roast leg of pork (US$7), creole mincemeat (US$6), or grilled pork steak (US$6). Open noon-10 p.m.

I've also heard good reports of the **Steak House,** an atmospheric colonial house where you may dine alfresco on a shady terrace, or inside, which is decorated with antique furnishings, swords, and model galleons. It specializes in steak, fish, and chicken dishes (US$15-25). **Restaurante El Dujo,** at the corner of Calle 16, also specializes in Cuban roasts. Grilled chicken and steaks are priced from US$4. It's open noon-1 a.m. Also try *La Barbacoa,* on Calle 64 and Avenida Primera, tel. 6-3435.

Italian

The **Pizzeria Capri** is very popular with locals. It serves basic spaghetti Napolitano (US$2) and unappetizing-looking pizzas (from US$3). **Kiki's Club,** on Carretera Kawama at Calle 5, tel. 6-4115, also serves basic Cuban pizzas, pastas, and *criollo* dishes for about US$5. It's closed on Sunday.

You may fare better in the **Troppo Ristorante,** next door to Hotel Tryp Paradiso, tel. 62996. It serves salads (US$3), spaghettis, and pizzas from US$4 and is open noon to midnight. There are two other Italian restaurants nearby—**Restaurante Venecia,** at the west end of Kawama, in a Spanish-style villa overlooking the beach, and *Club Alfredo,* tel. 6-4115, in Villa Tortuga on Avenida Kawama e/ Calles 6 y 7. Club Alfredo is ostensibly run by Canadians and is known for above-average pizzas. The elegant **La Trovalta Restaurant** is next to the Resort Internacional.

Oriental

I recommend the **Halong Restaurant,** in an old limestone villa on Camino del Mar and Calle 12, tel. 6-3787. It serves quasi-Vietnamese food against a backdrop of Vietnamese art. The menu includes spring rolls (US$3.50), fried rice with shrimp or lobster (US$5), lobster chop suey (US$9.25), and Tin Pan chicken (US$8.50). It's open 3-11 p.m.

Another Chinese restaurant is **Lai-Lai,** on Avenida de la Playa and Calle 18. It's open 7-11 p.m.

International

For ambience, consider the **Restaurante Las Américas,** on the ground floor of Xanadu, the former Du Pont mansion, tel. 63-856 or 66162. The restaurant specializes in French-style seafood and meats, such as lobster (US$39), fish sautéed with capers (US$13), seafood casserole (US$19), Chateaubriand tenderloin (US$32). It's like having dinner as the guest of a millionaire. The food is disappointing, however. Lunch and light snacks are served on the terrace. You can enjoy an aperitif at **Bar Solano,** in the basement. Open 10 a.m.-10 p.m.

Almost as enchanting is the chic **Restaurante La Fondue,** opposite the Hotel Cuatro Palmas, tel. 63-602. Elegant place settings and decor combine with classical music for a romantic note. The menu lists a large range of fondues using Cuban cheeses (US$22-30 for two). Special cheeses such as Gruyere, Sbrinz, and Gouda cost extra, per gram. (If, having dined far and wide in Cuba, you have reasonably concluded that Cuban cheese comes in one type and flavor, Rafael Pons, the welcoming manager, will happily edify you about the glories of cheese production in Cuba.) You can also order lobster and cheese (US$24), steak with cheese (US$14), and chicken with cheese (US$10). La Fondue has a good selection of wines. Open 1-11 p.m.

Supermarkets, Produce Markets
Varadero isn't geared to serve those catering for themselves, despite the proliferation of self-catering units. You'll find a bakery at Avenida Primera and Calle 43. You can buy Western foodstuffs and a minimal amount of fresh produce in the **El Cacique Shopping Center,** on Avenida Primera at Calle 62.

ENTERTAINMENT AND EVENTS

At night, the town is astir with Latin rhythms. The larger hotels all provide entertainment. Standard fare includes live bands, Afro-Cuban dance troupes, fashion shows, and competitions ranging from wet T-shirt contests to childish party games familiar to anyone who has vacationed at Butlin's or Club Med. More ritzy hotels host cabaret *espectáculos.* Many hotels also have their own discos. Nonguests are usually welcome.

Festivals and Events
Varadero's **Carnaval** was resurrected in 1995 and is held in mid-July. Don't expect the flair of Trinidad or Rio de Janeiro. Still, Varadero's home-grown street carnival is a colorful party with masquerades, music, merrymaking, and considerable licentiousness. A highlight is the selection of the "Butterfly" and "Papa Sol" from among the kings and queens chosen to represent specific hotels.

A **culture week** is traditionally held each second week in December, sponsored by the Ministry of Culture, Avenida Primera at Calle 23,

tel. 6-2793. It attracts artists from throughout Latin America. Every year, too, the **Varadero International Marathon** is held in November. And Cubans are shipped in from far and wide to celebrate the **May Day Parade,** each May 1.

Traditional Music and Dance
There's not much going on here, although many of the hotels provide Afro-Cuban shows. You can also check at the **Casa de la Cultura,** on Avenida Primera at Calle 35. The Parque Josone hosts a **Noche de Santería** each Friday at 9 p.m., with ritual dances of the mystical Cuban-Africa religion.

Bars and Discos
Take your pick of more than a dozen. Most are overly air-conditioned and play a mix of contemporary rock, hip-hop, world-beat, and Latin music. Discos don't get in the groove until 11 p.m. Most cost US$5 or less. The discos attract Cuban females (but few males), many of whom hang out by the entrance, hoping to entice a foreign male to pay their cover charge.

La Bamba, in the Hotel Tuxpán, tel. 6-6200, is the best disco in Varadero. Entrance costs US$10. **Havana Club,** next to the Hotel Cuatro Palmas on Avenida Primera, is another favorite, as is **La Salsa,** in the Hotel Puntarenas, and **La Pachenga,** beside the Hotel Aguazul. Others to try include **Rincón Latino,** in the Bella Costa, **Discoteca Caribbean Club,** in the Hotel Copey at Avenida Segunda y Calle 64, **Mi Salsa,** in Parque Josone, and **Disco Kastillito,** at Avenida de la Playa and Calle 49, tel. 6-3888. A newcomer is **Karaoke 440.** It gets packed. Entrance is US$2. Fortunately, karaoke is played only for a short time.

The open-air **Discoteca La Patana,** behind the Anfiteatro Varadero on the west side of the bridge into Varadero, is a less touristy option (Thurs.-Tues. 9 p.m.-3 a.m.; US$5, including two drinks). Farther west, near Marina Acua, is a fake pirate ship-cum-restaurant, **Discoteca El Galeón,** which doubles as a disco after 10 p.m.

There are very few bars. **Bar Beny,** on Camino del Mar e/ Calles 12 y 13, is open 24 hours. The most popular bar in town is **Bar Calle 13,** on Avenida Primera, catercorner to Hotel Aguazul and is best described as "foreigner meets girl."

Cabarets

Most of the larger tourist hotels host floor shows featuring kaleidoscopes of stiletto-heeled mulattas teasingly swirling their boas and behinds while musicians beat out sambas and salsa. Some of the shows are quite good.

Cabaret Continental, at the Hotel Varadero International, tel. 6-3011, is the best show in town. The cabaret (US$10, US$40 with dinner) is offered at 10:30 p.m. and is included in a "Night is a Feast" all-night cabaret, Tues.-Sun. 8:30 p.m.-3 a.m. I also recommend the **Cueva del Pirata,** tel. 66-7751, an emporium of exotica where an Afro-Cuban cabaret show takes place in an underground cave. It opens at 9 p.m. (US$15; closed Sunday). After midnight, a disco gets into full swing. It's east of town, at Km 11 on the Autopista Sur. Hotel transfers can be arranged (US$3).

The Meliá Varadero and Sol Palmeras also offer nightly cabarets, a Cuban tradition. Thus, locals have *theirs,* too: **Cabaret Anfiteatro Varadero,** in the Varadero Ampitheater, tel. 6-2169, on the mainland side of the bridge. It could well be the most spectacular cabaret in Varadero. Entrance for foreigners is US$10. It's followed by a disco. Open Wed.-Sun. 9 p.m.-3 a.m.

Cinemas

The Cine Varadero, on Avenida Primera and Calle 42, and the Cine Hicacos often have films in English at 6:30 p.m. (US$3). The movies range from camp classics such as *King Kong* to more prosaic fare such as *Fresa y Chocolate.*

Special Cultural Shows

Dolphins are the star performers at the **Delfinarium,** 400 meters east of Marina Chapelín. Shows are offered in a coral-rimmed lagoon at 11 a.m. daily (US$25, plus US$4 if you wish to take photographs). You can even swim with the dolphins—for US$5 extra.

SPORTS AND RECREATION

Most of the larger hotels have watersports and swimming pools. You'll have to pay for use of catamarans (about US$15 per hour), windsurfers (US$10 per hour), and jet skis and for water-skiing, para-sailing, etc. Many of the deluxe hotels also have tennis courts (expect to pay a US$2 court fee).

Scuba Diving

Nature takes the starring role in the seas off Varadero, a mecca for divers. The Varadero reef system extends from Matanzas Bay to the western extent of the Havana-Camagüey cay group. There are at least 25 acknowledged sites off Varadero, several with old wrecks. One of the best sites is the famous Blue Hole—*Ojo de Mégano*—an underwater cave 70 meters deep in the reefs near Cádiz Bay, east of Varadero.

Virgin forests of black coral are prevalent, especially at deeper levels. Hawksbill turtles are commonly seen. And there are more than 70 kinds of shells, including a massive and locally endemic species called *cobo.* The calm sea has little current, so turbidity is minimal. Even so, the diving here is not as good as elsewhere in Cuba.

Many of the upscale hotels have scuba diving facilities staffed by qualified dive instructors. The largest is at **Club Varadero. S'Cuba Dive Club Alfredo** is at Villa Tortuga #208, tel. 64-115 or tel./fax 33-7054, or, in Canada, Alfredo Werosta, 10708 142 St., Edmonton, Alberta. It offers full certification courses and resort courses for beginners. They have two Bauer compressors and an 18-passenger dive boat. Likewise, courses are offered by **Scuba Barracuda,** on Avenida Primera at Calle 58, tel. 6-3481, fax 66-7072, which also offers cave and night dives (US$40) and snorkeling (US$21).

Diving trips are also offered by **Puerto Sol,** tel. 56-3739 or 56-2203, from Marina Acua—US$35 for one dive, or US$65 for two dives including lunch—and **Marina Gaviota,** tel. 6-3712; similar prices. Marina Acua has an office on Avenida Kawama and Calles 3/4, tel. 66-8064.

Video Caribe, Av. 1 #6703, e/ 67 y 68, tel. 62-085, fax 33-7059, can videotape your underwater escapades or other watersport activities.

Snorkeling: All scuba outfitters rent fins, masks, and breathing tubes (about US$5). Most also offer snorkeling trips to the reefs, as do the three marinas (US$20).

Sporting Facilities

Golf: You can practice your swing at **Golf Club Las Américas,** at Xanadu, although the nine-hole course is threadbare. The club has a meagerly stocked caddie house pro-shop (open 8 a.m.-5 p.m.) and electric carts.

Parachuting: Varadero boasts the **International Parachuting Center,** or Centro Internacional de Paracaidismo, tel. 5-66-7265, fax 5-66-7260. It offers initiation courses, technical training, and jumps from various altitudes. The biggest attractions for novices is the tandem jump in a two-harness parachute with a professional trainer. All you need is a smidgen of courage and a desire to see Varadero as the frigate birds see it. The center is at the aerodrome on Vía Blanca, just west of the bridge into Varadero (open daily 8 a.m.-4 p.m.), reached via the dirt road opposite Marina Acua. The 10-minute fall (actual freefall lasts less than one minute) is made from a World War II-vintage Russian biplane and costs US$135.

Yacht Charters: A wide range of fishing boats and sleek yachts are available for charter at Marina Acua and Marina Chapelín. Rates vary according to season.

Sportfishing: Six-hour deep-sea sportfishing trips from Marina Acua cost US$300 for up to four people. Marina Chapelín, tel. 66-7093, and Marina Gaviota, tel. 6-3712, also offer four-hour sportfishing trips (US$250 and US$200 respectively, for four people). Every year in mid-June, Varadero hosts an **International Sportsfishing Tournament.** Entry costs US$200. For more information, contact Marina Acua.

Other Activities

There's a small **miniature golf** course on Avenida Primera e/ Calles 41 y 42 (US$1), **Horseback riding** is offered from several hotels, including Hotel Oasis.

There's an attractive **swimming pool** behind the beach at the west end of Avenida Kawama, 200 meters east of Hotel Tryp Paradiso. It was fully renovated in late 1995 and is popular with Cubans. Entrance is free. Facilities include changing rooms, plus a thatched bar and restaurant.

Restaurante Estrella, tel. 66-2649, in Parque Josone, has pool tables and a bowling alley (US$2).

SHOPPING

You'll find lots of stalls selling T-shirts, ceramics, maracas, music cassettes, etc., but there's also a good range of top-quality artwork. Most hotels have souvenir stores operated by the Cuban entity Caracol.

Stores and Boutiques

Centro Comercial de Caimán, opposite the Hotel Cuatro Palmas, is a commercial center with a fistful of boutiques, cosmetic stores, and other dollar-only stores. Other clothing boutiques are located two blocks farther east, and on Avenida Primera at Calle 45. You'll find several Caracol stores along Avenida Kawama selling Western clothing, swimwear, and touristy items. **United Colors of Benetton** even has a boutique, on Avenida Primera and Calle 39.

At press time, a large commercial complex was nearing completion between the Meliá Varadero and Meliá Los Américas hotels.

Photo Supplies

Photo Service has modestly stocked stores on Avenida Segunda at Calle 63, at Avenida Primera and Calle 42, and on Avenida de la Playa between Calles 43 and 44. The stores have a limited stock of film and batteries but also sell cameras (Zeniths and Canon EOS), including a wide range of instamatics. Open 9 a.m.-9 p.m.

Art and Craft Shops

Most hotels have small crafts and souvenir shops. Rumbos also operates mobile souvenir stalls along Avenida Primera. It's worth exploring farther afield, however, if you want real quality. A starting point should be the **Casa de la Artesanias Latinoamericano,** in front of the Hotel Siboney. Its superb range of goods from Latin America includes jewelry, jackets, shawls, belts, satchels, and erotic carvings. It's open 9 a.m.-7 p.m.

The **Boutique Artenucuo** (a rustic hut in front of the Hotel Copey) has an excellent array of jewelry. For truly world-class pottery and plates, ashtrays, and vases, head to **Taller de Cerámica Artística,** on Avenida Primera at Calle 59, tel. 62-703. Here you can watch local youths making pottery in a well-equipped modern workshop. Look for dining sets and individual plates by Osmany Betancourt, Alfredo Sosabravo, and Sergio Roque. Each is unique, painted by hand, and a steal at only US$40 each.

Next door is Varadero's **Galería de Arte,** with a range of wooden statues, paintings, and other artwork. Open 9 a.m.-7 p.m. Another good bet is **Barlovento,** a beachfront store on Calle 11, selling souvenirs, T-shirts, and postcards.

Bazar de los Orishas, on Avenida Primera e/ Calles 33 y 34, tel. 63-663, sells beads, dolls, fantastical wall hangings, jewelry, carvings, weavings, and tremendous leatherwork inspired by Afro-Cuban religious themes.

The airport has an excellent duty-free store selling everything from cigars and cassettes to "special mint" gold and silver coins and peso bills. You can even buy bongo drums (about US$150) and handmade saddles (US$350).

Cigar Stores

Most hotels have humidors where you can buy cigars. Habanos S.A. employs cigar rollers in the lobbies of most hotels (the cigars they make are sold under a generic Habanos label). Habanos recently opened a well-stocked cigar shop, **Casa del Habano,** at Avenida Primera, in the El Caimán shopping center, at Calle 61.

Bookshops and Music

Most hotel stores sell music cassettes and CDs, plus a limited range of Western newspapers and magazines. The only bookstore in town, however, is **Librería Hanoi,** which specializes in the usual range of social, historical, and political works. Fortunately, it has an excellent selection of Penguin classics in English. It also sells posters. Open Mon.-Sat. 9 a.m.-9 p.m. **ARTEX** also has a good music selection (open 9 a.m.-9 p.m.)

SERVICES

Banks and Moneychangers

Budget at least US$20 daily for meals and expenses—and double that would not be unusual.

As elsewhere, most hotels can cash traveler's checks or change small amounts of foreign currency. For larger sums, head for any of three banks. The **Banco Financiero Internacional,** Avenida Playa and Calle 32, offers a special service for tourists Mon.-Fri. 2-6 p.m. and Sat. 8:30 a.m.-noon. The bank is upstairs and is open daily 8 a.m.-12:30 p.m. and 1:30-7 p.m. The **Banco Nacional** is on Avenida Primera at Calle 36 (open 8 a.m.-3 p.m.). The **Banco Popular,** 50 meters south of Banco Nacional on Calle 36, can also change money and make advances against credit cards. It's open 8 a.m.-noon and 1:30-4:30 p.m.

There's also a **Casa de Cambio,** on Avenida las Américas and Calle C. Open Mon.-Fri. 9:30 a.m.-noon and 1-4 p.m. and Saturday 8:30 a.m.-noon. Believe it or not, if you hold American Express traveler's checks, you can cash them at Asistur.

There is virtually nothing for which you'll need pesos. Hence, you'll find very few people offering to change foreign currency for Cuban currency.

Post and Telecommunications

The larger hotels sell stamps and have mail boxes. The main post office is, peculiarly, in the gate house at Avenida as Américas and Avenida Primera. It has a fax, telex, DHL, and telephone service. Open 8 a.m.-8 p.m. There's another post office on Avenida Playa e/ Calles 39 and 40, and a third in the courtyard of the Hotel Copey.

You can send packages and letters by DHL express mail; the office is in front of Hotel Siboney at Avenida Primera and Calle 64, tel. 62103, fax 33-7020. It's located in the Servicio de Comunicaciones Internacionales, which also offers fax, telex, and telephone services. It's open 24 hours. The main Centro Telefónico is on Avenida Primera and Calle 30.

You can rent cellular telephones for US$7 a day from Cubacel, on Avenida Primera and Calle 26, tel. 80-9222, open Mon.-Fri. 8 a.m.-5 p.m. and Saturday 8 a.m.-noon. You'll pay a US$410 equipment deposit, US$100 deposit for each day of use, relevant charges for calls (US$2.45 per minute to the US), plus US90 cents per minute to receive and send. If you bring your own cellular phone, you can "purchase" a line here.

Hospitals

Clínica Internacional is a modern facility serving tourists at Avenida Primera and Calle 61, tel. 2122. A consultation costs US$20. A doctor and nurse are available 24 hours for hotel visits (US$40). The clinic has a pharmacy and can perform X-rays and laboratory tests. An ambulance is available. There are local pharmacies at Avenida Primera and Calle 28, tel. 62772, and Avenida Playa and Calle 44, tel. 62636.

There's a Sub-Aquatic Medical Center (Centro Médico Sub Acuático), tel. 52-2114, at Cárdenas, 10 km east of Varadero. It has a decompression chamber.

Other Services

The **police** station is at Avenida Primera between Calles 38 and 39. I'm not aware of any laundromats in Varadero. It's easy, however, to find a local willing to wash your clothes for a few dollars. A large public locker facility is beneath Coppelia, on Avenida Primera at Calle 44. The sole **Cupet gas station** in town is on the Autopista Sur, at Calle 17.

INFORMATION

The **Centro de Información Turístico** (Tourist Information Center) is at Avenida Primera and Calle 23. It's open 8 a.m.-8 p.m. and sells maps of Varadero and other cities. The *biblioteca* (public library) is on Calle 33 e/ Avenida Primera y 3.

Asistur, Asistencia al Viajoro, tel./fax 33-7277, at Calle 23 #101, e/ Avenidas Primera y Tercera, can provide medical assistance, insurance, cash advances, and legal advice, and help resolve other problems. It's the only place in Cuba where you may cash American Express traveler's checks. It's open Mon.-Fri. 9 a.m.-noon and 1:30-4:30 p.m. and Saturday 9 a.m.-noon.

Most hotel lobbies have a tour excursion and information desk, and the leading Cuban tour agencies also have offices where you can arrange flights and excursions. **Playa Azul** is opposite the Hotel Aguazúl, on Avenida Primera at Calle 14. **Gaviotatours,** is on Avenida Primera at Calle 26, tel. 66-7864; and **Cubatur,** at Calle 33, tel. 66-7269, fax 66-7048. **Havanatur,** tel. 66-7027,

---

VARADERO USEFUL TELEPHONE NUMBERS

Police	tel. 115
Ambulance	tel. 6-2950
Policlinica Internacional	tel. 6-2122
Airport	tel. 6-3016
Terminal de Ómnibus	tel. 6-2626

AIRLINES

Aerocaribbean	tel. 66-7096
Air Transat	tel. 66-7067
LTU Condor	tel. 66-7111
Martinair	tel. 66-7324

---

fax 66-7026, has its main office at Avenida de la Playa at Calle 37, and another office on Avenida las Américas, just east of Calle 64.

GETTING THERE

By Air

Cubana, tel. 5-66-7593, flies between Varadero and Baracoa (Tuesday and Friday), Cayo Coco (Tuesday, Thursday, Saturday, and Sunday), Holguín (Tuesday, Friday, and Saturday), and Santiago (daily except Tuesday and Thursday). **Aerovaradero,** tel. 5-3623, **Aerogaviota,** and **Aerocaribbean** (in Varadero, tel./fax 66-7096) also offer service to Varadero from Havana and other points in Cuba. Cubana flies to Varadero from Paris on Saturday and from Montréal and Toronto on Sunday.

Martinair (in Varadero, tel. 5-3624) operates flights from Amsterdam via Holguín on Saturday. In the UK, Regent Holidays offers charters using Martinair from £495 roundtrip. Varadero is also served by **Air Europa,** tel. 5-3617, and **LTU,** tel. 5-3611.

The **Juan Gualberto Gómez** airport, tel. 56-63016, is 16 km west of Varadero amid a landscape of scrub and yucca. A taxi ride will cost about US$25.

By Sea

The main marina is **Marina Acua,** tel. 66-3133, 66-7456, 56-3739, or 56-2203; HF-2790 or VHF-1668, at 23° 10'N, 81° 17'W, on the south side of Laguna Paso Malo, at the west end of the peninsula. It has berths for 60 vessels (US45 cents per foot per day), plus electricity, water, diesel, and gas. You enter via a narrow canal to the west of Varadero, immediately west of the twin hotels at the base of the peninsula.

A second, smaller marina—**Marina Chapelín,** tel. 6-3559 or 66-7093—lies eight km east of downtown Varadero, on the inside of the peninsula (channel 72 on VHF). Considerable investment has gone into the marina recently and it continues to expand. It features an attractive thatched bar and restaurant and full-service hookups. Crewed vessels can be chartered.

Near the end of the peninsula is **Marina Gaviota,** used mainly by the Cuban military and commercial concerns. It has dry-dock facilities, and pleasure craft can be rented, but foreign visitors are usually steered to the other marinas.

You should refer to Simon Charles' *Cruising Guide to Cuba.*

Taxis are available at the marinas to run you into town.

By Land

Most foreigners travel to Varadero aboard **minibuses** operated by Cuba's tour agencies. Transfers by minibus are available through Havanatur for about US$25 each way (any hotel tour desk can make the reservation for you). Locals, of course, travel by **public bus.** Bus no. 323 operates twice daily from Havana's main bus terminal at 4:50 a.m. and 3 p.m. (2 hours 45 minutes; six pesos). Your best bet may be to catch a bus or train to Matanzas or Cárdenas, and then take a local bus to Varadero from there.

A **taxi** from Havana costs about US$90 one-way.

Havanatur's **Tour & Travel,** Avenida 5 #8409 esq. 86, Miramar, Havana, tel. 33-3433, has a number of excursions to Varadero from Havana from US$27 (US$38 with lunch, US$135 overnight).

GETTING AROUND

By Air

Gaviota operates **Aerotaxi,** tel. 6-2929, using biplanes for excursions around Varadero (US$30 for 20 minutes; six passenger minimum) and to Cayo Largo (US$57 roundtrip), Trinidad (US$65), and as far afield as Pinar del Río (US$69). You can book through major hotels or directly at the Aerotaxi office, at Avenida Primera y 24, tel. 667540. You can even take a ride in a tiny seaplane from the Hotel Tryp Paradiso.

By Bus

Buses no. 47 and 48 run up and down Avenida Primera, as far west as Hotel Tryp Paradiso (10 centavos). Bus stops are clearly marked at regular intervals.

By Taxi

Tourist taxis hang around outside the major tourist hotels, most notably the Hotel Cuatro

Palmas. No journey between Calle 1 and Calle 64 should cost more than US$5. Beware of being overcharged by taxi drivers, especially at night. Official rates are US$1 plus US55 cents per km. You can call taxis from **Taxi OK,** tel. 66-7092, **Transgaviota,** tel. 66-7663, or **Turistaxi,** tel. 66-7344. State-run taxis are not permitted to take tourists.

Car, Motorcycle, and Bicycle Rentals

Varadero is well served by rental agencies. Reserve in advance or immediately upon arrival, as cars are often in short supply.

Cubacar, tel. 20-2188, and **Havanautos** have rental offices immediately east of Club Varadero. The main office of **Havanautos** is on Avenida Primera, e/ Calle 55 y 56, 50 meters west of Retiro Josone, tel. 66-7094; another office is located in the Hotel Kawama, a third on Avenida Primera, immediately north of Centro Comercial El Caiman, and a fourth at the airport, tel. 66-7300. **Cubanacán,** Calle 31, e/ Avenida 1ra and 3ra, tel. 63450, also rents cars.

Bicycle and Scooter Rental: Two-wheel travel is a perfect way to get around Varadero. Scooters and mountain bikes can be rented at several locations along Avenida Primera, most notably from opposite the entrance to Retiro Josone, on Avenida Primera (bicycles US$2 per hour; scooters US$9 one hour, US$12 two hours, US$15 three hours). Hotel Tryp Paradiso also rents mopeds and motorbikes (US$7.50 one hour, US$12 two hours, $15 three hours, US$4.50 each additional).

Horse-Drawn Cab

Dozens of *coches* trot along Avenida Primera and you'll have no problem locating one. Horse-drawn cabs gather outside Parque Josone. A leisurely exploration by pony-and-trap will cost US$4 per hour. You can ride the full length of Varadero for US$2.

Organized Excursions

Several tour companies offer overnight excursions from Varadero to Havana and other destinations.

Tour & Travel will help you get your bearings on a city tour (US$8). Their main office is at Avenida de la Playa #3606 e/ 36 y 37, tel. 66-3713, fax 66-7036. They also have offices at

Calle 31 and Avenida Primera, tel. 66-7154; in front of the Hotel Siboney on Avenida las Américas, tel. 63-509; and in the Hotel Kawama, tel. 66-7165. They're open 8 a.m.-8 p.m.

A 90-minute underwater journey is offered by **VaraSub,** a semi-submersible vessel that departs from the wharf at Hotel Tryp Paradiso. The vessel travels out to El Cayuelo, where you view the underwater world from large windows in the bowels of the 13.5-meter-long vessel. (I found the views disappointing.) Drinks (including rum cocktails) are included for US$35 (US$20 for children). You can book through any of the Tour & Travel offices or the Vara-Sub offices. A similar four-hour viewing experience is offered aboard the *Nautilo,* a glass-bottomed boat that sails from Marina Gaviota (US$25, including transfers).

Boating Excursions: Puertosol, tel. 6-3739, offers a range of excursions from Marina Acua, including a "seafari" to the Peninsula do Hicacos and Cayo Libertad and a "Caribbean Night" featuring dinner on Cayo Libertad, a santería ritual, and an Afro-Cuban *hechiceria* (US$49).

Cuba Nautica, tel. 66-7403, offers day trips daily at 10 a.m. (returning at 4 p.m.) for US$55, including cocktail, lunch, and snorkeling or diving. **Jolly Roger,** tel. 66-7565 or 66-7550, offers cruises by catamaran from Marina Chapelín. The all-day cruise lasts 9 a.m.-4:30 p.m. and sails to the cays of the Bahía de Cárdenas (US$70, including lunch).

GETTING AWAY

Buses depart the orderly Terminal de Ómnibus Interprovinciales at Autopista Sur and Calle 36. Departures for Havana are listed for 10:05 a.m. and 1:55 p.m. (two hours, 5.50 pesos) and for Santa Clara (three hours, eight pesos). However, foreigners are dissuaded from using buses departing Varadero, and you'll need to make reservations up to two weeks in advance. Buses to Matanzas depart hourly (two pesos); no reservations are needed.

Cárdenas is served hourly by bus no. 236, which departs from the Ómnibus de Cárdenas, next to the main bus station, and from Avenida Primera and Calle 13 (50 centavos).

By Taxi
Tourist taxis cost US55 cents per km—a costly getaway.

A slim bet is a *colectivo,* a communal taxis that can usually be found outside the bus terminal. It's illegal, however, for drivers to take foreigners, and fines are hefty. You're more likely to find a private car licensed as taxis (look for the yellow license plates). They, too, may not take foreigners, but many do (you'll have to cower behind the back seat each time you pass a policeman). Prices are negotiable. Expect to pay US$25 for a day trip to Cárdenas or Matanzas.

Hitching
If you want to try your luck hitching, stand by the traffic circle at the west end of Avenida Primera, near Calle 11, or on the Vía Blanca (for Havana). The official hitching point is about 400 meters west of the bridge, on the Vía Blanca for Matanzas. The Vía Blanca is busy with tourist traffic heading to Havana, so you should have good luck.

Organized Excursions
Tour & Travel, Avenida de la Playa #3606 e/ 36 y 37, tel. 66-3713, fax 66-7036; Calle 31 and Avenida Primera, tel. 66-7154; in front of the Hotel Siboney on Avenida las Américas, tel. 63-509; and in the Hotel Kawama, tel. 66-7165—all open 8 a.m.-8 p.m., has excursions to Matanzas (US$15) and the Bellamar Caves (US$10); Havana (US$79 including a cruise on *El Galeón,* US$115 including the Tropicana cabaret); Old Havana (US$44); Trinidad (US$60); Santiago (US$118); and elsewhere.

Rumbos, Compañía de Recreación y Turismo, Calle 32 y Av. 1, tel. 6-2506, fax 33-7034; and **Fantástico Tours,** Calle 39 #3901, esq. Avenida Primera, tel. 33-7062, fax 33-7061, also offer excursions to Havana, Matanzas, the Bay of Pigs, and destinations farther afield. Fantástico even has weekend excursions to Jamaica, Cancún, Nassau, and the Dominican Republic.

Cubanacán, tel. 66-7061, also has a wide range of excursions, as does the **Playazul Travel Agency,** Avenida Primera y Calle 13, Varadero, tel. 62384, fax 33-7034.

CÁRDENAS

The Peninsula de Hicacos forms a natural breakwater protecting the large Bahía de Cárdenas, whose southern shore is fringed with small oil derricks amid a desolate landscape covered with *marabú* scrub—stunted trees and henequin plantations. In their midst is the town of Cárdenas (pop. 75,000), a sleepy place a world away from the commercialism of Varadero, 10 km to the northwest.

The city was founded in 1828 as a place where settlers in the surrounding countryside could purchase supplies and sell their produce. Swampland was drained by canals and streets laid out like a chessboard. Many of the early population were refugees who fled Haiti following the Revolution. The town developed rapidly as a port serving the prosperous sugar-producing hinterland. Otherwise, Cárdenas has a lackluster history, punctuated by a singular event in 1850, when the Cuban flag was first flown here. That year, a Venezuelan adventurer called Narciso López came ashore with an invasion army to free the apathetic locals from Spanish rule and annex Cuba himself. Many of the 600 men that left New Orleans on 13 May 1850 were mercenaries from the state of Kentucky. Only six were Cubans. Although López's ragtag army captured the town, his meager force failed to rally local support and the invaders beat a hasty retreat. Cárdenas has forever since been called the "Flag City."

Cárdenas is hyped by several guidebooks for its architectural interest and, being close to Varadero, is favored for excursions. Alas, the town is in very tumbledown condition and can hardly make a good impression on day-trippers. A few pots of paint and whitewash would change the entire mood.

The town today derives its meager income from sugar and fish processing, the Arrachebala rum factory, and the burgeoning oil industry. A full-scale oil rig stands in the waters offshore, pumping black gold from deep beneath the bay. Still, the city is somnolent, seemingly awaiting the touch of a fairy godmother's wand to arouse it from sleep. Horse-drawn *coches* plod the streets, but cars—even 1950s-era American clunkers—are noticeably absent. In Cárdenas, the bicycle rules.

Columbus statue, Cárdenas

Sightseeing

The town has many examples of fine neoclassical architecture. An example is **Casa Natal de José Antonio Echevarría,** at Calle Genes #240, tel. 4919. The two-story house—now a museum—was built in 1873 and features a beautiful, hand-carved spiral wooden staircase. The house is named for an anti-Batista student leader, born here in 1932 and assassinated in 1957. The museum's top floor honors Echevarría and other Cárdenians martyred for the Revolution. Open Tues.-Sat. 8 a.m.-4 p.m. and Sunday 8 a.m.-noon; free.

The train station, at the base of Calle Concha, is a sky-blue, Moorish-style edifice of note. Another oddity is **Plaza Molokoff,** a two-story plaza that houses the *mercado agropecuaria* (public market). The market, made of iron, is built in the shape of a cross with a lofty metallic domed roof in Islamic style. Its wrought-iron balustrades are held aloft by colonnades. Molokoff refers to the "dome-like" crinoline skirts fashionable in the mid-19th century, when the market plaza was built.

Tiny **Parque Colón** is dominated by the **Catedral de la Concepción Inmaculada,** a beautiful old cathedral fronted by an impressive patinated statue of Columbus with a globe at his feet. The monument dates from 1858. Cárdenians, whose ancestors paid for it through donations, claim that it was the first statue to Columbus erected in Latin America. The church, built in 1846, has notable stained glass windows. The area around Parque Colón was last century known as La Dominica, which was linked by canal to the waterfront. The point became a wharf with the mayor's mansion, now the **Hotel Dominica.** The building is a national monument—it was here that Narciso López first raised the Cuban flag.

At the southwest end of Céspedes, a small fortress named for a revolutionary hero named Oscar María de Roja stands in the central median. It's now a popular café. There's a similar fortress at the west end of town, on Avenida 13 (Calzada) opposite the Cupet gas station.

Worth a browse, too, is the **Museo Oscar María de Roja,** in a beautiful restored colonial home at Calle Calzada #4. It's one of Cuba's oldest museums (founded in 1900) and contains an eclectic array of photographs and documents depicting the city's role in the wars of independence and the Revolution. It also houses a miscellany of butterflies and other bugs, including two fleas in dancing costumes, polished prehistoric axes, colonial weapons, and even a fountain-pen pistol that belonged to a Nazy spy who was captured in 1942. The *pièce majeure,* however, is a fabulously ornate 19th-century horse-drawn hearse, pure black baroque on wheels. Open Tues.-Sat. 1-6 p.m. and Sunday 9 a.m.-1 p.m. Entrance costs US$1.

Accommodations and Food

Hotel La Dominica, on Parque Colón, tel. 52-1502, is a basic 25-room hotel for Cubans. The ascetic rooms cost US$15 s, US$23 d. The restaurant downstairs overlooks the square. It was here in 1850 that the national flag was first raised in Cuba by Narciso López. You may have better luck at the **Hotel Europa,** almost cater-corner on the east side of Parque Colón, tel. 5638. This peso hotel reportedly charges a hefty US$15 or so to foreigners. Look for the colonial mansion at Avenida Céspedes #365.

You'll be hard-pressed to find anywhere exciting to eat. The best place seems to be the **Café La Cubanita,** a popular open-air eatery open 24 hours, on Avenida 5, one block southwest of Plaza Molokoff. Also check out the **Restaurante Las Palmas,** in an imposing mansion on Avenida Céspedes at Calle 16, tel. 4762, or the **Pizzeria La Bolognese** (formerly Pizzeria Castillo), on Céspedes and Calle 19. The former serves above-average *criollo* fare, the latter above-average pizzas (five pesos per slice). Two fast-food joints, **El Rápido,** Calle 12 and Avenida 3 Oeste, and **Los Almendros,** Avenida Céspedes and Calle 8, offer fried chicken, burgers, and pizzas. Alternately, try the **Hamburguesa Criolla,** on Avenida Céspedes and Calle 12, or the **Paladar Palmares,** on Céspedes and Calle 22.

The **Casa de las Infusiones,** next to the Hotel Europa on Parque Colón, serves tea and snacks—though (ahem) not up to English standards.

Entertainment and Events

Cárdenas has traditionally held a **culture week** in early March to honor the founding of the city. At other times of year, you can check out the **cabaret** held most nights at the Hotel Dominica (don't expect too much for your five pesos) or the one at the Restaurant Las Palmas, which is followed by a disco. The **Bar Colonial,** on Avenida 3, e/ Calles 11 y 12, seems to be the liveliest bar around. You'll find a **cinema** on Céspedes at Calle 14.

Services

Amazingly, Cárdenas is blessed with a **laundromat,** on Avenida Céspedes and Calle 7 (five pesos per load). There's a **post office** on Parque Colón (Mon.-Sat. 8 a.m.-6 p.m.) and a **Centro Telefónico** on Avenida Céspedes and Calle 13 (daily 7 a.m.-10:30 p.m.), where money-changers hang out.

The **hospital** is on Calle 13, midway to Varadero. The Centro Médico Sub Acuática is here and has a decompression chamber.

Photo Service has an outlet at Avenida Céspedes 568.

Need gas? There's a **Cupet gas station** at the west end of Calle 13 (Calzada), on the road to Varadero.

CÁRDENAS USEFUL
TELEPHONE NUMBERS

Police . . . . tel. 116
Ambulance . . . . tel. 196
Hospital . . . . tel. 52-4011
Railway Station . . . . tel. 52-2562
Terminal de Ómnibus . . . . tel. 52-1214
Taxi . . . . tel. 52-2528

Getting There and Away

By Bus: Buses 376 and 236 ostensibly run hourly between Varadero and Cárdenas, although the timetable is rarely followed. The journey takes about 30 minutes and costs 50 centavos. You can catch the bus in Varadero on Avenida Primera at Calle 12, or on Avenida de la Playa at Calle 35. Bus no. 376 for Varadero departs Cárdenas from Calle 14 and Avenida 8, no. 236 from the station at Calle 13 and Avenida 13 Oeste.

Bus no. 326 departs Havana's main bus terminal daily at 9 a.m. and 4 and 9:30 p.m. (three hours; seven pesos), depositing you at the main bus station in Cárdenas at Avenida Céspedes and Calle 21. Cárdenas is also served by buses daily from Matanzas, Santa Clara, Jovellanos, Colón, and Jagüey Grande. Buses tend to be sold out at least a week in advance.

By Taxi: You can reach Cárdenas by taxi from Varadero for about US$15. There are few taxis in Cárdenas, so if you plan on returning to Varadero, it is best to arrange a pick-up time with your driver.

By Train: A provincial rail line runs through town, connecting Cárdenas with Jovellanos and Colón (departures are in early morning). The station, tel. 330, is on Avenida 8 and Calle 5

Organized Excursion: Tour & Travel, Avenida de la Playa #3606 e/ 36 y 37, Varadero, tel. 66-7279, offers a city tour of Cárdenas and Varadero for US$12.

Getting Around

A ride in a horse-drawn *coche* is the way to explore. They tend to gather by Parque Colón. Your ride should cost one peso, the standard fare. Enterprising locals, however, are more interested in your dollars, and as a foreigner you'll be charged US$2 and up for a tour.

CENTRAL MATANZAS

Travelers have a choice of two main routes across central Matanzas—the Carretera Central and the Autopista. Of the towns described below, the first three—San Miguel de los Baños, Jovellanos, and Colón—are along the Carretera Central, while Jagüey Grande and Australia are along the Autopista.

From Havana, the Autopista runs ruler-straight east to west through south-central Matanzas province. The entire route is lined with farmland. There are no diversions to distract you until you reach Km 142 and the turnoff for Jagüey Grande, Australia, and the Zapata Peninsula. Dozens of people hitch rides at this major crossroads. The Autopista continues east, skirting northern Cienfuegos province en route to Santa Clara province. The only Cupet gas station along the Autopista is in Jagüey Grande. (There's another at Aguada de Pasajeros in Cienfuegos province.)

SAN MIGUEL DE LOS BAÑOS

San Miguel de los Baños is a little spa town of pretty villas hidden deep amid rolling hills. It's reached via a turnoff from the Carretera Central (route 3-N-1) at Coliseo, 37 km east of Matanzas, at the junction with route 3-101 to Cárdenas. The town's lofty setting makes it cool and airy. This, combined with the healing properties of its mineral waters, fostered the town's growth last century as a popular health spa. The gentry built villas here in neoclassical style, others erected homes with a distinctly French provincial feel, with filigreed balconies and gingerbread woodwork. Though some houses are tumbledown, the town is in reasonably good condition. Bougainvillea abounds, and sunflowers are popular garden adornments.

As you enter town, you'll pass the ornate **Balneario San Miguel** on your left, topped by Islamic-style turrets. Sadly, it's in slightly derelict condition (Cubanacán has plans to restore the *balneario*). A *custodio* and Islamic tiles. The marble-topped bar downstairs still functions, but water is no longer for sale—having been replaced by rum.

Pathways lead down the garden to outdoor *baños,* now disused. In the center is the grand baths, resembling Roman or Turkish baths, with flint stones inset in the walls in a crude mosaic. Sulfurous-smelling water still runs into a small sink, and it is not unusual to see locals filling their pails.

There's one hotel in town, the **Rincón del Daño,** terribly run-down but with great potential for restoration. Downstairs, the columned restau-

San Miguel
de Los Baños

rant retains its stucco work. It serves *criollo* food for pesos, but the hygiene is questionable.

JOVELLANOS TO COLÓN

The Carretera Central continues east past great fields of cane silvered by the fierce wind. Sixteen km east of Coliseo, you reach the small agricultural town of Jovellanos, whose main street (Calle 11) runs parallel to and two blocks north of the Carretera Central.

The town, which has a predominantly black population, is known as a center of Afro-Cuban music and dance, influenced by the Arara tribe from Benin, who arrived in the late 18th century via Haiti. Jovellanos has a small museum dealing with local affairs, plus a couple of basic restaurants.

The **Hotel Moderno,** Calle 11, e/ Av. 16 y 18, tel. 82837, can supply basic rooms (some with a/c) for seven pesos s, 8.40 pesos d. There's a **Cupet gas station** on the Carretera Central at the east end of town, with a dollars-only café. Bus no. 346 departs Havana's main bus terminal for Jovellanos at 2:10 p.m. (3.5 hours; 7 pesos).

South of Jovellanos, the 3-182 cuts southwest to **Pedro Betancourt,** a small and pleasant colonial town with a beautiful church at its core. Pedro Betancourt is the gateway to mile upon mile of citrus groves crisscrossed by ruler-straight roads and extending all the way south to the Austopista.

Colón

Colón, 33 km east of Jovellanos, is worth a quick browse. Its colonnaded streets are lined with tumbledown neoclassical structures, generating a sense that you've fallen into some sleepy 19th-century provincial setting.

COLÓN USEFUL TELEPHONE NUMBERS

Police	tel. 115
Ambulance	tel. 3-2125
Hospital	tel. 3-3011
Railway station	tel. 3-2758
Terminal de Ómnibus	tel. 3-2808

Colón is centered on **Parque de Libertad** two blocks south of the main street, **Máximo Gómez.** The park is fronted by some attractive buildings and surrounded by shade trees and a wide promenade. At its heart is a life-size, patinated bronze statue of the town's namesake Christopher Columbus (Cristóbal Colón), atop a pedestal with a lion at each diagonal.

There are two options where you can lay your head, the **Hotel Gran Caridad** and the **Hotel Santiago Cuba.** Both are on Máximo Gómez and offer rooms with private bathrooms (cold water only) for about 15 pesos.

Pickings are slim for the famished. **Restaurante Luzenye,** 50 yards southwest of the plaza, serves salads for one peso, pork steaks (15 pesos), snacks, and beer (US$1). There's a **Cupet gas station** on Gómez, one block west of Martí, and another outside town on the road (route 3-1-2) that leads south to Caliemete and the Autopista.

Colón lies on the main railway line from Havana to Santiago and is well served by trains. Local service runs between Colón and Cárdenas and Santa Clara. Buses also link Colón with Cárdenas, Jovellanos, and Matanzas (two hours; five pesos) several times daily, departing the bus terminal on Máximo Gómez. In town, the horse-drawn cab is king, although you'll find *colectivos* creaking along the dusty streets.

SOUTH TO THE AUTOPISTA

Route 3-1-2 leads *south* from Colón and the Carretera Central to Aguada del Pasajeros and the Autopista, via Calimete. It's a 22 km beeline past sugarcane and banana plantations shaded by thick stands of palms. The land is as flat as a billiard table. Agriculture is mechanized hereabouts, with few oxen in evidence. Tractors spread the red earth through the streets of **Calimete,** which has a 600-meter-long promenade on the east side of the main street lined by shade trees and lit at night by short, stubby lanterns. Calimete is a neat country town. Several *paladares* line the main street, including La Colonial, which serves *criollo* dishes.

Jagüey Grande

Jagüey Grande, along the Autopista, is an agricultural town and railhead encircled to the northwest by a vast citrus complex and to the north-east by sugarcane fields. If you spend any time here, check out the **Centro de Desarrollo de Artes Plasticos,** where you can view works of art in the making.

The **Hotel 9 de Mayo,** Calle 13, e/ Calle 56 y 58, tel. 2118, is a basic, modestly furnished pesos-only hotel in a colonial building. Rooms vary but are acceptable (12.05 pesos s, 12.56 pesos d). The eateries of choice are the **El Chino Restaurant,** facing the south side of the plaza, and **Paladar La Roca,** at Calle 11 #5013 (four blocks north of Jagüey Grande). There's a farmers' market on Calle 15, e/ Calles 54 y 56.

The **Cupet gas station** is at the junction of Calles 13 and 70, at the south end of town on the road that leads to the Autopista.

Warning: five miles east of Jagüey Grande, a railway track crosses the freeway. It's set in a deep hollow. *Slow down!* You can be upon it before you know it if you're not alert.

AUSTRALIA

Sugar Factory and Museum

Near the village of Australia, a huge sugar factory, Central Australia, looms over the sugarcane fields. Head south a half mile from the crossroads at Km 142. At the Y-fork, the road to the right leads to Playa Girón, the one to the left leads to the sugar factory and museum (there are no signs). You see the factory first, then hear the distant tooting of whistles and clanking of engines and carriages, which goes on around the clock.

Here, on the afternoon of 15 April 1961, Fidel Castro arrived to set up his military headquarters during the Bay of Pigs invasion. Castro, who knew that the sugar factory had the only telephone for miles around, directed his troops from the *central* before dashing off to lead *"un barraje infernal"* (an infernal barrage) of howitzers against the invaders attempting to break out of Playa Larga.

Remains of aircraft shot up in the fighting lie outside the administrative building, which is now a small **museum** open Mon.-Sat. 8 a.m.-5 p.m. and Sunday 8 a.m.-1 p.m.; entrance is US$1.

Bar El Bosque, just before the entrance to the sugar mill, is a spit-and-sawdust place where you may sip *aguardente* with the field- and factory-hands.

Finca Fiesta Campesina

In the same area, 400 yards south of the junction at Km 142, this traditional "peasant's farm" is a tourist contrivance but still an appealingly atmospheric stop. Open 24 hours, the place offers cockfights and a small zoo inhabited by deer, agoutis, snakes, and birds from parrots to owls. It also raises fruit trees. You can sample the fruits, excellent Cuban coffee (served in earthenware cups), and *guarapo* (sugarcane juice) crushed in a traditional trapiche. There's also a cigar shop and souvenir shop.

A thatched restaurant here serves *criollo* cuisine that includes *ajiaco,* a tasty *campesino* stew. Excellent! It has a **disco** on weekend nights, when the crowd is exclusively Cuban. There's no entrance fee. (There's another disco, in Australia village proper, that gets quite rowdy when the rum begins to flow.)

Bohio de Don Pedro

South of Finca Fiesta Campesina and part of the same facility is Bohio de Don Pedro, which reproduces a traditional peasant house—*bohio*—and is named for Don Pedro, an amiable *campesino* who manages the *finca.* Shade trees enhance the splendid aesthetic.

Bohio de Don Pedro is also one of Cuba's most endearing "hotels." There are seven rustic yet exquisite, roomy, thatched, all-log *bohio*-style cottages featuring terra-cotta tile floors, large bathrooms, TVs, ceiling fans, and small kitchenettes. It's a splendid bargain at US$18 s, US$25 d. Each has a veranda from where you can watch the chickens, horses, and other farm animals feasting and fornicating. Some cabins have loft bedrooms and sleep four people. A swimming pool and additional cabins are planned. The affable manager, Danilo Cañizo, says that he "accepts no responsibility for guests who do not want to go back home."

In the *bohio*'s rustic and atmospheric restaurant, Don Pedro's wife, Hildelias, serves tasty and filling *criollo* meals, including her husband's splendid home-baked bread (US$3 breakfast, US$10 lunch or dinner).

You can walk the 400 yards from Fiesta Campesina. If driving, the turnoff from the Autopista is 200 meters west of the turnoff for Playa Girón. Reservations can be made through Rumbos offices islandwide, tel. 59-2535.

There's an atmospheric restaurant and bar, *Pío Cua,* about two miles south of Australia.

The place is made of hardwoods and has a soaring thatched roof and lots of stained-glass windows. *Criollo* dishes cost about US$5. The restaurant is open noon-11:45 p.m., the bar and café 8 a.m.-11 p.m.

THE ZAPATA PENINSULA AND BAY OF PIGS

South of Australia, the sugarcane fields and dark-soiled miles of agro-industry abruptly end and the sawgrass, reed, and *marabú* brush begins, swaying like wheat in the wind. This swampland (the **Cienega de Zapata**) sweeps south to the Caribbean Sea, smothering the entire Zapata Peninsula, a great shoe-shaped extension jutting west into the Golfo de Batabanó. The 4,230-square-km landmass—Cuba's largest peninsula—is a region of limestone with flooded faults called *cenotes.* It is now a national park and Cuba's foremost wildlife reserve.

Zapata extends east and west to each side of a deep, finger-like bay, the Bahía de Cochinos—**Bay of Pigs.** Zapata is considered a sensitive region for more than ecological reasons, and the Cuban government keeps a tight rein on foreign visitation to the swamps. As yet, it is little utilized by ecotourists, through a handful of birders and fisherfolk are savvy to its allure. Only two roads lead into the park, and they are patrolled to ensure no unauthorized access—even to locals.

The entrance to the Zapata reserve is at Buena Ventura, two km west of Playa Larga, 32 km south of Australia. The only access is for specialist birders or hunters. You *must* hire a guide through Rumbos or at their facilities at Fiesta Finca Campesina or Bohio del Don Pedro. Guides cost US$53 for one person (less per person for two or more people). Bohio de Don Pedro will provide coolers at extra cost. Birding excursions are also offered from the Villa Playa Girón (US$20).

Be warned: large mosquitoes eagerly await your arrival. Take repellent!

HISTORY

Zapata was inhabited by pre-Columbian Indians. The Spanish *conquistadores* managed to destroy the local Taino Indian population before abandoning the region. It has remained a virtual no-man's-land ever since. Talk of draining the swamps was heard as early as 1854, but

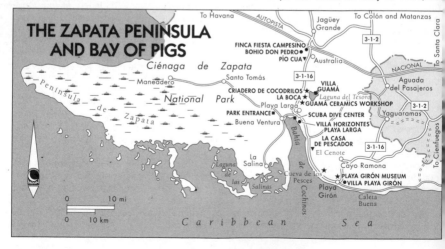

ZAPATA REGION USEFUL TELEPHONE NUMBERS

Police . . . . tel. 89-5107
Policlínico (Playa Girón). . . . . tel. 9-4196
Policlínico (Playa Larga) . . . . tel. 7116
Bus (Basé Girón). . . . . tel. 9-4134

nothing was done until 1912, when the American-owned Zapata Land Company was formed. The survey report found the swamps as inaccessible "as Stanley's Tenebrosa Africa . . . a place of fogs and death where alligators are absolute masters." Eventually, the company ran out of money.

The sparce population (about 8,000 souls inhabited Zapata on the eve of the Revolution) remained cut off from the rest of Cuba in conditions similar to those reported by Columbus when he landed in the Bahía de Cochinos in June 1494. Columbus reported seeing naked Indians carrying "in their hand a burning coal, and certain weeds for inhaling their smoke." The burning coal was charcoal.

Before the Revolution (the *cenagueros*—swamp people—refer to the Revolution as a milestone, as if it separated B.C. from A.D.), there had been no roads, no schools, no electricity. Charcoal-making was the major occupation of the impoverished population (charcoal is prized as a fuel for cooking). The austere, hardworking *carboneros* axed *marabú* and mangrove branches to a length of two feet, then stacked them against a teepee-shaped *horno de carbón,* a charcoal oven made of straw and earth, hollow at the center. The branches were covered in grass and ash and left to burn slowly for a week or so. The wood smoldered and, at the critical moment, was drowned with water. The *carboneros,* forever blackened by soot, staggered to Cienfuegos with sacks on their backs where, reportedly, one day's labor might sell for as little as two cents.

When Castro came to power, the area was still inaccessible. It is claimed that these unfortunate people—the poorest in Cuba—sometimes had to subsist on sugared water and sea snails. The *cenagueros* were among the first beneficiaries of the Revolution. The youthful

Castro government built highways of hard-packed limestone into the swamps. They also established the first schools, and more than 200 teachers from the national literacy campaign arrived. The indigent community of Cayo Ramón even got a hospital. Tourist bungalows went up at Girón. And an airport with a 4,100-foot runway was built. Today, *carboneros* still build their pungent ovens, but their charcoal now goes to town on trucks.

WILDLIFE

Cuba's most important wetland area is replete with wildlife. The diverse and complex ecosystems include marsh grass, mangrove thickets, and thickly wooded swamp forest of dense *marabú* bushes, with their inch-long thorns. It is claimed, biologically, to be a mirror of the Everglades of Florida (there are even beautifully banded *liguuc* snails, a kind of tree snail common in the Florida Everglades).

Zapata harbors more than 900 species of flora (including poisonous *guao* plants), 171 species of birds, 31 of reptiles, and 12 of mammals, including the pygmy *jutía* native to the Zapata swamp. The Río Hatiguanico harbors Cuba's largest population of manatees. There are freshwater turtles, many of which end up as fricassee, a popular dish among the marsh people. Iguanas will come up to you, totally fearless. And the alligator-gar *(manjuarí),* the most primitive of Cuban fish, is found in lagoons such as Laguna del Tesoro, as are crocodiles and caimans, a diminutive species of alligator. Crocodiles had been hunted to near-extinction during the past several centuries. Castro ordered them rounded up for breeding, saying, "When we have millions of them, we'll have an industry."

Crocodile tours can be arranged through Rumbos (one person US$53.50 by boat, including guide, US$74 double, or US$108 for four people), or at Bohio del Don Pedro.

Birds
Of Cuba's 22 endemic bird species, 18 inhabit the marshes. Zapata protects the bee hummingbird (the world's smallest bird) as well as an endemic tanager and *gallinuela de Santo Tomás,* the Zapata sparrow, Zapata rail, and Zapata wren, all of which are limited to Santo

Tomás lagoon. Cuba's national bird, the Cuban trogon or *tocororo,* is also found here, as is the long-tailed sparrow hawk, plus cormorants and a significant population of Cuban parrots.

Zapata is also a favorite stop for tens of thousands of migratory birds. The best time is October to April, when overwhelming numbers of birds flock in—sandhill cranes, great blue herons, tricolored herons, wood ibis (the only species of this family to be found in the Caribbean), and bitterns amid the muddy, pool-studded grasslands. Even flamingoes wade in the soupy lagoons.

There's an **International Bird-Watching Center** at Playa Larga. The best spot for birding is perhaps the hamlet of **Santo Tomás,** about 30 km west of Playa Larga, but there is splendid birding, too, just west of Playa Girón, where spoonbills, flamingoes, and ibis are easily seen by following trails of landfill (a guide is compulsory).

Fishing

Zapata has been isolated from fishing pressure since 1959, making this huge reserve as close to a virgin fishery as one can find in today's world. There are said to be places where you can catch the fish with your bare hands, the way the indigenous Indians did! Tarpon and bonefish are the species of choice. Bonefishing is most productive late fall through June; tarpon fishing peaks late February/early March through June. (Carp were also introduced, but they ate the grasses that supported the populations of bass and tilapia, so these species are fewer in number than elsewhere in Cuba.)

There are two distinct areas for fishing—Laguna de las Salinas, and the 200-meter-wide Río Hatiguanico and its tributaries. **Laguna de las Salinas** is a vast expanse of flats, watercourses, and islets on the southern shores of Zapata, at the western entrance to Bahía de Cochinos. The water contains sulfurous crystals. The dirt road is often flooded in places (then, you really get to see the crocodiles!). Vegetation includes the button tree, so small that it looks like a bonsai.

Laguna de las Salinas is famous for bonefish. Several well-traveled anglers consider Las Salinas the standard by which all other locations should be judged worldwide! Being shallow and firm-bottomed, it is ideal for wading and

CRABS!

Zapata's roads receive little traffic, except for swarms of *cangrejos* (crabs) scurrying across in springtime. Mid-March through April, giant land crabs emerge from the vegetation and swarm, legion upon legion, to meeting grounds where they gather for vast orgies and egg-laying parties. They move in such numbers that the main coast road (and those along much of the southern and eastern coasts of Cuba) becomes a veritable carpet of crushed crabs—and the fetid smell draws vultures to feast on the banquet.

In *Driving Through Cuba,* Carlo Gébler tells of driving around a corner and "suddenly the road ahead as far as we could see was strewn with the remains of crabs crushed flat onto the tarmac, thousands of them, a carpet of them, with hundreds of live ones crawling on top of the dead. . . . Through the open windows we heard the clacking of their claws on the tarmac as they ran across our path. Then came a noise like a Mib Mac styrofoam container exploding, and with horror we realised this was our first casualty. . . . From under the tyres came an almost continuous sound of their bodies exploding."

spotting tailing and cruising bonefish. Other species include *palometa* (also called permit), which can reach 20 pounds. Tarpon up to 40 pounds—ideal light-tackle adversaries—cruise the clear lagoons of the outer cays and will fight over a well-cast fly or plug as anglers drift the lagoons, watching for cruising tarpon and sight casting as the fish emerge from the mangroves or roll on the surface like trout in a stream in the midst of a heavy hatch.

The **Río Hatiguanico** and its mangrove-lined shores is famous for tarpon ("silver bullets") up to 30 pounds. The river also contains snook. Underpowered skiffs mean long periods getting to the best lagoons, but . . . wow! "My nerves were frazzled," recalls Gilberto Maxell, in *The Pan-Angler.* "Every cast was a strike, or so it seems, sometimes several tarpon hit the fly on the same retrieve."

In addition, the still waters of **Laguna del Tesoro** harbor trout, haddock, carp, native *biajacas,* tarpon, tilapia, and meter-long *manjuarí,* an antediluvian fish with a crocodilian head.

A Swede called Erland von Sneidern ("Big Swede") has been issued an exclusive right to operate fishing trips in Zapata. A US company, **Pan-Angling**, 180 N. Michigan Ave., Chicago, IL 60601, tel. (312) 263-0328, fax (312) 263-5246, arranges prepaid, all-inclusive tours, with stays at Bohio del Don Pedro. **Rumbos** also offers hunting and fishing excursions for groups of up to 10 people. Per-person prices vary according to number of anglers: three days costs US$1,275 (eight people) to US$1,500 (two people); six days costs US$2,250 to US$2,700. Three-hour fishing trips are also offered on Laguna del Tesoro from Villa Guamá.

LA BOCA DE GUAMA

La Boca, at the entrance to Laguna del Tesoro, 16 km south of Australia, is an important roadside stop of thatched *bohios* with numerous attractions and services. A five-km-long canal leads from here to the Villa Guamá resort, in the middle of the lagoon.

La Boca, tel. 2458, features an atmospheric bar and equally attractive restaurant; a well-stocked souvenir shop that sells film as well as a wide range of crafts; a crocodile farm; and the **Guamá Ceramics Workshop**, where you can watch bowls, masks, teapots, and kitchenware being made in Arawak style before being baked in huge brick kilns *(ornos)*. The director, Francisco Javier Ojeda, will be pleased to show you around.

There's a swimming pool, but it did not inspire confidence when I saw it. Rowboats can be hired during the day (US$2 per hour) for lazing on the lagoon.

La Boca Restaurant overlooks a lagoon full of water hyacinths. It serves *criollo* meals, including roast crocodile tail (US$7), a legendary aphrodisiac. You can buy *pipas* (coconut milk in its husk) and fresh-squeezed orange juice from stands inside the grounds of the crocodile farm.

Crocodile Farm
The *criadero de cocodrilos* is Cuba's most important crocodile farm, with more than 10,000 crocodiles. Pathways lead past souvenir stalls and little bars to the large, circular pens surrounding natural lagoons where crocodiles laze

in the sun. Raised wooden platforms provide vantage points to admire the awesome beasts lying still as death, jaws agape, hoping obviously for a careless visitor to stumble and fall into a pit. You can also see a "demonstration of crocodile capture" involving a docile two-meter-long youngster. The farm also has a **Breeding Center of Indigenous Ichthyofauna,** where scientists study local aquatic species, and a breeding center for parrots and deer.

Entrance costs US$3. Highly recommended.

LAGUNA DEL TESORO

Laguna del Tesoro (Treasure Lagoon) is a 16-square-km lake in which sportfishermen have caught record largemouth bass. The lake is named for the priceless religious objects that the Taino Indians supposedly threw into the water to hide them from the Spanish *conquistadores*. No gold has ever been recovered, but Indian artifacts have been raised from the lake and are now exhibited in the **Museo Guamá,** on an island in the middle of the lake.

The lake was one of Castro's favorite fishing spots. The Cuban leader spent many weekends in a bungalow that became known as "Fidel's Key." One day, lounging on his bed, he supposedly announced, "We're going to build a Tahitian village here!" And they did.

The revolutionary government dredged a canal network and created a series of islands featuring a replica Taino village, **Villa Guamá.** The 13 tiny islands are connected by hanging bridges and landscaped with hedgerows of fiery bottlebrush. One of the isles contains a mock Indian village and 32 life-size sculptures by Cuban sculptor Rita Longa, depicting Taino Indians engaged in daily activities.

You can ascend the staircase in the restaurant and emerge atop a *mirador* to survey the scene.

Tours of the lake are offered aboard a cruise boat—*Guamatur-2*—from Villa Guamá and La Boca.

Accommodations and Food
Villa Guamá, Laguna del Tesoro, Ciénaga de Zapata, Matanzas, tel. 59-7125 or 59-2979, has 59 adequate yet primitive thatched-roof octago-

nal *bohíos* with private baths, telephones, a/c, and TVs. Most are built on stilts above the water, and each has a private boat mooring. Castro used to stay in hut #33. There's a restaurant whose specialty is grilled crocodile, a bar, *cafetería,* nightclub, and the usual tourism bureau. The tranquillity is destroyed by excessively loud piped music by day and the disco by night. Also, if you forget your mosquito repellent, your stay may be misery. Rates are US$20 s, US$25 d low-season, US$25 s, US$30 d high-season.

Visitors can have lunch at the restaurant. Try the grilled crocodile, which has the texture and taste of chicken (US$6). Breakfasts are dismal.

Getting There: The facility is reached by an open-air tour boat that leaves La Boca for Villa Guamá at 10 a.m., noon, and 1 and 3 p.m. (US$5). Faster speedboats are available (US$7 per person). It's a good idea to have advance reservations for the resort if you intend taking the last boat (reports indicate that you may not be allowed to board without them).

Organized Excursions

Most Cuban tour companies include a visit to Laguna del Tesoro in their packages to Playa Girón. **Tour & Travel,** Avenida 5 #8409 esq. 86, Miramar, Havana, tel. 33-2433; or Avenida Playa #3606 e/ 36 y 37, Varadero, tel. 66-7279, has excursions from Havana for US$36 and from Varadero for US$43 or US$94, including overnight lodging.

THE BAY OF PIGS

Route 3-1-18 runs like a plumb line from Australia to Playa Larga, a small fishing village tucked into the head of Bahía de Cochinos. The fingerlike bay is 20 km long, with an average width of seven km. It is named for the local *cochinos cimarrones,* wild pigs, which once formed a staple diet for local Indians.

The name is known to every US citizen for the Bay of Pigs invasion, when about 1,300 heavily armed, CIA-trained Cuban exiles came ashore fully equipped to establish a beachhead and provoke a counterrevolution to topple the Castro regime.

A dirt road leads west from Playa Larga two km to the ramshackle hamlet of **Buena Ventu-**

ra. There's a guardpost here, at the entrance to the vast Zapata reserve. No one can proceed farther without a guide. Just beyond the guardpost, the road bifurcates. One road leads south to Laguna de las Salinas, the other leads west, to Santo Tomás and Maneadero (51 km). Aggressive mosquitoes replay the bombing runs by CIA B-26s. Take repellent!

A paved road runs south and east from Playa Larga to Playa Girón—where the beaches and diving are splendid—and thence to Cienfuegos.

PLAYA LARGA AND VICINITY

Playa Larga was one of the two main landing sites during the Bay of Pigs fiasco. A tourist haven has been salvaged from the bile. The village comprises a few fisherman's huts, military buildings, the International Bird-Watching Center, and a hotel facing a small cream-colored beach that stretches for half a mile. Shallow water provides for wading. The rectangular bay is shaped like a great swimming pool and, appropriately, has clear blue waters as warm and calm as bedtime milk. Nonetheless, it's not as attractive as Playa Girón, and local lads often pester tourists with sales pitches for guides and other services.

Accommodations and Food

Villa Horizontes Playa Larga, Playa Larga, Ciénega de Zapata, Matanzas, tel. 66-7542 or 59-7219, has 57 spacious, albeit modestly furnished, a/c rooms in *cabinas,* each with private bath, radio, small beds, tiny TV, and basic kitchenette. The cabins are widely spaced amid lawns and bougainvilleas (US$19 s, US$25 d in low season, US$23 s, US$30 d in high season). There's a restaurant, bar, *cafetería,* and nightclub. There's beach volleyball, and watersports include windsurfers. The Octopus Club features an **International Dive Center,** which is more modest than its grandiose name suggests. A local *paladar* offers lobster meals for US$10.

Getting There

Bus no. 353 ostensibly departs Havana daily for Playa Girón at 11:55 a.m. and passes by Playa Larga, but don't count on it. Bus no. 818 operates local service between Playa Larga and Playa Girón.

BAY OF PIGS

The Bay of Pigs invasion—Cubans call it the Battle of Girón or La Victoria (the victory)—was the brainchild of Richard Bissell, Deputy Director of the CIA. The plan was to infiltrate anti-Castro guerrillas onto the island so that they could link up with domestic opponents. The "Program of Covert Action Against the Castro Regime" called for creation of a Cuban government in exile, covert action in Cuba, and "a paramilitary force outside of Cuba for future guerrilla action." In August 1958, President Eisenhower approved a US$13 million budget with the proviso that "no US military personnel were to be used in a combat status."

Under a flexible mandate, Bissell radically expanded the original concept. The CIA borrowed officers from the armed services and created an air force that eventually numbered 80 US pilots. By the time President Kennedy was briefed, in November 1960, the plan had grown to include 1,500 men backed by a rebel air force of war-surplus B-26s and escorted by a US naval task force. Bissell didn't tell the president the true scale of the planned invasion. The "top brass" were left in the dark about the CIA's expansion into the navy and amphibious-warfare business.

The US Prepares to Invade

The CIA recruited Cuban exiles for the invasion force and used an abandoned naval base at Opa-Locka, outside Miami, to train the brigade. They were later moved to US military locations in Guatemala (replete with brothels to keep the *brigadistas* on camp) and Puerto Rico (in violation of US law). Meanwhile, a "government in exile" was chosen from within the *Frente,* a loose, feud-riven group of political exiles, many of them corrupt right-wing politicians nostalgic for Batista days. The group would be transformed into a provisional government once it had gained a military foothold in Cuba. Planes and ships circled Cuba, dropping off packages of small arms, ammunition, and demolition equipment to counterrevolutionaries in Cuba.

On 28 January 1960, Kennedy ordered the Joint Chief of Staffs to review the plans. The so-called "Trinidad Plan" called for an airborne assault and amphibious landing at Trinidad. Here, the invasion force could link up with guerrillas operating out of the nearby Escambray Mountains. The chiefs concluded it had a 30% chance of success and "that

ultimate success will depend upon . . . a sizable popular uprising or substantial follow-up forces." Kennedy rejected it as "too much like a World War II invasion."

Thus, Kennedy approved the second plan, for an invasion of the Bay of Pigs, more than 100 km west of the Escambray Mountains, where the brigade would land at three beaches 25 km apart and surrounded by swamps. The CIA assured Kennedy that the brigade could "melt" into the mountains. Moreover, "A great percentage of the [army] officers are believed ready to rebel against the government at a given moment, taking their troops with them," Bissell told Kennedy in an appallingly incorrect assessment.

In photos of Playa Girón taken by U-2 spy planes, the CIA's photo interpreter identified what he claimed was seaweed offshore. "They are coral heads," said Dr. Juan Sordo, a brigade member: "I know them. I have seen them." Another brigade member agreed. The water would be too shallow for the landing craft, he said. But the CIA wouldn't listen.

Nor did the CIA know that Castro knew the area intimately. In November 1960, Castro had inspected Girón, site of one of his pet projects: a new community that included a motel and recreation center. At one point he turned to a Cuban journalist and said, "You know, this is a great place for a landing. . . . We should place a fifty-caliber heavy machine gun here, just in case." Two weeks later, that machine gun fired the first shots against the invaders.

Cuba Prepares to Defend

Castro knew an invasion was imminent. Cuban police began to round up people suspected of counterrevolutionary activities. Four days before the invasion began, Castro ordered a battalion moved to the Bay of Pigs (the order took too long to process, and the battalion never arrived).

The invasion plan relied on eliminating the Cuban air force. The CIA wanted US air support; the State Department wanted it kept to a minimum so that the planes could later be claimed to have originated in Cuba (US involvement was supposed to be deniable). On April 15, two days before the invasion, B-26 bombers painted in Cuban air force colors struck Cuba's three military air bases.

Thus, Castro was fully forewarned. Worse, only five aircraft were destroyed, and Cuba still had at

(continues on next page)

BAY OF PIGS
(continued)

least three T-33-jet fighters and four British-made Sea Fury light-attack bombers. Castro turned the funeral for the seven persons killed into a stirring call for revolutionary defiance: "What the imperialists cannot forgive us for . . . is that we have made a socialist revolution under the nose of the United States." It was his first public characterization of the Revolution as socialist. The debacle thus created the conditions by which socialism became acceptable to a nation on the brink of invasion during a period when Cubans felt about *la revolución* the way US citizens would feel about the Declaration of Independence if it had been signed within recent memory.

The Invasion

The US Navy's aircraft carrier *Essex* and five destroyers were to escort six freighters carrying the Cuban fighters and their supplies. They moved in radio silence.

The landings began about 1:15 a.m. on 17 April at Playa Girón and Playa Larga. Landing craft (LCVPs) came roaring in. About 140 meters offshore, they hit the coral reefs the CIA had dismissed as seaweed. The brigade had to wade ashore. Meanwhile, the fiberglass boats used by the Second and Fifth Battalions capsized. The Cubans had installed tall, extremely bright lights right on the beach. "It looked like Coney Island," recalls Gray Lynch, the CIA point man who ended up directing the invasion. The brigade has also been told that "no communications existed within 20 miles of the beach." In fact, there was a radio station only 100 meters inland. By the time the brigade stormed it, Castro had been alerted.

Kennedy had approved taking the Cubans to the beaches; beyond that, they were on their own. Worried about repercussions at the UN, Kennedy ordered cancellation of a second strike designed to give the invasion force cover. With that decision, the operation was lost.

Castro set up headquarters in the Central Australia sugar mill and from there directed the Cuban defense. Castro, who displayed a remarkable control of events over the three days by telephone and handwritten messages, correctly guessed the enemy's plans.

He knew it was vital to deprive the invaders of their support ships before they could unload. As the exiles landed, Cuba's aircraft swooped down. Two supply ships containing ammunition and communications equipment, the *Houston* and *Río Escondido*, were sunk. Two other ammunition vessels (the *Atlántico* and *Caribe*) fled and had to be turned back by the USS *Eaton*. (The CIA had refused to outfit the ships with antiaircraft guns because it assumed no Cuban aircraft would survive the B-26 bombings.)

The brigade did, however, manage to unload World War II-era Sherman tanks. They fought the "battle of the rotunda" against Cuba's equally outdated Stalin tanks.

Despite the CIA's predictions, the local people ("armed only with M-52 Czech rifles," writes Peter Wyden in *Bay of Pigs*) defended their homeland until the first Cuban battalion of 900 student soldiers arrived in buses (half the cadet troops were killed when the convoy was strafed by the brigade's B-26s). Reinforcements poured in and encircled the invasion forces, and the fight became a simple matter of whittling away at the exiles.

A US jet-fighter squadron flew reconnaissance over the invasion but was forbidden to engage in combat. As the situation deteriorated, Kennedy came under increasing pressure to order US air strikes. He refused. By Tuesday, many of the *brigadista* pilots were "begging off" flying combat sorties. Hence, the CIA authorized its own US pilots to fly combat missions. In the final hours of the battle, six US pilots flew missions without President Kennedy's knowledge. Four were shot down and killed. The Cubans recovered the body of one of the pilots and found his dog tags (his corpse is still in a Havana morgue, waiting for the US government to claim it).

Abandoning the *Brigadistas*

"The military," writes Wyden, "*assumed* the President would order US intervention. The President *assumed* they knew he would refuse to escalate the miniature war." Instead, he ordered the Navy to remove the brigade from the beaches. The US destroyers advanced on the shore. Castro instinctively knew they were sailing in for an evacuation and ordered Cuban artillery not to fire. If the Cubans had fired on the destroyers and the vessels had claimed that they were merely patrolling in international waters, there could have been "transcendent consequences." (The Soviet Union had guaranteed to come to Cuba's military aid in the event she was attacked.)

The destroyers picked up those *brigadistas* who had made it back to sea, then sailed away, leaving the survivors to fend for themselves. The brigade had lost 114 men (the Cubans lost 161), but a further 1,189 were captured. Eventually, 1,091 prisoners were returned to the United States in exchange for US$53 million in food and medical supplies.

"You didn't get any help from us," Kennedy remarked to Eduardo Ferrer, one of the Brigade pilots at a ceremony at Miami's Orange Bowl, where each Brigade member received US$300 in cash. "No, Mr. President, but I expect it the next time," Ferrer replied. "You better believe that there's going to be a next time," the president told him. A month later, brigade members received mimeographed letters advising that no further "compensation" would be paid. The US government had washed its hands of the Cuban Brigade, leaving the exile community feeling doubly betrayed.

Playa Larga to Playa Girón

East of Playa Larga, the coast road hugs the Bay of Pigs. Solemn concrete monuments rise from the bush, each one standing at the site where a Cuban soldier (161 in all) fell defending his republic during the three-day battle in April 1961.

There are views of sugar-white beaches extending around the bay, which here is prized by pelicans. At **Caleta del Rosario**, about three km from Playa Larga, is a splendid little cove with a small beach and good swimming. It's popular with Cubans and has small cabins for rent, plus a café.

The route is also lined with *cenotes,* limestone sinkholes. Columbus discovered them and recorded that they contained subterranean streams with waters "so cold, and of such goodness and so sweet that no better could be found in the world." About eight km east of Playa Larga is **La Casa de Pescador,** a beautiful little ranchita restaurant overlooking a 20-meter-deep limestone sinkhole—**El Cenote**—filled with cool, pavonine waters. The place is exquisite. The grounds are landscaped, with hammocks slung between palms.

A short distance farther brings you to **Cueva de los Pesces.** This is one of the largest *cenotes,* 15 km from Playa Larga. The huge cave, 70 meters deep and formed by a flooded fault, is a superb spot for scuba diving, with labyrinthine halls teeming with fish.

The **Centro Recreativo** is three km east of Playa Larga. The facility is a resort for the military and their families.

PLAYA GIRÓN

Finally, you arrive at the spot where socialism and capitalism slugged it out. And what do you find? Vacationers from cool climates, lathered with suntan oil, splashing in the shallows where, 30-odd years before, blood and bullets mingled with sand on the beach. With the sun beating down on this idyllic spot, it is difficult to imagine the carnage and futility.

Playa Girón is a small *pueblo* of a few hundred people. It was named in honor of Gilbert Girón, a French pirate captured here by a Spanish captain, who sliced off the corsair's head and pickled it so as to claim a reward.

The community is centered on a wide-open square dominated by a huge billboard that reads, "Playa Girón—The First Rout Of Imperialism In Latin America." The beautiful white sand beach is enclosed within a concrete barrier *(rompeola),* which protects against any future wave of CIA-backed anti-Castroites foolish enough to come ashore. Nonetheless, it's a carbuncle on the coast. The beach is rocky below the waterline.

Playa Girón Museum

This superb museum gives an accurate portrayal of the drama of the revolutionary era. Black-and-white photographs confirm the appalling poverty of the local peasantry before the Revolution. Others profile the events preceding the invasion: the Agrarian Reform Law, the literacy campaign, and sabotage and other counterrevolutionary activity culminating in the act to which the museum is dedicated—the invasion of 15 April 1961 by 1,297 CIA-trained Cubans.

The whole story of the invasion (which in Cuba is called *la victoria*) is shown on maps that trace the evolution of the 72-hour battle. There are photographs, including gory pictures of civilians caught in the midst of explosions, and of all the martyrs—the "Heroes de Girón"—killed in the fighting (the youngest, Nelson Fernandez Estevez, was only 16 years old; the oldest, Juan Ruíz Serna, was 60). Note the photo of a young militiaman, Eduardo García Delgado, who wrote "Fidel" on a wall with his own blood before dying, facedown, with his hand on the L. And, of course, Fidel is there, leaping from his T-34 tank.

Other displays include weapons, and a superbly preserved Sea Fury fighter-aircraft, complete with rockets, which sits on the forecourt outside.

A frieze in the museum portrays the invaders as rich reactionaries bent on seizing back what the poor had gained. It lists the possessions that they owned prior to the revolution—over one million acres of land, 10,000 houses, 70 factories, 10 sugar mills, five mines, two banks, etc.

There are guides on hand to give you a blow-by-blow account. It's open daily 9 a.m.-noon and 1-6 p.m. Entrance costs US$2.

Scuba Diving

The waters off Playa Girón are noted for excellent diving, with abrupt ocean walls close to shore. There are many underwater caves. And gorgonians, sponges, and corals are abundant. **Playa Girón Scuba Diving Center** is located in the Villa Horizontes hotel. Initiation dives cost US$10. Single dives cost U$25, two dives U$42.

Accommodations

Villa Horizontes Playa Girón, tel. 59-4118, is like a miniature Butlin's holiday camp of the 1960s. The hotel, which is popular with Cubans, centers on an attractive, amoeba-shaped pool. The 292 a/c rooms in 196 bungalows are soulless affairs. They have private baths, radios,

and TVs and run US$27 s, US$36 d, US$60 t in high season. The buffet meals in the restaurant and *cafetería* are more appetizing than the venues themselves. Nonguests can also eat here (breakfast costs US$5, lunch and dinner cost US$10). Facilities include a disco, souvenir shop, and a tourist information desk that offers excursions to the crocodile farm at La Boca (US$27) and farther afield.

Across the road is the **Playa Girón Motel.** Its *cabañas* are popular with French Canadians. It has a swimming pool, bar, table-tennis, and the Dancing Lights Discotheque. The same prices apply.

Services

There's a launderette, pharmacy, and dollars-only shop opposite the museum. The post office and telegram office are 50 meters north of the museum.

Getting There and Around

Bus no. 353 departs Havana daily for Playa Girón at 11:55 a.m. and arrives at 5:30 p.m. (13 pesos). Bus no. 818 operates from Jagüey Grande to Playa Girón via Playa Larga. Buses also operate from Cienfuegos daily at 4 a.m. (5 a.m. on Sunday) and 3:30 p.m., although service may be unreliable.

Tour & Travel, Avenida 5 #8409 esq. 86, Miramar, Havana, tel. 33-2433; or Avenida Playa #3606 e/ 36 y 37, Varadero, tel. 66-7279, has excursions from Havana for US$36 and from Varadero for US$43 or US$94, including overnight accommodations.

Transauto has a car rental office opposite the Villa Horizontes, where you can rent also bicycles and mopeds.

EAST OF PLAYA GIRÓN

The paved coastal highway (Route 3-1-16) turns inland at Playa Girón and runs north, then east, 39 km through scrubland to Yaguaramas. Here, it connects with Route 3-1-2, which runs north to Aguada de Pasajeros and the Autopista and east to Cienfuegos, rising and dipping like a roller-coaster via Rodas and Conjogas.

You can continue east along the coast from Playa Girón by a blindingly white, hard-packed dirt road atop a raised coral shore. In springtime, the road is littered with dead crabs, which cross the road in their thousands. The stench of rotten crabmeat attracts vultures, who lope about like sinister undertakers, making great hay of the carnage.

Caleta Buena, eight km east of Playa Girón, is worth every inch of the drive. This small, exquisite coral cove contains a natural pool good for swimming. There are pocket-size beaches atop the coral platform, with red-tiled *ranchitas* for shade. The seabed is a multicolored garden of coral and sponges, ideal for snorkeling (US$3 for equipment rental) and diving (US$20). It is favored by Cubans and tour groups alike. Entrance costs US$1 (three pesos for Cubans).

East of Caleta Buena, the road deteriorates rapidly. The area is uninhabited. Eventually you'll reach a sharp curve, with a small cove to the right. The "main" route veers left and eventually leads to Yaguaramas. A narrow track straight ahead, however, will take you along virtually unexplored territory to Jaragua. This is adventure touring.

CIENFUEGOS AND VILLA CLARA
INTRODUCTION

Villa Clara and Cienfuegos provinces, east of Matanzas, are anchored by the Sierra del Escambray, which they almost encircle. Villa Clara, north of Cienfuegos, is skipped by most tourists, who whiz by along the Autopista or Carretera Central, bound for Oriente or the colonial city of Trinidad, in Sancti Spíritus province. Such haste is a pity, for you are likely to miss another colonial gem, Remedios, a tiny charmer caught in its own time warp. Remedios and neighboring villages east of Santa Clara—the provincial capital and an important industrial and university city—are renowned, too, for their *parrandas,* unique year-end carnival-style revelries that border on mayhem.

This eastern portion of the province is dominated by rolling uplands called the **Alturas de Santa Clara,** as photogenic and quintessentially Cuban in character as you'll find on the island—a medley of *bohíos,* ox-drawn ploughs, and royal palms, with the rolling land given to tobacco and cattle, and hazy mountains forming a fabulous backdrop. Villa Clara is second only to Pinar del Río as a center of tobacco produc-

tion, centered on the scenic **Vuelta Arriba** region, east of the provincial capital. However, sugar dominates the northern lowlands. (The few coastal towns have no appeal.)

South of Santa Clara, the Alturas rise gradually to the steep, pine-clad **Sierra del Escambray,** whose reservoirs supply towns for miles around. In the mountains, *campesinos* raise coffee. During the Revolutionary War, Che Guevara established a front in the Escambray and, on 28 December 1958, his rebel army swept down upon Santa Clara—the last battle of the Revolution before Batista fled Cuba. The Escambray were also a haven for counterrevolutionaries in the early years following the Revolution. Today, cool forests tantalize birders and hikers, with man-made lakes good for fishing, a famous health spa, and a cool, invigorating climate—the wettest in Cuba—to lure you away from the coast. To the south, rivers rush down from the mountains onto a narrow coastal plain, where tiny beaches lie in the cusp of rivermouths.

The mountains extend west into Cienfuegos province, which, despite being Cuba's second smallest, surpasses even Havana in industrial output. **Cienfuegos** city is a major port town and industrial center with notable architectural sights, a fine botanical garden, and the curiosity of a ghostly nuclear reactor.

The coastlines have few pleasing beaches and resorts (an exception is Rancho Luna, south of the city of Cienfuegos). However, the cays of the Archipiélago de Sabana, which lie sprinkled off the southern shore, boast untapped potential.

ALONG THE AUTOPISTA

The Autopista continues east from Matanzas province into Cienfuegos province. The turnoff for the city of Cienfuegos is at **Aguada del Pasajeros** (Passenger Watering Place), where there's a **Cupet gas station** alongside an appealing *ranchita* bar and restaurant, with an antique US steam engine displayed on the forecourt.

The road to Cienfuegos leads via Rojas, a few km northeast of which is **Ciego Montero Spring.** Much of the bottled mineral water sold in Cuba derives from this naturally carbonated spring, where there is a run-down spa-hotel and baths.

The freeway continues east beneath the northern border of Cienfuegos province, and atop the southern border of Santa Clara. East of Santa Clara, the scenery takes a dramatic turn as the Autopista cuts through the beautiful hills of the Alturas de Santa Clara, passes into Sancti Spíritus province, and peters out at Jatibonico.

The only accommodation beside the Autopista is the **Motel Las Jecas,** tel. 451432, two miles east of **Ranchuela,** on the outskirts of Santa Clara. The modest facility is quite pleasant as Cuban motels go and is very popular with Cubans. The *cabañas* cluster around a small pool (US$23 s/d).

Warning: The Autopista is in superb condition the whole way with the exception of just east of Ranchuelo, where the deteriorated section begins at a dangerous railway track that runs across the Autopista. You can't see the track in the shadow of a bridge that crosses the freeway (the track is on the bridge's eastern side). Slow down! And take note of any traffic crawling across the lines.

ALONG THE CARRETERA CENTRAL

A far more interesting route than the Autopista is the old Carretera Central through central Villa Clara. The route takes you through aged provincial towns, including **Santo Domingo.** Its venerable church is beautiful, displaying an intriguing amalgam of styles: red brick frontage with thick limestone columns inset into the wall, and a clock in the pediment topped by an octagonal bell tower containing a patinated bell. The tower is incongruously capped by Moorish mosaics.

About eight km west of Santa Clara, you'll pass through **Esperanza,** a cozy little town with an attractive old Spanish church.

There are no gas stations or other facitilities.

CIENFUEGOS

"'This must be one of the quietest ports in the world,'" Wormold writes to his sister in Graham Greene's Our Man in Havana. *"Just the pink and yellow street and a few cantinas and the big chimney of a sugar refinery. . . . The light here is wonderful just before the sun goes down: a long trickle of gold and the seabirds are dark patches on the pewter swell."*

Cienfuegos (pop. 105,000) is a city of commerce, as the numerous foreign vessels anchored in the bay attest. The city, 340 km east of Havana and 69 km southwest of Santa Clara, lies on the east side of the Bahía de Cienfuegos, a deep, vast bay with an umbilically narrow entrance and in which, as one 19th-century traveler remarked, "all the navies of the world could rendezvous and not crowd each other." It's Cuba's third-largest port and shelters a large fishing and shrimping fleet. International Influences (especially French) have

Archipiélag

BAÑOS DE ELGUEA ★

Playa el Salto y Ganuza

Corralillo

Itabo

Sierra Morena

Isabela de Sagua

4-011

Rancho Velóz

VILLA CLARA

4-13

4-241

CUPET GAS STATION ■

Sagua la Grande

To Matanzas

Presa Alacranes

CARRETERA

Los Arabos

Cascajal

CENTRAL

Manacas

4-13

Cifuentes

MATANZAS

To Matanzas and Havana

4-N1

San Diego del Valle

Jicotea

4-221

To Havana

CIENFUEGOS

CUPET GAS STATION ■

AUTOPISTA

NACIONAL

Esperanza

Sant Clar

Aguada de Pasajeros

Cartagena

Ranchuelo

4-474

Rodas

CIEGO MONTERO SPRING ★

La Ya Ya

Altur

Yaguaramas

4-112

Mataguá

Bahía de Cienfuegos

Cienfuegos

Cumanayagua

4-206

Manicaragua

4-4

Ciudad Nuclear

Pepito Tey

★ JARDÍN BOTÁNICO SOLEDAD

Sierra del Escambray

Presa del Hanabanilla

Castillo de Jagua

Pico San Juan (1140m) ▲

4-432

Valle de Yaguanabo

TOPES DE COLLANT ★ NATIONAL PARK

C a r i b b e a n   S e a

Trinidad

To Casilda

© MOON PUBLICATIONS, INC.

0   25 mi

0   25 km

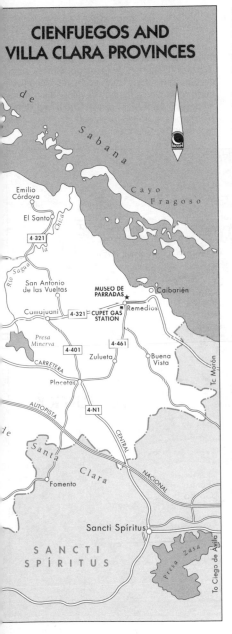

CIENFUEGOS AND VILLA CLARA PROVINCES

made themselves felt. Cienfuegos even had its own Chinatown (now long since devoid of Chinese people), west of Parque Martí on the edge of the port. The population contains a relatively small percentage of mulattoes and blacks.

Cienfuegos means "100 fires" and is sometimes written "100fuegos." Citizens call their town *La Perla del Sur* (the pearl of the south) or *La Linda Ciudad del Mar* (the beautiful city by the sea). The city's appeal lies partly in the European flavor of its colonial hub, with a wide Parisian-style boulevard and elegant colonnades. Still, Cienfuegos has neither the grace of Trinidad nor the flair of Havana. But there is an ambience that inspired Benny Moré, the celebrated Cuban *sonoro,* to sing, "Cienfuegos is the city I like best."

Cienfuegos is upbeat and lively. Classy, dollars-only boutiques have arrived. There's even a store selling computers. Alas, in October 1996, the city took the punch of Hurricane Lili full force on the snout. Virtually the entire population was left without electricity (as many as 15,000 electrical poles were torn up) or running water for several weeks.

ORIENTATION

Approaching from the Autopista, the two-lane highway enters the city from the north and widens into a broad boulevard, the **Paseo del Prado** (Calle 37), the city's main thoroughfare. At Avenida 46, the Prado becomes the **Malecón,** a wide seafront boulevard stretching south one km along a narrow peninsula ending at Punta Gorda, a once-exclusive residential district that recalls 1950s North American suburbia, with Detroit classics still parked in the driveways of mid-20th-century homes. Beyond Punta Gorda, hidden behind and south of the Hotel Jagua, is a short, slender isthmus lined with old French-style plantation homes.

The city is laid out in a perfect grid, with even-numbered *calles* running north-south, crossing odd-numbered *avenidas* running east-west.

The historic core is called **Pueblo Nuevo.** It is centered on Parque Martí, the main plaza, four blocks west of the Prado, along Avenidas 54 and 56. Avenida 54 (El Boulevard) is for pedestrians only between Calles 31 and 37. Avenida 56, the principal shopping street, is also called San Carlos. Pueblo Nuevo occupies the La Majagua Peninsula. Surrounding it is a "ring," built in the middle of this century with factories and Florida-style houses. The modern outskirts are composed of grim estates of *microbrigada*-built high-rise blocks.

If you want to bypass the town, you can do so on the six-lane carriageway, the Circunvalación, which swings north of the city.

HISTORY

Columbus supposedly discovered the bay in 1494. It was mapped a decade later by another explorer, Sebatián de Ocampo. Shortly after the Spanish settled Cuba and established their trade restrictions, the bay developed a thriving smuggling trade. Sir Francis Drake and Henry Morgan were among many cutthroat privateers who called for plunder.

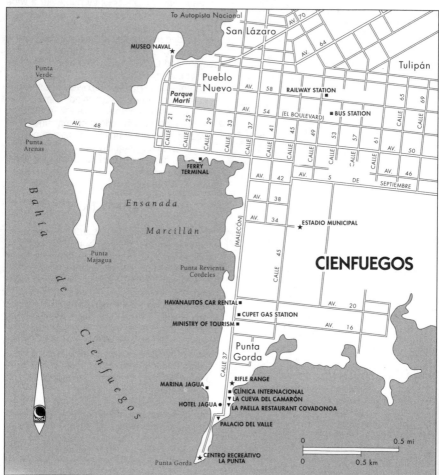

© MOON PUBLICATIONS INC

HISTORIC CIENFUEGOS (PUEBLO NUEVO)

Construction of a fortress—Castillo de Jagua—was begun in 1738 to protect the bay and to police illicit smuggling through the straits, though no town had yet developed. The town of Trinidad, established in 1518 a short distance east, had risen to prominence, eclipsing development of a rival city. Although a town plan was drawn up in 1796, it wasn't until 1817 that Louis D'Clouet, a French *émigré* from Louisiana (at the time, part of Spain's empire), devised a settlement scheme which he presented to Don José Cienfuego, the Spanish captain-general. The Spanish government would pay for the transportation of white colonists from Europe, and every male would receive a *caballería*, a 33-acre plot of land. The Spanish Cortés approved. By April 1819, the first 137 settlers arrived from Bordeaux and the Medoc to found a settlement they christened Fernandina de Jagua on the site of today's Cienfuegos. That hamlet was destroyed by a hurricane six years later but was rebuilt in 1831 and renamed Cienfuegos.

The city rapidly grew to wealth on the back of the deep-water harbor, a natural *entrepot* for locally grown sugar, tobacco, and fruit. As the port trade prospered, nearby Trinidad's trade declined, adding to Cienfuegos' glory. This was the heyday of lavish building, when wealthy merchants and plantation owners graced the city with a surfeit of stucco. The French influence can be felt to this day.

The city continued to prosper during the early 20th century and had an unremarkable history—until 5 September 1957, when young naval officers and sailors at the Cienfuegos Naval Base rebelled against the Batista regime and took control of the city's military and electrical installations (the electrical plant which they destroyed on the Prado and Avenida 48 is preserved as a monument). Members of Castro's revolutionary July 26th Movement—M-26—and students from the San Lorenzo School joined them. Batista's troops managed to recapture the city by nightfall.

Since the Revolution, the city's hinterland has witnessed significant growth, mostly to the west in Reparto O'Bourke, where a new port and massive industrial and residential complex was initiated in the 1980s. The oil refinery (the country's biggest), wheat mills, fertilizer plants, a steel mill, and the Tricontinental Bulk Sugar Shipping Terminal are spread along the bay.

THINGS TO SEE

Parque Martí

Most of Cienfuegos' buildings of note surround Parque Martí, on the ground where the founding of the first settlement was proclaimed on 22 April 1819. The *majagua* tree that once stood at the center has long since died and been replaced by a bandstand and gazebo.

The city's most prominent and illustrious sons are commemorated in bronze or stone, including a statue to José Martí, guarded by two marble lions. Note the triumphal arch on the west side, commemorating the establishment of the Cuban Republic in 1902 and unveiled on the day the Republic was constituted. There are benches for ruminating beneath shade trees. The plaza is worth visiting at night, when music and dance in the Casa de la Cultura occasionally spills into the square.

On the east side of the square is the **Catedral de la Purísima Concepción,** which dates from 1870. It has a splendid interior, at least by Cuban standards, with marble floors, and a pristine gilt Corinthian altar beneath a gothic vaulted ceiling. The beautiful stained-glass windows of the 12 apostles were brought from France following the revolution of 1789. The cathedral is a lively social setting on weekends. No reverential silence here!

On the north side is the **Teatro Tomás Terry.** This impressive theater, now officially known as the Cienfuegos Theater, was completed in 1895. It was named for a local sugar baron, a Venezuelan who had arrived penniless in Cuba in the mid-1800s. Terry apparently rose to great wealth by buying sick slaves for a pittance, nursing them back to health, and selling them for a whopping profit. He invested his money in a sugar estate, then in railroads and other profitable ventures. His family built the theater using materials and craftsmen imported from Europe.

Do peek inside. The proscenium is sumptuously decorated with laurel wreaths, lyres, trumpets, and a bas-relief centerpiece of Dionysius. Allegorical figures cling to the arch over the stage, and naked nymphs cavort across the ceiling, which, like the rest of the theater, desperately needs restoration. The auditorium, with its three-tiered balconies, is made entirely of Cuban hardwoods and can accommodate 900 people in old-fashioned, fold-down wooden seats. The theater floor can be raised to stage level to create a grand ballroom. Enrico Caruso, Sarah Bernhart, and the Bolshoi Ballet have performed here. The Nacional Ballet and Opera de Cuba still perform, bringing the bats from their hiding places to swoop harmlessly over the heads of the audience. Entrance costs US$1. There are guides.

Adjoining the theater is **Colegio San Lorenzo,** a handsome neoclassical building painted pastel blue and impressively fronted by thick columns.

Continuing your counterclockwise tour, you'll reach the **Casa de la Cultura,** on the west side, in the former home of another wealthy sugar baron. It has a *mirador* tower with fine views across the bay.

Several intriguing buildings occupy the south side. First is the former Spanish Club (the initials CE, inset in the pavement, stand for Club Español), now housing the **Museo Histórico.** The museum mostly commemorates local figures who fought in the War of Independence. It's open Tues.-Sun. 9 a.m.-5 p.m. Entrance costs US$1. Fifty meters east is the **Primero Palacio,** now the Poder Popular, the local government headquarters. The building was modeled in miniature on Havana's capitol and strongly influenced by North American architecture. It has a fine marble floor. Next to the Poder Popular is a fine bar and restaurant—the **Palatino**—whose shady terrace is supported by plump columns resembling milk bottles, amply demonstrating Cienfuegos's intriguing mix of architectural styles.

Paseo del Prado

Calle 37—the Prado—is lined its full length with plaques and busts honoring illustrious citizens, including a big white statue that Wormold in Graham Greene's *Our Man in Havana* thought looked in daylight like Queen Victoria.

The Prado remains a social center and in the cool evenings bustles with gossipy life, when citizens still promenade as in colonial days and bootblacks still shine shoes beneath the pink colonnades.

Farther south, along the Malecón, you can watch locals fishing in the bay from their rickety little boats made of polystyrene and assorted miscellany.

Palacio del Valle

Cienfuegos' architectural pride and joy is a palace at the tip of Punta Gorda. This architectural stunner—now a restaurant—originated as a modest home for a trader, Celestino Caceres. It passed out of his hands and was given as a wedding present to a member of the local Valle family, who added to it in virile Mughal style, with carved floral motifs, cupped arches, bulbous cupolas, and delicate arabesques.

The main dining room drips with ornate carvings, like Ellora or Ajanta in India, but without the erotic motif: the entire ceiling, columns and cornices are smothered in pre-cast carvings in Venetian alabaster. Another room is a replica in miniature of Versailles. There are even gothic flourishes. Note the mural of Magi on the Carrara marble staircase, then follow the corridors around to a spiral cast-iron staircase that will deposit you at a rooftop bar and windy *mirador*. It's open daily 10 a.m.-midnight, tel. 3021.

Other Sites

As of 1996, there was little to draw visitors to **Museo Naval,** situated on Cayo Loco on Calle 21 e/ Calles 60 y 62. The museum has a library containing important historical documents. It was here, in 1957, that naval officers rebelled against the Batista regime. The museum has recently undergone restoration and added exhibits, including naval vessels. Open Mon.-Sat. 8 a.m.-4 p.m.

Tomás Acea Cemetery is worth a browse for its impressive neoclassical structures and tombs. It is entered via a gate that is a scaled-down replica of the Parthenon, supported by 64 columns. The cemetery overlooks the bay from atop a bluff on the road to Rancho Luna.

There's another evocative cemetery—**Cementerio La Reina**—at the west end of Avenida 50 (from downtown, take Avenida 48, then turn right), and reached via the old and now seedy Barrio Chino, or Chinatown.

ACCOMMODATIONS

Cienfuegos has plenty of touts pushing *casas particulares*. Expect to pay US$10-15. Unless you're taken by somewhere immediately, check several before settling on a place.

Budget: The **Hotel Cierro de Oro,** at Calle 29 #5914, tel. 5757, accepts foreigners. A marble staircase fringed by ornate tilework leads up to 32 modest but perfectly adequate rooms for 10 pesos s, 18 d. They feature lofty ceilings, tiled floors, tall doors, and large bathrooms. Some of the a/c units I saw were broken, and rooms are slightly dingy, however.

The **Hotel Perla del Sur,** tel. 2-1531, also accepts foreigners. The 24 spacious rooms have a/c but are basic. They cost nine pesos s, 15 d. It's not inspiring but is perfectly adequate for the impecunious and has the advan-

Palacio del Valle

tage of location—on Calle 37 in the heart of downtown. You might also try **Hotel San Carlos,** a pesos-only hotel on Avenida 56 e/ Calles 39 y 41, which has an exceptionally pleasant atmosphere (and may reopen as a dollar hotel).

Moderate: The only designated tourist hotel in town is the **Hotel Jagua,** at the south end of Calle 37. It was renowned prior to the Revolution as a ritzy hotel-cum-gambling joint run by Batista's brother. Today, it is rather a characterless hotel, despite being in Cuba's elite Gran Caribe group. The a/c rooms are modestly furnished but large and well lighted, with attractive black-tile bathrooms. They have safes and TVs (US$40 s, US$50 d). Ask for a fifth-floor room, which offers fine views over Palacio Valle and the bay. Facilities include a tour desk, restaurant, small pool, boutique, and a nightly cabaret (disco) at 10 p.m.

Several tourist hotels are located a few km southeast of Cienfuegos, at Playa Rancho Luna and Pasacaballo.

FOOD

Cienfuegos has a much larger roster of cafés and restaurants than most Cuban cities. Some are quite good. The city even has its own cuisine, although you'll be hard-pressed to find it served. Anywhere other than touristy restaurants in and around Hotel Jagua, plan on dining by 7 p.m. (after that, the food tends to run out).

You'll be approached by touts attempting to interest you in *paladares.* Try **Romeo y Juliet,** on Calle 33 e/ Avenidas 60 y 58, or **Veronica,** on Calle 37 (Avenida 50).

Punta Gorda

If you haven't seen it by day, plan on dining at **Palacio de Valle,** tel. 3026. Its specialty is lobster prepared six different ways (US$9 and up). The lobsters are huge—a half-order should suffice. The food itself, served on real Chinaware, is mediocre. Ounce-for-ounce, your tiny ice cream may be the most expensive you'll ever eat (US$1.50). Carmen Iznaga, a niece of acclaimed writer Nicolás Guillén, plays an all-night medley of classical and modern pieces at a grand piano.

My favorite eatery is **Casa Garibeña,** Calle 35 #2004, e/ 20 y 24, tel. 3893, in an old seafront wooden house with full-length windows and a shady veranda. Rattan furniture, elegant settings, beautiful artwork, and an old tiled floor add to the romantic ambience. The manager, Miguel Angel Chivandi, is fastidious and welcoming. The predominantly *criollo* dishes (fish runs US$6, fried chicken US$3) are prepared with more care than in many places. The menu also includes filet mignon (US$7). The accomplished Trio del Caribeño plays soothing music.

Restaurante Caondo, in the Hotel Jagua, serves the usual *criollo* fare at inflated prices (US$15 for lobster, US$9 for fried chicken; even rice costs US$2 extra). Service is slow but enthusiastic. A duo of accomplished guitarists entertain most nights. Tasty paella is served at **La Paella Restaurante Covadonoa,** opposite the Hotel Jagua. It has views over the bay toward the Escambray. Decor plays on a nautical theme. It's open daily noon to 2:30 p.m., and 7-10:30 p.m. Immediately next door is **La Cueva del Camarón,** specializing in seafood.

Downtown

Downtown options include **Restaurante 1819,** in a colonial mansion replete with antiques. It's open weekdays 6:30 a.m.-9:30 p.m. and weekends for lunch. It features "Cuban Night" entertainment on Saturday nights. For quasi-Chinese food, try **Restaurante El Mandarin,** on the corner of Calle 37 and Avenida 60. It has suitably Chinese decor but a limited menu. Meals cost less than six pesos (open noon to 2:30 p.m. and 7-9:30 p.m.)

Along Calle 37, there are several tiny pizzerias (such as Restaurante la Veronica) selling slices of pizza for five pesos; try **Gioventa Pizzeria** e/ Avenida 52 y 54.

One of my favorite places is **Palatino,** a very handsome bar-cum-restaurant with an outside terrace overlooking Parque Martí. It's popular with tour groups. Also on Parque Martí, next to the cathedral, is the **Restaurante Polynesia,** with a Tahitian motif. The menu is *criollo* with hints of the South Seas (pineapple finds its way into chicken dishes, for example). Food quality is said to be above average. It's open 6:30-11 p.m.

Several popular cafés are located on Avenida 54, including the lively **Café Venecia, Café Que Bien,** and the **Restaurante El Everija.** The latter has been written up widely for its broad menu of seafoods and meats (US$8 and up). Reservations are said to be essential on Saturday nights, when the place has a cabaret.

Outside town (on the road to Rancho Luna), you'll find **Finca Isabela,** a hacienda-turned-restaurant. You can watch a cockfight before savoring your roast suckling pig washed down with a house cocktail.

If you're in need of caffeine, try **El Café,** where a glass of Cuban coffee and *agua mineral* each cost 20 centavos. **Coppelia,** on the Prado, is always a good bet for ice cream on a hot day. It's open 11 a.m.-11 p.m.

Warning: Don't buy shellfish from the fishermen who land their catch on the wharf. The bay is polluted.

ENTERTAINMENT AND EVENTS

Cienfuegos has an eclectic range of entertainment. A calendar of musical and artistic performances is posted in the door of the **Teatro Luna,** on Calle 37. With luck, there'll be a performance (anything from classical symphony to a live salsa band) at the **Teatro Tomás Terry** while you're in town. Entrance costs US$1, but you may be able to pay one peso, like a local.

A great place to meet locals is the **Café La Juvenil,** on Avenida 54. It features *ceñas* and *noches Cubanas,* with music and dancing; it gets packed. The **Casa de la Trova,** Avenida 16 at Calle 35, and the **Casa de la Cultura,** Calle 37 and Avenida 58, also host traditional performances. And **Teatro Guiñol,** on the Prado at Avenida 56, has music on weekends, plus kids' puppet shows on weekends at 10 a.m.

The **Beny Moré International Festival of Popular Music** is held here each August.

Bars

You can sup with locals in the dark, clubby bar beside the entrance to the **Hotel San Carlos,** where locals gather to gossip and down *aguardiente* for a couple of pesos a shot. The hotel's rooftop bar has good views over the city. A more salubrious place is (dollars-only) **Palatino,** on Parque Martí. It sells wines, beers, and rums.

Centro Recreativo La Punta in the park at the very tip of the peninsula is favored by young Cubans. There's a bar that plays popular Western music. It's open 10 a.m.-6 p.m. and 8 p.m.-1 a.m.

Discos

The laser-lit disco-cabaret in the Hotel Jagua reminds me of an ascetic workingmen's club or student union but is popular with young Cubans. If you like to dance to salsa and hip-hop, this is the place. Entry costs US$2.50, including one beer.

Tropizul is a popular open-air disco on the Prado at Avenida 48. It appeals to the younger crowd and begins to pack 'em in about midnight. Likewise, the **Aire Libre,** on Calle 37 and Avenida 56, attracts a full crowd. The doormen have been known to turn foreigners away (a dollar-bill-handshake should rectify things).

A "floating disco" (US$1) is offered 9 p.m. nightly from Marina Jagua aboard the "pleasure cruiser" *Linda Mar,* but forget it—the boat looks like an accident waiting to happen.

Other Entertainment

Fancy yourself a keen shot? Check out the rifle range 200 yards north of Hotel Jagua. Each shot costs a paltry five centavos.

Movies are shown at the **Cine Prado,** Calle 37 and Avenida 54, and **Cine Teatro Luisa,** Calle 37 and Avenida 50.

You can see artists at work in the **Maroya** art gallery, in the Bienes Fondo Cubano on Parque Martí, Avenida 54 #2506, tel. 3400. You can even have a caricature drawn. It's open Mon.-Sat. 8 a.m.-6 p.m.

SPORTS AND RECREATION

Puertosol, tel. 432-8195 or 432-6678, offers **fishing trips** (US$25) and **scuba diving** from Marina Jagua, on Punta Gorda. Initiation dives cost US$10. A single dive costs US$27, and a five-dive package is offered for US$108. Snorkeling excursions cost US$13.

Baseball games (and athletic meets) are hosted in the **Estadio Municipal,** at Calle 45 and Avenida 34, four blocks east of the Malecón. On weekends you can watch young boxers sparring in an open-air ring on the Prado between Avenidas 46 and 48. Watch your purse—it is easy to become transfixed by the pummeling the eager boxers (some as young as 10 years old) give each other.

SHOPPING

The store in Hotel Jagua has a meager choice of crafts. You'll find a larger selection of handmade ethnic crafts and clothing at **Publicigraf,** on Avenida 54; and in the ARTEX store in the foyer of the Teatro Tomás. Both also offer a selection of music cassettes and CDs. For artwork, check out the gallery next to the Museo de Historia, on the south side of Parque Martí. If you wish to buy classy designer clothing, try **Glamour,** a fashion boutique at the corner of Calle 35 and Avenida 56.

For books, try **Librería Dionisia,** at the corner of Calle 37 and Avenida 54. Adjoining it is a music store—**Discoteca**—where you can buy music cassettes and CDs. For cigars and rum, check out the **Tienda Ron y Tabacos,** in the La Cueva del Camaron restaurant, opposite Hotel Jagua.

CRIME AND SAFETY

Cienfuegos lacks the sleazy lowlife that drifts into port cities worldwide and is no less safe than other Cuban towns. Crime is little known. However, you should stay away from back alleys and cheap bars, where an excess of rum often leads to fisticuffs.

Expect to be importuned downtown by touts working on commission to get you to visit *paladares.* Many young males make a living off tourists walking the Malecón, especially near the Hotel Jagua. They'll try to interest you in changing dollars for pesos. Some are quite pushy.

INFORMATION AND SERVICES

The tourism bureau on the south side of Parque Martí is now closed—you are sent to the Hotel Jagua. The Ministry of Tourism has an administrative office on Calle 37 but does *not* act as an information bureau.

If you need legal advice, cash advances, medical attention, hospitalization, or other emer-

gency assistance, contact **Asistur,** in the Hotel Jagua, tel. 0432-6362 or 66-6190. You'll also find an official **Buro de Turismo** here (there's another in the Rancho Luna Hotel, out of town). **Consultoria Juridicia Internacional,** Avenida. 48 #2904, e/ 29 y 31, tel. 3732, fax 335082, also offers legal and other assistance, mostly for foreign businesses.

There's a small **postal service** in the Hotel Jagua, where you'll also find an international telephone and fax office. Downtown, there's a **post office** one block west of the Prado, at Avenida 56 and Calle 35; and a **Centro Telefónico** (open 24 hours) at Avenida 58 e/ Calles 41 y 43. **DHL,** in the Hotel Jagua, tel. 6554, offers express-mail service domestically and internationally. It's open weekdays 9 a.m.-6 p.m. and Saturday 8:30 a.m.-noon.

Banco Nacional has a branch at Avenida 56 and Calle 31, and **Banco Financiero Internacional** on the southeast corner of Parque Martí (open Mon.-Fri. 8 a.m.-3 p.m.). Foreigners are well served by the **Clínica Internacional,** Calle 37, e/ 2 y 4, tel. 7008, opposite the Hotel Jagua. It has a doctor and nurse on 24-hour call, plus a small pharmacy. Hotel visits cost US$40.

Need basic camera supplies? Try **Photo Service,** on Avenida 54 at Calle 33.

The **Cupet gas station** is on Calle 37 at Avenida 18, four blocks north of Hotel Jagua. You'll find another east of town just beyond the turnoff for Trinidad, on the road to Rancho Luna.

GETTING THERE

By Air: Domestic service is offered to **Aeropuerto Internacional Jaime Gónzalez,** tel. 5868, fax 33-5428, by Aerotaxi, Aerogaviota, and Aerocaribbean. Cubana does not fly to Cienfuegos. Royal Airlines has charter flights from Toronto three times a week in winter and weekly in summer. The airport is five km northeast of town, on the road to Caunao.

By Bus: Bus no. 411 for Cienfuegos departs Havana's main bus terminal at 5:45 and 7:10 a.m. and 12:20, 6, and 8:10 p.m. (17 pesos express, 14 pesos regular). Most buses take five hours via the Autopista and Aguada de Pasajeros. Demand far exceeds supply, and you should try to secure a reservation as far in advance as possible. There is also regular service from Santa Clara, Sancti Spíritus, and Camagüey.

The bus terminal is on Calle 49 e/ Avenida 56 y 58, six blocks east of the Prado.

By Train: Cienfuegos lies at the end of a branch line off the main Havana-Santiago railroad. The most recent check I made of the schedules indicates that trains operate from Havana to Cienfuegos daily at 10:15 a.m. and on Monday, Tuesday, and Saturday at 8:35 a.m. (US$11), but schedules are always liable to change. The train can take eight hours or more. Another option is to catch an *especial* from Havana to Santa Clara and then connect to Cienfuegos at 7:33 a.m. (train no. 206) and 5:27 p.m. (no. 208). Trains also operate to Cienfuegos from Sancti Spíritus daily at 4:30 a.m. and 2:09 p.m. The train station is on Calle 49 e/ Avenida 58 y 60.

By Cruise Ship: The 212-passenger *Meliá Don Juan* is based in Cienfuegos and operates three-, four-, and seven-day cruises to Santiago de Cuba, Jamaica, and the Cayman Islands. You can board the vessel in Grand Cayman or Montego Bay. (See "Getting There" in the On The Road chapter for more information.)

By Private Yacht: Marina Jagua, tel. 432-8195 or 432-6678, supposedly has moorings for 30 yachts, with water, electricity, and diesel. Berthing costs US$10 (flat rate). Its facilities are meager. Swim-aboard theft is said to be a problem. You must stop for clearance into the bay at the **Guárda Frontera** post, one km south of the Jagua fortress, on the western shores of the entrance channel. There's a US$30 fee to have a pilot on board (the authorities will tell you it's necessary, although you can argue otherwise with good cause).

Organized Tours: Tour & Travel, Avenida 5 #8409, Miramar, Havana, tel. 33-2433, includes Cienfuegos plus Varadero and Trinidad on a three-day tour from Havana (US$225). You can book at any hotel tour desk.

GETTING AROUND

Most attractions are concentrated downtown, a 30-minute walk from the Hotel Jagua into town. I walked most places. You may prefer wheels or hooves.

By Bus: Cienfuegos has a fairly good bus system. Journeys are a fixed 10 centavos. Bus no. 0 runs the length of the Prado and Malecón and stops outside the Hotel Jagua. Oddly, you need to buy tickets from a street kiosk before boarding downtown; ask a local where to buy a ticket.

By Taxi: Horse-drawn taxis *(mulos)* wait outside the bus terminal, the Hotel Jagua, and the train station. Downtown, horse taxis also congregate on Avenida 50 at the corner of Calle 37. Foreigners are now routinely charged US$1 or more for a ride from the Hotel Jagua (Cubans pay one peso). Longer trips are negotiable.

There are a few peso-taxis, who will try to charge you in dollars. Licensed dollar-only Tur-

Cienfuegos

istaxis are now the norm. You'll pay about US$2 between the Hotel Jagua and downtown. **Transtur,** Avenida 52, e/ Calle 29 y 31, operates Transtaxi, tel. 9-6256 or 9-6212.

By Car: You can rent a car from **Havanautos,** next to the Cupet station on Calle 37, tel. 335154. **Transtur** also offers rents cars.

By Ferry: A sea-taxi serves the merchant fleet anchored in the bay (see "Getting There" under "Castillo de Jagua," below).

Organized Excursions: Sightseeing cruises of the bay are offered by Puertosol from Marina Jagua (US$7 for one hour), including a stop at Jagua. You can also take an excursion to Playa Ancón for US$25, including lunch; a two-day excursion to the southern cays (US$350); or a three-day excursion to Cayo Largo (US$450).

Rumbos, Calle 20 #3905, e/ 39 y 41, Punta Gorda, tel. 9645, offers a city tour, as well as excursions to Trinidad, the Sierra del Escambray, the Valle de Yaguanabo, and other sites. **Viajes Altamira,** Avenida 56 #3110, e/ 31 y 33, tel. 3171, also offers a wide range of excursions. **Havanatur** has an office in the Hotel Rancho Luna, tel. 432-48131, fax 432-33-5057, south of town.

GETTING AWAY

Hitchhiking: There's a designated hitching point north of the city, opposite the university (bus no. 6 will take you there from the Prado).

By Bus: There are five buses daily to Havana, at 12:30 and 6 a.m., noon, and 2:30 and 7:30 p.m. You can make reservations in advance at the **Oficina de Reservaciones de Ómnibus Nacional,** at Calle 54 e/ Avenidas 35 y 37, tel. 6050 or 9358, which also has an information service. Buses also depart daily for Camagüey and Santiago at 5 p.m. Other buses depart for Trinidad at noon; Playa Girón at 4 a.m. (5 a.m. on Sunday) and 3:30 p.m.; for Santa Clara 10 times daily, beginning at 5 a.m.; and to Sancti Spíritus six times daily.

You can try for same-day service on local routes, but if you do, arrive first thing in the morning; you'll be given a ticket, then keep your fingers crossed that you can get on later that day. Long-distance routes are often booked solid days or even weeks in advance.

By Train: A train to Havana departs Cienfuegos daily at 11:30 p.m. (10:30 a.m. on Monday, Tuesday, and Saturday) and for Santa Clara and Sancti Spíritus daily at 4:39 a.m. and 2.34 p.m. (a two-hour journey). You may buy same-day tickets at the station, but don't count on it. However, foreigners now pay in dollars and get preferential service.

By Sea: The deluxe *Meliá Don Juan* cruise ship departs Cienfuegos each Monday for a four-day cruise to Cayman Brac, Santiago de Cuba, and Montego Bay (Jamaica). On Friday, it departs for a three-day cruise to Grand Cayman and Cayo Largo. Contact Meliá Hoteles in Varadero, tel. 5-66-7013, fax 5-66-7162.

VICINITY OF CIENFUEGOS

JARDÍN BOTÁNICO SOLEDAD

This splendid garden is about 10 km east of Cienfuegos, on the main coast road to Trinidad, between the communities of San Antón and Guaos. It was begun in 1899 by a New Englander, Edward Atkins, who owned vast sugar estates in the area and brought in Harvard botanists to develop hardier and more productive sugarcane strains. Later, Harvard University assumed control under a 99-year-lease, and a general collection making up one of the tropical world's finest botanical gardens—the Harvard Biological Laboratory—was amassed. Since the Revolution,

the garden has been maintained by the Cuban Academy of Science's Institute of Botany.

Pathways leads through the 94-hectare garden, reached along an avenue of royal palms. It harbors a collection of some 2,000 species, 70% of which are exotics, including rare tropical plants with important medicinal uses. A rare bamboo collection has 23 species. Of rubber trees, there are 89 species; of cactus, 400. The prize collection is the 307 varieties of palms—supposedly the world's largest. My favorite feature is a cactus-strewn rock garden shaped like Cuba.

The garden maintains its connections with the international botanical gardens, including with Harvard University, but the gardens are run-down and weeds are taking over. The facility includes a laboratory (in Harvard House) and library.

The garden is open daily 8 a.m.-4 p.m. Entrance costs US$2, including guided tour. Take your own snacks; the basic café serves drinks only.

The avenue of palms extends along the south side of the main road and leads to the Pepito Tey sugar factory, once owned by Atkins and today open for visits.

Getting There: The bus from Cienfuegos to Cumanayagua passes the garden. A taxi will cost about US$40 roundtrip.

PLAYA RANCHO LUNA AND PASACABELLO

A turnoff at San Antón leads southwest to the coast and the entrance to the Bahía de Cienfuogoo at Pasacabello. At the shore you'll come to a pleasant beach: Playa Rancho Luna, with calm, shallow turquoise waters; it's popular with Cubans and features a basic café and bar. The beach has no-see-ums (called *he-hin* locally) that emerge ravenous at dusk.

A road to the left at a T-junction at Rancho Luna leads to the Hotel Rancho Luna, fronting its own beach. To the right, the road follows the rocky coast eight km to Pasacabello, facing the Castillo de Jagua (22 km from Cienfuegos), across the 400-meter-wide mouth of the bay.

Watersports
You can choose from a wide range of watersports on Playa Rancho Luna. **Catamarans** (US$10 per hour) and **windsurfers** (US$5) can be rented. **Water-skiing** costs US$12 for 15 minutes. And **scuba diving** is available at the Rancho Luna Hotel to take you out to coral reefs in Las Playitas and Barrera *ensenada*. At least eight ships lie rotting on the seabed.

Accommodations
The **Hotel Pasacaballos,** tel. 9-6212, is operated by Islazul and is popular mostly with Cubans. Its situation is appealing: on a hill at the entrance of the bay, facing Jagua Castle. Alas, for some inexplicable reason, the rooms face the other way—another example of communist design gone awry.

The five-story hotel is decribed in its brochure as "the most beautiful hotel built since the Revolution and . . . probably the best hotel in all of Cuba." It looks like an enormous concrete block shipped in from Novosibirsk. Inside, the decor is orange and olive-green (hopefully, a facelift will have relieved your eyes of such a burden by the time you read this). A flying staircase of black marble leads to the rooms (US$20 s, US$24 d). It has a wide range of activities, from billiard contests to cocktail lessons. Bicycles can be rented for US$1 per hour.

Far better is the **Rancho Luna Hotel,** Carretera de Rancho Luna, Cienfuegos, tel. 434-48120, fax 33-5057, a staple of German and Canadian tour groups. It's an excellent facility with a huge pool and sundeck. Wide lawns fall to a wide golden-cand beach with shade trees, a ranchita bar and restaurant, and an array of watersports.

The 255 a/c double rooms feature private bath, radio, and telephone. Each costs US$29 s, US$38 d—a great bargain. There are also 12 suites. Mopeds, bicycles, cars, and horses can be rented, and there's a full panoply of watersports, including catamarans. The hotel also offers a range of excursions. Other facilities include three restaurants, a nightclub, and a scuba diving center.

A more intimate option is the **Hotel Faro Luna,** Carretera de Pasacaballos Km 18, Playa Rancho Luna, tel. 5502 and 48168, fax 335059, a stone's throw from the Rancho Luna. It has 14 a/c, modestly yet pleasantly decorated rooms with satellite TV. The hotel has a large swimming pool and restaurant.

Getting There
Buses depart daily from the Cienfuegos bus terminal at 11:20 a.m. and 5 and 8 p.m. (50 centavos; 45 minutes). A taxi will cost you about US$12. *Pesetero* ferries leave for Rancho Luna on a regular basis from the terminal on Avenida 46. Ferries to and from Cienfuegos connect Pasacabello with Jagua.

CASTILLO DE JAGUA

Across the bay from Pasacabello sits a 17th-century Spanish fort, Castillo de Jagua, guarding the entrance to the Bahía de Cienfuegos. The original fortress was expanded in the 18th century to defend against the English Royal Navy. Local lore says that the bay is protected by a ghost—the Blue Lady—who haunts the castle by night.

The small fortress overlooks a fishing village founded by immigrants from Mallorca and Valencia. It looks Portuguese and consists of delicate, whitewashed, red-tile-roofed houses perched above the water (some on stilts). Appropriately, it is called **Perché.** Fishing boats bob at anchor (note, too, the Batman-style Russian speedboat), and there's a tiny beach 200 meters south of the fortress.

A small museum is planned for the fortress, which today functions as a restaurant whose house special is *La Dama Azul,* tel. 096-402. The meals are said to be of reasonable quality.

Getting There
Ferries depart the wharf on Avenida 46 and Calle 29 in Cienfuegos at 6, 7, and 11 a.m. and 1, 3, and 5:30 p.m. (50 centavos). It's a slow, one-hour journey. The ferry wharf in Jagua is immediately below the fortress. A ferry also operates between Pasacabello, across the bay, but foreigners are reputedly often denied (one peso if you can board).

You can also get there by road. Exit Cienfuegos on Calle 37 past the industrial complexes. Keep the bay on your left. Drive carefully: the road is deeply potholed.

CIUDAD NUCLEAR

Up on the hill behind Jagua is a modern city, Ciudad Nuclear (Nuclear City), built in the 1980s to house workers constructing Cuba's first nuclear power station nearby at Juragua, atop the westernmost tip of the entrance to the Bahía de Cienfuegos. The half-completed reactor stands idle about two km west of town, where it rises menacingly, like a bubble, attended by a coterie of courtesan cranes.

A GLOW IN THE DARK

To friend and foe alike, it is "the monster"—the Juragua nuclear power station, near Cienfuegos. Construction began in 1983, when Soviet aid flowed freely. The initial project called for four reactors, but that has since been downsized to two 417,000 kilowatt reactors, either of which could supply up to 15% of Cuba's energy needs and save around two million tons of oil a year.

Construction was mothballed in September 1992, after Cuba announced it could not meet the financial terms set by the new Russian government. When construction ceased, assembly on one of the reactors was about 90% complete (the second reactor was about 20% complete).

A multinational study in 1995 gave the green light for the resumption of construction. In October 1995, Cuba signed an agreement with Russia's Atomic Energy Ministry (Minbas) to complete the plant, despite threats by the US Congress to sever aid to Russia. Minbas (which has sunk over US$1 billion into Juragua) agreed to provide US$350 million of the US$800 million needed for completion. Meanwhile, about 1,200 workers are still employed as maintenance crews to keep the reactors rust-free while awaiting the day when construction resumes.

Cuba has suggested creating an international consortium to conclude construction and operate the plant (French, German, and other partners would recover their investment from the sale to Cuba of the energy produced). Cuba has even invited the US to participate. Instead of seizing the opportunity to become involved in securing the safety of Juragua, the US seems determined to kill it.

Congress has held hearings dominated by anti-Cuba lobbyists, who claim that the plant will pose a serious threat to the safety of the United States (Juragua is 240 miles from Miami), although Florida has several nuclear reactors of its own. The US goverment says the project is flawed by faulty design and construction; Congress has portrayed the plant as similar to the Chernobyl plant which exploded in April 1986 in the Ukraine. However, the International Atomic Energy Agency (IAEA) has approved the project as safe. The Pentagon commissioned its own study in 1993 and agreed that Juragua is an advanced VVER-440 model, pressurized water-cooled reactor, wholly different in design from Chernoby's outdated graphite technology. The Geneva-based IAEA says it is similar to the world's most efficient reactor—the Russian-built VVER in Finland.

For now, the fields surrounding the plant are once more being plowed with oxen by farmers awaiting the day when the hum of energy surging from the reactors may turn the lights back on in Cuba.

The town is a dreary Soviet-built creation consisting of a dozen or so high-rise concrete apartment blocks with Cyrillic lettering painted on their mildewed façades. It's soulless and repulsive, despite the shopping centers and movie theater. Local inhabitants drown out the melancholy by setting up megawatt speakers in the streets for impromptu parties.

CIENFUEGOS TO TRINIDAD

Trinidad, Cuba's best-preserved colonial city, is 83 km east of Cienfuegos. The coast road dips and rises and is fabulously scenic. Ahead and to the north rise the Sierra del Escambray, saw-toothed and building ridge upon ridge. Below, in the rainshadow formed by the mountains, the road passes first through sugarcane fields, and the smell of molasses carries across the hummocky plains. The heat builds gradually. The land becomes increasingly arid, the sugarcane is replaced with parched savanna grazed by hardy cattle, and the *bohios* become noticeably simpler and aged.

Soon the mountain foothills narrow down to the roadway, squeezing it up against the coast, which boasts several twee little beaches.

About 50 km east of Cienfuegos, a road leads south to **Playa Ingles.** Here, you are deposited beside a beautiful and lonesome beach with fishing boats and a rustic hut that serves *refrescoes* and snacks to local fishermen.

Three km east of the turnoff for Playa Ingles, you'll cross the **Río Yaguanabo,** the first of several rivers whose mouths are set in deep gulleys and feature handsome, pocket-size beaches.

Accommodations and Food: There's a basic *campismo* at the east end of Playa Ingles. **Villa and Restaurante Yaguanabo,** at the mouth of the Río Yaguanabo, was closed for restoration at press time but will feature basic two-story villas (US$8 d) when it reopens.

VALLES DE MATAGUÁ AND YAGUANABO

At La Sierrita, about 30 km east of Cienfuegos, you can cut inland and ascend into the Sierra del Escambray via the valley of the Río Mataguá. It's a stupendously scenic route that rises past sheer-walled, cave-riddled limestone *mogotes,* at their most impressive near the town of **San Blas,** eight km east of La Sierrita. San Blas sits in the lee of great cliffs where huge stalactites and stalagmites are exposed in an open cave high atop the mountains. Bright red flame trees and bougainvillea in the valley add to the stunning effect.

The road winds and loops steeply until you are amid narrow valleys planted in coffee and bananas atop the *mogotes.* Look out for the gun slits in the cliffs at hairpin bends on the mountainside: they were used by Che Guevara's guerrillas to ambush Batista's troops.

Alternately, you can continue along the coast road and turn inland to follow the Río Yaguanabo through another stunningly scenic valley hemmed in to the north by the ragged southern slopes of the Escambray.

The road rises to Loma Palo Seco, the Yaguanabo Valley's highest point. There are waterfalls with cool ponds at their bases to discover amid the pastures, thicket, and dense woodlands. The highlight is **Cueva Martin Infierno,** boasting Latin America's largest stalagmite—67 meters tall—as well as mineralogical rarities such as gypsum flowers *(flores de yeso).*

Rumbos offers an excursion from Trinidad and Cienfuegos, including lunch at a cattle farm where you can sample homemade cheese.

SIERRA DEL ESCAMBRAY

The Sierra Escambray is Cuba's second-highest mountain range. The Escambray and adjacent ranges lie mostly within Cienfuegos province, descending gradually into Villa Clara province to the north, edging into Sancti Spíritus province to the east, and dropping steeply to the southern coast, deeply indented by rivers. The mountains reach 1,140 meters atop Pico San Juan. It is remarkable how much cooler it is up here, even on a summer day—ascending from the coastal lowlands, you will surely need a sweater (and you'll feel the heat mightily as you drop back down to the lowlands). Dark nimbus clouds can freshen during the morning and cold rain may fall while the surrounding lowlands bake, even in the "dry season." The region is the rainiest in Cuba, especially during the May-October rainy season.

The Escambray are a delight for birders and hikers. Guillermo Cabrera Infante wrote that in the Escambray, "The ground is covered with a herbaceous green carpet; the trees, bushes, and jungle run the whole gamut of green. Tree trunks are covered with a lichen that is like green rust . . . Thousands of pearls of raindrops drip from the leaves, and as you step, the grass sinks with a crackling watery sound."

In the late 1950s, these mountains were the site of a revolutionary front against Fulgencio Batista, led by Che Guevara. After the revolutionaries triumphed, in 1959, the Escambray hid another band of olive green-clad rebels, this time counterrevolutionaries who opposed Castro. The CIA helped finance and arm these resistance fighters, whom the Castro regime tagged "bandits." The resistance army had grown to at least 3,000 men by 1962—about as many men as Fidel had in the Sierra Maestra at his peak. The groups, however, were split into various rival groups of disgruntled revolutionaries, landowners, ex-Batista followers, and stubborn independent mountainfolk who opposed *fidelismo*. As a whole, they had no philosophical program other than to resist Castro. Castro formed counterinsurgency units called Battalions of Struggle Against Bandits. The "bandits" weren't eradicated until 1966. A museum in

Trinidad tells the communist government's version of *la lucha contra los bandidos* (although the *bandidos* are portrayed by the Cuban governments as representatives of the corrupt Batista regime, many were simple, honest *campesinos*).

UNEAC, the Cuban Union of Writers and Artists, has a retreat—El Catillito—high in the Escambray.

CUMANAYAGUA

Cumanayagua, 38 km east of Cienfuegos and midway to Manicaragua, is a small, pretty, seemingly prosperous, modern agricultural town with genteel whitewashed curbs. You can stop here to savor an ice cream at Coppelia. One km west of town is a T-junction with a road that encircles the western foothills of the Escambray. The road gradually rises through sweet-smelling citrus groves and meets the Cienfuegos-Trinidad coast road.

About 10 km east of Cumanayagua at **La Macagua,** just west of Ciro Redondo, a turnoff to the south leads to Lago Habanilla.

LAGO HABANILLA

This huge (32 square km) man-made lake fills what was once a deep valley on the northern slopes of the Escambray. The lake, which has an average depth of 35 meters and supplies water to Santa Clara and Cienfuegos, shimmers through every shade from pea-green to cobalt (depending on the mood of the weather) below its backdrop of pine-studded mountains. The lake is renowned for bass. Hunting is offered at an adjacent lake, **Lago Granizo.**

The folks in the hamlet of Hanabanilla make plastic recreation boats. The slopes are farmed by *campesinos* who grow malanga, tobacco, and coffee. The lakeshore curls like a jigsaw-puzzle piece, perfect for scenic boat trips from the dock of the Hotel Habanilla. A ferry (US$2) also takes passengers across the lake to the **Casa del Campesino,** where you can get a taste for the *campesino* lifestyle on this small working farm. You can also catch the boat that ferries *campesinos* and workers to and from remote hamlets on the steep slopes; it leaves from the tiny dock in Habanilla hamlet, reached by a side road just north of the dam and hydroelectric station below the hotel.

You can hire a guide to lead you to local caves.

Accommodations and Food

Sitting above the western lakeshore is the **Habanilla Hotel,** another Soviet complex designed without respect to its advantageous position— the restaurant, for example, looks out over . . . nothing! Otherwise, it's pleasant and popular with Cubans, who gather by the swimming pool and sundeck. The hotel has 125 a/c, modestly furnished rooms, each with private bath, telephone, and radio. Facilities include a restaurant, bar, *cafetería*, nightclub, swimming pool, shop, and tourism bureau. Rates are US$17 s, US$22 d in low season and US$26 s, US$31 d in high season.

I enjoyed a fresh-caught tilapia, superbly grilled and served with garlic, pickled cabbage, other condiments, and English-style chips (fries) in the hotel restaurant. The chefs will gladly prepare your fresh catch.

Lunch is also served at the **Río Negro Restaurante,** on the Casa de Campesino (see above) on the southern shores of the lake and featuring *bohios* surrounded by bougainvillea. Here you're fed *criollo* cuisine such as roast pork (the house speciality is chicken with pineapple; *pollo saltón à la piña*) and entertained by Afro-Cuban rhythms. The restaurant is reached by a steep trail.

MANICARAGUA TO TOPES DE COLLANTES

The most beautiful vistas in the Escambray are on the north-facing slopes, as you rise from Santa Clara or drop through the valleys east and north of Presa de Hanabanilla (Lake Hanabanilla) to the agricultural town of Manicaragua (pop. 80,000), 30 km south of Santa Clara and 30 km north of Topes de Collantes. The town is surrounded by rolling plains with hillocks resembling a basket of eggs. It's a classic Cuban landscape, with *bohios,* royal palms, and *guajiros* tending fields of tobacco with ox-drawn plows. There's nothing much to Manicaragua, though.

A road rises south of Manicuragua and climbs into the Escambray to Topes de Collantes. Midway between Manicuragua and Topes, you'll pass a T-junction at **Jibacoa,** where a road leads west to the southern end of Lake Hanabanilla.

Accommodations and Food: The **Hotel Escambray,** on the western side of Manicaragua, on the road to Cienfuegos, tel. 491548, has 20 basic, ill-lit rooms. It accepts foreigners and charges in pesos (seven pesos s, 10 d, 14 with a/c). It has a small restaurant and the El Rojito bar.

Manicaragua has several peso restaurants in the main square.

TOPES DE COLLANTES NATIONAL PARK

The Escambray's highest peaks and densest forests are protected in Topes de Collantes National Park, extending into Sancti Spíritus province, in the chain's southeast corner. The slopes are swathed in Caribbean pines and an abundance of ancient tree-ferns, bamboo, and eucalyptus. The area is tremendous for hiking; there are plenty of trails. Bring raingear and waterproof footwear. The views are fabulous during early evening, with silvered light filtering down through the clouds. The birdlife is rich and includes an abundance of parrots. The twisting roads are lined with billboards that say things such as, "To Care For Wildlife Is A Social Obligation."

At its heart, at a refreshingly cool 790 meters, is a spa-hotel complex dominated by a massive concrete structure—the Kurhotel—that you believe could only have been conceived by the Soviets but was in fact designed in 1936, when it served as a sanatorium for victims of tuberculosis. Following the Revolution, the disease was finally eradicated in Cuba. The structure was then sanitized and turned into a teacher-training facility. The complex, which includes smaller hotels, was developed as a resort area in the late 1970s, with a view to nature and health tourism—the swimming pool stays heated year-round.

The complex is mostly used by Cubans, especially those seeking post-operative rehabilitation or specialized therapies. It also attracts spa-vacationers from elsewhere in Latin America. Frankly, it holds little appeal unless you're seriously seeking physical therapy, such as medicinal herb treatments. Medicinal plants are grown in *viveros* in the valley below Los Helechos. Alas, the Special Period has taken its toll.

The road below the Hotel Los Helechos is now closed to traffic, but hikers still have access to trails.

Hiking

The two most important trails lead to two waterfalls—**Salto Vega Grande** and **Salto de Caburní,** (the latter, 75 meters high)—about four km northeast of the complex—a stiff hike. The trail to Caburní begins beside the Aparthotel, east of the Kurhotel. It leads steeply downhill, zigzagging in places.

Another trail leads south seven km to **Finca Cordina,** an erstwhile coffee estate that now serves as a post for birders and hikers. Special luncheons are laid on for tour groups, with roast suckling pig and a house cocktail made from rum, honey, and ginger. After a couple of toddies, you may feel brave enough to wallow in a pool of medicinal mud! The surrounding hills contain an extensive cave system, much of which remains unexplored. The trail begins below Los Helechos, from 400 meters along the road that leads east from Vina los Eucaliptus.

Accommodations and Food

The massive **Kurhotel** has a Stalinist aesthetic, with hints of art deco outside. A monstrous TV and radio transmitter looms over the massive hotel. By contrast, the lobby—reached via a stone staircase on a Siberian scale—is pleasantly welcoming, with lofty columns and ferns, and the rooms are satisfactory, with rattan furniture, floral prints, and attractive bathrooms. A TV, refrigerator, and telephone are standard. You could well wait forever for the two tiny elevators serving the 210 rooms and 16 suites. Rooms cost US$28 s, US$40 d in low-season

(US$2 more in high season); suites cost US$45 s, US$60 d (US$60 s, US$70 in high season). There are also apartments, due to open in 1997 following restoration. Each guest is issued a turquoise jogging suit. The hotel features its own TV station, Tele Caburni, and a thermal pool under a skylight in a separate building, where massage and therapeutic treatments are offered.

You'll *need* recuperative therapy after the dismal first impression of the **Hotel Los Helechos,** tel. 40180, though the facility, which hides in a cool valley below the Kurhotel, soon begins to warm. Rooms cost US$19 s, US$25 d. Take a room in the front, three-story blockhouse structure; the rest are poorly lit. There's a pleasant enough swimming pool and restaurant.

The **Hotel Serrano** and **Hotel Los Pinos** do not accept foreigners. Count your blessings.

I can't vouch for the quality of meals in the Kurhotel or Los Helechos. The only other restaurant nearby is a pizzeria with *mirador* a few miles south of Topes, on the road to Trinidad.

Getting There

By Bus: There's "bus" service (sometimes provided in an open-sided truck) to Topes from Trinidad, in Sancti Spíritus province, with departures on Monday and Sunday at 4 p.m. and Thursday at 6 a.m. Tour buses leave from the Motel Las Cuevas, in Trinidad. You may be able to talk your way aboard, but expect to pay tour excursion prices. Buses also travel to Topes from Manicuragua and from Santa Clara.

By Car: There are three routes to Topes de Collante. The most traveled is that from Trinidad, 21 km to the south (the turnoff from the coast road is five km west of Trinidad). The road, which is deeply potholed, rises in a steep switchback. If returning from Topes via this road, drive with utmost caution: the road also has huge corrugations and hairpin bends, often in combination—extremely dangerous!

A second road rises more gradually from Santa Clara via Manicaragua.

If coming from Cienfuegos, you should turn left at **La Sierrita.**

SANTA CLARA AND VICINITY

Santa Clara (pop. 175,000), 300 km east of Havana, is the provincial capital of Villa Clara. It is strategically located on the southern fringe of fertile plains, in the northern lee of the Escambray. The city was established within the confluence of the Ríos Bélico and Cubanicay in 1689 when residents of Remedios grew tired of constant pirate raids, pulled up stakes, and moved inland.

It straddles the Carretera Central at the gateway to the eastern provinces—a crucial strategic location at the center of Cuba. Hence, it functioned as a plum in Cuba's wars of independence. On 31 December 1958, Che Guevara's Rebel Army attacked the town and derailed a troop train carrying reinforcements and US armaments bound for Oriente. Two days later, the Rebel Army captured the city, which became known as *el último reducto de la tirania Batistiana* (the last fortress of Batista's tyranny). Within 24 hours, the dictator fled the island.

A half-day's sightseeing will suffice. Colonial charm remains in pockets, but Santa Clara has grown apace since the Revolution. Prior to 1959 there was only one factory of note: Coca-Cola's. As Minister of Industry, Che Guevara developed a soft spot for the city. Today, Santa Clara is an important industrial town. The suburbs contain many factories, including the largest textile mill in the country (built with Japanese help) and the Fábrica INPUD (established by Guevara), which makes refrigerators, stoves, and other household appliances. It has evolved, too, into a major center of learning, home to the University de las Villas, and the Ernesto "Che" Guevara Vocational School.

ORIENTATION

Santa Clara is a large city, and although laid out roughly in a rectilinear grid, it's complicated to get around. The city is encircled by a ring road *(circunvalación);* use it if you want to bypass the town.

The center of town is Parque Vidal. The Carretera Central enters town from the west and merges with Calle Marta Abreu, which runs to Parque Vidal (east of the square, Marta Abreu becomes Céspedes). Six blocks west of Parque Vidal (at the bridge over the Río Bélico), the Carretera swings south, then turns east again and exits town en route to Placetas. The main shopping street is Independencia, which runs parallel to Marta Abreu, one block north of Parque Vidal. Eastward, Independencia crosses the Río Cubanicay and (as Avenida de Libaración) leads to Remedios.

Máximo Gómez (also called Calle Cuba) and Luís Estévez (also called Calle Colón) run perpendicular to Abreu, on the west and east side of the park. Estévez leads north seven blocks to the railway station (beyond the tracks, it becomes Avenida Eduardo Chibás and leads to Sagua la Grande and the north coast).

THINGS TO SEE AND DO

Parque Vidal
A node of activity, this large paved square is rimmed by several buildings of note. It is named for the revolutionary hero Leoncio Vidal, who—according to a monument—was killed at this exact spot. A curiosity of the square is its double-wide sidewalk. In colonial days, this was divided by an iron fence, and whites perambulated on the inner half while blacks kept to the outside. In springtime, the park fairly blazes with pink blossoms of leafy *guasíma* trees and poinciana, full of sparrows and Cuban blackbirds caterwauling, honking, and chirping. The bandstand at its center is still used for concerts on weekends. Keeping her eye on things is a bronze effigy of Marta Abreu de Estévez (1845-1904), a local heroine and philanthropist who funded construction of the theater on the north side of the square.

The **Teatro la Caridad** was built in 1885 "for the poor of Santa Clara" but dedicated to the memory of Abreu's parents (her father was also a philanthropist, who funded the city's first free clinic and free primary school). Enrico Caruso considered it a fitting venue. Note the stunning muraled foyer.

Fifty meters east of the theater is the **Museo de Artes Decorativos,** featuring an eclectic array of stunning colonial antiques and furniture spanning styles from rococo and neoclassical to "imperial Cuban." Note the beautiful *ventrales* above the inner courtyard, and the so-called Empire Hall, with its delicate parquetry. Every room is sumptuously decorated with period pieces that would fetch princely sums at Sotheby's. It's open Mon.-Fri. 9 a.m.-5 p.m. and Saturday 1-9:30 p.m. Entrance costs US$1.

On the square's east side is the old **Palacio Provincial,** now housing the city *biblioteca* and with an imposing neoclassical frontage supported by Ionic columns. The building dates to 1922 and occupies the site of the original city hall. Opposite is the **Hotel Santa Clara Libre,** a glass and cement carbuncle where many of Batista's troops ensconced themselves in December 1958 and where a fierce battle ensued to dislodge them. (In 1969, Black Panther leader Huey Newton and his wife sought exile in Cuba and, asking to "live like the people," were sent to Santa Clara. The couple, however, ended up in a suite in the Santa Clara Libre.)

The **Casa de la Cultura** is on the square.

"Boulevard"

After exploring the plaza, walk north one block and amble this bustling pedestrian precinct along

Independencia (between Zayas to the west and Maceo to the east). It features an intriguing blend of colonial and 20th-century buildings and lively bars and cafés in Art Deco and antique Spanish styles. Midway along the Boulevard, at Luís Estévez, is the tiny, handsomely conceived **Plaza de las Arcadas,** whose trees (some intertwined with bougainvillea) are full of twittering birds.

Tren Blindado

The most fascinating sight in town is at the east end of Independencia, beyond the railway crossing. It was here on 29 December 1958 that rebel troops led by Che Guevara derailed one of Batista's troop trains. Four rust-colored carriages are preserved higgledy-piggledy in suspended animation as they came to rest after the train was run off the rails. There is an exhibit inside one of the carriages (open Tues.-Sun. 8 a.m.-noon and 3-7 p.m.; US$1; tel. 2-2758). The carriages are fronted by an obelisk with a plaque telling the tale of the 90-minute battle.

Plaza de la Revolución

The battle is commemorated at this impressive plaza on the west side of the city, at the west end of Marta Abreu. Looming over the wide hilltop plaza is a massive bronze statue of Che Guevara bearing his rifle. The effect is dramatic, especially during a fiery red sunset. The evocative granite edifice is guarded by gun-toting soldiers. Behind, a wall bears a relief of the Sierra del Escambray and the Tren Blindado. There is no sign to indicate it (the entrance is to the rear), but the podium contains the fascinating **Museo de la Revolución,** which worships the deeds of the rebel army and has a detailed account of the capture of Santa Clara in December 1958 (open Mon.-Sat. 8 a.m.-5 p.m. and Sunday 8 a.m.-noon; US$1).

Other Sites

Walk two blocks east of Parque Vidal and you'll reach the **Iglesia Buen Viaje,** a beautiful church where black slaves once gathered on the patio to hear services (since they weren't permitted in-

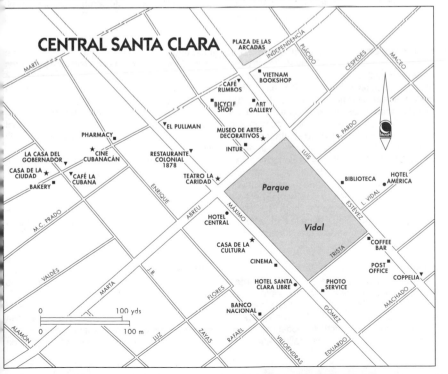

side). Another church of note is the **Iglesia del Carmen,** on Parque Tudury. This national monument dates to 1748.

If you want to further check out the history of Villa Clara, head to the impressive **Museo Provincial,** in the Escuela Abel Santamaría, at the north end of Calle Esquerra in the Reparto Osvaldo Herrera neighborhood. The site was formerly a military barracks (fulfilling Castro's dictum to turn all Batista's barracks into centers of learning). The museum is brimful of colonial furniture but is dedicated to the province's role in the wars of independence and the fight against Batista; it also features a large collection of weaponry spanning several centuries, plus a natural history exhibit downstairs. Open Tues.-Sat. 1-6 p.m. and Sunday 9 a.m.-1 p.m. (US$1).

ACCOMMODATIONS

The basic **Hotel América,** on Leon Vidal one block east of the main square, tel. 5451, has 28 rooms with fans for 10 pesos. Foreigners may be accepted, but expect to pay in dollars. The stately **Hotel Central,** 50 meters north of the Santa Clara Libre on Parque Vidal, tel. 2-2369, was closed for renovation at press time. It's operated by Islazul, which has a *carpeta* here (booking office tel. 5959). Intur also has an **Oficina de Reservaciones** on Lorda, next to the theater (open weekdays 8-11:30 a.m. and 1-4 p.m.). You may be able to book accommodations throughout the province at either office.

To be in the thick of things, check in at the **Santa Clara Libre,** tel. 27548, overlooking Parque Vidal. This modern, Soviet-style high-rise has 160 rooms—most with a/c, each with TV and telephone (US$18 s, US$24 d). There's a reasonable restaurant on the tenth floor and a rooftop bar above. You'll have to park your car on the square and should hire a volunteering local to guard it.

Upscale
The most appealing place is **Hotel Horizontes Los Caneyes,** Avenida de los Eucaliptos y Circunvalación de Santa Clara, Villa Clara, tel. 422-4512, fax 33-5009, about two km west of town. It has 91 a/c rooms in thatched, wooden, octagonal *cabañas* spread amid lawns, palms, and other shade trees in addition to bougainvilleas for color. The bungalows have terra-cotta tile floors, large bathrooms, refrigerators, and small TVs. Facilities include an attractive restaurant, *cafetería,* snack bar, disco, and small swimming pool. There's even a hairdresser and a rent-a-car and tourism bureau. Los Caneyes is popular with tour groups and is moderately lively. You'll need a sweater for the near-frigid restaurant. Breakfasts cost US$3, lunch and dinner typically about US$10. Los Caneyes is a bargain at US$24 s, US$32 d (US$32 s, US$40 high-season).

A similar concept—thatched cabins in a landscaped setting—is offered at **La Granjita,** Carretera Malez Km 2.5, Santa Clara, tel. 26059 or 26052, run by Cubanacán. The 24 rooms in bamboo, rattan, and thatch bungalows are pretty (a few older, concrete bungalows are less appealing) and feature TV, radio, and telephone, but—at US$35 s, US$45 d—are less of a bargain than Los Caneyes. There's a tennis court, pool, and restaurant. The facility is less utilized than Los Caneyes, with a more lonesome feel.

FOOD

First choice (for quality) is the restaurant in the **Hotel Los Caneyes,** though even the standards can vary. The top-floor restaurant in the **Hotel Santa Clara Libre** is nothing special, but at least it's guaranteed to have food (and views over the square). The **Restaurante Colonial 1878,** on Calle Máximo Gómez e/ Parque Vidal y Independencia, tel. 2-2428, also serves basic *criollo* fare.

Santa Clara is well blessed with private *paladares,* serving much better fare than the state-run restaurants do. Look for places lit up outside with Christmas lights. Ask around for recommendations **Restaurante Renacer,** is in a colonial home at Zayas #111 y Eduardo Machado y Tristá, tel. 2-2272.

There's a wide choice of bars and cafés selling snacks and drinks. The "Boulevard" has several lively options, including **El Pullman,** a colonial-period setting with patio seating under awnings (make sure you sit in the dollar-only section). **Rumbos** has a similarly popular café overlooking the Plaza de las Arcadas. My favorite is **La Casa del Gobernador,** at the corner of Zayas and Independencia. This colonial-era building, once the governor's house, is now a lofty-ceilinged bar. You can look down on life, so to speak, from the upstairs balcony. There's cabaret in the evening. Another favorite of locals is **La Cubana,** a café that also opens onto the "Boulevard."

For coffee, try the coffee bar on the southeast corner of the main square.

Craving something sweet? Check out Coppelia, one block south of the main square, on Calle Colón, for ice cream. There's a bakery opposite the Casa de la Ciudad, on Independencia.

ENTERTAINMENT AND EVENTS

Troubadors play most evenings (and weekend afternoons) at the **Casa de la Trova,** opposite the Coppelia on Calle Colón, one block southeast of Parque Vidal. Classical and other performances are also hosted on an ephemeral basis at **Teatro Caridad.** Look for the posters along the sides of Parque Vidal announcing upcoming events.

Band concerts are still occasionally held on weekends beneath the gazebo in Parque Vidal. They have been held less regularly since the onset of the Special Period.

There's a **cinema** on the west side of the main square, and another, **Cine Cubanacán,** next to La Casa on the "Boulevard." The latter shows several movies each day; entrance is one peso.

There's a **disco** in the Hotel Los Caneyes playing contemporary sounds from hip-hop and reggae to rock and Latin music. It attracts a few hip locals. Entrance is free to guests. To boogie with the locals, check out **Discoteca El Sotano,** on the west side of Parque Vidal, or **Cabaret Cacique.** I even saw posters advertising a "pajama party" at the **Discoteca Indiana!**

A nightly **cabaret** at La Casa del Gobernador, on Independencia, features comedians, occasional Tropicana-style dancing, and live musicians in the upstairs bar. Cabaret is also the forté of **Cabaret Cacique,** a huge *bohio* with great ambience, dark and moody. It's a five-minute walk west of Hotel Los Caneyes. Comedy (in Spanish) is big here, laden with typically Cuban transvestite humor. The crowd is all-Cuban. Meals are served. Entrance is US$1.

SPORTS AND RECREATION

Hunters and migratory waterfowl both flock to **Los Caneyes Game Reserve,** on the western outskirts of the city. Ducks and doves are favored species, although pheasant, quail, common snipe, fulvous tree duck, American coot, and guinea fowl are among the other beautiful species to be admired or killed. Hunting packages are offered through Horizontes, with accommodations at the Hotel Los Caneyes.

SERVICES AND INFORMATION

There are small information desks at both the Hotels Los Caneyes and La Granjita. The **Intur** tourist information office still functions; it's on Calle Lorda, one block north of the main square (open Mon.-Fri. 8-11:30 a.m. and 1-3:45 p.m.).

The **post office** is one block south of the square, on Colón. There's also a post office in the railway station. More reliable (albeit costly) is the express-mail service offered by **DHL,** which has an office at Colón #10, tel. 4626. It's open weekdays 9 a.m.-6 p.m. and Saturday 8:30 a.m.-noon.

You can make international calls from the tourist hotels, or from the **Centro Telefónico,** one block west of Parque Vidal, between Calle Marta Abreu and Independencia.

If you need to cash traveler's checks or obtain an advance against your credit card, head to the **Banco Nacional** on Calle Vidal, one block west of the square; another office is on Estévez. *Jiniteros* along Independencia can change dollars for pesos.

Photo Service has a meagerly stocked branch at 1 Gómez, one block south of Parque Vidal. Cyclists may find spare parts and assistance at a well-stocked **bicycle shop** at Independencia 54. The **Cupet gas station** is on the Carretera Central, nine blocks south of Calle Marta Abreu and Calle Cuba.

SHOPPING

Antique lovers may find some gems hidden behind the huge wooden doors of **Casa de la Ciu-**

dad, at the corner of Zayas and Independencia. For souvenirs, check out the arcade on Plaza de las Arcadas, which includes a store selling ceramics. You'll also find some intriguing experimental ceramics in the artisans' store inside the art gallery at 11 Luís Estévez. There's also a souvenir store at the Hotel Los Caneyes.

The **Vietnam Bookstore,** on Independencia e/ Plácido y Luís Estévez, is well stocked by Cuban standards, though I didn't see any English-language titles.

GETTING THERE AND AROUND

By Bus

Bus no. 400 departs for Santa Clara from Havana's main bus terminal at 6:20 a.m. and arrives at the **Terminal de Ómnibus Nacionales** at 8:55 p.m. (four hours; 15 pesos). The buses are usually sold out days in advance. Other bus service links Santa Clara with Sancti Spíritus, Remedios, Camagüey, Trinidad, and Santiago de Cuba. There are are least half a dozen buses daily to Cienfuegos.

The **Terminal de Ómnibus Interprovincial** is on the Carretera Central about 2.5 km west of the the city center. The municipal bus terminal is on Calle Marta Abreu, 10 blocks west of Parque Vidal. Licensed taxis and *colectivos* can usually be hailed from outside the stations.

The no. 11 bus runs between Parque Vidal and the Hotel Los Caneyes between 7 a.m. and 7 p.m. A taxi between the two points will cost about US$3. There are always taxis outside Los Caneyes. Otherwise, call 4512.

By Train

Santa Clara is on the main line between Havana and the Oriente and is served by most trains traveling between these destinations. Train no. 17 departs Havana at 2:20 p.m. for Santa Clara, arriving around midnight. Santa Clara is also served from Camagüey by no. 20 (departs 5:18 a.m.), Cienfuegos by no. 205 (departs 4:39 a.m.), and no. 207 (departs 2:34 p.m.) bound for Sancti Spíritus. Other trains stop here en route between Havana and Santiago de Cuba.

The railway station—Estación de Ferrocarriles—is at the northern end of Luís Estévez, seven blocks from Parque Vidal.

GETTING AWAY

By Bus

Ostensibly, buses depart Santa Clara's interprovincial terminal for Havana at 12:30 a.m. and 1:45 p.m. Buses also depart for Sancti Spíritus, Camagüey, Holguín, and Santiago de Cuba. A bus to Trinidad departs at 2:30 p.m.; another leaves for Manicaragua, where you can catch a separate bus to Trinidad.

By Train

Westbound trains depart Santa Clara for Havana (US$12) at 12:25 a.m. (train no. 8), 2:53 a.m. (no. 2), 8:43 a.m. (no. 4), 5:13 a.m. (no. 6), and 6:10 a.m. (no. 18); and for Cienfuegos at 7:33 a.m. (no. 206) and 5:27 p.m. (no. 208). Eastbound trains depart Santa Clara for Santiago (US$24) at 8:48 p.m. (no. 1); Bayamo and Manzanillo at 4:18 a.m. (no. 3); Camagüey at 11:27 p.m. (no. 5) and 3:12 p.m. (no. 19); Sancti Spíritus at 7:18 a.m. (no. 205), 2:37 p.m. (no. 7), and 5:29 p.m. (no. 207).

The station is on the north side of the tiny Plaza de los Mártires. You pay in dollars at the ticket office inside (the ticket office on the *south* side of the square is for locals paying in pesos). It's open daily, 24 hours.

SOUTH AND EAST OF SANTA CLARA

The main reason to pause in Villa Clara should be to admire the gentle Cuban landscapes of the Alturas de Santa Clara, which rise sensually to the south and east of the city. The hills and valleys are pocked with quaint timeworn villages and a quilt of tobacco fields tilled by oxen and tended by *guajiros* in straw hats and white linen field clothes. The region's mild climate and rich soils support some of the most productive *vegas* (tobacco fields) in Cuba.

Both the Autopista and Carretera Central pass through the region. The only place to eat along the Carretera east of Santa Clara is an attractive, thatch-roofed *paladar* on a hilltop about six km east of Santa Clara, midway to Manajanabo.

One of the most scenic drives in Cuba is the route directly south from Santa Clara to Manicaragua and into the foothills of the Sierra Escambray along route 4-474.

LA YA YA

This self-contained "model village" (named for a flowering tree that grows locally), 20 km south of Santa Clara, was apparently conceived by Fidel Castro and created in 1972. Before the Revolution, the local population scraped by growing sugarcane on small plots ill suited to the crop. The *campesinos* were offered apartments in exchange for their land, from which the state formed a dairy farming enterprise. Resistance from the peasantry was great—Castro's Agrarian Reform had given the peasants their own land only a decade before, and now the government wanted to take it back! Despite the plaudits that the government hands itself, there is nothing inspirational in the five-story, pretab apartment blocks (repeated all over the island). Still, the farmers now have electricity and hot water, which their old *bohios* lacked, and the inhabitants have traditionally paid no rent. It is interesting as a sociological curiosity.

PLACETAS TO ZULETA

East of Santa Clara, the Carretera Central runs through Placetas, a small agricultural town lent a Wild West feel by wide dusty streets and arcades such as those along the main street: Avenida de Gómez.

The village of Zulueta (pop. 11,000), 10 km north of Placetas, holds no great appeal except during the period leading up to New Year's, when rockets whiz through the streets and hand-held fireworks and "mortars" explode with a military boom as the townsfolk divide into two historic camps and vie with each other to see who can produce the best parade float and the loudest din (see the special topic "Parrandas"). In 1873, Julian Zulueta, one of Cuba's wealthiest sugar barons, laid a railroad to one of his mills. People in the hamlet of Guanijibes moved uphill and established a new settlement—La Loma—near the station. The *zulueteños* have ever since been divided into *guanijiberos* and *lomeros*. In 1894, they copied the citizenry of Remedios and held

ZULUETA USEFUL TELEPHONE NUMBERS
Police . . . . tel. 39-9114
Policlínica . . . . tel. 39-9218
Terminal de Ómnibus . . . . tel. 39-9188

their first *parranda*. After the Revolution, the parade floats took on revolutionary themes. Zulueta's *parranda* culminates on New Year's Eve.

The town's main street is Calle Real. Parque Armona, the main square, is ringed by important buildings—a church, movie theater, police station, assembly hall, and the homes of distinguished citizens. There's a **Casa de Cultura,** tel. 39-9219, on Martí.

Placetas also has its own *parranda*.

Accommodations, Food, and Services
The pesos-only **Hotel Placetas,** on Gómez, one block west of the plaza in Placetas, is very basic. There's a small pizzeria at the east end of Avenida de Gómez.

If you overnight and seek entertainment, there's a **cinema** on Falcon and a **cabaret** on Oeste.

You'll find a **post office** and **Centro Telefónico** facing each other on Gómez, west of the main plaza, plus a **Banco Nacional** on Avenida 1 Sur.

Getting There
Bus no. 448 departs Havana's main bus terminal at 6:40 a.m., arriving Placetas around noon (16 pesos). The **Terminal de Ómnibus,** tel. 8-2280, is on the main street.

Buses run to Zulueta from Santa Clara and Remedios. Bus no. 450 also departs Havana's main bus terminal daily at 11:40 a.m., arriving at around 5:15 p.m. (17 pesos). The terminal in Zulueta is at Avenida Eneida, tel. 39-9188.

SANTA CLARA TO REMEDIOS

From Santa Clara due east to Remedios, Route 4-231 dips and rises through tobacco country. The quintessentially Cuban landscapes are exceptionally photogenic. Midway, you pass through the unremarkable agricultural town of **Camajuani,** which, like Remedios and Zulueta, is famed for its year-end *parranda* (the rival sections of town are represented by a toad and a goat, depicted in roadside effigy at the entrance to town). The basic **Motel La Cañada** is here. Eight km west of Camajuani, on a slope by the side the of the road, is a delightful **Paladar Mi Bohio,** with tables and chairs outside beneath shade trees. It's a wonderful spot to stop for lunch or dinner.

REMEDIOS

This time-warp town whisks you back to a bygone era. It is one of the oldest towns in Cuba and has seen virtually no urban development this century. Remedios, 45 km northeast of Santa Clara, is also one of the most beautiful little towns (pop. 18,000) in Cuba, full of Spanish colonial charm. It has virtually none of the tourism of Trinidad and almost as much appeal. Unlike Trinidad, Remedios is on the flat. Neither does it have cobbled streets. But it is in a splendid state of preservation, with a graceful symmetry and charisma. The entire city was justifiably named a national monument in 1979.

Much of the pleasure is to be had in roaming the backstreets, especially in late afternoon and early evening, when the low sun glows richly against the pastel walls and the church bells ring through town, tolling the hour. There are few cars. Instead, bicycles and horse-drawn carriages wheel slowly through the narrow streets, where old men with cheroots and straw hats laze on rockers beneath red-tiled eaves. You might well be tempted to stay for a few days. I wouldn't blame you.

The time to visit is December, when the townsfolk feverishly begin preparing for their *parranda,* which, in Remedios, culminates on the last Saturday of the year. Then, the two sections of the city—El Carmen and San Salvador—compete with each other to make the most elaborate parade floats and the most deafening fireworks.

History

Remedios is one of the oldest of Cuban cities, founded in 1514 when a land grant was given to a *conquistador* named Vasco Porcallo de Figueroa. A city hall wasn't built, however, and supposedly for that reason the town was never acknowledged as one of the first seven cities,

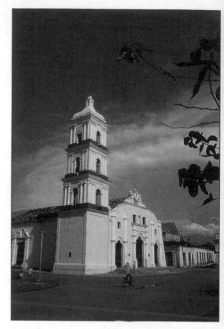

Remedios

despite its antiquity. It was originally named Santa Cruz de la Sabana and was situated closer to the shore. In 1544, it was moved a short distance inland to escape pirates. The town continued to come under constant attack and in 1578, the townsfolk uprooted again and founded a new settlement, which they renamed San Juan de los Remedios del Cayo. (Later that century, a group of citizens moved inland and founded Santa Clara, which grew to become the provincial capital. Apparently, the clique returned to Remedios to convince those that had remained to uproot and join them. They were rebuffed and ended up attacking and destroying the town!)

Sightseeing

The greatest pleasure in exploring Remedios is in letting serendipity reveal what it will. The obvious place to begin is **Plaza Martí,** the main square. The city fans out from here. The square (formerly Plaza de Isabel) is shaded by tall royal palms beneath which you can sit on marble and wrought-iron benches.

Dominating the square is the venerable **Iglesia de San Juan Batista.** One of Cuba's oldest churches, it dates from 1692, although extensions have since been added. Its pious exterior belies the splendor within, not least a carved cedar altar glimmering with 24-carat gold leaf, a statue of the Immaculate Virgin heavy with child, and—the *pièce de résistance*—a Moorish-style ceiling of carved mahogany, splendidly gabled and fluted, that had been sacrilegiously hidden behind plaster and was revealed only by a recent restoration. The cream and white church has an impressive bell tower with three stories (a bell in each). It was badly damaged by an earthquake in 1939 and restored over the ensuing 15 years at the behest of a local benefactor, who also donated European paintings.

The **Museo de la Música Alejandro García Caturla,** on the north side of Plaza Martí, recalls one of Cuba's foremost avant-garde composers. The house features beautiful green-tinted *mamparas*, period furniture, and many of Caturla's original manuscripts. The musical prodigy began writing music in 1920, when he was only 14. He was heavily influenced by the rhythms and sounds of Africa and fell under the sway of Stravinsky. The iconoclastic composer, born into a wealthy family, was moved by a concern for the poor and oppressed. His antiestablishment ways defied all conventions (for example, he married a black woman; when she died, he married her sister). The composer was a noted liberal and an incorruptible lawyer who rose to become judge for the city. Alas, he was assassinated in 1940 by a policeman who was due to come before him the next day for beating a woman to death. It has ever since been suspected that he was murdered in a government-inspired conspiracy (the day before his death, Caturla had cabled the Supreme Court of Cuba for protection; in 1939, he even composed a song predicting his own violent death).

One block west of the main square is the **Iglesia Bien Viaje,** a prim little church with a three-tiered bell-tower with a life-size figure of the Virgin Mary and Jesus in the "dove-hole." It is popular with the faithful among the local citizenry, who leave ex-votos by the door. Between the church and the main square is a tiny plaza with a marble statue of the Liberty-like Indian maiden hewn from the rock and dedicated by the people of Remedios to *"los mártires de la patria."*

The **Museo de las Parrandas,** on Calle Máximo Gómez #71, celebrates the history of the famous festivals unique to the region and contains costumes, flags, and banners, examples of homemade fireworks, and floats. Also displayed is the saxophone that belonged to Alejandro García Caturla and which he played in the *parrandas.* Open Tues.-Sat. 1-6 p.m. and Sunday 9 a.m.-1 p.m.

Haven't yet visited a cigar factory? Check out **Fábrica de Coronas** on Salado, tel. 39-5340, where you'll be given a guided tour.

Calle Andres del Río and Calle Maceo both feature exquisite buildings. The **Museo Histórico** is at Antonio Maceo #56 e/ Calles Carilla y Ariosa, in a beautiful colonial home replete with period furnishings.

Accommodations and Food

The **Hotel Mascotte,** tel. 395481, is a small grande-dame hotel with 14 simple rooms with lofty ceilings from US$15. Room 101 is best (US$21); it's full of impressive antiques, including a bed with a wraparound footboard and a tall headboard inlaid with dragons, plus a matching dresser and giant wardrobe. A plaque on the outside wall records that here on 1 February 1899, Máximo Gómez met with the special commission of US President William McKinley, Mr. Robert P. Porter. Here they negotiated the terms of the Mambí fighters' honorable discharge at the end of the Spanish-Cuban-American War. Gómez stayed in the handsome corner suite and slept in the same four-poster bed that visitos can sleep in.

Restaurante Las Arcadas, a simple, wood-paneled Spanish bodega-style eatery in the Hotel Mascotte, serves *criollo* cuisine (US$1-5). The dining room overlooks the main square and opens onto a flagstone patio with a well. My favorite place is the atmospheric **El Louvre,** now a touristy Rumbos café serving sandwiches and snacks, and coffee for 20 cents a cup. Next door is the **Refresquera La Fe,** serving *refrescoes* of mango and, when available, anise. Don't be fooled by the name or by the Chinese dragon on the wall of **La Joven China,** on the west side of the main square. The former Chinese restaurant is now a café serving snacks and *refrescoes.*

Entertainment and Events

During the last few weeks of the year, citizens get into high gear preparing their fireworks and

---

**REMEDIOS USEFUL
TELEPHONE NUMBERS**

Police . . . . tel. 39-5218
Ambulance. . . . . tel. 39-5149
Hospital . . . . tel. 39-5230
Terminal de Ómnibus. . . . . tel. 39-5185
Railway Station . . . . tel. 39-5129

---

floats for the annual *parranda,* which culminates on the last Saturday of the year. If you're in the area, don't miss it. Bring your earplugs and camera for a wild and racket-filled revelry you'll never forget.

You can also savor traditional music performed by troubadors at the **Casa de la Cultura,** one block east of the main square, at the corner of Gómez and José de Pena. Also check out the **Bienes Fondo de Culturales Cubano,** on the west side of the main square. Otherwise, there's not much action. Elderly citizens (mostly men) gather in the gloom of rustic bars to play dominoes and sip *aguardente.* Try **Las Leyendas** on south side of the main square, or the **Driver's Bar,** both popular hangouts. And maybe there's a performance at the **Teatro Ruben Matinez** at Camilo Cienfuegos #30, tel. 39-5364.

Services
The post office is at José Peña #101. You'll find a pharmacy on the southeast corner of the square, and a Cupet gas station on the west side of town, on the road to Santa Clara. For shopping, try the ARTEX store on Máximo Gómez.

Getting There and Away
Buses for Remedios leave Havana's main bus terminal daily. The Remedios bus station is on the west side of town, on the road to Santa Clara.

ALONG THE NORTH COAST

There is little to recommend along the north coast, as beaches are few and the scenery unimpressive. Still, a well-paved road (route 4-13) runs parallel to the shore, providing an easy, off-the-beaten-path route for travelers heading east or west between Varadero and, say, Cayo Coco or other spots along the coast. East of Caibarién—a down-at-heels coastal town of no appeal—you pass into Sancti Spíritus province.

Playa el Salto y Ganuza, immediately east of the pretty little village of **Coralillo,** is a scimitar-shaped beach, several km long, with white sand and thatched umbrellas for shade. The beach is a popular hangout for Cubans. There's a café at the far east end, but don't expect it to be open or to offer anything other than *bocaditos* (ham or Spam sandwiches). It is served by a railway that connects it with Santa Clara.

About six km farther east, just west of the pretty village of **Rancho Velóz,** a road leads north two km to **Playa la Panchita,** shown on some tourist maps as a "resort." Alas, this ugly strip of gray sand is backed by a down-at-heels fishing village and has no appeal. **Encrucijada,** 25 km due north of Santa Clara, was the birthplace of revolutionary heroes Abel Santamaría and Jesús Menéndez. Their houses are now museums dedicated to their memory.

East of Encrudijada, the 4-13 merges with route 4-321, which runs west to Santa Clara and east to Remedios.

Anglers might head to **Presa Alacranes,** about four km southwest of Sagua la Grande. This is the second-largest freshwater reservoir in Cuba. It boasts tremendous fishing for bass; the record catch is 15.7 pounds. There are two basic motels: **Motel La Roca,** on the north shore, and **Motel Amaro,** on the south shore. Fishing trips are offered from the Hotel Los Caneyes in Santa Clara.

There's a **Cupet gas station** in Sagua La Grande, at the junction of the roads for Varadero and Santa Clara.

Baños de Elguea (Elguea Thermal Spa)
These thermal baths, about three km northwest of Corralillo, are supplied by hyperthermal (up to 50° C) and hypermineralized springs containing bromine, sodium, radium, and sulfur. The waters, in shallow pools of varying temperature and potency, are good for treating rheumatism, skin ailments, and respiratory problems.

Accommodations: Horizontes Elguea Hotel & Spa, tel. 42-68-6290 or 68-6367, is promoted as a spa resort. The spa has traditionally served Cubans, who don't seem to mind the somewhat spartan conditions. However, the facilities have recently undergone a renovation. The hotel is dispiriting (one hopes that it, too, has gotten a full treatment). It has 139 a/c rooms with private baths, TVs, phones, and refrigerators (US$15 s, US$20 d). Facilities include volleyball, basketball, and tennis courts and a large swimming pool and sundeck. Mud therapy, massages, heliotherapy, electrotherapy, and physical excercise programs are offered. The hotel treatment even includes a visit to Cayo Blanquizal, whose highly sulfurous sands are supposedly very effective for natural beauty masks.

THE CAYS

Beach-fringed cays lie scattered like diamonds in the jade-colored waters all along the north coast. Fishermen use the cays, but there are no facilities.

The white sand beaches are untapped for tourism, and few snorkelers or scuba divers have as yet peered beneath the calm surface to discover a coral world more colorful than a casket of gems. The cays' landward shores are fringed by mangroves—havens for herons and other stilt-legged waders. And many of the cays are populated by iguanas and *jutías.* The largest cay is **Cayo Fragoso,** shaped like an arrowhead. A ship ran aground in the bight on the western side, and there it has rested and rusted since World War II—a perfect draw for scuba divers.

Before the onset of the Special Period, tiny **Cayo Conuco,** about one km offshore of Caibarién, was one of the most popular holiday spots for Cubans. There's a basic six-room hotel and a *campismo* with rustic wooden cabins overlooking the scintillating waters. The place has become very run-down in the past few years. Campers can set up tents (water, toilets, and showers are all present). A wooden dock grants boaters access. Horses can be rented. A boat leaves Caibarién for Cayo Conuco; it's a 15-minute journey.

About five km east of Caibarién, a causeway leads northeast from the coast road and leaps from tiny cay to tiny cay, ending at **Cayo Santa María** and **Marina Santa María.** Puertosol offers a series of six-hour **boat excursions,** including to Cayo el Mégano (US$30, including lunch). An eight-hour **scuba diving** trip to Ojo del Mégano costs US$50.

EAST OF CAIBARIÉN

The road east from Caibarién shuns the coast and skirts the scarp face of the **Sierra del Bamburanao,** a dramatic spur of steep, ruler-straight hills running parallel to the coast.

At **Mayijagua,** you can turn north 20 km to **Punta de Judas,** where there's an extensive cave system to be explored. Just west of Mayijagua is **San José del Lago,** a spa resort with a surprisingly pleasant hotel—**Motel San José**—for Cubans, and fully functional, too. It's centered on a mineral pool beneath tall palms. The modest *cabañas* cost about 25 pesos.

East of Mayijagua, the road rises onto the upper slopes of the Sierra, offering marvelous views down over the canefields, with scores of tiny cays—those of Ciego de Ávila province—floating in an azure sea to the north. You'll pass **Motel Aguazules,** which has *cabañas* for about 12 pesos, plus a swimming pool and a restaurant.

SANCTI SPÍRITUS
INTRODUCTION

The relatively small southeast corner of Western Cuba is mighty big in tourist appeal. The province is physically diverse and encompasses the beautiful eastern portion of the Sierra Escambrays, lush valleys, rolling plains, and a peninsula boasting the south coast's premier beach. Much of Sancti Spíritus province is cattle country. To the north, rolling hills flow down towards the coastal plains, with beach-lined cays beckoning offshore.

The city of Sancti Spíritus sits smack in the center of Cuba, on the eastern side of the Escambray and Sancti Spíritus mountains. Sancti Spíritus was one of the original seven cities founded by the Spanish in the 16th century. Despite being the provincial capital, the town is given short shrift by tourists. The limelight is stolen by another of the original seven cities— Trinidad, Cuba's best-preserved colonial city, nestled beneath the Escambray on the coastal plains of the Río Manatí. No visit to Cuba is complete without at least two days spent in this mellow charmer. It even has a great beach— Playa Ancón—close at hand.

Between Sancti Spíritus and Trinidad, you pass through the wide valley of the Río Manatí

and Valle de los Indigenos (Valley of the Sugar Mills), full of reminders of the heyday of sugar. The valley, and Trinidad, are both deservedly UNESCO World Heritage Sites.

Hunters, fisherfolk, and nature lovers are served by a number of wetland reserves. The southeastern lowland plains are inhospitably marshy and humid, with few villages or roads.

Sancti Spíritus province is also littered with battle sites from the War of Independence, including **Arroyo Blanco,** east of Sancti Spíritus, where in 1895 a young British officer named Winston Churchill narrowly avoided being killed by a rebel bullet that whizzed past his head, spawning his famous statement that "There is nothing more exhilarating than to be shot at without result." (Churchill was on a 10-week leave and, serving as war correspondent for the London *Daily Graphic,* had joined the forces of General Juárez Valdez, where he witnessed the Battle of La Reforma from the front lines.)

The Autopista, which runs 15 km north of the city of Sancti Spíritus, ends abruptly 20 km east of the city, at Jatibonico. There's a **policentro** (gas station) immediately east of the exit for Sancti Spíritus.

SANCTI SPÍRITUS AND VICINITY

Sancti Spíritus, 390 km east of Havana, is a modern city (pop. 100,000) laid out around a colonial core. It straddles the Carretera Central, which has helped boost the city's standing as the midway point between Havana and Santiago.

In 1895, Winston Churchill arrived in Sancti Spíritus. He loved the cigars but thought the city "a very second-rate place, and a most un-

healthy place" (an epidemic of yellow fever and smallpox was raging). It hasn't improved vastly since Churchill passed through, but it is worth at least a half-day visit.

Quaint cobbled streets and venerable houses with iron filigree and wide doors for carriages attest to the city's antiquity. Alas, though the cathedral is worth the trip for its photogenic po-

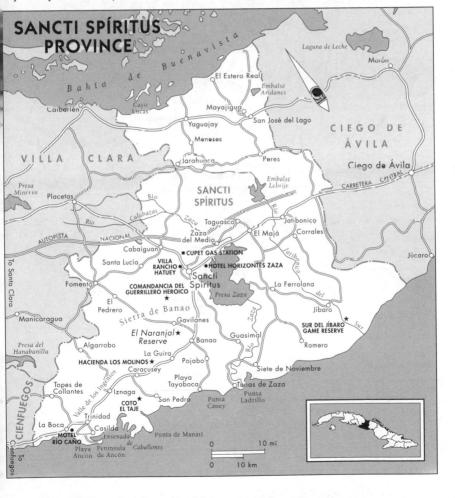

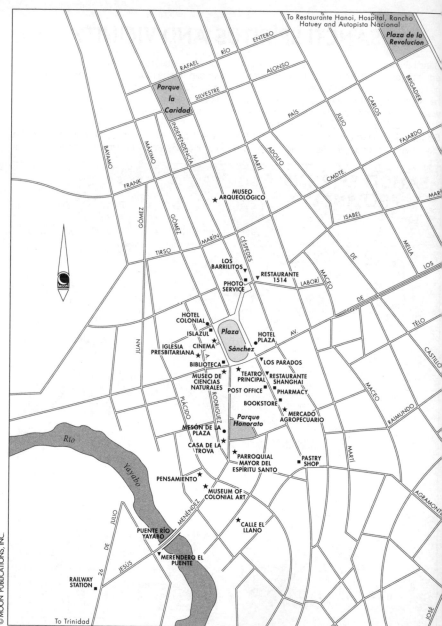

To Restaurante Hanoi, Hospital, Rancho
Hatuey and Autopista Nacional

Plaza de la
Revolución

RÍO ENTERO

RAFAEL

ALONSO

SILVESTRE

Parque
la
Caridad

BRIGADIER

PAÍS

CARLOS

FAJARDO

INDEPENDENCIA

JULIO

BAYAMO

MAXIMO

MARTÍ

ADOLFO

CMDTE.

FRANK

MARTÍ

GÓMEZ

ISABEL

GÓMEZ

MARÍN

MUSEO
ARQUEOLÓGICO

DE

MELLA

LOS

TIRSO

CÉSPEDES

LOS
BARRILITOS

RESTAURANTE
1514

LABORÍ

MACEO

DE

TÊLO

JUAN

PHOTO
SERVICE

CASTILLO

HOTEL
COLONIAL

Plaza
Sánchez

HOTEL
PLAZA

AV.

ISLAZUL

IGLESIA
PRESBITARIANA

CINEMA

BIBLIOTECA

LOS PARADOS

MUSEO DE
CIENCIAS
NATURALES

TEATRO
PRINCIPAL

RESTAURANTE
SHANGHAI

MACEO

POST OFFICE

PHARMACY

RAIMUNDO

PLÁCIDO

BOOKSTORE

RODRÍGUEZ

MESÓN DE LA
PLAZA

Parque
Honorato

MERCADO
AGROPECUARIO

CASA DE LA
TROVA

PARROQUIAL
MAYOR DEL
ESPÍRITU SANTO

PASTRY
SHOP

MARTÍ

Río
Yayabo

PENSAMIENTO

MUSEUM OF
COLONIAL ART

AGRAMONTE

MENÉNDEZ

CALLE EL
LLANO

DE
JULIO

PUENTE RÍO
YAYABO

26
DE

JESÚS

MERENDERO EL
PUENTE

RAILWAY
STATION

JOSÉ

To Trinidad

© MOON PUBLICATIONS, INC.

tential, most of the old town is forlorn and jaded. The outskirts are rimmed with industry and nondescript modern buildings, including a large paper mill fueled by bagasse from the sugar fields serving the nearby *central* at Uruguay—the country's largest sugar mill.

ORIENTATION

The city rises up the eastern bank of the Río Yayabo, centered on Plaza Sánchez (also called Plaza Central). The historic core lies immediately southwest of here, centered at the delightful Plaza de los Viejos and cathedral (Parroquial Mayor), at the heart of a tight little warren of narrow streets. Avenida Jesús Menéndez runs downhill two blocks to the river.

Newer sections north and east of Plaza Central form an uninspired assemblage of concrete and cement centered on the unremarkable **Plaza de la Revolución.** Streets are laid out in a grid, running northwest-southeast and northeast-southwest. The main street, Independencia, runs south to **Parque Honorato** and north to **Parque La Caridad,** each park home to a tiny church.

The most important east-west thoroughfare is **Avenida de los Mártires,** a broad boulevard that begins three blocks east of Parque Central. It crosses the equally wide **Bartolomé Maso,** which leads north through the modern city to the Autopista. South of the Avenida, Bartolomé Masó swings east and continues as the Carretera Central to Zaza and Ciego de Avila.

HISTORY

The settlement of Espíritu Santo was co-founded in 1514 by Diego Velasquez and Fernandez de Cordoba, who later rose to fame conquering the Yucatán. The city began life about six km from its current position. It was moved eight years later because the original site was plagued by biting ants.

The city prospered from cattle ranching and sugar. Its prominence attracted pirates, and during the late 16th and early 17th centuries it was ransacked and razed twice in a short span of years.

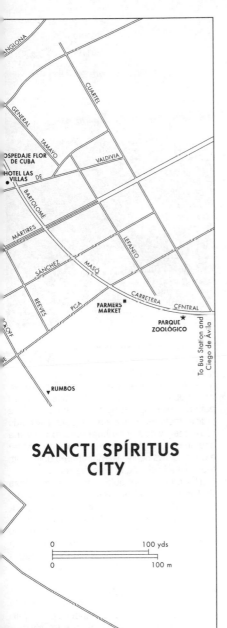

SANCTI SPÍRITUS CITY

0   100 yds

0   100 m

Unlike Trinidad, Sancti Spíritus never evolved as a center of culture. By the mid-19th century, after 400 years of Spanish rule, the city still lacked a library and museum (the university and other academic institutions arrived after the Revolution). Support for the independence cause was therefore strong, and the city contributed several leading military figures to the fight to end Spanish rule. A century later, Che Guevara established his headquarters nearby, in the Alturas de Sancti Spíritus, where citizens joined the Rebel Army.

THINGS TO SEE AND DO

Plaza Sánchez (Plaza Central)

Everything seems to happen around this large yet modest square, laid out in 1522 and named for Serafín Sánchez, a home-grown general in the War of Independence.

The square—a bustling meeting place, busy with traffic—has none of the charm or grandeur of main plazas elsewhere in Cuba. It is surrounded by undistinguished neoclassical buildings—the **biblioteca** (library) on the west side, the **Teatro Principal** on the south side. The latter was once resplendent, and could be so again with restoration.

There's a small **Museo de Ciencias Naturales** (also known locally as the Academy of Sciences), on the southwest corner of Parque Central, at Solano and Máximo Gómez. It's dedicated to Cuba's flora and fauna.

To the northeast, the plaza extends one block along Independencia and opens into a tiny square with a statue of another local hero, Judas Mártinez Moles (1861-1915).

Parroquial Mayor del Espíritú Santo

The small cathedral at Calles Placido and Menéndez is one of Cuba's oldest and best-preserved churches, maintained in near-pristine condition. The current church dates to 1680, when it replaced an earlier, wooden church built in 1612 but destroyed in a pirate raid. A solid gold cockerel that once adorned the church was pilfered, too. The triple-tiered tower wasn't completed until 1764, its cupola not until the middle of the 19th century. The bell still rings for Mass each Sunday, which seems mostly like an excuse for a secular binge.

Sancti Spíritus

The church is very simple inside, with minimal giltwork and an unimpressive altar. The ornately carved roof beams are splendid, however, with dropped gables carved and fitted in cross patterns and supporting a circular center. The crucifix looks like porcelain but is actually made of painted wood. The best time to view the church is during late afternoon, when its ocher exterior glows richly, like hammered gold, from the sunlight slanting in from the south.

The church overlooks the charming **Plaza de los Viejos,** to the west, and, to the north, the tiny **Plaza Honorato del Castillo,** honoring a local general in the War of Independence, yet highlighted by a statue of Rudesindo Antonio García Rojo, an eminent citizen in medicine and sciences. The tiny **Museo de la Esclavitud** is here; it's dedicated to the memory of slavery.

Museum of Colonial Art

One block south of the cathedral, at Plácido 64 (on the corner with Jesús Menéndez) is a perfectly preserved time capsule—the ornately decorated **Palacio del Valle-Iznaga**, which belonged to one of the wealthiest families in Cuba. The beautiful home is now a delightful museum, amply furnished with period decor. It's open Tues.-Fri. 1-10 p.m., Saturday 1-5 p.m., and Sunday 10 a.m.-4 p.m. Entrance costs US$1.

Puente Río Yayabo
Below Plácida, Jesús Menéndez crosses the Río Yayabo on a triple-arched bridge, built of cut stone in medieval style. It was begun in 1817 and is said to be the only colonial stone bridge still extant in Cuba.

Calle El Llano
El Llano is the most quintessentially colonial city street in Sancti Spíritu and one of very few that are still cobbled. This 100-meter-long street is lined with quaint houses painted pastel pink, canary, and blue, lent added grace by fancy wrought-iron balconies, hanging lanterns, and wooden *rejas* (turned grills).

Providing a touch of panache is a sea-green Plymouth Deluxe with a white roof, parked as if for a Hollywood movie. The 1934-vintage beauty has a whitewalled spare tire affixed to the trunk, which bears the words: "1934-PLY-MOUTH-1934."

Other Sites
Two blocks west of Parque Central, on Plácido, is a quaint little **Iglesia Presbitariana**, built last century by a small Scottish community.

Also worth a brief peek while browsing is the **Casa Natal Serafín Sánchez**, on Céspedes between Frank País and Tirso Marín, where the patriot-hero was born. A house across the street now houses the threadbare **Museo de Arqueológico.**

Sancti Spíritus' most unique site could be the **Casa de los Refranes** (House of Sayings), opposite the entrance to Rancho Villa Hatuey. It's dedicated to aphorisms profound and strange!

ACCOMMODATIONS

Budget
There are several pesos-only hotels. **Hotel Deportivos**, on Bartolomé Masó, north of the Circunvalación, is a faceless four-story building with basic utility furnishings. It accepts foreigners though it is the domain of Cubans. Rooms cost 20 pesos s, 30 d. Facilities include a swimming pool and *cafetería.*

The **Hospedaje Flor de Cuba**, on Bartolomé Masó just north of Avenida de los Mártires, and, nearby, **Hotel Las Villas**, tel. 23958, both look okay. Neither ostensibly accepts tourists, but a sob story could get you admitted. Likewise, the basic **Hotel Colonial**, one block north of Parque Central, at Máximo Gomez 23, tel. 25123, claims to be for Cubans only.

Foreigners are usually directed to **Hotel Los Laureles**, on Bartolomé Masó on the northern outskirts of town. It offers basic *cabañas* sprinkled throughout unkempt grounds (US$12 s, US$16 d). Some have TV, all have a/c, refrigerators, and telephones. It's a dour property serving a Cuban clientele. There's a pool and a mediocre restaurant.

Your best bet in town is the **Hotel Plaza**, an Islazul property in a restored colonial building on the east side of Parque Central. Rooms are small but lofty and cooled by fans (from US$7 s, US$10 d). You may be told that the hotel is full. I was. However, persistence, a tale of woe, or heaps of charm may lead to a room becoming magically available. The little lobby bar has appeal, but the restaurant has an abysmal menu.

Islazul has a regional booking office *(carpeta)*, next to the cinema on the west side of the plaza.

Moderate
Cubanacán operates the **Villa Rancho Hatuey**, Carretera Central Km 383, Sancti Spíritus, tel. 32-2-6015, by far the best place for miles. This charmer has 10 bungalows and 58 a/c rooms, all with color TVs and telephones (US$37 s, US$54 d, US$61 t). Attractive two-story apartments in contemporary Mediterranean style should be finished by the time you read this. The small but elegant restaurant serves a house buffet (breakfast US$3, lunch or dinner US$10). There's a small swimming pool and a terra-cotta-tile sundeck surrounded by palms and bougainvilleas—there's even a bowling alley! A lively cabaret is held featuring folkloric dances. Excursions include horseback-riding into the nearby mountains (US$10).

Your other option is the **Hotel Zaza**, 10 km east of town.

FOOD

Finding a good, wholesome meal is a withering experience. Your surest bet is the restaurant at **Villa Rancho Hatuey.**

If you're staying at the Hotel Plaza, you'll find several simple restaurants nearby, including **Los Parados,** one block south. **Restaurante 1514,** one block north, at the corner of Lavorri and Céspedes, serves *criollo* dishes in a dowdy colonial building full of dusty antiques (average price, 10 pesos). Craving a burger? Try **Los Barrilitos,** where a burger of unproven quality costs two pesos (10 cents)! It's on Céspedes, two blocks north of Parque Central.

For seafood, try the **Merendero El Puente,** on a houseboat moored beneath the old bridge at the bottom of Jesús Menéndez. A shrimp dish here costs US$6 (or 9 pesos). For meat dishes, try **Mesón de la Plaza,** on Plaza Honorato. Entrées cost less than 10 pesos (salads cost 80 centavos). I've been told by locals that the best place to eat is **Quinta Santarena,** which serves pork.

There are at least three quasi-Chinese restaurants: **Restaurante Shanghai,** on Independencia, one block south of Parque Central, and **Restaurante Yangset** and **Restaurante Hanoi,** both on Bartolomé Masó. All offer meals for about 10 pesos, but don't get your hopes up.

You'll find lots of snack stalls in front of Parque Diversiones, on Avenida de los Mártires (some sell cold *guarapo,* the refreshing sugarcane drink). You can buy fresh produce at the **mercado agropecuario** on the corner of Independencia and Honorato. There's a charming little **Dulcería el Capuchino** one block south where you can buy pastries, plus a *panadería* (bakery) at Máximo Gómez and Frank País.

ENTERTAINMENT

The liveliest and most popular place in town for live music and dancing is **Pensamiento,** next to the museum, on Plácido and Jesús Menéndez. You might also check out **Rumbos,** a dollars-only bar that gets packed with young Cubans. It's on Carlos Roboff, three blocks south of Avenida de los Mártires. At the corner of Roboff and Los Mártires is the **Palacio de los Salsas,** which has dancing on Friday and weekends, as does a club in the colonial building on Independencia and Agramonte. There's also a disco-cabaret at the Hotel Los Laureles (entrance costs 10 pesos).

The **Casa de la Trova,** on Máximo Gómez one block north of the cathedral, features occasional performances by *Coro de Clares* (Clear Choir), a local choral group. Watch, too, for classical and other music performances in the now faded **Teatro Principal.**

The main **cinema** is on the west side of Parque Central. A **sala video** in a private house on Céspedes, two blocks north of the plaza, also shows four films daily.

There's a **chess club** next to the cinema on the west side of the plaza. To keep kids amused, try the small children's park *(parque diversiones)* on Avenida de los Mártires or the small zoo three blocks south of the Avenida on Bartolomé Masó.

Baseball is played at **Estadio Victoria del Girón,** east of Plaza de la Revolución in Reparto Los Olivos.

SHOPPING

Shops are threadbare, and the trickle of tourists has not inspired local crafts. The tiny plaza on the north side of the main plaza has been turned into a miniature Petticoat Lane, with stalls selling everything from handicrafts to domestic knick-knacks.

The dowdy Spanish-language bookstore on Independencia, one block south of Parque Central, is limited to Latin American novels and works by the socialist pantheon.

SERVICES

The **hospital** is on Bartolomé Masó, opposite the Plaza de la Revolución. There are several **pharmacies** on Independencia, south of the main plaza, and at Bartolomé Maso 57.

The **post office** is on Independencia, one block south of the main plaza. **Photo Service** has a meagerly stocked outlet on Céspedes, one block north of Parque Central. There's a well-stocked **bicycle shop** on Independencia, one block north of the plaza. The *biblioteca* is on the west side of Parque Central.

Sancti Spíritus is one of the few cities with **public toilets,** one block west of Parque Central. Look for the mural of a man and woman in period costume painted on the wall. Your relief will cost you 10 centavos.

GETTING THERE

By Bus. Bus no. 453 departs Havana's main bus terminal for Sancti Spíritus at 4:15 a.m. and 3 and 4:05 p.m. (six hours; 19 pesos). The **Terminal Provincial de Ómnibus** in Sancti Spíritus is at the junction of Bartolomé Masó and the Circunvalación, east of town.

By Train: Train no. 7 leaves from Havana for Sancti Spíritus daily at 9:20 a.m. (minimum six hours; US$13.50) and from Cienfuegos at 4:39 a.m. and 2:34 p.m. Some *regular* trains take up to 15 hours to Sancti Spíritus. You can also catch the *especial* bound for Santiago; it stops at Guayos (15 km north of Sancti Spíritus), from where trains run to Sancti Spíritus (you may need to overnight in Guayos).

The **train station,** tel. 22405, is at the bottom of Avenida Jesús Menéndez, 400 yards south of the old arched bridge.

GETTING AROUND

Most people get around by **horse-drawn taxis,** which congregate around the main square and on Avenida de los Mártires, near the bus terminal. Ten pesos should get you anywhere you want to go, but as a foreigner, you may be charged in dollars. A few licensed tourist taxis also park here. **Colectivos** (shared taxis) are

few and far between but tend to congregate outside the bus terminals.

Excursions are available from the Rancho Villa Hatuey to the cigar factory in Cabaiguán, about 16 km north of Sancti Spiritus (US$5). You can also book an air tour by biplane (US$20). Havanautos has a **car rental** office in the Villa Rancho Hatuey.

GETTING AWAY

Hitchhiking: You can join the crowds of Cubans who gather at the official hitching points just east of the Terminal Provincial (eastbound) and along Bartolomé Masó (northbound).

By Bus: Buses depart the **Terminal Provincial** on Bartolomé Masó for Trinidad four times daily and for Havana twice daily. You can also catch buses to Camagüey, Holguín, and Santiago. Demand far outstrips supply.

Local buses serve nearby cities from the *terminal,* at Calle Sánchez and Carlos Roloff, one block south of Avenida de los Mártires, tel. 22162.

By Train: Train no. 8 departs Sancti Spíritus for Havana daily at 9:45 p.m. Trains depart for Cienfuegos at 4:30 a.m. (no. 206) and 2:09 p.m. (no. 208). Local trains operate from Cabaiguán to Tunas de Zaza, departing at 6:05 a.m. and 9:21 a.m. (returning at 5:17 a.m. and 3:30 p.m.), and from Tunas de Zaza to Zaza del Medio at 10:26 a.m. (returning at 5:13 p.m.)

PRESA ZAZA

This man-made lake, the largest in Cuba, has been created by a massive dam. The lake, immediately southeast of Sancti Spíritus, is studded with flooded forest and contains over 1,000 million cubic meters of water—and extraordinary numbers of trout and bass (the largest bass caught to date weighed 16.5 pounds). Marsh birds flock in from far and wide. Not surprisingly, Zaza is a favorite spot for birders, anglers, and hunters.

The lake is drained by the Río Zaza, which snakes south across the coastal plain to the Caribbean Sea, whose shores are choked by mangroves. At the rivermouth is **Tunas de Zaza,** a ramshackle place with a large fishing fleet. East toward the province of Ciego de Ávila, the marshy flatlands are sliced by canals that drain and feed vast acres of rice.

The **Copa Internacional de Pesca** is held here each September.

Hunting, Horseback Riding, and Fishing

The cost of hunting depends on the bird species but averages US$50 for 3.5 hours (three-person minimum). Fishing ranges upward of US$35 for the same period. Horseback-riding is also offered from the Hotel Zaza (US$20 for five hours).

Accommodations

The **Hotel Horizontes Zaza**, tel. 412-6012 or 412-5334, is a hunting and fishing lodge, but accepts all comers. The faceless, two-story, all-concrete hotel has 128 a/c rooms with private baths, telephones, and TVs (US$20 s, USR23 d). Most rooms enjoy views over the lake. Facilities include two bars, a restaurant, nightclub, swimming pool, games room, and store. Amazingly, neither fish nor duck are on the restaurant menu.

SUR DEL JIBARO GAME RESERVE

This hunting reserve lies in the middle of rice plantations and marshland on the banks of the Río Jatibónico. Migrant ducks, quail, white-crowned ringdove, mourning and white-winged doves, guinea fowl, and pheasant are offered up for hunters' enjoyment.

It is reached from the Carretera Central by turning south at Jatibónico, 29 km east of Sancti Spíritus. **Jatibónico** is an orderly town built around a huge sugar *central,* which pours a pall of black smoke over the town. Beyond Jatibónico, the Carretera Central continues east into Ciego de Ávila province.

SANCTI SPÍRITUS TO TRINIDAD

The road southwest from Sancti Spíritus to Trinidad rises, dips, and swings magnificently along the foothills of the Alturas de Banao, whose sheer, barren crags remind me of the Scottish highlands. Coffee is grown on the upper slopes; lower slopes are covered mostly with rough pasture grazed by ashen, humpbacked stock. Horses are still the staple mode of transport for *vaqueros* (cowboys) in straw hats, with machetes at their sides.

Che Guevara established his headquarters—**Comandancia del Guerrillero Heroico**—at El Pedrero, on the northern slopes (known as the Alturas de Sancti Spíritus), reached by a turnoff from the Trinidad road at the hamlet of **Las Brisas.** The route is fabulously scenic and offers good opportunities for birding and hiking.

Alturas de Banao

Just west of the village of **Banao,** a road leads south to the coast and **Playa Tayabacoa,** optimistically shown on maps as having a beach. You quickly drop down onto searingly hot coastal plains. Tomatoes are raised in the rich soil. Midway, south of **Pojabo,** the paved road ends; a rough dirt road continues to Playa Tayabacoa.

From Banao, you can follow the valley of the Río Banao north into the mountainous heights, where a virtually pristine and beautiful 3,050-hectare swath is protected in a reserve: **El Naranjal Area De Manejo Integral.** There are four separate ecosystems: semi-deciduous forest, tropical moist forest, rare cloud forest, and an endemic assembly associated with the free-standing limestone table-top formations called *mogotes.* The region is rich in flora, with more than 700 flowering plants (more than 100 of them endemic), including over 60 orchid species. Inevitably, the place is a paradise for birders—parrots are numerous. El Naranjal also harbors cave systems, waterfalls, and mineral pools.

Alcona S.A., Calle 42 #514, esq. Avenida 7, Playa, Havana, tel. 22-2526, fax 33-1532, a Cuban company specializing in nature tours, offers visits to El Naranjal with stays at **Casa del Guardabosques,** a rustic lodge in the Alto de la Sabina. It offers guided excursions. You can also rent horses to follow the Banao and Higuanojo Rivers to natural mineral springs.

VALLEY OF THE SUGAR MILLS (VALLE DE LOS INGENIOS)

West of Banoa, the Carretera de Sancti Spíritus drops spectacularly into the Valley of the Sugar Mills, also known as the Valle de los Ingenios and, more correctly, the Valle de San Luís. It is named for the many sugar mills (43 at its peak) that sprang up over the centuries to grind the cane produced by the valley's remarkably fertile soil. The valley was the most important sugar-producing region in early colonial days—a predominance that lasted into the 19th century, when the development of the *centrale* plantation system elsewhere in Cuba and the collapse of world sugar prices in the 1880s sounded a death knell for the valley's relatively primitive sugar factories. Many of the mills and estate houses remain, albeit mostly in ruins.

Like Trinidad, the valley has been declared a UNESCO Cultural Heritage Site.

Manaca-Iznaga Tower

No journey into the valley is complete without a visit to the quaint village of Iznaga, whose prim little railway station is a gem. The village, 14 km east of Trinidad, is most famous for the **Hacienda Iznaga** and its splendid tower, built 1835-45 by Alejo María del Carmen e Iznaga, once one of the wealthiest sugar planters in Cuba. According to legend, the tower was built as a wager. Alejo was to build a tower while his brother Pedro dug a well. The winner would be whoever went highest or deepest (no well has been found). It seems likely that it was once used by overseers to survey the fields and keep an eye on slaves, for the views from the top are panoramic.

The tower is 43.5 meters high. It has seven levels, each smaller than the one beneath. It

was recently restored to its original grandeur as a colonial monument (entry US$1). You can ascend the 136 steps with Sonia Recaudadora, the *custodia,* who will tell you the history of the tower and estate (a tip is appreciated).

The owner's farmhouse has also been beautifully restored and turned into a fabulous restaurant (see below). A horse-drawn carriage sits on the wide front porch, where mammoth doorways open into a lofty lobby replete with artwork, glass cases containing a miscellany of period costume, and maps of the valley properties of yesteryear.

Horseback Riding

Want to play the Marlboro man? A working cattle ranch, called **Hacienda Los Molinos,** welcomes guests seeking fun in the saddle. Guided horseback rides lead into the forested slopes of the Alturas de Sancti Spíritus (US$3 one hour, US$5 two hours, US$1 each additional hour). It's two km off the highway, a few km west of La Gúira, midway between Trinidad and Sancti Spíritus.

You can also go horseback riding, call 271 for reservations, at **Casa Guachinango,** 20 km east of Trinidad, a 200-year-old hacienda-turned-restaurant boasting a beautiful setting above the Río Ay.

Accommodations and Food

Hacienda Los Molinos has four rustic yet quaint rooms with ceiling fans in an old timber lodge (US$10 s, US$15 d, US$20 t). Meals are

guajiro, *Valle de Los Ingenios*

extra. Rumor is that you may be able to camp at **Casa Guachinango.** Both are occasional stops for tour buses.

The red-tiled, open-air **Bar el Mirador** is three km east of Trinidad, atop a hill—Mirador de la Loma—offering stunning views north over the valley and south along the coast. There's another thatched bar/restaurant—**Cafetería Los Molinos**—30 km east of Trinidad. Outshining both is Iznaga's **Alejo del Carmen e Iznaga's farmhouse,** which has been converted into an elegant and atmospheric bar and restaurant. Here you may dine on an outside terrace overlooking the valley. It serves breakfast, lunch, and dinner. The *criollo* food has been recommended.

Getting There

Sure, you can arrive by car. But I recommend you treat yourself to a journey aboard the local commuter train from Trinidad—a single diesel carriage, painted turquoise and white (see "Getting Around" and "Getting Away" in Trinidad). The tourist steam train from Trinidad stops for lunch at Iznaga, with a stop at Casa Guachinango.

COTO EL TAJE

About seven km east of Iznaga, a road leads south to the village of San Pedro. After four km you'll reach a turnoff for El Taje, a 15-square-km complex of lagoons and swamps favored by migratory birds. Blue-wing teal, shoveler, Bahamian pintail, and fulvous tree ducks are all present, as are other gamebirds. The area is popular with hunters (hunting is done from water-level or treetop blinds).

El Taje Lodge has seven a/c double rooms, all with private bathrooms and showers. There's a dining room, bar, recreation room with TV, plus a souvenir and hunting store.

Magna Outdoors, 50 Alness St. #200C, Downsview, Ontario M3J 2G9, tel. (416) 665-7174 or (800) 387-3717, fax (416) 665-8448, includes El Taja on a one-week hunting package from Toronto.

TRINIDAD

Trinidad (pop. 38,000) is tucked into the southwest corner of Sancti Spíritus province, in the lee of the Sierra del Escambray. It was the fourth of the seven cities founded by Diego de Velásquez, in 1514. Today, it is maintained as a living museum, just as the Spaniards left it in its period of greatest opulence. It is the crown jewel of Cuba's colonial cities and a must see on every traveler's list.

After the dour melancholy of most other Cuban cities, it's fantastic. No other city in Cuba is so well preserved—or so charming.

Trinidad

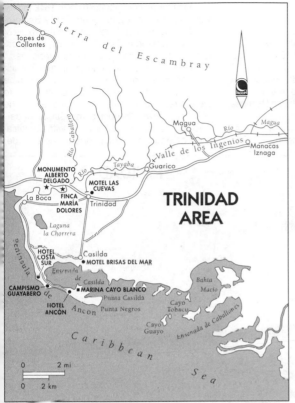

TRINIDAD AREA

ever, as in Havana), reflecting the town's heritage of 16th-century conquistadores, 17th-century corsairs, 18th-century smuggler-traders, and 19th-century sugar lords. The exquisite buildings are fronted by mahogany balustrades, fancy *rejas* (grills) of wrought iron and turned wooden rods, and massive wooden doors with *postigos* (small windows) that open to let the breezes flow through cool, tile-floored rooms connected by double-swing half-doors *(mamparas)* topped by *vitrales.*

No tinkering is allowed, for the entire city is a national monument, protected by law. The city sparkles after a recent restoration and is virtually devoid of touristic superstructure—concessions, billboards, souvenir shops.

Life in Trinidad

Even the life of Trinidad has been preserved in aspic. By day, mule-drawn carts and *vaqueros* on horseback clip-clop through the cobbled streets. Laughing children chase hoops through the plazas. And old folks rock gently beneath shady verandas, serenaded by twittering showbirds in bamboo cages—a Trinidad tradition. In Trinidad, people seem content to let time pass them by.

The town, 67 km southwest of Sancti Spíritus and 80 km east of Cienfuegos, reached its peak during the 19th-century sugar boom and seems to have been forsaken by history ever since. This time capsule is lent twin charms by its historical landmarks and its setting of great natural beauty, sitting astride a hill, where it catches the breezes and gazes out over the Caribbean against a backdrop of verdurous ring of mountains—the Topes de Collantes.

Its narrow, unmarked cobbled streets are paved with stones *(chinas pelonas)* shipped across the Atlantic as ballast or taken from the nearby river. The maze of streets is lined with terra-cotta-tile-roofed houses in soft pastel colors. Much of the architecture is neoclassical and baroque, with a Moorish flavor (there are no great palaces, how-

Life in Trinidad is lived in full view. By day, perspiring tour groups crawl along the cobbled streets, glancing inside living rooms full of antiques and knickknacks.

At night, the town is eerily still—silent but for the barking of dogs, the slap of dominoes, and the staccato voice of television. Then, the cool air flows downhill, the narrow alleys become refreshing channels, and it is a special joy to stroll the cobbled streets. By midnight, the entire town has bedded down and is still as death.

Petty thievery is said to be a greater problem here than in most other cities. Maybe. Maybe not. Still, take extra care of your valuables.

HISTORY

The initial settlement, named Villa de la Santísima Trinidad, was founded in 1514 by Diego de Velásquez on a site settled by the Taino Indians. The Spanish conquistadores found the native Indians panning for gold in the nearby rivers. The gold-hungry Spanish had high hopes, and, indeed, established a lucrative (but short-lived) gold mine that lent vigor to the young township and the wharves of nearby Casilda.

Hernán Cortés set up base here in 1518 to provision his expedition to conquer the Aztec empire for Spain. Soon, fleets bearing the spoils of Mexico gathered in Casilda, bringing new prosperity and eclipsing Trinidad's meager mines.

Trinidad was just far enough from the reach of Spanish authorities in Havana to develop a bustling commerce smuggling contraband to circumvent trade restrictions imposed by the Spanish Crown. Its position on Cuba's underbelly was also perfect for trade with Jamaica, the epicenter of the Caribbean slave trade.

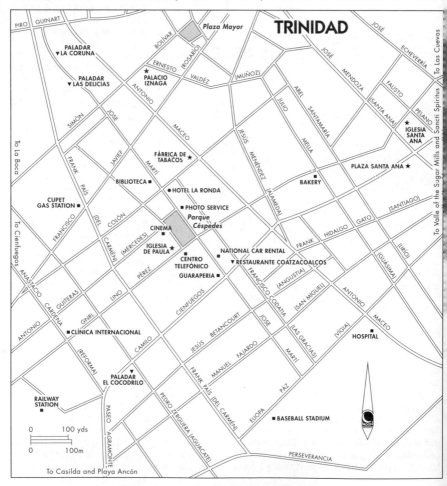

TRINIDAD

Trinidad grew prosperous importing slaves, many of whom were put to work locally, stimulating the sugar trade. A mild climate, fertile soil, and easy access to the Caribbean favored Trinidad's agricultural and commercial growth. Money poured in from the proceeds of sugar grown in the Valle de los Ingenios. When the English occupied Cuba, in 1762-3, Trinidad became a free port and prospered even further, entering its golden age.

Wealthy citizens built their sumptuous homes around the main square—Plaza Mayor—and along the adjoining streets (one owner petitioned the King of Spain for permission to embed coins in his floor; the king granted the wish on condition that the coins be laid sideways so that no one should walk on the monarch's face). Pianos from Berlin, sumptuous furniture from France, linens and lattices, and silverware from Colombia were unloaded here. Local craftsmen, too, reached their peak of perfection in the 19th century, and thriving industries developed in ceramics, gold, silver, and lace. Language schools and academies were even set up to prepare the children of the wealthy to complete their studies in Europe.

At first, the city created its own fleet to guard against pirates, but later decided to take the pirates to its bosom; many citizens prospered as victuallers to the sea-roving vagabonds, while some pirates bought property and settled in town.

By the early 19th century, Cienfuegos, with its vastly superior harbor, began to surpass Casilda, which had begun silting up. Trinidad began a steady decline, hastened by tumult in the slave trade and new competition from more advanced estates elsewhere in Cuba. Isolated from the Cuban mainstream, Trinidad foundered. By the turn of the 20th century, it was a down-at-heels little town. Only the faded beauty remained.

In the 1950s, Batista declared Trinidad a "jewel of colonial architecture." A preservation law was passed—a boon for latter-day tourism but regarded as a bane for the past 40 years, as development was prohibited and the city continued to stagnate in its own beauty (the construction of the Carretera Central, on the north side of the Sierra del Escambray, had already stolen the through traffic, ensuring that Trinidad would be preserved in its past).

The town was named a national monument in 1965. A Restoration Committee was established, and the city was divided into three zones, including a central core around Plaza Mayor that has been completely restored. In 1988, UNESCO named Trinidad a World Heritage Site.

ORIENTATION

Old Trinidad

There are two Trinidads. The original enclave takes up the northeast quarter, on the higher slopes. This cobbled quarter is bounded to the south by Calle Antonio Maceo and to the east by Calle Lino Pérez. At its heart is Plaza Mayor, at the top of Calle Simón Bolívar. It's a warren: some streets end at T-junctions, while others curl or bifurcate, one leading uphill while another drops sharply to another Y-fork or right angled bend. All this was meant to fool marauding pirates, but it does a pretty good job on visitors, too.

Many of the streets are known locally by older names—Calle Juan Manuel Márquez, for example, is better known as Amargura.

The streets are each sloped in a slight V, with gutters in the center. According to legend, the city's first governor had a right leg shorter than the other and could thereby be level when walking the streets by staying on the right-hand side.

The road from Cienfuegos (to the west) runs into Calle Piro Guinart, which leads uphill into the old city.

New Trinidad

Below the original settlement, encircling it to the west, south, and east, is a newer, albeit aged, nontouristy district laid out on a rough grid centered on Parque Céspedes. The main street is Calle José Martí, which runs north-south and is lined with shops and bars. **Calle Bolivar** (also called Desengaño) is the most important of the streets leading east to the *ciudad antigua*. One block south of Parque Céspeda is Calle Camilio Cienfuegos, a major thoroughfare leading east, uphill, to Plaza Santa Ana, the Motel Las Cuevas, and Sancti Spíritus.

At the base (west end) of Simón Bolívar is the road to La Boca; at the base of Camilio Cienfuegos is the road to Casilda and Playa Ancón.

WALKING TOUR OF PLAZA MAYOR

Trinidad is no place for a car—the central streets are closed to traffic by stone pillars and cannons stuck nose-first in the ground (the cannons served in colonial days to protect pedestrians as carriages turned the corners). You should walk the cobbled streets, and let serendipity be your guide.

Begin at **Plaza Mayor,** the heart of the origi-

nal settlement. At its center is a pretty park ringed with silver trellises, with shiny white wrought-iron benches beneath the shade of palms and hibiscus bowers. The immaculately restored plaza is adorned with small neoclassical statues—including two bronze greyhounds that would be at home in a Landseer painting—and pedestals topped by ceramic urns.

Plaza Mayor is ringed by a cathedral and four museums, all once the mansions of wealthy colonialists.

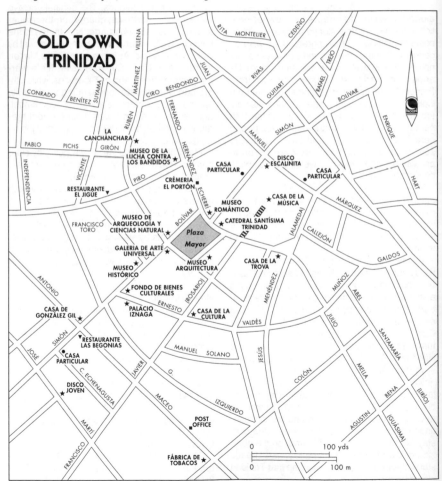

Catedral Santísima Trinidad

Begin your exploration on the plaza's southeast corner, at the surprisingly modest, almost ascetic cathedral, which was restored in 1996. It is more English than Spanish inside, with a Victorian-gothic vaulted ceiling and altar carved from mahogany and other hardwoods. The cathedral was rebuilt inside in 1894 on the spot where once stood the Parroquial Mayor, the original parish church. Hence, there's no baroque extravagance, although the carved statuary is intriguing, especially the 18th-century *Cristo de la Vera Cruz.*

Palacio Brunet

One block away, on the northwest corner, is a beautifully preserved, two-story, 18th-century mansion dating from 1741 (back then, it had only one story). Today it houses the **Museo Romántico**, which replicates the opulent original home. The dozen rooms are filled with with intriguing artwork, fabulous antiques, and potted plants in profusion. Note the solid carved-cedar ceiling, dating from 1770, and the *mediopunto* arches, also carved from cedar. The main staircase leads upstairs, where you can step out onto the bal-cony to admire the view down over the square. The stunning wrought-iron bed is the only heirloom of the Brunet family that originates from the house. Photographs are not allowed inside, but you can snap splendid scenes of the plaza from the balcony (traditionally, couples have their wedding pictures taken here). It's open Tues.-Sun. 9 a.m.-6 p.m. Entrance costs US$2.

Museo de Arqueología y Ciencias Naturales

Another impressive mansion, on the southwest corner of the plaza, at the corner of Bolívar and Martínez, today hosts the small Museum of Archaeology and Natural Sciences, exhibiting mostly Cuban fauna and flora. Natural history displays include glass cases filled with stuffed birds and animals, including a manatee and a *guaican,* a suction fish used by Taino Indians as a "hook" to catch other fish. There are also stuffed monkeys and representations of Stone Age man. A portion of the museum is devoted to the region's pre-Columbian peoples. The Indians called the region Guamuhaya, after which the museum is named. It's open daily except Saturday 9 a.m.-5 p.m. Entrance is US$1.

COLONIAL ARCHITECTURE

Cuba's colonial architecture can be divided into two categories: simple and grand. Colonial mansions and palaces—with their tall, generously proportioned rooms and shallow-stepped staircases, were usually built on two main floors (the lower floor for shops and warehouses, the upper floor for the family) with a mezzanine between them for the house servants. Life centered on the inner courtyard, hidden behind massive wooden doors often flanked by pillars.

Quintessentially Cuban features include:

Antepechos: ornamented window guards flush with the building façade

Entresuelo: a small window into the house slaves' mezzanine living quarters in colonial times

Lucetas: long rectangular windows that run along the edges of doorways and windows and usually contain stained or marbled glass.

Mamparas: double-swing half-doors that serve as room dividers or as partial outer doors to protect privacy while allowing ventilation. Some contain *persianas,* slatted blinds to keep out the sun.

Patio: An open space in the center of Spanish buildings—a Spanish adaption of the classic Moorish inner court—which permits air to circulate through the house. The patios of more grandiose buildings are surrounded by columned galleries.

Portales: galleried walkways protecting pedestrians from sun and rain. The grandest are supported by stone Tuscan columns and have vaulted ceilings and arches. Later, North American influences led to a more sober approach, with square wooden posts (à la the porch).

Postigos: small doors set at face level into massive wooden doors of Spanish homes

Rejas: wooden window screens of rippled, lathe-turned rods called *barrotes* (later *rejas* were made of metal)

Vitrales: arched windows of stained glass in geometric designs that fan out like peacock's tails and diffuse the sunlight, saturating a room with shifting color. A full 180-degree arch is called a *mediopunto.*

Museo de Arquitectura

Following the plaza counterclockwise past the Galeria de Arte Universal, on the south side, turn left onto the southeast side of the square. Here, in the **Casa de los Sánchez Iznaga,** is the Museum of Architecture, which tells the tale of the history of Trinidad's development. Maps, model structures, and sections of houses in miniature demonstrate city planning, colonial construction techniques, and the fine craftsmanship of the period. Out back, as in so many buildings in Trinidad, is a courtyard full of flower beds and blossoming fruit trees. Open Sat.-Thurs. 8 a.m.-5 p.m. (entrance costs US$1).

East of Plaza Mayor

Leaving Playa Mayor to the right of the cathedral, cobbled Calle Fernando Hernández (Cristo) leads past a wide staircase, which ascends to **Casa de la Música,** containing glass-case displays of old musical instruments. At the base of the steps is a handsome ocher-colored house—the **Mansión de los Conspiradores**— with an ornately woodworked balcony. On the other side of Cristo, opposite the mansion, is a home where Alexander Von Humbolt lived during his travels through Cuba in 1801.

Continuing one block east on Cristo brings you to the triangular **Plazuela de Segarta,** and Calle Jesús Menéndez, containing some of the oldest homes in the city, among them the **Casa de la Trova,** decorated with murals and dating to 1777.

North and West of Plaza Mayor

The **El Foturo District** comprises the blocks northwest of the plaza. In the 18th century, it was settled by foreign pirates, who were tolerated by Trinitarios (many of whom made a healthy living off the corsairs). At Ciro Redondo 261, for example, is a yellow house dating to 1754, built for Carlos Merlin, a French corsair. Nearby, on Calle Juan Márquez, are two houses with metal crosses on their exterior walls. They are two of 14 way-stops on the city's annual Easter religious procession.

A handsome tower one block west of the Museo Romántico guides you along Fernando Hernández Echarrí to Calle Pino Guinart and the **Antigua Convento de San Francisco de Asís.** You can ascend to the top of the bell tower for a view over the city. The tower *(torre)* and church are all that remain of the original convent. A paucity of noviates led to the convent's demise in the 19th century. The church was taken over by the government, and the convent was replaced by a baroque structure now housing the **Museo de la Lucha Contra Los Bandidos,** the Museum of the Fight Against Outlaws, which traces the campaign against the counterrevolutionary army in the Sierra del Escambray in the years following the Revolution. There are maps, black-and-white photographs, clothing and personal belongings of hero-soldiers, a CIA radio transmitter, and a small gunboat the agency donated to the counter-Castro cause. There is even a poster showing a boy shouldering a rifle. It reads, "My Mountains Will Never Be Taken!" The museum does *not* tell you that the guerrillas received considerable support from the local population. It's open Tues.-Sat. 9 a.m.-noon and 2-6 p.m., and Sunday 9 a.m.-1 p.m. Entrance costs US$1.

Follow Calle Pino Guinart uphill through **La Varanca,** a suburb of packed-earth streets and tiny houses of wattle and daub. The **Iglesia de la Popa** stands atop the steep hill and has splendid views over the city. It was built in 1726. Three bells, green with patina, hang over the door. It was closed when I last visited.

Walk back down Calle Piro Guinart and one block west of the convent you reach the **Plazuela Real del Jigúe,** a charming, tiny little triangular plaza (one block west of Plaza Mayor) with a calabash tree in the center. The tree, planted in 1929, is the youngest in a succession of trees kept alive since 1514, the year the Spanish celebrated their first Mass here. The colonial home (now Restaurante El Jigúe) fronting the plaza has a beautiful ceramic facia— a Trinitarian tradition.

Catercorner to El Jigúe, at Calle Piro Guinart 302, is the old town hall and jail, **Ayuntameinta y Carcel,** with a portion of the original stone-and-lime masonry exposed for view.

Southwest of Plaza Mayor

Calle Simón Bolívar leads downhill from Plaza Mayor. It is lined with former homes of once-important families, including the Palacio Cantero, whose Roman-style baths once amused 19th-century travelers, with a fountain that spouted *eau de cologne* for the ladies and gin for gents.

The Palacio, at the corner of Calle Francisco Toro, one block south of Plaza Mayor, today houses the **Museo Histórico.** The history of the city is revealed as you move through rooms furnished with rocking chairs, alabaster amphorae, marble-topped tables, and other antiques. Other intriguing exhibits include an antique bell, stocks for holding slaves, banknotes, and a magnificent scale model of the *Andrei Vishinsky,* which entered Trinidad harbor on 17 April 1960—the first Soviet ship to visit Cuba after the Revolution. Of course, the museum wouldn't be complete without exhibits honoring the 19th-century Cuban nationalist movement and the revolution that ousted Batista. Stairs lead up to a watchtower with a fine view over the city. It's open Mon.-Fri. 10 a.m.-6 p.m. and Sunday 9 a.m.-1 p.m.

A few steps away is the **Museo de Artes Decorativas,** in the former home of Ortiz de Zúñiga, an outfitter of pirate ships who rose to become Trinidad's mayor. Hernán Cortés supposedly lived here before his departure to conquer the Aztecs. Stroll downhill one block and you'll reach two other important colonial homes-turned-museums, **Palacio Iznaga,** and **Casa de González Gil.** Both are stuffed with antiques.

OTHER SIGHTS

The modest **Plaza Santa Ana,** at the top of Calle General Lino Pérez, is dominated by the ruins of **Iglesia Santa Ana.** On the east side is a beautifully restored ocher-colored colonial building containing a courtyard with a café, a bar, a specialty restaurant, and a store selling all things Che. It also has an artisans' gallery that includes a ceramic workshop.

The only site of major interest in the newer town is **Parque Céspedes,** on Calle José Martí and General Lino Pérez. It's a popular gathering spot for locals, who sit beneath an arbor of bougainvillea. On the southwest side is the **Iglesia de Paula,** containing some impressive carved wood and marble statuary. The main government buildings are here, too.

Fábrica De Tabacos, a small cigar factory on the corner of Colón and Macco, is one of Cuba's quaintest such *fábricas.* Entry is free.

ACCOMMODATIONS

Despite the town's popularity, hotel options are slim. Fortunately, Trinidad has plenty of *casas particulares* (this was the only city in the country where citizens were permitted to rent private rooms prior to the extension of the law throughout Cuba in 1996). This is the way to go! The *municipo* inspects the buildings and charges a monthly license fee. There are many to choose from, and the competition keeps prices low. Touts will approach you to offer you a room. It's best to compare several before making a choice—and don't forget to consider security (bars on the windows, for example, and locks on doors).

I opted for a large colonial home two blocks from the main plaza, at Juan Manuel Márquez #32B. It has a lounge, two bedrooms (each with double bed), a large kitchen (poorly stocked with utensils), lofty ceilings, and *three* TVs—for US$10 a day! Of all the *casas particulares* I've stayed in, this was my favorite outside Havana. Ask for Isabel or María Victoria.

Mariana Ruís also has a room (plus *paladar*) at Simón Bolívar #515, 50 yards northeast of the cathedral. You might try, too, the **Hostal,** at Simón Bolívar #312, tel. 4107, with three rooms, each for US$15, or the **Hospedaje,** with five rooms (also US$15) at Francisco Javier Zerquera #403, tel. 3818.

Others to consider include two colonial homes at Calle Martí #253, tel. 3142, and #335, tel. 4450. Your hosts may be happy to cook meals for US$5 or so.

Budget
The colonial-era **Hotel La Ronda,** on Martí near Parque Céspedes, planned to reopen in 1997 following a restoration and will charge about US$15 s, US$18 d for rooms. There's also a very basic option—the **Motel Brisas del Mar**—in Casilda, though it's a refuge of the desperate or impecunious.

Moderate
The **Motel Las Cuevas,** Finca Santa Ana, Trinidad, tel. 419-4013, is favored by tour groups. It has 84 a/c rooms with private baths, phones, and radios in bungalows that crawl up the hill-

side above town. The rooms are very modest (lumpy old mattresses and basic furniture are standard), though the setting is splendid. The restaurant and bar are in a huge thatched *bohio.* A swimming pool and shop are farther up the hill. There's also a tour desk, and car rental is available. It has lively entertainment each night. The motel is a touristy enclave. I recommend walking down into town (a 30-minute hike) at night to dine and engage with locals, not least because the food and service at the hotel are mediocre. Rates begin at US$30 s US$40 d.

FOOD

Trinidad has a fistful of atmospheric restaurants. After dusk, they lie fallow (few locals can afford the dollar prices, and the tourists have mostly departed Trinidad; those that remain dine in the Motel Cueva—a serious mistake). The waiters, expectantly standing beside their elegantly dressed tables, often go home without a single client having ventured in.

As elsewhere in Cuba, breakfasts are hard to come by. You can brave the meager buffet breakfast at **Motel Las Cuevas** for US$4. The motel restaurant reportedly serves a delicious house drink—*cascos de naranja*—made from syrup and boiled orange peel. A much better option is the buffet breakfast at the **Hotel Ancón** (see "Peninsula de Ancón," below).

My favorite restaurant is **Restaurante El Jigüe,** in a cool colonial home facing onto Plazuela Real del Jigúe. The wide menu features a filling *pollo el jigúe,* with spaghetti and cheese served in an earthenware dish (US$12). Most entrées cost less than US$10. I also enjoyed red snapper (complete with gruesome teeth and a sprig of mint sticking from its belly) at **Restaurante Las Begonias,** an elegant seafood restaurant lent a provincial French feel. It's on the corner of Antonio Maceo and Simón Bolívar. Dishes cost US$6 and up.

Another atmospheric option is **Mesón del Regidor,** which specializes in grilled meats and has an art gallery at the back. It's one block southwest of Plaza Mayor, on Simón Bolívar. The **Trinidad Colonial** at Maceo #55, tel. 2873, also serves high-quality *criollo* cuisine (averaging US$6).

Paladares. There are plenty to choose from near Plaza Mayor. Ask around. Those near Parque Céspedes include **Las Delicias,** Martí #409, and, opposite, **La Coruna,** and **El Cocodrilo** (at the bottom of Calle Cienfuegos), which does *not* serve crocodile, despite the stuffed beast outside. The atmospheric **Restaurante Coatzacoalcos,** on Calle Cienfuegos, is popular with locals.

There are lots of peso snack stalls selling *batidos* and finger food along Calle Martí near Parque Céspedes. Need a pick-me-up? Check out the *guarapería,* selling fresh-squeezed sugarcane juice at the corner of Cienfuegos and Martí—one of very few streetside *guaraperías* still extant in Cuba. Nearby are two houses advertising pizzas for five pesos a slice.

If the heat gets to you, indulge in an ice cream and soda from the **Crémeria El Portón,** west of Museo Romántico, or a delicious homemade lemonade at **Restaurante El Jigüe** (US65 cents). Closer to Parque Céspedes is an *heladería* next to Photo Service, on Calle Martí.

You'll find several tiny grocery stores in town, including **El Agabama,** at the corner of Julio Amelia and Camilo Cienfuegos.

ENTERTAINMENT AND EVENTS

Traditional Music and Dance

You'd expect a town such as Trinidad, pickled in time, to have heaps of traditional music. Visitors are not disappointed. Watch for performances by **Conjunto Folklórico de Trinidad,** which presents traditional Afro-Cuban dance routines. Genuine Afro-Cuban music is also a feature at the **Cabildo de San Antonio de los Congos Reales,** at Isidro Armenteros 168. This social club is strongly influenced by santería and is very colorful—the real McCoy!

Traditional music performances are also hosted at the **Casa de la Trova,** one block south of Plaza Mayor, at Calle Echerrí #29. Entrance is free. There'll be tourists there by day, paying dollar bills for beers. Go in the evening, when the mood shifts and locals gather to drink *aguardente* for two pesos a shot. It's normally open Tues.-Sun. 11 a.m.-2 p.m. and 8 p.m.-midnight on weekends.

The **Casa de la Cultura** also hosts traditional music (it's on Francisco Izquierda and Martínez Villena).

Cultural Festivals

Trinidad has long had a tradition for *madrugadas,* early-morning performances of regional songs sung in the streets. *Madrugadas* have died in recent years except during the town's weeklong *Fiesta de Cultura.*

Every Easter, a religous celebration—*El Recorrido del via Cruces* (the way of the cross)—is held; the devout follow a route through the old city, stopping at 14 sites marked with crosses.

Bars and Discos

There are plenty of locals bars to choose from. The most atmospheric is **La Canchánchara,** on Calle Rubén Martínez, tel. 4345. It features live music and is known for its house special, made of *aguardente* (raw rum), mineral water, honey, and lime (US$1.20).

About 50 meters farther west is **La Luna,** another popular and charming bar with adult locals.

The most popular place is **Disco Escalinita,** on Juan Manuel Márquez, behind the Casa de la Música. This open-air (roofless) disco is framed by red-brick walls and lit by ultraviolet lighting, adding to the attractive ambience. It plays world beat and modern pop music. Unfortunately, the techno beat pulses through the surrounding streets, making a miserable time of things for neighbors who want to sleep. Live bands also perform. Entrance costs US$2.

Your other option is **Disco Jóven,** at Martí #310.

Other Entertainment

The Motel Las Cuevas features special theme entertainment nightly at 10 p.m. for the tour-group crowd (a magician performs on Saturday; Monday and Wednesday are "Noches Campesina"; and Tuesday is "Afro-Cuban" night).

There's a **cinema** on the south side of Parque Cespedes.

SHOPPING

A good place to buy souvenirs, including jewelry and artwork, is the **ARTEX store,** beside the entrance to Museo Romántico. The widest options are offered by **Fondo de Bienes Culturales,** selling a splendid array of handicrafts, including wickerwork. Don't buy the coral pieces! The carvings, here, are relatively crude, as is most of the artwork, but the jewelry, and the animal figurines made of carved ox horn are splendid. It's one block south of Plaza Mayor, on Calle Simón Bolívar.

The best paintings are sold at the **Galería de Arte,** on the south side of Plaza Mayor. Its eclectic range runs the gamut of styles. Contemporary work is displayed downstairs; you'll find more traditional works upstairs.

You'll be approached on the street by touts selling trinket necklaces made from coffee beans, nuts, and various semi-precious stones. You can watch María Martinez Valdivia making her necklaces in her home at 277 Ciro Redondo (she sells them for as little as US20 cents apiece). Pennywhistles made of bamboo are another local craft item.

Much of the ceramic work is made at **El Alfarero Cerámica,** on the city's outskirts. There's also a **weaving factory** on Calle Bolívar, where straw hats and basketworks are produced.

The store in the **Casa de la Música** has a wide selection of Cuban music on cassettes and CDs. You'll find a Spanish-language bookstore next to the library, on Calle Martí between Colón and Francisco Javier Serquera.

INFORMATION AND SERVICES

There is no tourist information bureau in town. The tour desks at the Motel Cuevas and Hotel Ancón (see "Peninsula de Ancón," below) can provide basic information. You may be able to buy a detailed map of Trinidad in town (try the

---

TRINIDAD USEFUL TELEPHONE NUMBERS

Police	tel. 2168
Ambulance	tel. 2362
Hospital	tel. 3201
Railway station	tel. 3348
Terminal de Ómnibus	tel. 9-4448
Taxis	tel. 2214

ARTEX shop next to the Museo Romántico). Ediciones Geo publishes an accurate tourist map of Trinidad, Ancón, and Topes de Collantes.

The well-stocked **library** carries works almost exclusively on Cuba. It's open 8 a.m.-10 p.m.

There's a postal facility in the Motel Las Cuevas. The main **post office** is on the east side of Parque Céspedes. The **Centro Telefonico** is next door, open Mon.-Sat. 7:30 a.m.-noon and 1:30-5 p.m.).

The **Cupet gas station** is tucked into the corner of Frank País and Uzuerguera. A minimally stocked **Photo Service,**Martí # 222, has batteries, tape cassettes, film, and a few instamatic cameras.

Medical

If you need medical attention, you'll find the 24-hour **Clínica Internacional** at the bottom of Lino Pérez #103, on the corner of Anastasio Cárdenas. It has a small, reasonably stocked pharmacy as well as a doctor and nurse on hand. There's also a local 24-hour pharmacy at Martí #332.

CRIME AND SAFETY

The presence of so many tourists has given rise to petty thievery among adolescents. (Trinidad is the only town in the country where I've had anything stolen.) You will be importuned here by more children begging for *chiclets, un dolar,* or *plumas* (pens and pencils) than in other cities.

GETTING THERE

Despite its fame and importance, Trinidad is not well served by public transport.

By Air: Cubana offers flights on Monday and Friday at 7:30 a.m. to Trinidad from Havana (US$35).

By Bus: Bus no. 412 leaves daily from Havana's main terminal at 6 a.m., arriving at the terminal at Calles Gustavo Izquierda and Piro Guinart in Trinidad at 11:30 a.m. (21 pesos *especial,* 17 *regular;* you may be charged in dollars). Buses also operate from Cienfuegos daily at noon (1.20 pesos; one hour and 50 minutes)

and from Sancti Spíritus six times daily. You need to make reservations at least one day ahead, but don't count on a seat. Often the wait is several weeks!

By Train: Daily train service has been reinstated from Sancti Spíritus to Trinidad. If you're traveling from other cities, you'll have to connect in Sancti Spíritus. Trinidad's train station is at the bottom of Camilo Cienfuegos.

By Car: The Carretera Sur linking Cienfuegos with Sancti Spíritus runs through Trinidad.

Organized Tours: Tour & Travel, Avenida 5 #8409, Miramar, Havana, tel. 33-2433, includes Trinidad on a three-day tour from Havana (US$225), along with Cienfuegos and Varadero.

Trinidad is a staple of tours offered by international companies.In the US, the **Cuba Information Project,** 198 Broadway, Suite 800, New York, NY 10038, tel. (212) 227-3422, fax (212) 227-4859, offers a 10-day tour that traces the Spanish legacy in Trinidad and Sancti Spíritus. The midsummer trip costs US$1,200, including airfare. **Wings of the World** includes several days in Trinidad on its 10-day "Cultural Treasures" (US$2,495, including airfare from Bahamas) and weeklong "History Comes Alive" tours (US$1,795 including airfare). See "Activities" in the On The Road chapter.

GETTING AROUND

There is no public bus service in the old town. You must walk. Many streets are cobbled and uneven, the sidewalks are often high, the streets are poorly lit at night, and many are hilly.

A limited number of **horse-drawn taxis** operate through the new town. **Transauto** offers a car-and-driver taxi service from the Motel Las Cuevas (four hours cost US$30, eight hours US$55, 12 hours US$85), where it has a car rental office. **Nacional Rent-a-Car,** tel. 2577, has an office on Martí (between Cienfuegos and Perez).

A tourist train *(tren turistico)* runs to the town of Guachinango via the Valle de los Ingenios. It is organized by **Rumbos,** Calle G. Izquierdo, tel. 9-4204; Peninsula de Ancón, tel. 9-4414; Calle M. Gómez #23, tel. 9-2264. You'll travel in old railway carriages pulled by a World War I-era steam engine. Officially it departs Wednesday,

Friday, and Sunday, but I was told that departure time and cost depends on group needs and size. Individuals can buy tickets for the one-hour journey (US$13, or US$23 with lunch).

Rumbos and Aero-Gaviota also offer air tours by biplane for US$24. Rumbos also offers a **hiking** excursion along the El Nicho trail in the Sierra del Escambray and a horseback ride to La Vega Rancho. You can book through the tour office at Motel Las Cuevas, or in the Hotel Ancón.

For a tourist **taxi,** call 2479.

GETTING AWAY

By Bus: The bus to Havana leaves Trinidad daily at 2:30 p.m. Again, it is usually booked weeks in advance. Your best bet may be to take one of the buses that leave six times daily to Sancti Spíritus, then catch a train or bus from there. There's one bus to Cienfuegos, at 5 a.m. Buses to Topes de Collantes are scheduled thrice daily.

By Train: There's only one service—to Havana, via Sancti Spíritus and Santa Clara. It operates daily at 2:45 p.m. The ticket booth is open 7:30 a.m.-noon for advance purchase.

LA BOCA

La Boca is a quaint and slightly funky village with traditional *bohios,* five km west of Trinidad.

It appeals for its pocket-scale beaches amid coral coves favored by Trinitarios on weekends. The setting is marvelous, in the lee of the Sierra del Escambray.

It has been described by another writer as the place"the inhabitants of the area meet to relax in a lively congregation of music, flirting, and fistfights. They're far more interesting," he continues, "than the dowdy crowd of pale visitors from the north along the Ancón Peninsula, and you'll be made more welcome, too."

Rumbos has a small snack bar by the beach.

PENINSULA DE ANCÓN

The coast extends south of La Boca to a small point, **Punta María Aguilar,** beyond which a long narrow peninsula curls to the east, enclosing a mangrove-lined lagoon, the **Ensenada de Casilda.** From the inner side of the peninsula, you can watch a motley collection of homespun fishing boats made of planking and polystyrene, with crudely stitched canvas sails.

South of La Boca, the shore is mostly coral, interspersed with little beaches amid seagrape shrubs. Beyond Punta María Aguilar lies Playa Ancón, one of Cuba's premium beaches.

Ancón (hind leg) is named for a large rock that rises above Punta María Aguilar, resembles a horse's hind leg, and was a landmark for sailors. North of the point, you'll pass an army barracks with a billboard reading: *Por Nuestra Frontera*

Playa Ancón

El Enemigo No Pasará! (The Enemy Shall Not Pass Our Frontier). It's here with good reason. During planning for the invasion by Cuban exiles in spring 1961, Richard Bissel, the CIA director of operations, promoted Ancón as the preferred landing site. He advanced a combined airborne/amphibious assault. Kennedy rejected the idea as "too spectacular" and "too much like a World War II invasion." Instead, he settled for the Bay of Pigs—and a fiasco.

Playa Ancón, midway along the Ancón peninsula, provides the yin to Trinidad's yang. The four-km-long beach is fabulous, with sugary white sand and pavonine waters fringed with pines and palms. The sea is perfect for snorkeling: calm, crystal clear, with plenty of coral. Local youths stroll the beach selling polished seashells and jewelry carved from local hardwoods and endangered black coral.

Accommodations and Food

There's a basic campsite—**Campismo Guayabero**—at the west end of Playa Ancón.

There are two hotels. The larger, **Hotel Ancón,** Playa Ancón, Trinidad, tel. 419-4011, fax 667-7424, at the far southern end of the beach, has 279 rooms, all with a/c, private baths, telephones, and radios (US$50 s, US$75 d). The Soviet-style structure has been nicely upgraded. Facilities include a games room, cabaret, swimming pool, and tourism bureau, Photo Service shop, atmospheric restaurant with bamboo decor, and seven bars. Excursions are offered. The lively hotel is a favorite of charter tour groups and is a little enclave of Canadians, French, and Germans. There's a car rental service, but demand far exceeds supply.

The smaller, more intimate **Hotel Costa Sur,** at Punta María Aguilar, has its own little white sand beach with volleyball. The waters are shallow, albeit rocky. The hotel—a modestly appealing property—is popular with tour groups. The 131 a/c rooms and bungalows cost US$32 s, US$42 d. All have private baths, radios, and telephones. Facilities include a games room and volleyball and tennis courts, a pool, even a miniature rifle range. The hotel features scuba diving and offers a "Jungle Adventure" excursion into the Sierra del Escambray (US$30) and another to Zapata (US$20).

Both hotels have adequate restaurants. For ambience, you should eat at the gaily painted, thatched, **Grill Caribe,** on the beach 400 yards west of Hotel Ancón. It specializes in lobster. It's pricey, however—US$20 for a lobster meal!

Watersports and Excursions

The Hotel Ancón offers jet-skis, catamarans, and other watersports. Sportfishing (US$36), a six-hour "seafari" (US$35), and a nocturnal "cabaret at sea" (US$10) are available from Marina Cayo Blanco (see "Getting There and Around," below), as are excursions to Cayo Blanco (US$30) and nearby Cayo Macho (US$35). You can charter a sportfishing boat for four people (US$150 half-day, US$250 full day).

Scuba Diving: Ancón's offshore coral reefs have more than 30 dive spots and the added attraction of sunken vessels, concentrated at Cayo Blanco de Casilda and along the peninsula all the way to the mouth of the Río Guarabo, at La Boca. **Cayo Blanco,** nine km southeast of Ancón, is famous for its kaleidoscopic variety of corals, sea fans, sponges, and gorgonians.

Scuba diving is offered by both the Hotel Ancón and the Hotel Costa Sur, and by Puertosol at the Marina Cayo Blanco. Puertosol charges US$9 for an initiation dive (resort course) and US$30 per dive for certified divers (US$35 for night dives). You can arrange a 10-dive package for US$230. Instructors, compressors, and tanks are included.

Getting There and Around

Buses to La Boca leave Trinidad four times daily and continue to Playa Ancón. You may also be able to hop aboard the hotel workers' buses. A **taxi** between Trinidad and Ancón costs about US$11 one-way.

Transauto has a car rental office in the Hotel Ancón. It specializes in short-term rentals. A Daihatsu jeep, for example, costs US$13 for six hours or US$24 for 12 hours, plus US$8 insurance; a small Peugeot sedan costs US$20 for six hours, US$35 for 12. You can also rent **bicycles** at the Hotel Ancón. The ride to Trinidad is flat all the way as you wind through the salt lagoons (it's a hot ride, however; take water).

Marina Cayo Blanco, *Base Naútica,* tel. 419-4011 or 419-4414, lies within a cove in the Enseñada de Casilda, adjacent to the Hotel Ancón.

The marina has six moorings. Water, electricity, and diesel (US90 cents per liter) are available. Before berthing, you must first call in to clear Customs and Immigration across the bay at the ramshackle wharf of Casilda, where the process is said to be a dreary chore.

WEST OF TRINIDAD

The road west to Cienfuegos begins at the base of Calle Pino Guinart. It meets the coast at the mouth of the Río Caña, about seven km west of Trinidad. The turnoff for Topes de Collantes and the Sierra del Escambray is about four km west of Trinidad.

Finca María Dolores

This rustic *finca,* Carretera Circuito Sur, tel. 3581, is a contrived but appealing tourist attraction amid landscaped grounds on the banks of the Río Guaurabo, three km west of Trinidad. It's popular with tour groups. The representation of a traditional farm features an aviary, cockfights, milking, and other farm activities.

A turnoff from the coast road a stone's throw west of Finca María Dolores leads to a cave by the river, where **Monumento Alberto Delgado** recalls a Castroite killed during the counterrevolutionary war. Delgado was lynched by *bandidos* (counterrevolutionaries) after his identity as a spy for the Castro regime was discovered. Delgado's house (across the river, midway between Trinidad and La Boca) is open to visits.

Accommodations and Food

The *finca* offers accommodations in 20 small brick *cabañas,* each with a/c, hot water, and showers (US$8 s, US$15 d, US$21 t). The *criollo* meals are inexpensive (US$4-6 for pork and chicken dishes). You eat spit-roasted pig in a thatched restaurant, open to the sides, where folkloric shows featuring a *guateque* (a good ol' country hoe-down) are offered nightly at 9 p.m. (US$15, including dinner).

Motel Río Caño has little casitas beside the rivermouth (10 pesos). The basic facility caters primarily to Cubans but also accepts foreigners. The restaurant serves fish dishes for three pesos.

CIEGO DE ÁVILA AND CAMAGÜEY

INTRODUCTION

East of Sancti Spíritus, the Carretera Central passes through Ciego de Ávila and Camagüey, geographically similar provinces which together form the **central plains,** dominated along their axis by rolling savannas.

Ciego de Ávila is Cuba's least-populous province (pop. 390,000). Nevertheless, this dull, pancake-flat region is the nation's leading pineapple producer and among the top three producers of citrus, fruits, and vegetables (it is also important in the production of sugarcane), due to the quality of its soil and massive reserves of underground water. That said, almost three-fourths of the province is devoted to cattle.

There are few sights of natural or historical interest here, even in the only two towns of importance, Ciego de Ávila and, due north, Morón, gateway to important fishing and hunting preserves and Ciego de Ávila's star attraction—Cayo Coco and the other cays of Cayería del Norte.

Camagüey province is the nation's largest, though its population is also sparse. The grassy, honey-colored rolling plains are reminiscent of Montana (conveniently dismissing the silver-barked royal palm trees, which add a dramatic effect). Cattle *ganaderías* and cowboys make a poignant effect on the landscape.

The city of Camagüey far overshadows the town of Ciego de Ávila, and is behind only Havana and Trinidad for colonial charm, despite its industry and modern pretensions. Camagüey is a staging area, too, for access to the Cayería del Norte. From the city airport, pale *turistas* are bused to Playa Santa Lucía to pick up a tan on endless miles of secluded sand.

THE LAY OF THE LAND

The terrain of Ciego de Ávila is gentle plain; the average elevation of the land is less than 50 meters above sea level. Hence, there are few rivers and no distinguishing features. The wedge-shaped province (6,910 square km) is the narrowest point of Cuba—only 50 km from coast to coast. In Camagüey, the land broadens, bulging to the south like a pregnant cow. The land also rises along the central spine, forming an upland bounded to the north by a line of low mountains, the **Sierra de Cubitas,** beyond which lie coastal plains and the **Cayería del Norte,** low-lying, sandy coral islands that lie in a great line parallel to the coast, between 10 and 18 km from shore. Officially called the Archipiélago de Sabana-Camagüey, this sea-girt wilderness of coral reefs, cays, islands, and sheltered seas extends 470 km from the Península de Hicaco (Varadero) in the west to the Bahía de Nuevitas and Playa Santa Lucía in the east.

Ernest Hemingway actively pursued German submarines in these seas in the 1940s, immortalizing his adventures in his novel, *Islands in the Stream.* It is possible to follow the route of the novel's protagonists as they pursue the Nazis east-west along the cays, passing Confites, Paredón Grande, Coco, Guillermo, and on to Santa María. Papa was meticulous in his descriptions of landmarks, although he sometimes shifted their position.

The 400 or so cays are rimmed by stunning beaches, scintillatingly white as confectioner's sugar and dissolving into crystalline waters. They are separated from one another by narrow channels and from the coast by shallow lagoons. All but a few are inaccessible by road. Habitation is exceedingly sparse. And together they are among the least disturbed of all Cuba's terrain. Understandably, this maritime province is Cuba's next frontier for resort development. So far, that's been limited to Cayo Coco, Cayo Guillermo, and Santa Lucía, and a handful of mainland beaches.

The islands are mostly covered with low scrub (including mangroves), which forms a perfect habitat for wild pigs and iguanas and birds such as mockingbirds, nightingales, and woodpeckers. The briny lagoons are favored by pelicans, ibis, various duck species, and—the stars of the show—as many as 20,000 flamingoes, more by far than anywhere else in Cuba. They are all easily seen, especially on Cayos Coco, Guillermo, and Sabinal. Running along the northern edge of the cays are endless miles of coral reef—an underwater jungle of myriad colors, teeming with tropical fish that thrive in calm, transparent waters that remain 26-30° C year-round.

A paved road runs the entire length of the coast, paralleling it at an average distance of five km inland. It is mostly in good condition. Feeder roads connect it with the Carretera Central and provincial capitals, and by land bridges with Cayo Coco, Cayo Romano, and Cayo Sabinal.

Much of the coastal plain is covered with barren deciduous scrubland grazed by cattle; swampy marshland, perfect for birding or hunting; and lagoons, perfect for fishing. Elsewhere, the flatlands are drowned by vast undulating seas of green sugarcane.

Note: Conch shells are tempting items, shining and glossy pink, and local Cubans will attempt to sell them to you for almost nothing. *It's illegal.* Taking conch shells out of the county ostensibly requires a permit. More important, the conch population is under pressure. Shop with a conscience!

Camagüey

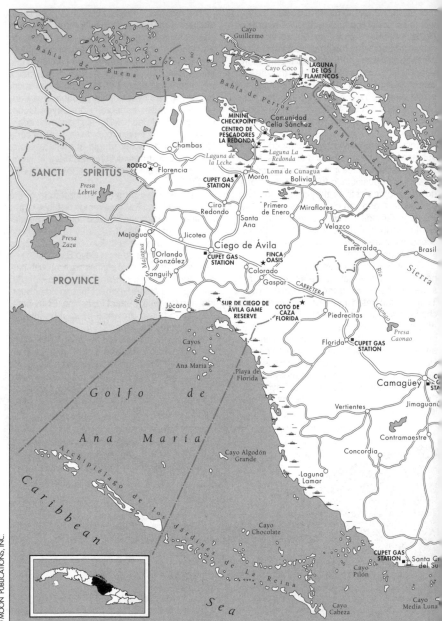

CIEGO DE ÁVILA AND CAMAGÜEY PROVINCES

The sparcely populated southern plains are covered almost entirely by marshland and swamps. There are few beaches. A slender archipelago—the **Járdines de la Reina**—lies off the southern coast, sprinkled east-west in a straight line across the Gulf of Santa Ana María. As yet, this paternoster of coral isles doesn't figure in Cuba's burgeoning tourism drive, despite fabulous beaches and birdlife, coral formations perfect for scuba diving, and shallow waters that offer plenty of angling delights.

Carretera Central to Ciego de Ávila

The Carretera Central runs through the south-central part of Ciego de Ávila province. It's a fairly boring drive, through plains awash with green, green sugarcane.

Immediately east of the Sancti Spíritus-Ciego de Ávila border is a turnoff for **Majagua.** This is a major junction, where lots of people wait for rides. There's a **Cupet gas station** here, with a large open-air restaurant.

The town is one mile south of the junction. Accommodations are available at **Cabañas del Río Majagua,** tel. 9249, hidden behind trees midway into town. It has a pleasing restaurant that overlooks a river and serves breakfast, lunch, and dinner. Modest a/c rooms are reached by a suspension bridge over the river; each has TV and two beds (26 pesos s, 30 d).

CIEGO DE ÁVILA AND VICINITY

The namesake capital city (pop. 80,000), 460 km east of Havana, is sleepy and unremarkable—the least inspirational of Cuba's provincial capitals (however, the locals—called Ávileños—are friendly). There's no need to stop except for curiosity's sake. The city is also known as "The Pineapple Town" for the local fields of pineapple (now looking neglected).

The first land grants locally were given in the mid-16th century, when the region was almost entirely forested. Gradually, cattle ranches were established. Local lore says that one of the earliest *hacienda*-owners was named Ávila. His property, established in 1538, occupied a large clearing, or *ciego,* and was used as a way-stop for travelers. A small settlement grew around it, named San Jeronimo de la Palma, but known locally as Ciego de Ávila. The city gained commercial prominence this century as an agricultural center.

Ciego de Ávila was also the site of one of the 43 forts along La Trocha, the great barrier built from coast to coast in the 1860s to forestall the rebel armies advancing west during the Ten Years' War of Independence. The line was strengthened by the Spanish general Valeriano Weyler during the second War of Independence, with a dyke paralleling the fence.

ORIENTATION AND SIGHTSEEING

The streets are laid out in a perfect grid. The Carretera Central (called Calle Chicho Valdés) runs east-west through the city. The main street is Independencia, running east-west two blocks north of Chicho Valdés.

The heart of affairs is **Parque Martí,** a pretty little square on the north side of Independencia and the west side of Marcial Gómez. It has a bust of the hero at its center. It was repaved in 1995 with the addition of Victorian-era lampposts and new seating beneath the shade trees. The most noteworthy structure is the **Poder Popular,** the old town hall, built in 1911. There are no other buildings of note.

The jewel of Ciego de Ávila is the **Teatro Principal,** one block south of Martí, on Joaquín Agüera and Honorario del Castillo. It is said to have been built at the whim of a local society figure, Angela Hernández Vida de Jiménez, who, between 1924 and 1927, reportedly spent 250,000 pesos on its construction. Its enormous hand-carved wooden doors open onto an elaborately decorated interior, a mix of imperial, baroque, and renaissance styles, with allegorical statuary, an oval grand marble staircase, and bronze chandeliers.

An old Spanish fort—**Fortín de la Trocha**—lies at the west end of Máximo Gómez, just beyond the railway tracks. It is the only one still standing of seven military towers built during the Ten Years' War of Independence. Today it houses a restaurant. Immediately west is the Instituto de Segunda Enseñanza, housing the modest **Museo Provincial,** tel. 28431 or 28128, open Tues.-Sun. 8 a.m.-noon and 1-5 p.m. Entrance costs US$1.

There's a small zoo **(Parque Zoológico)** at the east end of Independencia that has a half-dozen animals, including a zebra. It's a popular spot with Cuban families.

Into plants? Then head to **Borroto's Bio-Factory** town, where ornamental plants—including ficus, bougainvillea, bird of paradise, orchids, and the ixora—are grown for export. Carlos Borroto Nordlo, director of the complex (part of the Higher Institute of Agricultural Studies), will be delighted to show you the BioPlant Center and bio-factory.

ACCOMMODATIONS

Islazul operates the only two hotels in town. **Hotel Ciego de Ávila,** is on the Carretera Ceballos, two km northwest of downtown, tel. 2-8013. It's a faceless Eastern bloc-style building but pleasantly furnished. The 144 a/c rooms all have telephones and private baths (US$20 s, US$24 d in low season, US$25 s, US$30 d in peak season). There's a beauty parlor and barbershop, nightclub, and tourism bureau with rent-a-car service. Half of the city seems to flock to the swimming pool on weekends.

The **Hotel Santiago-Havana,** Independencia

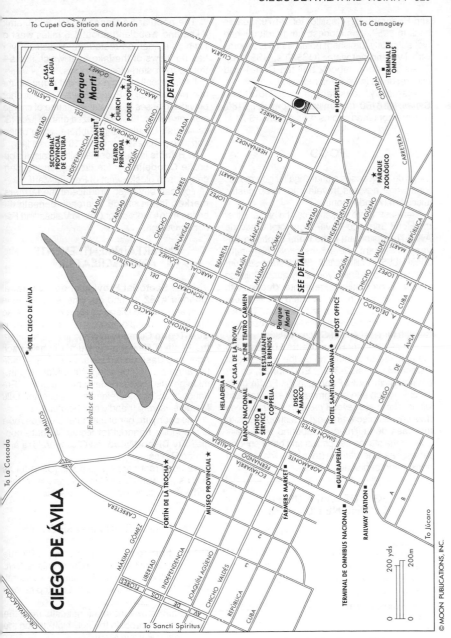

© MOON PUBLICATIONS, INC.

and Honorario del Castillo, tel. 2-5703, dates back to 1957. The modest, newly refurbished (yet still dourly furnished) hotel has 76 a/c rooms with TVs and hot water (US$20 s, US$25 d). There's a dark, moody bar (La Copa) and cabaret disco in La Cima nightclub.

Alternately, consider the basic **Motel Las Cañas,** tel. 8180, five km west of town, tel. 8180, with prefabricated cabins ranging US$16-21.

FOOD

Ciego de Ávila poses a challenge for gourmands (one writer advises travelers to "keep gastric juices firmly under control").

Breakfasts (unremarkable) can be had at either the Hotel Santiago-Havana or Hotel Ciego de Ávila. The restaurant in the **Hotel Santiago-Havana** is elegant and serves *criollo* dishes for about US$5. Tortillas cost US$2. Otherwise, your best option, assuming you enjoy quasi-Chinese cuisine, is probably **Restaurante Yiesen,** with suitably Chinese decor behind a circular door guarded by a huge "bronze" Buddha. There's even an authentic Oriental garden. The restaurant is at the far west end of Chicho Valdés.

You can also try **Restaurante Solaris,** atop the ugly red-brick building on the west side of Parque Martí, tel. 2-3424; **El Colonial** on Independencia; or **El Fuerte,** in the Fortín de la Trocha, which serves homemade sausage and wines. There are several *paladares.* Pizza slices (five pesos apiece) are sold at a shop opposite the Casa de la Trova on Libertad. And stalls outside the station sell pizzas and other snacks, *refrescoes,* and *batidos* (try a *pina fria,* an iced drink made of pineapple juice).

CIEGO DE ÁVILA USEFUL TELEPHONE NUMBERS

Police . . . . tel. 116
Ambulance
  (Red Cross/Cruz Roja) . . . . tel. 2-2582
Hospital . . . . tel. 2-4015
Airport (Reservations) . . . . tel. 2-5316
Railway Station . . . . tel. 2-3313
Terminal de Ómnibus . . . . tel. 2-5109
Taxi . . . . tel. 2-5238

The popular **La Cascada,** tel. 8539, amid lakes and woodland about 1.5 miles west of town, is a seafood restaurant. Ridiculously, it has no views of the lake over which it sits— thanks to frosted-glass windows.

If thirsty, call in at the **Casa del Agua,** on the northwest corner of Parque Martí. This little shop provides glasses of mineral water free of charge, plus refreshing, fresh-squeezed orange juice (30 centavos). Locals hang out here, while others pop in to purchase honey for 10 pesos a liter.

El Brindis is also popular with locals; it's opposite **Coppelia** (for ice cream), on Independencia, two blocks west of Parque Martí.

You can buy fresh produce at the **farmers' market,** in the shade of arches beneath the bridge at the junction of Chicho Valdés and Fernando Calleja.

ENTERTAINMENT, EVENTS, AND RECREATION

Visit the **Sectorial Provincial de Cultura,** at Libertad #162, to find out what's going on in town and around Ciego de Ávila province. Also on Libertad, two blocks west of Parque Martí, is **Cine-Teatro Carmen,** showing films, and where the Festival Nacional de Humor is held each April; and **Casa de la Trova,** which hosts traditional music and dancing Wed.-Mon. 6 p.m.-midnight (till 2 a.m. Friday and Saturday). Entrance is US$1 for foreigners. The director, Luís Morales, is very friendly and helpful.

The courtyard bar of the Hotel Ciego de Ávila is a popular hangout for locals. Want to boogie? Try **Disco Marco,** on Chicho Valdés and Simón Reyes.

You can rent horses and boats (US$1 for as long as you want) at La Cascada, an area of lake and woodland, two km west of town, tel. 7731.

INFORMATION AND SERVICES

The **post office** is two blocks south of Parque Martí, at Marcial Gómez and Chico Valdés. **DHL** has an office in the Hotel Ciego de Ávila, tel. 22573. It's open weekdays 9 a.m.-6 p.m. and Saturday 8:30 a.m.-noon.

You can make international calls from the **Centro Telefónico,** in the ugly high-rise on the west side of Parque Martí.

There's a **Banco Nacional** on Independencia at Simón Reyes, three blocks west of Parque Martí.

The city has a 565-bed, full-service teaching **hospital** (it specializes in orthopedics) at the east end of Máximo Gómez.

There's a **Photo Service** at Independencia, though you may find it stocking only a few batteries and film. The **Cupet gas station** is on the northeast outskirts of town, near the *circunvalación* on the road to Morón.

GETTING THERE AND AWAY

By Bus
Bus no. 504 departs Havana's main bus terminal at 12:40 and 8 p.m., arriving at 6:35 p.m. and 1:50 a.m., respectively (22 pesos). There are also regular buses to and from Camagüey, Sancti Spíritus, and other cities. The **Terminal de Ómnibus Nacional** is 1.5 km east of town, on the Carretera Central. The **Terminal de Ómnibus Municipal** is next to the railway station, at the west end of Calle Ciego de Ávila, three blocks south of Chicho Valdés.

By Train or Air
Ciego de Ávila is on the main east-west railroad between Havana and Santiago, and the *especial* between the two cities stops here. The second-class service is uncomfortable and not recommended. Reservations can be made 8 a.m.-noon and 2-4:30 p.m. There's a small café, but you'll fare better with the snack stalls outside. There's even a traditional *guarapería* selling fresh-squeezed sugarcane juice.

Weekly charter flights arrive at Ciego de Ávila from Montréal (Cubana) and Toronto (Canadian Airlines and Royal Airlines), bringing package tourists to the north coast resorts. Flights (US$35 one-way) depart the Máximo Gómez airport, tel. 683-2525, about 15 km north of town. A full-service facility, the airport is having its 3,500-meter runway extended to accommodate the rapid increase in foreign travelers arriving en route to the resort at Cayo Coco (even though in spring 1996, international flights began flying directly to Cayo Coco, stealing much of the business).

Cubana has an office at Calle Chicho Valdés #83 e/ Maceo y Honorario del Castillo, tel. 25316.

There's a smaller airstrip five km east of town, on the Carretera Central.

By Car
The east-west Carretera Central runs through the town center as Calle Chicho Valdés. For Morón, take Calle Marcial Gómez north past the main square to one block north of Calle Isabel; turning right onto the road leads you to the Carretera de Morón. For Júcaro, take Simón Reyes south to Calle D, then turn right to the railroad track; turn left and cross the railroad tracks after three blocks; immediately turn left onto Echevarria for Júcaro.

GETTING AROUND

Horse-drawn cabs rule the roads. They line up outside the train station. No ride should cost more than two or three pesos, although as a foreigner you may be charged in dollars.

You can rent cars from the **Havanautos** office in the Hotel Ciego de Ávila.

SOUTH AND EAST OF CIEGO DE ÁVILA

You can forego the South Coast without fear of skipping anything worth the drive. Hunters, however, might head for **Sur de Ciego de Ávila Game Reserve,** 40 km south of Ciego de Ávila. Its lagoons attract migratory ducks, doves, snipes, quail, and guinea fowl. Check with the tour desk in the Hotel Ciego de Ávila for more details.

A road leads south 20 km to the funky fishing village of **Júcaro,** gateway to the Járdines de la Reina. The road, potholed farther south, is as straight as a billiard cue—and the fields of sugarcane are as flat and green as a billiard table.

A hurricane came ashore at Júcaro in 1932, killing many people. The dead-end village looks as if it has never recovered. There are no restaurants or other facilities, just fading wooden shacks and browbeaten fishing boats. The railway line extends out onto the wharf but is today little used, the trade having been stolen by Palo Alto. A sugar-loading facility there allows visitors to watch freighters loading from the huge wharf—Embarcadero Palo Alto—which extends one mile out to sea (the turnoff is three km north of Júcaro). Tourist maps mark Playa Palo Alto as if it has some appeal. Alas, it's a tiny, unappetizing affair overgrown with washed-up seaweed.

Marina Júcaro: Puertosol operates this marina at Júcaro, tel. 332-98126, but it's no more than a rickety wharf with a gasoline pump (supposedly the six moorings also have electricity and water).

According to the Puertosol literature, **diving and fishing** are offered to the cays of the Járdines de la Reina using live-aboard vessels. Fly-fishing costs US$19 for four hours. Four-hour fishing trips by *lancha* cost US$49 (or US$79 by night). Deep-sea fishing is also available for US$79 (five hours).

Toward Camagüey Province

East of Ciego de Ávila, the Carretera Central continues almost ruler-straight eastward to Camagüey. There are few towns of any significance. Dozens of Cubans wait for rides at the crossroads at **Gaspar,** where there's a café.

Entering Camagüey, you'll pass through **Florida,** a relatively well-to-do town dominated by Centrale Argentina, one of three sugar factories in town. It belches black smoke—a grotesque counterpoint to the pretty colonnaded streets with central medians and columned *portales.*

Lake Porvenir (west of Florida) is renowned for its excellent bass fishing. Fishing trips are offered year-round. The lake is surrounded by the wetlands of Porvenir and Muñoz. The **Coto de Caza Florida** is a hunting preserve set amid lagoons flush with migrant ducks, doves, quail, guinea fowl, and pheasant. Hunting trips are offered from the Hotel Camagüey in Camagüey (US$42 per day, plus US$25 for a hunting permit, US$10 to rent a rifle, and US$10 per 25 cartridges). Or contact Horizontes, Calle L #456 e/ 25 y 27, Vedado, Havana, tel. 33-4042, fax 33-3722.

East of Florida, the landscape becomes more engaging as you begin a long, steady climb toward Camagüey. Sugarcane gives way to scrubland, then dairy country. Black-and-white cattle shelter under the wide, cool shade of spreading trees. Farther east still, royal palms also stud the landscape in great, evenly spaced swatches—beautiful.

You'll pass great cattle estates with names such as *Victoria de Girón.* There's a world-leading center for artificial insemination to the west of Camagüey city, which with its hinterland has traditionally had a thriving dairy industry. Camagüey was famed for its cheeses. Citizens boast how before the Revolution, local dairy farms were among the best in the world.

Accommodations and Food

Rumbos operates **Finca Oasis,** about 18 km east of Ciego de Ávila, three km before the turnoff for Gaspar. The facility, with its thatched *bohios,* attempts to re-create a traditional *campesino's* homestead. There are rabbits and guinea pigs in cages, and cattle, horses, and pigs in enclosures beneath the shade of mango trees. Accommodations in thatched cabins are planned for the future. For now, there's an appealing restaurant and bar where you can down a shot of invigorating *guarapo* (sugarcane juice). Horseback rides are available for US$1. You can even watch a cockfight (the cocks' spurs are clipped).

Rumbos also operates roadside cafés at Palma Dorado, three km east of Ciego de Ávila, and at El Centro, five km east of Finca Oasis.

The **Motel Itabo,** tel. 3366, is strangely located in the middle of agricultural land, one km north of the village of San Francisco, five km south of the Carretera Central on the road to Baragua. It has a restaurant and cabaret for the local villagers. The basic cement cabins have large rooms and feature a/c and large color TVs. You can't complain about the sagging beds for 14 pesos a night.

About 1.5 km east of Florida is the **Motel Florida,** which has tiny brick bungalows with thatched roofs, plus more substantial cabins for only six pesos. Each cabin has one double and one single bed. The bathrooms are funky.

Hotel Florida, Carratera Central Oeste, Km 536, Florida, tel. 5-3011, is a run-of-the-mill Soviet-style hotel operated by Islazul. The clientele is mostly Cuban. It has 72 a/c rooms with TVs, radios, and refrigerators (US$20 s, US$24 d). The staff provides good service. A very large and well-kept swimming pool is the center of activity, especially on weekends, when locals flock and the music blares. Come nightfall, the **Nightclub El Valle** is the happenin' place.

CAMAGÜEY

Camagüey (pop. 270,000) sits in the very center of the square-shaped province on a bluff above the vast plains 570 km east of Havana and 110 km east of Ciego de Ávila. It's Cuba's third-largest city. One of Cuba's four universities is here.

Camagüey is often overlooked by foreign visitors, although it's full of beautifully restored plazas that lend the city its nicknames, "City of Squares" and "Corinth of the Caribbean." Much of the city has justifiably been declared a national monument.

Camagüey lacks the heavy baroque architecture of Havana. Its style is simpler, more discreet. Even the homes of the wealthiest Camagüeyans were built without palatial adornments: the bourgeoisie built their homes around a courtyard patio surrounded by arches and galleries, or, in more modest abodes, with eaves supported by unembellished wooden columns. Always there was a *tinajón*, the big earthenware jars unique to the city and which lent it a third nickname: "City of the Tinajones."

It's a pleasure to walk the colonial streets, especially in late afternoon, when the sun gilds the façades like burnished copper; and at night, too, when light silvers the Spanish grills and façades of the the poorly lit streets, full of impending intrigue. In the dark, full of shadows, it is easy to imagine yourself cast back 200 years.

Camagüey can be explored in one day but is fully deserving of two.

HISTORY

Camagüey was one of the original seven settlements founded by Diego Velásquez, though the first buildings were erected in 1515 miles to the north, on the shores of Bahía de Nuevitas, when the city was known as Santa María del Puerto del Príncipe. The site was not well chosen. It lacked fresh water and came under constant attack from local Indians. It was finally moved to its present location, where it was built on the site of an Indian settlement (presumably, the Indians were murdered; In 1903, the city was renamed for the local chieftain, Camaguei).

The early settlers were beset with water shortages. The town's Catalonian potters therefore made giant earthenware amphori called *tinajones* to collect and store rainfall. Soon, the large red jars (up to 2.5 meters tall and 1.5 meters wide) were a standard item outside every home, partly buried in the earth or standing in the shade to keep them cool, but always under the gutters that channeled the rain from the eaves. Citizens began to compete with each other to boast the most *tinajones,* and demonstrate their wealth. Today they are used for decoration,

Camagüey

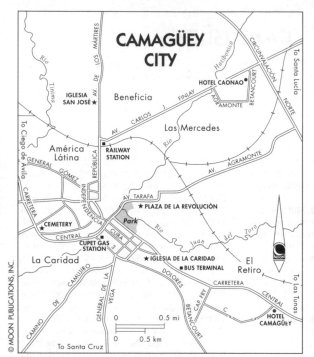

1871, "and its sons have had a greater or smaller share in almost every revolution that has taken place on the island." (US Marines even occupied the city 1917-23 to quell antigovernment unrest.)

The Camagüeyans' notoriety for insurrection did not translate to strong support for communism, however. True enough, its citizens vigorously opposed the Machado and Batista regimes, when student and worker strikes often crippled the city. It's also true that they supported the armies of Che Guevara and Camilo Cienfuegos when they entered the city in September 1958. But the province had been one of the most developed before the Revolution, and *fidelismo* apparently received little support from the independent-minded people of Camagüey. Hence it is claimed by some city residents that Fidel has been lukewarm to the city.

often containing a mariposa. Be careful—according to local legend, an outsider offered water from a *tinajón* by a local maiden will fall in love and never leave.

The city prospered from cattle raising and, later, sugar, which fostered a local slave-plantation economy. Descendants of the first Spanish settlers evolved into a modestly wealthy bourgeoisie that played a vital role in the national culture. The wealth attracted pirates, who often came ashore as small armies. The unfortunate city was sacked (and almost destroyed) twice during the 17th century—in 1688 and 1679. Today's labyrinthine street layout arose following this period and was designed to forestall such raids.

Many Camagüeyans were themselves notorious smugglers who went against the grain of Spanish authority. "This town has always been looked upon with suspicion by the authorities on account of the strong proclivities its people had for insurrection," wrote Samuel Hazard in

ORIENTATION

The city spreads east-west along the Carretera Central for more than 10 km. It is encircled by a circunvalación, a concrete dual-carriageway that carries virtually no traffic. The Carretera Central arcs south around the city center, then swings southeast as a broad boulevard called Avenida de la Libertad with, at the north end, a bridge—**Puente La Caridad**—over the Río Hatibonico, connecting the area of **La Caridad** to the old city (**Puente Hatibonico** is one block east).

Two plazas compete for status as the official center of town, but I use **Parque Agramonte** as the center. **Calle Martí** bisects the city east-west, passing the north side of Parque Agramonte and linking it to the Carretera Central to the west. **Calle Cisnero** runs north to south, connecting the square with Puente La

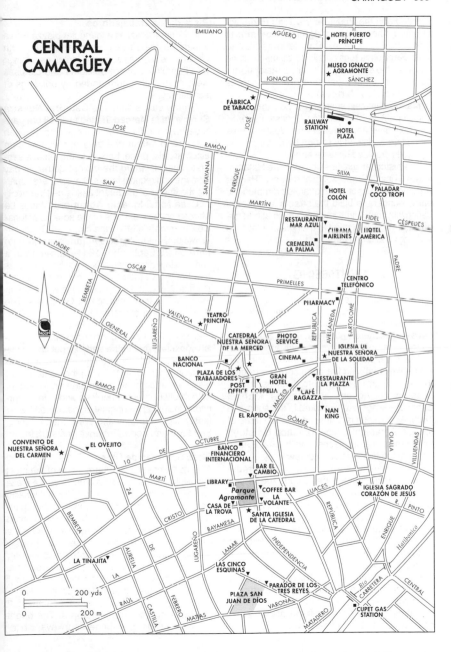

CENTRAL CAMAGÜEY

EMILIANO

AGÜERO

● HOTEL PUERTO PRÍNCIPE

● MUSEO IGNACIO AGRAMONTE

IGNACIO

SÁNCHEZ

★ FÁBRICA DE TABACO

JOSÉ

RAILWAY STATION

● HOTEL PLAZA

RAMÓN

JOSÉ

SANTAYANA

ENRIQUE

SAN

SILVA

MARTÍN

● HOTEL COLÓN

▼ PALADAR COCO TROPI

FIDEL

CÉSPEDES

RESTAURANTE MAR AZUL

CUBANA AIRLINES

HOTEL AMÉRICA

CREMERÍA LA PALMA

P'ADRE

OSCAR

PADRE

● CENTRO TELEFÓNICO

PRIMELLES

EEMBETA

GENERAL

LUGAREÑO

CURAREÑO

VALENCIA

■ PHARMACY

★ TEATRO PRINCIPAL

REPÚBLICA

AVELLANEDA

BARTOLOMÉ

CATEDRAL NUESTRA SEÑORA DE LA MERCED

PHOTO SERVICE

★ IGLESIA DE NUESTRA SEÑORA DE LA SOLEDAD

★ BANCO NACIONAL

CINEMA ■

RAMOS

PLAZA DE LOS TRABAJADORES

POST OFFICE ● COPPELIA

▼ GRAN HOTEL

▼ RESTAURANTE LA PIAZZA

MACEO

▼ CAFÉ RAGAZZA

EL RÁPIDO ▼

GÓMEZ

▼ NAN KING

CONVENTO DE NUESTRA SEÑORA DEL CARMEN ★

▼ EL OVEJITO

OCTUBRE

10

DE

■ BANCO FINANCIERO INTERNACIONAL

OLALLA

VILLUENDAS

MARTÍ

24

LIBRARY ■

Parque Agramonte

■ BAR EL CAMBIO

▼ COFFEE BAR LA VOLANTE

LUACES

★ IGLESIA SAGRADO CORAZÓN DE JESÚS

BEEMETA

CASA DE LA TROVA ▼

CRISTO

★ SANTA IGLESIA DE LA CATEDRAL

REPÚBLICA

R. PINTO

ENRIQUE

Hatibonico

LUGAREÑO

BAYAMESA

LA TINAJITA ▼

AURELIA

DE

LÁMAR

INDEPENDENCIA

0   200 yds

0   200 m

LA

RAÚL

CASTILLA

FEBRERO

MATÍAS

▼ LAS CINCO ESQUINAS

PLAZA SAN JUAN DE DIOS

▼ PARADOR DE LOS TRES REYES

VARONA

MATADERO

RÍO

CARRETERA

CENTRAL

■ CUPET GAS STATION

MOON

Caridad and the **Plaza de los Trabajadores,** the city's other focal point. **Ignacio Agramonte** feeds the Plaza de los Trabajadores east to west. **República** runs parallel to Cisneros, three blocks to the east, and is the city's major north-south thoroughfare (farther north it becomes **Avenida de los Mártires**).

Maceo, the main shopping street, links Martí and República. Maceo is now pedestrians-only, with boutiques and stores selling Western items for dollars and shoddy Cuban items for pesos. Maceo is crowded on weekends.

The historical core lies between the Hatibonico and Tinima Rivers, south and west of Parque Agramonte. Fear of pirate attacks prompted the early founders to build the streets in a meandering labyrinth, with some bearing off at odd angles and others meeting at a single point where invaders could be ambushed.

SIGHTSEEING

Parque Agramonte

A convenient starting point for a walking tour is this attractive plaza—a parade ground in colonial days—at Cisnero and Martí. The square has Victorian lamps, and its trees are ablaze with pink and yellow blossoms in spring. The tousled palms that stand at each corner, shading the square, are dedicated to local patriots— Joaquín de Aguero and Andres Manuel Sánchez—who were executed in the square in 1826. At its center is a life-size bronze statue of Ignacio Agramonte, mounted atop his steed and brandishing his machete, with a half-naked figure of the Indian maiden below.

The square is surrounded by venerable façades, including the beautifully preserved **Casa de la Trova,** on the west side, featuring stunning tilework and antiques and with a huge patio where musical recitals are given.

The **Catedral de Santa Iglesia** looms over the park on its south side. The cathedral was built in 1864 atop a predecessor, which had been established in 1530. In 1688, pirates led by the famous rogue Henry Morgan apparently locked the city fathers in the church and starved them until they coughed up the location of their treasures. It's worth a peek for its statuary and beamed roof over a narrow nave.

Plaza de los Trabajadores

The Workers' Plaza is a triangular piazza with a venerable ceiba tree at its heart. In the 19th century, the square frequently served as a miniature Pamplona, where bullfights and circuses were hosted. It is surrounded by buildings of eclectic styles.

On the east side is the **Catedral Nuestra Señora de la Merced,** dating to 1748 but partly destroyed by fire in 1906. It has recently been restored to former grandeur and contains an elaborate altarpiece. Look in to the left at a separate chapel, where the devout gather to pay homage and request favors at a silver altar bearing the image of the Infant Jesús de Prague.

Casa Natal Ignacio Agramonte faces La Merced on the west side of the square, at Ignacio Agramonte 459, on the corner of Candelaria. Major General Ignacio Agramonte was born here on 23 September 1841. Agramonte, a sugar-estate owner, led a brief yet intense life as head of the Camagüeyan rebel forces during the first War of Independence. He was killed in May 1873 at the Battle of Las Guasimas. The Spanish colonialists seized the Agramonte family assets, and turned the house into a tavern and boarding house. The house was the Spanish consulate during the early Republic.

The beautifully restored house opened as a museum on 11 May 1973, on the centenary of his death in combat. It contains an important art collection, plus mementoes and colonial furniture, including an original piano owned by the family. Open Monday and Wed.-Sat. 1-7 p.m., Sunday 8 am.-noon. Entrance costs US$1.

Plaza San Juan de Dios

The most impressive square—one of the most beautiful in all Cuba—is also known as the Plaza de Padre Olallo. It was here in 1873 that Ignacio Agramonte's corpse was brought by the Spanish and blown to pieces, and the remains burned as a public spectacle. On the west side is a beautiful blue-and-white house, still privately owned, where once lived poet and songwriter Antón Silvio Rodríguez. A bronze plaque on the wall has the words of his famous "El Mayor," which celebrates Agramonte in song.

The plaza is today a national monument. It has been magnificently restored. The bright pastel buildings have huge doorways, whitewashed steps, and beautifully turned *rejas* (wooden window grills). They date from the 18th century and reflect how the city must have looked at its prime, 200 years ago. Visit in late afternoon, when the glow of the fading sun gilds the square.

On the east side is the **Iglesia San Juan de Dios** (open Monday). Adjoining it is a fabulous building with a Moorish façade that was once a hospice and today houses the **Museo San Juan de Dios** and the headquarters of the Centro Provincial de Patrimonio, which is in charge of the city's restoration. It's open Mon.-Sat., 8 a.m.-5 p.m. (US$1)

The pink and yellow building on the north side is **Campaña de Toldeo**, now a restaurant highlighted by a stunning modernist wall mural.

Convento de Nuestra Señora del Carmen

This convent, built in 1825, could be beautiful if restored. It's mostly intact, and the tilework almost pristine, but the *ventrales* are shattered, the plaster much cracked, and the red-tile roof overgrown with ferns. It's on the north side of Martí, six blocks west of Parque Agramonte. Immediately east is a small plaza with cobbled streets and venerable houses painted in bright pastels.

Teatro Principal

Similarly begging for restoration is this once-exquisite theater. Camagüeyans (and tourist literature) claim that it is made entirely of marble, but it's not (not even *mostly*). A modest ocher exterior belies its fabulous interior, only hinted at by the lobby, with huge chandeliers reflected in faded full-length mirrors. Above, light filters through red and yellow *ventrales*. The theater was inaugurated in 1850, and such notables as Enrico Caruso have sung here. It is today the home of the Ballet of Camagüey.

Museum Ignacio Agramonte

This museum (also called the Museo Provincial) on Avenida de los Mártires, tel. 9-7231, is in a huge colonial structure dating from 1884 and formerly a garrison for Spanish cavalry. It later became the Hotel Camagüey, a flashy place that served the rail traffic. Today it exhibits an impressive and eclectic array of Cubana, from artwork, archaeology exhibits, and stuffed flora and fauna to historical records up to the Revolution. Open Tues.-Sat. 9 a.m.-5 p.m. and Sunday 8 a.m.-noon. Entrance costs US$1.

Casa Natal de Nicolás Guillén

Cuban poet Nicolás Guillén was born in this modest house on Calle Principe in 1902. A loyal nationalist and revolutionary and one of Latin America's foremost poets, Guillén was awarded the Lenin Peace Prize and also served as chairman of the National Union of Writers and Artists (UNEAC), which he helped found. Guillén died in 1989. The museum, opened in 1992, contains some of his personal possessions and a library of his works.

Casa Jesús Suárez Gayol

Fulfilling the city's image for revolutionary fervor is this museum, at Calle República 69, honoring the role of Camagüeyans in the Revolution. One such was Jesús Suárez, who was born in this house and died with Che Guevara in Bolivia in 1967. Open Tues.-Sat. 2-10 p.m. and Sunday 10 a.m.-1 p.m.

La Caridad

Several neoclassical buildings dominate the south side of the river, most impressively the **Instituto de Segunda Enseñanza.**

The spacious park southeast of the stone-and-metal **Puente Hatibonico,** which dates from 1773, is quiet and contemplative, with pathways leading past several prerevolutionary statues. It makes a pleasant respite from the bustling city streets.

Portales (colonnaded arcades) run the length of Avenida de la Libertad seven blocks to **Iglesia de la Caridad,** a simple red-tile-roofed, ocher-colored church dating to 1734. It guards an icon of Nuestra Señora de la Caridad (Our Lady of Charity), patroness of Camagüey.

Fábrica de Tabacos

To see cigars being hand-rolled, check out the tobacco factory at the north end of Enrique José Norte. Workers sit at rows of desks in a warehouse-scale room lit by neon lights. The factory receives few visitors, but Hernán Jaitalares will be happy to show you around. It's open for tourists daily, 8-11:30 a.m. and 1:30-4 p.m. Entrance is free, but you should tip Hernán.

Other Sites
One of the most overlooked sites is **Iglesia Sagardo Corazón de Jesús,** on the Plaza de Pablo Trias, two blocks east of Parque Agramonte. Its exterior is dull, but it is very beautiful within, with much marble and gold.

Another church—the tiny, neoclassical **Iglesia Santa Ana,** at the west end of Labrada, is closed (and badly in need of restoration). It dates from 1841. The red-brick **Iglesia Nuestra Señora de la Soledad** (dating from 1755) is similarly dilapidated. The baroque structure with thick bell tower stands at the corner of Agramonte and República. The splendidly frescoed interior is said to have an elaborate wood-beamed ceiling held aloft on massive square columns.

Also worth viewing are the ornate marble tombs in the **Cementerio** on the west side of the old town, south of **Iglesia Santo Cristo del Bien Viaje** at Crísto and the Carretera Central.

ACCOMMODATIONS

Travelers to Camagüey are well served by hotels, though none are anything to write home about. Several feature bargain prices.

Budget
Five km east of town is the **Motel La India,** a basic, pesos-only Cuban facility with recently restored cabins and new furniture.

In town, try the basic **Hotel Isla de Cuba,** on Oscar Primelles, one block west of República, a recently restored Islazul hotel with rooms for US$12 s and US$14 d. There's a TV lounge and restaurant. Three blocks north on República is **Hotel Colón,** where you'll pay US$12 s, US$14 d (US$18 s, US$20 d for an *"especial"* with a/c, TV, mini-bar and telephone). It has an atmospheric lobby with a mahogany bar featuring gilt Corinthian columns and a fabulous picture in stained glass depicting Columbus' landing.

Islazul also operates the **Hotel Puerto Príncipe,** tel. 82490, next to the Museo Ignacio Agramonte. It's a 1960s-era structure with pleasant, recently refurbished, spacious, high-ceilinged rooms with TVs, a/c, and double beds for US$20 s, US$22 d (US$24 s, US$28 d high-season). The restaurant is mediocre. Avoid the upper-floor rooms—the disco is above.

Your best bet is the **Hotel Plaza,** opposite the rail station at the top of República, tel. 82413, another recently restored and atmospheric Islazul hotel. The 67 a/c rooms have nice fabrics and TVs; US$20 s, US$24 d in low season and US$24 s, US$28 d in high season. The atmospheric *cafetería* and restaurant are both popular with locals.

If you've grown fond of Cuba's uninspired assembly-line hotels, try the **Hotel Camagüey,** on the Carretera Central, about four km southeast of downtown, tel. 71970. The 142 a/c rooms are adequate, but modestly furnished; US$17 s, US$23 d in low season, US$35 s, US$42d in high season. It has a pleasant courtyard bar and restaurant. Havanautos has a car rental office here. Hunting trips are offered to Laguna Porvenir and other game reserves. It also has six slightly pricier cabins.

The **Gran Hotel,** in a colonial building on Maceo #67, tel. 9-2093, closed for renovation in 1996 but promises to offer the most atmosphere in town when it reopens (as it may have by now), with 72 rooms in the US$20 range. It has a rooftop restaurant.

The **Hotel América,** tel. 8-2135, does not accept foreigners. Maybe next year? It's on Avellaneda.

If you don't mind being outside town, consider **Villa Tayabito,** off the Carretera, 8.5 km east of town, tel. 71939. This hotel doubles as an alcohol- and drug-addiction treatment center, boasting pleasant grounds and a panoply of activities, from horseback riding to a sauna and even a bowling alley. Modestly furnished rooms cost US$18 s, US$20 d. Cabins cost US$20 s, US$30 d.

Moderate
Cubanacán operates the **Villa Managuan,** surrounded by scrubland, about five km southeast of town on Camino de Guanabaquilla, just off the Carretera Central, tel. 72160 or 72017. It has 34 rooms in *cabinas* around a swimming pool surrounded by large *tinajones.* The restaurant is the high point—very elegant, with *ventrales* and chandeliers. It serves *criollo* food and has buffets when groups are in. There were no guests when I was there. It's very tranquil but overpriced at US$55 s/d, year-round. It has a large children's playground, and a cabaret at night.

FOOD

Dining in Camagüey is no problem. Fill your stomach here if you're traveling eastward into Oriente, where you can reasonably expect to lose weight. (Beer lovers should wash their meals down with **Tinima,** the local brew.)

Dollars Only

The three touristy options include **Campaña de Toledo,** tel. 95888, overlooking the Plaza de Padre Olallo. It's full of ambience, with terra-cotta tile floors and rustic furniture. You can dine under shady eaves in the courtyard out back. *Criollo* meals cost less than US$7. The house specialty is a corn-based stew called *ajiaco.* Next door, Rumbos also operates the dollars-only **Parador de los Tres Reyes,** with a similar setting and mood. It specializes in chorizo but has a large menu of *criollo* dishes and snacks. Equally atmospheric is **El Overjito,** at Calle Hermano Aguero #280, tel. 92540. The restaurant is said to specialize in lamb. Alas, when I last visited the menu was restricted to burgers (US$1), soups (US$2), salads, and a few *criollo* items.

El Rápido, Cuba's KFC-type fast-food café at the corner of Maceo and Gómez, serves hamburgers, fried chicken, and other fast foods (avoid the terrible pizza).

Peso Eateries

So where do the locals eat? Try **Nan King,** at República #222, tel. 95455, with suitably Chinese decor—fans, porcelain, and Buddhas—and a few Chinese dishes (average US$4), but mostly pizzas and *criollo* food. A shrimp entrée costs US$7. **Mar Azul Restaurant,** at the corner of República and Fidel Céspedes, has set meals for 12 pesos, including salad, *congrí, papas fritas,* and *bistec.* And **La Piazza,** catercorner to the Iglesia Nuestra Señora de la Soledad, is very popular. You can dine below at the counter or, more elegantly, on the upstairs balcony. The fare changes daily. Hamburgers cost two pesos! The restaurant in the **Hotel Plaza** is another favorite of locals, with good reason. You may still be able to pay in pesos. Check out the goat dishes. (I've not eaten at the **Hotel Camagüey,** but reports are that it's a dismal experience.)

Another hotel restaurant worth trying is in the Hotel Puerto Príncipe.

On Parque Agramonte, **La Volante** is housed in an old building with tall, wide-open windows offering views over the square. It serves basic *criollo* fare; nine pesos (50 cents) will buy fried chicken, beans and rice, and salad.

There are also several eateries north of town on the road to Nuevitas, including **El Pavito,** specializing in turkey dishes.

I haven't tried any *paladares,* but the **Coco Tropi** looks pleasant; it's at the corner of Bartolomé Masó and José Ramón Silva.

Snacks and Ice Cream

There are lots of small *heladerías* and cubbyholes selling *refrescoes* and snacks along República. You can also buy mineral water for one peso at **Agua de Tinajón,** at the corner of Fidel Céspedes. **Coppelia** (with entrances on Maceo and at the southwest corner of Plaza de la Trabajadores) is usually packed when open (Tues.-Sun. 3-10 p.m.), as is the **Cremería la Palma,** on República, and the open-air, dollar-only **Café Ragazza,** midway up Maceo.

There's a little coffee shop on the northeast corner of the main square selling cups of coffee for 90 centavos.

ENTERTAINMENT AND EVENTS

In early February, the **Jornadas de la Cultura Camagüeyana** celebrates the city's founding. **Carnival,** traditionally held around 26 July, may soon be resurrected. A religious festival is held on 8 September to honor Nuestra Señora de la Caridad, the city's patron saint.

The world-acclaimed **Camagüey Ballet,** founded shortly after the Revolution and often on tour, performs works from classical to contemporary at the Teatro Principal, as does the city's symphony orchestra.

The **Casa de la Trova,** at Calle Cisneros #171, on the west side of Parque Agramonte, has a bar in the rear courtyard where you can enjoy traditional music Tues.-Fri. 5-8:30 p.m. and weekends 8:30-11 p.m. (US$1). The famous folkloric group *Caidije* often visits from its base in Nuevitas. You may be able to hear them perform in the **Casa de Promoción Cultural,** opposite the Palacio de Justicia on Calle Cisneros #258. The center even presents jazz concerts now and then. A **puppet theater,** across the way at Cisneros #259, offers performances each Fri.-Sun. at 3 and 10 p.m.

Hotel Puerto Príncipe has a **cabaret** *espectáculo* and disco nightly at 9 p.m. (US$1). **Hotel Camagüey** also offers an "*espectáculo* under the stars" Thurs.-Sun at 9 p.m. Entrance costs US$2. The Hotel Camagüey, also features a fashion show and disco at 8:30 p.m. on Wednesday. **El Colonial,** on Agramonte, also has open-air cabaret, as does the Gran Hotel. The cabarets are followed by discos.

The movie-house 50 meters west of La Piazza restaurant shows several movies each day (most are timeless Hollywood classics).

My favorite watering hole is the atmospheric dollars-only **El Cambio,** on the northeast corner of the main square. The moody decor, old jukebox, popcorn machine, and lively music helps attract a young crowd late in the evening. It's the closest thing to a hangout you'll find. Beers cost US$1, but you can buy a bottle of rum for US$3, and a shot of cheap *aguardente* costs a mere 35 cents.

El Cinco Esquinas, on Plaza de San Juan, and **La Tinajita,** five blocks west, are good places to raise a glass with locals.

SHOPPING

Camagüey has few touristy shops. The *tinajones* are a bit hefty to take home as souvenirs, but you can buy miniatures, sometimes painted with Cuban landscapes. You can buy cigars at the **Fábrica de Tabaco** and honey from the honey factory (nine pesos a bottle), both on Enrique José Norte.

INFORMATION AND SERVICES

The main **post office** is on the south side of Plaza de las Trabajadores. There's another one and a **Centro Telefónico** next to each other on Avellaneda and Oscar Primelles; both are open 24 hours. You can also send letters and packages by express mail with **DHL** in the Hotel Camagüey, tel. 71542. It's open weekdays 9 a.m.-6 p.m. and Saturday 8:30 a.m.-noon.

CAMAGÜEY USEFUL TELEPHONE NUMBERS

Police . . . . tel. 116
Ambulance . . . . tel. 9-2860
Hospital . . . . tel. 8-3213
Airport . . . . tel. 9-2156 or 6-1010
Terminal de Ómnibus
    (Reservations) . . . . tel. 7-1602
Railway Station (Reservations) . . . . tel. 8-3214

There's a **Banco Nacional** on Plaza de los Trabajadores and a **Banco Financiero Internacional** two blocks south. You'll find locals exchanging dollars on Maceo and República.

There's no *clínica internacional.* However, there are several **hospitals,** and you'll find a 24-hour **pharmacy** on Avellaneda and Primelles. Servimed operates a medical facility—**Tayabito,** tel./fax 33-5548—for foreigners at Carretera Central Km 8.5. Tayabito specializes in rehabilitating alcoholics and drug addicts. Seven-day diagnostic programs are offered. Hospitalization programs last three months, including the first week with an accompanying person.

The **library** is Biblioteca Julio Mella, on Parque Agramonte. It occasionally sponsors art shows. **Photo Service** sells instamatic cameras, plus film and batteries. You'll find a travel agency—**Viajes Altamira,** in the Hotel Plaza, tel. 83551.

The only bookstore is **Librería Vietnam,** on República. It has the usual dismal array of Spanish-language socialist texts and novels.

There are two **Cupet gas stations** within 100 yards of each other on the Carratera Central, just west of Puente La Caridad.

GETTING THERE

By Bus
Bus no. 500 departs Havana's main bus terminal for Camagüey daily at 8:35 and 10:30 a.m. and 5:35 p.m. (seven hours; 27 pesos). There is also daily service from Báyamo, Cienfuegos, Holguín, Las Tunas, Santa Clara, Sancti Spíritus, and Santiago. The buses are generally sold out days or weeks in advance, but your dollar bills may win you preference.

By Air
Cubana has flights from Havana on Monday at 3:10 p.m., Tuesday, Thursday, Saturday, and Sunday at 9:30 a.m., Wednesday at 12:20 and 6 p.m., and Friday at 6 p.m. (US$60). Cubana also flies from Santiago. The Ignacio Agramonte airport is 14 km northeast of the city, on the road to Morón.

Air UK has weekly charter flights from London-Gatwick to Camagüey, and Royal Airlines offers charters from Toronto.

By Train
Camagüey is on the main railway between Havana and Santiago and is well served by trains. A train departs Havana for Camagüey daily at 6:35 p.m. You can also take trains from Santa Clara (no. 19, departing 3:12 p.m.) and Ciego de Ávila (no. 23, 6:10 a.m.). A train from Morón departs for Camagüey at 1:32 p.m. Sample fares include Havana, US$19.50; Santiago, US$13; Matanzas, US$16; Ciego de Ávila, US$3.50, Santa Clara, US$9; and Las Tunas, US$4.50. Foreigners can buy tickets the same day (Cubans need a minimum one-week notice) from the dollars-only office upstairs in the ticket office. Be sure to note the platform from which your train leaves.

GETTING AROUND

The city's historical core is for walking. The streets are too narrow and labyrinthine for buses and taxis. Nonetheless, **bus no. 10** plies a route between the Terminal de Ómnibus Municipales, near the train station on Avenida Carlos Finlay, and the historic quarter. You'll find **horse-drawn cabs** outside the rail station, and near the Iglesia de Nuestra Señora de la Soledad, on República. *Colectivo* taxis (called *piqueros* locally) hang out outside the rail and bus stations. For a tourist taxi, call 7-2428.

You can rent cars from **Havanautos,** in the Hotel Camagüey.

GETTING AWAY

By Bus
The Terminal de Ómnibuses Intermunicipales is two km southeast of town, on the Carretera Central, and is served by local buses (no. 2, 14, and 72). Buses operate to Havana four times daily, as well as to Ciego de Ávila, Cienfuegos, Holguín, Las Tunas, Manzanillo, Matanzas, Morón, Nuevitas, Santa Clara, Sancti Spíritus, Santiago, and other destinations. Tickets are usually sold many days in advance. Offer to pay in dollars and a seat may magically appear.

Buses and little commuter trains to Nuevitas, Santa Cruz del Sur, and other provincial destinations depart from the Terminal Ferro-Omnibus, next to the train station on Avenida Carlos Finlay.

By Air
Flights to Havana depart Camagüey's Ignacio Agramonte Airport, tel. 61000, on Monday at 5:20 p.m., Tuesday, Thursday, Saturday, and Sunday at 11:40 a.m., Wednesday at 2:30 and 8:15 p.m., and Friday at 8:20 p.m. The Cubana office is at República #400, tel. 91338, open Mon.-Fri. 8:15 a.m.-4 p.m. and Saturday 8:15-11 a.m. Avenida Carlos Finlay leads northeast from town to the airport and on to Nuevitas and Santa Lucía, on the north coast.

Bus no. 6 runs to the airport from Parque Finlay, opposite the Terminal Ferro-Ómnibus.

By Train
The Havana-bound train departs Camagüey at 11:30 p.m. Trains from Camagüey depart for Santa Clara at 5:18 a.m. (no. 20), Ciego de Ávila at 8 a.m. (no. 310), and Morón at 6:50 a.m. Other buses serve other destinations.

VICINITY OF CAMAGÜEY

MINAS

This small town, 37 km northeast of Camagüey, is a worthy stop en route to Santa Lucía, or in its own right for its violin factory (the only one in Cuba), at the east end of town. The factory—**Fábrica de Instrumentos Musicales**—was opened in 1976, when a guitar-maker named Álvaro Súarez Ravinal applied his 50 years of experience in making violins. Súarez, who wanted to pass his skills on to the next generation, gained the support of the Cuban Ministry of Culture. Guided by Súarez's genius, workers turn native hardwoods into elegantly curved violins, violas, and cellos. Guitars are also made here. Visitors are welcome (US$2; closed Sunday).

Minas lies in the lee of **Sierra De Camajan**, dramatically backdropped by cliffs up to 200 meters tall in river-carved limestone gorges called *cangliones* and resembling the *mogotes* of Pinar del Río. The most famous ravine is **Pasaje de Paredones,** a popular excursion spot for Cubans. Others are concentrated near Solá, in the Sierra de Cubitas, 60 km north of Camagüey, and near Belén, southeast of Camagüey.

SANTA CRUZ

South of Camagüey, the land slopes gradually downhill through parched savanna. Farther south, the land flattens out, and first sugarcane, then marshland replace pasture. In the distance you can see beach-fringed coral cays floating offshore. The road dead-ends at Santa Cruz, a lifeless town 75 km of Camagüey. The town trails south from its center (a circular square) for about three km to the Golfo de Guancanayabo. Watching the citizens lying beneath shady porches, wasting the hours, you sense that they are watching their lives pass them by.

The shorefront faces dirty, brown-stained water. There's no beach. At the eastern end, a rusting fishing fleet harbors at a **fish processing plant,** Combinado Pesquero Argeríco Lara.

Food and Services
You'll find a couple of basic peso restaurants, a pizzeria, and a **Coppelia** south of the square. There's a **Cupet gas station** 400 meters north of the main square, and a **Banco Nacional** on the square's southwest corner.

A bus runs from Camagüey (two hours; 2.50 pesos).

CAMAGÜEY TO GUÁIMARO

East of Camagüey is cattle country, parched in summer by a scowling wind that bows down the long flaxen grasses. The sun-struck cattle gather in the shade beneath lonesome trees festooned with epiphytes. The Carretera Central passes numerous ranches—*ganaderías*—worked by *vaqueros* with lassoes and machetes lashed to the flanks of their horses. There is only one town of note—Guáimaro—between Camagüey and the border with Las Tunas province.

Hacienda La Belén Reserve
Southeast of Camagüey is an upland area—the **Sierra Guaicanama-Najasa**—marked by *cangliones,* the dramatic, sheer-faced, free-standing hummocks (mini-mountains, really). The formations lie within the 4,000-hectare Hacienda La Belén Reserve, in Najasa Municipality. The turnoff is at Sibanicú, 42 km east of Camagüey.

The reserve has two distinct regions—undulating plains with scrub and semi-deciduous woodland, and tropical montane forest. It protects 110 species of higher plants (six are endangered), a rare cactus called *mamilaria* (found only here), large numbers of *jutías,* and at least 80 bird species, including parrots. The hacienda pastures are nibbled by exotic species such as black and Indian antelope. Hiking trails leads to several mineral springs with cool pools.

Accommodations: The reserve has a modern chalet for eight people. **Alcona S.A.,** tel. 22-2526, fax 33-1532, offers trips here. A weeklong package that includes two nights in Havana and five at Belén costs US$805 per person.

GUÁIMARO

Guáimaro, 65 km east of Camagüey, is a town of modest size (pop. 20,000) but historic importance. There's little of interest to see, except an intriguing statue in the town square—a round granite column with a carving of the Cuban flag wrapped around it and bronze plaques honoring local heroes of the War of Independence at its base. The monument commemorates the opening in April 1869 of the Constitutional Assembly, where the first Cuban constitution was drafted, Carlos Manuel de Céspedes elected President of the Free Republic of Cuba, and the abolition of slavery decreed. The building where the 1869 Assembly was held today houses the **Guáimaro History Museum.**

No specific mention of women's liberties was included in the Constitution, prompting a leading revolutionary and Camagüeyan, Ana Betancourt, to announce to the Assembly that, "You have destroyed the slavery of color by emancipating the slave. The moment of women's liberation has arrived." Betancourt and her husband, Ignacio Mora, fought side by side in battle and together edited *El Mambí,* the revolutionary newspaper. Mora was eventually shot, but Betancourt died a "free" woman in Madrid in 1901. Her ashes were brought from Spain on the 150th anniversary of her birth and deposited at the base of a monument outside the museum erected in her honor.

At the east end of town is a huge agricultural showground used for cattle fairs, including the Feria Exposición Ganaderia, held in February.

Accommodations, Food, and Services
The town has a few basic restaurants, plus the **Hotel Guáimaro,** tel. 82102, a 40-room Soviet-style motel with a pleasant restaurant a half-mile east of town. It accepts foreigners. Rooms cost 17 pesos (or US$17) and have TVs, refrigerators, and private baths (cold water only). East of Hotel Guáimaro, a dirt road leads uphill to **Centro Recreativo Las Colinas,** a large *ranchita* restaurant and bar dramatically perched atop the hill. It rents basic *cabañas.*

There's a **Cupet gas station** 400 meters west of the square.

JÁRDINES DE LA REINA

This chain of coral cays forms a barrier to the Golfo de Ana María beneath Ciego de Ávila province. Whoever named them the Járdines de la Reina (Garden of the Queens) had an eye for beauty. The archipelago contains literally hundreds of deserted cays, virtually all of them ringed by beautiful white sand beaches—sirens one and all.

The larger westernmost cays are called the "Twelve-Mile Labyrinth." An extensive coral reef runs along its southern shore, where marine turtles add to the attractions for scuba divers. Bright pink flamingoes can be seen wading in the briny shallows. There's a turtle farm on **Cayo Anclitas.**

This is virginal terrain, with no lodgings at press time. Appropriately, it is called Cuba's "Last Paradise." A hotel was supposedly being constructed at **Algodón Grande,** and another was begun on **Cayo Caguamas** but abandoned since the Special Period. The waters are fished by fleets, and you can buy more lobster than you can possibly eat.

Getting There
The only way to reach the cays is by boat from Marina Júcaro or aboard your own private yacht. Puertosol offers eight-hour **excursions** to Cayo Cana (US$39) or Cayo Algodones, plus one-hour excursions to Cayo Chocolate (US$12).

Simon Charles gives a good account of the passages in his book *Cruising Guide to Cuba.*

Scuba Diving: Puertosol offers scuba diving packages aboard live-aboard vessels and a small "floating hotel" that can accommodate 22 people. The per passenger cost of US$75 daily includes meals. Programs are seven or 14 days. One-day dives are also available. One dive costs US$27 (US$32 for night dives); two dives cost US$39. A full-day diving and fishing package is US$110 per person, including transfer from Júcaro. Transfers by launch cost US$5.

MORÓN AND VICINITY

Morón (pop. 50,000), 37 km due north of Ciego de Ávila and the gateway to Cayo Coco, is known as the City of the Rooster, a name bequeathed in the 18th century by settlers from Morón de la Frontera, in Andalusia, Spain. The immigrants recalled a 16th-century tale about an abusive official who conducted himself "like a gamecock" *(gallo)* and was finally beaten and expelled from the Andalusian town, where a monument of a plucked rooster was erected to recall the victory. In the 1950s, Morón's city fathers erected a rooster at the entrance to town. Fulgencio Batista was present for the unveiling. After the Revolution, an officer in the rebel army ordered the monument's destruction. In 1981, the city government decided to erect another cockerel in bronze at the foot of a clock tower fitted with an amplifier so that citizens (called Moronians) could hear the rooster crowing daily at 6 a.m. and 6 p.m. So can you, since it stands outside the entrance to the Hotel Morón.

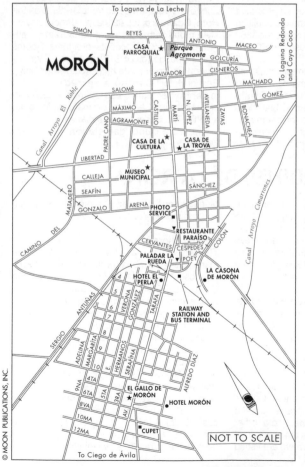

The city is enclosed to north and east by a vast quagmire of sedge, water, and reed in the path of major bird migration routes. It is beginning to prosper again from tourists en route to Cayo Coco and the hunting and fishing reserves north of town.

Orientation

Morón stretches north-south along the main street, Avenida Martí. South of the town center, Martí widens and becomes Avenida Tarafa, which leads south to Ciego de Ávila. Calle Libertad crosses Martí in the heart of town. It leads west to Chambas and east (via the Carretera Turiguanó) to Laguna la Redonda and Cayo Coco (most of the streets are one-way, and you'll enter Morón from these two destinations along Salomé Machado, which meets Martí three blocks north of Libertad).

Things to See and Do

The town has no distinguished sites, despite being full of colorful columns and colonnades.

Much of the city is dilapidated, including the semi-derelict **Iglesia de Lourdes** at **Parque Agramonte,** at the north end of Martí. The park is surrounded by pretty houses, including the **Casa Parroquial.** Morón also has two museums, a **Casa de la Cultura,** and a **Casa de Trovadores.** The **Municipal Museum,** on Castillo, one block west of Martí, displays more than 1,600 pieces of pre-Columbian culture. The Teutonic-style **railway station,** built in 1923, is also interesting.

East of Morón rises **Loma de Cunagua,** a strange hill shaped like Ayers Rock in Australia (but green instead of red).

Outside the city are the remains of one of a series of small forts known as **La Trocha de Júcaro.** The Spanish colonial army built the 50-km-wide barrier from Morón to Júcaro, on the south coast, at the narrowest point in Cuba. La Trocha featured a thick wooden barricade and 43 forts meant to stop the east-west progress of the rebel army under General Máximo Gómez. The area around Morón was the scene of heavy fighting, and the town itself was captured by rebel troops in 1876 (there's a memorial to the event outside the city).

Accommodations and Food
There are three hotels in town. The impecunious should head to the basic **Hotel El Perla,** tel. 3901, which has rooms for 16 pesos. It's on the main street, opposite the rail station.

Hotel Morón, Avenida Tarafa, tel. 3901, fax 3076, operated by Cubanacán, is a modest but acceptable recently renovated concrete two-story hotel with 144 rooms, eight of which are junior suites, all with satellite TV (US$30 s, US$39 d low-season, US$38 s, US$44 d high-season). Suites in *cabañas* cost US$60. Facilities include a tourism desk, massage salon, barber shop, swimming pool, bar, coffee shop, and disco. The hotel is a base for hunters.

Far more atmospheric is **La Casona de Morón,** Cristóbal Colón #41, Ciego de Ávila, tel. 33-4563, fax 33-5026, a Horizontes property also known as the International Hunting and Fishing Lodge La Rabiche. This colonial mansion has seven a/c rooms with private baths, TVs, and mini-bars (US$25 s, US$35 d). There's a bar, a grill, an elegant restaurant, and a swimming pool. You can have the contents of your bag frozen or prepared for dinner.

There are very few eateries in town. Try the restaurants in the Hotel Morón and La Casona del Morón. Rumbos has a café—**Club Ferroviario**—at the side of the railway station. **Paladar La Rueda** and **Restaurante Paraíso** look okay. The first is one block north of the railway station, the latter is on Martí, three blocks south of Libertad.

Entertainment and Events
The city hosts an annual "water carnival" that takes place in a canal leading to Laguna de la Leche. Musicians serenade the crowd while the city's prettiest young maidens row boats decorated with garlands of flowers.

The **Casa de Trovadores,** founded in 1981, is home to 30 musical groups and singers, and holds performances of traditional music, plus a *bolero* night and a children's *trova.* It's on Libertad, one block east of Martí. For hip-hopping nightlife, head to the **Discoteca Discoral,** in the Hotel Morón, or **La Cueva,** three km north of town on the road to Laguna de la Leche.

Services
The town boasts a modern 613-bed **hospital,** at the east end of Libertad. A mediocre stock of batteries and camera supplies can be had, with luck, at **Photo Service,** on Martí, three blocks south of Libertad.

The **Cupet gas station** is one block south of the Hotel Morón.

Getting There
By Bus: Bus no. 505 departs Havana for Morón daily at 10:05 a.m., arriving at 5:20 p.m. (24 pesos).

By Train: Morón is on the northern line that runs from Nuevitas to Santa Clara, with a branch line from Morón to Ciego de Ávila. Five trains

MORÓN USEFUL TELEPHONE NUMBERS

Police . . . . tel. 116
Ambulance . . . . tel. 3551
Hospital . . . . tel. 3531
Terminal de Ómnibus . . . . tel. 3774
Railway Station . . . . tel. 3683

daily serve Morón from Ciego de Ávila, including a second-class train (no. 312) departing at 9:41 p.m. Trains depart Camagüey for Morón daily at 8 a.m. (no. 310) and 6:50 p.m. (no. 312).

By Air: Cubana operates flights to Máximo Gómez airport, about 15 miles south of town, midway between Ciego de Ávila and Morón.

By Car: There are two routes from Ciego de Ávila—via the town of Villa and via Ciro Redondo. Both are well maintained.

Getting Around

Horse-drawn carriages congregate outside the railway station. You can also hire one outside the Hotel Morón for a ride around town.

Getting Away

By Bus: The bus station is next to the railway station, on Avenida Tarafa. Buses leave regularly for Ciego de Ávila, Havana, and elsewhere.

By Air: Cubana flights depart for Havana on Tuesday, Thursday, and Sunday at 9:55 a.m. and on Saturday at 9:55 a.m. and 2:55 p.m.

By Train: Trains depart the railway station for Ciego de Ávila at 12:05 (train no. 833) and 6:30 a.m. (no. 835) and 4:00 (no. 841) and 7:13 p.m., for Camagüey at 3:13 a.m. (no. 309) and 1:32 p.m. (no. 311), for Júcaro via Ciego de Avila at 4:50 a.m. (no. 323), for Santa Clara at 5:55 a.m. (no. 204), for Nuevitas at 6:20 a.m. (no. 325), and for Esmeralda at 8:10 p.m. (no. 327).

WEST OF MORÓN

Two km east of Chambas, a road leads north to the fishing village of **Punta Alegre,** where you can hire a boat to take you to Cayo Guillermo. The road ends at the village of **Máximo Gómez,** dominated by a large *central.* There's a modestly appealing beach, Playa Brisas del Mar.

Another road leads southwest from Chambas to **Florencia,** famous throughout Cuba as a center for horseback riding and rodeo. Rumbos offers a horseback excursion from here into the hills to a place called Boquerón, near where an enormous dam has been under construction for over a decade. The leisurely ride takes you past groves of bananas, palms, ceibas (silk-cotton trees), and guavas. For the last three

km, you pass beneath a rocky cliff. Once in Boquerón, you can swim in the cool river and enjoy a lunch of roast suckling pig.

LAGUNA DE LA LECHE

This 66.5-square-km lake, five km due north of Morón, is named for its milky complexion, which derives when deposits of gypsum and calcium carbonate are stirred up from the lakebed by breezes. The lake is chock-full of tilapia, carp, snook, and tarpon. It is fringed by mangroves and woodlands. Birdlife is abundant, including several thousand flamingos that occasionally fly in from the Bahía de Perros.

A recreation area lies at the southern shore, at **La Boca.** You can rent **rowboats** here. Rumbos operates **La Tarralloa** restaurant, which serves seafood and *criollo* dishes.

Getting There: From Morón, take Martí north to Parque Agramonte, turn right, then left on López

Aguachales de Falla Game Reserve

The lagoon is favored by bird-hunters. Aguachales, on the northwest shores of the lagoon, features seven small lakes surrounded by forest abounding in white-crowned pigeon, doves, ducks, quail, guinea fowl, and other gamebirds. Canals connect the lakes and lead to 24 shooting towers.

Hunting seasons are: wild pigeons, July 15 to September 15; migratory ducks, October 15 to March 15; quail, November to March; pigeons, September to March.

Hunting packages (US$85 per day) are offered from the Hotel Morón and La Casona de Morón.

LAGO LA REDONDA

Fourteen km north of Morón, on the road to Cayo Coco, you'll pass a turnoff for **Centro de Pescadores La Redonda,** a basic angling center on the shores of this large lagoon. The lake claims the largest concentrations of bass in Cuba and as such is an angler's paradise. Again, fishing programs are handled through the Hotel Morón and La Casona de Morón. I was quoted US$36 for spinning and casting; fly-fishing costs US$65. Prices include launch and guide, lunch, and morning and afternoon fishing.

The lagoon is connected to the Bahía de Perros and open sea by a canal. Private boaters can berth here. There are eight moorings with electricity and water, and gas is available.

There's a restaurant and a bar, whose barman makes great *mojitos*.

COMUNIDAD CELIA SÁNCHEZ

This eye-catching "Dutch village," atop a hillock rising above Isla de Turiguanó, 28 km north of Morón, makes you do a double take. The clique of 59 gable-roofed houses supported by timber-beam façades transports you lyrically back to Holland. The village is named for Fidel Castro's secretary, lover, and revolutionary alter-ego, who apparently conceived of the village, known locally as the Pueblo Holandés de Turiguanó. It nestles on the slopes of the Loma del Pavo.

Turiguanó was a US-owned private cattle estate before the Revolution. It was cut off from Morón by swampy marshes. In 1960-61, the land was expropriated, the swamps drained, a paved highway built, and modern houses in Dutch style built for the 30 or so families who lived here. New apartments have since been added, and other farmers resettled from other areas. The community serves as a cattle-rearing center for the island's high-yield native beef breed, the Santa Gertrudis.

The road swings 90 degrees to the east at Comunidad Celia Sánchez and continues five km to Playa La Tinaja, at the village of Manatí. One km east of Comunidad Celia Sánchez is the turnoff, to the left, for Cayo Coco.

CAYO COCO

This 364-square-km cay is a stunner, and not simply on account of its 21 km of superlative beaches and limpid waters. For both scuba divers and birders, it is a destination par excellence. The island is separated from the mainland by Bahía de Perros (Bay of Dogs) and joined to it by a man-made *tombolo* (land bridge). Cayo Coco is named for a bird, the roseate ibis, or *coco*.

The whiter-than-white beaches are divided into five separate sections, most importantly **Playa Palma Real** (Royal Palm Beach), where the island's only hotel is located. At least 12 additional properties are currently on the books, with a planned capacity of 13,000 hotel rooms under the existing tourism master plan.

Housing was also being built for employees, who at press time were being bussed daily from Morón, 18 miles away. US journalists often misrepresent this situation, criticizing it as "tourism apartheid." But the simple truth is that there is not, and never has been a Cuban settlement on the island, so the staff have to be brought in daily. The largely deserted island is inhabited by a few poor fishermen and charcoal-burners. As it happens, there's a *campismo* for Cubans at Playa Uva Caleta.

Cayo Coco was immortalized by Ernest Hemingway. The novelist gloried in waking up there early in the morning, to set sail with the sun at his back, advancing with an alert eye through a canal heading for a line of dark green keys rising out of the water till he was close enough to see their sandy beaches. In *Islands in the Stream,* his protagonist, Thomas Hudson, sets foot on the beach at Puerto Coco seeking traces of Nazi soldiers. Wandering farther inland, he discovers the lagoon where flamingos come to feed at high tide.

Cayo Coco has Cuba's largest flamingo colony, at least 2,000 strong (estimates vary widely—up to 10,000), concentrated between Punta Almácigo and Punta del Perro. The rose-pink birds seem to float atop the water, like mirages. Every day, they fly over the north end of the *tombolo* shortly after sunrise and again at dusk.

Flamingos are one of 158 bird species here, including the miniature hummingbird, Cuban cuckoo, ibis, herons, egrets, and sea-swallows. Migratory birds flock here, too, in vast numbers, and ducks and other waterfowl are common in the soupy shallows. The most prominent animals are *jabelí*—wild pigs—and endemic iguanas (if you don't see them in the wild, check 'em out in the iguana pit at Hotel Tryp). There are even deer. The island (90% of which is covered by scrub vegetation) is a protected reserve; no hunting is allowed.

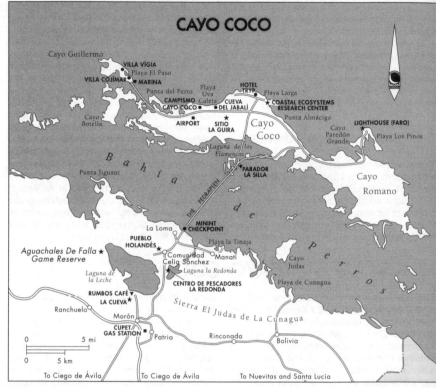

There are four nature trails, including to **Loma de Puerto sand dunes** and an **interpretive trail,** three km west of the Hotel Tryp.

THE *PEDRAPLEN*

Cayo Coco is connected by a 27-km land-bridge to the north coast of Cuba. The bridge, completed in 1988 and called the *Pedraplen,* is made of solid landfill and cuts the Bahía de Perros in two, preventing the natural flow of currents (with who-knows-what potential long-term effects for the ecology). Word is that the now-still waters are becoming nutrient-deficient and wildlife is already beginning to suffer.

MININT (Ministry of the Interior) has a security checkpoint at the entrance to the bridge.

It's a fabulous drive. On clear days, the transparent, mirror-calm waters reflect the clouds, mirages form, and the distant cays seem to float in midair, shimmering in the heat like a sort of dreamworld between hallucination and reality.

At its northern end, the road snakes along the cays that precede Cayo Coco, winding and looping past briny shallows in shades of pea-green and jade. Brine glistens in crusty patches picked over by herons and egrets. And gnarled trees (drowned in recent years) add to the dramatic effect.

Drive carefully. There are no barriers on the sides of the narrow road, which is deeply pot-holed in places, so one mistake and you'll be in the drink.

Eventually, you reach a traffic circle. The road to the right leads east to the marina and neighboring Cayo Romano and Cayo Paredon, where there are two lonely and beautiful beaches and a lighthouse. The road to the left leads west to the airport and Cayo Guillermo. The Hotel Tryp and main beaches are straight ahead; at the shore, there's a T-junction, with the hotel to the left. Turn right for Coastal Ecosystems Research Center and **Playa Las Coloradas,** a lonesome three-km-long beach.

Coastal Ecosystems Research Center
The center, opened in 1991, is part of Cuba's Academy of Sciences and employs a staff of 26 specialists responsible for preserving the biodiversity on the Sabana-Camagüey archipelago, including its 1,000 km of beachfront. The center is supported by the UN Development Program and the Caribbean Community. It also is studying the impact of cattle ranching in the region, plus the impacts of man on the ecology of Laguna La Redonda.

Visitors are welcome.

ACCOMMODATIONS

Campers may be able to pitch a tent at the *campismo* at Playa Uva Caleta, or at Playa Las Coloradas. Water is available.

At press time, a deluxe hotel was being built by Gran Caribe and a Spanish hotel company at Playa Las Coloradas. Until then, your sole option

is the **Hotel Tryp,** Cayo Coco, Ciego de Ávila, tel. 30-1311, fax 30-1386, or, in Havana, tel. 33-3202, fax 33-3292; in Spain, Tryp Hoteles, Mauricio Legendre 16, 28046 Madrid, tel. 315-32-46, fax 314-3156. This massive complex, formerly the Guitart Caya Coco Caribbean Village, sounds unappetizingly Russian. But *wow!* This world-class resort covers 6.7 hectares behind a four-km-long beach. A cobbled humpback bridge leads across an *estero* to an eye-pleasing, make-believe, contemporary interpretation of a colonial village.

The resort has 1,000 rooms in 85 two- and three-story Spanish villa-style units spread widely amid landscaped grounds that feature three large amoeba-shaped swimming pools. The rooms are nicely furnished, with cavernous bathrooms with large mirrors and heaps of marble. Each room has a/c, satellite TV, radio, mini-bar, and 24-hour room service.

It's a very popular and active hotel and has something missing in many Cuban resorts—vitality! The clientele is mostly Canadian, Argentinian, and French. A daily newsletter tells what daily activities are on.

You have a choice of an all-inclusive package or room-only. The former includes use of all facilities and watersports. All-inclusive rates range from US$87 s, US$166 d in low season to US$158 s, US$280 d in high season. A bed-and-breakfast rate is also offered. A three-star extension is to be built next door.

ERNEST HEMINGWAY, NAZI HUNTER

In May 1942, Ernest Hemingway showed up at the US embassy in Havana with a proposal to fit the *Pilar* out as a Q-boat, with .50-caliber machine guns, other armaments, and a trained crew with himself at the helm. The boat would navigate the cays off the north coast of Cuba, ostensibly collecting specimens on behalf of the American Museum of Natural History, but in fact on the lookout for Nazi U-boats, which Hemingway intended to engage and disable. The writer was "quite prepared to sacrifice his beloved vessel in exchange for the capture or sinking of an enemy submarine."

Hemingway's friend, Col. John W. Thornason Jr. was Chief of Naval Intelligence for Central America and pulled strings to get the plan approved. The

vessel was "camouflaged" and duly set out for the cays. Gregorio Fuentes—who from 1938 until the writer's death was in charge of the *Pilar*—went along and served as the model for Antonio in *Islands in the Stream,* Hemingway's novel based on his real-life adventures.

They patrolled for two years. Several times they located and reported the presence of Nazi submarines that the US naval or air force were later able to sink. Only once, off Cayo Mégano, did Hemingway come close to his dream: a U-boat suddenly surfaced while the *Pilar* was at anchor. Unfortunately, it dipped back below the surface and disappeared before Hemingway could get close.

FOOD

The Hotel Tryp has four restaurants (nonguests may be able to purchase a day-pass that includes meals). The menu in the Italian restaurant (which has a lively piano bar) isn't very inspired, and the food quality I thought mediocre.

On one of the little cays that precede Cayo Coco, about 16 km north of the MININT checkpoint, is **Parador La Silla,** a thatched wayside café and restaurant with a *mirador* from which you can watch the flamingoes make their daily pilgrimage. Rumbos has two other roadside cafés along the way to Cayo Guillermo and at the junction to Las Coloradas, where there's also a beachside restaurant selling seafood and fried chicken dishes.

The most atmospheric place is **Cueva del Jabalí,** five km west of the Hotel Tryp. The cave features a restaurant and bar, with tunnels leading to various rooms. It's open for dinner only.

ENTERTAINMENT AND EVENTS

Nightly entertainment at the Hotel Tryp includes theme parties, karaoke, and live bands. There's a disco.

A **cabaret *espectáculo*** is offered on Tuesday and Friday at 10 p.m. at the Cueva del Jabalí. Entrance is free. Excursions are available from the Hotel Tryp. Bring repellent; the mosquitoes are fierce.

SPORTS AND RECREATION

Watersports: The Hotel Tryp has a full range of watersports. They're included in the all-inclusive package; otherwise, you'll pay extra for a banana-boat ride and water-skiing (both US$5 for 15 minutes), snorkeling (US$15 for one hour), and catamaran and jet ski rental.

Scuba Diving: The offshore coral gardens are among the world's most diverse and beautiful, teeming with colorful fishes. There are 21 dive points between Caro Paredón in the east and Punta La Jaula to the west. Dolphins are frequently seen.

There's an international dive center at Marina Cayo Coco. A free introductory dive is offered.

Scuba diving costs US$27 for one dive, US$49 for two, US$40 for night dives. You can rent equipment here. A resort course costs US$60; open-water certification costs US$288.

Horseback Riding: Horseback excursions are offered from **Sitio La Güira,** a stable and nature facility that also has a thatched restaurant. Horses can also be rented at Playa Las Coloradas, where there's a restaurant and bar.

Sportfishing: Deep-sea fishing trips are offered from Marina Cayo Coco.

GETTING THERE

By Air: A 1,500-meter-long airstrip and tiny thatch-roofed airport opened in 1995. Cubana operates service from Havana and Santiago direct to Cayo Coco and Ciego de Avila. International charters may be operating directly to Cayo Coco by the time you read this.

From Canada: Royal Airlines operates direct flights from Toronto to Cayo Coco/Ciego de Ávila each Thursday mid-December through April. Charter packages offered by **Adventure Tours,** 111 Avenue Rd. #5000, Toronto, Ontario M5R 31B, begin at C$529, including airfare and accommodation.

By Sea: Puertosol runs **Marina Cayo Coco,** east of Punta Almágico, at the eastern half of the cay. It has electricity, water, and gas, plus a nautical store and restaurant. Servimar has a small supply vessel at hand to assist private yachters. You can call Servimar on VHF channel 16 for a boat to escort you through the shallows. Reportedly, there is no Guardia Frontera here.

GETTING AROUND

Bicycle, Moped, and Car Rental

You can hire bicycles, mopeds, and cars at Hotel Tryp. You really don't need a car if you're only interested in exploring the island. A bicycle or moped is a fun and simple way to go. Drive carefully in any event—some of the roads are covered with patches of sand and gravel.

Excursions

Rumbos offers a six-hour motorcycle excursion around Cayo Coco (known as "Cococross"). It also has horse-drawn buggy rides and an "eco-tour" to Cayo Guillermo by jeep (US$21).

The hotel offers a "seafari" that traces Hemingway's route aboard the *Pilar* as enumerated in *Islands in the Stream* and includes fishing and snorkeling (US$39). Sunset cruises (US$10) are offered from Parador La Silla, about 16 km north of the MININT checkpoint. And snorkeling excursions to Cayo Paredón are offered from the marina (US$25 including cocktails and lunch).

Excursions are also available from the Hotel Tryp to Morón (US$39), Havana (US$135), Santiago (US$119), and Nassau, the Bahamas (US$179) using a biplane operated by Aerotaxi. (Aerotaxi also has flights by biplane from the airstrip at Turiguanó, with flights to Santiago de Cuba, Trinidad, Varadero, and Havana).

CAYO GUILLERMO

This middle-size (18 square km) cay lies three km west of Cayo Coco, to which it is joined by an umbilical *pedraplen* elevated over the pavonine waters. The crossing is fabulous. The process of mangrove capture and cay development is wonderfully demonstrated along the drive from Cayo Coco. Snowy-white egrets and herons pick in the shallows, which are also favored by flamingoes.

The star attraction is chalky, five-km-long Playa El Paso. There are other beaches, including Playa del Medio and Playa Larga, at the far western end, where sand dunes pile up 15 meters high. At low tide, you can wade out for 400 meters or more on the sandbars.

Cayo Guillermo has been slated for major resort development (some 1,500 rooms are to be built). The inshore fishing is excellent: snapper, grouper, mackerel, and bonefish are the species of choice. Farther out, beaked marlin and swordfish run through the Old Bahama Channel—Hemingway's "great blue river." One of the first people to discover the charms of Cayo Guillermo was, in fact, the the great fisherman and novelist. ("On the inner side, gentlemen, is Guillermo. See how green she is and full of promise?" says Hemingway's alter ego and main character, Thomas Hudson, in *Islands in the Stream,* inviting his partners to discover the beauty of the place.) Papa is still fondly remembered by elderly fishermen in the Bahía de Perros, who regale visitors with tales of his exploits. Another admirer of Guillermo's charms was dictator Fulgencio Batista, who had a hideaway on now-deserted **Cayo Media Luna,** off the western tip.

You can also reach Cayo Guillermo by boat from the fishing village of Punta Alegre, 68 km northwest of Morón.

Accommodations
Villa Cojímar, Cayo Guillermo, Ciego de Ávila, tel. 30-1012, fax 33-5554, on Playa El Paso, is part of the Cuban Gran Caribe chain, jointly run by Venta Club of Italy, but open to all comers. Not surprisingly, the majority of guests are Italians. It's a beautiful low-rise property, with spacious lawns, 218 rooms, and two suites in small one- and two-story a/c *cabañas,* each with satellite TV, international phone, hair drier, safe deposit box (US$90 s, US$140 d, all-inclusive of meals, drinks, and watersports). Facilities include a tennis court and a soccer court. The Bodeguita del Guillermo restaurant beside the marina is smothered with graffiti in imitation of La Bodeguita de Medio, in Havana. The resort is being expanded to 750 rooms.

Another upscale hotel, the 264-room **Villa Vigía** (formerly the Villa Océano) was due to open in late 1996 after a total facelift. It is operated by Canadians.

Playa del Medio is scheduled to get a 500-room hotel of its own.

Watersports
Villa Cojímar has a watersport center, including jet skis, catamarans, and **scuba diving.** An initiation dive for beginners costs US$10. Certified divers can take guided dives for US$27. **Snorkeling** trips cost US$10. A full-day **deep-sea fishing** package costs US$250 including lunch (or US$150, for four hours without lunch) for up to four people.

"Seafari" boat excursions are also available from **Marina Cayo Guillermo,** tel. 332-1012, which consists of a lopsided wharf at the eastern tip of the cay. It has 10 moorings with water, electricity, diesel, and gasoline.

MORÓN TO NUEVITAS

The coast road continues east of Morón into Camagüey province through sugarcane country studded with huge *centrales* belching out inky black smoke. At **Esmeralda** (50 km east of Morón) is a road to/from the Carretera Central and Florida.

At **Brasil,** about 10 km east of Esmeralda, is the turnoff north to Cayo Romano.

East of Brasil, sugarcane gives way to poorly tended citrus orchards stretching mile upon mile. Between the groves are concrete, four-story housing blocks (each appointed with clinic and community center) about two km apart, offset from each other to either side of the ruler-straight road. East of **Cubitas,** the land is again farmed in sugarcane, the savanna grazed by gray cattle.

At **Lugareño** is a crossroads, with a road leading north to Cayo Sabinal and southwest to Minas and Camagüey.

CAYO ROMANO

Cayo Romano is the largest of the cays in the Archipiélago de Camagüey. The cay actually comprises *two* huge cays (the westernmost abuts Cayo Coco, from which it can be accessed by road), and more than a score of sandbars and tiny cays sprinkled like stardust offshore. They are all deserted and virtually unexplored, despite translucent waters that provide some of the best snorkeling and diving in the hemisphere.

Like the other cays, Cayo Romano is all mangroves and brine pools and endless beaches. Hemingway writes in *Islands in the Stream,* "Now it was there at its barest and most barren, jutting out like a scrubby desert. There were wild horses and wild cattle and wild hogs on that great key."

At press time there were no facilities whatsoever, though there was once a settlement called Versailles—"where Frenchmen had made their attempt at living on Romano. . . . Now all the frame buildings were abandoned but the one big house," Hemingway continues. "And one time when Thomas Hudson had gone in to

fill water, the dogs from the shacks were huddled with the pigs that had burrowed in the mud and dogs and pigs both were grey from a solid blanket of mosquitoes that covered them. It was a wonderful key when the east wind blew day and night. . . . It was country as unspoiled as when Columbus came to this coast. Then, when the wind dropped, the mosquitoes came in clouds from the marshes. To say they came in clouds, he thought, is not a metaphor. They truly came in clouds and they could bleed a man to death." Take repellent!

The road from Brasil reaches Cayo Romano via a 12-km-long land bridge and then leapfrogs to enchanting **Cayo Cruz,** a small, pencil-thin cay eight km north of Romano. Its north shore is an endless talc beach. Tiny **Cayo Confite** (setting for one of Fidel Castro's early adventures—see special topic) lies farther offshore, marking the northerly tip of a long barrier reef that arcs to the southeast all the way to Holguín province.

At press time, there were no facilities whatsoever on either Cayo Romano or Cayo Cruz. The government's tourism master plan, however, contemplates a maximum of 1,700 hotel rooms on Cayo Romano and 3,000 on Cayo Cruz.

CASTRO AND CAYO CONFITES

In 1947, a political adventurer and law student named Fidel Castro signed up for an expedition to overthrow President Trujillo of the Dominican Republic. Castro and about 1,200 other expeditionaries spent 57 days on Cayo Confites, a tiny and lonely cay a few km north of Cayo Romano. There the rag-tag army underwent military training beneath a blistering sun and unrelenting assault by mosquitoes.

When the whole affair was called off, Castro's battalion sailed anyway, aboard a small freighter called *Caridad.* The vessel was boarded by a Cuban cutter and ordered to turn back. Castro, apparently fearing that he was going to be murdered by rival figures on board, leapt overboard and swam nine miles to Saetía, at the mouth of Nipe Bay.

Cayo Guajaba, immediately east of Cayo Romano and west of Cayo Sabinal, is of no current interest to tourists, though there's a tiny hamlet on the western shore where adventuresome travelers may be able to find shelter in a humble shack. The cay is included in the government's master plan for tourism, but it will be many years before anything happens here.

Hemingway used Guajaba as his model for the fantasy Bahamian cay in which a Nazi submariner lies fatally wounded in *Islands in the Stream.*

CAYO SABINAL

Cayo Sabinal is the easternmost cay in the archipelago and one of my favorites. It is attached to the north coast of Camagüey by a hair's-breadth isthmus and encloses a great bay to the east, the Bahía de Nuevitas. It has 33 km of beaches protected by coral reefs. The offshore waters are prolific with gamefish and lobster. The entire island is virgin marshland, brush, and small pines, dotted with saucer-like pools filled with an unappetizing broth.

In all your explorations, you will pass only a couple of military posts and no more than a half-dozen humble *bohíos* belonging to impoverished charcoal-burners and fishermen. There are plenty of birds and iguanas, however, small deer *(venado),* and wild pigs called *jabali,* a relative of the peccary. The *jabali* resembles a massive-necked razorback hog; it grows to the size of a mid-scale hound. The myopic animal is sharp-toothed, excitable, and quite vicious if cornered. It marks its territory with a pungent oil emitted by a musk gland located on the hindquarters. It is well adapted to arid conditions such as those of the cays, where it survives by shoveling up roots and bugs with its hardy snout.

Sabinal is a major destination for hunters.

Things to See

Crossing the isthmus, you'll see snowy-white egrets, cranes, and flamingoes wading in the soupy shallows of **Laguna de las Flamencoes.** Don't be tempted to wander onto the mudflats in search of a close-up—you'll sink to your knees before your third stride.

At the far eastern end of Cayo Sabinal is a lighthouse—**Faro Colón**—built in the 19th century; and an even older fortress—**Fuerte San Hilario**—built to protect the entrance to Bahía de Nuevitas.

Hotels in Playa Santa Lucía arrange excursions to Faro Colón.

Beaches

There are three main beaches: Playa Brava to the west, Playa Los Pinos in the center, and Playa Bonita—perhaps the most beautiful of all—to the east. You can walk for two hours in virtually any direction and leave your Man Friday footprints the whole way in white sand. The reef lies within one km of shore—within wading distance of the whitecaps that mark the boundary between the jade shallows and the aquamarine blues of the Old Bahama Channel beyond.

The best place to spend your time is fantastically lonesome **Playa Los Pinos,** with sand as white as Cuban sugar, and sea shading from the shore through an ever-deepening palette of greens. The shallows are as warm and calm as bedtime milk. The beach has rustic accommodations and a restaurant. You can even rent windsurfers here to go scudding across the limpid lagoon. Occasionally, a small group of tourists may arrive for a day-visit from Santa Lucía, but more likely you will have the place to yourself.

A breeze blows ashore by day. After dusk, all is still but for the muffled wash of the surf breaking on the distant reef and the drone of mosquitoes, absent by day but voraciously hungry at night.

Accommodations and Food

There is only one place to stay on Cayo Sabinal. If you're seeking rustic yet handsome *cabañas* made of palm trunks and mangrove roots, with thatch for roof, then make haste to Playa Los Pinos, which has five huts on the beach. The simple and oh!-so-endearing property includes a bucolic open-air restaurant and is run by a warm-hearted old Cuban, Francisco, and his younger assistant, Tony. Cabins have simple bathrooms with showers (US$25 per person, including breakfast and dinner).

When I was there, I ordered a lunch of fresh fish. As if by magic, a local fishing boat arrived within minutes and I was able to peruse the catch of red snapper *(pargo)* and lobster and choose my own lunch.

Rumbos also operates a rustic restaurant and bar at Playa Brava (there's no accommodation).

Supposedly, Cubanacán and a Sint Maarten resort developer are jointly planning a 2,000-room resort on Cayo Sabinal. Another joint Cubanacán-Austrian project is a 2,400-room resort to be completed by 1998. The Cuban government reckons Sabinal has a potential capacity for 12,000 hotel rooms. *Ouch!*

Getting There
By Road: Cayo Sabinal is 65 km northeast of Camagüey and reached via a bridge over the Enseñada de Sabinal. The road was unpaved at press time. After a few miles, you reach a crossroads. Playa Brava is to the left. Playa Los Pinos is to the right; after about six km, turn left (the beach is about five km farther). Keep going straight for the lighthouse. In places, the narrow tracks are smothered in sand and hemmed in by vegetation.

Excursions: An excursion ferry operates between Santa Lucía and Cayo Sabinal (the journey takes 10 minutes). Jeep safaris also operate from Santa Lucía. Hunting trips to Sabinal are offered from virtually every major city and resort hotel in Cuba (check with tour agencies).

NUEVITAS

This major industrial town (pop. 35,000) sits astride a promontory that divides the vast Bahía de Nuevitas. The original provincial capital—Santa María del Puerto Príncipe—was built here in 1514 before being moved to a bank on the

---

NUEVITAS USEFUL TELEPHONE NUMBERS

Police . . . . tel. 116
Ambulance . . . . tel. 4-2227
Hospital . . . . tel. 4-3014

Río Caonao. Today, the ramshackle town center looks every bit as if it has suffered through a 30-odd-year embargo. An old wooden church (in need of repair) sits atop the hill that looms over the main square, where a huge cannon has cannonballs at its base. A baobab tree stands in the main square, where there's also a sturdy gold-domed church.

The town boasts a fish processing plant, a fertilizer factory, a cement factory, and the second-largest thermoelectric plant in Cuba. Together, they pour a horrible soup of pollutants into the bay. Palls of smoke rise from their stacks and are carried off by stiff breezes. A sugar-loading facility at the deep-water port (called Puerto Angola) handles the white gold produced in the province's 13 sugar mills.

The city is famous for **El Grupo de Caidije**, a folkloric group strongly influenced by Haitian music and dance, including a machete dance.

Accommodations, Food, and Services
One wonders why you would visit, but just in case. . . . The **Hotel Caonaba**, tel. 4-4265, is operated by Islazul and has a view over the bay. Rooms cost US$12 s, US$15 d. It's near a **Cupet gas station** as you enter town from the coast highway. For eats, try **Paladar Caribe Cuba**, one block west of the main street and two blocks south of the railway station at the end of the main street.

There's a **Banco Nacional** on Máximo Gómez.

Getting There
By Bus: Bus no. 525 departs Havana daily at 7 p.m., arriving Nuevitas at 4:55 a.m. (31 pesos).

By Train: Nuevitas is the easterly terminus of the rail line along the north coast. Train no. 325 departs Morón for Nuevitas at 6:20 a.m., arriving 12:41 a.m.

By Car: Nuevitas is three km north of the coast road and 65 km northeast of Camagüey and the Carretera Central. Nuevitas is also linked to Cayo Sabinal via a road of hardpacked dirt and rock, blindingly white, that runs along the western shore of the bay, with fetid salt marshes on both sides. The great morass smells like vomit. There is no sign of life except for comical black *toti* birds, and fawn doves dust-bathing in the road.

a vintage
Harley Davidson

NUEVITAS TO SANTA LUCÍA

East of Nuevitas the road is mostly in good condition, with occasional mammoth potholes. You pass through a spartan landscape of sagebrush savanna ranged by cattle. Bullrushes and water hyacinths thrive at waterholes, where flocks of egrets and herons gather.

Just west of **Camalote,** a turnoff leads northeast 26 km to Santa Lucía. Eight km along is **Finca Campesina,** a re-creation of a typical *campesino* farmstead, where you can take horseback rides and enjoy *criollo* meals.

There's a traffic circle where the road to Santa Lucía meets the coast. Santa Lucía is to the left. To the right, a dirt road leads east two miles past a military lookout post to **Punta Ganada,** which has a beautiful beach and a basic *campismo* for Cubans.

King Ranch

This working cattle ranch, just west of Camalote and the turn for Santa Lucía, was once owned by the owners of the famous King Ranch in Texas. The Castro regime expropriated the property, which today receives tourists. You can watch the workaday *vaqueros* herding cattle and getting coated with dust and manure. A rodeo provides entertainment, and horseback riding is offered. It has a restaurant, and a guest ranch can be rented

Visits are arranged through hotels in Santa Lucía.

SANTA LUCÍA

Just when you thought sand couldn't get any whiter or finer, or the sea a more brilliant blue, you arrive at Santa Lucía, 110 km east of Camagüey and 85 km north of Las Tunas. The beach (supposedly Cuba's third-longest) is virtually unbroken for an astounding 20 km, protected by an offshore coral reef. Sea grasses, however, have gained a foothold in places—rubber bathing shoes or sandals are a good idea.

Santa Lucía was popular with Cuban vacationers until the onset of the Special Period put a serious dent in everyone's budget. Today the resort is popular with Germans and Canadians and is widely touted in tourist literature as being "sophisticated." Forget the promotional hype. Santa Lucía is embryonic, with minimal infrastructure. Facilities are spread out over several kilometers, with stretches of grassy nothingness between them. At the west end is an ugly housing estate for Cubans, most of whom are employed in the hospitality industry or in the nearby saltworks. Many of the occupants derive a new income by renting rooms to Cuban vacationers and out-of-town girls seeking foreign boyfriends.

West of Santa Lucía is a funky fishing hamlet with its own beach and atmospheric restaurants.

Flamingoes occasionally flock to wallow by day in the lagoons behind the beach, then take off in a flash of bright pink at dusk.

ACCOMMODATIONS

The government's tourism master plan believes that Santa Lucía can support 7,000 hotel rooms. It will be years before it resembles Varadero. In midwinter, charter tour companies reserve large blocks of rooms. At Christmas and New Year's, Santa Lucía often sells out; if you're going then, I recommend a reservation.

Cuban families live in modest villas and huts widely dispersed along the seafront. You may be able to rent one if you ask around.

Hotel Mayanabo, Playa Santa María, Nuevitas, Camagüey, tel. 322-3-6184, operated by Cubanacán, is a Soviet-style building, dating from the 1970s. It was recently given an effective and handsome facelift. It has 201 red-tile-roofed a/c rooms, 12 suites, and 12 triple rooms, all with balconies, for US$73 per person, *all-inclusive*. There's a restaurant, bar, tennis court, swimming pool with shady palm-leaf umbrellas, and watersports.

Villa Tararaco, tel. 36222, is another Cubanacán motel-style property, with 30 rooms and one suite. It has undergone recent renovation.

Golden Tulip Villa Coral, tel. 36429, fax 335-043, is jointly operated by Golden Tulip (of the Netherlands) and Cubanacán. The 246 a/c rooms and 52 suites in two-story units, plus 12 bungalows, all have TVs, telephones, and mini-fridges. Rates are US$40 s, US$50 d, US$65 t with breakfast (low season), and US$72 for a bungalow. It has bicycle and horseback rides, watersports (including scuba diving), and an excursion desk. You can rent scooters and cars here. The buffet restaurant caters to Italian tastes with spaghetti and pizzas. There are two grill bars, a poolside bar, plus disco, where live entertainment and cabarets are hosted.

A more upscale and appealing option is **Golden Tulip Caracol,** Santa Lucía, Nuevitas, Camagüey, tel. 3-6302, or, in the UK, tel. (171) 924-4141; in the Netherlands, Golden Tulip International, P.O. Box 619, 1200 AP Hilversum, tel. 35-28-4588, fax 35-28-4681. It has 150 a/c

Camagüey

rooms and four suites, all with balconies and ocean views. The rooms are really small suites with large bedrooms and tiny lounges and that rarest find in Cuba—firm, comfy beds. You even get HBO and CNN on TV. Rooms cost US$45 s, US$60 d with breakfast (low-season)— bargain. Bicycle and horseback excursions are offered, and the resort has scuba diving.

At the top of the ladder is the **Hotel Cuatro Vientos,** a modern, 214-room hotel with a splendid aesthetic, operated jointly by Cubanacán and the Spanish Hotels C group, tel. 32-36493, fax 32-335433; in Spain, tel. 95-238-8877, fax 95-238-8744. This beautiful low-rise property combines a contemporary design with traditional thatch and lots of hardwoods. At its heart is a magnificent swimming pool with swim-up bar. Rates are US$70 s, US$110 d year-round, including breakfast and dinner.

In May 1996, Cuba and Italy penned an agreement to build a 200-room health resort called **Mediclub,** complete with beauty, cosmetology, and dental clinics.

FOOD

The hotels all have restaurants, and there are as yet few other options. Beachside restaurants include **Restaurante Las Brisas,** serving seafoods and *criollo* dishes, and **Restaurante Bonsai,** for quasi-Chinese food. Budget about US$5-8 for meals—double that for lobster. The **Restaurante Las Bahamas,** near the gas station, also serves *criollo* food. **Oasis** is an outdoor bar and restaurant serving country cooking, simple but good. Try the grilled pork steaks with red beans and rice.

I recommend a visit to Playa Los Cocos for lunch at one of the funky yet excellent seafood restaurants.

SPORTS AND RECREATION

Most of the hotels have watersports and beach volleyball. **Horseback rides** cost about US$5, more with a guide. The Marlin Dive Center offers yacht, catamaran, and sailboat rentals, plus waterskiing (US$10 for 15 minutes).

Santa Lucía offers great **sportfishing** and gamefishing, especially for *macabí* and *sábalo.* You can book a fishing excursion at Cuatro Vientes or Golden Tulip hotels for US$40.

Scuba Diving

The waters off Santa Lucía contain more than 15 dive sites. The warm waters support dozens of coral species and an infinity of gaudy fishes. Among the more exciting sites are **Sponge Paradise, Coral Tower,** and **Gorgonian Garden,** with their heaps of black coral and bright orange sponges hanging like garlands. There are also coral reefs in the shallow waters on the shore side of the drop, with plentiful queen conch, bright-colored starfish, and purple-lipped clams. Nurse sharks and barracudas occasionally pass by, but they are usually no problem.

The mouth of the entrance to the Bahía de Nuevitas is a ships' graveyard of wrecks, including the steamship *Mortera,* which sank in 1898, its prow resting at a depth of 20 feet. The hull is now encrusted with coral, and sharks, turtles, and other marine species live within.

The dive center of the Cuatro Vientes offers specialized courses for beginners, plus advanced courses, including night-diving and underwater video. Scuba diving is also offered at the Golden Tulip hotels.

SERVICES

There's a **Cupet gas station** at the east end of Santa Lucia. A doctor and nurse are on 24-hour duty at the **Clínica Internacional,** at the east end of Santa Lucía. Hotel visits cost US$40.

GETTING THERE AND AROUND

Bus no. 125 departs Havana's main bus terminal at 7:20 a.m., arriving Santa Lucía at 1 a.m. (10 pesos, foreigners may be charged US$10). The bus stop is near Villa Taraooo. Buses also operate from Las Tunas and Camagüey.

The nearest airport is in Las Tunas. A taxi from the airport will cost about US$50 one-way.

Santa Lucía is too spread out to explore on foot. The resort has only one street, which parallels the shore. **Horse-drawn carriages** ply the route (US$1 per person). **Taxis** charge about US$1 per km. You can hire a taxi for long-distance trips; expect to pay about US$80 roundtrip to Camagüey or Las Tunas.

Havanautos offers car rentals opposite Villa Tarataco. You can rent **bicycles and mopeds** from the major hotels.

Excursions: Fantástico Tours has tour desks in the hotels, plus an office farther east. It offer excursions far and wide. There are also excursions to Cayo Largo (US$130), but why bother? A jeep-safari to Cayo Sabinal costs US$25, including lunch at Playa Los Pinos.

Cubanacán offers excursions to the fishing village of La Boca by sea, with seafood lunch aboard. It also has a sunset cruise to La Boca, plus a snorkeling safari. You can also take an

---

SANTA LUCÍA USEFUL TELEPHONE NUMBERS

Police . . . . tel. 3-6225
Ambulance. tel. 3-6294

excursion to the rural village of Camalote, where you'll visit **Finca Adelaida** or King Ranch. Cubanacán also offers a trip to Camagüey; a nature excursion into the Cubitas Mountains; and two-day trips to Havana, Santiago de Cuba, and Trinidad. It even has a one-day trip to Jamaica.

Helicopter tours are also offered from the landing pad near the Hotel Villa Coral to La Belén Hunting Preserve (including horseback riding) and to Santiago de Cuba. A 20-minute flightseeing excursion of Santa Lucía costs about US$30.

Ostensibly, an excursion **ferry** operates from Santa Lucía to the lighthouse on Cayo Sabinal.

WEST OF SANTA LUCÍA

The coast road turns to dirt west of Santa Lucía and continues for three km to the funky fishing village of **La Boca.** This is a great place for travelers wanting to shun the tourist experience. The hamlet of ramshackle huts faces onto a cove with a beach—Playa de las Tararacos (also called Playa Coco)—where fishing nets are hung to dry.

The beach curves around the *estero,* growing more tantalizing with every yard. Diving is said to be superb just offshore.

The road continues west another km or so to the end of the peninsula, where Cayo Sabinal lies almost within shouting distance. There's no bridge; just a Guardia Frontera post.

Accommodations and Food
You can rent the modest *cabañas* at **Villa Panama.** Seafood eateries include the funky and atmospheric **Restaurante El Pescador, Lazo's Lobster House,** and **King Fish,** which has dishes for US$3 and up but charges a rather steep US$15 for lobster.

LAS TUNAS AND HOLGUÍN
INTRODUCTION

Las Tunas province is what you pass through en route to Holguín and elsewhere. The two namesake provincial capitals offer relatively little of tourist value. Las Tunas (or, more correctly, Victoria de las Tunas), is quaint and worth a quick browse. The city of Holguín isn't even quaint, though it does boast a good natural history museum, some colonial structures of interest, and, outside town, the Finca Mayabe, where you can buy a beer for a suds-supping donkey.

Most sites of tourist interest lie along Holguín's coast, where a few scintillating white beaches (most notably the resort of Guardalavaca) lie close to beautiful mountain ranges, the Sierra de Cristal and Sierra de Nipe. The area has been named a national park, a wilderness of pine forests laced by rugged mountain trails perfect for hikers and ecotourists. In a typically Cuban anomaly, ecotourists and hunters are both catered to on Cayo Saetia, an island resort and wildlife reserve near the Bay of Nipes where exotic beasts imported from Africa leave hoofprints in sugar-white Cuban sand.

History buffs may be enticed to Bahía Bariay, where Christopher Columbus first set foot on Cuban soil in 1492, and to Banes, site of the most important pre-Columbian finds in Cuba

(one-third of indigenous finds unearthed in Cuba to date have hailed from Holguín province). And how about Fidel Castro's birthplace and childhood home? Curious? Head to Birán.

THE LAY OF THE LAND

Las Tunas province forms a flat, narrow band across the island, broadening to the northeast. The capital city sits on a low-lying ridge (the Cuchilla Holguín) in the center of the province, on the eastern edge of the great plains that dominate central Cuba. It is dull, unvarying terrain, mostly farmed for sugar and cattle. The scenery begins to grow lusher and more interesting as you progress eastward toward Holguín, where stands of royal palms reappear and the vegetation closes in. The southern plains are swampy and of minimal tourist interest, although bonefish and tarpon provide challenging fishing in the coastal waters and lagoons.

Holguín itself is far more diverse. The capital city lies in the midst of the bulky western half of the province, with the Bay of Nipes its eastern flank. The province extends east from here in a panhandle along the north coast almost to Baracoa and the tip of the island. The narrow coastal plain is indented with neatly spaced, deep-pocket bays that are entered via narrow inlets. Here, towns such as Puerto Padre and Manatí have grown up around chemical works or sugar-loading facilities, but they serve no use for travelers. Much of the coast is covered with scrubby salt bushes atop raised coral shores.

Inland, Holguín has a classic Asian landscape—tall palms rising proudly above lime-green canefields and dun-colored cattle pastures, deep bottle-green woods far beyond, extending toward the sierras in the south. This is most splendidly seen in the mountain valleys that lie on the road from Banes to Guardalavaca.

Looming over eastern Holguín inland are mountains—the Sierra de Nipe, Sierra del Cristal, Cuchillas del Toa, and Alturas de Moa—that build to 1,200 meters. The mountains are the color of heated chrome, betraying the presence of precious mineral ores.

THE ECONOMY

Las Tunas relies on sugarcane and on cattle, which are raised in huge *ganaderias* named for revolutionary heroes. Tourism hasn't yet taken hold. Holguín province, Cuba's second-most populous, also evolved an important economy based on cattle (in the west), tobacco (in the center), sugar (in the north and east), and fruit. Tourism, however, is fast becoming a key income source for Holguín province, centered on Guardalavaca. The linchpin of the Holguín economy, however, is nickel, cobalt, and other mineral ores extracted from the Sierra Cristal and Sierra de Nipe and processed locally, most notably at the coastal town of Moa. The quarries are a veritable gold mine for the Cuban economy, with locally produced nickel accounting for about 15% of Cuba's export earnings.

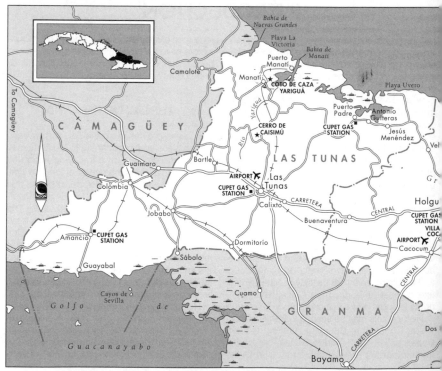

Che Guevara Nickel Plant, Moa

The region's economic history exemplifies the dilemmas and destructive forces imposed by US imperialism. Holguín province was a major center of rebellion during the wars of independence and suffered enormously. The vast sugarcane fields gradually fell into the hands of US corporations,

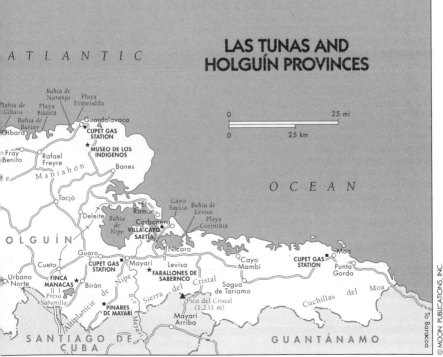

LAS TUNAS AND HOLGUÍN PROVINCES

ATLANTIC

Bahía de Naranjo
Playa Esmeralda
Bahía de Gibara
Playa Blanca
Bahía de Bariay
Guardalavaca
CUPET GAS STATION
Gibara
Fray Benito
Rafael Freyre
MUSEO DE LOS INDIGENOS
Banes
Maniabón
Tacajó
Deleite
El Ramón
Cayo Saetía
Bahía de Levisa
Playa Corinthia
Carbonero
Bahía de Nipe
VILLA CAYO SAETÍA
OLGUÍN
Guaro
Nicaro
OCEAN
Cueto
CUPET GAS STATION
Mayarí
Cayo Mambí
CUPET GAS STATION
Moa
Urbano Norte
FINCA MANACAS
Birán
Levisa
FARALLONES DE SABERNCO
Sagua de Tariamo
Punta Gorda
Presa Sabanilla
PINARES DE MAYARÍ
Río
Nipe
Sierra
del
Cristal
Pico del Cristal (1,231 m)
Cuchillas
del
Moa
Altiplanicie
de
Mayarí
Mayarí Arriba
SANTIAGO DE CUBA
GUANTÁNAMO
To Baracoa

0   25 mi
0   25 km

© MOON PUBLICATIONS, INC.

especially the United Fruit Company, which bought the land for a pittance following the devastation wrought by the wars. US companies came to dominate economic and political life in the region, and Cubans were under their sway. The US workers enjoyed a lifestyle of privilege that was denied Cuban workers, the majority of whom faced a harsh and marginalized existence.

Other US companies established mining ventures to extract the nickel, manganese, and iron ores. After the mining operations were nationalized, in 1960, Soviet money financed future expansion. Today, Canadian mining ventures have taken the lead.

Ironically, one of the few Cubans who *did* benefit economically was Fidel Castro's father, Ángel Castro, who leased lands from the United Fruit Company and grew to be relatively prosperous and powerful. The pitiful existence of the Cuban peasantry was not lost on the young Fidel, who witnessed the deleterious influence of US stewardship firsthand and who first agitated on workers' behalf as a boy—and on his father's estate!

THE CARRETERA CENTRAL

The Carretera Central cuts through the center of Las Tunas province. The road is lined with tamarind trees and is in good condition. There are Cupet gas stations in Florida and the city of Las Tunas. Before you blink, you pass into Holguín province. Immediately, the Carretera Central deteriorates, with sections badly in need of repair. There are no services along the road to Holguín, and only one town of significance—Buenaventura. The Carretera virtually doubles back at Holguín, where it turns southwest for Granma province.

LAS TUNAS AND VICINITY

Most guidebooks dismiss Las Tunas as a town to pass through. True, it wins no prizes for endless appeal. It's a small-time capital of a small-time province. That said, it's a cozy town, well kept and tidy, with a comfortable town center.

The town is officially known as La Victoria de las Tunas, a name bequeathed by the Spanish governor in 1869 to celebrate a victory over Cuban patriot forces in the War of Independence. Needless to say, the name took on a different import after the patriots kicked Spanish ass and captured the town in 1895. Two years later, the town was put to the torch by rebel forces as Spanish forces attempted to retake Las Tunas. Alas, the fire destroyed many of the original buildings, and the town today lacks edifices of historical or architectural note.

Las Tunas is famed for its terra-cotta ceramics, expressed in pieces of contemporary art scattered all over the city. The town has thus earned the nickname "City of Sculptures." Look for works by some of Cuba's leading artists, such as *Fountain of the Antilles,* with a woman's body shaped like Cuba at its center, by Rita Longa; and the powerful *Liberation of the People,* by Manuel Chong, opposite the Provincial Assembly building.

ORIENTATION

The town sits astride the Carretera Central, which enters from the west along Avenida 1ro de Enero, becomes Avenida Vicente García, which leads slightly uphill to the central square—Parque Vicente García—where it turns 90 degrees and runs southeast for Holguín as Calle Francisco Verona. A ring road *(circunvalación)* bypasses the town to the south.

The historic center is laid out in a rough grid, aligned northeast-southwest and centered on Parque García. The park lies at the top of Vicente García, between Calles Francisco Varona and Francisco Vega. Vicente García continues northeast as Ángel de la Guardia, which runs to the railway station, where it forks for the airport and Puerto Padre, on the north coast.

Avenida Lucas Ortíz (not to be confused with Lorenzo Ortíz) parallels Vicente García one block north and runs *from* the railway station westward (one-way) to merge with Vicente García. Most shops and sites of interest lie along these two roads.

LAS TUNAS CITY

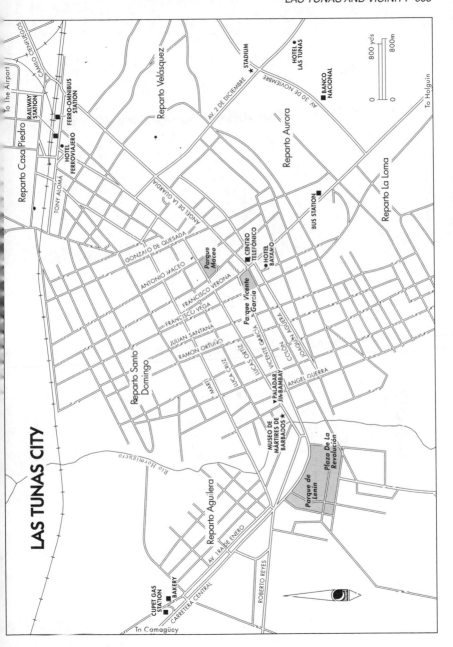

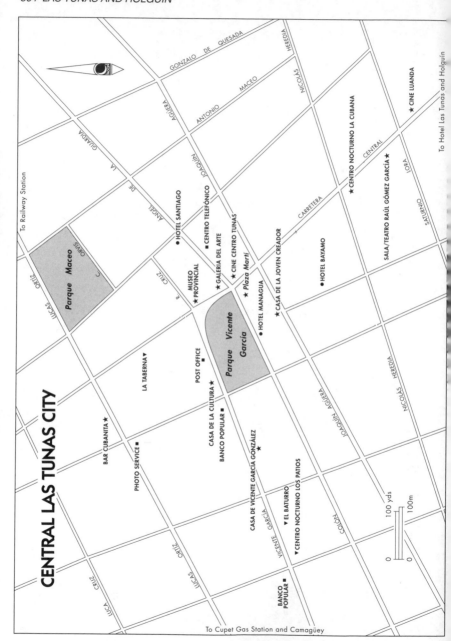

CENTRAL LAS TUNAS CITY

To Railway Station

Parque Maceo

C. ORFIS

LUCAS ORTIZ

CRUZ

LUCÍA

BAR CUBANITA ★

PHOTO SERVICE ■

LA TABERNA ▼

POST OFFICE ■

CASA DE LA CULTURA ★

BANCO POPULAR ■

CASA DE VICENTE GARCÍA GONZÁLEZ ★

VICENTE GARCÍA

LUCAS ORTIZ

▼ EL BATURRO

▼ CENTRO NOCTURNO LOS PATIOS

BANCO POPULAR ■

To Cupet Gas Station and Camagüey

GONZALO DE QUESADA

HEREDIA

ANTONIO

MACEO

NICOLÁS

LA GUARDIA

AGÜERA

JOAQUÍN

ANGEL DE LA CRUZ

R. CRUZ

● HOTEL SANTIAGO

★ CENTRO TELEFÓNICO

★ GALERÍA DEL ARTE

MUSEO ★ PROVINCIAL

★ CINE CENTRO TUNAS

★ Plaza Martí

Parque Vicente García

● HOTEL MANAGUA

★ CASA DE LA JOVEN CREADOR

★ CASA DE LA JUVENTUD

JOAQUÍN AGÜERA

NICOLÁS HEREDIA

COLÓN

CARRETERA

CENTRAL

LORA

SATURNINO

★ CENTRO NOCTURNO LA CUBANA

★ SALA/TEATRO RAÚL GÓMEZ GARCÍA

★ CINE LUANDA

● HOTEL BAYAMO

To Hotel Las Tunas and Holguín

0   100 yds
0   100m

SIGHTSEEING

Las Tunas's historic core can be explored on foot. The place to begin is the main square, **Parque Vicente García,** at the top of the main street and centered on an attractive marble statue of the local hero, Major General Vicente García González, who burned the city rather than let it fall into Spanish hands. It has granite seats beneath shady begonias. On the west side is an aged church, very small and simple yet in good condition.

Most buildings of interest lie along Avenida Vicente García, which is lined with columned colonnades. The houses west of Ramón Ortuño (two blocks west of the park) are in particularly good repair. Noteworthy among them is the **Casa del Vicente García González,** a restored colonial house where, on 26 September 1876, Vicente García González began the fire that burned the city. The building is now a museum telling the tale of the city and the War of Independence, leading to the town's immolation.

At the base of Vicente García is the tiny **Monumento de Mártires de Barbados,** a dramatic piece of contemporary art—an arc of metal pipes and bronze remnants welded into an arm and clenched fist. The monument is to the side of the small wooden house where lived Carlos Leyva González, Cuba's champion *florete* (fencer). Leyva died, along with his brother and the entire Cuban fencing team, when Cubana flight CUT-1201 was destroyed by a bomb en route to Georgetown, Barbados, on 6 October 1976. In all, 73 people died, including 57 Cubans, five Koreans, and 11 Guyanese. Right-wing Cuban-American exiles have been implicated in the terrorist act. The house is now a **museum** dedicated to the passengers who died. The museum showcases medals and diplomas won by Leyva and fellow *florete* Leonardo Mackenzie, as well as rapiers and a fencing suit. It's open daily 10 a.m.-6 p.m. (entrance costs US50 cents). Lather up with mosquito repellent before entering the museum.

Other parks of interest include **Parque Maceo,** on Calle Lucas Ortíz, one block northeast of Parque García, and the petite and attractive little **Plaza Martí,** one block east of Parque García.

The **Museo Provincial,** at the top of Vicente García, was closed for repair in mid-1996. There's also a **Museo Histórico** on General Menocal and Francisco Vega.

ACCOMMODATIONS

For its size and relative lack of importance, Las Tunas is suprisingly replete with hotels. Sure, the majority are basic, but still.

Budget
The place to stay is without a doubt the atmospheric **Hotel Bayamo,** on Lorenzo Ortíz one block south of Francisco Varona, tel. 4-4296. This pleasing historic hotel was recently renovated with bright (albeit modest) furnishings and modern art, including glazed terra-cotta ceramics. Some of the 23 rooms have a/c, others have fans (US$10 s, US$18 d, US$20 "matrimonial"). Alas, bathrooms are small and have cold water only. There's a bar and a twee little restaurant.

Other options include the pesos-only **Hotel Ferroviajero,** tel. 2601, in a colonial building directly opposite the *ferro-omni* station. It accepts foreigners; the rooms have *ventrales* and tall ceilings but are otherwise modest and somewhat run-down, with cold-water showers. Some have TVs. Rates range from 13 to 40 pesos. There's a basic restaurant.

A more basic option is **El Cornito,** tel. 45015, about 10 km east of town. It has 50 rustic, thatched, a/c *cabañas* amid palms and banyans on the banks of the Río Hormigo. Fishing and boating is offered, and the hotel hosts folk music concerts. Rates are about US$14 s, US$18 d. Avoid the musty motel rooms.

The very basic **Hotel Managua,** tel. 42743, overlooks the main square. It has rooms for 5 pesos.

The **Hotel Santiago,** tel. 4-3396, one block north of Parque García, was being restored in mid-1996 but looked like it would be appealing when completed.

Moderate
Most travelers stay at the **Hotel Las Tunas,** tel. 4-3893, one km east of town on Avenida de 2 Diciembre. The five-story neo-Stalinist prefab hotel sits atop a hillock a 20-minute walk east of

town. The views aren't particularly appealing, but the hotel is quite adequate. The 142 rooms have a/c, TVs, telephones, and refrigerators (US$23 s, US$34 d).

FOOD

Times change, but when I stayed (twice) at the Hotel Las Tunas, the menu was a wish list. I felt like snatching the flies for protein! The restaurant in the Hotel Bayamo is attractive.

Other alternatives include **Los Patios**, at Vicente García and Ramón Ortuno; it has a refectory-style dining area and serves burgers and snacks, plus beer for four pesos! Next to it is the basic but atmospheric **El Baturro**, where you can buy *refrescoes* served from a huge copper still.

There are several restaurants on Francisco Varona, one block west of the main plaza. The best is **La Taberna**, a dark, vaulted, red-brick tavern that serves burgers and snacks. **La Bodeguita**, next door, is similarly moody and pleasant and sells salads and *criollo* dishes, including fried chicken (US$4).

Café Quique Marina is renowned for its *caldosa*, a thick local stew combining chicken, banana, yucca, potato, and other vegetables. The place is named for Quique and Marina, its owners. It's on the Carratera Central, west of town.

You'll find lots of snack stalls outside the railway station, and there's a basic 24-hour café, **La Holguinera**, behind Plaza Martí. The town also has lots of *paladares*. Try **Paladar Jimbambay**, tel. 4-5104, on Lucas Ortíz one block east of the Museo de Mártires de Barbados.

ENTERTAINMENT AND EVENTS

Las Tunas is known for a festival called **Jornada Cucalambeana** (Cucalambé Folkloric Festival), when *trovadores* and songsters merge from all parts of Cuba to make merry in honor of Cristóbal Nápoles Fajardo (El Cucalambé), a native 19th-century poet known for his rhyming songs called *décimas*. It takes place at Motel El Cornito each June or July.

The **Galeria del Arte** has special exhibitions, as well as permanent displays. You might also check out the **Casa de la Cultura,** on the west side of Parque García.

There's a **disco** in the Hotel Las Tunas. **Cine Luanda,** on Francisco Varona, four blocks east of Parque García, has a disco Wed.-Sat. at 9 p.m. Next door is **Centro Nocturno la Cubana,** a modest but popular night spot with live music and dancing. Another popular spot is **Centro Nocturno Los Patios,** at Vicente García and Ramón Ortuño. It has a bar and dance area.

To sup with locals, try the dark and conspiratorial **Bar Cubanita.**

For movies, take your pick from between the **Cine Centro Tunas** and **Cine Luanda.** Immediately west is the **Sala/Teatro Raúl Gómez García,** which hosts classical and contemporary performances. Behind Plaza Martí is the **Casa de la Juven Creador,** where you can hear youths practicing song and dance routines.

SPORTS AND RECREATION

Watch for rodeos and festivities taking place in **Parque de Lenin,** where the Carretera Central merges with Avenida Vicente García. The park is also a fairground with mechanical rides.

Into boxing? Pugilists train at the **Gimnesio de Boxing,** at Angel Guerro, one block east of Vicente García. A large, modern stadium lies at the foot of the hill on Avenida 2 de Diciembre, 200 meters west of the Hotel Las Tunas. With luck, you may catch a baseball game here.

SHOPPING

ARTEX has a small store behind Plaza Martí selling crafts, music cassettes, T-shirts, and other souvenirs. A wider array of more authentic crafts, including *muñecitas* (dolls), miniature wooden horse-drawn coaches, and leather saddles and sandals, is displayed at **Cubartesania,** at Lucas Ortíz #238.

SERVICES

You can buy postage stamps and make international calls at the Hotel Las Tunas. The main **post office** is at the top of Vicente García, on the west

LAS TUNAS USEFUL TELEPHONE NUMBERS

Police	tel. 116
Ambulance	tel. 4-2073
Hospital	tel. 4-5012
Airport	tel. 4-3266
Terminal de Ómnibus	tel. 4-2444
Railway Station	tel. 4-2352

side of Parque García. Locals make international calls from the **Centro Telefónico** one block northeast of Parque García, on Ángel de la Guardia.

The **Banco Nacional** is handily situated 400 meters from the Hotel Las Tunas, on Avenida 30 de Noviembre. There are also two branches of **Banco Popular,** both on the west side of Vicente García, two blocks apart—one at Ramón Ortuño and the other at Francisco Vegas.

There's an **immigration office** next door to Casa de Vicente García González. Ostensibly, you can get your visa renewed here.

Cyclists will find a well-stocked **bicycle shop** next to the Casa de Vicente García González. You can buy batteries, film, and instamatic cameras at **Photo Service,** at the corner of Lucas Ortíz and Francisco Vega.

GETTING THERE AND AWAY

Las Tunas is on both the Carretera Central and the main rail line between Havana and Santiago.

By Bus
Bus no. 603 departs Havana's main bus terminal daily at 9 p.m., arriving around 7 a.m. the next day (28 pesos) at the **long-distance terminal,** one km from the Hotel Las Tunas, tel. 4-3801. It is relatively well organized and has plenty of seating.

Most buses traveling along the Carretera Central to whatever destination usually stop in Las Tunas. They are always oversold, however.

By Train
The orderly train station, is on Calle Terry Alomá, at the top of Lucas Ortíz and Ángel de la Guardia, tel. 4-2117. The journey between Ha-

vana and Las Tunas takes about 12 hours on the *especial.* Train fares to/from Las Tunas are: Camagüey, US$5; Ciego de Ávila, US$10; Guantánamo, US$11; Havana, US$27; Holguín, US$4; Santa Clara, US$16; and Santiago, US$9.

By Ferro-Ómnibus: Major towns throughout the province are linked to Las Tunas by a two-car commuter train—*ferro-ómnibus* or railtram—which leaves from a separate station adjacent to the main rail station.

Advance reservations are highly recommended; there's a specific time to make reservations for each train, usually the day before (check the schedule outside the station). Trains depart for Puerto Padre at 7:35 a.m. and 3:05 and 7:35 p.m. (1.50 pesos); Jesús Menéndez Monday, Friday, Saturday, and Sunday at 1:40 p.m. and Tues.-Thurs. at 7:30 a.m. (2 pesos); and Holguín at 4:30 a.m. and 12:30 p.m. (2.20 pesos).

By Air
Cubana serves Las Tunas from Havana on Monday and Thursday at 9:10 a.m. and Wednesday and Friday at 8 a.m. (US$65 one-way). Return flights depart the **Hermano Ameijeras Airport,** tel. 31-42484, in Las Tunas, at 11:35 a.m. and 10:35 a.m., respectively. The airport is on the northern edge of town, on Rafael Martínez (a taxi will cost about US$5 to/from town; a horse-drawn *coche* should cost about US$2). Flight schedules change frequently, so check well in advance. You'll need to secure reservations well in advance, too.

Cubana has an office on Lucas Ortíz, tel. 42702, open Monday, Wednesday, and Friday 7 a.m.-noon and Tuesday and Thursday 7 a.m.-2 p.m.

GETTING AROUND

You can walk everywhere in Las Tunas with relative ease. The Hotel Las Tunas is a 30-minute downhill walk.

You'll normally find a taxi outside the Hotel Las Tunas (expect to pay US$2 for a ride downtown). However, the locals all get around by horse-drawn *coches,* which gather outside the railway station. You'll be able to hop aboard anywhere in the city (one peso for locals; US$1 or more for foreigners).

THE SOUTH COAST

You'd be hard-pressed to find a reason to explore Las Tunas's slender south coast, most of which is farmed in sugar or rice and the rest of which is mostly virgin marshland.

If driving from Camagüey to Granma province and Santiago, you can bypass the city of Las Tunas via a paved road that leads from Guáimaro to Bayamo and cuts across the southern plains via the small agricultural town of Jobabo.

CERRO DE CAISIMÚ AND COTO DE CAZA YARIGUA

Cerro de Caisimú, 18 km due north of Las Tunas, is a pristine wilderness flush with guinea fowl, pigeons, and other game species. Much of the area is a hunting reserve. There's a basic hunting lodge on the hillside above the Yariguá and Gramal Rivers.

The Río Yariguá flows north to the Bahía de Manatí through a second reserve, the **Coto De Caza Yariguá.** This prize hunting preserve—also known as Manatí Hunting Preserve—is set amid 255 square km of marshland and saltwater estuaries adjacent to a huge rice-producing area. Bass fishing is also offered.

Accommodations

The lodge at Coto de Caza Yariguá has 13 a/c double *cabañas* with private baths. There's a hunting goods store, a restaurant, and a bar. It's run by Horizontes, Calle 23 #156 e/ N y O, Vedado, Havana, tel. 33-4142, fax 33-3161. Manatí is included in a weeklong hunting package offered by **Magna Outdoors,** 50 Alness St. #200C, Downsview, Ontario M3J 2G9, tel. (416) 665-7174 or (800) 387-3717, fax (416) 665-8448.

THE NORTH COAST OF LAS TUNAS

Las Tunas' north coast is something of an ugly duckling. However, it has a few beaches of note—even if, as yet, no resorts. Inland, the coastal plains are planted with sugar.

Roads radiate north from the city of Las Tunas to the two coastal towns of importance—Manatí and Puerto Padre. The coastal towns are also linked by a road that parallels the shore and connects with Camalote (gateway to Playa Santa Lucía, in Camagüey province) and Gibara (in Holguín province). The road between Camalote and Manatí is in lousy condition. The road north from Las Tunas to Manatí has similar problems, with huge potholes and plenty of them.

Manatí, 45 km northwest of Las Tunas, is a nondescript port town centered on a sugar *central.* Tourist maps show a road leading north from town to **Playa La Victoria** and **Puerto Manatí.** The road passes through miles of salty scrub and nothingness. Believe me, there's no reason to visit.

Puerto Padre (pop. 25,000), about 25 km east of Manatí, lies deep within a large pocket-bay shaped like a flask. Again, there's no reason to visit other than the **Cupet gas station.** Puerto Padre has an enormous sugar terminal called Carupano, on Cayo Juan Claro, just inside the bay (private yachters must report here before berthing at the dock at Puerto Padre, where there's a bar frequented by seamen and females hoping to be captains' mates).

You'll find several beautiful white sand beaches nearby, including (to the northwest) **Playa Covarrubias,** a four-km-long strip of silky white sands with turquoise waters protected by a coral reef. At the beach's eastern end is a rocky cliff offering views over the beach and tidelands. Covarrubias has been earmarked for development, with a total potential capacity of 5,000 hotel rooms.

About 20 km east of Puerto Padre, you pass through Jesús Menéndez and Loma, where a road leads north to **Playa Uvero** and **Playa La Herradura,** which lie to the east of the mouth of the bay. Both are glorious. They're backed by salt-encrusted *esteros.* Two modest hotels for Cubans were being restored at press time.

Some tourist maps show a road leading east along the coast from Playa Herradura via Punta Piedra de Mangle to Gibara, in Holguín province. It's a cartographer's fantasy.

HOLGUÍN AND VICINITY

Holguín, 775 km east of Havana and 200 km northwest of Santiago de Cuba, is the fourth-largest city in Cuba (pop. 195,000). It receives few tourists and is really a place to stop only in passing. The city is surrounded by cattle *fincas* and steep hills, which offer fine views over the city.

When Columbus landed in 1492 at Gibara, believing he had arrived in Asia, he apparently sent a small expedition inland to carry salutations to the Japanese emperor's court. Eventually, the explorers came across a large Indian village called *Cubanacán* (Center of Cuba), believed to have been near the current location of Holguín. Three decades later, a land grant was made to Capitán García Holguín, who built a settlement on the site of the Indian village (which had, naturally, been razed) and immodestly named the site San Isidoro de Holguín.

The center of town still contains single-story houses of Spanish provenance. Still, Holguín's colonial charm has been virtually suffocated in recent decades. Today, it is an industrial city that has expanded rapidly since the Revolution, when prefabricated concrete apartment blocks went up.

ORIENTATION

Star-shaped Holguín is an unassuming town that conveys an impression of being smaller than it really is—until you ascend the hills and

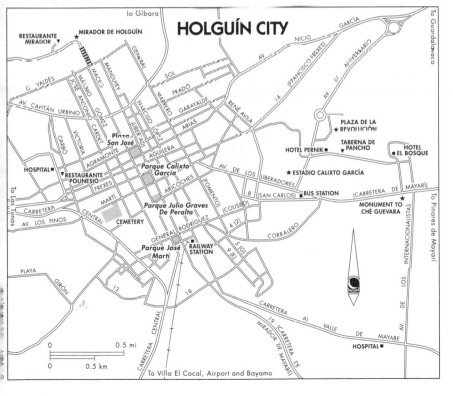

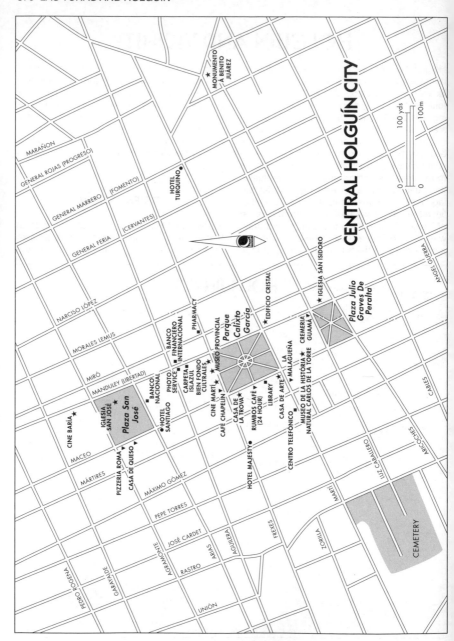

CENTRAL HOLGUÍN CITY

MONUMENTO A BENITO JUÁREZ ★

MARAÑON

GENERAL ROJAS (PROGRESO)

GENERAL MARRERO (FOMENTO)

HOTEL TURQUINO ●

(CERVANTES)

GENERAL FERIA

NARCISO LÓPEZ

MORALES LEMUS

MIRÓ

MANDULEY (LIBERTAD)

MACEO

MÁRTIRES

CINE BARIA ★

IGLESIA SAN JOSÉ ★
Plaza San José ★
● BANCO NACIONAL
● HOTEL SANTIAGO

PIZZERIA ROMA ▶
CASA DE QUESO ▶

MÁXIMO GÓMEZ

PEPE TORRES

JOSÉ CARDET

PEDRO ROGENA
GARAYALDE
AGRAMONTE
RASTRO
ARIAS
AGUILERA

UNIÓN

BANCO FINANCIERO INTERNACIONAL ■
PHOTO SERVICE ■
CARPETA ISLAZUL ■
BUEN FONDO DE UTRALES ■
PHARMACY ●

EDIFICIO CRISTAL ●

IGLESIA SAN ISIDORO ★

Plaza Julio Graves De Peralta

MUSEO PROVINCIAL ■
Parque Calixto García
CINE MARTÍ ▶
CAFÉ CHAPELÍN ▶
CASA DE LA TROVA ▶
RUMBOS CAFÉ (24 HOUR) ●
LIBRARY ■
CASA DE ARTE ■
LA MALAGUEÑA ★
CREMERÍA GUAMÁ ▶
CENTRO TELEFÓNICO ●
MUSEO DE LA HISTORIA ★
NATURAL CARLOS DE LA TORRE

HOTEL MAJESTY ●

FREXES

ZORILLA

MARTÍ

ANGEL GUERRA

CABLES

LUZ CABALLERO

ARICOCHES

CEMETERY

100 yds
100 m
0
0

gain an idea of its actual scale. The tight historic core is laid out in a near-perfect grid. At its heart is Parque Calixto García, bounded by Calles Frexes, Martí, Libertad (also known as Manduley), and Maceo. Most sites of importance lie within a few blocks of Parque García.

Frexes leads west from the park to the Carretera Central, which skirts downtown and swings southwest, heading away from the city for Bayamo and, eventually, Santiago. Frexes runs east from the square and links up with the road to Guardalavaca. Martí leads east and merges with Avenida de los Libertadores (lined with statues and monuments to revolutionary heroes), which leads east through the modern Plaza de la Revolución district. Other roads radiate out, like the spokes of a wheel, to Gibara, Pinares de Mayarí, and Finca Mayabe. The city is bypassed to the south by a ring road *(circunvalación)*.

SIGHTSEEING

Vicinity of Plaza Calixto García

The place to begin is the main square, Plaza Calixto García, known to locals as "el parque." The square has little visual appeal, but it is a pleasure to sit beneath the large shade trees and watch the activity. At its heart is a marble statue of General Calixto García, Holguín's most famous son, who was born in the simple house at Calle Miró #147, just off the square. Some of his personal effects are on view inside the museum.

The square also has the **Museo Provincial,** on the north side at Calle Frexes #198, with an eclectic range of historical artifacts and the usual photographs and displays recording the glories of the Revolution and the parts played by local inhabitants in Cuban contemporary history. It was formerly the Casino Español, where Spanish gentry caroused. One curiosity that locals enjoy telling is how the building (with its cage-like barred windows) became known as La Pariquera—the Parrot's Cage—supposedly after Spanish troops in their garish yellow, blue, and green uniforms barricaded themselves inside the building in 1868, when the town was besieged by General Calixto García's troops. The museum's pride and joy is a 35-cm-long pre-Columbian axe carved in the figurine shape of a human. The axe has become

view of Holguín

the provincial symbol. Open Mon.-Sat. noon-7 p.m. Entrance costs US$1.

Other historic buildings on the square house the library and the Bien Fondo Culturales (next to the museum), the Casa de la Trova, Casa de Arte, and, on the south side, the art deco Teatro Comandante Eddy Sunol.

Follow Maceo or Manduley south one block and you pass the **Museo de la História Natural Carlos de la Torre,** in an impressive neoclassical building strongly influenced by Moorish design. Note the beautiful ceramic tilework. The museum houses an eclectic array of dead animals and birds, including a stuffed manatee and a leatherback turtle, plus a dazzling collection of over 4,000 colorful polymite (snail) shells. It's open Tues.-Sat. 8 a.m.-6 p.m. and Sunday 8 a.m.-noon. Entrance costs US$1.

Plaza Julio Graves de Peralta

This small, attractive square, four blocks south of Parque Calixto García, is also known as Parque de San Isidoro. It is anchored by a marble statue of its namesake, looking remarkably like Karl Marx. At the northwest corner is a wall with a mural of a youthful Fidel holding a Soviet submachine-gun aloft, with other revolutionary heroes from the Americas to his right.

On the east side of Plaza Peralta is the **Iglesia San Isidoro,** dating from 1720 but restored in 1996. Its simple interior is entirely lacking in baroque or other typically Spanish colonial features, although the wooden ceiling is noteworthy.

Plaza San José
The most appealing and antique square is this quiet oasis two blocks north of Parque Calixto García and also known as Plaza Maceo. The reclusive cobbled square is surrounded by shade trees and simple colonial buildings. It is dominated on its east side by the beautiful **Iglesia José,** glowing incandescent in the Cuban light.

Mirador de Holguín
Looming over Holguín to the north is La Loma de la Cruz (Hill of the Cross), named for the cross that has stood here since 1790. The crest is dominated by a little castle-like structure. Inside is **The Pilgrim's Gallery,** selling crude paintings and ceramics. From here, you can look across the dry, barren plains towards the strange mountain formations known as *mogotes.*

Rumbos has a snack bar at the top of the steps. There's also a thatched restaurant with a *mirador* on the hilltop 200 meters farther west. You can climb the 450 or so steps that begin at the north end of Calle Maceo, 10 blocks north of Plaza San José. If the climb sounds demanding, don't worry—there are seats at regular intervals.

Fábrica de Órganos
This factory, also called Taller Polivalente, provides a fascinating peek at age-old Cuban craftsmanship as workers fashion organs and other musical instruments—a local tradition. A mile east of the base of La Loma, at Carretera de Gibara #301, it's the only organ factory in Cuba. Open weekdays 8 a.m.-4 p.m.

Plaza de la Revolución
The communists have built their own plaza, a wide-open concrete parking lot dominated by a huge frieze depicting important events in Cuba's history. The plaza, in a new *reparto* northeast of the city, can jam in 150,000-plus people. The plaza is dedicated to Calixto García, the homegrown hero of the War of Independence. His mausoleum is here; his remains were moved from Havana in 1980 (when the square was completed) to his native soil. His mother (also a patriot) is buried behind the plaza beneath a copse of shade trees, where a bronze monument features a faux-Cuban flag draped in the shape of Holguín province. By local custom, newlyweds deposit their bridal bouquets beneath the monument.

ACCOMMODATIONS

Budget
At the low end of the scale is the **Hotel Turquino,** at the east end of Calle Martí. This basic hotel for Cubans has rooms for 13 pesos s, 15 d (foreigners are allowed—but do expect to pay in dollars). A similar option is the **Hotel Majesty,** two blocks west of Plaza Calixto García, tel. 42-4322, with rooms for from eight to 30 pesos (Fidel Castro once slept in room 7). Alternately, in the same price range, try the **Hotel Praga,** at Calle López e/ Aguilera y Frexes, tel. 42-2665.

If the hotel receptionists turn you away, try making a reservation through the *carpeta* on the third floor of the Edificio Cristal on Plaza Calixto García.

Moderate
Horizontes' 202-room **Hotel Pernik,** on Avenida Dimitrov, near the Plaza de la Revolución, tel. 481011, is the principal tourist hotel in town. The hotel is named for the home town of Georgei (Jorge) Dimitrov, the first leader of communist Bulgaria, which helped finance construction. Rooms have a/c, TVs, and telephones. The hotel has a swimming pool, tennis court, and car rental. The restaurant is better than at most urban hotels of this type. Low-season prices are US$19 s, US$24 d in low season, US$25 s, US$32 d in high season.

The **Hotel El Bosque,** tel. 481012, is a more appealing option, about 400 meters farther east on Avenida Dimitrov. It has a restaurant, swimming pool, car rental, shops, and a disco, plus 69 a/c cabins set in pleasant grounds. Rates are about US$14 s, US$18 d in low season, US$20 s, US$27 d in high season.

Unless you need to be in town, the place to be is either the Finca Mayabe (see below) or Cubanacán's **Villa el Cocal,** on the Carretera Central, about six km south of town, tel. 461902. It has 40 rooms in beautiful two-story villas set amidst spacious gardens full of bougainvillea and birdsong (US$43 s, US$55 d year-round). At its heart is a pool and bar beside a huge spreading tree. The hotel boasts a large, atmospheric thatched restaurant. It serves a good buffet when tour groups are in.

FOOD

There is astonishingly little to recommend here. The restaurant at Hotel El Bosque is a disappointment; somewhat better is the one at Hotel Pernik, where there is a full menu of Cuban dishes, plus a pianist and saxophonist entertain.

If you have wheels, head out to **El Cocal,** the **Mirador de Holguín,** or **Finca Mayabe,** where the restaurants are atmospheric and the food quality (and the prices) are higher.

For private restaurants, try the **Polineslo,** on the 13th floor of a high-rise unit at Avonida Lenin e/ Garayalde y Agramonte, and the **Pico Cristal,** on the third floor of the commercial complex at the corner of Calle Libertad and Martí.

You can buy slices of pizza for five pesos apiece at **Pizzeria Roma,** at Calle Maceo and Agramonte, where there's also a basic **Casa de Queso** (House of Cheese), where, alas, the cupboard was bare when I last called by. You should have better luck at the **Café Chapelín,** on the main square, where Rumbos also operates a 24-hour café with a pleasant little courtyard and an arbor for shade.

The best place to buy snacks is in the parking lot of the baseball stadium, where dozens of stalls sell *batidos, refrescoes,* and all kinds of tidbits. Feeling the heat? Then head to **Cremería Guamá,** on Plaza Peralta for ice cream.

There are plenty of *paladares,* which are your best bet. Ask around.

ENTERTAINMENT AND EVENTS

Holguín is not known for its nightlife, but there are a few options available.

The Hotel Pernik has a **cabaret** featuring a magician, comedian, and singers. **La Malagueña** is a local bar popular for dominos and which also has a cabaret Mon.-Sun. from 9 p.m. For Tropicana-style open-air *cabaret espectáculo,* with sexy, sequined, stiletto-heeled mulattas, head to **Centro Nocturno,** three km east of town on the road to Las Tunas, Tues.-Sun. at 9 p.m.; US$10. A lesser *espectáculo* is in the **El Pétalo** disco, in the Hotel El Bosque, tel. 481012, US$5. The crowd is almost exclusively Cuban.

Traditional music and dance are performed at the **Casa de la Trova,** on the main square. Performances are also hosted in the **Teatro Comandante Eddy Sunol,** and the **Bien Fondo Culturales,** facing each other on the main square. The latter contains the **Galeria Bayado,** displaying experimental ceramics and art. Entertainment is offered on weekends, including a *Noches del Bayado* program on Friday at 9 p.m. The **Casa de Arte** houses the **Centro de Artes Plasticos,** where jazz concerts are held each Saturday at 9 p.m.

For movies, take your pick of the **Cine Martí,** on the north side of Parque Calixto García, or **Cine Baría,** on Manduley, one block north of Parque San José.

On Saturday evenings, check out Parque Céspedes, where an organist plays at 8 p.m. Worth a peek, too, is the **Casino de la Playa,** at Manduley and Cuba, where a professional organ group practices.

Every 3 May, a religious procession—**Romería de Mayo**—ascends to the top of Loma de la Cruz, where a Mass is held. The **Festival Internacional de Ballet** is held in November every even-numbered year; and the **Fiesta Iberoamericana de la Cultura,** in October, celebrates music, dance, and theater. A culture week is also held in mid-January.

SPORTS AND RECREATION

The huge Calixto García baseball and sports stadium, just west of the Hotel Pernik, is impressive. It can hold 30,000 spectators and is said to contain a **Baseball Museum.** With luck, you might catch a game.

SERVICES AND INFORMATION

There's an **Immigration office** at Calle Frexes #76 if you need to extend your stay. Open Mon.-Sat. 8 a.m.-2 p.m.

There's no tourist information bureau, but the various tourism-related offices in Edificio Pico de Cristal, on the southeast corner of Parque Calixto García, may be of help. These include the reservations office for Islazul hotels, tel. 42-4718, and, upstairs, the office of Cubana airlines, and the booking office for Campismo Popular.

The Hotel Pernik and El Bosque both have small postal facilities. You can also send letters and packages by express mail with **DHL** in the Hotel Pernik, tel. 481984. It's open weekdays 9 a.m.-6 p.m. and Saturday 8:30 a.m.-noon. The main **post office** is at Calles Agramonte and Maceo. All the tourist hotels have telephone facilities. There's a **Centro Telefónico** in the Pico Cristal building on the southeast corner of the main square. The main Centro Telefónico is two blocks west of the main square, on Martí (between Mártires and Máximo Gómez).

The *biblioteca* on Plaza Calixto García is also impressive. Its works are almost exlusively in Spanish and of a strongly socialist bent, as is the literature for sale at **Librería Rojena,** on the east side of the main square.

There are several hospitals. The main one is **Hospital Lenin,** tel. 42-3054, on the west side of town. The Hotel Pernik and Motel El Bosque have nurses.

Plaza Calixto García contains both a **Banco Nacional** and a **Banco Financiero Interna-**

cional. You can exchange US dollars for pesos with *jiniteros,* who hang out on Parque Calixto García.

The **Photo Service,** on Plaza Calixto García, sells from a meager stock of batteries, film, and instamatic cameras.

GETTING THERE

By Bus
Holguín is served daily by bus no. 610, which departs Havana's main bus terminal at 9:30 a.m. and 6:40 p.m. (12 hours; 36 pesos). Buses also serve Holguín from Bayamo, Camagüey, Las Tunas, and Santiago, but getting a seat is extremely difficult due to overbooking. The **Terminal Inter-Provinciales** is on the west side of town, on the Carretera Central at Calle 1 de Mayo. The **Terminal Municipales,** serving nearby towns, is eight blocks east.

Buses to/from Guardalavaca, Moa, Baracoa, and other towns east of Holguín arrive and depart from a separate terminal on Avenida de los Libertadores, south of the baseball stadium.

By Train
Surprisingly, Holguín is *not* on the main railway line, which passes 15 km south of town. The station is at Cacocum, from which a branch line serves Holguín's **Estación de Ferrocarriles,** south of town at Calle Pita (the ticket office for foreigners—where you must pay in dollars—is opposite the station). Allow plenty of time for connections. The *especial* trains that operate between Havana and Santiago stop here. Cacocum is also served from Las Tunas by train no. 431, departing at 1:10 p.m. and arriving Holguín at 4 p.m., and from Santiago by train no. 410, departing at 8:20 a.m. and arriving Cacocum at 11:35 a.m.

By Air
Cubana operates flights from Havana to Holguín on Monday and Saturday at 2:30 p.m., Tuesday and Thursday at 12:20 p.m., Wednesday and Friday at 3:30 p.m., and Sunday at 1:55 p.m. (US$79 one-way). Additional flights are offered on Tuesday (8:45 a.m.), Wednesday (11:35 a.m.) and Friday (3:15 p.m.). Schedules are subject to change.

HOLGUÍN USEFUL TELEPHONE NUMBERS

Police . . . . tel. 116
Ambulance . . . . tel. 48-1640
Hospital . . . . tel. 46-2011
Airport. . . . . tel. 46-2512
Railway Station . . . . tel. 42-2331

From Europe: Martinair operates a charter each Saturday during winter from Amsterdam to Holguín (fares from London via Holland begin at £495, depending on date of flight; contact Regent Holidays, 15 John St., Bristol BS1 2HR, tel. 1272-211711, fax 1272-254866). **Sunworld** offers charter flights from Gatwick, England, each Wednesday May through November. **Journey Latin America,** 14-16 Devonshire Rd., London W4 2HD, tel. (181) 747-8315, fax (181) 742-1312, offers a two-week fly-drive package from Havana to Holguín, based on a charter flight from Stansted to Havana on Thursday (from £1,279). LTV also flies from Düsseldorf. And Cubana has flights from Cologne.

From Canada: Regent Holidays and Air Transat offer charter flights to Holguín (Guardalavaca) from C$429 roundtrip.

GETTING AROUND

Buses run through most areas of the city (10 centavos *regular,* 40 centavos *especial*). Bus no. 16 connects the Hotel Pernik with downtown. Bus no. 3 runs from the terminal to the foot of Loma de la Cruz.

The favored mode of transport in town is the **tricycle rickshaw.** You should be able to get anywhere downtown for 10 pesos or US$1.

Havanatur has a **car rental** office at Carretera de Mayarí, Km 5.5, tel./fax 24-33 5467, and in Motel El Bosque. You can make reservations through tourist hotels.

Call 48-2398 for a tourist taxi.

GETTING AWAY

By Air
Cubana's flights to Havana depart Holguín on Monday and Saturday at 5:20 p.m., Tuesday and Thursday at 2:45 p.m., Wednesday and Friday at 6:20 p.m., and Sunday at 4:45 p.m. The **Frank País Airport** is south of town, tel. 24-43934. It is served by a bus from Calle Rodríguez, near the train station six blocks south of Parque Calixto García. A taxi costs about US$10.

Cubana has an office in the Pico Cristal building on Calle Libertad facing Parque Calixto García, tel. 425707.

By Train
Train no. 430 departs Cacocum for Havana at 8 a.m. (13 hours; US$31). Train no. 411 departs at 2:35 p.m. for Santiago (four hours; US$5). You can buy tickets at the Terminal Ferrocarril, on Calle Pita, eight blocks south of Plaza Calixto García.

FINCA MAYABE

Finca Mayabe is a "typical" *campesino's* farmstead high above the Mayabe Valley, eight km southeast of town.

The make-believe farm raises two dozen species of fruit trees. Enclosures hold turkeys, geese, and other farm animals. It even has a *yallah de gallos*—a cockpit—where you can watch cockfights. Horseback riding is also available. Just below the *bohio* is the **Mirador de Mayabe,** with a swimming pool and sundeck suspended over the cliff face, from where you can look down over the Valle de Mayabe, planted extensively with citrus groves.

The Finca's claim to fame, however, is a beer-loving burro called Pancho. The thirsty donkey has consumed, I was told, over 42,000 bottles of beer—at an average of eight per day (on one occasion, he guzzled 46!). He is given Monday off—presumably to sleep off his weekend hangover. Pancho (born in 1960) lives in a stall next to the bar, appropriately named Bar Burro.

Accommodations and Food
Finca Mayabe has 20 *cabañas* surrounded by palms and bougainvillea on the hilltop facing over the swimming pool and valley. The basic bungalows have radios and refrigerators (US$30). There's also a fully staffed villa for rent—**Casa de Pancho,** tel. 42-2160 or 42-5498, or c/o Islazul, Calle Libertad #126, Holguín, tel. 42-3512. This stunning house has four a/c double rooms decorated with pretty fabrics, modern furniture, and rattan wardrobes. Each room has a balcony, private bathroom, radio, color TV, and telephone (US$35 per room).

The facility includes a thatched restaurant and bar. The house specialty is sausage and pork cracklings. Seatings are supposedly at noon, 2, 6, and 8 p.m. A folkloric cabaret show is featured in the restaurant.

HOLGUÍN TO GRANMA PROVINCE

South of **Cacocum,** the province is flat as a lake, with savanna and sugar sharing the landscape. The little thatched *bohíos* are each in their own little garden fenced by tightly packed cactus shaped like candelabras and neatly and lovingly trimmed. South of **Baches,** the topiary work takes on real form, with little bushes clipped into rondels and cones. In the distance, the Sierra Maestra hovers luminously.

About 38 km south of Holguín is a sign for Granma province made of rocks and a gateway arch (the provincial boundary) supporting a large bronze bell.

Accommodations
About 13 km south of Holguín is the basic **Motel Los Pinos,** tel. 27216, a self-contained resort surrounded by pine groves and with a shop, dark bar, and basic restaurant. It's a lively place, popular with Cubans. Prices range 11-21 pesos per person, depending on the room.

NORTH OF HOLGUÍN

The landscape due north of Holguín is dominated by parched cattle country of little scenic interest, with a singular and noteworthy exception—the Grupo de Maniabon, a deeply dissected upland region of exquisite beauty. The coastal flatland is scrub-covered and indented with finger-like, marsh-fringed *esteros.* There are some splendid beaches.

GIBARA

Gibara (pop. 18,000), 28 km north of Holguín, is a dusty, time-encrusted fishing port that curls around a coral nipple jutting into the Bahía de Gibara. It was a major port in colonial days, when it was known as Villa Blanca. Rising over the flatlands inland is a flat-topped mountain, the *Silla de Gibara* (Saddle of Gibara), considered to be the hill described by Christopher Columbus in his journal when he first landed in Cuba, on 28 October 1492. (Citizens of Baracoa, in Guantánamo province, hotly defend their notion that Columbus landed *there* and that the mountain he described is their own El Yunque.) It is thought that the Genoese navigator first set foot in Cuba in the small bay **Bahía Bariay,** about 10 km east of town (see "Rafael Freyre," below).

The bay is enshrined in **Bahía Bariay National Park,** which encompasses over 30 beaches, numerous cays, and the low Grupo de Maniabon mountains.

There is very little to see, although you can gain a sense of Gibara's laid-back mood by walking the Malecón, a popular seafront promenade, where on weekends local couples still stroll arm in arm. Waves sweep in and break over the coral rocks. You may be surprised to find windsurfers and little sailboats in the breezy bay.

The streets rise steeply south and west of the pretty main plaza, which has a church with Byzantine-style cupolas and a stand of African oak trees. The church was recently restored. You might check out the **Museum of Colonial Art,** in a neoclassical mansion at Independencia 27, a short distance away. This former home of a tobacco-trading family boasts a modest collection of period furniture (open Tues.-Sat. 8 a.m.-noon and 1-5 p.m. and Sunday 8 a.m.-noon; US$1). Gibara also has a small **Museum of Natural History,** Independencio and Peralla, containing a large collection of shells and a miscellany of deceased wildlife (Tues.-Sat. 8 a.m.-noon and 1-5 p.m. and Sunday 8 a.m.-noon; US$1).

Don't be tempted to follow the coast road shown on maps as running west from Gibara to Playa Uvero and Playa La Herradura, in Las Tunas province—you can't get through without a sturdy 4WD and good fortune! Beyond the small community of **Caletones,** sand and coral smother the road, and you're soon amid the coral and mangroves, where the track forks. If you keep left you *may* eventually arrive at a river that can only be forded at low tide.

A small bus runs once daily between Holguín and Gibara. The bus stop is opposite the El Faro restaurant.

Accommodations and Food

There are no tourist hotels here. However, you are likely to be accepted, if grudgingly, at the pesos-only **Hotel Gibara, Hotel Río Luna,** near the town square, or **Hotel Bella Mar,** tel. 3-4206, on General Sartorio.

For eats, take your pick of two waterfront restaurants, the **Miramar,** Donato Mármol #13, tel. 24-34466, a peso eatery popular with locals, and the more impressive **Restaurante El Faro,** a dollars-only eatery run by Rumbos. Both serve *criollo* and seafood cuisine, when food is available. Nearby is the **Bar/Restaurante Villa Blanca,** which also has dramatic views along the coast.

RAFAEL FREYRE AND VICINITY

This ungainly town, 23 km east of Gibara, is dominated by the Rafael Freyre sugar *central.* From Holguín, route 6-241 dips and rises through cattle country punctuated by steep-faced conical limestone formations called *mogotes.*

The town lies a few km inland of **Bahía Bariay.** If you zigzag through town and go past the giant *central,* the road north will take you to the bay and aptly named **Playa Blanca,** where a commemorative plaque to Columbus marks the site thought to be that of the explorer's first landing with his three caravels from Hispaniola. There are two monuments, one on each side of the bay. The first is near the end of the road to Playa Blanca and simply declares this the "site of the first land-ing of Christopher Columbus in Cuba." The second, more recent, is reached by turning north at Frey Benito, four km west of Rafael Freyre.

The road ends at Playa Blanca. The beach is actually a grouping of pocket-size beaches in coral coves. A raised coral reef forms a natural seawall about 50 meters offshore—perfect for dips in calm, bathtub-warm, jade-colored waters.

Continuing east 10 km from Rafael Freyre, a turnoff leads north three km to **Playa Pesquero Nueva,** another beautiful white sand beach with a wide cove at its westernmost end. There's an abandoned *campismo* for Cubans.

Accommodations

The impecunious can stay in Rafael Freyre at the basic **Motel Guabanajay,** which has rooms for 12 and 25 pesos. **Cabaret Guabanajay,** next door, provides entertainment and booze.

Far better, though, is the 36-room **Hotel Don Lino,** tel. 4077, looking over a small but handsome beach at Playa Blanca. It is now under the management of the Canadian Delta Hotels group. Each a/c room has either one king-size or two double beds, a terrace, telephone, satellite TV, and ceiling fan. There's a freshwater pool and attractive *ranchón* restaurant, a gift shop, and recreational facilities. No children are permitted. It operates on an all-inclusive basis, with a free shuttle to the Delta Las Brisas hotel, whose facilities are "on the house." Contact Delta, in Cuba, tel. 33-6336; in Canada, tel. (800) 268-1133, fax (416) 926-7809; in the US, tel. (800) 877-1133.

GUARDALAVACA AND VICINITY

Guardalavaca (the name means "Watch the Cow") is a pocket-size resort about 70 km northeast of Holguín. It is billed as Cuba's second-largest resort, but don't be misled. It is as yet a small-fry and may come as a disappointment to tourists who are expecting more. Guardalavaca consisted at press time of five hotels, a fistful of small restaurants, a couple of artisans' shops, a disco, two car rental agencies, a grocery, and two fabulous beaches. Development was stalled by the onset of the Special Period.

The main beach—very popular with Cubans as well as tourists—runs westward in a curve from the Hotel Atlántico and has plenty of shady *ranchitas* and trees. It is almost 100 meters deep in places. A narrower, 400-meter-long beach fronts the Hotel Delta Las Brisas, to the east. The beachfront is landscaped with a beautiful walkway. Between the two beaches are a series of smaller beaches separated by coral outcrops. Roadside hibiscus add splashes of primary colors.

The resort is popular for scuba diving and snorkeling and is an ideal cut-rate package vacation spot.

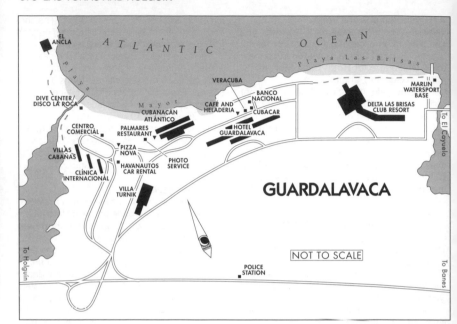

ACCOMMODATIONS

Self-Catering

If you're into self-catering, consider the **Villas Cabañas,** which offer modest bungalows with kitchenettes for about US$35.

Moderate

Take your pick from a trio of modest hotels, all run by Cubanacán.

Hotel Guardalavaca, tel. 30221, opened in 1991 in prefab concrete 100 yards inland from the beach. It has 225 pleasantly appointed a/c rooms with TVs, refrigerators, and 24-hour room service (US$45 s, US$60 d). The quality of the meals leaves much to be desired. Activity revolves around a huge swimming pool with a water slide and netball.

The **Cubanacán Atlántico,** tel. 30280, is similar, though a tad more upscale, with the advantage of a beachfront setting. Its 232 rooms and one suite all have a/c, TVs, and terraces (US$56 s, US$92 d, room only). Not all have ocean views. The hotel features a games room

beside the large swimming pool, car rental, a boutique, tourist bureau, and watersports, including scuba diving, sea kayaks, and windsurfing.

The most impressive is **Villas Turnik,** tel. 30195, also 100 yards inland but of striking contemporary design. It has 136 a/c rooms in gracious two-story villas around a swimming pool set in landscaped grounds. Each has a terrace, color TV, and telephone. There's a *ranchita* bar and an airy restaurant. It's a good bargain in low season at US$31 s, US$35 d (rates jump to US$61 s, US$101 d in high season).

Deluxe

Delta Hotels of Canada operates the sleek **Delta Las Brisas Club Resort,** 350 Bloor St. East #300, Toronto, Ontario M4W 1H4, tel. (416) 926-7800 or (800) 268-1133, fax (416) 926-7846; in Cuba, Calle 248 y Avenida 5, Santa Fe, Havana, tel. 33-6336. This four-star resort, with 230 rooms, three bars, and a watersports center, is one of Cuba's more handsome hotels. The decor is marvelous. It is fronted by its own virtually private section of beach and has a large pool in the shape of a figure eight, with a thatched swim-up bar in the middle. It also has a poolside entertainment center plus a choice of restaurants—including an Italian ristorante, an open-air *ranchón* grill, and a cappuccino café. Windsurfing, kayaking, sailing, water-skiing, and beach and pool volleyball are offered. The resort has a Kid's Kamp for children. Rooms cost US$85 per person, all-inclusive of drinks and meals. A bargain!

FOOD

When you tire of the meals in the Hotel Guardalavaca and Atlántico (where a so-so dinner costs a steep US$12 and the breakfast may make you groan), it's time to check out the handful of beachside eateries. They all serve mediocre cuisine.

El Cayuelo, on Carreteras de Banes, **El Patio,** and **El Ancla** specialize in seafood. The latter sits atop a coral outcrop at the west end of the main beach and serves fish dishes for US$6 and up (lobster costs US$13). **Pizza Nova** offers penne and fettuccine from US$6 and basic pizzas from US$5 (each extra item costs US$1, and shrimp adds US$4). Nearby is the **Palmares Restaurant,** a more elegant, breezy, bodega-style eatery serving pork, seafood, and *criollo* dishes from US$5. It's open noon-midnight.

You can buy **ice cream** from the *heladería* and snack bar opposite the Hotel Guardalavaca.

If you're catering yourself, Western groceries are available in the **Centro Comercial.**

SPORTS AND RECREATION

Horseback riding is offered at the stables south of Hotel Guardalavaca. You can book horseback rides at any of the hotels.

Marlin Watersport Base is on the jetty beside Delta Las Brisas, at the east end of the beach. It offers banana boat rides (US$5 for five minutes), water-skiing (US$15 for five minutes), jet-skiing (US$15 for 15 minutes), snorkeling (US$5 for one hour), and deep-sea fishing (US$250 for five hours). You can also rent small catamarans.

Scuba Diving
Guardalavaca is renowned for its superb diving opportunities, not least its riot of colorful

sponges (among the largest found anywhere in the Caribbean), deepwater gorgonians reaching the unusual length of six feet, and swordfish and barracudas slicing along an abrupt cliff known as "The Jump." Another exciting spot is Grouper Canyon, a fissure sheltering black and Nassau groupers.

Marlin Watersport Base charges US$36 for one dive (US$23 if you supply your own gear). There's another scuba-diving facility on the beach at the west end of Guardalavaca. Resort and certification courses are offered.

ENTERTAINMENT AND EVENTS

The nightly **cabaret** in the **Hotel Guardalavaca** is rather strained. You have to applaud the entertainers who put their all into getting the patrons in a dancing mood. The **Cubanacán Atlántico** hosts a more interesting cabaret, with comics and mime. **Fantástico Tours,** tel. 30114 or 30130, in the Delta Las Brisas, offers a night at Cabaret Nocturno, departing at 9 p.m.

All the hotel cabarets are followed by discos. *The* place to be, however, is **La Roca Disco,** at the west end of Guardalavaca. Its large dance floor is open on two sides, with seating beneath the stars and a terrace overlooking the beach. Marvelous! It gets full on weekends, when locals and tourists mingle. Entrance costs US$2.

La Dolce Vita disco, in the Delta Las Brisas hotel, is also ritzy but is utilized mostly by the hotel guests.

Aquarium
Want to watch Flipper flip? Then visit the aquarium enclosed in the midst of Bahía de Naranjo, about five km west of Guardalavaca. Here, sea lions and dolphins perform acrobatics at 10:30 a.m. and 2 p.m. (US$10, including entrance and dolphin show). Visitors can even swim with the dolphins (US$10 extra). All the hotels offer excursions.

ORGANIZED EXCURSIONS

Fantástico Tours, tel. 30114 or 30130, has a tour desk in the Delta Las Brisas. It offers a wide range of excursions, including one-day trips to Trinidad, Havana, and Baracoa and two-day trips to Havana and Baracoa. Fantástico even arranges one-day trips to Montego Bay, in Jamaica. It also has trips to Bahía Naranjo (see below), plus a "seafari" by boat to Playa Pesquero, and a five-hour deep-sea fishing trip, both sailing from the marina pier at 9 a.m.

Cubanacán offers a full-day excursion to Havana departing at 6:30 a.m., day excursions to Cayo Coco and Cayo Largo, Pinares de Mayarí, and Montego Bay in Jamaica, plus a two-day excursion to Baracoa and Santiago. You can also take a full-day excursion by bus to Cayo Saetia. Reservations are offered through the hotels.

Veracuba has an office opposite the Hotel Guardalavaca. It also offers excursions.

Marlin Watersport Base offers a "seafari" excursion along the coast (US$29, including lunch), as well as coast rides (US$10 per person per hour).

Helicopter Excursions: You can hop aboard a chopper for a bird's-eye view of Cuba on a day-trip to Santiago offered by Fantástico Tours, which also offers day-long helicopter trips to Cayo Saetía, departing at 7:30 a.m.

SHOPPING

The hotels all have souvenir stores selling artwork, T-shirts, rum, and cigars. You'll also find a range of jewelry, carvings, and other arts and crafts in the **artisans' store** in the Centro Comercial. Also check out the **Popular Art Bazaar** and **Cubartesania.**

SERVICES

The **post office** and **DHL** express international mail service are both located in the Delta Las Brisas. You can make international calls from any of the hotels.

You'll find a full-service **Banco Nacional** opposite the Hotel Guardalavaca, and a **Banco Financiero Internacional** in the Centro Comercial.

There's a **Clínica Internacional** specifically for foreigners, with a doctor and nurse on 24-hour call. It's at the far west end.

The **Cupet gas station** is one km west of town, on the main road to Holguín.

A **Photo Service** store next to the Palmares Restaurant sells batteries and film. **Massage** is available at the Hotel Delta Las Brisas (US$8 partial, US$18 full).

GETTING THERE AND AROUND

Guardalavaca has no airport. Flights arrive at Holguín, where transfers are offered (see "Getting There," under "Holguín," above). Buses operate from Holguín and Banes and drop off and depart opposite Villas Turnik. A taxi from Holguín will cost about US$40 one-way.

You can walk everywhere, since there is only the two-km-long beachfront road. You'll need wheels if you want to explore farther afield. I highly recommend touring the hills and valleys of the Grupo de Maniabon immediately southeast.

Havanautos has a car rental office beside the traffic circle at the west end; **Cubacar** has an office opposite the Hotel Guardalavaca. Mopeds *(mobilettes)* can also be rented from Cubacar (US$5 one hour, US$8 two hours, US$25 per day, US$100 per week). **Bicycles** can be rented at the Delta Las Brisas.

Taxis, including 4WD jeep-taxis, are available at the Cubacar office. Horse-drawn buggies run up and down the beachfront road (US$2 maximum). In addition, a local named Wilfredo Hidalgo rents his old Ford as a taxi.

BAHÍA DE NARANJO

A huge flask-shaped bay lies immediately west of Guardalavaca. The entire 400-hectare *estero* is a national park fringed by mangroves. A fish hatchery is located here. An aquarium is located in the midst of the bay (see above).

Playa Esmeralda lies just east of the mouth of the bay, three km west of Guardalavaca and reached by a separate road from the main highway. The powdery white sand beach is spectacular. Playa Esmeralda (formerly Playa Estero Ciego) is dominated by Gaviota's Sol Río del Lunes and Río del Mar hotels. You can gain access with a day-pass (good for the evening, too) for US$50, which includes use of all the facilities.

STILL PUFFING AWAY

Cuba maintains about 200 operating steam trains, all of them on sugar estates, with a concentration around Guardalavaca. Most date from the 1920s (the first Cuban railway was built by the British in 1837). The trains are kept going because the sugar mills operate only four to five months a year, providing plenty of time to overhaul the engines and keep them in good repair.

The road to Playa Esmeralda leads past a turnoff to the left pointing the way to **Mongo Vína,** where the eclectic attractions include a mini-zoo, cactus garden, medicinal garden, collection of caged birds, and typical *campesino* buildings. Trails lead down through the grounds to the *estero*'s edge, where you have a view across the lagoon to the aquarium.

Accommodations and Food

Sol Río del Lunes, Playa Estero Ciego, Bahía de los Naranjos, Guardalavaca, tel. 24-30102, fax 24-30126, is a splendid new property—one of Cuba's finest—on Playa Esmeralda. This all-inclusive hotel has 222 rooms and eight suites in four blocks set in beautifully landscaped grounds. It is operated jointly by Gaviota and Spain's Sol Meliá group. The rooms are large and nicely appointed, with satellite TV, telephones, and other modern conveniences. The property has its own nightclub and scuba diving center, plus a beachside restaurant. Rates are US$95 s, US$140 d in low season and US$110 s, US$170 d in high season, including all meals and drinks, entertainment and watersports (except motorized sports, such as jet skis, which are extra). You can purchase a day pass for US$50.

Sharing the beach is the **Sol Río Mar,** a virtually identical sister property that is *not* all-inclusive. Rooms cost US$45 s, US$55 d in low season and US$60 s, US$70 d in high season.

Mongo Vína serves *criollo* meals in its thatched restaurant. You can arrange ferry rides to Mongo Vína.

The **Base Naútica** has a two-story bungalow for rent on an island in the bay (US$70). It sleeps four people.

Base Naútica

There's a very small and basic **marina,** on the southern shore of the bay, two km west of the turnoff from the coast highway for Playa Esmeralda, tel. 25395 or 30115. A local Guarda Frontera provides clearance for private boaters (he or she can also call a taxi if you want to tour). Electricity and gasoline are available.

Boats leave for the aquarium on a regular basis from both Mongo Vína and Base Naútica.

GRUPO DE MANIABON

This dramatic upland region lies between Guardalavaca and Banes. Route 6-241 cuts through the region, leading you through quintessentially Cuban scenery, with tobacco fields plowed by oxen in the lee of rolling hills. The landscape is dominated by great rounded outcrops, with tousled royal palms, girthy silk-cotton trees, and bright red flamboyants rising over the pastures. The *bohios* here are hedged by neatly trimmed rows of cactus.

In the midst of the valley, on a hilltop midway between Guardalavaca and Banes, is the **Museo Chorro de Maita,** on the site of the largest aboriginal burial site thus far discovered in the Caribbean. It is thought that a large Indian village called Bani occupied the site. Almost 200 skeletons have been unearthed. The site is a national monument and very impressive. A gallery surrounds the burial ground within a building where the skeletons lie with arms crossed over chests in peaceful repose. Open Tues.-Sat. 9 a.m.-5 p.m. and Sunday 9 a.m.-1 p.m.; US$2.

BANES

Banes, 20 km southeast of Guardalavaca, is a small place (pop. 95,000) with a lot of history. Today it is a sleepy provincial town with a colonial core of mostly wooden houses surrounded by modern, concrete apartment blocks.

For much of this century, the town was run by the United Fruit Company, which owned virtually all the land in the region and had a massive sugar mill called Boston (since renamed Nicaragua) five km south of town. Jamaicans

BANES USEFUL TELEPHONE NUMBERS

Police . . . . tel. 116
Ambulance . . . . tel. 8-2727
Hospital . . . . tel. 8-3324
Terminal de Ómnibus . . . . . . tel. 8-2407

were imported to work the fields, and there are still a few locals who speak English and attempt to maintain their ancestors' traditions.

Fulgencio Batista was born here in 1901. His future archenemies, Fidel and Raúl Castro, were born nearby at Birán. As youths, the brothers would come into town in a red convertible to dance at the American Club. Here, on 12 October 1948, Fidel married Mirta Diaz-Balart, daughter of the wealthy mayor of Banes. (Fidel gave little time to his wife, and the marriage dissolved five years later.) Mirta's brother, Rafael, headed Batista's youth organization and in 1950 arranged a meeting for the young Fidel—already a well-known political activist—with Batista at the latter's sumptuous estate outside Havana. Rafael would later be named Batista's Minister of the Interior, in charge of the secret police (he fled Cuba after the Revolution; his son keeps the right-wing flame burning as a US congressman from Florida).

The only noteworthy site in town is the **Museo Indocubano** (Museum of Indian Civilization), on Calle General Marrero #305, tel. 2487. It exhibits a collection of shells, pottery, tools, carvings, statuary, and other artifacts and amazingly sophisticated jewelry, most importantly a small gold idol (thought to date from the 13th century and the first gold piece ever discovered in Cuba) wearing a feather headdress. There are also murals depicting the Indians and their ruin, rendered by artist José Martinez. Only a fraction of the collection of 14,000 indigenous pieces is on display. Open Tues.-Sat. noon-6 p.m. and Sunday 2-6 p.m. Entrance costs US$1.

The oblong plaza one block east of the museum has an eclectic range of intriguing buildings, most notably the art deco church—**Iglesia de Nuestra Señora de la Caridad**—where Fidel Castro got married.

You can follow the main road east from Banes along a rolling plateau planted in sugar. At the end is a handsome beach—**Playa Puerto Rico**—reached by following the dirt road to the left along the ugly coral shore. There's a basic *campismo* here, but, as usual, it hasn't any guests.

Accommodation and Food

If you end up here you can check in to the very basic pesos-only **Hotel Bani,** on General Marrero, or (a far better bet) the **Motel El Oasis,** tel. 3447. The latter, at the entrance to Banes, is one of the more pleasing motels for Cubans, with modest *cabañas* in nice grounds (18 pesos). Its restaurant and bar are popular with locals.

You'll find three pleasant-looking *paladares* near the Motel El Oasis, on the road into town. If thirsty, you can buy refreshing *batidos* made of

Banes

fruit and iced milk at **Casa del Batidos,** at the corner of Avenida Cárdenas and Bayamo.

Getting There
Buses operate between Holguín and Banes, where the bus terminal is at the east end of Calle Los Angeles. Bus no. 617 runs to Banes from Havana (40 pesos), and another afternoon bus goes to Holguín in time for the train to Havana.

MAYARÍ TO GUANTÁNAMO PROVINCE

MAYARÍ ABAJO

This medium-size town is 80 km east of Holguín, on the banks of the Río Mayarí. It lies in the midst of a fertile region encompassing the Bay of Nipes, at 50 square miles the largest pocket bay in Cuba (it was here, according to legend, that in 1608 three fishermen found the famous wooden statue of the Virgin of Charity that now resides in the basilica at El Cobre, in Santiago province.) The main coast road bypasses Mayarí, which is of no tourist interest except for the **Cupet gas station** in the town center.

The town, six km inland from the bay, was the subject of José Yglesia's *In the Fist of the Revolution,* in which the author documents the changes wrought since the Revolution. At the time of Fidel Castro's birth at Birán, the town and surrounding region were in the hands of the United Fruit Company, which had carved out a "veritable private fiefdom." Says author Ted Szulc, "The Mayarí region . . . featured probably greater American presence and control than any other place in Cuba."

United Fruit and its subsidiary, the Nipe Bay Company, bought 240,000 acres of land in the area following the Spanish-Cuban-American War. The town was a humble group of tumbledown shacks when the US company took over and transformed it into a bustling commercial center. The United Fruit Company built special housing for its US employees, complete with swimming pools and even a polo club. It also had its own police force to maintain order. But, writes Szulc in his biography *Fidel,* the "thousands of canecutters and mill workers lived with their families in miserable *bohíos* . . . usually earning less than one dollar a day (sometimes only forty or fifty cents, without food) during the four months of the annual *zafra,* or harvest. In the remaining months—the sinister 'dead-time'—

there was simply no work." This was the environment in which Fidel Castro grew up and which awakened his political consciousness.

In an impassioned speech in 1968, Fidel spoke of how "forests that covered all these hectares with precious woods and that were burned in the furnaces of the sugar mills, were worth many times—incomparably many times—this sum of money. They came with bulging pockets to a nation impoverished by thirty years of war to buy the best land of this country for less than six dollars the hectare."

Accommodations and Food
In town, the **Hotel Bitiri,** tel. 5-2589, serves Cubans. It has a swimming pool and 20 basic *cabinas,* plus a restaurant. Hardy travelers might be granted a room.

Several citizens operate *paladares.*

FINCA MANACAS

Fidel's birthplace was at Finca Manacas, at **Birán,** below the western foothills of the Altiplanicie de Nipe, 20 km southwest of Mayarí and 60 km southeast of Holguín. Fidel was born on 13 August 1926 in a two-story house on wooden pilings, with a cattle barn underneath. The property also contained a slaughterhouse, repair shop, store, bakery, and other facilities.

Castro's father, Ángel, began leasing land from the United Fruit Company in 1910, grew sugarcane to sell to their mills, hired labor, and gradually grew wealthy. His property grew to a 26,000-acre domain. Eventually, Fidel's father acquired forests and a sawmill in Pinares as well as a small nickel mine. Fidel, however, has worked to downplay his social privilege and prefers to exaggerate the simplicity of his background. Perhaps for this reason, the house is not marked on tourist maps or otherwise promoted. At press time, there were no road signs or markers.

Unfortunately, to visit the *finca,* you need a permit from the Communist Party headquarters, on the Plaza de la Revolución in Holguín, tel. 42-2224. However, you can drive up and peer through the gate, where a guard will eye you warily. Note the graves of Castro's parents, Ángel and Lina, to the right.

Getting There
From Holguín, take the Mayarí road. Turn south five km west of Cueto to Marcané. Turn east at the Central Loynaz Hechevarría. Birán is seven km farther, and Finca Las Manacas is four km beyond.

SIERRA CRISTAL

This vast mountain chain rises above the narrow coastal plain, climbing to the sharp-peaked **Pico de Cristal** (1,214 meters). The great mountainous bulk is deeply incised by rivers, which divides the Sierras into separate units. Largest of the rivers is the Río Mayarí. To the west of the valley is the soaring Altiplanicie de Nipe, a flat-topped, steep-sided massif that was the playground for Fidel Castro as a youth.

Integral Mountain Research Station
The Cuban Academy of Sciences has a scientific station at about 500 meters above sea level at Pinares de Mayarí. It was established in 1988 to research the mountain ecology and to evolve sustained development practices. It also serves as a meteorological station.

The mountain ecology is highly varied. Montane rainforest thrives adjacent to pine forest at these cool heights, where mists drift languidly through the branches. The Sierras harbor about 131 endemic mountain species, including orchid species that have adapted to dry conditions by producing neither flower nor leaf in order to conserve life in their roots.

Accommodations and Food
In the heart of the majestic mountains, 20 km south of Mayarí, is **Pinares de Mayarí,** an eco-resort operated by Cubanacán. It has 10 rustic, wooden, red-tile-roofed one-, two- and three-

bedroom cottages, plus 18 rooms, all made of pinewood (US$37 s, US44 d). All have private bathrooms (some with hot water). The recently renovated log cabins were originally built for Cuba's elite. There's an exercise room, steam baths, swimming pool, basketball, tennis, and even a baseball diamond. *Criollo* cuisine is served in the large open dining room with a soaring ceiling. Toads outnumber the guests.

Hiking and Horseback Rides
Horseback rides are available, and you can hire guides for hikes into the nearby forests and to the nearby El Gulyabo waterfall. You'll pass through four distinct ecological environments, from temperate forest to mountain rainforest. Signed stations point out features of the region. After hiking, you can enjoy tea brewed from herbs grown at the station.

Getting There
It's a pleasant and easy drive along a dirt road from Mayarí.

Cubanacán offers day-long excursions to Pinares from Guardalavaca. The company also includes two nights at Pinares de Mayarí (including mountain hiking, horseback riding, and a visit to the science station) in a seven-day ecotour from Santiago to Holguín, including time in the Sierra Maestra and Baconao reserve near Santiago.

Pinares is also included in an 11-day "environmental adventure" and eight-day bicycling adventure in Oriente offered in the US by **Wings of the World,** 1200 William St. #706, Buffalo, NY 14240, tel. (800) 465-8687.

FARALLONES DE SEBORUCO

About five km east from Mayarí, you'll pass a turnoff for the **Farallones de Seboruco,** a cavern system where indigenous Indian artifacts dating back 5,000 years have been found. The cave lies at the base of a hill and is 30 meters high, 500 meters long, and 300 meters wide.

CAYO SAETÍA

What an anomaly. This 42-square-km "island," forming the easternmost side of the entrance o the Bahía de Nipes, is stocked with exotic animals—ostrich, zebra, and antelope—imported for the hunting pleasure of top communist officials, for whom Cayo Saetía was until recent years a near-private vacation spot.

Cayo Saetía is an almost virgin island with white sand beaches as private as your innermost thoughts. It is ecologically important, with a patchwork of ecosystems ranging from mangrove swamps to evergreen forests harboring many endangered and endemic species. As is Cuba's quixotic way, the island is both a wildlife reserve and a hunting preserve where folks with weak (or over-inflated) egos can shoot harmless creatures. Jeep safaris and horseback riding are also available.

The eight-km-wide cay is linked to the mainland by a narrow isthmus.

Accommodations

The Villa Cayo Saetía complex, tel. 425350, has seven handsome yet rustic *cabañas* and a bar atop the hill. The hotel plays on the wildlife theme. The eyes of animals that wandered between crosshairs glower eerily as you pass by. The meals in the restaurant are said to be very good. You kill it, you eat it! Rooms cost a steep US$70 d.

Getting There and Away

Cayo Saetía is 20 minutes by helicopter from Guardalavaca (90 minutes by jeep). Tourist hotels in Santiago and elsewhere also offer excursions to Cayo Saetía, as does Havanatur.

Private boats can berth at the marina, on the southern side of the promontory at Saetía. There are officials to provide clearance.

MAYARÍ TO MOA

Route 6-123 parallels the shore and leads past a series of port towns that rely on the nickel and mineral-ore industries. The first of these is the important ore-processing town of **Nicaro,** 12 km east of Mayarí. There's no reason to digress the four km from the coast road to visit Nicaro, which sits atop a hill overlooking Cayo Saetía across the Bahía de Levisa.

Well worth the visit, however, is **Playa Corinthia,** a seemingly endless beach of purest

white sand shelving into turquoise shallows. There's nothing here—making it a perfect reclusive escape. The beach is backed by fir trees and perfect for camping. You can hear the muffled surf breaking on the reef 400 meters offshore. The beach is about eight km from the coast road, 25 km east of Mayarí.

Farther east, you pass the sugar-processing town of **Cayo Mambí** (five km north of the coast road). West of Cayo Mambí, great fields of sugarcane sweep down to the coast, rippling and silvered by breezes, like folds of green silk. East of Cayo Mambí the landscape takes an abrupt turn. The shore is lined with mangroves and the beaches are, with rare exception, a grim disappointment. Inland, the rolling hills cultivated with bananas and sugar and arable crops give way to miles of uninhabited, pine-smothered mountain slopes. The climate becomes drier, and the farther east you go, the more scrub takes over until soon, you are passing penurious hills scarred by years of human abuse.

MOA

Tall chimneys belching out smoke of every color—black, yellow, and white—provide plenty of warning that you've arrived at the coastal town of Moa, the center of Cuba's metal-ore industry. The first mines were set up by US companies before the Revolution (they were nationalized, of course, following the rancorous relations with Washington).

The town is smothered with red dust from the nearby nickel-ore processing plants, which dominate the local economy. The dour landscape is made worse by the *repartos* (neighborhoods) of ugly, Soviet-inspired, prefab concrete housing. It has been claimed (probably in

MOA USEFUL TELEPHONE NUMBERS

Police . . . . tel. 116
Ambulance . . . . tel. 6-6432
Hospital . . . . tel. 6-6012
Airport. . . . . tel. 6-7012
Terminal de Ómnibus . . . . tel. 6-6323

jest) that Cuban engineers would rather sacrifice their careers than work here.

A few miles east of Moa, you'll pass a huge ore processing plant—Empresa Comandante Ernesto Che Guevara (whose statue stands outside the gates). The modern plant was financed by the Soviet Union, the main customer for the processed ore (today, most of it heads to Canada; the Sherritt International Corporation has invested heavily). Much of what looks like smoke is actually metallic dust. It floats over the road and has settled on everything. You can taste it in your mouth. You'll pass leaking pipes along the roadside hissing and bubbling who knows what noxious stews from every joint. The landscape looks like the Somme, and, like the Somme, seems to speak only of horror and suffering! Huge pestilential lagoons of industrial waste lie within a stone's throw of the road. Drowned trees rise from them like witches' crooked fingers. Blood-red rivers pour effluents into a sea of deepest blue. Ugh. Try not to notice the children swimming and fishing in the polluted bay.

There's another processing plant about three km farther east, beyond the Río Guam, where there's a basic **campismo.**

If you must stay, the modern hilltop **Hotel Miraflores,** tel. 6-6103, has 140 rooms for US$17 s, US$23 d. Havanautos rents cars.

There's a **Cupet gas station** on the coast road, one km west of town.

Getting There

Bus no. 655 departs Havana's main bus terminal daily at 5:10 p.m., arriving (supposedly) around 8:10 a.m.

Cubana flies from Havana twice weekly (US$80 one-way) to Moa's Orestes Acosta Airport, three km east of town.

GRANMA
INTRODUCTION

Cuba's southwest corner makes up Granma province. It is a largely agricultural province (its economy is almost entirely based on sugar and rice production) with only two towns of size—Bayamo and Manzanillo. Nonetheless, the region abounds with sites of historical importance.

Throughout Cuba's history, the region has been a hotbed of rebellion, beginning in 1512, when Hatuey, the local Indian chieftain, rebelled against Spain. The citizens of Bayamo were from the outset at the forefront of the drive for independence, and the city, which became the capital of the provisional republic, is brimful of sites associated with the heady days when Cuba's *criollo* population fought to oust Spain. At La Demajagua, Carlos Céspedes freed his slaves and proclaimed Cuba's independence. And at Dos Ríos, in the northeast of the province, is the site where José Martí chose martyrdom in battle in 1895.

The region also became the first battleground in the revolutionary efforts to topple the Batista regime, initiated on 26 July 1953, when two dozen of Castro's rebels attacked the Bayamo garrison in concert with an attack on the Moncada barracks in Santiago. At Las Colorados, near the farthest tip of the province, is the site where Castro, Che Guevara, and 80 fellow revolutionaries came ashore in 1956 to set up their rebel army. (The province is named for the vessel—the *Granma*—in which the revolutionaries traveled from Mexico; prior to 1976, when the province was created, the region was part of Oriente).

Steep trails lead to sites of importance during the revolutionary war in the forested mountains, where an enormous swath is protected within Sierra Maestra Grand National Park. You can hike or take horseback trips and even ascend the trail to Pico Turquino, where there are staggering views south over the coast and north across the plains. Here, in Parque Nacional Pico Turquino, is La Plata, headquarters of the rebel army.

Pico Turquino, Cuba's highest peak (1,974 meters), looks down over the narrow southern shore, which provides an excellent—albeit adventurous—scenic drive past rocky bays and deserted beaches, with the mountains escalating to cloud-draped crescendoes.

Hunters and anglers flock to Viramas, in the marshy floodplain of the Río Cauto, which dominates the northern half of Granma province and swathes in fields of rice and sugarcane.

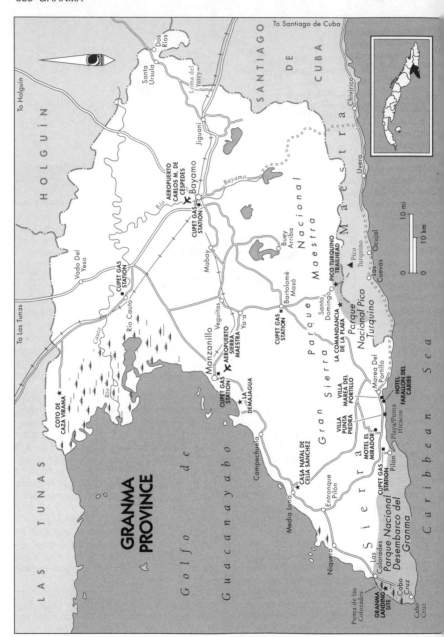

GRANMA PROVINCE

THE LAY OF THE LAND

The province is neatly divided into plains (to the north) and mountains (to the south). Granma comprises the floodplain of the Río Cauto (Cuba's longest river), which empties into the Golfo de Guanacayabo. Tributaries, most importantly the Río Bayamo, emerge from the Sierra Maestra and flow north to join the Cauto.

The Sierra Maestra massif runs about 140 km west-east from the tip of the island (Cabo Cruz) to the city of Santiago de Cuba; at its widest, it has a girth of 48 km. The spine *(firme)* averages 1,500 meters elevation and rises to Pico Turquino (1,974 meters). It is forbidding terrain. From the north, the mountains rise gradually, like a curve in a mathematical equation. From the south, the steep scarp face edges right up along the coast, extending ruler-straight with only the narrowest littoral at its base. Cuba's highest peaks lie within five km of the shore.

The province tapers southwestward to an arrow-tipped point piercing the Caribbean Sea, with the Gulf of Guanacayabo to the north. In the extreme southwest, an intriguing feature is the series of wide marine terraces uplifted from the sea eons ago and rising like a giant's staircase up the eastern flank of the Sierra Maestra.

CLIMATE

Granma province receives less rain and is hotter than elsewhere in Cuba. Perhaps only one-third of the cold fronts that sweep down over Cuba from the north reach this area, having spilled much of their rain in the mountains. Hence, the lowlands are relatively dry (agriculture has the upper hand only because of irrigation from the many rivers flooding down from the mountains).

In contrast, the north side of the Sierra Maestra has a moist micro-climate and is lushly foliated with forest. The south side lies in a rain-shadow; the foothills and narrow coastal plain is semi-desert favored only by thorny scrub and cactus.

BAYAMO

Bayamo (pop. 130,000) lies at the center of the province, immediately east of the Río Bayamo on the southern plains, in the lee of the Sierra Maestra, 130 km northwest of Santiago, and 05 km southwest of Holguín. The Carretera Central between Holguín and Santiago runs through Bayamo.

The town boasts a rich history. It was one of Cuba's first seven settlements (from here, Diego Velásquez set out to conquer the rest of Cuba) and the setting for remarkable events during the quest for independence from Spain. The city is called the "Birthplace of Cuban Nationality" and has earned the nickname "La Héroica." Much of the historic core is a national monument and is well worth a stop of a half-day or longer. The city also has a soft side. It is renowned as the birthplace of leading artists and writers and was once famous for its troubadors and swains who composed songs to their Juliets. The women of Bayamo are said to be as pretty as any in Cuba, inspiring "La Bayamesa," the most famous Cuban love song. You may prefer to tour by a horse-drawn carriage, which give cheap rides on Tuesday and Saturday.

HISTORY

The first Spanish settlement (the second in Cuba) was founded in 1513 as Villa de San Salvador de Bayamo by Diego Velázquez on a site—near contemporary Yara—then known as Las Ovejas. It was later moved to its present site.

Almost immediately, Diego Velásquez set to enslaving the aboriginal Indian population with cross and cutlass. Some Indians willingly subjugated themselves to Spanish rule. Others used guerrilla tactics to slay the strangers. The first Indian uprising occurred in 1528 and was ruthlessly suppressed. Soon, barbaric treatment and European epidemics had mown the aborigines down like a scythe. Black slaves began to arrive from Africa, increasingly so as sugar was planted, giving rise to a flourishing slave trade through the port of Manzanillo.

Cradle of Independence

As early as 1528, local landowners were developing a nationalistic spirit. That year, they called for more local control over affairs. Spain's monopolistic restrictions on trade led to a flourishing illicit trade, and Bayameses from all walks of life were active in contraband. Manufactured goods were landed from Europe in exchange for hides, indigo, tobacco, and precious woods. The Río Cauto became the most active waterway for smuggling in Cuba. When eight citizens were arrested and sentenced to death for smuggling in 1602, fellow citizens stormed the jail and freed them.

As with most cities, Bayamo was ransacked by pirates. In 1604, a force led by French pirate Gilbert Girón raided Bayamo and took hostage the Bishop of Cuba, Fray Juan de las Cabezas Altimirano. Rather than pay the ransom, the citizen-army stormed the pirate camp, killing the bishop in the process. However, they also managed to kill Girón. His head was proudly displayed in the main square.

By the 19th century, the *criollo* whites sensed that their interests were no longer those of the Spanish colonialists. These were boom days for sugar in Cuba. The planters of southeastern Cuba, however, were isolated, relatively poor, and struggling, unable to compete with modern plantations inaugurated farther west. Bayamo's bourgeoisie established masonic lodges (most prominently the Estrella Tropical) and in the 19th century their members were at the forefront of a swelling independence movement influenced by the American War of Independence and the revolutionary fervor then sweeping Europe.

The Cry of Yara

In 1867, Bayamo was a provincial town of perhaps 15,000 inhabitants, centered on Plaza Isabella II (today's Parque Céspedes). That year, following the coup that toppled Spain's Queen Isabella, the elite of Bayamo, led by Carlos Manuel Céspedes (1819-74), rose in revolt against the "motherland." As a young man, Céspedes, the owner of the La Demajagua sugar mill, south of Manzanillo, had been arrested several times for revolutionary activity. Céspedes organized chess clubs as a cover for his conspiratorial meetings. On 10 October 1868, he freed his slaves, enrolled them in his army, and, in an oration known as the *Grita de Yara* (Shout of Yara), declared an open revolt against Spain: independence or death.

The nationalists formed a revolutionary junta and, in open defiance of Spanish authority, played in the parochial church the martial hymn that would eventually become the Cuban national anthem, "To the battle, Bayameses!"

The rebellion spread quickly. With a small force of 147 men, Céspedes marched on Bayamo and captured it from Spanish forces on October 20. Soon, he had 1,200 men in his command. The actions sparked the War of Independence that swept the Oriente and central Cuba, ravaging the region for 10 long years. When Spanish troops captured Céspedes' son Oscar and offered to spare his life in exchange for the father's surrender, the father claimed that all Cubans were his sons and that he could not trade their freedom for that of one person. His son was promptly shot.

In January 1809, as Céspedes' army of mulattoes, freed slaves, and poor whites was attacking Holguín, Spanish troops were at Bayamo's doorstep. The rebellious citizens burned their beloved Bayamo to the ground rather than cede it to Spanish troops.

Alas, internal dissent arose among the revolutionary leadership. In 1873, Céspedes was removed from his position as President of the Republic in a meeting to which no one had bothered to invite him. He was cut down in a hail of bullets a year later—ambushed by the Spanish at San Lorenzo, where he had retreated to await a ship to take him to a life as a revolutionary in exile.

Spanish troops left Bayamo for a final time on 28 April 1898, when the city was captured by General Calixto García.

Modern Rebels

No more events of note occurred in Bayamo until 26 July 1953, when the army barracks were attacked by members of the 26th of July Movement. It was Castro's first open military challenge to Batista. At the time, there were no adequate communications between the military commands in Havana and Santiago, and the connecting highway from Holguín led through Bayamo. The attack on Bayamo was meant to

ecure the road and isolate the Oriente. Alas, the
1-man rebel unit, which attacked at 5:15 a.m.,
vas severely mauled by Batista's troops. The
ebels didn't realize that the gate in the fence,
pen during the day, was padlocked at night.
hey began firing on the barracks through the
arbed wire fence, and were cut down by ma-
hine-gun fire (12 rebels died).

ORIENTATION

3ayamo is laid out atop the eastern bluff of the
Río Bayamo, which flows in a deep ravine. The
istoric core sits immediately above the gorge.

The Carretera Central from Holguín enters

Bayamo from the northeast, skirts the eastern
side of town, then sweeps around to the southeast and becomes Avenida General Manuel
Cedeño, a wide boulevard lined with azalea and
oleander. It leads to Santiago. Avenida Perucho Figueredo leads off the Carretera Central
and runs due west to Barrio El Cristo, the historic
heart of the city. Avenida August Márquez leads
west from the junction of the Carretera Central
with Manuel Cedeño, to the foot of General García, which runs north to Barrio El Cristo. Calle
General Gárcia—the main business street—
becomes a pedestrians-only precinct during
business hours.

The old city is centered on Parque Céspedes, at the top of General García. Most of the

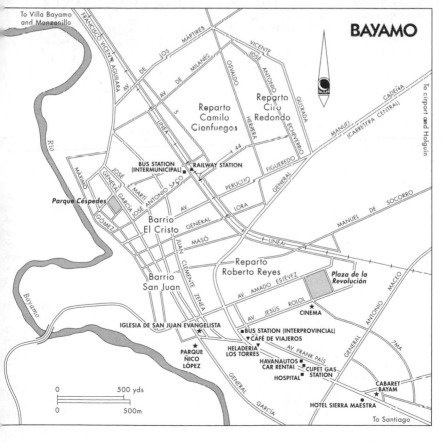

sites of interest are here. José Martí and Juan Clemente Zeneo parallel General García to the east. They merge into Avenida Francisco Vicente Aguilera, which begins one block north of Parque Céspedes and swings west over the ravine of the lily-choked Río Bayamo and leads to Manzanillo.

The grid-based modern city, built by micro-brigades, extends east of the old city. It is centered on the massive Plaza de la Revolución, on Avenida Jesús Rabi.

SIGHTSEEING

Parque Céspedes
This beautiful square is where the townsfolk congregate to schmooze and flirt. The square is surrounded by important buildings with balconies festooned with black grillwork, and exterior walls made up of a limestone base with an upper level of tilework. At its center is a granite column topped by a larger-than-life bronze statue of the "Father of Our Country," with motifs to each side depicting Céspedes' death at the hands of a firing squad and other scenes. The column is inscribed with the words, "We believe all men are created equal," and "Oscar is not my only son. I am the father of all Cubans who have died for the Revolution." There's also a bust of the local patriot Perucho Figueredo, inscribed with the words of the *himno nacional* (national anthem) which he wrote:

Al combate corre Bayameses
Que la patria os contempla orgullosa
No temáis una muerte gloriosa
Que morir por la patria es vivir

To the battle, run, Bayamases
Let the fatherland proudly observe you
Do not fear a glorious death
To die for the fatherland is to live

Céspedes was born on 18 April 1819 in a handsome two-story dwelling on the north side of the square. The house—**Casa de Carlos Manuel de Céspedes**—was one of only a fistful of houses to survive the fire of January 1869. Following independence, in 1898, the building served as a post office. It was opened as a mu-

church tower in Bayamo

seum in 1968, on the anniversary of the Declaration of Independence. Downstairs are letters, photographs, and maps tracing the history of Bayamo and of Céspedes' life. The ornately decorated upstairs bedrooms are full of his mahogany furniture, including a piano and a huge brass bed with headboard and footboard painted in Moorish scenes. The law books that filled his study are still there, as is the printing press on which Céspedes published his *Cubana Libre,* the first independent newspaper in Cuba. Open Tues.-Sat. noon-7 p.m. and Sunday 9 a.m.-1 p.m. Entrance costs US$1.

Next door is the **Museo Provincial,** on Calle Maceo #58, in a house where was born Manuel Muñoz Cedeño, composer of the *himno nacional,* "La Bayamesa." There are many exhibits from the colonial era, including the original score for the national anthem and eclectic miscellany such as a guitar and picture frame made from hundreds of different hardwoods. Open Tues.-Sat. 8 a.m.-6 p.m. and Sunday 9 a.m.-1 p.m.; US$1.

On the east side, is the house (now the **Poder Popular**) where, as president of the newly founded republic, Céspedes announced the abolition of slavery. Next to it is the **Casa de la Cultura.**

Plaza del Himno

Parque Céspedes opens to the northwest onto this charming plaza, dominated by the small **Catedral del Santísima Salvador,** also known as the Parroquial Mayor. The revolutionary national anthem was sung for the first time in the cathedral (by a choir of 12 women) during Corpus Christi celebrations on 11 June 1868, with the dumbfounded colonial governor in attendance. The ocher-colored church occupies the site of the original church, which was built in 1516, rebuilt in 1733, and rebuilt again following the fire of 1869. Its beautiful interior of stone and wood was lovingly restored in the 1970s, when it was declared a national monument.

On the north side of the cathedral is a separate chapel—**Capilla de la Dolorosa**—which dates back to 1630 and miraculously survived the fire. It is small and simple but with a *mudéjar* ceiling, a figure of Christ (now in a glass case), and a baroque altarpiece of gilt and laminated wood. The original flag, sewn by Céspedes' wife, is preserved here.

The tiny square also contains the **Casa de la Nacionalidad Cubana,** a quaint colonial building now housing the town historian's office. It is not open to the public, but the staff is eager to answer questions. A calendar of cultural activities is posted here.

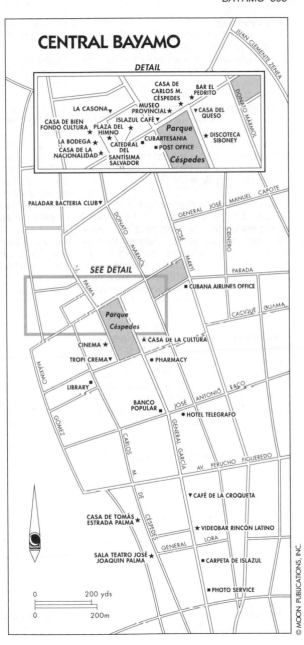

Calle Céspedes

This narrow street leads south from Plaza del Himno. It has several buildings of note, including, on the block south of Avenida Figueredo, the house where in 1835 was born Tomás Estrada Palma, the first president of Cuba following independence. It's not marked (he is considered a puppet of Washington), and today it houses an art gallery—the **Casa de las Artistas.** Céspedes lived briefly in the house across the street.

The ocher-colored **Sala Teatro José Joaquín Palma**—perhaps the prettiest building in the city—is also here. It is classically Spanish, with an overhanging balcony.

Iglesia de San Juan Evangelista

This ruined church, at the foot of Martí, at Avenida Augusta Márquez, was destroyed in the 1869 fire, though the bell tower (complete with bell) remains. The city's colonial cemetery, which also stood here, has likewise been destroyed, but the mausoleum of Joaquín Palma remains. Also here is the **Retablo de los Héroes,** portraying local patriots in stone. Carlos Manuel Céspedes is there in bas-relief. So, too, are revolutionary heroine Celia Sánchez and Frank País.

Immediately to the south is **Parque Ñico López** (also known as Plaza de la Patría), named for a revolutionary hero who, along with 24 other members of Fidel Castro's rebels, suicidally attacked Batista's troops here on 26 July 1953. López was one of the few survivors. There's a **museum** in the former officer's club on the west side of the square.

ACCOMMODATIONS

Budget

There are three budget options. The old-fashioned **Royalton Hotel,** on the west side of Céspedes Park, closed for renovation in mid-1996 but should be open again now and quite beautiful. **Hotel Telegrafo,** Saco #108, one block east of García, tel. 42-5510, is run by Islazul and functions as a hotel school. It was a bit rundown when I called by but will probably receive a facelift. Rooms cost US$10. **Hotel Central** is a peso hotel at Masó and García.

Islazul has reservations offices at General García #207 and Calle Mármol #120 e/ Avenidas

Francisco Vicente Aguilera y Antonio Maceo, tel. 42-5321 or 42-5105.

Moderate

The **Hotel Sierra Maestra,** Carretera Central Km 7.5, tel. 48-1013, is a big block-like structure built after the Revolution. It has a good reputation; however, my room had neither hot water nor a toilet seat, and the peace is regularly disturbed by the blaring piped music. Its 204 a/c rooms (18 in *cabañas*) all have private bathrooms, radios, phones, and TVs (US$28 s, US$34 d). Facilities include a nightclub, tourism bureau, car rental, post office, hairdresser, and an elegant restaurant. Alas, the food doesn't live up to the setting.

Villa Bayamo, Carretera de Manzanillo, Bayamo, tel. 42-3102, in the same price range, is a slightly more attractive place, six km outside Bayamo, on the road to Manzanillo. It has 34 a/c rooms with phones, TVs, radios, and refrigerators (US$15 d). Twelve of the rooms are in *cabinas* spread throughout the grounds (US$12). Its El Tamarindo restaurant specializes in roast pork. There's a swimming pool with bar, plus a small nightclub.

FOOD

The restaurant food in the Hotel Sierra Maestra is a third-rate disappointment. Unfortunately, the town isn't overflowing with other options. Here's a sad handful from which to choose: **Café de Viajeros,** a popular outdoor café outside the bus station on General Manuel Cedeño; **Islazul Café,** on the north side of Parque Céspedes, and **Casa de Queso,** off the northeast corner; and the tiny but atmospheric **La Casona,** on Plaza del Himno, selling *criollo* snacks and pastries. Craving Chinese food? Try **Chine Jai,** at Calle Zenea and Parada.

There are surprisingly few *paladares.* If you can get over the off-putting name, try **Paladar Bacteria Club,** on Mormól, two blocks north of Parque Céspedes.

For ice cream, try **Heladería Los Torres,** next to the main bus station; **La Tropical,** on General Gárcia; or **Tropi Crema,** a popular social gathering spot on Parque Céspedes' southwest corner. The latter also sell snacks. A fa-

BAYAMO TELEPHONE NUMBERS

Police . . . . tel. 116
Ambulance. tel. 185
Hospital . . . . tel. 42-5012
Airport (Reservations) . . . . tel. 42-3916
Terminal de Ómnibus
   (Reservations). . . . . tel. 42-4036
Railway Station
   (Reservations). . . . . tel. 42-3916

vorite *refresco* bar is the basic **Café de la Croqueta,** on García and Figueredo.

Craving a glass of milk? This rare (in Cuba) liquid is sold for a few pesos per pint from a large vat on the corner of Maceo and Cedeña (bring your own receptacle).

ENTERTAINMENT AND EVENTS

A celebration is held on 20 October in Parque Céspedes to celebrate the composition of the national anthem. Locals can't resist lending it a party atmosphere.

Traditional musical performances are offered at the **Sala Teatro José Joaquin Palma** and the **Casa de la Cultura,** on Parque Céspedes.

You can get your kicks at **Cabaret Bayamo,** opposite the Hotel Sierra Maestra and acclaimed as the largest indoor *espectáculo* in Cuba, featuring scantily costumed dancers. The dinner show costs US$30 including meal and drinks. A cabaret is also offered in the Hotel Sierra Maestra. It includes comedy, music, and dance routines, but no *espectáculo*. Entrance is US$1. There's a basic disco afterwards.

The modest disco in the Hotel Sierra Maestra is the happening place in town. You can also try **Discoteca Siboney,** on the northeast corner of Parque Céspedes. If you want to sup with locals, try **Bar El Pedrito,** on the northeast corner of Parque Céspedes, or the quaint **La Bodega,** next to the Casa de la Nacionalidad. The latter sells locally made wine.

The **cinema** is on the west side of the main square. On General García, you'll find the **Videobar Rincón Latino,** which shows movies Tues.-Sun. beginning at 7 p.m.

SHOPPING

The **Casa de Bien Fonda Cultura,** on Plaza del Himno, sells beautiful artwork, including stunning ceramics, hardwood lampshades, Daliesque paintings, and leather furniture. **Cubartesania** also stocks quality art, including wooden miniature horse-drawn cabs.

INFORMATION AND SERVICES

At press time, there was no tourist information bureau, although there's a small tour desk that serves as one in the Hotel Sierra Maestra. The hotel also has a post office, fax, and telephone office. The main **post office** is on the west side of Parque Céspedes (open Mon.-Sat. 9 a.m.-6 p.m.). You can make international calls from the **Centro Telefónico,** on Miguel Enrico Capote e/ Saco y Perucho Figueredo, open daily 7 a.m.-11 p.m.

You can change small amounts of money in the Hotel Sierra Maestra. There's a **Banco Nacional** on Estévez and a **Banco Popular** on García, one block south of Parque Céspedes.

The **hospital** is 400 meters north of the Hotel Sierra Maestra, on General Manuel Cedeño. There's a 24-hour **pharmacy** on the southeast corner of Parque Céspedes.

The **Cupet gas station** is on General Manuel Cedeño, one-half km west of the Hotel Sierra Maestra.

The **library** is in a tidy little colonial building on Carlos Manuel de Céspedes, one block south of the park. If you need camera batteries or film, try **Photo Service,** on General Gárcia.

GETTING THERE AND AWAY

By Bus

Bus no. 622 departs Havana's main bus terminal at 10 p.m. (12 hours; 36 pesos). All the buses from Santiago to major cities throughout Cuba stop in Bayamo. However, boarding here is difficult, as the buses are always full. The **Terminal de Ómnibus** is at the junction of General Manuel Cedeño and Augusta Márquez. Local buses leave from opposite the rail station.

By Air
At press time, Cubana offered service from Havana to Bayamo on Monday and Thursday at 8 a.m., alternate Fridays at 1:35 p.m., and alternate Saturdays and Sundays at 8:30 a.m. (US$59 one-way). Make your reservations as far in advance as possible. Return flights depart Bayamo on Monday and Thursday at 10:45 a.m., alternate Fridays at 4:15 p.m., and alternate Saturdays and Sundays at 11 a.m. **Cubana,** has a booking office in Bayamo at the corner of José Martí and Parada, tel. 423916.

The **Carlos Céspedes Airport,** tel. 23-43517, is four km north of town. **Aerotaxi** has a facility 400 meters farther north. A bus operates between the airport and the Terminal de Ómnibus.

By Train
Trains for Bayamo depart Havana daily at 11:20 p.m. and continue to Manzanillo. The return train departs Manzanillo at 11:10 p.m. The station is 1.5 km east of Parque Cespedes, at the end of Parada.

Organized Excursion
Bayamo is included in an eight-day guided bicycle tour of Granma province offered by a Canadian company, **MacQueen's Bicycle Tours,** 430 Queen St., Charlottetown, Prince Edward Island, Canada C1A 4E8, tel. (902) 368-2453 or (800) 969-2822, fax (902) 894-4547.

GETTING AROUND

Horse-drawn *coches* are everywhere, especially in droves outside the rail and bus terminals. One is also usually available outside the Hotel Sierra Maestra.

Havanautos has a car rental office behind the Cupet gas station, on Avenida General Cedeño.

BAYAMO TO SANTIAGO PROVINCE

The Carretera Central runs east from Bayamo across the Río Cauto floodplain. The road parallels the railroad, skipping over it several times west and east of **Jiguaní,** near where two battles were fought in the wars of independence. Beyond Jiguaní, the road rises gradually along the foothills of the Sierra Maestra before dropping to Contramaestre, in Santiago province. The Carretera bypasses south of Jiguaní.

JIGUANÍ TO DOS RÍOS

A minor road leads north from Jiguaní to Dos Ríos, one of Cuba's most hallowed yet rarely visited historical sites. Following the route, you might think that you have entered a different country. The region is an alluvial plain of rolling hills, dominated by giant cattle ranches. The first impression is of Cuba at its least welcoming—a vast, barren pan of white earth, burning hot in dry season, when a smoldering wind tears across the tableland and everything that walks, crawls, or flies gathers in the shade beneath tattered trees. It's like riding across the drought-stricken Sahel of Africa, with the cactus and thorny scrub nibbled upon by rust-colored goats and, farther north, around **Las Palmas,** herds of tough cattle.

Twenty km north of Jiguaní and a few hundred meters south of the village of **Santa Ursula,** you pass a junction with a road to the left leading 10 km to **Monumento Nacional La Jatia,** a former homestead of national hero José Martí. Keep straight for Dos Ríos. (The road to Dos Ríos begins at the northeast corner of the town square in Jiguaní.)

DOS RÍOS

Just beyond Santa Ursula, the road plummets into a steep valley bottom where villagers cool themselves in the river. Two hundred meters beyond the far rise is a turnoff to the right that leads one mile to Dos Ríos (Two Rivers), the holy site where José Martí, apostle of independence, national poet, indefatigable freedom fighter, and national hero, gave his life for the cause of independence.

On 11 April 1895, he had returned to Cuba from exile in the US. On 19 May, Generalíssimo

Máximo Gómez's troops exchanged shots with a small Spanish column. Martí, as nationalist leader (he had founded the Cuban Revolutionary Party in 1892), was a civilian among soldiers. Gómez halted and ordered Martí and his bodyguard to place themselves to the rear. Martí, however, took off down the riverbank towards the Spanish column. His bodyguard took off after him—but too late. Martí was hit in the neck by a bullet and fell from his horse without ever having drawn his gun. Martí, "seeking romantic death on the battlefield," had hurried forward to meet it. Revolutionary literature describes Martí as a hero who died fighting the enemy on the battlefield. The truth is that he committed suicide for the sake of martyrdom. Martí lives on in the Cuban psyche.

His memory is preserved at Dos Ríos by a simple 10-meter-tall obelisk of whitewashed concrete in a trim garden of lawns and royal palms. A stone wall bears a bronze bust of Martí and the words, "When my fall comes, all the sorrow of life will seem like sun and honey." A plaque on the monument says simply, "He died in this place on 19 May 1895."

LOMA DEL YAREY

A far more scenic route to Dos Ríos takes you over the massif of Loma del Yarey via a road that leads north from the Carretera Central, seven km east of Jiguaní. This road snakes up over the great *loma* (massif) before dropping back down to the plains. The views are stun-ning—as splendid as anywhere in Cuba. The lofty road gives you 360-degree views across the rolling plains laid out far below. To the south, mesas rise above the parched plains, with the serrated Sierra Maestra beyond. Looking down upon this austere landscape, shimmering, phantasmagorical in its infinity, conjures images of the wanderings of the demented Don Quixote across stark La Mancha. Indeed, the beauty is such that it is easy to come under its quixotic spell.

You *must* make this drive and stop for lunch or a beer at Villa el Yarey.

Accommodations and Food
Villa el Yarey, Jiguaní, tel. 66613, enjoys an enviable and breezy location atop Loma el Yarey. This Cubanacán property is elegant and well built of thatch and hardwood logs. The restaurant—perhaps the best in the province—serves quality *criollo* food. There are 14 cabins in two categories (US$20 s, US$30 d). Each has soaring thatched ceilings, terra-cotta floors, small single beds, TV, and large bathrooms. Some have a refrigerator. The cabins, reached via stone walkways, are set amid cactus and bushes and trees full of old man's beard dangling like fishermen's nets. Birdsong is everywhere. A swimming pool has been planned and may now be finished.

The lobby hints strongly of an African game lodge, on a small scale. It's a lofty log creation with twisting log staircase leading up to the bar, where breezes ease through the eaves. The manager claims you can see for 80 km.

WEST OF BAYAMO

VIRAMAS

Northwest of Bayamo, the Río Cauto and its tributaries have deposited vast acres of alluvial silt that are washed down to the Gulf of Guacanayabo. Near the rivermouth is a swampy zone with innumerable lagoons and canals full of water hyacinths. Much of the region has been drained and converted for large rice plantations. The rest is preserved as virgin swamp that attracts a Noah's ark's worth of endemic and migratory birds.

The lagoons of Viramas, north of the Río Cauto, are a hunting and fishing preserve where the largemouth-bass fishing is great and white-necked coots, guinea fowl, doves, and ducks flock. The hunting season runs from July 19 to April 26. The fishing season is November through June.

Accommodations
Viramas Hunting and Fishing Preserve, Carretera Vado del Yeso Km 32, Laguna, Viramas, tel. 25301, has 20 rooms in a main building and eight in four wood-and-thatch cabins. All have terraces, telephones, and mini-bars. Facilities include cleaning and cold storage, restaurant, bar, swimming pool, and a games room. Hunting and fishing gear can be rented, and guides are available. Contact Cubanacán, Avenida 146 and Calle 11, Apdo. Postal 16036, Havana, tel. 22-5511, fax 22-8382.

BAYAMO TO MANZANILLO

The road west from Bayamo to Manzanillo is one of the most dramatically scenic and varied routes in Cuba.

Fifteen km west of Bayamo you pass through **Mabay,** site of a victory for the rebel army during the War of Independence; a roadside monument honors the brilliant black general Antonio Maceo. Soon you are winding atop a deep gorge of the Río Yara, through pumpkin and banana fields, with the Sierra Maestra rising melodramatically to the south. Beyond **Veguitas,** whose entrance and exits are marked by busts of Martí, bananas are replaced with sugarcane, then scrubby pastureland grazed by cattle in the care of sombrero-wearing *vaqueros* (cowboys). The rustic *bohios* are here made of wattle-and-daub, with thatched roofs and squared-off gardens hedged with cactus fences as neatly trimmed as if by a barber's shears.

The only town of significance is **Yara,** where the first settlement was founded in 1513 by Diego Velásquez (it was later moved to the current site of Bayamo) and where, locals claim (incorrectly), the rebellious Indian chief Hatuey was burned at the stake. There's no reason to stop here unless you need to cash money at the **Banco Nacional.** If hungry, the advertisements for **Restaurante Joven Joven** may raise your hopes. However, I arrived at the *ranchita*-style restaurant to find that there was no food.

South of Yara, rice paddies stretch south toward the foothills of the Sierra Maestra and the town of **Bartolomé Masó,** dominated by a sugar *central.*

MANZANILLO

Manzanillo (pop. 105,000) is one of the most colorful of Cuban cities. Literally. Its buildings, albeit weatherworn and in no better repair than elsewhere, are at least painted in fresh pastels, adding vibrancy to the city's faded façade.

The city functions as a fishing port on the Gulf of Guanacayabo, where shrimp and lobster are landed. It also serves as a shipping port for sugar in the hinterland. The trade these days is legitimate, but not necessarily more enriching than in early colonial days, when Manzanillo was a smuggling port and a center of slave trading—beyond the reach of Spanish authorities.

It's a pleasure to wander the streets, where entrepreneurship seems recently to have taken greater hold than elsewhere (how can so many people make a living mending cigarette lighters and watches?). Many buildings have been influenced by Moorish design. I particularly like

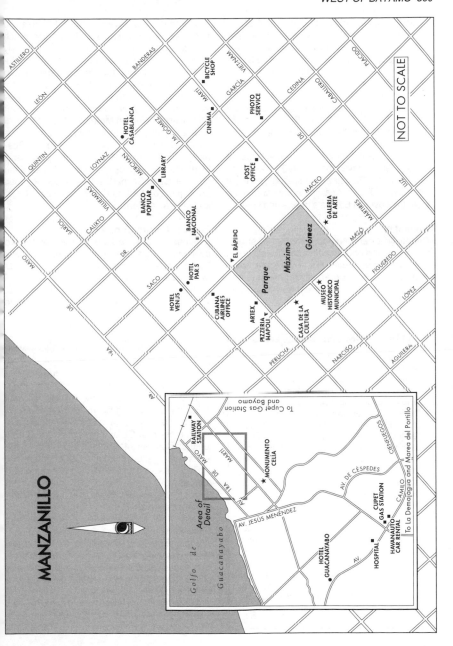

NOT TO SCALE

MANZANILLO

walking through Barrio de Oro, with its flyblown cobbled streets and rickety wooden houses where elders play dominoes or rock beneath sagging eaves with cactus growing between the faded roof tiles. Don't be surprised to chance upon a street organ being played—the tradition is strong here.

Offshore are the Manzanillo cays, the easternmost cays of the Járdines de la Reina archipelago, floating on the horizon like great gray-green carpets.

The city was the main underground base for Castro's rebel army in the late 1950s, when locally born Celia Sánchez coordinated the secret supply routes and information network from here, under the noses of Batista's troops and spies.

Orientation
Manzanillo extends along three km of shorefront on the Gulf of Guacanayabo. It is laid out in a grid and rises gradually from the shore to an escarpment, about one-half km inland (Manzanillo's streets run northwest-southeast and northeast-southwest).

FOR WHOM THE BELL TOLLS

Since independence, the La Demajagua bell had been entrusted to Manzanillo as a national shrine. In November 1947, the leftist city fathers refused a request by the corrupt President Grau to transport the bell to Havana to be rung at the following year's anniversary celebrations.

A young law student named Fidel Castro (already a prominent political figure) thought the bell would toll well for him. He arranged for the venerable 300-pound bell to be brought to Havana to be pealed in an antigovernment demonstration. Castro accompanied the bell from Manzanillo to Havana, to great popular fanfare. The bell was placed in the Gallery of Martyrs in the university, but disappeared overnight, presumably at the hands of Grau's police. Castro took to the airwaves denouncing the Grau government.

Several days later, the bell was delivered "anonymously" to President Grau and was immediately sent back to Manzanillo. The incident was over, but young Castro had achieved new fame as Cuba's most promising rising political star.

The road from Bayamo enters Manzanillo from the east, becoming Avenida Rosales, which runs to the shore. The shoreline is fronted by Avenida 1 de Mayo. It is paralleled five blocks inland by Avenida Martí. Both roads run west to Avenida Jesús Menéndez. The old city lies within this quadrangle. Modern construction extends south of Jesús Menéndez along a seafront boulevard, the forlorn **Malecón.**

The city is encircled by a ring road *(circunvalación),* which runs south from Avenida Rosales to the top of a hill before dropping down to the Malecón. Jesús Menéndez climbs inland (as Avenida de Céspedes) to meet the ring road at the junction for Las Coloradas, Cabo Cruz, and Marea del Portillo.

Parque Máximo Gómez
It all happens around this handsome square bounded by Martí, Maceo, Marchen, and Masó. Music is piped into the square, which has little stone sphinxes at each corner. It is ringed by tall royal palms and silver, Victorian-era lampposts. The most notable feature is an Islamic-style bandstand inlaid with cloisonné—very detailed, very pretty, and very out of place.

The buildings around the main square were being restored to glory in 1996. Of note are the Islamic-inspired building on the west side, now housing the **Tienda de Bienes Culturales,** and the **Casa de la Cultura,** on the south side, housed in an impressive Spanish-style colonial building with stunning tilework. Inside is a roofless courtyard that culminates in a fabulous ceramic mosaic of Columbus' landing and also features Don Quixote tilting at windmills. To the left is an art gallery displaying faded prints.

On the east side is the **Museo Histórico Municipal** (open Tues.-Sun. 8 a.m.-noon and 2-6 p.m.; entrance, US50 cents) and, next to it, the **Galería de Arte.**

Calle Martí
Seeking something serendipitous? Then follow Martí, watching for the splendid windows set high above the colonial building at the corner of Martí and Codina, and another building with a Moorish frontage at Martí #327.

At the southwestern end of Martí, beyond Avenida Jesús Menéndez, you enter Barrio de Oro, intriguing for a view of Manzanillo's parochial lifestyle. At the very least, stroll as far as Monumento Celia.

Monumento Celia

At Calle Caridad (on Martí, seven blocks southeast of the central plaza), a beautiful terra-cotta tile staircase climbs uphill to Avenida Placido. The houses to each side are graced with ceramic murals on the walls, and ceramic sunflowers are inset in the walkway. At the top is a striking ceramic monument to Celia Sánchez. Wreaths of cut flowers are kept at its base. It's very moving. To one side is an art gallery dedicated to the memory of *"Lo mas hermosa y autóctona flor de la Revolución"* (the most beautiful native flower of the Revolution), who died in 1980.

Accommodations

The **Hotel Venus** and **Hotel Paris,** both in colonial buildings on Avenida Valuendos, one block west and north of the main plaza, were completely restored in 1996 and should now have reopened as tourist hotels run by Islazul.

Monumento Celia

CELIA SÁNCHEZ

Celia Manduley Sánchez, an extremely intelligent woman and a dedicated revolutionary, was for many years the most important person in Fidel Castro's life.

Her father, Manuel Sánchez Silveira, was a doctor and an admirer of Martí; in 1953, father and daughter climbed to the top of Pico Turquino, where they erected a bust of the national hero. In time, she became dedicated to the ideals of Castro's 26th of July Movement, and was involved in propaganda and clandestine activities until she eventually joined Castro's guerrillas in the mountains. She set up the urban and peasant-based intelligence and supply networks based in Manzanillo, which she turned into a logistics center under the noses of Batista's spies.

Sánchez was 36 years old when she met Fidel for the first time, on 16 February 1957—the beginning of a 33-year association with the Cuban leader. She became his secretary, his "eyes and ears," and his lover. Celia was also his compass and kept Fidel in touch with the people. She was one of only a handful of people who could give him news and opinions he didn't want to hear. Her death from cancer in January 1980 profoundly shook him and removed from his life the only person with whom he could truly relax and be himself.

If they're not open yet, your only true budget option is **Hotel Casablanca,** on Calle Loynaz, four blocks north of the park. The desk clerk told me that foreigners are welcome. Rates start at four pesos (US20 cents) a room!

The town's only tourist hotel is the much-touted **Hotel Guayacayabo,** Avenida Camilo Cienfuegos, Manzanillo, tel. 5-4012, fax 62-34139, midway up a hill on the south side of the city, where it catches the breezes. It's another dreary-looking Soviet-style hotel with modest furniture. Most of the 112 a/c rooms face the ocean and have tiny balconies (US$24 s, US$30 d). Alas, when you fling open the curtains to take in the view, you discover only a peephole window—with frosted glass! Facilities include a solarium, video room, post office, rent-a-car, tour desk, and restaurant.

Food

The food in the restaurant of the Hotel Guacanayabo is unappetizing at best. Don't raise your hopes; even fried chicken was not available when I ate there. Perhaps they were stockpiling the chicken for the imminent opening of **El Rápido,** a KFC-style fast-food joint on the northwest corner of the plaza.

Unfortunately, Manzanillo has few other restaurants or *paladares,* and even the stoic locals are forced to choose the hotel when they want to go out to eat.

Locals gather in line at the **Pizzeria Napoli,** on the southwest corner of the main square. Slices cost five pesos.

Entertainment and Events

There's a bar and a disco in the Hotel Guacanayabo. The **Casa de la Cultura,** on the main square, holds occasional live music performances; the city claims to be the birthplace of *son,* and you can hear it performed here.

If boredom sets in, you might join the *vuejos* (old boys) who sitting around playing dominoes at the corner of Gómez and Benitez. They may look docile, but dominoes here is a fearfully strategic game (read Tom Miller's *Trading With The Enemy*).

Shopping and Services

You can buy crafts, music cassettes, and T-shirts at the **ARTEX** store on the west side of the main square.

A **Banco Nacional** and a **Banco Popular** both occupy the neoclassical granite building at the corner of Marchan and Cordina (before the Revolution, it belonged to the National City Bank of New York).

MANZANILLO USEFUL TELEPHONE NUMBERS

Police . . . . tel. 116
Ambulance . . . . tel. 118
Hospital . . . . tel. 5-4011
Airport (Reservations) . . . . tel. 5-2800
Railway Station
    (Reservations) . . . . tel. 5-3588
Terminal de Ómnibus
    (Reservations) . . . . tel. 5-2221

The **hospital** is atop the hill, on the ring road, one-half km east of Hotel Guacanayabo. The **Cupet gas station** is immediately east, at the junction for Media Luna and Marea del Portillo. There's another Cupet station about two km east of town, on the road to Bayamo.

There's a **Photo Service,** on Codina, east of Martí. In early 1996 it had a surprisingly wide stock of instamatic cameras, plus batteries and film. Bicyclists will find a well-stocked **bicycle shop** at Martí #284.

Getting There and Away

By Bus: Bus no. 626 departs Havana's main bus terminal daily at 8:30 p.m. (39 pesos). Supposedly, it's an 11-hour journey. Buses leave regularly from Bayamo.

By Air: Cubana operates flights to Manzanillo, departing Havana on Monday at 12:10 p.m. and alternate Sundays at 8:30 a.m. (US$59 one-way). Return flights leave Manzanillo on Monday at 2:35 p.m. and alternate Sundays at 11 a.m. Make reservations as far in advance as possible. Royal Airlines and Air Transat have charter flights to Manzanillo from Toronto. The Sierra Maestra Airport is 10 km south of town on the road to Cayo Espino.

The Cubana office is at Calle Maceo #70, e/ Marchan y Villuenda, tel. 2800.

By Train: Train no. 432 arrives Manzanillo from Havana at 3:45 p.m. (US$28). Trains also operate to Manzanillo from Bayamo at 6:22 a.m. (no. 434, originating in Jiguaní), 5:15 p.m. (no. 438), 10:24 a.m. (no. 408, originating in Santiago), and 2:32 p.m. (no. 436, originating in Jiguaní).

Trains depart Manzanillo for Havana at 9 p.m. (no. 433) and for Santiago at 2:10 p.m. (no. 409; US$5.75), Guantánamo (via Bayamo; US$1.70) at 5:05 a.m. (no. 439), and Jiguaní at 9:05 a.m. and 5:35 p.m. (no. 435 and 437).

The railway station is at the far northeast end of town, at the top end of Avenida Marchan. Note the statue honoring Jesús Menéndez, a local sugar workers' leader who was assassinated at this spot in 1948.

By Sea: There's a small enclosed harbor beside the Punta Caimanera light where private yachters can berth. Watch out for the wreck at the entrance! There's reportedly a ship's chandler (Provedora de Buques) downtown. It's run by Empresas Consignataria Mambisa, tel. 5-5470, who will deliver to the dock.

Getting Around
You can rent a car from **Havanautos,** tel. 5-2056, next to the Cupet gas station, on the ring road one-half km east of the Hotel Guanacayabo.

The Canadian company **MacQueen's Bicycle Tours,** 430 Queen St., Charlottetown, Prince Edward Island, Canada C1A 4E8, tel. (902) 368-2453 or (800) 969-2822, fax (902) 894-4547, offers an eight-day guided bicycle tour of Granma province beginning in Manzanillo and taking in the Yara, Bayamo, Dos Ríos, and the Sierra Maestra.

THE SIERRA MAESTRA

The Sierra Maestra hangs against the sky along the entire southern coast of Oriente, from the western foothills near Cabo Cruz eastward 130 km to Santiago de Cuba. At its broadest, it is 50 km north-south. Its spine—*el firme*—averages 4,500 feet in elevation. The towering massif gathers in serried ranges that precede one another in an immense chain, churning dark sea-green like the deepest water, and plumed with white clouds that conceal the highest peaks, including Pico Real del Turquino (1,974 meters), Cuba's tallest mountain and the node of the 17,450-hectare **Parque Nacional Pico Turquino,** in the very heart of the Sierra Maestra.

It is forbidding terrain plicated with steep ravines and boulder-strewn valleys. Every fold and depression is veined with shadow. "Ideal guerrilla territory," you may say to yourself, perusing the pleated ridges.

Even today, the mountains are sparsely inhabited. Cut off from civilization down on the plains, the hardy mountainfolk have traditionally eked out a subsistence living, supplemented by a meager income from coffee, carried on mules laden with wicker baskets.

Small schools, rural clinics, and farm cooperatives have been built over the past three decades, inestimably improving the lot of the local peasantry, whose support for the Revolution remains steadfast. Still, many people in these mountains are so poor that they can't even afford to get married, so they simply live together in simple thatched *bohios* hidden from view in the valleys and accessible only by trails.

FLORA AND FAUNA

These mountains, especially the region encompassed by Parque Nacional Pico Turquino,

are as important for their diversity of flora and fauna as for their historical importance. At least 100 species of plants are found nowhere else, and at least an additional 26 are peculiar to tiny enclaves within the park. Antediluvian tree ferns and wispy bamboo grow in patches. Fragile orchids cover the trunks of semi-deciduous montane forest and centenarian conifers. Higher up is cloud forest, festooned with old man's beard, bromeliads, ferns, and vines, fed by mists that swirl through the forest primeval. Pico Turquino is even tipped by sub-*páramo* above 1,900 meters, with wind-sculpted, contorted dwarf species on exposed ridges.

The calls of birds—including nightingales, woodpeckers, the *tocororo* (the national bird), and the tiny *passerine*—explode like gunshots in the green silence of the jungle. Hummingbirds are common. There are very few mammals, however, though wild pigs and *jutías* exist in small numbers. But there are especially large numbers of reptiles and amphibians, including three species of frog that are found only on Pico Turquino.

THE WAR IN THE MOUNTAINS

It is hard to imagine, as you watch groups of boys picking coffee beans, that amid the sweet peace of these green mountains war was waged. Between 1956 and 1959, this rugged terrain was the headquarters for Castro's rebel army. The mountains are replete with evidence of the struggle against Batista's troops. Many of the sites of importance can be reached by roads laid since the Revolution (en route, you'll pass billboards that announce where and under what circumstances columns of guerrillas crossed the road). However, rains regularly wash away sections of road, and you may need to negotiate boulders and deep crevices. Mules are the only reliable transportation past a certain point, where impassable streams stop your climb.

Fidel and Raúl Castro, Che Guevara, and a ragged band of survivors from the ill-fated *Granma* landing (see "Las Coloradas," below) stumbled into the Sierra Maestra in December 1956. Here, Fidel intended to establish and fashion a revolutionary army drawn from the peasantry and deal blows to the "army of tyranny"—a course of action that would eventually lead to the fall of the Batista regime. For the first six months, the famished, poorly armed band was constantly on the move. Its first goal was to stay alive and win the support of local peasants. "The story of how Castro was able to recover from a terrible initial defeat, regroup, fight, start winning against Batista units, and form an ultimately victorious rebel army is the story of the extraordinary support he received from Sierra Maestra peasants," writes Tad Szulc in *Fidel: A Critical Portrait*.

It wasn't difficult. Batista's troops tortured peasants, whose only hope out of destitution lay with a revolution. With rare exceptions, peasants rallied to the cause, providing shelter and serving as conduits for supplies. As news of the revolutionary front spread, peasants joined the rebel army in increasing numbers. "When a Rural Guard trooper visited a mountain house," recalls Argeo González, a merchant who ran supplies to the rebels, "he would receive bread, eat a chicken . . . take away a daughter if there was one there—but the rebels were different: they respected everything, and this was the basis of the confidence that they gained."

Gaining Ground

The initial year in the mountains was difficult. The tiny rebel band won small skirmishes with Batista's troops, but gained their major coup on 16 February 1957, when Herbert L. Matthews of the *New York Times* was led into the mountains to meet, the next day, with Castro. The rebel leader arranged a charade to convince his minuscule army, which was down to 18 men at the time, was large and had complete control of the Sierra Maestra. Matthews' report hit the newsstands on 24 February. It began, "Fidel Castro, the rebel leader of Cuba's youth, is alive and fighting hard and successfully in the rugged, almost impenetrable vastness of the Sierra Maestra." Batista had lifted censorship the week before, and Matthews' story ran as lead headlines in Cuba, creating a sensation that Castro milked by releasing his *Appeal to the People of Cuba,* a manifesto calling for violent uprising against the regime.

Castro had established a base at La Plata, on the northwest slope of Pico Turquino. The rebel army consolidated its control of the mountains throughout 1957. As the rebel force gathered strength, engagements became more intense. The first real battle occurred on 28 May, when Castro and a force of 80 men came down from the mountains and attacked a garrison at El Uvero, on the coast. They lost six men but gained two machine guns and 46 rifles.

On 12 July, Castro issued *The Sierra Maestra Manifesto,* in which he committed himself to "free, democractic elections" within one year of defeating Batista (Castro would, of course, renege on his promise in the euphoria of victory).

Meanwhile, the US government was re-arming the Batista regime in ignorance of the increasing strength of the anti-Batista movement. In 1958, it even re-armed Batista's warplanes at Guantánamo naval base; Castro would never forgive the US for supplying arms—including napalm, which was used to bomb peasant villages. (Interestingly, Castro received into his army three US citizens, all sons of servicemen at Guantánamo naval base.)

The communists in Cuba had shunned the Movement and gave Castro no help. By the end of 1957, they were rethinking their policy and came to the mountains for meetings (within a year, Raúl's army units would all be trained in Marxist theory, and Fidel had begun to swallow up or co-opt the party). The Venezuelan government supplied arms, as did other sympathizers. Many US citizens contributed money for the cause. In a dramatic twist, the *CIA* even began channeling funds to Castro's Movement—at least US$50,000 was delivered between November 1957 and mid-1958. The top-secret operation still remains classified by the US government.

Victory

In early 1958, the rebel army split into five separate units. Castro continued to lead from La Plata, Che Guevara held the northern slopes, Camilo Cienfuegos led a group on the plains near Bayamo, and Raúl Castro opened a new front in the mountains near Santiago. By spring the rebel army had control of most of the mountain regions of Oriente. The enemy was being denied more and more territory. And a radio station—Radio Rebelde—was set up to broadcast revolutionary messages, including Castro's *Total War* manifesto to the nation. All the while, Castro was kept abreast of rival groups in Havana and worked assiduously to maintain control of the opposition.

In May 1958, Batista launched an all-out attack—**Operation FF** *(Fin de Fidel)*—using air strikes, naval bombardments, and 10,000 troops. Batista's troops, however, were no match for Fidel's peasant-based rebel army, which knew "every path in the forest, every turn in the road, and every peasant's house in the immensely complicated terrain." To Fidel, "Every entrance to the Sierra Maestra is like the pass at Thermopylae, and every narrow passage becomes a death trap."

For three months they skirmished. By 19 June, Castro's troops were virtually surrounded atop their mountain retreat. The rebels rained mortars down into the valley, along with a psychological barrage of patriotic songs and exhortations blasted over loudspeakers to demoralize Batista's tired troops, many of whom deserted and switched sides (some were spies; when caught, they were summarily executed). Then, at the battle of Jigue, which lasted 10 days, Castro's rebels defeated a battalion whose commander, Major José Quevedo, joined the rebels. Batista's army collapsed and began to retreat in disarray.

By the time Batista's offensive collapsed, Castro and his meager force of about 320 peasant soldiers had captured tanks, along with hundreds of modern weapons. Radio Rebelde broadcast details of the victories to anxious Cubans. Castro then launched his counteroffensive. In August 1958, Castro's troops came down out of the mountains to seize, in swift order, Baire, Jiguaní, Maffo, Contramaestre, and Palma Soriano. On 2 January 1959, the rebel army entered Santiago de Cuba. Castro walked up the stairs of the Moncada barracks to accept the surrender of Batista's army in Oriente at the very site where he had initiated his armed insurrection six years before.

BARTOLOMÉ MASÓ TO PICO TURQUINO

Numerous roads and trails lead into the mountains. The traditional and most important gateway, however, is the town of Bartolomé Masó, at the very foothills of the mountains, 15 km south of Yara. From here, you can follow the valley of the Río Naguas eastward to **Los Lajales,** a working coffee *finca* in the village of San George.

South of Bartolomé Masó, the road climbs steadily and the vegetation grows thicker. The cement road winds ever more steeply uphill to **Providencia,** a little village in the lee of a river valley. A road to the left at a T-junction here leads to Santo Domingo and Parque Nacional Pico Turquino (the village is to the right). There is only silence, but for the occasional braying of a mule, birdsong, and the buzz of insects. Little *bohíos* cling to the precipitous slopes.

About eight km south of Providencia, the road dives sinuously to the Río Yara, where sits the village of **Santo Domingo.** From here, for the next five km, the road climbs at an ever-increasing gradient until you are forced to drop into first gear. The last hundred meters is a breathtakingly steep climb, with hairpin bends to boot. Eventually, you arrive at a parking lot (the end of the road), with views back down the mountains. You have arrived at **Alto del Naranjo,** the 950-meter-high gateway to Parque Nacional Pico Turquino. The drive is not for the faint-hearted. *Check your brakes beforehand.*

You cannot proceed beyond Villa Turística without permission, although there are no barriers (see "Permits and Guides," below).

Accommodations and Food
Villa Santo Domingo, Santo Domingo, Bartolomé Masó, Granma, tel. LD 375, or c/o Islazul, Calle Mármol #120, Bayamo, tel. 42-5321, is a demure complex on the banks of the Río Yara, at the base of the steep ascent to La Plata and Pico Turquino. The 20 attractive a/c *casas* are modestly decorated, each with two single beds and a refrigerator (US$24 s, US$26 d). There's a restaurant, bar, games room, video room, and tiny shop. The hotel is ideal for nature lovers and hikers, and you can even go horseback riding along the banks of the river. The

entrance is easily missed; it's on the left, just before the turnoff for the village.

Islazul also runs **Villa Balcón de la Sierra,** at Bartolomé Masó, Avenida Masó, Providencia, Bartolomé Masó, tel. 059-5180, or c/o Islazul. It's reportedly a similar property to Villa Santo Domingo and has 20 a/c rooms, a restaurant, bar, and swimming pool (US$15 d). Separate cabins cost US$22 d. The views are said to be splendid.

PICO TURQUINO AND VICINITY

Cuba's highest mountain (1,974 meters) looms over Santo Domingo. It's about 18 km to the summit, which is invariably swaddled in mulberry-colored clouds. It is reached via steep pathways that would stump anything without hooves.

Even here you cannot escape the Revolution. Pico Turquino is a revolutionary shrine. In 1952, Celia Sánchez and her liberal-minded father hiked up Turquino carrying a bust of José Martí, which they installed at the summit. In 1957, Sánchez made the same trek with the rebel army and a CBS news crew for an interview with Fidel beside the bust. It was Castro's first ascent of "El Pico." Che Guevara recorded how El Jefe checked his pocket altimeter to assure himself that Turquino was as high as the maps said it was (Castro never trusted anything or anybody).

La Comandancia de la Plata

Fidel named his rebel army headquarters in the Sierra Maestra after the river whose headwaters were near his camp on a spur ridge west of Pico Turquino. The camp occupied a large forest clearing atop the crest, reached only by a single tortuous narrow track—a tough climb over rocks and mud. The wooden structures were well hidden at the edge of the clearing and covered with branches to conceal them from air attacks.

Castro's house was built against the side of a ravine, with an escape route into the creek. It consisted of a bedroom with double bed for Fidel and his secretary, lover, and confidante, Celia Sánchez, plus an office for Celia, a kitchen, and a deck, where Castro received visitors.

In time, a small hospital (run by Che Guevara, who was a qualified doctor), a guest house, and a dental office were added. La Plata was also linked by field telephone to outlying rebel units and by radio to the rest of Cuba (a transmitter for Radio Rebelde loomed above the clearing).

The headquarters is preserved today as a museum. It is reached by a trail to the right from the car park high above Santo Domingo (it follows the ridgetop for three km). A wooden billboard points the way. *You must be accompanied by a guide.*

Hiking to Pico Turquino

Just as Edmund Hillary climbed Everest "because it was there," so Pico Turquino lures the intrepid who seek the satisfaction of reaching the summit of Cuba's highest peak. The trail begins from the car park. Wooden signs point the way to the summit, a 13-km hike. Don't even think of taking a 4WD. It looks like you can make it, but you can't get far.

About two km along is the humble little community of **La Plata.** Farther along is **La Mula,** the "base camp" at the trailhead for the peak. You and your guide normally set off about 3 a.m. for the climb to the peak, or shortly after. It's possible to attain the peak and hike back in one day, but it is extremely arduous. Far better is to stay in the tent camp, four km below the peak. A cook is usually on hand at the camp.

You can continue across the Sierra Maestra and down to Las Cuevas, on the south coast, via Pico Cuba and Pico Cardero. It's a three-day hike. You'll need to be prepared with sufficient food and adequate clothing. Alternately, you can tackle Pico Turquino from Las Cuevas, where you may be able to hire a guide.

The weather is unpredictable. Dress accordingly. Cold winds often kick up near the summit; the humidity and windchill factor can drop temperatures to near freezing. Rain is always a possibility, and short downpours are common in mid-afternoon. Fog is almost a daily occurrence at higher elevations, often forming in mid-morning. You better have warm clothing for nighttime, when temperatures near the summit plummet. With luck, you'll have fine weather the whole way.

Accommodations

Basic camp cabins are available at *campamento de Joaquín,* on the flank of Pico Turquino

(US$10 s/d). You can rent them at the Villa Turís-tica or through **Alcona S.A.,** Calle 42 #514, esq. Avenida 7, Playa, Havana, tel. 22-2526, fax 33-1532. You'll need to buy food in Santo Domingo.

There are shelters at 1,650 meters on Pico Cuba and at 600 meters at La Esmajagua, mid-way between Pico Cuba and Las Cuevas.

Permits and Guides
No one is allowed beyond Santo Domingo with-out a permit and a guide from the Villa Turística. A permit costs US$10 per person; guides cost US$5. You can also make arrangements through Alcona S.A., Calle 42 #514, esq. Aveni-da 7, Playa, Havana, tel. 22-2526, fax 33-1532, which can also arrange **horse rentals** for US$3.

Organized Tours
Alcona offers a six-day package that includes a visit to La Plata plus a hike to the top of Pico Turquino.

In the US, **Global Exchange,** 2017 Mission St., Room 303, San Francisco, CA 94110, tel. (415) 497-1994 or (800) 497-1994, fax (415) 255-7498, occasionally offers a two-week *Senderos de la Libertad* ecotour that follows the path taken by Castro, Guevara, Cienfue-gos, and other rebels.

MANZANILLO TO CABO CRUZ

The coastal plains of Granma province south of Manzanillo are awash in wave after wave of lime-green sugarcane, with the turquoise sea in beautiful counterpoint. Rising over this swell are sugar *centrales,* whose industry is all-con-suming. Great trolleys on wheels piled high with cut cane arrive through the night, when black smoke pours unseen from their spouts. The air is permeated by a thick, earthy scent of mo-lasses. Smoke-smudged workers slashing at the burnt cane with glinting machetes make a wondrous sight, as do ox-carts trundling down the road, spilling pieces of cane as they go.

pedes, José Martí, and Fidel Castro. On the right is the La Demajagua bell, the Cuban equivalent of the US Liberty Bell, which Cés-pedes rang at his estate to mark the opening shot in the 1868 War of Independence. The antique bell is inset in the wall, beyond which sugarcane still ripples in the breeze like sheets of green silk.

Getting There: La Demajagua is 13 km south of Manzanillo. Look for the huge poster of Cés-pedes and a patinated plaque beside the road, from where a side road leads two km to the monument.

LA DEMAJAGUA

La Demajagua was the sugar estate owned by Carlos Manuel Céspedes, the nationalist revolu-tionary who, on 10 October 1868, unilaterally freed his slaves and called for rebellion against Spain. His house (of which only the original floor remains) is now a museum, open 24 hours a day.

The eclectic displays include proclamations from the period, a copy of the original *Himno la Bayamesa* (the national anthem), and the rev-olutionary Flag of Céspedes. Glass cases con-tain ceramics and rusted agricultural implements and weaponry.

A stone path leads down to a monument of fieldstone in a walled amphitheater encircling two venerable trees and an old trapiche. Here a plaque bears inspirational words of Cés-

LA DEMAJAGUA TO LAS COLORADAS

There are three towns of modest importance south of La Demajagua: Campechuela, domi-nated by stockyards, and Media Luna and Ni-quero, both dominated by *centrales.* At Media Luna, there's the very basic **Hotel Plenlunio,** tel. 59-3425, with rooms for the hard-up at 15 pesos s, 20 pesos d. Just beyond the hotel is **Cabaret Salon Azul** and, next door, a simple green and white house—one of many gingerbread wooden houses in town—where Celia Sánchez, revo-lutionary heroine of Sierra Maestra, was born on 9 May 1920. Visitors are welcome. The mahogany tree in the backyard (full of fruit trees) was planted in 1980 by members of the Vencer-emos Brigade, US citizens who make annual pilgrimages to Cuba to work in the fields and demonstrate their support for *Fidelismo.*

Eight km south of Media Luna, at **Entronque Pilón,** is a turnoff leading east to Marea del Portillo and Santiago. Continue straight, however, and you'll arrive at **Niguero,** unique for its ramshackle buildings in French-colonial style, lending it a similarity to parts of New Orleans and Key West. Facilities include a **Banco Nacional** and a **Cupet gas station.**

Beyond Niguero, the road is in good condition all the way to **Playa Las Colorados** and Desembarco del Granma National Park, where it gives way to *piste* and the final few kilometers to Cabo Cruz. This is one of Cuba's poorest regions, attested to by the simple *bohios* of mud and thatch.

DESEMBARCO DEL GRANMA NATIONAL PARK

This park protects the southwesternmost tip of Cuba, from Cabo Cruz to Punta Hicacos, 40 km farther east. The park is named for the spot where Fidel and Raúl Castro, Che Guevara, and 79 other revolutionaries came ashore at the southern end of Playa las Coloradas on 2 December 1956. The narrow beach is named for its red-orange color. It's fringed by mangroves and has shallow waters good for wading. The site where Fidel fulfilled his promise to return from exile is marked by a monument. The area is more interesting visually, however, for its marvelous geomorphology and opportunities for nature-lovers.

The land stairsteps 507 meters up toward the Sierra Maestra in an orderly series of marine terraces left high and dry over the eons by receding sea levels. More than 80% of the park is covered by virgin woodland. The region lies is a rainshadow of the mountains. Floral and faunal species are distinct. Drier areas preserve cacti more than 400 years old. Two endemic species of note are the blue-headed quail dove and the Cuban amazon butterfly. Even endangered manatees are occasionally seen in the swampy coastal lagoons.

The park is well served by nature trails. Morlotte-Fustete Trail leads to the **Morlotte Hole,** a cavern that drops impressively more than 70 meters. Nearby is the **Fustete Cave,** which extends for several miles, and the **Bojeo Cave,** the country's largest underwater system. The **Guafe Trail** is said to feature remains of Taino Indian culture.

I strongly recommend hiring a guide, which can be arranged at the **Interpretation Center** at Cabo Cruz, where an underwater tour of the coral reef is also available (the marinelife supposedly includes massive colonies of conchs).

Monumento de Desembarcadero

The exact spot where the *Granma* ran aground is one km south of the hamlet of Las Colorados. The site is a national monument consisting of a replica of the *Granma* (under a canopy) and a bunker-like concrete structure from where Fidel can address the crowd assembled in the equally dismal plaza.

Below the "bunker" is a small air-conditioned room, empty but for a large black-and-white photo of a young Fidel in the mangroves and, next to it (in a none-too-subtle piece of hero worship), a quote by Bertolt Brecht:

There are men who fight for a day, and they are good. There are others that fight a year, and they are better. There are some who fight many years, and they are very good. But there are those who fight all their life; those are the indispensable ones.

A map shows the route of the *desembarcaderos* into the Sierra Maestras.

A cement pathway, enclosed in parts by a tunnel of foliage, leads through the mangroves to the exact spot where the *Granma* bogged down. A pier extends partway into the crystalclear, turquoise water. Otherwise there is nothing to indicate that this place was the pivotal point for the success of Castro's long-dreamed revolution.

A large café below the "pontification platform" raises your hopes for refreshment, but apparently it is open only on the anniversary of the landing on 2 December, or when tour groups are expected. It features a green-marble bartop, 20 meters wide.

Accommodations

There are 13 simple cabins at Playa Las Colorados (US$7.50 small, US$10 large). Larger

THE *GRANMA* LANDING

Shortly after midnight on 25 November 1956, Castro and his revolutionaries set off from Tuxpán, Mexico, sailing without lights for Cuba. The 1,235-mile crossing was hellish. The *Granma* had been designed to carry 25 passengers. Battered by heavy seas and with a burden of 82 heavily-armed men and supplies, the vessel lurched laboriously toward Cuba, which Castro had planned to reach in five days. Batista's army and navy were on alert. Castro figured they would not patrol far from shore, hence he planned a route 170 miles offshore, beyond reach of Cuban surveillance.

In the violent seas the men, packed in like sardines, became seasick. The boat rose and dropped from beneath them. In the open, the drizzle began to turn into a cold, penetrating rain. Castro smelled victory, but to the men on the slippery decks the smell in the air was vomit. Then one engine failed and the boat slowed, falling two days behind schedule. Castro ordered rationing: for the last two days there was neither water nor food—which was probably just as well.

On November 30, the scheduled date for landing, Celia Sánchez had gathered five trucks and several dozen supporters at the beach near Las Coloradas. They were to meet the rebels and transport them to Media Luna, where they would seize arms from Batista's troops and move into the Sierra Maestra, where sympathetic peasants were waiting to receive them.

At dawn on December 2, the ship ran aground at low tide, two km south of the planned landing site at Playa Las Coloradas. Two hours later, just after dawn, Fidel Castro stood on *terra firma* alongside 81 men, with minimal equipment, no food, and no contact with the Movement ashore. "This wasn't a landing, it was a shipwreck," Che Guevara later recalled.

The motley group set out towards the safety of the Sierra Maestra none too soon. Within two hours of landing, *Granma* had been sighted and a bombardment of the mangroves began. Batista's military commander foolishly announced to the press that the rebels had been ambushed and captured or killed, "annihilating 40 members of the supreme command of the revolutionary 26th of July Movement—among them its chief, Fidel Castro." The United Press bureau sent the news around the world. Meanwhile, the exhausted, half-starved rebels moved unseen and unscathed.

On 5 December, however, the rebels were betrayed by their guide and ambushed by Batista's troops. Only 16 of the survivors eventually managed to meet up, including Fidel, Raúl, and Che.

Thinking that the danger was over, Batista canceled his search-and-destroy missions and withdrew his forces. On 13 December, Castro's meager force finally made contact with a peasant member of the 26th of July Movement, and with that, word was out that Fidel had survived. That day, 20 peasants joined the rebel army. Aided by an efficient communications network and intense loyalty from the Sierra peasants, the rebel unit was passed from homestead to homestead as they moved deeper into the mountains, and safety.

---

cabins have air conditioning, showers, and refrigerator. There's a simple restaurant and bar.

CABO CRUZ

The lonesome road south from Los Colorados begins to dip and rise through dense scrubland. After about 10 km, you pass **Sendero Arqueológico Natural El Guage,** a trail that leads into the mangroves and scrub. The road twists around a lagoon (Laguna Guafes), where wading birds jab for crustaceous food, and then you emerge atop a cliff overlooking a lagoon and the Caribbean Sea—miraculously blue and jade, with a reef where the waves break 100 meters offshore. You have arrived at the end of the road, at Cabo Cruz, the southwesterly tip of Cuba.

The ramshackle fishing village nestles on the rocky shoreline. It is inordinately pretty, albeit impoverished. The road is lined with conch shells. Bougainvillea adds a splash of color. And the mud-and-stone *bohios* are painted in pretty pastels. The road winds past the fishing cooperative to an old limestone lighthouse, built in 1877 and today containing a small museum. Pigs grub at the water's edge.

Simon Charles gives an excellent account of sailing conditions around Cabo Cruz in his book *Cruising Guide to Cuba*.

lighthouse,
Cabo Cruz

THE SOUTH COAST

If you get half a chance, make the drive along the south coast. You won't regret it for scenic beauty and a sense of adventure. The journey begins in earnest east of Marea del Portillo, 40 km east of Entronque Pilón, where the road fades to rough dirt and stone. Landslides occasionally block the long, lonesome road, which periodically climbs over great headlands before sweeping back down to the coast. It's one of the most magnificent drives in all Cuba. The teal-blue sea is your constant companion, with mountains pushing up close on the other side. There are no villages or habitations for miles, and no services whatsoever. Drive with utmost caution. Bulldozers are at work along this 42-km-long section, and I suspect it will be a few years before the pavement is finished—in parts, you may find yourself climbing up and slithering down steep scree-covered slopes.

In springtime, giant land crabs march up and down the cliffs in a paroxysm of egg-laying. Amazingly, the battalions even scale vertical cliffs, often several hundred feet above the shore. The base of the steepest cliffs become graveyards that are a veritable potlatch of crabmeat for vultures. Drive with care, for the broken shells include sharp pincers that do everlasting damage to tires. This is no place for a puncture.

The road is a true enduro course as far west as the bridge over the Río Macio, which marks the border with Santiago de Cuba province, and the beginning of another paved section. East from here the scenery keeps getting better, with magnificent seascapes reminiscent in parts of California's central coast, or even that of the Côte d'Azur.

I saw perhaps no more than two dozen cars in the 200 miles between Niquero and Santiago. You'll pass beaches of variegated colors. Some are gloriously white, such as Cayo Blanco and Playa Hicaco. Those of Marea del Portillo are dark gray. To cap it all, there are even several superb resorts tucked along the coast, like pieces of pirate treasure.

Getting There

There are only two ways to reach the south coast from Granma province. The easiest is from Entronque Pilón, on the Golfo de Guacanaybo. A road leads inland from here, rising slowly yet dramatically up the western foothills of the Sierra Maestra. The scenery is stunning and quintessentially Cuban, with tufts of royal palms shading *bohios* and tilled fields sugar and other crops. Beyond the villages of **Sevilla** and **El Guaímaro,** the road drops sharply down through a narrow pass to emerge on the coastal plains above Pilón.

A second, infrequently traveled route, is via Bartolomé Masó, from where a road leads up over the western flank of the mountains via **San Lorenzo** and **La Habanita.** It drops down to Marea del Portillo, where the true adventure begins (see below).

No buses run along the coast east of Pilón.

PILÓN

Pilón sits in a bowl ringed on three sides by mountains and on the fourth by the Caribbean Sea. The land west of Pilón is smothered in sugarcane and the town is eclipsed by a huge sugar *central.* This is the last greenery you'll see for a while; east of Pilón, the land lies in the rain shadow of the Sierra Maestra and is virtually desert. Tall cactus appear, and goats and white zebu cattle graze hungrily amid stony pastures in the lee of penurious hills.

The dusty sugar and fishing town has nothing to recommend it, except the **Museo Celia Sánchez,** dealing with the area's aboriginal history and the revolutionary literacy campaign, as well as Celia Sánchez's life. The revolutionary heroine briefly lived in Pilón and utilized it as a secondary base for her underground supply network for the rebel army.

Offshore are reefs and countless little coral islets rimmed by tantalizing golden sand. Boaters are offered a wharf inside the protective reefs, where fishing boats berth, but there are only minimal facilities.

Accommodations and Services

There's a fleabag—**Hotel Caribe**—but you may be able to rent a cheap flyblown room from locals. There's a **Cupet gas station** at the entrance to town. Fill up here—this is the last station before Santiago, about 200 km to the east.

MAREA DEL PORTILLO

Fifteen km east of Pilón the mountains shelve gently to a wide scimitar bay rimmed by a deep two-km-wide beach. The beach is of fine gray-brown sand and small pebbles, and when wet it resembles soil. It's appealing, but not enough to linger day after day. A small down-at-heels fishing village is hidden within a cove at the northeast end of the bay, where range upon range of

mountains seem to be clambering down to the sea. The setting is sublime.

Four hotels are oases amid this barren landscape. As recently as 1993, when there was just one hotel, the tourist facilities were reserved for Cubans in summer and foreigners in winter. Now, Marea del Portillo is a year-round favorite of Canadian and European charter groups.

Private yachters can harbor in the cove.

Accommodations

Villa Punta Piedra, tel. 59-4421, is a Cubanacán hotel four miles east of Pilón. The modern Spanish-style complex has pretty villas in a landscaped setting looking down over the coast through the palms. Air-conditioned rooms are sizable and have full-length windows with views. It's a bargain at US$20 s/d, though you fare better at the hotels below. There's a little beach below. The restaurant wasn't functioning when I called by, though it has a bar and café with a terrace, also with coastal views.

Villa Marea del Portillo, tel. 59-4002, is another Cubanacán property, built to Western standards and operated by Commonwealth (Canada) Hotels. It, too, is a bargain—at US$40 (with all meals included). The rooms are splendid: large, beautifully furnished in contemporary vogue, and with full-length glass doors opening onto the beach. Bathrooms, too, are impressive. Cuisine also attains high standards. There are 70 rooms and four suites in the main building, plus 56 bungalows, all with a/c, terraces, and ocean views. Suites and bungalows have TVs. Cabaret is offered poolside for the predominantly Canadian clientele.

Better yet is the **Hotel Farallon del Caribe,** tel. 59-4032, an ultramodern, four-story, all-inclusive resort also run jointly by Cubanacán and Commonwealth. It sits above the Villa Marea and is of eye-catching contemporary design. Hardwoods abound. There are low-slung leather chairs on airy, wide-open terraces, plentiful Spanish tiles, and huge glass frontages enfolding a curved swimming pool crossed by a footbridge. At every turn there are splendid vistas over the bay. You can't lose at US$50 per person, including all meals and drinks. Each of the 140 double rooms has a TV. A full range of facilities and recreation is offered—even bingo.

A fourth option, **Motel El Mirador,** tel. 59-4365, sits on the mountainside, immediately north of Marea del Portillo. It has four simple cabins (US$10 d) and a thatch-roofed restaurant.

Watersports and Services

Both the Villa Marea and Hotel Farallon have full ranges of watersports. The dive program is run by a Canadian company, **Dive Adventures,** tel. (416) 424-4247 or (800) 567-6284.

There's a doctor and nurse available 24 hours at the Villa Marea del Portillo, where **Havanautos** has a car rental facility. You can also rent scooters (US$10 for four hours).

Organized Excursions

Cubanacán, tel. 59-4088, offers excursions, including a two-hour trip to the Pilón sugar mill, a day-tour to Bayamo and Manzanillo, and one- and two-day excursions to Santiago de Cuba (from US$69). **Fantástico** offers excursions to the *Granma* landing site at Las Colorados (US$35) and to the Las Yagrumas waterfall (US$29).

You can also book an excursion to Cayo Portillito, offered Tuesday and Thursday 9 a.m.-3 p.m. The "Oyster Farm" package includes a transfer by rowboat, 12 oysters, and a glass of white wine (US$8).

MAREA DEL PORTILLO TO CHIVIRICO

East of Marea del Portillo, the mountains close in on the shore, beetling down to a sea the color of peacock feathers, and waves crash ashore. The road hugs the coast the whole way. The road fades to dirt and scree, switchbacking in places over steep headlands, and continuing in terrible shape as far as the Río Macio, the border with Santiago province, 40 km miles from Marea. After rains, flash floods rip down through the foothills, washing great boulders onto the riverbeds that are normally dry as a bone. The road is often blocked.

Thirty km east of Marea del Portillo, you cross the mouth of the Río La Plata. It was here, on 28 May 1957, that Castro's rebel army first came down from the Sierra Maestra to attack a small garrison of Batista's Rural Guard. A small museum—**Museo de La Plata**—has an exhibit (open Tues.-Sat.; US$1). It's off the road, beside the river.

There's a small yet attractive dark sand beach seven km farther at **Las Cuevas,** though there are no services whatsoever. Several other pleasing pocket-size beaches lie hidden in coves. At **Bella Pluma** is a small cream-colored beach and settlement in the lee of a rivermouth (you are 109 km from Santiago).

Offshore, just east of **Ocujal** and the mouth of the Río Turquino, is a wartime wreck of the Spanish ironclad cruiser *Colón,* sunk in 1898 by the US Navy. The wreck rests on a submarine shelf at a mere 20 meters, only 35 meters from shore. Its gun turrets are still in place. Ocujal lies directly beneath Pico Turquino, whose summit is less than five km from the shore.

You can rent basic cabins at **Campismo La Mula,** at Ocujal.

There are several rustic fishing communities tucked into paradisiacal bays, including **Uvero,** the closest thing to a town. It's the first place to buy food. There's an *alimentario* (grocery), a basic restaurant, and stalls selling *refrescoes.*

Hiking to Pico Turquino

The small community of **Las Cuevas** is the start of a steep, arduous trail to Pico Turquino, which looms to the north. A crude map posted beside the road and trailhead shows campsites at 600 meters from the shore at Gumajacua, at Pico Cuba, and elsewhere along the 6.7 km-long trail.

CHIVIRICO

Almost 100 km east of Marea del Portillo, you reach civilization. Chivirico is a small fishing village protected within an enclosed cove in the lee of a steep peninsula. The dusty town is the incongruous setting for three of Cuba's finest upscale hotels. To the west of town is a long brown sand beach that gets thronged by locals.

One mile east of town is **Cayo Damas,** lying 200 meters offshore. It has a teeny-weeny beach where fishing boats lie at anchor. Nearby, too, are the Bat Caves, **Las Cuevas del Murciélagos,** full of harmless bats.

The main street has a cinema, two restaurants, and shopping center, where, with luck, you might find toiletries and other essentials (your best bet, however, is the shop in the Delta Sierra Mar Club Hotel).

Accommodations

Moderate: Motel Guamá, tel. 2-6125, is an attractive little place frequented by Cubans. It sits atop a headland two km east of Chivirico, with small red-brick-and-stone villas on stilts on the hillside (US$25 s, US$30 d). Each has a wooden balcony with views over the bay. There's a basic restaurant and bar.

Upscale: Far more salubrious is the **Delta Sierra Mar Club Hotel,** 350 Bloor St. East #300, Toronto, Ontario M4W 1H4, tel. (416) 926-7892 or (800) 268-1133, or, in Cuba, Calle 248 y Avenida 5, Santa Fe, Havana, tel. 33-6336, a beautiful 200-room oceanfront property on a hillside overlooking Playa Sevilla Guamá, 10 km east of Chivirico. First impressions are of the spacious and breezy lobby opening onto a wide terrace and swimming pool high above the beach, with views along the coast and mountains. *Ventrales* (stained-glass windows above alcoves) diffuse colors onto the white tiles. There are three blocks of rooms, which are furnished in upscale fabrics; US$70 s, US$120 includes all meals and rum-based drinks. Facilities include two restaurants, five bars, and a well-stocked upscale boutique. There's even an a/c fitness room down by the beach (ringed by a protective reef). The action takes place by the huge pool, which has a water slide and swim-up bar, and games of volleyball and aquacize. There's a Kid's Kamp for children. Cycling, sailing, snorkeling, tennis, banana-boat rides, and windsurfing are offered at extra cost. The hotel caters mostly to Canadians and is one of the liveliest hotels on the island. Highly recommended.

Another upscale and far more intimate option is **Hotel Delta Los Gallones,** tel. 2-6160, a 34-room property perched perfectly atop a headland with views along the entire coast and the village of Chivirico. It's a cozy little place with a contemporary Spanish feel, centered on a small swimming pool and sundeck. The charming restaurant overlooks the pool. Rooms are spacious, with king-size beds, hardwood ceilings, tile floors, and balconies (US$70 s, US$120 d, including all meals and drinks). Facilities include a game room, basic fitness center, sauna, and dive shop. The hotel is a popular scuba-diving resort (the wrecks of five Spanish galleons lie nearby). A 296-step staircase leads to the private beach. Guests can also use the facilities of the Delta Sierra Mar.

Food

You are welcome to call in at the **Hotel Los Gallones** for lunch. The pretty restaurant serves simple fare: burgers (US$3), pasta bolognesa (US$3.50), pizza (US$3), etc. A set dinner is served nightly (US$11). Nonguests are also welcome to eat at **Delta Sierra Mar,** where the cuisine, including buffet lunch and dinner, is first-rate.

There are two pesos-only restaurants in Chivirico, plus stalls where you can buy a refreshing *batido* or fruit juice, and you'll need it—the coast is searing hot.

Excursions

Fishing and horseback riding are available at the upscale hotels, as are a jeep safari (US$35); excursions to Santiago (US$27) and the Tropicana nightclub (US$50); helicopter trips to El Saltón (US$89), in the mountains; and excursions to Jamaica (US$169) and nearby Cayo Saetia (US$99). The Delta Sierra Mar also offers excursions to Las Cuevas del Murcielagos (US$10).

Scuba Diving

The two hotels offer scuba-diving trips to the offshore coral reefs and even to the submerged wreck of the *Colón,* near Ocujal.

CHIVIRICO USEFUL TELEPHONE NUMBERS

Police	tel. 2-6116
Ambulance	tel. 2-6123
Policlínica	tel. 2-6123
Terminal de Ómnibus	tel. 2-639

SANTIAGO DE CUBA
INTRODUCTION

Santiago de Cuba province is one of the most interesting and beautiful regions in the country. Santiago de Cuba, the cosmopolitan capital city of irresistible charm, is well and truly on the tourist map, exceeded in popularity only by Havana and Varadero. Deservedly. It is the second-largest city in Cuba, distinctive in mood, and teeming with sites of historical and cultural interest.

Relatively few tourists travel far from Santiago de Cuba, however, despite the many attractions. Excursion staples include Parque Bacanao, a short drive east along the coast and which includes a cactus garden, an aquarium, the prehistoric world of Valle de la Prehistoria, and Gran Piedra National Park, reached by a circuitous road that leads through cool pine forest to a splendid garden perched atop a peak at over 1,200 meters. Another well-known haunt is the holy shrine of El Cobre. Diminutive beaches lie hidden in sheltered coves. There's even a crocodile farm.

Farther afield lies intriguing mountain terrain in which you, the intrepid explorer, may well be the first foreigner to pass by in a week or a month. The Sierra Maestra to the west and the remote Sierra de Cristal to the north lure hikers and birders, as well as anyone interested in revolutionary history. Santiago claims to be the Cradle of the Revolution. The first charge of machete-wielding *Mambís* was at Baire, in 1868; Carlos Manuel de Céspedes was killed at San Lorenzo in 1874; the attack on Machado's troops occurred at San Luís in 1933; and, in 1953, Fidel Castro's attack on Batista's barracks took place at Moncada, in the city of Santiago, initiating the Revolution that would, six years later, bring him to power.

The province has a lighthearted side, too. The people carry themselves here with a certain lassitude. They also speak in a lilting tongue with a musical tone. The *c*s and *d*s are swallowed, and French and African words appear, a legacy of the many French and Haitian families that settled here in the late 18th century.

Santiago (and adjacent Guantánamo province) has the highest percentage of African blood in Cuba. Though the traditional architecture is mostly Spanish, the faces are mostly black—often with jade green eyes betraying hints of European blood. Santiagueros are lovers of music and dance—*muy festivante* in mood, as Santiago's lively annual *Carnaval* attests.

LAY OF THE LAND

The greater part of the province is mountainous and sparsely populated. The majestic Sierra Maestra builds west of Santiago, rearing up like a great, crocodile-backed sea beast and extending along the coast as far as the westernmost tip of Granma province. East of the city, an elevated plateau extends for miles, slanting gradually to the sea, with a great serrated whaleback of mountains—the tall *Cordillera de la Gran Piedra*—behind. Behind these rise the Sierra de Baracoa and Sierra Cristal, extending into Holguín and Guantánamo provinces—wild and uncharted territory where Raúl Castro set up the Second Front of the rebel army in 1958.

Eastern Cuba is still rising from the sea, and temblors are common. Santiago and other cities in Oriente have survived several large earthquakes, most recently in 1942.

Santiago's beaches are small and intimate, tucked into little bays backed by mountains.

CLIMATE

The climate of Santiago province is much hotter than farther west. Relief may be found in the mountains and at beaches where breezes ease the heat. In general, temperature and rainfall vary according to altitude: cooling and wetter on higher slopes. Santiago de Cuba sits within a bowl surrounded by mountains that form windbreaks. Temperatures within the bowl can rise to withering heights in summer. The average temperature is 80° F. The average annual precipitation is 40 inches. The rainiest season is May to October.

SANTIAGO DE CUBA CITY

INTRODUCTION

Santiago, home of rum and revolution, has an ongoing rivalry with Havana, its larger historical counterpoint. It can make one claim that Havana cannot: in 1994, Santiago de Cuba (pop. 375,000) was awarded the highest distinction conferred by the International Confederation of Tourism Journalists and Writers—the *Manzana de Oro* (Golden Apple), the Oscar of tourism, awarded once a year to cities or entities considered the most oustanding in touristic value. Santiago de Cuba is only the second city in the Americas to have won the distinction (the first was Cartagena, in Colombia). Personally, I think this is stretching things a bit far, but there is no doubt that Santiago has a unique, enigmatic appeal. Not least are its 14 or so museums, broad tree-lined boulevards, and intimate squares, its life syncopated with hoofbeats and the squeak of carriage wheels and trucks that bounce up and down the streets to the rhythm of the rumba on the radio.

Bucolic residential areas are replete with colonnaded houses lining tree-shaded boulevards. Closer in to the historic center are older, rustic, tile-roofed dwellings graced by fancy forged-iron railings, weathered timbers, shady hanging balconies, turned wooden *rejas*, Moorish balustrades, and façades painted in faded tropical pastels. The immediate sense is one of grace and charm. Adding to the latter are the cacti growing profusely from red-tile roofs, fulfilling an Oriente superstition that a cactus will keep away the evil eye. If a Santiaguero lets his or her cactus die, a year of bad luck will follow.

Santiago's main shopping streets are still lit up at night by neon signs of the capitalist era—adding, even in its modernity, another layer of times past. Much remains as it was in the 1950s, when Graham Greene wrote that the night "was hot and humid, and the greenery hung dark and heavy in the pallid light of half-strength lamps." Greene noted how "abandoned the streets of Santiago were after dark," with the shutters closed behind iron grilles, and how his protagonist, Wormold, gets roughed up in the shadowy streets by two policemen. But those were the bad old days under Batista. (Greene had arrived in Santiago in 1958 to research his book and agreed to carry a suitcase full of supplies to Castro, whom he was going to interview in the Sierra Maestra. Unfortunately, the interview fell through. He recalls his tension-filled times in Santiago in his autobiographical *Ways of Escape*.)

Santiago is the most Africanized of Cuba's cities. The city and surrounding region were a clearinghouse for nationalities: its east-facing position and proximity to Jamaica and Haiti fostered close links between the city and the two Caribbean islands. (It is sometimes referred to as "Cuba's most Caribbean city.") The majority of the 30,000 or so French planters and merchants who fled Haiti following the revolution in 1791 chose to settle in and around Santiago, stitching their habits and customs onto the cultural quilt of the city. Many French planters also established coffee estates in the surrounding mountains, adding to the city's importance for trade. (Santiago attracts many French tourists, drawn by the city's historical connections to France.)

Eventually, black Haitians came also, as workers. The rich racial mixture has produced some of the most exciting music, art and architecture in the Caribbean. In fact, Santiago has been more of a melting pot than other Cuban cities. The potpourri of influences can be felt to this day.

The proud Santiagueros never tire of telling you about their noble rebelliousness, their long history of revolt against authority. Santiago is the "Hero of the Republic of Cuba," the "Hero City," the *capital moral de la Revolución.*

The port city is also a major industrial center: the distilleries of the original Bacardi rum are here, as are a chemical factory, oil refinery, and electricity generating plant belting out smoke and pouring disgusting effluvia into the bay.

Plan at least a two-day stay, more if you want to explore all the museums and sites fully. By serendipitously strolling, you'll discover streets that are still cobbled and lined with gas lamps (such as San Basilio). You'll need transport for outlying sites (an excursion tour is a good idea).

HISTORY

Diego Velásquez founded the city in 1514 and named it for the King of Spain's patron saint, St. Jago. The city was named the Cuban capital and grew rapidly on the strength of trade inspired by its splendid harbor. Its first *capitan-general* was none other than Hernán Cortéz, soon to be conqueror of Mexico. Other famous *conquistadores* resided here, as well, including Francisco Pizarro (conqueror of Peru), Don

Pedro de Alvarado (founder of Guatemala), and Juan Ponce de León (colonizer of Puerto Rico).

Many of the original buildings still stand, including Velázquez's own sturdy home, financed by wealth from nearby copper mines at El Cobre. Small quantities of gold were also discovered locally.

Santiago's Fall and Rise

Santiago remained capital of Cuba for less than 40 years, until February 1553, when the governor transferred his residence to Havana because "in the said town is the confluence of all the trade of the island." Santiago had lost its advantage. Shortly thereafter, the El Cobre mine closed and the city diminished in size to only several hundred people. The city was subsequently damaged by earthquakes (most severely in 1580) and razed by pirates, including the French buccaneer

Jacques de Sores, who held a group of prominent Santiaguerans hostage for a ransom of 80,000 doubloons. The pirate Henry Morgan also captured the city, in 1662, after taking the Morro Castle from the rear.

Spanish settlers from Jamaica boosted Santiago's numbers when the island was seized by the English, in 1655. And at the close of the century (when Santiago's population approached 10,000), a massive influx of French émigrés from Haiti doubled the city population and added new vitality. Another boost in fortunes came in 1793, when Spanish authorities granted Santiago an *asamiento* (unlimited license) to import slaves to be sold to sugar plantations elsewhere on the island. Countless West African slaves gained their first look at the New World as they stepped shackled and confused into the harsh light on Santiago's wharfs.

The Heroes' City

Santiago has always had a reputation as a liberal city, dating to 1836, when city fathers proclaimed local elections in defiance of the governor in Havana. Governor Tacón won the battle, but Santiago had asserted an autonomy that propelled it to the forefront in the evolving quest for independence. Antonio Maceo (the Bronze Titan), a mulatto—mixed African and Spanish—who rose to become second-in-command of the patriot army during the two wars of independence, hailed from Santiago. Santiago, however, was never taken. Instead, it became a kind of concentration camp, held by Spanish troops and enclosed within acres of booby traps and barbed wire.

Santiago was thrust into the military spotlight again in 1898, when the United States entered the fray. On July 1, the US troops reached the

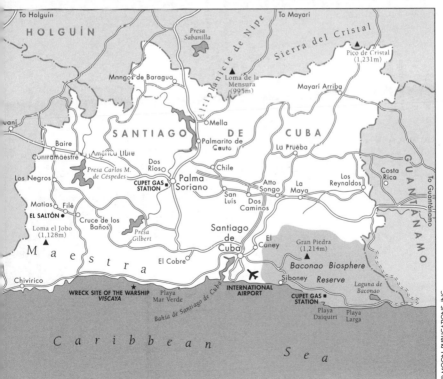

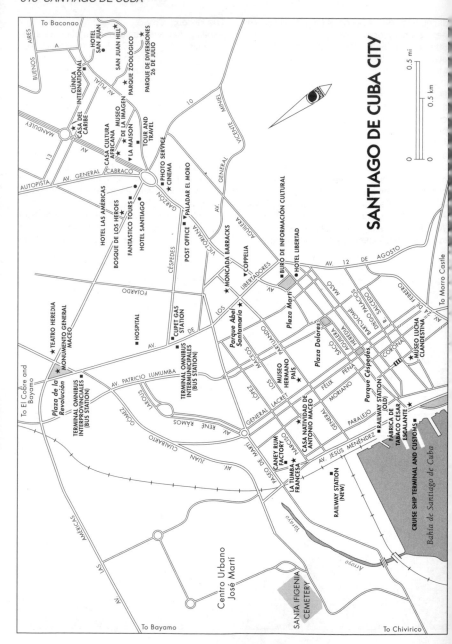

SANTIAGO DE CUBA CITY

0.5 mi

0.5 km

outskirts of Santiago and the defenses atop San Juan Hill that protected the city. Throughout the morning, the US artillery softened up the Spanish defenders before about 3,000 US and Cuban troops—one infantry and two cavalry regiments, including Teddy Roosevelt and the Rough Riders—stormed the hill under cover of punishing fire from Gatling guns.

In portraits, Roosevelt is portrayed leading the charge on a white horse, but it is thought that he himself was on foot. Though Roosevelt's part has been vastly overblown by US history texts, the victory (at a cost of 223 US soldiers and 102 Spanish troops) sealed the war. The Spanish navy, meanwhile, had gathered in Santiago harbor. On 3 July, it attempted to escape. A battle ensued. Several Spanish vessels were immediately sunk. Others grounded or were sunk as they raced west along the coast (the Spanish admiral had to swim ashore).

The Spanish surrender was signed on San Juan Hill on 17 July. The Spanish flag came down and in its place rose . . . the Stars and Stripes. Uncle Sam took the prize for himself, to his eternal shame and Cuba's eternal chagrin.

The 20th Century

To its credit, the US military government initiated extensive construction projects, including hospitals, schools, and roads. Money talks louder than good intentions, however: US forces came ashore in 1912 and again in 1917 (US marines were stationed in Oriente from 1917 to 1923) to protect US sugar growers and mining interests from labor unrest and political insurgency. Hence, as a major industrial and intellectual center, Santiago became a hotbed of revolutionary activity during the decades prior to 1950.

The opening shots in Castro's revolution were fired here on 26 July 1953, when the hot-blooded 26-year-old lawyer and his followers attacked the Moncada Barracks at dawn in an attempt to seize arms and inspire a general uprising.

Moncada was originally built as a fortress by the Spanish, surrounded by crenellated walls. Castro had studied the barracks plans for months and concluded that the fort could be rushed through the southeastern gate. The commandos would then fan out through the barracks with newly seized weapons. Since there were more volunteers than arms, only 123 men attacked Moncada (at the last minute, two men had refused to go). Their motley firearms comprised a few .44-caliber sawed-off Winchester rifles, hunting shotguns, a single M-1 rifle, a single Browning submachine gun, and assorted sporting rifles.

At five a.m. on Sunday, July 26, the young men sang the national anthem. Then, dressed in brown Cuban Army uniforms, they set out crammed inside 16 cars, with Castro in the fifth car—a brand-new 1953 Buick sedan. The third car, containing Raúl (leading a second commando), took a wrong turn and arrived at his target—the Palace of Justice—after the fighting had begun. Another car had a flat tire and a third car also took a wrong turn, which reduced the fighting force to 105 men.

At first, the attack went acording to plan. The sentinels were taken by surprise and disarmed. As the commandos rushed into the barracks, an Army patrol appeared. Fidel gunned his car but it hit the curb obliquely and stalled. Gunfire erupted. The alarm bells were sounded. Then a volley of machine-gun fire sprayed the rebels, who were forced to retreat. The battle lasted less than 30 minutes. Only eight rebels were killed in combat, but 61 others were caught and tortured to death (the Batista regime wanted no surviving prisoners).

Batista's army, which lost 19 soldiers, claimed that Moncada was attacked by "between 400 and 500 men, equipped with the most modern instruments of war," and that Castro's men had been gunned down at Moncada. A photographer, however, managed to get photos of the tortured *Fidelistas,* and Marta Rojas, then a young journalist for *Bohemia,* smuggled the film to Havana in her brassiere. The gruesome photos were printed five days later, exposing Batista's lie and unleashing a wave of disgust.

The failed and seemingly suicidal attack lent legitimacy to Castro's 26th of July Movement (M-26-7), the revolutionary group that evolved in subsequent years as the preeminent opposition body working to topple Batista. Santiago became a hotbed of underground rebellion. Assassinations and summary executions were common. It reached a crescendo on 30 November 1956, when a 22-year-old Santiago teacher named Frank País led a group of M-26-7 rebels in a daring attack on the police headquarters in Santiago, timed to coincide with the landing of the *Granma* bringing Castro and other revolutionaries from exile in Mexico. After the fiasco, Batista's henchmen initiated a campaign of indiscriminate murders. Frank País was shot on the street on 30 July 1958. His funeral erupted into a massive protest led by Santiago's mothers. The city workers went on strike, inspiring similar protests throughout Cuba.

On 2 January 1959, two days after Batista fled the island, Fidel Castro and his Rebel Army arrived in Santiago to accept the surrender of Batista's general. Castro gave his victory speech in Céspedes Park.

The postrevolutionary years have seen a massive expansion. An oil refinery was built north of the city, along with a power-generating plant, a huge textile mill, a cement factory, and massive port expansion. The suburbs grew rapidly, most notably in Reparto José Martí, northwest of the city (this giant housing complex was begun in 1965 to replace the San Pedro slums), where micro-brigades built large apartment blocks, community centers, health clinics, and gardens. The complex is a staple of many tour excursions.

The city has suffered greatly since the onset of the Special Period in 1990 (when I visited in 1994, it was clearly down on its knees but has bounced back considerably in recent years. A few stores have opened selling auto parts, household electrical appliances, and computers. There's even a shop selling *paint*—a first for Cuba!

ORIENTATION

Santiago is built on hills on the east side of the Bahía de Santiago de Cuba. The old town falls gently toward the bay so that you can look down the streets upon the red-tile roofs of the historic quarter.

Historic Quarter
The narrow, bustling streets are roughly arranged in a grid. At its heart is Parque Céspedes, bounded by Félix Pena and Lacret (north-south) and Aguilera and Heredia (east-west). Aguilera and Heredia fall westward seven blocks to Avenida Jesús Menéndez, which runs along the harborfront and broadens to the south

into a wide boulevard with a grassy central median: Parque Alameda. The main shopping streets are Aguilera and Sacó, one block north. (Most streets in the city center have both modern and older names—Aguilera is also known as Marina, Sacó as Enramada.)

Aguilera leads east from Parque Céspedes uphill to Plaza de Martí, a major hub on the eastern edge of the historic quarter. The wide Avenida Victoriano Garzón winds northeast from Plaza de Martí to an all-important traffic circle—**Parque Ferreiro**—at the junction with Avenida Las Américas. Five major spokes fan out from this hub.

A broad boulevard—Avenida de Libertadores—begins two blocks east of Plaza de Martí and leads north past the Moncada Barracks to Plaza de la Revolución. (It continues north as the Carretera Central to El Cobre, Bayamo, and Havana.) Avenida 12 de Agosto leads south from Plaza de Martí to the airport and Morro Castle.

Around Parque Ferreiro
Avenida las Américas runs northwest from Paque Ferreiro past the Hotel Las Américas and Hotel Santiago to Plaza de la Revolución. Avenida Manduley leads north from the traffic circle into the residential Reparto Vista Alegre district, where the nouveau riche had their art-nouveau mansions. Garón continues northeast from the traffic circle as Avenida Pujol (Carratera Siboney) to San Juan Hill, the Hotel San Juan, and Baconao; and Avenida General Cabrera also leads north from the traffic circle through Vista Alega to the Autopista Nacional. The Autopista leads north from the city for 22 km before petering out in the middle of nowhere.

THE HISTORIC QUARTER

Parque Céspedes
Formerly known as Plaza de Armas, this square is the undisputed center of Santiago de Cuba. The compact plaza is ringed with gas lamps, metal grills, and tall shade trees. It is crowded with important buildings and has at its center a stone statue of the square's namesake hero, who is buried in Santiago.

A lively flood of humanity ebbs and flows, lending Parque Céspedes a cosmopolitan air. The tour buses are thick around the main square, attracting *jiniteros* and *jiniteras* eagerly eyeing the foreigners entering and leaving the Hotel Casa Grande. At night it is awash with activity, when youth gather to smooch and converse. A tradition here is for small children to be given rides in little carts pulled by billy goats.

The beautiful white colonial building on the north side is the **Poder Popular** (or Ayuntamiento), former headquarters of the Spanish colonial-governor. The first building to occupy the site was made of wood and palm thatch and was first occupied by Hernán Córtes. The current structure dates from the 1950s and is based on a design from 1783 that inspired the prize-winning project for a municipal government house. Its antecedent, built in 1855, was toppled by an earthquake and had housed the US military government during Cuba's occupation. It was from the overhanging balcony with deep sky-blue *rejas* that Fidel Castro gave the victory speech on 2 January 1959, after he entered town following Batista's flight from Cuba. The Ayuntamiento houses the town hall.

Dominating the plaza is the cathedral—**Santa Ifigenia Basílica Metropolitana**—raised on a pedestal on the southern side. The peach-colored cathedral is the fourth building to occupy the site. The original was begun in 1528. The current edifice dates to 1922, although its nave is held aloft by walls erected in 1810. Much of the interior decoration has been beautifully restored, including choirstalls handcarved in precious hardwoods. Its ecclesiastical treasures and documents are displayed in a small museum. The remains of Diego Velásquez are entombed within. Between the church's twin towers is a statue of the Angel of the Annunciation holding a trumpet. The entrance is to the west side. The best place to admire the cathedral is from the rooftop bar of the Hotel Casa Grande.

On the park's west side is **La Casa de Don Diego Velásquez**, the former home of Cuba's first colonizer. It dates from 1516 and is claimed to be the oldest house in Cuba. The splendid and sombre Spanish mansion is fronted by dark wooden Moorish window grills and shutters, looking like they were transported from Yemen. Cuba's oldest house is in remarkably good condition. Velásquez lived upstairs. A gold foundry was maintained downstairs (it is still there, in the rear).

The house, which subsequently served as a Masonic lodge and hotel, today contains the **Museo Colonial** (or Museo de Artes Decorativas), with separate rooms that concentrate on two periods—the 16th and 18th centuries. It is full of period furniture, tapestries, crystalware, and artwork. It's open Mon.-Sat. 9 a.m.-4:30 p.m. and Sunday 9 a.m.-1 p.m. Entrance costs US$1.

Calle Heredia

The cultural heart of the city is Calle Heredia, extending east three blocks from the southeast corner of Parque Céspedes. It is replete with places of interest and resounds with the tap of clave and the beat of the drum. The street has traditionally been closed to traffic on weekend evenings, when it hosts a cultural fair drawing troubadors, clowns, mimes, and revelers from far and wide.

Your first stop should be the **Casa de la Trova** at Heredia #208, one block east of Parque Céspedes. What a tragedy has befallen this once-cozy institution, which until 1995 was a tremendously atmospheric place, dark and moody, the air thick with smoke and charged with cheers from the audience. A thoughtless remake has destroyed all the charm. The dark wooden swing doors and paneling are gone, as is the nostalgic photo collection, replaced with the art of local musical heroes, such as the Trio Matamoros. At least the musicians are still as good as ever, and their haunting melodies and plaintive *boleros* of the *trova* still reverberate down the street. The troubadors take pride in performing for the love of it—the music is played and the songs are sung with more passion than you are every likely to hear again.

If thirsty, nip next door to the **Casa de Vino** to sample the locally made wines and cheeses.

One block east of Casa de la Trova (between Hartmann and Pío Rosado) is **Casa Heredia,** the birthplace of the 19th-century poet José María Heredia (1803-39), the first Cuban poet to champion independence. The house is furnished in colonial fashion and displays works by Heredia and other Cuban authors. Open Tues.-Sun. 8 a.m.-5 p.m.

One block farther, on the north side of Heredia, is the **Museo de Carnaval,** which tells the history of Santiago's colorful carnival. Some of the outlandish costumes are on display. Folkloric shows are sometimes hosted here. It's open

Tues.-Sun. 9 a.m.-5 p.m. and Saturday 9 a.m.-9 p.m. (and possibly Monday by request). Entrance is US$1.

Continue to the next block, where stands the **Jesuit Dolores College,** where Fidel Castro was educated as a youth. It was one of the most profound intellectual influences in his life. (Fidel had earlier been enrolled in Santiago's Marist brother's La Salle school, a private establishment for boys from affluent families. There, he established a reputation as a tempestuous tyke, according to teachers' reports.)

Plaza Dolores

The most enchanting of Santiago's squares is this delightful little plaza fringed by quaint colonial buildings. It was formerly a religious center and market (its name is taken from the church—Nuestra Señora de los Dolores—that looms over the square). The teeny park is shaded by tamarind trees, bougainvillea, and hibiscus and has wrought-iron seats surrounding a marble column bearing a larger-than-life bronze statue of Francisco Vicente Aguilera, who was born in Bayamo in 1821 and died in New York in 1877.

Plaza de Martí

This small plaza is laid out at the top of Aguilera, on the eastern fringe of the old city. It's a pretty plaza. At its center is a thick phallic column topped with a bulbous red cone. Large cannons sit at the base. A bust of Martí is at the southern end of the park, which has plenty of shade trees. The original plaza was built in 1860 as the Spanish army parade ground and execution spot for Cuban patriots.

Museo Lucha Clandestina

The Museum of the Underground Fight is dedicated to telling the tale of the 26th of July Movement. The museum is housed in the old police station that was attacked by revolutionaries led by Frank País on 30 November 1956. The building is one of Santiago's most splendidly restored colonial houses. Open Tues.-Sat. 9 a.m.-5 p.m. and Sunday 9 a.m.-3 p.m. (entrance, US$1).

The museum sits above **Calle Padre Pico** in an area known as **Loma del Intendente,** settled in the late 18th century by French citizens fleeing Haiti. Its streets are lined with 16th-century houses. Calle Padre Pico is a wide staircase that joins the upper and lower parts of the city.

(Santiagueros gather beneath the shady eaves to play dominoes, gossip, or strum guitars.) Touristy hype urges you to climb the steps for a privileged view over Santiago. Females may receive a lift from unsolicited compliments—locals say that the steps make women undulate, and it has become a tradition for men to praise their movement with clever poetic phrases. Three members of the 26th of July Movement were killed on the steps of Padre Pico during the attack on police headquarters.

To reach the museum, follow the road (Calle Rabi) lined by a crenellated wall that curves uphill from the top of the stairs.

You should return to Parque Céspedes via Calle Corona—one block east of Padre Pico—where, at Bartolomé Masó, you'll pass beneath arches that open to **Balcón de Velásquez,** a plaza offering splendid views over the city.

Museo Bacardi

This museum, at Calle Pío Rosado, e/ Aguilera and Heredia, was founded by Emilio Bacardi Moreau in 1899. A member of the expatriate and anti-Castroite Bacardi rum family, Emilio, patriot writer and mayor of Santiago, is in good

graces; he was imprisoned in the Morro Castle for his revolutionary activities last century. The museum is housed in a huge neoclassical edifice with Corinthian columns and statues and is out of place in the heart of Santiago's oldest quarter, but it makes nonetheless for a dramatic effect.

The splendid museum has three floors. The first contains a superb array of colonial artifacts, including slave shackles and stocks, and eclectic miscellany from a printing press to a boomerang. Most impressive, however, is the huge array of antique daggers, blunderbusses, rifles, pistols, and the personal effects of leading 19th-century heroes. There's even a casket-shaped wooden torpedo used by the Mambís and driven by two little engines and propellers.

The second floor is an art gallery, including 19th-century and contemporary works by leading figures. Note the bronze sculptures at the rear.

The basement, entered by a separate door off Aguilera, has a small but impressive display of pre-Columbian artifacts from throughout the Americas, including colorful feather headdresses, a shrunken head *(cabeza reducido),* pottery shards, and—most interesting of all—two Peruvian mummies folded up and squashed as if to fit in a box for mailing. There's even an Egyptian mummy and a mummified baby crocodile, both disgustingly blackened, as if pan-baked in engine oil.

The museum is open Tues.-Sat. 9 a.m.-8:30 p.m., Sunday 9 a.m.-3:30 p.m., and Monday 3-7:30 p.m. Entrance costs US$2. (Prepare to be disconcerted by being followed around step by step by museum guards.)

Casa Natal de Antonio Maceo

If you're interested in Cuban history, call in at the little house at Calle Maceo #207 e/ Corona y Rastro, the birthplace of Antonio Maceo, a mulatto who rose to become second in command of the Liberation Army during the wars of independence. Maceo was born here on 14 June 1845. The fearless leader and brilliant tactician refused to accept the treaty ending the Ten Years' War of Independence in 1878 (his act is known as the Protest of Baragua). He fought on for several months until fleeing into exile. He returned with José Martí in April 1895 and led a rebel army all the way to Pinar del Río before being killed in battle on 7 December 1895.

The house was built between 1800 and 1830 with wood-paneled floors and walls of intertwined flexible twigs covered with lime and sand, commonly used to mitigate damage from earthquakes. The house is now a museum. It's open Mon.-Sun. 8 a.m.-6:30 p.m. Entrance US$1.

Museo Abel Santamaría

This museum, at Calle Trinidad and Carretera Central, is in the former home of one of Cuba's most revered heroes. A confidante of Fidel Castro and his designated successor in the revolutionary movement, Santamaría helped organize the attack on the Moncada barracks. He led a contingent that captured the hospital across the street. Santamaría and his men continued to snipe at the barracks, unaware that the attack had failed.

Batista's troops stormed the hospital, where Santamaría and his 23 men had taken to bed, pretending to be patients (his sister, Haydee, was one of the attackers and pretended to be a nurse). They were betrayed and ruthlessly tortured. Haydee's fiancé, Boris Luís, was beaten to death on the spot with rifle butts. Abel was brutally tortured and died later that day. Open Mon.-Sat. 8 a.m.-noon and 2-6 p.m. and Sunday 9 a.m.-8 p.m.

Museo Hermanos País

The house at Avenida General Banderas #266 e/ Trinidad y Habana is where the revolutionary heroes Frank and José País were born. Frank, a teacher, was instrumental in running Castro's 26th of July Movement in Havana during the mid-1950s and became the movement's principal leader in Oriente, providing logistical support to the rebel army in the mountains. He led the ill-fated attack on the police headquarters in Santiago on 30 November 1956, timed to coincide with the *Granma* landing. José was shot and killed in June 1957, and Frank was assassinated by police agents one month later.

Caney Rum Factory

This factory, at the north end of Avenida Jesús Menéndez, at Gonzalo de Quesada, is the oldest rum factory in Cuba. It was built in 1868 by the Bacardi family and nationalized in 1959, after which the Cuban government continued to make rum under the Bacardi title. Bacardi sued. The International Court of the Hague found in favor of Bacardi, which had set up shop in Puerto Rico.

Ever since, the rum produced here has been sold as "Havana Club." (The Bacardi corporation's lawyers helped write the Helms-Burton bill, signed into US law in March 1996; the law gives the company the right to sue anyone, domestic or foreign, "trafficking in stolen property," meaning goods produced at the factory, and including the right to sue for the Havana Club label.) A warehouse across the railway tracks stores 42,000 casks, many of which have gathered dust for 15 years.

view from the Hotel Casa Grande, Santiago de Cuba

Guided tours have been offered in the past (I've paid US$10, including free samples), but latest report was that tours are no longer offered. No cameras are allowed in any case. There's a tasting room and a gift store selling rum. Supposedly, this is the only place in the country where you can buy rum matured for more than 15 years. Try the Ron Paticruzados—"Crossed Legs Rum"—which Santiagueros swear is the best drink with which to keep cool in the sweltering heat. Open Mon.-Sat. 9 a.m.-6 p.m. and Sunday 9 a.m.-noon.

Fábrica de Tabaco César Escalante

Do visit the cigar factory on Avenida Jesús Menéndez and the foot of Bartolomé Masó. Here you can watch men and women rolling, snipping, and pressing fine Cuban cigars. They're happy to pose for your camera. It's open Mon.-Sat 7 a.m. 5 p.m. Entrance is free.

NORTH OF PLAZA MARTÍ

Moncada Barracks

Don't miss Santiago's most famous and worthy site. This former military barracks was a linchpin in Batista's control of the Oriente. Moncada has a medieval countenance, with its castellated ocher-colored walls and its turrets with gun slits all around. It seems badly out of place in the heart of the city, on Calle Carlos Aponte, a 10-minute walk from the Hotel Santiago.

The site is renowed for the fateful day on 26 July 1953, when Fidel Castro and 79 poorly armed cohorts dressed in Cuban Army uniforms stormed the barracks.

After the Revolution, Moncada was turned into a school, the Ciudad Escolar 26 de Julio. A portion of the main building near the entrance gate is riddled with bullet holes. They're not the originals however; Batista's troops filled those in. Castro apparently had the holes redone using photographs.

This section today houses a superb museum that tells the tale of the attack, the Revolution, and subsequent history. One wall has the names of the 61 rebels and nine innocent civilians murdered to fulfill Batista's promise to kill 70 people in retaliation for the attack. There's a large-scale model of the barracks showing the attack. Prolific weaponry includes Castro's personal sharpshooter rifle. Blood-stained uniforms hang inside glass cabinets. A separate room is dedicated to José Martí, and outside you'll find a light blue truck driven by a farmer—Juan Liezan—who picked up Castro and helped save his life.

Open Mon.-Sat 8 a.m.-6 p.m. and Sunday 8 a.m.-noon. Entrance costs US$2.

Parque Abel Santamaría

On the west side of Avenida de Libertadores, opposite Moncada, is a Mount Rushmore in miniature—a huge granite cube atop a column and carved with the faces of Abel Santamaría and

Moncada Barracks

José Martí. The third side has six swords, and the fourth a star and the words *Morir por la Patria es Vivir* (Died so the Nation Could Live). A fountain seems to hold the cube aloft magically.

Note how the wide, tree-lined boulevard is lined with bronze busts of revolutionary heroes atop cement columns.

Bosque de los Héroes

This small park sits atop a rise opposite the Hotel Santiago on Avenida Las Américas. At first the monument looks totally uninspired: simple building blocks arranged higgledy-piggledy. However, on the east side are engravings of revolutionary heroes carved into the marble tableaux. Center place goes to Fidel, with José Martí, Celia Sánchez, and other to each side. The rest of the park is totally unkempt, and the bamboo bushes are used as toilets by Santiagueros. Watch where you step!

Plaza de la Revolución

This wide-open plaza, at the junction of Avenida Las Américas and Avenida de los Libertadores, is dominated by a massive monument to Antonio Maceo, the hero-general of the War of Independence. Maceo was nicknamed the Bronze Titan, and the mammoth statue of the general on a rearing horse is appropriately cast in bronze. An eternal flame flickers in a marble-lined bowl cut into the base. Soaring, rust-colored, crystal-shaped metal sculptures are set obliquely into the ground like great pikes.

There's a museum—**Sala Deposición Holgrafía**—beneath the mound. It tells of Maceo's life and of the War of the Independence—and uses nothing but holograms. Entrance costs US$1.

REPARTO VISTA ALEGRE

This leafy residential district is bounded on the south by Avenida de las Américas and on the east by Avenida Pujol (Carretera Siboney). Avenida Manduley runs through the center of Vista Alegre and is lined with shade trees, bougainvilleas, and once-upscale villas of varying ages and styles. Note the grand three-story, pink, neo-baroque house with white columns

that stands at the corner of Calle 9. This is the **Casa de Don Pepe Bosch**. It was once owned by a Mambí general. It is now a Young Pioneer's School and has a Soviet MiG fighter jet in the playground.

Museo de la Imagen

This museum, at the corner of Calle 5 and Calle 8, was established by famed cameraman Bernabá Muñiz (affectionately known as "Bebo"), who gained his first screen credit when he captured on film a man who decided to play Tarzan—naked—down Avenida de los Misiones in Havana. He went on to such accomplishments as filming Fulgencio Batista's coup d'etat in 1952, the surrender of the Moncada barracks to the revolutionaries in 1959, and the victory parade by tank with Fidel from Santiago to Havana.

His Musem of Images features almost 500 photographic, film, and TV cameras—everything from CIA espionage cameras to a stereoscopic viewfinder from 1872. The museum also contains a library of over 200 feature films, newsreels, and documentaries dating back to 1926.

Casa Cultura Africana

Cuba's African legacy comes alive in this exquisite museum on Avenida Manduley e/ Calles 3 y 5. It is full of marvelous carvings and weavings from the various tribes of Africa. Entrance costs US$1.

San Juan Hill

Loma San Juan rises on the east side of Avenida Pujol to a pleasant park shaded by palms. Every US schoolchild knows that Teddy Roosevelt and his Rough Riders valiantly defeated the Spanish here, but the hill hardly lives up to its legend, being astonishingly small and unprepossessing.

Today, the landscaped park contains various monuments and cannons. Plaques tell the tale of the War of Independence. There's a Tomb of the Unknown *Mambí,* the independence fighters. One memorial is dedicated to Cuban revolutionaries and "the generous American soldiers who sealed a covenant of liberty and fraternity between the two nations." There is no monument, however, to Roosevelt and his Rough Riders, perhaps in payback for the fact that the Cuban liberationists who helped storm the hill weren't even invited to the surrender ceremony.

The huge spreading ceiba tree beneath which the treaty with Spain was signed on 16 July 1898 still stands at the entrance to the park.

VICINITY OF MORRO CASTLE

Morro Castle

Santiago's most impressive structure is poised ominously atop the cliffs at the narrow entrance to Santiago Bay, about 14 km south of Santiago. This enormous piece of military architecture—a minotaur's maze of stairways and dungeons—was begun in 1640. It was designed by an Italian engineer, Antonelli, who also designed the Morro castle in Havana. The Morro was rebuilt and strengthened in 1664, after the English pirate Henry Morgan reduced it to rubble. It was recently restored using coral chunks and red brick alongside the much-worn original limestone

Morro Castle

blocks. The effect is not lost, however, and you still gain a full sense of the power of the Morro.

You enter via a narrow drawbridge over a deep moat glazed with colored colonial tiles—marvelous! Guides will lead you through the passageways (don't forget to tip) and to such sites as the powder magazine (still full of cannonballs, and a tread for hauling them to the batteries), and the chapel, which still has its original pews and a large wooden statue of Christ on the cross beneath a sky-blue ceiling. There are cannons everywhere. Note the gutters designed to channel rainwater into a deep well in the lower courtyard.

The castle now houses the **Museum of Piracy.** It features excellent displays on piracy, colonialism, and slavery. There are old blunderbusses, muskets, cutlasses, and Toledo blades in glass cases. Contemporary piracy isn't forgotten—one room informs visitors of Operation Mongoose (the CIA's no-holds-barred efforts to destabilize the Castro regime).

Getting There: The Morro is signed from Santiago. Follow Avenida 12 de Agosot south from Plaza de Marte. This leads to Carretera del Morro dual-carriageway and a traffic circle, about seven km south of Santiago. You'll reach a Y-junction. The road to the left leads to Morro Castle.

Alternately, you can follow the bayfront Carretera Turística, which begins at the southern end of Avenida Jesús Menéndez. This serpentine road follows the bayshore to Punta Gorda and snakes in and out of inlets until you emerge atop the cliffs immediately east of the castle.

Tour & Travel (see "Getting Around," below) offers excursions to Morro (US$19), including in conjunction with other attractions.

Punta Gorda

This slender peninsula lies between Morro Castle and town, with the Marina Marlin at the tip. It was once fashionable with Santiago's upper class, who had their fine old wooden homes here. Most of the houses still stand, albeit in dilapidated condition. A large statue of the revolutionary hero Frank País holding an M-15 carbine looms over the point in **Parque Frank País.** The park is well maintained.

Cayo Granma

The Morro and Punta Gorda look out over a little island in the bay; less than one km offshore, it looks as if it has been magically transferred from the Mediterranean. It was once a summer getaway for rich Santiago families. Today it is a small fishermen's colony. Little rowboats are berthed beneath the eaves of quaint red-tiled waterfront houses that ring the isle.

No cars run through the narrow streets that lead up to a church atop the hill. There's a beach—**Playa Socapa**—and a tiny tree-shaded plaza, where locals gather to play dominoes.

There are no hotels. If you can get a local to rent you a room (no problem), this would be a fantastic place to ease back. The **Restaurante El Cayo** sits over the bay and serves seafood and *criollo* dishes.

Getting There: A small ferry leaves regularly from the Alameda wharf in Santiago. The departure times are erratic. A passenger ferry serves Cayo Granma from Marina Marlin about four times daily; US$3 for tourists. A local ferry (10 centavos) also leaves from an obscure point called Punta Puntilla, directly opposite Cayo Granma, below Morro Castle. You can reach it by following the Carretera Turística or by following the road to the right at the Y-fork described in the directions for getting to Morro Castle.

OTHER SITES

Fortress De Yarayó
Four hundred meters north of the rum factory on Avenida Jesús Menéndez, across Paseo de Martí, is a twee little ocher-colored fortress (the first of 116 that the Spanish built around Santiago) with wooden turrets and gun slits. Originally it stood on the banks of the Río Yarayó, which today flows beneath the ground, unseen.

From here, Avenida Crombet leads west to Repart José Martí and Santa Ifigenia Cemetery.

Santa Ifigenia Cemetery
This inspired cemetery is indeed hallowed ground. Its grand entrance is dominated by a gateway dedicated to Cuban soldiers who died fighting in Angola. Just beyond is the splendid tomb of José Martí beneath a crenellated hexagonal tower (each side represents one of the six original provinces of Cuba). Marble steps lead down to a circular mausoleum suffused in soft light—designed so that the sun would always shine on his coffin. The casket is draped with the Cuban flag.

Narrow walkways lined with palms lead past scores of marble tombs, some simple, many grand, adorned with angels, cherubs, and other statues. The cemetery also contains the graves of Carlos Manuel Céspedes, Emilio Bacardi, Tomás Estrada Palma (Cuba's first president), and heroes of the attack on the Moncada barracks (look for the red and black flags on their graves). Heroes of the War of Independence are entombed in a tiny castle.

Before the Revolution, the cemetery was segregated by race and social position. The poor folks' section, as you may expect, is to the rear. Entrance costs US$1, including a guide.

For Botanists and Archaeologists
Santiago's **Jardín Botánico**—botanic garden—is run by the Cuban Academy of Sciences and contains a library and laboratories in addition to its specimen trees and plants. The garden is about two km northeast of the Hotel Santiago, to the right, off the Carretera Siboney.

Cuba's flora and fauna and aboriginal cultures are also displayed at the small **Museo Arqueológico,** in the University de Oriente, on the Carretera Central, north of town.

DANGERS AND ANNOYANCES

Becaues it is an industrial city, Santiago was especially hard hit by the collapse of the Soviet Union. The situation has improved radically, but the *jiniteros* are still more openly aggressive than elsewhere on the island, and you may be regularly accosted by "professional" hustlers who see tourists as the best opportunity around. Many approach quite shamelessly and simply demand, "Give me one dollar!" Try getting rid of them with a civil, *"No moleste, por favor"* ("Don't bother me, please") before switching to something stronger.

ACCOMMODATIONS

Many Cubans rent out *casas particulares* in their homes to tourists. They're not hard to find:

touts will approach you in the street (especially around Parque Céspedes). Alternately, try the **Casa del Caribe,** tel. 4-2285, which arranges room-stays for foreign students; it's at the corner of Calles 13 and 5, in Vista Alegre. Compare several places. Most owners will be happy to cook for you for, say, US$5 a meal. Prices are on a par with Havana—between US$15 and US$25 a night.

There are also several hotels outside town near Morro Castle.

Budget

The **Hotel Rex,** one block north of Plaza de Martí, tel. 2-6314, was scheduled to reopen in 1997 with rooms for about US$14. A group of revolutionaries met here prior to assembling at Granjita Siboney for the attack on Moncada in 1953, according to the bronze plaque on the wall outside.

Nearby, the **Hotel Libertad,** tel. 23080, on the east side of Plaza Martí, has rudimentarily furnished a/c rooms for US$9 s, US$12 d. It's in need of renovation, as the lobby's faded furniture suggests.

The impecunious might try the **Hotel Bayamo,** on Saco one block northeast of Parque Céspedes, tel. 2-8435. It has rooms for 10 pesos. However, it's in need of a good cleaning. The receptionist told me that it won't accept foreigners—a standard line. Officially, the **Hotel Venus,** one block east of Parque Céspedes at San Félix #658, tel. 2-2178, also doesn't accept foreigners, but try your luck anyway—it has rooms from 15 pesos. Amazingly, it is claimed that the daiquiri was christened at the hotel bar (but don't bother going for curiosity's sake).

Also consider the modern **Hotel Deportivo,** behind the sports stadium on Avenida Las Américas, tel. 4-2146. It has 84 rooms with TVs for US$15 and up.

Lastly, consider a place known as **M.E.S.** (or **Hotel Universario**), on the edge of Reparto Vista Alegre, on Calle 7 at Calle Terrazas, behind the Hotel Las Américas, tel. 4-2398, or, in Havana, tel. 33-5011. It's a hostel for students and teachers, with shared bathrooms. The rooms are adequate (US$12 per person), and there's a restaurant.

Islazul has a booking office on Hartmann, one block east of Parque Céspedes.

Moderate

A modest bargain is the **Hotel Las Américas,** Avenida de las Américas y Avenida General Cebreco, tel. 226-42011, across from the Hotel Santiago. It's an adequate, albeit uninspired Horizontes property with 68 a/c rooms, all with satellite TVs, phones, and radios (US$30 s, US$23 d, US$36 t). The hotel has two restaurants and a bar, plus the Havana Club disco. Car rental is available.

I can recommend the **Hotel San Juan,** Avenida Siboney y Calle 13, tel. 4-2478, fax 33-5015, formerly Motel Leningrado, on the south side of San Juan Hill. The 112 rooms are in villa-style blocks (take an upstairs room with a lofty ceiling to help dissipate the heat). Each has a large satellite TV, modern (albeit modest) furniture, safety box, and large, newly renovated bathrooms. Facilities include a swimming pool, boutique, tour desk, and car rental. There's a restaurant and nightclub adjoining the hotel. The hotel is popular with European tour groups. Rates are US$25 s, US$35 d low-season and US$30 s, US$40 d high-season.

The place to be is undoubtedly the **Hotel Casa Grande,** splendidly situated on Parque Céspedes. Wormold stayed here in Graham Greene's *Our Man in Havana,* and he thought it "a hotel of real spies, real police-informers and real rebel agents." It lost its sheen following the Revolution and just a few years ago was described as "an establishment so magnificent in its squalor that it seems born out of an opium smoker's vision." All that has changed. The hotel has since been restored and is now operated by Gran Caribe. It has 58 rooms, including three junior suites (one for guests with disabilities), all with a/c, telephones, and satellite TV. Many rooms have splendid antique reproductions in walnut, including double beds with inlaid hardwood headboards. Suites even have gold silk fabrics. The prices are very reasonable: US$42 s, US$54 d, US$65 suite. The city's bourgeoisie used to sit on its first-floor veranda to sip rum, smoke Havanas, and watch the flood of life through the colonial plaza. Today, you can do the same. It is one of the most atmospheric of Cuban hotels, lent a Parisian feel by its red-and-white awnings.

Gaviota runs a *protocolo* called **Villa Gaviota** in the quiet Vista Alegre area at the end of Avenida Manduley #502 e/ Calles 19 y 21, tel. 4-1598 or 4-

1368. It features 13 three- to five-bedroom bungalows. There's a swimming pool, store, and a restaurant that specializes in game dishes (when available). Rates are US$24 s, US$29 d in low season and US$30 s, US$ 40 d in high season.

On the southern outskirts of town is **Hotel Versalles,** Alturas de Versalles Km 1, Carretera del Morro, tel. 91016 or 91504, just two km from the airport. It's a gracious property with a hilltop location and cabins spread throughout the landscaped grounds. It's very quiet and offers fine views over Santiago. The 46 rooms, 14 bungalows, and one villa all have a/c, balconies, telephones, refrigerators, and TVs (US$44 s, US$57 d low-season and US$48 s, US$67 d high-season). Facilities include a swimming pool and disco. Excursions are offered. It's somewhat lonesome, especially since tour groups have decamped to more central hotels.

A far better option is **Hotel Balcón del Caribe,** an Islazul property that should now be finished with a full renovation and have rooms for US$25 s, US$32 d and *cabañas* with ocean views for US$39 s/d. Cabins and rooms sit above the cliffs near the Morro Castle and face the deep blue, endless ocean. A great spot if you don't mind being far from town.

El Rancho Hotel, is beside the Carretera Central, on the hillside four km north of town, tel. 29040. It has 32 small, modestly furnished a/c *cabañas* for US$20 s, US$24 d in low season and US$23 s, US$30 d in high season.

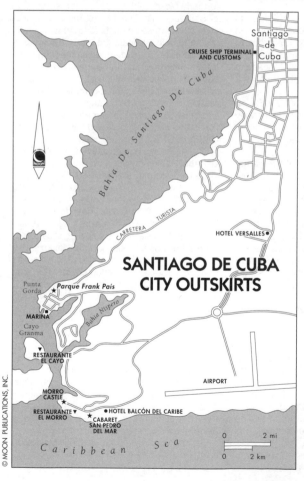

Upscale
You'll either love or hate the architecture of the **Hotel Santiago,** Avenida de las Américas e/ Cuarta y Manduley, tel. 4-2634 or 4-2612, fax 4-1756, a 15-story modernist structure with an exterior that is all plate-glass and metal girders painted blood-red and blue. It has been castigated by many writers. I find it attractive. The supposedly five-star hotel (run by Cubanacán) has 270 rooms plus three suites and 30 junior suites. The spacious rooms are done up in complimentary beige and mauve, with ultramodern furniture (handmade in Cuba) of rose-colored tropical hardwoods, Sony TVs and telephones, and bathrooms big enough for a house party and featuring piping-hot water. A panoply of facilities includes a jacuzzi, sauna and massage,

a small gym, three swimming pools and a solarium, beauty parlor, and barber shop. Rates are US$84 s, US$121 d.

FOOD

Santiagueros have their own cuisine, though these days creative dishes are as hard to find here as elsewhere in provincial Cuba. Most popular of Oriente's homegrown cuisine is roast suckling pig served with *congri*-style rice, seasoned yucca, tomato, and lettuce, followed by a stewed fruit in syrup. Look for *prú*, a refreshing soft drink concocted from fruit, herbs, roots, and sugar.

There are few local restaurants of note. Your best bet may be to head down to Plaza Dolores. Better-known restaurants are best booked in advance through the tourist desk in your hotel.

The water is barely potable. Stick to bottled water.

Paladares

Santiago is surprisingly weak on private restaurants. Keep your eye out for Christmas lights, the *paladares'* universal advertisement. **Paladar El Morro** is 600 meters southwest of Hotel Santiago on Avenida Victoriano Galzon. I had a huge (albeit mediocre) meal of lobster, salad, *congrí*, plantain, and beer for US$12.

Ask around. Locals will point you to the best *paladares*.

Hotel Restaurants

Most restaurants worth recommending serve the tourist trade. They're expensive. The **Restaurante Las Columnas,** in the Hotel Santiago, can set you back US$20 a person in two mouthfuls!

Some of the finest (albeit not prize-winning) cuisine in town is served at the **Restaurante Casa Grande,** in the hotel of that name on Parque Céspedes. The elegant setting is helped along by live classical music and a complimentary house special of rum, lemonade, and tamarind. Set meals cost US$11 and US$20. À la carte dishes, such as grilled fish, cost about US$6. Cuisine is *criollo* with a hint of the Continent.

Skip the **Las Terrazas** restaurant, in front of the Hotel San Juan. It serves mediocre buffet meals. Dinner costs US$12—about three times what it's worth. Same for breakfast.

For Dollars Only

My favorite eatery—**El Morro Restaurant**—is out of town, near Morro Castle. It is splendidly set atop the cliffs, with fabulous views along the coast. You dine on a terra-cotta-tiled terrace shaded by a gazebo covered by trumpetvine. Dark colonial furniture and goat-hide chairs add to the ambience, as do serenades by a trio of troubadors. A typical lunch (US$10) features an appetizer of pickled runner beans and cucumbers, and tasty entrée of pork, steak, or fish served with rice and cucumber and fried plantain. The staff is conscientious. It's a favorite with tour groups.

Another touristy favorite is **Tocororo,** housed in a colonial mansion with a splendid aesthetic sense on Avenida Manduley, tel. 41410. Choose indoor or outdoor dining. Shrimp costs US$8 upward, and lobster double that. A similar option is **La Maison,** also on Manduley. Seafoods are expensive, but you can order fried chicken, sandwiches, or pizza for US$4 and up. The menu features lobster and grilled fish of mediocre quality (US$5-20). A US$15 package includes dinner and the famous fashion show, plus comedians and magicians, who are likely to pull you up on stage.

Plaza Dolores has several good options. On the northwest corner is **Restaurante Don Antonio,** tel. 52205, in a beautifully restored colonial building. It's very elegant and has windows wide-open to the plaza. It serves *criollo* dishes (US$3-8). Next door is **La Perla del Dragon,** not surprisingly serving Chinese cuisine (entrées average US$10). **La Restaurante Terracina,** tel. 52307, is an upscale Italian restaurant with contemporary decor. Alas, the pizzas (US$2-6) are mediocre. The menu includes mussels (US$2) and scallops (US$7). On the south side, the elegant **Café Matamoros,** serves burgers and spaghetti for less than US$4. **Restaurante Mar-Init** specializes in seafoods. Finally, here, Rumbos has an outdoor café on the northwest corner.

If you want to combine dinner with a *cabaret espectáculo,* consider **Cabaret San Pedro del Mar,** tel. 91011 or 91506, outside town near Morro Castle. Dinner costs about US$5, US$15 with the show.

Local Favorites

Taberna Dolores is a colorful old bar and restaurant on Plaza Dolores. It's very popular with locals and has an open courtyard out back serving *criollo* food.

The much-touted **Santiago 1900,** San Basilico e/ Pio Rosado y Hartmann, is also popular with Cubans. The restaurant is in a mansion that once belonged to the Bacardi family. It has an outdoor patio beneath an arbor around a fountain where you may dine on overpriced *criollo* food (US$6 and up). It is said to offer veal, rabbit, and turkey, but none of that was available when I last tried it. Nearby is the **Casa del Vino** (formerly Casa del Queso), on Calle Heredia, serving wines and cheeses plus more substantial fare. Supposedly it operates in strict hourly shifts, by reservation.

Needing pizza? Try **Pizzeria Fontana,** on the corner of Lacret and Sacó. I'm told that the pizza is very good by Cuban standards.

If you can, make time for the ferry ride to Cayo Damas (across the bay) and a meal at the simple seafood **Restaurante El Cayo,** on the eastern side of the island. It boasts a lovely view. Try the lobster or prawns. **Palador El Marlin** offers an alternative.

Cafés and Snacks

Two atmospheric places to sip coffee are the little café on the corner of Calles Santo Tomás and Entramada and the atmospheric **La Isabelica,** a favorite of locals, in a 300-year-old house at the corner of Aguilera and Calvario, facing Plaza Dolores.

Another curious delight is the **Casa de Té,** on Aguilera, on the northeast corner of Parque Céspedes—"a small room with wobbling tables and a filthy floor. The tea was Russian, stewed black and drunk sweet," Carlos Gebler recorded (unfairly) in *Driving Through Cuba.* The menu includes Asian teas, mint teas, and *"plantas medicinales"* for 10 centavos a cup. However, few, if any, will be available.

Regardless of circumstance, there's always ice cream to be had at **Coppelia,** a true Cuban treat at the corner of Avenida de los Libertadores and Avenida Garzón. The world-class ice cream is served in aluminum bowls delivered speedily to your table. The bowl will be whisked away before the last spoonful touches your lips. Two big scoops costs 35 centavos. You pay first, then get your ticket and wait in line. Those ahead of you will probably be scattered all about, but everyone seems to know when their turn is due. As a foreigner, you may be ushered to the front (as I was) and served without the rigmarole, but expect to be charged in dollars. Downtown, you can buy ice cream from the *heladería* below the cathedral on Félix Pena.

Self-Catering

Buying your own food is no easier here than elsewhere in Cuba. For produce and meats, try the farmers' market at Aguilera and Padres Pico. You can buy Western goods at any Tienda Panamericano, Cupet gas station, or in the stores of the Hotel Santiago. Also try the hard-currency supermarket on Plaza de Martí, which includes a bakery. If heading into town from Morro Castle, call in at the Centro Comercial, at the entrance to the international airport.

ENTERTAINMENT AND EVENTS

Santiago is Cuba's second most dynamic city, with cultural activities and nightlife to keep you entertained for a month. The first few years of the Special Period knocked the wind out of its sails, but it has bounced back with new vigor. The city is known for its musical traditions and has also given rise to some of Cuba's most important modern rock groups.

A monthly tabloid called *Perfil de Santiago* lists forthcoming events.

Festivals and Events

The Ministerio del Cultura, Carniceria #461, tel. 7935, can supply a list of events. If you can, time your visit for **Carnival** (recently renamed the **Festival del Caribe**), in late July, when everyone in town downs shots of *aguardente* and gets caught up in the street rumbas and conga lines. The center of carnival activities is the area of La Trocha, near the harbour at the southern end of Avenida Jesús Menéndez, around Avenida 24 de Febrero.

The celebration was resurrected in 1995 after a three-year hiatus and is today encouraged as a celebration of Caribbean culture. It traditionally runs from 22 to 28 July, focused on the 26 July public holiday that marks the day in 1953 when, under the cover of carnival, Fidel Castro's revolutionaries attacked the Moncada barracks. Its roots, however, go much further back.

In August, people converge in Parque Céspedes for the Festival of *Pregón,* arriving in carriages smothered with flowers and dressed in traditional costume to compete in the improvisation of verse and song in the tradition of the old street vendors.

Traditional Music and Dance

Santiago's **Casa de la Trova,** on Calle Heredia, is the island's most famous. The *trova* tradition of romantic ballads was born here. The form mingles Spanish guitar, African percussion, and ballads that hauntingly tell of the struggles of traditional life. Many famous Cuban musicians perform here. The mood is still strong but has been diluted by a blasphemous facelift. Wednesday and Saturday evenings are traditionally the best times to go.

Traditional music and dance performances are also offered at the **Teatro Guignol,** where a children's puppet theater *(Teatro Muñecos)* has traditionally been offered. Also watch for performances by **La Tumba Francesa** and **Grupo Folklórico,** two groups that render traditional Afro-Cuban music and dance.

The **Alliance Française,** tel. 4-1503, the French-language school, at Calle 6 and Calle 11 in Vista Alegre, also hosts *tumba francesa,* plus cultural exhibitions playing on the town's French links. Free films are shown on Friday at 6 p.m. Also check out the **Casa de la Cultura,** at General Lacret #651 on weekends, when it hosts folkloric dancing (US$5).

Among the more exciting performances are those of **Ballet Folklórico Cutumba,** tel. 2-25860, a world-famous Afro-Cuban dance group that has a workshop on Saco e/ Corona y Padre Pico. They give performances of *columbia, conga oriental, tumba francesa,* and other dance styles each Sunday at 10:30 a.m. (US$3), but you can call in to see practice sessions held Tues.-Sun.

Another acclaimed troupe, **Conjunto Folklórico de Oriente,** is at Hartmann #407.

Caribbean Music & Dance Programs, 1611 Telegraph Ave., Suite 808, Oakland, CA 94612, tel. (510) 444-7173, fax (510) 444-5412, e-mail caribmusic@igc.apc.org or http://www.arana.com/caribmusic, offers weeklong study workshops in

Santiago to coincide with the Festival del Caribe. Programs in 1996 included "Cuban and Haitiano Folkloric Music and Dance" and "Son and Changuí Music."

Cabarets

As elsewhere in Cuba, the Las Vegas-style *cabaret espectáculo* is a local tradition. Several venues cater to tourists, but there are also less fancy cabarets for the locals.

If you ever need convincing that Cubans know how to put on a show, head to the **Tropicana,** four km northeast of town. Evening excursions are offered by all the tourist hotels. There are two shows per evening Wed.-Sat. (the first, beginning at 9 p.m., is the most spectacular; admission is US$30, including drink). Performers include Desi Arnez-type crooners in white suits, male dancers in tight spandex, and, most prominently, females in high heels, fanciful feathers, and bikinis that amount to no more than two dots and dash. Perhaps 100 dancers appear in a never ending parade of elaborate costumes. Colored floodlights reveal feathered mulattas high amid the palm trees on the hills to each side, quivering and cooing like denizens of an exotic harem. There are three bars and a restaurant.

Tour & Travel, beneath the Hotel Casa Grande on Parque Céspedes, tel. 8-6152; Calle 8 #54 e/ 1 y 3, Rpto. Vista Alegre, tel. 43603 or 41237; or Aeropuerto Antonio Maceo, tel. 01773, offers a Tropicana package (US$50), including meal and drinks.

Cabaret San Pedro del Mar, tel. 91011 or 91506, outside town near Morro Castle, also offers an *espectáculo* on a much smaller scale Fri.-Mon. at 9 p.m. (US$10). The cabaret takes place on a Mediterranean-style white terrace high above the ocean. You can dine here, too.

La Maison, on Avenida Manduley (one block north of Parque Ferreiro), tel. 41117 or 43965, fax 335083, offers a less fanciful night out. A fashion show is held each evening at 10 p.m., with male and female models displaying everything from swimwear to evening dress. The show is usually followed by a cabaret featuring a magician's act and a song-and-dance show. It all takes place in an outdoor patio. The old mansion contains a series of boutiques selling import goods—clothing, jewelry, cosmetics, etc. Note

CARNIVAL!

Carnival in Santiago de Cuba has been performed since the 19th century, when it was an Easter celebration. Originally it was called the Fiesta de las Mamarrachos (Festival of the Nincompoops), when slaves were given time off and the opportunity to release their pent-up energies and frustrations in a celebration full of sinister and sexual content. The celebration was bound irrevocably to the secret societies of ancient Africa, transformed in Cuba into neighborhood societies called *carabalí*. They would vie with one another to produce the most colorful and elaborate processions *(comparsas)* led by a frenzied melée of fife, drum, and maracas. There are representations of the *orishas* in the *comparsas* and characters representing the various gods lead the way. Since each *comparsa* comes from a different neighborhood, each dance and tune varies.

The hour-glass drums of the ancestors begin to pound out their *tun q'tu q'tu q'-tun* rhythm, which builds each day as the city becomes gripped by a collective frenzy. The wail of Chinese cornets *(corneta China)* adds to the racket. Young and old alike rush to join the conga lines full of clowns and celebrants in colonial period dress.

Carnival provides a release from the melancholy of much of life. Everyone participates. It all culminates in a carefully choreographed orgy of dance.

The main procession takes place on Avenida Jesús Menéndez, where stands are erected for spectators. The conga lines are followed by floats (sponsored by various Cuban agencies) graced by girls (*luceros*—morning stars) in riotous feathers and sequined bikinis or outrageous dresses. Huge *papier-mâché* heads supported by dancing Cubans bash into each other. Every year there's a different theme, and contestants are judged on originality and popularity.

Watching Rehearsals
The *carabalís* rehearse all year long, normally on Tuesday and Friday evenings. Visitors are welcome to drop in and watch their rehearsals. *Carabalí Izuama,* the oldest group, has a studio on Calle Pío Rosado e/ Los Maceo and San Antonio; *Carabalí Olugo* is at Trocha 496. *La Tumba Francesca* is another group, formed by Haitian émigrés (its workshop is at Los Maceo 501 and San Bartolomé). **Tour & Travel** can arrange visits, as can the tour desks of the major hotels.

the stunning paintings and bronze busts and statues in the lobby. Entrance costs US$5, including one drink. Tell them you're having dinner and the entrance fee will usually be dropped. **Tour & Travel** (see above) offers a *"Noche Especial"* at La Maison (US$15).

Nearby on Manduley is **Cabaret Soroa,** a far less ritzy Tropicana for the local populace. It's popular with young Cuban couples and is followed by a disco. **Las Terrazas** also has a cabaret (disco, comedy, and magic act) and dancing to live music on weekends, as does the rooftop bar of the **Hotel Casa Grande,** on Parque Céspedes (US$10).

Classical Performances
The huge, modernist **Teatro Heredia,** by the Plaza de la Revolución on Avenida de Las Américas, hosts classical performances and poetry readings on an infrequent basis. Its café has live music. **Poetry readings** are also given each Friday evening at UNEAC (Union of Writers and Artists of Cuba), in the Casa Heredia.

And the Poder Popular purportedly puts on opera every Saturday night.

Bars and Discos
The first place to bend your elbow should be the 15th-floor bar of the Hotel Santiago for the stunning views of the city. The bill will dent your wallet, as it will in the rooftop bar of the Hotel Casa Grande (also with a marvelous view)—or downstairs at the veranda bar, which compensates with views down over Parque Céspedes. In the evening, a magician called Antonio sometimes shows up and performs free tricks on patrons before heading up to the rooftop bar to perform in the cabaret.

The most popular dance spot is **Disco Espanta Sueños,** tel. 42634, next to the Hotel Santiago. The disco has a state-of-the-art multiple-screen video setup, lighting, and pumped-in fog. The hip youth of Santiago flock here. Entrance is free for guests, 30 pesos for locals (including free drinks), and US$5 for foreign nonguests. Supposedly, there are special fees for guests at other hotels. You bump and grind on a stainless steel dance floor. Beers cost US$3. Closed Monday.

A second option is the **Disco Havana Club,** across the road, next to the Hotel Las Américas (US$3); a third is the outdoor disco hosted on weekends at the Hotel San Juan. All are popular with Cuban youth. A disco is also held each Saturday night at **Casa del Estudiante,** next to the Casa de la Trova on Calle Heredia. Entrance costs US$4. Live music and dance is also featured on Sunday nights.

Nearby, the **Bar Claqueta,** at Félix Pena #654 has dancing and live music.

Other Entertainment
The main movie-house is **Cine Rialto,** on Félix Pena, one block south of the main square. Also try **Cine Cuba,** at Saco #304, and **Cine Latinoamericano,** at Avenida Victoriano Garzón #390.

SPORTS AND RECREATION

There's a sports facility at the north end of Avenida de las Américas, opposite Plaza de la Revolución. The baseball stadium—**Estadio Guillermón Moncada**—is also on Avenida de las Américas, at Calle E. The tour desks may be able to tell you when a baseball game is happening (usually Tues.-Thurs. evenings and Saturday and Sunday at 1:30 p.m., Nov.-March).

For Children
Kids will probably enjoy the **Parque Zoológico,** immediately west of the Hotel San Juan. Animals from most continents are represented, including mandrills, baboons, and other monkeys. It's open Tues.-Sun. 10 a.m.-5 p.m. Entrance costs US$1 (US40 cents children).

Nearby, at the foot of San Juan Hill, is the **Parque de Diversiones 26 de Julio** amusement park, a large fairground with rides that has recently been refurbished.

Watersports and Excursions
Marina Marlin, tel. 91446, at Punta Gorda, offers a range of recreational watersports, including sportfishing charters for US$130 for four

passengers. It also offers panoramic bay excursions (US$5) and six-hour "seafaris" to Guamá (US$30 including lunch) and Playa Daiquiri and Baconao (US$25 including lunch). Another excursion includes Morro Castle (US$20). You can can charter sportfishing boats, yachts, and a motor launch.

A young fellow named Merino rents his sportfishing boat for casual tourist trips inside the harbour and for deep-sea fishing trips outside. Ask at the marina (formerly Marina Caribe Oriental), operated by Puertosol S.A.

SHOPPING

All the hotels have souvenir shops selling the usual range of T-shirts, music tapes, *muñecas* (dolls), and musical instruments. Santiago's stores close on Monday, with a few exceptions.

Tour & Travel beneath the Hotel Casa Grande on Parque Céspedes, tel. 8-6152; Calle 8 #54 e/ 1 y 3, Rpto. Vista Alegre, tel. 43603 or 41237; or Aeropuerto Antonio Maceo, tel. 91773, offers a shopping tour (US$18).

Arts and Crafts
Take your pick. The largest art and craft shop is on the corner of Calles San Pedro and San Basilio. **Cubartesania** has a store at Bartolomé Masó and Félix Pena selling quality arts and crafts. You'll also find an **ARTEX** shop in the Casa de la Trova, on Calle Heredia (a real trove of serendipity for shoppers). Outside, artisans sell crude carvings and paintings and jewelry from streetside stalls.

Galería Oriente, on the east side of Parque Céspedes, has a wide range of quality art, with separate rooms dedicated to the work of students and their professors. The former tend to be more experimental, with Salvador Dali's influence strongly present and a sense of exasperation in many works. You'll need an official receipt to export any artwork bought in Cuba.

A shop below the cathedral on Céspedes Square sells books, records, and crafts.

Check out **La Minerva,** a small antique shop on Heredia and Pío Rosado. Consider heading out to **El Oasis,** a small village dedicated to the production of arts and crafts.

Rum and Cigars

Sure, you can buy these in the hotel stores, but I say go to the source. For rum, visit the rum factory on Avenida Jesús Menéndez e/ San Antonio y San Ricardo. The tasting room sells Havana Club, Ron Varadero, and Ron Matusalem (US$4.75-8.10 a liter). Here, too, is the only place in Cuba where you can buy 25-year-old rum in special porcelain bottles.

The cigar factory is also on Jesús Menéndez, 0.5 km farther south, at the foot of Masó.

SERVICES AND INFORMATION

Money

The tourist hotels can cash traveler's checks, as can the banks, although there are surprisingly few of these for such a large city. You can cash traveler's checks and get advances against credit cards (except those issued by US banks) at **Banco Financiero Internacional,** on the northwest corner of Parque Céspedes (open weekdays 8 a.m.-3 p.m.), and at **Banco Nacional,** which has a branch on the northeast corner of Parque Céspedes. If you want pesos, you'll find plenty of *jiniteros* hanging out outside the Hotel Santiago and in Parque Céspedes. They'll approach you to change US dollars at the going black-market rate (be discreet; there are usually police hanging around).

Medical

Tourists have their own medical facilities, provided by the **Clínica Internacional,** on Calle 13 one block north of Carretera Siboney, opposite the entrance to Hotel San Juan, tel. 42589. A doctor and nurse are on permanent duty (US$20 per consultation) and will make hotel visits for US$30. The clinic has a modestly stocked pharmacy, an ambulance, and beds in the event that you need an overnight stay.

In a pinch, you can use Santiago's several hospitals or policlínicos, where service is free. However, given Cuba's dire shortage of medicines, you should refrain from doing so unless you are willing to give a donation.

Post and Telecommunications

All the tourist hotels have post and international telephone facilities. The main post office is at the corner of Hartmann and Heredia, one block east of Parque Céspedes. The telegraph office is also here.

You can make international calls from the Centro de Llamados Internacionales in the arcade beneath the cathedral on the south side of Parque Céspedes. In the same facility is DHL, tel. 7795, from where you can send express letters and packages both domestically and overseas. It's open weekdays 9 a.m.-6 p.m. and Saturday 8:30 a.m.-noon.

Other Services

Cyclists will find a well-stocked **bicycle store** selling parts at the corner of Saco and Hartmann.

There are **Cupet gas stations** at the junction of Avenida de Céspedes and Avenida de los Libertadores, and, two km farther north, on the road to Bayamo.

TOURIST INFORMATION

The hotels have tour information desks. **Rumbos** maintains a *buro de turismo* across from the entrance to the Hotel Casa Grande on Parque Céspedes; it arranges excursions (including to the Tropicana nightclub) and issues train tickets (open 8 a.m.-8 p.m.).

The **Carpeta Central,** below the cathedral on General Lacret between Heredia and Bartolomé Masó, makes reservations for peso hotels. Similarly, the **Oficina de Reservaciones de Turismo Parque Baconao,** at Sacó #455, makes reservations for Cuban *campismos* along the coast east of town.

Maps

Look for the tourist guide *Guía Turística Santiago de Cuba.* This 250-page booklet has the

---

SANTIAGO USEFUL TELEPHONE NUMBERS

Police	tel. 116
Ambulance	tel. 2-2848
Hospital	tel. 2-6571
Railway Station	tel. 5-2143
Terminal de Ómnibus	tel. 2-3050

most detailed maps available, as well as brief information on sites of tourist interest. Well-thumbed copies are for sale at bookstores and street stalls. You may be able to find outdated copies of *Mapas Turística,* published by various government agencies.

Libraries
The Biblioteca Elvira Cape is at Heredia #259, between Pío Rosado and Hartmann. It has a section devoted to opera music, replete with listening booths.

Travelers' Assistance
Asistur, has an office in the Hotel Santiago, on Avenida de las Américas and Calle M, tel. 33-5015, ext. 3128, fax 33-5805, and another beneath the Hotel Casa Grande, on Parque Cespedes, tel. 63-8284 or 62-5519, fax 33-8087. This agency can provide travelers with legal advice, help arrange a doctor's visit or other medical attention, and assist with cash advances and other matters.

Visa Extensions
You can obtain an extension *(paroga)* from the Immigration office at Calle San Vacilio# 412 e/ Carbarrio and Carniceria, or at Avenida Raúl Pujol #10, 200 meters east of the Hotel Santiago. You'll need your passport and tourist card, of course. Once approved, you have to pay US$25 at the tour desk in the Hotel Santiago, then return to Immigration to receive the extension.

Bookstores
Most hotel stores carry a fistful of English-language coffee-table books, novels, and pro-Revolution texts. For Spanish-language books hyping the glories of the Revolution, check out the large bookstore at Sacó #356 or Librería Vietnam, at Aguilera #567.

GETTING THERE

By Car
From Bayamo, you can enter via the Carretera Central or the three-lane, concrete Autopista, which begins just east of Palma Soriana. It has no lane markings, but, fortunately, neither does it have much traffic. Watch for cattle crossing the freeway, ox-carts, pedestrians, and bicycles.

The road from Guantánamo enters Santiago at Parque Ferreiro. And a rough dirt road from Marea del Portillo follows the south coast and enters Santiago from the west.

By Bus
Bus no. 600 departs Havana's main bus terminal daily at 12:30 and 7:35 p.m. (14 hours; 42 pesos). As always, the buses are usually booked solid weeks in advance. The experience is for masochists. You arrive at the **Terminal de Ómnibus Interprovinciales,** at the north end of Avenida de los Libertadores and Calle 9, where taxis and *colectivos* await.

By Air
Cubana has at least three flights daily from Havana to Santiago (90 minutes; US$80 one-way). The schedule is complicated, with different departure times for each day. It is also subject to change, and delays can be interminable. Cubana also offers service between Santiago and Baracoa (Sunday) and Varadero (daily except Tuesday and Thursday).

Well-scrubbed and uncrowded **Antonio Maceo International Airport,** tel. 226-911014, is eight km south of Santiago. Local bus service (no. 211 or 213) operates between downtown, opposite the hospital on Avenida de los Libertadores, and the airport. There are taxis (about US$10 one-way), and a radio dispatcher to keep things orderly. A minibus transfer from the airport to downtown costs US$15 roundtrip, US$10 one-way, and can be arranged through Havanatur, Calle 8 #54, e/ 1 y 3, Rpto. Vista Alegre, tel. 43603, fax 33-5083.

From Europe: LTU operates charters from Düsseldorf and Munich. Cubana flies to Santiago from Paris in conjunction with AOM French Airlines. Other package tour operators offer charters (see the On The Road chapter for more details).

From Canada: November through April, **Regent Holidays** offers weekly charter flights from Toronto to Santiago using Air Transat (from C$369 air-only roundtrip, depending on dates). Weeklong packages begin at C$659, including accommodations and airfare. **Fiesta Sun** also offers weekly charters from Toronto, with fares from CAN$399 depending on dates.

From Jamaica: Sunholiday, tel. (809) 979-6672, fax (809) 979-6672, offers flights from Montego Bay to Santiago each Thursday (US$165 roundtrip, US$148 one-way, US$179 including a one-day tour package, returning to Jamaica that evening). **Inter-Caribe,** 11½ Ardenne Rd., Kingston 10, tel. (809) 978-2150, has a three-day excursion (from US$239, including airfare), and weeklong packages (from US$387) to Santiago from Kingston each Friday and Sunday morning. Prices include sightseeing.

By Train

An express train departs daily from Havana for Santiago at 4:25 p.m. Brace yourself for a melée when the Havana train arrives. The venerable train station abuts the harbor on Avenida Jesús Menéndez, at the foot of Sánchez Echuverria, but a glitzy new railway station should now be operating, one km north of the existing station.

By Sea

Private Boat: Private yachters can arrive at **Marina Marlin** (formerly Marina Caribe Oriental), at Punta Gorda. The funky little place has moorings for six boats. Power and diesel are available, plus showers and bathrooms. Plans for a restaurant had not materialized in spring 1996, but there's a Cuban pesos-only restaurant a short distance from the marina.

The marina offices are in the old wooden building at the rear. The staff can call a taxi, arrange rental cars, and help resolve any difficulties with officialdom. If you need supplies, try the Cubalse shop, north of the Hotel Santiago, or the *diplotienda* by the airport, a few miles east of the marina. Customs and Immigration is very friendly. A taxi ride into town will cost about US$12.

Cruise Ship: Costa Cruceros includes Santiago on its year-round weeklong cruises from the Dominican Republic. The cruise ship—*Costa Playa*—arrives midafternoon each Wednesday and departs in the wee hours of Thursday morning. Sightseeing excursions, including the Tropicana nightclub, are offered. The *Meliá Don Juan,* which offers deluxe three, four- and seven-day cruises from Cienfuegos, also calls in to Santiago de Cuba every Wednesday, arriving at 10 a.m. and departing at 6 p.m. Excursions in and around Santiago are offered.

(The *Carribean Queen,* which offered cruise service from Jamaica, was discontinued in 1995. A new cruise-ship facility is being touted.)

By Organized Tour

All the leading tour operators in Havana, Varadero, and other prime resort areas offer excursions to Santiago (see relevant chapters).

Wings of the World, 1200 William St. #706, Buffalo, NY 14240, tel. (800) 465-8687, includes Santiago as the focus of several organized tours from the US, including an 11-day "envi-

Monument to Antonio Maceo, Santiago

ronmental adventure" and an eight-day cycling adventure.

A Canadian company, **MacQueen's Bicycle Tours,** 430 Queen St., Charlottetown, Prince Edward Island, Canada C1A 4E8, tel. (902) 368-2453 or (800) 969-2822, fax (902) 894-4547, offers an eight-day guided bicycle tour from Santiago. The itinerary includes Baconao Park, Gran Piedra, the Sierra Maestra, and parts of Granma province (C$1,599 including roundtrip airfare from Toronto).

GETTING AROUND

By Bus
Buses serve most of the city (fare is 20 centavos). Bus no. 1 runs between Parque Céspedes and both the interprovincial and intermunicipal bus terminals. There's a third bus depot **Estación de Transporte Serrano,** serving local traffic on the harborfront, opposite the train station. Buses are exceedingly crowded.

Taxis
Taxis hang out below the cathedral on the south side of Parque Céspedes and outside the tourist hotels. A taxi between the Hotel Santiago or Hotel San Juan and Parque Céspedes should cost about US$3. Horse-drawn *coches* cost one peso or US$1. Call 9-1012 or 3-1398 for a tourist taxi.

By Car
A car is fine for the outer suburbs but, in town, forget it. The streets in the center are too narrow and congestion too much to contemplate. **Havanautos** has facilities at the Hotel Las Américas, tel. 8-6160, and at the airport, tel. 9-1773 or 8-6161. **Transtaxi** has an office beneath the Hotel Casa Grande, on Parque Céspedes.

A Cuban named Jorge will drive your around town in his 112-hp 1930 Phaeton with the canvas top, which parks outside the entrance to the Hotel Casa Grande. He charges US$12 for a city tour. You can even rent a motorcycle with sidecar around Parque Céspedes (no more than US$2 or US$5 to Morro Castle).

Excursions
Tour & Travel has an office beneath the Hotel Casa Grande on Parque Céspedes, tel. 8-6152;

and other offices at Calle 8 #54 e/ 1 y 3, Rpto. Vista Alegre, tel. 43603 or 41237; and Aeropuerto Antonio Maceo, tel. 91773. It offers a city tour (US$10) and shopping tour (US$8). It also has a wide range of excursions farther afield (see below). **Cubanacán** also offers a city tour, as does **Fantástico Tours,** which has an office in the airport.

GETTING AWAY

By Bus
Buses operate between Santiago and outlying destinations and as far as Guantánamo and Manzanillo from the **Terminal de Ómnibus Municipales,** at the corner of Avenida de los Libertadores and Calle 4. Long-distance buses operate from the **Terminal de Ómnibus Interprovinciales,** at the north end of Avenida de los Libertadores and Calle 9.

Buses for El Cobre, Siboney, and other destinations within a one-hour striking distance leave from the Estación de Intermunicipales Serrano, on Avenida Jesús Menéndez, opposite the railway station.

Peso-only *colectivos* also operate from the bus stations.

By Air
Flights operate to Havana at least three times daily (see "Getting There," above), and to Camagüey, Baracoa, Moa, and other destinations. You need to book as many days in advance as possible.

The airport has a restaurant and bar above the departure lounge. You can also sip your Havana Club rum in an old Cubana DC-8 converted into a bar. Other facilities include a Havanautos car rental office, a Fantástico Tours office, and shops outside the airport parking lot.

The Cubana office is beneath the Hotel Casa Grande on Parque Céspedes, tel. 24156 or 22290. They also have an office in the Hotel Santiago.

By Train
You can buy tickets at the train station. Reservations can also be made and tickets purchased at the **Ferrocarril de Cuba** office, at Calle Aguilera #565 (open Mon.-Fri. 8 a.m.-4 p.m. and Sat-

urday 8 a.m.-noon). Sample destinations and fares include Bayamo, US$4.50; Camagüey, $13; Guantánamo, US$4; Havana, US$35; Holguín, US$5; Manzanillo, US$6; and Matanzas, US$32.

Excursions

Tour & Travel, beneath the Hotel Casa Grande on Parque Céspedes, tel. 8-6152; Calle 8 #54 e/ 1 y 3, Rpto. Vista Alegre, tel. 43603 or 41237; or Aeropuerto Antonio Maceo, tel. 91773, offers day excursions to Baconao (US$30) and Gran Piedra (US$15, including lunch), Playa Daiquiri (US$22), El Cobre (US$8), El Cobre and Morro Castle (US$14), Baracoa (US$55, including lunch), and Cayo Saetía (US$61). **Cubanacán** also offers excursions to El Cobre, Baconao, and Gran Piedra, as well as to Havana and Varadero, and even a one-day junket to Jamaica.

Visits to the *mirador* overlooking the US naval base at Guantánamo can be arranged at Villa Gaviota.

NORTH AND WEST OF SANTIAGO

EL COBRE

The small town of El Cobre, 20 km northwest of Santiago, takes its name from the large copper mine that the Spanish established in the mid-1500s, run by German engineers. By the end of the century the mine was providing Havana's artilleryworks' entire supply of copper. In 1630, it was abandoned, and the African slave-miners were unilaterally freed.

A century later, the mine was reopened by Colonel Don Pedro Jiménez, governor of Santiago, who put the slaves' descendants back to work. It is said that the Virgin de la Caridad del Cobre (see below) eventually interceded on their behalf. The slaves were officially declared free in 1782. The mine continued in operation throughout the 19th century.

The town sits in a valley surrounded by the Sierra de Cobre, the easternmost spur of the Sierra Maestra. The valley is scarred by the huge open-pit mine. Dominating the town from atop a small hillock is the ocher-colored, red-domed, triple-towered Basílica del Cobre.

Basílica del Cobre

The church—Cuba's only basilica is imposing atop its lofty pedestal, although it can hardly compete with St. Paul's or Notre Dame. It is famed—and worth a visit—for its chapel full of propitiary offerings, and as the shrine to La Virgen de la Caridad (Virgin of Charity), patron saint of Cuba, to whom miraculous powers are ascribed.

The church is called the "Cuban Lourdes." Once a year, thousands of devoted Cubans make their way along the winding road, many shuffling along on their knees, crawling painfully uphill to fulfill a promise made to the saint at some difficult moment in their lives. The unlucky fisherman in Ernest Hemingway's *Old Man and the Sea* promises to "make a pilgrimage to the Virgin de Cobre" if he wins his battle with the massive marlin. In 1952, Hemingway dedicated his Nobel Prize for Literature to the Virgin, placing it in her shrine, which also has a small gold figure presented by Fidel Castro's mother, Lina Ruz—the maid who married the boss—perhaps asking favor and protection for Fidel and his brother, Raúl. On 6 May 1988, two men stole Hemingway's Nobel medallion. The culprits (and the medal) were found several days later, to much public fanfare. Today, the medal is in the custody of the Archbishop of Santiago.

The main entrance is reached via a steep staircase lined with old lamps. More usual is to enter at the rear, from the car park. Touts will rush forward to sell you iron pyrite (fool's gold) culled from the residue of the nearby mine. "*¡Es reál!*" they say, attemping to put a small piece in your hand. The church lobby—the Salon of Miracles—contains a small chapel with a silver altar crowded with votive candles and flowers. To left and right are tables with dolls, bottles, and a motley miscellany of objects you might find in your grandmother's parlor. The two centuries of ex-votos ("all the heaped and abandoned hopes of Cuba laid before its patron saint," wrote Pico Iyer) include war mementoes that narrate Cuba's history from the struggle for independence from Spain to the conflict in Angola (amazingly, the medals of men who fought *against* the Revolution lie side-by-side with those given by men who fought to defend it at the Bay of Pigs). On the walls hang scores of silver adornment and little *milagros* of limbs and other body parts.

The main church is plain except for its large marble altarpiece and the stained-glass windows in the upper reaches of the arched nave, which is bathed in soft, colored light. Choral groups often perform here. The **Virgen de la Caridad del Cobre** resides in effigy in an a/c glass case in a niche in the wall above and to the right of the altar. You can view her up close by taking a staircase marked *Subida*. The virgin's figure, clad in a golden cloak and crown, is surrounded by a sea of flowers, and the entire shrine is suffused with narcotic scents. On saint's day, the church warden presses a button and, as if by magic, she turns to face the rapt audience.

The church is open daily 6:30 a.m.-6 p.m. Masses *(misas)* are offered Mon.-Sat. (except Wednesday) at 8 a.m., on the eighth day and the first Thursday of each month at 8 p.m., and Sunday at 8 and 10 a.m. and 4:30 p.m.

Note: In 1993, the church was briefly closed to foreigners after tourists forced their way inside to take photographs during a religious service. Common decency dictates that you honor any restrictions and local customs.

Accommodations and Food

The *Hospedaje El Cobre,* tel. 3-6246, for pilgrims, in an old mansion behind the church, has 16 basic rooms where foreigners are welcome when space allows (10 pesos d per night). You can also bunk in a dormitory (four pesos). The place is appropriately ascetic but has fine views. There's a refectory serving basic fare for a pittance at 7:30 a.m., 11:30 a.m., and 6:30 p.m. To make reservations, you can write Hermana Carmen Robles, Hospedaje El Cobre, Santiago de Cuba.

There are a couple of basic restaurants and snack stalls down the hill in town.

Getting There

Exiting Santiago, take either Avenida de los Libertadores or Avenida de los Américas, which leads to the Carretera Central. Follow this uphill past the university en route to Bayamo. The turnoff for El Cobre is signed, 16 km northwest of Santiago. Bus no. 2 operates four times daily to El Cobre from the Terminal Ómnibus Intermunicipales.

A taxi from Santiago will cost about US$30 roundtrip.

Tour & Travel, beneath the Hotel Casa Grande on Parque Céspedes, tel. 8-6152; Calle 8 #54 e/ 1 y 3, Rpto. Vista Alegre, tel. 43603 or 41237; or Aeropuerto Antonio Maceo, tel. 91773, offers excursions to El Cobre (US$8) and in conjunction with visits to Morro Castle and Gran Piedra.

EL COBRE TO GRANMA PROVINCE

The Carretera Central continues northwest through **Palma Soriano,** an unappealing town with the virtue of possessing a **Cupet gas station.** Two miles west of town, there's a face-

---

THE LEGEND OF THE BLACK VIRGIN

The 17th-century image of the black madonna was supposedly found by two fishermen and their young slave, Juan Moreno, in the Bay of Nipe in 1608. According to legend, the three fishermen (the "three Juans") were caught in a tropical storm and doomed to die when the figurine appeared, floating atop a board that read *"Yo Soy la Virgen de la Caridad,"* "I am the Virgin of Charity." It was the very statue that, according to legend, had been given to an Indian chief by a *conquistador,* Alonso de Ojeda, in 1510, but had been set adrift on a raft when jealous chiefs tried to seize it.

The fishermen survived. Pope Benedicto XV declared her the Patron Saint of Cuba on 10 May 1916.

The Virgin is represented in effigy in churches all over the island, usually depicting her standing atop the waves, with the three fishermen gazing in awe from their little boat. In santería, the Afro-Cuban religion, she is *Ochún,* the powerful goddess of sensuality.

---

less motel catering to Cubans. There's a hotel and restaurant nearby called **Mirador Valle de Tallabe,** tel. 2594, which offers splendid views down the valley, in the Altos de los Coquitos.

This area is one of rolling hills and parched rangeland. Approaching **Contramaestra,** 72 km northwest of Santiago, the land is sweeping, with wide rolling plains (very scenic) planted in sugar and shaded by clumps of baobab trees. The town itself is attractive, with whitewashed curbstones and shady sidewalks. A curiosity (for its name) is the *central* called **Free America,** just outside town. Should you be tempted to stay in the area, you'll find basic rooms at the pesos-only **Hotel Luanda** and **Hotel Praga.**

There is little evidence to suggest that a century ago, these flatlands were stained with the blood of *Mambís* and Spanish troops.

SIERRA MAESTRA

The easternmost spurs of the Sierra Maestra rise sharply south of Palma Soriano and Contramaestra. It is a thrilling adventure to climb the Sierra Maestra by car to gain an impression of peasant lifestyle and locate some of the sites associated with Che Guevara's Rebel Army.

At the village of **Cruce de los Baños,** 25 km south of Contramaestra (and the highest point reached by paved roads), you'll find one of the guerrilla headquarters—now a camp for Exploradores, revolutionary Cuba's version of the Boy Scouts.

About 32,000 people live in the vicinity, though at first sight you would imagine it deserted, with its rocky terrain and dense vegetation. Beyond Cruce, the deeply rutted dirt roads are used only by adults on mules and by donkeys laden with coffee beans, making your arrival at **El Saltón** all the more breathtaking. Here, you'll find a natural pool and picture-perfect cascades nestled in a valley high in the mountains west of Cruce.

Accommodations

El Saltón is an eco-lodge run by Delta Hotels of Canada, 350 Bloor St. East #300, Toronto, Ontario M4W 1H4, tel. (416) 926-7800 or (800) 268-1133, fax (416) 926-7846, or, in Cuba, Carretera a Filé, Contramaestra, or Calle 248 y Avenida 5, Santa Fe, Havana, tel. 33-6336. The facility was built in the 1970s as an anti-stress center for the Cuban elite. It still offers massage, sauna, and whirlpool, as well as hikes and horseback rides (US$2 per hour). Accommodations are in 22 double rooms in four separate buildings (US$37 s, US$44 d). There's an open-sided dining area where, after dinner, the lively band plays and locals gather to join in the dancing with guests. It's three km south of Filé.

Getting There

Buses operate into the Sierras from the Estación de Transporte Serrano, on the harborfront in Santiago.

Anyone with a 4WD vehicle and the requisite *cojones* can tackle the steep and exceedingly rugged dirt road that crosses the Sierra Maestra from Río Seco, on the south coast. Allow several hours.

El Saltón is included as a stop on a seven-day "eco-tour" offered by Cubanacán; on an 11-day tour "From Mountains to Forest" tour offered from the US by **Wings of the World,** 1200 William St. #706, Buffalo, NY 14240, tel. (800) 465-8687; and on an eight-day mountain-bike tour of Oriente offered by **MacQueen's Bicycle Tours,** 430 Queen St., Charlottetown, Prince Edward Island, Canada C1A 4E8, tel. (902) 368-2453 or (800) 969-2822, fax (902) 894-4547.

SANTIAGO TO CHIVIRICO

The drive west along the coast from Santiago is magnificent, with the sinuous road pushed right to the shoreline by the Sierra Maestra plummeting down to a crashing sea. The road becomes gradually more lonesome as you pass rustic fishing villages tucked into paradisiacal bays. There are several evocations of history, including the ruins of a Spanish fort.

Playa Mar Verde, 17 km west of Santiago, is a beach popular with city dwellers. You might do a double-take as you pass through **Asseredero,** about 32 km west of Santiago—in the harbor is the wreck of the Spanish-American warship *Viscaya,* scuttled by the US navy on 3 July 1898, when the Spanish navy attempted to break out of Santiago harbor. The cruiser's forward guns point skyward above the water. (There are other wrecks in the shallow bay of Nima-Nima, 10 km west of Santiago.)

The only town is **Chivirico,** about 80 km west of Santiago. Here you'll find two splendid foreign-operated hotels with top-notch facilities and knockout views.

West of Chivirico, the mountains *really* make their presence felt. The searing heat builds. Arable plots give way to parched pastures and cacti begin to appear. The road deteriorates as you pass into Granma province en route to Marea del Portillo, with its own top-notch resorts. After tempests, the unpaved road may be washed out.

SIERRA DEL CRISTAL

You could well be the first foreigner in a week to journey into the Sierra Cristal, a rugged, mineral-rich mountain region northeast of Santiago. It's a spectacular drive. French coffee planters established estates here in the 19th century, though the region remained remote until the Revolution, when a paved road was built and community facilities arrived.

The only town of note is **Mayarí Arriba,** enfolded by peaks, 55 km northeast of Santiago. Céspedes established his revolutionary government here in the 1860s, and the town was so remote that Raúl Castro established his military headquarters here when he opened the Second Front in 1958.

Batista's air force utilized the US base at Guantánamo for raids into the mountains, where they used napalm bombs on peasant villages. A small **Museum of the Second Front** recalls those days. Open daily except Monday 9 a.m.-6 p.m.

From Santiago, follow the Autopista Nacional north and exit at Boniato for El Cristo and **Alto Songo,** a crossroads town in the foothills of the mountains. From here, a road leads north to Mayarí Arriba.

SANTIAGO TO GUANTÁNAMO PROVINCE

The main road turns east at Alto Songo and rises along the northern foothills of the Gran Piedra Mountains. It's a beautifully scenic drive past rolling sugarcane fields. Beyond **La Maya,** the land takes on a different look, becoming more lushly tropical. About 10 miles east of La Maya, you'll pass a sheer scarp slope, strangely striated, and smothered in vegetation.

The area is pitted with pockets of poverty. One sees hovels—a rare sight in Cuba, more reminiscent of the backwaters of Jamaica or Mexico—amid the fields of coffee and bananas and arable crops. Farther along, you pass rows of bottle-green coffee bushes beneath tall shade trees smothered in epiphytes.

The boundary with Guantánamo province is about 25 km east of Alto Songo. As you drop onto the flatlands of the Cuenca de Guantánamo the road opens up into wide freeway for the last 20 km into town.

BACONAO BIOSPHERE RESERVE

The area immediately east of Santiago is replete with attractions and deserves at least a full day. The region is encompassed by the 32,400-hectacre Baconao Biosphere Reserve, which officially begins at San Juan Hill, in the eastern suburbs of Santiago, and extends east 40 km to Laguna Baconao and the border with Guantánamo province. The Sierra de la Gran Piedra forms a steep east-west backbone through the reserve, which includes parts of two other zones: the Santiago Reserve, extending along the coast; and the remote *altiplano* of Santa María de Loreto, north of Gran Piedra. The park contains many places of historical interest, including revolutionary shrines and coffee plantations established by the French settlers who came from Haiti in the 19th century. It features wildlife refuges, natural monuments, beaches, and museums.

It is reached via the Carretera Siboney, which, after passing through the suburbs, is lined with 26 monuments to the heroes of the Moncada attack. Each has a plaque with a simple inscription that tells the hero's name, occupation, and how he died. They're signposted by blue markers and are numbered in order.

Getting There: Tour & Travel, beneath the Hotel Casa Grande on Parque Céspedes, tel. 8-6152; Calle 8 #54 c/ 1 y 3, Rpto. Vista Alegre, tel. 43603 or 41237; or Aeropuerto Antonio Maceo, tel. 91773, offers several excursions to Baconao from US$30, including Gran Piedra and other attractions. A transfer to Baconao with Havanatur's Tour & Travel costs US$18 roundtrip (US$12 one-way). Baconao is also the highlight of an eight-day mountain-bike tour of Oriente offered by **MacQueen's Bicycle Tours,** 430 Queen St., Charlottetown, Prince Edward Island, Canada C1A 4E8, tel. (902) 368-2453 or (800) 969-2822, fax (902) 894-4547. The itinerary includes a thrilling downhill ride from the top of Gran Piedra!

Wildlife

During the first half of this century, North American mining companies deforested much of the terrain. Extensive areas have also been felled for coffee and charcoal production—and, more recently, for cattle ranching. Still, there is incredible potential (as yet untapped) for hikers, birders, and other ecotourists.

The park was named by UNESCO for its biodiversity. Baconao harbors more than 6,000 species of higher plants. By one account, 51.6% are endemic (this seems high; another official source says there are 138 species of endemic plants, of which three are rare and three more are endangered) The north-sloping faces are more lushly forested due to higher rainfall. There are also more than 800 insect species, 29 reptile species, 60 bird species, and 19 mammal species.

Monument to Heroes of Moncada, Baconao

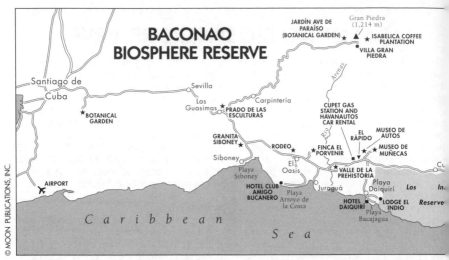

Of these, at least 102 are endemic to the region. Almost half of the bird species are native.

This is a protected area (though it includes a hunting reserve). Signs along the road read "Cuidad de Insectas" (Care for the Insects).

PRADO DE LAS ESCULTURAS

Just beyond **Sevilla** (so named because it was settled by immigrants from Sevilla in Spain), you'll reach a T-junction at Las Guasimas, eight miles from Santiago. To the left, on a rise overlooking the road, is a sculpture garden amid a large park of wide-spreading trees and rocks. Most of the metal and rock pieces are ungainly contemporary works. It's open daily 7 a.m.-4:30 p.m. (entrance costs US$1).

GRAN PIEDRA NATIONAL PARK

The road past Prado de las Esculturas winds up through ravines, growing ever steeper and more serpentine until it deposits you at the top of Gran Piedra (1,214 meters). The road (in moderately poor condition) winds and loops uphill for 14 km. You pass through several ecosystems. Below is lush and thick with forest. As you climb, the vegetation opens out, becoming more scrubby, and the views grow more dramatic. Suddenly you emerge on a ridge with a view down the mountains to the north. It's noticeably crisper and cooler up here, where clouds hover, swirling through the ancient tree ferns and tall pines and bamboo. The road follows the ridgecrest, giving views of the Atlantic far off to the north and the Caribbean below to the right.

After about 14 km, you arrive at a narrow bridge. Here, a dirt road winds 400 meters downhill to Jardín Ave de Paraíso. A half-mile beyond the bridge is a restaurant and hotel at 1,150 meters elevation. From the restaurant, a 454-step stairway leads up to the **Gran Piedra** (Great Rock), where you can climb a steel ladder onto the rock itself for a spectacular view down the mountainside. On a clear day, you can see the Blue Mountains in Jamaica; and by night, the lights of Port-au-Spain, Haiti.

Fidel Castro and 18 other survivors of the Moncada barracks attack on 26 July 1953 fled into these mountains. On August 1 he was taken prisoner by a Rural Guard contingent. Castro was lucky. The troops wanted to kill him, but the squad commander, Lt. Pedro Manuel Sarría Tartabull, guaranteed Castro's life (in 1957, Sarría was court-martialed and jailed. After the success of the Revolution he was named a Hero of the Revolution and later became a captain in the Revolutionary Army).

Jardín Ave de Paraíso

What a surprise to discover this gem, falling down the hillside in billowing waves. It's bloomin' lovely up here! This 45-hectare garden was created in 1960 on a former coffee plantation to raise flowers for hotels and for the celebration of the coming-of-age *Quince* of 15-year-old girls. The garden is a riot of color and scents (difficult to dampen in even the wettest of weather). The chief gardener, Nilsys Dominquez Mora, will gladly show you around her cherished garden—a veritable Sissinghurst in the mountains. Like England's Sissinghurst, Ave de Paraíso is laid out as a series of interlocking, juxtaposed gardens, each with its own color scheme, surrounded by neatly clipped topiary hedges. Without extremes of conditions or temperature, the climate encourages an immense variety of plants: amaryllis grow with carnations, *salvia roja* spring up beside daisies, blood-red dahlias thrive beside the garden's namesake "bird of paradise," almost overwhelming with their vivid oranges, blues, and purples. There are potting sheds, too, full of begonias and anthuriums, plus a prim little courtyard with a small café and *floreria* (flower shop). where you can buy a huge floral display for US$25. Entrance costs US$1.

Isabelica Coffee Plantation

Two km east of Gran Piedra is the remains of a coffee plantation and manor built by Victor Constantin Couson, a French immigrant fleeing Haiti during the slave rebellion of 1792. The estate was named Isabelica, after his slave lover. In 1961, it was turned into a museum. The renovated two-story *finca* exhibits farming implements and furniture. The coffee-crushing wheel can still be seen. Trails lead through the now-overgrown estate and forests. It's open Tues.-Sun. 8 a.m.-4 p.m. (US$1).

The road is badly deteriorated.

Accommodations and Food

Villa Gran Piedra, Carretera de la Gran Piedra, Km 14, tel. 5-224 or 5913, is an eco-lodge operated by Cubanacán and Delta Hotels of Canada. Its 22 rustic red-brick cottages spread along the ridgecrest—a spectacular setting! The cottages (US$37 s, US$44 d) are pleasant, with a lounge, tiny kitchen, nice bathrooms, and mezzanine bedroom. The cabins are a popular romantic retreat for Cubans. The old stone-and-timber lodge is today a restaurant and bar.

Getting There

Tour & Travel, beneath the Hotel Casa Grande on Parque Céspedes, tel. 8-6152; Calle 8 #54 e/ 1 y 3, Rpto. Vista Alegre, tel. 43603 or 41237; or Aeropuerto Antonio Maceo, tel. 91773, offers excursions to Gran Piedra (US$25). Gran Piedra is also a highlight of an 11-day "environmental adventure" offered in the US by **Wings of the World,** 1200 William St. #706, Buffalo, NY 14240, tel. (800) 465-8687.

A taxi from Santiago will cost about US$35 roundtrip. A freelance chauffeur will charge half that.

GRANITA SIBONEY

About two km south of Las Guasimas is Granjita Siboney, the red-tile-roofed farmhouse from which Fidel and his loyal cohorts gathered in preparation for their attack on the Moncada Barracks. They sang the national anthem in whispers and at five o'clock on the morning of Sunday, 26 July 1953, Castro and 123 fellow rebels set out.

A pathway lined with palms leads to the entrance, which is riddled with large bullet holes. Otherwise there is little to indicate that this site is of such historical import. Today it is a museum displaying weapons, blood-stained uniforms, and even the rebels' shopping lists. Newspaper clippings tell the tale of horrific torture. (Six of the attackers died in the attack; the rest died in captivity, tortured in cold-blooded murder. Batista's henchmen then took the already-dead revolutionaries to Granita Siboney, laid them on the porch and inside the house, then blasted them with gunfire to give the impression that they had been caught plotting and were shot in a battle.) Note the well to the side of the house where rifles were hidden in the weeks preceding the attack.

The museum is open daily, 9 a.m.-5 p.m.; entrance costs US$1.

The **Centennial Gallery,** 200 meters farther along on the right, is an exhibition hall containing a display of revolutionary paintings.

Getting There: Bus no. 214 operates from Santiago's Terminal de Ómnibus Municipales on Avenida Pujol. It travels past Granjita Siboney to Playa Siboney.

PLAYA SIBONEY

The little village of Siboney lies in a sheltered bay with a nice beach encusped by coral rocks. You can wade out at the eastern end, where the beach extends out to sea. It's a favorite with Cubans, not tourists, and a great place to relax with the locals. The village has heaps of charm. Many of the old wooden houses are built on stilts.

Accommodations and Food
A well-known figure, Marlene Pérez, tel. 39-219, rents two upstairs rooms with fans in her waterfront house on Avenida de Serano (US$15 d); she'll also cook for you.

Otherwise, there's **Villa Siboney,** tel. 39-261, with cabins and rooms behind the beach. The **Mar Azul** serves *comida criollo.*

EL OASIS (EL CRUCERO)

The road to the left at the T-junction immediately south of Granjita Siboney leads east to Laguna Baconao. About three km along you

pass through El Oasis, a pretty little hamlet of fieldstone cottages that form the **Comunidad Artistas Oasis,** an artist's community where 10 families produce artwork of the highest quality—sculpture, ceramic masks, and paintings. At its heart is the Art Shop (don't mistake this for the souvenir store, just off the road). Check out the beautiful masks made by Mariano Frometa, and the erotic ceramic sculptures of Eduardo Troche.

Accommodations, Food, and Entertainment
On the north side of the main road is a large rodeo grounds that attracts *campesinas* from far and wide. The rodeo is overlooked by a large thatched restaurant and bar—**Finca Guajira Rodeo**—where you can dine on *criollo* cuisine (dollars only) while watching the action if your timing is good. Rodeos are given on Tuesday, Thursday, Saturday, and Sunday at 2:30 p.m. (US$5). Horseback rides are offered. You can sometimes rent an apartment in El Oasis from local artists. Ask around.

PLAYA ARROYO DE LA COSTA AND PLAYA BUCANERO

A side road leads south from the rodeo to Playa Arroyo, another small, pretty cove popular with Cubans. The road continues two km west along the coral cliff to Playa Bucanero, a magnificent golden sand beach backed by limestone cliffs—the private reserve of the Hotel Bucanero.

About three km east of El Oasis, another road leads south to **Playa Jaragua.** A sign points the way to Villa Turística Jaragua, but this facility serves as a resort for the military.

Accommodations
You can make reservations (essential) for this and similar *campismos* in Parque Baconao at the **Oficina de Reservaciones de Turismo Parque Baconao,** at Sacó #455 in Santiago.

Hotel Club Amigo Bucanero, Carretera de Baconao Km 4, Arroyo La Costa, tel. 5-224 or 9-1484, is an attractive 200-room all-inclusive resort run by Cubanacán. The facilities stretch almost one km atop the coral terrace and are served by three swimming pools. The spacious rooms feature natural stone walls and are cool and atmospheric (US$84 s, US$134 d). Wide balconies overlook the ocean. The resort, which is popular with German and Canadian tour groups, also has *casas* for three and four people (US$201). There's a restaurant, boutique, and tour desk, and an atmospheric restaurant and bar built on log stilts behind the beach. Watersports, excursions, and car rental are available.

Weeklong charter package rates offered by **Adventure Tours,** 111 Avenue Rd., Suite 500, Toronto, Ontario M5R 318, begin at C$649 (including airfare from Toronto).

FINCA EL PORVENIR

Midway between El Oasis and the turnoff for Playa Juragua, a rutted dirt road to the left leads uphill one mile to the community of La Poseta, where a natural spring empties into a large bathing pool. It's very scenic and a popular spot on weekends for locals who come to cool off, sunbathe, and smooch and dance. *Criollo* dishes prepared on an outside grill are served at a handsome stone-and-bamboo restaurant.

When I first called here, in 1994, the place was known only to locals. Now it's on the tourist route—excursions are even arranged from Santiago through Rumbos (which now runs the facility).

VALLE DE LA PREHISTORIA

It's a shock to find a Tyrannosaurus Rex prowling the valley of the Río Arenas, about six km east of El Rodeo. But there he is, in stalking pose, head down, tail up, eyes seeming to flick back and forth malevolently. The ferocious-looking dinosaur is one of dozens of life-size reptiles that lurk in a lush, natural setting. Apatosaurus (the erstwhile Brontosaurus) is there, wallowing in a pool (which dries out in the dry season). There are even woolly mammoths and a Pterodactyl, with wings outspread atop a nearby hillock. Real-life goats nibble contentedly amid the fearsome make-believe beasts.

The lifelike critters are made of metal rings and beams covered with cement. Scientists say the last of the great dinosaurs disappeared 65

million years ago. If so, the prehistoric monsters are enjoying a renaissance that eclipses even Elvis' 1968 comeback tour.

No bones about it, the Valle de la Prehistoria is a must-visit. Entrance costs US$1 per person. Alas, you're charged US$1 extra if you wish to photograph the dinosaurs (US$5 for video filming).

Don't leave before checking out the **Museo de Ciencias Naturales,** a natural-history museum full of butterflies, polymite snails, and impressive re-creations of mangrove and other marine environments replete with stuffed animals and birds. There's no charge, but tip the guides, who give a lively presentation.

MUSEO DE AUTOS AND MUSEO DE MUÑECAS

Dowagers from the heyday of Detroit and Coventry are on view at this Auto Museum, run by Roberto Pérez Mirabent, tel. 39197 or 41064, 26 km east of Santiago. Roberto puts the spit and polish to about three dozen cars, from a 1934 Model-T Ford to a 1960 Lincoln Continental, a '58 Thunderbird, and singer Beny Moré's Cadillac. There's even a Jaguar 2.4 sedan from the 1960s. Most are in reasonably good condition. The cars are protected under galvanized tin roofs and can be viewed close-up from the pathway.

The **Toy Car Museum,** across the street, contains scores of tiny toy cars, from the earliest models to modern-day productions. Separate cases are dedicated to fire trucks, ambulances, racing cars, etc. It's a fabulous collection.

The grounds include a tiny Museo de Muñecas **(Doll Museum)** with an equally impressive collection of dolls, most dressed in national costumes, from all over the world, arranged by region and country.

Entrance costs US$1 and includes entrance to the Toy Car Museum and Museo de Muñecas.

Food and Services

An attractive a/c restaurant next to the doll museum serves quality *criollo* food. A lunch of pickled cabbage and avocado appetizer, grilled pork chops or fish, and dessert of cheese and tasty guava jam costs US$8. You can eat outside under an arbor of vines while being serenaded by three guitarists. For burgers or fried chicken, try the **El Rápido** fast-food café beside the Cupet gas station.

Between the doll and car museums is the **Centro de Información,** plus an **ARTEX shop,** selling maps, postcards, arts and crafts, and a wide range of cassettes. There's a **Cupet gas station** at the entrance to the auto museum. The Cupet facility also includes a **Havanautos** car rental office, plus a **Tour & Travel** office, where you can book excursions farther afield.

Roberto, the museum manager, hopes to provide a taxi service venture using antique cars from the museum.

PLAYA DAIQUIRÍ

Yes, this place lent its name to the famous drink. It was here that Teddy Roosevelt and his Rough Riders disembarked in 1898 during the Spanish-American War and that US marines landed in 1912 and 1917 to quell a series of strikes in Santiago and Guantánamo.

The hamlet of Daiquirí consists of a half-dozen *bohios* that once housed workers at the old copper mine. Today, it is dominated by a Cubanacán hotel overlooking the 400-meter-wide beach of unappealing gray sand overgrown with vegetation. Don't be dismayed, however: the road continues east through the resort for one km to **Playa Bacajagua,** a beautiful golden sand beach within the deep cleft of a rivermouth. There's an attractive *ranchita*-style bar and restaurant behind Playa Bacajagua, which has volleyball.

Casual visitors are charged US$2 for a day visit.

Accommodations

Cubanacán's **Hotel Daiquirí,** Carretera de Baconao Km 25, Daiquirí, tel. 2-4849 or 2-4724, is a bit run-down—not least the unappealing swimming pool. It has 94 rooms (US$35 s, US$45 d) and one suite, plus 62 bungalows that line the clifftop (US$55 for three people, US$60 for four), all with a/c, terraces, radios, telephones, and refrigerators. Facilities include a restaurant, grill, bar, games and video rooms, a tennis court, and volleyball on the beach. Scuba diving is offered, and watersports include sailing and catamarans. Scooters and bicycles can be rented.

Getting There

The turnoff for Daiquirí is 100 meters east of the Cupet gas station by the Museo de Autos. You can visit Daiquirí on excursions from Santiago offered by **Tour & Travel,** beneath the Hotel Casa Grande on Parque Céspedes, tel. 8-6152; Calle 8 #54 e/ 1 y 3, Rpto. Vista Alegre, tel. 43603 or 41237; or Aeropuerto Antonio Maceo, tel. 91773.

EAST OF PLAYA DAIQUIRÍ

A series of tourist attractions of modest interest lie speckled along the coast road between Playa Daiquirí and Laguna Baconao. This section of coastline is renowned for the zillions of giant land crabs that scurry across the road in springtime to pursue their mating and egg-laying urges. A fair percentage are squashed by traffic.

About eight km east of the turnoff for Daiquirí, you'll come to a bend in the road with a huge, brightly colored mosaic of a *tocororo,* the national bird of Cuba, inlaid in the hillside. A few km beyond is **Playa Larga,** a pebbly beach of little appeal. It has a pool and basic stone *cabañas* utilized by Cuban workers on holiday. You may be able to rent one.

Beyond Playa Larga, a massive limestone plateau shoulders up against the coast. The land here is covered with scrubland and tall cacti, most spectacularly featured in the **Jardín de Cactos,** a small but impressive cactus garden set into the hillside just beyond the modestly appealing **Playa Sigua.**

Caza El Indio

This hunting preserve, Cubanacán El Indio, Carretera de Baconao Km 25, Dairquirí, extends east from Daiquirí to Playa Larga. Deer are the game of choice. Hunting trips can be arranged through Cubanacán at the Hotel Santiago, in Santiago, or in Havana, tel. 22-5551 or 4-1476. Excursions are offered to a pre-Columbian Indian burial site.

A basic lodge has seven rustic yet pleasant rooms and one suite of wood and thatch, plus a restaurant, grill, and bar.

The highlight is the 15-meter-wide dolphin pool into which you may plop to play tag with Flipper (US$5). There's a show theater, too, where a lone and venerable sea lion performs tricks alongside dolphins daily except Monday at 10 and 11.30 a.m.

Entrance costs US$3 (one peso for Cubans).

Accommodations

Cubanacán Sierramar, at Playa Verraco, is a modest beach resort utilized mainly by Canadians. It has 200 rooms, including six suites.

Cubanacán also operates **El Colibri,** Carretera Baconao Km 25, tel. 226-24-849 or 226-2-4735; or c/o Delta Resorts, 350 Bloor St. East #300, Toronto, Ontario M4W 1H4, tel. (416) 926-7892 or (800) 268-1133; in Cuba, Calle 248 y Avenida 5, Santa Fe, Havana, tel. 33-6336. El Colibri is a rustic but handsome eco-lodge with 12 one- and two-bedroom wooden cabins overlooking mountain or ocean, best enjoyed from your balcony (US$37 s, US$44 d). This cozy and quiet retreat is nestled above its own cove, with a thatched dining room overlooking the Caribbean. A stone staircase under an archway of flowering thumbergia leads to a small pool and cascade. The place also has a tour desk and small boutiques.

Another good option is **Delta Balneario del Sol Club Resort,** on Playa Larga, Carretera de Baconao #350, Km 24, tel. 6005; or c/o Delta Resorts 350 Bloor St. East #300, Toronto, Ontario M4W 1H4, tel. (416) 926-7892 or (800) 268-1133. This all-inclusive, three-star resort is also a joint venture between Canada's Delta Hotels & Resorts and Cubanacán. It has 125 rooms, most with private balconies and ocean views, set amid a cacti and rock garden (about US$40 s, US$60 d). Facilities include a thatched *bohio*-style entertainment center, three bars, a buffet dining room, games room, and dance hall. It features magicians and other performances by day and night and has volleyball and tennis. Rocks prevent swimming directly in front of the hotel, but a sandy beach lies a short walk away. There's also a swimming pool, plus a natural saltwater tidal pool enclosed by a sea wall. The resort offers scuba diving and snorkeling excursions.

In similar vein is the **Club LTI Carisol,** tel. 8519-7601, in Havana, tel. 33-5011, an attractive beachfront property at Playa Cazonal, run by

---

THE DAIQUIRI

The daiquiri is named for a Cuban hamlet 16 miles east of Santiago, near a copper mine where the mining firm's chief engineer, Jennings S. Cox, first created the now world-famous cocktail that Hemingway immortalized in his novels. Cox had arrived in 1898, shortly after the Spanish-American War, to find workers at the mines anxious about putatively malarial drinking water. Cox added a heartening tot of local Bacardi rum to boiled water, then decided to give his mixture added snap and smoothness by introducing lime juice and sugar.

The concoction was soon duplicated, and within no time had moved on to conquer every high-life watering hole in Havana. It is still most notably associated with El Floridita, where Hemingway's words can still be seen scrawled on the wall: "My Mojito In La Bodeguita" (My Daiquiri In El Floridita).

Shaved—frappéd—ice, which gave the drink its final touch of enchantment, was added by Constante Ribailagua, El Floridita's bartender, in the 1920s. The frozen daiquiris, "the great ones that Constante made," wrote Hemingway, "had no taste of alcohol and felt, as you drank them, the way downhill glacier skiing feels running through powder snow and, after the sixth and eighth, felt like downhill glacier skiing feels when you are running unroped."

A daiquiri should include all of Cox's original ingredients (minus the water, of course). It may be shaken and strained, or frappéd to a loose sherbet in a blender and served in a cocktail glass or poured over the rocks in an old-fashioned glass. The "Papa Special" which Constante made for Hemingway contained a double dose of rum, no sugar, and a half-ounce of grapefruit juice.

Acuario Bacanao

It's quite a surprise to come across this dolphinarium and aquatic park in the middle of nowhere. When I visited, moray eels, thresher sharks, and hawksbill turtles were housed in filthy tanks that lacked coral or other re-creations of natural environments. Very sad! There's a walk-through glass tunnel enveloped by a tank containing a motley collection of fish.

the German LTI-International Hotels, in association with Cubanacán. Understandably, it is popular with Germans. It backs a three-km-long white sand beach. There are 166 a/c rooms in twin-level bungalows, all with terraces, satellite TV, and telephones. Only 56 look out over the sea; the rest have mountain views. The self-contained property has everything from scuba diving and watersports to a boutique, disco, and bicycle and car rental. The prices are very reasonable—US$38 s, US$56 d.

Hotel Los Corales Carretera de Baconao, Playa Cazonal, tel. 2-2126 or 2-7191, or, in Havana, tel. 33-5011, is another LTI property, two km east of Carisol at Playa Cazonal. It, too, is a joint venture with Cubanacán and is popular with German tour groups. It's slightly more elegant than its sister property. It has 116 rooms in twin-level blocks and 28 rooms in seven villas. All have a/c, terraces, radios, and telephones. It, too, has a wide range of facilities, including tennis, scuba diving, and other watersports. Excursions and car rentals are offered. Prices are the same.

The University Hotel (near LTI Carisol) is where Cubans study the hows and wherefores of the hospitality industry. It might take foreign guests.

Food

Non-guests can eat at the LTI hotels listed above. Buffet breakfasts cost US$8.50, buffet dinners US$12.50.

Playa Sigua is famous for two restaurants—**Casa del Pedro el Cojo** (Lame Peter's House), tel. 398160 or 398140, and **Los Corales.** The former, on the roadside, is noted for its roast pork dishes. The latter, looming above the road, specializes in seafoods.

Scuba Diving

There is good diving in a "marine garden" called *El Mundo de Fantasía* (World of Fantasy), which features three sunken ships as well as fabulous coral. Scuba diving is offered through both LTI hotels and the Delta Balneario del Sol.

Getting There and Away

There's bus service from Playa Cazonal to Santiago (US$10) that departs at 9 a.m.; it returns at 4 p.m., departing from outside the Hotel Libertad on Plaza de Marte.

LAGUNA DE BACONAO

Three km east of Club Carisol is Laguna de Baconao, a large circular lagoon encusped by mountain slopes. The small hamlet of **Baconao** lies on its eastern side, at the end of the paved road. On the southwestern shore, 400 meters from the paved road, is a **Criadero de Crocodrilos,** a "crocodile farm" with a series of cages in which aggressive Cuban crocodiles are penned for your viewing pleasure. The crocs are bred here merely as a tourist attraction, according to the caretaker, who takes pleasure in irritating the beasts with a pole to get them thrashing.

The lake itself contains only a few crocs. Plans were afoot to turn it into a marine-sport lagoon. Boat trips are offered (US$2). It enjoys an enviable backdrop of dramatically ridged mountains.

Atop a rise, thatched **La Casa Rolando** restaurant proffers fabulous views across the lake. You can dine on *criollo* dishes for US$3 upward.

A rough road leads east into Guantánamo province.

GUANTÁNAMO

Guantánamo. The name reverberates around the world. Everyone knows it as a US naval base and a humiliating thorn in the side of Castro's Cuba. Actually, you will not find the base displayed on Cuban maps of the province or the bay from which the contentious US naval facility takes its name. With a little preplanning, yes, you *can* get to see the base from military *miradors.*

If Cuba has an untamed, undiscovered quarter, it is here. The wild eastern shore and secluded mountains of Guantánamo province offer fantastic but as yet untapped opportunities for hiking, whitewater rafting, and ecotourism. The region retains a wild feel, so much so that the indigenous Indian population here, and only here, managed to avoid total devastation by Spanish *conquistadores.* Runaway slaves—*cimarrones*—also managed to eke out a living in the remote fastness, safe from Spanish troops.

The region has long been one of Cuba's poorest provinces due to its remote location and relative lack of tillable land. Guantánamo was chosen for its remoteness by José Martí and other revolutionary leaders returning from exile in 1895 to lead the second War of Independence. Most of the province remained terra incognito until the late 18th century, when

French settlers arrived from Sainte Domingue (Haiti) following the slave rebellion, bringing their coffee-growing skills to the mountains. The end of slavery in the late 19th century attracted migrant workers from Jamaica, Haiti, and other Caribbean islands.

Traces of the indigenous culture also linger. Baracoans—residents of the province's remote second city—wear it on their faces. The Oriente was peopled by the Taino Indians on the eve of Columbus' supposed arrival on this coast. The Taino's arrival in Cuba is said to have preceded Columbus' visit by no more than a century. There are many poorly excavated pre-Columbian sites, especially around Baracoa (a ball court similar to those of the Mayan culture has been discovered recently).

Baracoans attempt to boost their city's image (in fact, it is charming and needs no boosting) by claiming that Columbus first set foot in Cuba here and left a wooden cross (now on view in the town's cathedral) as a memento—the oldest Old World relic in the New World. Whatever the truth, it's undisputed that the first Spanish *conquistadores* who came on Columbus' heels established the first town in Cuba at Baracoa, and it retains its aged colonial feel in a setting that any other city would die for. It is one of the most endearing towns in Cuba.

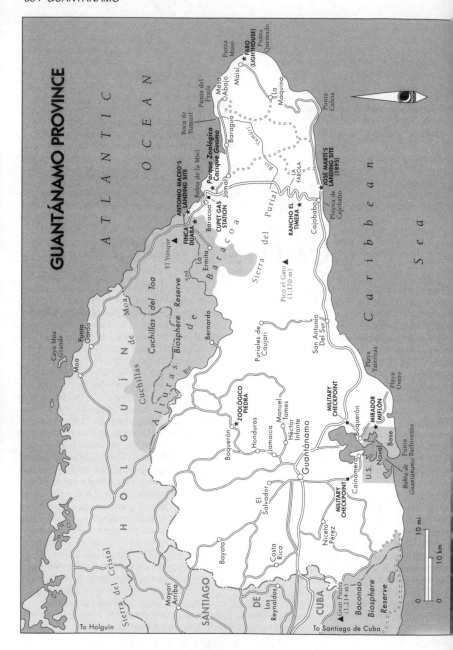

GUANTÁNAMO PROVINCE

THE LAY OF THE LAND

Guantánamo province tapers eastward to a rounded tip—Punta de Maisí—at the easternmost point of the island. The province is almost wholly mountainous. Except for a great scalloped bowl surrounding the town of Guantánamo, the lushly forested uplands push up against a thread-thin coastal plain. Much of the mountain terrain remains swathed in prime forest. Today, a great part of the mountain region is protected within Cuchilla del Toa Biosphere Reserve. Few foreign travelers ever make the journey into these wildlife-rich mountains harboring rare plant and bird species and polymites—snails that haul fabulously colored shells on their backs. Portions remain virtually unexplored.

The northeast coast and north-facing mountains around Baracoa makes up the rainiest region in Cuba, with precipitation ranging from 200 cm in the coastal zone to 360 cm in the upper Toa river valley and majestic heights of the Sierra Sagua-Baracoa. By contrast, valleys along the southern coast are pockets of aridity, and cacti grow in the lee of Cuba's wettest slopes.

GUANTÁNAMO AND VICINITY

Guantánamo, 82 km east of Santiago, is a large city (pop. 180,000) at the head of a deep bay of the same name and some 25 km north of the naval base (the base lies at the mouth of the bay, which opens up like the cloud of a nuclear explosion). The city is spread out on a broad plain surrounded by a meniscus of mountains. In *Driving Through Cuba*, Carlo Gebler describes it as a "depressed city of miserable, low houses and railway marshalling yards filled with decrepit rolling stock." True, the city has grown rapidly in the past three decades, adding soulless concrete carbuncles and vast acreages of jerry-built brick-and-breeze-block housing to the colonial core. There are many hovels, too, giving an impression of a city in Mexico or India.

But the colonial heart of the city has several buildings of interest. And the people are warm and lively. Much of the population is descended from Jamaican and Haitian immigrants who arrived in the 1920s to work in the sugar fields. Others arrived from Barbados, St. Kitts, and other islands. The connections are strong—so much so that there are a British West Indian Welfare Center (an association for English-speaking descendants, locally called *Ingleses*—Englishmen) and a Haitian cultural center—Tumba Francesa—that works to keep alive the traditions and anomalous culture (Haitians are called *Franceses*—Frenchmen). Non-Spanish-speaking travelers can take heart—many Ingleses speak fluent English.

There's a local saying that the "sun rises in Guantánamo" (the island's easternmost city), meaning that things in Cuba happen first here. Baloney! It's a somnolent place, except when serious friction occurs between Cuba and the United States and the city gears up for a worst-case scenario. Given the proximity of the US naval base, you'd expect a strong military presence. The town center has more than its fair share of senior officers toting briefcases. The grunts are billeted on the outskirts of town in several military bases and a military school. It is not unusual to see platoons in camouflage dress. I even saw an active platoon of women soldiers in full battle gear marching by, reminding me of something Tom Miller had written: "They all wore earrings, flowers in their hair, and wide smiles. Cuba has a lovely army."

Most locals seem to have nothing better to do than rock on their porches, waiting wistfully for something to happen. Local citizens even watch an armed forces television station piped in from the US naval base.

The salt industry is important locally (most of Cuba's salt originates here).

HISTORY

In 1494, Columbus anchored in Guantánamo Bay during his second voyage to the New World. He called it Puerto Grande (the exact site where he landed, Fisherman's Point, lies within the

GUANTÁNAMO US NAVAL BASE

Guantánamo (GITMO) is the oldest US overseas military base. It's also the only one located in a communist country—and a constant thorn in the side of Cuban-US relations.

Since 1903, the US has held an indefinite lease on the property, which it claimed as a prize at the end of the Cuban-Spanish-American War. Uncle Sam dictated the peace terms. The Platt Amendment stated that "to enable the United States to maintain the independence of Cuba, and to protect the people thereof . . . the Cuban Government will sell or lease to the United States the lands necessary for coaling or naval stations." The 45 square miles of land and water were formally handed over to the US in ceremonies aboard the USS *Kearsarge*, anchored in the bay, on 10 December 1903.

In the original lease, the US agreed to pay Cuba the sum of US$2,000 in gold per year. In 1934, when gold coins were discontinued, the rent was upped to US$4,085 (14 cents an acre), payable by US Treasury check. The first rent check that Uncle Sam paid to Castro's regime, in 1959, was cashed. Since then, Fidel has kept the unclaimed checks in a drawer in his office desk. The checks remain valid.

The Platt Amendment was dropped in 1934, and a new treaty was signed. Although it confirmed Cuba's "ultimate sovereignty," the treaty stipulated that the lease would be indefinite and can be terminated only by mutual agreement of both parties (or if the US decides to pull out). "As a result," writes Tom Miller, "the United States is in the enviable position of an imperious tenant who establishes the rent, controls the lease, and ignores the landlord."

The gates between the base and Cuba were closed on 1 January 1959 and have not been reopened. It served as a detention center for refugees fleeing Haiti's political crisis in 1992. Two years later, it housed more than 20,000 *balseros*, who were later returned to Cuba.

Life on the Base

The base occupies both sides of the entrance to the bay, which is inhabited by endangered manatees and marine turtles (iguanas roam on land; the iguana is the unofficial GITMO mascot). The Naval Air Station (NAS) is located on the western side of the bay and separated by four km of water from the naval station, on the east side. Hence, the bay is crisscrossed by helicopters, boats, and an hourly ferry. The treaty guarantees free access to the waters to Cuban vessels and those of Cuba's trading partners heading in and out of the Cuban port of Boqueron, and in the past it was not unusual to see Soviet warships sailing through the US base. An Anti-Air Warfare Center monitors Cuban traffic.

Today, 7,000 US servicemen and their dependents live here amid the comforts of a small midwestern town. There are five swimming pools, four outdoor movie houses, 400 miles of paved road, and a golf course. McDonald's even has a concession (the only one in Cuba). Another 7,000 civilians also work here, including 800 Jamaican laborers and 87 Cubans who chose to remain following the Revolution (they receive rent-free housing and have their own community center). A dwindling number of Cubans (fewer than two dozen today) also "commute" to work daily through the base's North East Gate—"the last unfrozen trickle in our icy relations."

In 1964, the Cuban government cut off the base's water supply from the Yateras River. It was replaced with a seawater desalinization plant that today provides 3,000,000 gallons of fresh water daily, along with electrical power (the plant originally was located at Point Loma, California, and was dismantled and shipped in entirety to Guantánamo, where it was rebuilt).

The facility is ringed by the largest US minefield in the world, laid down during the Cuban Missile Crisis of 1962. The minefield lies behind barbed wire and is clearly marked with red triangular warning signs in English and Spanish. Nonetheless, each year many young Cubans risk death to reach a "paradise" promised by radio and television stations broadcasting from the base. An average of 137 Cuban "fence-jumpers" made the crossing every year between 1964 (when records began) and 1992, when the figure leapt upward. The United States publicly accuses Cuba of using weapons to stop people from swimming to the base. Cuba denies the charges and says that US troops routinely provoke "clashes."

Most of the fenceline incidents seem to have been provoked by wayward US marines taking potshots at Cuban patrols. One such incident, in the summer of 1986, led to the death of a private who snitched on a marine firing over the fence and died following a beating by 10 fellow marines (the episode was eventually fashioned into the play *A Few Good Men,* which later became the movie starring Demi Moore, Tom Cruise, and Jack Nicholson).

Castro asserts that, "The naval base has only served to offend the honor of our nation." He has proposed to make it a regional medical center for all the Caribbean when and if Uncle Sam relinquishes his hold.

US naval base). The area remained unsettled and undeveloped during the first centuries of colonial government, so much so that the English even attempted to settle the area in 1741. The city got its real start in the years following the rebellion in Haiti, when French exiles claimed a

stake. The only event of note took place in 1871, when General Máximo Gómez and his troops stormed the city during the War of Independence. They were followed in June 1898 by US marines during the Spanish-Cuban-American War—but they haven't left yet! In 1903, Uncle

GUANTÁNAMO CITY

To Santiago
CASA DE LOS ENSUEÑOS
Rio Banc
RESTAURANTE CARIBE
HOTEL GUANTÁNAMO
Plaza de la Revolución
Rio Guaso
To Baracoa
BUS STATION
HAVANAUTOS CAR RENTAL
HOSPITAL
PASEO (AV. ESTUDIANTES)
RAILWAY STATION
CUPET GAS STATION
MÁXIMO GÓMEZ
PEDRO PÉREZ
JESÚS DEL SOL
CINEMA
BRITISH WEST INDIAN WELFARE CENTER
IGUAZUL HQ
RESTAURANTE LA ORIENTALE
5 DEL PRADO
FLOR CROMBET
BARTOLOMÉ MASÓ
Parque Martí
BERNACE VERONA
AV. CAMILO CIENFUEGOS
CENTRAL
To Santiago
CARRETERA
MININT
Rio Guaso
CALLE PINTO
HOSPITAL
To Caimanera
0   0.5 mi
0   0.5 km

© MOON PUBLICATIONS, INC.

Sam confirmed Cuba's independence, subject to US supervision under the Platt Amendment, which secured Guantánamo as a US coaling station. Although the Platt Amendment was terminated in 1934, the US government kept the lease on the base, and Guantánamo became the stepping stone for US marines to meddle in Cuban affairs throughout this century.

The town developed a near-total economic dependency on the base, which employed hundreds of Cuban workers. Unfortunately, prostitution was the major industry. Says an early guidebook, "The flourishing prostitution business passed from generation to generation like titles to land, and it was not unusual to find three generations of women in service to the base." Other women flocked from all over Cuba to bed down with monied marines. During the 1950s, many of the prostitutes supported Castro's rebel army. "They would get rifles, bullets, grenades. The sailors had to pay twice, first with weapons, and then a lot of the prostitutes insisted on being paid in cash, too," author Tom Miller was told by Nydia Sarabia, who had helped run *red de mujeres*, the women's network during the Revolution. The *guantanameras'* support for Fidel was understandable: wage rates were at subsistence levels, poverty was endemic, and education near nil.

In 1958, Revolution closed in on Guantánamo. Raúl Castro set up base in the mountains. In June, Raúl's troops took 24 Gitmo servicemen captive in an attempt to force Batista's air force to stop bombing his units and peasant communities in the mountain war zone. Fidel ordered the hostages released, and the air attacks resumed. The base was never attacked by Castro's rebel army.

ORIENTATION

Guantánamo is laid out in a near-perfect grid. It is approached from Santiago de Cuba by a four-lane highway that enters town from the northwest (note the regular exit ramps that dead-end into each side: the highway is intended to serve as a runway for military aircraft in the event that Cuba has to defend itself from a US invasion; the side "roads" are meant to store warplanes).

The old Carretera Central enters town farther south and becomes Avenida Camilo Cienfuegos, a wide boulevard that runs east to the

southern edge of the historic downtown. The center of town is Parque Martí, six blocks north of Camilo Cienfuegos, between Pedro Pérez and Calixto García (north-south) and Aguilera and Flor Crombet (east-west).

Paralleling Camilo Cienfuegos is Paseo (Avenida Estudiantes), a major shopping street 11 blocks north. Paseo leads west to the Reparto Caribe, where the Hotel Guantánamo, ministry buildings, and modern high-rise apartments are concentrated. It is centered on Plaza de la Revolución, on Calle 6.

The old city lies on the west bank of the Río Bano. Calle 5 de Prado (four blocks south of Paseo) leads east across the river for Baracoa. Calle Pinto runs south from the west end of Camilo Cienfuegos for Caimanera. A ring road *(circunvalación)* runs north of the city.

SIGHTSEEING

Parque Martí
Most of what little there is to see surrounds this attractive and cozy little square with its pretty, well-preserved, ocher-colored church—**Iglesia Parroquia de Santa Catalina**—on the north side. Where US sailors once paraded with floozies, bench seats today offer a chance to sit and watch the ebb and flow of a more parochial life. In springtime, laburnum trees blaze with harmonious yellow and purple blossoms.

While here, take a stroll north along Calixto García to **Plaza del Mercado,** built last century to house the original agricultural market and still used for that purpose. It's the city's most intriguing building: a pink neoclassical structure, with columns and pediments.

Calixto García also leads south five blocks to the **Parque Zoológico,** at Ramón Pinto. The zoo's complement of wildlife includes a few geese, ducks, and other fowl, and—one of the saddest sights in all Cuba—two fully grown African lions kept in a diminutive cage.

Plaza de la Revolución
This huge, barren square faces the Hotel Guantánamo. Its two high notes are billboards touting the achievements of Karl Marx and Friedrich Engels and the **Monument to Heroes.** Steps lead up to a huge concrete structure with the faces of

Martí Monument and Plaza de la Revolución

Martí, Maceo, and other heroes from the War of Independence and later wars. The monument is illumined at night by dazzling arc lights. The bones of Los Mártires de Angola (Cuban military personnel who died fighting in Angola) are interred here. Military ceremonies are often held.

Museo Municipal
The streets immediately west of Parque Martí are lined with humble yet venerable houses, including the local museum, at Aguilera and Martí. The building dates from 1862 and was once a prison. The museum contains artifacts and lithographs portraying life from the pre-Columbian through the revolutionary eras. It's open daily 8 a.m.-noon and 2-6 p.m. Entrance costs US$1.

ACCOMMODATIONS

Budget
It may be possible to stay at the basic **Hotel Martí,** on Calixto García (one block north of Parque Martí), tel. 32-2456, if you have both pesos and persuasive powers. Rooms cost 11-20 pesos. Similar standards apply at the **Hotel Brasil,** tel. 32-2080, one block south of Parque Martí on Calixto García.

Moderate
Islazul has three hotels in town catering to both Cubans and tourists, plus Hotel Caimanera, on the bay.

Hotel Guantánamo, Calle 13 e/ Calles Ahogado y Oeste, tel. 32-6015, is a standard Soviet-style two-block structure on with 124 mediocre yet adequate rooms (US$24 s, US$30 d). The hotel is professionally run by Pedro (Peter) Hope, a gifted former professor who demonstrates a keen intellect and sense of marketing. The restaurant serves the usual dismal (and overpriced) Islazul faro, though the bread, ice cream, and service are good. Facilities include a tour desk, swimming pool, disco, and store.

Check this out. **Casa de los Ensueños** is a beautiful two-story villa in 1960s Miami style in Reparto Caribe. Light pours in through large, louvered windows, illuminating a lounge containing handsome contemporary furniture, a stereo system, and even a grand piano. The three bedrooms are more modestly decorated. The villa, which can sleep up to eight people, is staffed by a maid, barman, and cook. Cost is US$18 s, US$28 d, US$35 suite, including the staff (on call 24 hours). What a bargain! Meals are extra. There's a small courtyard, and a spiral staircase leads up to a small sundeck. The villa is sometimes rented out at nominal cost to Cubans for birthdays and other special occasions. (Such a "humanistic approach to tourism" is typical: Islazul also hosts local indigents and people with disabilities at the Hotel Guantánamo.)

Villa La Lupe, three miles north of town on the banks of the Río Bano, tel. 32-6112, is a tranquil option but for the noise from the lively poolside bar. The hotel has 50 graciously appointed rooms with large bedrooms, most in two-story *cabañas* (US$14 s, US$18 d low-season; US$17 s, US$22 d high-season). Take an upstairs room with lofty ceilings. All have a/c, TVs, and refrigerators. Some have mini-bars. There are also two suites with connecting bedrooms overlooking the river (US$22 per room). A small restaurant overhangs a weir and has a shady patio beneath a huge

CENTRAL GUANTÁNAMO CITY

tree festooned with epiphytes Islazul may by now have acted on plans to introduce kayaking

FOOD

Mother Hubbard would feel at home in Guantánamo. There are numerous peso restaurants and cafés, but during my last visit virtually every pantry was bare.

Alas, the restaurant of the Hotel Guantánamo leaves much to be desired. An alternative option is the rooftop (9th floor) **Restaurante Caribe** atop a high-rise apartment complex immediately west of the Hotel Guantánamo.

Downtown, basic *criollo* meals are promised at the 24-hour **Café Sol**, next to the Casa de la Cultura on Parque Martí; at **Café Americana**, on the northeast corner; and at **Café Las Antillas**, on the corner of Camilo Cienfuegos and Pérez. **Hamburguesa La Avellenada** serves a kind of burger (10 pesos), and five pesos will buy you a slice of pizza at **Pizzeria Holguin** facing Parque Martí.

You might have better luck at a **paladare**, such as **Restaurante La Orientale**, in a colonial-era home four blocks north of the plaza.

Thirsting for coffee? Try **Casa La Indiana**, on the south side of Parque Martí; **Casa de Café**, on Pérez, two blocks south of the park; or **Casa de Chocolate**, one block southeast on Calixto García.

Coppelia serves excellent ice cream for 2.50 pesos a bowl (in the contemporary building at the corner of Pérez and Bernace Verona).

GUANTANAMERA . . . GUAJIRA GUANTANAMERA!

"Guajira Guantanamera" has become a kind of signature tune of Cuba. Everywhere you go, you'll hear it played by troubadors. It was written in 1928 by Joseío Fernández (1908-1979), who at the time was in love with a woman from Guantánamo. When the song was first played on the radio, in 1934, it became an overnight hit. In 1962, Cuban musician Háctor Angulo went to New York to study and added the words of José Martí's *versos sencillos* (simple verses) to Fernández's melody. Popular folk-singer Pete Seeger performed Angulo's version at Carnegie Hall and launched it to international fame.

ENTERTAINMENT AND EVENTS

Traditional Music and Dance

The **British West Indian Welfare Center,** Serafin Sánchez #663, e/ Paseo y Narciso López, tel. 32-5297, hosts music and dance sessions featuring Caribbean forms such as *changuí* (an antecedent of *son*). Two blocks south is **Tumba Francesa,** a similar assocation representing the descendants of Haitian immigrants. The center is named for the music and dance styles evolved by Haitians. The Hotel Guantánamo offers picnics that include *changuí* music and dance in the backyard of a farmer's house (US$15). **Havanatur** has group excursions to Tumba Francesa.

Also try the **Casa de la Cultura,** on the west side of Parque Martí.

Watch for performances by Elio Revé and his Orquestra Revé, a local (and world-famous) exponent of *son-changuí.*

Other Entertainment

A cabaret including an *espectáculo* is featured on Friday nights and weekends at the Hotel Guantánamo, which also has a disco Tues.-Sun. **Club Nevada,** a rough-and-ready hangout for *Ingleses,* also reportedly has cabaret followed by a disco.

There's a **cinema** on the southeast corner of Parque Martí showing camp classics—such as *King Kong*—and Schwarzenegger films. Entrance costs one peso.

SERVICES

The **hospital** is half a km south of town, on the road to Caimanera. You'll find **pharmacies** on Pérez and Bartolomé Masó, on the northeast corner of Parque Martí, and on Paseo.

You can cash traveler's checks in the Hotel Guantánamo and at **Banco Nacional,** at Calixto García and Bartolomé Masó, and **Banco Popular,** one block east.

There's a **Photo Service** outlet one block south of Parque Martí, on Calixto García. You can buy batteries and film.

The **Cupet gas station** is 200 meters east of the bridge over the Río Bano, on the road to Baracoa.

GETTING THERE AND AWAY

By Bus

Bus no. 640 leaves Havana daily for Guantánamo at 3:30 p.m., arriving about 7:15 a.m. next morning (46 pesos). The modern bus terminal is inconveniently located about four km west of downtown, on the road from Santiago. Buses depart from here for most major cities via Santiago. Reservations are booked solid for weeks in advance.

You can try *colectivos* (communal taxis), here, too.

By Air

The small **Mariana Grajales Airport,** tel. 21-33564, is 12 km east of town. It is served by Fokker-27s from Havana; Cubana flies on Monday, Thursday, Saturday, and Sunday at 6 a.m., Tuesday and Friday at 7:35 a.m., and Wednes-

GUANTÁNAMO USEFUL TELEPHONE NUMBERS

Police	tel. 116
Ambulance	tel. 32-5720
Hospital	tel. 32-6013
Airport (Reservations)	tel. 32-4782
Terminal de Ómnibus (Reservations)	tel. 32-3713

day at 9:30 a.m. (US$60). Return flights to Havana depart Guantánamo on Monday, Thursday, Saturday, and Sunday at 9:15 a.m., Tuesday and Friday at 11:25 a.m., and Wednesday at 12:35 p.m.

You'll need to make reservations as far in advance as possible. Cubana has an office at Calle Calixto García #817, e/ Prado y Aguilera, tel. 34533.

By Train
The train station is an art deco structure on Pedro Pérez, one block east of Paseo. A train departs Santiago daily for Guantánamo at 1:35 p.m. (four hours; US$4).

By Organized Tour
Havanatur's **Tour & Travel** offers excursions to Guantánamo from Santiago de Cuba (see "Getting Away" in the Santiago de Cuba chapter). The town is also included on an eight-day bicycling adventure in Oriente offered in the US by **Wings of the World,** 1200 William St. #706, Buffalo, NY 14240, tel. (800) 465-8687.

GETTING AROUND

There are plenty of horse-drawn carriages. With luck, you'll be charged in pesos (no more than 10 pesos anywhere in town; you should be able to go anywhere for US$2). Buses run along main streets, but they are invariably crowded. Bus no. 9 runs past the Hotel Guantánamo.

Havanautos has a car rental office on the east side of town, beside the Cupet gas station.

CAIMANERA

Caimanera is a small town 22 km south of Guantánamo, on a peninsula on the west shore of the bay. Surrounded by salt flats, it is a modern town, almost totally rebuilt since the Revolution, with soulless concrete apartment blocks abutting older wooden houses. Today, its economy is based on salt and fishing and the Frontera Brigada military complex.

Before the Revolution, many Caimaneros worked on the US naval base, while Caimaneras

---

CAIMANERA USEFUL TELEPHONE NUMBERS

Police . . . . tel. 9-9116
Hospital . . . . tel. 9-9128
Railway Station . . . . tel. 9-9242

---

worked in the strip joints and brothels that were the town's staple industry. Many of the former are due pensions, but Uncle Sam, the ol' skinflint, won't pay them their due—approximately US$5 million, according to author Tom Miller—unless they renounce their Cuban citizenship.

There's a **museum** that tells of the negative toll of the naval base. It is heavily slanted toward proving "enemy provocation" and contains photos of Cubans killed, others showing marines schmoozing with Cuban women at the fence, and even one of a marine sticking his naked butt at the camera.

From the Hotel Caimanera, with its three-story observation tower, you can look out past Cuban watchtowers and, farther back, the US watchtowers clearly ringing the naval base that Castro has called "a dagger plunged in the heart of Cuban soil."

The main *mirador*—Mirador Miflón—is on the *east* side of the bay, near Boquerón.

There's a police barrier just before Caimanera. Residents hold special permits. Caimanera is a restricted military zone. At press time, you needed advance permission from the **Ministero del Interior** (MININT) to visit Caimanera or the Mirador Miflón. Things may have changed by the time you read this.

The MININT office is on Calle José Martí, three blocks south of Avenida Camilo Cienfuegos. Here, I was told that visitors *must* obtain a permit in advance through MINREX (the Ministry of Foreign Relations), in Havana. However, this, too, seems flexible. If you follow this route, it can take forever. Far easier is to arrange a permit or excursion through the Villa Gaviota, tel. 41598; Hotel Santiago, tel. 42634; or a tour agency in Santiago or Havana. The Hotel Guantánamo was planning to offer guided tours, with accommodations at the Hotel Caimanera.

Getting to the US naval base itself is out of the question. The transit point from Caimanera to the base has been closed since 1961. Civilians must request permission from the US Navy and, if granted, fly down on the charter flights from Norfolk, Virginia.

Accommodations and Food

The **Hotel Caimanera,** Loma Norte, Caimanera, tel. 99-414, sits atop a low hillock in the center of town. It has 19 attractive a/c rooms with TVs and VCRs, plus a restaurant, café, bar, and swimming pool with a water slide (US$24 s, US$30 d). You can order a *mojito,* put your feet up, and look out over the US base, which blazes brightly at night like a miniature Las Vegas. When I last called by, tourists weren't being allowed (probably because of the tensions that arose in February 1996), but policy toward admitting foreigners seems to change.

Getting There

By Train: Trains depart Guantánamo for Caimanera at 5:40 and 10:45 a.m. and 2:15 and 5:10 p.m. (50 minutes). You can always try sneaking on board without a permit.

By Sea: Believe it or not, US (and other) skippers can sail right past the US naval base and into the Cuban-controlled harbor and port of Caimanera. Private yachters are not really made welcome (US naval vessels may also board and search your vessel when you pass through the straits), and the hassle may not be worth it.

Excursions: Islazul has been hoping to arrange group packages from the Hotel Guantánamo, with an overnight at Hotel Caimanera. Day excursions were planned for US$12 per person, including lunch; a guide (US$3 per person extra) is obligatory. Call and check.

MIRADOR MIFLÓN

On the east side of Guantánamo Bay, opposite Caimanera, are several military bases and two Cuban naval facilities—Glorieta and Boquerón. The area is off-limits to foreigners without a permit. The area abounds in cacti. Many were planted in the 1960s to form a natural barrier (as much to stop Cubans from defecting as to stop

US troops from attacking, claims one author); it's now called the Cactus Curtain.

The coastal plain rises to a north-south escarpment of the Sierra del Maquey with a meniscus of tall hills at the southern end overlooking the US installation. The Cuban military finds it a perfect vantage point and has a military command center buried deep beneath the mountain. The major lookout point—El Mirador Miflón (US marines call it "Castro's Bunker")—is here, on the south side of a hill called Loma Malones. Few foreigners are granted access to this *mirador,* which is normally reserved for VIPs. Still, permits are sometimes granted. Visitors are sometimes shown the bunker, which contains a diorama of the base. The camouflaged *mirador,* reached via a stairway, has a restaurant from where you can look right down on the US base. Cuban soldiers may even lend you their high-powered Soviet binoculars.

Getting There

Just east of Glorieta, at the turnoff for Boquerón, is a military post and barrier. You'll need a permit. It is 14 km from here through scrubland and cacti to Mirador Miflón. Excursions to Miflón are also offered by **Villa Gaviota,** in Santiago, which may be able to arrange an individual permit, with guide.

The **Vietnam Veterans of America Association** offers an annual trip to Cuba each November. Past trips have featured visits to Miflón. Trip members usually receive the VIP treatment (see "Veterans Tours" in the section on "Special Interest Travel" in the On The Road chapter for further information.)

ZOOLÓGICO PIEDRA

The "stone zoo" features a menagerie of wild animals from around the world—lions, tapirs, hippopotamus, elephants, and other species—hewn from huge limestone blocks with hammer and chisel by a coffee farmer, Angel Iñigo. Iñigo has carved more than 100 animals that he had seen only in photographs in books.

The zoo is near the village of Boquerón (not to be mistaken for the port on the east side of Guantánamo Bay), in the middle heights of the mountains of Yatueras, 25 km northeast of Guantánamo.

To get there, follow the road for Jamaica from the Cupet gas station on the east side of Guan-tánamo. Continue straight past Honduras (other villages north of Guantánamo are named for neighboring countries, including Costa Rica, El Salvador, and Paraguay).

GUANTÁNAMO TO BARACOA

Immediately east of the turnoff for Mirador Miflón, the coast road rises up a two-km-long hill where you have your only views back down over the milky bay towards Cainamera. The land for several miles is virtually uninhabited. Don't be tempted to part the barbed-wire fence and go hiking over the scrub-covered upland in search of a view of the base. Signs warn that you should not trespass; *Obey them! Much of the area is strewn with land mines.*

Beyond the crest, the road drops to the coast and you suddenly emerge at a beach—**Playa Yateritas**—in a wide bay. The golden beach is popular with Cuban schoolchildren and residents of Guantánamo on weekends, when the place can get lively. The calm turquoise waters are perfect for a refreshing dip. There are thatched *ranchitas* for shade, and a basic restaurant. Basic *cabañas* can be rented.

Just beyond Playa Yateritas is **Tortuguilla**, a truly rustic one-street village that fringes the coral clifftop. It would be a great place to rent a room with local fishermen for a few days of reclusive, offbeat escape. Bougainvillea and cactus add to the away-from-it-all charm.

For the next few miles, you'll pass little coves cut into the raised coral shore, with pellucid waters and tiny beaches as private as your innermost thoughts. The coast grows more dramatic, with mountains rising ahead. There are few villages. **San Antonio del Sur** is an exception. This small town has a tiny museum and a Casa de la Cultura on a main street lined with topiary and shrubs. Nearby, inland, is **Avre Mariana**, a mountain with a scarp face said to be the best launch platform for hang-gliding in the Oriente. Islazul is planning to offer hang-gliding packages from the Hotel Guantánamo.

Beyond the pleasant little village of **Imias**, the terrain turns to semi-desert, with scrub-covered hills and valley bottoms filled with orchards and oases of palms.

CAJOBABO

Cajobabo, 45 km east of Guantánamo, is hallowed ground. Here, José Martí, Máximo Gómez,

and four other prominent patriots put ashore in a small rowboat on 11 April 1895 after years of exile. You can't miss the site: a huge roadside billboard has a picture of the sextet rowing ashore.

There are two beaches. The first fronts Campismo Playita Cajobabo, at the end of the tiny hamlet, where there's a simple store and cantina. It's lonesome, except when schoolchildren are here on vacation. The shingle beach is unattractive. Hence, the preferred bathing spot is the rivermouth. There's a tiny **museum** glorifying Martí's party and their respective deeds. It's 200 meters east of the *campismo* (look for the simple *bohios* along the foreshore). **Campismo Playita Cajobabo** has simple concrete *cabañas* (six pesos d) and a café selling *refrescoes* and snacks.

The beach where Martí and his troupe landed is two km farther east, past the museum, reached via a steep headland. There's nothing here, not even a plaque to mark the landing. It's a contemplative place where you can sit and listen to the hiss of the sea on the shingle.

The road continues east to Punta Miasí.

Excursions
Horizontes offers a group excursion—"The Beginning of Cuba"—from Baracoa to Cajobabo and including Maisí.

CAJOBABO TO BARACOA

Immediately beyond Cajobabo, the road turns north and climbs into the **Sierra del Purial** along La Farola (the Beacon), built since the Revolution to link Baracoa with the rest of Cuba. This scenic highway spirals over precipitous peaks and through deep ravines and is sometimes called "Cuba's roller coaster."

On the north side of the bridge over the Río Ojo, a sign points the way to **Rancho El Timera**, where Martí spent some time after his landing at Cajobabo. It's a rough five-km ride uphill along a dirt track to the farmstead.

La Farola hugs the mountainside, twisting and curling uphill through the valley of the Yumurí and Ojo Rivers, carpeted with palms like

Moroccan oases. Farther up, the scenery resembles the fir-clad canyons of Colorado. The road is a marvelous piece of engineering that includes 11 bridges suspended on the mountainside by columns. The road narrows with the ascent, the bends growing tighter, the views more dramatic and wide-ranging. Soon you are climbing through pine forests amid the most non-Cuban landscapes in Cuba.

Thoughtfully, near the summit is a *mirador* platform beside the road, then the summit ridge, smothered in pine and firs and with noticeably cooler air blowing up from the north. There's a tiny café here—**Alto de Coltillo**—with a *mirador,* where you can savor a *refresco* or coffee.

Beyond Alto de Coltillo, the road drops through a moist valley brimful of banana trees until you emerge by the sea at Baracoa.

Warning: Drive with care—particularly in the rainy season, when the road is subject to small landslides. It's unlit at night, when you should drive with extreme caution.

BARACOA AND VICINITY

Isolation breeds individuality. Baracoa is both isolated and individual, so much so that the town has even been likened to Macondo in Gabriel García Márquez's surrealistic novel *One Hundred Years of Solitude.* Five centuries have passed, but the place has lost none of the exquisite beauty that so impressed Columbus. It is still "wonderfully beautiful countryside . . . not flat, but diversified by hill and vale, the most lovely scene in the world."

Baracoa is an Indian word meaning "highlands" (it is also sometimes translated as meaning "where the sea begins"). The somnolent town is nestled hard up against the ocean beneath rugged mountains, most notably the great hulking mass of El Yunque (the Anvil), a huge flat-topped mesa. This being Cuba's rainiest region, Baracoa is surrounded by fruitful countryside; the uplands are smothered in humid tropical forests festooned with epiphytes. Much of the mountainous region is protected within Cuchilla del Toa Biosphere Reserve—a last refuge of the ivory-billed woodpecker and the *amique,* an insectivorous mammal (both species are endangered). This area is as far off the beaten track as you can get in Cuba, and your arrival will be somewhat of a precedent. Birders, hikers—check it out.

The fecund mountains are cut into deep valleys by rivers spilling onto the narrow coastal plain. Several of the rivers have precipitous lower courses that one day will surely be touted as classic whitewater runs. The Toa is the biggest. It was scouted in the 1970s by my friend Richard Bangs of Sobek Expeditions (California), with a view to operating commercial whitewater trips, but for years the tumbling waters were untapped. Whitewater trips are now offered by Horizontes Hotels.

There are miles of dark sand beaches east of Baracoa as far as the mouth of the Río Yumurí. Maritime terraces also rise along the east, most noticeably south of Punta Maisí, the remote easternmost tip of Cuba—a great adventure to reach.

Unlike the rest of Cuba, the region has no history of slave plantations or of African slaves. The Indians suffered greatly at the hands of the Spanish. But they were never killed off, as elsewhere in Cuba. Baracoans proudly point out those who have Indian blood, identified by their short stature, light, olive-brown skins, and squared-off faces.

POLYMITES

Polymita pictas is a species of tiny snail unique to the Baracoa region. This diminutive critter is much sought by collectors for its Joseph's Coat of Many Colors.

According to an Indian legend, the snails' shells were originally colorless. One snail, while slooooowly roaming the region, was taken by the area's lush beauty and asked the mountains for some of their green. Then he admired the sky and asked for some blue. When he saw the golden sands, he asked for a splash of yellow, and for jade and turquoise from the sea. And that's how the polymites get their colors, which are as unique to each individual polymite as fingerprints are to humans.

BARACOA

On 27 October 1492, approaching Cuban shores for the first time, Christopher Columbus saw "a high, square-shaped mountain, which looked like an island." He called it Puerto Santo. For centuries, it was widely accepted that the mountain he saw was El Yunque. It is now thought, however, that Columbus was actually describing a similar flat-topped mountain near Gibara, many miles to the west (don't argue the case with a Baracoan, however; they're staunchly partisan on the subject). The town plays unashamedly on the Columbus tradition, most notably that it was here that the explorer planted a large wooden cross on the beach. The bar in the Hotel El Castillo serves a rum-and-coconut-milk cocktail called El Yunque, and the name Puerto Santo now belongs to a modern luxury hotel at the spot where Columbus purportedly landed.

The city (pop. 65,000) lies 200 km east of Santiago and 120 km east of Guantánamo and is really miles from anywhere. The town has a greater simplicity, a less hurried pace, less of a revolutionary fervor than other parts of the island. It is altogether less sophisticated than Santiago de Cuba or Guantánamo, but it is full of delightful surprises. Baracoa looks and feels antique, with its little fortresses and its streets lined with venerable wooden edifices, rickety and humbled with age, with red-tiled eaves supported on ancient timber frames (the Cuban government has initiated a restoration project). The streets are virtually devoid of cars or other traffic. The fastest thing in town are the youngsters chasing hoops or flying kites, a local tradition. Watch for César Paumier Frómeta walking his pig along the Malecón.

HISTORY

Baracoa was the first of the seven cities founded by Don Diego Velásquez de Cuellar. As such, it is the oldest colonial city in the Americas. The town retains the pioneering atmosphere of 1510, when Velásquez arrived fresh from Spain with 300 men and founded La Villa de Nuestra Señora de la Asunción. The indigenous Taino population resisted the strange cutthroat proselytes who came dressed in leathers and metal helmets and breast-plates. A Dominican-born chief named Hatuey rallied the Tainos in a rebellion against Spanish enslavement. The city, the first capital of Cuba, was besieged and burned. The Spanish managed to hold out for three months before repelling the Indians and capturing Hatuey. The noble "savage" was burned at the stake. (Before putting flame to the pyre, the Spaniards offered Hatuey an option—redemption in Heaven by renouncing his pagan practices and accepting a Christian God, or a life in Hell. He replied that if all Christians were as wicked as Diego Velásquez's men, he would rather not go to Heaven. To hell with him!)

Alas, its inauspicious geographical circumstance did little to favor the settlement. Baracoa was remote and surrounded by mountains. After five years, Santiago de Cuba, with its vastly superior harbor, was proclaimed the new capital. Baracoa limped along based on a limited agricultural economy that produced yucca, coffee, cocao, and maize. The mountainous terrain precluded the land's being planted in precious sugar.

Between 1739 and 1742, the Spanish authorities erected three fortresses to protect the city from invasion by English forces, including pirates. Nonetheless, the town languished in limbo for the next two centuries, without road or rail link to the rest of Cuba. Baracoa was briefly in the spotlight in the wars of Independence: in 1877, the rebel army under General Antonio Maceo besieged the city (when Maceo returned from exile in 1895, he put ashore just west of town). The city produced its own legendary *Mambí* fighters, including Luz Palomares, a woman who went into battle with machete in hand.

The city remained underdeveloped during this century. A long-touted highway was supposed to connect Baracoa with Moa and, hence, the rest of Cuba. It was never built. When Panama disease blighted the local banana industry in the late 1940s, Baracoans called a general strike to protest the Cuban government's indifference. The Cuban government responded by remaining indifferent. The town's status changed significantly with the Revolution. Health clinics and doctors arrived (up from four to 150), along with schools, cultural institutions, and sports centers. And a road—La Farola—was built over

the mountains, linking Baracoa finally with Santiago and the rest of Cuba.

ORIENTATION

Baracoa curves around the wide Bahía de Miel
(Honey Bay) within the cusp of high mountains, including a line of hills known as La Bella Dormiente
(Sleeping Beauty), for reasons which are obvious when you look at them. The road from Santiago enters town from the east, via the modern
section of Soviet-style apartment houses, fronted
by the bay, which is fed at its eastern end by the
Río Miel (it is claimed locally that if you bathe in its
waters at midnight, you will fall in love and return
to Baracoa). The bay is lined by a sweeping beach
of shingly gray sand, **La Playita.**

The old city lies farther west, on a rocky terrace at the tip of which is the inlet of Porto Santo
opening into a flask-shaped harbor. The town is
only a few blocks wide, with roads (still laid out in
its colonial guise) running parallel to the shore.
The ugly shorefront boulevard is the wind-swept
Malecón, lined to the west by hideous concrete
housing blocks. The most important street is
Calle José Martí, two blocks inland.

Both the Malecón and Martí run east-west
from Fuerte Matachín, the tiny fortress at the
east end of town, to Fortaleza de La Punta, at
the west end. Avenida Primero de Abril curls
south around the harbour and continues to the
airport and, eventually, Holguín province.

SIGHTSEEING

A good place to begin your serendipitous sightseeing is Fuerte Matachín. From here, you can
walk west, taking in all the sites of interest within half a day. Stop to admire virtually any house
and the owners will probably invite you inside.
(Why, you may ask, do Baracoans place elephant statuettes with their rear ends facing the
door? Supposedly it brings good luck).

Fuerte Matachín

This tiny fortress, which dates to 1802, guards
the eastern entrance to the old town. The
fortress is in good condition and has low, thick
walls topped with cannons in embrasures.

The storehouse in the fortress courtyard
today houses the **Museo Matachín,** tel. 2122,
run by Alejandro Hartmann Matos, the city historian, whose passion for his subject is infectious. The glass cases are arranged in chrono-
logical order tracing the history of the region
since pre-Columbian days. It tells of the bar-
barities enacted on the indigenous population by
the Spanish; the pirates' dastardly deeds (and
those of the slave-and-sugar era); and the period when French coffee planters settled the
surrounding hills. The museum also displays
memorabilia from the War of Independence
and in praise of the Revolution's achievements.
It's open daily 8 a.m.-noon and 2-6 p.m. Entrance costs US$1.

On the fort's north side is a small plaza with
shady cedar trees and a large **Statue of Columbus** (made of what looks like baked mud) with a
large cross beside it. Outside the fortress entrance is a bronze bust of **General Antonio
Maceo.**

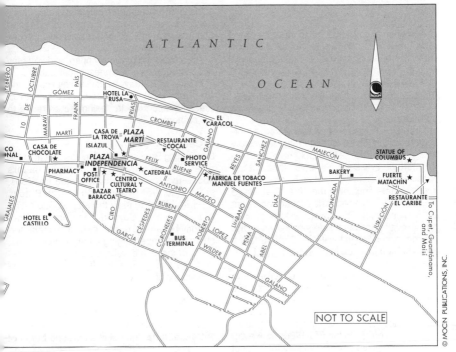

© MOON PUBLICATIONS, INC.

The round tower—**Torreón de Toa**—immediately south of the fort served as a Spanish Customs checkpoint to quash the contraband trade. The house at Calle Juración #49 (opposite the tower) claims to be the oldest colonial home in the Americas. The home has been added to over ensuing centuries and there's nothing to distinguish it from any other.

Fábrica de Tabaco Manuel Fuentes

This intimate tobacco "factory" overlooks a triangular plaza at the corner of Roberto Reyes and José Martí, four blocks west of Fuerte Matachín. The harmonious plaza has a pleasing bucolic feel. It is ringed by colonial houses with simple verandas.

The *fábrica* is inside a pretty blue house on the south side. Visitors are welcome. Inside, two rows of men and women sit side by side, tenderly rolling and pressing fat cigars for local consumption. A blackboard shows production

goals and achievements. It's open weekdays, 7 a.m.-noon and 2-5 p.m. Entrance is free.

Plaza Martí

This little hive of activity, at José Martí and Ciro Frias, is where locals gather to gossip and flirt, have their shoes shined, or peruse the stalls selling cosmetics and domestic knicknacks. You *must* visit at night, when locals gather to watch the communal TV that by day is kept locked safely inside a box atop a pedestal.

From here, follow Ciro Frias one block south to Plaza Independencia.

Plaza Independencia

This triangular plaza is home to the most impressive buildings in town, most notably the **Catedral Nuestra Señora de la Asunción,** an ocher-colored edifice dating from 1805 on the site of an earlier church, which was destroyed by pirates in 1652. Masses are held here each weekend by the young, bearded priest, Father Valentín Sanz.

The church is famous not so much for its interior, which is quite simple, but for the **Cruz de la Parra**—supposedly the oldest European relic in the Americas. It is on display inside a glass case. With luck, you may even be allowed to touch the relic (miraculous powers are ascribed to it), which Columbus himself may have touched.

Dr. Alejandro Hartman Matos, Baracoa's official historian, loves to tell the tale—possibly true, probably not—of how Columbus supposedly left the cross upright amid stones at the harbor entrance in 1492. Most Baracoans believe the tale, including the detail that Diego Velásquez's expeditionaries found the cross in 1510 and used it to convert the aborigines. It has forever since been safeguarded within the church, according to local lore. Carbon-dating analysis confirms that it is indeed about 500 years old.

The dark, well-worn, meter-tall cross has been whittled away through the years by zealous souvenir hunters and has acquired a deep, well-rubbed luster (along with some silver ornamentation added to stop worshippers pilfering splinters as souvenirs). In the mid-1980s, however, one sliver traveled back to Belgium for perusal by experts from the Royal Museum of Central Africa, who determined that the cross hadn't traveled from the Old World, but was instead made of *Coccoloba diversifolia,* a native hardwood of the seagrape family that grows abundantly around Baracoa. Even so, the legend endures. Perhaps Columbus whittled the cross himself in Cuba!

Alas, the church is rarely open, and you may need to search out the priest or caretaker.

A **bust of Hatuey,** the Indian chief called the "first Cuba rebel," stands proudly in the center of Plaza Independencia, facing the entrance to the cathedral.

El Castillo

Dominating Baracoa is this fortress built atop the rocky marine terrace that looms 40 meters above the city. It was constructed in 1730s, during the War of Jenkins' Ear with Britain, when the English navy threatened Cuba. The fort—known as Castillo Seboruco—subsequently became a prison. It recently metamorphosed again, emerging as an upscale hotel. Parts of the castle walls, including a turret, remain. It's a magnificent location offering a bird's-eye view of the city.

Fortaleza de la Punta

This small semicircular fort (at the west end of José Martí) was built in 1803 to guard the harbor entrance. It has gun slits all around but is of only modest interest and has no cannons. The courtyard now houses the Restaurante Guamá. To the left, a pathway leads down to the water's edge, with a "secret" boat slip where messengers could be dispatched. You half-expect

street scene, Baracoa

Errol Flynn to appear, dressed in his swash-buckling best.

Other Sites

There's a **Fábrica de Cucurucho** near the Hotel Porto Santo; it makes a sweet sugar-and-coconut candy called *cucurucho,* sold only here. And you can watch chocolate being made at the **Casa de Chocolate,** at Calle Antonio Maceo #121, two blocks north of El Castillo (open 7 a.m.-9:45 p.m.).

There's even a small zoo—**Parque Zoológica Cacique Guama**—seven km east of Baracoa. I haven't been in, but the gatekeeper told me that it contains monkeys, a hippo, a lion, birds, crocodiles, rodent-like *jutías,* and a near extinct relative, the *almiquí,* indigenous to eastern Cuba. Entrance costs 20 centavos.

For a souvenir snapshot of Fidel, head to the **Taller de Sarcófagos,** at Calle José Martí #300, where a coffin maker called Felipe is a dead ringer for *El Comandante.* You can even seek out the *real* Fidel Castro (well, a real Fidel Castro), a disarming mustachioed chap who lives on Calle Máximo Gómez (believe it or not, this Fidel also has a younger brother named Raúl).

ACCOMMODATIONS

Budget

The **Hotel La Rusa,** Máximo Gómez #161, Baracoa, tel. 4-3011, is an endearing little place facing the Malecón. It once belonged to a Russian woman, Mima Rubenskaya, who inspired the character Vera in Alejo Carpentier's novel *The Rite of Spring.* She fled the Soviet Union in 1917 and settled in Baracoa long before *it* turned communist. She is reputed to have belonged to Castro's M-26 (if you want to know more about her, check out the museum in the Fuerte Matechín). After her death in 1979, the property was converted into a hotel (Fidel Castro and Che Guevara both stayed here, apparently, as did Errol Flynn). It was renovated in 1992. It has 13 simple a/c rooms with louvered windows (overlooking the ocean) and small but nicely restored bathrooms (US$14 s, US$18 d). There's a small bar and open-air restaurant with seafront views.

An alternative is the simple **Hotel Plaza,** tel. 4-2252, hidden away up a flight of steps on the south side of Plaza Martí. At last report, rooms cost about US$20.

Moderate

Though twice the price of La Rusa, you get five times your money's worth at **Hotel Castillo,** Calixto García, Loma del Paraíso, Baracoa, tel. 214-2103, 2115, or 2147, in a contemporary structure built in Spanish-colonial style atop the foundations of El Castillo, overlooking the town and reached by a winding driveway or a steep 85-step staircase. It's one of my favorite Cuban hotels. It is run by Horizontes and was formerly the Hotel Sanguily. The 35 a/c rooms are colonial style, with lofty ceilings, terra-cotta-tiled floors, private baths, telephones, and furniture carved from cedar by local craftsmen (the mattresses should be retired, however). There's a TV lounge in the lobby. The swimming pool and sundeck provide great places to relax, as well as stupendous views towards El Yunque. The bodega-style restaurant serves *criollo* dishes with a Baracoan flavor. The hotel is popular with tour groups. It's a tremendous bargain at US$19 s, US$25 d low-season and US$28 s, US$35 d high-season.

On the north side of the bay, a taxi ride or long walk from town, is the **Hotel Horizontes Porto Santo,** Carretera del Aeropuerto, Baracoa, tel. 214-3578 or 3590. The hotel is centered on an amoeba-shaped pool with views over the bay. It is neither as lively nor as appealing as the El Castillo. The 36 a/c rooms and 24 *cabañas* cost US$21 s, US$28 d (low-season). Facilities include a restaurant, two bars, a shop, tennis court, and car rental.

FOOD

Its regional cuisine is reason enough to visit Baracoa. Try the *paladares* at Calle Ruber López #47 e/ Céspedes y Coroneles Galano, or **Maribel's,** at Calle Máximo Gómez #104. At either, US$10 will buy a filling meal of local specialities. Maribel's has rocking chairs for postprandial recuperation.

Your next best bet is the restaurant in the **Hotel Castillo.** The menu is extensive and favors local dishes. The fish and shellfish dishes are prepared in coconut sauce that includes annato seeds, coriander, onion, hot pepper, oregano, and salt. The lobster is also splendid—as it should be for US$25. But don't be fooled into thinking that the *chicken casserole* is anything other than fried chicken.

Another good bet for regional cuisine is the **Restaurante Guamá,** in the Fortaleza de la Punta, where you can sit beneath wide eaves on a terra-cotta tile terrace. But get there early. Once, when I called by for dinner at 7:10 p.m., they had already run out of food.

Restaurante Cocal is popular with locals, though the peso eatery was serving only ham and Spam sandwiches and *refrescoes* when I called by. Still, it's a good place to sit and watch street life, as is **Café Baracoa,** at Maceo #129, one block west of Plaza Hatuey (it serves tortillas, *congrí,* and snacks). Other popular options are **El Caribe,** overlooking the beach be-

hind the Fuente Matachín, and **El Caracol,** on the Malecón e/ Limbano Sánchez y Coroneles Galano. The latter, which is also known as Baturro, serves a lobster enchilada and fried bananas.

Want pizza? Three pesos will buy you a slice of *picadillo* pizza (ground beef with olives and raisins) *and* a shot of rum at **Pizzería Isernia,** at Calle Flor Crombet #175. Open 10 a.m.-9:40 p.m.

Refreshments

The **Casa del Batidos,** down near the port, sells *batidos* and *refrescoes* for 20 centavos—a perfect cure for impending heat stroke! You can buy ice cream and a drink of local chocolate or coffee at the **Casa del Chocolate** (open 7:20 a.m.-9:40 p.m.), which may have bars of chocolate for sale. If not, you can find "black market" chocolate (two bars for US$1).

The perfect thing on a hot day is sno-cone or a zapote-flavored ice cream sold in a cone made with a waffle-iron (one peso). Try Luís Gamboa Borges at Calle José Martí #171.

Bakeries

There are several bakeries, including **Panadería La Mia** and **Panadería El Triunfo,** one and two blocks west of Fuerte Matachín, respectively. Try the delicious *pudin de boniato* (made from sugar, coconut milk, and sweet potato), the spongy biscuits called *panquecitos,* or the deep-fried pastry (made from the flour of the yucca root) called *buñuelo,* from **Arnaldo's,** at Calle José Martí #212. All cost one peso, which will also buy five *yemitas,* sweet balls made with chocolate, coconut, and sugar; or a delicious *turrón de coco,* a baked bar of grated coconut mixed with milk and sugar.

THE LOCAL FLAVOR

Baracoa is acclaimed for its original cuisine—almost unknown in the rest of the country. Coconut is a staple of local menus. It finds its way into such local delicacies as *bacán* (a tortilla made of baked plantain paste mixed with coconut milk, wrapped in banana leaves, and filled with spiced pork); *cucurucho,* an ambrosial pudding made of shredded coconut mixed with papaya, orange, nuts, and sugar or honey and wrapped in palm leaves; and *frangollo,* a dish of green bananas toasted and mashed.

I like *calalú,* a spinach-like vegetable simmered in coconut milk.

For drinks, try *chorote,* a tasty chocolate drink thickened with cornstarch (the region around Baracoa is also known for growing cacao, from which the townsfolk make chocolate). Also try the local drink called *sacoco,* a concoction of rum and coconut milk served in green coconuts; and the less appetizing *pru,* a drink made from pine needles and sugar syrup introduced from Haiti by French planters in the mid-19th century.

Local fishermen also net a local oddity, *tetí,* a tiny red fish that migrates like salmon up the Río Toa. The fish arrive at the mouth of the river enveloped in a gelatinous cocoon that splits apart on contact with freshwater. *Tetí* is eaten raw with cocktail sauce, like shrimp.

ENTERTAINMENT

Half the town populace seems to gather in Plaza Martí at 7 p.m. every night to watch the TV that by day is locked inside its case atop a stand in the plaza (most residents of Baracoa have their own televisions; the public TV serves when power is cut in particular neighborhoods to conserve energy; at press time, each of the town's four sectors had a weekly four-hour blackout). Saturday nights are best, when the movie double bill lasts until 2 a.m.

On Sunday, you can head to the square to take on one of the local kids at chess. Be wary if young Andrés Pierra challenges you—he's the local star and can often be seen completing against six opponents *at a time.*

Traditional Music and Dance
The **Casa de la Trova,** on Calle Antonio Maceo #149 e/ Ciro Frías y Pelayo Cuervo, is a great place to sample local music played by troubadors. Open daily 10 p.m.-2 a.m.; entrance costs US$1. Alternately, head to the **Casa de la Cultura,** on Calle Antonio Maceo e/ Frank País y Maravi, tel. 3627, where locals perform adaptations of Cuban *son* known as *el nengen* and *el kiriba.* Live Afro-Cuban performances are also given at night at the **Galería Yara.**

Bars and Discos
The *mirador* bar at the **Hotel El Castillo** is an upscale bar with the benefit of fine views and occasional live music. For local color, descend into town and the Casa de la Trova and adjacent bar. The **School of Gastronomy** *(Escuela de Gastronomía),* on Calle Antonio Maceo, has a bar run by students and open to the public.

You can shake some booty with local youth at the **Centro Nocturno,** next to the Casa de Chocolate; or at **Noches de Praga,** where the crowd swings to salsa, *son,* and imported disco (entrance costs five pesos, the same as a beer or shot of rum). Every Friday, Saturday, and Sunday night, an open-air disco—*Fiesta calle-jera*—is set up (the location varies weekly; bring your own drinks). The youngsters love it, but you have to pity everyone else. The designated street is cordoned off and lit with Christmas lights, the boom-box music reverberates until well past midnight, and only the dead can sleep.

Other Entertainment
Still trying to catch up on 1950s camp classics? Check out the **Centro Cultural y Teatro** cinema (one peso), on the south side of Plaza Independencia. Films show most evenings, cartoons on Saturday mornings.

The plaza is also the setting for an intriguing battle every Sunday morning, when the church choir tries to drown out the jazz riffs of the state-sponsored municipal band!

A **Semana de la Cultura**—culture week—is held the first week of April.

SHOPPING

Baracoa boasts several artists of note, including Pedro Sabo, a famous native painter who records life in Baracao in monochrome and riotous color. If you're interested in buying pictures by Baracoan artists, ask for Alejandro Hartmann at the museum; he has a collection of local native paintings and knows all the artists in the area.

Galería Yara, in the **Bien Fonda Cultura,** on Antonio Maceo two blocks west of the cathedral, has paintings, clothing, and simple carvings. Most are crude, but there are a few gems, especially of jewelry of ebony and coconut. The **Bazar Baracoa,** two blocks east, sells higher-quality art (especially ceramics) from throughout Cuba, though the selection is small.

You might also check out the house of Pelay Alvarez López at Félix Ruenes #25. Alvarez makes furniture and carvings from precious hardwoods, often inlaid with mother-of-pearl.

SERVICES AND INFORMATION

Information
There are tour information desks in the Hotel El Castillo and Hotel Porto Santo. There's an Agencia Reservaciones Turismo at Calle Antonio Maceo #149, tel. 2337, where you can make hotel and other reservations for elsewhere in Cuba. The staff is helpful. Open Mon.-Fri., 8 a.m.-noon and 2-6 p.m., and Saturday 8 a.m.-noon.

Library
The Biblioteca Raúl Gómez García, at Calle José Martí #130, tel. 3300, has over 20,000 books, though few in English.

Money
You can cash traveler's checks and change foreign currency at the Hotel El Castillo or Hotel Porto Santo or at the Banco Nacional on Antonio Maceo, one block west of 10 de Octubre.

Post and Telecommunications

You can make international telephone calls from the Hotel El Castillo or Hotel Porto Santo; you can also buy stamps and mail postcards. There's a post office—*Correos y Comunicaciones*—on the south side of Plaza Independencia at Calle Antonio Maceo #136 (open daily 8 a.m.-10 p.m.); you can also make telephone calls from here.

Medical Services

The hospital is two km east of town (supplies are limited; consider donating sheets and other necessities). There's a pharmacy on Antonio Maceo, one block west of the cathedral. If your teeth need attention, head to the Clínica Estomatólogica, at Calle Antonio Maceo #82 (open Mon.-Sat. 24 hours). Even foreigners are treated *free,* supposedly. Should you need sex counseling, head to the Centro de Educación Sexual y Planificación at José Martí #316.

Other Services

You'll find a Cupet gas station five km east of town, just before the turnoff for Punta Maisí. The police station is on Calle Antonio Maceo.

SPORTS AND RECREATION

You may be able to catch a **baseball game** in the large stadium east of town. **Whitewater rafting** trips were being planned on the Río Toa and may be available from Hotel El Castillo by the time you read this.

Senior citizens passing through might pop into the **Círculo de Abuelos** (Grandparents' Society), which meets daily for calisthenics at 5 p.m. on Calle Antonio Maceo.

To find out how computer-literate the Baracoans are head to the **Joven Club de Computación,** Calle José Martí #217, tel. 3587, which offers free computer classes to all Baracoans, using IBM computers. Foreigners are welcome.

GETTING THERE AND AWAY

By Car

Baracoa is reached by a pothole-riddled road from the west and, from the east, by Cuba's most dramatic causeway—La Farola.

BARACOA USEFUL TELEPHONE NUMBERS

Police	tel. 116
Ambulance	tel. 4-2472
Hospital	tel. 4-2502
Airport (reservations)	tel. 4-2171

By Bus

Bus no. 641 departs Havana's main bus terminal every other day at 11 a.m., depositing you 20 hours later at the interprovincial bus station in Baracoa at Los Mártires and José Martí (53 pesos). The municipal (local) bus station is at the junction of Coroneles, Galano, and Rubio López; buses for Guantánamo, Santiago, and Moa depart from here. Buses for Havana depart Baracoa at 7:30 p.m. (arriving 3 p.m. next day); at least 24 hours reservation usually required. Buses to Santiago depart daily at 1:50 p.m., but you'll normally need to book a week in advance.

By Train

Baracoa is not served by rail. However, an express bus service *(Espresso Ferrocarríl)* to the Guantánamo rail station leaves from down by the port. Buy your ticket early.

By Air

Supposedly, **Cubana** operates flights from Havana on Tuesday and Friday at 6 a.m. and Sunday at 6:30 a.m. (US$78). Return flights depart Baracoa at 10:20 and 10:45 a.m. respectively. There are also flights between Baracoa and Santiago de Cuba on Tuesday (US$20). You can take a biplane to Maisí from here (US$16 roundtrip).

Gustavo Rizo Airport, tel. 21-42216, is on the west side of the bay. The Cubana office is at Calle José Martí #181, tel. 42171 or 2261. Open Mon.-Fri. 8 a.m.-noon and 2-5 p.m.

Organized Excursions

Tour & Travel, Calle 8 #54 e/ 1 y 3, Rpto. Vista Alegre, Santiago, tel. 43603 or 41237, or Aeropuerto Antonio Maceo, tel. 91773, offers excursions to Baracoa from Santiago (US$55 or US$99 overnight). **Hoteles Horizontes,** Calle 23 #156 e/ N y O, Vedado, Havana, tel. 33-4142, fax 33-3161, features Baracoa on a one-week tour, "Horizons at Dawn," that originates in Havana and includes sightseeing in Santiago.

GETTING AROUND

Baracoa is small enough to walk everywhere. You'll need wheels, however, to visit Porto Santo or locations farther afield.

You'll find one or two **horse-drawn carriages** *(coches)* departing the main square and following a fixed route (one peso). You may be able to rent **bicycles** from the Hotel El Castillo, where **taxis** also hang out in the courtyard (others can be found outside the hospital). Eduardo Navarro ("El Ruso") leaves his bicycle—the one with a red ribbon—in front of the Casa de la Cultura at Calle Antonio Maceo #120. Anyone is free to borrow it as long as they return it undamaged.

Plenty of locals are willing to rent their **private vehicles.** Look out for Nildo Ortíz Machado's super-long limo-Lada, which follows a fixed route through town. You might want to pass on Oscar Granada's offer, however; he's a renowned speedster and his Lada is called the "Death Car."

BARACOA TO HOLGUÍN PROVINCE

The coast west of Baracoa is a lonesome region, hemmed in by the steep faced **Alturas de Baracoa.** A road hugs the coast and leads to Holguín province. Most is dirt (rocky in places), deeply rutted and potholed for the first 25 km, where a newly paved road begins. The border with Holguín province is delineated as if by Mother Nature's whimsy. To the east it is lushly tropical; to the west, the penurious land is covered in scrub and pine.

Immediately west of Baracoa, you cross the wide, brown Río Macaguaní, which runs into Bahía de Miel. At the mouth of the **Río Duaba,** five km west of Baracoa, is a long black sand beach where the mulatto general Antonio Maceo and 22 compatriots landed in April 1895 and, beyond, the site where he fought his first battle. He is honored by a roadside bust. There's a grove nearby where shards of pottery demonstrate the pre-Columbian presence of Indians. You can turn inland here and follow a dirt road

one km to **Finca Duaba,** a rustic *bohio* serving *criollo* meals beneath the shade of palms and plantains. Horseback riding is offered, and you may be able to hire a guide for hikes into the nearby mountains. Open Tues.-Sun. noon-4 p.m. I advise reservations through the Hotel El Castillo or Islazul office on Plaza Independencia.

Five km farther west you cross the Río Toa, with banks smothered in virgin rainforest. You can turn inland and follow the deep ravine into the vast biosphere reserve.

Cuchillas del Toa Biosphere Reserve

This 127,500-hectare reserve encompasses most of the ranges of the Alturas de Sagua-Baracoa, Cuchillas de Toa, and Cuchillas de Moa, and rises from sea level to 1,139 meters elevation. The region (one of the oldest geologically in Cuba) is composed mostly of igneous rocks, etched by rivers into countless knife-edged ridges *(ouchillas)* that rise like islands in a rainforest sea.

Two protected nature reserves—Jaguaní and Cupeyal del Norte—take up most of the region, which owes its origin in part to a single bird species. Here, the large ivory-billed woodpecker exists in isolation. They were once common throughout the American South, but logging has since devastated their habitat, and they have not been seen in the US since the 1940s. The bird was considered extinct until the mid-1980s, when it was identified in these mountains. The sightings resulted in the Cuban government's establishing a 220-square-km protection area. Logging was banned, and a highway was rerouted. Impressive! With luck (lots of it) you may see an ivory-billed woodpecker in the valley of the Ríos Yarey and Jiguaní, which feed the Río Toa. Whatever, the forests are filled with the chirps and sqawks of more than a score of bird species.

The reserve has a great diversity of climate types and corresponding ecosystems. It protects the richest fauna in Cuba, including more endemic species of flora than anywhere else in Cuba—more than 100, including several types of palms and the colorful *ocujé,* or Santa María tree. Much of the area is composed of rainforest bordered by brushwood and Cuban pine, a perfect habitat for the ivory-billed woodpecker and its cousin, the endemic and endangered royal woodpecker. Cockatoos inhabit the rainforests.

These mountains are also known for the polymite, a rare and singularly beautiful snail species (well, at least the shell is beautiful).

The most dramatic formation is **El Yunque**, the spectacular table-top mountain (575 meters) that dominates the landscape southwest of Baracoa. It resembles the square-topped *tepuís* of Venezuela and seems to float above the surrounding hills. This sheer-sided giant is the remains of a mighty plateau that once extended across the entire area. Over time, the plateau was eroded, leaving El Yunque as a giant monument to its existence. It was a god-like presence for the Taino Indians.

Mists flow down from the summit in the dawn hours, and it glows like hot coals at dusk, when the setting sun pours over the red rocky walls like molten lava. El Yunque is a lonely outpost of life with its own unique flora and fauna—a result of isolation over millions of years. From its summit, waterfalls tumble down, washing away soil and mineral nutrients. The soils are thin, and the oases of orchids, lichen, mosses, and forest seem to survive on water and air alone. Little exploration has been done amid this "roofless Hades," and many new species await discovery atop the often mist-shrouded plateau.

Getting There: You can drive to El Yunque's summit: turn left—west—half a km south of the Río Duaba and follow the road to La Ermita. The road climbs steeply to a lookout point, where you can gaze down on the tumbling waters of the Río Duaba. **Excursions** can be arranged through the Hotel El Castillo, tel. 214-2103, and Hotel Porto Santo, tel. 214-3578, in Baracoa. **Alcona S.A.,** Calle 42 #514, Havana, tel. 22-2526, fax 33-1532, specializes in nature tourism and can arrange guided excursions.

Accommodations and Food

If you long for your own lonesome house miles from anywhere, check out **Villa Maguana,** about 28 km west of Baracoa, nestling in its own little cove with a scintillatingly white beach with shade trees. This reclusive charmer has four a/c rooms, modestly furnished with double beds and TVs. Blazing light pours in through wide windows. There's also a lounge with TV, and a shady veranda with rockers. The house comes with cook and maid (US$19 s, US$25 d;

Meals are extra). Reservations can be made through Islazul offices.

At El Yunque, you can **camp** at a basic *campismo,* which also has basic huts (US$5 d). Book through the **Reservaciones de Campismo** office in Baracoa, at Calle José Martí #225, tel. 2776; open Tues.-Thurs. 8 a.m.-noon and 2-6 p.m.

Kayaking and Whitewater Rafting

The Río Tao and its tributaries have tempestuous rapids and a tremendous future for kayaking and whitewater rafting. Whitewater rafting trips can be arranged through Horizontes, Calle 23 #56, Vedado, Havana, tel. 33-4142, fax 33-3161, or c/o the Hotel El Castillo and Hotel Porto Santo, in Baracoa.

BARACOA TO PUNTA MAISÍ

If you want to visit the easternmost point of Cuba, you can take the coast road east from Baracoa. It begins five km south of town, at **Jobo Dulce,** and follows a windy course inland via the hamlet of Jamal up hill and down dale, touching the coast again 20 km east of Baracoa at **Baragua.** Baragua is famous for its long, ruler-straight silver sand beach backed by palms.

Beyond Baragua, the road passes through a cleft in the vertical cliffs spanned by a natural arch called **Túnel de los Alemanes** (Germans' Tunnel). A stone's throw beyond, you emerge at **Abra de Yumurí,** a ramshackle village where the road deposits you at the side of the rivermouth, where the Río Yumurí cuts through a deep canyon and meets the hissing breakers of the Atlantic. Upriver, the Yumurí narrows into a steep-faced gorge (where the fishing is said to be good).

A 100-meter-wide wooden bridge across the river got completely washed away by a storm in spring 1996. Locals cross the river in rowboats. Cars can drive across the beach and pebbly rivermouth at low tide. Touts will be there to encourage you to cross, so that they can earn a few dollars hauling you through the deep sand (a 4WD should be able to make it; a small, less adaptable vehicle should not attempt this crossing without several folks to assist you). On the east bank of the river, the badly potholed road

*lighthouse,
Punta Maisí*

CHRISTOPHER P. BAKER

continues along the coast, then rises sharply inland to **La Maquina,** 22 km beyond Abra de Yumurí. La Maquina, on the cooler eastern slope of the Meseta de Maisí, is the center of a coffee-growing region.

Alternate Routes to La Maquina

If you have doubts about the river crossing at Yumurí, consider following a route over the mountains from Jamal to La Maquina. You should do this only if you have a firm sense of adventure—and a sturdy 4WD. The route deteriorates into a gravel and scree-covered track best described as steeper than a dentist's bill and with twice as many cavities. In places, it is washed out entirely, and there are several small rivers to ford. There are several bifurcations, no signs, and scant habitation. Eventually (with luck), you'll emerge at La Maquina.

The easiest—albeit longest—and most spectacular route is via the coast road from Cojababo (reached from Baracoa via La Farola. From Cojababo, a road follows the coast eastward, passing through semi-desert in the lee of a series of lofty marine terraces. These massive coral cliffs were raised from the ocean eons ago and have since been eroded, exposing caves displaying stalagmites and stalactites suspended as if in midair. The paved road is badly deteriorated. It continues level for a while, then snakes sharply uphill onto the next limestone plateau, each of which is several hundred feet high. The coastal vistas build dramatically. You then pass through sea-green coffee farms and emerge at La Maquina.

PUNTA MAISÍ

La Maquina looks down over a vast circular plain spread out like a fan and overgrown with scrub and cacti. Far below, you might be able to make out the lighthouse at Punta Maisí, the easternmost tip of Cuba. Here, you can experience daybreak 40 minutes before it occurs in Havana. (Actually, Punta Quemado, five km south of Punta Maisí, is fractionally farther east, but it's accessible only by a stiff hike along the thorn-covered coral clifftop.) Maisí consists of no more than the *faro* (lighthouse) and a few miserable shacks. There is nowhere to stay, and no facilities, although you might have some luck in La Maquina.

Getting There

You can take a sightseeing trip by biplane from the Baracoa airstrip (US$16 roundtrip). Or, if driving, a rugged, much eroded track of red earth descends from La Maquina onto the plain. The distance is deceptive: the lighthouse looks close at hand but is actually 12 km away. Eventually you reach Land's End, 1,280 km from Havana.

CUBAN SPANISH

Learning the basics of Spanish will aid your travels considerably. In key tourist destinations, however, you should be able to get along fine without it. Most Cubans are well educated and English is widely spoken in Havana, and the number of English-speakers is growing rapidly. (For example, English is now required of all university students and hotel staff. Most larger hotels have bilingual desk staffs, and English is widely spoken by the staff of car rental agencies and tour companies.) Cubans are exceedingly keen to practice their English and you will be approached often by such individuals. Many Cubans know at least the basics of one other European language (a surprising number are fluent in French and, of course, Russian). Away from the tourist path, far fewer people speak English.

Use that as an excuse to learn some Spanish. Cubans warm quickly to those who make an effort to speak their language. Don't be bashful. Use what Spanish you know and you'll be surprised how quickly you become familiar with the language.

Pronunciation

Castilian Spanish, with its lisping "c"s and "z"s, is the Spanish of Spain, not Latin America (Cubans do not lisp their "c"s and "z"s; they pronounce the letters more like an "s," as do Andalusians and most other Latin Americans). In its literary form, Cuban Spanish is pure, classical Castilian. Alas, in its spoken form Cuban Spanish is the most difficult to understand in all of Latin America. Cubans have lent their own renditions to the Spanish sound: like a zebra that is not quite a horse, Cuban Spanish is white but with black stripes.

Cubans speak more briskly than other Latin Americans, blurring their rapid-fire words together. The diction of Cuba is lazy and unclear. The letter "s," for example, is usually swallowed altogether, especially in plurals. The final consonants of words are also often deleted, as are dipthongs such as "d" and, often, the entire last syllable of words ("If they dropped any more syllables, they would be speechless," suggests author Tom Miller). Regional variants exist, too. I find the Spanish of the Oriente a bit slower and less confusing. Around Baracoa, the idiom of the Indians endures.

Cubanisms to Know

Cubans are long-winded and full of flowery, passionate, rhetorical flourishes. Fidel Castro didn't inherit his penchant for long speeches from dour taciturn Galicia—it's a purely Cuban characteristic.

Cubans also spice up the language with little affectations and teasing endearments—*piropos*—given and taken among themselves without offense.

Many English (or "American") words have found their way into Cuban diction. Cubans go to *besbol* and today eat *hamburgesas*.

Formal courtesies are rarely used when greeting someone.

Since the Revolution, everyone is a *compañero* or *compañera* (*señor* and *señora* are considered too bourgeois).

The swallowed "s"s are apparently accumulated for use in restaurants, where they are released to get the server's attention—*"S-s-s-s-s-st!"* Because of this, a restaurant with bad service can sound like a pit-full of snakes.

Confusingly, *ciao!* (used as a long-term goodbye) is also used as a greeting in casual passing—the equivalent of "Hi!" You will also be asked *¿Como anda?*, meaning "How goes it?"

A common courtesy when paying a call on someone, especially in the countryside, is to call out *"Upe!"* from outside the house to let him or her know you're there. As you enter, you should say *"Con permiso"* ("With your permission").

Language Study Programs

The Universities of Havana and Matanzas offer intensive Spanish language courses for foreigners. The courses (from beginner to advanced) include at least a modicum of workshops or lectures on Cuban culture. The norm is three to five hours of instruction daily, more in intensive courses. Classes are best arranged from abroad via one of the following organizations or Cubatur.

In the U.K., the **School of Latin American Spanish,** Docklands Enterprise Centre, 11 Marshalsea Rd., London SE1 1EP, tel. (171) 357-8793, offers seven-week summer courses in Cuba, with options for regular and intensive courses.

In the U.S., **Global Exchange,** 2017 Mission St., Suite 303, San Francisco, CA 94110, tel. (415) 497-1994 or (800) 497-1994, fax (415) 255-7498, offers language study at the José Martí Language Center in Miramar. The **Cuba Information Project,** 198 Broadway, Suite 800, New York, NY 10038, tel. (212) 227-3422, fax (212) 227-4859, offers two- and four-week "Study Spanish and Cuban Culture" programs at the University of Havana. The trips are open to all levels, from beginners to advanced; in 1996, trips were offered in July.

SPANISH PHRASEBOOK

PRONUNCIATION GUIDE

Consonants

c   as c in cat, before a, o, or u; like s before e or i
d   as d in dog, except between vowels, then like th in that
g   before e or i, like the ch in Scottish loch; elsewhere like g in get
h   always silent
j   like the English h in hotel, but stronger
ll like the y in yellow
ñ   like the ni in onion
r   always pronounced as strong r
rr trilled r
v   similar to the b in boy (not as English v)
y   similar to English, but with a slight j sound. When y stands alone it is
    pronounced like the e in me.
z   like s in same
b, f, k, l, m, n, p, q, s, t, w, x, z as in English

Vowels

a   as in father, but shorter
e   as in hen
i   as in machine
o   as in phone
u   usually as in rule; when it follows a q the u is silent; when it follows an h or g
    its pronounced like w, except when it comes between g and e or i, when it's
    also silent

NUMBERS

0	cero	11	once	40	cuarenta
1 (masculine)	uno	12	doce	50	cincuenta
1 (feminine)	una	13	trece	60	sesenta
2	dos	14	catorce	70	setenta
3	tres	15	quince	80	ochenta
4	cuatro	16	diez y seis	90	noventa
5	cinco	17	diez y siete	100	cien
6	seis	18	diez y ocho	101	ciento y uno
7	siete	19	diez y nueve	200	doscientos
8	ocho	20	veinte	1,000	mil
9	nueve	21	viente y uno	10,000	diez mil
10	diez	30	treinta		

DAYS OF THE WEEK

Sunday — *domingo*
Monday — *lunes*
Tuesday — *martes*
Wednesday — *miércoles*
Thursday — *jueves*
Friday — *viernes*
Saturday — *sábado*

TIME

What time is it? — *¿Qué hora es?*
one o'clock — *la una*
two o'clock — *las dos*
at two o'clock — *a las dos*
ten past three — *las tres y diez*
six a.m. — *las seis a la mañana*
six p.m. — *las seis a la tarde*
today — *hoy*
tomorrow, morning
    — *mañana, la mañana*
yesterday — *ayer*
week — *semana*
month — *mes*
year — *año*
last night — *la noche pasada*
next day — *el próximo día*

USEFUL WORDS AND PHRASES

Hello. — *Hola.*
Good morning. — *Buenos días.*
Good afternoon. — *Buenas tardes.*
Good evening. — *Buenas noches.*
How are you? — *¿Cómo está?*
Fine. — *Muy bien.*
And you? — *¿Y usted?*
So-so. — *Así así.*
Thank you. — *Gracias.*
Thank you very much. — *Muchas gracias.*
You're very kind.
    — *Usted es muy amable.*
You're welcome; literally, "It's nothing."
    — *De nada.*
yes — *sí*
no — *no*
I don't know. — *Yo no sé.*
it's fine; okay — *está bien*
good; okay — *bueno*
please — *por favor*
Pleased to meet you. — *Mucho gusto.*
excuse me (physical) — *perdóneme*
excuse me (speech) — *discúlpeme*
I'm sorry. — *Lo siento.*
goodbye — *adiós*

see you later; literally, "until later"
    — *hasta luego*
more — *más*
less — *menos*
better — *mejor*
much — *mucho*
a little — *un poco*
large — *grande*
small — *pequeño*
quick — *rápido*
slowly — *despacio*
bad — *malo*
difficult — *difícil*
easy — *fácil*
He/She/It is gone; as in "She left," "He's gone" — *Ya se fue.*
I don't speak Spanish well.
    — *No hablo bien español.*
I don't understand. — *No entiendo.*
How do you say . . . in Spanish?
    — *¿Cómo se dice . . . en español?*
Do you understand English?
    — *¿Entiende el inglés?*
Is English spoken here? (Does anyone here speak English?)
    — *¿Se habla inglés aquí?*

TERMS OF ADDRESS

I — *yo*
you (formal) — *usted*
you (familiar) — *tú*
he/him — *él*
she/her — *ella*
we/us — *nosotros*
you (plural) — *ustedes*
they/them (all males or mixed gender) — *ellos*
they/them (all females) — *ellas*

Mr., sir — *señor*
Mrs., madam — *señora*
Miss, young lady — *señorita*
wife — *esposa*
husband — *marido* or *esposo*
friend — *amigo* (male), *amiga* (female)
sweetheart — *novio* (male), *novia* (female)
son, daughter — *hijo, hija*
brother, sister — *hermano, hermana*
father, mother — *padre, madre*

GETTING AROUND

Where is . . . ? — *¿Dónde está . . . ?*
How far is it to . . .?
 — *¿Qué tan lejos está a . . . ?*
from . . . to . . . — *de . . . a . . .*
highway — *la carretera*
road — *el camino*
street — *la calle*
block — *la cuadra*
kilometer — *kilómetro*

mile (commonly used near the U.S. border) — *milla*
north — *el norte*
south — *el sur*
west — *el oeste*
east — *el este*
straight ahead — *al derecho* or *adelante*
to the right — *a la derecha*
to the left — *a la izquierda*

ACCOMMODATIONS

Can I (we) see a room?
 — *¿Puedo (podemos) ver un cuarto?*
What is the rate? — *¿Cuál es el precio?*
a single room — *un cuarto sencillo*
a double room — *un cuarto doble*
key — *llave*
bathroom — *retrete* or *lavabo*
bath — *baño*

hot water — *agua caliente*
cold water — *agua fría*
towel — *toalla*
soap — *jabón*
toilet paper — *papel higiénico*
air conditioning — *aire acondicionado*
fan — *abanico, ventilador*
blanket — *cubierta* or *manta*

PUBLIC TRANSPORT

bus stop — *la parada del autobús*
main bus terminal
 — *la central camionera*
railway station
 — *la estación de ferrocarril*
airport — *el aeropuerto*
ferry terminal
 — *la terminal del transbordador*

I want a ticket to . . .
 — *Quiero un boleto a . . .*
I want to get off at . . .
 — *Quiero bajar en . . .*
Here, please. — *Aquí, por favor.*
Where is this bus going?
 — *¿Dónde va este autobús?*
roundtrip — *ida y vuelta*
What do I owe? — *¿Cuánto le debo?*

FOOD

menu — *lista, menú*
glass — *taza*
fork — *tenedor*
knife — *cuchillo*
spoon — *cuchara, cucharita*
napkin — *servilleta*
soft drink — *refresco*
coffee, cream — *café, crema*
tea — *té*
sugar — *azúcar*
drinking water — *agua pura, agua potable*
bottled carbonated water — *agua mineral*
bottled uncarbonated water — *agua sin gas*
beer — *cerveza*
wine — *vino*
milk — *leche*
juice — *jugo*
eggs — *huevos*
bread — *pan*

watermelon — *sandía*
banana — *plátano*
apple — *manzana*
orange — *naranja*
meat (without) — *carne (sin)*
beef — *carne de res*
chicken — *pollo*
fish — *pescado*
shellfish — *camarones, mariscos*
fried — *frito*
roasted — *asada*
barbecue, barbecued
    — *barbacoa, al carbón*
breakfast — *desayuno*
lunch — *almuerzo*
dinner (often eaten in late afternoon)
    — *comida*
dinner, or a late night snack — *cena*
the check — *la cuenta*

MAKING PURCHASES

I need . . . — *Necesito . . .*
I want . . . — *Deseo . . .* or *Quiero . . .*
I would like . . . (more polite) — *Quisiera
    . . .*
How much does it cost? — *¿Cuánto cuesta?*
What's the exchange rate?
    — *¿Cuál es el tipo de cambio?*

Can I see . . . ? — *¿Puedo ver . . . ?*
this one — *ésta/ésto*
expensive — *caro*
cheap — *barato*
cheaper — *más barato*
too much — *demasiado*

HEALTH

Help me please. — *Ayúdeme por favor.*
I am ill. — *Estoy enfermo.*
pain — *dolor*
fever — *fiebre*
stomache ache — *dolor de estómago*
vomiting — *vomitar*

diarrhea — *diarrea*
drugstore — *farmacia*
medicine — *medicina*
pill, tablet — *pastilla*
birth control pills — *pastillas contraceptivos*
condoms — *contraceptivas*

BOOKLIST

GENERAL AND COFFEE-TABLE

Barclay, Juliet (photographs by Martin Charles). *Havana: Portrait of a City*. London: Cassell, 1993. A well-researched and abundantly illustrated coffee-table volume especially emphasizing the city's history. Written in a lively, readable style.

Calder, Simon and Emily Hatchwell. *Cuba: A Guide to the People, Politics and Culture*. London: Latin America Bureau, 1995. A slender yet thoughtful and insightful overview of Cuba.

García, Cristina and Joshua Greene. *Cars of Cuba*. New York: Harry N. Abrams, 1995. A splendid book with color photographs of 53 lovingly maintained beauties from the heyday of Detroit. It also features a lively introduction.

Graetz, Rick. *Cuba: The Land, The People*. Helena, MT: American Geographic Publishing, 1990. A slender coffee-table book that shows Cuba's diverse beauty with stunning visual imagery. Meager text.

Graetz, Rick. *Havana: The City, The People*. Helena, MT: American Geographic Publishing, 1991. A tribute to Havana in full-color photography that captures the spirit of the 500-year-old city. Minimal text.

Halperin, Maurice. *Return to Havana*. Nashville, TN: Vanderbilt University Press, 1994. An engaging and scathing personal essay on contemporary Cuba by a professor who taught in Havana and worked for Cuba's Ministry of Foreign Trade in the 1960s.

Kufeld, Adam. *Cuba*. New York: W. W. Norton, 1994. A stunning photographic portrait of Cuba depicting all aspects of life. The book is enhanced by an Tom Miller's introduction ("Kufeld has achieved that rare perspective of looking at Cuba from the inside out, and in doing so he has given us a gentle look at a hard place").

Lewis, Barry and Peter Marshall. *Into Cuba*. New York: Alfred Van Der Marck Editions, 1985. An evocative and richly illustrated coffee-table book widely available in Cuba.

Matthews, Herbert L. *Cuba*. New York: Macmillan Publishing, 1964. Written during the McCarthy era, this book reveals Matthews as no Castro sympathizer (despite that reputation). On the whole, a balanced look at the young Revolution.

Michener, James and John Kings. *Six Days in Havana*. Austin, TX: University of Texas Press, 1989. A wonderful read regaling the noted novelist's brief but emotionally touching week in Havana. Beautifully illustrated.

Núñez Jiménez, Antonio. *The Journey of the Havana Cigar*. Havana: Empresa Cubana del Tabaco, 1995. A large-volume treatise on the history of Cuban cigars lavishly illustrated with glossy photos.

Rudolf, James, ed. *Cuba: A Country Study*. Washington, D.C.: Government Printing Office (write to: Superintendent of Documents, Government Printing Office, Washington, DC 20402). Part of the US Government Area Handbook Studies. A surprisingly balanced general study of Cuba, with detailed sections on history, economics, and politics.

Sapieha, Nicolas. *Old Havana, Cuba*. London: Tauris Parke Books, 1990. A beautifully illustrated coffee-table book accompanied by lively text.

Smith, Wayne (photographs by Michael Reagan). *Portrait of Cuba*. Atlanta, GA: Turner

Publishing, 1991. A succinct, lucid, and entertaining profile on contemporary Cuba told by a noted expert. This splendid coffee-table book is superbly illustrated.

Stout, Nancy and Jorge Rigau. *Havana.* Rizzoli, New York, 1994. A stunning coffee-table book that captures the mood of the city in color and black-and-white photography; superb text and essays add to the photographic perspectives on Havana's cultural and architectural history.

Walker, Evans. *Havana.* Pantheon, New York, 1989. A reissue of the classic collection of black-and-white photographs depicting life in Cuba in the 1930s, first published in 1933.

Williams, Stephen. *Cuba: The Land, The History, The People, The Culture.* Philadelphia, PA: Running Press Books, 1994. A richly evocative, lavishly illustrated coffee-table book with a concise and enlivened text.

ART AND CULTURE

Behar, Ruth, ed. *Bridges to Cuba/Puentes á Cuba.* Ann Arbor, MI: University of Michigan Press, 1995. An evocative and sometimes moving anthology of essays, poetry, and fiction providing perspectives on contemporary Cuba from within Cuba and throughout the Cuban disapora.

Cabrera, Lydia. *El monte . . . notas sobre las religiones, la magia, las supersticiones, y el folklore de los negros criollos y el pueblo de Cuba.* Ediciones Universal. A compulsory work for understanding the identity and impact of African cultures on Cuba.

Camnitzer, Luís. *New Art of Cuba.* Austin, TX: University of Texas Press, 1994. Profiles the work of 40 young Cubans who formed part of the first generaton of postrevolutionary artists.

Geldof, Lynn. *Cubans: Voices of Change.* New York: St. Martin's Press, 1991. Interviews with Cubans representing the spectrum of viewpoints and backgrounds.

Lewis, Oscar, Ruth M. Lewis, and Susan M. Rigdon. *Four Men: Living the Revolution, An Oral History of Contemporary Cuba.* Urbana, IL: University of Illinois Press, 1977.

Montejo, Esteban. *The Autobiography of a Runaway Slave.* Newark, NJ: Pantheon, 1968 (edited by Miguel Barnet).

Moore, Carlos. *Castro, the Blacks, and Africa.* Los Angeles: Center for Afro-American Studies, University of California, 1988.

Stubbs, Jean and Pedro Pérez Sarduy, ed. *AfroCuba: An Anthology of Cuban Writing on Race, Politics and Culture.* New York: Ocean Press/Center for Cuban Studies, 1993. An anthology of black Cuban writing on aspects of "Afrocuba," including essays, poetry, and extracts from novels.

Timerman, Jacobo. *Cuba: A Journey.* New York: Knopf, 1990. A passionate, provocative, sometimes scathing, report of a recent journey through Cuba by a man who suffered torture at the hands of right-wing Argentinian extremists and who formerly idealized Cuba as a model socialist state.

FICTION

Carpentier, Alejo. *Reasons of State.* Havana: Writers and Readers. A novelistic tour de force, alive with wit and erudition, about the despotic head of state of an unnamed Latin American country in the early days of the 20th century.

Cabrera Infante, Guillermo. *Three Trapped Tigers.* New York: Avon, 1985. A poignant and comic novel, described as "a vernacular, elegiac masterpiece," which captures the essence of life in Havana before the ascendance of Castro. Written by an "enemy of the state" who has lived in embittered exile since 1962.

García, Cristina. *Dreaming in Cuban.* New York: Ballantine Books, 1992. A brilliant, poignant, languid, and sensual tale of a family divided politically and geographically by the Cuban revolution and the generational fissures that open on each side: in Cuba, between an ardently pro-Castro grandmother and a daughter who retreats into santería; in America, between another, militantly anti-Castro daughter and her own rebellious punk-artist daughter, who mocks her obsession.

Greene, Graham. *Our Man in Havana.* New York: Penguin, 1971. The story of Wormold, a conservative British vacuum-cleaner salesman in prerevolutionary Havana. Recruited by British intelligence, Wormold finds little information to pass on, and so invents it. Full of the sensuality of Havana and the tensions of Batista's last days.

Hemingway, Ernest. *Islands in the Stream.* New York: Harper Collins, 1970. An exciting triptych. The second and third parts are set in Cuba during the war and draw heavily on the author's own experience hinting Nazi U-boats at sea.

Hemingway, Ernest. *The Old Man and the Sea.* New York: Scribner's, 1952. The simple yet profound story of an unlucky Cuban fisherman, the slim novel won the author the Nobel Prize for Literature.

Hemingway, Ernest. *To Have and Have Not.* New York: Macmillan Publishing, 1937. The dramatic, brutal tale of running contraband between Cuba and Key West.

Iyer, Pico. *Cuba in the Night.* New York: Alfred A. Knopf, 1995. A slow-moving story of a love affair between a globe-trotting photojournalist and a young Cuban woman. The spirit of José Martí hovers over the trysts and political musings. Set in Cuba during the Special Period, the author unduly stresses an atmosphere of negativity.

HISTORY AND POLITICS

Aguila, Juan M. del. *Cuba: Dilemnas of a Revolution.* Boulder, CO: Westview Press, 1994. An up-to-date, well-balanced review of the history and contemporary reality of Cuba.

Benjamin, Jules R. *The United States and the Origins of the Cuban Revolution.* Princeton, NJ: Princeton University Press, 1990. A superb study explaining how Cuba and the United States arrived at the traumatic rupture in their relations.

Benjamin, Medea, ed. *Cuba: A Current Issues Reader.* San Francisco: Global Exchange, 1994. A compilation of recent articles on a wide range of Cuban topics.

Bonachea, Rolando and Nelson Valdés. *Cuba in Revolution.* New York: Anchor Books, 1972. A collection of essays by noted academics, providing a comprehensive, many-sided overview of the Cuban Revolution and the issues it raises.

Bonachea, Rolando and Nelson Valdés. *Selected Works of Ernesto Guevara.* Cambridge, MA: M.I.T. Press, 1969.

Castro, Fidel. *Che: A Memoir by Fidel Castro,* Melbourne, Australia: Ocean Press, 1983. Fidel's candid account of his relationship with Che Guevara documents the man, the revolutionary, the thinker, and the Argentine-born doctor's extraordinary bond with Cuba.

Eckstein, Susan. *Back from the Future: Cuba under Castro.* Princeton, NJ: Princeton University Press, 1994. A well-reasoned and balanced attempt to provide a broad overview of Castro's Cuba. Eckstein contends that Cuba is less rigidly Marxist than presented and that a revisionist view is needed.

Franqui, Carlos. *Family Portrait with Fidel.* New York: Vintage Books, 1985. An insider's look at how the Sovietization of the Cuban Revolution occurred and precisely what goals Fidel Castro had in mind. The author debunks myths and provides startling revelations.

Gray, Richard Butler. *José Martí, Cuban Patriot.* Gainesville, FL: University of Florida Press, 1962.

Halebsky, Sandor and Kirk, John, eds. *Cuba in Transition: Crisis and Transformation.* Westview Press, 1992.

Halperin, Maurice. *The Taming of Fidel Castro.* Berkeley, CA: University of California Press, 1981.

Johnson, Haynes. *The Bay of Pigs.* New York: Norton, 1964. Writing in collaboration with leaders of the Brigade, Haynes provides both perspectives in this masterful, encyclopedic work.

Kennedy, Robert F. *Thirteen Days: A Memoir of the Cuban Missile Crisis.* New York: Norton, 1969.

Kenner, Martin and James Petras. *Fidel Castro Speaks.* New York: Penguin Books, 1969. A collection of 16 of Castro's most important speeches, made between his seizure of power in 1959 and 1968.

Lockwood, Lee. *Castro's Cuba, Cuba's Fidel.* Boulder, CO: Westview Press, 1990.

Martí, José. *Inside the Monster: Writings on the United States and American Imperialism.* New York: Monthly Review Press, 1975 (Phillip S. Foener, ed.). Essential prose works of the late-19th-century activist, literary man, and national hero, who has exercised a lasting influence on the politics of 20th-century Cuba.

Mesa-Lago, Carmelo, ed. *Cuba After the Cold War.* Pittsburgh, PA: University of Pittsburgh, 1993.

Meyer, Karl E. and Tad Szulc. *The Cuban Invasion.* New York: Praeger, 1962. A shrewd and fascinating interpretation of the Bay of Pigs.

Oppenheimer, Andres. *Castro's Final Hour.* New York: Simon & Schuster, 1992. A sobering, in-depth expose of the uglier side of both Fidel Castro and the state system, including controversial topics such as drug trading. This book is anathema in Cuba.

Ortíz, Fernando. *Cuban Counterpoint: Tobacco and Sugar.* New York: Alfred A. Knopf, 1947. A seminal work on the decisiveness of tobacco and sugar in Cuban history.

Patterson, Thomas G. *Contesting Castro: The United States and the Triumph of the Cuban Revolution.* New York: Oxford University Press, 1994.

Pérez, Louis A. *Cuba: Between Reform and Revolution.* New York: Oxford University Press, 1988.

Pérez-Stable, Marifeli. *The Cuban Revolution: Origins, Course, and Legacy.* New York: Oxford University Press, 1993. A negative review of the past four decades that closes with a polemic offering a damning accusation of a revolution betrayed.

Quirk, Robert E. *Fidel Castro.* New York: W.W. Norton, 1993. A detailed, none-too-complimentary profile of the Cuban leader.

Schulz, Donald, ed. *Cuba and the Future.* Westport, CT: Greenwood Press, 1994. A series of essays analysizing Cuba's contemporary economic and political dilemnas.

Smith, Wayne. *The Closest of Enemies.* New York: W.W. Norton, 1987.

Stubbs, Jean. *Cuba: The Test of Time.* London: Latin American Bureau, 1989. A comprehensive overview of Cuban economics, politics, religion, and social structure.

Szulc, Tad. *Fidel: A Critical Portrait.* New York: Morrow, 1986. A riveting profile of the astounding life of this larger-than-life figure. The book is full of never-before-revealed tidbits. A marvelous read.

Thomas, Hugh. *Cuba: The Pursuit of Freedom, 1726-1969.* New York: Harper & Row, 1971. A seminal work—called a "magisterial conspectus of Cuban history"—tracing the evolution of conditions that eventually engendered the Revolution.

Thomas, Hugh. *The Cuban Revolution.* London: Weidenfeld and Nicolson, 1986. The definitive work on the Revolution offering a brilliant analysis of all aspects of the country's diverse and tragic history.

Wyden, Peter. *Bay of Pigs: The Untold Story.* New York: Simon and Schuster, 1979. An in-depth and riveting exposé of the CIA's ill-conceived mission to topple Castro.

Yglesias, José. *In the Fist of the Revolution.* New York: Pantheon, 1968.

TRAVEL GUIDES

Calder, Simon and Emily Hatchwell. *Cuba: Travellers Survival Kit.* Oxford, England: Vacation Work, 1993. A detailed book packed with useful information strongly oriented to British travelers.

Cameron, Sarah and Ben Box. *Caribbean Island Handbook.* Trade & Travel, 1992. An astounding amount of nuts-and-bolts information is packed into its 34-page Cuba section.

Charles, Simon. *The Cruising Guide to Cuba.* St. Petersburg, FL: Cruising Guide Publications, 1994. Invaluable reference guide for every sailor wishing to charter sailing or motorized craft. Charles gives it to you straight. His goal is "to seek only to ensure the safe passage of all who would use the seas to travel where they will."

Coe, Andrew. *Cuba.* Lincolnwood: NTC Publishing, 1995. Lavishly illustrated and evocatively written. Strong background and succinct regional overviews. Limited practical information.

Cure, Karen, ed. *Fodor's Cuba.* New York: Fodor's, 1995. A concise guidebook. Strong regional chapters, but minimal treatment of background material. Translated from Italian with limited regard for North American travelers.

Helmhausen, Ole. *Practical Travel: Cuba.* Cologne, Germany: Hayit, 1994. Pocket-size guide arranged alphabetically.

Mawer, Fred. *Berlitz's Pocket Guides: Cuba.* Oxford, England: Berlitz, 1996. A tiny guide-book packed with succinct information and lively discourse.

McManus, Jane. *Getting to Know Cuba—A Travel Guide.* New York: St. Martin's Press, 1989. Pocket-size guide written by a US journalist and long-time resident of Havana.

Núñez Jiménez, Antonio. *Tourist Guide of Cuba.* Rome: Ediciones Gianni Constantino, 1990. Pocket-size guidebook more suited to package tourists. Widely available in Cuba.

Perrottet, Tony and Joann Biondi. *Insight Guides—Cuba.* Hong Kong: APA Publications, 1995. Lavishly illustrated. Detailed introductory material and succinct regional overviews.

Williams, Diana. *Diving and Snorkeling Guide to Cuba.* Houston, TX: Pisces Books, 1996. A concise guide to the best diving spots in Cuba.

TRAVEL LITERATURE

Baker, Christopher P. *Mi Moto Fidel: Motorcycling through Castro's Cuba.* (forthcoming). Riveting and self-deprecating tales of the author's 11,000-km adventure by motorcycle through Cuba.

Gébler, Carlo. *Driving Through Cuba.* New York: Simon & Schuster, 1988. The tale of a three-month sojourn through Cuba by car. Full of wry, often acerbic, commentary. Strong historical analyses, but incomplete and at times naive interpretations of Cuban society.

Hazard, Samuel. *Cuba with Pen and Pencil.* Hartford, CT: Hartford Publishing, 1871.

Iyer, Pico. *Falling off the Map.* New York: Alfred A. Knopf, 1993. Presents a far rosier picture than the author's dour novel *Cuba in the Night.*

Miller, Tom. *Trading with the Enemy: A Yankee Travels Through Castro's Cuba.* New York: Atheneum, 1992. A fabulous travelogue told by a famous author who lived in Cuba for almost a year. Thoughtful, engaging, insightful, compassionate, and told in rich narrative.

Samuelson, Arnold. *With Hemingway: A Year in Key West and Cuba*. Maine: Thorndike Press, 1984. The true-life tale of a young Midwestern farm boy who wanted to become a writer and was hired to guard Hemingway's *Pilar*. For a year he accompanied "E.H." on fishing excursions around Key West and Cuba, recording this diary, in which he captures Hemingway "off-guard and all-too-human."

OTHER

Agee, Philip. *Inside the Company; CIA Diary*. New York: Bantam Books, 1975. This sobering work details the mission to discredit Cuba, including dirty tricks—disinformation campaigns, bombings, political assassinations, etc.—employed by the CIA against Latin America leftists. Told by a CIA "deep-cover" agent who eventually resigned because he "finally undestood how much suffering [the CIA] was causing."

Benjamin, Medea and Peter Rosset. *The Greening of the Revolution*. Melbourne: Ocean Press, 1994. A detailed account of Cuba's turn to a system of organic agriculture told by two noted authorities on the subject.

Benjamin, Medea, Joseph Collins, and Michael Scott. *No Free Lunch: Food and Revolution in Cuba*. San Francisco: Institute for Food and Development Policy, 1984.

Cabrera Infante, Guillermo. *¡Mea Cuba!* New York: Farrar Straus Giroux, 1994. An acerbic, indignant, raw, wistful, and brilliant set of essays in which the author pours out his bile at the Castro regime.

Clark, Susannah and John Miller. *Chronicles Abroad: Havana*. San Francisco: Chronicle Books, 1996. Short essays and extracts on Cuba (not just Havana), by such authors as Graham Greene, Ernest Hemingway, Mario Puzo, and Fidel Castro.

Cruz, Mary. *Cuba and Hemingway on the Great Blue River*. Havana: Editorial José Martí, 1994. A splendid critical study of Hemingway's writings in which the author presents the theory that Hemingway's works reflect core tenets of Cuban ideology.

Fuentes, Norberto. *Hemingway in Cuba*. Secaucus, NY: Lyle Stuart, 1984. The seminal, lavishly illustrated study of the Nobel Prize winner's years in Cuba.

Hemingway, Gregory. *Papa, A Personal Memory*. New York: Pocket Books, 1976. A funny, serious, and touching account of the author's childhood, including a long period in Cuba with his father, Ernest Hemingway.

LaFray, Joyce. *¡Cuba Cocina!* New York: Hearst Books, 1994. A sweeping compilation of Cuban rooipos, both classic and *nuevo cubano*, from both Floridian Cuban restaurants and such famous Havana restaurants as Bodeguita del Medio. Should be compulsory reading in Cuba.

Murray, Mary. *Cruel and Unusual Punishment: The US Blockade Against Cuba*. Melbourne: Ocean Press, 1992. Details the US embargo from its inception in 1960 to today. Presents Cuba's perspectives.

Rius. *Cuba for Beginners: An Illustrated Guide for Americans*. New York: Pathfinder Press, 1970. The Mexican caricaturist presents the internationalist view of Cuba-US relations with comic inventiveness. Hilarious depictions of Uncle Sam's machinations and misadventures.

Senzel, Howard. *Baseball and the Cold War*. New York: Harcourt Brace Jovanovich, 1977.

Thurston, Charles W. *In From the Cold: How to do Business With Cuba*. New York: Journal of Commerce, 1995. Detailed information on current opportunities in sectors ranging from agriculture to transportation. Lists of useful Cuban, US, and foreign private and public-sector contacts.

Walker, Alice. *In Search of Our Mother's Gardens.* New York: Harcourt Books, 1983. This biography of experiences includes a chapter in which the noted novelist and activist explores her feelings about and recounts her experiences in Cuba.

VIDEOS

Cuba. An 80-minute video that looks at the lives of Cubans. (US$25, plus US$2 shipping, from John Holod, 140 Mullan Road West, Superior, MI 59872).

Cuba Va: The Challenge of the Next Generation. A fascinating 60-minute documentary released in 1993 captures the vigor and diversity of Cuban youth—the politically committed and the alienated—who express their divergent perspectives on the Revolution, the Special Period, and the future. Copies cost US$95 from Cuba Va Video Project, 12 Liberty St., San Francisco, CA 94110, tel. (415) 282-1812, fax (415) 282-1798.

Gay Cuba. This one-hour documentary takes a candid look at one of Cuba's most controversial human rights issues: the treatment of the gay and lesbian people in Cuba since the Revolution. Order from Frameline, 346 Ninth St., San Francisco, CA 94103, tel. (415) 703-8654, fax (415) 861-1404, e-mail frameline@aol.com; http://www.frameline.org.

Workers Democracy in Cuba. A 30-minute video records the 17th National Congress of the Cuban Workers Federation, in April 1996; US$25, plus US$3 postage, from International Peace for Cuba Appeal, 2489 Mission St. #28, San Francisco, CA 94110, tel. (415) 821-7575, fax (415) 821-5782.

Havana Nagila: The Jews of Cuba. An hour-long look at the history of Jews in Cuba during five centuries. Copies can be ordered from Schnitzki & Stone, 819 W. Roseburg Ave. #240, Modesto, CA 95350, tel. (209) 575-1775, fax (209) 575-1404.

INDEX

Page numbers in *italics* indicate maps.

Parque Nacional Peninsula de Guanahacabibes: 402; Sierra del Rosarios Biosphere Reserve 377, 378-380; trees 11-13; Zapata Peninsula 461-463
Florencia: 546
Florida: 532
flowers: 13-14
folklore: 127-128
Fondo Cubano de Bienes Culturales: 132, 259, 315
food: 142-148; *see also specific place*
Ford, Gerald: 44-45
Fortaleza de la Punta: 670
Fortín de la Trocha: 528
Fortress de Yarayó: 628
fruits: 146
Fuente de la India Noble Habana: 264
Fuente de los Leones: 255
Fuentes, Gregorio: 345
Fuerte Matachín: 668
Fuerte San Hilario: 553
Fulbright, J. William: 49, 50
Fund for Educational and Cultural Development: 132
Fustete Cave: 608

G
Gabinete de la Archeología: 243
Gaitán, Jorge Eliécer: *66*
galleries: 126, 309; Artesanías Para Turismo Taller 259; Asociación Cubana de Aretesana Artistas 316; Casa de las Américas 316; Casa de las Artista 594; Casa de los Condes de Jaruco 315; Centro de Desarollo de Artes Visuales; Centro Provincional Artes Plástico Galería 391; Centro Wilfredo Lam 316; Galería de Arte Provincial (Matanzas) 430; Galería de la Cosona 315; Galería de la Plaza Vieja 315; Galería del Arte (Las Tunas) 566; Galería del Arte (Trinidad) 519; Galería del Arte Amelia Peláez 350; Galería del Centro Gallego 315; Galería Forma 309, 315; Galería Francisco Javier Baez 309; Galería Habana 309; Galería Haydee Santamaría 279, 309; Galería Horacio Ruíz 309, 316; Galería Kahlo 271; Galería La Acacia 309, 312, 315; Galería Mariano 316; Galería Mariano Rodríguez 344; Galería Oriente 635; Galería Pequeño Formato 259; Galería Plaza Vieja 309; Galería Roberto

Diago 309; Galería tor Manuel 249; Galería UNEAC 309; Galería Victor Manuel 309, 315; Galería Yara 673; Instituto Superior de Arte 354; Lester's Art Studio 384; Nelson Domínguez Experimental Graphics Art Gallery 246-247; Palacio de Artesanía Cubana 316; Taller de Alberto 384; Taller de Fibras 384; Taller de Pintura 315-316; Taller de Seregráfia Rene Portocarrero 309; Taller Experimental de la Gráfica 246, 309, 315
Galería de Arte (Manzanillo): 600
Galería de Arte (Varadero): 449
Galería de Arte Provincial (Matanzas): 430
Galería de la Cosona: 315
Galería de la Plaza Vieja: 315
Galería del Arte (Las Tunas): 566
Galería del Arte (Trinidad): 519
Galería del Arte Amelia Peláez: 350
Galería del Centro Gallego: 315
Galería Exposición: 318
Galería Forma: 309, 315
Galería Francisco Javier Baez: 309
Galería Habana: 309
Galería Haydee Santamaría: 279, 309
Galería Horacio Ruíz: 309, 316
Galería Kahlo: 271
Galería la Acacia: 309, 312, 315
Galería Mariano: 316
Galería Mariano Rodríguez: 344
Galería Oriente: 635
Galería Pequeno Formato: 259
Galería Plaza Vieja: 309
Galería Roberto Diago: 309
Galería tor Manuel: 249
Galería UNEAC: 309
Galería Victor Manuel: 309, 315
Galería Yara: 673
García, Calixto: 571, 590
García, Cristina: 233
García González, Vicente: 565
gasoline: 182, 183-184, 333
Gaspar: 532
gay travelers: 196-197
Gellhorn, Martha: 349
genetic engineering: 326
geography: 1-5, 6-7, 392-393; *see also specific place*
George III of England: 237
giardiasis: 205
Gibara: 576

Reciprocal Trade Agreement: 39
recreation: 116-124, 122-123; bicycling 116;
  birdwatching 117; fishing 117-119; golf
  119; hiking 119; hunting 119-120; sailing
  120-121; sports 123-124
Refugio de Fauna los Indios: 415
Refugio de Saturno: 435
Regla: 347-348
religion: 103-106; Christianity 103-104;
  Judaism 105-106; Santería 104-105
Remedios: 495-498
Remington, Frederic: 34
rentals: car 185-187
Reparto Matanzas: 429
Reparto Vista Alegre: 626
reptiles: 17-19
Retablo de los Héroes: 594
Río Bacunayagua: 371
Río Bayamo: 589
Río Bélico: 489
Río Caiguanabo: 386
Río Carragua: 386
Río Cauto: 589, 596
Río Cubanicay: 489
Río Duaba: 675, 676
Río Hatibonico: 534
Río Hatiguanico: 462
Río Jiguaní: 675
Río La Plata: 612
Río Macaguani: 675
Río Macio: 610, 612
Río Manatí: 500
Río Matafuá: 485
Río Miel: 668
Río Ojo: 665
Río San Juan: 425
Río Toa: 675
Río Turquino: 612
Río Yaguanabo: 485
Río Yara: 598
Río Yarey: 675
Río Yayabo: 503
Río Yumurí: 425, 665, 676
Río Zaza: 507
rivers: 5; *see also specific place; specific river*
  (río)
Robaina, Roberto: 71
Rodríguez, Carlos Rafael: 39
Rojas, Marta: 619
Rojo, Rudesindo Antonio García: 504
roller skating: 312

Romeo y Julieta: 267
Romería de Maya: 573
Roosevelt, Teddy: 619, 626-627, 650
Roosevelt, Theodore: 34
Root, Elihu: 35
Rosenberg, Julius and Ethel: 282
Rosenberg Monument: 282
Rough Riders: 619, 626-627, 650
Ruinas de San Pedro y Santa Catalina: 383
rum: 148, 320, 636; Casa de Ron 320;
  Taberna del Galeón 320; *see also specific
  place*
rumba: 128
running: 311
Ruz, Lina: 641

S
Sábado de Rumba: 303
safety: 208-211, 331
sailing: 120-121
Sala Desposición Holgrafía: 626
Sala Teatro José Joaquín Palma: 594
salsa: 129
salt: 655
Salto de Caburní: 488
Salto Vega Grande: 488
San Antonio de los Baños: 366-367
San Antonio del Sur: 665
San Blas: 485
San Cayetano: 378
Sánchez, Andres Manuel: 536
Sánchez, Celia: 43-50, 279, 547, 594, 600,
  606, 607, 609, 626; Monumento á Celia
  Sánchez 350; Monumento Celia 601;
  Museo Celia Sánchez 611
Sancti Spíritus City: 501-507
Sancti Spíritus Province: 500-523, *501, 502-
  503,* 511, 512, 514; Introduction 500-501;
  Sancti Spíritus City and Vicinity 501-510;
  Trinidad 510-523
San Diego de los Baños: 372, 378, 385
Sandino: *400*
San Francisco de Paula: 349
San José de Lago: 499
San Juan Hill: 619, 626-627
San Juan River Trail: 383
San Juan y Martínez: 399
San Luís: 399
San Miguel: 424
San Miguel de los Baños: 457-458
Santa Clara: 489-494, *490, 491*

ABOUT THE AUTHOR

CHRISTOPHER P. BAKER was born and raised in Yorkshire, England. After receiving a B.A. (Honours) in Geography at University College, London (including two Sahara research expeditions and an exchange program at Krakow University, Poland), he earned M.A. degrees in Latin American Studies from Liverpool University and in Education from the Institute of Education, London University. He began his writing career in 1978 as a contributing editor on Latin America for *Land and Liberty,* a London-based political journal. In 1980, he received a Scripps-Howard Foundation Scholarship in Journalism to attend the University of California, Berkeley. Since 1983 he has made his living as a professional travel and natural-sciences writer. His byline has appeared in publications as diverse as *Newsweek, National Wildlife, Islands, Elle, Esquire,* and *The Los Angeles Times,* and he has also written for such outlets as the BBC and The Discovery Channel. For seven years, Baker was president of British Pride Tours, which he founded. He has escorted group tours to New Zealand, Hong Kong, Korea, England, and Cuba. He appears frequently on radio and television talk shows, and as a guest lecturer aboard cruise ships throughout the Caribbean and farther afield. His other books include Moon Publications' *Costa Rica Handbook, Travel Bug Guide to California, Passport Illustrated Guide to Jamaica,* and *Mi Moto Fidel: Motorcycling through Castro's Cuba.* He has also contributed chapters to *I Should Have Stayed Home, Traveler's Tales: Food,* and *Traveler's Tales: Romance.* Baker is a member of the Society of American Travel Writers and has been honored with several awards for outstanding writing, among them the prestigious Lowell Thomas Travel Journalism Award (four times, including "Best Travel News Investigative Reporter") and the 1995 Benjamin Franklin Award for "Best Travel Guide" for *Costa Rica Handbook.* He lives in California.

NOTES

MOON TRAVEL HANDBOOKS
THE IDEAL TRAVELING COMPANIONS

Moon Travel Handbooks provide focused, comprehensive coverage of distinct destinations all over the world. Our goal is to give travelers all the background and practical information they'll need for an extraordinary travel experience.

Every Handbook begins with an in-depth essay about the land, the people, their history, art, politics, and social concerns—an entire bookcase of cultural insight and introductory information in one portable volume. We also provide accurate, up-to-date coverage of all the practicalities: language, currency, transportation, accommodations, food, and entertainment. And Moon's maps are legendary, covering not only cities and highways, but parks and trails that are often difficult to find in other sources.

On the following pages is a complete list of Handbooks, covering North America and Hawaii, Mexico, Central America and the Caribbean, and Asia and the Pacific. To purchase Moon Travel Handbooks, please check your local bookstore or order by phone: (800) 345-5473 Monday-Friday 8 a.m.-5 p.m. PST. If you are calling from outside of the United States the number is (916) 345-5473.

NORTH AMERICA AND HAWAII

"These domestic guides convey the same sense of exoticism that their foreign counterparts do, making home-country travel seem like far-flung adventure."
—*Sierra Magazine*

Alaska-Yukon Handbook	**$17.95**
Deke Castleman and Don Pitcher	500 pages, 92 maps
Alberta and the Northwest Territories Handbook	**$17.95**
Andrew Hempstead and Nadina Purdon	497 pages, 72 maps
Arizona Traveler's Handbook	**$17.95**
Bill Weir and Robert Blake	486 pages, 54 maps
Atlantic Canada Handbook	**$17.95**
Nan Drosdick and Mark Morris	436 pages, 61 maps
Big Island of Hawaii Handbook	**$13.95**
J.D. Bisignani	349 pages, 23 maps
British Columbia Handbook	**$15.95**
Jane King	375 pages, 69 maps
Colorado Handbook	**$18.95**
Stephen Metzger	447 pages, 59 maps
Georgia Handbook	**$17.95**
Kap Stann	360 pages, 50 maps
Hawaii Handbook	**$19.95**
J.D. Bisignani	1004 pages, 90 maps
Honolulu-Waikiki Handbook	**$14.95**
J.D. Bisignani	365 pages, 20 maps
Idaho Handbook	**$18.95**
Don Root	582 pages, 42 maps
Kauai Handbook	**$15.95**
J.D. Bisignani	330 pages, 23 maps
Maui Handbook	**$14.95**
J.D. Bisignani	393 pages, 35 maps
Montana Handbook	**$17.95**
Judy Jewell and W.C. McRae	454 pages, 52 maps
Nevada Handbook	**$16.95**
Deke Castleman	473 pages, 40 maps
New Mexico Handbook	**$15.95**
Stephen Metzger	337 pages, 47 maps
New York City Handbook	**$13.95**
Christiane Bird	295 pages, 20 maps
New York Handbook	**$19.95**
Christiane Bird	760 pages, 95 maps
Northern California Handbook	**$19.95**
Kim Weir	779 pages, 50 maps
Oregon Handbook	**$16.95**
Stuart Warren and Ted Long Ishikawa	520 pages, 33 maps

Road Trip USA	**$22.50**
Jamie Jensen	786 pages, 165 maps
Southern California Handbook	**$19.95**
Kim Weir	600 pages, 30 maps
Tennessee Handbook	**$17.95**
Jeff Bradley	490 pages, 44 maps
Texas Handbook	**$17.95**
Joe Cummings	598 pages, 70 maps
Utah Handbook	**$17.95**
Bill Weir and W.C. McRae	456 pages, 40 maps
Washington Handbook	**$19.95**
Don Pitcher	630 pages, 113 maps
Wisconsin Handbook	**$18.95**
Thomas Huhti	580 pages, 69 maps
Wyoming Handbook	**$17.95**
Don Pitcher	581 pages, 80 maps

ASIA AND THE PACIFIC

"Scores of maps, detailed practical info down to business hours of small-town libraries. You can't beat the Asian titles for sheer heft. (The) series is sort of an American Lonely Planet, with better writing but fewer titles. (The) individual voice of researchers comes through."

—Travel & Leisure

Australia Handbook	**$21.95**
Marael Johnson, Andrew Hempstead, and Nadina Purdon	944 pages, 141 maps
Bali Handbook	**$19.95**
Bill Dalton	715 pages, 54 maps
Bangkok Handbook	**$13.95**
Michael Buckley	221 pages, 30 maps
Fiji Islands Handbook	**$13.95**
David Stanley	275 pages, 38 maps
Hong Kong Handbook	**$15.95**
Kerry Moran	347 pages, 49 maps
Indonesia Handbook	**$25.00**
Bill Dalton	1,351 pages, 249 maps
Japan Handbook	**$22.50**
J.D. Bisignani	952 pages, 213 maps
Micronesia Handbook	**$14.95**
Neil M. Levy	311 pages, 70 maps
Nepal Handbook	**$18.95**
Kerry Moran	466 pages, 51 maps

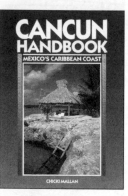

New Zealand Handbook	**$19.9**
Jane King	595 pages, 81 map
Outback Australia Handbook	**$18.9**
Marael Johnson	424 pages, 57 map
Pakistan Hanbdbook	**$19.9**
Isobel Shaw	660 pages, 85 map
Philippines Handbook	**$17.9**
Peter Harper and Laurie Fullerton	638 pages, 116 map
Singapore Handbook	**$15.9**
Carl Parkes	300 pages, 29 maps
Southeast Asia Handbook	**$21.9**
Carl Parkes	1,103 pages, 196 maps
South Korea Handbook	**$19.9**
Robert Nilsen	824 pages, 141 maps
South Pacific Handbook	**$22.9**
David Stanley	913 pages, 147 maps
Tahiti-Polynesia Handbook	**$13.9**
David Stanley	243 pages, 35 maps
Thailand Handbook	**$19.9**
Carl Parkes	834 pages, 142 maps
Tibet Handbook	**$30.0**
Victor Chan	1103 pages, 216 maps
VIetnam, Cambodia & Laos Handbook	**$18.95**
Michael Buckley	691 pages, 112 maps

MEXICO, CENTRAL AMERICA, AND THE CARIBBEAN

"Travel guides published by Moon Publications are uniformly just as they are advertised: 'informative, entertaining, highly practical.' They satisfy all the needs of travelers on the road. At the same time they are colorful and educational enough to be enjoyed by those whose travel is confined to armchair-bound wishes and dreams." —*Worldviews*

Baja Handbook	**$15.95**
Joe Cummings	362 pages, 44 maps
Belize Handbook	**$15.95**
Chicki Mallan	363 pages, 45 maps
Cabo Handbook	**$14.95**
Joe Cummings	205 pages, 18 maps
Cancún Handbook	**$13.95**
Chicki Mallan	254 pages, 25 maps
Caribbean Handbook	**$16.95**
Karl Luntta	384 pages, 56 maps

entral Mexico Handbook	**$15.95**
Chicki Mallan	391 pages, 63 maps
osta Rica Handbook	**$19.95**
Christopher P. Baker	750 pages, 74 maps
uba Handbook	**$19.95**
Christopher P. Baker	650 pages, 70 maps
ominican Republic Handbook	**$15.95**
Gaylord Dold	350 pages, 24 maps
onduras Handbook	**$15.95**
Chris Humphrey	350 pages, 40 maps
amaica Handbook	**$15.95**
Karl Luntta	312 pages, 17 maps
lexico Handbook	**$21.95**
Joe Cummings and Chicki Mallan	1,457 pages, 232 maps
lorthern Mexico Handbook	**$16.95**
Joe Cummings	500 pages, 68 maps
acific Mexico Handbook	**$17.95**
Bruce Whipperman	483 pages, 69 maps
uerto Vallarta Handbook	**$14.95**
Bruce Whipperman	285 pages, 36 maps
irgin Islands Handbook	**$13.95**
Karl Luntta	230 pages, 19 maps
ucatan Peninsula Handbook	**$15.95**
Chicki Mallan	397 pages, 62 maps

OTHER GREAT TITLES FROM MOON

"For hardy wanderers, few guides come more highly
recommended than the Handbooks. They include
good maps, steer clear of fluff and flackery, and offer
plenty of money-saving tips. They also give you the
kind of information that visitors to strange lands—on
any budget—need to survive."

—*US News & World Report*

Moon Handbook	**$10.00**
Carl Koppeschaar	141 pages, 8 maps
Moscow-St. Petersburg Handbook	**$13.95**
Masha Nordbye	259 pages, 16 maps
The Practical Nomad	**$17.95**
Edward Hasbrouck	575 pages
Staying Healthy in Asia, Africa, and Latin America	**$11.95**
Dirk Schroeder	197 pages, 4 maps

WHERE TO BUY MOON TRAVEL HANDBOOKS

BOOKSTORES AND LIBRARIES: Moon Travel Handbooks are sold worldwide. Please contact our sales manager for a list of wholesalers and distributors in your area.

TRAVELERS: We would like to have Moon Travel Handbooks available throughout the world. Please ask your bookstore to write or call us for ordering information. If your bookstore will not order our guides for you, please contact us for a free catalog.

> **Moon Travel Handbooks**
> **P.O. Box 3040**
> **Chico, CA 95927-3040 U.S.A.**
> **tel.: (800) 345-5473, outside the U.S. (916) 345-5473**
> **fax: (916) 345-6751**
> **e-mail: travel@moon.com**

IMPORTANT ORDERING INFORMATION

PRICES: All prices are subject to change. We always ship the most current edition. We will let you know if there is a price increase on the book you order.

SHIPPING AND HANDLING OPTIONS: Domestic UPS or USPS first class (allow 10 working days for delivery): $3.50 for the first item, 50 cents for each additional item.

EXCEPTIONS: *Road Trip USA, Tibet Handbook, Mexico Handbook,* and *Indonesia Handbook* shipping $4.50; $1.00 for each additional *Road Trip USA, Tibet Handbook, Mexico Handbook,* and *Indonesia Handbook.*

Moonbelt shipping is $1.50 for one, 50 cents for each additional belt.

Add $2.00 for same-day handling.

UPS 2nd Day Air or Printed Airmail requires a special quote.

International Surface Bookrate 8-12 weeks delivery: $3.00 for the first item, $1.00 for each additional item. Note: Moon Publications cannot guarantee international surface bookrate shipping. Moon recommends sending international orders via air mail, which requires a special quote.

FOREIGN ORDERS: Orders that originate outside the U.S.A. must be paid for with an international money order, a check in U.S. currency drawn on a major U.S. bank based in the U.S.A., or Visa or MasterCard.

TELEPHONE ORDERS: We accept Visa or MasterCard payments. Minimum order is US$15. Call in your order: (800) 345-5473, 8 a.m.-5 p.m. Pacific standard time. Outside the U.S. the number is (916) 345-5473.

ORDER FORM

Prices are subject to change without notice. Be sure to call (800) 345-5473,
or (916) 345-5473 from outside the U.S. 8 a.m.–5 p.m. PST for current prices and editions,
or for the name of the bookstore nearest you that carries Moon Travel Handbooks.
(See important ordering information on preceding page.)

Name: _____ Date: _____

Street: _____

City: _____ Daytime Phone: _____

State or Country: _____ Zip Code: _____

QUANTITY	TITLE	PRICE
	Taxable Total_____	
	Sales Tax (7.25%) for California Residents_____	
	Shipping & Handling_____	
	TOTAL_____	

Ship: ☐ UPS (no P.O. Boxes) ☐ 1st class ☐ International surface mail

Ship to: ☐ address above ☐ other _____

_____

Make checks payable to: **MOON TRAVEL HANDBOOKS**, P.O. Box 3040, Chico, CA 95927-3040
U.S.A. We accept Visa and MasterCard. **To Order**: Call in your Visa or MasterCard number, or send
a written order with your Visa or MasterCard number and expiration date clearly written.

Card Number: ☐ **Visa** ☐ **MasterCard**

☐ ☐ ☐ ☐ ☐ ☐ ☐ ☐ ☐ ☐ ☐ ☐ ☐ ☐ ☐ ☐

Exact Name on Card: _____

Expiration date:_____

Signature: _____

MOONBELT

A new concept in moneybelts. Made of heavy-duty Cordura nylon, the Moonbelt offers maximum protection for your money and important papers. This pouch, designed for all-weather comfort, slips under your shirt or waistband, rendering it virtually undetectable and inaccessible to pickpockets. It features a one-inch high-test quick-release buckle so there's no more fumbling around for the strap or repeated adjustments. This handy plastic buckle opens and closes with a touch but won't come undone until you want it to. Moonbelts accommodate traveler's checks, passports, cash, photos, etc. Size 5 x 9 inches. Available in black only. **$8.95**

www.moon.com

MOON
PUBLICATIONS

Welcome to <u>Moon Travel Handbooks</u>, publishers of comprehensive travel guides to <u>North America</u>, <u>Mexico</u>, <u>Central America and the Caribbean</u>, <u>Asia</u>, and the <u>Pacific Islands</u>. We're always on the lookout for new ideas, so please feel free to e-mail any comments and suggestions about these exhibits to <u>travel@moon.com</u>.

If you like Moon Travel Handbooks, you'll enjoy our travel information center on the World Wide Web (WWW), loaded with interactive exhibits designed especially for the Internet.

Our featured exhibit contains the complete text of *Road Trip USA*, a travel guide to the "blue highways" that crisscross America between the interstates, published in paperback in 1996. The WWW version contains a large, scrollable point-and-click imagemap with links to hundreds of original entries; a sophisticated network of links to other major U.S. Internet sites; and a running commentary from our online readers contributing their own travel tips on small towns, roadside attractions, regional foods, and interesting places to stay.

Other attractions on Moon's web site include:

- Excerpted hypertext adaptations of Moon's bestselling *New Zealand Handbook, Costa Rica Handbook,* and *Big Island of Hawaii Handbook*

- The complete 75-page introduction to *Staying Healthy in Asia, Africa, and Latin America,* as well as the *Trans-Cultural Study Guide,* both coproduced with Volunteers in Asia

- The complete, annotated bibliographies from Moon's Handbooks to Japan, South Korea, Thailand, the Philippines, Indonesia, Australia, and New Zealand

- Current and back issues of Moon's free newsletter, *Travel Matters*

- Updates on the latest titles and editions to join the Moon Travel Handbook series

Come visit us at: **http://www.moon.com**

U.S.~METRIC CONVERSION

1 inch = 2.54 centimeters (cm)
1 foot = .304 meters (m)
1 mile = 1.6093 kilometers (km)
1 km = .6214 miles
1 fathom = 1.8288 m
1 chain = 20.1168 m
1 furlong = 201.168 m
1 acre = .4047 hectares
1 sq km = 100 hectares
1 sq mile = 2.59 square km
1 ounce = 28.35 grams
1 pound = .4536 kilograms
1 short ton = .90718 metric ton
1 short ton = 2000 pounds
1 long ton = 1.016 metric tons
1 long ton = 2240 pounds
1 metric ton = 1000 kilograms
1 quart = .94635 liters
1 US gallon = 3.7854 liters
1 Imperial gallon = 4.5459 liters
1 nautical mile = 1.852 km

To compute celsius temperatures, subtract 32 from Fahrenheit and divide by 1.8. To go the other way, multiply celsius by 1.8 and add 32.

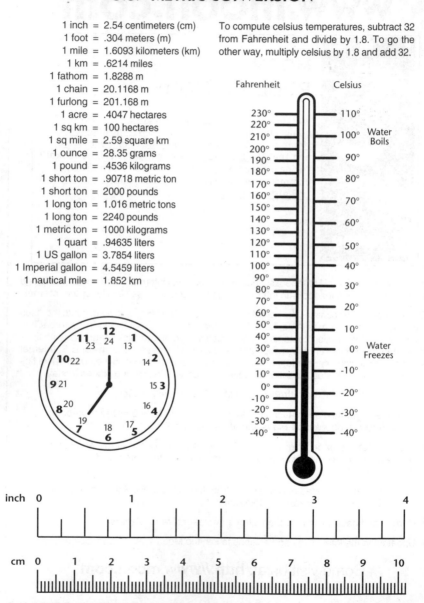